HANDBOOK OF
LATIN AMERICAN STUDIES
No. 41

A Selective and Annotated Guide to Recent Publications
in Anthropology, Economics, Education, Geography,
Government and Politics, International Relations, and Sociology

VOLUME 42 WILL BE DEVOTED TO THE HUMANITIES:
ART, FOLKLORE, HISTORY, LANGUAGE, LITERATURE, MUSIC, AND PHILOSOPHY

EDITORIAL NOTE: Comments concerning the *Handbook of Latin American Studies*
should be sent directly to the Editor, *Handbook of Latin American Studies*,
Hispanic Division, Library of Congress, Washington, D.C. 20540.

HANDBOOK OF LATIN AMERICAN STUDIES: NO. 41

SOCIAL SCIENCES

Prepared by a Number of Scholars
for the Hispanic Division of The Library of Congress

Edited by DOLORES MOYANO MARTIN

1979

UNIVERSITY OF TEXAS PRESS   *Austin and London*

International Standard Book Number 0-292-73013-6
Library of Congress Catalog Card Number 36-32633

CONTRIBUTING EDITORS

Philip B. Taylor, Jr., *University of Houston*, GOVERNMENT AND POLITICS
Agnes E. Toward, *Southwest Educational Development Laboratory, Austin, Texas*,
    EDUCATION
Nelson P. Valdés, *University of New Mexico, Albuquerque*, SOCIOLOGY
Carlos H. Waisman, *University of California, San Diego*, SOCIOLOGY
Alan C. Wares, *Summer Institute of Linguistics, Dallas*, ANTHROPOLOGY
Hasso von Winning, *Southwest Museum, Los Angeles*, ANTHROPOLOGY
Jan Peter Wogart, *World Bank*, ECONOMICS

HUMANITIES

Earl M. Aldrich, Jr., *University of Wisconsin, Madison*, LITERATURE
Jean A. Barman, *University of British Columbia*, HISTORY
Roderick J. Barman, *University of British Columbia*, HISTORY
Juan Bruce-Novoa, *Yale University*, LITERATURE
David Bushnell, *University of Florida*, HISTORY
Edward E. Calnek, *University of Rochester*, HISTORY
D. Lincoln Canfield, *Southern Illinois University at Carbondale*, LANGUAGES
Carlos J. Cano, *University of South Florida*, LITERATURE
Donald E. Chipman, *North Texas State University, Denton*, HISTORY
Don M. Coerver, *Texas Christian University*, HISTORY
Michael Conniff, *University of New Mexico, Albuquerque*, HISTORY
Edith B. Couturier, *The Newberry Library*, HISTORY
Lisa E. Davis, *York College*, LITERATURE
Maria Angélica Lopes Guimaraes Dean, *University of Wisconsin, Parkside*,
    LITERATURE
Ralph E. Dimmick, *General Secretariat, Organization of American States*,
    LITERATURE
Rubén A. Gamboa, *Mills College*, LITERATURE
Naomi M. Garrett, *West Virginia State College*, LITERATURE
Cedomil Goić, *The University of Michigan*, LITERATURE
Roberto González Echevarría, *Yale University*, LITERATURE
Richard E. Greenleaf, *Tulane University*, HISTORY
Oscar Hahn, *University of Iowa*, LITERATURE
Michael T. Hamerly, HISTORY
John R. Hébert, *Library of Congress*, BIBLIOGRAPHY AND GENERAL WORKS
Carlos R. Hortas, *Yale University*, LITERATURE
Ann Hagerman Johnson, *University of California, Davis*, HISTORY
Djelal Kadir, *Purdue University*, LITERATURE
Franklin W. Knight, *Johns Hopkins University*, HISTORY
David Lagmanovich, *The Catholic University of America*, LITERATURE
Pedro Lastra, *State University of New York at Stony Brook*, LITERATURE
Asunción Lavrin, *Howard University*, HISTORY
James B. Lynch, Jr., *University of Maryland, College Park*, ART
Murdo J. MacLeod, *University of Pittsburgh*, HISTORY
Wilson Martins, *New York University*, LITERATURE
Carolyn Morrow, *University of Utah*, LITERATURE
Gerald M. Moser, *Pennsylvania State University*, LITERATURE
Robert J. Mullen, *University of Texas, San Antonio*, ART
John V. Murra, *Cornell University*, HISTORY

José Neistein, *Brazilian American Cultural Institute, Washington*, ART
Betty T. Osiek, *Southern Illinois University at Edwardsville*, LITERATURE
José Miguel Oviedo, *Indiana University*, LITERATURE
Margaret S. Peden, *University of Missouri*, LITERATURE
Vincent C. Peloso, *Howard University*, HISTORY
Humberto M. Rasi, *Andrews University*, LITERATURE
Daniel R. Reedy, *University of Kentucky*, LITERATURE
James D. Riley, *The Catholic University of America*, HISTORY
Eliana Rivero, *The University of Arizona*, LITERATURE
Alexandrino E. Severino, *Vanderbilt University*, LITERATURE
Nicolas Shumway, *Yale University*, LITERATURE
Merle E. Simmons, *Indiana University*, LITERATURE
Saúl Sosnowski, *University of Maryland, College Park*, LITERATURE
Hobart A. Spalding, Jr., *Brooklyn College*, HISTORY
Robert Stevenson, *University of California, Los Angeles*, MUSIC
Juan Carlos Torchia-Estrada, *General Secretariat, Organization of American States*,
    PHILOSOPHY
John Hoyt Williams, *Indiana State University*, HISTORY
Benjamin M. Woodbridge, Jr., *University of California, Berkeley*, LITERATURE
George Woodyard, *University of Kansas*, LITERATURE
Thomas C. Wright, *University of Nevada*, HISTORY
Winthrop R. Wright, *University of Maryland, College Park*, HISTORY

Foreign Corresponding Editors

Marcello Carmagnani, *Università di Torino, Italy*, ITALIAN LANGUAGE
Lino Gómez-Canedo, *Franciscan Academy, Washington*, COLONIAL HISTORY
Wolf Grabendorff, *Lateinamerikareferat, Stiftung, Wissenschaft und Politik,
    Ebenhauser/Isar, Federal Republic of Germany*, GERMAN SOCIAL SCIENCE
    MATERIAL
Manfred Kossok, *Karl-Marx-Universitaet, Leipzig, German Democratic Republic*,
    GERMAN SOCIAL SCIENCE MATERIAL
Magnus Mörner, *Latinamerika-institutet i Stockholm, Sweden*, SCANDINAVIAN
    LANGUAGES
Wilhelm Stegmann, *Ibero-Amerikanisches Institut, Berlin-Lankwich, Federal Re-
    public of Germany*, GERMAN LANGUAGE

Special Contributing Editors

Robert V. Allen, *Library of Congress*, RUSSIAN LANGUAGE
Georgette M. Dorn, *Library of Congress*, GERMAN AND HUNGARIAN LANGUAGES
George J. Kovtun, *Library of Congress*, CZECH LANGUAGE
Maurice A. Lubin, *Howard University*, HAITIAN MATERIAL
Renata V. Shaw, *Library of Congress*, SCANDINAVIAN AND GERMAN LANGUAGES

CONTENTS

INTERNATIONAL RELATIONS

SOCIOLOGY

INDEXES

EDITOR'S NOTE

I. GENERAL TRENDS

In *HLAS 40* we noted that the increasing sophistication of Latin American scholarship coincided with the growing interest of European and other extra-hemispheric scholars in the region. This trend is most noticeable in the Geography section of this volume which includes several important West German studies of Mexico and Japanese works on Brazil. In other fields such as Mesoamerican archaeology this is not the trend, and English-language publications by American authors continue to outnumber those in Spanish, German, and French by more than three to one. The growing interest of the Japanese in Latin America, first mentioned in the Andean ethnohistory section of *HLAS 40*, is the most notable development. In 1979, the first interdisciplinary meeting of Latin Americanists in Japan was held at Tsukuba University. The topic was "The Latin American Environment and Development."

The study of the Latin American environment is a dominant theme of this volume. Works on the subject encompass a wide spectrum of multidisciplinary issues ranging from man's use and abuse of the environment to the latter's relationship to the structure of forest tribes to the effect environmental considerations have on the formulation of government policies. A major concern of many works is the need to integrate environmental assessments with government policies on economic development, population, and internal migration.

The need for studying the process of policy formulation by Latin American governments is emphasized by both economists and political scientists who also underscore the need for evaluating whether government policies for national, urban or rural development adopted in the 1960s and 1970s attained the desired goals (see p. 231–335). The tone of many critical reexaminations of such development policies is, in the words of a contributor to this volume, "far from optimistic" (see p. 544). It is also interesting to observe that studies of dependency theory which dominated much of the literature of the 1970s are on the wane, a change noted in this volume by both economists and political scientists. Instead, the growing concentration on case studies of specific countries may lead to a better understanding of the many varieties and degrees of dependency rather than to the ideological assertions of the 1970s.

Concurrent with the interest in the Latin American environment is the study of populations, particularly the twin phenomena of population movements and the urbanization process. Urban research is a leading topic in geography, Latin American cities being among the most rapidly growing in the world. Anthropologists have, in the words of contributors to this volume, "migrated to the cities in the footsteps of their subjects" (see p. 107), a trend that is yielding much interesting research. Some notable studies have appeared in recent years which describe how migrants have responded to the opportunities and tribulations of city life. The most sophisticated, comprehensive and interdisciplinary treatment of Mexican urban growth appeared in 1976 and is highly praised by both economist and geographer (see items 2975 and 5372). In Brazil, there is much concern over unchecked urbanization and attendant environmental and social problems but, in contrast to Mexico, no specific work is singled out for praise as a landmark study in more than one field. The volume of literature devoted to Colombian urban areas is "staggering," to quote two social scientists who contribute to this volume (see p. 629). Symptomatic of the growing interest in urbanization are the increasing numbers of symposia on topics that range from the development of precolumbian centers to current problems of overpopulation and social disruption.

A growing sophistication in the study of Latin American populations is also evident in this volume. The section, formerly titled Physical Anthropology, a name which indicated the predominantly anatomical-morphological orientation of the field's earliest practitioners, is renamed Biological Anthropology (see p. 191). This new title reflects the increasing expansion of the field and the continuous exploration of new types of data on human evolution and biological variation through research in genetics, biochemistry, hematology and serology, immunology, physiology, nutrition, epidemiology, environmental ecology, sociobiology, etc.

Finally, the study of agriculture continues to command much attention and ranges from analysis of contemporary problems to the nature of precolumbian Maya farming. The latter became the subject of intense research in the 1970s, extending the antiquity of Maya sedentary settlements to 2500 BC (see p. 33).

II. REGIONAL TRENDS

Mexico:

A recent major work on Mexican urbanization, singled out for praise twice in this volume (see items 2975 and 5372), is indicative of Mexico's leadership in many fields of the social sciences. Other examples of this leadership are studies of foreign policy and histories of bilateral relations, both of which have increased in number since Mexican archival sources became available to scholars. In Mesoamerican archaeology the collaboration of art historians and archaeologists has provided a new and important perspective on the classic period (see p. 33).

Caribbean and Central America:

Interest in the Caribbean, noted in the Editor's Note to *HLAS 39* and *HLAS 40*, continues. The question of the Panama Canal has generated a flood of publications, many of them United States government documents. In sociocultural anthropology there has been a notable increase in the number of works by scholars from the region, a promising development for the future of Caribbean social science. Very little has been accomplished in the area of comparative politics, a regrettable lack given recent political development in Central America (see p. 467). Fidel Castro's support of African revolutionaries has stimulated much interest in Cuban foreign policy, an area partly neglected until now. The section on education in this volume notes that the literature on Cuba is the "most interesting" and attributes this to "the Cuban social experiment" (see p. 340). The Cuban economy is the subject of some rigorous analysis, and a three-volume history of the Cuban sugar mill, singled out as "excellent" by the ethnologist in *HLAS 39:1239*, and praised as a "landmark" by the historians in *HLAS 40:2985*, is once again commended in this volume by the sociologist as a "classic" (see item 9175).

Andean Countries:

In Venezuela, there has been notable progress in economic research, particularly by Venezuelans themselves, a trend first noted in *HLAS 39*. In contrast, there has been little progress in such an important field as the study of the country's foreign policy and international relations, two surprisingly neglected topics given Venezuela's active role in world affairs as well as in OPEC, the UN and the OAS. Colombia has become such a research mecca that, according to two contributors to this volume, one is tempted to assume that for every five persons walking the streets of Colombian cities, two are social scientists engaged in field-work (see p. 629). Notwithstanding this upsurge of interest in Colombia, very little has been published on the most significant phenomenon to affect the country in recent years: the drug traffic (principally marihuana and cocaine), which has replaced coffee as the number one export. There are no studies on how these commodities are affecting the country's economy, its political system or its society (see p. 489).

The notable improvement in the quality of publications issuing from Peru, a trend noted by historians, social scientists and literary critics in the three previous volumes of *HLAS*, has now leveled off. The volume of material on Chilean politics is as formidable as before, but one detects a more reflective tone and a more detached perspective in studies of the Allende period, especially in works about the economy prior to the 1973 coup. Studies of the economy since the military's takeover remain highly polarized (see p. 289).

The River Plate Countries:

Much of the literature on Argentine politics and sociology was published outside of the country and, of works published in-country, about half are journalistic books or essays on general questions (see p. 639). Economic research on Argentina, however, shows surprising depth and breadth and is represented best in serial articles published by professional journals (see p. 308). Unfortunately, the state of social science research in Paraguay and Uruguay is far from satisfactory (see p. 300).

Brazil:

Like Mexico, Brazil continues to generate an astonishing number of quality studies by nationals and foreigners alike. This is especially true for regions such as the Amazon, the Northeast and Rio Grande do Sul and in fields such as ethnology, sociology, geography, political science, and most notably economics where government policies and development strategies have become the subject of rigorous scrutiny and ardent debate. In contrast to other countries of the southern cone, there is now in Brazil a new climate of openness and free discussion which favors the public examination of issues. This augurs well for the future of Brazilian social sciences.

III. SPECIAL DEVELOPMENTS

On January 15, 1979, William E. Carter, professor of anthropology at the University of Florida and former Director of the University's Center for Latin American Studies, was appointed Chief of the Hispanic Division of the Library of Congress. Dr. Carter has performed anthropological and inter-disciplinary research in Costa Rica, Guatemala, Peru, Chile, Bolivia, Argentina and Uruguay. His publications include *The first book of South America* (1972), *Bolivia: a profile* (1971), *New lands and old traditions: Kekchi cultivators in the Guatemalan lowlands* (1969), *Aymara communities and the Bolivian Agrarian Reform* (1965), *Brazil: anthropological perspectives* (1979), and *Chronic cannabis users in Costa Rica* (1980). Most recently Dr. Carter served as principal investigator of a project focusing on traditional coca use in Bolivia sponsored by the National Institute on Drug Abuse of the U.S. In selecting Dr. Carter, the Library was assisted by a committee of scholars in Hispanic studies. The appointment of Dr. Carter has given the *Handbook* staff the benefit of his interdisciplinary scholarship, editorial skills and administrative experience.

On May 15, 1979, the Library of Congress signed a contract with the University of Texas Press for the publication of the *Handbook*. This volume 41 is the first to be

published by this press, an institution with a long and successful record of collaboration with the Hispanic Division of the Library of Congress, having published many
noted works edited by the Division including the 16-volume *Handbook of Middle
American Indians* and the two-volume *Latin American history: essays on its study
and teaching.* The first 13 volumes of the *Handbook* were published by Harvard
University Press, five of them under the editorship of Lewis Hanke, who brought the
series to the Library of Congress in 1939. In 1951, the University of Florida Press took
over publication with volume 14 and continued for the next 28 years through volume
40 (1978). As we announce this change of publishers it is with deep regret that we
must report the loss of William B. Harvey, former Director of the University of Florida
Press, who died on October 23, 1979. Mr. Harvey was a dedicated supporter of the
Handbook during the 10 years he presided over the publication of volumes 29
through 39 or from 1967 through 1977. He will be missed by all members of the
Handbook staff who were familiar with his kindness and enthusiasm.

Also on May 15,.1979, the *Handbook*'s Advisory Board met at the Library of
Congress and among the topics discussed were: the automation of the *Handbook*,
other area bibliographies published by the Library of Congress, and the possibility of
issuing paperback reprints of individual *Handbook* sections. The Sociology and Economics sections of volume 39 were reviewed by Advisory Board members, and their
recommendations will be incorporated in volume 43.

The importance of government publications for the study of the social sciences
in Latin America cannot be overemphasized. Principal publishers of economic and
social science research are government agencies of countries as diverse as Cuba,
Brazil, Venezuela, Peru and Chile. A new unit of the Library of Congress—The
Hispanic Acquisitions Project or HAP—is greatly facilitating the receipt of such
materials. The Project's goal is to improve the comprehensiveness and currency of the
Library's receipts of publications issued in all of the Western Hemisphere south of the
United States as well as in Spain and Portugal. To attain this goal, the Project assumed
responsibility for a variety of operations formerly divided between the Library's Order
and Exchange and Gift Divisions. Because of the Project's use of innovative procedures, its greatly expanded range of bibliographic sources, and its current
acquisitions control file of more than 25,000 titles, the number of monographs and
serials received at the *Handbook* office has increased greatly, especially from Mexico,
Cuba, Haiti, Peru, Chile, and Uruguay. The Project's greatest success has been in
Haiti, where a local contract agent acquired, in the short space of 15 months, some
527 monographs and almost 900 serial issues, thereby virtually completing the
Library's collections of important Haitian publications issued during the past five
years. The Project's 1980–81 program calls for intensive attention to Puerto Rico, the
Dominican Republic and the River Plate area.

IV. CHANGES IN VOLUME 41

Anthropology:
Norman Hammond (Rutgers University) collaborated with Hasso von Winning
in the preparation of the section on Mesoamerican archaeology. Cynthia A. Cone
(Hamline University) and Frank C. Miller (University of Minnesota) annotated the
material on Middle American ethnology. The section devoted to Physical Anthropology has been renamed Biological Anthropology, the reasons for the change
being noted by R. A. Halberstein in his introduction (see p. 191).

Economics
Markos Mamalakis (University of Wisconsin, Milwaukee) reviewed the litera-

ture of a new section devoted to Chile and Peru. Michael L. Cook (Texas A&M University) was responsible for another new section that covers Bolivia, Paraguay, and Uruguay. Dennis J. Mahar (The World Bank) collaborated with Peter T. Knight in the preparation of the section on Brazil.

Geography:

Gary S. Elbow (Texas Tech University) assumed the responsibility for reviewing materials on Mexico and Guatemala for the section on Middle America.

Sociology:

Nelson P. Valdés (University of New Mexico, Albuquerque) annotated the literature for a new section on the Caribbean and the Guianas.

Subject Index:

The thesaurus of this volume on the social sciences has been expanded to include more economic terms (e.g., Fiscal Reform, Foreign Investment, Monetary Policy, Private Enterprise, Public Enterprise, Tariffs and Trade Policy, etc.). The term INDIGENOUS PEOPLES substitutes the former term INDIANS. The names of indigenous groups are listed separately.

Numbering:

The standardized numbering system adopted in *HLAS 39* (see p. xii–xiii) continues with this volume.

Other Changes:

Changes in the editorial staff of the *Handbook*, the administrative officers of the Library of Congress, membership of the Advisory Board, and publisher are reflected in the title page of the present volume.

Washington, December 1979   Dolores Moyano Martin

HANDBOOK OF
LATIN AMERICAN STUDIES
No. 41

BIBLIOGRAPHY AND GENERAL WORKS

JOHN R. HÉBERT, Hispanic Division, Library of Congress

THERE HAS BEEN AN INCREASE, of great significance to the research community, in the number of useful tools designed to facilitate research in various fields of Latin American studies such as collection guides, subject bibliographies, catalogues of new acquisitions, national bibliographies, and indexing projects. The more worthwhile contributions among them are noted in this essay.

There is continued interest in the development and continued publication of national bibliographies, crucial tools for the development of collections. In addition, many of these bibliographies conveniently list new journals including mailing address and cost. The new and impressive annual *CARICOM Bibliography* (item **8**) prepared by the Caribbean Community Library is worthy of note and lists currently published monographs in the English-speaking Caribbean. Another new work is the *Bibliografía Nacional* of Peru (item **6**) produced by the National Library and providing monthly information on Peruvian imprints. Finally, the Cuban National Library will publish supplements in order to complete the missing years of its *Bibliografía Cubana* (i.e., 1924–36, item **10**).

Several general bibliographies and substantial catalogues of Latin American materials have appeared. The new annual *Bibliographic Guide to Latin American Studies 1978* (item **66**) lists publications catalogued in 1978 by the Benson Latin American Collection at the Univ. of Texas and by the Library of Congress. The six-volume *Catálogo de autores de la colección peruana* prepared by the Peruvian National Library and produced by G.K. Hall came out in 1979 (item **91**). The first bibliographies of bibliographies to appear are the supplement to Arthur Gropp's *A bibliography of Latin American bibliographies: social sciences and humanities* (item **2**) and the useful annual publication of SALALM's Committee on Bibliography, the *Annual report on Latin American and Caribbean bibliographic activities* (item **4**). The latter publication lists more than 430 contributions to bibliographic compilations and contains an instructive essay by Juan Freudenthal on the development of national bibliographies in the West Indies.

A number of useful and complementary subject bibliographies and reference works should be noted. The following deal with racial and ethnic groups: Henrique Alves' *Bibliografia afro-brasileira* (item **9295**); Robert Conrad's *Brazilian slavery* (item **24**); Fundação Cultural de Maranhão's *O negro no Maranhão* (item **29**); Dorothy Porter's *Afro-Braziliana* (item **41**); Jalil Sued Badillo's *Bibliografía antropológica para el estudio de los pueblos indígenas en el Caribe* (item **48**); Gerard Nagelkerke's *Bibliografisch Overzicht van de Indianen in Suriname* (item **39**); Martin Sable's *Latin American Jewry: a research guide* (item **45**); and Diane Herrera's *Puerto Rican and other minority groups in the continental United States* (item **32**).

The question of territorial disputes in the hemisphere has stimulated numerous bibliographic projects; e.g., the controversy between Chile and Argentina over the Beagle Channel is partially addressed in Nicolás Matijevich's preliminary *Bibliografía sobre el Canal de Beagle* (item **37**); Argentine sovereignty over the Islas Malvinas and a portion of Antarctica is the subject of a work by the Argentine Ministry of Culture and Education (item **8736**); boundary concerns of Venezuela and Colombia are described in item **8774**; and Lewis Tambs offers general perspective of boundary disputes and other issues in *Latin American geopolitics: a basic bibliography* (item **8601**).

National politics, political parties and political philosophies continue to generate much bibliographic interest. Of particular merit are CIDAL's *Bibliografía demócrata-cristiana latinoamericana* (item **7008**) and José Ferrer Benimeli's *Bibliografía de la masonería* (item **26**). Three crucial Latin American political movements and ideologies of the 20th-century are the subjects of bibliographic scrutiny: Dominique Ferre's *Le peronisme* (item **25**) considers Argentine political activity in the last four decades; Ignacio González-Polo's *Bibliografía general de las agrupaciones y partidos políticos mexicanos 1910–1970* (item **30**) and Verónica Vázquez' *Selección bibliográfica sobre los principales partidos políticos mexicanos 1906–1970* (item **7148**) consider the country's dominant political party and other competing groups. Harry Vanden's bibliographical essay on Mariátegui in the *Latin American Research Review* (item **14**) examines the impact of the Peruvian thinker on political philosophy. These compilations provide a broad introduction to the wealth of documentation available on each subject for the interested researcher.

Well conceived and executed bibliographies on literary topics continue to appear. David Foster considers 19th and 20th-century Chilean writers in his *Chilean literature* (item **28**) while Aida Prátici de Fernández cites provincial writings in her *Guía bibliográfica de la literatura de Mendoza* (item **43**). The belated recognition and impact of Latin American writers on the English-speaking world is noted by Bradley Shaw in his *Latin American literature in English: 1975–1978* (item **47**) and by Patricia and Juan Freudenthal in their *Index to anthologies of Latin American literature in English translation* (item **110**).

The increasing number of indexing projects underway is a recent and important development in Latin American studies. These cooperative labor-saving undertakings should lead to more thorough and definitive research. Among the new catalogues and indexes are Brazil's IBICT-produced *Catálogo colectivo de publicações periódicas em ciências sociais e humanidades* (item **67**) which lists over 14,400 serial titles located in nearly 800 Brazilian research collections; *Indice CENATE: catálogo de teses universitárias brasileiras* (item **82**); and *CLADINDEX: Resúmen de documentos CEPAL/ILPES* (item **102**) which lists more than 850 UN publications issued between 1970–76. Examples of the wealth of indexing of serials and documents are *Documentación socioeconómica centroamericana* (item **106**) prepared by the Centro de Documentación Económica y Social de Centroamerica (CEDESC) of the Confederación Universitaria Centroamericana (CSUCA) in San Pedro, Costa Rica; the *Hispanic American Periodical Index 1976* (item **104**) which indexes over 200 journals related to Latin American studies; *Indice de ciências sociais* (item **119**) of the Instituto Universitário de Pesquisas do Rio de Janeiro; and Manuel de Jesús Roa Santana's *Indice de publicaciones periódicas de universidades dominicanas* (item **135**) which indexes issues of seven Dominican journals appearing between 1971–77.

Several new guides to collections will be of use to researchers. The colonial Latin American manuscripts and transcripts of the Obadiah Rich collection at the New York Public Library have been identified in a 1978 publication by Edwin Brownrigg (item **68**); Mexican archival materials in the magnificent collections of the Genealogical Society of Utah have been microfilmed as well as listed in a *Preliminary survey* *of the Mexican collection* by Susan Cottler and others (item **72**); and Esperanza Rodríguez de Lebrija's *Indice analítico de la guía de Archivo Histórico de Hacienda* (item **94**) describes the relevant portion of the Mexican general archives. Finally, there is an indispensable work for the scholar seeking guidance and information on the numerous Latin American resources of the city of Washington: Michael Grow's recent guide (item **116**) sponsored by the Woodrow Wilson International Center for Scholars.

A new subsection introduced in this *HLAS*, "New Serial Titles," responds to a need expressed by several scholars. This first attempt offers a highly selected listing with the hope that additional titles will appear in future volumes. For that reason, we welcome comments and suggestions from readers and users of the "Bibliography and General Works Section."

GENERAL BIBLIOGRAPHIES

1   *Amérique Latine.* Bulletin analytique de documentation. Groupe de Recherches sur l'Amérique Latine (GRAL), Toulouse, France; Groupe de Recherches et d'Études Economiques et Sociales sur l'Amérique Latine (GRESAL), Grenoble, France; and Centre des Recherches Cientifiques, Institut des Hautes Études de l'Amérique Latine (IHEAL), Paris. No. O, déc. 1978–. Paris.

An analyzed listing of 196 selected works appearing between 1975 and 1978 on ecology and Indian medicine, indigenous migrations, integration of people, industrialization politics, mass communication and the literature of Peru and Mexico. Listing of journals reviewed, and subject and author indexes are provided.

2   **Cordeiro, Daniel Raposo; Solena V. Bryant; Haydée N. Piedracueva;** and **Barbara Hadely Stein** *eds.* A bibliography of Latin American bibliographies: social sciences and humanities. Metuchen. N.J., The Scarecrow Press, 1979. 272 p.

This supplement to Arthur Gropp's 1968 and 1976 bibliographies of Latin American bibliographies lists publications, both monographs and articles, appearing between 1969 and 1974. A total of 1750 entries are arranged within 36 subject headings, with a prevalence of works of biography and libraries and archives. Subject and author indexes are provided. A useful reference tool.

3   **Nederlandse Stichting vöor Culturele Samenwerking met Suriname en de Nederlandse Antillen.** Nederlandse Antillen. Amsterdam, 1975. 271 p.

Listing of publications, arranged by subject, related to the history, culture, geography, economy, sociology, and politics of the islands. Author and subject indexes are included.

4   **Piedracueva, Haydée.** Annual report on Latin American and Caribbean bibliographic activities, 1979. Austin, Tex., SALALM Secretariat, 1979. 48 p. (XXIV SALALM working paper, A-2) (mimeo)

Consists of three parts: 1) a state-of-the-art article by Juan Freudenthal, entitled "Toward a Current National Bibliography in the West Indies"; 2) a selected list of recent bibliographies on Latin American and Caribbean topics, arranged by broad subject categories; and 3) a section on works in progress. Author and subject indexes are included. Lists 438 books and articles. Submitted to the XXIV Seminar on the Acquisition of Latin American Library Materials, University of California, at Los Angeles, 17–22 June 1979.

NATIONAL BIBLIOGRAPHIES

5   *Anuario Bibliográfico Uruguayo de 1977.* Biblioteca Nacional. 1978–. Montevideo.

Over 950 new monographic and 688 periodical titles are given in this bibliography (169 p.). Includes separate listings of works and periodicals of foreign authors and institutions published in the country and an author index.

6   *Bibliografía Nacional.* Libros, artículos de revistas y periódicos. Biblioteca Nacional. No. 7, julio 1979–. Lima.

A monthly listing (62 p.), arranged by

subject, of Peruvian imprints deposited in the National Library and articles gleaned from Peruvian periodicals. Separate listings of monographs and articles. Also includes onomastic and thematic indexes and a key to journals analyzed. A subscription to the monthly update is available from the library for US $12.00 per year.

7 *Boletim Bibliográfico da Biblioteca Nacional.* Biblioteca Nacional. Vol. 23, No. 1, Trimestre No. 1, 1978–. Rio.

A listing of over 1300 Brazilian publications mainly from 1977, arranged in order by Dewey Decimal Classification. An author index and a listing of acronyms used are included.

8 *The CARICOM Bibliography.* Caribbean Community, Secretariat, Library. Vol. 1, 1977 [and] Vol. 2, 1978–. Georgetown.

Listing of materials currently published in the Caribbean Community (CARICOM) member territories (i.e., Antigua, Bahamas, Barbados, Belize, Dominica, Grenada, Guyana, Jamaica, Montserrat, St. Kitts/Nevis/Anguilla, St. Lucia, St. Vincent, Trinidad and Tobago). Periodicals (unless a first issue or an annual report) and certain government publications (e.g., bills, gazettes, debates) are not included. Material arranged in two sections: by subject arrangement and author/title/series arrangement. Listings of vol. 1 (210 p.) are augmented in vol. 2 (522 p.). List of publishers and their addresses given. Cost: $6.00 per year. This work is a major reference and acquisitions tool for scholarly research on the English-speaking Caribbean.

9 **Dulzaides Serrate, Marta** and **Elena Graupera Arango** *comps.* Bibliografía cubana: 1976. La Habana, Biblioteca Nacional José Martí, 1978. 373 p.

Contains citations for 662 monographic and pamphlet titles published in Cuba in 1976, 183 titles from 1969–75 not previously listed, and 57 works by Cubans published abroad. Also includes separate sections for posters, exhibit catalogs, cinema, discography, postal stamps, and new serials. Each section has titles arranged in alphabetical order by subject; each section contains separate author and general indices. Bio-bibliographies for Félix B. Caignet Salomón (1892–76); Dulce María Escalona Almeida (1901–76); Raimundo Lazo (1904–76); José Lezama Lima (1910–76); Juan Ernesto Pérez

de la Riva (1913–76); and Gonzalo de Quesada y Miranda (1900–76) appear. The section on posters (604 listed) provides an insight to Cuban mass education/promotion interests.

10 ———; ———; and Elena Cabeiro Gil *comps.* Bibliografía cubana: 1921–1924. La Habana, Biblioteca Nacional José Martí [and] Editorial Orbe, 1978. 185 p.

The second installment in the National Library's effort to complete the missing years of the Cuban bibliography (i.e., 1917–36). To date the bibliography from 1917–24 has appeared. Each year appears separately in alphabetical order. A publisher's index and a separate analytical index are provided.

Elogio y bibliografía de Rómulo Ferrero Rebagliati. See item **4544.**

11 *Guyanese National Bibliography.* National Library of Guyana. Jan./Dec. 1978–. Georgetown.

Subject and alphabetical lists of new books and non-book materials published in Guyana during the year. The bibliography is based on materials deposited at the National Library. Acts, bills, legislation and parliamentary debates appear in appendix. Provides author, title, and series indexes and a list of Guyanese publishers. Political party publications are also included.

COLLECTIVE AND PERSONAL BIBLIOGRAPHIES

12 *Informaciones.* Número especial en conmemoración del bicentenario del nacimiento del General Don José de San Martín, 1778–1978. Univ. Nacional de La Plata, Biblioteca Pública. Pts. 1/5, feb./junio 1978–. La Plata, Arg.

Special issue (112 p.) lists over 1600 works on San Martín contained in the collection of the 16 libraries of the Univ. de La Plata. Works (i.e., monographs, articles, papers) are presented in alphabetical order by author. No index appears.

13 **Lovera de Sola, Roberto J.** *comp.* José Luis Salcedo-Bastardo. Caracas, Academia Nacional de la Historia, Depto. de Investigaciones, 1975. 201 p. (Col. Bibliográfica, 4)

Provides bio-bibliographical information of the noted Venezuelan writer, José Luis Salcedo-Bastardo. Contains separate listings of his contributions: monographs, pamphlet articles, and other writings and presentations. Periodicals in which he collaborated are identified. General and title indexes appear. A fitting honor for this prominent Bolivarian writer.

14 Vanden, Harry E. Mariátegui: marxismo, comunismo, and other bibliographic notes (LARR, 14:3, 1979, p. 61–86)

Discusses Aprista and leftist views regarding José Carlos Mariátegui. Works by Peruvians, North Americans, and other Latin Americans regarding the figure appear in the review article. Monographs and articles by and about Mariátegui appear in an appended bibliography.

SUBJECT BIBLIOGRAPHIES

15 Alberich, José. Bibliografía anglo-hispánica 1801–1850: ensayo bibliográfico de libros y folletos relativos a España e Hispanoamérica impresos en Inglaterra en la primera mitad del siglo diecinueve. Oxford, UK, Dolphin Book, 1978. 197 p.

The author has identified more than 1600 titles published about Spain and Latin America, between 1801 and 1850. Dictionaries, grammars, bibliographies, literature (some in translation) and history and travel are especially listed. Onomastic, title, and geographic indexes are included.

Alves, Henrique Losinskas *comp.* Bibliografía afro-brasileira: estudos sobre o negro. See item **9295**.

Argentina. Ministerio de Cultura y Educación. Dirección de Bibliotecas Populares. Soberanía: contribución bibliográfica a la afirmación de derechos argentinos sobre las Malvinas, Islas y Sector Antártico. See item **8763**.

Bahía (state), *Brazil.* **Secretaria das Minas e Energia.** Bibliografia comentada da geologia da Bahia: 1817–1975. See item **5595**.

16 Ban, Ibuki. Bibliografía de publicaciones japonesas sobre América Latina. Tokyo, Sofia Univ., Instituto Iberoamericano, 1978. 38 p.

Lists 239 monographs and serial articles on Latin America published in 1977 in the Japanese language and held at Sofia Univ. library. Reflects a 30 percent reduction in the number of items from 1976 to 1977. Contains a breakdown of the number of articles by country and discipline. The majority of the works listed deal with Brazil, Mexico, Argentina, Chile, Peru and Cuba in descending order of representation. Approximately 10 percent of the items are translations. Includes index of contents of journals and authors.

Beretta, Pier Luigi. Contributo per una bibliografía geográfica del Rio Grande do Sul, Brasile. See item **5602**.

Bernard, Charles L. Fischer. Notas para una bibliografía sobre la Isla de Pascua: 1923–1972. See item **688**.

17 Bibliografía Económica de México. Indice general. Banco de México, Subdirección de Investigación Económica y Bancaria. Vol. 1, 1976–. México.

Cites recent publications on economics issued in Mexico. Entries are divided into 10 main sections: general reference, methodology (economics), economic theory, history, economic activity, organization of production, demography, services, money and finance, and social economy. Works are further divided by subject in each main section. Entries are not numbered; contains no index.

18 Bibliografía Histórica Mexicana: 1976–1978. El Colegio de México, Centro de Estudios Históricos. No. 10, 1979–. México.

A listing of nearly 1100 works (monographs, articles, documents, etc.) on various aspects of Mexican history, e.g., general, precolonial, national, regional, and the history of science, law, diplomacy, education, ideas, politics, religious, social, and bibliographies in Mexico. Contains selective annotations. General index included. Masterful bibliographic work by María del Carmen Velázquez.

Bibliografía sobre la frontera entre Venezuela y Colombia. See item **8774**.

Bozzoli de Wille, María. Bibliografía antropológica de Costa Rica. See items **528** and **886**.

Brazil. Ministério da Agricultura. Secretaria Geral. Coordenação de Informação Rural. Bibliografía de café. See item **5604**.

19   **Briggs, Lucy Therina.** A critical survey of the literature on the Aymara language (LARR, 14:3, 1979, p. 87–105)
Discusses major bibliographical sources, prelinguistic and linguistic studies for Aymara. Colonial period and current efforts appear.

20   **Bryant, Shasta M.** A selective bibliography of bibliographies of Hispanic American literature. 2. ed. Austin, Univ. of Texas, Institute of Latin American Studies, 1976. 100 p. (Guides and bibliographies series, 8)
An alphabetical listing of 662 bibliographies useful to the student of Hispanic-American literature. Greatly expanded coverage over the 1966 first ed. General index included.

Buenos Aires (prov.), *Arg.* **Ministerio de Educación. Instituto de Bibliografía.** Bibliografía argentina. See item **4371.**

21   **Campbell, Leon G.** Recent research on Andean peasant revolts, 1750–1820 (LARR, 14:1, 1979, p. 3–49)
Essay describes briefly the various revolts of the period, capped by that of José Gabriel Túpac Amaru in 1780, and considers recent research on the theme. Appended bibliography identifies primary and secondary sources for the further study of peasant revolts.

22   **Cardozo, Lubio.** Historia de los estudios bibliográficos humanísticos latino-americanos. Caracas, Academia Nacional de la Historia, 1978. 93 p. (El libro menor, 5)
An essay on selected bibliographic works compiled since the 17th century to describe publications on Latin America in general, and on individual nations and subjects. Contributions by Hispanic, North American, and other authors are described in separate segments. A useful listing and description of over 100 publications.

Carrasco Puente, Rafael. Bibliografía del Istmo de Tehuantepec. See item **5339.**

23   **Carvajal, Manuel J.** Bibliography of poverty and related topics in Costa Rica. Washington, Agency for International Development, Bureau for Latin America and the Caribbean, Rural Development Division, 1979. 329 p. (Working document series. Costa Rica. General working paper, 1)

A listing of over 2000 publications useful to the study of poverty-related issues in Costa Rica written mainly in the past 20 years. Excludes works in which "excessive emphasis on technical aspects clouds potential poverty or income distribution implications." Works are classified into 17 disciplines and 10 formats of presentation, (i.e., government publications, theses, conference papers, etc.). Also includes indexes to subjects, authors, geographical places, and institutions.

Centro de Información, Documentación y Análisis Latinoamericano (CIDAL), *Caracas.* Bibliografía demócrata-Cristiana latino-americana. See item **7008.**

Centro Paraguayo de Estudios Sociológicos, *Asunción.* **Centro Paraguayo de Documentación Social. Grupo de Trabajo de Migraciones Internas.** Las migraciones en América Latina: bibliografía. See item **9012.**

24   **Conrad, Robert.** Brazilian slavery. Boston, Mass., G.K. Hall, 1977. 163 p.
Lists 994 published bibliographies, research aids, monographs and articles related primarily to African slavery in Brazil, although items on Amerindians are included. Emphasizes 19th-century slave trade, slavery, and the abolition process. Also notes publications on the subject which appeared during the colonial period. Includes author index.

25   **Ferré, Dominique** *comp.* Le peronisme: bibliographie. Rennes, France, Univ. d'Haute Bretagne, Centre d'Études Hispaniques et Hispano-Américaines, 1978. 79 l.
Provides references to 734 monographs and articles related to all phases of Peronism. Chapters on the Infame Decade (1930s) the 1943 revolution, Peronism in power 1943–55, and Argentina 1955–76 appear. Author and analytical indexes and French locations of works cited are included.

26   **Ferrer Benimeli, José Antonio.** Bibliografía de la masonería: introducción histórico-crítica. 2. ed. Madrid, Fundación Universitaria Española, 1978. 603 p.
This second ed. of a 1974 publication practically doubles its bibliographic content, providing 6060 entries related to the history of Masonry. Separate chapters are devoted to the origins, history, enemies, and national lodges of the organization. Especially useful to the Latin Americanist are entries found on

p. 78–86, p. 308–316, and p. 508–516. The latter group consists of a listing of Latin American masonic journals. Author introduces the work with a well-documented bibliographical essay on all phases of the movement, (see p. 35–133). Geographic, subject and onomastic indexes are provided.

Ferris, Elizabeth G. The Andean Pact: a selected bibliography. See item **2810**.

Figueroa, Patricio and **Lucrecia Roca.** Bibliografía para la historia de la educación chilena. See item **4405**.

Fischer Bernard, Charles N. Notas para una bibliografía sobre la Isla de Pascua: 1923–1972. See item **5468**.

27 **Foster, David William.** An annotated registry of scholarly journals in Hispanic studies (RIB, 28:2, abril/junio 1978, p. 131–147)

Lists 76 Hispanic-oriented journals or those of general interest and Romance studies in which Hispanic studies are well represented. As determined by the author, emphasis has been on scholarly journals and those general journals that satisfy prevailing scholarly criteria. This registry can also be used as a helpful guide to those interested in submitting manuscripts for publication. This article updates the author's previous article "Bibliografía Anotada de Revistas de Actualidad dentro del Campo de la Literatura y de Interés para los Hispanistas" in *La Torre* (67, enero/marzo 1970, p. 125–147).

28 ———. Chilean literature: a working bibliography of secondary sources. Boston, Mass., G.K. Hall, 1978. 236 p. (A reference publication in Latin American studies)

A listing of bibliographies, critical books and essays on 46 Chilean authors, chosen for their historical and esthetic importance and on the basis of available critical references. Some 300 journals were consulted for contributions useful to scholarly research and opinion. Items in magazines, dailies, and literary supplements have been excluded. A separate general reference section and the index to critics enhance the publication. A useful research tool.

29 **Fundação Cultural do Maranhão,** *São Luis, Brazil.* O negro no Maranhão: bibliografia. São Luis, Brazil, 1978. 19 p.

A brief but useful listing of 55 works pertaining to the religion, social institutions, and the history of blacks in Maranhão. Selected entries receive informative annotations. For complementary work, see item **9295**.

García-Rendueles, Manuel A. Bibliografía de la familia lingüística jibaroana. See item **1363**.

30 **González-Polo, Ignacio** *comp.* Bibliografía general de las agrupaciones y partidos políticos mexicanos: 1910–1970. México, Reforma Política, Ediciones de la *Gaceta Informativa de la Comisión Federal Electoral*, 1978. 317 p. (Serie bibliografías)

Identifies over 1800 items divided into groupings: essays and studies on political parties; literature published by the parties. The latter group of materials is presented in chronological order by party. An analytical index provides subject, short title and author access to the publications. A valuable reference tool.

Hartmann, Thekla Olga. Contribuições em língua alemã para a etnologia do Brasil: 1966–1976. See item **1153**.

31 **Hernández de Caldas, Angela.** Bibliografía agro-industrial de Colombia: un catálogo colectivo. Bogotá, Fundación Mariano Ospina Pérez, 1978. 222 p.

This useful list of 3142 citations on Colombian agriculture was compiled after review of publications in 109 Colombian libraries and documentation centers. Locations of individual works are given. Author, geographic and scientific name of plant indexes appear. Items are arranged in alphabetical order within sections on the wide range of agricultural activity in the country, e.g., fertilizers, oils and fats, cotton, sugar, coffee, crops, agro-industry. Researchers involved in the social aspects of agriculture in the country should find the publication indispensable.

32 **Herrera, Diane** *ed.* Puerto Ricans and other minority groups in the continental United States: an annotated bibliography. With a foreword and supplemental bibliography by Francesco Cordasco. Detroit, Mich., Blaine Ethridge Books, 1979. 397 p.

An annotated listing of over 2100 citations to publications related primarily to Puerto Rican and other Hispanic groups' experiences in the educational system of the continental US. Includes sections on bilingual/bicultural education, linguistic studies, special education and teacher attitudes as well as a chapter related to general experiences of Hispanics in the continental US. An expanded ed. of *Puerto Ricans in the United States: review of the literature* (1973).

33 Highfield, Arnold R. and **Max Bumgarner.** A bibliography of articles on the Danish West Indies and the United States Virgin Islands in The New York Times: 1867–1975. Gainesville, University Presses of Florida, Center for Latin American Studies *for the* Caribbean Research Institute, College of the Virgin Islands, 1978. 209 p. (Caribbean Research Institute occasional paper, 1)

A chronological listing of articles. Topical access to entries provided in an index. Compilers feel that this newspaper contains valuable information for research on the Virgin Islands.

Jiménez, Roberto and **P. Zeballos.** América Latina y el mundo desarrollado: bibliografía comentada sobre relaciones de dependencia. See items **2844** and **8551.**

34 Kendall, Aubyn. The art and archaeology for pre-columbian Middle America: an annotated bibliography of works in English. Boston, Mass., G.K. Hall, 1977. 324 p. (A reference publication in Latin American studies)

Lists nearly 2150 entries divided into separate sections of books and periodicals. Works on precolumbian art, art history, art criticism, archaeological findings, as well as related material such as epigraphy, literature, codices, religion and ethnology published no later than Dec. 1976 appear. Location of copy examined is given. A selective list of dissertations and a topical geographical and cultural index are included. The precolumbian Mexican works listed in the author's 1973 publication (see *HLAS 37:639*) are incorporated here. For archaeologist's comment, see item **309.**

35 Krumpe, Paul F. The world remote sensing bibliographic index: a comprehensive geographic index bibliography to remote-sensing site investigations of natural and agricultural resources throughout the world. Fairfax, Va., Tensor Industries, 1976. 619 p.

Geography index bibliography of over 4000 references on remote sensing. Citations from Jan. 1970–Aug. 1977 are arranged within 14 major disciplines among more than 150 geographic areas, states, and countries. Designed as an integrated reference guide for use in remote sensing and environmental education, training, applications research, analysis, and technology transfer. Publications on individual Latin American countries appear. Useful guide for social scientists.

Laureani, Camila. Bibliografía y piezas originales de la Isla de Pascua existentes en la Sede Central de la Congregación de los SS. CC. de Picpus-Roma. See item **696.**

Lombardi de Almirati, Olga and **Blanca Martínez Gil** *comps.* Bibliografía uruguaya sobre educación. See item **4557.**

36 Markman, Sidney David. Colonial Central America: a bibliography. Tempe, Arizona State Univ., Center for Latin American studies, 1977. 345 p.

This bibliography lists more than 2250 items pertaining to colonial Central America. It is divided into eight distinct sections: 1) works produced during the colonial period; 2) works produced on the subject during the national period; 3) general art and architectural history; 4) Central American art and architecture; 5) bibliography; 6) documentary sources; 7) maps and plans; and 8) documents in the Archivo General del Gobierno (Guatemala City). The latter chapter is a listing of pertinent documents culled from the card index in the Guatemala archive. The locations of items cited appear. Includes index to authors, people, places, and subjects. A valuable introduction to Central American research.

Marshall, Trevor G. *comp.* A bibliography of the Commonwealth Caribbean peasantry: 1838–1974. See item **1062.**

37 Matijevic, Nicolás. Bibliografía sobre el Canal de Beagle: primera contribución. Bahía Blanca, Arg., Univ. Nacional del Sur, Depto. de Ciencias Sociales, 1978. 26 p.

Lists 310 titles published mainly in Argentina related to the Beagle Channel question affecting Chilean-Argentine relations. Most of the works cited were printed between 1977 and 1978 and appeared in national newspapers and magazines. A useful listing for one side of a delicate matter.

38 *Mexico: Artículos Clasificados.* UNAM, Facultad de Ciencias Políticas y Sociales, Centro de Documentación. Vol. 1, No. 1, 1978–. México.

An annotated monthly index to Mexican and foreign serial articles pertaining to Mexican international relations, political science, sociology, communications, public administration, and economics. Subject access by discipline is given. The journals (and issues) reviewed each month are listed. New documents received by the documentation center are also given.

39 **Nagelkerke, Gerard A.** Bibliografisch Overzicht van de Indianen in Suriname (Bibliographical survey of the Indians of Surinam). Leiden, The Netherlands, Royal Institute of Linguistics and Anthropology, Caribbean Dept., 1977. 55 p.

A ground breaking bibliography, containing 391 listings, on the native Indians of Surinam. Compiled largely from works contained in the Royal Institute of Linguistics and Anthropology in Leiden; items from that collection are noted. Includes an onomastic index. A brief historical background to Surinam and the Indians has been provided by the compiler. For anthropologist's comment, see item **1179**.

Pachón, Consuelo de. Bibliografía sobre grupos indígenas. See item **1181**.

Pagán Perdomo, Dato. Bibliografía sumaria sobre el arte rupestre del Caribe. See item **506**.

40 **Paraná** (state), *Brazil.* **Secretaria do Estado do Planejamento. Coordenadora de Informações Técnicas.** Catálogo de estudos sobre o Paraná. v. 1/3. Curitiba, Brazil, 1977. 3 v. (334, 329, 249 p.)

Listing of more than 2550 official publications, including articles, research papers, and pamphlets on Paraná state, issued between 1970–77. Volumes cover works by the state agencies for education, culture, public security, finance, industry, commerce, and agriculture. Entries are listed by title, subject, and geographical area; includes completed and in-progress studies. Final vol. 4, is in preparation.

Pennano, Guido. Economía política del caucho en el Perú: una aproximación bibliográfica. See item **3273**.

41 **Porter, Dorothy B.** *comp.* Afro-Braziliana: a working bibliography. Boston,

Mass., G.K. Hall, 1978. 294 p.

A selected listing of over 5200 items written by Afro-Brazilians on the history, culture, literature and social conditions of Brazil. Author defines Afro-Brazilian as those persons "who have been described in the Brazilian literature as *homen de côr, mulatto, Negro, pardo, preta, filha,* and *filho de escravos* and persons said to have '*uma gota de sangue preto*'." Publications listed are found in US repositories, mainly the Library of Congress, Columbus Memorial Library (OAS), and the Moorland-Spingarn Research Center (Howard Univ.); library location of items listed is given. Writings of selected Afro-Brazilian authors, including critical and bio graphical references, are contained in a separate section. Includes introductory notes and general index.

42 **Posnett, N.W.** and **P.M. Reilly.** Dominica. Surrey, UK, Ministry of Overseas Development, Land Resources Division, 1978. 74 p. (Land resources bibliography, 12)

Selected list of key works on Dominica's land resources. Separate sections on agriculture, climatology, cultural studies, economics, forestry, land tenure, population, and water resources appear. Does not include index.

43 **Prátici de Fernández, Aída.** Guía bibliográfica de la literatura de Mendoza. Mendoza, Arg., Univ. Nacional de Cuyo, Facultad de Filosofía y Letras, 1977. 30 p.

Compilation of literary works on Mendoza in the faculty's library. Author and title indexes are included.

Richardson, James B., III. A bibliography of archaeology, pleistocene geology, and ecology of the departments of Piura and Tumbes, Peru. See item **828**.

44 **Rodríguez Masís, René.** Selección de la obra *La costa atlántica de Nicaragua* (BNBD, 26, nov./dic. 1978, p. 112–144)

A selection of 163 current articles on Nicaragua's east coast, mainly from the Nicaraguan newspapers *La Prensa* and *Novedades.* Entries are arranged by subject.

45 **Sable, Martin Howard.** Latin American Jewry: a research guide. Cincinnati, Ohio, Hebrew Union College Press, 1978. 633 p. (Bibliographica Judaica, 6)

Contains a broad selection of scholarly and popular materials covering almost all aspects of the impact of Jewry in and on Latin America and its individual nations, regions and places from 1492 to 1974. Includes a directory of 433 periodical titles and a listing of general associations and organizations. This path-breaking bibliography of over 4420 items is a valuable addition to any research collection.

46 Saco, María Luisa. Fuentes para el estudio del arte peruano precolombino. Lima, Retablo de Papel, 1978. 261 p.

Bibliographical essay on the study of precolumbian Peruvian art. Refers to the 16th and 17th-century chronicles and 18th to 20th-century travels, studies and investigations. Pioneering efforts of Max Uhle and Julio C. Tello (begun in the late 19th century) are discussed. Final chapter provides a chronological classification to the ancient cultures of Peru. Onomastic, toponymic, and culture/style indexes are included.

Sánchez de Sánchez, Ofelia. Bibliografía anotada de las tesis sobre ingeniería forestal presentadas en la Universidad Distrital Francisco José de Caldas. See item **5518.**

47 Shaw, Bradley A. Latin American literature in English: 1975–1978. N.Y., Center for Inter-American Relations, 1979. 23 p. (Supplement to *Review 24*.)

A comprehensive list of US and British (only partially) books on Spanish American and Brazilian fiction, poetry, drama, or the literary essay in English translation. The list is a supplement to Shaw's *Latin American literature in English translation: an annotated bibliography* (N.Y., 1976). Works are divided into four sections: anthologies, individual works, additions, reprints of anthologies.

48 Sued Badillo, Jalil. Bibliografía para el estudio de los pueblos indígenas en el Caribe. Santo Domingo, Fundación García-Arévalo, 1977. 579 p. (Investigaciones, 8)

Includes works on indigenous groups in the Caribbean region, which encompasses the islands and the nearby continental areas. Each item is presented in separate sections on discipline (i.e., archaeology, ethnology, geography, history and linguistics) and by geographic location (e.g., Cuba, Hispaniola, Costa Rica). Each unique item appears at least twice in the bibliography. A useful working tool.

Sullivan, William M. and **Winfield J. Burggraaf** *comps.* El petróleo en Venezuela: una bibliografía. See item **3177.**

Tambs, Lewis A. Latin American geopolitics: a basic bibliography. See item **8601.**

49 Tantaleán Arbulú, Javier and **Augusto Pérez-Rosas Cáceres.** Referencias bibliográficas para el estudio de la economía peruana: 1830–1977. Lima, Consejo Nacional de Investigación, Fundación Friedrich Ebert, 1978. 244 p.

A listing of over 5900 items appearing in alphabetical order on the subject published since 1830. Directories to national and foreign institutional sources of information and a broad subject index are included. A brief overview, entitled "Historia Económica," prepared by Javier Tantaleán, places Peru's economic history in historical perspective.

50 United Nations. Comisión Económica para América Latina (CEPAL). **Biblioteca.** Bibliografía sobre la pobreza. Santiago, 1978. (E/CEPAL/LIB, 16 junio 1978)

A working list of 878 publications regarding the subject located in six institutional (mainly CEPAL or ECLA) libraries in Santiago. Subject, author and geographic location indexes are provided. The subject, poverty, is treated broadly in theme and geographic terms; compilation does not list primarily works specifically on Latin America.

51 ——. ——. Centro Latinoamericano de Documentación Económica y Social (CLADES). Bibliografía sobre promoción de exportaciones. Santiago, 1973. 371 p. (CLADES/BBG/7)

A listing of the titles of a small collection of works, more or less 800 items, published between 1969–71, used for consultation in the work of the promotion of exports program of ECLA. A subject index, using key-word-out-of-context (KWOX) arrangement, and an author index provide access to the material.

52 ——. ——. ——. Interpretaciones sociológicas y sociopolíticas del desarrollo de América Latina: bibliografía de 25 años. Santiago, 1975. 2 v. (658 p.) (Continuous pagination) (CLADES/BBG/8)

This listing of about 1500 entries concerns the politics and sociology of development and provides coverage in a variety of related subjects. Emphasizes social and cultural anthropology, economic development, social theory, sociological studies and the politics of development. The majority (85 percent) of entries was gleaned from information sources located in Santiago.

Valdéz Illescas, Raquel Yolanda. Bibliografía sobre el recurso agua en Guatemala. See item **5324.**

Vázquez, Verónica. Selección bibliográfica sobre los principales partidos políticos mexicanos: 1906–1970. See item **7148.**

Vescelius, Gary S. A bibliography of Virgin Islands archaeology. See item **523.**

53 Viñaza, Cipriano Muñoz y Manzano, *conde de la.* Bibliografía española de lenguas indígenas de América: Madrid, 1892. facsim. ed. Madrid, Atlas, 1977. 427 p.

A facsim. ed. of the famous 1892 work with preliminary notes on it and its compiler prepared by Carmelo Sáenz de Santa María (Instituto Gonzalo Fernández de Oviedo). A listing of 1188 works, including grammars, vocabularies, catechisms, sermons, etc., in Spanish and Portuguese, are divided into three sections: 1) imprints with exact dates; 2) imprints with century of publication known; and 3) imprints without known dates. Also includes indexes providing access to works by language, author, translator, and censors.

Vogt, Evon Z. Bibliography of the Harvard Chiapas Project: the first twenty years, 1957–1977. See item **983.**

Wagner, Erika and **Walter Coppens.** Quinta bibliografía antropológica reciente sobre Venezuela. See item **1209.**

54 Wilkinson, Audine. The Caribbean sugar industry: a select bibliography. Cave Hill, Barbados, Univ. of the West Indies, Institute of Social and Economic Research, Eastern Caribbean, 1976. 87 p. (Occasional bibliography series, 4)

Sugar has been the single most important product of the Caribbean since its Europeanization. This bibliography focuses on the historic, economic, agronomic, and technical aspects of the sugar industry; it includes references to books, chapters of books, articles, official and non-official documents, and theses. Items are classified according to territory and within each territory by subject. Locations of items listed are given.

LIBRARY SCIENCE AND SERVICES

55 Annual Conference of the Association of Caribbean University and Research Libraries, *III, Caracas, 1971.* Los recursos bibliotecarios para la investigación en el Caribe: documentos oficiales (Library resources for research in the Caribbean: official documents). San Juan, P.R., Association of Caribbean University and Research Libraries (ACURIL), 1978. 459 p., plates, tables.

As the title implies, this collection of papers presented at the ACURIL Meeting held in Caracas, Venezuela, in 1971, provides brief but useful assessments of the collections of various Caribbean research institutions in fields of the social sciences, political sciences, economics, education, law, medicine, agriculture, and literature. The information provided should be of value to those embarking on research on or in the area.

56 Congreso Nacional de Archivos de la República Argentina, *I, Buenos Aires, 1977.* Primer Congreso Nacional de Archivos de la República Argentina (Revista del Archivo General de la Nación [B.A.] 6:6, 1977, p. 66–182)

This is a record of the proceedings of the I National Congress of Argentine Archives held in B.A., 24–27 Aug. 1977. Contents describe sessions devoted to archival personnel, selection and classification of documents, archive administration, coordination among Argentine archives, and archives and modern technology.

57 Congresso Brasileiro de Biblioteconomia e Documentação, *VIII, Brasília, 1975.* A responsabilidade social da biblioteca no plano setorial da educação: pt. 1. Brasília, Associação dos Bibliotecarios do Distrito Federal [and] Univ. de Brasília, Faculdade de Estudos Sociais Aplicados, Depto. de Biblioteconomia, 1977. 575 p., tables (Revista de Biblioteconomia de Brasília, 5:1)

Pt. 1 of this report consists of brief summaries of papers presented at the Brazilian National Congress of Librarianship and Documentation. While most of the efforts pertain to national librarianship activities, universal themes (e.g., automation of serial records, development of library systems in Latin America, national research libraries, medical/scientific libraries, library education and universal bibliographic control) are discussed in single papers or in large group sessions. The entire volume provides an impressive array of contributions to the field of library science.

58 ————, *IX, Porto Alegre, Brazil, 1977.* Anais. v. 1, Temário libre. Porto Alegre, Brazil, n.p., 1977. 707 p., tables.

Contains a wide range of presentations relating to library science in general and in Brazil. Provides sections on technical processing, reference, documentation, library publications, university libraries, library systems, specialized libraries (e.g., science, law, agricultural), and the professional associations for librarians. Also includes articles devoted to library activities of some form at SUDENE, PETROBRÁS, the universities of Rio Grande and São Paulo and municipal libraries in São Paulo, Pernambuco and Paraná. Author and subject indexes are given.

59 García-Carranza, Araceli; Melba Arce; and Carmen Fernández Ballester. Las características tipológicas de la Biblioteca Nacional de Cuba en el período 1959–1976 (BNJM/R, 20:1, enero/abril 1978, p. 5–52, bibl., tables)

Detailed review of the development of the National Library of Cuba, especially since 1959. The article describes the variety of its programs and special subject collections (e.g., the periodical and newspaper collections, the international document collections, the map and atlas collection, manuscripts, visual arts, music, and the Cuban collection). In addition, the outreach programs of the Library, especially related to library development in the country, are described (e.g., cataloging, book buying, and bookmobile programs that further consolidate the Cuban library network). An informative contribution.

60 Jackson, William Vernon. Cooperation in Latin America (Library Trends [Univ. of Illinois, Library School, Urbana] 24:2, Oct. 1975, p. 379–397)

Describes cooperative library programs in Latin America, with specific regional and general area examples. A useful assessment of progress during early phases of program developments.

61 Jamaica. National Council on Libraries, Archives and Documentation Services. Plan for a national documentation, information and library system for Jamaica. Kingston, 1978. 83 p., illus.

Sets forth particular goals for a national system for library development in Jamaica. Includes nine working papers that reflect on various aspects of information and documentation plans (e.g., archives and records management, university library, data bases and automation, and publishing and production).

62 *El Papiro.* Organo de la Asociación Dominicana de Bibliotecarios (ASODOBI). No. 10, oct./dic. 1978–. Santo Domingo.

Quarterly journal of the Dominican Librarians Assn. contains useful information and news of library activities in the Dominican Republic. Available from: ASODOBI, Biblioteca Nacional, Calle César Nicolás Penson, Santo Domingo, Dominican Republic.

63 São Paulo (state), *Brazil.* **Secretaria da Cultura, Ciência e Tecnologia. Departamento de Artes e Ciências Humanas. Divisão de Bibliotecas.** Guia das bibliotecas do Estado de São Paulo, 1978. 399 p.

Lists libraries in the state by function (e.g., public, school, university and specialized). Also provides information on size of collection, readership, cataloging system and directors. Includes geographical and alphabetical indexes. The work was designed to identify and qualify the various state libraries in order to facilitate the study of current needs.

64 Vieira, Anna da Soledade and Etelvina Lima. A pós-graduação em biblioteconomia e a formação de uma liderança nacional (The role of post-graduate programs to develop national leadership in the library profession in Brazil) (Revista da Escola de Biblioteconomia [Univ. Federal de Minas Gerais, Belo Horizonte, Brazil] 6:1, março 1977, p. 125–135, bibl.)

Addresses the issue of the inefficient preparation of librarians in Brazil, citing poor educational objectives and a lack of recognition in formal library education. Proposes the implementation of post-graduate programs which would develop professional leadership and create a national policy for library education.

ACQUISITIONS, COLLECTIONS, CATALOGS

65 Abella, Rosa; Amelia Mederos; and Haydée Piedracueva *comps.* Index to the SALALM progress reports; 1956–1970. Amherst, Mass., Seminar on the Acquisition of Latin American Library Materials (SALALM), Secretariat, 1975. 163 p.

A valuable key to the wealth of information, of historical and current use, con-- tained in the annual reports of the first 15 years of SALALM's existence. The index provides access to the record of SALALM activities or to information on a specific topic of collection development, bibliographic compilation, acquisition methodology, and library science on or in Latin America.

66 Bibliographic guide to Latin American studies, 1978. v. 1, A–E; v. 2, F–O; v. 3, P–Z. Boston, Mass., G.K. Hall, 1979. 3 v. (656, 598, 565 p.)

Lists publications catalogued in 1978, regardless of publication date, by the Benson Latin American Collection, Univ. of Texas, supplemented by publications catalogued by the Library of Congress. Records from the Univ. of Texas' OCLC tapes and from the Library of Congress' MARC data base were used. All languages are represented in the guide, including Latin American Indian dialects. Book and non-book materials appear. Entries are arranged in alphabetical order by author, title, subject, and geographical location. The publication serves as the annual supplement to the *Catalog of the Latin American Collection of the University of Texas at Austin* (1969, supplements, 1971, 1973, 1975 and 1977).

67 Brazil. Conselho Nacional de Desenvolvimento Científico e Tecnológico. **Instituto Brasileiro de Informação em Ciência e Tecnologia** (IBICT). Catálogo colectivo de publicações periódicas em ciências sociais e humanidades. v. 1, A–H. v. 2, I–Z. Rio, 1978. 2 v. (738 p.) (Continuous pagination)

An impressive listing of over 14,400 serial titles obtained from the records of nearly 800 research collections in Brazil. Lists more than Latin American related titles.

————. **Ministério da Fazenda. Departamento de Administração. Divisão de Documentação.** Indicador das publicações do Ministério da Fazenda: 1968–1974. See item **3446.**

68 Brownrigg, Edwin Blake. Colonial Latin American manuscripts and transcripts in the Obadiah Rich Collection: an inventory and index. N.Y., The New York Public Library and Reader Books, 1978. 159 p.

This listing of the original and transcribed manuscripts in the Obadiah Rich collection in the New York Public Library serves as a useful guide for all research libraries. The collection contains items of interest from discovery to the 19th century, with emphasis in the mid-16th century and portions of the 17th and 18th centuries. The collection contains 103 separate sets with approximately 31,380 folio leaves. Name and chronological indexes are included.

69 Caron, Aimery. Inventory of French documents pertaining to the US Virgin Islands: 1642 to 1737. St. Thomas, US Virgin Islands, Bureau of Libraries, Museums and Archaeological Services, Dept. of Conservation and Cultural Affairs, 1978. 62 p. (Occasional paper, 3)

Inventory of documents found at the St. Thomas (Virgin Islands) Public Library and the Archives Nationales, Paris, in five series: $C^{10}D$, Box 2, Colonies, St. Croix; $F^3$58, Colonies, Virgin Islands; $C^{10}B$, Box 2, Colonies, St. Christopher; B, Colonies; C8A, Colonies; Martinique. Items are arranged in chronological order and provide the appropriate series locations. Includes personal names index.

70 Carvalho, Thereza de Sá; María Lucas Mattos and Margarida Querimurê Edelweiss Braga. Catálogo da Biblioteca Frederico Edelweiss. v. 1. Salvador, Brazil, Univ. Federal da Bahia, Centro de Estudos Baianos, 1975. 184 p., facsims.

Vol. 1 of a proposed multi-volume catalog of the 18,600 title Frederico Edelweiss library at the Bahian Univ. Items are arranged into broad disciplinary categories; a separate group of entries, Tupiguarani studies, appear initially.

71 Casa de las Américas, *La Habana.* **Biblioteca José A. Echevarría.** Bibliografía de Chile. La Habana, Editorial Orbe, 1977. 195 p.

Separate listings of books and periodicals on Chile contained in the collections of the Cuban Biblioteca José Antonio Echevarría. Books are arranged in alphabetical order by subject; Chilean periodicals appear in one alphabetical listing with holdings indicated.

Colombia. Ministerio de Educación Nacional. Instituto Colombiano para el Fomento de

la Educación Superior (ICFES). División de Documentación y Fomento Bibliotecario. Catálogo de tesis de la región central: ciencias biomédicas. See item **1644**.

72   Cottler, Susan M.; Roger M. Haigh; and Shirley A. Weathers. Preliminary survey of the Mexican Collection. Salt Lake City, Univ. of Utah Press, 1978. 163 p. (Finding aids to the microfilmed manuscript collection of the Genealogical Society of Utah, 1)

This is the first in a series of finding aids intended to make known and to increase usage of the extensive microfilm collections of manuscript materials on Latin America in the Society's holdings. The bulk of material filmed consists of civil and parish-registry records of births, marriages, deaths, etc., as well as Church administrative records, maps, letters, factory and guild records, and immigrant materials. The series will include preliminary surveys (as this one of Mexico), descriptive inventories and bibliographic guides (as the planned guide to the Casa de Morelos, the Library of the Archdiocese of Michoacan). This guide to Mexican materials identifies the 105,584 rolls of microfilm in the Society's collections providing Church-record coverage from the late-17th century to the 20th century and civil records from the mid-19th century to the present. Information given includes geographic locations of records and coverage and number of microfilm reels. Material is presented in geographic location in alphabetical order by state. An invaluable guide.

Documentação Amazônica: catálogo colectivo. See item **5619**.

73   Dorantes, Alma; José María Muriá; and Jaime Olveda. Inventario e índice de las misceláneas de la Biblioteca Pública del Estado de Jalisco. v. 1/3. Guadalajara, Mex., INAH, Centro Regional de Occidente, 1978. 3 v. (404, 260, 386 p.) (Col. Científica. Historia, 64)

A calendar to the contents of 810 miscellaneous collections in the Public Library of the Jalisco state, Mex. Includes pamphlets, political manifestos and decrees, pastoral letters, theses, essays, and separates from periodicals. Vast majority of the material is from the 19th century. A personal and geographic names index provides only access to inventory.

74   Dorn, Georgette M. Luso-Hispanic recordings at the Library of Congress (LARR, 14:2, Summer 1979, p. 174–179).

Describes the history, current activities, and research uses of the unique Archive of Hispanic Literature on Tape maintained in the Library's Hispanic Division. Among its more than 400 recordings are contributions by Pablo Neruda, Gabriela Mistral, Miguel Angel Asturias, Juan Ramón Jiménez, Vicente Aleixandre, Jorge Luis Borges, Nicolás Guillén, Jorge Amado, Gabriel García Márquez, Mario Vargas Llosa and Julio Cortázar. For additional information on the archive, see *The Archive of Hispanic Literature on Tape: A Descriptive Guide* (1974) annotated in *HLAS 36:14*.

75   Ecuador. Superintendencia de Bancos. Dirección de Información. Centro de Documentación. Biblioteca. Catálogo colectivo de publicaciones periódicas. Quito, 1978. 32 p.

Second ed. of a popular work related to documentation on banking, securities and other financial matters. Supplies information on center's holdings of journals, frequency of publication, and location of publisher.

76   Fontes, Lucy Gonçalves. Relação das coleções de documentos dos séculos XVIII e XIX existentes na cidade de Tiradentes (Lists of 18th and 19th century document collections in the city of Tiradentes, Minas Gerais, Brasil) (Revista da Escola de Biblioteconomia [Univ. Federal de Minas Gerais, Belo Horizonte, Brazil] 6:1, março 1977, p. 67–77)

Surveys the 18th and 19th-century document collections in the parish and municipal archives of Tiradentes, Minas Gerais, Brazil. Each contains valuable information on the history of this prosperous gold-mining town and important center of Church influence. Announces the future publication of catalogues for the Arquivo Paroquial de Tiradentes and the Arquivo da Câmara Municipal de São José del Rei.

77   Fundação Getúlio Vargas, Rio. Instituto de Documentação. Biblioteca. Guia de publicações da FGV: 1944–1974. Rio, 1974. 538 p.

A listing of 30 years of productive research at the Fundação Getúlio Vargas (i.e., books, pamphlets, articles, studies, reports, etc.). More than 1250 publications are noted; access is facilitated through author, subject, and title indexes. Includes a list of abbreviations and acronyms. The diversity of publications attests to the wide variety of subjects encompassed by FGV research.

78 García del Pino, César and Alicia Melis Cappa. Catálogo parcial de los fondos de la sección XI, Cuba, del Archivo General de Indias. La Habana, Editorial Orbe, 1978. 215 p.

An initial listing of Cuban materials in 322 legajos of the 2375 legajo Papeles de Cuba in Seville's Archivo General de Indias (AGI). Items are presented in numerical order within legajo. Includes title and date listing of Cuban maps and plans in Sec. XVI of the AGI. Separate general, personal names, and ships indexes are included.

79 Gorman de Alzate, Martha and Ximena Espinosa de Bermeo comps. Guía de editoriales, distribuidoras y librerías de Bogotá. Bogotá, Centro Regional para el Fomento del Libro en América Latina (CERLAL), 1977. 214 p.

This directory of 216 bookstores, publishers and distributors fulfills a need for those wishing to acquire Colombian materials. Includes list of publication outlets for specific foreign and domestic publishers, index to specialized book-dealers, and the basic questionnaire used to compile the volume's information. Updates the preliminary work prepared by the compilers and described in HLAS 39:78.

80 Guía de editores de idioma español: 1977. B.A., Turner Ediciones, 1977. 120 p.

A useful alphabetical listing of publishers in the Spanish language which includes under each publisher a listing of disciplinary specialities. Also provides an index of directors.

81 Herrmann, André and Gustav Siebenmann. Verzeichnis der Spanien, Portugal und Lateinamerika betreffenden Schweizer Hochschulschriften aus dem Gebiet der Geistes- und Sozialwissenschaften: 1897–1977: Habilitationsschriften (Tesis de doctorado y otras publicaciones universitarias realizadas en las Universidades de Suiza sobre temas de ciencias humanas y sociales refe-

rentes a España, Portugal e Iberoamérica: 1897–1977) (Iberoromania [Zeitschrift für die iberoromanischen Sprachen und Literaturen in Europa und Amerika, Max Niemeyer Verlag, Tübingen, FRG] 1 [Neue Folge] 1978, p. 118–130)

A selected listing of doctoral theses, inaugural lectures, and other university publications presented in nine Swiss universities since 1897. Only lists works in the humanities and social sciences of Spain, Portugal and Latin America.

82 Indice CENATE. Catálogo de teses universitarias brasileiras (Indice CENATE. Catalogue of Brazilian university theses). Informações, Microformas e Sistemas, Centro Nacional de Teses. Vol. 1, No. 2, 1977–. São Paulo.

A non-cumulative listing of 133 theses by Brazilians which are available on microfilm. Includes separate subject, author, institutional, and English-language indexes. Also notes offerings of microfilm or xerographic reproductions of selected catalogues, journals, out-of-print works, government publications, and musical scores. Theses as of 1978 are available from University Microfilms, Ann Arbor, Mich.

83 Mesa, Rosa Quintero comp. Latin American serial documents: a holding list. v. 7, Chile; v. 8, Ecuador; v. 9, Paraguay; v. 10, Peru; v. 11, Uruguay. Ann Arbor, Mich. Xerox University Microfilms 1973. 5 v. (327, 142, 61, 273, 169 p.)

This is a major bibliographical and research tool which provides access to government document holdings in 16 US university libraries, the New York Public Library and the Library of Congress. Documents listed include publications of the judicial, executive, or legislative branches of these five countries and their national museums, libraries, and universities as well as autonomous agencies organized or financed by all five governments. For vols. 1–6, see HLAS 31:48–50, HLAS 33:85, and HLAS 34:72–73. Volumes for Venezuela, Costa Rica, El Salvador, Guatemala, Honduras, Nicaragua, Panama, and Dominican Republic-Haiti (one volume) are projected.

84 Mundo Lo, Sara de comp. Colombian serial publications in the University of Illinois Library at Urbana-Champaign. Aus-

tin, Texas, Seminar on the Acquisition of
Latin American Library Materials (SALALM),
Secretariat, 1978. 130 p.

A checklist of the more than 500 current and ceased Colombian serial titles (with
holdings) available at the Univ. of Illinois.
Monographic serial titles identified as in the
library are also given. A synoptic history of
Colombian serials bibliographies as well as
an annotated bibliography of works consulted
in compiling the checklist have been appended. The collection of Colombian laws and
government annual reports date to the early
19th century; seven numbers of *El Alacrán*,
satirical periodical published by Germán
Gutiérrez de Piñeres and Joaquín Pablo Posada
in 1849, appear in their original form. The
work was prepared as a contribution to the XX
Seminar on the Acquisition of Latin American Library Materials (SALALM) held in
Bogotá, June 1975.

85 Nuevo León (state), *Mexico*. **Oficilía
Mayor. Dirección del Registro Civil. Archivo General del Estado. Asuntos Eclesiásticos.** Indice y catálogos de la Sección Asuntos
Eclesiásticos existentes en el Archivo General del Estado: 1568–1874. Monterey, Mex.,
1979. 48 p.

A calendar of the contents of the ecclesiastical section of the state archives. The
eight boxes of material described contain indispensable information for the study of
church and state relations in Nuevo León. A
names' index is included.

**86 Organization of American States. Sec-
retaría General.** Catálogo de informes y
documentos técnicos de la OEA: 1974–
1976. Washington, 1977. 127 p. (SG/Ser.
A/III.1 rev. 1 1974–1976)

Includes citations for technical reports
and studies which were issued in 1974–76
and not included in the Official Records Series
or offered for sale in the Catalog of Publications. Includes technical reports from services, studies prepared under contract, final
reports of seminars and workshops, papers
presented by OAS staff members at national
and international meetings, external studies
and technical reports, theses or studies prepared by OAS fellowship holders. An author-
title-subject index appears.

87 ———. ———. Catálogo de informes
y documentos técnicos de la OEA:

Suplemento 1977. Washington, 1978. 89 p.
(SG/Ser. A/III.1 Supl. 1977)

The first annual supplement to the
1974–76 catálogo described in item **86**.

88 ———. ———. Documentos oficiales
de la Organización de los Estados
Americanos. v. 16, Indice analítico: enero/dic.
1975. Washington, 1978. 160 p. (OEA/Ser.
Z/II.1)

Invaluable index to the general list of
documents published in 1975 by the OAS.
Access through subject, personal names, and
geographic location is provided.

89 ———. ———. Documentos oficiales
de la Organización de los Estados
Americanos. v. 17, Lista general de documentos: enero/dic. 1976; v. 18, Lista general de
documentos: enero/dic. 1977. Washington,
1978/1979. 2 v. (196, 219 p.) (OEA/Ser.Z/I.1)

A series arrangement of OAS documents, including those of limited and general
distribution, which appeared in 1976 and
1977. The table of contents provides access to
material through the series. A list of acronyms precedes the compilation.

90 Pagán Jiménez, Neida. Los recursos
bibliotecarios sobre el Caribe en Puerto
Rico. Austin, SALALM Secretariat, Univ. of
Texas Library, 1979. 14 p., bibl., (XXIV SAL-
ALM Working Paper B-3) (mimeo)

Briefly describes the collections of important institutional, academic, governmental, and public libraries in Puerto Rico
pertaining to the Caribbean. Descriptions of
the Caribbean Regional Library and the General Library of Puerto Rico are especially
useful to the researcher. The paper was submitted to the XXIV Seminar on the Acquisition of Latin American Library Materials,
UCLA, 17–22 June 1979.

91 Peru. Biblioteca Nacional. Catálogo
de autores de la Colección Peruana. v.
1/5, Libros y folletos; v. 6, Publicaciones periódicas: mapas y planos. Boston, Mass., G.K.
Hall, 1979. 6 v. (809, 835, 785, 725, 783,
762 p.)

Vols. 1/5 represent 424 years of bibliographic production from 1553–1977 and
include listing of books, pamphlets, theses,
maps and serials housed in the National Library of Peru. Vol. 6 is a listing, by geographical location in alphabetical order, of

the nearly 1400 maps in the collections of the National Library. Main strengths are in 20th-century general maps and city plans. These volumes include a wide variety of languages and native dialects in addition to the collection of Paul Rivet, the French anthropologist. Also part of the Biblioteca's Colección Peruana but not identified separately are the collections of Félix Cipriano, Coronel Zegarra, Raúl Porras Barrenechea, Ricardo Palma, Luis Alayza y Paz Soldán, José María Eguren and Agustín P. Justo. No subject access is provided. This is an impressive collection of materials on and by Peruvians, especially in view of the fact that the Library and its collections were destroyed in 1943 and had to be recollected.

92 Placer, Xavier and **Nellie Figueira** *comps.* Publicações da Biblioteca Nacional: catálogo, 1873–1974. Rio, Biblioteca Nacional, 1975. 128 p., illus. (Col. Rodolfo García. Série B: catálogos e bibliografias)

A listing of the 531 titles of books, pamphlets, periodicals, albums and a map published by the Brazilian National Library since 1873. The publications cover the breadth of the Library's collections and include works in the fields of literature, history, biography, geography, music, iconography, folklore, botany, administration, and legislation. Provides multiple access to publications through the onomastic index.

93 Pouncey, Lorene. The Library Convent of Ocopa (LARR, 8:3, 1978, p. 147–154, illus.)

A brief description of the library of the 250 year old Franciscan Monastery at Ocopa, Peru. This outstanding catalogued collection of more than 20,000 Latin and Spanish titles from the 16th to the 18th century covers the fields of history, geography, philosophy science, medicine, literature, religion and theology.

94 Rodríguez de Lebrija, Esperanza. Indice analítico de la guía del Archivo Histórico de Hacienda. México, Archivo General de la Nación, Archivo Histórico de Hacienda, 1975 [i.e. 1976]. 511 p. (Col. Documental, 2)

A convenient index to the *Guía del Archivo Histórico de Hacienda: siglos XVI-XIX* compiled by Agustín Hernández in 1940. Provides access by subject, proper names,

geographic entities, collections and legajos and also includes dates of documentation.

95 Sánchez Quell, Hipólito. Los 50,000 documentos paraguayos llevados al Brasil. Asunción, Comuneros, 1976. 163 p.

An impassioned plea by a Paraguayan historian for the return of the Paraguayan archival material confiscated by the Brazilians during the War of the Triple Alliance, sent to Rio Branco in 1869, and now in the Brazilian National Library. Lists major portions of this collection. Compilation is based on *Catálogo de la colección Visconde de Río Branco*, Rio, 1950.

96 Tejerina Carreras, Ignacio G. El Archivo del Arzobispado de Córdoba: breve guía para el conocimiento de la documentación existente (JPHC/R, 5, 1977, p. 147–172)

A brief account of records found in the Archives of the Archdiocese of Córdoba (Arg.) and the dioceses of Río Cuarto, Villa María, San Francisco and Cruz del Eje from as early as 1566 to the mid-20th century. Among the material are parish records of baptisms, confirmations, matrimonies and deaths; various registers; account books; communications of bishops and other religious; and administrative matters. A useful introduction to important research materials. For further information, the researcher should consult Aurelio Tanodi's "Guía de los Archivos de Córdoba" (see *HLAS 32:2630a*).

97 Velazquez, María del Carmen. Bibliographical essay: the Colección SepSetentas (AAFH/TAM, 35:3, Jan. 1979, p. 373–390)

A general review of the composition of the 315 volumes of the Colección SepSetentas published by the Mexican Dept. of Public Education during the 1970–76 presidential term of Luis Echeverría. While the quality of the publications is uneven, the collection includes impressive works on historical, anthropological, sociological, economic and geographic themes. Works on the 19th-century history of Mexico were most popular. The review article also includes a listing of the titles published and the size of each printing.

98 Yhmoff Cabrera, Jesús. Catálogo de obras manuscritas en Latín de la Biblioteca Nacional de México. México, UNAM,

Instituto de Investigaciones Bibliográficas, 1975. 459 p., plates, tables (Serie guías, 4)

A valuable and impressive identification of some 648 Latin manuscripts (1573–1798) found in the National Library of México. The number of items increases chronologically with the most abundant found in the 18th century. Manuscripts by Jesuits are most common with theological treatises by Diego Marín de Alcázar, Juan Diego de Ledesma and Antonio Núñez among the best. The catalog provides author, title, location, full citation, and a synopsis of each manuscript; materials are presented in alphabetical order by author. Topographical, chronological (including items without year or dates), depositories prior to the National Library, subject, and names of persons and sites indexes facilitate use of catalog.

REFERENCE WORKS & RESEARCH

99   Avilés, Jimmy. Publicaciones periódicas de Granada (BNBD, 8, nov./dic. 1975, p. 14–18)

A record of 30 periodicals published in Granada, Nicaragua, during various times since 1907. Provides, where available, the dates of the first and last number, known examples, editors and major contributors.

Borisov, Eugenio Filippovich and others. Diccionario de economía política. See item 2769.

100   Brow, Bill H. Directory of Latin Americanists in Kansas: 1978–1979. Lawrence, The Univ. of Kansas, Tri-University Center of Latin American Studies, 1979. 1 v. (Unpaged)

A listing of 300 specialists affiliated with colleges and universities in Kansas who have a professional involvement with Latin America. Includes institution, faculty standing, academic degree, and teaching and research areas of interest for each person.

101   Civeira Taboada, Miguel and María Elena Bribiesca. Guía descriptiva de los ramos que constituyen el Archivo General de la Nación. México, Archivo General de la Nación, Depto. de Publicaciones, 1977, 124 l.

An alphabetical listing of the various collections of the archives; a total of 159 collections are listed and described briefly.

Relationships of materials throughout the publication are indicated by references. The work is not indexed.

102   Cladinex. Resúmen de documentos CEPAL/ILPES. Organización de las Naciones Unidas. Comisión Económica para América Latina (CEPAL), Centro Latino-americano de Documentación Económica y Social (CEDES). Vol. 1, No. 1, 1977–. Santiago.

Lists over 850 publications of CEPAL and ILPES issued 1970–76, and divided into two parts: "Resúmenes" and "Índice." Includes indexes on subject, author, institutions, title, geographic location, series, and conferences. Work is designed to disseminate the thought of CEPAL (ECLA) throughout the area and to contribute to the transfer and the exchange of socioeconomic information of the region. There are plans to publish indexes at more frequent intervals.

103   Coffin, Jean Hawkins and Crystal Graham. Latin American studies research guide. Bloomington, Indiana Univ., Latin American Studies Program, 1978. 139 p. (Latin American studies working papers, 8)

Intended as a guide to selected reference sources which will serve as starting points for research in Latin American studies. Chapters are divided according to disciplines. Includes author/title index.

104   Cox, Barbara ed. HAPI: Hispanic American Periodicals Index, 1976. Los Angeles, Univ. of California, UCLA Latin American Center Publications, 1979. 608 p.

This annual listing provides separate subject and author access to all articles appearing in more than 200 journals containing contributions on Latin America. Only the pure and technical sciences have been excluded. Journals included in this volume were published in 1976, although some bear earlier dates because of delayed or irregular publication schedules. An international panel of indexers perform the compilation task. Journals published in Latin America are indexed in full; only articles on Latin America in journals from other regions appear. Spanish and Portuguese translations of subject headings are given. Lists journals reviewed. An important bibliographic tool for access to journal articles.

105 Cuba. Ministerio de Cultura. Biblioteca Nacional José Martí. Departamento de Hemeroteca e Información de Humanidades. El Equipo Bibliográfico Carlos M. Trelles. Indice general de publicaciones periódicas cubanas. t. 5, Humanidades y ciencias sociales. La Habana, 1977. 329 p.

Vol. 5 in a series of indexes to periodical articles lists more than 4300 articles appearing in 1973 (some in 1972) in 67 Cuban serials. The section on social sciences and general contain 2790 entries alone. Citations are arranged by subject within each section; separate sections on social sciences and general; folklore, linguistics and literature; writers, poets, newspapermen, novelists, songwriters; plastic arts; interviews, etc., with artists; cinema; music and ballet; interviews, etc., with singers, musicians, dancers; sports and sport figures appear. Includes an author index. Articles listed are not necessarily about Cuba or Cubans.

106 *Documentación Socioeconómica Centroamericana.* Confederación Universitaria Centroamericana (CSUCA), Programa Centroamericano de Ciencias Sociales, Centro de Documentación Económica y Social de Centroamérica (CEDESC). No. 1, dic. 1978–. San José.

Prepared by the Centro de Documentación Económica y Social de Centroamérica (CEDESC) to disseminate information contained in the publications of its collection on the economic and social development of Central America. Materials are keyed through a subject index. As part of its continuing effort, CEDESC provides computerized bibliographies and photocopies of documents in its holdings. It also continues to develop its collection of important documents related to the Central American region.

107 El Salvador. Ministerio de Obras Públicas. Instituto Geográfico Nacional Pablo Arnoldo Guzmán. Guía para investigadores: República de El Salvador. San Salvador, Instituto Panamericano de Geografía e Historia, 1977. 81 p., illus., maps.

Useful listing of 756 works related to the physical, economic, and human geography of the country. Provides keys to completed topographical and cadastral mapping and aerial photography by scale. An important update to earlier OAS inventory.

108 Emprêsa Brasileira de Pesquisa Agropecuária (EMBRAPA). Departamento de Informação (DID). Siglas agropecuárias brasileiras. Brasília, 1977. 308 p.

A listing, by alphabetical order of acronym, of 1591 entities in Brazil concerned with agricultural matters. A useful reference tool.

Ferraro, Oscar. Datos y estudios sobre educación en el Paraguay. See item **4537**.

109 Freudenthal, Juan R. Caribbean acronym list. Austin, SALALM Secretariat [and] Univ. of Texas, Latin American Collection, 1979, 6 p. (XXIV SALALM Working Paper, C-4) (mimeo)

Lists 61 acronyms related to Caribbean bibliography, library science, and documentation in alphabetical sequence. Entries are provided with historical and descriptive annotations and are cross-referenced. The paper was submitted to the XXIV Seminar on the Acquisition of Latin American Library Materials, Univ. of California, Los Angeles, 17–22 June 1979.

110 ——— and Patricia M. Freudenthal *eds. and comps.* Index to anthologies of Latin American literature in English translation. Boston, Mass., G.K. Hall, 1977. 199 p., bibl.

This is an index to 116 anthologies of Latin American literature translated into English. It identifies the efforts of 1122 Spanish American and Brazilian writers. Authors born on or after 1850 appear. Translator and geographic indexes are included. An annotated and selective readings list accompanies the work.

111 Friedemann, Nina S. de and Jaime Arocha *comps.* Bibliografía anotada y directorio de antropólogos colombianos. Bogotá, Sociedad Antropológica de Colombia, 1979. 441 p.

Lists in chronological order and by author publications by practicing professional Colombian anthropologists. Each entry is given extensive annotation. Subject and subfield indexes are included. Includes a directory of Colombian anthropologists, defined as degree-holding and residents of the country for at least 10 years, with biographical and bibliographical information. The work is introduced by a useful essay on the methodology employed in the preparation of the bibliography and a brief analysis of Colombian anthropological research.

112 Gardini, Marília Júnia de Almeida. Fontes de informação cartográfica no Brasil (Sources of cartographic information in Brasil) (Revista da Escola de Biblioteconomia [Univ. Federal de Minas Gerais, Belo Horizonte, Brazil] 6:1, março 1977, p. 45–65, bibl.)

Defines the relationship between the mapped area and the total area of Brazil. Notes sources of cartographic information in Brazil, produced by federal, state and private bodies. Includes indication of various types of maps published.

113 González Gisbert, Manuel. El catecismo de indios de Cuenca (El Libro Español [Instituto Nacional del Libro Español, Madrid] 247, julio 1978, p. 355–358, plates)

A brief but informative description of the rare and thought to be lost catechism. It was one of the earliest printed works in South America.

114 Gordillo y Ortiz, Octavio. Diccionario biográfico de Chiapas. México, B. Costa-Amic Editor, 1977. 295 p.

Contains biographical and bibliographical information on over 300 individuals identified with the Chiapas region. This is a well researched and useful compilation.

115 Graham, Ann Hartness. Subject guide to statistics in the Presidential Reports of the Brazilian provinces: 1830–1889. Austin, The Univ. of Texas, Institute of Latin American Studies, 1977. 454 p. (Guides and bibliographies series, 9)

The guide lists nearly 1100 annual reports, arranged chronologically by province. They were originally delivered by Brazilian presidents to the opening session of 20 provincial legislatures. An index, providing state access to the wide range of subjects found in the reports, is a necessary addition. Author indicates the library sources for all items listed.

116 Grow, Michael. Scholars' guide to Washington D.C.: Latin American and Caribbean studies. Washington, Smithsonian Institution Press, Woodrow Wilson International Center for Scholars, Latin American Program, 1979. 346 p.

An indispensable reference tool for those interested in utilizing the rich resources of Washington. Separate sections examine collections and organizations. Among collections described are libraries, archives and manuscript depositories, art-film-music-and map collections, and data banks. The section on organizations describes public and private entities which are related to Latin America and are potential sources of information or assistance to researchers. The *Guide's* topical coverage concentrates on the disciplines of the social sciences and humanities, although the fields of science and technology are included where relevant. The geographic scope includes not only Iberic Latin America but also former and current Caribbean possessions of European nations. Coverage does not include research resources for Chicano or Hispanic-American studies.

117 Hallewell, Laurence ed. Latin American bibliography. London, Univ. of London, Institute of Latin American Studies *for the* SCONUL Latin American Group, 1978. 227 p.

An introductory guide to research in Latin American topics. Contains references to general works, topically arranged in chapters, useful to the beginning Latin American researcher.

118 Hernández, Manuel comp. Indice general de los números 31–101 de la revista *Cultura Universitaria* de la U.C.V., mayo 1952–diciembre 1975. Mérida, Univ. de los Andes, Facultad de Humanidades y Educación, Instituto de Investigaciones Literarias Gonzálo Picón Febres, 1978. 413 p.

Provides subject and author access to the 71 issues of a journal published by the Univ. Central de Venezuela, Cultura Universitaria. Most popular type of articles appearing are in literature (i.e., poetry, novel, literary criticism).

119 *Indice de Ciências Sociais.* Instituto Universitario de Pesquisas do Rio de Janeiro. Ano 1, No. 1, julho 1979–. Rio.

Principal objective of this journal is to abstract scholarly articles on sociology and political science in order to facilitate research. The articles are by national authors on Brazil, Latin America, current affairs on matters dated no earlier than 1930. Items cited have appeared no earlier than six months prior to publication of the index. Also includes indexes by subject, author, key-word in title, and periodicals. Entries in this number were gleaned from 14 Brazilian scholarly journals.

120 Inventario dos documentos relativos ao Brasil existentes na Biblioteca Nacional de Lisboa (BRBN/A, 97, 1977, p. 9–284)

This is the fourth inventory of Brazilian materials housed in Portugal's National Library. For previous ones, see other issues of Anais da Biblioteca Nacional (Rio, vol. 75, p. 1534–1692 and vol. 93, p. 1693–1702, p. 1723–1825). Material is presented in chronological order with locations provided. Also includes onomastic index.

121 **Kutscher, Gerdt.** Berlín como Centro de Estudios Americanistas: ensayo bio-bibliográfico. Berlin, FRG, Ibero-Amerikanisches Institut, 1976. 72 p., bibl., tables (Indiana Beiheft, 7)

A bio-bibliographic record of the efforts of German specialists who have studied Latin America since Baron von Humboldt. This work is an amplified version of the author's 1966 article, which appeared in the Jahrbuch der Stiftung Preussischer Kulturbesitz (vol. 4).

Lambert, Claire M. ed. and comp. Village studies: data analysis and bibliography. See item **9032.**

122 Latin America in Books. Univ. of New Orleans, Dept. of Anthropology and Geography. Vol. 2, No. 1, Jan. 1979–. New Orleans, La.

Lists works published in 1978 in the US on Latin American themes. Titles, with a selected number annotated, are arranged into broad subjects; there is no country access. Future issues will feature US publications released within five months of this bibliography; articles on Latin American bibliography are anticipated.

123 **León de Leal, Magdalena.** Personas interesadas en la problemática femenina en Perú, Argentina, Brasil y Venezuela (LARR, 14:1, 1979, p. 134–144)

Provides information on researchers and institutions engaged in research on the subject. The type of research in progress is indicated.

124 **Lindvall, Karen.** Research in Mexico City: a guide to selected libraries and research centers. San Diego, Univ. of Califor-

nia, Instructional Services Dept., 1977. 45 p.

Describes 15 libraries and research centers for the study of Mexican history and literature, their location and access to them. Useful introductory guide.

125 **Louis, Dionel** and **Michèle Montas.** Bibliographie: 1957–1977; index des textes et articles parus dans Conjonctions (IFH/C, 138, mai 1978, p. 97–135)

An index to articles on arts and letters, bibliography, culture and societies, economics and development, history (documents), language and education, and science and technology appearing in Haiti's leading intellectual journal between 1957 and 1977. Prominent among the contributions are those made by Max Bissainthe (bibliography), Pradel Pompilus (literature) and Roger Gaillard (culture).

126 **Marcus, Joyce** and **Ronald Spores.** The Handbook of Middle American Indians: a retrospective look (AAA/AA, 80:1, March 1978, p. 85–100)

This is a thorough review of the multivolume Handbook of Middle American Indians (vols. 1/16) which provides not only an assessment of the content and preparation of the individual volumes but also information on the history of the project and its realization. The reviewers consider the work a valuable addition to the study of the field and propose the compilation of regular supplements which would identify new trends and activities.

127 **Mazzei de Grazia, Leonardo.** Un artículo inédito de Don Guillermo Feliú Cruz: presentación de un libro útil a la bibliografía chilena (Revista de Historia [Univ. de Concepción, Chile] Instituto de Antropología, Historia y Geografía, 2:2, 1977, p. 43–55)

A posthumous printing of Guillermo Feliú Cruz' article, "Presentación . . . ," on the origins and development of Chilean national bibliographical efforts. The author describes the groundbreaking efforts of Ramón Briseño in 1862 and 1879, the extraordinary output of José Toribio Medina in the late 19th and early 20th century, and the appearance of the Anuario de la Prensa from 1886. A useful summary of the subject.

128 **Mevis, René** comp. Inventory of Caribbean studies: an overview of social research on the Caribbean conducted by

Antillean, Dutch and Surinamese scholars in the period 1945–1973. Leiden, The Netherlands, Royal Institute of Linguistics and Anthropology, Caribbean Dept. 1974. 181 p., bibl.

A record of Dutch production on the Caribbean. Includes: 1) listing of specialists in the Netherlands, the Netherlands Antilles, and Surinam; 2) social research from 1945–73 and works in progress; 3) bibliography of Caribbean studies in the social sciences; and 4) unpublished graduate theses in the field by Antillean, Dutch and Surinamese students. Research in the Netherlands was mainly in economic, socio-historical, sociological and anthropological fields; economic research has shown the most vigorous growth. A useful record of the state of the art in the Netherlands. For anthropologist's comment, see *HLAS 37:1262.*

129   Miranda, Alvaro comp. *Revista de las Indias:* 1936–1950. Bogotá, Instituto Colombiano de Cultura, 1978. 469 p. (Col. Autores nacionales. Serie las revistas)

A potpourri of selections taken from various issues of the noted Colombian intellectual journal which was founded in July 1936 and ended in Dec. 1950. Includes articles by German Arciniegas; Abelardo Forero Benavides; Rafael Maya; Gonzalo París Lozano; Gustavo Samper; and a final article by Jorge Zalamea on the "Piedras y Cielo" group.

Montoya, Amanda; Juan María Hidalgo and **Ernestina Rojas de C.** Indice colombiano de educación: 1905–1973. See item **4437.**

130   Nicaragua. Instituto Geográfico Nacional. Guía de recursos básicos para estudios de desarrollo en Nicaragua. Managua, Instituto Panamericano de Geografía e Historia, 1977. 86 p., maps.

Describes and provides key to aerial photography, geologic, topographic and planimetric mapping, by scale. Includes listing of works on the physical, economic and human geography of the country. An important update to the earlier OAS inventory.

Parker, Franklin and **Betty June Parker** eds. and *comps.* Education in Puerto Rico and of Puerto Ricans in the U.S.A.: abstracts of American doctoral dissertations. See item **4554.**

131   Personalities Caribbean: the international guide to who's who in the West Indies, Bahamas and Bermuda, 1977/1978. 6. ed. Kingston, 1977. 1064 p.

Useful biographical guide to selected individuals of the Caribbean, Bahamas and Bermuda. A classification by professions appears after each island listing.

132   Posada, Joaquín de. Anuario de familias cubanas: directorio internacional. San Juan, P.R., Art Printing, 1977. 1353 p., illus.

A biannual listing of Cuban families living in exile; professions, addresses of residences, and family complements are given.

133   *Referativa.* Ministerio de Educación, Centro de Documentación e Información Pedagógica. Año 2, No. 4, enero/abril 1975–. La Habana.

Provides abstracts of selected articles on education. Cites many East European journals and includes subject and author indexes.

134   Ríos, José. Breve biografía de intelectuales uruguayos. Montevideo, Talleres Gráficos de Shera'a, 1978. 125 p.

Provides useful data on a selected group of Uruguayan writers, artists, musicians, historians and newspapermen. Lacks any indication of the criteria applied in the selection of those listed.

135   Roa Santana, Manuel de Jesús comp. Indice de publicaciones periódicas de universidades dominicanas. Santo Domingo, Instituto Tecnológico de Santo Domingo, 1978. 152 p. (Serie bibliográfica, 1)

Provides subject and author access to articles in seven journals, the Dominican Republic: *Aula; Ciencia; Ciencia y Sociedad; Derecho y Política; Eme Eme; Revista de la Facultad de Ciencias Agronómicas y Veterinarias;* and *Pequeño Universo de la Facultad de Humanidades.* Covers period 1971–July 1977. The appendixes list publications by the following: INTEC; Univ. Autónoma de Santo Domingo; Univ. Católica; Univ. Central del Este; and Univ. Pedro Henríquez Ureña.

136   Rodríguez Masís, René and **Antonio Acevedo E.** Indice selectivo de la prensa literaria: mayo 1972–agosto 1978 (BNBD, 25, sept./oct. 1978, p. 95–192)

Indexes 1346 articles in *La Prensa Literaria*, a supplement to the daily newspaper *La Prensa* (Managua). Thematic and onomastic indexes facilitate research. A useful overview to literary themes in Nicaragua, Central America and Latin America during the past six years.

137   Sable, Martin Howard. A guide to nonprint materials for Latin American studies. Detroit, Mich., Blaine Ethridge Books, 1979. 141 p.

This useful introductory work to nonprint material presents relevant guides and descriptions along three divisions: 1) general reference tools; 2) guides and aids for the study of Latin America with concern to nonprint materials; and 3) items dealing wholly with Latin America and its individual nations. Notes guides to films, slides, photographs, phonorecords, paintings, multi-media sets, maps, microforms and US museum collections. Entries are annotated.

138   Seckinger, Ron and F.W.O. Morton. Social science libraries in greater Rio de Janeiro (LARR, 14:3, 1979, p. 180–201)

Describes 64 research libraries, providing useful information on collection sizes, hours of service, personnel, and copying facilities. All libraries listed are open to the public. Two newspaper archives and another which is a research center are included because of their particular value to the social sciences. All institutions are located in Rio, except for two in Niterói and one in Petrópolis.

Sociedad Geográfica de Colombia, *Bogotá.* Indice por autores del *Boletín de la Sociedad Geográfica de Colombia* del No. 1 al No. 100: 1903–1973. See item 5523.

139   Spain. Instituto de Cultura Hispánica. Centro Iberoamericano de Cooperación Universitaria y Científica. Guía de estudios superiores de Iberoamerica. Madrid, Ediciones Cultura Hispánica, 1973. 508 p.

A useful listing of the institutions of higher education in Latin America, by country, and the disciplines taught. Also includes index that classifies institutions by disciplines.

140   United Nations. Comisión Económica para la América Latina (CEPAL). Centro Latinoamericano de Documentación Eco-

nómica y Social (CLADES). Directorio del medio ambiente en América Latina y el Caribe: versión preliminar. Santiago, 1976. 122 p. (CLADES/Ins. 6 agosto 1976)

A listing by country of institutional and governmental associations related to environmental matters which answers the growing interest in the region's environmental problems and which will facilitate communication among specialists. Provides complete addresses of most of the institutions listed.

141   United States. Central Intelligence Agency. National Foreign Assessment Center. Directory of the Cuban Government and Mass Organizations: a reference aid. Washington, 1977. 129 p., map (CR77-16183)

Guide to the administrative structure of the Cuban government and various official and mass organizations with names of incumbent key personalities. Information current as of Oct. 1977. Supersedes CIA's March 1974 list.

142   ———. Department of Agriculture. Latin American Branch. International Economics Division. Economics, Statistics and Cooperatives Service. Indices of agricultural production for the Western Hemisphere excluding the United States and Cuba: 1969 through 1978. Washington, 1979. 33 p. (Statistical bulletin, 622)

A compilation of useful statistical data on food and agricultural production in the Western Hemisphere and within individual nations. Includes data on production by commodity, value and indices of total agricultural and food production from 1969–78 for 22 Latin American nations.

143   Whittingham W. L. and L. Bushy. Economic activity in Caribbean countries: 1976. Santiago, Economic Commission for Latin America (ECLA), Office for the Caribbean, 1977. 1 v. (Various pagings) tables (ECLA/CARIB 77/5)

The report is an attempt to analyze and to disseminate information on current economic trends and developments in the Caribbean Community and to identify the determinants of those trends. Includes general assessment of activities and separate economic surveys (or "country notes") for the Bahamas, Grenada, Surinam, Barbados, Belize, Guyana, Jamaica, Trinidad & Tobago, and the West Indies Associated States. Efforts are underway to include data on Cuba, the Dominican Republic and Haiti in subsequent issues. Although the report is hampered by the unavailability of certain information and the narrow scope of the statistics collected, it provides a myriad of useful data.

144 Woods, Richard D. and **Grace Alvarez-Altman.** Spanish surnames in the Southwestern United States: a dictionary. Boston, Mass., G.K. Hall, 1978. 154 p.

Provides definitions and origins of popular selected Spanish surnames of the US Southwest. A useful introductory reference work.

145 Wright, Ione S. and **Lisa M. Nekhom.** Historical dictionary of Argentina. Metuchen, N.J., Scarecrow Press, 1978. 1113 p., bibl., maps (Latin American historical dictionaries, 17)

Excellent reference tool for specialists and generalists. Source for brief descriptions of figures, events and places important in the history and culture of the country. Includes a chronology of past presidents and an informative bibliography.

GENERAL WORKS

146 Belize. Independence Secretariat. Belize: new nation in Central America. Belize, 1972. 72 p., facsim., illus., maps, plates, tables.

Short introduction to Belize covering geographical, socioeconomic, and political aspects. [A. Suárez]

147 Black, Jan Knippers and others. Area handbook for Cuba. 2. ed. Washington, The American Univ., Foreign Area Studies, 1976. 550 p., bibl., illus., maps (DA Pam 550–152)

This updated version of the popular 1971 publication chronicles major administrative, diplomatic and commercial transformations experienced in Cuba by 1976. Separate bibliographies containing works on social, political, economic, and national security topics include mainly current publications. A useful general work.

148 Blutstein, Howard I. and others. El Salvador: a country study. Washington, The American Univ., Foreign Area Studies,

1979. 260 p., bibl., illus., maps (DA Pam 550-150)

This reprinting of the 1970 handbook of El Salvador follows the format of other volumes in the area handbook series. No new information on development in the 1970s has been added.

149 Brasseur, Gérard. La Guyane Française: un bilan de trente années. Paris, Secrétariat Général du Gouvernement, Direction de la Documentation Française, 1978. 184 p., bibl., maps, tables (Notes et études documentaires, 4497/4498)

An informative general work providing insights to geography, administrative and financial organization, and economic and social activities of French Guiana. The political and economic data are especially useful. A necessary addition to the literature on the area.

150 Cau, Jean and **Jacques Bost** *comps.* Nagel encyclopédie de voyage: Brésil. 13. ed. Geneva, Les Editiones Nagel, 1978. 450 p., fold. maps, maps.

An informative tourist guide that provides an introduction to Brazilian culture through its history, art, geography, administrative divisions, folklore, etc. Sections of the guide are devoted to descriptions of the states or regions and major cities. Includes key maps of city centers and of the country in general, useful addresses in each major city, and a selected list of hotels.

Coleção Nosso Brazil: Estudos Sociais. See item **5614.**

151 Cozean, Jon D. Latin America 1979. Washington, Stryker-Post, 1979. 107 p. (World today series)

Presents general overviews of Latin American and national issues. Brief descriptions of each country are provided. Useful introductory reference.

Educación U.P.B. See item **4315.**

Ensaios de Opinião. See item **7532.**

Figueiredo, Napoleão. Amazônia: tempo e gente. See item **1141.**

Haiti. Institut Haitien de Statistique. Départmente des Finances et des Affaires Économiques. Guide économique de la Republique d'Haiti. See item **3032.**

152   *Latin America Ronshu.* Univ. Sofia,
      Sociedad Japonesa de Ciencias Sociales
de Latinoamérica. No. 11/12, 1978–. Tokyo.
   Japanese language journal devoted to
Latin America which includes a wide range of
articles on the social sciences. Compiled by
Yasuhiko Sano and Yoichi Ishii.

153   **Manigat, Leslie F.** *ed.* The Caribbean
      Yearbook of international relations:
1976. Leiden, The Netherlands, A.W. Sijthoff
[and] IIR-UWI, Port of Spain, 1977. 613 p.
   The second annual review of the Caribbean's international relations. Includes
studies on the region's problems, issues and
debates, book reviews and selected documents
on international relations. Provides a combination of current information and reflective
thoughts on this theme. Excellent source of
information.

154   **Martínez, José Luis.** Los estudios nor-
      teamericanos sobre México (CM/D, 86,
marzo/abril 1979, p. 12–14)
   Basis of the article is the record of US
doctoral dissertations on Mexican themes produced between 1961–77. Almost 25 percent
of dissertations produced during the period on
Latin American themes pertained to Mexico and concentrated in history, literature and
anthropology. Martínez desires a great exchange of information among scholars involved in research projects on Mexico.

Rivarola, María Magdalena. Datos y estudios
sobre la vivienda en el Paraguay. See item
9290.

155   **Rocky Mountain Council on Latin
      American Studies,** *XXV, Tucson, Ari-
zona,* 1977. Proceedings. Lincoln, Univ. of
Nebraska, 1977. 224 p.
   Contains 27 papers presented at the
XXV annual meeting. The brief presentations,
introductory in most cases, cover a diversity
of subjects, including business and legal topics; management; modernization, political
theory, revolution; literature, poetry, drama;
history, historiography; and anthropology.

156   **Rodríguez-Buckingham, Antonio.** The
      establishment, production, and equip-
ment of the first printing press in South
America (Harvard Library Bulletin [Cam-
bridge, Mass.] 26:3, July 1978, p. 342–354)
   The first printing in South America and
in Peru began after Antonio Ricardo arrived

in Lima in 1581 from Mexico. This is a brief
account of the activities of Ricardo in Peru,
the circumstances surrounding the establishment of the first printing shop in Lima and
some of the characteristics and the nature of
its equipment. Books, holy pictures and playing cards were printed by this first press.

157   **Seminar on the Acquisition of Latin
      American Library Materials (SALALM),**
XXIII, London, 1978. Latin American studies in Europe: final report and working papers.
Austin, Texas, Seminar on the Acquisition
of Latin American Library Material (SAL-
ALM), Secretariat, 1979. 343 p., tables.
   This account of the activities of the
SALALM meeting held in London in July
1978 provides a current review of Latin American studies programs in Europe. Of additional interest are the working papers by
William Glade, Harold Blakemore and Magnus Mörner on the status of Latin American
studies in the US, Europe and the Association
of Latin American Historians in Europe, respectively. The segment on the development
and current status of Latin American studies
in the UK, in which the programs at Oxford,
Cambridge, Essex, Glasgow, Liverpool and
London are described by their respective directors is especially useful. This publication
addresses a wide range of Latin American
interests.

LIST OF NEW SERIAL TITLES

Cladinex. See item **102.**

158   *Cuadernos de Marcha.* Año 1, No. 1,
      2. época, mayo/junio 1979–. México.
   Contributions by Uruguayan exiles;
current Latin American activities and Uruguayan politics. Formerly published in Montevideo (Talleres Gráficos 33). Bimonthly
publication edited by Carlos Quijano. Annual
subscription: $18.00(U.S.), $12.00(Latin
America). Address: Avenida Revolución 1123,
desp. 4, México 19, D.F. Mexico.

*Documentación Socioeconómica Cen-
troamericana.* See item **106.**

159   *Economía.* Pontificia Univ. Católica
      del Perú, Depto. de Economía. Vol. 1,
No. 1, dic. 1977–. Lima.

160   *Estudios.* Instituto de Estudios Eco-
      nómicos sobre la Realidad Argentina y

Latinoamericana. Año 1, No. 1, enero/feb. 1978–. Córdoba, Arg.

161 *Estudios Rurales Latinoamericanos.* Consejo Latinoamericano de Ciencias Sociales (CLACSO), Comisión de Estudios Rurales. Vol. 1, No. 1, enero/abril 1978–. Bogotá.

162 *Ethnic Groups.* Gordon and Breach. Vol. 1, 1977–. N.Y.

163 *Iberoromania.* Zeitschrift für die iberoromanischen Sprachen und Literaturen in Europe und Amerika. Max Niemeyer Verlag. No. 1, 1978–. Tübingen, FRG.

Indice de Ciências Sociais. See item **119**.

164 *Informaciones Arqueológicas.* Ediciones Catequil. Vol. 1, 1977–. Lima.

164a *Latin American Indian Literatures.* Univ. of Pittsburgh, Dept. of Hispanic Languages and Center for International Studies, Center for Latin American Studies, Vol. 1, No. 1, Spring 1077–. Pittsburgh, Pa.

165 *The Latin American Times.* José Font Castro. Vol. 1, No. 1, April 1979–. Bogotá.

Purpose of this new independent monthly is to increase awareness of the political, economic, social, and cultural realities of Latin America throughout the English-speaking world. Edited by Leopoldo Villar Borda. Address: IPC, P.O.Box 1301, FDR Station, New York, N.Y. 10022.

165a *Medical Anthropology.* Vol. 1, No. 1, Winter 1977–. Redgrave. Pleasantville, N.Y.

México: Artículos Clasificados. See item **38**.

166 *Nueva Ciencia.* Univ. Central de Venezuela, Facultad de Economía, Instituto de Investigaciones. Año 1, No. 1, enero/dic. 1975–. Caracas.

167 *Resenha de Política Exterior do Brasil.* Revista trimestral. Ministério das Relações Exteriores. Ano 1, No. 1, março/junho 1974–. Brasília.

168 *Revista Coahuilense de Historia.* Colegio Coahuilense de Investigaciones Históricas. Año 1, No. 1, mayo/junio 1978–. Saltillo, Mex.

Contains historical essays, reproduction of key state documents, calendars to manuscripts and bibliographical reviews. Five issues to date. Address: Apartado Postal 648, Saltillo, Coahuila, Mexico.

169 *Temática Dos Mil.* Revista de pensamiento. Año 1, No. 1, julio 1977–. B.A.

A second reappearance of the journal *Revista de Derecho Social*, which in the 1930s was edited by Francisco José Figuerola who appears as founder and writes a preface. This issue contains 20 articles (total length 158 p.) of widely varying length and seriousness, and in a wide variety of disciplines from international law to cultural anthropology. There is a marked Christian orientation to a number of them (i.e., conservative), although the Church has no obvious relationship to it. Significant articles include: Jorge Reinaldo Vanossi "La Democracia Política y la Democracia Social" p. 13–30; Salvador F. Busacca "Las Ideas: Fuerza de Nuestro Tiempo" p. 113–148. [P.B. Taylor, Jr.]

170 *Universidad.* Divulgación filosófica, científica y artística. Univ. Autónoma de Querétaro. Vol. 1, No. 1, oct. 1978–. Querétaro, Méx.

Articles on psychology, history, science, social science, and music appear. 100.00 pesos annually. Address: Universidad Autónoma de Querétaro, Centro Universitario, Cerro de las Campanas, Querétaro, Qro., Mexico.

171 *Yax-kin.* Instituto Hondureño de Antropología e Historia. Vol. 1, No. 1, oct. 1975–. Tegucigalpa.

JOURNAL ABBREVIATIONS BIBLIOGRAPHY AND GENERAL WORKS

AAA/AA American Anthropologist. American Anthropological Association. Washington.

AAFH/TAM The Americas. A quarterly publication of inter-American cultural history. Academy of American Franciscan History. Washington.

BNBD Boletín Nicaragüense de Bibliografía y Documentación. Banco Central de Nicaragua, Biblioteca. Managua.

BNJM/R Revista de la Biblioteca Nacional José Martí. La Habana.

BRBN/A Anais da Biblioteca Nacional. Divisão de Obras Raras e Publicações. Rio.

CM/D Diálogos. Artes/Letras/Ciencias humanas. El Colegio de México. México.

IFH/C Conjonction. Institut Français d'Haïti. Port-au-Prince.

JPHC/R Revista de la Junta Provincial de Historia de Córdoba. Archivo Histórico Monseñor P. Cabrera. Córdoba, Arg.

LARR Latin American Research Review. Univ. of North Carolina Press *for the* Latin American Studies Association. Chapel Hill.

RIB Revista Interamericana de Bibliografía [Inter-American Review of Bibliography]. Organization of American States. Washington.

ANTHROPOLOGY

GENERAL

251 Aguirre Beltrán, Gonzalo. Regiones de refugio: el desarrollo de la comunidad y el proceso dominical en mestizo América. México, Secretaría de Educación Pública, Instituto Nacional Indigenista, 1967. 366 p., bibl. (Col. SEP/INI, 17)

An ambitious theoretical synthesis concerning the position of marginal peoples in the plural societies of Latin America. After treating ecology, technology, dual economies, caste and class, the distribution of power, and ideology, the author closes with a summary of his views about *indigenismo*. (Although an extremely important book, it was never reviewed in *HLAS*). [F.C. Miller]

Centro Paraguayo de Estudios Sociológicos, Asunción. Centro Paraguayo de Documentación Social. Grupo de Trabajo de Migraciones Internas. Las migraciones en América Latina: bibliografía. See item **9012.**

252 Cordy–Collins, Alana and **Jean Stern** eds. Pre–columbian art history: selected readings. Palo Alto, Calif., Peek Publications, 1977. 519 p., bibl., illus.

Contains 33 interpretative articles on architecture, sculptures, ceramics, and textiles from Mexico, Middle and South America. Most of the papers appeared fairly recently, others were written for this volume (see item **302**). [H. von Winning]

Cornelius, Wayne A. and **Robert V. Kemper** eds. Metropolitan Latin America: the challenge and the response. See item **9016.**

Dobkin de Ríos, Marlene. Una teoría transcultural del uso de los alucinógenos de origen vegetal. See item **1650.**

253 Fogelson, Raymond D. and **Richard N. Adams** eds. The anthropology of power: ethnographic studies from Asia, Oceania, and the New World. N.Y., Academic Press, 1977. 429 p.

This collection of papers treats the many domains in which anthropologists have analyzed the nature and exercise of power, ranging from village politics to shamanistic performances. For reviews of specific papers see items **913, 921, 925** and **948.** [F.C. Miller]

254 Gil Elorduy, Julieta. Sobre arte y sociedad indígena en Sudamérica (ARMEX, 22:186, p. 61–69, plates)

Societal characteristics and art objects of contemporary indigenous groups in South America. Hunting societies (mainly Argentina and Chile) produce painted skins, textiles. Wide range of objects among five major agricultural groups: feathers, fibers, ceramics, masks. Marginal cultural areas include Araucanos (Chile)—textiles, silver ceramics; Cuná (Panama)—colored fabrics (molas), adornments, wood figures, fibers. Bibliography. Ten illustrations. A generalized but compact overview of material otherwise somewhat difficult to come by. [R.J. Mullen]

255 International Congress of Americanists, XLII, Paris, 1976. Actes. v. 1, Généralités. v. 2, Social time and social space in lowland Southamerican societies. v. 3, Les mouvements indiens paisans aux XVIII, XVIX, XX siècles. v. 4, Organización social y complimentalidad económica en los Andes Centrales. v. 5, Écologie, démographie, et acculturation. Paris, Société des Americanistes, Musée de l'Homme, 1977/1980. 5 v. (592, 622, 362, 645, 364 p.) bibl., illus., maps, plates, tables.

256 Jennings, Jesse D. ed. Ancient native Americans. San Francisco, Calif., W.H. Freeman, 1978. 698 p., bibl., illus., maps.

Volume which replaces the 1964 Jennings and Norbeck's book *Prehistoric man in the New World* (see *HLAS 27:150*). Includes some of the same contributors and 13 chapters which cover peopling of New World from Alaska to the Andes, Lowland South America, the Antilles, with a special chapter on pre–columbian Transoceanic contacts. Some bad errors in typesetting can cause confusion on understanding some maps and plate captions. See items **565, 567, 570** and **818**. [B. Meggers & C. Evans]

Lambert, Claire M. *ed.* and *comp.* Village studies: data analysis and bibliography. See item **9032**.

257 Land, Lewis K. *ed.* Pre–columbian art from the Land collection. San Francisco, California Academy of Sciences [and] L.K. Land, 1979. 272 p., bibl., col. plates, illus., maps, tables.

Sumptuous exhibition catalog with scholarly introductions to subareas and extensive descriptions of 156 outstanding, mainly ceramic, objects from Mesoamerica, by H. B. Nicholson; and 61 items from the Intermediate and Andean areas, by Alana Cordy–Collins. [H. von Winning]

Leacock, Eleanor. Women, development, and anthropological facts and fictions. See item **9033**.

Moreno Fraginals, Manuel *ed.* Africa en América Latina. See item **9035**.

Pescatello, Ann M. *ed.* Old roots in new lands: historical and anthropological perspectives on black experiences in the Americas. See *HLAS 40:2214*.

258 Reed, Charles A. *ed.* Origins of agriculture. The Hague, Mouton, 1977. 1017 p., bibl., illus. (World anthropology)

Papers prepared for the IX International Congress of Anthropological and Ethnological Sciences held in Chicago in 1973. For reviews of specific papers see items **566, 577**, and **811**.

Ribeiro, Darcy. Os protagonistas do drama indígena. See item **1187**.

Rowe, John Howland. Indian tribes of South America. See item **5732**.

259 Taylor, R.E. and **C.W. Meighan** *eds.* Chronologies in New World archaeology. N.Y., Academic Press, 1978. 587 p., bibl., illus. (Studies in archaeology)

First chapter deals with advances in dating methods in New World archaeology and is followed by 13 chapters containing detailed chronologies for most culture areas (with some gaps) for the entire continent. Concluded by a summary scan by Gordon R. Willey. For specific coverage see items **322, 357, 511, 536, 574–575** and **700**.

260 Wilbert, Johannes *ed.* Enculturation in Latin America: an anthology. Los Angeles, Univ. of California, UCLA Latin American Center Publications, 1976. 421 p., bibl. (UCLA Latin American studies, 37)

A diverse and interesting collection of papers, strong on ethnographic description but with relatively little theoretical discussion. For reviews of specific papers see items **916, 922, 954, 975, 1210, 1212–1213, 1216, 1261, 1318** and **1389**. [F.C. Miller]

ARCHAEOLOGY: Mesoamerica

HASSO VON WINNING, *Consultant in Mesoamerican Archaeology, Southwest Museum*
NORMAN HAMMOND, *Associate Professor of Archaeology, Douglass College, Rutgers University*

A SPECTACULAR DISCOVERY WAS MADE in the heart of Mexico City, Feb. 1978, when a trench dug for laying a telephone cable led to a monumental, perfectly preserved stone carving depicting the dismembered goddess Coyolxauhqui. Consequently a major exploration and reconstruction project was initiated at the site of the Templo Mayor in the ceremonial precinct of the ancient Aztec capital (item **397**).

Fruitful cooperation between art historians and archaeologists has resulted in a new perspective of the middle span in the long-lasting classic period. Esther Pasztory's "Middle Classic Mesoamerica: A.D. 400–700" (item **331**) contains many important contributions on art, architecture, religion, ceremonialism and interregional contacts that establish the validity and usefulness of this new concept.

"Central place" is another term that occurs for the first time in titles in this *Handbook* section and should therefore be briefly explained. It is essentially an economic model based on a spatial concept formulated to explain how the movement of goods and services can determine a hierarchy of settlements. The modified version of this model has become a useful tool in anthropological research (for a detailed exposition of it, see items **271** and **352**).

Trade, communication routes and cultural contact continue to be an important concern for Mesoamericanists who can now avail themselves of a major reference work on these subjects (item **313**). Of interest to all anthropologists is the volume "Chronologies in New World archaeology," edited by R.E. Taylor and Clement W. Meighan (item **259**) in which some 140 p. are devoted to Mesoamerica.

A momentous Festschrift in memory of Sir Eric Thompson, edited by Norman Hammond, covers in 25 papers a wide range of Maya proper and Maya-related topics (item **295**). The thorny problem of Transpacific contacts has been critically reviewed by Balajar Mundkur, with comments by various scholars, some of whom hold divergent views (item **320**). Despite the proliferating number of conferences and symposia, relatively few contributions appear in print. Notable exceptions are listed in items **276, 381,** and *HLAS 39:254.* A volume on the III Mesa Redonda at Palenque is in press.

It might be of interest to note that among the publications annotated in this section, 158 were written in English, 51 in Spanish, 12 in German, three in French, and one in Russian.

CURRENT RESEARCH: Barbara L. Stark reported extensively on field work in progress in *American Antiquity* (42:2, April 1977, p. 272–281, and 43:3, July 1978, p. 511–519). Two newsletters have been launched: one by the Misión Arqueológica y Etnológica Francesa en México (address: Virreyes 135, México 10, D.F.) entitled *Boletín Informativo* (1, Oct. 1978); the other has been issued by Berthold Riese (address: Katharinenstr. 20, D-1000 Berlin 37) and is entitled *Mexicon* (1:1, March 1979, 12 p.). A stimulating appraisal of recent research, its trends and future needs, has been written by Michael D. Coe (item **280**).

MAYA RESEARCH: A contribution of several significant trends is noted, most of which concern the processes of development of Maya civilization, particularly at an economic and social level. The examination of the collapse of classic Maya civilization begun in the early 1970s (see *HLAS 37:612*) has been matched by a similar work (item **261**) on the origins of Maya civilization, in which the complexity of late formative Maya culture is emphasized, particularly in regions far from the Peten-Campeche "heartland" such as Belize; heartland primacy in the development of a complex society is seen to be, in part at least, the result of research concentrated there because of the impressive classic sites.

The antiquity of sedentary settlement in the Maya lowlands has been extended (item **404**) to 2500 BC in calendar years (2000 b.c. in radiocarbon years; see R.M. Clark's article in *Antiquity,* 49, 1975, for the correlation). The ceramic, artifactual and architectural tradition was already distinctively ancestral to later formative Maya culture. The economy was based on maize cultivation in addition to root and other crops as well as on the hunting of deer and other animals. Apart from the Cuello site in Belize, early formative pottery of the Swasey ceramic complex has been recognized at several sites in Campeche, Yucatan and Belize.

Because of the mapping of Tikal in the late 1960s, the nature of Maya agriculture became the subject of intense investigation and discussion in the mid-1970s. The "milpa model" of a rural peasantry carving new fields from the bush each year in an extensive, low-pressure swiddening mode of production began to clash with the observed settlement-pattern evidence. The latter had been replaced by a model encompassing intensive cultivation techniques including short-fallowing, permanent field demarcation, and the construction of artificial facilities such as hillside terracing and swamped-bottom raised fields. This emerging synthesis of opinion is exemplified by the Harrison and Turner volume (item **296**) based on a 1976 symposium held in Paris by the International Congress of Americanists (item **255**).

There has been further progress in the study of Maya trade in minerals, including obsidian, volcanic ash (item **445**), and jade, and in the Mexican turquoise trade (item **284**), using neutron-activation and X-ray fluorescence analysis. Site reports continue to appear, including vol. 2 of the Seibal series (item **456**), three volumes on Chalchuapa (item **441**), and single volumes on Chantuto (item **361**) and Lubaantun (item **293**). Preliminary articles have appeared on the major projects at Quirigua, and Lamanai, by D.M. Pendergast in the *Newsletter of the Royal Ontario Museum* (144, May 1977, and 163, Dec. 1978), and at Abaj Takalik (item **291**) with reports on the research therein. Four additional fascicules of the Corpus of Maya Hieroglyphic Inscriptions have been published (item **464**).

The looting and destruction of Maya sites in Guatemala, Mexico, and Belize continues, and several authors base much of their scholarly output entirely on material from such illegal excavation.

OBITUARY. Linton Satterthwaite passed away at age 81, on 11 March 1978. He was field director of the University Museum, Univ. of Pennsylvania, excavations at Piedras Negras and epigrapher for the Tikal Project. Dennis E. Puleston, a young Mayanist, was killed by lightning on the Castillo at Chichén Itzá, 29 June 1978. Robert Wauchope died on 27 Jan. 1979, at age 69. He was director of the Middle American Research Institute at Tulane Univ. and general editor of the 16-volume *Handbook of Middle American Indians*.

GENERAL

261 Adams, Richard E.W. *ed.* The origins of Maya civilization. Albuquerque, Univ. of New Mexico Press, 1977. 465 p., bibl., illus., maps, plates, tables (A School of American Research book. Advanced seminar series)

Six data base chapters on the formative-early classic sequence in different parts of the Maya lowlands are followed by three external comparative sections dealing with the immediate western neighbors of the Maya (Olmec, Mixe-Zoque, Izapa). Cultural-ecology and stress/warfare models are among others in an interpretive section which concludes with a synthesis of all chapters by G.R.

Willey. The book leaves the factual basis of the Maya rise to civilization clear, but the process still obscure. [NH]

262 ———— and **Woodruff D. Smith.** Apocalyptic visions: the Maya Collapse and medieval Europe (AIA/A, 30:5, Sept. 1977, p. 292–301, illus., map)

Draws parallels between the 9th-century AD Maya collapse and the historical collapse of 14th-century Europe; invokes population factors as possible cause. [NH]

263 Asaro, F.; H.V. Michel; R. Sidrys; and **F. Stross.** High-precision chemical characterization of major obsidian sources in Guatemala (SAA/AA, 43:3, July 1978, p. 436–443, tables)

Detailed analysis of El Chayal obsidian source together with fresh data on Tajumulco, Ixtepeque and Rio Pixcaya sources. Close matching of El Chayal and Ixtepeque sources with archaeological obsidians from southern Belize was achieved. [NH]

264 Aveni, Anthony F. ed. Native American astronomy. Austin, Univ. of Texas Press, 1977. 286 p., bibl., illus., maps, plates, tables.

A sequel to "Archaeoastronomy" (see *HLAS 39:252*), this volume contains nine essays dealing with Mesoamerican astronomical knowledge and practices evident in calendrics, Maya inscriptions, Mixtec and Dresden codices, architecture and city planning. Five papers deal with North America and one with the Inca calendar. [HvW]

264a ——— and Horst Hartung. Tres observatorios astronómicos mayas en la península de Yucatán (AI/I, 3:3, May/June 1978, p. 136–142)

Three circular buildings on raised platform—the Caracol at Chichen Itza, the Caracol at Mayapan, and the Castillo at Paalmul Playa (Q.R.) are compared in structure and orientation and concluded to all be part of a network of astronomical observatories. [NH]

265 ———; ———; and Beth Buckingham. The pecked cross symbol in ancient Mesoamerica (AAAS/S, 202:4365, 20 Oct. 1978, p. 267–279, illus., plates, tables)

Possibly of Teotihuacan origin, this design was pecked in floors of buildings or on horizontal rock surfaces. Authors describe 29 examples, ranging from the Tropic of Cancer to the Peten. Their orientation and meaning (as architect's benchmarks at Teotihuacan) are discussed in terms of Mesoamerican cosmological-calendrical concepts, and with reference to the patolli game. [HvW]

266 Ball, Joseph W. The rise of the northern Maya chiefdoms: a sociopolitical analysis: pt. 2 (CEM/ECM, 10, 1976/1977, p. 209–222)

Interprets the consequences of the nonuniform, gradual introduction and selective absorption of classic Maya elements from the south. Pt. 1 (see item 261, p. 101–132) deals with the culture history of the northern lowlands from the first occupation in the 6th century BC through the end of the

preclassic in the 3rd century AD. [HvW]

267 ——— and E. Wyllys Andrews, V. Preclassic architecture at Becan, Campeche, Mexico. New Orleans, La., Tulane Univ., Middle American Research Institute, 1978. 17 p., bibl., illus., plates (Occasional paper, 3)

Description of Structures XXVII and IV-sub, with other traces of late formative construction. [NH]

267a Bandelier, Adolf Francis Alphonse. Report of an archaeological tour in Mexico in 1881. Millwood, N.Y., Kraus Reprint, 1976. 326 p., illus., map, plates, tables.

Reprint of the 1884 ed. published for the Institute by Cupples, Upham in Boston which was issued as v. 2 of "Papers of the Archaeological Institute of America, American series." Descriptions of the journey from Tampico to Mexico City and its major sculptures, of Cholula and vicinity, and of Mitla. [HvW]

268 Becker, Marshall Joseph. Moieties in ancient Mesoamerica: inferences on Teotihuacan social structure (SAIS/AIQ, 2:3, Autumn 1975, p. 217–236; 2:4, Winter 1975/1976, p. 315–330, bibl., illus., table)

Certain aspects in Teotihuacan iconography possibly refer to political moieties in charge of external and internal affairs of the city. [HvW]

269 Benson, Elizabeth P. The Maya world. N.Y., Thomas Y. Crowell, 1977. 176 p., bibl., illus., maps, plates.

Revised ed. of a 1967 popular work. [NH]

270 Blanton, Richard E. and others. Monte Alban: settlement patterns at the ancient Zapotec capital. N.Y., Academic Press, 1978. 451 p., bibl., fold. map, maps, plates, tables.

Traces the development of Monte Albán as a regional political capital, based on settlement distribution, architectural features and ceramics, with conclusions on population size, social systems and exterior relations (109 p.). Appendices (328 p.) by five authors contain detailed survey data, tabulations and computer print-outs. Includes index. [HvW]

271 Bove, Frederick J. Laguna de los Cerros: an Olmec central place (Journal of New World Archaeology [Univ. of California, Institute of Archaeology, Los Angeles] 2:3, Jan. 1978, p. 33–43, illus., maps, tables)

Useful synthesis of Olmec studies with discussions of theories concerning the territorial, political, and economic development. Pottery analysis and other evidence suggest that Laguna de los Cerros, in the Tuxtla region, may be the earliest major Olmec site known. [HvW]

272 **Braniff, Beatriz.** La posibilidad de comercio y colonización en el noroeste de México, vista desde Mesoamérica (SMA/RMEA, 23:2, julio 1977, p. 229–246, illus.)

Reviews the cultural contacts and trade relations of Mesoamerica with northwestern Mexico and outlines the causes for expansion and retraction of the northern frontier in terms of changes in climate, agriculture, natural resources, trade and political organization. [HvW]

273 **Braun, Barbara.** Ball game paraphernalia in the Cotzumalhuapa style (MV/BA, 25, 1977, p. 421–457, illus.)

Description of extant material and argument for variable function, practical, ritual and symbolic, at different times of use. [NH]

274 **Broda, Johanna.** Cosmovisión y estructura de poder en el México prehispánico (FAIC/CPPT, 15, 1978, p. 165–172)

Stresses the importance of solar observations and the agricultural calendar for justification of political power by the priest-rulers of Teotihuacan and Monte Albán. Extraordinary Mexican (Aztec) concern with rituals governed by a calendar is based on this earlier ideology and was adapted to a military society to assure political and economic control over resources. [HvW]

275 **Brotherston, Gordon.** Mesoamerican description of Space I: myths, stars and maps, and architecture [and] Mesoamerican description of Space II: signs for direction (IAA, 1:1, 1975, p. 279–305; 2:1, 1976, p. 39–61, illus., tables)

Article published in two installments reviews directional symbolism and related calendar signs, colors, deities in Maya and Mexican codices, myths, and architecture. Traditional cosmological interpretations are challenged. Considerable irregularities are noted among symbols for north and south that suggest a higher order for the east-west horizon. Since time and space are inseparable, cosmic space was conceptualized by the Maya only between the east and west and therefore the Maya system offers a new perspective for the Mesoamerican calendar and writing systems. [HvW]

276 **Browman, David L.** ed. Cultural continuity in Mesoamerica. The Hague, Mouton, 1978. 438 p., bibl., illus., tables (World anthropology)

Papers presented at the IX International Congress of Anthropological and Ethnological Sciences, Chicago, 1973, covering earliest artifacts (Valsequillo), early maize, exchange networks (five papers); ethnographic analogy in Maya archaeology (three papers); Olmec mythology, classic iconography, Aztec writing (six), and three papers on the northern frontier, the Antilles and Costa Rica. [HvW]

277 **Carlson, John V.** The case for geomagnetic alignments of precolumbian Mesoamerican sites: the Maya (UNC/K, 10:2, June 1977, p. 67–88, illus.)

A serious investigation of factual evidence and speculative ideas concerning geomagnetic site orientations, archaeomagnetism, and possible analogies with Chinese geomancy ("fengshui," a divinatory art for orienting buildings in harmony with cosmic forces). [HvW]

278 **Casasola, Luis.** Notas sobre las relaciones prehispánicas entre El Salvador y la costa de Veracruz, México (CEM/ECM, 10, 1976/1977, p. 115–138, illus.)

Reviews archaeological and ethnohistorical evidence for continuous influx of objects and ideas from the Gulf coast into Salvador since the middle preclassic, attributed in part to Pipil migrations. Refers to a late classic Xipe cult exemplified by ceramic figures from Cihuatlán and Lake Guija. [HvW]

279 **Charlton, Thomas H.** Teotihuacan, Tepeapulco, and obsidian exploitation (AAAS/S, 200:4347, 16 June 1978, p. 1227–1236, maps, table)

Presents a resource exploitation model based on investigations of obsidian quarries, workshops, and trade routes developed under Teotihuacan control. Stresses the importance of non-agricultural production and distribution systems that contributed to the political expansion of Teotihuacan, Toltecs, and Aztecs. [HvW]

280 Coe, Michael D. Archaeology today: the New World (in New perspectives in Canadian archaeology. Edited by A.G. McKay. Ottawa, The Royal Society of Canada, 1977, p. 23–38)

Appraisal of methods and accomplishments in recent research in Mesoamerica and the Andean area. New trends are noted, even among adherents of the "New Archaeology," with increased concern for ideological (mainly religious) systems. Interest in historical archaeology (early European settlers in US and Canada) is a heuristically promising trend. [HvW]

281 ———. Mexico. N.Y., Praeger, 1977. 216 p., bibl., illus., maps, plates.

Second revised and expanded ed. (for first ed., 1962, see *HLAS 27:204a*). [HvW]

282 Cohodas, Marvin. Diverse architectural styles and the ball game cult: the late middle classic period in Yucatan (in Pasztory, Esther *ed.* Middle Classic Mesoamerica: A.D. 400–700 [see item 331] p. 86–107, illus.)

Considers the late middle classic ball player sculptures in the Maya lowlands coeval with those in Yucatan. Challenges widely accepted ethnohistorical interpretations that assign Toltec Chichén Itzá to the postclassic and proposes a middle classic date for the coexistence of four architectural styles in central Yucatan (Puuc, Maya Chichén, Toltec Chichén, and Regional). Distinguishes a terminal middle classic (ca. 690–720) in Chichén Itzá, when Puuc influence is prominent and a new martial cult is introduced. [HvW]

283 Davis, Whitney. So-called jaguar-human copulation scenes in Olmec art (SAA/AA, 43:3, July 1978, p. 453–457)

Rejects specifically mythological interpretations and considers jaguar and were-jaguar motifs as allegorical themes. [HvW]

284 Earle, Timothy K. and **Jonathan E. Ericson** *eds.* Exchange systems in prehistory. N.Y., Academic Press, 1977. 274 p., illus., tables.

Papers from two SAA symposia in 1973 and 1975, some of which deal with Meso-

american topics, as with Weigand et al on the analysis of Mexican turquoise trade, and Hammond et al on the source characterization of Maya jade. [NH]

284a Foncerrada de Molina, Marta. El enano en la plástica maya (IIE/A, 45, 1976, p. 45–57, illus.)

A compilation of dwarf representations in classic Maya art suggests that they were court officials of high status, indicated by their attire, with special administrative or ritualistic-divinatory functions, and perhaps also court jesters. [HvW]

285 Fox, John W. Quiche conquest: centralism and regionalism in highland Guatemala state development. Albuquerque, Univ. of New Mexico Press, 1978. 322 p., maps.

Study of late postclassic Quiché Maya urbanism from archaeological and ethnohistoric evidence, documenting shifts in settlement pattern and distribution of power. [NH]

286 Freidel, David A. Culture areas and interaction spheres: contrasting approaches to the emergence of civilization in the Maya lowlands (SAA/AA, 44:1, Jan. 1979, p. 36–54, illus., maps)

Criticizes single- and multiple-core models for rise and spread of classic Maya civilization, and argues for its emergence through the increasing complexity of regional networks; the argument is based on his excavations at Cerros, Belize, a site which does not fit the "core" models but which can be fitted into a regional interaction model; also a useful summary of the Cerros discoveries. [NH]

287 Fuente, Beatriz de la. Los hombres de piedra: escultura olmeca. México, UNAM, 1977. 390 p., bibl., map, plates.

Systematic study of formal and intrinsic qualities of over 100 Olmec monumental sculptures in the Veracruz/Tabasco area, dating 1300–400 BC. General and local style characteristics are defined under three categories: human (which predominate), animal, and composite representations. Stylistic sequences for monuments at San Lorenzo (the oldest "classic" style) and La Venta are outlined and select major monuments from other sites discussed. Concludes that the figurations express an integrated homocentric system intended to preserve in stone those images and primordial concepts that were held sacred. For data on size, present location, etc., see her "Catálogo" (*HLAS 37:713*). For a more detailed study of Monument 77, La Venta, see "Sobre una Escultura Olmeca Recientemente Encontrada en La Venta, Tabasco" in *Anales del Instituto de Investigaciones Estéticas* (UNAM, 13:45, 1976, p. 31–43, illus.)

288 García Cook, A. and **B. Leonor Merino C.** Notas sobre caminos y rutas de intercambio al este de la Cuenca de México (FAIC/CPPT, 14, 1977, p. 71–82, illus., maps)
Detailed study of characteristics and distribution of settlements, in terms of size, sociopolitical and economic importance, in northwest Tlaxcala and in the Apan region to the northeast. These settlements are mapped for each of six phases (proto-Teotihuacan through Contact) to infer changes in major and minor communications routes. [HvW]

289 Gendrop, Paul. Les mayas. Paris, Presses Universitaires de France, 1978. 127 p., bibl., illus. (Col. Encyclopédique, 1734)
Up-to-date popular account of Maya civilization in French. [HvW]

290 ———. Quince ciudades mayas. México, UNAM, Dirección General de Publicaciones, 1977. 67 p., illus., map, plates (Col. de arte, 31)
Reviews the development of ceremonial architecture and related sculptural art, with comparisons of characteristics among the seven major regional art styles. Profusely illustrated. [HvW]

291 Graham, John Allen. Studies in ancient Mesoamerica III. Berkeley, Calif., Univ. of California, Archaeological Research Facility, Dept. of Anthropology, 1978. 114 p., illus., maps (Contribution, 36)
Consists of eight papers (one on Peru) including the 1976 Abaj Takalik preliminary report and site map; a report on a Cycle 10 sculpture from Chinaja, A.V. (B. Dillon); the excavation of seven unlooted Colima tombs (in 1940) at El Manchon (I. Kelly); description of a newly-discovered sculpture at Morelia, Escuintla (J. Clark); a Maya planetary observation (Fox and Justeson); a study of double images and two-headed compound creatures

(J. Quirarte). For *Studies in ancient Mesoamerica II*, see *HLAS 39:311*. [NH]

292 Grove, David C. The central Mexican preclassic: Is there really disagreement? (SAA/AA, 42:3, Oct. 1977, p. 634–636)
Clarifies his position concerning Olmec manifestations in central highland Mexico. [HvW]

293 Hammond, Norman. Lubaantun: a classic Maya realm. Cambridge, Mass., Harvard Univ., Peabody Museum of Archaeology and Ethnology, 1975. 428 p., bibl., illus., maps, tables (Monographs, 2)
Description of 1970 excavations at small ceremonial precinct in southern Belize, with resumé of previous work; demonstrates late foundation of site in C8 AD and places it within a regional geographical and economic framework. Detailed appendices describe excavations, pottery, artifacts, human remains. [NH]

294 ———. Sir Eric Thompson, 1898–1975 (SAA/AA, 42:2, April 1977, p. 180–190, illus.)
Obituary and bibliography (265 items) of noted Maya scholar. For addendum, see *American Antiquity* (43:1, 1978, p. 103). [NH]

295 ——— ed. Social process in Maya prehistory: studies in honour of Sir Eric Thompson. N.Y., Academic Press, 1977. 609 p., bibl., illus.
Twenty-five papers, including biographical sketch (with many illustrations) and bibliography (select) of Thompson. Topics include presentation of data bases from early formative to postclassic, discussions of raised-field agriculture, catalog of metalwork and several further examinations of the classic Maya collapse. [NH]

296 Harrison, Peter D. and **B.L. Turner, II** eds. Prehispanic Maya agriculture. Albuquerque, Univ. of New Mexico Press, 1978. 414 p., bibl., illus., maps, tables.
Seventeen articles on the revolution in knowledge of ancient Maya subsistence and intensive farming techniques include summaries by the editors, G.R. Willey and D.R. Harris. Important codification of new data and ideas. [NH]

297 Hartung, Horst. Teotihuacan, eine Metropole im alten Mexiko (Deutsche

Bauzeitung [Stuttgart, FRG] 6, 1978, p. 42–49, illus.)

Observations on environmental integration in urban planning at Teotihuacan. [HvW]

298 Hay, Clarence L. and others eds. The Maya and their neighbors. N.Y., Cooper Square, 1973. 606 p., bibl., fold. maps, illus., maps, plates, tables (Library of Latin-American history & culture)

Reprint of the famous and scarce Tozzer homenaje, including some papers which are still of prime importance. [NH]

299 Healan, Dan M. Architectural implications of daily life in ancient Tollan, Hidalgo (World Archaeology [Routledge & Kegan Paul, London] 9:2, 1977, p. 140–156, illus.)

Description of 21 domestic house groups with inferences on their occupants and their economic and ritual specializations. [HvW]

300 Hellmuth, Nicholas. Teotihuacan art in the Escuintla, Guatemala region (in Pasztory, Esther ed. Middle classic Mesoamerica: A.D. 400–700 [see item **331**] p. 71–85, illus.)

Description of incensarios and molded relief pottery, the iconography of which is a blend of several foreign and local art styles. [HvW]

301 Hester, Thomas R. and **Norman Hammond** eds. Maya lithic studies: papers from the 1976 Belize Field Symposium. San Antonio, Univ. of Texas, Center for Archaeological Research, 1976. 190 p., illus., maps., tables (Special publications, 4)

Symposium collection of 14 papers on chipped-chert and obsidian technology, production methods and trade. [NH]

302 Heyden, Doris. The year sign in ancient Mexico: a hypothesis as to its origin and meaning (in Cordy-Collins, A. and J. Stern. Pre-columbian art history: selected readings [see item **252**] p. 213–237, illus.)

Traces the occurrences and development of the imbricated trapeze-and-ray sign from Teotihuacan to the Aztecs and interprets, from contextual associations, its changes in form and meaning. [HvW]

303 Hirth, Kenneth G. Interregional trade and the formation of prehistoric gate-

way communities (SAA/AA, 43:1, Jan. 1978, p. 35–45, maps)

Presents a model, based on data from middle formative Chalcatzingo, that relates Mesoamerican long distance and local trade to the growth of market centers ("gateway communities"). [HvW]

304 ———. Problems in data recovery and measurement in settlement archaeology (Journal of Field Archaeology [Boston Univ.] 5:2, Summer 1978, p. 125–131)

Gauges "the effect of different types of surface disturbance on the recoverability of cultural debris" (author) with reference to a survey area on the Río Amatzinac, Morelos, Mex. [NH]

305 Holien, Thomas and **Robert B. Pickering.** Analogues in classic period Chalchihuites culture to late Mesoamerican ceremonialism (in Pasztory, Esther ed. Middle classic Mesoamerica: A.D. 400–700 [see item **331**] p. 145–157, illus.)

Contents of an exceptional early classic interment in Zacatecas appears to be related to a Tezcatlipoca ritual; and analogues to the postclassic Toxcatl sacrifice are discussed. [HvW]

306 Hunter, C. Bruce. A guide to ancient Mexican ruins. Norman, Univ. of Oklahoma Press, 1977. 261 p., bibl., illus., maps, plates.

Adequate descriptions with good site maps and up-to-date historical background. For volume on Maya ruins see HLAS 39:328. [HvW]

307 Jones, Grant D. ed. Anthropology and history in Yucatan. Austin, Univ. of Texas Press, 1977. 344 p, bibl., maps, tables.

Contents mainly 19th-century AD history, but two papers are important for archaeologists: 1) the proposal for a "Chan Maya" cultural and linguistic subgroup (Sir Eric Thompson); 2) the publication of the Pérez Probanza of 1654–56 and the Matrícula of Tipu (Belize) (France V. Scholes and Sir Eric Thompson). The other papers, though less relevant, are good and important for their own field. [NH]

308 Kampen, M.E. Classic Veracruz grotesques and sacrificial iconography (RAI/M, 13:1, March 1978, new series, p. 116–126, bibl., plates)

Discusses the participation of three gods: the vampire bat, ghoulish vulture, and pulque rabbit, in blood sacrifices on Tajin Ball Court panels and on *hachas* and *palmas*. Suggests connections of classic Veracruz symbolism and Aztec gods. [HvW]

309 Kendall, Aubyn. The art and archaeology of precolumbian Middle America: an annotated bibliography of works in English. Boston, Mass., G.K. Hall, 1977. 324 p. (Reference publications in Latin American studies)

Lists books and periodicals separately; appendix lists doctoral dissertations. [HvW]

310 Krumbach, Helmut. Heilbäder bei den Maya und Azteken (SJUG, 28:2, 1977, p. 145–156)

Archaeological and ethnohistorical evidence of the sweat bath and its therapeutical use. [HvW]

311 Kubler, George. Aspects of classic Maya rulership on two inscribed vessels. Washington, Dumbarton Oaks, Trustees for Harvard Univ., 1977. 60 p., bibl., illus., plates, tables (Studies in pre-columbian art and archaeology, 18)

Stylistic and epigraphic analysis of an onyx bowl of unknown provenance (looted), at Dumbarton Oaks, and the Initial Series Vase excavated at Uaxactun. [NH]

312 ———. Renascence and disjunction in the art of Mesoamerican antiquity (Ornament VIA III [Univ. of Pennsylvania, Graduate School of Fine Arts, Philadelphia] 1977, p. 31–39, illus.)

Commentary on the proposition that "continuous form does not predicate continuous meaning and that continuity of form or of meaning does not necessarily imply continuity of culture." Elucidated with examples of architectural details and figural representations of central Mexico and the Maya area. [HvW]

313 Lee, Thomas A. and **Carlos Navarrete** *eds.* Mesoamerican communication routes and cultural contacts. Provo, Utah, Brigham Young Univ., 1978. 265 p., bibl., illus., maps, tables (New World Archaeological Foundation papers, 40)

Contains 21 papers on archaeological and ethnohistorical evidence for interregional prehispanic and colonial period trade and communication systems. Includes detailed maps and descriptions of routes and deals with specific topics such as maritime trade, market systems, military intervention, and the relation between trade and cultural processes. See also item **288**. [HvW]

314 Limbrey, S. Tlapacoya: problems of interpretation of lake margin sediments at an early occupations site in the basin of Mexico (*in* Davidson, D.A. and M.L. Shackley *eds.* Geoarchaeology: earth science and the past. Boulder, Colo., Westview Press, 1976, p. 213–226, tables)

Defines the sedimentary sequence and the composition of the beach where "a group of hunting people were present, some 22,000 years ago," adding that this date "could not be regarded as controversial although it was the earliest in Mexico." [HvW]

315 Litvak King, Jaime. El factor de comunicación en el contacto norte-sur de Mesoamérica: una teoría sobre la función del Valle de Oaxaca en el Clásico (UNAM/AA, 14, 1977, p. 13–20)

Presents a model of trade networks between the Valley of Mexico and the Maya area and discusses consequences of route changes for Monte Albán. [HvW]

Malmstrom, Vincent H. Izapa: cultural hearth of the Olmecs? See item **5356**.

Mathewson, Kent. Maya urban genesis reconsidered: trade and intensive agriculture as primary factors. See item **5357**.

316 Matos Moctezuma, Eduardo. The Tula chronology: a revision (*in* Pasztory, Esther *ed.* Middle classic Mesoamerica: A.D. 400–700 [see item **331**] p. 172–177, illus., maps)

Teohihuacan (Metepec phase AD 650–750) ceramics were recently found in the fill of the Tula Chico Plaza, the oldest of the site. Furthermore, 13 classic sites in the macro-area suggest that "the Tula area had been under Teotihuacan control." [HvW]

317 Mendoza, Rubén G. World view and the monolithic temples of Malinalco, Mexico: iconography and analogy in precolumbian architecture (SA/J, 64, 1977, p. 63–80, illus.)

The numerical symbolism of architectural features and the iconography of the sculptures are explained in terms of ethnohistory as relevant to a Nahua cosmic scheme.

The round temple symbolizes the concept of the sun's transits through the 13 heavens. [HvW]

318 Miller, Arthur G. A brief outline of the artistic evidence for classic period cultural contact between Maya lowlands and central Mexican highlands (*in* Pasztory, Esther *ed.* Middle classic Mesoamerica: A.D. 400–700 [see item **331**] p. 62–70, illus.)

Cites iconographic motifs in architecture, mural painting and ceramics that demonstrate cross-cultural artistic and intellectual contact. [HvW]

319 Montoliu, María. Algunos aspectos del venado en la religión de los mayas de Yucatán (CEM/ECM, 10, 1976/1977, p. 149–172, illus.)

On the ritual functions of the deer in Maya art, religion, and folklore. [HvW]

320 Mundkur, Balaji. The alleged diffusion of Hindu divine symbols into precolumbian Mesoamerica: a critique (UC/CA, 19:3, Sept. 1978, p. 541–583, bibl., illus., tables)

Rejects the theses by Kirchhoff, Kelley, and Barthel who affirm that Hindu influences are evident in Mesoamerican religious-astronomical-calendric symbolism. Argues that their comparisons are "superficial and intrinsically contradictory" and "chronologically incompatible with historical events," and that astronomical-astrological beliefs developed independently in the New World. Includes comments by 16 scholars with author's reply. [HvW]

321 Muser, Curt *comp.* Facts and artifacts of ancient Middle America. N.Y., E.P. Dutton, 1978. 212 p., bibl., colored plates, illus., maps, tables.

A glossary of over 2500 terms used in the archaeology and art history of precolumbian Mexico and Central America. [HvW]

322 Nicholson, H.B. Western Mesoamerica: A.D. 900–1520 (*in* Taylor, R.E. and C.W. Meighan *eds.* Chronologies in New World archaeology [see item **259**] p. 285–329, bibl.)

Concise review and evaluation of numerous regional dated native histories which contribute substantially to greater chronological precision of archaeological sequences, particularly for events after AD

1370. The methodological complexities are discussed, including the problems of the different native year counts. See item **357**. [HvW]

323 Niederberger, Christine. Early sedentary economy in the basin of Mexico (AAAS/S, 203:4376, 12. Jan. 1979, p. 131–142, illus., maps, tables)

Revised and condensed version of author's Zohapilco report (see *HLAS 39:480*) with emphasis on food procurement, settlement, and lithic artifacts of the earliest periods (6000–2000 BC). Comparable early occupations in Tamaulipas and the Tehuacan Valley differ in many aspects because of their environment and lower altitude. [HvW]

324 Noguera, Eduardo. Representación de invertebrados en culturas prehispánicas (UNAM/AA, 14, 1977, p. 127–153, illus.)

Insects in prehispanic art and their religious and cultural significance. [HvW]

325 Norman, V. Garth. Izapa sculpture: pt. 2, Text. Provo, Utah, Brigham Young Univ., 1976. 360 p., illus. (New World Archaeological Foundation papers, 30)

The pendant to Norman's 1973 album of Izapa sculpture illustrations, with 'descriptive analyses', thematic analyses and conclusions. [NH]

326 Ortiz de Montella, Bernard R. Aztec cannibalism: an ecological necessity? (AAAS/S, 200:4342, 12 May 1978, p. 611–617, illus.)

Refutes Harner's (see *HLAS 39:318*) contentions that human sacrifice was a response to population pressure and famine. Instead, protein supply was adequate and cannibalism motivated by religion. [HvW]

327 Paddock, John. The middle classic period in Oaxaca (*in* Pasztory, Esther *ed.* Middle classic Mesoamerica: A.D. 400–700 [see item **331**] p. 45–62, illus.)

In a cogent synthesis of Valley of Oaxaca and Mixteca sites Paddock lends support to Parson's middle classic concept (*ibid.* p. 25–34) by expanding the latter's stylistic trait list to reconcile seemingly conflicting interpretations in chronology. [HvW]

328 Parsons, Lee A. The peripheral coastal lowlands and the middle Classic period (*in* Pasztory, Esther *ed.* Middle classic Mesoamerica: A.D. 400–700 [see item **331**] p. 25–34, map)

Defines "Peripheral Coastal Lowlands" as a corridor along the Gulf coast, across the Isthmus and along the Pacific coast to El Salvador, to be considered a separate environmental and cultural unit between the Mexican highlands and Maya lowlands. Reviews classic Veracruz/Cotzumalhuapa relationships, mainly in terms of art and architecture. [HvW]

329 Pasztory, Esther. Artistic traditions of the middle classic period (*in* Pasztory, Esther *ed.* Middle classic Mesoamerica: A.D. 400–700 [see item **331**] p. 108–142, illus.)

Detailed and perceptive exposition of characteristics, developments and interrelationships of iconography, art styles and architecture in the Central Mexican highlands, Maya lowlands and peripheral coastal lowlands. Differentiates phenomena of the early and the late middle classic with reference to preceeding and following periods. [HvW]

330 ———. Historical synthesis of the middle classic period (*in* Pasztory, Esther *ed.* Middle classic Mesoamerica: A.D. 400–700 [see item **331**] p. 3–22, map, table)

Defines as middle classic the 300 year period of intense cross-cultural communication. An early phase (400–550) witnessed the greatest Teotihuacan influence which, in the late phase (550–700) yielded to the rise of centers peripheral to Teotihuacan (Cholula, Xochicalco, Tula) and other coastal lowland centers. The historical events are discussed in terms of socio-political changes and artistic innovations and eclecticism. [HvW]

331 ——— *ed.* Middle classic Mesoamerica: A.D. 400–700. Foreword by Gordon F. Ekholm. N.Y., Columbia Univ. Press, 1978. 197 p., bibls., illus., maps, tables.

The three centuries are considered a crucial period of innovation and brilliant achievements, preceded and followed by a higher degree of regional isolation. Archaeologists and art historians have therefore introduced the middle classic concept to highlight the period between early and late classic. The 11 articles are annotated separately (see items **282, 300, 305, 316, 318, 327–330, 344** and **350**). [HvW]

332 Piña Chan, Román. Divagaciones en torno a Teotenango (UAEM/H, 1:1, enero/marzo 1976, p. 60–71, illus., plates)

Traces the history of the occupants of Teotenango and of the Toluca Valley utilizing archaeological and ethnohistorical data. [HvW]

333 Pohorilenco, Anatole. On the question of Olmec deities (Journal of New World Archaeology [Univ. of California, Institute of Archaeology, Los Angeles, 2:1, April 1977, p. 1–16, illus.)

Constructive critique of Joralemon's identification of Olmec images as prototypes of postclassic deities. Credits the Olmecs with developing a composite representational system which was adopted by all subsequent cultures. But suspected Olmec/postclassic continuities may only reflect similarity of form, not of content or meaning. [HvW]

334 Pollard, Helen Perlstein. An analysis of urban zoning and planning at prehispanic Tzintzuntzan (APS/P, 121:1, Feb. 1977, p. 46–69, illus., maps)

Five categories of zones within late postclassic Tzintzuntzan are described; these indicate the planning of individual structures and of activity zones, but no overall planning of the settlement. Suggests that the capital of the Tarascan state was an administrative city. [HvW]

335 Potter, David F. Maya architecture of the Central Yucatan Peninsula: Mexico. Edited by Jennifer S.H. Brown and E. Wyllys Andrews, V. New Orleans, La., Tulane Univ., Middle American Research Institute, 1977. 118 p., bibl., fold. table, illus., map, plates, tables (Publication, 44)

Argues for a fusion of the Rio Bec and Chenes styles, into a Central Yucatecan style of ca. AD 600–900. A major data base is the site of Becan, Campeche. [NH]

336 Price, Barbara J. Shifts in production and organization: a cluster-interaction model (UC/CA, 18:2, June 1977, p. 209–233)

Synthetic study of causes in intensification and shifts in mode of production, with implications for shifts in mode of social organization. Postulates that regular causal processes operate, at the determined level in cultural evolution, in a lawful way. Although based on Mexican cultures, "the model (presented) should be applicable to Peru, to Mesopotamia, and probably to China." [HvW]

337 Puleston, Dennis. The people of the Cayman/Crocodile: riparian agriculture and the origins of aquatic motifs in ancient Maya iconography (*in* Montequin, François-Auguste de. Aspects of ancient Maya civilization. St. Paul, Minn., Hamline Univ. 1976, p. 1–25)

Use of aquatic animal/plant imagery in Maya art derives from early use of raised-field agriculture. [NH]

338 Rathje, William L. and **Jeremy A. Sabloff.** A model of ports-of-trade (CEM/ECM, 10, 1976/1977, p. 81–90)

The model defines the political-mercantile and mythical-religious factors with comparisons between the classical Mediterranean island of Delos and the island of Cozumel at Spanish contact in 1517. [HvW]

339 Renfrew, Colin. Trajectory discontinuity and morphogenesis: the implications of catastrophe theory for archaeology (SAA/AA, 43:2, April 1978, p. 203–222, illus.)

Discussion of discontinuity in cultural systems and descriptive analysis using Thom's catastrophe theory is illustrated by *inter alia* the Classic Maya collapse, compared with that of Mycenaean Greece and other Old World examples. [NH]

340 Reunión de Antropología e Historia del Noroeste, *I, Hermosillo, Mex., 1974.* Sonora: antropología del desierto. Edited by Beatriz Braniff C. and Richard S. Felger. México, Secretaría de Educación Pública (SEP), Centro Regional del Noroeste [and] Instituto Nacional de Antropología e Historia (INAH), 1976. 592 p., bibl., maps (Col. Científica diversa, 27)

Covers paleoecology, geography, ethnography, history and includes six papers on regional archaeological topics. [HvW]

341 Rice, Don S. Middle preclassic Maya settlement in the central Maya lowlands (Journal of Field Archaeology [Boston Univ.] 3:4, 1976, p. 425–445, illus., maps)

Survey of lake region of Yaxha-Sacnab using random transects indicates occupation by 1000 b.c., using lake resources but living on forested uplands. Population increase led to greater social complexity and a more formal

political structure with Yaxha as primate site. [NH]

342 Riley, Carroll L. and **Basil C. Hedrick** *eds.* Across the Chichimec sea: papers in honor of J. Charles Kelley. Foreword by Charles DiPeso. Carbondale, Southern Illinois Press, 1978. 318 p., bibl., maps, tables.

Title expresses metaphorically the arid area in northern Mexico and the southwestern US. The 18 papers range from archaeological and ethnohistorical interpretive syntheses to specific regional topics and highlight culture contact and trade with Mesoamerica. [HvW]

343 Ruz Lhuillier, Alberto. Semblanza de John Eric Sidney Thompson: 1898–1975 (CEM/ECM, 10, 1976/1977, p. 317–335, bibl.)

Biographical sketch of the late doyen of Maya archaeology with a lengthy bibliography. [HvW]

344 Sanders, William T. Ethnographic analogy and the Teotihuacan horizon style (*in* Pasztory, Esther ed. Middle classic Mesoamerica: A.D. 400–700 [see item **331**] p. 35–44, illus.)

Archaeological evidence at Kaminaljuyú and comparison with the Aztec merchant class suggest that Teotihuacan created a commercial, not a political, empire and controlled trade throughout Mesoamerica. [HvW]

345 ———. Resource utilization and political evolution in the Teotihuacan valley (*in* Hill, James N. ed. Explanation of prehistoric change. Albuquerque, Univ. of New Mexico Press, 1977, p. 231–257, maps [A School of American Research book])

Reconstruction of ecological processes, from the formative to Aztec period, in terms of land use patterns and population changes. Throughout the evolution of Teotihuacan irrigation was a crucial factor. Paper presented at the VII Seminar sponsored by the School of American Research, held in Santa Fe, N. Mex., April 1970. [HvW]

346 ——— and **David Webster.** Unilinealism, multilinealism, and the evolution of complex societies (*in* Redman, Charles and others eds. Social anthropology: beyond subsistence and dating. N.Y., Academic Press, 1978, p. 249–302)

The case examples from Mesoamerica

deal specifically with Highland Guatemala, Highland Oaxaca, Basin of Mexico, the Olmec, and Lowland Maya. [HvW]

347 ―――― and **Joseph W. Michels** eds. Teotihuacan and Kaminaljuyu: a study in prehistoric culture contact. University Park, Pennsylvania State Univ. Press, 1977. 467 p., bibl., illus., maps (Monograph series on Kaminaljuyu)

Of the six papers, by various authors, two report on excavations at Kaminaljuyú 1969–72, and four analyze and interpret the evidence for cultural interaction between the two sites. [HvW]

348 **Seler, Eduard.** Observations and studies in the ruins of Palenque. Edited by John Bartman and George Kubler. Pebble Beach, Calif., Robert Louis Stevenson School, Precolumbian Art Research, 1977. 92 p., illus., maps, plates.

Translation, by Gisela Morgner, of Seler's 1915 *Beobachtungen und Studien in den Ruinen von Palenque.* Useful also for the numerous illustrations. [HvW]

349 **Serra, Mari Carmen** and **Yoko Sugiura.** Las costumbres funerarias como indicador de la estructura social en el formativo mesoamericano (UNAM/AA, 14, 1977, p. 21–36)

Theoretical considerations for evaluating archaeological data of burials to determine aspects of formative period social structure in Mesoamerica. [HvW]

350 **Sharp, Rosemary.** Architecture as interelite communication in preconquest Oaxaca, Veracruz, and Yucatan (*in* Pasztory, Esther ed. Middle classic Mesoamerica: A.D. 400–700 [see item **331**] p. 158–171, illus.)

Reviews occurrences and development of the step-fret motif which, because of widespread use in major buildings is considered "a means of intercommunication between the elites of Oaxaca, Veracruz, and northern Yucatan." [HvW]

351 **Sheets, Payson D.** Ilopango volcano and the Maya protoclassic. Carbondale, Southern Illinois Univ., Univ. Museum, 1976. 78 1., bibl., illus., maps, plates, tables (University museum studies, 9)

Argues that the protoclassic eruption of Ilopango created refugees whose migration to the Maya lowlands sparked off the rise of classic civilization. Useful technical study of the extent of tephra fall from the Ilopango eruption. [NH]

352 **Smith, Michael E.** The Aztec marketing system and settlement patterns in the valley of Mexico: a central place analysis (SAA/AA, 44:1, Jan. 1979, p. 110–125, illus.)

This analysis indicates that commercial factors were of primary importance in the development of settlements in the Valley of Mexico. Furthermore, political, ecological, and agricultural determinants are discussed to explain deviations from the ideal central place model. [HvW]

353 **Stark, Barbara L.** and **Barbara Voorhies** eds. Prehistorical coastal adaptations: the economy and ecology of maritime Middle America. N.Y., Academic Press, 1978. 313 p., bibls., illus., maps, plates, tables (Studies in archaeology)

Ten articles report on recent research of subsistence, procurement and settlement patterns in coastal habitats whose cultural evolution differs markedly from that of adjacent lowlands. William T. Sanders included a comprehensive critique and the editors comment on past and future research. Includes index. [HvW]

354 **Stresser-Péan, Guy.** San Antonio Nogalar, la sierra de Tamaulipas et la frontière Nord-Est de la Mésoamérique. Preface by Ignacio Bernal. Mexico, Mission Archéologique et Ethnologique Française au Mexique, 1977. 905 p., bibl., maps, plates (Etudes mésoamericaines, 3)

Well illustrated report of excavations at an early classic site re-occupied from the postclassic to the present. Detailed discussions of architectural features, ceramics, artifacts, and of contacts with central highland Mexico, the Huasteca, and southeastern United States. Scholarly utilization of copious ethnohistorical, linguistic, and modern ethnographic data provide the fullest account, so far, of the culture history from this northeastern frontier region of Mesoamerica. [HvW]

355 **Stuart, George E.** and **Gene S. Stuart.** The mysterious Maya. Washington, National Geographic Society, 1977. 200 p., illus.

Popular, accurate and up-to-date description of Maya archaeology and ethnology, with many fine color plates. [NH]

356 Tichy, Franz. Altamerikanische Orientierungssysteme im Siedlungsbild der Gegenwart (UEN/LS, 1, März 1976, p. 135–168, illus., tables)

Further observations on concepts of time and space as organizing principles in architecture and settlement plans, derived from viceregal and modern evidence. See both *HLAS 39:365–366* and author's "El Calendario Solar como Principio de Organización del Espacio para Poblaciones y Lugares Sagrados in *Comunicaciones Proyecto Puebla-Tlaxcala* (15, 1978, p. 153–163, illus.), which stresses solar observations at different latitudes in Mesoamerica. [HvW]

357 Tolstoy, Paul. Western Mesoamerica before A.D. 900 (*in* Taylor, R.E. and C.W. Meighan eds. Chronologies in New World archaeology [see item **259**] p. 241–284, bibl.)

Discussion and synthesis of many regional chronologies with emphasis on the Central Highlands, particularly the Basin of Mexico and Valley of Tehuacan. These provide a finely calibrated and well anchored master sequence. See also item **322**. [HvW]

358 ——— and others. Early sedentary communities of the basin of Mexico (Journal of Field Archaeology [Boston Univ.] 4:1, Spring 1977, p. 91–106, map, tables)

Data on human occupation between 1200–500 BC and summary of their culture history. Recommends a balanced approach in regard to historical and processual aspects for interpretation of past events. [HvW]

359 Tschohl, Peter and others. Catálogo arqueológico y etnohistórico de Puebla-Tlaxcala, Mexico. v. 2, Ch-O. Köln, FRG, Proyecto Puebla-Tlaxcala, 1977. 676 p., bibl., illus., maps, plates.

Vol. 2 of a comprehensive and very detailed alphabetical site catalogue (letters Ch to O) with copious archaeological and ethnohistorical data and valuable bibliographical cross references. For vol. 1, see *HLAS 37:677*. [HvW]

360 Turner, B.L., II. Agricultura prehistórica intensiva en las tierras bajas de los mayas (III/AI, 38:1, enero/marzo 1978, p. 105–124, bibl., illus.)

Reiteration in Spanish of the principal points of the author's article in *Science* (185, 1974, p. 118–124), viz. that land demarcation by terracing indicates a permanence and intensity hitherto unsuspected for ancient Maya agriculture. Subsumed into Harrison and Turner's *Prehispanic Maya agriculture* (see item **296**). [NH]

361 Voorhies, Barbara. The Chantuto people: an archaic period society of the Chiapas Littoral, Mexico. Provo, Utah, Brigham Young Univ., 1976. 146 p., map, tables, illus. (New World Archaeological Foundation papers, 41)

Description of field work in the earliest sites of the Soconusco Coast, occupied ca. 3000–2000 b.c. by exploiters of coastal resources. Important. [NH]

362 Whitecotten, Joseph W. The Zapotecs: princes, priests and peasants. Norman, Univ. of Oklahoma Press, 1977. 338 p., bibl., illus., maps, plates, tables (The civilization of the American Indian series)

Summary of the prehispanic cultural history of Oaxaca and of Monte Albán in particular, based on latest archaeological and ethnohistorical data. Covers also the viceregal and modern periods. For ethnohistorian's comment, see *HLAS 40:2020*. [HvW]

363 Willey, Gordon R.; Richard M. Leventhal; and **William L. Fash, Jr.** Maya settlement in the Copan valley (AIA/A, 31:4, July 1978, p. 32–43, illus., map)

Summary of recent Harvard project including excavation of elite residences near Copan ceremonial precinct. [NH]

364 Wuthenau, Alexander von. Unexpected faces in ancient America: 1500 BC–AD 1500, the historical testimony of precolumbian artists. N.Y., Crown, 1975. 240 p., bibl., plates.

"This book stresses the fact that the Semites and Negroes formed an integrated part of the early American population . . . " (p. 204). According to the author, ethnic diffusion from many parts of the world is evident in physical aspects, dress and ornaments portrayed in sculptures and ceramics of virtually every Mesoamerican culture and period. [HvW]

365 Yadeun, Juan. Arqueología de la arqueología (SMA/RMEA, 24:2, julio 1978, p. 152–191, bibl.)

Based on a summary review of over 300 articles of 14 Round Table Conferences,

organized by the Sociedad Mexicana de
Antropología between 1941–76, the author
evaluates the archaeological accomplishments, the institutions and personnel involved, and their procedures and methodology,
pointing out various trends. Refuting commentaries by Eduardo Matos Moctezuma,
Jaima Litvak King, Lorenzo Ochoa, Miguel
Messmacher (p. 193–212). [HvW]

EXCAVATIONS AND ARTIFACTS

366 Acosta, Jorge. Exploraciones en el Palenque: durante 1972 [y] Temporada
1973–1974 (INAH/A, 5 [7. época] 1974/1975
[i.e. 1975] p. 5–62, illus.)
    Detailed report (in two parts but in
same issue) on extensive restorations of the
Palace, Temple of the Inscriptions, Temple
XIV, Templo Encantado, and the North
Group, with descriptions of tombs, burials,
and associated artifacts. [HvW]

367 Agrinier, Pierre. A sacrificial mass
burial at Miramar, Chiapas, Mexico.
Provo, Utah, Brigham Young Univ., 1978. 52
p., illus., map (New World Archaeological
Foundation papers, 42)
    A small platform at the center of this
small site in the Grijalva basin covered remains of 24 persons in positions suggesting *in
situ* execution. The sacrifice has many associated ladle censers and other pottery
indicating a middle classic date, and the author suggests an association of the sacrifice
with the total eclipse of AD 565; religious
syncretism of local and foreign elements is
also suggested. [NH]

368 Aguilera, Carmen. El arte oficial te-
nochca, su significación social. México,
UNAM, Instituto de Investigaciones Estéticas, 1977. 168 p., bibl., illus. (Cuadernos
de historia de arte, 5)
    Historical perspective of the role of
Aztec rulers in the creation of major and
minor works of art for state and religious
functions, procurement of raw materials, organization of artisans, and related ritualism.
[HvW]

369 Anders, Ferdinand. Der altmex-
ikanische Federmosaikschild in Wien
(MVW/AV, 32, 1978, p. 67–88, illus., table)
    Description of materials and manufac-

ture of the best preserved Mexican feather
mosaic shield ("Blue Coyote") in the Vienna
Museum, with notes of the history of this and
other objects sent to Europe after the Conquest. [HvW]

370 Arnold, Dean E. and Bruce F. Bohor.
An ancient clay mine at Yo'K'at,
Yucatan (SAA/AA, 42:4, Oct. 1977, p. 575–
582, illus.)
    Contemporary clay-mine has associated
sherd tool dating to AD 800–1000, suggesting ancient use also. [NH]

371 Ashmore, Wendy and Robert J. Sharer.
Excavations at Quiriguá, Guatemala:
the ascent of an elite Maya center (AIA/A,
31:6, Nov./Dec. 1977, p. 10–19, illus., map)
    Resumé of excavations with numerous
illustrations. [NH]

372 Ball, Joseph W. The archaeological ceramics of Becan, Campeche, Mexico.
New Orleans, La., Tulane Univ., Middle
American Research Institute, 1977. 190 p., illus., maps, tables (Publication, 43)
    Description and exegesis of the first
major ceramic sequence for the central Maya
lowlands. Important source work and analysis.
[NH]

373 Benson, Elizabeth P. Mexico, 100th
century BC–20th century AD: rich collections of art open at two Smithsonian
museums (Smithsonian [Washington] 9:2,
May 1978, p. 52–63, illus.)
    Introduction to a traveling exhibit (see
item 403). Important for large photograph of a
monumental Aztec relief (three m. diam.) of
the dismembered Moon Goddess Coyolxauhqui, discovered Feb. 1978 in Mexico City.
[HvW]

374 Bruder, Claus J. Die Phallus-
Darstellung bei den Maya: ein
Fruchtbarkeits-Symbol (Ethnologia Americana
[Düsseldorfer Institut für Amerikanische
Völkerkunde, Düsseldorf, FRG] 14:5, Jan./Feb.
1978, p. 809–815, illus.)
    Whereas postclassic phallic sculptures
in the northern Maya area are attributed to
Gulf Coast influences, a compilation of classic
Maya sculptures shows their use as fertility
symbols already between AD 300–900.
[HvW]

375 Cabrera Castro, Rubén. Trabajos de
rescate arqueológico en la región de

Chicayán, Ver. (INAH/B, 2:19, oct./dic. 1976, p. 3–12, illus.)

Salvage explorations in the Huasteca Veracruzana. 31 sites were located and 6 classic sites excavated, with Teotihuacan style pottery and simple masonry architecture. [HvW]

376 Castro-Leal, Marcia and **Lorenzo Ochoa.** El Ixtepete como um ejemplo de desarrollo cultural en el occidente de México (INAH/A, 5 [7. época] 1974/1975 [i.e. 1976] p. 121–154, illus.)

Exploration of a late classic building complex near Guadalajara, with description of ceramics and discussion of socio-political developments in the valley. Previously postulated Teotihuacan influence has not been substantiated. [HvW]

377 Charlton, Thomas H.; David C. Grove; and **Philip K. Hopke.** The Paredón, Mexico: obsidian source and early formative exchange (AAAS/S, 201:4358, 1 Sept. 1978, p. 807–809, illus.)

Description of trace element analyses of obsidian from a previously unrecognized source and its implications for trade in central Mexico. [HvW]

378 Coe, Michael D. Lords of the underworld: masterpieces of classic Maya ceramics. Princeton, N.J., Princeton Univ. Press for the Art Museum, 1978. 142 p., illus.

Catalogue raisoné of an exhibition of looted Maya vessels of undeclared provenance, further illustrating Coe's chthonic interpretation of Maya vase-painting of his book The Maya scribe and his world (see HLAS 37:800); the exhibition celebrates the Art Museum's acquisition of one of the principal pieces in the exhibition. Technically interesting color roll-out photographs by J. Kerr. [NH]

379 Comunicaciones Proyecto Puebla-Tlaxcala. Fundación Alemana para la Investigación Científica, No. 13, 1976–. Puebla, Mex.

Contains following articles on archaeology: Thomas R. Wheaton's "La Cerámica Clásica del Area de Huejotzingo, Pue." (p. 25–32). Classification of regional surface collections with conclusions on population distribution. Konrad Tyrakowski's "Poblamiento y Despoblamiento en la Región Central de la Cuenca de Puebla-Tlaxcala, México" (p. 37–

40) Notes on continuities of netlike settlement patterns from prehispanic through viceregal periods. Angel García Cook's "Notas sobre las Orejeras de Cerámica en Tlaxcala" (p. 41–48) Regional and temporal distribution of over 900 solid and hollow ear disks and their cultural significance. Patricio Dávila C. and Diana Z. de Dávila's "Periodificación de Elementos Culturales para el Area del Proyecto Arqueológico Cuauhtinchán" (p. 85–98) Reconnaissance of a 1200 km² region and middle preclassic through early colonial ceramic sequence. [HvW]

380 ———. ———. No. 14, 1977–. Puebla, Mex.

Contains following articles on archaeology: Patricio Dávila's "Una Ruta 'Teotihuacana' al Sur de Puebla" (p. 53–56, map) A string of production centers with Teotihuacan style ceramics and architectural elements are part of a trade network. A. García Cook and Elía del Carmen Trejo's "Lo Teotihuacano en Tlaxcala" (p. 57–70, maps) Comprehensive evaluation of Teotihuacan elements in Tlaxcala and adjacent regions with conclusions on their distribution and duration, and the cultural, political, and commercial impact of the metropolis and of its Teotihuacan residents abroad. A. García Cook and B. Leonor Merino C.'s "Notas sobre Caminos y Rutas de Intercambio al Este de la Cuenca de México" (p. 71–83, maps) See item **288.** Monika Tesch's "Figurillas de Acatepec, Puebla" (p. 87–90, illus.) On local occurrences of preclassic figurines. [HvW]

381 ———. ———. No. 15, 1978–. Puebla, Mex.

For articles on archaeology, see items **274, 356, 392** and **396.** [HvW]

382 Diehl, Richard A. and **Edward G. Stroh, Jr.** Tecali vessel manufacturing débris at Tollan, Mexico (SAA/AA, 43:1, Jan. 1978, p. 73–79, illus.)

Observations on the reuse of drill cores from travertine vessels in a residential zone at Tula. [HvW]

383 Dillon, Brian D. Salinas de los Nueve Cerros, Guatemala: preliminary archaeological investigations. Socorro, N.Mex., Ballena Press, 1977. 94 p., bibl., illus., maps (Studies in Mesoamerican art, archaeology and ethnohistory, 2)

Description of protoclassic-terminal

classic salt-making site and ceremonial precinct on the border of the Maya lowlands and
highlands, with late preclassic origins. [NH]

384 Doppee, Michèle and **Michel Grau-
lich.** Une grande statue en terre cuite
du Veracruz—Mexique—aux Musées Royaux
d'Art et d'Histoire (Bulletin de Musées
Royaux d'Art et d'Histoire [Bruxelles] 48:6,
1976, p. 35–48, bibl., illus., plates)
     A large ceramic Veracruz figure in the
Brussels Museum is compared with others in
Europe and Mexico, and identified as Xochi-
quetzal. [HvW]

385 Drennan, Robert D. Excavations at
Quachilco: a report on the 1977 season
of the Palo Blanco Project in the Tehuacan
Valley. Ann Arbor, Univ. of Michigan, Museum of Anthropology, 1978. 81 p., bibl., illus.
(Technical reports, 7. Research reports in archaeology: contribution, 3)
     Summary descriptions and preliminary
assessment of a large "central place" with
substantial remains of public or ceremonial
architecture. Text in English and Spanish.
[HvW]

386 Eaton, Jack D. and **Joseph W. Ball.**
Studies in the archaeology of coastal
Yucatan and Campeche, Mexico. New Orleans, La., Tulane Univ., Middle American
Research Institute, 1978. 146 p., illus., maps,
tables (Publication, 46)
     Two studies: 1) Archaeological Survey
of the Yucatan-Campeche Coast (JDE); 2) Archaeological Pottery of the Yucatan-Campeche Coast (JWB). Survey runs from Isla del
Carmen to Isla Blanca near Puerto Juárez; ceramic sequence runs from late formative to
colonial. [NH]

387 Ericson, J.E. and **J. Kimberlin.** Obsidian sources, chemical characterization,
and hydration rates in West Mexico (Archeometry [Oxford Univ.] 19:2, 1977, p. 157–
166)
     Identification of obsidian sources and
preliminary information of hydration rates of
artifacts from different sources. [HvW]

388 Feuchtwanger, Franz. Tlatilco: Be-
trachtungen über Fundplatz und Funde
(MV/BA, 24, 1976, p. 389–427, illus.)
     Comments by a knowledgeable col-
lector on the region and art of Tlatilco with
descriptions of outstanding figurines reminiscent of Olmec monuments. [HvW]

389 Folan, William J. Coba, Quintana
Roo, Mexico: an analysis of a prehispanic and contemporary source of sascab
(SAA/AA, 43:1, Jan. 1978, p. 79–85, illus.,
map)
     Many sources of ancient *sascab* were
found at Coba, a major Maya site. Extraction
technology can be deduced and it is suggested
that exhausted pits were used for horticulture. [NH]

390 Foncerrada de Molina, Marta. The
Cacaxtla murals: an example of cultural contact? (IAA, 4:2, 1978, p. 141–160,
bibl., illus., plates)
     Recently discovered murals in Tlaxcala
are probably epiclassic (8th–10th century)
and represent a regional eclectic art style. Its
Maya elements (however glyphs are lacking)
may have been introduced by Chontal Putún
traders, possibly accompanied by Maya artists.
[HvW]

391 ———. El comerciante en la cerámica
pintada del clásico tardío maya: 600–
900 D.C. (*in* Del arte: homenaje a Justino
Fernández. México, UNAM, Instituto de Investigaciones Estéticas, 1977, p. 45–52, illus.)
     Defines the characteristics of a class of
human figures, on polychrome vases, that
depict merchants in a natural setting (i.e. not
in the Underworld nor as deities) for the purpose of designating their social rank. [HvW]

392 ———. Reflexiones en torno a la pintura mural de Cacaxtla (FAIC/CPPT, 15,
1978, p. 103–130, illus.)
     Further discussion of the stylistic pe-
culiarities of the murals, particularly of their
Teotihuacan-derived elements. Numerous line
drawings of the masked personages and of
the gory battle scenes. For a more comprehensive treatment of artistic and cultural
backgrounds, see "La Pintura Mural en Cacaxtla" *Anales del Instituto de Investigaciones
Estéticas* (UNAM, 13:46, 1978, p. 5–20, illus.). [HvW]

393 Franco Carrasco, José Luis. Arte prehispánico de México, cerámica, piedra,
metales. México, Edición Lito Offset Fersa,
1973. 21 p., plates.
     Unusual specimens from various re-
gions selected from an important private
collection in Mexico. Text in Spanish, English, and French. Includes 129 plates, many
in color. Not for public sale. [HvW]

394 Freidel, David A. Monumental Mayan mask in northern Belize (Journal of Field Archaeology [Boston Univ.] 4:4, Winter 1977, p. 488–491, illus., map)

Brief record of late formative polychrome stucco mask, one of four on front of a small pyramid at Cerros, Belize. [NH]

395 Furst, Peter T. The ninth level: funerary art from ancient Mesoamerica, selections from the Gerald and Hope Solomons collection. Iowa City, Univ. of Iowa, Museum of Art, 1978. 126 p., bibl., illus.

Exhibition catalogue of figural art from West Mexico, Chupicuaro, Veracruz and Jaina published on the occasion of an exhibition at the Univ. of Iowa Art Museum 14 April–27 Aug. 1978. Furst provides the archaeological background and deals in particular with the pervasive cosmological-religious symbolism. [HvW]

396 García Cook, Angel. Tlaxcala: poblamiento prehispánico (FAIC/CPPT, 15, 1978, p. 49–84, maps)

Archaeological synthesis of the cultural sequence, 1700 BC to AD, based on the extensive annotated literature in the author's "Bibliografía Comentada del Proyecto Puebla-Tlaxcala" in *Comunicaciones* (13, 1976, p. 49–84). [HvW]

397 ——— and Raúl M. Arana A. Rescate arqueológico del monolito Coyolxauhqui: informe preliminar. México, Instituto Nacional de Antropología e Historia (INAH), 1978. 94 p., illus.

Detailed account of the excavation and consolidation of an eight-ton discoidal sculpture discovered by the stairs of a substructure of the Templo Mayor, and attributed to the reign of Axayacatl, AD 1470–1485/87. The remarkably well preserved relief depicts the decapitated and dismembered female deity Coyolxauhqui, sister of Huitzilopochtli. A great variety of associated offerings includes painted deity statues, obsidian, gold, bone and shell artifacts, and many Mezcala style sculptures. Study provides folded plans and appendices. [HvW]

398 Gifford, James C. Prehistoric pottery analysis and the ceramics of Barton Ramie in the Belize Valley. Cambridge, Mass., Harvard Univ., Peabody Museum of Archaeology and Ethnology, 1976. 359 p., bibl., illus., tables (Memoirs, 18)

Posthumous garnering (by C. Gifford, M. Kirkpatrick, R. Sharer and others) of Gifford's theoretical work on Maya pottery and the description of the Barton Ramie sequence. A major contribution to Maya ceramic studies. [NH]

399 Goldstein, Marilyn. The ceremonial role of the Maya flanged censer (RAI/M, 12:3/4, Dec. 1977, p. 405–420, bibl., illus., plates)

Ornament on Maya censers has connotations of rain, fertility, and health, suggesting motives for the burning of incense in them. [NH]

400 Graham, John A. Discoveries at Abaj Takalik, Guatemala (AIA/A, 30:3, May 1977, p. 197–198, illus., map)

Summary of 1976 discoveries of very early Maya sculpture, with final paragraph on 1977 finds. [NH]

401 Gussinyer, Jordi and Alejandro Martínez Muriel. Una figurilla olmeca en un entierro del horizonte clásico (CEM/ECM, 10, 1976/1977, p. 69–80, illus., map)

An Olmec greenstone figurine was found in a burial urn at La Angostura, Chiapas. It had been accidentally discovered by the builders of a late classic construction who ceremoniously re-buried it. For a description of other discoveries and salvage operations 1972–73 in this region see: Jordi Gussinyer's "Tercera Temporada del Salvamiento Arqueológico en la Presa de la Angostura, Chiapas" in *Anales* (INAH, 5:53, 1976, p. 63–84, illus.). [HvW]

402 Gutiérrez Solana, Nelly and Susan K. Hamilton. Las esculturas en terracota de El Zapotal, Veracruz. México, UNAM, Instituto de Investigaciones Estéticas, 1977. 251 p., bibl., illus., plates (Cuadernos de historia de arte, 6)

Over 400 large ceramic figures have been excavated at this late classic ceremonial site in central Veracruz. Forty-four of the more spectacular figures, including a monumental unfired Death God sculpture, are described in terms of formal and aesthetic qualities, iconographic attributes, and religious themes. [HvW]

403 Hammer, Olga and Jeanne D'Andrea *eds.* Treasures of Mexico from the Mexican national museums: an exhibition presented by the Armand Hammer Foundation. Los Angeles, Calif., Los Angeles County Museum of Art, 1978. 206 p., bibl., illus., plates.

Consists of 100 prehispanic masterpieces (p. 62–112), viceregal, and 19th and 20th-century art. Includes an introduction on art history by Octavio Paz "El arte de México: Materia y Sentido" (p. 12–23) which appeared in English and Spanish in *Americas* (30:9, Sept. 1978, p. 13–22). See also item 373. [HvW]

404 Hammond, Norman and others. The earliest lowland Maya?: definition of the Swasey phase (SAA/AA, 44:1, Jan. 1979, p. 92–110, illus.)

Presents evidence from the Cuello site, Belize, for an early formative of 2000–1000 b.c. (2500–1300 BC) in the eastern Maya lowlands, under heads of Chronology, Ceramics, Lithics, Architecture, Funerary Practices, Human Remains, Economy, External Contacts. Summary indicates a sedentary farming society with pottery, lithics and building in a tradition ancestral to the known Maya formative. [NH]

405 ——— and others. Maya formative radiocarbon dates from Belize (NWJS, 267, p. 608–610, table)

Presents 16 further radiocarbon dates from the Cuello, Belize, site to substantiate the proposed early formative chronology (see *Nature*, 260, p. 579–581). [NH]

406 Hester, Thomas R. Archaeological studies of Mesoamerican obsidian. Socorro, N. Mex., Ballena Press, 1978. 210 p., bibl., illus., tables (Studies in Mesoamerican art, archaeology and ethnohistory, 3)

Seventeen papers, including translations of early studies on obsidian artifacts, quarries, technology, and trace elements analyses. Hydration dating is not included. Useful bibliography. [HvW]

407 Hirth, Kenneth G. Toltec-Mazapan influence in eastern Morelos, Mexico (Journal of New World Archaeology [Univ. of California, Institute of Archaeology, Los Angeles] 2:1, April 1977, p. 40–46, illus., map)

Abundant ceramics and three sculptured relief fragments (two of these are described and illustrated), indicate strong Toltec influence in the Amatzinac River re-

gion during the middle post-classic or late Toltec phase. [HvW]

408 Hurtado de Mendoza, Luis and **William A. Jester.** Obsidian sources in Guatemala: a regional approach (SAA/AA, 43:3, July 1978, p. 424–435, maps, tables)

Attempt to group obsidian outcrops into source systems. [NH]

409 Ichon, Alain. A late postclassic sweathouse in the highlands of Guatemala (SAA/AA, 42:2, April 1977, p. 203–209, illus.)

Rectangular sweathouse with reservoir, drain and hearth at site of Los Cimientos-Chustum, El Quiché, is similar to lowland classic sweathouse, different from the single known highland example at Paraíso. [NH]

410 Joesink-Mandeville, L.R.V. The significance of Mani Cenote, Yucatan, in the prehistory of Middle America (SEM/E, 41:1/4, 1976, p. 146–164, maps, illus., plate)

Reasserts the importance of Brainerd's Mani work and its probable middle formative (ca. 800 BC date); detailed assessment of monopod bottles. [NH]

411 Johnson, Irmgard Weitlaner. Weft-wrap openwork techniques in archaeological and contemporary textiles of Mexico (Textile Museum Journal [Washington] 4:3, 1976, p. 63–72, illus.)

Description of a unique postclassic cotton textile from Durango and evidence of survival, in Oaxaca until recently, of the same weaving technique. [HvW]

412 Kelly, Isabel T. Archaeological research in Colima, Mexico (Research Reports: 1969 Projects [National Geographic Society, Washington] 1978, p. 307–311, illus.)

Reports radiocarbon date 160 BC for local ceramics at the Colima/Michoacan border "that equate, in the Armeria Basin, with the Ortices phase." Cites C-14 date 1450 BC for Capacha cinctured vessels (illustrated), noting close resemblances with El Opeño tomb sherds of 1500 BC. Capacha, the earliest phase in Colima, shows some generic resemblances with even earlier material from coastal Ecuador (see *HLAS 29:1203*) and with the some centuries more recent "Tlatilco style," but suggests no Olmec ties. [HvW]

413 ———. Seven Colima tombs: an interpretation of ceramic context (*in*

Graham, John Allen. Studies in ancient Mesoamerica III [see item 291] p. 1–26, illus.)

Evidence of re-use of these shaft tombs and revised ceramic sequence. The much cited Ortices phase is late preclassic, followed by Comala (early classic), and Colima phase (large hollow effigies, middle classic). [HvW]

414 **Macazaga Ordoño, César.** Coyolxauhqui, la diosa de la luna. México, Editorial Cosmos, 1978. 63 p., bibl., illus.

Popular description of the moon goddess and her cult prompted by the discovery, in Mexico City, of a large relief sculpture bearing her image. Includes glossary. [HvW]

415 **McClung de Tapia, Emily.** Recientes estudios paleoetnobotánicos en Teotihuacan, México (UNAM/AA, 14, 1977, p. 49–61)

Plant remains from various excavations have been identified and their relevance for subsistence and economic patterns is discussed. [HvW]

416 **Mason, Roger D.** and others. An archaeological survey on the Xoxocotlan piedmont, Oaxaca, Mexico (SAA/AA, 42:4, Oct. 1977, p. 567–575, map, table)

Investigation of a late formative irrigation system and settlements on the southeastern slopes of Monte Albán. [HvW]

417 **Mayer, Karl Herbert.** Maya monuments: sculptures of unknown provenance in Europe. Ramona, Calif., Acoma Books, 1978. 103 p., plates.

Catalog with ample descriptions of 51 stone carvings, including stelae, in private and museum collections in Belgium, France, Germany, Holland, Sweden and Switzerland. Includes 55 full-page photographs. [HvW]

418 ———. The mushroom stones of Mesoamerica. Ramona, Calif., Acoma Books, 1977. 46 p., bibl., plates.

English translation of *HLAS 39:468*. [HvW]

419 **Meighan, Clement W.** Empirical determination of obsidian hydration rates from archaeological evidence (*in* Taylor, R.E. *ed.* Advances in obsidian glass studies, archaeological and geochemical perspectives. Park Ridge, N.J., Noyes Press, 1976, p. 106–119, bibl., tables)

Discussion of procedure, problems and advantages of this dating method with reference to the Amapa (Nayarit) chronology. See also the article by Fred H. Stross and others "Chemical and Archaeological Studies of Mesoamerican Obsidians" in the same work edited by R.E. Taylor *Advances in obsidian glass studies* (see above citation, p. 240–258, bibl., tables). [HvW]

420 **Mercer, Henry C.** The hill-caves of Yucatan. Norman, Univ. of Oklahoma Press, 1975. 183 p., illus., map.

Valuable reprint (the original 1896 edition was largely destroyed by fire) of an honest but unsuccessful search for Early Man in the Puuc limestone caves. Thompson's introduction is a useful updating and expansion of his 1959 Termer Festschrift paper, and includes previously unpublished photographs of Maya cave paintings. [NH]

421 **Moholy-Nagy, Hattula.** The utilization of *Pomacea* snails at Tikal, Guatemala (SAA/AA, 43:1, Jan. 1978, p. 65–73, illus., tables)

The edible snail *Pomacea flagellata* (Say) was eaten throughout the history of Tikal, most heavily during periods of growth and decline. During early classic florescence it was more frequently deposited as an offering than at other times. Its economic importance was marginal. [NH]

422 **Moser, Christopher L.** The head-effigies of the Mixteca Baja (UNC/K, 10:2, June 1977, p. 1–15, illus., map)

Description, classification, and probable function of 42 Thin Orange, middle classic effigies from Oaxaca. [HvW]

423 ———. Ñuiñe writing and iconography of the Mixteca Baja. Nashville, Tenn., Vanderbilt Univ., 1977. 245 p., bibl., illus., maps, plates, tables (Publications in anthropology, 19)

Descriptive catalog of stone reliefs and ceramic urns pertaining to a middle classic (AD 400–700) regional eclectic art style of Oaxaca. Compilation of a dictionary of 139 motifs and symbols led to recognition of calendar signs, personal and place names, possible deities, and iconographic themes. [HvW]

424 ———. The wheel problem in ancient Mesoamerica (UNC/K, 10:1, March 1977, p. 59–63)

Evaluates arguments that account for the non-existence of vehicular transport. [HvW]

425 Muller, Florencia. La iconografía de la cerámica de Cholula (SMA/RMEA, 23:2, julio 1977, p. 155–177, illus.)

List of naturalistic and symbolic motifs on Cholula and Cholulteca pottery with discussion of their occurrences during seven phases (AD 200–1500). [HvW]

426 Navarrete, Carlos. Chinkultic, Chiapas: trabajos realizados en 1976 (INAH/B, 2:19, oct./dic. 1976, p. 43–58, illus.)

Exploration and consolidation of the ball court and other structures of this much looted late classic center. See *HLAS 39:477* for 1975 explorations. [HvW]

427 Nelson, Fred W. and others. Preliminary studies of the trace element composition of obsidian artifacts from northern Campeche, Mexico (SAA/AA, 42:2, April 1977, p. 209–225, illus., map, tables)

Obsidians from Edzna, Dzibilnocac and Santa Rosa Xtampak were analyzed by X-ray fluorescence; most came from the El Chayal source in Guatemala, with some preclassic samples from San Martin Jilotepeque near Chayal and some from Ixtepeque. A possible route down the Usumacinta is suggested, and another overland via northeast Peten. [NH]

428 Ochoa, Lorenzo. Notas preliminares sobre el proyecto: arqueología de las tierras bajas noroccidentales del área maya (CEM/ECM, 1976/1977, p. 41–52, illus., maps)

Survey of the riverine Tabasco-Campeche region, where over 70 minor sites were located. Includes two detailed site maps. [HvW]

429 Pasztory, Esther. Aztec stone sculpture. N.Y., The Center for Inter-American Relations, 1976. 1 v. (Unpaged) illus.

Selections from five New York City museums, described and illustrated with a historical introduction. [HvW]

430 ———. The Xochicalco stelae and a middle classic deity triad in Mesoamerica (*in* Congreso Internacional de la Historia del Arte, XXIII, Granada, Spain, 1973. España ante el Mediterráneo y el Atlántico: actas. Granada, Spain, Univ. de Granada, Depto. de Historia del Arte, 1976, v. 1, p. 185–215, illus.)

Penetrating interpretations of symbolism and esoteric connotation of the three Xochicalco stelae with comparisons of triadic representations at Palenque, El Tajín, and Bilbao. Notwithstanding regional iconographic differences, a common theme is perceptible, concerned with major events of the agricultural cycle. [HvW]

431 Pendergast, David M. Royal Ontario Museum excavations: finds at Lamanai, Belize (AIA/A, 30:2, March 1977, p. 129–131, illus.)

Summary of 1976 excavations of major Maya site, including also Franciscan church. Continuation of "postclassic" pottery tradition after 1644 is an important chronological revision. [NH]

432 Piña Chan, Román. Teotenango: segundo informe de exploraciones arqueológicas. Toluca, Mex., Gobierno del Estado de México, Dirección de Turismo, 1969/1975. 75 p., plates.

Exploration and reconstruction of ceremonial structures of the late classic/early postclassic fortified Matlatzinca center which consists of extensive terraces, platforms, and a ball court. Third session was initiated 1973. [HvW]

433 Pring, Duncan C. The dating of Teotihuacan contact at Altun Ha: the new evidence (SAA/AA, 42:4, Oct. 1977, p. 626–628)

Pendergast's assertion of early (protoclassic period) Teotihuacan contact is challenged on the ceramic evidence and placed later, in the early classic. New evidence from Nohmul, Belize, also confirms the contemporaneity of Floral Park and Chicanel ceramics in the southern Maya lowlands, the two complexes, according to author, "performing different functions within an increasingly complex Maya society." [NH]

434 Rattray, Evelyn C. Seriación de cerámica teotihuacana (UNAM/AA, 14, 1977, p. 37–48, tables)

Describes application of Meighan's three-pole seriation method which was found valuable for the current revision of the Teotihuacan ceramic sequence. [HvW]

435 **Rice, Prudence M.** Whiteware pottery production in the valley of Guatemala: specialization and resource utilization (Journal of Field Archaeology [Boston Univ.] 4:2, Summer 1977, p. 221–233, maps)

Chemical analysis of several clay sources of white clay enables their differential exploitation through time and space and for differing types of vessel to be discerned over the period from 500 b.c. to the present day. [NH]

436 **Sanders, William T.** and **Robert S. Santley.** A prehispanic irrigation system near Santa Clara Xalostoc in the Basin of Mexico (SAA/AA, 42:4, Oct. 1977, p. 582–588, illus.)

Recognition of stratified canals tentatively attributed to a Teotihuacan (pre-Coyotlatelco) occupation. [HvW]

437 ——— and others. The Teotihuacan Valley Project, final report: the formative period occupation of the valley. v. 2, pt. 1, Text and tables; pt. 2, Plates and figures. University Park, Pennsylvania State Univ., Dept. of Anthropology, 1975. 579 p., bibl., illus. (Occasional papers in anthropology, 10)

Detailed description of surveys and excavations at four major sites, with ceramic and artifactual analyses, and discussion of characteristics of the Patlachique Range that relate to formative settlement. Copiously illustrated. For vol. 1, see *HLAS 35:696*. [HvW]

438 **Schmidt, Peter J.** Postclassic finds in the Cayo District, Belize (CEM/ECM, 10, 1976/1977, p. 103–114, illus.)

An assemblage of censers and copal from ceremonies held in the Agouti Cave (Uchentzub) is discussed in terms of linkages with Tikal and Yucatan, and offers clues on regional population movements in the southern Maya lowlands during the early and the late postclassic. [HvW]

439 **Schmidt S., Paul.** Rasgos característicos del área maya en Guerrero: una posible interpretación (UNAM/AA, 14, 1977, p. 63–73, illus., maps)

Sporadic occurrences of Maya traits in Guerrero (Fine Orange ware, corbeled vaults, stelae, etc.) may be attributed to Putun (Chontal Maya) traders. [HvW]

440 **Sharer, Robert J.** Archaeology and history at Quirigua, Guatemala (Journal of Field Archaeology [Boston Univ.] 5:1, Spring 1978, p. 51–70, illus., maps, tables)

Summarizes recent excavations (to 1977) and discusses identified rulers of Quirigua and their monuments. [NH]

441 ——— ed. The prehistory of Chalchuapa, El Salvador. Philadelphia, Univ. of Pennsylvania Press, 1978. 3 v. (194, 211, 226 p.)

Final report on excavations at a major Maya site of the southeast highland zone. [NH]

442 **Sheets, Payson D.** Analysis of chipped stone artifacts in southern Mesoamerica: an assessment (LARR, 12:1, 1977, p. 139–158, bibl., tables)

Historiography of a branch of Mesoamerican archaeology, focussed on the Maya but with comparative material from elsewhere. [NH]

443 **Shook, Edwin M.** and **Marion Popenoe Hatch.** The ruins of El Balsamo, Department of Escuintla, Guatemala. Los Angeles, Univ. of California, Institute of Archaeology, 1978. 37 p., bibl., illus., plates (Journal of New World Archaeology, 3:1)

Reconnaissance survey of an important middle preclassic site with material related to that of neighboring Monte Alto. The pottery is described in detail. [HvW]

444 **Sidrys, Raymond.** Trace-element analysis of obsidian articles artifacts from Portezuelo, Mexico (Journal of New World Archaeology [Univ. of California, Institute of Archaeology, Los Angeles] 2:1, April 1977, p. 47–51)

Commentary on obsidian imports from Otumba, Pachuca, and distant Michoacan, and their cultural implications. [HvW]

445 **Simmons, Michael P.** and **Gerald F. Brem.** The analysis and distribution of volcanic ash-tempered pottery in the lowland Maya area (SAA/AA, 44:1, Jan. 1979, p. 79–91, illus., maps)

Volcanic ash as a tempering agent in pottery from Belize, Petén, Palenque and northern Yucatán suggests the import of ash from highland Guatemala/Salvador. The trade routes indicated by obsidian analysis would have been equally feasible for the ash trade, which however ceases with the fall of Chichen Itza. [NH]

446 **Sosa Vega, Constanza.** Artefactos en piedra pulida del México prehispánico (INAH/A, 5 [7. época] 1974/1975 [i.e. 1976] p. 209–270, illus., tables)

Very detailed classification of grooved axes and similar artifacts in terms of surface features and their use. Includes numerous frequency tables and maps indicating spatial and temporal distributions. [HvW]

447 **Spranz, Bodo; D.E. Dumond; and P.P. Hilbert.** Die Pyramiden vom Cerro Xochitecatl, Tlaxcala, Mexico. Wiesbaden, FRG, Franz Steiner Verlag, 1978. 109 p., bibl., fold. maps, illus., maps, plates, tables (Das Mexiko-Projekt der Deutschen Forschungsgemeinschaft, 12)

Descriptions of preclassic ceramics from hillside test pits and discovery, in the hilltop pyramids, of pottery and figurine offerings pertaining to the Teotihuacan-Toltec transition (AD 750–900). Many figurines show attributes to deities in Codex Borgia. [HvW]

448 **Stoltman, James B.** Lithic artifacts from a complex society: the chipped stone tools of Becan, Campeche, Mexico. New Orleans, La., Tulane Univ., Middle American Research Institute, 1978. 30 p., bibl., plates, tables (Occasional paper, 2)

Analysis of some 8200 chipped chert and obsidian artifacts of which some 7950 were flakes, only 400 of them retouched; ca. 150 pieces were obsidian. Analysis is morphological only, without use-wear or trace-element studies. [NH]

449 **Tellenbach, Michael.** Algunas observaciones sobre la "Estela C" y su complemento, la "Estela Covarrubias," de Tres Zapotes, Veracruz (IAI/I, 4, 1977, p. 63–76, illus.)

Comparative study of the reliefs on the recently discovered upper section of Stela C found by Stirling in 1939. With clear photographs and reconstruction drawings of both sides. For a popular account of the discovery see Ronald S. Callvert's "Olmec Head-Hunting in Mexico" in *Explorer's Journal* (56:1, March 1978, p. 26–31, illus.). [HvW]

450 **Tommasi de Magrelli, Wanda.** La cerámica funeraria de Teotenango: la cultura del Valle de Toluca. México, Biblioteca Enciclopédica del Estado de México, 1978. 206 p., bibl., illus., maps, plates (Biblioteca Enciclopédica del Estado de México, 61)

Historical background of the Toluca Valley culture (inappropriately known as Matlatzinca according to the author) and classification of 14th-century pottery from burials in the ceremonial plaza of this fortified urban center. Includes chart and appendix. [HvW]

451 **Velasco M., Margarita** and **Rosa Brambila.** Trabajos de rescate arqueológico en La Negreta, Querétaro (SMA/RMEA, 24:1, marzo 1978, p. 53–74, illus.)

Salvage excavations at a classic site in the Bajío, with abundant lithic artifacts and pottery from Michoacan, Guanajuato, and Teotihuacan. [HvW]

452 **von Winning, Hasso.** Human-mask pectorals on Teotihuacan figurines (SM/M, 52:1, Jan./March 1978, p. 11–16, illus.)

Identifies these figurines iconographically as representations of dead warriors. [HvW]

453 ———. The old fire god and his symbolism at Teotihuacan (IAI/I, 4, 1977, p. 7–61, illus.)

Identification of designs on Teotihuacan ceramics, sculptures and mural paintings. [HvW]

454 **Webster, David.** Three walled sites of the northern Maya lowlands (Journal of Field Archaeology [Boston Univ.] 5:4, Winter 1978, p. 375–390, illus., maps)

Describes prehispanic walls of Coba, Dzonot Ake and Chacchob and links them to Puuc expansion AD 900–1000, with continued later expansion at a lower level of intensity. [NH]

455 **Wilk, Richard.** Microscopic analysis of chipped stone tools from Barton Ramie, British Honduras (CEM/ECM, 10, 1976/1977, p. 53–68, illus.)

Preliminary classification and notes on selected tools from middle preclassic through early postclassic house mounds. [HvW]

456 **Willey, Gordon R.** *ed.* Excavations at Seibal, Department of Peten, Guatemala. Cambridge, Mass., Harvard Univ., Peabody Museum of Archaeology and Ethnology, 1978. 250 p., bibl., illus., maps, tables (Memoirs, 14:1/3)

Consists of three studies: 1) Gordon R. Willey's "The Artifacts;" 2) Gair Tourtellot III, Jeremy A. Sabloff and Robert Sharick's "A Reconnaissance of Cancuen;" and 3) Gair Tourtellot III, Norman Hammond, and Richard M. Rose's "A Brief Reconnaissance of Itzan." The first work is a descriptive and comparative account of the Seibal artifacts, with several technical chapters by other authors including obsidian analysis and use-wear. The second and third studies describe subsidiary reconnaissance carried out by Seibal Project staff, the first substantial, the second preliminary. [NH]

457 Winter, Marcus C. Dos fechas de carbón 14 de la época I de Monte Albán, Oaxaca. México, Instituto Nacional de Antropología e Historia (INAH), Centro Regional de Oaxaca, 1978. 13 p., illus., tables (Estudios de antropología e historia, 7)

Classification of pottery associated with radiocarbon samples that provide a 600–400 BC range for the early phase of period 1. The pottery of the preceding Rosario phase is classified by the author in his monograph *Cerámica de la fase Rosario encontrada en dos pozos tronco-cónicos en el sitio de Tierras Largas, Valle de Oaxaca, México* (México, INAH, Centro Regional de Oaxaca, 1976, 22 p., illus.). [HvW]

NATIVE SOURCES

458 Barthel, Thomas S. Die Mayahieroglyphe "Gesang" (IAI/I, 4, 1977, p. 95–104)

Interprets the phonetic value of T 507 ("spotted kan," maize) as *kay* (song, to sing) and *kaayah* (to trade, sell). Comments on homophonic equivalences, epigraphic varieties and associations, and on ritual connotations in various thematic contexts. [HvW]

459 ———. A Tuebingen key to Maya glyphs: on the occasion of the quincentennial anniversary of the Eberhard Karls University (MLV/T, 26, Nov. 1977, p. 97–102, tables)

List of about 150 affixes and 150 main signs with their proposed equivalents in Maya lowland and highland languages, or in English. [HvW]

460 ———. Untersuchungen zur Grossen Göttin der Maya (DGV/ZE, 102:1, 1977, p. 44–102)

This "Investigation of the Great Goddess" is a lucid and penetrating interpretation of the numerous aspects, names, and functions of the Moon Goddess and of related themes (e.g. sacred bundles, serpent associations, directional and sequential ordering schemes, etc.), based on colonial sources, codices, epigraphy and iconography. Like Dütting's "Great Goddess" (see *HLAS 39:298*), Barthel's article also contains numerous transcriptions of glyphic texts, and both articles, being complementary, represent the most detailed and comprehensive coverage of the subject since Eric Thompson's writings. [HvW]

461 Caso, Alfonso. Reyes y reinos de la Mixteca. México, Fondo de Cultura Económica, 1977. 246 p., col. plates, illus., map (Sección de obras de antropología)

Caso's final work, published posthumously with the collaboration of Ignacio Bernal, is a major synthesis of numerous Mixtec regional dynastic histories, based on his pioneering interpretations of pictorial manuscripts and maps. Appendices include genealogical charts, listing places and events with their Mixtec/Christian dates. Includes appendices. [HvW]

462 Closs, Michael P. The initial series on Stela 5 at Pixoy (SAA/AA, 43:4, Oct. 1978, p. 690–694, illus.)

Interpretation of a recently discovered inscription, notable for its unorthodox usage of the moon sign. For a similar interpretation, see Berthold Riese's "Eine Unorthodoxe Maya Initial Serie auf Stela 5 aus Pixoy, Campeche" in *Ethnologica Americana* (Düsseldorf, FRG, 15:3, Sept./Okt. 1978, p. 862–863, illus.) See also Karl H. Meyer and Berthold Riese's "Ein Inschriftenfund in Playa del Carmen, Mexico" in the same issue of *Ethnologica* (p. 859–861, illus.). [HvW]

463 Gates, William. An outline dictionary of Maya glyphs. N.Y., Dover, 1978. 204 p., illus., tables.

Useful reprint of 1931 work. Original scarce. Arguable scholarly value. Modified by the addition of "Glyph Studies," 1932. [NH]

464 Graham, Ian. The art of Maya hieroglyphic writing. Cambridge, Mass.,

Harvard Univ., Peabody Museum of Archaeology and Ethnology, 1971. 63 p., illus.

Catalogue of an exhibition, N.Y., 1971. [NH]

465 ——— and **Eric von Euw.** Corpus of Maya hieroglyphic inscriptions. v. 2, pt. 2, Naranjo, Chunhuitz, Xuanantunich; v. 3, pt. 1/2, Yaxchilan; v. 4, pt. 1, Pixoy, Tzum, Itzimte; v. 5, pt. 1, Xultun. Cambridge, Mass., Harvard Univ., Peabody Museum of Archaeology and Ethnology, 1977/1979. 4 v. (58, 125, 67, 62 p.)

For review of v. 1 and v. 2, pt. 1, see *HLAS 39:542-543* of this major endeavor, maintaining the superlative standards of the first parts. A fundamental contribution. [NH]

466 **Knorozov, Iurii V.** Ieroglificheskie rukopisi Maiia (The hieroglyphic manuscripts of the Maya). Leningrad, USSR, Izdatel'stvo Nauka, 1975. 272 p., illus.

Description of pictorial elements and phonetic transcription of the glyphs in Dresden, Paris, Madrid, and Grolier, with translation into Russian. Includes commentary with details about these manuscripts, the circumstances of their composition, and the aims they were intended to serve. [HvW (based on summary by Robert V. Allen)]

467 **McDonald, Andrew J.** Two middle preclassic engraved monuments at Tzutzuculi on the Chiapas coast of Mexico (SAA/AA, 42:2, Oct. 1977, p. 560-566, illus.)

Two Olmec-style engraved boulders were found set on each side of the south stair of Mound 4; the site layout is compared to that of La Venta. C14 assays suggest a data ca. 600-400 b.c. [NH]

468 **Nicholson, H.B.** The deity 9 Wind "Ehecatl Quetzalcoatl" in the Mixteca

pictorials (UCLA/JLAL, 4:1, Summer 1978, p. 61-92, illus.)

Detailed exposition, with sober evaluation of previous research, of numerous depictions of this deity that corresponds iconographically to the central Mexican Ehecatl-Quetzalcoatl, and that may have been the direct lineal ancestor of Mixtec royalty. [HvW]

469 **Pahl, Gary W.** The inscriptions of Río Amarillo and Los Higos: secondary centers of the southeastern Maya frontier (UCLA/JLAL, 3:1, Summer 1977, p. 133-154, bibl., illus., maps, tables)

Documents appearance of emblem glyphs around 9.17.0.0.0. in secondary sites of the Copan region, suggesting increasing independence of Copan. [NH]

470 **Schalén, C.** On the possible astronomical nature of Maya inscriptions (SEM/E, 42:1/2, 1977, p. 69-73, table)

Commentary on the Thompson-Ludendorff controversy relating to this subject. [HvW]

471 **Troike, Nancy P.** Fundamental changes in the interpretation of the Mixtec codices (SAA/AA, 43:4, Oct. 1978, p. 553-568)

Report on work in progress or completed since 1974, by various researchers, aimed at revisions, with new interpretations, of the contents of the pictorial manuscripts. Troike advises that "almost everything now in print concerning the Mixtec codices is out-of-date and inaccurate." See also Eva Hunt's "The Provenience and Contents of the Porfirio Díaz and Fernández Leal Codices: Some New Data and Analysis" also in *American Antiquity* (43:4, Oct. 1978, p. 673-690, map, tables). [HvW]

ARCHAEOLOGY: Caribbean Area

W. JERALD KENNEDY, *Assistant Professor of Anthropology, Florida Atlantic University*

IN THE LAST TWO YEARS we have seen steady, continuing work both in Caribbean and Central American archaeology. Although space limitations do not allow for exhaustive treatment, it is hoped that this bibliography will serve as a useful guide to the literature in the field.

CARIBBEAN: Caribbeanists will miss Oswaldo Ignacio Morales-Patiño, well-known Cuban anthropologist who died in July 1978. His obituary and bibliography will be published in the *Journal of the Virgin Islands Archaeological Society* (6, 1979).

Ongoing research in the Caribbean is noted by Charles Hoffman in "Research Notes" (see *American Antiquity*, 43:3, 1978, p. 530). Several regional chronological syntheses of Caribbean prehistory are most welcome additions to the archaeological literature. See especially those by Rouse (item **511**), Meggers and Evans (item **501**), Harris (item **492**), and Sears and Sullivan (item **514**).

Publications and reports have appeared about excavations of sites in Venezuela, the Dominican Republic, the Bahamas, Haiti, Puerto Rico, the Virgin Islands, Dominique, St. Kitts, Trinidad, Tobago, Curaçao, and Cuba.

Two bibliographies are most welcome additions to the Caribbean archaeological literature, Perdomo's on petroglyphs and rock art (item **506**) and Vescelius' on the archaeology of the Virgin Islands (item **523**).

Two important professional conferences were held in 1978. The VII International Congress for the Study of Pre-Columbian Cultures of the Lesser Antilles in Caracas, and the Symposium on the Archaeology of the Caribbean in Ponce, P.R., which honored Antonio Ramos Ramírez.

CENTRAL AMERICA: The quality of archaeological research conducted in Central America over the past two years is also impressive. Richard Cooke spells out the varied research projects underway in the region, noting, among others, the work of Espinosa and Magnus in Nicaragua; Michael Snarskis and Fred Lange in Costa Rica; and Olga Linares in Panama (see "Research Notes," *American Antiquity,* 43:3, 1978, p. 510–530).

As in the Caribbean, several excellent regional syntheses have been published in the last two years. Haberland and Myers deal with the general region of lower Central America and the Intermediate Region (items **536** and **551**). Others concern more specific areas such as Helms and Magnus on coastal Nicaragua (items **538** and **548**); Stone's excellent update of Costa Rican prehistory (item **559**); and Linares and Cook on Panama (items **531** and **544**).

Several articles employ content analysis of ceramic and other non-utilitarian decorated artifacts in an attempt to better understand varied aspects of precolumbian cultures. See, for example, Helms (item **539**), Fonseca (item **535**) and Linares (item **546**).

Maria Bozzoli's Costa Rican bibliography has an extensive archaeology section which should be of use to specialists (item **528**) while the books by Casimir and Ferrero could be used as textbooks (items **530** and **533**).

Other themes noted are articles dealing with extra-regional contacts (items **534** and **553**) and subsistence patterns (items **542, 547, 549**).

Several unpublished but significant works should also be acknowledged:

MASTER'S THESES

Einhaus, Catherine Shelton. A technological and functional analysis of stone tools from Isle Palenque, Panama. Temple Univ., 1978.

DOCTORAL DISSERTATIONS

Alegría, Ricardo. Ball courts and ceremonial plazas in the West Indies. Harvard Univ., 1977.

Snarskis, Michael. The archaeology of the Atlantic Watershed of Costa Rica. Columbia Univ., 1978.

ANTILLES

472 Alegría, Ricardo E. La primera exposición de piezas arqueológicas y el establecimiento del primer museo en Puerto Rico (ICP/R, 17:64, julio/sept. 1974, p. 37–42, illus.)

The article describes artifacts that were exhibited during the first public exposition of Puerto Rico and the establishment of the first museum in 1854 in Puerto Rico.

473 Arvelo B., Lillian. Tucuragua: un yacimiento aruquinoide del Orinoco Medio (*in* International Congress for the Study of Pre-Columbian Cultures of the Lesser Antilles, *VII, Montreal, Canada, 1978* [see item **495**] p. 27–37, bibl., plates)

A preliminary report on recent investigations of Tucuragua, a site in the Middle Orinoco region of Venezuela. While poorly preserved, artifacts reveal the culture cultivated both manioc and maize. Ceramic elements are typically Arauquinoid within Period IV (AD 1000–AD 1500). A single C14 date from this site was AD 1385.

474 Bentz, Pedro J. Borrell. Buceando tras los taínos (MHD/B, 7:11, sept. 1978, p. 17–26, plates)

Descriptive report on an investigation of cave sites in the vicinity of Macao, Dominican Republic. The artifacts encountered in this survey are discussed.

475 Chanlatte Baik, Luis A. Cultura igneri: investigaciones arqueológicas en Guayanilla, Puerto Rico. pt. 1, Tecla II. Santo Domingo, Museo del Hombre Dominicano, 1976. 168 p., bibl., illus., maps, plates, tables (Serie investigaciones, 5)

An excellent, well illustrated monograph dealing with archaeological investigations in Guayanilla, Puerto Rico. The author presents data from Tecla II site. Ceramics, bone, shell, stone, and other artifacts are described by level at this Ostionoid Period site.

476 Dacal Moure, Ramón. Artefactos de concha en las comunidades aborígenes cubanas. La Habana, Univ. de La Habana, Museo Antropológico Montane, 1978. 114 p., bibl., illus., tables (Publicación, 5)

The author examines shell artifacts found in Cuba. Nine hundred and fifty-five specimens from the Montane Museum of Anthropology are classified according to use.

Techniques of manufacture are also covered. Well illustrated.

477 Dávila y Dávila, Ovidio. Analysis of the lithic materials of the Savanne Carrée No. 2 site, Fort Liberté region in Haiti (MHD/B, 7:10, mayo 1978, p. 202–226, bibl., illus., maps, table)

A preliminary study of a lithic assemblage from the Savanne Carré No. 2 site in the Fort Liberté region in Haiti. Utilizing statistical techniques, an analytical and typological study is presented.

478 Dick, Kenneth C. Aboriginal and early Spanish names of some Caribbean, Circum-Caribbean islands and cays (Virgin Islands Archaeological Society Journal [St. Thomas, US Virgin Islands] 4, 1977, p. 17–41, tables)

An informative article which deals with the aboriginal etymology and early Spanish terms for various place names in the Circum-Caribbean area.

479 Escardo, Mauricio E. Who were the inhabitants of the Virgin Islands at the time of Columbus' arrival? (*in* International Congress for the Study of Pre-Columbian Cultures of the Lesser Antilles, *VII, Montreal, Canada, 1978* [see item **495**] p. 245–257, bibl.)

Using ethnohistoric documents an attempt is made to establish who inhabited the Virgin Islands at the time of first contact by the Europeans. The conclusion tentatively reached is that neither Arawak nor Island Carib were present but rather another ethnic group whose origins are unknown.

480 Figueredo, Alfredo E. Prehistoric ethnozoology of the Virgin Islands (*in* International Congress for the Study of Pre-Columbian Cultures of the Lesser Antilles, *VII, Montreal, Canada, 1978* [see item **495**] p. 39–45, bibl.)

The author examines the faunal species found principally in an archaeological context (neo-Indian) in the Virgin Islands. He attempts to catalogue these animals which were used as food, pets, etc., along with the various microenvironments they inhabited.

481 ——— and Stephen D. Glazier. A revised aboriginal ethnohistory of Trinidad (*in* International Congress for the Study of Pre-Columbian Cultures of the Lesser Antilles, VII, Montreal, Canada, 1978 [see item 495] p. 259–262, bibl.)

The authors suggest that aboriginal Trinidad in the 16th century had various Carib-speaking Indians along with true Arawakan and possibly Salivan-speaking peoples. Culture traits appear to be more akin to mainland Guianas Tropical Forest groups rather than Circum-Caribbean.

482 **Fortuna, Luis.** Análisis polínico de Santa Abajo (MHD/B, 7:10, mayo 1978, p. 125–130, bibl.)

Results of palynological studies from Sanate Abajo, an Ostionoid Period site in the Dominican Republic. A general ecological profile of the area is reconstructed as well as a discussion and listing of various plants that were utilized.

483 ———. Informe sobre la flora actual en los alrededores del yacimiento arqueológico del paraje Sanate Abajo en el municipio de Higucy, provincia de la Altagracia (MHD/B, 7:10, mayo 1978, p. 131–132)

A short report on the present floral assemblage found in the environs of the Sanate Abajo site. Thirty-two separate genera were observed.

484 **Galicia, Fulvia Nieves de.** Banador: un sitio arqueológico del Bajo Orinoco (in International Congress for the Study of Pre-Columbian Cultures of the Lesser Antilles, VII, Montreal, Canada, 1978 [see item 495] p. 71–80, bibl., plates)

A brief article dealing with Banador, a site in the Lower Orinoco in Venezuela. The author believes this to be a unique site in the region, based on the appearance of typical (for the area) corrugated ceramics. It is suggested that these influences diffused from northwest Colombia through the Lake Maracaibo area or perhaps the Amazonian region of Brazil.

485 **García Arévalo, Manuel Antonio.** Influencia de la dieta indo-hispánica en la cerámica taína (in International Congress for the Study of Pre-Columbian Cultures of the Lesser Antilles, VII, Montreal, Canada, 1978 [see item 495] p. 263–267, bibl., illus., plate)

A discussion of changes in ceramic form and design among the Taino during the colonial period. The author believes that a more abundant use of meat and cereal grains plus food preparation techniques introduced by the Spanish were in large part responsible for changes noted in ceramics during this period.

486 ——— and **Julia Tavares.** Presentación (MHD/B, 7:10, mayo 1978, p. 31–44, plates)

A general discussion of recent archaeological findings from Sanate, a multicomponent site in Altagracia province, Dominican Republic. The earliest ceramic levels are Ostionoid related with C14 dates of AD 1050. Upper occupation levels suggest a transition, perhaps an intermediate phase between Ostionoid and Chicoid ceramic styles.

487 **Glazier, Stephen D.** Trade and warfare in protohistoric Trinidad (in International Congress for the Study of Pre-Columbian Cultures of the Lesser Antilles, VII, Montreal, Canada, 1978 [see item 495] p. 279–282, bibl.)

A brief article on trade and warfare in Trinidad after the arrival of Columbus. The author sees both as endemic to this island and draws parallels that were found among other neolithic type swiddeners.

488 **Goodwin, R. Christopher** and **Cyd Heymann.** St. Kitts salvage archeology (EJ, 55:1, March 1977, p. 20–23, plates)

Authors give a brief report on salvage excavations of the Sugar Factory Pier site on the island of St. Kitts. The site of Saladoid people reflects an occupation beginning around AD 120 and terminating around AD 650. Cultural deprivation beginning about AD 400 is reflected in ceramics being of poor quality. Attempts to explain this cultural decline lead to a consideration of dietary stress and protein deficiency as the likely causal factor.

489 **Gullick, C.J.M.R.** Black Carib origins and early society (in International Congress for the Study of Pre-Columbian Cultures of the Lesser Antilles, VII, Montreal, Canada, 1978 [see item 495] p. 283–289, bibl.)

By using ethnohistoric documents the author pursues the question of the roots of black Carib society. Gullick concludes they were very likely a Maroon people, i.e. runaway slaves, but differing from other Maroon peoples by exhibiting more Amerindian cultural traits.

490 Hall, Shirley Michelene. Restos alimenticios (MHD/B, 7:10, mayo 1978, p. 95–124, bibl., illus., plates, tables)

Results of 1978 excavations at the Ostionoid Period site of Sanate Abajo. The focus is on subsistence patterns and diet of the local population. A detailed analysis, by level, of percentages of various species of shell fish utilized is of interest. A C14 date of AD 1050 is noted.

491 Handler, Jerome S. The Bird-Man: a Jamaican Arawak wooden idol (Jamaica Journal [Institute of Jamaica, Kingston] 11:3/4, March 1978, p. 25–29, bibl., plates)

A general description and analysis of three unique Arawakan carved wooden figures from Jamaica. The author feels the "so-called Bird Man" figure was likely a Zemi, perhaps associated with plant protection and growth.

492 Harris, Peter. A revised chronological framework for ceramic Trinidad and Tobago (in International Congress for the Study of Pre-Columbian Cultures of the Lesser Antilles, VII, Montreal, Canada, 1978 [see item 495] p. 47–63, bibl.)

Recent archaeological findings necessitate a revision of the temporal framework for Trinidad and Tobago. The proposed new chronology is based on recent findings in the Lesser Antilles. The author spells out the new data and notes that four traditions appear to affect Trinidad and Tobago through time.

493 Hatt, Gudmun. Notas sobre la arqueología de Santo Domingo (MHD/B, 7:11, sept. 1978, p. 221–240, bibl., illus., map, plates)

Reprinting of an early article originally published in 1932 by Gudmun Hatt, a pioneer in Caribbean archaeology, who recounts his observations on a trip to the Dominican Republic in 1923.

494 Hummelinck, P. Wagenaar. Rotstekeningen van Curaçao, Aruba en Bonaire (NWIG, 49:1/2, Nov. 1972, p. 1–66, illus., maps, plates, tables)

A description of petroglyphs, principally from the island of Bonaire. Petroglyphs from Aruba and Curaçao are also reported.

495 International Congress for the Study of Pre-Columbian Cultures of the Lesser Antilles, VII, Montreal, Canada, 1978. Proceedings. Montreal, Can., Univ. de

Montreal, Centre de Recherches Caraïbes, 1978. 349 p.

Papers from the conference are reviewed separately in this section and entered under each author's name, see items 473, 479–481, 484–485, 487, 489, 492, 498, 508–509, 512–513, 516, 518–519, 524–525, 752–753, 859, 864, 870 and 872–874.

496 Jiménez Lambertus, Abelardo. Representación simbólica de la tortuga mítica en el arte cerámico taíno (MHD/B, 7:11, sept. 1978, p. 63–76, plates)

The turtle in Taino mythology and its presence in Taino ceramics is discussed. Several symbolic motifs are suggested.

497 Kay, Katheryne. Sculptured stone from St. Thomas, U.S. Virgin Islands (Virgin Islands Archaeological Society Journal [St. Thomas, US Virgin Islands] 3, 1976, p. 15–18, plates)

Author briefly reports on two unique carved stone artifacts from St. Thomas. One, a petaloid celt with a carved human face; the other, an "Elbow Stone," carved in low relief with a geometric design. The author feels stone sculpture is a valid indicator of periods of vigorous artistic and intellectual activity.

498 Kerby, I.A. Earle. Some notes of interest to the archaeology of the Antilles (in International Congress for the Study of Pre-Columbian Cultures of the Lesser Antilles, VII, Montreal, Canada, 1978 [see item 495] p. 65–67)

The author briefly discusses the source and use of rubber, vegetal emetics, ritual enemas, three pointed stones and white on red ceramic decoration in the Caribbean.

499 Kozlowski, Janusz. Las industrias de la piedra tallada de Cuba en el contexto del Caribe. La Habana, Academia de Ciencias de Cuba, Instituto de Ciencias Sociales, 1975. 35 p., bibl., illus., tables (Serie arqueológica, 5)

Research conducted on Cuban lithic materials in collections at the Univ. of Oriente, Montane Museum of Havana Univ. and the Institute of Archaeology. A tentative classification is given along with details on manufacturing techniques. Lithic industries are presented by geographical area, chronology and origins. Well illustrated.

500 Manón Arredondo, Manuel J. Importancia arqueológica de los ingenios indohispánicos de las Antillas (MHD/B, 7:10, mayo 1978, p. 139–164, bibl., maps, plates)

The author discusses the significance in pursuing archaeological studies of early 16th and 17th-century sugar mills and factories in the Antilles which to date have been neglected. A specific early sugarcane industrial complex in the Dominican Republic is covered.

501 Meggers, Betty J. and **Clifford Evans.** Las tierras bajas de Suramérica y las Antillas (Estudios Arqueológicos [Centro de Investigaciones Arqueológicas. Ediciones de la Univ. Católica, Quito] 1977, p. 11–69, bibl., maps)

An excellent and important summary of the present archaeological knowledge covering the area west of Cuba to Tierra del Fuego from the Atlantic to the Andes. The authors present a time-space framework from 5000 BC to AD 1500 in four major regions: 1) the southern lowlands of South America; 2) the coastal band of the Amazon; 3) Venezuela; and 4) the Antilles. Consideration is given to the movements of people and diffusion route vectors through time.

502 Morbán Laucer, Fernando and **Abelardo Jiménez Lambertus.** Enterramientos humanos localizados en Sanate (MHD/B, 7:10, mayo 1978, p. 75–93, bibl., plates)

Discussion of human osteological materials and associated lithic artifacts from three burials excavated in the vicinity of Sanate, Altagracia province, Dominican Republic. The burials are placed in the Ostionoid Period between AD 820–AD 1050.

503 Myers, Robert A. Ethnohistorical vs. ecological considerations: the case of Dominica's Amerindians (in International Congress for the Study of Pre-Columbian Cultures of the Lesser Antilles, VII, Montreal, Canada, 1978 [see item **495**] p. 325–342, bibl., illus.)

Ethnohistoric records, artifact collections and other data are presented to refute earlier reports that Dominica, due to lack of adequate food sources was at best a temporary place of settlement for early Amerindians.

504 Nicholson, Desmond N. The importance of sea-levels Caribbean archaeology (Virgin Islands Archaeological Society Journal [St. Thomas, US Virgin Islands] 3, 1976, p. 19–21, bibl., maps)

A brief discussion of types of sea-level change with implications for Caribbean archaeology. The author cites recent changes of sea level and shorelines of Antigua caused by tectonic movements, erosion and subsequent sedimentation. As a result, archaeological sites will be found some distance from the present shoreline while others closer to shore may be heavily covered by sand and sediments. Less recent sea-level changes are also considered. Causal factors produce eustatic changes brought about by alternate melting and build up of glacial areas. Many early lithic sites are presently submerged.

505 Ortega, Elpidio. Informe sobre investigaciones arqueológicas realizadas en la región este del país, zona costera desde Macao a Punta Espada (MHD/B, 7:11, sept. 1978, p. 76–105, bibl., maps, plates)

A brief discussion of the results of an archaeological reconnaissance from Macao al Cabo to Punta Espada in the Dominican Republic. Four sites are tested in this study. Two time periods were delineated; Period I was characterized by Ostionoid ceramics, Period II was typically Chicoid ceramics.

506 Pagán Perdomo, Dato. Bibliografía sumaria sobre el arte rupestre del Caribe (MHD/B, 7:11, sept. 1978, p. 107–130)

An extensive bibliography which compiles the principal publications covering petroglyphs and rock art in the Caribbean.

507 Pena Sosa, Santiago. Aspectos arqueológicos de Río San Juan (MHD/B, 7:11, sept. 1978, p. 131–140, bibl., plates)

Discussion of an archaeological site in the Municipio Río San Juan, Dominican Republic. At least two occupation levels were noted, the earlier possessing ceramics of the Ostionoid series, the later one, Meillacoid. Artifacts and ecological configurations are discussed. It is felt that the occupants of the site subsisted mainly on fish and collecting.

508 Robinson, Linda Sickler. Modified Oliva shells from the Virgin Islands: a morphological study (in International Congress for the Study of Pre-Columbian Cultures of the Lesser Antilles, VII, Montreal, Canada, 1978 [see item **495**] p. 169–187, bibl., tables)

A preliminary report examining 84 modified Oliva shell ornaments from collections in the Virgin Islands. The focus of the article was to consider the use of the Oliva shell as ornaments and any cultural differences in their selection and modification. Admitting to a relatively small sample; the author deals principally with an analysis of attributes of the modified shells.

509 Roget, Henry Petitjean. Reconnaissance archéologique a l'Ile de la Dominique, West Indies (*in* International Congress for the Study of Pre-Columbian Cultures of the Lesser Antilles, *VII, Montreal, Canada, 1978* [see item **495**] p. 81–97, bibl., maps, plates)

The article summarizes 24 archaeological sites found on the island of Dominique.

510 Rouse, Irving. Objetivos de la investigación arqueológica en el Caribe (MHD/B, 7:11, sept. 1978, p. 11–15)

A brief summary article which traces the direction of interests in Caribbean archaeology since the early 1900s to present day.

511 —— **and Louis Allaire.** Caribbean (*in* Taylor, R.E. and C.W. Meighan *eds.* Chronologies in New World archaeology [see item **259**] p. 431–481, bibl., tables)

A key article on the Caribbean culture area which summarizes current data (up to 1977) in order to establish a chronological framework for the Caribbean. The author synthesizes local archaeological complexes through time in the Orinoco River region, Venezuelan llanos, the Caribbean mountains, the Coastal region, the Lesser and Greater Antilles. A complete listing of C14 dates and chronologies of each region is presented.

512 Ruiz, Kay Tarble de. Comparación estilística entre la cerámica de Langunillas, estado Zulia y Santa Ana, estado Trujillo, Venezuela nor-occidental (*in* International Congress for the Study of Pre-Columbian Cultures of the Lesser Antilles, *VII, Montreal, Canada, 1978* [see item **495**] p. 190–194, bibl.)

The article compared ceramics from two sites in Venezuela; Lagunillas in the state of Zulia, and Santa Ana in the state of Trujillo. C14 dates between 480 BC and 210 BC suggest a Period II placement (1000 BC–AD 300). While the author notes ceramic dif-ferences between these sites she suggests the commonalities are much greater.

513 Sanoja, Mario. Proyecto Orinoco: excavación en el sitio arqueológico de los Castillos de Guyana, Territorio Federal Delta Amacuro, Venezuela (*in* International Congress for the Study of Pre-Columbian Cultures of the Lesser Antilles, *VII, Montreal, Canada, 1978* [see item **495**] p. 157–168, bibl., maps, plates)

A brief discussion of excavations and the importance of the Castillo de Guyana site. The fortress built circa AD 1600 by the Spanish is considered in terms of a most important civil and military base.

514 Sears, William H. and Shaun O. Sullivan. Bahamas prehistory (SAA/AA, 43:1, Jan. 1978, p. 3–25, bibl., map, plate, tables)

Important article on Bahamian prehistory resulting from archaeological survey and test excavations of 53 sites. Previous work in Bahamian archaeology is covered as is a description of artifacts both ceramic and non-ceramic. Site distribution and comparison between various zones are treated which suggest movements of Antillian Arawak people to secure salt with a local cultural tradition emerging around AD 1000. Shortly theraafter this tradition spreads to the central Bahamian islands. Ecological factors are considered to explain these movements and their direction.

515 Sued-Badillo, Jalil. La mujer indígena y su sociedad. Río Piedras, P.R., El Gazir, 1975. 17 p., bibl., plates.

Utilizing both ethnohistoric documents and artifactual evidence, the author describes the role and position of women in various facets of Caribbean and Arawakan culture in precolumbian times.

516 Sutty, Lesley A. A study of shells and shelled objects from six precolumbian sites in the Grenadines of St. Vincent and Grenada (*in* International Congress for the Study of Pre-Columbian Cultures of the Lesser Antilles, *VII, Montreal, Canada, 1978* [see item **495**] p. 195–210, bibl., plates)

The article examines and describes worked shell artifacts from six sites in the Grenadines of Arawak and Carib occupation. The question of whether the origins of worked shell were Caliviny/Carib is pursued.

517 Valdez A., María Luisa. Nuevos petroglifos localizados en la Cordillera Central, República Dominicana (MHD/B, 7:10, mayo 1978, p. 227–238, bibl., plates)

A description of several new petroglyphs found in the region of Los Huesos, La Vega province in central Dominican Republic. The author concludes these were likely made by groups of Taino and feels that they reflect some relationship with ceremonialism.

518 Vargas Arenas, Iraida. Puerto Santo: un nuevo sitio arqueológico en la costa oriental de Venezuela (in International Congress for the Study of Pre-Columbian Cultures of the Lesser Antilles, VII, Montreal, Canada, 1978 [see item 495] p. 211–220, bibl., plates)

A report describing the site of Puerto Santo, in the state of Sucre, Venezuela. Ceramics of both Barrancoid and Saladoid traditions. The author believes data suggests diffusion of these groups from the Middle and Lower Orinoco toward the coast of Venezuela beginning about the time of Christ up to 500 AD.

519 ——— and Mario Sanoja. Comparaciones entre la arqueología del Bajo y Medio Orinoco (in International Congress for the Study of Pre-Columbian Cultures of the Lesser Antilles, VII, Montreal, Canada, 1978 [see item 495] p. 221–229, bibl., plates)

The author argues that the Barrancoid and Ronquinoid traditions represent independent developments. Giving a date of 655 BC from the site of La Gruta the same strata indicate marked differences between ceramic of Ronquin and Barrancas styles.

520 Vega Boyrie, Bernardo. El lambi en nuestra cultura prehispánica (MHD/B, 7:10, mayo 1978, p. 173–183, plates)

Elaboration on the widespread utilization of the Strombus Gigas shell fish and its importance in the aboriginal cultures of Hispaniola. Various uses such as a food source, musical instrument, a material for utilitarian implements, ornaments and as a magical-religious element are discussed.

521 ———. Pictografías. Santo Domingo, Museo del Hombre Dominicano, 1976. 44 p., plates.

Illustrated booklet which discusses and compares varied precolumbian picto-graphs found in cave sites in the Dominican Republic.

522 Veloz Maggiolo, Marcio. Variantes productivas de la agricultores precolombinos antillanos (MHD/B, 7:11, sept. 1978, p. 177–183, bibl.)

A discussion of three economic subsistence modes in the Antilles in prehistoric time. Proto-agriculture, tropical and proto-theocratic modes of production and their variants are discussed.

523 Vescelius, Gary S. A bibliography of Virgin Islands archaeology (Virgin Islands Archaeological Society Journal [St. Thomas, US Virgin Islands] 4, 1977, p.1–16)

A comprehensive bibliography of published and unpublished materials dealing with the archaeology of the Virgin Islands.

524 Winter, John. A note on Bahamian griddles (in International Congress for the Study of Pre-Columbian Cultures of the Lesser Antilles, VII, Montreal, Canada, 1978 [see item 495] p. 231–236, bibl., illus.)

A short article which examines a variety of griddles found in the Bahamas. The focus is on the comparison of manufacturing techniques, surface wear and impressions in an attempt to elicit their use.

525 ———. Preliminary work from the McKay site on Crooked Island (in International Congress for the Study of Pre-Columbian Cultures of the Lesser Antilles, VII, Montreal, Canada, 1978 [see item 495] p. 237–242, bibl., illus.)

Discussion of preliminary archaeological investigations of the McKay site on Crooked Island. While the main body of artifacts suggest native Bahamian origins some ceramics reflect Chicoid and Meillacoid derivation. As both are found in the same strata co-existence of these two traditions is inferred. C14 dates suggest to the author that Chicoid influence was present in the Bahamas by AD 1250.

CENTRAL AMERICA

526 Accola, Richard M. Análisis de la difracción de rayos X: su aplicación experimental en el estudio de la cerámica poliocromada de Nicoya, Costa Rica (MNCR/V,

3:1/2, 1977, p. 37–45, bibl., map, plate, table)

A utilization of the x-ray diffraction technique on Mora Polychrome, a Middle Period (AD 800–1200) ceramic in Costa Rica. In hopes of ascertaining whether these ceramics were made in various "centers" or of "local" manufacture the author concludes: 1) ceramics from the area of Bahía Salinas are not from the same interaction sphere of Playa Panamá and Nosara in the Nicoya Peninsula; 2) two varieties of Mora Polychrome appear to be manufactured in a single center and were being traded to Playa Panamá and Nosara but not with the Salinas site; and 3) other Mora Polychrome varieties reflect local manufacture and were made in various areas.

527 Balser S., Carlos. El jade de Costa Rica: un album arqueológico con reproducciones en color (an archaeological picture book with color reproductions). Textos en español e inglés con 1 mapa. San José, Litografía Lehmann, 1974. 88 p., bibl., map, plates.

A handbook on precolumbian "jade" artifacts found in Costa Rica. The author describes and illustrates jade of foreign styles, those exhibiting Mayan incision, and local styles from Guanacaste and the Atlantic Watershed regions. Well illustrated, in Spanish and English.

528 Bozzoli de Wille, María E. Bibliografía antropológica de Costa Rica (BBAA, 38:47, 1976, p. 63–82)

A bibliography of publications dealing with the anthropology of Costa Rica, including archaeology. The reference work covers the years 1969–75.

529 Brook, Frederico and **Vittoro Minardi** eds. Arte precolombiana: Costa Rica/Panamá, catálogo. Roma, Instituto Italo-Latinoamericana, 1976. 1 v. (Unpaged) bibl., maps, plates, tables.

An illustrated book dealing with selected aspects of precolumbian art in Panama and Costa Rica. Predominantly ceramics and stone work of selected cultures.

530 Casimir de Brizuela, Gladys. Síntesis de arqueología. Prefacio de Mario A. Stoute Hassán. Panamá, Univ. de Panamá, Editorial Universitaria (EUPAN), 1973. 221 p., illus., maps, tables (Serie: arte)

A summary of Panamanian archaeol-

ogy from Paleo-Indian times to contact period. The archaeological regions of Darién, Coclé, Parita, Veraguas, and Chiriquí are covered.

531 Cooke, Richard G. and **Marcela Camargo R.** Arqueología (USMLA/LA, 6:9, nov. 1977, p. 115–172, bibl., maps)

A good historical review of the archaeology of the Coclé in Panama. C14 dates allow for the development of a chronology extending from 10,000 BC to contact period. Recent field work focusing on ecological problems and the development of agriculture in the region is covered.

532 Espinosa Estrada, Jorge. Excavaciones arqueológicas en El Bosque. Managua, Ministerio de Obras Públicas, Instituto Geográfico Nacional, Depto. de Antropología e Historia, 1976. 70 p., bibl., fold. illus., fold. maps, fold. plate, fold. table, illus., maps, plates, tables (Informe, 1)

An important monograph treating the first Paleo-Indian site found in northern Nicaragua and perhaps one of the oldest archaeological sites in America. Six C14 dates ranging from 32,000 BP to 18,100 BP were obtained.

533 Ferrero Acosta, Luis. Costa Rica precolombina: arqueología, etnología, tecnología, arte. San José, Editorial Costa Rica, 1975. 446 p., bibl., illus., maps, plates, tables (Biblioteca patria, 6)

Part of Editorial Costa Rica's collection dealing with the cultural heritage of Costa Rica. The book, well suited as an introduction to Costa Rican prehistory, is well organized as a textbook. Chapters on general archaeological concepts, archaeological regions, technology, esthetics, and art.

534 Fonseca Z., Oscar M. and **James B. Richardson, III.** South American and Mayan cultural contacts at the Las Huacas site, Costa Rica (Annals of Carnegie Museum [Pittsburgh, Pa.] 47:13, Sept. 1978, p. 299–317, bibl., plates, tables)

The article deals with a number of artifacts found in the Hartman Collection (1903) in the Carnegie Museum of Natural History. The specific artifacts described are llama effigies, mirror backs, a face pendant and reptilian effigy. The conclusion reached is that both South American and Mayan contacts existed during precolumbian times.

535 ———— and **Richard Scaglion.** Stylistic analysis of stone pendants from Las Huacas burial ground, Northwestern Costa Rica (Annals of Carnegie Museum [Pittsburgh, Pa.] 47:12, Sept. 1978, p. 281–298, bibl., illus., plates, tables)

Using the Hartman Costa Rican Collection, the authors employ a stylistic seriation analysis of stone pendants representing three bird categories—harpy eagles, three-dimensional quetzals, and two-dimensional quetzals. Scalograms revealed an artistic sequence for the stonework found at Las Huacas in the Nicoya Peninsula. A chronology for this sequence is presented.

536 **Haberland, Wolfgang.** Lower Central America (*in* Taylor, R.E. and C.W. Meighan *eds.* Chronologies in New World archaeology [see item **259**] p. 395–430, bibl., tables)

An excellent summary, up to 1973, of Lower Central American archaeology. The author covers its history, the present status of archaeological knowledge and suggests future research. C14 dates and regional chronologies in the area make this an extremely important article.

537 **Healy, Paul F.** Excavations at Río Claro, northeast Honduras: preliminary report (Journal of Field Archaeology [Boston Univ.] 5:1, Spring 1978, p. 15–29)

Author's preliminary reports on excavations of site H-CN-12, Río Claro in northeast Honduras. Dated between AD 1000–AD 1530. Author alludes to Lower Central American and Mesoamerican artifactual similarities. Site may be the ethnohistorical chiefdom center, Papayeca.

538 **Helms, Mary W.** Coastal adaptations as contact phenomena among the Miskito and Cuná Indians of lower Central America (*in* Stark, Barbara L. *ed.* Prehistoric coastal adaptations: the economy and ecology of maritime Middle America [see item **353**] p. 121–149, maps)

A regional assessment of settlement patterns and subsistence strategies among the contemporary coastal Miskito and Cuná Indians is considered. The author also reconstructs their prehistoric and early historic settlement patterns and concludes a diachronic approach is necessary to adequately understand the nature of the coastal adaptations.

539 ————. Iguanas and crocodilians in tropical American mythology and iconography with special reference to Panama (UCLA/JLAL, 3:1, 1977, p. 51–132, bibl., plates, tables)

The author interprets a select group of iconographic motifs found on polychrome ceramic wares and gold artifacts from precolumbian Panama. Emphasis is on analyzing art, myths, and chants of contemporary San Blas Cuná as well as other descendents of precolumbian populations. The commonly depicted crested crocodile god is seen as an *iguana* associated with ancient Panamanian cosmology and political ideology. Finally an examination of the role of the iguana in Classic Mayan cosmology is reviewed in this extremely interesting article.

540 **Ichon, Alain.** Tipos de sepultura precolombina en el sur de la Península de Azuero. Traducción de Reina Torres de Araúz. Panamá, Instituto Nacional de Cultura, Dirección Nacional de Patrimonio Histórico, 1975. 91 p., fold. tables, illus., maps, plates, tables.

The author discusses precolumbian burial practices in the southern part of Azuero Peninsula, Panama. Information is based on 1968–69 excavations in the region of Tonosí, principally the El India and La Canaza sites. Artifacts found in association with the burials are discussed.

541 **Kennedy, William J.** A Middle Period lithic tool assemblage from the Atlantic watershed region, Costa Rica (MNCR/V, 4:1, 1978, p. 43–56, bibl., maps, plates, tables)

A preliminary study of the utilitarian stone tools found at the Monte Cristo site in Costa Rica.

542 **Lange, Frederick W.** Coastal settlement in Northwestern Costa Rica (*in* Stark, Barbara L. *ed.* Prehistoric coastal adaptations: the economy and ecology of maritime Middle America [see item **353**] p. 101–119, bibl., maps)

A synthesis of settlement locations and subsistence patterns found in Northwest Costa Rica during precolumbian times. A time-space regional framework is presented. Consideration is given to population growth, trade, over exploitation of local fauna as important factors of culture change in this area.

543 ———. Estudios arqueológicos en el
Valle de Nosara, Guanacaste, Costa
Rica (MNCR/V, 3:1/2, 1977, p. 27–36, bibl.,
map, plate)
   A preliminary survey of the Nosara Valley on the Nicoya Peninsula, Costa Rica.
Twenty-six sites were located and data suggests heavy occupation during the Middle
Polychrome Period (AD 800–1200) with little
indication of earlier or later occupation. Extra areal contacts and trade relations are
treated.

544 **Linares, Olga F.** Adaptive strategies in
western Panama (World Archaeology
[Routledge & Kegan Paul, London] 8:3, Feb.
1977, p. 305–319, bibl., maps)
   Applying a biological concept (adaptive
radiation) to cultural phenomena, the author
compares two allotropic types of tropical forest agricultural lists in western Panama. The
possible effects of vegaculture and seed culture are examined in relation to their social
and political organization. The model presented has significance when dealing with
prehistoric population phenomena such as migration, colonization, population change and
adaptation in the humid versus seasonal
tropics.

545 ———. Animals that were bad to eat
were good to compete with: an analysis
of the Conte style from ancient Panama (in
Young, Philip and James Howe eds. Ritual and
symbol in native Central America. Eugene,
Univ. of Oregon, 1976, p. 1–20, bibl., illus.
[Anthropological papers, 9])
   Drawing heavily upon Lévi-Strauss, the
author creatively argues that the precolumbian Conte iconography functioned sym-
bolically to maintain individual and collective
statuses as well as to promote status change
by warfare and competitive display. Iconographic "symbol power" is seen by the
association of aggressive animals and individuals with equivalent roles.

546 ———. Ecology and the arts in ancient Panama on the development of
social rank and symbolism in the central provinces. Washington, Dumbarton Oaks, Trustees for Harvard Univ., 1977. 86 p., bibl., illus.,
maps, plates (Studies in pre-columbian art
and archaeology, 17)
   An excellent monograph dealing with
Cocle art as a product of human adjustments

to a specific environment in Veraguas and Cocle provinces. Utilizing both published and
unpublished materials, the author examines
Cocles art as a rich symbolic system which
gives insights in varied spheres of political and
social life of the prehistoric populations in
this region.

547 ———. "Garden hunting" in the
American tropics (Human Ecology
[Plenum, N.Y.] 4:4, 1976, p. 331–349, bibl.,
illus., map, tables)
   This article, focusing on faunal analysis in a prehistoric context, considers the
mammalian "harvesting" pattern found in the
Bocas del Toro region of Panama. Archaeological evidence suggests that wild animals
feeding regularly on domesticated crops were
hunted in the local gardens and cultivated
fields. As the gardens and cultivated fields
artificially increased the biomass of certain
mammalian forms, the author believes this
strategy may have functioned as a substitution
for animal domestication.

548 **Magnus, Richard W.** La costa atlántica
de Nicaragua (BNBD, 16, marzo/abril
1977, p. 1–6, illus.)
   Summary results of excavations by the
author conducted between 1971–77 in the
Atlantic Coast of Nicaragua; an area little
known archaeologically. The article treats
four ceramic traditions beginning 400 BC and
ending AD 765. C14 dates, ceramic types
and illustrations.

549 ———. The prehistoric and modern
subsistence patterns of the Atlantic
coast of Nicaragua: a comparison (in Stark,
Barbara L. ed. Prehistoric coastal adaptations:
the economy and ecology of maritime Middle America [see item 353] p. 61–79, bibl.,
maps, tables)
   Excellent comparison of modern and
prehistoric subsistence system and settlement
patterns of sites on the Atlantic Coast of
Nicaragua. The author suggests that data indicate a marked difference between prehistoric
and posthispanic procurement systems. Data
suggests the former to be central villages in a
riverine ecosystem and fishing stations on
the coast while the latter exhibit primary
coastal villages and inland agricultural
stations.

550 **Meléndez Ch., Carlos.** Papel de los
zopilotes en la religión de los indios del

Pacífico sur de Costa Rica (AGHCR/A, 1967/1969, p. 79–87, bibl.)

Using ethnohistoric documents and myth analyses of contemporary Bribri Indians in the Talamanca region, an attempt is made to resolve the question of whether precolumbian indigenous artifacts with bird motifs were indeed eagles. The author concludes that, in his opinion, the so-called "Eagles of Gold" were in fact representations of turkey buzzards.

551 Myers, Thomas P. Formative Period interaction spheres in the intermediate area: archaeology of Central America and adjacent South America (*in* Browman, David L. *ed.* Advances in Andean archaeology [see item **767**] p. 203–234, bibl., map, tables)

An excellent article in which the author presents evidence of several distinctive ceramic traditions in the Intermediate Area before 2000 BC. Origins and diffusion vectors of the Puerto Hormiga, Carinated Bow, Rancho Peludo and Pacific Coast ceramic traditions are discussed.

552 Ranere, Anthony J. and **Pat Hansell.** Early subsistence patterns along the Pacific coast of central Panama (*in* Stark, Barbara L. *ed.* Prehistoric coastal adaptations: the economy and ecology of maritime Middle America [see item **353**] p. 43–58, bibl.)

A reconstruction of procurement patterns in central Panama. The authors compare subsistence patterns of coastal and interior piedmont sites during the preceramic and early ceramic times (5000–1000 BC). Data suggests coastal peoples utilized aquatic resources while those sites located more inland seem to be campsites where plant collecting and the hunting of terrestrial animals were the predominant activities. Maize agriculture does not appear in these early subsistence patterns and when such complexes are found, they are situated in different environmental zones than the preceramic and early ceramic sites.

553 Reyes Mazzoni, Roberto R. Posibles influencias epi-Teotihuacanas en petroglifos de Honduras (MNCR/V, 3:1/2, 1977, p. 47–65, bibl., map, plates)

The author describes a group of petroglyphs from Honduras. He analyzes their symbolic content and stylistic affinities with Mexican cultures.

554 Rouse, Irving. Patrones y procesos en la arqueología de las Antillas (MHD/B, 7:10, mayo 1978, p. 185–199, bibl.)

The author believes that there has been a false dichotomy created with so-called "New Archaeology" and "Old Archaeology." Using Antillean prehistory as a model for his thesis, he argues that both foci are interdependent and important for the understanding of past cultures.

555 Snarskis, Michael J. Turrialba: a Paleo-Indian quarry and workshop site in eastern Costa Rica (SAA/AA, 33:1, Jan. 1979, p. 125–138, bibl., map, plates)

Excellent discussion of the first Paleo-Indian site found in eastern Costa Rica. The Turrialba site, a multicomponent quarry has yielded 18 fluted projectile points and other lithic material. Both North and South American types of Paleo-Indian points were noted.

556 ———. Turrialba, 9-FG-T: un sitio paleoindio en el este de Costa Rica (MNCR/V, 3:1/2, 1977, p. 13–27, bibl., maps, plates)

An important article treating the first Paleo-Indian site reported in Costa Rica. A multicomponent site in eastern Costa Rica revealed 17 fluted points in the Clovis tradition, one fishtail point and a variety of scrapers and tool types often associated with Paleo-Indian sites. The author believes these date between 7000–8000 BC.

557 ———; Héctor Gamboa P.; and **Oscar Fonseca Z.** El mastodonte de tibias, Costa Rica (MNCR/V, 3:1/2, 1977, p. 1–12, bibl., map, plates)

Report of a salvage excavation in the vicinity of San José in which a Pleistocene mastadon was found. No artifactual materials were found in association with the mammal.

558 Soto M., Ana Z. Técnicas del jade precolombino costarricense (Troquel [Banco Central de Costa Rica, San José] 5, 1976, p. 17–20)

A brief description of jade technology in precolumbian Costa Rica.

559 Stone, Doris. Precolumbian man in Costa Rica. Cambridge, Mass., Harvard Univ., Peabody Museum Press, 1977. 238 p., bibl., illus., maps, plates.

A companion volume to her *Precolumbian man finds Central America* (1976), the grand lady of Central American archaeology presents a thoroughly readable synthesis of Costa Rican prehistory. Based on detailed and current research, some of it still unpublished, both the professional and "armchair" archaeologist will enjoy this book.

560 Torres de Araúz, Reina. Arte precolombino de Panamá. 2. ed. Panamá, Instituto Nacional de Cultura y Deportes, Dirección de Patrimonio Histórico, 1972. 95 p., bibl., illus., map, plates, table.

The author gives a general overview of Panamanian prehistory followed by well-illustrated chapters which treat ceramics, gold work, semi-precious stone ornaments, bone and shell ritual objects, and lithic sculpture. The book, which serves as an introduction to Panamanian precolumbian art, does not attempt a detailed treatment of these artifacts, nor does it deal critically with spatial and temporal considerations.

561 Trujillo, Guillermo. Diseños autóctonos: aves y fauna marina en la cerámica pre-hispánica panameña. 2. ed. Prólogo de Carlos M. Gasteazoro. Panamá, Univ. de Panamá, Editorial Universitaria (EUPAN), 1976. 49 p. illus. (Sección: arte)

A book of illustrations showing precolumbian ceramic designs of birds, crabs, shrimp and fish.

ARCHAEOLOGY: South America

CLIFFORD EVANS, Curator, South American Archaeology, Department of Anthropology, Smithsonian Institution
BETTY J. MEGGERS, Research Associate, Department of Anthropology, Smithsonian Institution

ALTHOUGH STRICTER CRITERIA for the inclusion of entries have been applied in this volume, the continued growth of published literature is such that almost the same number of items are annotated here as were in *HLAS 39*.

There has been an increase in "readers" or "compendia" with chapters by separate authors. Therefore, when an entire volume concerns one subject, only the single entry is provided. This is the case with Rogger Ravines' compilation of classic studies of various aspects of precolumbian technology (item **827**). All 40 chapters have been published previously. Those in English have been translated into Spanish, others are classics long out-of-print or obscure references not easily available. Ravines introduces each section with an essay which puts the material in perspective and context. The publisher, Instituto de Estudios Peruanos, of the Instituto de Investigación Tecnológica Industrial y de Normas Técnicas, is to be congratulated for this fourth volume in the series "Fuentes e Investigaciones para la Historia del Perú."

Another collection of articles worthy of mention is entitled *Jornadas Peruano-Bolivianas de Estudios Científicos del Altiplano Boliviano y del Sur del Perú* (item **495**), a new series of the Biblioteca Paceña, La Paz, Bolivia.

Several major summaries of aspects of New World archaeology would have been more useful had the editors consulted professional South American archaeologists or asked Latin Americans rather than US scholars to prepare chapters. For example, the Taylor and Meighan volume, *Chronologies in New World Archaeology* (item **259**), has only one chapter by a Latin American archaeologist, Lautaro Núñez on Chile (item **700**). Moreover, although Willey's summary chapter (item **575**) is interesting and attempts a fair presentation of different positions, areas such as Peru, Ecuador, Venezuela, and Brazil, deserve more detailed coverage. The same shortcomings are apparent in Alan Bryan's volume, *Early man in America from a circum-Pacific perspective* (item **563**), and in Jesse D. Jenning's *Ancient native Americans* (item **256**), which replaces the well-known Jennings and Norbeck book, *Prehistoric man in the New World*, published in 1964. Unfortunately, the chapter on "The Evolution of Andean Civilization" by Michael Moseley (item **818**), deals almost exclusively with Peru.

Volumes in the "World Anthropology Series" continue to appear, but are so costly that few Latin American libraries or scholars will be able to afford them. It is most unfortunate that many papers in this series—all of them delivered in 1973 in Chicago at the IXth International Congress of Anthropological and Ethnological Sciences—are already out-of-date. Thus, *Advances in Andean archaeology*, edited by David L. Browman, which appeared in 1978 (item **767**), is disappointing. New discoveries and data have accumulated during the past six years, but other evidence is missing because of the small representation of Latin American archaeologists whose extensive data remain unpublished due to lack of funds. Failure to invite these Latin American archaeologists to contribute to compendia, readers and summary volumes is as unfortunate as the failure of the US authors to cite their publications.

The trend noted above about lack of funds preventing established serials from appearing regularly, is evident in this compilation. To mention a few examples: the last issue available for São Paulo's *Revista do Museu Paulista* was Vol. 24, 1977; for Lima's *Revista del Museo Nacional de Antropología y Arqueología* was Vol. 42, 1975 (distributed in the US in 1977); and for B.A.'s *Relaciones de la Sociedad Argentina de Antropología* was Vol. 10, 1976 (received in the US in early 1978).

Fortunately, there is some good news in this regard. Although some journals have disappeared and others are delayed, some new ones have appeared and one hopes they will continue beyond the first issue. They are: *Revista Chilena de Antropología* (Univ. de Chile, Facultad de Ciencias Humanas, Depto. de Antropología, Santiago, No. 1, 1978); *Cadernos de Arqueologia* (Univ. Federal do Paraná, Museu de Arqueologia e Artes Populares, Paranaguá, Brazil, Ano 1, No. 1, 1976); *Informaciones Arqueológicas* (Ediciones Catequil, Lima, No. 1, 1977); *Arqueología en América Latina* (Huancayo, Perú, Vol. 1, No. 1, marzo 1978); *Boletín del Museo del Oro* (Banco de la República, Bogotá, Año 1, enero/abril 1978).

The publication of well-illustrated monographs with detailed descriptions of the site, excavations, and artifacts has always been a problem in Latin America. In some cases, shortage of money has been resolved by using Itek or mimeograph reproduction (see items **841** and **868**). Of outstanding significance are two reports on the Archaeological Project at Itaipú, a hydroelectric dam and plant under construction on the Paraná River, whose construction budget financed the field research, study, and publication of the material (items **642–643**). This was due to a successful public relations and educational campaign conducted by Brazilian archaeologist Igor Chmyz. Indeed, the Itaipú Project plans to construct a local museum featuring the natural and archaeological history of the area. This could set a precedent for future hydroelectric dam projects in Brazil and other South American countries.

Several US archaeologists working in Peru published final monographs. Unfortunately, Grieder is an art historian and his approach excludes questions of interest to archaeologists (item **794**). Isbell's *The rural foundation for urbanism: economic and stylistic interaction between rural and urban communities in eighth-century Peru* (item **800**) not only provides full descriptive data of the excavations and classification of materials, usable for future comparative studies by any archaeologists, but attempts to formulate broader concepts. His analysis of the socioeconomic, sociopolitical, and socioreligious influence of Wari on a particular region of the Central Peruvian Andes constitutes an important addition to general anthropological theory. The Misión Científica Española en Hispanoamérica directed by José Alcina Franch published the results of the extensive archaeological research conducted 1968–71 at Chinchero, Cuzco Valley, Peru, in two volumes, one on architecture, the other on pottery and other materials (item **758**).

Another large publication of outstanding importance is *Areas da Amazônia legal brasileira para pesquisa e cadastro de sítios arqueológicos* (item **682**). In it, Mário F. Simões and Fernanda Araujo-Costa describe the method for recording archaeological sites used since 1965 under the Programa Nacional de Pesquisas Arqueológicas (PRONAPA), and since 1976 for the ongoing Programa Nacional de Pesquisas Arqueológicas na Bacia Amazônica (PRONAPABA). Large foldout maps of each state show the boundaries dividing the regions and the code letters which identify them. Fully half of the text is devoted to a listing of all the archaeological sites reported up to 1977, incorporating them into the system of site designation, and providing brief descriptions and bibliographic references. The recording system and the publication itself should serve as models for other countries in Latin America.

GENERAL

562 Alcina Franch, José. L'art précolombien. Paris, Editions d'Art Lucien Mazenod, 1978. 613 p., bibl., illus.

Magnificent art edition by Mazenod includes superb black-and-white and color plates and architectural plans for all precolumbian cultures south of the US border. Four chapters are of outstanding interest to South Americanists: "Research on Pre-Columbian Art;" "Chavín Art;" "Classic Period of the Andes;" and "Principal Archaeological Sites." Specimens in major museums of the world never before illustrated in books of this sort are presented and this makes the volume important for archaeologist and art historian alike.

563 Bryan, Alan Lyle ed. Early man in America from a circum-Pacific perspective. Edmonton, Canada, Univ. of Alberta, Dept. of Anthropology, 1978. 327 p., bibl., illus., maps (Occasional papers, 1)

Bryan organized a symposium at the XIII Pacific Science Conference in Vancouver, 1975, with papers from 13 countries covering the Pacific rim plus Argentina, Brazil and Venezuela. Some additional papers were solicited for the volume. Arranged into six parts: 1) General theory and introduction; 2) Asia; 3) North America; 4) Central America; 5) South America; and 6) a final synthesis by Alan Bryan. Useful volume but with surprising gaps: certain fundamental sites, their artifact assemblages, and significant researchers are missing. The handling of South America, as a whole, is very weak.

564 Gardini, Walter. Influencias de Asia en las culturas precolombinas: estado actual de las investigaciones. B.A., Univ. del Salvador, Escuela de Estudios Orientales, Instituto Latino Americano de Investigaciones Comparadas "Oriente-Occidente," 1978. 202 p., bibl., illus. (Col. Oriente-Occidente)

Book is divided into chapters on origin, development and present state of research on the subject of the title. Encompasses a discussion of the Heine-Geldern's school; an examination of research based on the comparison of religious and philosophical concepts; works published in last decade; and finally, chapters on the comparative method. Excellent and objective summary of the entire topic.

565 Jett, Stephen C. Precolumbian transoceanic contacts (*in* Jennings, Jesse D. ed. Ancient native Americans [see item **256**] p. 593–650, bibl., illus.)

The best summary to date of important diffusionist theories and how some of them fit the ancient Americas into the broader chronological and geographical frames of world history.

566 Lathrap, Donald W. Our father the cayman, our mother the gourd: Spinden revisited, or a unitary model for the emergence of agriculture in the New World (*in* Reed, Charles A. ed. Origins of agriculture [see item **258**] p. 713–751, bibl., illus.)

The author reproduces his theory on the origin of agriculture in the Amazonian lowlands and northern Colombia by using bottle-gourd, manioc, and cayman relationships of Olmec and Chavín, the instability of house gardens in lowlands, etc.

567 Lynch, Thomas F. The South American Paleo-Indians (in Jennings, Jesse D. ed. Ancient native Americans [see item **256**] p. 455–489, bibl., illus.)

Discusses the questionable pre-projectile point stage, Paleo-Indian antecedents in Central America, entry into South America and reconstruction of Paleo-Indian subsistence. Unfortunately, this most recent summary of the topic in English leaves out a lot of ongoing work and new data from the work of South American archaeologists.

568 Meggers, Betty J. Fluctuación vegetacional y adaptación cultural prehistórica en Amazonia: algunos correlaciones tentativas (SAA/R, 10, 1976, p. 11–26, bibl., maps)

Spanish translation of *HLAS 39:695* on tropical refugia model and its tentative correlation with archaeological data and reconstruction of man's distribution in Amazon. (Bernardo Dougherty translated the article.)

569 ———— and **Clifford Evans.** Aspectos arqueológicos de las tierras bajas de Suramérica y las Antillas (Cuadernos del Cendia [Univ. Autónoma de Santo Domingo] 258:4, 1978, p. 1–40, bibl., maps)

The more accurate of two Spanish versions (see also item **571**) of the English chapter (item **570**). Maps and sequence charts are reproduced but not the illustrations of the English version. However, one map, Figure 4, of the location of sites and complexes from 2000–1000 BC was bound out-of-order in the booklet. The caption is correct. Translation by Bernardo Dougherty.

570 ———— and ————. Lowland South America and the Antilles (in Jennings, Jesse D. ed. Ancient native Americans [see item **256**] p. 543–591, bibl., illus.)

Space allocation by editor Jennings gave only a single chapter to the largest region. Hence, data are highly concentrated. Presented in nonceramic traditions for area as a whole with maps in a chronological review into periods of 5000–3000 BC; 3000–2000 BC; 2000–1000 BC; 1000–0 BC; AD 0–500;

AD 500–1000; AD 1000–1500; with final overall interpretation of some general patterns and their significance. Credit given to use of unpublished results of field-work from 15 Latin American scholars. For Spanish translations, see items **569** and **571**.

571 ———— and ————. Las tierras bajas de Suramérica y las Antillas (Estudios Arqueológicos [Univ. Católica, Centro de Investigaciones Arqueológicas, Quito] 5:17, Sept. 1977, p. 11–71, bibl., maps)

One of two Spanish versions (see item **569**) of the English chapter (see item **256**). Includes maps and charts but none of the illustrations of the English version. Mixup of captions and maps makes it difficult to follow argument (e.g., Map, Figure 3 is actually Figure 4-2000–1000 BC; Map, Figure 4 is actually Figure 6-0–500 AD; Map, Figure 6 is actually Figure 3-3000–2000 BC). Article was translated by Pedro I. Porras.

Myers, Thomas P. Formative Period interaction spheres in the intermediate area: archaeology of Central America and adjacent South America. See item **551**.

572 Pickersgill, Barbara and **Charles B. Heiser, Jr.** Origins and distributions of plants domesticated in the New World tropics (in Browman, David L. ed. Advances in Andean archaeology [see item **767**] p. 133–165, bibl.)

Very detailed summary of the problem of plant domestication which provides the most recent data from archaeological materials. Experts who consult this chapter will realize that, unfortunately, the state of our knowledge regarding many species has not advanced much and that little good and hard data have been added to Sauer's summary of 1959. The authors comment extensively on the interdependence and interconnection of Mexico and South America with regard to the domestication of certain plants.

573 Smith, C. Earle, Jr. Recent evidence in support of the tropical origin of New World crops (in Crop Resources. N.Y., Academic Press, 1977, p. 79–95)

Summarizes families of plants with New World origins, and their supporting archaeological data from South America, Middle America, and Mexico.

574 Taylor, R.E. Dating methods in New World archaeology (in Taylor, R.E. and

C.W. Meighan *eds.* Chronologies in New World archaeology [see item **259**] p. 1–27, bibl.)

Good summary which uses New World examples to illustrate status of dating methods for archaeology, advances in radiocarbon dating, obsidian hydration dating, experimental methods of amino-acid dating and flourine diffusion dating. Includes an excellent bibliography.

575 Willey, Gordon R. A summary scan (*in* Taylor, R.E. and C.W. Meighan *eds.* Chronologies in New World archaeology [see item **259**] p. 513–563, bibl.)

Summary chapter of the whole book (item **259**) which deals with North America, Central America, Mexico, and Caribbean with only one chapter on South America, i.e. on Chile (see item **700**). However, Willey's comments in this chapter do cover Colombia, Amazonia, Ecuador, Peru, Bolivia, northern Chile, the remainder of the southern Andes, the Chaco, the Pampean area, and the Fueguian area with an extensive bibliography through 1975. A good summary which offers the pros and cons of agruments on dating complexes and sequences in various areas. Since he uses only published sources, he lacks the advantage of hundreds of C14 dates from Brazil, Peru, Chile, Venezuela, and Ecuador that are in the work in progress of Latin American archaeologists.

576 Wing, Elizabeth S. Animal domestication in the Andes (*in* Browman, David L. *ed.* Advances in Andean archaeology [see item **767**] p. 167–188, bibl., maps)

Summarizes data, especially on guinea pig, dog, and camelids, from many archaeological sites. Sees three important stages: 1) 9000–6000 BP, when there was a great dependence on guinea pigs; 2) 6000–3000 BP, when both guinea pigs and camelids underwent domestication; and 3) 3000 BP to conquest period, when there developed a greater dependence on domesticated animals than on wild game.

577 Wright, Herbert E., Jr. Environmental changes and the origin of agriculture in the Old and New Worlds (*in* Reed, Charles A. *ed.* Origins of agriculture [see item **258**] p. 281–318, bibl., illus.)

Specifically discusses Chile, Colombia, and Peru, especially the reconstruction past of climate in Colombia by Van der Ham-

men. After warming up in the Andean area from 16,000 to 10,000 years ago, man became more dependent on plants and their domestication.

ARGENTINA

578 Berberian, Eduardo E. El problema de la expansión de la cultura de Tiwanaku en el Noroeste Argentino (*in* Jornadas Peruano-Bolivianas de Estudio Científico del Altiplano Boliviano y del Sur del Peru, I, La Paz, 1975. Arqueología en Bolivia y Perú [see item **619**] t. 2, p. 171–179, bibl.)

On the basis of many publications, summarizes the degree and extent of Tiahuanaco influence in northwest Argentina.

579 Borello, Maria Angélica. El sitio incaico de Costa de Reyes, Tinogasta, Provincia de Catamarca (MEMDA/E, 20:83, julio/dic. 1974, p. 35–40, bibl., illus.)

Proof of Inca expansion into this area of Northwest Argentina.

580 Caggiano, Maria Amanda. Contribución a la arqueología del Delta del Paraná (Sapiens [Museo Arqueológico Oswaldo F.A. Menghin, Chivilcoy, Provincia Buenos Aires] 1, 1977, p. 17–30, bibl., illus.)

Data on excavation of Site I.L.1, in Entre Ríos province near Paraná Guazú and Paraná Ibicuy. Describes material and illustrates sherds and bone-tools.

581 Cardich, Augusto. Las culturas pleistocénicas y post-pleistocénicas de Los Toldos y bosquejo de la prehistoria de Sudamérica (*in* Obra del Centenario del Museo de La Plata. La Plata, Arg., Museo de La Plata, 1977, t. 2, 149–172, bibl., illus.)

Brief report on archaeological sequence of lithic materials from Cave 3, Los Toldos, Santa Cruz province in Patagonia, with four distinct levels; the oldest date 12,600 BP and the most recent from 4500 BP to historic times. Includes illustrations of artifact types. Of importance to anyone interested in Paleo-Indian studies (see also *HLAS 37:868*).

——. Recent excavations at Lauricocha, Central Andes, and Los Toldos, Patagonia. See item **774.**

582 Chapman, Anne and **Thomas R. Hester.** New data on the archaeology of the

Huash, Tierra del Fuego (SA/J, 62, 1973, p. 185–208, bibl., illus., map)

In 1964–65, Chapman and Annette Laming-Emperaire conducted work on Isla Grande in eastern Tierra del Fuego. This article describes and defines the archaeology from those sites with excellent photographs. The authors also provide the ethnographic background of present-day groups drawing comparisons with artifacts and subsistence patterns. C14 dates of 850± 70 years ago. Important article.

583 **Cigliano, Eduardo Mario** and **Rodolfo A. Raffino.** Un modelo de poblamiento en el Noroeste Argentino: período de los desarrollos regionales (in Obra del Centenario del Museo de La Plata. La Plata, Arg., Museo de La Plata, 1977, t. 2, p. 1–25, bibl., illus.)

Describes an ecological model of pre-columbian settlement of Northwest Argentina in the 13th–15th centuries and how indigenous communities exploited different environments. This article further expands ideas already expressed in HLAS 35:794 and HLAS 37:870 and 889.

584 ————; ————; and **Horacio A. Calandra.** La aldea formativa de Las Cuevas, Provincia de Salta (SAA/R, 10 [nueva serie] 1976, p. 73–131, bibl., illus.)

Detailed account of materials from site, including profiles of pottery, photographs, line-drawings of designs, and charts showing persistence and change in frequency of artifacts through the time sequence of the site, of about 600 BC to AD 400.

585 **Curzio, Damiana E.** Consideraciones tipológicas del contexto óseo de Cueva Las Buitreras, Provincia de Santa Cruz (SAA/R, 10 [nueva serie] 1976, p. 293–307, bibl., illus.)

Very good study of the actual bones found at a site in Santa Cruz prov., which could benefit from the application of new techniques of experimental archaeology on bones. The site's finds were typed into: bones broken showing no further use, broken bones used in some way, wastage, and reused bones.

586 **Dougherty, Bernardo.** Análisis de la variación cerámica en el complejo San Francisco (in Obra del Centenario del Museo de La Plata. La Plata, Arg., Museo de La Plata, 1977, t. 2, p. 237–252, bibl., illus.)

Item 587 discusses a cultural ecological approach to the area; this one deals with the pottery. Specialists should consult this article where author includes charts indicating the change in frequency of types throughout time from his excavations.

587 ————. Análisis de la variación medioambiental en la subregión arqueológica de San Francisco, región de las selvas occidentales, subárea del Noroeste Argentino (MEMDA/E, 20:81, julio/dic. 1974, p. 1–11, bibl., map)

Cultural ecological approach to region. See item 586 for pottery study from this area.

588 **Fernández, Jorge.** Arqueología de la Cueva de el Toro, Departamento Susques, Jujuy (SAA/R, 10 [nueva serie] 1976, p. 43–65, bibl., illus.)

Describes the artifacts from different levels, from pottery in upper to lower with only lithic materials, including rock art on walls of cave. Estimates lower levels at 800–6000 years ago on comparative method of lithic technology without any C14 dates.

589 ————. Excavación arqueológica en abrigos del Río Despensas, Puna de Jujuy (MEMDA/E, 22:85, julio/dic. 1975, p. 1–10, illus.)

Lithic materials including a variety of projectile points from stratigraphic excavations. No date available on associated materials.

590 **Fernández Distel, Alicia.** Pestos vegetales de etapa arcaica en yacimientos del Noroeste de la República Argentina, Provincia de Jujuy (MEMDA/E, 22:86, julio/dic. 1975, p. 11–24, bibl., illus.)

Summary article on vegetal remains from Archaic period sites in Northwest Argentina which shows some evidence of incipient agriculture. Study includes important data for archaeo-botanical studies of South America.

591 ————. Reciente fechado radiocarbónico para una entidad agro-alfarera tardía en la Quebrada de Huamahuaca, Jujuy (SAA/R, 10 [nueva serie] 1976, p. 167–172, bibl., illus.)

Regional Florescent of the Huamahuaca Culture has a new date of AD 1300 that fits well into others of same culture of AD 1360, 1330, 1280, and 1290.

592 González, Alberto Rex. Arte precolombino de la Argentina: introducción a su historia cultural. B.A., Filmediciones Valero, 1977. 469 p., bibl., illus., maps.

Excellent study of the precolumbian cultures of Argentina. Superb color and black-and-white plates make this the best illustrated volume on the subject. The text permits one to understand the various cultures, their place in time, their interrelationships, and their evolution. Art historians will find this book as useful as those interested in the prehistory of South America.

593 Gradin, Carlos J.; Carlos A. Aschero; and Ana M. Aguerre. Investigaciones arqueológicas en la Cueva de las Manos, Estancia Alto Río Pinturas, Provincia de Santa Cruz (SAA/R, 10 [nueva serie] 1976, p. 201–271, bibl., illus.)

Reports on cave with hunting scenes and negative painting of hands in different colors and includes excellent line drawings of stone materials. Compares this series of caves and their contents with those in Los Toldos, Patagonia. Of extreme importance for specialist in Paleo-Indian and Archaic periods.

594 Gramajo de Martínez Moreno, Amalia J. La primitiva ciudad de San Miguel de Tucumán de Ibatín: estudio histórico-arqueológico (SAA/R, 10 [nueva serie] 1976, p. 141–165, bibl., illus.)

Historical and archaeological approach to the study of Spanish town founded in 1565.

595 Kirbus, Federico B. Historia de la arqueología argentina. Ilustraciones originales de Luis Juárez. B.A., Editorial La Barca Gráfica, 1976. 93 p., illus., maps, plates, tables (Ciencia. Col. Historia y Arqueología)

An excellent summary of archaeology in Argentina from 1880 to present with good illustrations, cross indexed in various ways, with special emphasis on sites and museums in Northwest Argentina.

596 Lorandi, Ana María and others. La fase Las Lomas de la tradición cultural Chaco-Santiagueña (MEMDA/E, 21:84, enero/junio 1975, p. 1–12, bibl., illus.)

Authors believe four phases can be defined for the Santiago del Estero area. This article provides detailed discussion on the Las Lomas phase dating from ca. AD 1000–1200

within the Chaco-Santiagueña tradition which lasts from AD 1000–1650.

597 Lorenzi, Mónica de and Pío Pablo Díaz. La ocupación incaica en el sector septentrional del Valle Calchaquí (Estudios de Arqueología [Museo Arqueológico de Chachi, Arg.] 2, 1973 [i.e. 1977] p. 45–59, bibl.)

Defines Inca occupation of Calchaquí Valley, Salta prov., with detailed information on pottery. Unfortunately, no illustrations.

598 Millán de Palavecino, María Delia. Esquema de los tejidos prehispánicos de la Puna (SAA/R, 10 [nueva serie] 1976, p. 67–71, illus.)

Conclusions based upon study of 500 specimens from archaeological context in the Puna. Textile experts should consult this article.

Núñez A., Lautaro; Vjera Zlatar M.; and Patricio Núñez H. Relaciones transandinas entre Noroeste Argentino y Norte Chileno. See item **701**.

599 Núñez Regueiro, Víctor A. Considerations on the periodizations of Northwest Argentina (in Browman, David L. ed. Advances in Andean archaeology [see item 767] p. 453–484, bibl., map)

Discusses the different efforts to set up time sequences for area, and then gives a very clearcut sequence in stages: 1) Foraging, 13,000–500 BC; 2) Producing, 500 BC–AD 1536; and 3) Stage of European Trade Expansion, post AD 1536.

600 Pastore, Marta Angela. Industrias arcaicas del Mallin San Francisco, Provincia de Neuquén (SAA/R, 10 [nueva serie] 1976, p. 185–192, bibl., illus.)

Long occupation of site from lithic complex of 9,000 to 10,000 years ago, based on comparative typology and not C14, to 2700–2200 years BP.

601 Pérez, José Antonio. Concerning the archaeology of the Huamahuaca Quebrada (in Browman, David L. ed. Advances in Andean archaeology [see item 767] p. 513–524, map, bibl.)

This Quebrada in Northwest Argentina has generated extreme interest since Ambrosetti first discussed it in 1908. Author summarizes present knowledge and provides a sequence and radiocarbon dates.

602 Perrotta, Elana and **Clara Podestá.** Contribution to the San José and Santa María cultures, Northwest Argentina (*in* Browman, David L. *ed.* Advances in Andean archaeology [see item 767] p. 525–551, bibl., illus.)

By consulting the appendix, which includes the distribution of each phase and shape of urns in the Santa María phase, one can understand what typifies each phase. Authors also discuss other cultural traits and provide as well a good general summary of the time sequences and settlement patterns.

603 Puppo, Giancarlo. Arte argentino antes de la dominación hispánica (Argentine art before the Hispanic domination). Foreword by Alberto Rex González. English translation by Diana Zambomi. B.A., Hualfin Ediciones Edicolor, 1979. 275 p., bibl., col. plates, map, plates.

This volume has a unique feature. It is printed bilingually with English and Spanish on the same page as each illustration. The introduction also appears in both languages. The chronological chart sets the scientific framework and the chapters are arranged according to well-known cultures, such as La Candelaria, Tafí, La Ciénaga, Condorhuasi, etc. Moreover, the presentation of this book will appeal to artists and art historians as well as to pre-columbian experts. The photographs in both color and black-and-white are superb and depict pottery, metal, stone artifacts, etc. Over 60 percent of the material illustrated has never appeared in either article or book. This work complements another excellent study (see item 592).

604 Raffino, Rodolfo A. Las aldeas del formativo inferior de la Quebrada del Toro, Provincia de Salta, Argentina (*in* Obra del Centenario del Museo de La Plata. La Plata, Arg., Museo de La Plata, 1977, t. 2, p. 253–299, bibl., illus.)

Describes formative period development in this region by showing excellent data on ceramic analysis, sequences, inventory of tombs, settlement patterns. This article should be consulted by experts. See also *HLAS 35:793a* and *794* and *HLAS 37:889.*

605 Sanguinetti de Bórmida, Amalia C. Excavaciones prehistóricas en La Cueva de Las Buitreras, Provincia de Santa Cruz (SAA/R, 10 [nueva serie] 1976, p. 271–292, bibl., illus.)

Site has three distinct occupations: 1) the earliest with horse, guanaco, Mylodon; 2) a Middle Horizon; and 3) a late one of seasonal use of site. No C14 dates available. Anyone interested in these hunting cultures in southern South America and their relationships to Andes should look up this article.

606 Tarragó, Myriam Noemí. Paleoecology of the Calchaquí Valley, Salta Province, Argentina (*in* Browman, David L. *ed.* Advances in Andean archaeology [see item 767] p. 458–512, bibl., illus.)

An excellent discussion of settlement patterns of this valley, from earliest occupation to post-Spanish contact, in terms of an ecological approach.

607 ——— and Pío Pablo Díaz. Sitios arqueológicos del Valle Calchaquí (Estudios de Arqueología [Museo Arqueológico de Cachi, Arg.] 2, 1973 [i.e. 1977] p. 63–71)

Detailed listing of sites for Calchaquí Valley, Salta prov., with location, type of site, period.

608 Tonni, Eduardo P. and **José H. Laza.** Paleoetnozoología del área de la Quebrada del Toro, Provincia de Salta (SAA/R, 10 [nueva serie] 1976, p. 131–140, bibl., illus.)

Identifies more than 100 individuals of distinct taxa of fauna with breakdown by sites and genus and species. Paleo-zoologists and archaeo-zoologists should consult the article.

609 Weber, Ronald L. A seriation of the late prehistoric Santa María culture of Northwestern Argentina (Fieldana: Anthropology [Field Museum of Natural History, Chicago, Ill.] 68:2, Jan. 1978, p. 49–98, bibl., illus.)

Seriation on stylistic grounds of Santa María burial urns from a collection in the Field Museum of Natural History. Correlates seriation with radiocarbon dates for region. Specialists in Argentine archaeology should consult this article because of the excellent illustrations and results.

BOLIVIA

610 Arellano López, Jorge. La cerámica de las tumbas de Iskanwaya. La Paz, Instituto Nacional de Arqueología (INAR),

Centro de Investigaciones Arqueológicas de Is-kanwaya, 1975. 24 p., bibl., illus., plates (Publicación, 8)

Detailed description with drawings and photographs of pottery from tombs of the small city of Iskanwaya, which is basically El Molle culture with indirect Inca influence. This article also appeared in *Arqueología en Bolivia y Perú* (see item 619).

611 ———. Determinación del anti-plástico en algunas cerámicas pre-colombinas de Bolivia y Perú (*in* Jornadas Peruano-Bolivianas de Estudio Científico del Altiplano Boliviano y del Sur del Perú, I, *La Paz, 1975*. Arqueología en Bolivia y Perú [see item 619] t. 2, p. 75–101, bibl., illus., map)

Thin section studies of temper of pre-columbian sherds include detailed mineralogi-cal analysis of sherds from Tiahuanaco, Mollo, Chiripa, Inca, and Peruvian cultures of Para-cas, Chancay, and Chavín.

612 **Avila Salinas, Waldo.** Análisis es-pectrográfico semicuantitativo de al-gunas obsidianas de Bolivia, Argentina, Perú y Chile. La Paz, Instituto Nacional de Ar-queología (INAR) [and] Ministerio de Educa-ción y Cultura, Instituto Boliviano de Cultura, 1975. 19 p., bibl., illus., tables (Publicación, 14)

Emission spectographic analysis of ob-sidians, mostly from Bolivia with a few from Argentina, Peru, and Chile.

613 ———. Elementos trazas de algunas obsidianas bolivianas. La Paz, Centro de Investigaciones Arqueológicas, 1975. 16 p., bibl., illus., tables (Publicación, 4. Nueva serie)

Emission spectographic studies of obsi-dian artifacts and natural outcrops of ob-sidian indicate the famous obsidian flow of Sorasora not used in precolumbian times and the sources of obsidians found at Tiahua-naco and La Hoya not known. More research needed.

614 **Baptista, Mariano.** Tiwanaku. Chur, Switzerland, Plata Publishing, 1975. 48 p., illus., maps, plates (Plata histories)

Popular summary of the history of ex-ploration and investigation of Tiahuanaco for the tourist and layman. The volume is poorly illustrated with an inadequate selection of photos of site, architecture, objects.

Browman, David L. Toward the develop-ment of the Tiahuanaco/Tiwanaku state. See item 766.

615 **Bruhn, Jan G.; Bo Holmstedt; Jan-Erik Lindgren; and S. Henry Wassén.** The tobacco from Niño Korin: identification of nicotine in a Bolivian archaeological collec-tion (EM/A, 1976, p. 45–48, bibl., illus., plate)

Collection of classic Tiahuanaco mate-rial from the Niño Korin site, Saavedra prov., La Paz dept. Consists of assemblage of pre-columbian medicine man's paraphernalia which dates around AD 315 by C14. It is believed that the preserved tobacco is the oldest ever found in a South American archae-ological site. See *HLAS 35:821* for a detailed description of the artifacts.

Congreso Peruano: El Hombre y la Cultura Andina, III, Lima, 1977. El hombre y la cultura andina. See item 782.

616 **Cordero Miranda, Gregoria.** Descubri-miento de una estela lítica en Chiripá (*in* Jornadas Peruano-Bolivianas de Estudio Científico del Altiplano Boliviano y del Sur del Perú, I, La Paz, 1975. Arqueología en Bolivia y Perú [see item 619] t. 2, p. 229–232, bibl.)

Describes a stela from Chiripá.

Gade, Daniel W. and **Roberto Ríos.** La Cha-quitaclla: herramienta indígena sudamericana. See item 792.

617 **Girault, Luis.** Las ruinas de Chullpa Pata de la comunidad de Kallamarka (*in* Jornadas Peruano-Bolivianas de Estudio Científico del Altiplano Boliviano y del Sur del Perú, I, La Paz, 1975. Arqueología en Bolivia y Perú [see item 619] t. 2, p. 181–210, illus., maps)

Author clarifies controversy over this site involving work by others and his own.

618 **González, Alberto Rex** and **Antonio Cravotto.** Estudio arqueológico e inven-tario de las ruinas de Inkallajta. Paris, UNESCO, 1977. 106 p., bibl., illus., maps (In-forme técnico, PP/1975–76/3.311.6)

Report prepared to assist UNESCO member states in the conservation and pre-sentation of a ruin for public use as a tourist attraction. The ruin is located at Inkallajta, Carrasco prov., Cochabamba dept., near the small town of Pocona, at an altitude of 2929–

3100 m. on an old road from Cochabamba to Santa Cruz. The study is divided into two parts, one prepared by the archaeologist González, the other by the architect Cravotto.

Guidoni, Enrico and **Roberto Magni.** Monuments to civilization: the Andes. See item **796.**

619 Jornadas Peruano-Bolivianas de Estudio Científico del Altiplano Boliviano y del Sur del Peru, I, *La Paz, 1975.* Arqueología en Bolivia y Perú. t. 2. La Paz, Editorial Casa Municipal de la Cultura Franz Tamayo, 1977. 443 p., bibls., illus., maps (Biblioteca Paceña. Nueva Serie)

Proceedings of a conference which consists of five volumes published 1976–78. Unfortunately, at press time, only vol. 2, *Arqueología en Bolivia y Perú,* was available for review. This volume consists of 21 chapters, including a few reprinted from other sources commemorating the sesquicentennial of the founding of the Republic of Bolivia (18–24 July 1975). Each of the articles on precolumbian archaeology is entered separately under the author's name (see items **611, 616–617, 620–624, 838** and **848**).

620 Kornfield, William J. El lugar de Viscachani dentro del precerámico andino (*in* Jornadas Peruano-Bolivianas de Estudio Científico del Altiplano Boliviano y del Sur del Perú, I, La Paz, 1975. Arqueología en Bolivia y Perú [see item **619**] t. 2, p. 325–333, bibl.)

Author provides history of archaeology of this site, stresses the importance of South America in early lithic cultures and points to the need for further scientific excavations at this site in order to overcome theories strictly based on typology.

621 Kuljis M., Danilo. Aplicación del método de hidratación de la obsidiana a una muestra de Iskanwaya (*in* Jornadas Peruano-Bolivianas de Estudio Científico del Altiplano Boliviano y del Sur del Perú, I, La Paz, 1975. Arqueología en Bolivia y Perú [see item **619**] t. 2, p. 225–227, bibl.)

Author reports hydration thickness of 2.50–2.54 of an obsidian artifact from this Molle culture site. He uses rate C of Friedman and Smith scale and dates it at AD 1425. See also item **610.**

622 Piú Salazar, Percy Antonio. Quellata: un sitio precerámico en el altiplano puneño (*in* Jornadas Peruano-Bolivianas de Estudio Científico del Altiplano Boliviano y del Sur del Perú, I, La Paz, 1975. Arqueología en Bolivia y Perú [see item **619**] t. 2, p. 361–374, bibl., illus.)

Variety of lithic artifacts suggests that this area was used over long period by hunters and gatherers on high altiplano. Classifies material by form.

623 Portugal Ortiz, Max and **Maks Portugal Zamora.** Investigaciones arqueológicas en el Valle de Tiwanaku (*in* Jornadas Peruano-Bolivianas de Estudio Científico del Altiplano Boliviano y del Sur del Perú, I, La Paz, 1975. Arqueología en Bolivia y Perú [see item **619**] t. 2, p. 243–283, bibl., illus., map)

Work at Qallamarka shows Tiahuanaco III occupation and definition of a black pottery type associated with typical Tiahuanaco III pottery. Illustrates and describes the new pottery style.

624 Portugal Zamora, Maks. Estudio arqueológico de Copacabana (*in* Jornadas Peruano-Bolivianas de Estudio Científico del Altiplano Boliviano y del Sur del Perú, I, La Paz, 1975. Arqueología en Bolivia y Perú [see item **619**] t. 2, p. 285–323, bibl., illus.)

Study of peninsula of Copacabana in Lake Titicaca and the islands ties it in with Epoch III of Tiahuanaco.

BRAZIL

625 Andreatta, Margarida Davina. Projeto arqueológico anhanguera, Estado de Goiás, Missão 1976 (MP/R, 24 [nova série] 1977, p. 111–129, bibl., illus.)

Polished axes with corrugated, painted and other types of pottery. No comparative discussion given but has some resemblances to Tupiguarani tradition.

626 Anthonioz, Sydney and **Suzana Monzon.** Les representations sexuelles dans l'art rupestre brésilien (MH/OM, 17:1, Spring 1977, p. 31–38, bibl., figures, plates)

Very crudely-drawn sexual representations are depicted on rockshelter painted art from sites in Minas Gerais and Piauí. Authors believe they are probably associated with fertility rites. Without dating them, the article suggests some could be related to Lapa Vermelha in Lagoa Santa region of 3720± 120 years ago.

627 Barbosa, Altair Sales; Pedro Ignacio Schmitz; and Avelino Fernandes de Miranda. Projeto Centro-Sul de Goiás: fase complementar, comunicação prévia (Anuário de Divulgação Científica [Univ. Católica de Goiás, Instituto Goiano de Pré-História e Antropologia, Goiânia, Brazil] 1976/1977, p. 45–60, bibl., illus.)

Data on survey of three areas in Goiás. Important for specialist in Brazilian archaeology.

628 ———; ———; and ———. Um sitio paleoindio no medio-norte de Goiás (Anuário de Divulgação Científica [Univ. Católica de Goiás, Instituto Goiano de Pré-História e Antropologia, Goiânia, Brazil] 1976/1977, p. 21–55, bibl., illus., maps)

Sitio Manuel Alves Borges, GO-NI-49, near town of Urualina produced lithic materials and a C14 date of 10,750± 300 BP. Experts in Paleo-Indian of South America should consult this article.

629 Beck, Anamaría. O problema do conhecimento histórico dos sambaquis do litoral do Brasil (Anais do Museu de Antropologia [Univ. Federal de Santa Catarina, Florianópolis, Brazil] 7:7, dez. 1974 [i.e. 1977] p. 27–66, bibl.)

Reviews history of knowledge about shell middens from historical records of missionaries, travelers, and chroniclers of the 16th, 17th, and 18th centuries. Covers pre-scientific and scientific stages, the interrelated use of shell-midden archaeology with geomorphology and reconstruction of paleoclimates and rise and fall of sea level, destruction of shell middens, and present-day situation. Bibliography includes 105 references.

630 Beltrão, Maria da Conceição de Moraes Coutinho. Ocupação pré-histórica: aspectos culturais, geológicos e paleontológicos; coveniência de abordagem interdisciplinar (UFP/CA 2:2, 1977, p. 50–92, bibl.)

Generalizes on the value of an interdisciplinary approach to the study of Brazil's prehistory.

631 ———. Pré-história do Estado do Rio de Janeiro. Rio, Forense-Universitária,

Instituto Estadual do Livro, 1978. 276 p., bibl., illus.

Selective inventory of archaeological sites, annotated bibliography, and description of collections and research, past and present, conducted by the staff of the Museu Nacional. Useful as a compilation of data not readily accessible to specialists.

632 Bigarella, João José. Considerações a respeito das variações de nivel do mar e datações radiométricas (UFP/CA, 1:1, 1976, p. 105–118, bibl.)

Discusses sea-level changes and their relationship to archaeological sites, especially along the southern coast of Brazil. Extremely good summary of available data.

633 Bombin, Miguel and Alan L. Bryan. New perspectives on early man in south-western Rio Grande do Sul, Brazil (in Bryan, Alan ed. Early man in America from a circum-Pacific perspective [see item **563**] p. 301–302, bibl.)

Authors should have asked the archaeologist who did the field work on the Uruguay River to write an article for the volume instead of trying to summarize the data themselves. Sequence runs from 10,000–12,000 years ago to later lithic traditions from 5000–2500 years ago, when drier conditions prevailed.

634 Breitinger, Roland. Die Felsgravuren von Inga (MLV/T, 26, Nov. 1977, p. 109–116, illus., plates)

Describes an elaborate pictograph known as Itacoatiaria de Inga and located 10 km. south of the road from Campina Grande to João Pessao in Paraíba state.

635 Brochado, José Proenza. Alimentação na floresta tropical. Porto Alegre, Brazil, Univ. Federal do Rio Grande do Sul, Instituto de Filosofia e Ciências Humanas, 1977. 103 p., bibl. (Caderno, 2)

An ethnographic analogy which concerns the reconstruction of manioc use in the tropical forest. Discusses indirect evidence from archaeology as well as how various forms of griddles are related to the preparation of manioc. Includes tables on use of manioc by different tribes compiled from various volumes of the *Handbook of South American Indians*, edited by Julian Steward, and which are extremely useful.

636 Bryan, Alan L. and Maria da Conceição de Moraes Coutinho Beltrão. An early stratified sequence near Rio Claro, East Central São Paulo state, Brazil (*in* Bryan, Alan L. ed. Early man in America from a circum-Pacific perspective [see item 563] p. 303–305, bibl., illus.)

Authors summarize stratigraphic situation at Alice Boer site where lithic materials and C14 dates include an early one which, according to original information from C14 lab, cannot be clearly defined as in association with an occupation layer. Authors plead for more excavation at the site.

637 Chiara, Wilma. Contribuição da antropologia para a interpretação dos resultados de pesquisas em arqueología préhistórica (*in* Coletânea de estudos em homenagem a Annette Laming-Emperaire [see item 645] v. 2, p. 245–274, bibl.)

Author stresses importance of archaeologists using ethnographic data to interpret their finds, especially in Brazil. Exemplifies point by using Kraho Indians.

638 Chymz, Igor. Arqueologia e história da Vila Espanhola de Ciudad Real do Guaira (UFP/CA, 1:1, 1976, p. 7–103, bibl., illus., maps)

Excellent combination of archaeological excavation, analysis and description of pottery into types, seriation of pottery into sequences and discussion of ethnohistorical and archival records of the Spanish city of Ciudad Real do Guairá on the margins of the Paraná and Piquirí Rivers. City founded 1556–57. Superb example of how historical archaeology can be applied to Brazil.

639 ———. Contatos interétnicos verificados en sitios arqueológicos no Estado do Paraná, Brasil (UNCIA/HC, 3:2, abril 1977, p. 5–19, bibl., map)

On the basis of archaeological ceramic phases and traditions, author shows the dispersion of these over parts of Paraná.

640 ———. O ocorrência de sítio arqueológico com pontas-de-projétil no litoral paranaense: nota prévia sobre o sítio PR P 31: Ribeirão (Anais [Academia Brasileira de Ciências, Rio] 47, 1975, p. 81–89, bibl., illus.)

Describes preceramic site in Distrito Alexandra, Município Paranaguá, Paraná state, partially excavated in 1974. Consists mainly

of stemmed projectile points, ovate points, bifaces, etc. Author provides no actual date but correlates finds with Bituruna Phase of middle Iguaçú River and with sea rise at around 4100–4800 years ago.

641 ———. Pesquisas paleoetnográficas efetuadas no Vale do Rio Paranapanema, Paraná, São Paulo. Paranaguá, Brazil, Univ. Federal do Paraná, 1977. 219 p., bibl., illus., maps (Boletim de psicologia e antropologia, 5)

Monograph on the archaeology conducted in middle Rio Paranapanema from 1964 onward, partially reported in PRONAPA progress reports. Includes excellent detailed presentation of material, with precise descriptions, photographs, line drawings, profiles, etc., of pottery and other artifacts. Anyone interested in Brazilian archaeology should look up this monograph for comparative data.

642 ———. Projeto Arqueológico Itaipú: primeiro relatório das pesquisas realizadas na área de Itaipú, 1975/1976. Curitiba, Brazil, Convênio Itaipú [and] Ministério de Educação e Cultura, Instituto do Patrimônio Histórico e Artístico Nacional (MEC/IPHAN), 1976. 105 p., bibl., illus., maps.

The construction of an hydroelectric dam at Itaipú financed the archaeology of the Paraná River area, a little above the mouth of its tributary, the Iguaçú River. This was the result of an agreement between the Empresa Binacional Itaipú and the Ministério de Educação e Cultura under the direction of its Instituto do Patrimônio Histórico e Artístico Nacional (IPHAN). Author divides this report into sites and phases classified according to materials, profiles of pottery, etc. Finally, a closing chapter provides preliminary conclusions as to how these finds fit into the overall archaeology of Brazil. For report on the second year (1976–77), see item 643.

643 ———. Projeto Arqueológico Itaipú: segundo relatório das pesquisas realizadas na área de Itaipú, 1976/1977. Curitiba, Brazil, Convenio Itaipú [and] Ministério de Educação e Cultura, Instituto do Patrimônio Histórico e Artístico Nacional (MEC/IPHAN), 1977. 150 p., bibl., illus., maps.

For report on the first year of this salvage archaeology project, see item 642. This report on the second year has better format and reproduction quality. It presents the cultural material according to the system established by PRONAPA from 1965–73 and relates the material to other complexes in Brazil. Experts should consult these two reports.

644 ——— *ed.* Terminologia arqueológica brasileira para a cerâmica (UFP/CA, 1:1, 1976, p. 119–148, bibl., illus.)

Revised and expanded terminology for Brazilian archaeology originally prepared in 1964 and published in 1965 (see *HLAS 29:1083*).

645 Coletânea de estudos em homenagem a Annette Laming-Emperaire. São Paulo, Univ. de São Paulo, Museu Paulista, Fundo de Pesquisas, 1978. 383 p., bibl., illus., maps (Col. Museu Paulista. Série ensaios, 2)

Consists of 12 papers on ethnology and archaeology prepared in honor of anthropologist Annette Laming-Emperaire who died in 1977 while conducting field work in Brazil. All of the papers on archaeological topics are annotated in this section and entered under the author's name.

646 **Colombel, Pierre.** Método de decalque em arte rupestre aplicado no estudo de sítios da região de Lagoa Santa, Estado de Minas Gerais, Brasil (MP/R, 24 [nova série] 1977, p. 175–197, bibl., illus.)

By describing the technique for collecting rock-paintings in the Lagoa Santa region, the author insures accurate laboratory study which will prevent distortions and allow for realistic interpretations.

647 **Cunha, Fausto Luiz de Souza** and **Martha Locks Guimarães.** Posição geológica do homem de Lagoa Santa no Grande Abrigo da Lapa Vermelha Emperaire, Pedro Leopoldo, Estado de Minas Gerais (*in* Coletânea de estudos em homenagem a Annette Laming-Emperaire [see item **645**] v. 2, p. 275–305, bibl., illus., map.)

Using paleontological data, archaeological data and C14 dates, authors establish a sequence of the Pleistocene and Holocene deposits in this site. They conclude that the human skeletal material is from the same Holocene age but distributed in different levels. Also includes study of small vertebrate fauna.

648 **DeBoer, Warren.** Observations of collections of ancient ceramics from the Altamira area, State of Pará, Brazil (UNC/ED, 2:2, July 1977, p. 1–9, bibl., illus.)

Describes material collected from 21 archaeological sites by Nigel Smith in 1972–74 in the Altamira area along the Trans-Amazon Highway, between Marabá and Itaitubá, and deposited in Belém's Museu Goeldi. Because the illustrations show a peculiar mixture of corrugated ware reminiscent of Tupiguarani tradition and yet figurines more reminiscent of Tapajós style, one would recommend that a specialist look at these materials before they are placed into known ceramic complexes.

649 **Dias, Ondemar.** Evolução da cultura em Minas Gerais e no Rio de Janeiro (Anuário de Divulgação Científica [Univ. Católica de Goiás, Instituto Goiano de Pré-História e Antropologia, Goiânia, Brazil] 1976/1977, p. 110–130, bibl.)

Using C14 dates, author gives a brief summary of development for various precolumbian cultures in the states of Minas Gerais and Rio.

650 **Eble, Alroino B.** and **Maria C. Scatamacchia.** Sítio cerâmico Tupi-Guaraní no Vale do Itajaí, SC-VI-69 (Anais do Museu de Antropologia [Univ. Federal de Santa Catarina, Florianópolis, Brazil] 7:7, dez. 1974 [i.e. 1977] p. 67–79, bibl., illus.)

Describes pottery and illustrates forms of 811 sherds from site that is typically Tupiguarani in tradition in an area which up to this time was marginal to main distribution of this phase (see *HLAS 37:906–906a*).

651 **Figueiredo, Napoleão.** Amazônia: tempo e gente. Belém, Brazil, Prefeitura Municipal de Belém, 1977. 152 p., bibl.

Chap. 2, "O Reencontro das Culturas," deals with the archaeological reconstruction of the prehistoric cultures using four ceramic traditions. Also discusses the history of archaeology in Amazonia in three periods: 1) "Pioneer," up to 1948; 2) "Systematic" from 1948 onward; and 3) "Integration" beginning in 1962 with work of Simões at Museu Goeldi to present.

652 **Guidon, Niède.** A análise da arte pre-histórica: problemas metodológicas (*in* Coletânea de estudos em homenagem a Annette Laming-Emperaire [see item **645**] v. 2, p. 123–143, bibl., illus.)

Describes techniques for copying, cataloguing and photographing rock-paintings and how painting techniques are studied and classified. Examples are drawn from paintings on rock shelter in Toca de Morcego, southeastern Piauí state. Also includes chemical analysis of pigments of the Varzea Grande style.

653 Kneip, Lina Maria. Pescadores e coletores pré-históricos do Litoral de Cabo Frio, Rio de Janeiro. São Paulo, Univ. de São Paulo, Museu Paulista, 1977. 167 p., bibl., illus. (Col. Museu Paulista. Série de arqueologia, 5)

Describes archaeological excavations, artifacts, burials from Sambaquí do Forte, Cabo Frio, Rio state. Includes appendices on faunal analysis, soil studies and morphological study of skeletal materials. This work adds to our knowledge of shell-midden sites in Brazil.

654 ———. Projeto Sítio Arqueológico de Tres Vendas, Araruama, Estado do Rio de Janeiro (in Coletânea de estudos em homenagem a Annette Laming-Emperaire [see item **645**] v. 2, p. 145–169, bibl., illus., map)

Study of prehistoric ceramic site which extends into historical times, stressing the need for interdisciplinary study. Author identifies clay and temper as coming from local area and fitting into the Tupiguarani tradition.

655 Laroche, Armand François. Contribuições a arqueologia pernambucana: os sítios arqueológicos do Monte de Angico. Bom Jardim, Brazil, Gabinete de História Natural, 1977. 130 p., bibl., illus.

Description of sites, principally caves and rock shelters, in the Município de Bom Jardim. Has series of C14 dates from 4650± 150 years BP to 300± 80 BP. Relates his ceramic materials to Pedro do Caboclo tradition of Calderon's in Bahia.

656 ———. Contribuição para a pré-história pernambucana. Recife, Brazil, Governo do Estado de Pernambuco, Secretaria de Educação e Cultura, 1975. 49 p., bibl., illus., maps, plates.

Description of archaeological research, especially in the Município de Bom Jardin, which includes summary discussion of phases with C14 dates of 8400 BP to 450 BP. Because this area is so little known, this study should be of importance to anyone working in Brazilian archaeology.

657 Maranca, Silvia. Considerações gerais sobre a distribuição da indústria lítica e

cerámica do sítio Aldeia da Queimada Nova, Estado do Piauí (MP/R, 24 [nova série] 1977, p. 199–211, bibl.)

Discusses site in terms of data from independent studies on lithic and ceramic materials in effort to get a better interpretation of site as a whole.

658 ———. Salvamento em sítios arqueológicos do Estado de São Paulo: Projeto Ilha Solteira (in Coletânea de estudos em homenagem a Annette Laming-Emperaire [see item **645**] v. 2, p. 171–193, bibl., map)

Study of site in the northwest part of São Paulo state describes pottery and lithic materials. Attributes material to Tupiguarani tradition.

659 Mello, Elisa Botelho de and **Arminda Mendonça de Souza.** O sambaqui do Saracuruná (Nheengatu [Cadernos brasileiros de arqueologia e indigenismo, Instituto Superior de Cultura Brasileira, Rio] 1:1, jan./fev. 1977, p. 43–58, bibl., illus.)

Reports on archaeological excavations in small part of site still undamaged, on Saracuruná River in Rio state. Authors establish a relation to two later phases of the Rio das Pedrinhas shell midden and, for the upper levels, to pottery of the late Tupiguarani tradition at time of European contact.

660 Miller, Tom O., Jr. Tecnologia cerâmica dos Caingang paulistas. Curitiba, Brazil, Archivos do Muscu Paranaense, 1978. 51 p., bibl., illus. (Nova série etnologia, 2)

Of interest to archaeologists will be this surviving pottery technique of the Caingang Indians, central São Paulo state, which shows surface-treatment techniques defined in the prehistoric Casa de Pedra tradition. Main differences between the archaeological and contemporary materials lies in the temper, the lesser skill and technique of the historic material and the greater skill of vessel form and rim in the contemporary which borrows from the styles of modern Brazilian society.

661 ———. Tecnologia lítica arqueológica: arqueologia experimental no Brasil (Anais do Museu de Antropologia [Univ. Federal de Santa Catarina, Florianópolis, Brazil] 7:8, junho 1975 [i.e. 1978] p. 7–124, bibl., illus., plates)

82 / Handbook of Latin American Studies

Detailed discussion of the technology used for making stone artifacts, based on experimental work. Includes glossary and extensive drawings and photographs.

662 Moehlecke, Silvia; Pedro Ignacio Schmitz; Altair Sales Barbosa; and Irmhild Wüst. Sítios petroglifos: nos Projetos Alto Tocantins e Alto Araguaia, Goiás (Anuário de Divulgação Científica [Univ. Católica de Goiás, Instituto Goiano de Pré-História e Antropologia, Goiânia, Brazil] 1976/1977, p. 61–109, bibl., illus.)

Study of five sites with petroglyphs which classifies and describes them in detail with good line drawings.

663 Moraes, Agueda Vilhena de. Estudo da industria lítica proveniente da primeira campanha de escavações 1971, no sítio Almeida, município de Tejupá, Estado de São Paulo. São Paulo, Univ. de São Paulo, Museu Paulista, 1977. 145 p., bibl., illus. (Col. Museu Paulista. Série de arqueologia, 4)

Some "artifacts" illustrated as scrapers are merely stages in the manufacture of other tools. Describes material from lowest levels, only stone, to upper ones which include lithic material and ceramics.

664 Morais, José Luiz de. A região do sítio lítico de Jataí, Estado de São Paulo: uma tentativa de abordagem geológica e geomorfológica em arqueologia brasileira (in Coletânea de estudos em homenagem a Annette Laming-Emperaire [see item 645] v. 2, p. 307–324, bibl., map)

Results of archaeological studies made at sites along the middle Pardo River utilizing geomorphology for interpretations.

665 Myazaki, Nobue. Cerâmica Waurá: mundança de tipos (in Coletânea de estudos em homenagem a Annette Laming-Emperaire [see item 645] v. 2, p. 223–243, bibl., illus., map)

Study of modern pottery-making among Waurá and Mehináku Indians in Xingú Park during 1971–72 which compares their pottery to specimens collected earlier and located in the Paulista Museum. Author notes a general trend toward simplification of form and decoration. Of interest to archaeologist for possible relation to area's prehistoric pottery.

666 Orssich, Adam. Observações arqueológicas em sambaquis (UFP/CA, 2:2, 1977, p. 61–67)

General observations on shell-midden sites of Brazil. This article was originally published in the Revista de Antropologia (Univ. de São Paulo, 2:1, July 1954).

667 ———. O sambaqui do Araújo II: nota prévia (UFP/CA, 2:2, 1977, p. 11–61, bibl., illus.)

A modified English version of this article appeared in American Antiquity (April 1956, see HLAS 20:320).

668 ———. Traçoes de habitação nos sambaquis (UFP/CA, 2:2, 1977, p. 69–71)

The author died in 1968 and this article was published posthumously from the manuscript without modification. Orssich comments on the possibility of finding evidence of habitation structures if shell middens are carefully excavated.

669 Orssich, Elfriede Stadler. A propósito de sepulturas em sambaquis (UFP/CA, 2:2, 1977, p. 73–76)

Discusses the use of some shell-mounds as cemeteries. Originally published in Revista de Antropologia (Univ. de São Paulo, 2:1, July 1954).

670 Pallestrini, Luciana. Camargo 76, município de Pirajú, Estado de São Paulo (MP/R, 24 [nova série] 1977, p. 83–110, bibl., illus.)

Article describes a variety of lithic materials and artifacts from stratigraphically excavated site betweeen the confluence of Paranapanema and Araras Rivers.

671 ———. Interpretation of buried structures: coastal sites of the state of São Paulo, Brazil (in Browman, David L. ed. Advances in Andean archaeology [see item 767] p. 291–300, bibl., illus.)

Author discusses the application to shell-middens, since 1960, of excavation techniques developed by A. Leroi-Gourhan of the College de France. She compares lithic and bone industries in some shell-middens and notes how they differ in the number of burials and patterns of habitation.

672 ——— and **Philomena Chiara.** Indústria lítica de Camargo 76, Município de Pirajú, Estado de São Paulo (in Coletânea de estudos em homenagem a Annette Laming-Emperaire [see item 645] v. 2, p. 83–122, bibl., illus., map)

Using Leroi-Gourhan's French technique of excavation in natural levels, authors classify lithic artifacts into 31 types. Specialists in nonceramic levels of Brazil should consult this article which includes excellent line drawings of artifacts.

673 Pereira Júnior, José Anthero. Pesquisas arqueológicas no "Patio do Colégio" (IHGSP/R, 72, 1975, p. 3–17, bibl.)

Archaeological investigations in the patio of the Colegio do Convento e Igreja dos Jesuitas, São Paulo, to reconstruct history of Jesuits in this area.

674 Prous, André. Les sculptures zoomorphes du sud brésilien et de l'Uruguay. Paris, École des Hautes Études en Sciences Sociales, 1977. 177 p., bibl., illus. (Cahiers d'archéologie d'Amérique du Sud, 5)

Analysis of some 200 stone sculptures from shell-middens in Uruguay and southern Brazil, including classification into types, methods of manufacture, art and style, fauna represented, regional variation, and dating. Useful compilation of information on this enigmatic archaeological artifact.

675 —— and **Walter Piazza.** Documents pour la préhistoire du Brésil méridional. pt. 2, L'État de Santa Catarina. Paris, École des Hautes Études en Sciences Sociales, 1977. 178 p., bibl., illus. (Cahiers d'archéologie d'Amérique du Sud, 4)

Summary of state of knowledge of archaeology in Santa Catarina, with emphasis on nonceramic sites. Geography, history of research, major cultural divisions, and relations between groups are discussed briefly. Detailed descriptions are provided for 50 sites, principally shell-middens and rock paintings. The annotated bibliography is a useful reference.

676 Ribeiro, Pedro Augusto Mentz. A arte rupestre no sul do Brasil (Revista do CEPA [Associação Pro-Ensino, Centro de Ensino e Pesquisas Arqueológicas, Santa Cruz do Sul, Brazil] 7, agôsto 1978, p. 1–27, bibl., illus., map)

Pictographs (paintings) form a single tradition in Paraná state showing relations to that of Minas Gerais. Petroglyphs along the coast of Santa Catarina state and on the high mesas of Rio Grande do Sul state form distinct traditions. Author believes pictographs are older than petroglyphs but does not believe it is possible to determine an absolute date.

677 ——. Cerâmica Tupiguarani do Vale do Rio Pardo (Revista do CEPA [Associação Pro-Ensino, Centro de Ensino e Pesquisas Arqueológicas, Santa Cruz do Sul, Brazil] 6, 1978, p. 1–54, bibl., illus., maps, plates)

Very important report for additional data on the Tupiguarani tradition. Includes detailed description of sites and artifacts with drawings, profiles and excellent photographs of pottery and other artifacts. Creates three phases of Tupiguarani tradition with the most recent being transitional to the Neo-Brazilian.

678 ——; **Catharina Torrano Ribeiro;** and **Itela da Silveira.** A occorrência de zoólitos no Planalto Meridional: Barros Cassal, Rio Grande do Sul, Brasil (Revista do CEPA [Associação Pro-Ensino, Centro de Ensino de Pesquisas Arqueológicas, Santa Cruz do Sul, Brazil] 5, 1977, p. 5–37, bibl., illus.)

Describes a pecked and polished zoolith in the form of a bird or a tortoise which was found in the excavation of a site along the Rio Pardo in the Brazilian interior. It was found with a variety of percussion-struck flakes, cores, bifaces, etc. Of interest because most of these zooliths come from shell-middens.

679 Rohr, João Alfredo. O sítio arqueológico do Pântano do Sul: SC-F-10. Florianópolis, Brazil, Programa de Apoio Editorial, 197?. 114 p., bibl., illus. (Col. Cultura catarinense. Série ciência)

Detailed description of excavations and artifacts from site on southeast tip of Isla de Santa Catarina, part of which has shell-midden refuse. C14 date of 4460 years ago. Includes many illustrations of the artifact complex. Specialists should consult this article.

680 Schmitz, Pedro Ignacio. Arqueologia de Goiás: sequencia cultural e datações de C14 (Anuário de Divulgação Científica [Univ. Católica de Goiás, Instituto Goiano de Préhistoria e Antropologia, Goiânia, Brazil] 1976/1977, p. 21–44, bibl., map)

Evaluation of C14 dates in terms of phases of various periods for Goiás.

681 Silveira, Itela da and others. Arqueologia no Planalto Meridional entre os Vales dos Rios Jacuí e Pardo, Rio Grande do Sul: nota prévia. Santa Cruz do Sul, Brazil,

Associação Pró-Ensino, Centro de Ensino e Pesquisas Arqueológicas (CEPA), 1978. 29 p., bibl., illus., tables (Publicação avulsa, 1)

Surveyed 26 sites and classified the material into a new phase of the preceramic Humaitá tradition, called Pinhal Phase, and added further information on sites with ceramics of the Taquara tradition (Erveiras Phase) and the Tupiguarani tradition, Corrugated subtradition (Carinjho Phase).

682 Simões, Mario F. and Fernando Araújo-Costa. Areas da Amazônia legal brasileira para pesquisas e cadastro de sítios arqueológicos. Belém, Brazil, Museu Paranaense Emílio Goeldi, 1978. 160 p., bibl., illus. (Publicações avulsas, 30)

Extremely useful reference work which includes a catalog of Amazônia's known and registered sites (current as of Dec. 1977 and legally approved by MEC's Instituto do Patrimônio Histórico e Artístico Nacional in 1968). Describes the sites and cultures, lists their names and bibliographic references, and notes the system of site denomination and their trinomial designation. A similar volume in the same format should be published for all of Brazil.

683 Simonsen, Iluska. Alguns sítios arqueológicos de Goiás: notas prévias. Goiânia, Brazil, Univ. Federal do Estado do Goiás, Museu Antropológico, 1975. 80 p., bibl., illus., plates.

Describes series of sites and rock-shelters in central Goiás with lithic materials. Good photos and line drawings. Important for specialist in Paleo-Indian and Archaic of South America. Sites need careful stratigraphic excavation.

684 ——— and Acary de Passos Oliveira. Cerâmica da Lagoa Miararré: notas prévias. Goiâna, Brazil, Univ. Federal do Estado do Goiás, Museu Antropológico, 1976. 67 p., bibl., illus., map, plates.

Pottery from Lake Miararré in the National Park of the Xingú, about 4 km. west of Lake Ipavú. Present-day Indians of area disclaim having made the materials. Interesting series of modeled figurines, fish, animals and geometric patterns. Archaeological affiliations unknown. Tempered with sponge spicules (cauixi).

685 Souza, Alfredo Mendonça de. Pré-história de Paratí (Nheengatu [Cadernos brasileiros de arqueologia e indigenismo, Instituto Superior de Cultura Brasileira, Rio] 1:2, março/abril 1977, p. 47–90, bibl., illus.)

Study of Bay of Ilha Grande on the southernmost part of Rio state, adjacent to São Paulo state. Fifty sites were studied along with ethnohistorical sources. Shell-middens were placed in Mambucaba Phase with two subdivisions followed by Pequeré Phase. The most important subsistence pattern in this phase was hunting even though shell-fish gathering and fishing continued. This was followed by simple pottery, the Jabaquara Phase. Only one site had Tupiguarani tradition material. Neo-Brasileira Phase, called Parati, was established.

CHILE

686 Benavente Aninat, María Antonia. Chiuchíu 200: poblado agroalfarero temprano (Revista Chilena de Antropología [Univ. de Chile, Depto. de Antropología, Santiago] 1, 1978, p. 5–15, bibl., illus.)

Additional information on this complex in the Atacama desert (see *HLAS* 39:810–811).

687 Berenguer Rodríguez, José. La problemática Tiwanaku en Chile: visión retrospectiva (Revista Chilena de Antropología [Univ. de Chile, Depto. de Antropología, Santiago] 1, 1978, p. 17–40, bibl.)

Summary of work on the problem of Tiahuanaco influence in Chile, ranging from the first paper on the subject (Latcham's in 1908) to the present, with complete bibliography. Concludes that research on the topic having been fortuitous rather than problem-oriented, progress in understanding the degree and extent of this influence has been minimal.

688 Bernard, Charles L. Fischer. Notas para una bibliografía sobre la Isla de Pascua: 1923–1972 (BBAA, 37:46, 1974/1975, p. 101–124)

Bibliography of 213 entries published 1923–72 and cross-indexed by year of publication and by author. Follows Gusinde's lengthy bibliography published in 1920 and 1922.

689 Dillehay, Tom D. and **Américo Gordon.** Estudio del material lítico excavado en Padre Las Casas, Provincia de Cautín, IX Región, Chile (Revista de Antropología [Univ. de Chile, Depto. de Antropología, Santiago] 1, 1978, p. 41–49, bibl., illus.)

Pure description of lithic material from site with no attempt at interpretation and without available date. Argues material is not a quarry or workshop site for making stone-tools but surmises wood or vegetal materials were worked with these artifacts.

690 Druss, Mark. Computer analysis of Chiuchíu complex settlement patterns (UNC/ED, 2:3, Oct. 1977, p. 51–73, bibl.)

Chiuchíu complex, final preceramic phase of the Middle Rio Loa sequence of Atacama Desert, circa 2700–1600 BC of Lanning's scheme. Computer analysis of settlement patterns and environmental variables of 70 sites supports author's hypothesis that settlement pattern of this non-ceramic group is related to variation in environmental conditions from wet-to-dry and dry-to-wet periods. An amazing computer exercise which merely proves the obvious.

691 Durán S., Eliana. Estudios de los tipos cerámicos del sitio Padre Las Casas, Provincia de Cautín, IX Región, Chile (Revista Chilena de Antropología [Univ. de Chile, Depto. de Antropología, Santiago] 1, 1978, p.51–59, bibl., illus.)

Describes pottery from burial into various types. C14 dates are AD 1280± 80.

692 Gordon, Américo. Urna y canoa funerarias: una sepultura doble excavada en Padre Las Casas, Provincia de Cautín, IX Región, Chile (Revista Chilena de Antropología [Univ. de Chile, Depto. de Antropología, Santiago] 1, 1978, p. 61–80, bibl., illus.)

Describes burial associated materials excavated in a salvage operation.

693 Iribarren Charlin, Jorge. Dos yacimientos arqueológicos de la cultura El Molle: Agua Amarga, III Región, Atacama. La Serena, Chile, Museo Arqueológico, 1978. 27 p., bibl., plates (Contribución arqueológica, 9)

Manuscript completed in 1976 was not published until 1978. Author describes with good line drawings artifact material from habitation site in Agua Amarga, not far from Vallenar, and associated cemetery site with five burials, all of El Molle culture.

694 ———. Manifestations of Inca culture in two provinces of Chile (in Browman, David L. ed. Advances in Andean archaeology [see item 767] p. 443–448, bibl.)

Author uses Inca roads, pottery decoration and form, settlement patterns, forts and metallurgy in order to show the strength of Inca culture in Atacama and Coquimbo provs., especially in the Valleys of Copiapó, Huasco, Coquimbo, and Maule.

695 Johnson, L. Lewis. The Aguas Verdes Industry of Northern Chile (in Browman, David L. ed. Advances in Andean archaeology [see item 767] p. 7–39, bibl., illus.)

Study of quarry waste from two sites at Aguas Verdes complex in Central Loa region; dates material by seriation with other areas as around 8000–7000 BC. Develops a theoretical model of stone-tool manufacture based on study of quarry waste and value of flint-knapping experience combined with a multivariant analysis for understanding lithic technology. States that model indicates how study of quarry waste can give insights into process of manufacture and nature of tools.

696 Laureani, Camila. Bibliografía y piezas originales de la Isla de Pascua existentes en la Sede Central de la Congregación de los SS. CC. de Picpus-Roma (Aisthesis [Revista chilena de investigaciones estéticas, Pontificia Univ. Católica de Chile, Instituto de Estética, Santiago] 10, 1978, p. 81–106)

Lists brief description and catalog number of 49 artifacts from Easter Island which are located at the Sede Central of the Congregación de los Sagrados Corazones de Picpus in Rome. Also lists a bibliography of 249 items on Easter Island indicating their location.

697 Molinero, José Ramón. Ilha de Páscoa: o mistério das estatuas tombadas. São Paulo, Global Editora, 1976. 111 p., plates.

Brief description of history of discovery and exploration of Easter Island including a purely philosophical, almost occult, discussion of the large stone figures. Of no scientific value.

698 Moreno P., Patricio. Informe sobre trabajo de arte rupestre realizado en el sitio Compe-1, Quebrada de Camiña, Tarapacá (Serie Documentos de Trabajo [Univ. de Chile, Depto. de Ciencias Sociales, Grupo de Arqueología y Museos, Sede Antofagasta] 6, 1975, p. 30–34, illus.)

Describes over 200 petroglyphs and painted pictographs from Valley of Camiña, sector Llalañuzco, at an altitude of ca. 2,200 m.

699 Núñez A., Lautaro. L'évolution millénaire d'une vallée: peuplement et ressources a Tarapacá (AESC, 5/6, sept./déc. 1978, p. 906–920)

Human use of the Tarapacá Valley of northern Chile from 5000 BC to present, contrasting the aboriginal adaptation in harmony with the environment and the recent mineral exploitation and absentee ownership. Abandonment of the ancient pattern of transhumance between the upper and lower valley has led through a brief period of prosperity (18th–19th centuries) to the present state of population decline and poverty.

700 ———. Northern Chile (*in* Taylor, R.E. and C.W. Meighan *eds.* Chronologies in New World archaeology [see item 259] p. 483–511, bibl.)

Gives history of chronological research in Chile and analyzes present situation. Unfortunately, the article was written in 1972 and not brought up to date. Of historic interest exclusively.

701 ———; **Vjera Zlatar M.;** and **Patricio Núñez H.** Relaciones transandinas entre Noroeste Argentino y Norte Chileno: período cerámico (Serie Documentos de Trabajo [Univ. de Chile, Depto. de Ciencias Sociales, Grupo de Arqueología y Museos, Sede Antofagasta] 6, 1975, p. 1–24, bibl.)

Good summary on the subject of relations between two areas during all ceramic periods, with detailed bibliography for specialists.

702 Salazar Ramírez, Jaime. Conservación de objetos arqueológicos del Norte de Chile: a propósito de la restauración de un cerámico Chiza Modelado. (Serie Documentos de Trabajo [Univ. de Chile, Depto. de Ciencias Sociales, Grupo de Arquelogía y Museos, Sede Antofagasta] 6, 1975, p. 25–29, bibl., illus.)

Pleads for the need to create a conservation laboratory for all the materials excavated in North Chile. Specifically discusses and illustrates reconstruction from sherds of a double vessel.

703 Stehberg Landsberger, Rubén. La fortaleza de Chena y su relación con la ocupación incaica de Chile Central. Santiago, Museo Nacional de Historia Natural, 1976. 37 p., bibl., fold. map, illus., plates, tables (Publicación ocasional, 23)

Good illustrations and descriptions of pottery and architecture clearly showing the strength of Inca occupation in Central Chile, with good historical account of all the investigators who have visited the site and made observations.

704 ———. Primeros fechados RC-14 de los pueblos portadores de cerámica en la zona central de Chile (Revista Chilena de Antropologia [Univ. de Chile, Depto. de Antropología, Santiago] 1, 1978, p. 81–84, bibl.)

Dates of 180 BC and AD 430 for the early ceramic period in central coast and AD 900 for Cemetery of Aconcagua Salmón dating the end of Molle II here.

705 Thomas Winter, Carlos. Estudio arqueológico del poblamiento prehispánico tardío de Chiu-Chiu (Revista Chilena de Antropología [Univ. de Chile, Depto. de Antropología, Santiago] 1, 1978, p. 85–104, bibl., illus.)

Attempts a settlement-pattern study of this site and surrounding land available for agriculture. Describes layout of prehistoric defense walls, living areas, cemetery.

706 True, Delbert L. and **Lautaro Núñez A.** Un piso habitacional temprano en el Norte de Chile (UCC/NG, 1:2, dic. 1974, p. 155–166, bibl., illus., map, plates, table)

Floor of pithouse in Quebrada de Tarapacá uncovered in 1966–67 dating ca. 4480 BC of a nonceramic lithic complex of hunting and gathering group. See also *HLAS 39:841– 842.*

COLOMBIA

707 Alzate Amaya, Fernando. Dos conchales de la costa atlántica colombiana (UA/U, 51:197, abril/junio 1976, p. 65–73, bibl.)

Compares type of shell-midden and artifacts from Conchal de Barlovento and Caimán Nuevo and suggests seasonal use of site as area for exploiting marine food resources.

708 Angulo Valdés, Carlos. Arqueología de La Ciénaga Grande de Santa Marta. Bogotá, Banco de la República, Fundación de Investigaciones Arqueológicas Nacionales, 1978. 172 p., bibl., illus.

Detailed monograph on the archaeology of the Ciénaga Grande where author worked for years with well-illustrated plates of pottery, and lithic artifacts, description of pottery types, seriated sequences and carbon dates. Indicates a long sequence from Puerto Hormiga Phase of ca. 3000 BC to Historic Period. Specialists should consult monograph for it is the first detailed archaeological study of this part of the North Coast of Colombia.

709 Arango Cano, Jesús. Cerámica quimbaya y calima. Bogotá, Plaza & Janes, 1976. 97 p., bibl., col. plates, plates.

Of value because of the photographs in color and black-and-white of many pieces from Quimbaya and Calima cultures never before illustrated. Experts interested in "negative-resist" painting in South America should look at this volume.

710 Bernal Andrade, Leovigildo. San Agustín: testimonio de piedra sobre el origen del hombre. Bogotá, Gráficas Leipzig, 1976. 167 p., plates.

Illustrates all the anthropozoomorphic figures of San Agustín plus others and argues for evolutionary development of man. Of no scientific value.

711 Bray, Warwick. Investigaciones arqueológicas en el Valle del Calima: informe preliminar (Cespedesia [Boletín científico, Depto. del Valle del Cauca, Colombia] 5:17/18, enero/junio 1976, p. 47–54, bibl., illus.)

Describes material excavated in 1962 of Calima style.

712 ——— and **M. Edward Moseley.** Una secuencia arqueológica en las vecindades de Buga, Colombia (Cespedesia [Boletín científico, Depto. del Valle del Cauca, Colombia] 5:17/18, enero/junio 1976, p. 55–78, bibl., illus.)

Originally published in English in *Ñawpa Pacha* (7/8, 1969/1970). Includes C14 dates as an appendix.

713 Bruhns, Karen Olson. Ancient pottery of the Middle Cauca Valley, Colombia (Cespedesia [Boletín científico, Depto. del Valle del Cauca, Colombia] 5:17/18, enero/junio 1976, p. 101–196, bibl., illus.)

Summary of the author's work on the Middle Cauca for her thesis and more recent research conducted in 1969/1970. She divided the area into eight groups according to surface decoration and form. Specialists in Andean archaeology should consult this article.

714 ———. La Salina de los Quingos: nueva información sobre el intercambio prehispánico de sal (Cespedesia [Boletín científico, Depto. del Valle del Cauca, Colombia] 5:17/18, enero/junio 1976, p. 89–100, bibl., illus.)

Author insists that there is evidence in this area of salt manufacture and trade center in the last period just before European contact.

715 ———; **Oscar Osorio Gómez;** and **Ole Christiansen.** A projectile point from the Department of Quindio, Colombia (IAS/ÑP, 14, 1976, p. 69–72, illus.)

Authors argue that there is proof of Paleo-Indian occupation of Colombia on the basis of an isolated find of chipped point with tapering stem and corner notches. Authors' assumption is based solely on morphology of point without other proof.

716 Chaves Mendoza, Alvaro. Máscara precolombina. Bogotá, Ediciones Zazacuabi, 1977. 55 p., bibl., map, plates (Colombia: arte y cultura)

Describes precolumbian metal and pottery masks from Colombia, discusses their function as known from ethnological dates, and compares them with those from other parts of the New World.

717 Correal Urrego, Gonzalo. Investigaciones arqueológicas sobre la etapa lítica en Colombia (Boletín [Banco de la República, Museo del Oro, Bogotá] 1, enero/abril 1978, p. 45–50)

Summary of research on Atlantic Coast and Magdalena Valley in collaboration with palynologist Van der Hammen on lithic horizon. Establishes two new C14 dates of 10,000± 40 and 7640 years ago.

718 Gamboa Hinestrosa, Pablo. San Agustín. Bogotá, Ediciones Zazacuabi, 1975. 32 p., bibl., illus. (Colombia: arte y cultura)

Popular account of San Agustín stone sculpture.

719 Grass, Antonio. La marca mágica (The magic mark): diseño precolombino colombiano. Translated by Roberto A. Cartagena. Fotografías de Luis Fernando Barriga. Bogotá, The Author [and] Centro Colombo-Americano, n.d. 243 p., illus., map.

Description of design motifs taken from stone and pottery stamps from collections in the Museo del Oro of the Banco de la República. Spanish and English text.

720 Guaqueros y coleccionistas: cerámica precolombina. Bogotá, Centro Colombo-Americano, 1977. 1 v. (Unpaged) plates.

Excellent photographs of pottery from all regions of Colombia in private collections. Of value because some pieces have never been illustrated before, especially Tolima and Colima. Unfortunately, all of these items were dug up by professional grave robbers.

721 Hildebrand, Elizabeth R. von. La manufactura del budare entre la tribu Tanimuka, Amazonia, Colombia (ICA/RCA, 20, 1976, p. 177–200, bibl., illus.)

Modern ethnological study of pottery-griddle making is useful to archaeologist because of the process described. Shows how base gets a leaf impression and gives idea of size and variety of shapes.

722 ———. Resultados preliminares del reconocimiento del sitio arqueológico de La Pedrera, Comisaría del Amazonas, Colombia (ICA/RCA, 20, 1976, p. 145–176, bibl., illus.)

Excavations on the Caqueta River produced ceramic materials with modeled adornos, negative paintings, incision, fiber tempered. Preliminary comparison permits author to relate this material to Hilbert's, along the Japura river, and to Napo elements in eastern Ecuador.

723 Hurt, Wesley R.; Thomas van der Hammen; and Gonzalo Correal Urrego. The El Abra rockshelters, Sabana de Bogotá, Colombia, South America. Bloomington, Indiana Univ. Museum, 1976. 28 p., bibl., illus. (Occasional papers and monographs, 2)

A report on the 1969 season which discusses only lithic materials and recommended to experts in Paleo-Indian and Archaic Periods. Nevertheless, the comparative sections are poor because Hurt accepts lithic cultures in Ecuador and Peru whose ages are not proven or which are actually workshop refuse of quarry sites without any proof of antiquity.

724 Murdy, Carson N. La economía y densidad de población en los asentamientos de la cultura tairona en la árida zona litoral de la Sierra Nevada de Santa Marta (in Congreso Nacional de Historiadores y Antropólogos, I, Santa Marta, Colombia, 1975. Memorias. Medellín, Colombia, Editorial Argemiro Salazar, 1976, p. 122–143, bibl., maps, plates, tables)

A good ecological analysis of subsistence-pattern Tairona culture along the coast and their relationship to the sea and dry tropical region of the Sierra Nevada de Santa Marta mountains. Author estimates the population density of these sites as much lower than interior Tairona sites.

725 Sampson, E.H.; S.J. Fleming; and W. Bray. Edad de la cerámica colombiana del Estilo Yotoco, revelada por thermoluminescencia (Cespedesia [Boletín científico, Depto. del Valle del Cauca, Colombia] 5:17/18, enero/junio 1976, p. 79–88, illus.)

Authors tested material of negative painted style and compared them with C14 dates for culture. They found that although a difference of 200 years between the two methods was one of the errors, it was not serious enough to cause problems. Specialists should consult this article.

726 Schrimpff, Marianne Cardale de. Informe preliminar sobre una mochila muisca hallada en la región de Pisba (Boletín [Banco de la República, Museo del Oro, Bogotá] 1, enero/abril 1978, p. 18–21, bibl., illus.)

Double cloth bag with geometric design of brown-and-white cotton from cave in zone of Paramo de Pisba, northeast of city of Tunja, Boyacá dept. First example of double cloth from Colombia.

727 ———. Investigaciones arqueológicas en la zona de Pubenza, Tocaima, Cundinamarca (ICA/RCA, 20, 1976, p. 335–496, bibl., illus.)

Detailed description of archaeology done at Pubenza, where the Bogota River joins the Magdalena, with classification of lithic materials and pottery. Specialists should consult article for detailed data, drawings, and good illustrations. The type Pubenza Red Banded is widespread in area and author perceives it as indication of widespread occupation beginning around AD 1000 and lasting until conquest times and wonders if the sites with later material are remains of the Panche Indians which the Spanish found in this area.

728 Silva Celis, Eliécer. Elementos arqueológicos procedentes de las montañas de Pisba (Boletín [Banco de la República, Museo del Oro, Bogotá] 1, enero/abril 1978, p. 22–29, illus.)

See item **726.** Describes entire find of mummy and textiles, basketry, gourds, etc., with the burial. Position and method of wrapping mummy similar to those of Paracas in Peru. This is a most unique preservation not normally found in Colombia or brought to a museum, since usually the bundle is looted.

729 Uribe Alarcón, María Victoria. Relaciones pre-hispánicas entre la costa del Pacífico y el altiplano nariñense, Colombia (ICA/RCA, 20, 1976, p. 11–24, bibl., illus.)

From fieldwork in Ipiales Municipio, Nariño dept., established Capuli style and relates it to Río Chota, Esmeraldas prov., Ecuador.

730 Wassén, Henry. Un estudio arqueológico en la Cordillera Occidental de Colombia (Cespedesia [Boletín científico, Depto. del Valle del Cauca, Colombia] 5:17/18, enero/junio 1976, p. 9–45, bibl., illus.)

Reprint of long out-of-print article which appeared in English in 1944 in *Revista Colombia.* Includes detailed discussion of archaeological excavations and finds made by Wassén in Cauca Valley in 1935. Andean specialists should consult this article.

ECUADOR

731 Baumann, Peter. Valdivia: die Entdeckung der ältesten Kultur Amerikas. Hamburg, FGR, Hoffman und Campe, 1978. 276 p., bibl., col. plates, illus., map, plates, table.

Of no scientific value. This is a dramatic account of the discovery of the oldest culture in the New World, Valdivia in Ecuador, with comments on each investigator coupled with author's romanticized comments. Includes pictures of many other precolumbian Ecuadorian cultures. A postscript chapter by Otto Zeries discusses the jaguar, cayman and eagle and the problem of the relations between Andean and Amazonian motifs.

732 Bonifaz, Emilio. Cazadores prehistóricos del Ilalo. Quito, The Author, 1979. 115 p., bibl., illus.

As a big-game hunter, the author presents his ideas of how Paleo-Indians used the artifacts of El Ilalo (see item **733**) to obtain various animals and birds for food.

733 ———. Obsidianas del Paleo-Indio de la región del Ilalo. Quito, The Author, 1977. 104 p., bibl., illus.

Most complete publication of Bonifaz's collections includes good line drawings and presents his interpretations—as hunter not archaeologist—of obsidian points, flakes, scrapers, etc. These are from the El Ilalo area of highland Ecuador and include hydration measurements and dates of specimens tested. See also *HLAS 35:897, HLAS 39:880,* and item **732.**

734 Di Capua, Constanza. Las Cabezas Trofeo: un rasgo cultural en la cerámica de La Tolita and de Jama-Coaque (Antropología Ecuatoriana [Casa de la Cultura Ecuatoriana, Quito] 1:1, 1978, p. 72–164, bibl., illus.)

Author compares the ceramic heads from La Tolita and Jama-Coaque cultures and indicates that the same holes were drilled for carrying. The 60 such heads she examined did not come from figurines but are complete, naturalistic modeling. Compares them with a trophy skull from La Tolita. She thinks some Jama-Coaque examples show shrinking. She also makes comparison beyond Ecuador. Includes good illustrative material.

735 Echeverría A., José H. Contribución al conocimiento arqueológico de la Provincia de Pichincha: sitios Chilibulo y Chillogallo (Estudios Arqueológicos [Univ. Católica, Centro de Investigaciones Arqueológicas, Quito] 1977, p. 181–225, bibl., illus.)

Consists of main chapters taken from thesis and includes excellent illustrations. Specialists should consult this article.

736 Holm, Olaf. Lanzas silvadoras (Estudios Arqueológicos [Univ. Católica, Centro de Investigaciones Arqueológicas, Quito] 1977, p. 71–88, bibl., illus.

Ethnographic and archaeological evidence for use of lance with lance point and whistling device.

737 Jaramillo Paredes, Mario. Estudio histórico sobre Ingapirca. Quito, Pontificia Univ. Católica del Ecuador, Centro de Publicaciones, 1976. 171 p., bibl., illus., maps, plates.

Good summary with photographs and ground plans of the earliest to most recent work on the Inca site of Ingapirca in Cañar prov., Ecuador.

738 McEwan, Gordon F. and D. Bruce Dickson. Valdivia, Jomon fisherman, and the nature of the North Pacific: some nautical problems with Meggers, Evans, and Estrada's (1965) transoceanic contact thesis (SAA/AA, 43:3, July 1978, p. 362–371, bibl., illus.)

Does not like the suggestion due to the mechanics of the voyage, type of craft, surface currents, and survival problems of the "crew." However, in conclusion, does not rule out possiblity of Transpacific contacts at Valdivia or other parts of world. Authors' qualifications for argument is that senior author is a former merchant marine sailor.

739 Meyers, Albert. Die Inka in Ekuador: Untersuchungen anhand ihrer materiellen Hinterlassenschaft. Bonn, Bonner Amerikanistische Studien, 1976. 186 p., bibl., illus., maps (Bonner Amerikanistische studien, 6)

Originally presented as the author's thesis, Bonn, 1973. Monograph based on author's Ph.D. dissertation (Univ. of Bonn, 1973) consists of a study of Inca influence in Ecuador which compares it with that in Peru. Author based his observations on the study of some surface collections, limited excavations, extensive study of museum collections, and chroniclers data. Very thorough study and of importance to Andeanists interested in Inca expansion, theoretical problems of the state, etc. Includes Spanish summary (13 p.).

740 Mino Grijalva, Manuel. Algunos problemas arqueológicos en la Sierra Norte del Ecuador: Carchi (Estudios Arqueológicos [Univ. Católica, Centro de Investigaciones Arqueológicas, Quito] 1977, p. 161–180, bibl.)

Reviews all the different interpretations of Carchi culture based upon Jijón y Caamaño's first definition and the earlier work begun by González Suárez, Verneau, and Rivet.

741 Myers, Thomas P. Un entierro en la Hacienda Santa Lucía (Sarance [Revista del Instituto Otavaleño de Antropología, Otavalo, Ecua.] 6, dic. 1978, p. 90–102, bibl., illus.)

Describes burial and associated ceramics: two tall tripod vessels and one double jar, ring-based. They do not fit the usual types found in this area from the Tolas period.

742 Plaza Schuller, Fernando. El complejo de fortalezas de Pambamarca: contribución al estudio de la arquitectura militar prehispánica en la Sierra Norte del Ecuador; segundo informe preliminar. Otavalo, Ecua., Instituto Otavaleño de Antropología, 1977. 53 p., bibl., illus., map (Serie arqueología, 3)

Partial results of an Instituto project devoted to the study of Inca influence in the Andean area of Ecuador and based on detailed study of 14 out of a total 17 forts in Pichincha prov.

743 Porras G., Pedro I. Arqueología de la Cueva de los Tayos. Quito, Pontificia Univ. Católica, Centro de Publicaciones, 1978. 83 p., bibl., illus., maps.

The interdisciplinary study of this cave was made possible by the Ecuadorian military forces which facilitated access to the area and descent into the cave. It is located in the Cordillera del Cóndor, on the right bank of the Huangus (Coangos) River, a tributary of the Santiago River, Morona-Santiago prov. The author illustrates, describes, and compares the pottery, shell and stone objects, seem to have been placed in the cave as special offerings over long periods of time.

744 ———. Fase Alausi (Estudios Arqueológicos [Univ. Católica, Centro de Investigaciones Arqueológicas, Quito] 1977, p. 89–160, bibl., illus., map)

Detailed description of pottery with photographs and drawings and seriation charts based on the study of 19 different strata cuts in sites in Alausi area. This zone is a natural route of contact between highlands, coast and tropical forest. Porras compares it with Machalilla, Cerro Narrío, and Macas. Andeanists should look up this article for details.

745 Raddatz, Corinna. Kleidung und Schmuck im Vorkolumbischen Esmeraldas. Bremen, FRG, Übersee-Museum, 1977. 107 p., illus., maps (Veröffentlichungen aus dem Ubersee-Museum Bremen, D:1)

Study of 1095 pottery figurine fragments from private collections and museums, most of which are in Europe. Author established description and typology of dress and ornament of these precolumbian materials from Esmeraldas prov. and north Manabí. Makes no comparisons beyond Ecuador but includes good drawings. Important for specialists. Provides summary in Spanish (10 p.).

746 Stothert, Karen E. Proyecto Paleoindio: informe preliminar. Guayaquil, Ecua., Banco Central, Museo Antropológico, 1977. 24 p., illus.

Discusses excavation of Site 80 on Santa Elena Peninsula in 1977 which produced burials without pottery but a few wood, shell and bone artifacts. Earlier excavations by Lanning in 1971 named this complex Las Vegas with C14 dates of 6650± 200 and 5650± 100 as Paleo-Indian. This study also appeared as an article (without illustrations) in *El Dorado* (Univ. of Northern Colorado, Greeley, 2:2, July 1977, p. 27–36).

747 Tesoros del Ecuador: arte precolombino y colonial: exposición, salas de exposiciones de la Dirección General del Patrimonio Artístico y Cultural. Madrid, Patronato Nacional de Museos, 1976. 120 p., bibl., col. plates, maps, plates.

Guide to the traveling exhibit of the collection of the Banco Central del Ecuador. It includes outstanding color and black-and-white photographs which give an excellent idea of the variety of ceramic materials known by the precolumbian cultures of Ecuador. For the French translation of this guide, see *Richesses de l'Equateur; art précolombien et colonial* (Paris, Petit Palais, 1973, 124 p.).

748 Uzcátegui Andrade, Byron. Investigaciones arqueológicas en Achupallas, un sitio al sur oriente de la Provincia de Chim-

borazo (Estudios Arqueológicos [Univ. Católica, Centro de Investigaciones Arqueológicas, Quito] 1977, p. 227–258, bibl., illus.)

Sees occupation of area from formative period through Inca. Illustrates material with line drawings and also shows rim profiles.

749 Vilhena Vialou, Agueda. Utensílios pré-históricos do Equador: estudo tipológico (*in* Coletânea de estudos em homenagem a Annette Laming-Emperaire [see item **645**] p. 195–221, bibl., illus.)

Describes 107 items from Bonifaz's collections sent by him for study to the Institut de Paléontologie Humaine, Paris. Classifies them in terms of chipping, from simplest artifact to most elaborate. See item **732**.

THE GUIANAS

750 Boomert, A. and **S.B. Kroonenberg.** Manufacture and trade of stone artifacts in prehistoric Surinam (Ex Horreo [Univ. van Amsterdam Albert Egges Giffen, Instituut voor Prae-en Protohistoire] 4, 1977, p. 9–46, bibl., illus., map)

Discusses the distinctive ceramic styles as well as axes, adzes, chisels, and flakes from sites in the Brownsberg/Afobaka area of the coastal plain of Surinam. Authors relate the pottery found in Guyana's Koriabo Phase defined by Evans and Meggers (see *HLAS* 23:447). Authors generalize on trade routes and the trade of stone axes in precolumbian times and among the 20th-century Akuriyo Indians of southeastern Surinam. This is an extremely important article which shows how crucial this area is for the basic archaeological research of South America as a whole.

751 Bubberman, F.C. Rotstekeningen in de Sipaliwinisavanne: een bijdrage tot de archeologie can Zuid-Suriname (NWIG, 49:3, Nov. 1973, p. 129–142, bibl., plates)

Describes petroglyphs on Surinam side of watershed between various tributaries, a small one of the Sipaliwini, another of the Corantyne and Brazilian Paru de Oeste, and a third one of the Cuminá. Author also found a few flakes and scattered pottery, stated to be of historical Taruma Indians. Attempts to relate these finds to published literature on

Guyana and Amapa Territory, Brazil. Includes short English summary.

752 Petitjean Roget, Hugues. Decouverte du site de Gros-Montagne, Guyane (in International Congress for the Study of Pre-Columbian Cultures of the Lesser Antilles, VII, Montreal, Canada, 1978. Proceedings [see item **495**] p. 149–155, illus.)

Author describes sherds and vessels of polychrome (red on white slip) which he found further inland in a rock shelter located in a small range on the Oyapock River's north side at the Gros-Montagne site near the village of Ouanary (see also item **753**). These finds are apparently another example of Serra Painted material of the Aristé Phase of Amapa Territory (in Brazilian Guiana, see item **751**). Unfortunately, article lacks illustrations. No mention of European trade goods.

753 Roy, Dominique. Decouverte du site de jarre Indien, Guyane (in International Congress for the Study of Pre-Columbian Cultures of the Lesser Antilles, VII, Montreal, Canada, 1978. Proceedings [see item **495**] p. 137–147, bibl., illus.)

Author describes red-on-white slip vessel found with European trade goods on the French Guiana side of the Oyapock River's mouth. Although the author does not mention it nor cite the bibliographic reference, the specimen found is an excellent example, in decoration and form, of the Serra Painted of the Aristé Phase established by Meggers and Evans for the Amapá Territory (in Brazilian Guiana, see *HLAS 21:278*).

754 Versteeg, A.H. A distinctive kind of pottery in Western Surinam (Mededelingen [Surinaáms Museum, Paramaribo] 23/24, June 1978, p. 15–26, bibl., maps, plates)

Discusses pottery from precolumbian site on the Kaurikreek, a tributary of the Courantyne River, which forms the border between Surinam and Guyana. Pottery's temper consists of quartz, chalcedony, laterite, and kaolin particles, in contrast to usual quartz temper for Surinam. The most common decoration is appliqué in a wide variety of geometric patterns but appearing in less than one percent of the sherds. There is no clear-cut affiliation with known cultures from Guyana or Brazil but then this area is unknown archaeologically which points to the need for more work in this region. Article

includes good photographs and experts should consult it.

755 ———. The proposed rescue of threatened petroglyphs in Surinam (Mededelingen [Surinaáms Museum, Paramaribo] 23/24, June 1978, p. 27–30, illus. map)

The establishment of the Kabalebo Hydroelectric Plant in western Surinam will flood petroglyphs and archaeological sites. Author recommends the removal of rocks to Paramaribo's Museum and the creation of a local park similar to the one in Guadeloupe.

PERU

756 Aguerre, Roberto. Gli Incas: uomini delle altezze. Milano, Italy, Fratelli Fabbri Editori, 1975. 151 p., bibl., col. plates, illus., maps, plates.

Popular account in Italian of the Inca which includes an interesting combination of reproduction drawings from the chronicles of Garcilaso de la Vega, color and black-and-white photos of Inca ruins as well as modern Indians and modern murals.

757 Aguila Ríos, Aura Inés del. Informe inicial sobre las excavaciones en Selva Sur, Departamento de Madre de Diós, Lago Sandoval (PUCIRA/BSA, 15:16, 1974/1975, p. 139–158, bibl., illus.)

Brief description of pottery with incised, modeled and painted tradition, possibly related to lowland Bolivia and Amazon cultures.

758 Alcina Franch, José and others. Arqueología de Chinchero. v. 1, La arquitectura; v. 2, Cerámica y otros materiales. Madrid, Ministerio de Asuntos Exteriores, 1976. 2 v. (166, 144 p.) bibl., illus., maps, plates (Memorias de la Misión Científica Española en Hispanoamérica, 2/3)

Vol. 1, on Chinchero's architecture, reports the archaeology conducted by the Spanish government in the Chinchero region, a Cuzco valley on the right side of the Urubamba River. The sequence begins ca. 2000 BC through the Inca period AD 1534. A detailed text is illustrated with excellent photos and ground plans of buildings, terraces, pavement, walls, and ceremonial structures. Vol. 2, on Chinchero ceramics, contains excellent line drawings and some photos of specimens, most of which date from the pre-

Inca period of AD 1200–1480 through the Inca, colonial and republican eras (1835–1970).

759 Alfaro de Lanzone, Lidia. Una somera prospección en Huayuri, Quebrada de Santa Cruz, Ica (PUCIRA/BSA, 15/16, 1974/1975, p. 83–106, bibl., illus.)
Preliminary survey.

760 Amano, Yoshitaro and **Yukihiro Tsunoyama.** Textiles of the pre-Incaic Period: catalog of the Amano Collection. Lima, Amano Museum, 1978? 312 p., illus., plates.
Excellent publication of the Amano collection in Lima, principally of materials from the Chancay Valley. Most outstanding are the patterns woven in gauze.

Arellano López, Jorge. Determinación del antiplástico en algunas cerámicas precolombinas de Bolivia y Perú. See item **611.**

761 Bankes, George. Peru before Pizzaro. Oxford, UK, Phaidon Press, 1977. 208 p., bibl., col. plates, illus., maps, plates.
Good introductory book on Peru for the layman. Extends from precolumbian background to modern survivals of weaving, pottery and agricultural techniques. Good color and black-and-white photos. Will easily replace popular out-of-print volumes such as G.H.S. Bushnell's *Peru* (in the Ancient Peoples and Places series) or J. Alden Mason's *Ancient civilizations of Peru.*

762 Benavides Calle, Mario. Yacimientos arqueológicos en Ayacucho. Presentación de Enrique González Carré. Ayacucho, Perú, Univ. Nacional de San Cristóbal de Huamanga, Depto. Académico de Ciencias Histórico-Sociales, 1976. 237 p., bibl., illus., maps (Fuentes para la antropología e historia de Huamanga, 2)
Catalog with maps and a few line drawings of archaeological sites in Ayacucho dept. with detailed location and description of site, history of discovery and, when known, the time period.

763 Benson, Elizabeth P. The bag with the ruffled top: some problems of identification in Moche Art (UCLA/JLAL, 4:1, 1977, p. 29–47, bibl., illus.)
An effort to interpret the symbolism of Moche pottery. Author discusses four types of bags (runner bags, lap bags, coca bags, and

bags with ruffled tops) and notes different associations, showing that ruffled-top bag was never associated with runner bag.

764 Bonavia, Duccio. Ecological factors affecting the urban transformation in the last centuries of the pre-columbian era (in Browman, David L. ed. Advances in Andean archaeology [see item **767**] p. 393–410, bibl.)
Points out how in spite of the extent of knowledge of Andean archaeology, there is very little data on the urban development which began perhaps as long ago as the Early Intermediate Period, expanded during Middle Horizon, and flowered in the Inca Period.

765 Browman, David L. External relationships of the early horizon ceramic style from the Jauja-Huancayo basin, Junin (El Dorado [Univ. of Northern Colorado, Greeley] 2:1, March 1977, p. 1–23, bibl., illus.)
Study based on surface collections and excavations made in 1968–69 at 305 sites in the Jauja-Huancayo sector of the Mantaro River drainage. Author refers readers to the more detailed treatment of the subject in his Ph.D. dissertation (Harvard Univ., 1970). He attributes the pervasive integration between coast and highlands evident from ceramic traditions, use of copper, etc., to trading caravans using llamas.

766 ———. Toward the development of the Tiahuanaco/Tiwanaku state (in Browman, David L. ed. Advances in Andean archaeology [see item **767**] p. 327–349, bibl., illus.)
Attempts to discuss the origins and relations of the Andean Domain of Tiahuanaco, the postulated capital and religious mecca of the second great Andean empire. Classic Tiahuanaco coalesced from many expanding economic networks around AD 300–400, beginning with an elaborate expansion of technological, engineering, and architectural skills, flowering in a religious art style, and culminating in Huari, Peru, around AD 550 which became a forceful political center. The more peaceful spread of religious ideas to Bolivia and Chile was also closely related to the economic network. Finally, the author comments on the Bolivian Federation, after Huari's collapse.

767 ———. ed. Advances in Andean archaeology. The Hague, Mouton, 1978. 580 p., bibl., illus. (World anthropology)

Browman edited these papers which were delivered at an Andean seminar during the IX International Congress of Anthropological and Ethnological Sciences held in Chicago in 1973. Although these papers did not go to press until 1976 (published in 1978), no bibliographic references are more recent than the Congress' date of 1973. Of 23 chapters, each by a different author, 20 deal with South American archaeology and are entered separately under each author's name (see items 551, 572, 576, 599, 601–602, 606, 671, 694–695, 764, 766, 781, 791, 795, 807, 812, 861 and 871).

768 Bruhns, Karen Olsen. Chavin butterflies: a tentative interpretation (IAS/ÑP, 15, 1977, p. 39–48, bibl., illus.)

Perceives possible depiction of butterflies or moths in some of Chavin relief drawings as representing various "winged" things. Author's interesting art approach is worthy of further study as well as the cooperation of entomologists.

769 ———. The moon animal in northern Peruvian art and culture (IAS/ÑP, 14, 1976, p. 21–40, bibl., illus.)

Discusses how motifs of the moon animals are of minor importance when compared to other animals in Moche pantheon. She discusses those from Moche III or later and shows relationships to the Recuay Moon Animal.

770 Bueno Mendoza, Alberto. Cajamarquilla y Pachacamac: dos ciudades de la costa central del Perú (BBAA, 37:46, 1974/1975, p. 171–201, illus., maps, plates)

Describes and defines, with good photos and drawings, two sites which author regards as examples of urbanism in precolumbian Peru.

771 Burger, Richard L. The Moche sources of archaism in Chimu ceramics (IAS/ÑP, 14, 1976, p. 95–104, bibl., illus.)

Author uses four examples of Chimu potters imitating Moche iconographic themes in order to show how the esthetic tastes of a later culture determine the degree of copying and modification.

772 Cabrera Darquea, Javier. El mensaje de las piedras grabadas de Ica. Lima, INTI-Sol Editores, 1976. 372 p., map, plates, table (Col. Documentos)

Discusses the documentation of a private collector about the carved stones from Ica with a variety of modern drawings. Offers no proof of the precolumbian origins of any of the illustrated items. This publication is of value because it exemplifies the falsification in the presentation of material which is characteristic of certain books on precolumbian topics designed for gullible readers. Of no scientific value.

773 Cárdenas Martín, Mercedes. Vasijas del intermedio temprano en la Sierra de Lima (PUCIRA/BSA, 15/16, 1974/1975, p. 37–52, bibl., illus., map)

Describes pottery from Early Intermediate Period sites of Chacla and Collata between headwaters of the Chillón and Rimac Rivers.

774 Cardich, Augusto. Recent excavations at Lauricocha, Central Andes, and Los Toldos, Patagonia (in Bryan, Alan ed. Early man in America from a circum-Pacific perspective. [see item 563] p. 296–300, bibl., illus.)

Brief summary in English of recent work on these two Paleo-Indian complexes (see also HLAS 39:912 and HLAS 37:868).

775 ———. Vegetales y recolecta en Lauricocha: algunas inferencias sobre asentamientos y subsistencias preagrícolas en los Andes centrales (SAA/R, 10 [nueva serie] 1976, p. 27–41, bibl., illus.)

An excellent attempt to reconstruct the subsistence pattern of these early hunters and gatherers. Includes detailed listing of plant remains with complete identification. Role of Lauricocha as subcenter of domestication of camelids.

776 ———; L. Cardich; and D. Rank. Datierung der jungpleistozänen Vereisung Lauricocha in den Peruanischen Anden (GV/GR, 66, June 1977, p. 446–454, bibl., illus., map)

Notes how radiocarbon dating of organic matter in glacial deposits confirms the date of Paleo-Indian in area and also that there were glacial advances and retreats from mountain chain of Raura and the region of Lauricocha.

777 Casana R., Teodoro and others. Restos arqueológicos de la Provincia de Canta. Lima, Imprenta del Colegio Militar Leoncio

Prado, 1976. 238 p., fold. map, map, plates.
Description of precolumbian ruins in Canta prov., Lima dept., on the headwaters of the Chillón and Chancay Rivers, Andean Cordillera. Includes summary and photographs of stone architecture of chullpas, associated structures and urban centers but lacks modern archaeological information.

778   Cauchat, Claude. Additional observations on the Paijan Complex (IAS/ÑP, 16, 1978, p. 51–64, bibl., illus.)
This re-review of studies of an early lithic complex should be read in conjunction with *HLAS 39:914.*

779   Chahud, Carlos E. and Rómulo A. Ríos. The archaic sites of Waraqu-Machay, Huancavelica, Perú (Arqueología en América Latina [Boletín trimestral dedicado a los estudios arqueológicos en América Latina en el Caribe, Huancayo, Perú] 1:1, March 1978, p. 13–19, bibl., illus.)
Describes preceramic complex of lithic tools in association with pictographs located at 4000-4200 m. of Archaic Period probably around 5000–7000 years ago.

780   Cohen, Mark Nathan. Archaeological plant remains from the central coast of Peru (IAS/ÑP, 16, 1978, p. 23–50, bibl., map)
Detailed analysis of plant remains from 1961–71 excavations made in lower portion of Chillón Valley and adjoining the Ancón region, written in 1973 and revised in 1977 with some corrections of earlier reports. Archaeo-botanists should consult this article which offers a full listing of plant taxa and time periods.

781   ——. Population pressure and the origins of agriculture: an archaeological example from the coast of Peru (*in* Browman, David L. *ed.* Advances in Andean archaeology [see item 767] p. 91–132, bibl., maps)
Notes conclusions derived from author's intensive archaeological work on plant-remains in the Chillón Valley and adjoining Ancón region. He reconstructs the type of population and existing techniques for exploiting food sources and notes how population pressure and limited resources "forced" the beginnings of agriculture. On the basis of comparative information, Cohen expands his theory to Peru as a whole and finally to the

world. Tables offer supporting evidence of various plants used by man at different time periods. This same article is available in two other books: Charles A. Reed's *Origins of agriculture* (The Hague, Mouton, 1977, p. 135–177, bibl., maps) and Stephen Polgar's *Population ecology and social evolution* (The Hague, Mouton, 1975, p. 79–121, bibl.).

782   Congreso Peruano: El Hombre y la Cultura Andina, *III,* Lima, 1977. El hombre y la cultura andina. Edited by Ramiro Matos M. Lima, Comisión del Congreso Peruano, Secretaría General, 1978. 2 v. (826 p.) (Continuous pagination) bibl., illus., maps.
Papers delivered at an organized symposium of the III Congreso Peruano: El Hombre y la Cultura Andina held 31 Jan.–5 Feb. 1977 in Lima, under the auspices of the Univ. Nacional Mayor de San Marcos' Programa Académico de Arqueología. Collection was published in June 1978 by the Secretary General of the Congress' Commission.

783   Conklin, William J. The revolutionary weaving inventions of the Early Horizon (IAS/ÑP, 16, 1978, p. 1–12, bibl., illus.)
Discusses how during Chavin times, disappearing twining traditions were replaced by looping, wrapping, discontinuous weft, tapestry, and possibly double cloth. Moreover, the introduction of plant fibers such as *Furcraea* (like a century plant) and camelid hair strongly support author's application of the term "revolutionary" to the history of Andean weaving. Includes excellent photographs and description. Article should be consulted by all those interested in precolumbian weaving.

784   Conrad, Geoffrey W. Models of compromise in settlement pattern studies: an example from coastal Peru (World Archaeology [Routledge & Kegan Paul, London] 9:3, Feb. 1978, p. 281–298, bibl., maps)
Theoretical article shows how settlement patterns of complex societies, which require compromises among several determinants, do not apply necessarily to another culture or region. Author compares precolumbian data of Moche Period from Viru Valley with data from Santa and Nepeña Valleys. Andean specialists as well as those interested in anthropological-archaeological theory should read this study with care.

785 DeBoer, Warren R.; Eric Ross; Jane Ross; and Marie Veale. Two ceramic collections from the Río Huasaga, Northern Peru: their place in the prehistory of the upper Amazon (El Dorado [A newsletter-bulletin on South American anthropology, Univ. of Northern Colorado, Greeley] 2:2, July 1977, p. 10–26, bibl., illus.)

Notes how Kaminun Style is almost identical to Porras' Pastaza Phase on Ecuadorian side of Huasaga (see *HLAS 39:897*). Anatico Style resembles Evans and Meggers' Napo Phase in decoration (see *HLAS 31:1585*).

786 Dillehay, Tom D. Pre-Hispanic resource sharing in the Central Andes (AAAS/S, 204, 6 April 1979, p. 24–31, bibl., illus., map)

Author shows how a peaceful intergroup exploitation of a unique ecological zone occurred from about 800 BC to AD 1534, on the basis of archaeological research conducted at the Huancayo Alto site, in the Chillón River's Middle Valley, an area of subtropical bushy desert. A very important article, which goes beyond pure description, to discuss ecological, interpretive archaeology. This is a revised and expanded version of item 787.

787 ———. Tawantinsuyu integration of the Chillón Valley, Peru: a case of Inca geo-political mastery (Journal of Field Archaeology [Boston Univ.] 4:4, Winter 1977, p. 397–405, map)

Discusses how structures built in lower Chillón Valley gave the Inca power to control the coast and lower mountain range from a minimum of sites.

788 Donnan, Christopher B. Moche art of Peru: precolumbian symbolic communication. Los Angeles, Univ. of California, Museum of Culture History, 1978. 206 p., bibl., illus., map.

Originally published in 1976 as *Moche art and iconography* (see *HLAS 39:922*), this is a revised edition issued to accompany an exhibition of Moche materials from private collections and public museums. Excellent volume which illustrates heretofore unpublished specimens. Recommended to all scholars interested in archaeology, art history, symbolism and iconography of precolumbian cultures.

789 ——— and **Carol J. Mackey.** Ancient burial patterns of the Moche Valley, Peru. Austin, Univ. of Texas Press, 1978. 412 p., bibl., illus., maps, plates, tables.

Description of Moche Valley burial patterns from 103 grave-sites excavated principally in 1969–72 and ranging in time from Initial Period to Chimú-Inca with the majority occurring in Moche Phase IV and Early Chimú. Each burial is described in detail indicating location, grave construction, individuals involved, and grave goods. Although the archaeology is well presented, the study lacks any physical anthropology which diminishes the value and utility of the data.

790 Eisleb, Dieter. Altperuanische kulturen. v. 2, Nasca. Berlin, FRG, Museum für Völkerkunde, 1977. 153 p., col. plates, plates (Neue Folge, 34. Abteilung amerikanische Archäologie, 4)

Vol. 2 of a series which began in 1975 (see *HLAS 39:924*) in order to describe Peruvian materials in the Berlin Museum für Völkerkunde. This volume, devoted to Nasca items, illustrates much material heretofore unpublished.

791 Engel, Frederic. Toward a typology of architecture and urbanism in the precolumbian Andes (*in* Browman, David L. *ed.* Advances in Andean archaeology [see item 767] p. 411–441, bibl., illus.)

In order to standardize discussion of architectural, ecological and geographical characteristics of precolumbian sites, author introduces architectural terms and technological features with excellent line drawings. Those working on architectural features of precolumbian sites are well advised to consult this article.

792 Gade, Daniel W. and **Roberto Ríos.** La Chaquitaclla: herramienta indígena sudamericana (III/AI, 36:2, abril/junio 1976, p. 359–374, bibl., illus., map, tables)

Discusses archaeological precolumbian origin of the Andean foot-plow (*taclla*) in terms of its modern survival. This highly efficient tool is still widely used and very much a part of Andean Indians' way of life, particularly in southern Peru and northern Bolivia, at altitudes of 3600 m. and above.

793 Gasparini, Graziano and **Luise Margolies.** Arquitectura inka. Caracas,

Univ. Central de Venezuela, Facultad de Arquitectura y Urbanismo, Centro de Investigaciones Históricas y Estéticas, 1977. 357 p., bibl., illus., maps, plans.

Two architects analyze Inca architecture explaining techniques for joining corners, making roof peaks, windows, doors, etc. Illustrated with superb black-and-white and color photos and architectural plans.

794   Grieder, Terence. The art and archaeology of Pashash. Austin, Univ. of Texas Press, 1978. 268 p., bibl., illus., maps.

Detailed description of excavations and artifacts recovered from Pashash site at 3255 m. in North Peru at headwaters of the Cabaña and Pallasca Rivers. Author approaches this mass of Recuay-style material from the point of view of history of art. Includes excellent color and black-and-white photographs, drawings, and ceramic profiles. Experts should consult this volume because of the extensive illustrations of Recuay material. However, author's art historian's approach, evident in his interpretive chapter "Society and Symbolism in Ancient Pashash," will not be easily accepted by anthropological archaeologists.

795   Grollig, Francis X. Cerro Sechín: medical anthropology's inauguration in Peru? (*in* Browman, David L. *ed.* Advances in Andean archaeology [see item **767**] p. 351–369, bibl., illus.)

After discussing whether or not Cerro Sechín is Chavín, author leaves the question open but accepts a date of 3500 years BP. He then proceeds to describe the figures on stonecarvings which show dismembered parts of human body as well as anatomical inventory including stomach, vertebrae, and intestines. This is a good English summary of the topic. For an article in Spanish on the same subject but by a different author, see item **823**.

796   Guidoni, Enrico and Roberto Magni. Monuments to civilization: the Andes. 2. ed. N.Y., Grossett and Dunlap, 1977. 189 p., bibl., illus., maps, plates, tables.

Superb, dramatic photographic presentation of the precolumbian ruins of the Andes which range from the Paleo-Indian hunting stage through the Inca era. This ed. is not revised (1. ed. 1972). Includes good general summaries and serves as a good introduction for interested laymen and young people.

797   Huapaya Manco, Cirilo and Lorenzo Roselló Truel. Informe preliminar sobre sitios sin cerámica en la Isla San Lorenzo, Callao, Peru (PUCIRA/BSA, 15/16, 1974/1975, p. 13–28, bibl., illus., map)

Authors believe complex of artifacts, without pottery, suggests there was fishing, gathering of shellfish and fire-making with sticks on this island.

798   Hyslop, John. Hilltop cities in Peru (AIA/A, 30:4, July 1977, p. 218–225, illus.)

Popular account of architectural features of precolumbian cities occupied circa AD 1100–1400 in Lupaca part of Lake Titicaca. Comments on the cultural influences which came into the area around 1100 together with the Aymara.

799   Illescas Cook, Guillermo. Astrónomos en el antiguo Perú: sobre los conocimientos astronómicos de los antiguos pueblos del Perú. Prólogo de Víctor A. Estremadoyro R. Lima, Kosmos Editores, 1976. 190 p., bibl., illus., maps, plates, table.

Good compendium in Spanish of arguments that the large figures on the Nasca Plains are related to precolumbian peoples understanding and observations of constellations and other astronomical phenomena.

800   Isbell, William Harris. The rural foundation for urbanism: economic and stylistic interaction between rural and urban communities in eighth-century Peru. Urbana, Univ. of Illinois Press, 1977. 188 p., bibl., illus., map, plates, tables (Illinois studies in anthropology, 10)

Detailed monograph on archaeological work conducted in 1969 in the San Miguel Valley, along a tributary of the Pampas River in the central Andes, especially at the Jargampata site. Author attempts to relate this site of ca. AD 550–825 to the Wari and their economic and socio-political influence. The work includes careful description of artifacts with photos and drawings which are valuable for comparative studies. The author's broader interpretations are interesting and convincingly presented. An important study for experts.

801   ——— and Katharina J. Schreiber. Was Huari a state? (SAA/AA, 43:3, July 1978, p. 372–389, bibl., illus.)

Includes the same data and conclusions as Isbell's 1977 book (see item **800**.) Although authors believe Huari achieved state government, they hedge by saying that state formation is not like pristine formation in Mesopotamia.

Jornadas Peruano-Bolivianas de Estudio Científico del Altiplano Boliviano y del Sur del Perú, *I, La Paz, 1975*. Arqueología en Bolivia y Perú. See item **619**.

802 Kauffmann Doig, Federico. Comportamiento sexual en el antiguo Perú. Lima, Kimpaktos G.S. Editores, 1978. 191 p., col. plates.

Compilation of precolumbian Peruvian materials showing sexual organs, positions of intercourse, and other representations of sexual practices.

803 Kaulicke, Peter. Reflexiones sobre la arqueología de la Sierra de Lima (PUCIRA/BSA, 15/16, 1974/1975, p. 29–36, bibl.)

Discusses the importance of the lower coastal range to agricultural exploitation, especially during the Middle Periods and later.

804 Keatinge, Richard W. The Pacatnamú textiles (AIA/A, 31:2, March/April 1978, p. 30–41, illus.)

Describes textiles from ceremonial center of Pacatnamú, near mouth of Jequetepeque River, North Coast, Peru. Author traveled to Germany and studies collections in Ubbelohde-Doering's home and Museum für Völkerkunde in Munich, as he had done for his earlier work in 1937–63. Includes superb color photographs of textiles showing iconography. They suggest close relationships to Pachacamac during Middle Horizon and Late Intermediate Period.

805 ———. Religious forms and secular functions: the expansion of state bureaucracies as reflected in prehistoric architecture on the Peruvian north coast (NYAS/A, 293, 15 July 1977, p. 229–245, bibl., illus., maps, tables)

Author defines Pacatnamu in Jequetepeque Valley as the ceremonial center of a theocratically oriented regional state. Discusses the evolution, development and maintenance of such a center.

806 Lavallée Danièle and **Michèle Julien.** Les éstablissements asto à l'époque pré-

hispanique. v. 1. Lima, Institut Français d'Études Andines, 1973. 143 p., bibl., fold. map, illus., plates, tables (Travaux de l'Institut Français d'Études Andines, 15. Recherche interdisciplinaire sur les populations andines. Project, ACL-1)

Important monographic presentation for Andean specialists of archaeological studies in the Asto region, high Andean sites along the headwaters of the Mantaro and Vilcamayo Rivers, central Andes. Most sites are clearly late Inca occupation. Includes appendices (one by Schoenwetter on pollen, one by Poulain on fauna) as well as summaries in English and Spanish.

807 Linares Málaga, Eloy. Prehistory and petroglyphs in southern Peru (*in* Browman, David L. *ed.* Advances in Andean archaelogy [see item **767**] p. 371–391, bibl., illus.)

Comments on 58 sites, 34 with petroglyphs, 12 with pictographs, two with geoglyphs (large geometrical figures covering ground), and 10 with cave-tradition mobile art (work on stone, bone, horn, etc.). Suggests a chronology beginning as early as 7600 BC.

808 López, Lorenzo Elaido and **Sebastián Chantal Caillavet.** La pajcha inka: ejemplares del Museo de América de Madrid (IGFO/RI, 36:145/146, julio/dic. 1976, p. 271–297, bibl., plates)

Describes and comments on these peculiarly shaped vessels showing a long handle with a canal and found in collections of Madrid's Museo de América. Expands Rebecca Carrión Cachot's original work on the subject (1955).

809 Lumbreras, Luis Guillermo. Excavaciones en el Templo Antiguo de Chavín, Sector R: informe de la sexta campaña (IAS/ÑP, 15, 1977, p. 1–38, bibl., illus.)

Report on excavations at Chavín de Huantar Temple from 1966–72. Includes important drawings and photos for specialist.

810 Lyon, Patricia J. Female supernaturals in ancient Peru (IAS/ÑP, 16, 1978, p. 99–140, bibl., illus.)

Author suggests there were female supernaturals in the precolumbian pantheon from Early Horizon III Period onward into Inca Empire and uses illustrative material from pottery, stone and wood carvings of various Peruvian periods.

811 **MacNeish, Richard S.** The beginning of agriculture in Central Peru (*in* Reed, Charles A. *ed.* Origins of agriculture [see item **258**] p. 753–801, bibl., illus.)

Author perceives highland region as source of and center for the domestication of plants which were taken to the coast. The article is packed with data he gathered on the Ayacucho Project. Specialists should consult this article.

812 **Matos Mendieta, Ramiro.** The cultural and ecological context of the Mantaro Valley during the Formative Period (*in* Browman, David L. *ed.* Advances in Andean archaeology [see item **767**] p. 307–325, bibl.)

Long-range program which requires combined study of puna and Mantaro Valley because of the interchanges of products and access to resources at different levels. Author considers that the most important period of study was one of transition from nomadic harvesting of wild crops and hunting to sedentary agriculture. He stresses an ecological approach, especially in the role of microenvironments of the Andean area. Good compendium in English of Matos' work.

813 **Matsuzawa, Tsugio.** The Formative site of Las Haldas, Peru: architecture, chronology, and economy (SAA/AA, 43:3, Oct. 1978, p. 652–673, bibl., illus., plates)

The 1958 and 1969 Tokyo Univ. expeditions to Las Haldas revealed that the temple complex was not preceramic and that the whole area was a slow buildup. Article includes good data from pottery study, architecture, C14 dating, and problem approach to the site. Author believes main subsistence was marine and that there is need of further study of the type of work force which built such a temple in the Formative Period. The article, published in Japan in 1974, was translated into English by Izumi Shimada. The translation makes available to most scholars not only data which would have remained otherwise inaccessible but a very important article in Andean archaeology.

814 **Menzel, Dorothy.** The archaeology of ancient Peru and the work of Max Uhle. Berkeley, Univ. of California, Robert H. Lowie Museum of Anthropology, 1977. 135 p., bibl., illus.

Consists of text prepared in 1974 for an exhibit of Uhle's collection held at the R.H. Lowie Museum. An historically important contribution which points to the importance of Uhle's data and collections. Includes excellent illustrations. Specialists should consult this work.

815 **Milla Villena, Carlos.** Evidencias de una cultura local en la Sierra de Lima (PUCIRA/BSA, 15/16, 1974/1975, p. 53–74, bibl., illus., map)

Author uses ethnohistorical and archaeological data to argue that there was a local precolumbian cultural development from the Formative to Inca periods in the Rimac and Santa Eulalia Valleys.

816 **Moorehead, Elisabeth L.** Highland Inca agriculture in adobe (IAS/ÑP, 16, 1978, p. 65–94, bibl., illus.)

Study of adobe construction in highlands dating from the Inca period. Since most other studies deal with stone construction, this one has unusual significance. This research is related to the PER-39 Project sponsored by the UN and the Peruvian government.

817 **Morris, Craig.** The archaeological study of Andean exchange systems (*in* Redman, Charles L. *ed.* Social archaeology beyond subsistence and dating. N.Y., Academic Press, 1978, p. 315–327, bibl.)

Author uses results of combined archaeological, ethnohistorical and chroniclers' records of Inca occupation at Huanaco Pampa, central highland Peru, in order to show how archaeology can verify the elaborate distribution of goods, ware-housing, and related administration activities during Inca times (see also *HLAS 37: 1030b* and *HLAS 39:961*).

818 **Moseley, Michael E.** The evolution of Andean civilization (*in* Jennings, Jesse D. *ed.* Ancient native Americans [see item **256**] p. 491–541, bibl., illus.)

Misleading title should state "Andean Peru" for only a few lines are devoted to other Andean countries (i.e., Ecuador, Bolivia, Chile and Colombia). In addition to describing some general archaeological sites and sequences, author discusses his ideas concerning the origins and development of societies and institutions in this area to better explain evolutionary processes affecting the dynamics of civilization.

819 ———. Peru's golden treasures: an essay on five ancient styles. Contributor: Robert A. Feldman. Chicago, Ill., Field Museum of Natural History, 1978. 75 p., bibl., col. plates, illus., map, plates, tables.

Catalog of Miguel Mujica Gallo's Museo del Oro in Peru with commentary about sites and cultures of Ancient Peru and based upon collection of the Museo's gold specimens loaned for exhibit to various US museums. Includes good photos, especially useful for those who do not know the collection in Peru nor publications in Spanish.

820 **Myers, Thomas P.** Mat impressed pottery from Yarinacocha, Peru (IAS/ÑP, 14, 1976, p. 61–68, bibl., illus.)

Discusses modern ethnographic examples of placing clay on a mat while making pottery and how this is related to archaeological material.

821 **O'Neale, Lila M.** Notes on pottery making in highland Peru (IAS/ÑP, 14, 1976, p. 41–60, illus.)

Of interest to archaeologists, this article describes pottery-making in Ayacucho's Huancayo district observed by the author in early 1940s. Her observations, not published until now, on the use of moldes (foundation disks) are important.

822 **Ossa, Paul P.** Paiján in early Andean prehistory: the Moche Valley evidence (in Bryan, Alan ed. Early man in America from a circum-Pacific perspective [see item 563] p. 290–295, bibl., map)

Author defines the Paiján complex in the Chicama Valley and from La Cumbre and the Chirimac shelter in the Moche Valley and provides a series of dates between 10,000–12,000 years ago. He compares the lithic typology found with that of other complexes in South America and concludes that there were three distinct lithic traditions of Andean hunter-gatherers in Paleo-Indian times.

823 **Paredes Ruiz, Víctor M.** Sechín: posible centro de conocimientos anatómicos y de disección en el Antiguo Perú. n.p., Gráfica Comercial, 1975. 32 p., bibl., illus., plates.

Interprets the famous stone carvings of Sechín, Casma Valley, as indication of a precolumbian knowledge of human anatomy and surgical knowledge. Since these carvings have had many different interpretations, one more adds to the total picture. Proof of any theory will never be available.

824 **Pires-Ferreira, Edgardo; Jane Wheeler Pires-Ferreira; and Peter Kaulicke.** Utilización de animales durante el período precerámico en la Cueva de Uchcumachay y otros sitios de los Andes Centrales del Perú (SA/J, 64, 1977, p. 149–154, bibl.)

Study of faunal remains according to levels of several sites in the central Andes and excavated by Ramiro Matos M. Specialists should consult the article and table because they report interesting changes in fauna from Paleo-Indian horizon, through Late Archaic (preceramic) or 10,000 to 1750 BC.

825 **Ramos de Cox, Josefina.** Informe preliminar sobre el proyecto de arqueología y computación del material del Complejo Pando (PUCIRA/BSA, 15/16, 1974/1975, p. 7–12, bibl., illus., map)

Data on efforts to standardize classification and computerize information on pottery forms from a series of sites in Lima area, south of the San Marcos Univ. campus.

826 **Ravines, Rogger.** Excavaciones en Ayapata, Huancavelica, Perú (IAS/ÑP, 15, 1977, p. 49–100, bibl., illus.

Detailed description of excavations and artifacts found between 1967–69 at this site and especially a Middle Horizon votive offering. Pottery shows an interesting mixture of Tiahuanaco, Nasca, Pachacamac, and Ayacucho Huari motifs. Important study for Andean specialists.

827 ——— comp. Tecnología andina. Prólogo de José Matos Mar. Lima, Instituto de Estudios Peruanos [and] Instituto de Investigación Tecnológica, Industrial y de Normas Técnicas, 1978. 821 p., bibls., illus., maps, plates, tables (Fuentes e investigaciones para la historia del Perú, 4)

A superb compilation for Spanish-reading audience of classic, long out-of-print articles not available in Spanish until now. Includes an introduction to the volume as a whole and one to each of the 10 chapters: 1) Natural Resources of the Andes; 2) Agriculture and Irrigation; 3) Storage and Food [i.e., Diet]; 4) Textile Craft; Pottery; 6) Metallurgy; 7) Construction and House Types; 8) Transportation and Communication; 9) Medicine and Surgery; and 10) Statistical [i.e., Recordings] Technology. The volume ends with a general bibliography on technology; the references of the original articles; and a short vitae about each author. This compilation is recommended both as a teaching tool and as an excellent introduction for the educated layman. It should encourage students to realize the importance of technological studies for Andean archaeology.

828   **Richardson, James B., III.** A bibliography of archaeology, pleistocene geology, and ecology of the departments of Piura and Tumbes, Peru (LARR, 12:1, 1977, p. 123–137, bibl., map)

Extremely useful bibliographic compilation of both old and new references in many languages.

829   ———. Early man on the Peruvian north coast: early maritime exploitation and the Pleistocene and Holocene environment (in Bryan, Alan ed. Early man in America from a circum-Pacific perspective [see item 563] p. 274–289, bibl., illus., map)

Author reports the results of intensive study conducted in 1971–72 of Talara Tar seeps in Peru's northwest coast. He located 10 main camp-sites and two scattered finds on the outwash slopes of the Amotape Mountains. Author illustrates the quartzite assemblage, discusses climatic changes in the Pleistocene-Holocene, and reconstructs subsistence patterns from 10,000 to 5,000 years ago. He sees hunters obtaining animals as they come for water in the Tar seep areas and then changing to more use of mangrove resources at 8,000 with the drying up of the region ca 5,000 years ago.

830   **Ríos, Marcela** and **Enrique Retamozo.** Objetos de metal procedentes de la Isla de San Lorenzo (MNAA/A, 17, 1978, p. 1–98, bibl., illus.)

Study of objects found by Max Uhle in graves he excavated in 1906–11 in the Isla de San Lorenzo, in front of Callao, and which are now located in Lima's Museo Nacional. Authors include Uhle's catalog which lists pottery, textiles, bones, metal (mostly silver with a little gold), etc.

831   **Rivera Dorado, Miguel.** La cerámica inca de Chinchero, Perú (IAI/I, 4, 1977, p. 139–158, bibl., illus.)

With excellent line drawings, author defines the Inca pottery of Chinchero, Cuzco dept. (for full reports, see items 562 and 758.

832   **Roe, Peter G.** Archaism, form and decoration: an ethnographic and archeological case study from the Peruvian montaña (IAS/ÑP, 14, 1976, p. 73–94, bibl., illus.)

Using ethnographic materials and relating them to archaeology, author concludes that both pottery form and surface decoration are important and must be considered not as isolated factors but together with other variables in reconstructing culture history.

833   **Rossel Castro, P. Alberto.** Arqueología sur del Perú: áreas—Valles de Ica y La Hoya de Río Grande de Naska. Prólogo de Luis E. Valcárcel. Lima, Editorial Universo, 1977. 368 p., illus., maps, music, plates, tables.

Good general summary with photographs, drawings, maps and charts of archaeology of the Ica Valley and mouth of Nasca. Author's terminology, however, does not coincide with most recent usage of Lumbreras and others (see HLAS 37:1026a).

834   **Rowe, John H.** El arte religioso del Cuzco en el Horizonte Temprano (IAS/ÑP, 14, 1976, p. 1–20, bibl., illus.)

Describes and compares motifs of Oberti metal disc and other metal objects from the Cuzco area in Echenique's collection.

835   **Ruiz Estrada, Arturo.** Las chullpas de Qaqsi (PUCIRA/BSA, 15/16, 1974/1975, p. 107–116, bibl., illus.)

Chullpas near town of Puno.

836   ———. Las ruinas de Tuich, Departamento de Amazonas (Informaciones Arqueológicas [Ediciones Catequil, Lima] 1, 1977, p. 5–22, bibl., illus.)

Pottery relates site to period more recent than Cajamarca III. Architecture suggests the Regional States period of 12th–15th century.

837   **Sanders, William T.** Pikillakta en la historia cultural andina (Arqueología de América Latina [Boletín trimestral dedicado a los estudios arqueológicos en América Latina y el Caribe, Huancayo, Peru] 1:1, March 1978, p. 3–12, bibl., illus.)

Describes ruin of some 700 structures which cover about 50 hectares. It is found at 3200 m. on a ridge about 30 km. from Cuzco, near a small lake and the town of Huarcapay. Sanders interprets it as one of the large cities created by Huari expansion, which developed out of a small pueblo.

838 Santos Ramírez, René. Presencia de Wari en el Valle de Siguas (in Jornadas Peruano-Bolivianas de Estudio Científico del Altiplano Boliviano y del Sur del Perú, I, La Paz, 1975. Arqueología en Bolivia y Perú [see item 619] t. 2, p. 393–409, bibl., illus., map)

Discusses Valley of Siguas, Arequipa dept., and ceramics which show clear Wari (i.e., Huari) influence.

839 Schaedel, Richard P. The Huaca Pintada of Illimo (AIA/A, 31:1, Jan./Feb. 1978, p. 27–37, illus.)

Reconstruction of painted mural on Peru's North Coast, north of Chiclayo, derived from Brunings' original notes, photos and other accounts. Excellent job of archival research. Most significant reconstruction of a maritime iconography of about AD 600–700. Excellent photographs and line drawings.

840 Shady, Ruth and Hermilio Rosas. El Horizonte Medio en Chota: prestigio de la cultura Cajamarca y su relación con el Imperio Huari (MNAA/A, 16, 1977, p. 1–73, bibl., illus.)

Excellent illustrations and descriptive material of Middle Horizon pottery from Chota, excavated in 1968 and 1971. Relates material to northern Cursive style and discusses role of Cajamarca and Huari cultures. These extremely significant interpretations should be read by specialists in Andean archaeology and by those interested in the origins of the State.

841 —— and ——. Notas sobre enterramientos subterráneos de Chota, Cajamarca (Informaciones Arqueológicas [Ediciones Catequil, Lima] 1, 1977, p. 23–47, bibl., illus.)

Describes negative painted vessels and copper ax with burial. Shows relationships both to Recuay and to coast during Regional Developmental period.

842 Sharon, Douglas and Christopher B. Donnan. The magic cactus: ethnoarchaeological continuity in Peru (AIA/A, 30:6, Nov. 1977, p. 374–381, illus.)

With good illustrations of precolumbian textiles, pottery, stone sculpture, authors show the depiction of the San Pedro cactus (Trichocereus pachanoi) and how the modern inhabitants of Coastal Peru still employ shamanic healing processes using this hallucinogenic cactus. Excellent example of how

the use of ethnographic data can facilitate the interpretation of archaeological depiction.

843 Shimada, Izumi. Economy of a prehistoric urban context: commodity and labor flow at Moche V Pampa Grande, Peru (SAA/AA, 43:4, p. 569–592, bibl., illus.)

Special study conducted by teams from the Royal Ontario Museum of the urban context at Pampa Grande which was last occupied by Moche V population at ca. AD 600–700. The teams followed a contiguous room excavation in an attempt to develop a structural-functional approach to the site. Author sees the site as consisting of many dispersed areas of low-output craft production, where the labor force commuted from elsewhere bringing food from spatially separated kitchens. Important for those interested in precolumbian urbanism of the Andean regions.

844 Silva Sifuentes, Jorge E. Chavín de Huantar: un complejo multifuncional. Lima, Univ. Nacional Mayor de San Marcos, Gabinete de Arqueología, 1978. 31 p., bibl., illus., map (Serie investigaciones, 1)

Proposes that Chavín de Huantar served not merely as a ceremonial center but that it also had functions connected with the storage of exotic materials in specific areas (i.e., pottery in one, textiles in another, food in a third one, etc.). Suggests a stronger socioeconomic-political role even if based on a ceremonial foundation.

845 Silverman de Mayer, Helaine. Estilo y estado: el problema de la cultura Nasca (Informaciones Arqueológicas [Ediciones Catequil, Lima] 1, 1977, p. 49–78, bibl., illus.)

Believes that conclusions about the state and a dominant religious cult are based on inadequate data.

846 Stothert, Karen E. Preparing a mummy bundle: note on a late burial from Ancón, Peru (IAS/ÑP, 16, 1978, p. 13–22, bibl., illus.)

Article about a mummy bale enclosed in a rope net-bag found in a vandalized tomb near Ancón, possibly Area 6 of Ancón Necropolis. The analysis by Eve Yarberry briefly describes opening of bundle, its contents, technique of rope net.

847 Tabío C., Ernesto E. Prehistoria de la costa del Perú. La Habana, Academia de Ciencias de Cuba, 1977. 268 p., bibl., illus., maps.

Based on the author's personal experiences in Peru (1953–60), this book describes travel along the entire coastline, its prehistory, collections and excavations. Unfortunately, the study is slightly outdated with references only to the late 1960s. Includes a few illustrations of pottery specimens, none of architectural features.

848 Tapia Pineda, Félix B. Cerámica Tiwanacota en Puno (*in* Jornadas Peruano-Bolivianas de Estudio Científico del Altiplano Boliviano y del Sur del Perú, I, La Paz, 1975. Arqueología en Bolivia y Perú [see item **619**] t. 2, p. 339–360, bibl., illus.)

Describes vessels and keros of pottery from city of Puno as good Tiahuanaco.

849 ———. Contribuciones al estudio de la cultura precolombina en el altiplano peruano. La Paz, Instituto Nacional de Arqueología, 1976. 20 p., bibl. (Publicación, 16)

General summary pleading for better understanding of relationships between Tiahuanaco and Pukara which can only be attained with more work at Pukara.

850 ———. Visión panorámica de la cultura en el altiplano peruano. La Paz, Instituto Nacional de Arqueología, 1976. 31 p., bibl. (Publicación, 21)

Summarizes work to date on prehistoric cultures of the Peruvian altiplano and indicates the importance of interpreting the sociocultural, sociopolitical and socioeconomic development in ecological terms.

851 Thatcher, John P., Jr. A Middle Horizon IB cache from Huamachuco, North Highlands, Peru (IAS/ÑP, 15, 1977, p. 101–110, bibl., illus.)

Cache of pottery shows that Huamachuco was under Huari influence during Middle Horizon IB Period.

852 Topic, John R. and Theresa Lange Topic. Prehistoric fortification systems of northern Peru (UC/CA, 19:3, Sept. 1978, p. 618–619)

Authors examine, from the point of view of pure defense, the construction of great walls and fortresses in the Moche and Viru Valleys, taking into account the lack of associated large refuse accumulations.

853 Trimborn, Hermann. Sama (DGV/ZE, 100:1/2, 1975, p. 290–299, bibl., illus., map, plates)

Report on the results of excavations along the Sama and Caplina Rivers in Tacna, adjacent to the Chilean border. They reveal strong Inca influence in area and upon a sequence of local cultures.

854 Vreeland, James. Ancient Andean textiles: clothes for the dead (AIA/A, 30:3, May 1977, p. 166–178, illus.)

Good popular account, with superb color photos, of mummy bundles from the Peruvian coast. Exemplifies how a detailed study of textiles can tell much about precolumbian cultures.

855 Weiss, Pedro. El perro peruano sin pelo: perro chino, viringo, ccala o ccalato. Lima, Museo Nacional de Antropología y Arqueología, 1976. p. 34–54, bibl., illus., plates (Serie paleobiología, 1)

Commentary on present day hairless dogs and those shown in archaeological remains, especially Chimú and Chancay cultures. This article was also published in *Acta Herediana* (Univ. Peruana Cayetano Heredia, 3:1, Sept. 1970).

856 West, Michael. Early watertable farming on the north coast of Peru (SAA/AA, 44:1, Jan. 1979, p. 138–144, bibl., illus.)

Describes simple watertable farming plots in Viru Valley, North coast, Peru from Early Intermediate Period. Believes that specialized segments of one community did fishing while others engaged in this type of farming. Pollen studies show that separate field systems were used for *Zea*, *Leguminosae*, and *Solonaceae*.

857 Wheeler Pires-Ferreira, Jane; Edgardo Pires-Ferreira; and **Peter Kaulicke.** Domesticación de los camélidos en los Andes Centrales durante el período precerámico: un modelo (SA/J, 64, 1977, p. 155–165, bibl.)

After analyzing faunal remains from five cave sites in the Puna de Junín, Central Andes, the authors establish a model for man. They perceive him as going from generalized to specialized hunting of camelids, gradually moving into control of camelids in semi-domestication and, finally, attaining controlled herding in specific pastures.

URUGUAY

858 Boretto Ovalle, René. Intento de cronología relativa de los sitios arqueológicos del área de Salto Grande: interpretación de gráficos de seriación. Fray Bentos, Uru., Museo Nacional de Historia Natural, 1976. 6 p., bibl., tables.

Attempt to apply the quantitative method of ceramic analysis to the Salto Grande area of Uruguay, and interpretation of results.

VENEZUELA

859 Arévalo B., Lilliam. Tucuragua, un yacimiento aruquinoide del Orinoco Medio (*in* International Congress for the Study of Pre-Columbian Cultures of the Lesser Antilles, VII, Montreal, Canada, 1978. Proceedings [see item **495**] p. 29–38, bibl., illus.)

Preliminary account of work at site of typical Arauquin materials in Bolivar state. Excellent photographs.

860 Delgado, Rafael. Los petroglifos venezolanos. Caracas, Monte Avila Editores, 1976 [i.e. 1977]. 472 p., bibl., illus., plates (Col. Estudios)

Well illustrated work. Unfortunately, it includes little proof of author's classification and lacks a discussion of relationships, both customary in most petroglyph studies.

861 Denevan, William M. and Alberta Zucchi. Ridged-field excavations in the central Orinoco llanos, Venezuela (*in* Browman, David L. ed. Advances in Andean archaeology [see item **767**] p. 235–245, bibl., illus.)

Report on ongoing research. Concludes that ridged fields in Venezuela's western plains are manmade and precolumbian in origin, dating around AD 1000. Their surface was raised in order to allow for cultivation in regions that were periodically flooded. Authors estimate that only a relatively dense population, not dependent on shifting agriculture, could have created them. The article also speculates on direct cultural links of such fields in the Andes, lowland Bolivia, and the Amazonian and Orinoco plains.

862 Martín, Carlos Alberto. Arqueología de la Cueva el Zamuro, Estado Por-

tuguesa, Venezuela (Boletín de la Sociedad Venezolana de Espeleología [Caracas] 7:14, oct. 1976, p. 181–197, bibl., illus.)

Materials from cave site on Rio Saguás, Portuguesa state, described as a burial site with Tocuyanoid style pottery.

863 Medina, Luis J. Acerca de la agricultura prehispánica de Venezuela (VANH/B, 60:237, enero/marzo 1977, p. 61–78, bibl., tables)

Using archaeological, historical, ethnographic and biological data, author provides a list of plants used in precolumbian times. Includes full botanical identification and discussion of different types of agriculture practiced in each region during similar periods.

864 Nieves de Galicia, Fulvia. Bañador: un sitio arqueológico del Bajo Orinoco (*in* International Congress for the Study of Pre-Columbian Cultures of the Lesser Antilles, VII, Montreal, Canada, 1978. Proceedings [see item **495**] p. 71–80, bibl., illus.)

Pottery from site in the lower Orinoco does not resemble materials usually found therein. Corrugated decoration is similar to materials from Colombia, Guyana, and Brazil and suggests possible relationship with Tupi-Guarani tradition of Brazil.

865 Perera, Miguel Angel. El estudio de las placas líticas del occidente de Venezuela: algunos proposiciones para el análisis integral de un objeto cultural. Caracas, The Author, 1977. 116 p., bibl., illus., maps.

Everything you wish to know about winged stone placques from Venezuela's Andean regions, including excellent measurements, photos and descriptions. Author used computer in order to assist him in classifying and trying to determine a meaningful cluster. He compares these placques with similar materials in Panama, Costa Rica, Colombia. Despite this thorough study, we still lack an exact definition of their meaning and use. See item **866** for shorter version.

866 ———. Las placas líticas de los Andes Venezolanos y su origen mesoamericano (BBAA, 37:46, 1974/1975, p. 125–135, bibl., illus.)

Short version of item **865** without detailed information.

867 ———; Ernesto Borges; and Carlos A. Martín. Arima, un cementerio histórico de la Alta Guajira (Boletín de la Sociedad Venezolana de Espeleología [Caracas] 8:15, abril 1977, p. 51–66, bibl., illus.)

Detailed description with photos of cemetery, with bones in good condition and pottery with fingertip punctate and fingernail imbricated, probably of 16th century and related to Guajira Indians. Survival of earlier traditions probable.

868 **Sanoja Obediente, Mario.** Las culturas formativas del Oriente de Venezuela. Caracas, Univ. Central de Venezuela, Proyecto Orinoco, 1977. 542 p., bibl., illus., maps, (Monografía, 3)

Complete monograph on sites excavated on Orinoco of the Barrancoid tradition. The introduction discusses historical information and environmental conditions. Both phases, Barrancas and Macapaima, are described in detail with well illustrated artifacts and pottery. Seriation charts support author's sequences and are correlated with C14 dates. This is a highly significant study which all archaeologists interested in South America and the Caribbean should consult.

869 ———. Nuevas fechas de radiocarbón para la Cueva de el Elefante, Estado Bolívar, Venezuela (Boletín de la Sociedad Venezolana de Espeleología [Caracas] 8:15, abril 1977, p. 47–50, bibl., illus.)

Two new dates of 2440±85 and 2320±100 years BP date the lower levels where only flake artifacts of jasper occur. In upper levels, pottery probably belongs to Barrancoid or Arauquinoid styles. Pictographs cannot be correlated with these proposed occupations although they classify into two styles, one geometric and one with figures.

870 ———. Proyecto Orinoco: excavación en el sitio arqueológico de Los Castillos de Guayana, Territorio Federal Delta Amacuro, Venezuela (in International Congress for the Study of Pre-Columbian Cultures of the Lesser Antilles, VII, Montreal, Canada, 1978. Proceedings [see item 495] p. 157–168, bibl., illus.)

Reports on the archaeology of Spanish fort constructed about AD 1600 with a sequence of Indian occupation of ca. AD 1300, up to modern conversion of the site into a military post of the Venezuelan army.

871 ——— and **Iraida Vargas Arenas.** The formative cultures of the Venezuela

Oriente (in Browman, David L. ed. Advances in Andean archaeology [see item 767] p. 259–276, bibl., map)

Good summary of authors' points of view based upon evidence of pottery, C14 dates, and lots of unpublished data only available in Venezuela.

872 **Tarble de Ruiz, Kay.** Comparación estilística entre la cerámica de Lagunillas, Estado Zulia y Santa Ana, Estado Trujillo, Venezuela Nor-Occidental (in International Congress for the Study of Pre-Columbian Cultures of the Lesser Antilles, VII, Montreal, Canada, 1978 [see item 495] p. 189–197, bibl.)

See *HLAS 39:1007a–1008* for detailed information and good illustrations on the study subject. This presentation is highly generalized.

873 **Vargas Arenas, Iraida.** Puerto Santo: un nuevo sitio arqueológico en la costa oriental de Venezuela (in International Congress for the Study of Pre-Columbian Cultures of the Lesser Antilles, VI, Montreal, Canada, 1978. Proceedings [see item 495] p. 211–220, bibl., illus.)

Site on Carúpano-Río Caribe road, Sucre state, produced classic Barrancoid adornos and sherds painted in red and white on natural surface and white on red typical of Saladoid tradition. C14 date of AD 425± 80.

874 ——— and **Mario Sanoja Obediente.** Comparaciones entre la arqueología del Bajo y Medio Orinoco (in International Congress for the Study of Pre-Columbian Cultures of the Lesser Antilles, VII, Montreal Canada, 1978. Proceedings [see item 495] p. 221–230, bibl., illus.)

Good, short and clear summary of the two areas of the Orinoco, as interpreted by Vargas and Sanoja with reference to La Gruta and Las Barrancas Sites and including opinions of Roosevelt, Cruxent and Rouse. South American specialists should consult this article.

875 **Wagner, Erika.** Los Andes venezolanos: arqueología y ecología cultural (IAA, 4:1, 1978, p. 81–91, bibl.)

Summary of precolumbian history of Venezuelan Andes which developed in three district cultural patterns: Andean, Sub-Andean, and Tropical North-Andean. Also discusses ceramic complexes that are related to all three.

876 ———. Campoma: una encrucijada cultural en el Oriente venezolano (Revista Líneas [Compañía Anónima de Electricidad de Caracas] 241, mayo 1977, p. 16–21, bibl., illus.)

Study of a site near Campoma, in eastern part of Sucre state, reveals cultural relationships in precolumbian times to Lesser Antilles and sites on the west, along Venezuela's northern coast and Arauquin in Orinoco.

877 ———. La prehistoria de la Cuenca de Maracaibo (*in* Unidad y variedad: ensayos en homenaje a José M. Cruxent. Caracas, Instituto Venezolano de Investigaciones Científicas [IVIC], Centro de Estudios Avanzados, 1978, p. 329–348, bibl.)

Review of history of archaeology in Lake Maracaibo area. Summarizes periods and 25 C14 dates.

878 **Zucchi, Alberta.** Caño Caroní: un grupo prehispánico de la Selva de los Llanos de Barinas. Caracas, Univ. Central de Venezuela, Facultad de Ciencias Económicas y Sociales, División de Publicaciones, 1975 [i.e. 1976]. 101 p., bibl., illus., maps, plates, tables (Col. Antropología, 5)

Monographic presentation of Caño Caroní culture of plains of Western Venezuela from AD 1000–1400 believed to be an advanced group of Carib origin. Detailed description includes drawings, sherd profiles and photos of sherd pottery and other artifacts. Important article for specialists.

ETHNOLOGY: Middle America

CYNTHIA A. CONE, *Associate Professor of Anthropology, Hamline University*
FRANK C. MILLER, *Professor of Anthropology, University of Minnesota*

RECENT RESEARCH IN MIDDLE AMERICA has carried on and extended the classical themes of work in that region, and has introduced some promising new emphases. The largest number of works, and some of the most important, deal with the economics and the social relations of production. Gudeman's analysis of agricultural production in a subsistence economy in Panama is a notable theoretical advance in anthropological economics (item **919**). Climo's study of *ejidos* in Yucatán (item **897**), a fine example of controlled comparison, shows that some anthropologists recognize the need to examine administrative strategies and the impact of government policies. Stavenhagen and his coworkers continue their penetrating work on agrarian structure in Mexico and the implications of capitalist agricultural development (item **976**). Carol Smith applies and extends dependency theory in her study of regional underdevelopment in Guatemala (item **972**).

While some Marxist-influenced approaches raise a substantial challenge to earlier interpretations, others sometimes seem to be a ritualistic exercise that contribute little but a new terminology (see items **896, 908,** and **946**). As an all-purpose explanatory principle, "dependent capitalism" is as fashionable as the "age-area hypothesis" or "pattern saturation" used to be. It is well to keep in mind that Latin America in general and Middle America in particular contain many varieties of capitalism that are related in different ways to their "peripheries," and the dynamics of these systems deserve some careful comparative scrutiny.

The lively tradition of symbolic analysis also continues to produce provocative statements. El Guindi, Helms, Hirschfeld, and Vogt treat various aspects of expressive culture with respect for the materials and with a finely-honed ethnographic imagination (items **920–921, 924–927** and **983–984**). Laughlin again presents a domain of Tzotzil ethnography with a poet's touch (item **937**), and Haviland raises gossip to a high art (item **923**). Huichol art is beautifully photographed and presented with insight in item **885**.

The biennium marks the 20th anniversary of the Harvard Chiapas project. Initiated in 1957 by Vogt, this project has set a new standard for ethnography and continues to produce a stream of excellent publications (see items **923, 937, 983– 984** and **987**).

Another significant anniversary occurred in 1976: the 25th anniversary of the Centro Coordinador Tzeltal-Tzotzil, the first regional center of the Instituto Nacional Indigenista. Its program is described and analyzed by Aguirre Beltrán, Köhler, and Nahmad Sitton (items **879, 935** and **949**).

In the footsteps of their subjects, anthropologists have migrated to the cities; and the movement is producing some substantial dividends in research. Recent notable research on Mexico City includes the work of Arizpe, Kemper, and Lomnitz, testimony to the creative response by migrants to the opportunities and tribulations of city life (items **881, 933** and **939–940**).

As in other parts of the world, women and their roles have been substantially neglected in anthropology. Publications during the past two years are beginning to redress the balance (items **881, 896, 903, 905, 909, 912** and **956**).

Another domain long neglected is politics and power. Middle Americanists have pursued their interest in the production of goods and the interpretation of symbols largely without regard for the political context, particularly on a regional level. The few articles on political processes are a step (but not a long enough step) in the right direction (items **913, 920–921, 925, 946, 948** and **981**). Friedrich is one of the rare anthropologists to realize the possibilities of research on local-level politics in Middle America, and the second edition of his classic on agrarian revolt is most welcome (item **914**).

879 Aguirre Beltrán, Gonzálo and others.
El indigenismo en acción: XXV aniversario del Centro Coordinador Indigenista Tzeltal-Tzotzil. México, Instituto Nacional Indigenista, 1976. 270 p., illus., map, plates, tables (Col. SEP/INI, 44)

The Instituto Nacional Indigenista (INI) of Mexico operates one of the world's most comprehensive development programs specifically concerned with a cultural minority. The program began in the Highlands of Chiapas in 1951 and has expanded to virtually all areas of significant Indian population in Mexico. In this 25th anniversary volume, Alfonso Villa Rojas presents a brief but vivid account of exploitation of the Indians before the coming of INI. Aguirre Beltrán discusses the structure and function of the coordinating centers, and other authors discuss the program, with the most space devoted to education. There are also personal accounts by 12 Indian change agents, and many valuable tables of statistics.

880 Appleby, Gordon. Here a market, there a market, and nowhere any system: a review of marketing studies in Oaxaca, Mexico (UP/PS, 6:3, July 1977, p. 87–94, bibl.)

A thorough critique of the comprehensive research on Oaxacan markets by Beals (see *HLAS 39:1019*) and Cook and Diskin (see *HLAS 39:1040*). The author argues that these investigators have failed to define regional units carefully, to conceptualize the system as a whole, and to take into account the functioning of the capitalist system on the national and international levels.

881 Arizpe S., Lourdes. Indígenas en la ciudad de México. México, Secretaría de Educación Pública, 1975. 157 p., bibl., map, plates, tables (SepSetentas, 182)

Theoretically sophisticated study of Mazahua, Nahua, and Otomí women vendors and beggars, popularly called "Marías" in Mexico City. Field work was conducted both in the city and in home villages. The author argues that the problem is a result of the urban socio-economic structure and not a matter of cultural differences, and that cultural integration would not eliminate the poverty of the "Marías."

882 Armas Molina, Miguel. La cultura pipil de Centroamérica. 2. ed. San Salvador, Ministerio de Educación, Dirección de Publicaciones, 1976. 72 p., illus., map, plates.

A general account of the Pipil culture of Central America. It is believed that the Pipil arrived from Central Mexico and settled along the Pacific coast from Guatemala to Nicaragua, about the eighth century. They belong to the ethnic group called Nahua from whom they obtained their writing and numeration systems, and also show Totonac, Olmec, and Toltec cultural influences. Besides hunting and fishing, the Pipil economic system is based on the cultivation of corn. The religious system is composed of a number of deities, and involves the practice of human sacrifice.

883 Barlett, Peggy. El caso puriscaleno y el mecanismo de la evolución agrícola (MNCR/V, 4:1, 1978, bibl., tables) Spanish version of *HLAS 39:1017.*

884 Beals, Ralph L. Sonoran fantasy or coming of age? (AAA/AA, 80:2, June 1978, p. 355–362, bibl.)

A respected senior anthropologist explains in no uncertain terms why he does not agree with Wilk's appreciation (see item **988**) of Castaneda's books about Don Juan (see *HLAS 31:1729*), in what ways the books fail to meet the accepted canons for anthropological research, and why he believes that Castaneda's "alternate reality" exists only for Castaneda and perhaps his followers.

885 Berrin, Kathleen ed. Art of the Huichol Indians. N.Y., Harry N. Abrams, Inc. for the Fine Arts Museums of San Francisco, 1978. 212 p., bibl., map, plates.

A beautifully produced volume on Huichol art forms that is exceptional in its attempt to present those forms within cultural and psychological contexts. "Contexts" is the appropriate word, for the articles present diverse academic viewpoints of Huichol reality as well as highly individualistic Huichol perceptions. Though the articles are primarily the work of anthropologists, also

included are essays by a psychiatrist and a psychic adventurer.

886 Bozzoli de Wille, María. Bibliografía antropológica de Costa Rica (BBAA, 38:47, 1976, p. 63–82)

A general and comprehensive bibliography, principally of the years 1969–75, and including papers presented at conferences. See also item **528.**

887 ———. Narraciones bribris (MNCR/V, 2:2, 1977, p. 165–199, bibl.)

Bribri narratives fall into two large classes: 1) ritual cures and others which may be told only at night; and 2) those which may be related at any time. All are said to have been revealed by the gods to the first shamans. Narratives of the second group are discussed here. Bribri texts with Spanish translations.

888 Braniff C., Beatriz and **Richard S. Felger** comps. Sonora: antropología del desierto (in Reunión de Antropología e Historia del Noroeste, I, México, 1976. México, Instituto Nacional de Antropología e Historia, Centro Regional del Noroeste, 1976. 592 p., bibl., maps, tables [Col. Científica diversa, 27])

Ecology, archaeology, and ethnography of the state of Sonora, Mex.

889 Bryce-Laporte, Roy Simón. Religión folklórica y negros antillanos en la zona del Canal de Panamá: estudio de un incidente y su contexto (INC/RNC, 5, 1976, p. 61–80, bibl.)

The role of Afro-Antillean folk religion and magic in resolving a dispute in a segregated black community adjacent to Balboa.

890 Bunch, Roland and **Roger Bunch.** The highland Maya: patterns of life and clothing in Indian Guatemala. Visalia, Calif., Josten's, 1977. 99 p., bibl., map, plates.

Sometimes stereotyped, sometimes insightful, non-technical treatment. Illustrated with many exceptional color plates.

891 Butterworth, Douglas. Selectivity of out-migration from a Mixtec community (UA, 6:2, Summer 1977, p. 129–139, bibl., tables)

Out-migrants from a Mixtec town are found to be wealthier, better educated, Spanish-speaking and more cosmopolitan than those who remain. Individuals high in rank on these attributes are more likely to move to large metropolitan centers.

892 Carrasco Pizana, Pedro. El catolicismo popular de los tarascos. México, Secretaría de Educación Pública, Dirección General de Divulgación, 1976. 213 p., bibl. (SepSetentas, 298)

The bulk of this book is a Spanish version of the author's 1949 doctoral dissertation at Columbia Univ. published in 1952 by the Middle American Research Institute at Tulane. When first published, this work was a pioneering analysis of religion and social conflict. Also includes Spanish version of an article (see *HLAS 35:1040*) criticizing van Zantwijk's claims about precolumbian survivals in Tarascan religion.

893 Carter, William E. and Paul L. Doughty. Social and cultural aspects of *cannabis* use in Costa Rica (NYAS/A, 282, 1976, p. 2–17, bibl., table)

A carefully conducted and illuminating study of long-term, male marijuana users in San José. After interviewing and examining a larger sample, the authors constructed a matched sample of 41 users and a like number of nonusers from the lower middle and working classes. The users smoked an average of 9.6 joints a day, some as many as 40 a day. Behavioral differences are attributed to differing experiences during socialization; not to marijuana use. The users feel that *cannabis* helps them cope with daily life, and do not perceive any problems with it other than cost and the growing harrassment by police. The authors conclude that there is no evidence that chronic use of the drug itself interferes with normal functioning.

894 Chambers, Erve. Modern Mesoamerica: the politics of identity (AAA/AA, 79:1, March 1977, p. 92–97, bibl.)

This useful review article on seven recent community studies in Mexico and one in Guatemala (including *HLAS 37:1134*, *HLAS 39:1048* and *1113*) asserts that change and modernization are still inadequately conceptualized, even after 40 years of research in the area.

895 Chance, John K. Race and class in colonial Oaxaca. Stanford, Calif., Stanford Univ. Press, 1978. 250 p., bibl., maps, tables.

The *sistema de castas* of colonial New Spain has commonly been interpreted in terms of the European concept of "estates," relatively rigid social strata defined by legally-based rights and obligations. Chance rejects the estate model because it cannot account for the variety and complexity of stratification in the city of Oaxaca and because, in assuming a high degree of normative consensus, it neglects the political coercion and economic interdependence which hold colonial societies together. In concentrating on the criteria of rank rather than the definition of strata, the author follows Weber's notions of class, status, and power. During the first century after the conquest, rank depended of course on ethnic identity, but beyond that primarily on political power, especially one's ability to garner favors from the Crown. After 1630, wealth became more important as a criterion of rank, a tendency reinforced in succeeding centuries by the development of capitalism in Mexico. This is a book whose importance is enforced by a careful grounding of the theoretical argument in empirical data. For historian's comment, see *HLAS 40:2486*.

896 Chinchilla, Norma S. Familia, economía y trabajo de la mujer en Guatemala (CM/DE, 34, 1978, p. 99–113, bibl., tables)

After asserting that the Marxist tradition is the only hope for a theory to explain the effects of economic change on the family, the author concludes that the productive function of the family has declined with the penetration of capitalism. The census and survey data presented are useful but are not an adequate basis for the conclusions.

897 Climo, Jacob. Collective farming in northern and southern Yucatán, Mexico: ecological and administrative determinants of success and failure (AAA/AE, 5:2, May 1978, p. 191–206, bibl., tables)

An exemplary instance of the ecological-society perspective on technological change (see item **968**) and the method of controlled comparison. National administrative policies for communal farms (*ejidos*) are uniform throughout the country, particularly in their tendency to foster capital dependency on federal agencies. They vary in actual implementation because of local differences. The northern region has a finite land base where only one crop, *henequen*, can be profitably grown. A state monopoly regulates its production and marketing, fostering a paternalistic alliance betwen the *ejidatarios* and those with large private landholdings. In contrast, the ecological features of the southern zone are conducive to expansion. Moreover, the *ejidatarios* have had access to development loans for the preparation of new lands, agricultural extension agents, considerable support from the Instituto Nacional Indigenista, and greater independence from private landowners. The rapid economic growth and relative solvency of the southern mixed-farming *ejidos* stand in sharp contrast to the stagnant *henequen* production.

898 Cook, Scott. Value, price and simple commodity production: Zapotec stoneworkers (JPS, 3:4, July 1976, p. 395–427, chart)

Cook begins with a detailed discussion of the concepts of "commodity" and of "simple commodity production" in the work of Marx and his interpreters in order to explore the utility of the Marxian labor theory of value in the examination of precapitalist production. Its application to the Zapotec stoneworking industry illuminates the structure of production relations through market exchange, and indicates the mechanisms through which prices are adjusted over the long run to maintain equivalences among the embodied labor values of various types of commodities.

899 Crumrine, N. Ross. The Mayo Indians of Sonora: a people who refuse to die. Foreword by Edward H. Spicer. Tucson, Univ. of Arizona Press, 1977. 167 p., illus., maps, plates.

A general ethnography is followed by an analysis of Mayo revivalism and the maintenance of cultural identity, interpreted in terms of Victor Turner's concept of liminality and cetain structuralist notions. In contrast to Erasmus, who sees the Mayo as peasants, Crumrine emphasizes their ethnic separateness.

900 ——— and M. Louise Crumrine. Ritual symbolism in folk and ritual drama: the Mayo Indian San Cayetano Velación, Sonora, Mexico (AFS/JAF, 90:355, Jan./March 1977, p. 8–28, plates)

Concerned with ritual symbols and their relation to sociocultural conditions, the authors employ Victor Turner's analytical framework in a comprehensive examination of rituals associated with San Cayetano, a popular Mayo Indian trickster-like saint. He is seen to mediate between the Mayo and *mestizo* political and economic sources of power. Historically a puritanical and pious figure, San Cayetano is now a drunkard and prone to violence, befitting the Mayo's perception of *mestizo* power and personality.

901 Davis, Enriqueta and Freddy Enrique Blanco. El problema del indio en Panamá (III/AI, 38:1, enero/marzo 1978, p. 97–103)

This brief discussion of Indian policy in Panama claims, without presenting evidence, that legislation has tended to guarantee the continuity of Indian cultures.

902 Dennis, Philip A. and Douglas Uzzell. Corporate and individual inter-village relations in the Valley of Oaxaca (UP/E, 17:3, July 1978, p. 313–324, bibl.)

The corporate community based on communal land tenure and often involved in inter-village feuding is contrasted to the economic strategies of individuals who maintain social networks that extend beyond the village and often the region. From colonial times the village has served to minimize peasant losses while at the same time wealth-leveling mechanisms require that economic gain be sought beyond its boundaries. Capitalist penetration has stimulated network formation but the village continues to function as an elastic labor pool.

903 Díaz Ronner, Lucila M. and María Elena Muñoz Castellanos. La mujer asalariada en el sector agrícola (III/AI, 38:2, abril/junio 1978, p. 327–339)

The Mexican agrarian structure consists of a dynamic commercial sector and a peasant or traditional sector where survival becomes increasingly difficult, so that both men and women must seek wage work in order to meet the needs of the family. The empirical evidence comes from interviews with 185 day laborers, both male and female and overwhelmingly landless, in the vineyards of Aguascalientes, Mex.

904 Dinerman, Ina R. Economic alliances in a Mexican regional economy (UP/E, 17, 1, Jan. 1978, p. 53–64, bibl.)

In the Tarascan town of Ihuatzio on the shores of Lake Pátzcuaro, the major source of cash is the sale of *petates* (rush mats) in the Pátzcuaro market. The author attempts to demonstrate that the quality of interpersonal relations is shaped by the dominant characteristics of the marketplace: erratic supply, unpredictable demand, indeterminant prices. She holds that this approach is superior to Foster's model of the "dyadic contract" (see *HLAS 25:428* and *HLAS 27:905*). Except for a few prices, no quantitative data are presented, so the argument hinges on internal consistency and ethnographic persuasiveness.

905 ———. Ritual y realidad: auto-imagen de las mujeres tarascas sobre su papel económico (III/AI, 8:3, 1978, p. 569–597, bibl., illus.)

A study, all too rare, of community rituals from the point of view of female participants. In Huecorio, Michoacán state, Mex., as elsewhere, these rituals convey many messages about the social order and the proper role of women. A brief analysis of the role of female vendors concludes that they accept their economic position as inferior to *mestizas*, but claim superior social values.

906 **Downing, Theodore E.** Ecodevelopment: an alternative future (SAA/HO, 37:2, Summer 1978, p. 213–218, bibl.)

A provocative description of the goals of an alternative development strategy emphasizing community self-sufficiency, equitable relations of production and marketing, conservation of non-renewable resources and rational exploitation of renewable resources. This concept of development, formulated by the UN Environment Programme, is the theoretical basis for the Centro de Ecodesarrollo in México. Downing describes the Centro's project to design and execute such a strategy in the Mexican coffee industry.

907 ———. Partible inheritance and land fragmentation in a Oaxacan village (SAA/HO, 36:3, Fall 1977, p. 235–243, bibl., illus., tables)

A Zapotec and Spanish-speaking village in the Valley of Oaxaca has all of the conditions leading to high fragmentation; and yet there is less of it than would be expected. The reasons are that 1) larger holdings are less likely to be fragmented; 2) some consolidation takes place; and 3) 10 percent of land transfers involve only one heir.

908 **Durand, Pierre.** Société paysanne et lutte des classes au Mexique. Montréal, Canada, Les Presses de l'Univ. de Montréal, 1975. 257 p., bibl., maps, tables.

An ethnography, interpreted within the framework of French Marxism, of Nanacatlan, a Totonac village in the Northern Sierra of the state of Puebla, Mex. The author argues that three modes of production—feudal, mercantile, and capitalist—exist, and that the capitalist mode is dominant. Whether or not one accepts the Marxist interpretations, the data about the ideology of egalitarianism and the realities of stratification are useful.

909 **Elmendorf, Mary Lindsay.** Nine Mayan women: a village faces change. N.Y., Halstead Press *for* Schenkman Publishing Co., 1976. 159 p., bibl., plates.

Expanded version of *HLAS 37:1129*.

910 **Estrada, Alvaro.** Vida de María Sabina: la sabia de los hongos; con la traducción de cantos chamánicos mazatecos, cantados por María Sabina. México, Siglo XXI, 1977. 164 p., facsim., plates.

María Sabina relates the story of her life, including her personal experience with the *niños santos* (hallucinogenic mushrooms), which led her to become the best known shaman in Mazateca culture. She explains the important role these mushrooms play in the religious system, and how their mystical power has been destroyed with the intrusion of foreigners, who have failed to understand the proper use and significant value of the mushrooms in Mazateca culture.

911 **Favre, Henri.** L'indigénisme mexicain (FDD/NED [Problèmes d'Amérique Latine, 42] 4338/4340, 2 déc. 1976, p. 67–84, bibl., maps, tables)

A summary of the situation of Indians in Mexico and a history of *indigenismo*. The role of the Instituto Nacional Indigenista and criticisms of its program are discussed.

912 **Flores Andino, Francisco A.** El Departamento de Gracias a Dios y la mujer indígena miskita (YAXKIN, 1:1, oct. 1975, p. 23–30, plate)

The life cycle of Miskito women, customs concerning menstruation and infidelity, household maintenance, and typical foods.

913 Fried, Jacob. Two orders of authority and power in Tarahumara society (*in* Fogelson, Raymond D. and Richard N. Adams. The anthropology of power: ethnographic studies from Asia, Oceania, and the New World [see item **253**] p. 263–269, bibl.)

Asserts that the Tarahumara borrowed complex notions of power from the Jesuits and have maintained them alongside aboriginal ideas, without attempting a synthesis.

914 Friedrich, Paul. Agrarian revolt in a Mexican village. Chicago, Ill., Univ. of Chicago Press, 1977. 162 p., illus., maps, plates.

Second edition of a superb book (see *HLAS 33:1310*), with a new preface and a supplementary bibliography on agrarian reform and local-level politics.

915 Fuente, Julio de la. Yalalag: una villa serrana zapoteca. México, Instituto Nacional Indigenista, 1977. 381 p. (Clásicos de la antropología mexicana, 2)

A reissue of a classic monograph of Middle American ethnography (see *HLAS 15:376*)

916 Furst, Peter T. and **Marina Anguiano.** "To Fly as Birds:" myth and ritual as agents of enculturation among the Huichol Indians of Mexico (*in* Wilbert, Johannes *ed.* Enculturation in Latin America: an anthology [see item **260**] p. 95–181, bibl.)

A brief history of the impact of European contact on the Huichol reveals that, though not impervious to Western culture, their rituals and beliefs remain largely intact. These include an elaborate children's ceremony conducted annually by the local shaman at the time of the ripening of the first foods. The chants, less abbreviated in style than those intended mainly for adults, provide children with a mental map of the sacred places and events of the peyote pilgrimage, images obtained through children's vicarious flights as birds. The article contains descriptions of four major myths as well as the role of shamans as background for three different and complementary versions of the children's ceremony.

917 García Mora, Carlos. La migración indígena a la Ciudad de México (III/AI, 37:3, julio/sept. 1977, p. 657–669, bibl.)

After reviewing a series of works on the Mazahua by Iwanska (including *HLAS 35:1065*) and on Indian migrants in Mexico City by Arizpe (see item **881**), the author considers suggested solutions for the problems posed by the migrants. He holds that it would be naïve to recommend solutions requiring structural changes that are unlikely, given the present distribution of power in Mexico.

918 Gates, Marilyn. Measuring peasant attitudes to modernization: a projective method (UC/CA, 17:4, Dec. 1976, p. 641–665, bibl., illus., plates)

A photographic technique for eliciting attitudes was designed and administered to 68 men from five agrarian communities in northern Campeche, Mex., the site of an internationally financed small-scale irrigation project. The approach demonstrates that the use of photographs is a good way to get people to express their opinions, but falls into the trap of assuming that a better understanding of peasant attitudes would produce a less traumatic introduction to modern agriculture.

Ginzbarg, Steven. Plantas medicinales de los indios bribris y cabécar. See item **1652**.

919 Gudeman, Stephen. The demise of a rural economy: from subsistence to capitalism in a Latin American village. London, Routledge and Kegan Paul, 1978. 176 p., bibl., illus., map, tables.

An eye-opening antidote to the mind-numbing debates of the formalists and substantivists, whose stultifying preoccupation with exchange has blinded them to the basic facts of life: the production of goods and the reproduction of workers. After a lucid discussion of labor, labor value, subsistence, and surplus in the thinking of Ricardo, Marx, and the neoclassical economists, Gudeman confronts the issue with which none has dealt adequately: the distribution of the product and the constitution of the surplus. The bulk of the book is an analysis of the subsistence economy of a Panamanian village (see *HLAS 39:1071–1073*) and the beginning of its demise with the shift to sugar cane. A brilliant application of theory to data.

920 el-Guindi, Fadwa. Lore and structure: Todos Santos in the Zapotec system (UCLA/JLAL, 3:1, Summer 1977, p. 3–18, bibl., tables)

Lucid analysis of the Zapotec All Saints ritual when the dead return to visit their living families. In a series of reciprocal exchanges only the dead receive without giving. This is a result of the dead as a mediating category creating the structures of kin relationship of which they are no longer a part.

921 ———. The structural correlates of power in Zapotec ritual (*in* Fogelson, Raymond D. and Richard N. Adams. The anthropology of power: ethnographic studies from Asia, Oceania, and the New World [see item **253**] p. 299–307, bibl.)

A set of transformational rules constitutes a "grammar" of ritual which defines the nature of power in the ritual process.

922 **Hatley, Nancy Brennan.** Cooperativism and enculturation among the Cuna Indians of San Blas (*in* Wilbert, Johannes *ed.* Enculturation in Latin America: an anthology [see item **260**] p. 67–94, bibl.)

Actually two separate papers: a description of a successful Cuna cooperative and a discussion of socialization practices. The traditional labor organization is described as providing the basis for *sociedades*, economic organizations that call not only for cooperative labor, but also the accumulation of capital. The Mola Co-op added a further dimension of more complex decision-making. The author attributes the success of cooperative projects to the groundwork laid in the development and reinforcement of cooperative behavior in children. The reverse can just as easily be argued. Societies with effective cooperative adult groups may be apt to nuture similar behavior in children. Other factors must be considered as well. It would not be possible for the Mola Cooperative to succeed without the economic opportunities provided by markets beyond the Cuna islands.

923 **Haviland, John Beard.** Gossip, reputation, and knowledge in Zinacantan. Chicago, Ill., Univ. of Chicago Press, 1977. 264 p., bibl., plates.

Placing his material in a rich cultural context and treating it in fascinating detail, the author shows how gossip allows people to examine the rules they live by, to redefine the conditions for application, and to manipulate interpretations for personal ends.

924 **Helms, Mary W.** Iguanas and crocodilians in tropical American mythology and iconography with special reference to Panama (UCLA/JLAL, 3:1, Summer 1977, p. 51–132, bibl., illus., tables)

Argues that the iconographic motifs on ancient Panamanian polychrome ceramics and gold pieces, generally thought to depict crocodilians, in fact represent iguanas, possibly a key symbol associated with the ruling elites of precolumbian chiefdoms. This conclusion is reached through extensive use of symbolic structural analysis of myths and charts of contemporary San Blas Cuna, considered in the wider context of Central and South American myths and cosmologies.

925 ———. Power structure in Middle America (*in* Fogelson, Raymond D. and Richard N. Adams. The anthropology of power: ethnographic studies from Asia, Oceania, and the New World [see item **253**] p. 245–261, bibl., illus., maps)

Maintains that consistent structural patterns can be perceived in heartland-hinterland relations within Middle America broadly defined, from precolumbian times to present.

926 **Hirschfeld, Lawrence A.** Art in Cunaland: ideology and cultural adaptation (RAI/M, 12:1, April 1977, p. 104–123, bibl., tables)

A fascinating, original analysis of the formal coincidence of Cuna aesthetic and political economic structure which moves beyond symbolic structural analysis as an end in itself. Art is perceived as a logically structured domain of preserved possibilities providing a potentially adaptive response to changing circumstances. The structural relations among the major Cuna arts, three forms of chants and the construction of *molas* (designs of reverse appliqué for women's blouses), are examined to reveal how the genesis of the latter as a novel art form developed in conjunction with extensive changes in Cuna political economy in the 19th century. Despite extensive contact with European capitalistic economy and a shift from communal to individual land ownership and cash cropping, the Cuna have been able to maintain a near equality in the distribution of wealth. They have achieved this through inheritance patterns which disperse wealth; cooperatives which make joint purchases; the internal restriction of credit so that only the village as a whole can operate as creditor; and through the channeling of surplus cash into non-productive rituals and goods, thus insuring that differential production of surplus cannot become the basis for permanent economic stratification. The features of the *mola* fulfill the structural dictates of the pre-existent aesthetic structure.

927 ———. Cuna aesthetics: a quantitative analysis (UP/E, 16:2, april 1977, p. 147–166, bibl., tables)

A pioneering attempt at using quantitative techniques in the analysis of ethnic art forms. Stepwise regression is employed to obtain an abstract set of ethno-aesthetic norms from preferences expressed by Cuna woman for photographs of *molas*. Two sets of norms were obtained: those for personal preferences and those for perceived salability. (*Molas* are sold only to outsiders.) In evaluation of their own wardrobes, a mixture of both sets of criteria appears to apply. Since *molas* are worn before they are sold, women may be combining, in a dialectical fashion, the two divergent sets of norms, producing salable articles while at the same time maintaining the integrity of a traditional art form.

928 Hunn, Eugene S. Tzeltal folk zoology: the classification of discontinuities in nature. N.Y., Academic Press, 1977. 400 p., bibl., tables.

This analysis of data from Tenejapa, Chiapas, is the first comprehensive treatment of any folk zoological system. Over 500 taxa are organized into five hierarchical levels. The author develops measures for the correspondence between folk and scientific systems, and proposes a generative model of classification.

929 Icaza Saldaña, Teresita. La mujer chocoe de Bayamón: observaciones de campo realizadas en la localidad de Bayamón, Provincia de Darién, 1976 (USMLA/LA, 6:8, mayo 1977, p. 53–85, tables)

An excellent description of Chocoe women in Bayamón, past and present. The development of communal living in Bayamón was one of the causes for women's role to change. Today, Chocoe women experience a wider range of sociability, which gives them access to cooperatives for the improvement of their economic system. Also they have taken part in the political meetings of the community; not in the sense of proposing or taking the initiative, but in approving or disapproving what the men propose.

930 Jäcklein, Klaus. Un pueblo popoloca. México, Instituto Nacional Indigenista, 1974. 323 p., bibl., maps, plates, tables (Col. SEP/INI, 25)

Spanish version of Jäcklein's *San Felipe Otlaltepec* (item 931).

931 ———. San Felipe Otlaltepec: Beiträge zur Ethnoanalyse der Popoloca de Puebla, Mexiko. Göppingen, FRG, Verlag Alfred Kümmerle, 1970. 295 p., bibl., maps, tables, plates.

An ethnography with no special theoretical focus, encompassing economic, political, and social organization, formal education, religion and curing (not previously reviewed in the *Handbook*).

Johnson, Kirsten. Disintegration of a traditional resource-use complex: the Otomí of the Mezquital Valley, Hidalgo, Mexico. See item 5352.

932 Kelly, John C. A social anthropology of education: the case of Chiapas (CAE/AEQ, 8:4, Nov. 1977, p. 210–220, bibl.)

Though in need of editing and a less muddled application of theory, this description of the schools in two regions of Chiapas contains anecdotal material that effectively demonstrates one of the authors arguments—schools as institutions need to be understood within the larger context of political and economic structures.

933 Kemper, Robert V. Migration and adaptation: Tzintzuntzan peasants in Mexico City. Beverly Hills, Calif., Sage Publications, 1977. 221 p., bibl., maps, plates, tables.

Longitudinal data adds much to the study of migration. Making use of George Foster's information from the village of Tzintzuntzan, Michoacán, since 1945 and his own from Mexico City since 1969, Kemper is able to document the increasing involvement of Tzintzuntenös in urban life, an involvement that appears to be primarily a successful one.

934 Köhler, Ulrich. Cambio cultural dirigido en los Altos de Chiapas. México, Instituto Nacional Indigenista, 1975. 394 p., bibl., maps, plates, tables (Col. SEP/INI, 42)

Spanish version of *HLAS 35:1069.*

935 ———. Vorläufer der heutigen Menschen und Weltalter: Diskussion eines Mythos auf Maya-Tzotzil (PMK, 23, 1977, p. 265–276, bibl.)

Myths collected in San Pablo Chalchihuitán, Chiapas, are variants of a widespread Mesoamerican myth about the precursors of contemporary human beings.

936 **Kurtz, Donald V.** and **Margaret Showman.** The *tanda*: a rotating credit association in Mexico (UP/E, 17:1, Jan. 1978, p. 65–74, bibl., table)

Clifford Geertz suggested in his comparative study of credit associations, that they promote economic development by serving as a bridge between peasant and merchant attitudes toward money. In contrast to the commercially-oriented associations reported for Africa and Asia, these *tandas* are consumer-oriented. Both blue and white-collar members use them primarily to save for consumer purchases, although some white collar people use them for educational purposes.

937 **Laughlin, Robert M.** Of cabbages and kings: tales from Zinacantan. Washington, Smithsonian Institution Press, 1977. 427 p., bibl., maps, plates (Smithsonian contributions to anthropology, 23)

"For those who eagerly anticipate a scholarly feast. . . . where each delicacy is assigned an elegantly mysterious name. . . . Instead, at their feet will be placed a bowl of peasant soup" (p. 1). Peasant fare it may be, but it is served with grace and erudition. A collection of 173 tales, myths, and reminiscences by eight men and one woman. The Tzotzil texts and free English translations are accompanied by linguistic and ethnographic commentary.

938 **Littlefield, Alice.** Exploitation and the expansion of capitalism: the case of the hammock industry of Yucatán (AAA/AE, 5:3, Aug. 1978, p. 495–508, bibl., tables)

In an examination of the cottage production of hammocks in Yucatán, Mex., the author effectively applies Marx's formula for rate of surplus-value to measure exploitation in a traditional noncapitalist industry currently being incorporated into the global capitalist system. Polanyi, Dalton, and others are criticized for overemphasizing exchange and neglecting production.

939 **Lomnitz, Larissa Adler de.** Cómo sobreviven los marginados. México, Siglo XXI, 1975. 229 p., bibl., illus., plates, tables.

An important contribution to the understanding of shantytowns. This study of a squatter settlement in Mexico City emphasizes how people use their local resources of kinship, *compadrazgo,* and friendship in the unremitting struggle for survival. The author offers many sensitive insights into the workings of what economists euphemistically call the "informal sector" of the urban labor market.

940 ———. Networks and marginality: life in a Mexican shantytown. N.Y., Academic Press, 1977. 230 p., bibl., illus., maps, plates, tables.

English version of item **939.**

941 **Marcus, Joyce** and **Ronald Spores.** The *Handbook of Middle American Indians:* a retrospective look (AAA/AA, 80:1, March 1978, p. 85–100, bibl.)

A detailed and even-handed reconsideration of a widely-used work. The authors are particularly critical of the lack of substantive synthesis in some volumes and, in others, the failure to rise above the "timeworn 'buddy system'" so frequently used in edited works. Overall, they recognize the notable achievements of the *Handbook,* and especially the work of General Editor Robert Wauchope and Associate Editor Margaret A L. Harrison.

942 **Máximo Miranda, Luis.** Un comentario al margen de la Fase Auristanación del estudio de Roberto de la Guardia (LNB/L, 245, julio 1976, p. 37–49, bibl., map)

Describes Roberto de la Guardia's study of the development and struggle for survival of the cultural group called Castelauros, product of three mixed races (Leuca, Melanoderma, Xantoderma). They occupy the Auristan territory of Panama and have encountered a series of territorial problems with other cultural groups of Panama, even when they created in 1903 their own state called the Panama Republic, which gave them political power over these groups.

943 **McGoodwin, James R.** No matter how we asked them they convinced us that they suffer (SAA/HO, 37:4, Winter 1978, p. 378–383, bibl., tables)

The Redfield-Lewis disagreements about Tepoztlan inspired this effort to examine what the residents of Teacapan, Sinaloa, suffer from and enjoy in life. A minor instance of what C. Wright Mills called "abstracted empiricism," this article offers no significant insights into the human condition in Sinaloa.

944 Miller, Frank C. and Rolf Sartorious. Population policy and public goods (PU/PPA, 8:2, Winter 1979, p. 148–174, bibl.)

In this unusual collaboration between an anthropologist and a philosopher, the theory of public goods is applied to some issues in population policy. Public goods are those which are freely available to all, even to those who do not contribute toward providing them. Asserting that reduced population growth is a public good, the authors examine the conditions under which considerations of rationality and morality would impel individuals to limit family size. They illustrate their argument with Mexican data, and argue that a more equitable distribution of the benefits of development would furnish the incentives required for voluntary limitation of family size.

945 Molina, Virginia. San Bartolomé de los Llanos: una urbanización frenada. México, Instituto Nacional de Antropología e Historia, Centro de Investigaciones Superiores, 1976. 239 p.

In this *Ladino* and Tzotzil town near the Grijalva River valley in Chiapas, the rate of urbanization has slowed greatly as a result of displacement of peasant communities by the rising waters of a new reservoir on the river. The historical background and the economic role of the town as a regional center are considered.

946 Montoya Briones, José de Jesús. Estructura de poder y desarrollo social en la sierra de Hidalgo (III/AI, 38:3, julio/sept. 1978, p. 599–605, bibl.)

A brief summary of economy and society in the Huastec area of Hidalgo, Mex., holds that despotic regional bosses who gained power during the Revolution of 1910, have nurtured misery and exploitation. This situation is portrayed as an example of the unequal development that is characteristic of dependent capitalism.

947 Murphy, Arthur D. and Alex Stepick. Economic and social integration among

urban peasants (SAA/HO, 37:4, Winter 1978, p. 394–397, bibl., table)

A brief presentation of a system model of goals conditioned by varying environments and activities in a peasant village and two settlements on the outskirts of the city of Oaxaca, Mex. The claim that this model offers a better explanation of urban migration and adaptation than does the familiar rural-urban dichotomy, is not supported by any conclusive evidence.

948 Nader, Laura. Powerlessness in Zapotec and United States societies (*in* Fogelson, Raymond D. and Richard N. Adams. The anthropology of power: ethnographic studies from Asia, Oceania, and the New World [see item 253] p. 309–324, bibl.)

Thought-provoking comparison of reactions to feelings of injustice and to failures to resolve small complaints.

949 Nahmad Sitton, Salomon. Perspectives and the future of Mexican applied anthropology (SAA/HO, 36:3, Fall 1977, p. 316–318, bibl.)

Mexican views about the proper role of anthropology, as expressed by the Deputy Director of the Instituto Nacional Indigenista, the world's leading agency for applied anthropology. The goals of Mexican anthropology are increased human welfare, social justice, and harmonious ethnic pluralism.

950 Nash, June. Bajo la mirada de los antepasados: creencias y comportamiento en una comunidad Maya. México, Instituto Indigenista Interamericano, 1975. 393 p., bibl., map, tables (Ediciones especiales, 71)

Spanish version of item **951.**

951 ———. In the eyes of the ancestors: belief and behavior in a Maya community. New Haven, Conn., Yale Univ. Press, 1970. 368 p., bibl., figures, map, plates, tables.

This exemplary problem-focussed ethnography of the Tzeltal *municipio* of Amatenango del Valle (published in 1970 but never annotated in *HLAS*) concludes that social stability depends upon the efficiency of procedures for adjusting conflict, the ability to validate innovations in terms of existing values, and the effectiveness of procedures for transforming old political roles into ceremonial posts.

952 Nolasco, Margarita. Zonas marginadas con problemas de lengua en el

Estado de Oaxaca (III/AI, 38:3, julio/sept. 1978, p. 541–567, map, tables)

Recent studies show that, except for isolated jungle groups, Indians are part of a national society. Yet there is a great variation in degree of marginality which is measured in the state of Oaxaca by seven indicators such as dispersion of population, proportion of monolinguals, illiteracy, and occupational structure. The author argues that ethnic revival movements should be a part of a more general fight against marginality.

953 Novelo, Victoria. Artesanías y capitalismo en México. México, Instituto Nacional de Antropología e Historia, Centro de Investigaciones Superiores, 1976. 270 p.

Examines the controversies that have arisen as traditional handicrafts have become more incorporated into national and international markets. Analyzes the operations of the markets and the role of government regulation and efforts to promote craft production.

954 O'Brien, Linda L. Music education and innovation in a traditional Tzutuhil-Maya community (*in* Wilbert, Johannes *ed.* Enculturation in Latin America: an anthology [see item **260**] p. 377–393, bibl.)

Employed in the parish of Santiago Atitlán by American Catholic priests to develop and teach a mass based on indigenous Tzutuhil musical styles, the author found insuperable difficulties in creating something that was acceptable to both the Indians and the priests. She went on to examine innovation and tradition in Tzutuhil music. Music plays an important role as an integral part of a host of rituals that are part of the life cycle and the calendrical year. Musicians learn their skill through imitation and improvisation. For that reason, despite the emphasis on the traditional nature of music—its origins and the skills to perform have their source in the ancestral supernaturals—contemporary ritual music is influenced by African, Spanish and other Western sources. Alien forms are analogously identified with traditional ones and the integrity of Tzutuhil music continues.

955 Olien, Michael D. The adaptation of West Indian blacks to North American and Hispanic culture in Costa Rica (*in* Pescatello, Ann M. *ed.* Old roots in new lands [see *HLAS 40:2214*] p. 132–156, bibl., maps, plates, tables)

An historical study of the ethnic relations of blacks in Costa Rica, who though small in comparison to the total population (less than two percent), constitute over 33 percent of the people in the coastal province of Limón. West Indians were brought to Costa Rica to build railroads and remained to work on the banana plantations of the United Fruit Co. As a result of the collapse of the plantations by 1942 and the civil revolution of 1948, positions of power in Limón are now held by Spanish-speaking whites rather than North American administrators, requiring that blacks make rapid cultural adaptations. Structurally their position changed as well for they became citizens, many of them landholders, rather than foreign laborers.

956 Olson, Jon L. Women and social change in a Mexican town (UNM/JAR, 33:1, Spring 1977, p. 73–88, bibl., table)

Because of temporary labor migration by men, women have become increasingly self-sufficient in Mina, a small town in Nuevo León, Mex. The formal and informal networks formed by women gave them the power base for electing a woman mayor, a rare event in Mexico. The data are presented in terms of Evalyn Michaelson and Walter Goldschmidt's analysis of sex roles in three peasant structural types.

957 O'Nell, Carl W. and Nancy D. O'Nell. A cross-cultural comparison of aggression in dreams: Zapotecs and Americans (IJSP, 23:1, Spring 1977, p. 35–41, bibl., tables)

In comparing types of aggressive behavior in Zapotec dreams with American dreams, the authors find many similarities. Males tend to display more aggression and experience higher levels of physical aggression in both groups. There is less age and sex variation in dreamed aggression among the Zapotecs and it is markedly more physical than verbal. No attempt is made to explain the similarities and differences.

958 Parnell, Philip. Village or state? Competitive legal systems in a Mexican judicial district (*in* Nader, Laura and Harry F. Todd, Jr. *eds.* The disputing process: law in ten socieites. N.Y., Columbia Univ. Press, 1978, p. 315–350)

In the Zapotec judicial district of Loani, Oaxaca, state and local legal systems compete. The analysis is built around two cases:

the murder of a political boss and the "unlikely death" of a husband.

959 Pettersen, Carmen L. The Maya of Guatemala: their life and dress. Guatemala, Ixchel Museum, 1976. 274 p., illus., plates.

A handsome volume in "coffee-table" format, and yet a valuable ethnographic work on traditional dress. Illustrated with line drawings and 60 full-page reproductions of paintings by the author. Distributed by Univ. of Washington Press.

960 Plattner, Stuart M. Occupation and kinship in a developing society (SAA/HO, 37:1, Spring 1978, p. 77–83, bibl., illus., tables)

A comparison of kin networks among female pork vendors and male wage laborers in a *barrio* of San Cristóbal de Las Casas, Chiapas, Mex., reveals that the pork vendors' networks are somewhat denser and considerably more closely knit. These differences are consistent with the nature of each occupation; for kinship among vendors plays a more active role in cooperation and in the exclusion of outsiders.

961 Pollnac, Richard B. and **John J. Poggie, Jr.** Economic gratification orientations among small-scale fishermen in Panama and Puerto Rico (SAA/HO, 37:4, Winter 1978, 355–367, bibl., maps, tables)

Economic gratification, measured by asking respondents what they would do with gifts or inheritances, is related to relative security, opportunity structure, and situational factors such as boat ownership. Many investigators have considered deferred gratification to be a key variable in development, yet there is no general theory to explain the results reported here.

962 Pozas Arciniega, Ricardo. Chamula. México, Instituto Nacional Indigenista, 1977. 2 v. (401, 250 p.) (Clásicos de la antropología mexicana, 1)

A reissue of *HLAS 24:683*. This important monograph on the most populous Tzotzil municipio preceded the recent wave of research in the Highlands of Chiapas, Mex., and its reissue is most welcome.

963 Prestán Simón, Arnulfo. El rescate del alma en la sociedad Kuna (III/AI, 37:3, julio/sept. 1977, p. 749–758, bibl.)

Concepts of the soul, theories of disease, diagnosis, and curing among the San Blas Cuna.

964 Raymond, Nathaniel C. Remembrance of things past: hacendados and ejidatarios in Yucatán, Mexico (SAA/HO, 36:4, Winter 1977, p. 371–375, bibl., tables)

The expressed desire of both the old landowning class and the beneficiaries of the land reform to return to the good old days is interpreted as a desire to escape the conflicts of the present, as measured by the types and numbers of complaints presented to *ejido* officials.

965 Reina, Rubén E.; Norman B. Schwartz; and Edwards Foulks. Aculturación, modernidad, y personalidad en Chinautla, Guatemala (III/AI, 37:3, julio/sept. 1977, p. 615–641, bibl.)

Thematic Apperception Tests (TATs) administered to samples of Indians and Ladinos in 1955 revealed psychological similarities of a kind not noted in comparisons of these groups elsewhere in Mesoamerica. The similarities are interpreted in the light of interethnic relations in the community, the possibilities of social mobility, and the modernizing tendencies of both groups.

966 Richardson, Miles. La plaza como lugar social: el papel del lugar en el encuentro humano (MNCR/V, 4:1, 1978, p. 1–20, bibl., illus., maps, plates)

Community *plazas* in Costa Rica from colonial times to the present are analyzed in terms of the concept of "social place," where recurring micro-dramas of human interaction occur.

Rubel, Arthur J. and **J. Gettelfinger-Krejci.** The use of hallucinogenic mushrooms for diagnostic purposes among some highland Chinantecs. See item **1668.**

967 Sánchez de Almeida, María Eugenia and **Eduardo Almeida Acosta.** Experiencia comunitaria en San Miguel Tzinacapan (III/AI, 38:3, julio/sept. 1978, p. 607–630, bibl.)

Some specialists of urban origin—teachers, sociologists, a horticulturalist, a nurse and a priest, among others—are conducting a project of directed change in a Nahuatl-speaking community. The general goals are to integrate Indian and national identity and improve material conditions. The evaluation of the project presents only anecdotal evidence of changes in attitudes, and little evidence of changes in material conditions.

Sandstrom, Alan R. The image of disease: medical practices of Nahua Indians of the Huasteca. See item **1669**.

968 Schwartz, Norman B. Community development and cultural change in Latin America (in Siegel, Bernard J.; Alan R. Beals; and Stephen A. Tyler eds. Annual review of anthropology. v. 7. Palo Alto, Calif., Annual Reviews Inc., 1978, p. 235–261, bibl.)

A large portion of the literature on community studies in Latin America concerns Mexico and Guatemala, and much of this research has been influential in the development of a focus on the local community not as an entity unto itself but as an integral part of a wider environment—in the broad ecological-social sense of the term. In this review article, the author elucidates the implications of the two approaches, both the research conclusions they are likely to inspire (e.g., community development studies locate development failures within the community or in the change agent's ignorance of the culture) and the direction they offer to the disciplines. The consideration of ecological factors, regional, national, and global power structures, and intracommunity diversity as explanatory variables may ultimately lead anthropologists into political involvement they have heretofore generally avoided.

969 ———. Drinking patterns, drunks and maturity in a Petén town, Guatemala (SOCIOL, 28:1, p. 35–53, bibl., tables)

Social, cultural and psychological variables are used to explain drinking patterns and problem drinkers in a town of some 1500 people. When, where and with whom one drinks is related to sex (women rarely participate), occupation, residence patterns, stage of the life cycle, and the atomistic social structure. Marital and social status in conjunction with unusual relations with the father are linked to problem drinkers.

970 Sexton, James D. Protestantism and modernization in two Guatemalan towns (AAA/AE, 5:2, May 1978, p. 280–302, bibl., tables)

A specific focus leads to a more productive analysis of the kinds of data examined in item **971**. The growing number of Protes-

tant converts in two towns appear more modern by a number of measures than believers in traditional folk Catholicism. Religious affiliation is not posited as a cause or effect but a concomitant change linked to high social status, the acceptance of both Westernized material culture and the Spanish language, superior political knowledge, and a rejection of traditional and fatalistic beliefs. This is especially the case in the less Indian and more developed of the two, presumably offering more opportunities and reinforcement for individual modernization.

971 ——— and **Clyde M. Woods.** Development and modernization among highland Maya: a comparative analysis of ten Guatemalan towns (SAA/HO, 36:2, Summer 1977, p. 156–172, bibl., tables)

In the mode of traditional community development studies, the authors examine correlations of a host of indicators of modernization such as wealth, religious affiliation, occupational aspirations and exposure (e.g., literacy, travel) with the developmental ranks of ten towns. Though statistically sophisticated, little is revealed concerning the processes involved. There is no theoretical justification for the items used to define community development and no information concerning the magnitude of population differences.

Simeon, George. Illness and curing in a Guatemalan village: a study of ethno-medicine. See item **1670**.

972 Smith, Carol A. Beyond dependency theory: national and regional patterns of underdevelopment in Guatemala (AAA/AE, 5:3, Aug. 1978, p. 574–617, bibl., tables)

In this important and carefully argued paper which examines the effects of coffee production in western Guatemala on the nation and region, the author orchestrates three versions of dependency theory: 1) metropole-satellite (Gunder-Frank, Stavenhagen); 2) periphery-marginalization (Sunkel and Paz, Roberts, Portes and Walton); and 3) core-periphery (Wallerstein). Smith concludes that the underdevelopment of Western Guatemala did not originate in export-crop dependency but emerged with capitalistic agriculture which made the mass of the population dependent on wage labor. Capitalist relations of production could only develop through the demise of the old metropole-urban satellite structure which effectively prevented competition through the political administration of market towns. Coffee production funded a vast expansion in the production and trading enterprises of already existing merchants and producers in the regional core. Effective use is made of census data to trace population growth, and occupational characteristics.

973 Smith, Waldemar R. Class and ethnicity in the fields of the Tzotzil (UP/PS, 6:2, April 1977, p. 51–56, bibl.)

While commending certain aspects of George Collier's analysis of the land and ethnicity in the Highlands of Chiapas (see *HLAS 39:1038*), Smith argues that he fails to take sufficiently into account the pattern of agricultural development in Chiapas and the role of Indian labor therein.

974 ————. The fiesta system and economic change. N.Y., Columbia Univ. Press, 1977. 194 p., bibl., plates, tables.

A somewhat stridently written, but stimulating analysis of the fiesta system in four Mayan communities in Guatemala. Smith takes issue with previous interpretations, particularly those emphasizing the stabilizing, integrative functions of fiesta rituals. He maintains that the fiesta system is not so much a cause of community stability and cohesiveness, but a response to economic restrictions and social exclusion. Access to economic opportunities as in the case of San Pedro, or an insufficient local subsistence base as in San Marcos, lead to organizational tactics to reduce individual costs of ritual. Though Smith argues for the necessity of regional studies, he is perfectly willing to generalize from single cases when it suits his purposes. His work should provoke even more comprehensive, historical examinations of the subject.

975 Sorenson, E. Richard; Kalman Muller; and Nicolas Vaczek. The context of Huichol enculturation: a preliminary report (*in* Wilbert, Johannes ed. Enculturation in Latin America: an anthology [see item **260**], p. 183–190, bibl.)

An account of the advantages of using film in anthropological research, followed by a brief description of Huichol child-rearing which emphasizes the role of religious ritual. Little of this description appears to utilize film data, but the analysis of the film is

clearly in the early stages and may prove, as it did with respect to the Fore of New Guinea, to be of considerable interest.

976 Stavenhagen, Rodolfo and others. Capitalismo y campesinado en México: estudios de la realidad campesina. México, Instituto Nacional de Antropología e Historia, 1976. 246 p.

An extremely important book that deserves to be read by all who would understand the effects of agricultural development on Mexican peasants. The familiar "inputs" of modern agriculture—new varieties of seed, fertilizer, pesticides, and herbicides—have created a highly productive sector that expands at the expense of traditional agriculturalists. These authors examine both modes of production and relations of production and criticize the anthropological approaches that fail to appreciate, after all these years, how the peasants are being incorporated into the capitalist system.

977 Swetnam, John. Class-based and community-based ritual organization in Latin America (UP/E, 17:4, Oct. 1978, p. 425–438, bibl., tables)

Contrasts Indian religious organizations (*cofradías*) with the *ladino* counterpart (*hermandades*). Examination of a brotherhood of the patron saint of the marketplace in Antigua, Guatemala, suggests a distinction of "class-based" compared to "community-based" religious organizations. The former involves lifelong rather than rotating membership and comparatively small expenditures.

978 Thomas, John S. Kinship and wealth in a Maya community (SAA/HO, 37:1, Spring 1978, p. 24–28, bibl., table)

Using Beauchamp's measure of centrality, the author finds a close association between high kinship involvement and family wealth among swidden agriculturalists. Efforts of the Instituto Nacional Indigenista to introduce coffee, pig, and cattle production enhance cooperating kin units.

979 Torres de Araúz, Reina. Las culturas indígenas panameñas en el momento de la conquista (UP/HC, 3:2, abril 1977, p. 69–96, bibl.)

The composition and distribution of Indian cultures at the time of the conquest, with some information about intergroup relations in succeeding centuries. The author maintains that it is not possible to identify the cultures found by the Spaniards with those of today.

————. La leyenda de los indios blancos del Darién y su influencia en la etnografía istmeña y en la historia política. See *HLAS* 40:2924.

980 Turner, Paul R. Intensive agriculture among the Highland Tzeltals (UP/E, 16:2, April 1977, p. 167–174, bibl.)

An application of two models to swidden agriculture in Corralito, Oxchuc municipality, Chiapas State, Mex. The static model views *milpa* farming as a specialized adaptation to a specific environment, while the dynamic one, views it as a step toward intensive cultivation which is taken in response to population pressures. Though the former appears to apply in this instance, the author skirts the burgeoning literature on the complexities of innovation and is working with a very short time span.

981 Vélez I., Carlos G. Amigos políticos o amigos sociales: the politics of putting someone in your pocket (SAA/HO, 37:4, Winter 1978, p. 368–377, bibl.)

Local cultural brokers whose power is based on traditional forms of bossism, *compadrazgo*, and friendship, play an important role in the Mexican political system. Vélez analyzes a dispute in Ciudad Netzahualcóyotl Izcalli, the squatter settlement on the outskirts of Mexico City that is now, with over one million inhabitants, one of Mexico's largest cities. The handling of the dispute is a fine example of how the Mexican system operates.

982 Villa Rojas, Alfonso. El proceso de integración nacional entre los mayas de Quintana Roo (III/AI, 37:4, oct./dic. 1977. p. 883–906, bibl., map, plates)

In 1935–1936, Villa Rojas did a study of the Mayas of Quintana Roo and found they were still practicing their rituals and maintaining their traditional life style. In 1977, he encountered many changes due to national integration. The effects of roads, education, and the destruction of forests on several different communities are discussed.

983 Vogt, Evon Z. Bibliography of the Harvard Chiapas Project: the first twenty years, 1957–1977. Cambridge, Mass., Harvard

Univ., Peabody Museum of Archaeology and Ethnology, 1978. 75 p., map, plates.

For over twenty years Prof. Vogt has directed perhaps the most remarkable research project in the history of Middle American ethnology, documented here in a publication record of impressive depth and scope. Also included is an account of research design and of high and low points in the field work.

984 ————. On the symbolic meaning of percussion in Zinacanteco ritual (UNM/JAR, 33:3, Fall 1977, p. 231–244, bibl.)

In a provocative paper inspired by Rodney Needham's hypothesis of a universal link between percussion and transition in social life, Vogt examines the wide array of percussive sounds in Zinacanteco ritual. His observations generally confirm the hypothesis and reveal that percussion is a matter of considerable symbolic complexity. Fireworks, for instance, mark transitions in ritual life, serve as signaling devices, punctuate the passage of solar time in the universe, and symbolize highly significant aspects of the natural world. Life cycle and curing rituals, not being congruent with the solar calendar, do not involve fireworks except as recently influenced by the *ladino* "fiesta complex."

985 Warren, Kay B. The symbolism of subordination: Indian identity in a Guatemalan town. Austin, Univ. of Texas Press, 1978. 209 p., bibl., plates.

San Andrés Semetabaj overlooks Lake Atitlán in Guatemala and is inhabited by Cakchiquel Indians and Ladinos. The influences of Acción Católica and national development projects have given a segment of the Indian population a new view of ethnic subordination. This symbolic analysis of the process avoids the basic questions: to what extent are self-conceptions of identity a reflection of material conditions and social realities, or to what extent do they define such realities?

986 Wasserstrom, Robert. The exchange of saints in Zinacantan: the socioeconomic bases of religious change in southern Mexico (UP/E, 17:2, April 1978, p. 197–210, bibl., maps, tables)

Agricultural expansion in the form of lowland sharecropping and the Pan-American highway are seen as responsible for alterations in the *cargo* system that undermine the traditional hierarchies. Ties to the municipal center are loosened when hamlets build their own chapels. The associated rituals and offices emphasize cooperation rather than legitimizing hierarchical status. Whether these changes have been made in an attempt to restrain inequalities created by modernization, as the author suggests, or to release funds once encumbered in religious ritual for capitalist operations, is an open question.

987 ———. Land and labor in central Chiapas: a regional analysis (SP/DC, 8:4, Oct. 1977, p. 441–463, bibl., map, tables)
After surveying the development of commercial agriculture in Chiapas after 1821, the author compares the differing ways that tenant farmers from Zinacantan and day laborers from Chamula have been incorporated into the commercial sector. An analysis of class relations and conflicting interests is contrasted to Aguirre Beltrán's (see item **879**) and George Collier's ecological metaphors of marginality (see *HLAS 39:1038*).

988 Wilk, Stan. Castaneda: coming of age in Sonora (AAA/AA, 79:1, March 1977, p. 84–91, bibl.)
Explains why the author believes that Castaneda's writings about Don Juan (see *HLAS 31:1729*) should be considered serious anthropological documents about shamanism. Ralph Beals emphatically disagrees (see item **884**).

989 Wilker, Gene C. Patla at Ajalpan: a barter system in the Tehuacán Valley of Mexico (UNM/JAR, 33:1, Spring 1977, p. 89–98, bibl., map, plates)
In the barter section of the periodic

market, small amounts of valley-grown maize and vegetables are exchanged for hill products such as fruit. Many vendors prefer barter to cash sales, and the author concludes that the system is efficient.

990 Young, James C. Illness categories and action strategies in a Tarascan town (AAA/AE, 5:1, Feb. 1978, p. 81–97, bibl., illus., tables)
In Pichátaro, Michoacán, Mex., formal eliciting procedures yielded 34 terms for illness and 43 attributes. Hierarchical clustering techniques then produced an organization of the data that is roughly analogous to the taxonomies of ethnosemantics. The underlying distinctions that appear to organize the data are internal locus of cause, seriousness, and life-stage of the victim. Although the "hot-cold" distinction is important in treatment, it is not so pervasive in the system as other research in Mexico has suggested.

991 Young, Kate. Economía campesina, unidad doméstica y migración (III/AI, 38:2, abril/junio 1978, p. 280–302, bibl., tables)
A critique of migration research in Latin America, illustrated by an analysis of cityward migration from two villages in the Sierra Zapoteca, Oaxaca, Mex. Since 1930 the region has been gradually integrated into the national economy. The author maintains that the inability of the urban industrial sector to absorb displaced rural labor is a feature of unequal capitalist development and that attitudes toward sex roles in Mexico make women vulnerable to economic exploitation.

ETHNOLOGY: West Indies

LAMBROS COMITAS, *Professor of Anthropology and Education, Teachers College, Columbia University and Director, Institute of Latin American and Iberian Studies, Columbia University*

GIVEN THE DIVERSITY OF THE CARIBBEAN and the uneven distribution of research activities in the area, it has been sometimes difficult to maintain a reasonable geographic balance or coverage in this section. This does not appear to be a problem in this issue. For the current review period, annotations of publications by social and cultural anthropologists or by others on anthropologically pertinent themes are provided for 26 discrete territories (Antigua, Bahamas, Barbados, Belize,

Bermuda, British Virgin Islands, Carriacou, Cayman Islands, Costa Rica, Cuba, Dominica, Dominican Republic, Grenada, Guadeloupe, Guyana, Haiti, Honduras, Jamaica, Martinique, Nicaragua, Panama, Puerto Rico, St. Lucia, St. Vincent, Surinam and Trinidad], for a number of publications dealing with Commonwealth or general Caribbean themes as well as for a limited few on West Indians abroad. In this issue, the single territory claiming by far the largest number of annotated publications is Jamaica, a fact which has several possible explanations but which nonetheless lends credence to a perhaps apocryphal statement attributed to the present Prime Minister of Jamaica that his country is the most studied but least understood in the Caribbean, if not the world. Whatever the reason, other territories are well represented in this issue, particularly Guyana, Surinam, Barbados, Haiti, Puerto Rico and the Dominican Republic.

As indicated in volumes 35, 37 and 39 of the *HLAS*, Caribbean sociocultural anthropology continues to be eclectic in its theoretical and methodological approaches, certainly no single "school" or position appear to be dominant. The problem orientation of researchers seems to be increasingly, although in no way completely, focused on socially relevant and practical concerns. In *HLAS 39*, I stated that there was good reason to suspect that the near future would see an acceleration of research on problems of physical and mental health, local level politics, urban life, and the middle class and elites. This has come to pass. And moreover, this review period is noteworthy for the number of publications by scholars from the region itself, a trend which argues well for the future of anthropology and social science in the Caribbean. Of particular interest in this regard are two publications: *La antropología en la República Dominicana: una evaluación* (item 998) and Lindsay's collection *Methodology and change: problems of applied social science research techniques in the Commonwealth Caribbean* (item 1056).

Although the publications cited in this issue cover a very wide range of topics, nearly half can be placed into five gross categories or fields of interest.

I. *Mating, marriage, household and family*

For publications on this general theme, see Angrosino on sexual politics in the Trinidadian East Indian family (item 997); Gardner and Podolefsky on conjugal patterns in Dominica (item 1026); Goldberg on household in Grand Cayman (item 1030); Jones on Barbadian family planning (item 1042); Marks and Römer's collection on family and kinship (item 1088); Otterbein and Otterbein on the developmental cycle in Andros (item 1075); Pierce on Nengre kinship and residence (item 1076); Roberts and Sinclair on women in Jamaica (item 1082); Rubenstein on diachronic inference and lower-class Afro-Caribbean marriage (item 1085) and on incest and effigy hanging in St. Vincent (item 1086); Stoffle on Barbadian mate selection and family formation (items 1093–1094); Sutton and Makiesky-Barrow on social inequality and sexual status in Barbados (item 1095); Vazquez-Geffroy on preferred consanguineal marriage in the Dominican Republic (item 1099); and, of Voydanoff and Rodman on marital careers in Trinidad (item 1101).

II. *Religion and magic*

For publications on Haitian vodun see Acquaviva (item 993); Bebel-Gisler and Hurbon (item 1004); Dorsainvil (item 1018); Kerboull (item 1044); Lescot (item 1054); and Lowenthal (item 1057). For religious practices of black people in the New World, see Simpson (item 1091) and for Jamaican practices refer to Barrett (item 1002). Puerto Rican spiritism is covered by Koss (items 1047–1048). Massé deals with the Seventh Day Adventist movement in Martinique (item 1063); and, Thoden van Velzen focuses on the Gaan Gadu movement in Surinam (item 1097). Related to this general category are five publications on various aspects of life among the Jamaica Rastafarians by: Barrett (item **1001**); Davis and Simon (item **1017**): Dreher and Rogers (item **1019**); Nicholas (item **1072**); and, Reckford (item **1080**).

III. *Immigration and Emigration*

The theme of migration is important in the following publications: Bowen on social change in the British Virgin Islands (item **1010**); Bryce-Laporte and Mortimer on Caribbean immigration to the US (item **1011a**); Clarke's collection on Caribbean social relations (item **1012**); Foner on Jamaicans in London (item **1024**); Hendrick's Spanish-language version of the Dominican Diaspora (item **1039**); Hill's account of the impact of migration on Carriacou (item **1040**); Koch on Jamaicans in Costa Rica (item **1045**); and, Lamur and Speckmann's collection on the adaptation of Caribbean migrants in the metropoles (item **1052**).

IV. *Middle-Class and Elites Studies*

Alexander deals with the culture of race among the Jamaican middle class (item **995**); Bell appraises elite performance of Jamaican elites with regard to egalitarian values (item **1006**); Bell and Gibson survey Jamaican elites' attitudes toward global alignments (item **1007**); Gilloire and others study social class structure in the French Antilles with particular emphasis on the white upper class (item **1028**); Holzberg discusses political economy, ethnicity and the Jewish segment in Jamaica (item **1041**); Manning deals with Bermudian politics (item **1059**) and the impact of Canadian cultural symbolism on Bermudian political thought (item **1060**); and Robinson and Bell assess Jamaican elites' attitudes towards political independence (item **1083**).

V. *Health and Medicine*

Aho and Minott focus on the relation of folk and western medicine in Trinidad (item **994**); Beet and Sterman deal with male absenteeism and nutrition among the Matawai Bush Negroes (item **1005**); Bordes and Couture give a lively account of public health and community development in Haiti (item **1009**); Colson examines the treatment of sickness among the Akawaio (item **1013**); and, Lieberman and Dressler analyze bilingualism and cognition of disease terms in St. Lucia (item **1055**).

In closing, I should make special mention of the recent books of two of the most respected and prolific scholars of Caribbean culture, George Eaton Simpson's *Black religions in the New World* (item **1091**) and Douglas Taylor's *Languages of the West Indies* (item **1096**). Simpson and Taylor, between the two of them, have devoted more than 80 years to Caribbean research. Their two books, which combine careful thought with unparalled experience, will be valued by colleagues and students.

I am indebted to Georganne Chapin for her valuable contribution to the preparation of this section.

992 Abrahams, Roger. The West Indian tea meeting: an essay in civilization (*in* Pescatello, Ann M. *ed.* Old roots in new lands [see *HLAS 40:2214*] p. 173–208)

With particular reference to "tea meetings" on Nevis and St. Vincent, author provides a thorough review of the history and the development of this institution in the British Caribbean. Introduced by Methodist missionaries into the region in order to facilitate the teaching of Euro-Christian modes of worship, "it soon became one of the most important focal community events in which the very excesses of the African style which it set out to counteract were soon incorporated into its performance. . . . " As in other syncretisms, African structural patterns were central to the West Indian 'tea meeting' even though some, if not many, of the elements used were European in origin. For sociologist's comment, see item **9133**.

993 Acquaviva, Marcus Claudio. Vodu: religião e magia negra no Haiti. Prefácio de Aurélio M. G. de Abreu. São Paulo, Nosso

Brasil, 1976? 31 p., bibl., illus. (Cadernos antigos, 1)

In this brief Brazilian work on "religion and black magic in Haiti," the author sketches the syncretic vodou tradition, describes some of the more sensational elements of Haitian native religion, and refers to the historically volatile position of vodou in Caribbean politics.

994 Aho, William R. and Kimlan Minott.
Creole and doctor medicine: folk beliefs, practices, and orientations to modern medicine in a rural and an industrial suburban setting in Trinidad and Tobago, The West Indies (Social Science and Medicine [N.Y.] 11:5, March 1977, p. 349–355, tables)

A survey of 77 mothers (38 from rural Blanchisseuse and 39 from suburban Laventille), two traditional healers and two district nurses on their beliefs about childhood illnesses and attitudes toward modern, scientific medicine. Hot-cold view of the nature, causes, and treatment of illness presented as well as one supernatural illness and its treatment by traditional healers (*maljo*, or Evil Eye). Controlling for residence, the following four hypotheses are tested: more rural than suburban mothers would assign Creole (folk) causes to illness; self-treatment would be listed in more instances of reported illness by rural than by suburban mothers; creole cures are used in more instances of reported illness by rural than by suburban mothers; and, more rural than suburban mothers have an unfavorable attitude toward modern doctor medicine. The first two hypotheses are not supported by data, the third and fourth are.

995 Alexander, Jack. The culture of race in middle-class Kingston, Jamaica (AAA/AE, 4:3, Aug. 1977, p. 413–435, bibl., tables)

Data generated from sets of interviews with 11 core and 14 subsidiary informants (all drawn from the several segments of the urban middle class) who were asked to talk about their family life. In essence, five categories of racial terms, usually "white," "fair," "brown," "dark," and "black," were used to describe relatives. Additional categories were used which refine understanding of the basic system, these include: different labels for a single category; labels for subcategories; labels for categories of persons defined as Jamaicans but not on the white-black continuum;

labels for persons defined as of other nationality; and, historical terms. Significance of race analyzed by isolating seven major themes and showing their interrelationships. These themes include the relation of race to a hierarchy of social honor; justification of this hierarchy; relation of race to solidarity, to class, and to the mythological charter for the society. Author concludes by arguing that to suppose that the idea of race refers informants simply to physical characteristics or to an inherent physical hierarchy is wrong. Rather it refers them through their bodies to a historical hierarchy and solidarity of race that has been constantly fragmented by a historical process of mixture.

996 Anderson, W.W. and R.W. Grant. Political socialisation among adolescents in school: a comparative study of Barbados, Guyana and Trinidad (UWI/SES, 26:2, June 1977, p. 217–233, tables)

Results of survey administered to 539 secondary school students in the three countries in order to ascertain, empirically, their political perspectives. Aside from basic demographic data, information was elicited as to students' level of cognition of the political system in their respective countries, of the Caribbean Common Market, and of trade unions. Another section was devoted to attitudes and perceptions to politics and elections, economy, education, national service, their country's ability to feed, clothe, and house itself, trade unions, independence etc. "Though differing emphases and focuses have emerged in individual issues and questions, no conclusive case can be made for an identifiable or distinct pattern of differences among these territories. But this is not to say that at the cognitive and attitudinal levels there was complete similarity."

997 Angrosino, Michael V. Sexual politics in the East Indian family in Trinidad (UPR/CS, 16:1, April 1976, p. 44–66)

Based on data collected in a predominantly East Indian village, author analyzes the Trinidadian Indian family "in its two apparently contradictory aspects:" as a market of separate Indian ethnic identity; and, as an institution developed in the West Indian setting and; therefore, a factor in the adaptation of the Indian group to the local setting. Sections devoted to the Indian family; its historical development in Trinidad; family life in estate days; family life in post-estate days; sexual politics, marriage, and maintenance of family system; and, concomitants of and implications in changes of family style. Concludes that the Trinidadian Indian family contains definite survivals or retentions of ancient forms but its structure has undergone substantial changes due to social, economic, and political developments in Trinidad as a whole. For sociologist's comment, see item 9135.

998 La antropología en la República Dominicana: una evaluación. Santo Domingo, Asociación para el Desarrollo, 1978. 74 p.

A collection of five papers presented at the 1977 meeting held to discuss the current position of social anthropology in the Dominican Republic as well as the need for applying anthropological research to local conditions and problems. In "Toward a Dominican Anthropology," Martha Ellen Davis notes that sociocultural anthropology in the Dominican Republic has always been "imported." The consequences of this, she points out, are, first, that certain aspects of this anthropology do not belong to or fit the Dominican situation and, second, that the theoretical and practical problems of the discipline are then also imported. Some of the problems outlined include: 1) the focus upon personal or institutional interests, rather than quality and morality; 2) a mistaken scientific (or so-call "objective") perspective; 3) poorly conceived themes and priorities which ignore critical problems; and 4) the alienation of the human being, lack of communication with the people. The author posits that enthusiasm, a desire to explore new ideas and theories, and self-awareness in the anthropologist are necessary elements in the formation of a new anthropology which will be more relevant to the Dominican situation. Local institutional resources for developing such an anthropology are described. An emphasis on "total system" is advocated, in order for the investigator to understand the history of social significance of social phenomena with uniquely Dominican characteristics. In "Perspectives and Strategies for an Applied Anthropology in the Dominican Republic," Luciana Castillo outlines some general ideas concerning the discipline of applied anthropology and proceeds to explore major areas in which applied research is

needed. These include community studies and works which focus on social organization, medicine and public health, industry, education, politics, and linguistics. Particular research strategies which address sociocultural and technological change are reviewed. Some suggestions are offered for the coordination of research efforts which would have specific relevance for the Dominican situation, rather than simply reflect the European/colonialist perspective dominant in contemporary social science. The third article, "Folklore: Problems, Methods, Priorities," is a brief review of work conducted in the area of Dominican folklore. The author, Fradique Lizardo, outlines different approaches to the study of folklore and distinguishes between material, social, and mental-spiritual folklore. Noting the disappearance of rural folk traditions, the scarcity of interested social scientists, and the need for the Dominican people to know their own folklore, the author criticizes the newly popular "pseudo-folklore" and calls for official government support for the training of competent folklorists. The fourth and fifth papers address general concerns of anthropology as a social science. In "The Science of Anthropology," Wendaline Rodríguez Vélez reviews the historical roots of the discipline, describes the four divisions with the field, and outlines the "anthropological paradigm"—methodologies and perspectives. In "New Trends in Anthropology," Euribíades Concepción Reynoso discusses the shift from traditional social anthropology, which dealt primarily with simple or "primitive" societies (systems), to an anthropology which focuses on complex socieites and social change (process). New methodology and an emphasis on applied aspects of the discipline are among the phenomena described.

999 **Bailey, Wilma.** Social control in the pre-emancipation society of Kingston, Jamaica (CEDLA/B, 24, junio 1978, p. 97–110)

Author debates the validity of Colin Clarke's conclusions in his *Kingston, Jamaica: urban growth and social change 1692–1962* that cohesion in Jamaica depended upon force or the threat of force given a social structure of incompatible institutional systems. Examines conflicts in pre-Emancipation Kingston (specifically the Jewish challenge, the colored challenge, and the slaves) in order to assess whether conflicts in a stratified society can arise from increasing adherence to a common value system. Concludes that the underlying cause of conflict "was the determination of all under-privileged sectors to secure wider participation in a society to which they were becoming adjusted, and of the ruling class to preserve, at all cost, an exclusive right to power."

1000 Barbados. National Commission on the Status of Women. Report of the National Commission on the Status of Women in Barbados. St. Michael, Barbados, The Barbados Government Printing Office, 1978. 3 v. (1218 p.) (Continuous pagination) tables.

The report of a Commission established by the Government in 1976 and empowered to inquire into the many areas affecting the position of women in Barbados. Of intrinsic contextual value to social scientists, the formal report, presented in vol. 1, deals with historical background, traditional attitudes, women and the law, education, women and employment, health, family, and a series of "miscellaneous" issues. Two accompanying volumes present authored background papers and reports on education, demographic aspects of employment, a survey of variables and attitudes related to work, marriage, maintenance, divorce, matrimonial property, estate duty law and sexual discrimination, women and the criminal law, income tax law, citizenship, guardianship, labor laws, employment placing and promotion of women in public service and in the private sector, historical background to the position of Barbadian women in 1977, role of women in society, mental health, physical health, trends in family life, the one-parent family, women in politics and public life, women in the church, abortion, and the contribution of women.

1001 Barrett, Leonard E. The Rastafarians: sounds of cultural dissonance. Introduction by C. Eric Lincoln. Boston, Mass., Beacon Press, 1977. 257 p., bibl.

A study of the emergence and development of Rastafarianism in Jamaica from 1930 to present. Author attempts to demonstrate that the Rastafarian movement has rejected most of what is considered typically Jamaican although assimilating much of the native religious culture; to show the impact of cultural deprivation and what can result when members of a society are denied opportunities to perform normally expected cul-

tural roles; and, to examine the nature and dynamics of a millenarian—messianic movement and its function and impact on a typical Caribbean community. Of particular interest to the specialist is the second half of the book which deals with Rastafarian beliefs, rituals and symbols; the routinization of the movement between 1961 and 1971; dissonance and consonance; and, the future of the movement.

1002 ——. The sun and the drum: African roots in Jamaican folk tradition. Kingston, Sangster's Book Stores Ltd. *in association with* Heinemann Educational Books, London, 1976. 128 p., bibl., plates.

A book for the non-specialist which includes chapters on the African roots of the author's Jamaican heritage; proverbs, sayings, signs, and omens; healing and medicine; and witchcraft and psychic phenomena.

1003 Basso, Ellen B. *ed.* Carib-speaking Indians: culture, society and language. Contributors: Nelly Arvelo-Jiménez and others. Tucson, The Univ. of Arizona Press, 1977. 122 p., bibls., illus., maps, plates, tables (Anthropological papers, 28)

An outgrowth of a meeting of Carib specialists, this compact book contains 10 focused, topical essays on extant Carib-speaking groups in northern South America. The first three are comparative and classificatory in their orientation: Ellen B. Basso deals with the status of Carib ethnography, including location and estimated populations of the several groups; Marshall Durbin surveys the issues and problems of the study of the Carib language family; and, Peter G. Rivière examines the general structural principles derivable from Carib systems of kinship classification and rules for spouse selection. The five middle essays are on ethnographic aspects of individual tribes: Audrey Butt Colson deals with the Akawaio shaman and the symbolic content of Akawaio shamanism and Guyana; Helmut Schindler examines seven folktales of the Carijona for those characteristics of tribal ideology embedded in them; Lee Drummund discusses the social history of the word "Carib," the way it acquires new meaning and importance, and the process through which people attach labels and evaluations to themselves and others; Jean-Paul Dumont analyzes the system of proper names along the Panare of Venezuelan Guiana; and, Ellen B.

Basso discusses its relationships between the dietary categories and cosmology of the Kalapalo from the Upper Xingu. The last two essays address themselves to problems of social organization and adaptive strategy: Nelly Arvelo-Jiménez studies the process of village formation among the Ye'cuana; and, Peter Kloos deals with causes of death among the Surinamese Akariyo and how these causes are related to social, cultural, and ecological characteristics.

1004 Bebel-Gisler, Dany and **Laënnec Hurbon.** Cultures et pouvoir dans la Caraïbe: langue créole, vaudou, sectes religieuses en Guadeloupe et en Haïti. Paris, Librarie-Editions L'Harmattan, 1975. 140 p.

Cultures and power in the Caribbean: Creole language, vodou, religious sects in Guadeloupe and Haiti. Dependence on France and the US, the miserable conditions of the peasantry and the agricultural proletariat, and the exportation of manpower are three fundamental similarities which characterize Haitian and Guadeloupean society. This book examines the relationship between culture and political power in the two regions. The first section, which focuses on language, is written in Creole. The second section, which addresses questions of cultural domination, religion, and social class and political struggle, is written in French.

1005 Beet, Chris de and **Miriam Sterman.**
Male absenteeism and nutrition: factors affecting fertility in Matawai Bush Negro society (NWIG, 52:3/4, June 1978, p. 131–163, bibl., illus., plates, tables)

Although children are highly valued in Matawai society, fertility levels are low. Authors utilize demographic data in order to understand discrepancy between motivation and actual reproductive performance and "put forward some hypotheses which relate nutritional deficiencies to reproductive instability, considering the role of men in the agricultural and ecological cycle as an intermediate variable." Of methodological interest is the study of seasonal variations in Matawai births, an undertaking which facilitated the discovery of variables influencing the probability of birth and conception.

1006 Bell, Wendell. Inequality in independent Jamaica: a preliminary appraisal of elite performance (RRI, 7:2, Summer 1977, p. 294–308, table)

Author attempts to reach objective of appraisal of elite performance by assessing the fate of egalitarian values since independence (through data generated on Jamaican leaders in surveys given in 1958, 1961–62, and 1974); and by appraising some aspects of Jamaican inequality by examining social legislation, social indicators, and beliefs of leaders themselves. Concludes that appraisal must remain ambiguous: Jamaican leaders seem increasingly committed to equality, considerable social legislation is aimed at equality, educational levels have generally been raised, and the very poor may be absolutely better off than before independence. However, economic inequalities remain, widespread poverty continues, and the middle and upper classes may have benefitted more than the lower classes from post-independence policies.

1007 ——— and J. William Gibson, Jr. Independent Jamaica faces the outside world (International Studies Quarterly [Sage for International Studies Assn., Beverly Hills, Calif.] 22:1, March 1978, p. 5–48, bibl., illus., tables)

A 1974 follow-up study of attitudes toward global alignments among 83 Jamaican leaders, 12 years after independence, compared with data generated in a 1962 study. It was found that favorable attitudes toward Jamaica's alignment with the West dramatically declined in favor of alignment with the Third World. Attitudes about this subject differed by the social characteristics and differential roles of the leaders in the sample.

1008 Bolland, Nigel and **Assad Shoman.**
Land in Belize, 1765–1871. Mona, Jam., Univ. of the West Indies, Institute of Social and Economic Research, 1977. 142 p., bibl., tables (Law and society in the Caribbean, 6)

This monograph examines the development of the Belizean land tenure system between 1765 and 1871. Dividing their presentation into four chapters (the foundation of the settlement, 1765–1817; the settler monopoly, 1817–38; emancipation to Crown Colony, 1838–71; and, the legacy), the authors indicate that the principal factors affecting the development of the land tenure system include the demands of the colonial market, the territory's constitutional situation, and the patterns of land use. "By 1871, these factors had created the monopolistic structure of land ownership and distribution that remains to this day a paramount feature of the political economy of Belize. This structure is antagonistic to the possibility of changing the persistent underdevelopment that characterizes the economy of Belize, efforts to achieve agricultural development within this structure having consistently failed."

1009 Bordes, Ary and **Andrea Couture.** For the people, for a change: bringing health to the families of Haiti. Boston, Mass., Beacon Press, 1978. 299 p., plates.

An interesting, personalized account of the work of Dr. Ary Bordes, leading Haitian practitioner of public health medicine and exponent of community development. Of particular value to the applied social scientist.

1010 Bowen, W. Errol. Development, immigration and politics in a pre-industrial society: a study of social change in the British Virgin Islands in the 1960s (UPR/CS, 16:1, April 1976, p. 67–85)

An examination of the interplay of three sets of changes during the critical decade of the 1960s: 1) the economic development of the islands and their transformation from a pre-industrial state; 2) the relatively large-scale immigration from other Caribbean territories and the United Kingdom; and 3) the transition from formal colonialism to a more representative type of politics. Changes include an emerging class structure, a landless, wage-laboring, black stratum and a marked increase in the number of white residence. The implications of these changes are likely to be many and varied particularly in the areas of politics, industrial relations, social services, and race relations.

1011 Brana-Shute, Gary. Some aspects of youthful identity management in a Paramaribo Creole neighborhood (NWIG, 53:1/2, Sept. 1978, p. 1–20, bibl.)

Description and analysis of aspects of identity management and status maintenance among lower-income, urban youth in Surinam. Applying Peter Wilson's concepts of "reputation" and "respectability" as well as others derived from the work of Erving Goffman, author focuses on "streetcorners," or those contexts where young males, "with individual style and 'flair', act out public dramas that are supportive of reputation which they perceive to be unvalued or unrecognized

by persons of more 'respectable' society." A useful addition to the literature of the urban Caribbean.

Bryce-Laporte, Roy Simón. Religión folklórica y negros antillanos en la zona del Canal de Panamá. See item **889.**

1011a —— and **Delores M. Mortimer** *eds.* Caribbean immigration to the United States. Washington, Smithsonian Institution, Research Institute on Immigration and Ethnic Studies, 1976. 257 p. (RIIES occasional papers, 1)

The following papers, primarily by Caribbean immigrant scholars, deal with various aspects of Caribbean migration to the United States: Roy S. Bryce-Laporte's "The United States' Role in Caribbean Migration: Background to the Problem;" Hilbourne A. Watson's "International Migration and the Political Economy of Underdevelopment: Aspects of the Commonwealth Caribbean Situation;" Ransford W. Palmer's "Migration from the Caribbean to the States: the Economic Status of the Immigrants;" Dennis Forsythe's "Black Immigrants and the American Ethos: Theories and Observations;" Centro de Estudios Puertorriqueños, CUNY "Puerto Ricans in the U.S.: Growth and Differentiation of a Community;" Pierre-Michel Fontaine's "Haitian Immigrants in Boston: a Commentary;" Joyce Bennett Justus' "West Indians in Los Angeles: Community and Identity;" Theodore A. Bremner's "The Caribbean Expatriate: Barriers to Returning: Perspectives of the Natural Scientist;" Edwin H. Daniel's "Perspectives on the Total Utilization of Manpower and the Caribbean Expatriate: Barriers to Returning;" Rawle Farley's "Professional Migration: the Brain Drain from the West Indies to Africa: Abbreviated Remarks;" Delores M. Mortimer's "Caribbeans in America: Some Further Perspectives on their Lives;" Roy S. Bryce-Laporte's "Caribbean Migration to the United States: Some Tentative Conclusions;" Christine Davidson and Hubert Charles' "Caribbean Migration to the U.S.: a Selective Bibliography;" and Roy S. Bryce-Laporte and Carmen H. Allende's "Research Note on the U.S. Virgin Islands."

1012 Clarke, Colin G. Caribbean social relations. Liverpool, U.K., The Univ. of Liverpool, Centre for Latin-American Studies, 1978. 95 p., illus., maps, tables (Monograph series, 8)

This monograph includes five edited versions of papers presented at a symposium on Caribbean social relations at the Univ. of Liverpool in May 1975. An introduction to the monograph titled "West Indians at Home and Abroad" is presented by Colin G. Clarke followed by: David Nicholls' "Caste, Class and Colour in Haiti;" Stephanie Goodenough's well illustrated "Race, Status and Ecology in the Port of Spain, Trinidad;" Bridget Leach's "Activity Space and Social Relations: Young People in Basseterre, St. Kitts;" Elizabeth M. Thomas-Hope's "The Establishment of a Migration Tradition: British West Indian Movements to the Hispanic Caribbean in the Century after Emancipation;" and, David Lowenthal's "West Indian Emigrants Overseas."

1013 Colson, Audrey Butt. Binary opposition and the treatment of sickness among the Akawaio (*in* Loudon, J.B. *ed.* Social anthropology and medicine. London, Academic Press, 1976, p. 422–499, bibl. [A.S.A. monograph, 13])

A detailed article which deals with the basic principles underlying the selection and application of medicinal substances for the cure of sickness among the Akawaio Carib-speakers of the Upper Mazaruni District of Guyana. In addition, reference is made to those aspects of ritual blowing which illustrate the same basic concepts as the medicines. Sections are devoted to: onset of illness; fasting and dieting; charms and cures; curing medicines and their preparation; hot cures and the hot category; frightening away sickness; bitter cures; the cold-sweet category; harmony and balance through use of binary oppositions; spirit activity; and, the mediate state.

1014 Comitas, Lambros. The complete Caribbeana 1900–1975: a bibliographic guide to the scholarly literature. v. 1/4. Millwood, N.Y., KTO Press, 1977. 4 v. (2193 p.) (Continuous pagination)

A four-volume comprehensive bibliography, organized from an anthropological perspective, which includes citations of over 17,000 books, monographs, journal articles, conference proceedings, masters and doctoral theses, and reports and pamphlets, published during this century. Divided into 63 subject chapters and extensively cross-referenced, this bibliography covers Surinam, French Guiana, Guyana, Belize, Bermuda, The Bahamas and all the islands of the Antillean archipelago, with the exception of Haiti and the Spanish-speaking territories. English translations of all foreign language titles are provided as well as codes which indicate the geographical region(s) dealt with in each work cited and the library in which each can be found. Author and geographical indexes appear as a separate volume. For bibliographer's comment, see *HLAS* 40:6.

1015 Cross, Malcolm. Problems and prospects for Caribbean social research (CEDLA/B, 22, June 1977, p. 92–111, bibl.)

Keeping within the four substantive areas of inquiry (race relations and racial categorization; studies of West Indian family and conjugal forms; fertility and fertility limitation; and, internal and external migration) considered by Lloyd Braithwaite in his 1957 review of social research in the English-speaking Caribbean, the author attempts a critical/constructive assessment of selected accomplishments of the last 20 years.

1016 D'Allaire, Micheline. Le Centre de Recherches Caraïbes (RRI, 7:1, Spring 1977, p. 118–222)

A short history of the Center for Caribbean Research in Martinique founded, in part, through the efforts of anthropologists from the Univ. of Montreal. Objectives, resources, and publications of this center are reviewed.

1017 Davis, Stephen and **Peter Simon.** Reggae bloodlines: in search of the music and culture of Jamaica. Garden City, N.Y., Anchor Press Doubleday, 1977. 216 p., plates.

Beautifully illustrated with Peter Simon's photographs, this informative, non-scientific book deals with Jamaican reggae music and its socio-cultural context.

1018 Dorsainvil, Justin Chrysostome. Vodou et névros. Port-au-Prince, Editions Fardin, 1975. 175 p. (Bibliothèque haitienne)

Vodou and neurosis. The author stands by his assertions originally made in 1913 (this 1975 ed. is a reprint of a revision [Port-au-Prince, Imprimerie La Presse, 1931] *not* of the original 1913 work) that vodou possession is a phenomenon wholly explainable by psycho-biological factors.

1019 Dreher, M.C. and **C.M. Rogers.** Getting high: ganja man and his socioeconomic milieu (UPR/CS, 16:2, July 1976, p. 219–231)

Study compares and contrasts the kinds of behavior and the degrees of participation related to marijuana use among Rastafarians in an urban "yard" in Kingston and members of a Pentecostal revivalist sect in a rural mountain village of Jamaica. A detailed description of both groupings particularly with reference to their position on ganja (marijuana) is prefaced by a listing of their gross, or contextual, differences and similarities. A marked dichotomy in ganja-related attitude and behavior between Rastafarians and Pentecostals were formed which supports authors' hypothesis that patterns of ganja use vary and are dependent on specific social and economic pressures rather than on the pharmacological properties of the substance itself. Authors conclude that there is no single explanation for behavior centering on cannabis usage.

1020 Drummond, Lee. Structure and process in the interpretation of South American myth: the Arawak dog spirit people (AAA/AA, 79:4, Dec. 1977, p. 842–868, bibl., illus.)

Utilizing a synchronic clan origin myth collected from an Arawak of the upper Pomeroon River, Guyana, author elegantly explores complementarities and contradictions in the two major approaches to the study of symbolic systems—the structuralist and processual (also labeled contextual, performative, or interpretive). Objective is to demonstrate "the possibilities and impossibilities of bringing both approaches to bear on what seem to be fundamental issues at the present state of myth studies."

1021 Duncan, Ronald J. The people of Puerto Rico and the "culturing system" concept (RRI, 8:1, Spring 1978, p. 59–64)

A contribution to a symposium that reconsidered The people of Puerto Rico (see HLAS 20:497) 25 years after its completion, this article rejects the evolutionism and typologizing of Steward as no longer adequate and proposes the "culturing system" concept as a new and potentially productive thrust (i.e., a concept of behavior that can incorporate innovative and generative dimensions into an overall ecology of behavior; the real-

ization of behaviors by individuals based on their own experience and the influences of the physical and social environments). For other contributions on the subject, see items **1068, 1079, 1084, 1100** and **1105.**

1022 Epple, George M. Technological change in a Grenada W.I. fishery, 1950–70 (in Smith, M. Estellie ed. Those who live from the sea. St. Paul, West Publishing Co., 1977, p. 173–193, bibl., maps [American Ethnological Society monograph, 62])

Examination of the impact of the change from oar- and sail-powered to inboard engine fishing craft on other dimensions of a fishery near Grenville, Grenada. Demographic, economic, technological, social, and organizational changes were noted, all of which created the "take-off" conditions that led to the formation of a fishermen's marketing cooperative. Analysis is based on an ecological perspective which views the fishery as a system consisting of natural resources, physical environment, and a human-cultural component.

1023 Figueroa, Peter M.E. and **Ganga Persuad** eds. Sociology of education: a Caribbean reader. Oxford, Oxford Univ. Press, 1976. 284 p., bibl., tables.

Given current anthropological interest in the problems of Caribbean education, this collection of 14 articles (nine previously printed and five for the first time) should prove a valuable research source: Peter M.E. Figueroa and Ganga Persuad's "Sociology, Education and Change;" George L. Beckford's "Plantation Society: Toward a General Theory of Caribbean Society;" Errol Miller's "Education and Society in Jamaica;" Samuel Bowles' "Cuban Education and the Revolutionary Ideology;" Ganga Persuad's "The Hidden Curriculum in Teacher Education and Schooling;" and "School Authority Pattern and Students' Social Development in Jamaican Primary Schools;" Sherry Keith's "Socialization in the Jamaican Primary School: a Study of Teacher Evaluation and Student Participation;" Peter M.E. Figueroa's "Values and Academic Achievement among High School Boys in Kingston, Jamaica;" Ahamad Baksh's "The Mobility of Degree Level Graduates of the University of Guyana;" Malcolm Cross and Allan M. Schwartzbaum's "Social Mobility and Secondary School Selection in Trinidad and Tobago;" P.B. Dyer's "The Effect of the Home on the School in Trinidad;" L.H.E. Reid's "School and Environmental Factors in Jamaica;" Edward P.G. Seaga's "Parent Teacher Relationships in a Jamaican Village;" and Martin Carnoy's "Is Compensatory Education Possible?"

1024 Foner, Nancy. Jamaica farewell: Jamaican migrants in London. Berkeley, Univ. of California Press, 1978. 262 p., bibl., tables.

Based on data generated from a structured interview administered to a non-random sample of 110 Jamaican migrants in London in 1973, this book examines how various types of status change affect the lives of these transplated West Indians. The study "explores how Jamaicans' mobility experiences, or the structural aspects of status change, affect their reactions to life in London. It also examines the cultural aspects of status change—how Jamaican migrants perceive their own and others' social position, and how they perceive changes in their own position in England. What the analysis of these perceptions shows is that the symbolic meaning of various status criteria seems to have shifted in the move to England—indeed, a new set of cultural values is beginning to emerge."

1025 Gabriel, Mesmin. Conscience-de-soi du negre dans la culture. v. 2. Port-au-Prince, Imprimerie des Antilles, 1976. 500 p.

In this series of articles on black consciousness (originally published in the 1950s in Haitian newspapers), the author attempts to integrate the nature-culture perspectives in black thought. Asserting that "political, economic and social problems (of modern civilization) are only a facade which masks the true problem, which is spiritual," Gabriel criticizes white interpretations of African history and culture, discusses the heterogeneous elements in black culture and consciousness, and calls for a philosophical reorientation in modern society. This reorientation, following the order of black consciousness, would reverse the "modern" supremacy of science over human consciousness and wisdom and would, according to the author, result in true humanism and harmony.

1026 Gardner, Richard E. and Aaron M. Podolefsky. Some further considerations on West Indian conjugal patterns (UP/E,

16:3, July 1977, p. 299–308, bibl., tables)

Based on a random sampling of 337 male household heads from within and around Portsmouth, Dominica, this article critically examines M.G. Smith's contention that marriage occupies a different position in the life cycle of West Indian peasants and proletariats. After comparing sub-samples of individuals classified as peasants and as proletariats, the authors find that marriage for both categories is often delayed until the middle to later years of life. "As such, the findings do not support Smith's contention that West Indian peasants and proletariats are characterized by a lack of common regard for Christian marriage."

1027 ——— and Jane E. Tinkler. Some normative aspects of friendship in Dominica, West Indies: a preliminary analysis (Anthropology [State Univ. of New York, Dept. of Anthropology, Stonybrook] 1:2, Dec. 1977, p. 147–155)

A study of the behaviors and sentiments Dominican males find rewarding in close or "bosom" friendship. Based on textual analysis of 86 interviews constructed to elicit how respondents construe their world of friendship, the authors find that the instrumental aspects and the emotional or affective aspects of close friendship are inextricably bound together. Concludes that the fundamental categories for an understanding of friendship are concern and caring.

1028 Gilloire, Augustin and others. Reproduction des hierarchies sociales et action de l'ètat: le cas des Antilles Françaises. Paris, Commissariat General du Plan, Groupe de Recherches sur l'Organisation et le Milieu des Sociétés de la Caraïbe, 1978? 329 p., bibl., tables.

A study of the perpetuation of the social class structure in the French Antilles, particularly Martinique. It is noted that Martinique's failure to industrialize, rather than being a cultural or ecological problem as it is often held, is actually due to her social structure, since large-scale agriculture (and hence economic power) has always been in the hands of a dominant few. The study briefly analyzes the history of Martinican society and the "departmental" status of the French Antilles. Development policy and the economic role played by the "Grands Blancs" are then explored. Examples of social strategies and intra-class alliances within the dominant group, and evidence of this group's links with the state administration are presented. Finally, an attempt is made to describe the Beke group, and its position in the class structure and the changing economic situation.

1029 Girvan, Norman. Aspects of the political economy of race in the Caribbean and the Americas: a preliminary interpretation. Mona, Jam., Univ. of the West Indies, Institute of Social and Economic Research (ISER), 1975. 33 l., bibl. (Working paper, 7)

An essay on the historical development of the Americas with specific reference to the major racial groups involved as context for observations about the political economy of racial exploitation and the nature of the resistance this provoked. Short sections devoted to the colonial period, to the 19th century, and to contemporary developments are provided.

————. White magic: the Caribbean and modern technology. See item **9158.**

1030 Goldberg, Richard S. The concept of household in East End, Grand Cayman (SEM/E, 41:1/4, 1976, p. 116–132, tables)

Combining the terminologies of Edith Clarke and Nancie Solien, author sorts Cayman households into the following types: 1) family households; 2) denuded family households; 3) nonlocalized family households; 4) single person households; and 5) sibling households. Concept of household headship discussed and following Romney and D'Andrade's kinship algebra for use in the componential analysis of kinship terminology, author provides a quasi-algebraic presentation for a typology of household organization which "allows one to see simply and straightforwardly that the various 'types' are permutations of each other. . . . Because the typology represents a set of transformations, it can be seen that the developmental cycle of household organization which is modeled by the typology is indeed systematic."

1031 Graham, Sara and **Derek Gordon.** The stratification system and occupational mobility in Guyana: two essays. Mona, Jam., Univ. of the West Indies, Institute of Social and Economic Research, 1977. 161 p., bibl., tables.

The first and longest essay in this book is contributed by Graham who deals with the issue of intergenerational mobility. It is hypothesized that occupational status is influenced by factors such as age, racial or ethnic group, educational attainment, religious affiliation, migration and family background. Her analysis, however, based on a survey of 1,043 Guyanese-born male household heads in Georgetown, indicates the overwhelming influence of educational attainment on occupational status and occupational mobility within and between generations. Nevertheless, access to different types of educational institutions and educational attainment were strongly associated with the provider's occupational status and race, thereby severely limiting the fluidity of the stratification system. Gordon, making use of the same data base, deals with the process of occupational attainment through path analysis. One of his more important conclusions is that ethnic relations permeate the economic structure of Guyanese society and particularly the division of labor, but are not so all-pervasive as to form the only principle of social structure.

1032 Green, Edward C. Social control in tribal Afro-America (CUA/AQ, 50:3, July 1977, p. 107–116, bibl.)

Description and analysis of law and social control among the acephalous Matawai, a "tribally-organized" group of Maroons in Surinam. Relying heavily on Radcliffe-Brown's usage and typology of sanctions, author describes the several patterns for regulating behavior and resolving conflict including the use of *kutus* or deliberative councils, types of direct retaliations or self-help, gossip among other diffuse sanctions, and magico-religious sanctions. Matawai system of self-control judged to be more efficient means of social control than national external controls would be. Clusters of variables contribute to the effectiveness of Matawai sanctions, i.e., ideological homogeneity, size of community, kinship, religion, and constancy of interaction. Predictions given as possible changes in the self-control system over the next two generations.

1033 Greene, John Edward. Race vs politics in Guyana: political cleavages and political mobilisation in the 1968 general election. Kingston, Jam., Univ. of the West Indies, Institute of Social and Economic Research (ISER), 1974. 198 p., bibl., tables.

Utilizing aggregate data and a survey of 1,000 Guyanese electors and 106 party activists, this political science study of the 1968 general election in Guyana is of interest to anthropologists and others. "It argues while racial cleavage within the society is the single most important determinant of political behaviour, party organisation provides the motive force behind 'the people's choice' . . . the study shows that between 1953 . . . and 1968, party identification and political mobilisation had shifted from those based on class antagonism to those based on racial disaffection. However, the change in the electoral machinery—from a system of plurality voting to proportional representation—has forced parties to reform their campaign strategy. The emphasis is on votes gained rather than on seats won. As a result, the local party organisations have become important sources of electoral mobilisation." The political system of Guyana has not disintegrated partly because a marginal element is willing to identify across racial boundaries, partly because political patronage is used as bait to attract support across racial lines, and due to a small group of 'political dissenters' whose ideal is to broaden the base of political support in terms of class rather than of race.

1034 Handler, Jerome S.; Frederick W. Lange; and Robert V. Riordan. Plantation slavery in Barbados: an archaeological and historical investigation. Cambridge, Mass., Harvard Univ. Press, 1978. 368 p., bibl., illus., tables.

Utilizing the approaches of archaeology, history and ethnography, this study focuses on Newton plantation in Christ Church parish and on an apparent slave cemetery on this site. Newton and its slave population is examined within the broader framework of Barbadian slavery: the skeletal and cultural evidence from the cemetery is detailed and compared with available historical and ethnographic information; all data are then used to discuss slave mortuary patterns as well as the culture history of Barbadian slaves; and, a final chapter considers "the relationship between conventionally defined historical archaeology and ethnohistory as methodological approaches to slave culture."

1035 Haynes, Lilith M. The sociology of local names of plants in Guyana, South

America (LING, 193, June 1977, p. 87–101, illus., tables)

Drawing on a data base of names given by respondents to 592 specimens of Guyanese flora as well as the uses to which these specimens were put, author examines the nature of sharing in those names of plants given by more than one respondent. Objective is to delineate the nature and extent of multilingual language choice and the treatment of these flora by the segment of Guyanese society most cognizant of it in order to further clarify societal and linguistic interrelation and diversity in Guyana. Analysis concentrates on responses by racial and socioeconomic groups.

1036 Helly, Denise. Idéologie et ethnicité: les Chinois Macao à Cuba: 1847–1886. Montréal, Canada, Les Presses de l'Univ. de Montréal, 1979. 345 p., bibl., maps, tables.

Nineteenth-century Chinese immigration to Cuba is the subject of this work. Noting that the Chinese developed into an "ethnic" group within Cuba, while the blacks imported as slaves did not manifest "ethnicity," the author proceeds to examine: the different social mechanisms operative in the demographic displacement of the two populations; and, the social conditions which contributed to the formation of Chinese ethnicity. The history of Cuban agriculture, the development of sugar as a monocrop through the utilization of black slave labor, and the importation of the Chinese as a solution to the problems posed by the end of slavery are detailed. Based on data from archival sources, a description is presented of the living and working conditions of the black slaves and the Chinese laborers, with an emphasis placed on the economic, occupational, legal, racial and cultural criteria by which the Creole Cubans viewed the Chinese newcomers. The social significance of these criteria is explored through an analysis of Cuban Creole ideology. The author then proposes a definition of the ideological process which permits among one group the development of ethnic identity, while discouraging such a development among another.

1037 Helman, Albert ed. Cultureel mozaïek van Suriname. Met medewerking van Mevr. E. Abendanon-Hymans and others. Technische redactie van J.W. Bennebroek

Gravenhorst. Zutphen, The Netherlands, Walburg Pers, 1977. 447 p., maps, plates.

A collection of writings on various aspects of the cultural mosaic of Surinam. Among many contributors are W.F.L. Buschkens, G. Hesselink, Harry Hoetink, P. Kloos, Lou Lichtveld, A.J.A. Quintus Bosz, and J. van Raalte.

1038 Helms, Mary W. Negro or Indian?: the changing identity of a frontier population (in Pescatello, Ann M. ed. Old roots in new lands [see HLAS 40:2214] p. 157–172, bibl., map)

A review of Euro-American travel accounts, missionary reports and government documents from the late 17th century to present as well as ethnographic and ethnohistorical evidence dealing with the Miskito population of eastern Nicaragua and Honduras. Objective is to explore the question of why the Miskito are considered "Indian" in some accounts but a variant of "Negro" in others. Concludes that "the Miskito appear to be an example of a racially mixed American Indian-Afro-American 'colonial tribe' . . . which over the centuries has gradually become generally identified more as 'Indian' than as 'Negro' by outside observers. This changing identification can be understood to be largely the result of the changing relationships between the Miskito and various other coastal and Central American peoples over the last 300 years. It is also significant that very few traits of contemporary Miskito culture appear to be distinctly based on an African heritage, the New World slavery experience, or West Indian Negro cultures."

1039 Hendricks, Glenn. Los dominicanos ausentes: un pueblo en transición. Santo Domingo, Editora Alfa y Omega, 1978. 318 p., bibl., tables.

A translation into Spanish of Hendrick's book The Dominican Diaspora: from the Dominican Republic to New York City—villagers in transition, published in 1974 (see HLAS 37:1243). This version contains a new introduction and an epilogue which reports on field work in the Dominican village by the author in 1977 after an absence of eight years.

1040 Hill, Donald R. The impact of migration on the metropolitan and folk society of Carriacou, Grenada. N.Y., American Museum of Natural History, 1977. 1 v. (Various pagings) bibl., illus., maps, plates, tables (Anthropological papers of the American Museum of Natural History, 54:2)

This useful monograph on Carriacou delineates the interrelation between the metropolitan institutions of the society and the local folk order as well as describes Carriacou social organization with particular reference to labor migration. Separate chapters are devoted to: the development of the social structure; pattern of migration; sources and uses of money; local sources of employment; the land and the sea; marriage, keeping, and friending; the household; descent; the church calendar; magic and supernatural manipulation; "Maroons," "Sacrifices," "Thanksgivings" and related rituals; the ritual cycle for the dead; and, the Big Drum Dance. "Although the social organization and culture of Carriacou is constantly changing, the social structure has remained remarkably stable due to migration and the family system by which migrants are supported and in turn support relatives in Carriacou."

1041 Holzberg, Carol S. The social organization of Jamaican political economy: ethnicity and the Jewish segment (Ethnic Groups [Gordon and Breach, N.Y.] 1, 1977, p. 319–336)

An examination of the factors that explain the disproportionate success of the Jamaican Jewish population (0.025 percent of the total national population but 24 percent of the national entrepreneurial elite). Author argues a study of the local political economy based on gross racial categories minimizes the important input of cultural factors and the significant role that ethnicity plays in the differential success of Jamaica's white population segments. Jamaican Jewish social organization, "cultural forms," and intraethnic links are posited as elements explaining the continuing success of this group.

1042 Jones, H.R. Metropolitan dominance and family planning in Barbados (UWI/SES, 26:3, Sept. 1977, p. 327–338, illus., tables)

A demonstration of how metropolitan (major urban area) dominance in family planning exists in an island as small as Barbados and a consideration of some of the policy implications of this regional imbalance.

1043 Justus, Joyce Bennett. Language and national integration: the Jamaican case (UP/E, 17:1, Jan. 1978, p. 39–51, bibl.)

An essay utilizing data on the relationships between Jamaican Standard English and Jamaican Patois in which author argues that where large segments of the population are bilingual, bilingualism, stable diglossia, and language switching may be occurring simultaneously; and, where political and social integration have preceded cultural integration, or are developing at a more rapid pace, language diversity may in fact be maintained. Given the trend away from monolingualism toward bilingualism, Jamaican Patois, the first language of the majority, will increase in prestige and will cease to be an indicator of social class.

1044 Kerboull, Jean. Voodoo and magic practices. Translated from the French by John Shaw. London, Barrie and Jenkins Ltd., 1978. 192 p., bibl.

This book, by a missionary priest argues that although voodoo religion is strongly inspired by African practices and beliefs, voodoo magic is inspired by French magic which itself is rooted in a long European tradition with origins in Asia. "Of course, I would not go so far as to maintain that the French alone have taught the Haitians their magic. However, they were certainly the initiators, as we shall see; and at the very least they reactivated the dormant aptitude for magic which was in the Haitians."

1045 Koch, Charles W. Jamaican blacks and their descendants in Costa Rica (UWI/SES, 26:3, Sept. 1977, p. 339–361, bibl., illus., tables)

A short but nevertheless detailed social history of Jamaican blacks in Costa Rica with particular reference to the Atlantic Zone, a part of Limón prov. Emphasis placed on the economic causes and social consequences of the migrations. Considerable attention paid to black-white relationships, racist policies, and somewhat unexpected by-products of these policies in the contemporary period.

1046 Kopytoff, Barbara Klamon. The early political development of Jamaican Maroon societies (William and Mary Quarterly [College of William and Mary, Institute of Early American History and Culture, Williamsburg, Va.] 35:2, April 1978, p. 287–307, map)

A discussion of the organizational development of the Windward and Leeward Maroons and the differences between them. Author "stresses the critical importance of an early formative period, a period of structural 'looseness' and of maximum flexibility and creativity in setting out the broad outlines of the maroons' social order."

1047 Koss, Joan D. Religion and science divinely related: a case history of spiritism in Puerto Rico (UPR/CS, 16:1, April 1976, p. 22–43)

A review of the history of Spiritism as a healing system and social movement from its European genesis to its manifestation and development in Puerto Rico. Often disparaged, and considered as superstition and witchcraft, it is the author's contention that if Spiritism had not been blocked in its evolution by 'Euro-American' cultural imperialism in the medical sciences," it might well have developed into a prestigious, more systematic and organized social movement. Bulk of paper deals with the history of Spiritism in Puerto Rico from 1856 and 1890 when it was introduced and disseminated; from 1891 to 1930 when the movement for autonomy from Spain was rife and American occupation was imposed; and from 1930 to present when modern medicine reached ascendancy and Spiritism lost legitimacy.

1048 ———. Social process, healing, and self-defeat among Puerto Rican spiritists (AAA/AE, 4:3, Aug. 1977, p. 453–469, bibl.)

Discussion of the long-term effect of spiritualist cult social process on individuals who become healing mediums. Author contends that while spirit cults may have initial positive therapeutic effects on clients, a longitudinal examination indicates that cult socialization may reverse initial benefits and that, consequently, not all cults are equally effective in promoting and maintaining lasting personal transformations in healers. Short sections offer detail on the background of cultists in Philadelphia and San Juan; basis of spiritism in Puerto Rico; belief system; spiritist ritual; beliefs and cures; cult structure and organization (statuses and role sets, role recruitment, dynamics and cult organization); and transformation in ritual states. See also item **1656.**

1049 Krute-Georges, Eugenia. Algunos aspectos socioeconómicos de los modelos productivos y distributivos en tres communidades de pescadores en el suroeste de la República Dominicana (*in* Seminario Nacional sobre Pesca de Subsistencia, I, Santo Domingo, 1978. Seminario nacional sobre pesca de subsistencia. Santo Domingo, Amigo del Hogar *for* Catholic Relief Services, 1978, p. 73–84)

An anthropological study comparing the production and distribution of fish among fishing populations in three southwestern Dominican communities—Barahona, Pedernales and Puerto Palenque. An understanding of these patterns is considered key for the appropriate formulation of development programs for fishermen. Study communities form a rough rural to urban continuum and each manifests distinctive occupational and economic opportunities. Author concludes that one of the most important factors for the socioeconomic well being of fishermen is the prevailing system of fish marketing. And this system, in turn, is the consequence of several factors which may vary community by community. The most important of these is the size and structure of local demand; proximity and accessibility of important markets; and, the availability and accessibility of means of preserving and storing the catches.

1050 Labelle, Micheline. Idéologie de couleur et classes sociales en Haïti. Montréal, Canada, Les Presses de l'Univ. de Montréal, 1978. 393 p., bibl., tables.

This book explores the relationship between the ideology of color and social class in Haiti. The socioeconomic history of Haiti as a dependent nation is discussed, with particular attention given to the question of color in Haitian history. Current socioeconomic and demographic structure of the country is described. The author's research, which includes a quantified analysis of extensive interviews on attitudes toward color, is then presented. Haitian classificatory color terminology is explained. Separate analyses are offered of responses by the mulatto bourgeoisie, the black petit-bourgeoisie, and well-to-do, "middle" and poor peasants to questions concerning normative and stereotypic perceptions in the areas of somatic image, economic condition, honesty, sexuality, and capacity for intellectual versus manual work.

The reciprocal effects of the ideology of color and sociopolitical stratification are noted.

1051 Lacey, Terry. Violence and politics in Jamaica 1960–70: internal security in a developing country. London, Frank Cass, 1977. 184 p., tables.

A case study of the problems related to the maintenance of internal security in Jamaica between 1960 and 1970 which concentrates on violence, riots and civil disorders and the responses of the security forces, government and political elites. Author argues that political violence during this period was functional to the political system; it was rooted in the social and economic system. Such violence cannot be repressed by force but only by drastic change in the economic and social order of the nation.

1052 Lamur, Humphrey E. and **John D. Speckmann,** *eds.* Adaptation of migrants from the Caribbean in the European and American metropolis. Amsterdam, Univ. of Amsterdam, Dept. of Anthropology and Non-Western Sociology [and] Royal Institue of Linguistics and Anthropology, Dept. of Caribbean Studies, Leiden, 1978. 201 p.

The following are selected papers presented at the symposium on problems of adaptation of Caribbean migrants held at the XXXIV Annual Meeting of the Society for Applied Anthropology in Amsterdam, March 1975: David Lowenthal's "West Indian Emigrants Overseas;" Delroy M. Louden's "Adjustment of West Indian Migrants to Britain;" Ceri Peach's "Spatial Distribution and the Assimilation of West Indian Immigrants in British Cities;" Daniel Lawrence's "Caribbean Immigrants and Race Relations in Nottingham;" Nancy Foner's "The Meaning of Education to Jamaicans at Home and in London;" Joyce Bennett Justus' "Strategies for Survival: West Indians in Los Angeles;" Glenn L. Hendricks' "The Phenomenon of Migrant Illegality: the Case of Dominicans in New York;" Emerson Douyon's "Les Immigrants Haitiens à Montréal;" Julie Lirus' "Identité Culturelle chez les Martiniquais;" Jean Galap's "Violence et Culture aux Antilles Françaises;" A.J.F. Kobben's "The Impact of Political Events on a Research Project;" and W.E. Biervliet's "The Hustler Culture of Young Unemployed Surinamers."

1053 LeFranc, E.R.-M. The co-operative movement in Jamaica: an exercise in social control (UWI/SES, 27:1, March 1978, p. 21–43, bibl., tables)

An essay which attempts to explore some of the reasons for the failure of most co-operative efforts in Jamaica. Useful review of the co-operative movement on the island is provided as well as the responses of the peasantry to this movement. Concludes with the negative assessment that the introduction of service-oriented co-operative organization into conditions of underdevelopment and impoverishment will not result in significant social and economic changes. If a Jamaican co-operative survived at all, the following consequences were almost inevitable: individualization and internal division, the sharpening of distinctions between management and labor or the transformation of co-op into a government-supported or owned agency for patronage and welfare.

1054 Lescot, Elie. Avant L'Oubli: christianisme et paganisme en Haïti et autres lieux. Port-au-Prince, Imprimerie H. Deschamps, 1974. 532 p., bibl., facsims., plates.

"Christianity and paganism in Haiti and other places." A religious history of Haiti, this work essentially describes the institutionalization of the Catholic Church and, to a lesser extent, the interaction between the Church and folk religious traditions (i.e., vodou).

1055 Lieberman, Dena and **William W. Dressler.** Bilingualism and cognition of St. Lucian disease terms (Medical Anthropology [Society for Medical Anthropology, Washington] 1:1, Winter 1977, p. 81–110, illus., tables)

Based on interviews of an opportunistic sample of 62 bilingual English and Patois speakers, an examination of whether intracultural variation exists with regard to the cognition of disease terms and the linguistic and sociocultural correlates of this possible bilingual variation. Cognitive mapping technique is used to determine the cognition of a set of terms and multivariate data analysis indicated variation related to language proficiency. When speaking English, the Patois dominant sub-sample manifested a cognitive model similar to the English dominant sub-sample, but when speaking Patois, the Patois dominant sub-sample manifested a model similar to that of monolingual Patois speakers. "Thus, it would seem that individuals in the PD group keep their two languages psychologically distinct and use different categories of meaning when speaking these languages. However, the ED group manifests similar models in both languages."

1056 Lindsay, Louis ed. Methodology and change: problems of applied social science research techniques in the Commonwealth Caribbean. Mona, Jam., Univ. of the West Indies, Institute of Social and Economic Research (ISER), 1978. 370 p. (Working paper, 14)

Proceedings of a multidisciplinary seminar held in Jamaica in May 1975. Participants were members of the Faculty of Social Sciences at the Univ. of the West Indies engaged in research sponsored by the Institute of Social and Economic Research. Objective of the seminar was to discuss, without the use of formal papers, the problems the participants were encountering as social scientists coming to grips with the realities of life and living in the Caribbean. While the informal presentations are of uneven quality, these proceedings provide valuable insight into the perspectives and orientations of West Indian scholars involved with West Indian research. For sociologist's comment, see item **9172.**

1057 Lowenthal, Ira P. Ritual performance and religious experience: a service for the gods in southern Haiti (UNM/JAR, 34:3, Fall 1978, p. 392–414, bibl.)

"Offertory ritual in Haitian voodoo is examined from the point of view of the participants . . . Such a view highlights spirit possession and acoustic/kinetic performance as the most salient features of ritual within this religious system . . . It is argued that previous analyses of voodoo tend to fragment and/or objectify this fundamental ritual process. A perspective which confronts the act of worship on its own terms, as a coherent and meaningful event in the religious lives of the faithful, leads to a reformulation of some traditional anthropological questions concerning the culture-history, function, and psychological significance of Haitian voodoo."

1058 Malefijt, Annemarie de Waal. Commentary (CEDLA/B, 22, June 1977, p. 83–91)

Commentary on Sidney Mintz's article "North American Contributions to Caribbean Studies" (see item 1066), and further discussion on the theme.

1059 **Manning, Frank E.** Bermudian politics in transition: race, voting, and public opinion. Hamilton, Bermuda, Island Press, 1978. 231 p., bibl., plates, tables.

A valuable work by an anthropologist long associated with research on Bermuda. In essence, book is based on analyses of two surveys: one, drawn from an informal street sample, was taken 25 days after the important elections of 1976; the second and more extensive one taken two months later, utilized a stratified random cluster sample from selected residential areas. Organized into two lengthy substantive sections, one on the political process and the other on issues and sentiments this study "explores the complex process that gave Bermuda's black Opposition a fifty percent gain of parliamentary seats in 1976, split the ranks of Government, toppled the Premier, sparked a major riot in 1977 and generated a mass momentum that endangers a white-controlled colonial order that has endured for more than three centuries."

1060 ———. The big brother: Canadian cultural symbolism and Bermudian political thought (RRI, 7:1, Spring 1977, p. 60–72)

This article deals with two facets of Canadian-Bermudian linkage. The first is the presence in Bermuda of a series of Canadian religious, educational and prestige symbols; the second is the development of Bermudian support for a future political relationship with Canada. The pragmatic rationale for the latter is explored.

1061 ———. Carnival in Antigua: Caribbean sea (AI/A, 73:1/2, 1978, p. 191–204, bibl.)

Description and analysis of the Antigua Carnival, one of the new Carnivals that have sprung up in Antillean territories. Held in Aug., it commemorates the official date of Emancipation. Following a succinct detailing of Carnival organization and events, author posits that its social context is formed by two opposing processes: the political movement toward national sovereignty; and, the economic movement toward increasing dependency on foreign tourism. Utilizing a symbolic anthropological approach, he argues that Carnival in Antigua reconciles these antithetical forces by associating symbols of one process with those of the other. "This symbolic association works to promote political nationalism by lending it stylistic and sensual appeal, and to indicate that the material wealth of the tourist environment can be part of a native cultural order. Integrating foreign wealth and material glamor into an indigenous expressive idiom, Carnival is analogous to revitalization movements, especially those of the Cargo Cult variety."

1062 **Marshall, Trevor G.** *comp.* A bibliography of the Commonwealth Caribbean peasantry: 1838–1974. Preface by Joycelin Massiah. Cave Hill, Barbados, Univ. of the West Indies, Institute of Social and Economic Research (ISER), 1975. 47 l. (Occasional bibliography series, 3)

A not overly-exhaustive bibliography divided into two sections: the first includes items dealing with the Commonwealth Caribbean in general, the second contains citations to studies dealing with individual territories.

1063 **Massé, Raymond.** Les Adventistes du Septième Jour aux Antilles française: anthropologie d'une espérance millénariste. Martinique, Univ. de Montréal, Centre de Recherches Caraïbes, 1978. 107 p., bibl., tables.

The history, organization, and social significance of the Seventh Day Adventist movement in Martinique are examined in this book. Author links the growing force of the movement with rapid social and political change, in the process of which the always disenfranchised poor population has found itself even more alienated. Seventh Day Adventism, as it has evolved in Martinique, has strong traditional folk religious elements, such as exorcism, combined with elements of millenarian Christianity. Thus, holds the author, conversion to Adventism can serve a socially reintegrative function, self-affirmation, for the individual. Ironically, Massé concludes, because it channels political and social discontent into religious millenialism (people "working to prepare for the coming of Christ"), Seventh Day Adventism in Martinique actually represents another neo-colonialist intrusion into the lives of the oppressed Martinican population.

1064 Menezes, Mary Noel. British policy towards the Amerindians in British Guiana: 1803–1873. Oxford, UK, Clarendon Press, 1977. 326 p., bibl., maps.

From documents in the National Archives in Guyana and the Colonial Office Records in London, author traces the formation and development of policy toward the Guyanese Amerindians from the Dutch and the British practice of distributing subsidies for capturing runaway slaves to protective control through Postholders, Protectors of Indians, and Superintendents of Rivers and Creeks to Indian slavery and the role of missionaries. No simple definition of British policy towards the Indian exists. "In general, it was a conglomerate of the policy of liberal and conservative, pro-and anti-humanitarian members of the Colonial Office, of sugar-minded and money-grubbing members of the Combined Court, of interested and uninterested officials, and of zealous missionaries . . . Indian policy, if it can be so called, was a blend of humanitarian idealism and economic realism."

1065 Midgett, Douglas. West Indian version: literature, history, and identity (in Pescatello, Ann M. ed. Old roots in new lands [see HLAS 40:2214] p. 209–242, bibl.)

A contribution to the growing literature on the confounded issue of identity in the West Indies. Author applies the approaches of Ali Mazrui to cultural engineering, ("the process of constructing institutions and ideologies that will enable new nations . . . to embark on nationhood with integrity and sense of purpose") in examining the writing of West Indian history and creative literature. Discussion of literature focuses on five broad themes West Indian writers have stressed. And, on history, the geographical focus is on St. Lucia and Jamaica.

1066 Mintz, Sidney W. North American anthropological contributions to Caribbean studies (CEDLA/B, 22, June 1977, p. 68–82)

A concise review of North American anthropology in the Caribbean with particular attention devoted to the contributions of Martha Beckwith, Melville and Frances Herskovits, Julian Steward, William H. Davenport, Erika Bourguignon, Anthony Lauria, Chandra Jayawardena, Peter J. Wil-

son, and Richard Price. Theoretical and problem developments emphasized.

1067 ———. A note on Useem's "Peasant Involvement in the Cuban Revolution" (JPS, 5:4, July 1978, p. 482–484)

Deploring the lack of knowledge about the role played by rural people in Cuban Revolution, the author, using Useem's article in the *Journal of Peasant Studies* as backdrop, poses the question of who were "the peasants" in pre-Castro Cuba.

1068 ———. The role of Puerto Rico in modern social science (RRI, 8:1, Spring 1978, p. 5–16)

A contribution to a symposium that reconsidered Steward's *The people of Puerto Rico* (see HLAS 20:497) 25 years after its completion, this article argues, utilizing the last quarter of a century as context and the work of the Steward team as a point of departure, "that the development of the social sciences in Puerto Rico has been a continuous, if irregular process; that Puerto Rico's character as a society has resulted in innovations in anthropology and the other social sciences, some of them holding rich promise; and that the time has clearly come when Puerto Rico's scholars need not rely on anyone else in contention with scholars from elsewhere, least of all from the mainland United States."

1069 Moore, Brian L. The retention of caste notions among the Indian immigrants in British Guiana during the nineteenth century (CSSH, 19:1, Jan. 1977, p. 96–107)

Argues that the caste system was not transmitted to, or retained in, British Guiana with traditional authenticity but, nevertheless, caste notions are retained centering around traditional concepts of prestige and status. A modified version of caste categories with attendant ranking system was established which was understood and accepted by Indian immigrants in general. This modified concept of caste was the reference point for the social reorganization of the immigrant population which served also as the mechanism for adjustment on a "rational" basis to the existing framework of the plantation society.

Moreno Fraginals, Manuel. El ingenio: complejo económico social cubano del azúcar. See item **9175.**

1070 **Murch, Arvin W.** Martinique in transition: some implications of secondary modernization in a dependent society (RRI, 7:2, Summer 1977, p. 207–215)

Despite the "artificial modernization" of the island's social and economic infrastructure, "Martinique's present development is shot through with tensions that are in part common to all developing societies and in part a reflection of its own peculiar contradictions. The outcome of this transition is far from certain, except that it will produce a society and a people very different from what they once were, and an association with France that if it does not differ in form, will at least rest on a different basis."

Nagelkerke, G.A. *comp.* Bibliographie overzicht van de Indianer in Suriname: 1700–1977. See item **1179**.

1071 **Nettleford, Rex M.** Caribbean cultural identity: the case of Jamaica; an essay in cultural dynamics. Kingston, Institute of Jamaica, 1978. 239 p., plates.

By the noted Jamaican educator and creative artist, this wide-ranging and informative book deals primarily with the Caribbean problem of identity with an emphasis on "cultural pluralism" and "Eurocentricity." The following themes structure and integrate the work: cultural pluralism and national unity; the preservation and further development of cultural values; the cultural dimension of development; and, the possibility of cultural integration and co-operation between the Anglophone Caribbean and the wider Caribbean and Latin America. Particularly recommended to those interested in the perspectives of an articulate and intelligent participant and observer of the contemporary Caribbean reality.

1072 **Nicholas, Tracy.** Rastafari: a way of life. Garden City, N.Y., Anchor Books, 1979. 92 p., plates.

Of interest to anthropologists, this handsome book of text and over 70 unnumbered pages of photographs by a writer and a photographer sketches the development of Rastafarianism in Jamaica and contributes useful material on Rasta world view, terminology, theocratic government, ganja, dreadlocks, food preferences, relations between the sexes, "grounation," and the arts. Bill Sparrow's photographs are aesthetic as well as informative.

1073 **Norton, Ann.** Shanties and skyscrapers: growth and structure of modern Kingston. Mona, Jam., Univ. of the West Indies, Institute of Social and Economic Research (ISER), 1978. 108 p., bibl., maps, tables (Working paper, 13)

The modern population growth of the metropolitan Kingston area has been accompanied by extensive suburban expansion of low density housing of North American style, apartment blocks, and "town house" complexes. This modernization is less impressive when viewed against a growing housing problem, worsening living conditions in the inner city and tenement areas, and the growing number of squatter settlements. Author, a geographer, describes the spatial characteristics of the residential structure of the metropolitan area.

1074 **Omoruyi, Omo.** Exploring pattern of alignment in a plural society: Guyana case (SOCIOL, 27:1, 1977, p. 35–63, tables)

Using a modified variant of the Bogardus technique for measuring social distance, students were tested in a mixed school, in one with an East Indian student body, and in one with an African descended population. It was hypothesized (and confirmed) that children in mixed schools will reduce their expressed social distance towards persons who differ from them in race and religion; and, that the reduction in the expressed social distance will increase with the number of years spent in mixed school. A major finding was that subjects tended to express the least social distance toward the stimulus person that combined the subjects' race and religion. For example, Indian Hindus would accept Indian Hindus for the closest form of relationship, etc. When it came to ordering other stimulus persons on a preference order, Hindu children preferred Christians over Muslims; Muslim children preferred Christians over Hindus and Christian children preferred Muslims over Hindus.

1075 **Otterbein, Keith F.** and **Charlotte Swenson Otterbein.** A stochastic process analysis of the development cycle of the Andros household (UP/E, 16:4, Oct. 1977, p. 415–425, bibl., tables)

Based on three censuses taken in 1961, 1968, and 1975 of a small community in The Bahamas, this methodologically interesting article reports the results of two stochastic process analyses of changes in household types. This analytic procedure hypothesizes that if data, organized by type, are available for two time periods, future points in time can be predicted. The first stochastic analysis utilized household types generated by a non-stochastic approach and resulted in a redefinition of major household types. The second used the newly defined major types and "the results, using both actual and projected distributions, indicated no changes in trends . . ."

Philippe, Jeanne. Bilinguisme, syncretisme religieux dans la vocabulaire des troubles mentaux en Haiti. See item **1664.**

1076 Pierce, B. Edward. The historical context of Nengre kinship and residence: ethnohistory of the family organization of lower status Creoles in Paramaribo (*in* Pescatello, Ann M. *ed.* Old roots in new lands [see *HLAS 40:2214*] p. 107–131, tables)

Author opens essay by detailing contemporary patterns and variations of conjugal, domestic and residence patterns of Nengre families. The section which follows places synchronic data into historical perspective through the description and analysis of the sociohistorical development of the colony with particular emphasis on the slave system. Concludes by suggesting that factors affecting Nengre family organization can be subsumed within the following categories: African cultural survivals of a general nature which have subsequently operated to selectively filter adaptive responses at a deep structural level; Euro-American acculturation in general and Dutch cultural influence in particular which have become increasingly significant in the post-emancipation period; and historical events, phenomena, and ecological and demographic factors that are unique to Surinam. Cultural impact of other, small ethnic groups in Surinam on Nengre family organization is minimal.

1077 Pollak-Eltz, Angelina. Instituciones de ayuda mutua en Africa Occidental y entre afroamericanos (BBAA, 38:47, 1976, p. 185–206, bibl.)

Structure and functions of various originally African mutual-aid institutions which persist among blacks in the Americas are examined. Rotating credit institutions, funeral/burial societies, organized agricultural

groups, and a variety of secular "brotherhoods" (e.g., *cofradías*) are some of these phenomena which continue to manifest their African roots, although adapting to local situations. In present-day Africa and the Americas, such institutions often evolve into formal entities organized around particular interests (some agricultural cooperatives in Latin America are examples of this), thus keeping pace with socioeconomic change.

1078 Pollnac, Richard B. and **John J. Poggie, Jr.** Economic gratification orientations among small-scale fishermen in Panama and Puerto Rico (SAA/HO, 37:4, Winter 1978, p. 355–367, illus., tables)

Based on interviews with 123 Panamanian fishermen and 111 adult Puerto Rican males, this paper tests a number of hypotheses concerning the correlates of economic gratification orientations. "Periodicity, relative security, optimism, and opportunity structure are proposed as general factors influencing economic gratification orientations. Adaptation to the occupational subculture of fishing is also found to be an important variable. Sub-sample differences indicate that perceived socioeconomic progress, age, income from fishing, boat ownership, and having a fisherman father are situationally influenced determinants of gratification orientations."

1079 Ramírez, Rafael L. Treinta años de antropología en Puerto Rico (RRI, 8:1, Spring 1978, p. 37–49)

A contribution to a symposium that reconsidered Steward's *The people of Puerto Rico* (see *HLAS 20:497*) 25 years after its completion, this article analyzes the principal tendencies in Puerto Rican anthropology during the decades of the 1940s and 1950s and the impact of the publication on research which followed on Puerto Rican society and culture. The state of the discipline on the island is described as well as the theoretical orientations which prevail and the present-day position or situation of Puerto Rican anthropologists in their society.

1080 Reckord, Verena. Rastafarian music: an introductory study (Jamaica Journal [Institute of Jamaica, Kingston] 11:1/2, 1977, p. 3–13, plates)

This short article deals with a description of three Rasta drum types (bass, Fundeh, and Repeater); Rasta "ridims" or popular patterns; the possible relationship of Rasta music to Burru music and to Kumina music; the functions of Rasta music; borrowing; and, the influence of Rasta music on local pop music.

1081 Rivero de la Calle, Manuel. Primer centenario de la fundación de la Sociedad Antropológica de la Isla de Cuba (BNJM/R, 19[68]:3, sept./dic. 1977, p. 165–168)

This short article marks the 100th anniversary of the founding of the Cuban Anthropological Society with a brief review of anthropology in Cuba. In the 14 years (1877–91) in which the society was active, most of its work consisted of studies on race and psychology, including strong interest in anthropometric measurement. At present in Cuba, a number of anthropologists are to be found in universities and other research institutions with interests in both social and physical anthropology. Post-revolutionary concerns of the government, such as physiological growth and development of Cuban youth and social progress, are some of the areas in which anthropological research is presently being applied.

1082 Roberts, George W. and Sonja A. Sinclair. Women in Jamaica: patterns of reproduction and family. Introduction by Vera Rubin. Millwood, N.Y., KTO Press, 1978. 346 p., illus., tables.

Based on extensive survey data collected by the authors as well as previously published material, this book deals with the position of women in Jamaica with particular focus on reproductive performance and family relationships. It examines the formation and properties of family union types (common law and visiting); aspects of the menstrual cycle; knowledge of reproduction and menstruation; pregnancy wastage; infant mortality; breastfeeding; position of children living away from mother; and, characteristics of women with large families and with small families. Concluding chapter provides a succinct enumeration of the major findings as well as discussions of their medical, social and demographic implications.

1083 Robinson, Robert V. and Wendell Bell. Attitudes towards political independence in Jamaica after twelve years of nationhood (BJS, 29:2, June 1978, p. 208–233, illus., tables)

A 1974 follow-up study of 83 Jamaican leaders after 12 years of nationhood. Authors conclude that attitudes toward political independence, compared with those collected in 1962, have become considerably more favorable. The 1962 study identified three basic types of leaders (True Nationalists, Acquiescing Nationalists and Colonialists); the 1974 study indicated the development of a new category of leaders labelled Restive Nationalists, elites who thought that political independence had not gone far enough in producing structural changes. This latter category is considered to be possibly a bell-weather group. For political scientist's comment, see item **7237.**

1084 Roseberry, William. Historical materialism and *The people of Puerto Rico* (RRI, 8:1, Spring 1978, p. 26–36)

A contribution to a symposium that reconsidered *The people of Puerto Rico* (see *HLAS 20:497*) 25 years after its completion, this article attempts to analyze the work "in the context of the recent convergence of marxism and anthropology." While granting the continuing significance of the publication, author contends that Steward and his team did not carry their cultural historical approach to its logical conclusion. "Although they saw that their communities existed within a capitalist society, they did not make the necessary methodological adjustments."

1085 Rubenstein, Hymie. Diachronic inference and the pattern of lower-class Afro-Caribbean marriage (UWI/SES, 26:2, June 1977, p. 202–216, bibl., tables)

Utilizing field data collected in St. Vincent, author argues "that a serious methodological error has been committed in the analysis of the quantitative data upon which statements of the relationship between mating types over time have been based. This error involves the uncritical transformation of a pattern of synchronic distribution of mating into a pattern along a time axis." Three sources of error: "age lag," "population overlap," and "replacement" may well be obscuring the understanding of patterns of mating in black Caribbean communities.

1086 ——. Incest, effigy hanging, and biculturation in a West Indian village (AAA/AE, 3:4, Nov. 1976, p. 765–781, bibl.)

Focus of paper is the institutionalized,

ceremonial reaction (mock trial and effigy hanging) to breaches of the incest taboo in a St. Vincent village. Two cases of "hangings" are described and analyzed. These relatively infrequent Vincentian events, it is argued, combine aspects of society-wide norms and institutions with rural, lower-class values and customs. Specifically, the "hanging" is viewed by the author as an example of bi-culturation (participation in two cultural traditions) and as a creative response of the Vincentian lower class to their exclusion from participation in mainstream institutions. Biculturation is posited as a more potent analytic concept than social class or plural society for understanding societies such as St. Vincent. Adaptive significance of "hanging" is explored through the slander, family business, gossip ("commess"), speech performance, prestige, sex ("nature"), and views of mainstream institutions expressed by villagers.

1087 Sanders, Andrew. American Indian or West Indian: the case of the coastal Amerindians of Guyana (UPR/CS, 16:2, July 1976, p. 117–144, bibl.)

A very useful examination and review of the relationship of coastal Amerindian society and culture to that of aboriginal tropical forest Amerindians and to lower-class Afro-Guyanese Creoles. A brief account of traditional Amerindian culture prefaces a detailed account of contemporary coastal Amerindian patterns in comparison with those of the encompassing Creole society. The ultimate substantive section explores those historical factors that affected Amerindian society and which were instrumental in producing the present situation. Author argues that the problem of Amerindian development in Guyana is not just a function of geographical location and community structure but is integrally involved with Guyanese social stratification, "and because of this Guyana's 'Amerindian problem' is a truly Guyanese problem and is part of Guyana's colonial heritage."

1088 Seminar of the Committee on Family Research of the International Sociological Association, XIV, Curaçao, 1975. Family and kinship in Middle America and the Caribbean. Edited by Arnaud F. Marks and René A. Römer. Curaçao, Univ. of the Netherlands Antilles, Institute of Higher Studies [and] Royal Institute of Linguistics and Anthropol-

ogy, Leiden, The Netherlands, 1978. 672 p., bibl., maps, tables.

Proceedings of the XIV Seminar of the Committee on Family Research of the International Sociological Association, Curaçao, Sept. 1975. Volume is divided into four sections: family, social structure and change; migration and the family; matrifocality; and, sexual behavior: Ira R. Abrams' "Modernization and Changing Patterns of Domestic Group Development in a Belizean Maya Community: the Usefulness of the Diachronic Approach;" Joseph J. Gross' "Marriage and 'Family' among the Maya;" Annemarie de Waal-Malefijt's "Respect Patterns and Change among the Javanese Family of Surinam;" Antonio T. Díaz-Royo's "Dignidad and Respeto: Two Core Themes in the Traditional Puerto Rican Family Culture;" Arnaud F. Marks' "Institutionalization of Marriage and the Family in Curaçao;" Siegfried Tecla and Raymond Römer's "Fertility Trends in the Netherlands Antilles;" Harry M. Lasker and Fred L. Strodtbeck's "Stratification and Ego Development in Curaçao;" Hebe M.C. Vessuri's "Family, Kinship and Work among Rural Proletarians in Tucumán, Argentina;" William E. Carter and William R. True's "Family and Kinship among the San José Working Class;" John P. Hawkins' "Ethnicity, Economy and Residence Rules; Class Differences in Domestic Systems in Western Highland Guatemala;" Raymond T. Smith's "Class Differences in West Indian Kinship: a Genealogical Exploration;" Luise Margolies and Marie Martilde Suárez' "The Peasant Family in the Venezuelan Andes;" Richard Frucht's "Household in Crisis: the Failure of Petty Agricultural Production in Nevis, West Indies;" Angelina Pollak-Eltz' "The Black Family in Venezuela;" Frank C.R. Pollard and J. Wilburg's "Family Organization in a Squatter Settlement in Guyana;" Michel S. Laguerre's "The Impact of Migration on the Haitian Family and Household Organization;" Serge Larose's "The Haitian Lakou: Land, Family and Ritual;" Lear Mathews and S.C. Lee's "Matrifocality Reconsidered: the Case of the Rural Afro-Guyanese Family;" Rae L. Blumberg's "The Political Economy of the Mother-Child Family Revisited;" Stanford N. Gerber's "Further Reflections on the Concept of Matrifocality and its Consequences for Social Science Research;" Robert F. Winch's

"Inferring Minimum Structure from Function: or Did the Bureaucracy Create the Mother-Child Family?;" Kathleen J. Adams' "Taking a Lover among the Carib;" and Leanor B. Johnson's "Sexual Patterns of Southern Blacks: a University Sample Viewed in Cross-Cultural Perspective."

Sharpe, Kenneth Evan. El campesino de la sierra: el problema de vivir. See item **9186.**

1089 ———. Peasant politics: struggle in a Dominican village. Baltimore, Md., The Johns Hopkins Univ. Press, 1977. 263 p., bibl., illus., tables (Johns Hopkins studies in Atlantic history and culture)

A valuable study of "how a group of Dominican peasants . . . came to believe that they could and should take action against the economic control exercised over them, and how they did so." The book is divided into two parts: the first deals with the life led by the peasants in this mountainous community in the Dominican Republic, the kinds of economic controls exerted by middlemen, and the efforts to organize a cooperative; the second part is theoretical in orientation and is particularly focused on questions of ideology.

Sheppard, Jill. A historical sketch of the poor whites of Barbados: from indentured servants to redlegs. See item **9187.**

1090 ———. The "Redlegs" of Barbados: their origins and history. Foreword by Sir Philip Sherlock. Millwood, N.Y., KTO Press, 1977. 147 p., bibl., plates, tables (The Caribbean, historical and cultural perspectives)

This first full study devoted to the origins and history of the "redleg" or "poor white" population of Barbados is of interest and value to Caribbean specialists. It traces the development of this unusual West Indian category of person from an initial period of indenture (1627–1703) through a transitional period (1704–1839) of social tranformation into "poor white" and to the problems faced after emancipation and into the 20th century. For historian's comment, see *HLAS 40:2954.*

1091 Simpson, George Eaton. Black religions in the New World. N.Y., Columbia Univ. Press, 1978. 415 p., bibl., illus., maps, tables.

Major contribution by one of the leading authorities on black religious expression and organization in the New World. Simpson utilized a variety of sources as well as revisions of his own prolific publications to discuss slavery, freedom, and the religions of blacks in the New World; blacks in the historical churches of the Caribbean; neo-African religions and ancestral cults of the Caribbean and South America; revivalist and other cults of the Caribbean; blacks in the historical churches, Pentecostalism, and Spiritualism in South America; neo-African and African-derived religions of South America; blacks in the historical churches of the US and Canada; and sect and cult among blacks in North America and Britain. The remarkable geographical and comparative coverage provided by this work marks it as a most valuable reference for all serious researchers in the field.

1092 Sio, Arnold A. Race, colour, and miscegenation: the free coloured of Jamaica and Barbados (UPR/CS, 16:1, April 1976, p. 5–21)

Discussion of the similarities and differences in the legal, political, economic, and social aspects of the status of the free colored in Jamaica and Barbados up to the time of the emancipation of the slaves as well as a consideration of the racial aspect of the status of the free colored in the two colonies. Winthrop Jordan's position on the free colored in his *White over black* is used as a point of analytic departure. For sociologist's comment, see item **9188.**

1093 Stoffle, Richard W. Family and industry: mate selection and family formation among Barbadian industrial workers (RRI, 7:2, Summer 1977, p. 276–293, bibl., tables)

An analysis of the relationship between new industry and the "traditional West Indian family system" in Barbados. Sections deal with the process of family formation; establishing a union; and industry and family formation. Author emphasizes the existence of a formerly unanalyzed aspect of mate selection which Barbadians in his study population call "meeting by passing."

1094 ———. Industrial impact of family formation in Barbados, West Indies (UP/E, 16:3, July 1977, p. 253–267, bibl., tables)

After a review of the diachronic features of family formation in Barbados and the processes of establishing a union (how Barbadians meet and the selection of a mate), author focuses on the relationship between new industry on the island and the traditional family system. Based on data generated from interviews with 120 industrial employed families and long-term participant-observation, he concludes that nascent industrialization in Barbados has caused changes in family patterns toward rather than away from traditional ideal norms, results which run counter to the hypothesis that "the transition from agricultural to industrial modes of production will weaken traditional family patterns."

Stone, Carl. Class and institutionalization of two-party politics in Jamaica. See item **7238.**

————. Urban social movements in post-war Jamaica. See item **7240.**

———— and **Aggrey Brown** eds. Essays on power and change in Jamaica. See item **7241.**

1095 Sutton, Constance and **Susan Makiesky-Barrow.** Social inequality and sexual status in Barbados (in Schlegel, Alice ed. Sexual stratification: a cross-cultural view. N.Y., Columbia Univ. Press, 1977, p. 292–325, tables)

With a focus on one rural community studied in the late 1950s and the early 1970s, authors consider both its historical and contemporaneous nature with reference to the participation of the sexes in familial and non-domestic realms of activity; the relative autonomy of women and men and the bases by which they acquire status and prestige; the significance attached to motherhood and its influence on women's economic dependence and independence; the cultural conceptions of sex roles and identities; and, the effects of recent changes on the balance of power between the sexes. Women in Barbados are both more autonomous and more highly regarded than in western industrial societies, due primarily to the historic sexual division of labor on slave plantations which produced few differences in the "public" economic participation between the sexes and to the social cleavage between free whites and slave blacks which minimize the impact of the ideologies of the superordinate segment and permitted slaves some autonomy in retaining and developing distinct patterns and concepts about sex roles.

1096 Taylor, Douglas. Languages of the West Indies. Foreword by Sidney W.

Mintz and Dell Hymes. Baltimore, Md., The Johns Hopkins Univ. Press, 1977. 278 p., bibl., tables (John Hopkins studies in Atlantic history and culture)

Based on more than 40 years of linguistic and ethnographic research in the Caribbean, this very welcome book by the noted linguist deals with two different but related themes: the history of the language of the Island-Caribs of the Lesser Antilles; and, the origins and character of Caribbean Creole language forms. In the following order, he discusses the dead Amerindian languages of the West Indies (Nepuyo, Shebayo, Yao, Taino) and the living languages (Arawak, Island-Carib); the phonology, grammatical outline, and vocabulary of Island Carib; form and function of Karina loanwords in Island-Carib; the Caribbean Creoles; Saramaccan and some other Creoles; a grammatical survey of Caribbean Creoles; an outline of Dominican Creole; and social aspects of Creole languages.

1097 Thoden van Velzen, H.U.E. The origins of the Gaan Gadu movement of the Bush Negroes of Surinam (NWIG, 52:3/4, June 1978, p. 81–140, bibl., plates)

An essay focused on the origins of probably the most successful religious movement among the Bush Negros of the interior. Author carefully reviews the two major theoretical positions of early writers on the subject—those that stressed continuity, "explaining events as the outcome of a power struggle between two Djuka leaders which was compounded by the interventions of the colonial administration" as well as those with an opposing set of interpretations which argue a revolutionary break in the religious history of the Djuka Bush Negroes. The bulk of this lengthy and informative article is devoted to new material drawn from archival and oral sources.

1098 Tramm, Madeleine Lorch. Multinationals in Third World development: the case of Jamaica's bauxite industry (UWI/CQ, 23:4, Dec. 1977, p. 1–16, bibl.)

An essay, based on primary source material drawn mainly from the Mandeville area, on the effects of bauxite-alumina multinationals in Jamaica on economic growth and social mobility. With a theoretical emphasis on the concepts of mobility, class and status, author concludes that the impact of the operations of these multinationals is more negative than positive. Although economic development, linked to a world system, has credited some economic growth and opportunities for social mobility among Jamaicans, it has not been accompanied by any considerable social progress.

1099 Vázquez-Geffroy, Margaret. La dispensa borra consanguinidad: preferred consanguineal marriage in a Dominican peasant community (UWI/CQ, 16:2, July 1976, p. 232–239)

Despite Roman Catholic prohibitions against close kin marriage, an unusually high rate of preferred consanguineal marriage requiring Church dispensations were found. From 1827 to present, one-third of unions recorded in parish required such dispensations. The occurrence of this pattern, which transformed the Church prohibition into a positive sanction, is related to the economic marginality of available land, scattered resources, and the usefulness of consanguineal marriages in the management of common land. With changes in the local economy, the frequency of this marriage pattern has begun to decrease.

1100 Velázquez, René. Julian H. Steward's perspective on Puerto Rico (RRI, 8:1, Spring 1978, p. 50–58)

A contribution to a symposium that reconsidered *The people of Puerto Rico* (see *HLAS 20:497*) 25 years after its completion, this article, by a historian, critically examines the principal theoretical concepts utilized by Steward in this publication as well as "patronizing attitudes, and serious misrepresentations of Puerto Rican cultural traits and of the relations between the anthropologist and the people studied." Finds that the book, while still the most complete analysis of Puerto Rican culture, is now a historical document and should be considered in the context of the development of anthropological theory.

1101 Voydanoff, Patricia and **Hyman Rodman.** Marital careers in Trinidad (WRU/JMF, 40:1, Feb. 1978, p. 157–163, bibl., tables)

Data presented on marital careers of 176 lower-class respondents in a non-probability sample. Respondents report on 595 "friending" (extra-residential visiting relationships), 229 "living" (non-legal marriage) and 80 married unions. Frequency and sequencing of these three types are given and analyzed. "Friending" relationships were found to be most frequently followed by "living" and marriage but the sequencing of marital unions indicates movements toward more stable relationships within partnerships and throughout the respondent's marital career. Authors argue that their data should help resolve the controversy about normative status and behavior patterning of the different types of marital unions in Caribbean societies.

1102 Walker, Malcolm T. and **Jim Hanson.** The voluntary associations of Villalta: failure with a purpose (SAA/HO, 37:1, Spring 1978, p. 64–68)

Drawing on data from a community in the Dominican Republic, authors argue that the existence of voluntary organizations and the seeming responsiveness of people to new ideas and change are not necessarily indicators of modernization. Associations in Villalta "are mostly dramatic enactments of the moment; they come and go. Their continued existence is usually a paper one solely for the sake of appearance. Contrary to the suggestions of many investigators, associations (in Villalta at any rate) are neither effective nor are they a significant part of the community's organizational structure."

1103 Wessman, James W. The sugar cane hacienda in the agrarian structure of southwestern Puerto Rico in 1902 (RRI, 8:1, Spring 1978, p. 99–115, map, tables)

Author utilizes José Ferreras Págan's *Biografía de la riquezas de Puerto Rico* to provide an informative essay on agrarian structure in southwestern Puerto Rico. Focusing on sugar cane haciendas and mills, the author attempts to demonstrate the value of the *Biografía* as a historiographic source as well as to describe the social and material conditions of rural Puerto Rico at the onset of the American occupation.

1104 Whitten, Norman E. *comp.* LAAG contributions to Afro-American ethnohistory in Latin America and the Caribbean. Washington, American Anthropological Association, Latin American Anthropology Group (AAA/LAAG), 1976. 66 p., bibl., tables (Contributions of the LAAG, 1)

This first publication of the Latin American Anthropology Group consists of six articles originally presented, apparently with one exception, at a 1975 symposium. All six, including the reprint of Gonzalo Aquirre Beltrán's 1952 essay on ethnohistory in the study of the black population in Mexico, are of interest to students of the Caribbean area: Michael D. Olien deals with US attempts before and during the Civil War to settle American blacks in several regions of the New World; John Stewart describes the voluntary migration of American black Baptists (The Merikins) to Trinidad; Michel S. Laguerre focuses on the historical-ecological development of a black neighborhood in Port-au-Prince from slave and Maroon settlement to a contemporary ghetto; Evelyn M. Hutz and B. Edward Pierce deal, in detail, with the perception of ethnicity among the Nengre (Afro-Creole proletariat) of Surinam; and, Johannes Wilbert argues the commonality of Afro-Caribbean kinship symbolism of direct West African ancestry and traces the influence of this complex among the Goajiro Indians of Colombia and Venezuela.

1105 Wolf, Eric R. Remarks on *The people of Puerto Rico* (RRI, 8:1, Spring 1978, p. 17–25)
A contribution to a symposium that reconsidered *The people of Puerto Rico* (see *HLAS 20:497*) 25 years after its completion,

this article discusses the key theoretical positions utilized by Steward and his team in the original study and indicates, in retrospect, the major shortcomings of the work and of Steward's orientation: the stress on social relations of work to the neglect of social relations of production; the flawed use of the concept of levels of sociocultural integration; and, the lack of any formulation of what is now called dependency theory.

1106 Young, Ruth C. The structural context of the Caribbean tourist industry: a comparative study (UC/EDCC, 25:4, July 1977, p. 657–672, tables)
Utilizing statistical and published data on tourism in 29 Caribbean islands, this paper tests the hypothesis that new economic, social, and political phenomena will tend to adapt to and ape the structural characteristics of the societies into which they are introduced. Specifically, tourist institutions in the more rigid or "plantation" types of Caribbean societies will develop along similarly rigid lines and that in the more flexible, democratic, or socially progressive islands, the industry will be a widespread phenomenon. Scales and indices of many sub-patterns of the tourist industry are constructed and principal components analysis is used as a method of data reduction.

ETHNOLOGY: South America, Lowlands

SETH LEACOCK, *Professor of Anthropology, University of Connecticut*

UNTIL QUITE RECENTLY, OUR KNOWLEDGE of lowland South American Indians was extremely limited. Not only did few controversies arise among scholars in the field, but when arguments did occur, there was a tendency to abandon them for lack of evidence. With the great increase in research over the past decade, the data available for testing hypotheses have multiplied several times over. Old controversies have been revived, new ones are developing, and the whole field of South American ethnology has been revitalized.

One of the major current debates deals with the relationship between the structure of tropical forest tribes and their environment. The traditional view has been that the size, location and permanence of tropical forest villages were determined by the availability of protein in the form of game animals and fish. Warfare was explained as a means whereby human populations were kept far enough apart so that protein sources were not over-exploited (see *HLAS 39:1331*). Several scholars have recently challenged this view, arguing specifically that these arguments do not apply to the Yanomamo (items **1169** and **1192**). Fortunately more and more field-workers are collecting accurate data relating to protein consumption, and the debate now hinges more on quantitative data than on guess and assumption as in the past (see items 1111, 1119, 1158 and 1169).

Other disputes are on a smaller scale. The intricacies of Gê kinship organization are the subject of continued debate, and Matta has recently published a major monograph in which he takes issue with earlier reports on the Apinayé (item 1174). There is still open disagreement about the structure of Canela society, with Crocker (item 1132) and Lave (item 1164) taking opposite positions on the issue of matrilineality. A growing dispute over whether or not all Yanomamo subtribes have unilineal descent groups may be resolved by an agreement that there is in fact considerable variation among the subtribes (items 1168, 1186 and 1199).

Among the less controversial and basically descriptive works that have appeared recently, two major monographs deal with Upper Xingu tribes. Gregor's study of the Mehinaku (item 1145) and Agostinho's study of Kamayura ritual (item 1108) make the Upper Xingu area one of the best known in South America. Another noteworthy monograph has been published by Morey and Metzger, who studied different groups of Guahibo and then combined their findings in a single short book (item 1176). There has been a remarkable amount of recent research in the Northwest Amazon region. Although thus far only preliminary reports have appeared, major contributions to our understanding of that area can be expected soon (see items 1117, 1122, 1143, 1147–1148, 1156–1157, 1160 and 1178).

Responding to a challenge by Baldus, who published his version of Tapirapé culture several years ago (HLAS 35:1225), Wagley has written a complete monograph on the same tribe (item 1208). In addition to material provided in a number of earlier publications, Wagley has added data obtained during the course of several recent visits.

Topically, Clastres has written an interesting comparative study of political institutions among tropical forest tribes, concentrating on the role of the chief (item 1126). Another topic that has received an unusual amount of attention is kinship (items 1121, 1131, 1135, 1143, 1148, 1175, 1197, 1201 and 1218). In part, this reflects the ever-growing number of scholars who are using a structuralist approach and who deal with kinship primarily as part of the ideological system. It might be noted in passing that among lowland South American ethnologists generally, structuralism continues to be far and away the most popular analytic perspective.

Although the number of articles dealing primarily with the current political situation of Indian groups has declined somewhat, there is obviously still a keen interest in the future of lowland tribes (see item 1142, 1149, 1165, 1170, 1187, 1191 and 1200). Several articles deal with the plight of Brazilian Indians, as does Wagley's book mentioned above, and opinions both pro and con are expressed regarding FUNAI, the Brazilian Indian Service (see items 1109, 1125, 1183).

1107 Adams, Kathleen J. Oblique marriage among the Barama River Caribs (in International Congress of Americanists, XLII, Paris, 1976. Actas [see item 255] v. 2, p. 11–17, bibl.)

Account of several unusual marriage practices among group of acculturated Carib-speakers of northern Guyana.

1108 Agostinho, Pedro. Kwaríp: mito e ritual no alto Xingú. São Paulo, Editora da Univ. de São Paulo (EDUSP) [and] Editora Pedagógica e Universitária (EPU), 1974. 209 p., bibl., plates.

Detailed description of Kwaríp, the major ritual of the Upper Xingu tribes (central Brazil). Based on observations among the

Kamayura, study is major contribution to knowledge of Upper Xingu ceremonial life and religion. See items **1120** and **1145**.

1109 *América Indígena.* Instituto Indigenista Interamericano. Vol. 37, No. 1, enero/marzo 1977–. México.

Special issue devoted to Brazilian Indians and the Brazilian Indian Service: FUNAI (Fundação Nacional do Indio). Editorial generally favorable to FUNAI is followed by articles by FUNAI director, other FUNAI staff members, and several Brazilian anthropologists. Most articles deal with political and economic obstacles to effective assistance programs. For comments critical of FUNAI, see items **1125** and **1183**.

1110 Arcand, Bernard. The logic of kinship, an example from the Cuiva (*in* International Congress of Americanists, XLII, Paris, 1976. Actas [see item **255**] v. 2, p. 19–34, bibl., tables)

Detailed analysis of the kinship terminology of the Cuiva, described as hunting and gathering tribe of eastern Colombia.

1111 Arhem, Kaj. Fishing and hunting among the Makuna (EM/A, 1976, p. 27–44, bibl., maps, tables)

Detailed analysis of time devoted to hunting and fishing, and amount of game and fish obtained, among the Makuna of eastern Colombia. Author concludes that protein in diet is adequate and resources probably underexploited. See items **1119, 1158** and **1169**.

1112 Barandiaran, Daniel de and **Aushi Walalam.** Los hijos de la luna: monografía antropológica sobre los indios sanemá-yanoama. Caracas, Ediciones del Congreso de la República, 1974. 134 p., bibl., plates.

Primarily a collection of spectacular full-page photographs, this book also contains popular account of Sanemá-Yanoama culture (southern Venezuela).

1113 Bartolome, Leopoldo. Movimientos milenaristas de los aborígenes chaqueños entre 1905 y 1933 (UCNSA/SA, 7:1/2, 1972, p. 107–120, bibl.)

Significant addition to our knowledge of millenarian movements in South America. Author describes several such movements that have occurred in the Chaco since 1905, concludes that similar movements are likely to continue. See item **1198**.

Basso, Ellen B. *ed.* Carib-speaking Indians: culture, society and language. See item **1003**.

1115 Becker, Itala Irene Basile. O índio Kaingáng no Rio Grande do Sul. São Leopoldo, Brazil, Univ. do Vale do Rio dos Sinos, Instituto Anchietano de Pesquisas, 1976. 331 p., bibl., plates, tables (Pesquisas: antropologia, 29)

Ethnohistorical account of the Kaingang of southern Brazil. Most information provided in form of unedited excerpts from sources.

1116 Beltrão, Luiz. O índio, um mito brasileiro. Petrópolis, Brazil, Editora Vozes, 1977. 328 p., bibl., illus. (Estudos brasileiros, 6)

Comprehensive analysis, by a journalist, of articles concerning Indians which appeared in 10 Brazilian newspapers between 1973–75. Contains useful data on current treatment of Indian populations by FUNAI, the Brazilian Indian Service.

1117 Bidou, Patrice. Naître et être Tatuyo (*in* International Congress of Americanists, XLII, Paris, 1976. Actas [see item **255**] v. 2, p. 105–120, bibl.)

Structuralist analysis of beliefs concerning birth and certain features of the kinship system among the Tatuyo (Tukano-speakers) of the Northwest Amazon. See item **1147**.

1118 Brumbaugh, Robert C. Kinship analysis: methods, results, and the Sirionó demonstration case (KITLV/B, 134:1, 1978, p. 1–29, bibl., illus.)

Author compares structuralist analysis of Sirionó kinship terminology with transformational analysis, concludes that structuralist analysis is more useful. Also speculates about origin of Sirionó kinship system.

1119 Campos, Roberta. Producción de pesca y caza de una aldea Shipibo en el Río Pisqui (CAAAP/AP, 1:2, julio 1977, p. 53–74, bibl., illus., table)

In addition to describing hunting and fishing techniques, author also presents data on all game and fish taken over eight month period in Shipibo village (eastern Peru). For similar data from another area, see item **1111**.

1120 Carneiro, Robert L. Recent observations on shamanism and witchcraft among the Kuikuru Indians of central Brazil (NYAS/A, 293, 15 July 1977, p. 215–228)

Welcome addition to growing body of data on religious behavior among Upper Xingu tribes. Author considers in detail initiation of shaman and pervasive fear of sorcery among the Kuikuru, Carib-speaking tribe of the area. See items **1108** and **1145**.

1121 Casevitz, France-Marie. Du proche au loin, étude du fonctionnement des systèmes de la parenté et de l'alliance Matsiguenga (in International Congress of Americanists, XLII, Paris, 1976. Actas [see item **255**] v. 2, p. 121–140, bibl., tables)

Detailed analysis of the kinship terminology, patterns of marriage, and factors influencing residence among the Matsiguenga of eastern Peru.

1122 Centlivres, P.; J. Gasche; and A. Lourteig comps. Culture sur brûlis et évolution du milieu forestier en Amazonie du Nord-Ouest. Neuchâtel, Switzerland, Univ. de Neuchâtel, Institut d'Etnologie avec l'aide de la Société Suisse des Sciences Humaines, 1976. 171 p., tables.

Series of preliminary reports by researchers who conducted several expeditions to the Northwest Amazon region between 1969–74. Reports focus on slash-and-burn agriculture. See item **1178**.

1123 Chase-Sardi, Miguel and others. Proyecto marandú (UCNSA/SA, 9:1/2, 1974, p. 205–233)

Description of remarkable aid program intended to instruct Paraguayan Indians in ways of legally defending themselves. Program abolished in 1975 with arrest of Chase-Sardi and other participants. See *HLAS 39:1279*.

1124 Chaumeil, J. and **J.P. Chaumeil.** El rol de los instrumentos de música sagrados en la producción alimenticia de los yagua del noroeste peruano (CAAAP/AP, 1:2, julio 1977, p. 101–120, illus., plate)

Authors discuss relationship between hunting and ritual among the Yagua of northeastern Peru and present detailed description of sacred instruments used in ceremonies.

1125 Chiappino, Jean. The Brazilian indigenous problem and policy: the Aripuana Park. Copenhagen, International Work Group for Indigenous Affairs (IWGIA) [and] Documentation and Information Center for Indigenous Affairs in the Amazon Region

(AMAZIND), Geneva, 1975. 28 p., map (AMAZIND/IWGIA document, 19)

Report of five months spent with the Surui and Cinta Larga in the Aripuana reservation (southern Brazil). Author charges that the Brazilian Indian Service (FUNAI) has done little to protect Indians from settlers and introduced diseases. See items **1109** and **1183**.

1126 Clastres, Pierre. Society against the state: the leader as servant and the humane uses of power among the Indians of the Americas. Translated by Robert Hurley in collaboration with Abe Stein. N.Y., Urizen Books, 1977. 186 p.

In interesting attempt to generalize about political organization of tropical forest tribes, author argues that typical chief was without power and led by example and generosity. References to specific tribes are sometimes vague and out of date. Most details come from author's work with Guayaki (Aché). See *HLAS 37:1331*.

1127 Cocco, Luigi. Parima: dove la terra no accoglie i morti. Roma, Librería Ateneo Salesiano, 1975. 558 p., plates (Diari e memorie, 2)

Based on 15 years experience, this massive monograph by Salesian missionary contains wealth of data on Yanomami of southern Venezuela. Especially good on subsistence and life cycle, book contains remarkable number of excellent photographs. Published originally (1972) in Spanish with title *Iyewei–teri: quince años entre los yanomamos*.

1128 Colombia. Ministerio de Gobierno. Dirección General de Integración y Desarrollo de la Comunidad. División Operativa de Asuntos Indígenas. Instituto Lingüístico de Verano. Aspectos de la cultura material de grupos étnicos de Colombia. t. 1. Lomalinda, Colombia, 1973. 335 p., bibl., illus., plates.

Prepared by members of the Summer Institute of Linguistics, book contains chapters on 20 indigenous groups, mostly in tropical rain forest. Descriptions stress material culture, but book is useful primarily as report of current situation of populations described.

Colson, Audrey Butt. Binary opposition and the treatment of sickness among the Akawaio. See item **1013**.

Conaway, Mary Ellen. Circular migration in Venezuelan frontier areas. See item 5568.

1129 Constanzo, Giorgio. I Piaroa. Pisa, Italy, Pacini Editore, 1977. 257 p., bibl., illus., maps, plates.

Ethnographic analysis of the Piaroa Indians of the Orinoco region in Venezuela. Of particular interest is the chapter on the dissolution of Piaroa culture. [M. Carmagnani]

1130 Crocker, J. Christopher. The mirrored self: identity and ritual inversion among the Eastern Bororo (UP/E, 16:2, April 1977, p. 129–145, bibl.)

Analysis of social and personal identity among the Bororo of central Brazil. Relationships of clans and sub-clans, associated animals and rituals, life-cycle observances, and funeral practices are discussed in detail from a structuralist perspective. See item 1205.

1131 ———. Why are the Bororo matrilineal? (in International Congress of Americanists, XLII, Paris, 1976. Actas [see item 255] v. 2, p. 245–258, bibl.)

Author argues that the Bororo have erroneously been described as "matrilineal," then presents interpretation that uxorilocal residence and matrilineal corporate groups are balanced by a patrilateral ceremonial emphasis.

1132 Crocker, William H. Canela "group" recruitment and perpetuity: incipient "unilineality?" (in International Congress of Americanists, XLII, Paris, 1976. Actas [see item 255] v. 2, p. 259–275, bibl.)

Discussion of evidence suggesting that the Canela of central Brazil once had well-defined matrilineal descent groups. Author emphasizes kinship terminology, beliefs about transmission of blood, and stress on matrilines as supporting this conclusion. See item 1164.

1133 Cromack, Robert E. Relaciones entre el alimento y el ciclo vital en el grupo Cashinahua (PEMN/R, 41, 1975., p. 423–432)

Based primarily on texts collected in 1914 and between 1956–64, study stresses conservative aspects of Cashinahua (eastern Peru) practices associated with the life cycle.

1134 Cunha, Manuela Carneiro da. Espace funéraire, eschatologie et culte des ancêtres: encore le problème des paradigmes africains (in International Congress of Americanists, XLII, Paris, 1976. Actas [see item 255] v. 2, p. 277–295, bibl.)

Description and interpretation of beliefs concerning death and the soul among the Krahó, a Gê-speaking tribe of central Brazil.

Denevan, William M. The aboriginal population of Amazonia. See item 5618.

1135 Dietschy, Hans. Espace social et "affiliation par sexe" au Brésil central: Karajá, Tapirapé, Apinayé, Mundurucú (in International Congress of Americanists, XLII, Paris, 1976. Actas [see item 255] v. 2, p. 297–308, bibl.)

Elaborate analysis of unusual form of organization found among the Karajá of central Brazil in which males and females belong to different units. Comparative material on neighboring tribes is included.

1136 Diniz, Edson Soares. Relações interindividuais entre os Kaypó-Gorotíre (MP/R, 23, 1975, p. 85–108, bibl., illus.)

Sketch of kinship system of the Kayapó-Gorotíre of central Brazil. Variations in behavior and use of kin terms is explained as result of bringing together several Gê-speaking sub-tribes on one reservation.

1137 Dornstauder, João Evangelista. Como pacifiquei os Rikbáktsa. São Leopoldo, Brazil, Univ. do Vale do Rio dos Sinos, Instituto Anchietano de Pesquisas, 1975. 192 p., bibl., maps (Pesquisas: história, 17)

Written by Jesuit missionary, book gives intimate portrait of relationships among missionaries, rubber collectors, and the Rikbáktsa (Canoeiro) and other Indian groups in Mato Grosso in the 1950s.

1138 Dreyfus, Simone. Territoire et résidence chez les Caribes insulaires au XVIIème siécle (in International Congress of Americanists, XLII, Paris, 1976. Actas [see item 255] v. 2, p. 35–46, bibl., map)

Historical account of the Carib-speaking groups inhabiting the Lesser Antilles in the 17th century, based on few and probably unreliable sources.

Drummond, Lee. Structure and process in the interpretation of South American myth: the Arawak dog spirit people. See item 1020.

1140 Fernández Distel, Alicia Ana. La decoración pintada aplicada a elementos de tela de corteza, entre los indígenas mashco de la Amazonia peruana (MVW/AV, 30, 1976, p. 5–30, bibl., illus., plates, tables)

Detailed description of items made of bark cloth by the Mashco of eastern Peru. Includes list of meanings associated with design elements.

1141 Figueiredo, Napoleão. Amazônia: tempo e gente. Belém, Brazil, Secretaria Municipal de Educação e Cultura, 1977. 152 p., bibl., maps.

Author deals broadly with the three major traditions that have been combined to produce modern Amazonian culture: Indian, African, and Portuguese. Especially useful for extensive bibliography of early Brazilian sources.

1142 Friedemann, Nina S. de comp. Tierra, tradición y poder en Colombia: enfoques antropológicos. Bogotá, Instituto Colombiano de Cultura, Subdirección de Comunicaciones Culturales, 1976. 171 p., bibl., fold. map, illus., plates (Biblioteca básica colombiana)

Collection of articles, of which the following contain useful ethnographic information: Robert V. Morey "Los Guahibo: Colonos Antiguos en la Frontera Nueva" p. 39–61, Stephen Beckerman "Los Bari: sus Reacciones frente a la Contracción de sus Tierras" p. 65–83.

1143 Gasché, Jürg. Les fondements de l'organisation sociales des indiens Witoto et l'illusion exogamique (in International Congress of Americanists, XLII, Paris, 1976. Actas [see item 255] v. 2, p. 141–161, bibl., tables)

First comprehensive account of kinship system of the Witoto, a Northwest Amazon tribe long known but never before intensively studied. Basic unit of society is localized patrilineal lineage. See item 1122.

1144 Goldman, Irving. Time, space, and descent: the Cubeo example (in International Congress of Americanists, XLII, Paris, 1976. Actas [see item 255] v. 2, p. 175–183, bibl.)

Analysis of Cubeo origin myths as these relate to the general structure of the society.

1145 Gregor, Thomas. Mehinaku: the drama of daily life in a Brazilian Indian village. Chicago, Ill., Univ. of Chicago Press, 1977. 382 p., bibl., illus., plates, tables.

Another excellent monograph dealing with Upper Xingu tribe (central Brazil), study stresses patterns of daily life and role playing at expense of formal descriptions of institutions. Based on 18 months fieldwork, work treats all aspects of Mehinaku culture, and is especially good on extra-marital sexual activity and shamanism. See items 1108 and 1120.

1146 Gros, Christian. La fin d'une autonomie indienne: le cas de indiens Tatuyo du Pirá-Paraná, Amazonie colombienne (CDAL, 15, 1977, p. 113–146, bibl., map)

Analysis of ways in which the Tatuyo (Tukano) have become dependent on manufactured goods and thus lost their autonomy. Trade goods are acquired through selling artifacts or manioc flour, collecting rubber, or engaging in wage labor.

1147 ———. Introduction de nouveaux outils et changement sociaux: le cas des indiens Tatuyo du Vaupés, Colombie (CDAL, 13/14, 1976, p. 189–235, map)

Author describes subsistence activities of the Tukano-speaking Tatuyo of southeastern Colombia, then discusses impact of introduction of steel tools on division of labor by sex. See item 1117.

1148 Guyot, Mireille. Structure et évolution chez les indiens Bora et Miraña, Amazonie colombienne (in International Congress of Americanists, XLII, Paris, 1976. Actas [see item 255] v. 2, p. 164–173, bibl., tables)

Analysis of kinship terminology and major features of kinship organization among the Bora and Miraña of the Northwest Amazon region.

1149 Haller, Franz and **Fritz Trupp.** Tieflandindianer in der Erdölkultur (OLI/ZLW, 12, 1977, p. 136–147, bibl., map, table)

Discussion of probable effects of oil production and increasing pressure from settlers and missionaries on indigenous populations of eastern Ecuador. Includes good map of location of remaining tribal groups, with population estimates.

1150 Hames, Raymond and **Ilene L. Hames.** Ye'kwana basketry: its cultural context (FSCN/A, 44, 1976, p. 3–58, bibl., illus., plates, tables)

Detailed description of Ye'kwana (Makiritare) baskets, together with discussion of relationship of basketry to mythology, art, division of labor, ecology, life cycle, and trade.

1151 Hartmann, Günther. Litjoko: Puppen der Karaja, Brasilien. Berlin, FRG, Staatliche Museen Preussischer Kulturbesitz, Museum für Völkerkunde, 1973. 133 p., bibl., illus., plates, tables (Veroffentlichungen des Museums für Völkerkunde, neue Folge, 23. Abteilung amerikanische Naturvölker, 3)

Elaborate analysis of figurines made by the Karajá of central Brazil and now housed in the Museum für Völkerkunde, Berlin. Well illustrated.

1152 Hartmann, Thekla Olga. A contribuição da iconografia para o conhecimento de índios brasileiros do século XIX. São Paulo, Univ. de São Paulo, 1975. 229 p., bibl., illus., plates (Col. Museu Paulista. Série de etnologia, 1)

Author discusses ethnographic content of sketches and paintings of Brazilian Indians made by artists associated with major expeditions of the 19th century. Many illustrations.

1153 ———. Contribuições em língua alemã para a etnologia do Brasil: 1966–1976 (MP/R, 24, 1977, p. 213–243)

Useful annotated bibliography of ethnographic studies of Brazilian Indians published in German between 1966 and 1976.

1154 Heath, Ernest Gerald and Vilma Chiara. Brazilian Indian archery: a preliminary ethno-toxological study of the archery of the Brazilian Indians. Manchester, UK, Victoria Univ., Manchester Museum [and] The Simon Archery Foundation, 1977. 188 p., bibl., map, plates.

Detailed account of the manufacture and use of bows and arrows by Brazilian Indians.

1155 Henley, Paul. Wanai: aspectos del pasado y del presente del grupo indígena mapoyo (FSCN/A, 42, 1975, p. 29–55, bibl., maps, plates, tables)

Brief report on the Mapoyo, a small, acculturated tribal group located between the Panare and Piaroa in the Orinoco Basin.

1156 Hugh-Jones, Christine. Skin and soul: the round and the straight, social time and social space in Pirá-Paraná society (in International Congress of Americanists, XLII, Paris, 1976. Actas [see item 255] v. 2, p. 185–204, tables)

Structuralist analysis of conceptions concerning reproduction, houses, the earth, and the body among the Barasana (Tucano sub-group) of the Northwest Amazon. See item **1157**.

1157 Hugh-Jones, Stephen. Like the leaves on the forest floor; space and time in Barasana ritual (in International Congress of Americanists, XLII, Paris, 1976. Actas [see item **255**] v. 2, p. 205–215, bibl.)

Author describes major ritual of the Barasana (Tucano sub-group) and relates it to social structure. Like most of their neighbors in the Vaupés region (Northwest Amazon), the Barasana are organized into localized patrilineal descent groups. See item **1156**.

1158 Isacsson, Sven-Erik. Observations on Chocó slash-mulch culture (EM/A, 1975, p. 20–48, bibl., illus., maps, plates, tables)

Study of subsistence activities among group of Emberá of northwestern Colombia. Author presents quantitative data on time devoted to horticulture, hunting, fishing, and other activities, as well as record of food intake, for five-week period. See items **1111** and **1119**.

1159 Jacopin, Pierre-Yves. La parole et la différence ou l'entrée des blancs dans la mythologie des indiens Yukuna (SSA/B, 41, 1977, p. 5–19, bibl.)

Structuralist analysis of a myth told by the Yukuna of southeastern Colombia. Author provides brief sketch of Yukuna culture.

1160 ———. Quelques effets du temps mythologique (in International Congress of Americanists, XLII, Paris, 1976. Actas [see item **255**] v. 2, p. 217–232, bibl.)

Author analyzes a myth of the Yukuna (Northwest Amazon) in order to clarify their conception of preferred patterns of marriage (sister exchange).

1161 Kensinger, Kenneth M. Cashinahua notions of social time and social space (in International Congress of Americanists, XLII, Paris, 1976. Actas [see item **255**] v. 2, p. 233–244, bibl., tables)

Author examines notions of ideal village organization held by the Cashinahua of eastern Peru, then shows how these conceptions influence actual village structure.

1162 ———— and others. The Cashinahua of Eastern Peru. Edited by Jan Powell Dwyer. Providence, R.I., Brown Univ., The Haffenreffer Museum of Anthropology, 1975. 238 p., bibl., illus., plates, tables (Studies in anthropology and material culture, 1)

Primarily a detailed study of material culture, book includes sketch of Cashinahua culture (Kenneth M. Kensinger), chapters on weaving (Helen Tanner), ceramics (Susan G. Ferguson), and graphic art and design (Alice Dawson), and a catalogue of the Cashinahua collection at the Haffenreffer Museum (Phyllis Rabineau). Many superb illustrations accompany text.

1163 Kramer, Betty Jo. Las implicaciones ecológicas de la agricultura de los urarina (CAAAP/AP, 1:2, julio 1977, p. 75–86, bibl.)

Description of unusual form of slash-and-burn technique used by Urarina of northern Peru. Plantains are planted first, then forest felled. After burning, which does not damage plantains, additional crops are planted.

1164 Lave, Jean. Eastern Timbira moiety systems in time and space: a complex structure (in International Congress of Americanists, XLII, Paris, 1976. Actas [see item 255] v. 2, p. 309–321, bibl., tables)

Structuralist analysis of moiety systems of the Ramkokamekra of central Brazil, based on earlier work of Nimuendajú and recent study of related group. Presence of matrilineal descent groups is denied. See item **1132**.

1165 Lepargneur, François Hubert. L'avenir des indiens du Brésil. Paris, Les Éditions du Cerf, 1975. 176 p. (Col. Terres du feu)

General discussion, based on limited sources, of past and future of Brazilian Indians. Author expresses tempered pessimism.

1166 Lind, Ulf. Zur Heilkunde der Ayoré-Indianer im Chaco Boreal (SJUG, 28:2, 1977, p. 122–134, bibl.)

Detailed account of beliefs associated with illness, therapy, and shamanism among the Ayoré of northwestern Paraguay.

1167 Lindblad, Jan. Stenålder och vita indianer. Stockholm, Bonnier, 1977. 188 p., illus.

In this book entitled *Stone age and white Indians*, Swedish zoologist and photographer Lindblad once again writes on the jungles of southern Surinam. This time he deals with the Waiana and the small tribal group of Acuris/Waiadekudes, the "white Indians" who were "discovered" in 1968. Though Lindblad's magnificent photos are more eloquent than his text, his account of the Acuris deserves attention. It is a very sad story told with remarkable fairness. [M. Mörner]

1168 Lizot, Jacques. Descendance et affinité chez les Yanomami: antinomie et complémentarité (in International Congress of Americanists, XLII, Paris, 1976. Actas [see item **255**] v. 2, p. 55–70, bibl., tables)

Joining argument concerning kinship systems of Yanomamo subtribes, author presents data to demonstrate that central Yanomami have patrilineal descent groups. See items **1186** and **1199**.

1169 ————. Population, resources and warfare among the Yanomami (RAI/M, 12:3/4, Dec. 1977, p. 497–517, bibl., tables)

Using data obtained during extensive fieldwork, author argues that warfare among the Yanomami (southern Venezuela) cannot be explained in terms of competition for hunting territories. Data presented to show that protein is abundant also have bearing on arguments concerning relationship between available protein, settlement size, and cultural complexity among tropical forest tribes. See items **1111, 1119, 1158** and **1192**.

1170 ————. The Yanomami in the face of ethnocide. Copenhagen, International Work Group for Indigenous Affairs (IWGIA), 1976. 36 p., bibl., maps (IWGIA document, 22)

Brief but poignant description of effect of missionaries on the Yanomami during period of fieldwork by author.

1171 Lukesch, Anton. Bearded Indians of the tropical forest: the Asuriní of the Ipiaçaba, notes and observations on the first contact and living together. Graz, Austria, Akademische Druck- u. Verlagsanstalt, 1976. 143 p., bibl., illus., maps, plates.

Popular account of brief visit to the Asuriní of central Brazil.

1172 McDonald, David R. Food taboos: a primitive environmental protection agency, South America (AI/A, 72:5/6, 1977, p. 734–748, bibl., tables)

Author discusses possibility that food taboos serve to conserve populations of certain game animals in lowland South America. Tribes of tropical forest are compared with savanna tribes. Lack of data allows only tentative positive conclusions. See item **1192**.

1173 Massajoli, Pierleone and **Mario Mattioni.** I Palikur della Guyana Francese (IGM/U, 56:4, luglio/agosto 1976, p. 625–672, plates)

First substantial report dealing with the Palikur of northeastern French Guiana to appear in 50 years. Only material culture and subsistence activities are described, these have changed very little.

1174 Matta, Roberto da. Um mundo dividido: a estrutura social dos índios Apinayé. Petrópolis, Brazil, Editora Vozes, 1976. 254 p., bibl., illus., plates (Col. Antropologia, 10)

Long awaited monograph by member of Harvard-Central Brazil Research Project (see *HLAS 35:1292*). Deals in detail with social structure of the Apinayé, correcting earlier account of Nimuendajú. Author also provides general formulation of basic similarities said to underly superficial differences found among Gê-speaking tribes.

Melatti, Delvair Montagner. Aspectos da organização social dos Kaingáng Paulistas. See item **9351**.

Mendoza, Angela. Indianische Bauern in Zentralkolumbien, Gutavita-Tuá. See *HLAS 40:2074*.

Menezes, Mary Noel. British policy towards the Amerindians in British Guiana: 1803–1873. See item **1064**.

1175 Menget, Patrick. Adresse et référence dans la classification social Txicão (*in* International Congress of Americanists, XLII, Paris, 1976. Actas [see item **255**] v. 2, p. 323–339, bibl., tables)

Detailed analysis of kinship terminology of the Txicão, a Carib-speaking tribe now living in the Xingu National Park.

1176 Morey, Robert V. and **Donald J. Metzger.** The Guahibo: people of the savanna. Wien, Univ. Wien, Institut für Völkerkunde, 1974. 147 p., map (Acta etnologica et linguistica, 31. Series americana, 7)

Brief but comprehensive ethnography of the Guahibo (Colombia-Venezuela border). Authors studied different groups of Guahibo for relatively short periods (about six months), then combined their findings to produce a single monograph.

1177 Münzel, Mark. Schrumpfkopf-Macher? Jíbaro-Indianer in Südamerika. Frankfurt am Main, FRG, Museum für Völkerkunde, 1977. 424 p., illus., maps, plates, tables (Roter Faden zur Ausstellung, 4)

Popular account, designed to accompany museum exhibit, of history and culture of the Jívaro (eastern Ecuador). Includes extensive data on current changes, based on recent research.

1178 Musée d'Ethnographie de Neuchâtel, *Switzerland.* Amazonie nord-ouest. Neuchâtel, Switzerland, 1975. 99 p., plates.

Elaborate preliminary report of three expeditions to northwest Amazonia (southern Colombia) between 1969–74. Tribes studied by Swiss, French, Colombian and Peruvian anthropologists, zoologists and geographers included Yukuna, Witoto, Bora, Yagua and Secoya. See item **1122**.

1179 Nagelkerke, G.A. *comp.* Bibliographisch overzicht van de Indianen in Suriname: 1700–1977 (Bibliographical survey of the Indians of Surinam: 1700–1977). Leiden, The Netherlands, Royal Instituut voor Taal-, Land- en Volkenkunde, Caraïbische Afdeling, 1977. 55 p., bibl.

Comprehensive bibliography of works dealing with the Indians of Surinam.

1180 Oliveira, Adélia Engrácia de. A terminologia de parentesco Mura-Pirahã (MPEG/B [nova série: antropologia] 66, fev. 1978, p. 1–33, bibl., map, tables)

Author describes kinship terminology of Pirahã, one of few remaining Mura subgroups. Simplicity of generation-type terminology is stressed. See item **1190**.

1181 Pachón, Consuelo de. Bibliografía sobre grupos indígenas. Bogotá, Ministerio de Gobierno, 1977? 91 l., map.

Bibliography, arranged by tribe, of works dealing with Indians of Colombia. Not exhaustive.

1182 Perrin, Michel. L'extraordinaire et le quotidien: mythes ou fantasmes goajiro? (FSCN/A, 44, 1976, p. 59–114, bibl.)

Analysis of 18 tales (presented in French) collected among the Goajiro of the Guajira peninsula. Author suggests that content (sex, hunger) involves projection of basic problems of Goajiro existence.

Prance, Ghillean T.; D.G. Campbell; and B.W. Nelson. The ethnobotany of the Paumarí Indians. See item **1665.**

1183 Price, P. David. Acculturation, social assistance and political context: the Nambiquara in Brazil (in International Congress of Americanists, XLII, Paris, 1976. Actas [see item 255] v. 2, p. 603–609, bibl.)

Account of efforts to assist the Nambiquara by anthropologist who was hired by FUNAI (Brazilian Indian Service). Conflicts with local financial interests and lack of support by FUNAI brought the program to a halt after two years. See items **1109** and **1125.**

1184 ———. Real toads in imaginary gardens: Aspelin vs. Lévi-Strauss on Nambiquara nomadism (KITLV/B, 134:1, 1978, p. 149–161, tables)

Author supports Aspelin's argument that Nambiquara are not seasonally nomadic as claimed by Lévi-Strauss (see *HLAS 39:1288*).

1185 Ramos, Alcida R. Mundurucú: social change or false problem? (AAA/AE, 5:4, Nov. 1978, p. 675–689, bibl.)

Author questions earlier interpretation of Mundurucú social structure which emphasized disharmony between descent (patrilineal) and residence (uxorilocal). Comparison with the Sanumá and other tribes suggests that Mundurucú organization was not unusual and also not the result of recent change.

1186 ——— and Bruce Albert. Yanomama descent and affinity: the Sanumá/Yanomam contrast (in International Congress of Americanists, XLII, Paris, 1976. Actas [see item 255] v. 2, p. 71–90, bibl., map, tables)

Detailed comparison of kinship systems of the Sanumá and Yanomam (southern Venezuela). Although both are Yanomamo subtribes the Sanumá have unilineal descent groups whereas the Yanomam are bilateral. Other differences are stressed. See items **1168** and **1199.**

1187 Ribeiro, Darcy. Os protagonistas do drama indígena (VOZES, 71:6, agosto 1976, p. 5–20)

General treatment of the past and future of indigenous populations of the Americas by one of their most persistent champions. Includes an appeal to anthropologists to support the cause of the Indians.

1188 Riester, Jürgen. En busca de la Loma Santa. La Paz, Editorial Los Amigos del Libro, 1976. 375 p., bibl., illus., maps, plate, tables.

Described as popular account of tribes of eastern Bolivia, book actually contains considerable ethnographic detail, especially concerning the Ayoréode, Chiquitano, Pauserna-Guarasug'wé, and Chimane. Good bibliography.

1189 ———. Indians of eastern Bolivia: aspects of their present situation. Copenhagen, International Work Group for Indigenous Affairs (IWGIA), 1975. 71 p., bibl., tables (IWGIA document, 18)

Brief survey of remaining tribal groups in eastern Bolivia, with estimates of how long each group will retain its identity. Predictions are not optimistic.

1190 Rodrigues, Ivelise and Adélia Engrácia de Oliveira. Alguns aspectos da ergologia Mura-Pirahã (MPEG/B [nova série: antropologia] 65, jan. 1977, p. 1–47, bibl., illus., maps, plates)

Brief description of material culture of the Pirahã, a Mura subgroup living near the middle Madeira (southwestern Brazil). See item **1180.**

1191 Rodríguez, Nemesio J. Oppression in Argentina: the Mataco case. Copenhagen, International Work Group for Indigenous Affairs (IWGIA), 1975. 39 p., map (IWGIA document, 21)

Brief account of current situation of the Mataco (central Chaco). Clashes with encroaching settlers and indifference of local authorities are emphasized.

1192 Ross, Eric Barry. Food taboos, diet and hunting strategy: the adaptation to animals in Amazon cultural ecology, with CA comment (UC/CA, 19:1, March 1978, p. 1–36, bibl., tables)

Author argues that food taboos of Amazonian Indians are ecologically determined.

Settlement size and permanence, and availability of fish are seen as major variables. This article and appended critical comments of other scholars comprise excellent survey of current debate over relationship of ecology and culture in Amazon Basin. See items 1111, 1119, 1158 and 1169.

1193 Santos, Juana Elbein dos. Os Nágô e a morte: Páde, Ásésé e o culto Égun na Bahia. Petrópolis, Brazil, Vozes, 1976. 244 p., bibl. (Col. Mestrado, 4)

Based on research in Brazil and in Nigeria, book presents elaborate interpretation of beliefs and rituals associated with death. Exactly who holds these beliefs is not made clear, but presumably beliefs originated in Africa and are found among members of most conservative Afro-Brazilian cults in Bahia.

1194 Santos, Sílvio Coelho dos. Educação e sociedades tribais. Porto Alegre, Brazil, Editora Movimento, 1975. 92 p., bibl., plates (Col. Documentos brasileiros, 6)

Brief account of educational situation among acculturated tribes of southern Brazil (Kaingang, Xokleng, Guarani, Xetá). Author urges use of bilingual instruction and makes other recommendations for change.

1195 Seeger, Anthony. Fixed points on arcs in circles: the temporal, processual aspect of Suyá space and society (in International Congress of Americanists, XLII, Paris, 1976. Actas [see item 255] v. 2, p. 342–359, bibl., map, tables)

Structuralist analysis of Suyá society (central Brazil) in which author stresses village form, residential units, and place names.

1196 Shaver, Harold. Los campa-nomatsiguenga de la Amazonía peruana y su cosmología (CIF/FA, 20, junio/dic. 1975, p. 49–53)

Brief account of Campa beliefs relating to after-life and major supernatural beings. For more extensive account, see HLAS 39:1406.

1197 Spell, Patsy Jean Adams and **Patricia Woods de Townsend.** Estructura y conflicto en el matrimonio de los indios culina de la Amazonia peruana (CIF/FA, 20, junio/dic. 1975, p. 139–160, bibl., tables)

Detailed analysis of kinship terminology, patterns of marriage, and sources of marital discord among the Culina of eastern Peru.

1198 Susnik, Branislava. Dimensiones migratorias y pautas culturales de los pueblos del Gran Chaco y de su periferia (UCNSA/SA, 7:1/2, 1972, p. 85–105, bibl.)

Detailed historical account of extensive movements of Chaco tribes after arrival of Europeans.

1199 Taylor, Kenneth I. Raiding, dueling and descent group membership among the Sanumá (in International Congress of Americanists, XLII, Paris, 1976. Actas [see item 255] v. 2, p. 91–104, bibl., tables)

Description of unusual system of differential participation in dueling according to lineage membership among the Sanumá (Yanomamo subtribe). Author uses data to support argument that Sanumá have patrilineal descent groups. See items 1168 and 1186.

1200 Temple, Dominique. Répression au Paraguay: l'exemple du Projet Marandu et la détention de Miguel Chase-Sardi (in International Congress of Americanists, XLII, Paris, 1976. Actas [see item 255] v. 2, p. 612–622)

Account of several projects designed to assist the Indians of Paraguay and their subsequent suppression by the government. For further details concerning the Marandu Project, see item 1123.

1201 Thomas, David John. Demografía, parentesco y comercio entre los indios pemón (VMJ/BIV, 17:13 [nueva época] enero/dic. 1976, p. 73–140, map, tables)

Elaborate analysis of Pemón kinship system (eastern Venezuela). Author deals not only with general patterns of kinship terminology and marriage, but also describes regional variations.

1202 ———. El movimiento religioso de San Miguel entre los pemón (FSCN/A, 43, 1976, p. 3–52, bibl., tables)

Account of origin and development of religious movement among the Pemón. Combining ideas from shamanism, Catholicism, and earlier syncretistic religious beliefs, leaders of movement stress purification and visions of San Miguel or God.

1203 Vidal, Lux Boelitz. As categorias de idade como sistema de classificação e controle demográfico de grupos entre os Xikrin do Catete e de como são manipuladas em diferentes contextos (MP/R, 23, 1975, p. 129–142, bibl.)

Description of ways in which age-grades among the Kayapó-Xikrin have been modified to fit new conditions created by establishment of Indian Post.

1204 ———. Morte e vida de uma sociedade indígena brasileira: os Kayapó-Xikrin do Rio Cateté. São Paulo, Editora da Univ. de São Paulo [and] Editora de Humanismo, Ciência e Tecnologia (HUCITEC), 1977. 268 p., bibl., illus.

Welcome addition to knowledge of Gê-speaking tribes of central Brazil. Based on limited fieldwork, study deals with all aspects of culture of Kayapó-Xikrin, with emphasis on age-grade organization, kinship, and ritual.

1205 Viertler, Renate Brigitte. As aldeias Bororo: alguns aspectos de sua organizaçao social. São Paulo, Univ. de São Paulo, 1976. 294 p., bibl., illus.

Based largely on the literature, study deals in detail with names, clan and moiety organization, and marriage among the Bororo of central Brazil. Excessive use of Bororo terms detracts from usefulness. See item 1130.

1206 Villamañán, Adolfo de. Cosmovisión y religiosidad de los barí (FSCN/A, 42, 1975, p. 3–27)

Brief account of religious beliefs of the Barí of western Venezuela. Includes description of major ceremonies and rituals associated with treatment of disease.

1207 Wagley, Charles. Time and the Tapirapé (in International Congress of Americanists, XLII, Paris, 1976. Actas [see item 255] v. 2, p. 369–377, bibl.)

Discussion of ways in which the Tapirapé of Central Brazil conceive of and measure time.

1208 ———. Welcome of tears: the Tapirapé Indians of Central Brazil. N.Y., Oxford Univ. Press, 1977. 328 p., bibl., plates.

Author did major fieldwork in 1939–40, has visited the Tapirapé repeatedly since. Present complete ethnography supplements numerous earlier publications, adds data on recent changes, and presents sketches of individual Tapirapé. Final chapter deals with "tragedy of the Brazilian Indians."

1209 Wagner, Erika and Walter Coppens. Quinta bibliografía antropológica re-

ciente sobre Venezuela (FSCN/A, 43, 1976, p. 53–64)

Brief bibliography of recent publications (1973–76) by anthropologists working in Venezuela.

1210 Watson, Lawrence C. The education of the cacique in Guajiro society and its functional implications (in Wilbert, Johannes ed. Enculturation in Latin America: an anthology [see item 260] p. 289–302, bibl. Reprint. See HLAS 35:1330.

1211 ———. Formal education in Calinatá: learning and the role of the Western school in a Guajiro community (CUA/AQ, 50:2, April 1977, p. 91–98, bibl., table)

Discussion of Guajiro attitudes toward formal education. Schools tend to be utilized if traditional values are not threatened.

1212 ———. Urbanization, cognition, and socialization of educational values: the case of the Guajiro Indians in Venezuela (in Wilbert, Johannes ed. Enculturation in Latin America: an anthology [see item 260] p. 395–414, bibl.)

Study of Guajiro women and children as they adapt to urban environment of Maracaibo, Ven. Adaptation is measured in terms of learning appropriate values, especially those dealing with status and the significance of formal education.

1213 Watson-Franke, Maria-Barbara. To learn for tomorrow: enculturation of girls and its social importance among the Guajiro of Venezuela (in Wilbert, Johannes ed. Enculturation in Latin America: an anthology [see item 260] p. 191–211, bibl.)

Author describes traditional treatment of girls at puberty among the Guajiro (Guajira Peninsula). Girls were isolated for two–five years, taught weaving and other skills.

1214 Whitten, Norman E., Jr. Ecological imagery and cultural adaptability: the Canelos Quichua of eastern Ecuador (AAA/AA, 80:4, Dec. 1978, p. 836–859, bibl.)

Elaborate symbolic interpretation of Canelos Quichua cosmology and ritual. Beliefs and rituals are said to enable the Canelos Quichua to express resistance to impinging social and cultural pressures and to adapt to dramatic ecological changes.

1215 Wilbert, Johannes. Metafísica del tabaco entre los indios de Suramérica

(UCAB/M, 5, 1976, p. 181–235, bibl.)

Survey of use of tobacco by South American Indians is followed by detailed account of beliefs associated with shamanism among the Warao (Orinoco delta). Based on research conducted over many years, description of shamanism stresses initiation experiences and use of tobacco to induce trance. See *HLAS 37:1413*.

1216 ————. To become a maker of canoes: an essay in Warao enculturation (*in* Wilbert, Johannes *ed*. Enculturation in Latin America: an anthology [see item **260**] p. 303–358, bibl., illus., tables)

Detailed account of canoe making among the Warao. Description follows life cycle of canoe maker, stressing social and religious concomitants as well as technical details of manufacture.

1217 Wise, Mary Ruth; Eugene E. Loos and **Patricia Davis.** Filosofía y métodos del Instituto Lingüístico de Verano (*in* International Congress of Americanists, XLII, Paris, 1976. Actas [see item **255**] v. 2, 499–525)

Outline of basic philosophy and methodology of Summer Institute of Linguistics, especially with reference to activities in eastern Peru. Evangelizing orientation is admitted and defended.

1218 Wistrand de Robinson, Lili M. Notas etnográficas sobre los cashibo (CIF/FA, 23, junio 1977, p. 117–144, bibl., illus.)

Brief ethnographic account of the Cashibo of eastern Peru, including good treatment of kinship terminology.

1219 Zarur, George. Parentesco: ritual e economia no Alto Xingu. Rio, Fundação Nacional do Indio (FUNAI), 1975. 97 p.

Survey of some major features of social organization of the Upper Xingu tribes. Kinship terminology of the Aweti included. See items **1108** and **1145**.

1220 Zerries, Otto. Die Bedeutung des Federschmuckes des südamerikanischen Schamanen und dessen Beziehung zur Vogelwelt (PMK, 23, 1977, p. 277–326, bibl., maps, plates)

Exhaustive survey of descriptions of South American shamanistic practices in which feather ornaments were utilized and birds were considered to have supernatural attributes. Some sources used uncritically. Conclusions regarding history of beliefs highly speculative.

ETHNOLOGY: South America, Highlands

LESLIE ANN BROWNRIGG, *AMARU IV Cooperative, Inc., Washington*

BECAUSE OF SPACE LIMITATIONS, this introduction will be brief in order to list theses and dissertations of interest to Andean ethnologists. A list was last published in this section in *HLAS 37* (see p. 129–131). Dissertations are now the single most important source of new ethnographic information on the peoples of the Andes.

We welcome the appearance of a new journal, *Antropología Andina*, published by the Centro de Estudios Andinos Cuzco (Apartado 582, Cuzco, Peru); the publications by Andeanists in the American Anthropological Association's journal *American Ethnologist*, the assumption of the editorship of *América Indígena* by the Peruvian anthropologist, Enrique Mayer. These developments should improve access to publication outlets for the amassed backlog of data and analyses which are indicated by the volume of dissertations.

A format change is introduced in this volume. Citations are arranged by country, then alphabetically by author in the manner of the "Archaeology: South America" section. The theses and dissertations listed below are similarly organized. Several publications included in this section have been annotated by William E. Carter or Steven A. Romanoff. These are identified by the respective contributor's initials.

Special appreciation is due to the *HLAS* staff, authors and publishers who supplied materials for review and suggestions.

MASTER'S THESES

COLOMBIA

Binder Schlager, Hildegard. La religiosidad del moreno de la costa cáucana del Pacífico. Univ. de Santo Tomás de Aquino, Cauca, Colombia, 1975.

PERU

Bischoffshausen H., Gustavo. Algunos aportes sobre las denominaciones quechuas de color. Univ. Nacional Mayor de San Marcos, Lima, 1976.

Palacios Ríos, Félix. "Hiwasha Uywa Uywataña Uka Uywaha Hiwasaru Uyusitu:" los pastores aymara de Chichillapi. Pontificia Univ. Católica del Perú, Lima, 1977.

Palomino Flores, Salvador. El sistema de oposiciones en la comunidad sarhua. Univ. Nacional de San Cristóbal de Huamanaga, Ayacucho, Perú, 1970.

Pinto R., Edmundo G. Estructura y función en la comunidad de Tomanga. Univ. Nacional de San Cristóbal de Huamanga, Ayacucho, Perú, 1970.

DOCTORAL DISSERTATIONS

ARGENTINA

Whiteford, John Hunter. Urbanization of rural proletarians: Bolivian migrant workers in northwest Argentina. Univ. of Texas at Austin, 1975. (Microfilm Order No. 75-16,756)

BOLIVIA

Buechler, Judith-Maria. Peasant marketing and social revolution in the State of La Paz, Bolivia. McGill Univ., 1972. (Order from the National Library of Canada, Ottawa)

Dutt, James S. Altitude and fertility: the Bolivian case. Pennsylvania State Univ., 1976. (Microfilm Order No. 76-24,759)

Miracle, Andrew W., Jr. The effects of cultural perception on Aymara schooling. Univ. of Florida, 1976. (Microfilm Order No. 77-1137)

Mariscotti de Görlitz, Ana María. Pachamama Santa Tierra: contribución al estudio de la religión autóctona en los Andes centro-meridionales. Univ. Märburg, FRG, 1975.

Stearman, Allyn MacLean. The highland migrant in lowland Bolivia: regional migration and the Department of Santa Cruz. Univ. of Florida, 1976. (Microfilm Order No. 77-8221)

Weiss, Andrew Simon. Peasant adaptation to urban life in highland Bolivia. Yale Univ., 1975. (Microfilm Order No. 76-14,571)

Widerkehr, Doris E. Bolivia's nationalized mines: a comparison of a cooperative and a state-managed community. New York Univ., 1975. (Microfilm Order No. 75-22,936)

CHILE

Hartwig, Vera. Die Indianer-Agrarfrage in Chile bis 1970. Karl-Marx-Univ., Berlin, GDR, 1971.

Manning, Alice Elizabeth. Calama: patterns of interaction in a Chilean city. Columbia Univ., 1975. (Microfilm Order No. 76-12,767)

Melville, Margarita Bradford. The Mapuche of Chile: their values and changing culture. American Univ., 1976. (Microfilm Order No. 76-26,209)

Melville, Thomas Robert. The nature of Mapuche social power. American Univ., 1976. (Microfilm Order No. 76-26,208)

COLOMBIA

Arocha, Jaime. "La Violencia" in Monteverde: environmental and economic determinants of homicide in a coffee-growing *municipio.* Columbia Univ., 1975. (Microfilm Order No. 76-12,800)

Browner, Carole. Poor women's fertility decisions: illegal abortions in Cali, Colombia. Univ. of California at Berkeley, 1976. (Microfilm Order No. 77-15,621)

Foster, Donald Ward. Survival strategies of low income households in a Colombia City. Univ. of Illinois at Urbana-Champaign, 1975. (Microfilm Order No. 75-24,303)

Hollenbach, Margaret Gloria. Culture and madness: a Colombian case study. Univ. of Washington, 1977. (Microfilm Order No. 78-14,444)

Kagan, Mary Dianne. Being old in Bojacá: a case study of aging in a Colombian peasant village. Univ. of California at Riverside, 1976. (Microfilm Order No. 76-19,586)

Nalven, Joseph Gilbert. The politics of urban growth: a case study of community formation in Cali, Colombia. Univ. of California at San Diego, 1978. (Microfilm Order No. 78-14,990)

Roberts, Ralph Leon, III. Migration and colonization in Colombian Amazonia: agrarian reform or neo-latifundismo. Syracuse Univ., 1975. (Microfilm Order No. 76-7711)

Stipek, George. Sociocultural responses to modernization among the Colombian Emberá. State Univ. of New York at Binghamton, 1976. (Microfilm Order No. 76-17,356)

ECUADOR

Belote, Linda Smith. Prejudice and pride: Indian-white relations in Saraguro, Ecuador. Univ. of Illinois at Urbana-Champaign, 1978. (Microfilm Order No. 78-20,902)

Brownrigg, Leslie Ann. The *nobles* of Cuenca: the agrarian elite of southern Ecuador. Columbia Univ., 1972. (Microfilm Order No. 75-25,656)

Fintzelberg, Nicholas Milton. The form, meaning and function of a *duende* legend in Santa Elena Peninsula, Ecuador. Univ. of California at Los Angeles, 1975. (Microfilm Order No. 76-7840)

Middleton, De Wright Ray. Form and process: a study of urban social relations in Manta, Ecuador. Univ. of Washington, 1972. (Microfilm Order No. 72-24,232)

Scrimshaw, Susan Crosby. Culture, environment and family size: a study of urban im-migrants in Guayaquil, Ecuador. Columbia Univ., 1974. (Microfilm Order No. 75-16,136)

Walter, Lynn Ellen. Interaction and organization in an Ecuadorian Indian highland community. Univ. of Wisconsin at Madison, 1976. (Microfilm Order No. 77-6632)

Weinstock, Steven. The adaptation of Otavalo Indians to urban and industrial life in Quito, Ecuador. Cornell Univ., 1973. (Microfilm Order No. 74-6363)

PERU

Appleby, Gordon. Exploration and its aftermath: the spatio-economic evolution of the regional marketing system in highland Puno, Peru. Stanford Univ., 1978. (Microfilm Order No. 79-05,814)

Anderson, Jeanine Marie. The middle class women in the family and the community: Lima, Peru. Cornell Univ., 1978. (Microfilm Order No. 78-17,783)

Beall, Cynthia M. The effects of high altitude on growth, morbidity and mortality of Peruvian infants. Pennsylvania State Univ., 1976. (Microfilm Order No. 77-9759)

Bode, Barbara. Explanation in the 1970 earthquake in the Peruvian Andes. Tulane Univ., 1974.

Bolton, Ralph Lamar, II. Aggression in Qolla society. Cornell Univ., 1972. (Microfilm Order No. 73-338)

Burchard, Roderick E. Myths of the sacred leaf: ecological perspectives of coca and peasant biocultural adaptation in Peru. Indiana Univ., 1976. (Microfilm Order No. 77-1871)

DeWind, Andrian W., Jr. Peasants become miners: the evolution of industrial mining systems in Peru. Columbia Univ., 1977. (Microfilm Order No. 78-02,298)

Gitlitz, John S. Hacienda, comunidad and peasant protest in northern Peru. Univ. of North Carolina at Chapel Hill, 1975.

Gow, David Drummond. The gods and social change in the high Andes. Univ. of Wisconsin at Madison, 1976. (Microfilm Order No. 76-29,915)

Haas, Jere Douglas. Altitudinal variation and infant growth and development in Peru. Pennsylvania State Univ., 1973. (Microfilm Order No. 74-20,921)

Hafer, R.F. The people up the hill: individual progress without village participation in Pariamarca, Cajamarca, Peru. Indiana Univ., 1971.

Hoff, Charles Jay. Preliminary observations of altitudinal variation in the physical growth and development of Peruvian Quechua. Pennsylvania State Univ., 1972. (Microfilm Order No. 72-33,175)

Horton, Douglas Earl. Haciendas and cooperatives: a study of estate reorganization, land reform and new reform enterprises in Peru. Cornell Univ., 1976. (Available from Latin American Studies Program Dissertations Series No. 67)

Lewellen, Theodore Charles. The Aymara in transition: economy and religion in a Peruvian peasant community. Univ. of Colorado at Boulder, 1976. (Microfilm Order No. 77-24,248)

Lobo, Susan Bloom. Kin relationships and the process of urbanization in the squatter settlements of Lima, Peru. Univ. of Arizona, 1977. (Microfilm Order No. 77-18,588)

Mayer, Enrique Jose. Reciprocity, self-sufficiency and market relations in a contemporary community in the Central Andes of Peru. Cornell Univ., 1974. (Microfilm Order No. 75-1621)

Núñez del Prado, Daisy L. Parentesco y organización social quechua a traves de una comunidad. Univ. Nacional de San Antonio Abad del Cusco, Perú, 1974.

Osterling, Jorge Pablo. Migration and adaptation of Huayopampino peasants in Lima, Peru. Univ. of California at Berkeley, 1978. (Microfilm Order No. 79-04568)

Sharon, Douglas. The symbol system of a north Peruvian Shaman. Univ. of California at Los Angeles, 1974.

Smith, Margo Lane. Institutionalized servitude: the female domestic servant in Lima, Peru. Indiana Univ., 1972. (Microfilm Order No. 72-10,007)

Wagner, Catherine A. Coca, chicha and trago: private and communal rituals in a Quechua community. Univ. of Illinois at Urbana-Champaign, 1978.

Wallace, James Macauley, III. Schooling in highland Peru: the impact of formal education on a peasant community. Indiana Univ., 1975. (Microfilm Order No. 75-23,436)

Walton, Nyle K. Human spatial organization in an Andean valley: the Callejón de Huaylas, Peru. Univ. of Georgia, 1974.

Webster, Steven S. The social organization of a native Andean community. Univ. of Washington at Seattle, 1972. (Microfilm Order No. 72-28,679)

Zednick, Gerhard Viktor. Language and culture retention in a German/Peruvian contact situation. Univ. of Texas at Austin, 1977. (Microfilm Order No. 77-29,124)

VENEZUELA

Conaway, Mary Ellen. Still Guahibo, still moving: a study of circular migration and marginality in Venezuela. Univ. of Pittsburgh, 1976. (Microfilm Order No. 77-2995)

Goulet, Jean-Guy. Guajiro social organization and religion. Yale Univ., 1978. (Microfilm Order No. 78-19,004)

Roseberry, William Clinton. Social class and social process in the Venezuelan Andes. Univ. of Connecticut at Storrs, 1977. (Microfilm Order No. 78-06,145)

GENERAL

1221 Bolton, Ralph and Enrique Mayer *eds.* Andean kinship and marriage. Washington, American Anthropological Association, 1977. 298 p., bibl., illus., maps (A special publication of the American Anthropological Association, 7)

The editors are to be congratulated for publishing these important technical studies, long circulated among specialists. Many articles were reviewed as symposium papers in *HLAS* 35:1352, 1362, 1375, 1422, and 1504. A summary of the themes by Lambert (see item **1225**) and a reaction by Casaverde (item **1222**) are annotated below. Other articles in the collection include items **1235, 1279, 1302** and **1305**. The "References Cited" (p. 282–292) is an important bibliographic tool in itself.

1222 Casaverde, Juvenal R. Comunidad andina y descendencia (III/AI, 38:1, enero/marzo 1978, p. 15–41, bibl.)

Reanalyzes the kinship studies published in item **1221**. Identifies the thematic problem in several articles as an underemphasis on the *ayllu* and *comunidad* and an overemphasis on the egocentric kindred.

1223 Hulshof, Josée. La coca en la medicina tradicional andina (AI, 38:4, oct./dic. 1978, p. 837–846)

Very brief discussion of the magical and medicinal uses of coca. The biochemist author argues that pharmacological properties of cocaine can best explain the medicinal use of the coca leaf. [WEC]

1224 Isbell, Billie Jean and Fredy Amílcar Roncalla Fernández. The ontogenesis of metaphor: riddle games among Quechua speakers seen as cognitive discovery procedures (UCLA/JLAL, 3:1, Summer 1977, p. 19–49, bibl., tables)

Isbell and Roncalla Fernández' approach to Quechua riddles is to set forth the "structure" and "transformations" of riddles as an exercise in symbolic, cognitive analysis. Compare to Bolton, item **1280**.

1225 Lambert, Bernd. Bilaterality in the Andes (*in* Bolton, Ralph and Enrique Mayer *eds.* Andean kinship and marriage [see item **1221**] p. 1–27, bibl.)

With reference to the collected articles but to few other treatments of Andean kinship, Lambert notes themes such as the strong collateral sibling/sibling-in-law bonds. He detects a lineage-like mechanism in the inheritance of some private goods. A postulation of lineage-like structure ignores transmission of goods produced by women through women, deemphasizes strategic resources held in common by the corporate transgenerational *comunidad* or *ayllu*, evades consideration of the impact of Spanish law and bilateral kin reckoning on the variety of Andean kinship systems and does not distinguish the social and ecological context of those systems where certain classes of wealth are private rather than communal.

1226 Mariscotti de Görlitz, Ana Maria. Der Kult der Pachamama und die Autochthone Religiosität in den Zentral und Nördlichen Süd-Anden (ZMR, 62:2, April 1978, p. 81–100)

A blaze of theoretical atavism emerges from this conflagration of data on the "autochthonous" Pachamama cult from a "heartland" (*kulturkreis*?) between Cajamarca, Peru, and Jujuy prov., Arg. Is the Andean world prepared to learn that their Pachamama is merely a variant of a Frazierian vegetation earth goddess? Or that they substitute iconographically a vicuña for the black dog guardian of the gate of hell in their dualist lunar/underworld goddess *gestalt*? The method of picking appropriate data out of context mimics that of the theoretical mentors of the piece: Frazier, Father Wilheim Schmidt and R.T. Zuidema in his structuralist excesses.

1227 Naranjo, Plutarco. Etnobotánica de la ayahuasca (SGL/B, 94, julio/dic. 1975, p. 24–33)

Juxtaposes reports of Jíbaro, Cayapa, Tucano, Zaparo, Piojes and ethnohistoric Inca ritual and use of hallucinogenic substances with an overly simple and conjectural "history" of myth as the spiritualization of natural phenomena. The term "god" is singularly misapplied to a variety of numina from different cosmologies.

1228 Zorrilla Eguren, Javier. El hombre andino y su relación mágico-religiosa con la coca (AI, 38:4, oct./dic. 1978, p. 867–874)

Brief note on symbolic uses of coca, based on secondary sources. [WEC]

1229 Zubritskii, Iurii Aleksandrovich. Inki-Kechua; osnovnye etapy istorii naroda (The Inca-Quechua; basic stages in the history of the people). Moscow, Izdatel'stvo "Nauka," 1975. 191 p.

A history of the Quechua people from their origins to the present, examining developments from the Marxist point of view. Broadly footnoted, and supplied with bibliography. Based in part on author's own research among the Quechua. [R.V. Allen]

ARGENTINA

1230 García, Alicia Irene and Clara Angela Armentano. La Feria de Simoca: mercado regional (UNT/H, 18:24, 1977, p. 135–150, bibl., map, plates)

Presents ethnography, ethnohistory and economics of a Saturday market at Simoca, 50 km. southwest of Tucumán, Arg. Details what regional produce and artisanal products are centralized for sale and redistribution. Geographical hinterlands are mapped. Historical and subannual fluctuations in the volume of goods exchanged are noted.

1231 Lafón, Ciro René. Antropología argentina. B.A., Editorial Bonum, 1977. 190 p., bibl., maps.

Important, systematic classification of the remaining groups in Argentina which maintain indigenous (pre-Hispanic) cultural traits, phrased in terms of historic and ongoing social change. The typology distinguishes *altiplano andino* cultural areas (e.g., Quebrada de Huamahuaca, the valleys of Calchaquíes, and frontier zones), the old Guaraní and Vaquerías mission, criollos and neo-criollo groups near rural industrial areas.

BOLIVIA

1232 Albó, Xavier. El mundo de la coca en Coripata, Bolivia (AI, 38:4, oct./dic. 1978, p. 939–969)

Author examines the conditions of coca production in Coripata, a town in the Yungas region of Bolivia. Production is in the hands of small farmers, and wage workers are rare. The economics of production are discussed and the conclusion reached that most profits accrue to the middleman. Most coca produced in the region is for traditional consumption, and the cocaine connection is weak. [WEC]

1233 Ayma Rojas, Donato. El ayllu en las comunidades del Departamento de

Oruro (Educación Popular [Instituto de Investigación Cultural para la Educación Popular, Oruro, Bol.] 8:2, 1977, p. 34–40, map)

This valuable communication is part of an ongoing study by the educational *promoter* of INDICEP.

1234 Bastien, Joseph W. Mountain of the Condor: the metaphor and ritual in an Andean ayllu. St. Paul, Minn., West Publishing Co., 1977. 227 p., bibl., maps, plates (Monograph of the American Ethnological Society, 64)

The rituals and beliefs associated with the sacred mountain Kaata by the villagers living on its slope frame a study of the underlying symbol patterns of a Qollahuaya (Kallawaya) Aymara-speaking community. Rituals of birth, first haircutting, marriage, healing and mourning are detailed. Concludes that "the telluric quality of Andean shrines enables them to be metaphors of the ecological order."

1235 Carter, William E. Trial marriage in the Andes? (*in* Bolton, Ralph and Enrique Mayer *eds.* Andean kinship and marriage [see item **1221**] p. 177–216)

A new look at trial marriage suggesting that, rather than being trial in character, it is an integral part of an interlocking series of rituals, all of which are essential for sealing the marriage bond. Illustrated with a detailed account of the Bolivian Aymara ceremonial marriage cycle. [WEC]

1236 ———— and **Mauricio Mamani P.** Patrones del uso de la coca en Bolivia (AI, 38:4, oct./dic. 1978, p. 905–937)

Summary report of the results of the first year of a two-and-one half year team project focusing on traditional coca use in Bolivia. Results of a nationwide survey are presented. Of the surveyed population 92 percent used coca in some form or other. Mean household consumption was 10.13 ounces per week for the sample as a whole, and 17.16 ounces for the households of miners. In general coca use is associated with the assumption of adult status, and is not disappearing. [WEC]

1237 Cason, Marjorie and **Adele Cahlander.** The art of Bolivian highland weaving. N.Y., Watson-Guptill Publications, 1976. 216 p., bibl., illus., plates.

Aimed at an audience of craft weavers, this well-illustrated book explains how to weave with techniques common in Bolivia —three color warp-faced double cloth, a *chuspa*, three span warp floats and the like. The weaver authors documented the techniques well enough to reproduce them after only a few months fieldwork. Rather than present the materials in any ethnographic context, the authors focus on the objects and how each can be produced.

1238 Cereceda, Verónica. Mundo quechua. Cochabamba, Bol., Editorial Serrano, 1978. 93 p., plate.

Observations and generalizations on topics of native religion based on the study of three "ayllus;" the Jukumanis of Chukiuta; the Laymes (Laymis) of their "capital" town, Qalaqala; and the Qallawayllas (Kallawayas) of Banderani, Oruro.

1239 La cultura quechua (Educación Popular [Instituto de Investigación Cultural para la Educación Popular, Oruro, Bol.] 8:2, 1977, p. 21–28)

Basic ethnological concepts have been incorporated into this quasi-official statement by educational workers in Oruro, Bol. Their view of Quechua and Inca history is one among alternatives, but the outline of the social organization, social groupings, social problems, political authority structure and religious and ritual aspects of Quechua culture in Oruro contains sound observations.

1240 Girault, Luis. La cultura kallawaya (*in* Mesa Redonda sobre Expresiones de la Cultura Boliviana en el Lapso 1925–1974, La Paz, 1975. Dualismo o pluralismo cultural en Bolivia [see item **1245**] v. 1, p. 59–72)

The Kallawaya—a distinct ethnic group of folk curers and herbalists—are traced through historical and contemporary accounts of their activities. Author describes their prodigious ethnobotanical knowledge of plants from the high plateau, mountains, subtropical plains, tropical forests and valleys.

1241 Harris, Olivia. Laymis y machas: temas culturales del Norte Potosí (*in* Mesa Redonda sobre Expresiones de la Cultura Boliviana en el Lapso 1925–1974, La Paz, 1975. Dualismo o pluralismo cultural en Bolivia [see item **1245**] v. 1, p. 73–82, bibl.)

The Quechua-speaking Machas and Aymara-speaking Laymis are regarded as distinct ethnic groups in Potosí, displaying many overlaps in traits of social organization and ritual inspite of sharp differences in authority structure and ideology.

1242 Higgins, Kitty and David Kenny. Bolivian highland weaving of the 18th, 19th and 20th centuries. Toronto, The Canadian Museum of Carpets and Textiles, 1978. 29 p., bibl., illus., maps, plates.

This catalogue from an exhibit of Bolivian textiles largely collected by the authors contains many debatable ethnographic observations, but provides valuable excerpts from more technical studies of Andean weaving and a translation of Louis Girault's 1969 section on Bolivian textile dyes from his *Textiles boliviens*. Plates are unfortunately in black and white; dates assigned to pieces are doubtful.

1243 Lavaud, Jean-Pierre. Compérage, stratification sociales et rapport de pouvoir: un enquete à La Paz (CDAL, 13/14, 1976, p. 103–125, bibl.)

Vertical *compadrazgo* is explored at the level of La Paz professionals and bureaucrats in government posts. Godparent sponsorship of marriages and baptisms formalizes patron-client relationships which Lavaud deems essential for political career in Bolivia. Strategies of choice are highly politicized. In the case histories presented, the godfathers make their clients into functionaires to support them within the bureaucracy. Allies, not achievement, build careers.

1243a Léons, Madeline Barbara. The economic networks of Bolivian political brokers: revolutionary road to fame and fortune (*in* Halperin, Rhoda and James Dow eds. Peasant livelihood: studies in economic anthropology and cultural ecology. N.Y., St. Martin's Press, 1977, p. 102–116, table)

Case study sketches the career of a political boss (*caudillo, cacique*) of the Bolivian south yungas: his economic teamwork with a brother-in-law—another storeowner/coca buyer/moneylender—manages a large local clientele of debtors repaying loans in cash crops, labor and political support.

1244 Leons, William. Pluralism and mobility in a Bolivian community (UNC/ED, 2:3, Oct. 1977, p. 36–50, bibl.)

Leons here defends his adoption of a model of plural society to interpret his Bolivian data from Chicaloma, in the south

yungas. He chooses his words more cautiously than in his previous article (see *HLAS 39:1509*) but still relies solely upon plural society theorists—M.G. Smith, J.C. Mitchell, B.N. Colby and P.L. Van den Berghe.

1245 Mesa Redonda sobre Expresiones de la Cultura Boliviana en el Lapso 1925–1974, *La Paz, 1975.* Dualismo o pluralismo cultural en Bolivia. t. 1. Coordinated by Carlos Ponce Sangines. La Paz, Casa Municipal de la Cultural Franz Tamayo, 1975. 186 p., bibl., maps (Biblioteca paceña: nueva serie)

A series of lectures on the theme of Bolivian cultural variations presented by Bolivian and foreign researchers. See items **1240** and **1241** for two articles of special interest.

1246 La missione evangēlizzatrice. Verso una chiesa aymara (Quaderni Asnal [Associazione per gli Studi e la Documentazione dei Problemi Socio-Religiosi dell'America Latina, Roma] 4:19, maggio/giugno, p. 1–86, maps)

Overview of religious organizations in Ingavi, Los Andes, Murillo and Sud Yungas in La Paz dept. with a focus on the Aymara community of Laja.

1247 Montaño Aragón, Mário. Antropología cultural boliviana. La Paz, Editorial Casa Municipal de la Cultura Franz Tamayo, 1977. 262 p., illus.

Best described as a high-school level textbook rather than a monograph, the book presents conventional understandings among national Bolivian anthropologists of the various cultures of their nation.

Smith, Hubert. A filmmaker's journal: Bolivia. See *HLAS 40:965*.

Smith, Stephen M. Labor exploitation on pre-1952 haciendas in the lower valley of Cochabamba, Bolivia. See item **3317**.

Stearman, Allyn MacLean. The highland migrant in lowland Bolivia: multiple resource migration and the horizontal archipelago. See item **5454**.

1248 Vidaurre Retamoso, Enrique. Los indomables: semblanza de un indio chiriguano y su raza. La Paz, Biblioteca Popular Boliviana de Ultima Hora, 1977. 202 p., bibl.

Embedded in what is largely a history of military engagments involving the Chiriguanos are tidbits of ethnographic data. Reprints Riester's section on the Chiriguano from *En busca de la Loma Santa* (p. 193–198).

CHILE

1249 Berdichewsky, Bernardo. La ceremonia religiosa del Ñillatun entre los araucanos del Cono Sur (UNC/ED, 2:3, Oct. 1977, p. 1–26, bibl., maps)

Presents and analyzes fieldwork conducted in southern Chile, in the area of Lakes Villarrica and Calafquén among communities in 1965 and 1967. The central Ñillatun ceremonies are minutely described; analysis of the symbolism and function of the Ñillatun is in clear continuity with a tradition of similar analyses among Chilean ethnologists cited in the study.

1250 ———. Reducciones araucanas y su incorporación en el modo de producción capitalista. Lima, Univ. Nacional Mayor de San Marcos, 1977. 63 p., bibl. (Seminario de historia rural andina) (mimeo)

Spanish translation of "The Agrarian Reform in Chile and its Impact on Indigenous Araucanian Communities," originally published in a compilation edited by Elías Sevilla-Casas *Western expansion and indigenous peoples: the heritage of Las Casas* (The Hague, Mouton, 1976).

1251 Berglund, Staffan. The national integration of Mapuche ethnical minority in Chile. Stockholm, Almquist & Wiksell International, 1977. 228 p., bibl., illus., maps.

Based on fieldwork conducted Aug. 1972–Jan. 1973, in Cautín and Malleco provs., Chile, and among enclaves of Mapuche migrants in urban areas, the study documents the perspective of the Unidad Popular government that land reform is critical to the Mapuche. More interesting than the ethnography of the Mapuche are the author's defense of the UP government's development activities and policy toward the Mapuche.

1252 Hartwig, Vera. Die Indianer-Agrarfrage in Chile bis 1970. Berlin, GDR, n.p., 1976. 1 v. (Unpaged)

East German analysis of the historical aspects of the Mapuche problem in Chile. Includes statistics and legislation. [M. Kossok]

1253 Kessel, Juan Van. Los conjuntos de bailes religiosos del Norte Grande: análisis del censo practicado en 1973 (UCC/NG, 1:2, dic. 1974, p. 211–216, tables)

Comparison of censuses made among religious festival dance groups in 1969 and 1973 shows an across-the-board increase in dance group participation in northern Chile urban areas of Tarapacá and Antofagasta.

1254 Martínez S., Gabriel. El sistema de los uywiris en Isluga (*in* Niemeyer F., Hans *ed.* Homenaje al Dr. Gustavo le Paige, S.J. Santiago, Univ. del Norte, 1976, p. 255–327, bibl., maps, tables)

First-rate analysis of the symbolism of space—ethnogeographical, social and mythical—among a population of about 2,000 Aymara speakers in a dozen communities in the altiplano of north Chile contiguous to Oruro, Bol., gives special emphasis to the various mountain spirits.

Núñez A., Lautaro. L'évolution millénaire d'une vallée: peuplement et ressources a Tarapacá. See item **699.**

COLOMBIA

1255 Abello Santana, Consuelo and **Francisco Avella E.** Asentamientos humanos de la Sierra Nevada: prueba de una metodología (*in* Congreso Nacional de Historiadores y Antropólogos, I, Santa Marta, Colombia, 1975. Memorias. Medellín, Colombia, Editorial Argemiro Salazar, 1976, p. 69–92, bibl., map, plate)

The authors describe settlement patterns in the warm, temperate and cold zones of the northern slopes of the Sierra Nevada in Colombia, in order to sketch the agricultural production of peasant colonists, agricultural enterprises, sponsored colonization, established peasants, and indigenous peoples—principally the Kogi but also the Arhuacos (Ijka) and Arasarios (Sanka). The colonists, struggling to make a decent living, settle in the lower and middle zones, displacing indigenous people. The process is ecologically unstable, often resulting in eroded grasslands of poor quality, a familiar situation for the east slopes of the Andes today. [SAR]

1256 Friedemann, Nina S. *ed.* Tierra, tradición y poder en Colombia: enfoques antropológicos. Bogotá, Instituto Colombiano de Cultura, Subdirección de Comunicaciones Culturales, 1976. 171 p., bibl., maps, plates (Biblioteca básica colombiana)

This attractive publication of a 1974 symposium on anthropology in Colombia treats land rights and power dynamics among the following groups: peasants of the central cordillera Cauca Valley (Elías Sevilla-Casas and Nina S. Friedemann); peasants of the eastern cordillera (Ronald J. Duncan); the Guahibo (Robert V. Morey); the Embera (Sven-Erik Isacsson); and the Bari (Stephen Beckerman).

1257 Havens, A.E. and William Flinn.
Green revolution technology and community development: the limits of action projects (UC/EDCC, 23, 1975, p. 469–481, illus.)

Gives Colombian case examples of "careless technology" in agricultural peasant production.

1258 López Méndez, Harold. Guambia.
Bogotá, Instituto Colombiano de Cultura, Subdirección de Comunicaciones Culturales, División de Publicaciones, 1976. 120 p., illus., map, plates (Serie publicaciones especiales colcultura)

Photographs of the Guambian people of the Cauca Valley are of ethnographic interest; the text is weak and promotes stereotypes.

1259 Ochiai, Inés. El contexto cultural de la coca entre los indios kogi (III/AI, 38:1, enero/marzo 1978, p. 43–49, bibl.)

Sketches briefly how the Colombian Kogi produce and use coca leaves, noting how coca use is part of the masculine Kogi ideal of life. For Kogi men, the priests (mamá) act as intermediaries between the ancestors and men. In these rituals and as a symbol of male initiation and male sexuality, coca leaves are central. Ochiai discusses how non-Kogi advocates of coca eradication ignore the cultural context of coca leaf use among the Kogi. [SAR]

1260 Reichel-Dolmatoff, Gerardo. La antropología patrocinada por la Gobernación del Magdalena (in Congreso Nacional de Historiadores y Antropólogos, I, Santa Marta, Colombia, 1975. Memorias. Medellín, Colombia, Editorial Argemiro Salazar, 1976, p. 98–103, bibl., plates)

Presents useful background for the many works that Reichel-Dolmatoff and Alicia Dussan de Reichel have written on the ethnography and archaeology of Magdalena prov., Colombia, the better known of which concern the Kogi and Tairona cultures. The author reflects upon the four years of fieldwork from which the 53 works listed in a bibliography derive. [SAR]

1261 ———. Training for the priesthood among the Kogi of Colombia (in Wilbert, Johannes ed. Enculturation in Latin America: an anthology [see item 260] p. 265–288, bibl.)

Living in small settlements disrupted by exogeneous influences, the Kogi maintain ceremonial centers and a special group of ritual specialists in the Sierra Nevada de Santa Marta, Colombia. The article describes how Kogi priests (mamá) train postulates in their esoteric knowledge during an 18-year period of apprenticeship. The training is strikingly elaborate, strict and removed from ordinary Kogi routine. [SAR]

1262 Sanmiguel, Inés. Relación económica indígena colono-campesino en la Vertiente Norte de la Sierra Nevada de Santa María (in Congreso Nacional de Historiadores y Antropólogos, I, Santa Marta, Colombia, 1975. Memorias. Medellín, Colombia, Editorial Argemiro Salazar, 1976, p. 112–115)

This too brief article sketches the relation of some 2,000 Kogi censused in the Garavito and San Miguel River basins to the peasant colonists who are displacing them from the best lands. The Kogi supply colonists with agricultural good and labor in return for manufactured objects, salt and particularly rum. Urban intermediaries control the flow of manufactured goods into and export crops out of the area, binding colonists and Kogi in perpetual debt through high-price mark-ups. [SAR]

1263 Stipek, George, Jr. Relaciones inter-étnicas en el Chocó colombiano (UA/U, 50:193, enero/marzo 1975, p. 75–81, bibl.)

Proposes that interethnic compadrazgo and fear of harmful magic and trade between the Amerind Emberá and peasant blacks residing in the tropical forest Chaco of western Colombia help the Emberá maintain "ethnic identity." Ethnographic details combined with an analysis of social distance mechanisms are instructive, but do not support Stipek's projection of what might happen in the absence of the institutions. [SAR]

1264 Torres Márquez, Vicencio. Los indígenas arhuacos y "la vida de la civilización." Bogotá, Librería y Editorial América Latina, 1978. 130 p., illus.

The author, himself an Arhuaco educated at a Capuchin mission, describes aspects of the Sierra Nevada (Colombia) Arhuaco, Kakatukua, Antanquero and other native groups. The history of land encroachment by the Capuchins in Santa Marta, the struggle for native rights, formal agreements made among Arhuaco and Kogi leaders and Arhuaco world view are well reported. The author's perspective as a militant in native struggles influenced by and working with Kogi priests lends unique insights.

ECUADOR

1265 Agro, Robert Joseph. La pasada del huagra: el ritual para la fertilidad entre los indios cañaris del Azuay y otros elementos afines a este (CCE/RA, 5, 1974, p. 89–100, illus.)

A "*huagra*" is a man carrying a large *zambo* squash, chasing people as though he were a mad bull. Agro interprets this burlesque game, held in the context of a feast sponsored by a domestic unit, as a fertility-anxiety ritual. Though the symbolism is clear (the bull image, seed distributions, "altares" of imported food), these feasts are scheduled. Agro's correlation of the timing with lack or profusion of rainfall is, however, incidental.

1266 Belote, Jim and Linda Belote. The limitation of obligation in Saraguro kinship (*in* Bolton, Ralph and Enrique Mayer *eds.* Andean kinship and marriage [see item 1221 and *HLAS 35:1352*] p. 106–116)

Brief discussion of an ego-centric kin system in the highlands of southern Ecuador. The wealthy tend to limit their obligation networks more than do the poor, but even the latter regularly discard kin who, theoretically, could form part of such networks. [WEC]

1267 ——— and ———. El sistema de cargos de fiestas en Saraguro (*in* Naranjo, Marcelo F.; José I. Pereira V.; and Norman E. Whitten, Jr. *eds.* Temas sobre la continuidad y

adaptación cultural ecuatoriana [see item 1274] p. 47–73, bibl., illus.)

Compares the ritual and agricultural calendars, and the range of annual climatological cycles to analyze important analogues. The event structure and social organization of religious festivals is detailed for Carnaval, Semana Santa, Santa Cruz (May 3), La Virgen Auxiliadora de Shindar, Corpus Cristi, San Pedro, La Virgen de Tránsito, La Virgen de las Mercedes and Navidad/Tres Reyes. Festivals falling between March and June are related to harvests in the upland Loja prov. base settlements of the Saraguro ethnic group, while the Sept. Mercedes Festival concentrates some highland base communities with Saraguro colonists from the lowland, eastern zones (see also *HLAS 35:1352*).

1268 Brownrigg, Leslie Ann. Areas y mecanismos de control de la elite regional (UP/EA, 8:14, 1978, p. 63–74, bibl.)

Extends relevant characteristics of the social, spatial and economic organization of the Cuenca resident elite of southern highland Ecuador to analyze political and economic behaviors of similar regional elite groups in Peru and Bolivia. The thesis hinges upon resources controlled or obtained through political actions of segments of each regional elite group.

1269 ———. Variaciones del parentesco cañari (Naranjo, Marcelo F.; José I. Pereira V.; and Norman E. Whitten, Jr. *eds.* Temas sobre la continuidad y adaptación cultural ecuatoriana [see item 1274] p. 25–44, bibl.)

Ritual kinship as a mechanism to reinforce preexisting consanguineal and affinal relations is explored in cases from Azuayan and Cañar Cañari communities. Ritual kinship relations are established not only at life-passage rites celebrated by Catholic events (baptism, marriage) but also more clearly indigenous events: cutting of the umbilicus and a ritual battle, the *pukara*. Patterns of birth-order naming, generational naming, mixed Spanish-Quechua terminological systems, gender-specific terminology and non-patronymic surname inheritance are among the traits discussed.

1270 Casagrande, Joseph B. Estrategias para sobrevivir: los indígenas de la sierra (*in* Naranjo, Marcelo F.; José I. Pereira V.; and Norman E. Whitten, Jr. *eds.* Temas sobre la

continuidad y adaptación cultural ecuatoriana [see item **1274**] p. 77–104, bibl.)
Translation of *HLAS 37:1447*. See also *HLAS 39:1443*.

1271 ———. Looms of Otavalo (AMNH/NH, 86:8, Oct. 1977, p. 48–59, plates)
Popular presentation with brilliant photographs by Victor Engelbert of weaving as the theme of Otavalan society.

1272 Krener, Eva. Juncal: en indianerkommunei, Ecuador. Copenhagen, Nationalmuseet, 1977. 128 p., illus., map, plates.
The photoethnography is as evocative as the popularly presented text (in Danish) is provocative with discoveries made during the author's community study of a freehold village of Cañari near Cañar in southern highland Ecuador. This is the first book on an Andean topic to be included in a series of popular ethnographies published by the Danish National Museum.

1273 Middleton, De Wright Ray. Choice and strategy in an urban compadrazgo (AAA/AE, 2:3, 1975, p. 461–475, bibl., illus.)
Qualitative and some quantitative data on choice of godparents in terms of family development cycle and geographical variables is presented from Barrio Tarqui, a former fisherman's barrio in Manta, Ecua.

1274 Naranjo, Marcelo F.; José I. Pereira V.; and Norman E. Whitten, Jr. *eds.* Temas sobre continuidad y adaptación cultural ecuatoriana. Quito, Ediciones de la Univ. Católica, 1977. 213 p., bibl., tables.
Contains items **1267**, **1269**, and item **1270** (a translation of *HLAS 37:1447*), and an ethnohistory of ethnic adaptation in the Ecuadorian Oriente by Naranjo.

1275 Scheller, Ulf and others. Artesanía folclórica en el Ecuador. Guayaquil, Cromos Cia. Ltda., 1973? 64 p., bibl., col. plates, maps, plates.
A *Foxfire* from Ecuador! the collective effort of Guayaquil high school class, their teachers, and the photographers Jean Claude Constant and Wulf Weiss, inspired by Ulf Scheller. Topics include Shuara (Jívaro) ceramics, bread sculptures, *rondador* flutes, Otavalan, Cañari, Salasacan and Azuayan textiles, wood sculpture, mirambas, "Panama" hats and other weavings in straw. A light and lovely book, highly recommended for cultural appreciation.

1276 Whitten, Norman E., Jr. Etnocidio ecuatoriano y etnogénesis indígena: resurgencia amazónica ante la colonización (*in* Naranjo, Marcelo, F.; José I. Pereira V.; and Norman E. Whitten, Jr. *eds.* Temas sobre la continuidad y adaptación cultural ecuatoriana, 1977 [see item **1274**] p. 171–213, bibl.)
Translation of item *HLAS 39:1576*.

PERU

1277 Arguedas, José María *ed.* Señores e indios: acerca de la cultura quechua, 1976. Introduction by Angel Rama. Montevideo, Arca Editorial, 1976. 259 p., bibl.
Presents a selection of newspaper articles on folkloric themes and extracts from longer studies by Arguedas between 1940 and 1969. Angel Rama's introductory comments, heavily influenced by Lévi-Strauss, provide a literary and theoretical context for the Arguedas vignettes.

1278 Bode, Barbara. Disaster, social structure, and myth in the Peruvian Andes: the genesis of an explanation (NYAS/A, 293, 15 July 1977, p. 246–274)
"Culture! More culture, until we evolutionize man!" broadcasted Radio Huascarán daily as relief workers of various stripes flocked to Ancash. Bode reports with sharp insight the remarks and social dramas which indicated the ideologies struggling to revitalize the disaster area. Mythic beliefs, religion, social organization and politics were outlined by the tragedy. Of the great outpouring of selective explanations and rationalizations, Bode has chosen those which best describe the underlying and emerging social structure. Her feat is as delightful as it is sobering.

1279 Bolton, Ralph. The Qolla marriage process (*in* Bolton, Ralph and Enrique Mayer *eds.* Andean kinship and marriage [see item **1221**] p. 217–238)
The concept of marriage presented here is that of a complex sequence of interactions and decisions rather than of an event. An outline of the major steps and alternatives in the decision process is given, along with manifest reasons for choosing one course of action over another at each of the decision points. [WEC]

1280 ——. Riddling and responsibility in highland Peru (AAA/AE, 4:3, Aug. 1977, p. 497–516, bibl., tables)

Quechua riddles experienced a minor vogue in the pages of *American Ethnologist* (see item **1224**). Bolton introduced a sampling technique and a control group of American children to "measure" such matters as riddling ability and the correlation of interest in riddling with parental nagging, a plus or minus.

1281 —— and **Charlene Bolton.** Concepción, embarazo y alumbramiento en una aldea qolla (Antropología Andina [Centro de Estudios Andinos, Cuzco, Peru] 1/2, 1976, p. 58–74, bibl.)

First and second-person accounts of unusual or difficult pregnancies of cases from a Puno village are inadequate for the generalizations drawn.

1282 **Brush, Stephen B.** Kinship and land use in a northern sierra community (*in* Bolton, Ralph and Enrique Mayer *eds.* Andean kinship and marriage [see item **1221** and *HLAS 39:1362*] p. 136–152)

Discussion of five different reciprocal relationships as these relate to a broad subsistence base consisting of seven recognized ecological zones. Six case studies illustrate the underlying structure. [WEC]

1283 ——. Man's use of an Andean ecosystem (Human Ecology [Plenum, N.Y.] 4:2, 1976, p. 147–166, bibl., illus., maps)

Describes the natural and crop zonation of Uchucmarca Valley (see *HLAS 37:1436* and the author's 1973 dissertation) and includes a life zone map (Tosi's model) and crop-zone map. Based on his own and other works, Brush reports that four major crop zones are distinguished by Andean subsistence farmers: 1) lowland tropical; 2) temperate grain; 3) cool potato-tuber; and 4) natural pastures. Brush asserts that types of exploitation and socio-economic features of communities vary with distance between zones, and with altitude and gradient (see *HLAS 37:1438* for another treatment of this theory).

1284 ——. Mountain, field and family: the economy and human ecology of an Andean valley. Philadelphia, Univ. of Pennsylvania Press, 1977. 1 v. (Unpaged) bibl., illus., maps.

A major monographic presentation of the Uchucmarca, Peruvian community (see *HLAS 37:1438* and the author's dissertation).

1285 **Burchard, Roderick E.** Una nueva perspectiva sobre la masticación de la coca (AI, 38:4, oct./dic. 1978, p. 809–835)

Argues for an ecgonine-model of coca chewing to replace the traditional cocaine model. Burchard suggests, as he has in other publications, that the chewing of coca leaf may be an important cultural mechanism for blood glucose homeostatis and carbohydrate utilization. [WEC]

1286 **Cáceres, Baldomero.** La coca, el mundo andino y los extirpadores de idolatrías del siglo XX (AI, 38:4, oct./dic. 1978, p. 769–785)

Briefly chronicles the rise and fall of coca and cocaine as legal drugs in Europe and the US. Argues that Peruvian opposition to the coca habit rises out of a confusion of coca with cocaine and out of deep rooted anti-Indian prejudice. [WEC]

1287 **Camino, Alejandro.** Trueque: correrías e intercambios entre los quechuas andinos y los piro y machiguenga de la montaña peruana (Amazonia Peruana [Centro Amazónico de Antropología y Aplicación Práctica, Lima] 1:2, julio 1977, p. 123–140, bibl.)

This excellent study traces the ethnohistory of interaction among the Machiguenga of the upper Urubamba, the Piro-Chontaquiros of the lower Urubamba and highland Andean settlements in the Cuzco area, Peru. Political anthropologists may find value in the argument that redistributive chiefs (*curacas*) arose as a response of the Machiguenga to annual invasions of their territory by the Piro-Chontaquiros' trading expedition rather than as leaders for rubber gathering and slave raiding. Level of detail parallels Oberem's.

1288 **Carlin Arce, Jorge.** Antología documental del Departamento de Tumbes. Lima, Talleres de la Imprenta del Ministerio de Guerra, 1977. 339 p., illus., maps, plates.

Retired from Army service in Tumbes, Carlin Arce has assembled his second volume of documents concerning the history and ethnology of Peru's northern border department. The third section (p. 209–245) compiled vintage articles on "folkloric aspects" which are of ethnological interest.

1289 Christinat, Jean Louis. Conception, grossesse, naissance et soins post-partum dans une communauté indienne des Andes péruviennes (SSA/B, 40, 1976, p. 5–17)

Transcriptions of fascinating and frank conversations between the anthropologist and his elderly *comadre*, "Rita" of Chia community, Puno, concerning sexual topics: conception and customs of intercourse, pregnancy, and birth. An introduction and ample footnotes put the information in context.

1290 Cuche, Denys. La mort des dieux africains et les religions noires au Pérou (Death of African gods and black religions in Peru) (CNRS/ASR, 22[43]:1, jan./mars 1977, p. 77–91)

Applies Roger Bastide's thesis to suggest that African religious concepts were submerged through syncretism and survive only as minor magical notions in Peru. The demographics put African belief systems at a disadvantage.

1291 Custred, Glynn. Peasant kinship, subsistence and economics in a high altitude Andean environment (*in* Bolton, Ralph and Enrique Mayer eds. Andean kinship and marriage [see item **1221** and *HLAS* 35:1375] p. 117–135)

Custred describes the bilateral kin system of a Quechua-speaking community in Cuzco dept. Post marital residential patterns are preferably virilocal and labor is recruited basically from siblings and their children. In the case of scarce land resources, joint ownership is maintained by male siblings and their male children. [WEC]

1292 Della Santa, Elizabeth. Aspects folkloriques de la vie agricole à Arequipa, Pérou (SSA/B, 37, 1973, p. 15–24, illus., plates)

Tools and rituals of Arequipa agriculture are noted briefly.

1293 Earls, John and **Irene Silverblatt.** El matrimonio y la autoconstrucción de alianzas en Sarhua (IFEA/B, 6:1/2, 1977, p. 63–70, bibl., illus.)

Resumé and conclusions of a longer, yet unpublished ethnography of the marriage ceremonialism of Sarhua, a village in Ayacucho, Peru.

1294 Favre, Henri. The dynamics of Indian peasant society and migration to coastal plantations in central Peru (*in* Duncan, Kenneth; Ian Rutledge; and Colin Harding eds. Land and labour in Latin America [see *HLAS* 40:2156] p. 253–267, map)

Northern Huancavelica descendants of the Asto or Anqara ethnic group seized on late 19th-century wage opportunities in Cañete cotton plantations to finance agricultural colonization of the high (3,800 m.) plateau. Villages were organized to secede from the administrative control of older towns. This study delves into an understudied type of Andean colonization directed to bringing higher altitude zones into production.

1295 Flores Ochoa, Jorge A. Enga, Engaychu, Illa y Khuya Rumi: aspectos mágico-religiosos entre pastores (SA/J, 63, 1974/1976, p. 245–261, bibl., illus.)

This work represents a major breakthrough in explanation of a fragment of Andean ethnography often noted: the use of amulets (often of stone) in rituals to increase animals. A major ethnozoological classification is noted, between animals which are wild (*salga*) and those which are domesticated (*uywa*); the latter are subdivided between wool-bearers (*millmayuq*) and non-wool bearing such as cows or horses. Ceremonialism and mythological beliefs vary according to this classification.

1296 ——— and Yemira D. Najar Vizcarra. El likira: intermediario ambulante en la Cordillera de Canchis (Antropología Andina [Centro de Estudios Andinos, Cuzco, Perú] 1/2, 1976, p. 125–135, bibl., map)

Likira are peddlers, who carry staples (trago, noodles, candles, matches, bread, sugar, maize, ají, etc.) to remote communities to barter, preferably for wool, skins or ch'uno in Canchis, southern Peru. The masculine article of the title is somewhat inappropriate as many of the likira peddlers are women.

1297 Fonseca Martel, César. Diferenciación campesina en los Andes peruanos (Discusión Antropológica [Univ. Nacional Mayor de San Marcos, Lima] 2:2, 1976, p. 1–20, bibl.)

Perhaps the cardinal distinction between anthropological studies and those of economists and many rural sociologists is a view of the "peasant" as differentiated by ecological adaptations, distinct local labor organizations and unique technologies. Drawing upon his own experience and the literature, the author begins a categorization of differences among the peasant "masses" of Peru.

1298 Gagliano, Joseph A. La medicina popular y la coca en el Perú: un análisis histórico de actitudes (AI, 38:4, oct./dic. 1978, p. 789–805)

Highlights in the history of the coca debate, beginning with the Spanish conquest. Opponents to coca use have argued that it historically impeded the Christianization of the Indians, that it has led to crime and degeneration, that it militates against assimilation, and that it is a narcotic drug. Over the centuries, however, the opinion that has prevailed is that coca has adaptive value for Andean peasants as a stimulant, medicine, and cultural symbol. [WEC]

1299 Gasparini, Graziano and **Luise Margolies.** Arquitectura doméstica (in Arquitectura inka. Caracas, Univ. Central de Venezuela, Facultad de Arquitectura y Urbanismo, Centro de Investigaciones Históricas y Estéticas, 1977, p. 137–199, illus., plates)

This chapter, within the most detailed study to date of Inca architecture, examines the modern vernacular forms and construction technology of Andean peasant housing to interpret ancient ruins. Contemporary wall construction, roof forms and circular house foundations—which survive among the Chipaya of Oruro, Bolivia as *putuku*—are spotlighted.

1300 González Carre, Enrique and **Virgilio Galdo Gutiérrez.** Introducción al procedo de socialización andina. Ayacucho, Perú, Univ. Nacional de San Cristóbal de Huamanga, 1976. 209 p., illus. (mimeo)

Essays on rites of passage (birth, haircutting, puberty, marriage and death) drawn in part on studies by the authors, and by Lorenzo Huertas Vallejo, Luis Millones, Aníbal Ponce, Efraín Morote Best and Blas Valera. Typed, mimeo format—buried for all effective purposes in an edition limited to 1,000.

1301 Hafer, Fritz. Village of commuters: ten years of change in North Highland, Peru (UNC/ED, 2:3, Oct. 1977, p. 74–87, bibl.)

A preliminary research report on the Cajamarca, Peru, community of Pariamarca, this study notes the effects of USAID and Belgian foreign development aid on a 1972–80 Peruvian plan for model village development. The author's baseline research derives from his dissertation at Indian Univ. *The people up the hill: individual progress without village participation in Pariamarca, Cajamarca, Peru* (1971).

1302 Hickman, John M. and **William T. Stuart.** Descent, alliance, and moiety in Chucuito, Peru: an explanatory sketch of Aymara social organization (in Bolton, Ralph and Enrique Mayer eds. Andean kinship and marriage [see item **1221**] p. 43–59)

Aymara social organization is analyzed from the standpoint of descent, alliance, and moiety. The conclusions are that interlocking descent and alliance systems are reflected in kinship terminology and operate through mechanisms of parallel transmission of property and kinship status. Of the moiety structure there are only surviving vestiges. [WEC]

1303 Isbell, Billie Jean. "Those who love me:" an analysis of Andean kinship and reciprocity within a ritual context (in Bolton, Ralph and Enrique Mayer eds. Andean kinship and marriage [see item **1221** and *HLAS 35:1422*] p. 81–105)

Using as her prime example the ritual cleaning of the irrigation canals, Isbell examines the various expectations that an individual has of his relatives. She distinguishes between kin-based and public institutional reciprocity, and points out that the greatest donations are expected of a male ego's male generation mates and his affines. [WEC]

1304 Lewellen, Ted. Peasants in transition: the changing economy of the Peruvian Aymara: a general systems approach. Boulder, Colo., Westview Press, 1978. 195 p., bibl., illus., maps, tables.

Study of three Aymara-speaking communities on the Lake Titicaca island of Soqa develops the author's dissertation. Questionnaire methodology points to the rise of an "Adventist elite," and 18 percent minority of families who are demonstrably more entrepreneurial, wealthier, and occupy positions of civil authority. Static study skips back to

Weber for an analysis rather than to the history of communities' dynamics.

1305 Long, Norman. Commerce and kinship in the Peruvian highland (*in* Bolton, Ralph and Enrique Mayer *eds.* Andean kinship and marriage [see item **1221**] p. 153–176)

Deals with the mechanisms used in the management of sibling and affinal relationships by individuals operating commercial enterprises. The basic argument is that entrepreneurial behavior should be examined from both the transactional and normative points of view. [WEC]

1306 ———. Intermediaries and brokers in highland Peru (Dyn [Durham Univ., Anthropological Society, Durham, U.K.] 3, 1975, p. 19–28, bibl.)

Long-distance traders in southern Peru.

1307 Malengreau, Jacques. Integration, aliénation et mythe de progrès dans une zone andine du Nord péruvien (ULB/RIS, 1, 1977, p. 101–136)

Notes from a fascinating corner of Peru—Ongara, Luya and Chachapoyas provs. in northeast Amazonas dept.—sketch a grim tale of ecological and economic displacement of peasant communities as the region is progressively integrated into the Peruvian national economy.

1308 Marzal, Manuel Maria. Estudios sobre religión campesina. Lima, Pontificia Univ. Católica del Perú, 1977. 306 p., bibl., illus.

Three studies summarize the author's earlier work on Ayaviri in southern Peru previously reported in *Allpanchis*; present a sympathetic view of culturally Andean marriage practices based on data from modern Puno and the chronicles; and outline a Joaquim Wach style religious sociology of Lower Piura, Peru.

1309 Mayer, Enrique. Beyond the nuclear family (*in* Bolton, Ralph and Enrique Mayer *eds.* Andean kinship and marriage [see item **1221**] p. 60–80)

Explores the relationship between kinship, alliance, and the recruitment of labor in the Quechua speaking community of Tangor, Pasco, Peru. Mayer argues that kinship reckoning is based on the nuclear family unit, not the individual. Most relatives are

categorized as either *masha* or *lumtshuy*, i.e. related affinally through either daughter or son. Alliance predominates over lineage in situations of resource abundance. [WEC]

1310 ———. El uso social de la coca en el mundo andino: contribución a un debate y toma de posición (AI, 38:4, oct./dic. 1978, p. 849–865)

Mayer discusses the economic and social functions of coca leaf consumption by the Andean peoples of Peru. Coca is seen as a luxury good used to create and maintain ties of friendship, as well as to symbolize group solidarity. As a luxury good coca may be replaced by alcohol, but as a cultural symbol it is irreplaceable. [WEC]

1310a Mitchell, William P. Irrigation farming in the Andes: evolutionary implications (*in* Halperin, Rhoda and James Dow *eds.* Peasant livelihood: studies in economic anthropology and cultural ecology. N.Y., St. Martin's Press, 1977, p. 36–59, tables)

Revision of *HLAS 39:1520* introduces new data concerning crops for crop cycles of planting and irrigation timing.

1311 Oliver-Smith, Anthony. Disaster rehabilitation and social change in Yungay, Peru (SAA/HO, 36:1, Spring 1977, p. 5–13, bibl.)

Parables of Peruvian social life lie in these reports of post-earthquake social reorganization: the resentment of middle and upper-class townsmen towards the egalitarian distribution of disaster relief; the rise of a stratified folk taxonomy of "need." The act of petitioning food to support workers reconstructing public works led to the fission and formalization of new political recognition for some communities. The introduction of payment in food for work had the effect of weakening communal work traditions.

1312 ———. Traditional agriculture, central places, and post-disaster urban relocation in Peru (AAA/AE, 4:1, Feb. 1977, p. 102–116, bibl., maps, tables)

Draws upon the theories of Darrell E. LaLone, Nyle K. Walton, Bruce Trigger, and David Grove among others to apply central place concepts to resettlement patterns after the May 1970 earthquake in the Callejón de Huaylas. Crop schedules, urban facilities and hinterland/center relationships are among the data analyzed to demonstrate the logic of population relocation.

1312a Orlove, Benjamin Sebastian. Against a definition of peasantries: agrarian production in Andean Peru (*in* Halperin, Rhoda and James Dow *eds*. Peasant livelihood: studies in economic anthropology and cultural ecology. N.Y., St. Martin's Press, 1977, p. 22–35)

Describes strategies for maximizing pasture resources in Espinar prov., Peru: occasional cultivation of *oca*, *olluco* or potatoes in the dung compost of animal corrals, digging shallow depressions to promote early rainy season grass growth, planting in furrows to promote wild grass regeneration in fallow cycles and the important rotation of sections between long fallow use for pasture and shorter term cultivation—a system known by a variety of terms: *laymi* (Quecha), *suerte* (Spanish), *aynoka* (Aymara).

1313 ———. Alpacas, sheep, and men: the wool export economy and regional society in southern Peru. N.Y., Academic Press, 1977. 270 p., bibl., maps, plates, tables.

This monograph stands alone as a fully realized study of the cultural ecology of an Andean micro-region in the economic environment of the world market system. The export commodity, wool, articulates a hierarchy of different orders of sociopolitical organization, from the pastoral communities of the high puna through English and other international brokers. The complexities and contradictions are explored in a smooth literary style, warm with humanizing anecdotes drawn from Orlove's understanding of and sympathy with the people of the Sicuani, Peru, area. Includes glossary and index.

1313a ———. Inequality among peasants: the forms and uses of reciprocal exchange in Andean Peru (*in* Halperin, Rhoda and James Dow *eds*. Peasant livelihood: studies in economic anthropology and cultural ecology. N.Y., St. Martin's Press, 1977, p. 201–214)

Discusses cases of ayni and mink'a reciprocal exchanges to demonstrate how individuals use these social forms to their own economic advantage. However, the characterization of these forms as an alternative to the market economy prevents an analysis of how market values penetrate and distort equality in reciprocal exchanges.

1314 ———. Integration through production: the use of zonation in Espinar (AAA/AE, 4:1, Feb. 1977, p. 84–101, bibl., maps)

The agriculturalists of Espinar prov. in southern Peru manage two differentiated ecozones: 1) a lower slope where tubers, grains and other crops are cultivated; and 2) a high altitude zone where llamas, alpacas, sheep and some cattle, horses, and donkeys are pastured. Herding is transhumant. The practices described of planting lower zone areas also used as corrals and of digging moisture retaining *quochawinas* and furrows demonstrate the interrelated use of the lower zone for both cultivation and for pasture. For geographer's comment, see item **5552**.

1315 ———. Surimana: decaímiento de una zona y decadencia de un pueblo (Antropología Andina [Centro de Estudios Andinos, Cuzco, Peru] 1/2, 1976, p. 75–106, bibl., illus., maps)

This could be retitled "The Surimana By-Pass." Details including maps, sketch the decline of a region, as new transportation routes based on roads and vehicular technology regrouped trade networks away from Surimana and towards the now fast-growing Sicuani in southern Peru.

1316 Saco Miró Quesada, Alfredo. Incas sin tierra. Lima, Pontificia Univ. del Perú, Programa de Ciencias Sociales, Taller de Investigación Rural, 1977. 113 p., illus. (mimeo)

First publication of a 1940s study. Discusses status of landlessness from Inca times through colonial period and focuses on cases from La Oroya, Chicama, and especially the Casa Grande hacienda. Reifies the *comunidad indígena* as romanticized by Castro Pozo to the reobtainable, egalitarian ideal.

1317 Sánchez Farfán, Jorge. Autoridades tradicionales en algunas comunidades del Cusco (Antropología Andina [Centro de Estudios Andinos, Cuzco, Peru] 1/2, 1976, p. 136–155, bibl.)

Role rungs in what Mesoamericanists call the "ladder" of politico-religious *cargos* are described for Viacha, P'isac, Calca and near-by communities. Civil authority roles were much eroded in their importance by the long influence of townsmen and landlords; religious roles gained halos of civil authority.

1318 Sharon, Douglas. Becoming a *curandero* in Peru (*in* Wilbert, Johannes ed. Enculturation in Latin America: an anthology [see item **260**] p. 359–375, bibl.)

Provides the personal biography of the folk-curer Eduardo of Trujillo to emphasize his calling and training. Eduardo's curing practices were the subject of Sharon's dissertation, other articles and a book (see item **1319**). Eduardo's life story is as fascinating as Borges' fiction.

1319 ———. Wizard of the four winds: a shaman's story. N.Y., The Free Press, 1978. 222 p., bibl., illus., plates.

The "shaman's story" occupies few pages and has been told before in earlier publications; the rest consists of analysis and analogies, setting Eduardo, the Peruvian Trujillo shaman, in the context of the literature on shamanism and cosmology in South and Mesoamerica.

1320 Soto Quijano, Clemente; Arturo Urbano San Martín; and Zenón E. Vargas Morales. Empobrecimiento absoluto y relativo: Paramonga. Lima, Univ. Nacional Mayor de San Marcos, 1977. 112 p., bibl., illus. (Seminario histórico rural andina) (mimeo)

W.R. Grade company archives and a questionnaire administered to workers at Paramonga are combined to demonstrate the thesis that laborers at Paramonga have suffered an absolute decline in income and a relative decline in standard of living, despite agrarian reform.

1321 Stein, William W. Modernización y retroceso del mito: diagnosis por medio de la magia y curación en el pueblo de Vicos, Perú (III/AI, 37:3, julio/sept. 1977, p. 671–747, table)

In another tour-de-force reanalysis of the Peru-Cornell Vicos archives, Stein analyzes health. Chronic malnutrition, parasites (in 99 percent of the population), frequent skin, eye and gastrointestinal or respiratory ailments and periodic epidemics are the dismal parameters of health among Viscosinos. Explanations include the usual Andean folk illness-bad air, *susto*, soul consumption by ancient ghosts and cures—jungle herbs, transferring injuries to guinea pigs. Vicosinos pay small fortunes for useless cures to folkhealers and physicians alike. They prefer "preventative" health rituals, tribute payment to

potential disease wielding forces. Comparisons of medical examinations with cases documented in terms of folk taxonomies and folk cures reveal the fallacy of folk disease ideology.

1322 ———. A test of Peru's "Indian problem" through the use of a personal document (Papers in Anthropology [Univ. of Oklahoma, Dept. of Anthropology, Norman] 18:2, 1977, p. 103–125, bibl.)

Stein quotes a number of leading scholars' definitions of the "Indian problem" (Spaulding, Pike, Davies, Malpica, Mariátegui, Mayer, Cotler, Quijano, Piel, Valcárcel, Pease, et. al.) but gives the last work to a Vicosino: "Julián Colonia," who, on the basis of his own personal experience, says: "I think the *mishtis* are the same as we are except they know how to read and speak Spanish, have more opportunities to get money . . . while we spend every day working in the fields just to exist."

1323 Urton, Gary. Beasts and geometry: some constellations of the Peruvian quechuas (AI/A, 73:1/2, 1978, p. 32–40, bibl., illus.)

Preliminary report names, locates and characterizes the single stars, star-to-star constellations and "black," or silhouette, constellations based on data from native Quechua in three Cuzco, Peru, area villages.

1324 Van den Berghe, Pierre L. El Cargo de las Animas: mortuary rituals and the cargo system in highland Peru (CUA/AQ, 51:2, April 1978, p. 129–136, bibl.)

Report concerns one case of ritual disinterment and reinterment of a corpse by the deceased's primary relatives, acting in a *mayordomío de las ánimas*, during All Souls Day observances in San Jerónimo, Cuzco, Peru.

1325 Wagner, Catherine A. Coca y estructura cultural en los Andes peruanos (IPA/AP, 9, 1976, p. 193–223, bibl., illus.)

Presents an understanding of the etiquette of chewing coca in Sonqo community, Cuzco dept., Peru. Coca chewing evokes Quechua concepts concerning sacred places, time and the nature of the *ayllu* as a neighborhood. Coca chewing is simultaneously a social and ritual act which requires deference and courtesies to place spirits and to one's human companions.

1326 **Webster, Steven S.** Kinship and affinity in a native Quechua community (*in* Bolton, Ralph and Enrique Mayer *eds.* Andean kinship and marriage [see item 1221 and *HLAS* 35:1504] p. 28–42)

Discusses cognatic kin groupings and affinal alliances as adaptive strategies for handling resource fluctuation and scarcity. The article contains clear kinship charts, and touches on the incorporation and reinterpretation of Spanish kin terms by Andean society. [WEC]

1327 **Williams, Lyndon S.** Land use intensity and farm size in highland Cuzco, Peru (JDA, 11, Jan. 1977, p. 185–203)

Suggests that the redistribution of land on large estates in highland Cuzco will lead to more intensive land use. At the same time, land formerly worked by the recipients of the redistributed land will presumably be worked less intensively.

1328 **Winterhalder, Bruce; Robert Larsen; and R. Brooke Thomas.** Dung as an essential resource in a highland Peruvian community (Human Ecology [Plenum, N.Y.] 1:2, April 1974, p. 89–104, bibl., illus., map, tables)

Dung is critical as a source of fuel and of fertilizer, particularly on higher altitude fields rotated into production after long fallows. Authors estimate 134 hectars of grazing land can support 25 sheep, 10 cattle and 38 llamas which in turn would provide sufficient dung for a single family's dung requirements. Data based on Nuñoa, Peru.

1329 **Zuidema, R.T.** The Inca kinship system: a new theoretical view (*in* Bolton, Ralph and Enrique Mayer *eds.* Andean kinship and marriage [see item 1221] p. 240–281)

Discusses the structure of Inca kin terminology, the structure of different social contexts, and the use of a given kin term or equation in a specific social context. Problems found in ethnohistorical sources dealing with the Cuzco kinship system at the time of the Spanish conquest are found to be similar to those characteristic of contemporary Quechua kinship systems. [WEC]

VENEZUELA

1330 *Montalbán.* Univ. Católica Andrés Bello, Facultad de Humanidades y Educación, Instituto Humanístico de Investigación. No. 7, 1977–. Caracas.

Massive issue (985 p.) of journal *Montalbán* devoted to transcriptions of documents relating to the indigenous peoples of Venezuela, from royal cédulas of the colonial period through modern decrees, court decisions, treaties, etc. Represents a gold mine of unanalyzed data presented as follows:

Cesáreo de Armellada "Fuero Indígena Venezolano" p. 7–424

Carmela Bentivenga de Napolitano "Compilación y Prólogo: Cedulario Indígena Venezolano, 1501–1812" p. 425–754

Joaquín Gabaldón Márquez "Compilación y Prólogo: Fuero Indígena Venezolano" p. 755–984.

LINGUISTICS

ALAN C. WARES, *Bibliographer, Summer Institute of Linguistics*

SOCIOLINGUISTIC STUDIES IN RECENT YEARS have included research in bilingualism in Mexico (items 1347 and 1407) and Paraguay (item 1352), in criminal jargon in Peru (item 1341), and in regional Spanish of Peru (item 1411) and of Chile (item 1336). The way in which politics impinges upon linguistics is apparent in discussions of the "oppressed" languages of Peru and Bolivia (item 1331), in the government-approved alphabets of Guatemala (item 1358), and in the teaching of Spanish to speakers of minority languages in Mexico by using the "direct method" (item 1344). Perhaps anticipating the eventual disappearance of minority languages, the Investigation Center for Social Integration in Mexico has begun an archival program for preserving something of the linguistic heritage of that country (items 1354, 1377 and 1408).

Language description continues to be the theme of many of the works in this section. Two works have been written on Mataco, a language of Argentina (items **1432** and **1434**), and two on the Barasano of Colombia (items **1360** and **1424**). Comparative studies of Uto-Aztecan (items **1346** and **1380**) are worth mentioning. The works of 16th-century writers continue to be of interest as shown by the republication of Basalenque's grammar of Matlatzinca (item **1340**) and the consideration of Lugo's grammar of Mosca (item **1334**).

It is fitting to mention here the death of Edward Moser, ethnographer and linguist of the Summer Institute of Linguistics whose study of the language and culture of the Seri Indians of Sonora, Mexico, extended over a quarter of a century.

1331 Albó, Xavier. El futuro de los idiomas oprimidos en Los Andes. Lima, Univ. Nacional Mayor de San Marcos, Centro de Investigación de Lingüística Aplicada, 1977. 28 l., bibl., table (Documento, 33)

"Oppressed languages" refers to large language groups of little prestige, as Quechua and Aymara in Peru and Bolivia, where native speakers of these were obliged to learn Spanish to gain standing in the community. Gives historical sketch of language policies in these countries from the 16th century to the present and considers dilemmas in planning for the future.

1332 ———. Idiomas, escuelas y radios en Bolivia. Lima, Univ. Nacional Mayor de San Marcos, Centro de Investigación de Lingüística Aplicada, 1977. 55 l., bibl., map, tables (Documento, 35)

Radio stations in the Quechua- and Aymara-speaking areas of Bolivia customarily schedule up to four hours a day of broadcasting in these languages. These vernacular programs are having a psychological effect on speakers of these "oppressed languages" in giving them a respect for their mother tongue.

1333 Albores, Beatriz A. Trilingüismo y prestigio en un pueblo náhuatl del estado de México (UNAM/AL, 14, 1976, p. 239–254, tables)

Sociolinguistic study of a Spanish-and-Nahuatl speaking town (Jalatlalco) and an Otomí town (Tilapa), situated across the street from each other in the state of Mexico, Mex.

1334 Alvar, Manuel. La gramática mosca de Fray Bernardo de Lugo (ICC/T, 32:3, sept./dic. 1977, p. 461–500)

Misunderstanding the Chibcha word for "people" (*muisca*), the early Spanish chroniclers called them *Mosca*. Bernardo de Lugo learned their language and described it,

following the customary Latin model, in the early 17th century. Alvar discusses the phonetic value of symbols used by Lugo and compares Lugo's work with another grammar of Chibcha edited by E. Uricoechea and published in 1871. Although it once numbered close to a million speakers, the language became extinct in the 18th century.

1335 Arango M., Francisco. Lenguas indígenas del Vaupés: pequeño diccionario. Medellín, Colombia, Museo Etnográfico Miguel Angel Builes, 1973. 29 p., tables.

Comparative 528-item vocabularies of Tucano, Desano, Carapana, Guanano, Piratapuya, and Cubeo, Tucanoan languages of Colombia. Although there is no introduction to explain the orthography or the relationships of the languages to each other, this might prove a useful work for comparative studies in this field.

1336 Araya, Guillermo and others. Atlas lingüístico-etnográfico del sur de Chile, Alesuch. t. 1. Valdivia, Univ. Austral de Chile, Instituto de Filología [and] Editorial Andrés Bello, 1973. 1 v. (Unpaged) illus., maps.

Consists of more than 300 maps of five provinces of Chile, each map representing some Spanish word or expression with its variations in different localities.

1337 Barrera Marin, Alfredo; Alfredo Barrera Vázquez; and Rosa María López Franco. Nomenclatura etnobotánica maya: una interpretación taxonómica. Colaboraciones especiales de Alma D.L. Orozco Segovia and others. México, Secretaría de Educación Pública (SEP), Instituto Nacional de Antropología e Historia, Centro Regional del Sureste, 1976. 537 p., bibl., illus., tables (Col. Científica, 36: etnología)

Four glossaries related to the eth- nobotany of the Yucatán peninsula, Mexico. Glossary A lists Mayan words used in connection with work in the fields (242 items); B lists Mayan names of plants with their scientific Latin names (1721 items); C lists the scientific plant names with their Mayan equivalent (909 items); and D lists plants with a religio-magic significance and those related to ancient Mayan deities (not numbered). Includes chapter on etymology of Mayan plant names and analysis of the data.

1338 Barrera Vázquez, Alfredo. La familia lingüística mayana (UY/R, 20:116, marzo/abril 1978, p. 39–47)

Mayan languages began to diversify some 3,000 years ago, judging from lexicostatistical data, having originated in the highlands of Guatemala about 1,000 years before that. Subdivisions are discussed as in a previous article (see item **1339**).

1339 ———. El gran diccionario maya en preparación (UY/R, 19:114, nov./dic. 1977, p. 76–83)

Mayan languages may be subdivided into four groups, viz., Huastecan, Maya proper (of the Yucatán Peninsula); Cholan (including Chol, Chontal, Tzeltal, Tzotzil, and Tojolabal); and Quichean. A comprehensive Mayan dictionary, begun in 1974, takes all these into consideration.

1340 Basalenque, Diego de. Arte y vocabulario de la lengua matlaltzinga vuelto a la castellana. Versión paleográfica de María Elena Bribiesca S. Estudio preliminar de Leonardo Manrique C. México, Biblioteca Enciclopedica del Estado de México, 1975. 324 p., facsims. (Biblioteca, 33)

New edition of 16th-century grammar of Matlatzinca, and Otopamean language of the state of Mexico, Mex., of about 2,000 speakers. A monumental work, although based on the Latin model.

Basso, Ellen B. ed. Carib-speaking Indians: culture, society and language. See item **1003**.

Bebel-Gisler, Dany and **Laënnec Hurbon.** Cultures et pouvoir dans la Caraïbe: langue créole, vaudou, sectes religieuses en Guadeloupe et en Haïti. See item **1004**.

1341 Bendezú Neyra, Guillermo E. Vocabulario hampesco. Ayacucho, Perú, Ediciones Kuntur, 1975. 159 p.

Dictionary of jargon used by the criminal classes of Peru. Incomplete, in that entries are from A to G only.

1342 Berlin, Brent. Sumario de la primera expedición etnobotánica al Río Alto Marañón, Departamento de Amazonas, Perú (Amazonia Peruana [Centro Amazónico de Antropología y Aplicación Práctica, Lima] 1:2, julio 1977, p. 87–100, bibl.)

Results of a study of plant use by Aguaruna Indians of the western Upper Marañón River area of Peru suggest a well-developed classification system for the plants used in the area. Lists Indian names of 62 plants and their varieties.

Bozzoli de Wille, María. Narraciones bribris. See item **887**.

1343 Bravo, Domingo A. Diccionario castellano-quichua santiagueño. B.A., EUDEBA, 1977. 158 p., bibl.

Vocabulary of the Santiago del Estero (Argentina) dialect of Quechua, consisting of about 12,000 entries.

1344 Bravo Ahuja, Gloria. Los materiales didácticos para la enseñanza del español a los indígenas mexicanos. v. 1, De la conquista a la revolución; v. 2, Las cartillas, pt. 1, Evaluación y crítica; v. 3, Las cartillas, pt. 2, Evaluación y crítica; v. 4, Propuesta de una planeación lingüística. México, Secretaría de Educación Pública (SEP), 1976. 4 v. (135, 190, 147, 220 p.) facsims., illus., plates, tables (SepSetentas, 312/315)

Examines literacy methods designed for Mexican Indians from the 16th century to the present and finds fault with them for not teaching Spanish. Uses illustrations of many primers published by the Instituto Lingüístico de Verano (Summer Institute of Linguistics in Mexico) and tables of statistics to reinforce this criticism. Vol. 4 describes the goals of the Institute of Investigation and Social Integration of the State of Oaxaca which the author established while her husband (later appointed Mexico's Minister of Education) was Governor of Oaxaca. Favors the direct method of teaching Spanish to the Indians of Mexico.

Briggs, Luch Therina. A critical survey of the literature on the Aymara language. See item **19**.

1345 Cadogan, León. En torno al "guaraní paraguayano" o "coloquial" (UTIEH/C, 14, 1970, p. 31–41)

Claims that many works on Guaraní do not deal with the language of the rural indigenes but with *guaraní culto*, a hybrid of Spanish and Guaraní. Lists 49 corrections to be made in Gregores and Suárez's *Description of colloquial Guaraní* (see *HLAS 31:2342*).

1346 Campbell, Lyle and **Ronald W. Langacker.** Proto-Aztecan vowels: pts. 1/3 (IU/IJAL, 44:1, April 1978, p. 85–102, bibl., illus., tables; 44:3, July 1978, p. 197–210, tables; 44:4, Oct. 1978, p. 262–279)

Data from Pochutec, an extinct Uto-Aztecan language of Oaxaca, Mex., seem to indicate that Pochutec was coordinate with General Aztec, a reconstruction from other Uto-Aztecan languages of Mexico and San Salvador. In pt. 1 of this three-part study, vowel correspondences listed by Boas (1912) are re-examined and new sets of correspondences made. Proto-Uto-Aztecan fifth vowel is reconstructed as **i rather than **e. Pt. 2 proposes two subgroupings of Uto-Aztecan languages: Southern Uto-Aztecan (Pimic, Taracahitic, Corachol, and Aztecan) and Aztecan-Corachol as a subfamily. Proto-Aztecan developed from Proto-Uto-Aztecan through a series of 11 changes, according to this hypothesis. Pt. 3 cites Aztecan cognate sets (198) and Uto-Aztecan cognate sets (89) in support of reconstructed forms of Proto-Aztecan and Proto-Uto-Aztecan.

1347 Cárdenas de Mella, María Cristina. Bilingüismo y biculturalismo (UC/A, 33, abril 1978, p. 125–145, tables)

Although language may be considered a product of culture, there are instances of people living in different cultures but speaking the same language and also of people speaking different languages but sharing the same culture. Meaning in various contexts is discussed in terms of the "signifying" (*significante*) and the "signified" (*significado*).

1348 Casad, Eugene H. Location and direction in Cora discourse (IU/AL, 19:5, May 1977, p. 216–241, bibl., tables)

Native speakers of Cora, a Uto-Aztecan language of western Mexico, use particles, adverbs, prefixes of verbs of motion and position, and stems of motion verbs to indicate the three basic orientations of the locative-directional system of their language. These orientations are a referential boundary that the speaker has in mind, distance, and position relative to a slope.

1349 Castillo Mathieu, Nicolás del. Léxico caribe en el Caribe Insular: pts. 1/2 (ICC/T, 32:2, mayo/agosto 1977, p. 316–373, bibl.; 32:3, sept./dic. 1977, p. 544–652, bibl.)

Pt. 1 of this two-part article examines the comparative vocabulary of Carib languages, with a consideration of their relationships and language classification. Pt. 2 lists lexical entries from various sources, comparing items from island Carib with those from Carib languages of South America.

1350 Clark, Lawrence E. Linguistic acculturation in Sayula Popoluca (IU/IJAL, 43:2, April 1977, p. 128–138, tables)

Discusses phonological changes in Sayula Popoluca due to contact with Spanish since the conquest of Mexico. Proposes 15 rules to account for changes. Lists 44 borrowed words from the earliest period of contact (1520–1650) and 25 from the second (1650–1900). Borrowings during the past three quarters of a century were too numerous to list.

1351 Córdova, Carlos J. Cestmir Luokotka y la clasificación de las lenguas aborígenes del Ecuador (CCE/CHA, 24:41, 1974, p. 173–183)

Lists corrections to be made in Loukotka's *Classification of the South American Indian languages*, especially as regards the location of several Ecuadorian Indian tribes and their state of civilization. Mentions particularly the Jívaros and the Aucas, among whom profound sociological changes have taken place in recent decades.

1352 Corvalán, Grazziella. Estudios sociolingüísticos en el Paraguay. 2. ed. Asunción, Centro Paraguayo de Estudios Sociológicos [and] Centro Paraguayo de Documentación Social, 1976. 32 p. (Serie bibliográfica)

Bibliography of works dealing with Guaraní, bilingualism, and attitudes toward language in Paraguay.

1353 Crawford, James M. Nominalization in Cocopa (*in* Hokan-Yuman Languages Workshop, Salt Lake City, 1977. Proceedings of the 1977 Hokan-Yuman Languages Workshop, held at University of Utah, Salt Lake City, June 21–23, 1977 [see item **1375**] p. 43–53, tables)

Nouns in Cocopa (a Yuman language of Mexico and Arizona) may be formed from verbs by prefixing k ^{w}- or ʔa-. The former has definite reference ("the one who . . ."); the latter indefinite ("someone who . . .").

1354 Daly, John and **Margarita Holland de Daly** *comps.* Mixteco: Santa María Peñoles, Oaxaca. México, Centro de Investigación para la Integración Social, 1977. 153 p., bibl., map, tables (Archivo de lenguas indígenas de México, 3)

Describes the phonology of the Peñoles dialect of Mixtec, followed by language text, a translation of 594 Spanish sentences, and a 17-page lexicon.

1355 Delgaty, Alfa Hurley de and **Agustín Ruiz Sánchez** *comps.* Diccionario tzotzil de San Andrés, con variaciones dialectales: tzotzil-español, español-tzotzil. México, Instituto Lingüístico de Verano, 1978. 481 p., bibl, illus., maps, tables (Serie de vocabularios y diccionarios indígenas Mariano Silva y Aceves, 22)

Although based mainly on the San Andrés dialect of Tzotzil (a Mayan language of Chiapas, Mexico, of more than 100,000 speakers), this dictionary includes variations from Chamula, Chenalhó, Ixtapa, and Zinacantán. References to the Huixtán dialect are not included, as the variations are more numerous than for the other dialects. In addition to the Tzotzil-Spanish section (6,000 entries) and the Spanish-Tzotzil (4,000 entries), there is a 70-page description of the grammar of Tzotzil.

1356 Edwards, Walter F. A preliminary sketch of Arekuna—Carib—phonology (IU/IJAL, 44:3, July 1978, p. 223–227, tables)

Distinctive feature analysis of vowels and consonants of Arekuna, a Carib language of Guayana (100 speakers), Venezuela (14,000), and Brazil (1,500).

1357 Fernández Arévalos, Evelio. Presupuestos para una "política lingüística" en el Paraguay (UTIEH/C, 14, 1970, p. 23–29)

General discussion of language and culture, with some observations on Guaraní and Spanish in Paraguay.

1358 Fleming, Ilah *comp.* Alfabeto de las lenguas mayances. Guatemala, Instituto Indigenista Nacional, 1977. 125 p., illus., tables.

Presents alphabets approved officially by the Ministry of Education of Guatemala for writing 20 indigenous languages of that country. Includes explanation of the symbols and diacritics used as well as a glossary of linguistic terms.

1359 ———— and **Ronald K. Dennis.** Tol—Jicaque: phonology (IU/IJAL, 43:2, April 1977, p. 121–127, tables)

Tol has 20 consonant phonemes, six vowels, two semivowels, and stress. There are three sets of voiceless stops: plain, aspirated, and glottalized. Tol is a Hokan language of Honduras.

1360 Franco García, Germán and **José Raúl Monguí Sánchez.** Gramática yebamasa: lingüística aplicada. Informante y recolectora de datos de Bertha Díaz. Bogotá, Univ. Social Católica de La Salle, Depto. de Idiomas, 1975. 237 p., map, tables.

Phonology, morphology, syntax, and lexicon of Yebámasá (also known as Barasano), an Eastern Tucanoan language of Colombia, spoken as a lingua franca by several tribes of that country. Phonemic system consists of 15 consonants and five vowels in addition to nasalization, which may occur with any of the vowels. Lexicon includes almost 8000 items.

1361 García de León, Antonio. Los elementos del Tzotzil colonial y moderno. México, UNAM, Coordinación de Humanidades, 1971. 107 p., bibl., map, tables (Centro de estudios mayas. Serie cuadernos, 7)

Brief discussion of colonial works on Tzotzil (a Mayan language of Chiapas, Mex.), followed by an extensive treatment of the phonology (21 consonants, five vowels) and grammar, a list of lexical elements, a Spanish-Tzotzil vocabulary, and an analyzed colonial text.

1362 ————. El trabajo educativo y su relación con algunos aspectos de sociolingüística (INAH/A, 5:53, 1974/1975, p. 155–170, bibl.)

Argues that little has been done in Mexico in using indigenous languages in education, owing to capitalist exploitation. Presents linguistic data on class markers and on colors in Chol, a Mayan language of Chiapas, Mex.

1363 García-Rendueles, Manuel A. Bibliografía de la familia lingüística jibaroana (Amazonia Peruana [Centro Amazónico de Antropología y Aplicación Práctica, Lima] 1:2, julio 1977, p. 171–178)

Selective bibliography of indigenous groups of Peru of the Jivaroan language family.

1364 Geoffroy Rivas, Pedro. Fonología del Masiewalli de náhuatl de Tetelcingo (MNDJG/A, 42/48, 1968/1975, p. 83–99, bibl., tables)

Presents phonology and selected vocabulary of the Tetelcingo (Morelos, Mex.) dialect of Nahuatl.

1365 Golbert de Goodbar, Perla. Epu peñiwen (los dos hermanos): cuento tradicional araucano. Transcripción fonológica, traducción y análisis. B.A., Centro de Investigaciones en Ciencias de la Educación (CICE), Sección Lenguas Indígenas, 1975. 184 p., plate (Documento de trabajo, 9)

Folklore text, with translation and morphological analysis, in Araucano, an Araucanian language of 40,000 speakers in Argentina; the same language is called Mapuche in Chile, where there are 200,000 speakers.

1366 Grajeda Challco, Braulio and Asís Orlando Vela Flores. Gramática quechua: enciclopedia de gramática quechua integral. Lima, Ediciones Instituto Superior de Quechua del Perú (INSUQ), 1976. 273 p., bibl., tables.

Describes Quechua in terms of Latin grammar.

1367 Griffiths, Glyn and Cynthia Griffiths. Aspectos da língua Kadiwéu. Brasília, Summer Institute of Linguistics, 1976. 200 p., tables (Série Lingüística, 6)

Classification of Kadiwéu, hitherto uncertain, may be effected as a result of these linguistic studies which are based on intermittent field work between 1958 and 1974. There are about 500 speakers of this language, living in the southern part of the state of Mato Grosso, Brazil. Titles of the articles, the first five of which bear the name of the first author only, are: "A Estrutura de Dois Estilos Discursivos na Língua Kadiwéu" p. 7–34; "O Elemento Interrogativo em Kadiwéu" p.

35–41; "Verbos Kadiwéus" p. 42–97; "O Sistema Pronominal na Língua Kadiwéu" p. 98–108; "Substantivos Kadiwéu" p. 109–129; "Relatório Fonêmico do Kadiwéu" p. 130–156; "Formulário dos Vocabulários Padrões para Estudos Comparativos Preliminares nas Línguas Indígenas Brasileiras" p. 157–200.

1368 Grimes, Joseph E. *ed.* Papers on discourse. Dallas, Tex., Summer Institute of Linguistics, 1978. 389 p., bibl., tables (Summer Institute of Linguistics publications in linguistics and related fields, 51)

Extended field seminars in various parts of the world resulted in 33 articles on discourse analysis of indigenous languages. There are six general groupings of the articles: 1) Morphology and Discourse; 2a) Theme-Oriented Referential Strategies; 2b) Sequence-Oriented Referential Strategies; 3) Overall Structure; 4) Particles; 5) Linkage; and 6) Special Signals. Only one of these articles deals with a language of Latin America (see item **1423**).

1369 Groth, Christa. *Here* and *there* in Canamarí (IU/AL, 19:5, May 1977, p. 203–215, tables)

Spatial deictic adverbs, verbs of direction and trajectory, and directional suffixes are used as indications of orientation in Canamarí, a Brazilian Indian language of approximately 850 speakers.

1370 Hardman, Martha J. Proto-jaqui: reconstrucción del sistema de personas gramaticales (PEMN/R, 41, 1975, p. 433–456)

Comparison of verb forms of Aymara, Jaqaru, and Kawki leads to reconstruction of 13 pronominal suffixes in the "proto" form of these languages (see *HLAS 39:1657*). Two major and seven minor rules account for the development of modern forms.

1371 Hasler, Juan A. Datos acerca del pipil de los tuxtlas (INAH/B, 17, abril/junio 1976, p. 9–18)

Presents phonological and brief morphological analysis of a dialect of Nahuatl spoken in the vicinity of San Andrés Tuxtla, Veracruz, Mexico. Vocabulary includes several words borrowed from Popoluca.

1372 Heath, Jeffrey. Uto-Aztecan morphophonemics (IU/IJAL, 43:1, Jan. 1977, p. 27–36, table)

Discusses morphophonemic processes

(reduplication, stress alteration, "hardening," and others) in Proto-Northern- and Proto-Southern-Uto-Aztecan which developed from Proto-Uto-Aztecan.

1373 ———. Uto-Aztecan *na-class verbs (IU/IJAL, 44:3, July 1978, p. 211–222, tables)

Reconstructs main morphological features of *na-class for Proto-Uto-Aztecan and for Proto-Northern- and Proto-Southern-Uto-Aztecan. This class has bisyllabic roots and thematic variation, the themes being stem-grade *CV'CV- or reduplicated CV-CVCV-plus one or more thematic suffixes.

1374 Hill, Jane and **Kenneth Hill.** Language death and relexification in Tlaxcalan Nahuatl (LING, 191, 1977, p. 55–69, bibl., map)

Describes methods and results of survey of indigenous language use in the state of Tlaxcala, Mex. Deficient in their understanding of Spanish, Indians nevertheless use many borrowed words, but feel that their native language, Nahuatl, has been "spoiled" by the mixture. This relexification contributes to the death of the language, "Indianness" being expressed now in other ways than by the use of Nahuatl.

1375 Hokan-Yuman Languages Workshop, *Salt Lake City, 1977.* Proceedings of the 1977 Hokan-Yuman Languages Workshop, held at University of Utah, Salt Lake City, June 21–23, 1977. Edited by James E. Redden. Carbondale, Southern Illinois Univ., Dept. of Linguistics, 1977. 92 p., bibl. (Occasional papers on linguistics, 2)

Yuman and Hokan languages are spoken by relatively small groups of Indians scattered over a wide area extending from the Colorado River in the southwestern US to southern Mesoamerica. Of the seven articles included in this collection, three pertain specifically to indigenous languages of Mexico (see items **1353, 1400** and **1436**).

1376 Hollenbach, Fernando and **Elena E. de Hollenbach** comps. Trique: San Juan Copala, Oaxaca. Oaxaca, Mex., Instituto de Investigación e Integración Social del Estado de Oaxaca, 1975. 157 p., bibl., tables (Archivo de lenguas indígenas del estado de Oaxaca, 2)

Description of Trique phonology, followed by analyzed language text, a translation of 594 Spanish sentences, and a brief lex-

icon. Trique is a Mixtecan language of the state of Oaxaca, Mex.

1377 Jamieson, Allan and **Ernesto Tejeda** comps. Mazateco: Chiquihuitlán, Oaxaca. México, Centro de Investigación para la Integración Social, 1978. 151 p., bibl., map, tables (Archivo de lenguas indígenas de México, 5)

Describes phonology of Chiquihuitlán Mazatec, with analyzed language text and translation of more than 600 Spanish sentences and a brief lexicon.

Justus, Joyce Bennett. Language and national integration: the Jamaican case. See item **1043**.

1378 Key, Mary Ritchie. Araucanian genetic relationships (IU/IJAL, 44:4, Oct. 1978, p. 280–293, bibl., tables)

Describes phonology of Mapuche (an Araucanian language of Chile and Argentina of a quarter of a million speakers altogether) and finds correspondences with Tacanan and Panoan languages of Bolivia and Peru. Some of the cognate forms cited are from documents of the colonial era.

1379 Kondo, Víctor. A tagmemic description of Guahibo: sentence to morpheme. Bogotá, Ministerio de Gobierno, Instituto Lingüístico de Verano, 1975. 139 l., tables.

Grammatical analysis of Guahibo, a Guahiban language of Colombia and Venezuela, of about 20,000 speakers.

1380 Langacker, Ronald W. The syntax of postpositions in Uto-Aztecan (IU/IJAL, 43:1, Jan. 1977, p. 11–21, bibl., tables)

Data from 15 Uto-Aztecan languages are examined and syntactic reconstruction attempted. Development of postpositions needs study "before we can determine what portions of what postpositions can validly be compared for purposes of reconstruction."

1381 ——— ed. An overview of Uto-Aztecan grammar. v. 1, Studies in Uto-Aztecan grammar. Dallas, Tex., Summer Institute of Linguistics [and] Univ. of Texas, Arlington, 1977. 199 p., bibl., table (Publications in linguistics, 56)

General introduction to a three-volume set of grammatical sketches that results from a workshop on Uto-Aztecan languages sponsored by the Summer Institute of Linguistics in Mexico. Articles in the two following volumes are expected to provide material for comparative studies in Uto-Aztecan languages.

1382 Lastra de Suárez, Yolanda and **Fernando Horcasitas.** El náhuatl en el oriente del Estado de México (UNAM/AA, 14, 1977, p. 165–226, bibl., plates, tables)

Describes search for speakers of Nahuatl in 31 municipalities of the eastern part of the state of Mexico and compares results with number of speakers recorded in the 1970 census, as in an earlier study carried out in the Federal District (see *HLAS 39:1680*). Maps indicate areas of phonological, morphological, and lexical distinctions. Appendix includes 15 word lists, sentences, and two brief texts.

1383 *Latin American Indian Literatures.* Univ. of Pittsburgh, Dept. of Hispanic Languages and Center for International Studies, Center for Latin American Studies. Vol. 1, No. 1, Spring 1977–. Pittsburgh, Pa.

Indigenous literatures of Latin America will be the theme of this new journal whose first issue consists of two articles, three book reviews, a bibliography of recent works on the subject, and a collection of brief items.

Laughlin, Robert M. Of cabbages and kings: tales from Zinacantan. See item **937**.

1384 Lefebvre, Claire. Linguistic survey of Cuzco Quechua: sampling procedures and data collection (IJ/AL, 18:7, Oct. 1976, p. 328–339, bibl., tables)

Describes methods of gathering and recording linguistic data in Cuzco, Peru, where Quechua is widely spoken or understood by all social classes.

1385 Levinsohn, Stephen. Una gramática pedagógica del inga. pt. 1. Traducción de Raul Mongui. Bogotá, Ministerio de Gobierno, Dirección General de Integración y Desarrollo de la Comunidad, División Operativa de Asuntos Indígenas, Instituto Lingüístico de Verano, 1974. 85 l.

Traditional type of grammar of Inga, a Quechumaran language of Colombia, in 20 lessons, with vocabulary.

Lieberman, Dena and **William W. Dressler.** Bilingualism and cognition of St. Lucian disease terms. See item **1055**.

1386 Lionnet, A. Relaciones del varojío con el mayo y el tarahumar (UNAM/AA, 14, 1977, p. 227–242, tables)

Comparison of Northern, Central, and Western dialects of Varojío with Mayo (all Uto-Aztecan languages of northern Mexico) results in a "Prototaracahita" from which developed Mayo and Tarahumara. On this hypothesis the author shows how the present-day languages may have developed.

1387 Lizarralde, Roberto. Vocabulario barí: listado de 200 ítemes de Morris Swadesh (BBAA, 38:47, 1976, p. 207–215, tables)

Phonology of Barí (a Chibchan language of Venezuela also known as Motilón) consists of 19 consonant phonemes, six vowels, and three tones. Word list includes 100 items in addition to the 100-word lexicostatistical list of Morris Swadesh.

1388 Loos B., Eugenio *ed.* Materiales para estudios fonológicos. t. 1/2. Yarinacocha, Perú, Instituto Lingüístico de Verano, 1976. 2 v. (263, 218 l.) (Documento de trabajo, 9)

Lists of words, phrases, and paradigms of 16 indigenous languages of Peru, with Spanish translation. The languages are: Bora, Cashibo, Campa Ashaninca, Quechua Pestaza, Katukina, Piro, Capanahua, Cashinahua, Tashiro, Mayoruna, Culina, Quechua Ancash, Urarina, Orejón, Yagua, and Huitoto Murui.

1389 McCosker, Sandra. San Blas Cuna Indian lullabies: a means of informal learning (*in* Wilbert, Johannes *ed.* Enculturation in Latin America: an anthology [see item 260] p. 29–66, bibl., music, plates, tables)

Among the Cuna Indians of Panama, lullabies are used to teach infants and young children acceptable behavior as well as to induce sleep. Appendix includes texts of 13 lullabies in Cuna, which is considered to be a Chibchan language, although with some features of Arawakan. For musicologist's comment, see *HLAS 40:9074*.

1390 McLeod, Ruth and **Valerie Mitchell.** Aspectos da língua Xavante. Tradução de Mary I. Daniel. Brasília, Summer Institute of Linguistics, 1977. 228 p.

Pedagogical grammar of Xavante, a Jê language of Mato Grosso, Brazil.

1391 Martín, Eusebia Herminia. Aymara syntactic relationals and derivational verb suffixes (IU/IJAL, 44:2, April 1978, p. 131–136, tables)

Describes reflexive (-si-), human causative (-ya-), beneficiary (-rapi-), and prejudicial (-raqa-) suffixes of Aymara verbs in combination with substantive suffixes indicating a complementary relation between substantive and verb.

1392 Martínez, Fernando Antonio. A propósito de una gramática chibcha (ICC/T, 32:1, enero/abril 1977, p. 1–23)

Posthumous review of a 17th-century grammar of Chibcha (a presumably extinct Chibchan language of Colombia), the manuscript of which was discovered in the library of the Royal Palace in Madrid and published in 1965. Discusses probable author and the relationship of this manuscript to others of the same era dealing with the same language.

1393 Mercer, José Luiz. Notas dialetológicas sobre Guaraqueçaba (UFP/EB, 2:3, 1977, p. 35–63, bibl., tables)

Study of the phonology, grammar, and lexicon of speakers of Portuguese in Guaraqueçaba (an isolated region of the state of Paraná, Brazil), where the language has developed with little influence from the rest of the country.

1394 Merrifield, William R. ed. Studies in Otomanguean phonology. Dallas, Tex., Summer Institute of Linguistics [and] Univ. of Texas, Arlington, 1977. 180 p., tables (Publications in linguistics, 54)

Various aspects of phonology of Otomanguean languages of Mexico are dealt with in eight articles by members of the Summer Institute of Linguistics. Individual titles are: John Daly "A Problem in Tone Analysis" p. 3–20. Joanne North and Jäna Shields "Silacayoapan Mixtec Phonology" p. 21–33. Barbara E. Hollenbach "Phonetic vs. Phonemic Correspondence in Two Trique Dialects" p. 35–67. Sharon Stark and Polly Machin "Stress and Tone in Tlacoyalco Popoloca" p. 69–92. Allan R. Jamieson "Chiquihuitlan Mazatec Phonology" p. 93–105. Allan R. Jamieson "Chiquihuitlan Mazatec Tone" p. 107–136. Larry Lyman and Rosemary Lyman "Choapan Zapotec Phonology" p. 137–161. Ted E. Jones and Lyle M. Knudson "Guelavía Zapotec Phonemes" p. 163–180.

1395 Mixco, Mauricio J. The innovation of /h, hʷ/ in Kiliwa (IU/IJAL, 43:3, July 1977, p. 167–175, table)

In several Yuman languages (e.g., Paipai, Walapai, Mohave), /h, hʷ/ have developed from protoforms x and xʷ. Kiliwa, however, has developed /h, hʷ/ as phonemes in addition to /x, xʷ/, which are reflexes of the Proto-Yuman phonemes.

1396 ———. The linguistic affiliation of the Ñakepa and Yakawal of Lower California (IU/IJAL, 43:3, July 1977, p. 189–200, tables)

Examination of field notes made by J.P. Harrington in the 1920s leads to the conclusion that the languages he labeled Yakakwal and Ñakipa are Paipai and Kiliwa respectively. These are Yuman languages of Lower California.

1397 Mock, Carol comp. Chocho: Santa Catarina Ocotlán, Oaxaca. México, Centro de Investigación para la Integración Social, 1977. 175 p., map, tables (Archivo de lenguas indígenas de México, 4)

Describes phonology and morphophonemics of Chocho, with analyzed language text, a translation of more than 600 Spanish sentences, and a brief lexicon. Chocho is a Popolocan language of the state of Oaxaca, Mex.

1398 Monserrat, Ruth Maria Fonini. Prefixos pessoais em aweti. Recomeço de L. de Castro Faria. Rio, Univ. Federal do Rio de Janeiro [and] Museu Nacional, 1976. 16 p., tables (Lingüística, 3)

Describes person prefixes of verbs, statives, and nouns of Aweti, a Tupí-Guaraní language of Brazil. "Statives" are transitory states of the subject of the sentence as in "It is hot" or "He is sad."

1399 Morínigo, Marcos A. Impacto del español sobre el guaraní (in Homenaje al Instituto de Filología y Literaturas Hispánicas Dr. Amado Alonso en su Cincuentenario, 1923–1973. B.A., Editorial Fernando García Cambeiro, 1975, p. 283–294)

Following the Spanish conquest in 1537 of what is now the Republic of Paraguay, the Guaraní Indians accepted European culture and religion but retained their own language, adapting it to their new sociocultural surroundings. Bilingualism flourished even among the offspring of Spanish-

Indian unions and, as colonization was not strongly promoted, initiative in colonial life remained in the hands of the *criollos* whose social position was not affected by their speaking their mother tongue. As a result, Paraguay has remained prominently bilingual (see *HLAS 37:1853*).

1400 Moser, Mary B. Articles in Seri (*in* Hokan-Yuman Languages Workshop, Salt Lake City, 1977. Proceedings of the 1977 Hokan-Yuman Languages Workshop, held at University of Utah, Salt Lake City, June 21– 23, 1977 [see item **1375**] p. 67–89)

Seri articles are definite, indefinite, and general. The first two agree in number with the nouns they modify and occur at the end of the entire noun phrase. There is close phonological and semantic relationship between the definite article and certain verbs (be, be sitting, be standing, be lying).

1401 ———. Switch reference in Seri (IU/IJAL, 44:2, April 1978, p. 113–120)

Subject change in Seri subordinate clauses is marked by either of two forms of the auxiliary -a(a) 'be', ta (future), or ma (past). This corresponds to similar markers in other Hokan languages. Seri is a Hokan language of about 440 speakers living along the coast of Sonora, Mex., mainly in Punta Chueca and El Desemboque.

1402 Mosonyi, Esteban Emilio. El lugar de las lenguas y literaturas indígenas en el contexto de la literatura venezolana (UZ/R, 57, enero/dic. 1977, p. 111–124)

Indigenous languages and literature merit inclusion in the catalogue of national literature of Spanish-American countries.

1403 Naula Guacho, Juan and **Donald H. Burns.** Bosquejo gramatical del quichua de Chimborazo: un estudio de la fonología, morfología y sintaxis del quichua de la Provincia de Chimborazo basado en textos de la literatura oral y tradicional de la zona. Quito, n.p., 1975. 202 p., tables.

Analysis of phonology, morphology, syntax, clause, sentence, and discourse of the Chimborazo (Ecuador) dialect of Quichua, with lexicon. Includes texts with interlinear literal translation and separate free translation.

1404 Oltrogge, David. Proto Jicaque-Subtiaba-Tequistlateco: a comparative reconstruction (*in* Oltrogge, David and Calvin R. Rensch *eds.* Two studies in Middle American comparative linguistics. Dallas, Tex., Summer Institute of Linguistics, 1977, p. 1– 52, bibl., tables [Publications in linguistics, 55])

Sound correspondences between Jicaque and Subtiaba and between Jicaque and Tequistlatec show that the three languages have a common origin, possibly related to the Otomanguean languages. Subtiaba is an extinct language formerly spoken in Nicaragua; Jicaque is an indigenous language of Honduras; and Tequistlatec (also known as Chontal of Oaxaca) is a Hokan language of southern Mexico.

1405 Parker, Gary J. Diccionario polilectal del quechua de Ancash. Lima, Univ. Nacional Mayor de San Marcos, Centro de Investigación de Lingüística Aplicada, 1975. 145 l. (Documento de trabajo, 31)

Vocabulary of the Ancash (Peru) dialect of Quechua of more than 3,000 items, with indicators of dialect(s) in which the same form is found. This comparison is confined to Peruvian dialects of Quechua.

1406 Paula, Ruth Wallace de García. Harmonia vocálica nos afixos de posse na língua Kaxuyâna (SBPL/RBL, 3:2, 1976, p. 42– 50, bibl.)

Discusses vowel harmony in possessive affixes of Kaxuyâna, a Carib language of Brazil. This harmony, which may be essentially vocalic although in some cases determined by both consonant and vowel, occurs with first person plural possessive prefixes and with possessive suffixes.

1407 Paulín de Siade, Georgina. Los indígenas bilingües de México frente a la castellanización. México, UNAM, Instituto de Investigaciones Sociales, 1974. 131 p., tables.

Sociolinguistic study of attitudes of indigenous Mexican bilinguals toward their mother tongue and toward Spanish, based to a large extent on interviews with individuals who have had considerable contact with members of the Summer Institute of Linguistics.

Perrin, Michel. L'extraordinaire et le quotidien: mythes ou fantasmes goajiro? See item **1182**.

1408 Pickett, Velma and **Virginia Embrey** *comps*. Zapoteco del Istmo: Juchitán,

Oaxaca. Oaxaca, Mex., Instituto de Investigación e Integración Social del Estado de Oaxaca, 1974. 139 p., tables (Archivo de lenguas indígenas del estado de Oaxaca, 1)

Describes phonology of Isthmus Zapotec (an Otomanguean language of southern Mexico), followed by analyzed language text and a translation of 593 Spanish sentences and a 13-page lexicon.

1409 Pottier, Bernard. La situation linguistique du Paraguay (UTIEH/C, 14, 1970, p. 43–50, map)

Lists indigenous languages of Paraguay along with documentary sources. Four dialects of Guaraní are: Paraguayan Guaraní, used by the majority of the population; Paikaiová, Chiripá; and Mbya, the last three of these having little contact with Spanish.

1410 Quesada Castillo, Félix. Léxico del quechua de Cajamarca. Lima, Univ. Nacional Mayor de San Marcos, Centro de Investigación de Lingüística Aplicada, 1976. 142 l. (Documento de trabajo, 32)

Vocabulary of about 2,000 entries in the Cajamarca (Peru) dialect of Quechua (see *HLAS 39:1733*).

1411 Ramírez, Luis Hernán and others. Proyecto del *Atlas lingüístico y etnográfico del Perú*. Lima, INIDE, Ediciones Previas, 1974. 52 p., fold. map, maps, tables.

Outlines goals and methods to be followed in gathering data for a linguistic and ethnographic survey of Peru, a project which is estimated to take no longer than eight years.

1412 Rensch, Calvin R. Classification of the Otomanguean languages and the position of Tlapaned (*in* Oltrogge, David and Calvin R. Rensch *eds.* Two studies in Middle American comparative linguistics. Dallas, Tex., Summer Institute of Linguistics, 1977, p. 53–108, bibl., tables [Publications in linguistics, 55])

Traces development of classification of Otomanguean languages over the past century, reconstructs phonology of proto-Otomanguean (POM), and compares reflexes of POM forms with Tlapanec, concluding that the latter is most like proto-Zapotecan. Tlapanec is an indigenous language of the state of Guerrero, Mex.

Ribeiro, José and others. Esboço de um atlas lingüístico de Minas Gerais. See item **5770.**

1413 Robertson, John S. A phonological reconstruction of the ergative third-person singular pronoun of common Mayan (IU/IJAL, 43:3, July 1977, p. 201–210, tables)

Present-day Mayan languages have such a variety of ergative third-person singular pronouns that they seem to be unrelated to any possible protoform of which they are reflexes. Careful study of language data, however, brings out evidence to the contrary.

1414 ——. A proposed revision in Mayan subgrouping (IU/IJAL, 43:2, April 1977, p. 105–120, tables, illus.)

Presents evidence for rejecting Kaufman's grouping of Chuj and Toholabal together (see *HLAS 39:1671*), and suggests that Toholabal is a member of the Chol-Tzeltal branch of the Mayan language family and that Chuj is a member of the Kanjobalan branch.

1415 Romaina, Amelia and Joaquina Romaina. Quimisha Yohuan Xení: cuentos folklóricos de los capanahua. Revisadas por Manuel Huaninche. Traducción y recopilación de Thelma Schoolland. Yarinacocha, Perú, Instituto Lingüístico de Verano, 1976. 34 p., illus. (Comunidades y culturas peruanas, 6)

Folklore text in Capanhua, a Panoan language of about 400 speakers in eastern Peru (and possibly Brazil).

1416 Rowan, Orland and Phyllis Rowan *comps.* Dicionário Parecis-Português e Português-Parecis. Brasília, Summer Institute of Linguistics, 1978. 161 p.

Vocabulary of about 2,500 items in Parecis, an Arawakan language of some 450 speakers living in the State of Mato Grosso, Brazil.

1417 Sánchez A., Micaela and Olga Castro G. Lenguas de Panamá. t. 3, pt. 1, Una gramática pedagógica del waunana. Edited by Reinaldo Binder. Panamá, Instituto Nacional de Cultura, Dirección del Patrimonio Histórico [and] Instituto Lingüístico de Verano, 1977. 175 p., bibl., tables.

Description of Waunana, a Macro-Chibchan language of Colombia and Panama, in 16 lessons, with vocabulary.

1418 Sánchez-Marco, Francisco. Acercamiento histórico a la sociolingüística. Prólogo de Nicholas A. Hopkins and J. Kathryn Josserand. México, Instituto Nacional de Antropología e Historia (INAH), 1976. 263 p., bibl.

Concise account of the development of the science of linguistics in North America and in Europe and of the related discipline of sociolinguistics since the mid-20th century. With its ample bibliography, this makes an excellent introduction to the study of sociolinguistics.

1419 Santos, Emmanoel. Mobilidade social e atitudes lingüísticas. Apresentação de Yonne de Freitas Leite. Rio, Univ. Federal do Rio de Janeiro [and] Museu Nacional, 1976. 11 p., bibl. (Lingüística, 4)

Sociolinguistic study of adolescent students' correlation of phonological variables in their native Portuguese with difference in social status in Rio, using techniques developed by Labov in a similar study in N.Y.

1420 Saquic Calel, Felipe Rosalío. Primer curso de quiché: método práctico para aprender el idioma mayoritario de la República de Guatemala. Guatemala, Instituto Lingüístico de Verano, 1975. 183 p., tables.

Ten lessons in Quiché, a Mayan language of Guatemala, consisting mainly of paradigms, vocabulary, and sentences in Quiché and Spanish. In some cases the Quiché and Spanish sentences are in parallel columns on a page, but in others the translation may follow a block of 20 or 30 sentences, making it awkward to find the translation of a particular sentence.

1421 Schram, Judith L. and Eunice V. Pike. Vowel fusion in Mazatec of Jalapa de Díaz (IU/IJAL, 44:4, Oct. 1978, p. 257–261)

Vowels in Mazatec of Jalapa de Díaz (Oaxaca, Mex.) are conditioned by one another as well as by alveopalatal consonants. Various kinds of vowel fusion, described and illustrated, throw light on irregular verb forms of Huautla Mazatec, a neighboring dialect.

1422 Série Lingüística. Summer Institute of Linguistics. No. 5, 1976–. Brasília.

Ten articles of a descriptive nature on indigenous languages of Brazil, reflecting various linguistic models. Individual titles are: Helen E. Waller "A Conjunção Nhũm na Narrativa Apinajé" p. 7–29. Peter K.E. Kingston "Sufixos Referenciais e o Elemento Nominal na Língua Mamaindé" p. 31–81. Rose Dobson "Repetição em Kayabí" p. 83–105. Menno Kroeker "Condicionamento Múltiplo de Vogais na Língua Nambikuára" p. 107–130. Meinke Saelzer "Fonologia Provisória da Língua Kamayurá" p. 131–170. James Y. Kakumasu "Gramática Gerativa Preliminar de Língua Urubú" p. 171–197. Shirley Chapman "Significado e Função de Margens Verbais na Língua Paumarí" p. 199–230. Miriam Abbott "Estrutura Oracional da Língua Makúxi" p. 231–266. Cathy Ann Hodsdon "Análise de Cláusulas Semânticas na Língua Makúsi" p. 267–300. Linda Koopman "Cláusulas Semânticas na Língua Apinajé" p. 301–330.

1423 Sheffler, Margaret. Munduruků discourse (in Grimes, Joseph E. ed. Papers on discourse [see item **1368**] p. 119–142, table)

Primary content of discourse in Munduruků (a Tupí language of Pará, Brazil, of about 1500 speakers) has a reference system that identifies participants, indicates target relationships, and links events. Secondary content provides background against which the narrative is told.

1424 Smith, Richard D. Gramática tagmémica del barasano del sur. Traducción de Paulina Piedrahita. Bogotá, Ministerio de Gobierno [and] Instituto Lingüístico de Verano, 1976. 101 p., bibl., tables.

Grammatical analysis of discourse of Southern Barasano, a Tucanoan language of Colombia, using the tagmemic model. Includes lexicon of about 450 items.

1425 Stark, Louisa R. and Pieter C. Muysken. Diccionario español-quicha, quichua-español. Presentación de Segundo E. Moreno Yánez. Quito, Banco Central del Ecuador, Los Museos [and] Archivo Histórico del Guayas, Guayaquil, Ecua., 1977. 366 p., illus. (Publicaciones de los museos del Banco Central del Ecuador, 1)

Comparative vocabulary compiled from 14 dialects of Quechua spoken in Ecuador (where the preferred spelling is *Quichua*). Entries in the Spanish-Quichua section show lexical variations from dialect to dialect and those in the Quichua-Spanish section show semantic variations for a given Quichua word. Scholarly work.

1426 Suárez, Jorge A. Estudios huaves. México, Instituto Nacional de Antropología e Historia (INAH), Depto. de

Lingüística, 1975. 181 p., bibl., tables (Col. Científica, 22: lingüística)

Studies of several dialects of Huave, an as yet unclassified indigenous language of southern Mexico, were used to reconstruct the phonology and morphology of a proto form of the language. Examines possible affiliation with Algonquian languages, with Mixe-Zoque, and with Mayan. Discusses hypothesis of Oto-Manguean relationship.

1427 ———. La posición lingüística del mosetén, del panotacana y del arahuaco (UNAM/AA, 14, 1977, p. 243–255, bibl.)

Finds points of comparison in vocabularies of Moseten and Uru (languages of Bolivia) and in those of Pano-Tanoan and Arawakan (language families of Bolivia and of Peru respectively). Questions classifications of Greenberg and of Swadesh regarding languages of these families.

1428 Taack, George H. Maya script and Maya language: new data with regard to the phoneme /H'/ (IU/AL, 19:6, Sept. 1977, p. 280–302, bibl., illus., tables)

Discusses representation of phonemes /h'/ and /h/ in Mayan hieroglyphs. (Both were voiceless aspirates, the latter being so soft as to be almost inaudible.) This involves glyphs representing VC suffixes which occasionally function as CVC.

1429 Tangol, Nicasio. Diccionario etimológico chilote. Notula mínima de Mario Ferreccio Podestá. Santiago, Editorial Nascimento, 1976. 139 p., bibl.

Dictionary of the speech of the inhabitants of Chiloé, in the archipelago south of Chile. The language is Spanish, strongly influenced by Mapuche, an indigenous Araucanian language of Chile.

1430 Taylor, Douglas. Four consonantal patterns in Northern Arawakan (IU/IJAL, 44:2, April 1978, p. 121–130, tables)

Discusses sound correspondences among four Arawakan languages: Taino, Island Carib, Arawak, and Guajiro.

———. Languages of the West Indies. See item 1096.

1431 Tibón, Gutierre. Historia del nombre y de la fundación de México. México, Fondo de Cultura Económica, 1975. 877 p., bibl., illus., maps, plates (Sección de obras de historia)

Copiously documented (with 2185 footnotes and 22 pages of bibliography) collection of history and legend of precolumbian and colonial Mexico. Seems a useful reference work.

1432 Tovar Llorente, Antonio. Estudiando una lengua indígena: el mataco (in Jornadas Americanistas, III, Valladolid, Spain, 1974. Estudios sobre política indigenista española en América [see HLAS 40:2298] v. 1, p. 247–255)

Analyzes phonology of Mataco (an indigenous language of the Argentine Chaco) as consisting of nine vowel phonemes (six oral, three nasal), 23 consonants, and two semivowels (see HLAS 39:1770). Discusses grammar very briefly.

1433 Uribe Villegas, Oscar. Los hablantes de idiomas indomexicanos según el censo de 1970 (UNAM/RMS, 38:2, abril/junio 1976, p. 413–432, maps)

Reviews data on speakers of indigenous languages in the 1970 Mexico census (which lists only 30 languages), and ranks them in order of number of speakers, with Nahuatl and Maya being the most numerous. No mention is made of some languages (e.g., Chontal of Tabasco, Lacandón) nor of mutually unintelligible dialects of major languages (e.g., Highland and Isthmus Zapotec).

1434 Viñas Urquiza, María Teresa. Lengua mataca. t. 1/2. B.A., Univ. de Buenos Aires, Facultad de Filosofía y Letras, Centro de Estudios Lingüísticos, 1974. 2 v. (165, 143 p.) bibl., plates, tables (Archivo de lenguas precolombinas, 2)

Outlines phonology, morphology, and syntax of Mataco, an indigenous language of Argentina, Paraguay, and the Bolivian Chaco. Includes texts and a lexicon of about 1000 items (see HLAS 39:1774).

Viñaza, Cipriano Muñoz y Manzano, conde de la. Bibliografía española de lenguas indígenas de América: Madrid, 1892. See item 53.

1435 Waltz, Nathan. Hablemos el guanano: gramática pedagógica guanano-castellano. Bogotá, Ministerio de Gobierno, Dirección General de Integración y Desarrollo de la Comunidad, División Operativa de Asuntos Indígenas, Instituto Lingüístico de Verano, 1976. 139 l., tables.

Consists of 12 lessons, with dialogues,

vocabulary, examples of points of grammar, and exercises, designed to teach Guanano, a Tucanoan language of Colombia, to non-native speakers.

1436 Waterhouse, Viola and **Muriel Parrott.**
Oaxaca Chontal noun inflection and classification (in Hokan-Yuman Languages Workshop, Salt Lake City, 1977. Proceedings of the 1977 Hokan-Yuman Languages Workshop, held at University of Utah, Salt Lake City, June 21–23, 1977 [see item **1375**] p. 54–66)
Oaxaca Chontal nouns are inflected for specification, possession, and plural by sets of prefixes attached to noun stems. Free stems may be prefixed directly by the definite article prefix; bound stems have an intervening a-. Grammatical gender of animate vs. inanimate determines the choice of the definite article prefix set.

1437 Weber, David J. Los sufijos posesivos en el quechua del Huallaga, Huanuco. Yarinacocha, Perú, Instituto Lingüístico de Verano, 1976. 61 l., bibl., tables (Documento de trabajo, 12)

Distinguishes possessive suffixes from other phonologically similar suffixes of Quechua and describes their usage in conjunction with subordinate verbs, the genitive construction and its use, and adverbial relations (geographical and temporal). Amply illustrated with expressions from the Huánuco (Peru) dialect of Quechua (see *HLAS 39:1776–1777*).

Wise, Mary Ruth; Eugene E. Loos and **Patricia Davis.** Filosofía y métodos del Instituto Lingüístico de Verano. See item **1217**.

1438 Yapita, Juan de Dios. Vocabulario castellano—inglés—aymara. Oruro, Bol., Editorial I.N. D.I.C.E.P., 1974. 48 p., tables.
Orthography of Aymara words in this vocabulary follows the three-vowel (a, i, u,) phonemic system of the language, as in *uraqi* [orake] "soil, ground," in contrast to orthographies that are adapted to Spanish pronunciation. Glottalized stops are indicated by an apostrophe following the stop, and aspirated stops by a double quotation mark in the same position. Back velar stop is *q* and fricative is *x*.

BIOLOGICAL ANTHROPOLOGY

R.A. HALBERSTEIN, *Associate Professor, Department of Anthropology and Department of Epidemiology and Public Health, University of Miami*

THE NEW TITLE OF THIS SECTION reflects the increasing expansion of the field and the continuous exploration of new types of data relevant to the study of human evolution and biological variation. The previous title "Physical Anthropology" stemmed from the predominantly anatomical-morphological orientation of the field's earliest practitioners. In addition to physical characteristics, anthropologists have more recently investigated numerous other sources of data on human biology and evolution including genetics, biochemistry, hematology and serology, immunology, physiology, nutrition, epidemiology, biodemography, environmental ecology, sociobiology, etc. All the above approaches are embodied in the references compiled below.

Research and publications on biological anthropology in Latin America have steadily accelerated over the past few years. For example, in *HLAS 37* (1975) there were 24 items from the two major journals in the field: *American Journal of Physical Anthropology* and *Human Biology*. The same two publications accounted for 33 entries in *HLAS 39* (1977). In the present edition there are 41 items from these two serials. Twenty-nine new doctoral dissertations have appeared on the biological anthropology of Latin American populations, and they are listed below. Seven new scientific journals in biological anthropology and closely related disciplines have been established in the past two years: 1) *Culture, Medicine and Psychiatry* (Reidel,

Dordrecht, The Netherlands); 2) *Ethology and Sociobiology* (Elsevier-North Holland, N.Y.); 3) *Journal of Behavioral Medicine* (Plenum, N.Y.); 4) *Journal of Ethnopharmacology* (Elsevier-Sequoia, Lausanne, Switerzerland); 5) *Journal of Social and Biological Structures* (Academic Press, London); 6) *Studies in Human Sociobiology* (Academic Press, N.Y.); and 7) *Medical Anthropology* (Redgrave Press, Pleasantville, N.Y.).

The references annotated below are divided into the following categories: Paleoanthropology; Population Studies: Biodemography; Population Studies: Genetics; Human Adaptation and Variation; Human Development; and Epidemiological Anthropology.

PALEOANTHROPOLOGY

The selections under this heading deal with the fossilized and mummified human remains of prehistoric populations from Mexico, Peru, Bolivia, Ecuador, Colombia, and Chile. Craniometry, dental morphology, post-cranial osteological variation, and paleopathology are the major topics addressed. Heyerdahl's new book (item **1453**) should renew speculation on the possible role of prehistoric transoceanic contact in the evolution of Central and South American populations. Also lively and controversial are Harner's new theories on the functional (and nutritional) significance of ritualized human sacrifice among the ancient Aztecs (items **1451–1452**).

POPULATION STUDIES:
BIODEMOGRAPHY

The biodemographic research chronicled in this section represents the results of work conducted in 14 different Latin American countries. Fertility, mortality, and patterns of migration and mate selection are investigated. Specialized subjects include the effects of inbreeding on population biology, the relationship between contraceptive practices and reproductive wastage, rural-urban variations in fertility and mortality, etc. The collection of papers on Latin American historical demography edited by Denevan (item **1472**) is an important new contribution to the literature in this field.

POPULATION STUDIES:
GENETICS

The major theme of this section is the evolutionary application of population genetics data. Various Latin American populations (from 23 different countries) are compared with respect to simply inherited, discrete polymorphic genetic traits—blood groups, red-blood cell and serum proteins, enzymes, HLA antigens, PTC taste sensitivity, dermatoglyphics, and dental characteristics. Of special interest are the linguistic and geographic correlates of genetic distance and diversity (items **1510, 1513, 1515** and **1520–1521**). Other articles deal with the genetics of isolate populations, twin studies, hemoglobin polymorphisms, intragroup vs. intergroup variation, and the covariation and interrelationships of different genetic marker systems in Latin America.

HUMAN ADAPTATION AND VARIATION

Human adaptation to hot climates and to high altitude environments is currently being examined in Latin America. The selection by Neel and others (item **1583**) summarizes the highlights of extensive interdisciplinary research on the biosocial adaptations of the tropical Yanomama Indians of South America. In the high altitude research, attention is focused upon respiratory and cardiovascular charcteristics, adaptive anatomical features (e.g., enlarged chest), work capacity, and biomedical and nutritional phenomena. The insightful paper by Baker (item **1562**) realistically sets forth some of the methodological problems in this area.

Also included here are publications on quantitative, continuous biological variables in Latin American groups—skin color, head shape, stature, anthropometric measurements, facial structure, etc.

HUMAN DEVELOPMENT

The selections on human development in Latin America are concerned with longitudinal and cross-sectional growth studies, nutritional evaluations of typical diets, the relationship of diseases and growth, the biological effects of nutritional deficiencies, and the utilization of synthetic foods and supplements. This work is based upon a variety of different methods and sources of data—anthropometry, biochemistry, hematology, metabolism, hair structure, age of menarche, and radiographic indicators of skeletal development. The multiple biological aspects of nutritional stress in Guatemala are well-illustrated in the detailed monograph by Mata (item **1624**). The volumes by Hakim, Solimano (item **1609**) and Winikoff (item **1635**) deal with the socioeconomic and political ramifications of nutritional stress and its alleviation in Latin America.

EPIDEMIOLOGICAL ANTHROPOLOGY

Materials cited here pertain to medical anthropology, particularly the examination of traditional medical systems and healing practices in indigenous Latin American societies. Several articles describe medicinal plant usage, and the following reports indicate that the native use of local plant-derived medicaments generally has been curatively successful and highly adaptive in Latin America: Arenas (item **1637**); Moreno Azorero (item **1638**); Bandoni (item **1639**); Dobkin de Ríos (item **1650**); Ginzberg (item **1652**); Halberstein and Saunders (item **1654**); and Wong (item **1671**). Other writers have considered the role of shamanism and witchcraft in traditional Latin American healing dynamics (items **1321, 1643** and **1669–1670**) and public health problems in modern Latin America (items **1642, 1647, 1649, 1651, 1655** and **1660**). The field study by Woods in Guatemala (item **1672**) is an instructive example of an effective anthropological analysis of medical modernization and acculturation.

RECENT DOCTORAL DISSERTATIONS
Biological Anthropology in Latin America (1976–78)

Beall, Cynthia. The effects of high altitude on growth, morbidity, and mortality of Peruvian infants. Pennsylvania State Univ., 1976.

Bogin, Barry. Periodic rhythm in the rates of growth in height and weight of Guatemalan children and its relation to season of the year. Temple Univ., 1977.

Browner, Carole. Poor woman's fertility decisions: illegal abortion in Cali, Colombia. Univ. of California at Berkeley, 1976.

Cheng, Anthony H. Effect of age upon protein utilization in human subjects. Univ. of Rhode Island, 1976.

Clement, Susan. Medicine in Panchimalco: a symbolic and thematic analysis of an El Salvadorian medical system. Univ. of Wisconsin, 1978.

Conway, Frederick. Pentacostalism in the context of Haitian religion and health practice. American Univ., 1978.

Graziano, Joseph. Sociocultural determinants of fertility: social mobility and fertility decline in Caracas, Venezuela. Univ. of Colorado, 1977.

Gwynn, Eunice. Family well-being, fertility, and childhood nutrition: a comparative study between migrant and native families in Guadalajara, Mexico. Cornell Univ., 1977.

Harrison, Sarah. Determinants of nuptiality and fertility in a small population. Pennsylvania State Univ., 1977.

Heggenhougen, H.K. Health care for the edge of the world: Indian campesinos as health workers in Chimaltenango, Guatemala. New School for Social Research, 1977.

Hughey, David. The effects of mating patterns on the genetic structure and microevolution of Grand Cayman, British West Indies. Univ. of Pittsburgh, 1977.

Johnson, Allan. The prevalence and etiology of the nutritional anemias in Guyana. Cornell Univ., 1978.

Kautz, Robert. Late Pleistocene paleoclimate and human adaptation on the western flank of the Peruvian Andes. Univ. of California at Davis, 1976.

Lawrence, Trude. Physical and social deviants: a study of health-related attitudes, perceptions, and practices within a San Blas Cuna Village, Panama. Univ. of North Carolina, 1977.

Leslie, Paul. Mating structure and the genetics of small human populations. Pennsylvania State Univ., 1977.

Low, Setha. The meaning of *nervios*: social organization of urban health care in San José, Costa Rica. Univ. of California at Berkeley, 1976.

Lutes, Steven. Alcohol use among the Yaqui Indians of Potam, Sonora, Mexico. Univ. of Kansas, 1977.

Marchione, Thomas. Health and nutrition in self-reliant national development: an evaluation of the Jamaican Community Health Aide Programme. Univ. of Connecticut, 1977.

Midgett, Douglas. West Indian migration and adaptation in St. Lucia and London. Univ. of Illinois, 1977.

Milton, Katherine. The foraging strategy of the Howler monkey in the tropical forest of Barro Colorado Island, Panama. New York Univ., 1977.

Mittermeier, Russell. Distribution, synecology and conservation of Surinam monkeys. Harvard Univ., 1977.

Page, John. Costa Rican marijuana smokers and the amotivational syndrome hypothesis. Univ. of Florida, 1976.

Pastron, Allen. Aspects of witchcraft and shamanism in a Tarahumara Indian community of northern Mexico. Univ. of California at Berkeley, 1977.

Reagan, Patricia. The utilization of modern health services by Aymara Indians living in Chiquito, Peru. Univ. of Illinois, 1978.

Roberts, Peggy. The composition of the Costa Rican population: some evidence from history, genetics, and morphology. Univ. of Colorado, 1978.

Seims, Sara. A cohort analysis of fertility decline in Barbados. Univ. of Pennsylvania, 1978.

Stinson, Sara. Child growth, mortality and the adaptive value of children in rural Bolivia. Univ. of Michigan, 1978.

Urdaneta, María Luisa. Fertility regulation practices of two groups of Mexican American women in an urban setting. Southern Methodist Univ., 1976.

Young, James. Health care in Pichataro: medical decision-making in a Tarascan town of Michoacan, Mexico. Univ. of California at Riverside, 1978.

PALEOANTHROPOLOGY

1439 Adovasio, J. M. and G. F. Fry. Prehistoric psychotropic drug use in northeastern Mexico and Trans-Pecos Texas (SEB/EB, 30:1, Jan./March 1976, p. 94–96, bibl.)

Use of psychotropic drugs traced back 10,000 years before the present in northeastern Mexico. Data from some 20 sites suggest prehistoric use of red or mescal bean, peyote, and a third type of psychotropic plant called monilla (or Mexican buckeye).

1440 Allison, Marvin J. and others. ABO blood groups in Chilean and Peruvian mummies: pt. 2, Results of agglutination-inhibition technique (AJPA, 49:1, July 1978, p. 139–142, bibl., map, table)

ABO blood group phenotypes determined in mummies from Peru and Chile dating back 5,000 years ago using the agglutination-inhibition technique. Population relationships among sample groups are postulated.

1441 Basto Girón, Luis J. Salud y enfermedad en el campesino del siglo XVII. Presentación de Honorio Pinto H. Lima, Univ. Nacional Mayor de San Marcos, Seminario de Historia Rural Andina, 1977. 165 p., bibl., fold. table.

Study of native medical systems of early Peruvian groups. "Folk" concepts of disease and etiology are discussed, including *mal de ojo, mal de viejo,* etc. Therapeutic measures featured divination, sacrifice, bloodletting, and use of musical instruments and medicaments. Healing substances derived from plant, animal, and mineral sources.

1442 Benfer, Robert A. and others. Mineral analysis of ancient Peruvian hair (AJPA, 48:3, March 1978, p. 277–282, bibl., plates, tables)

Nine samples of hair from prehistoric Peruvians dating back to 8,800 years ago examined by means of scanning electron microscope. Trace metal composition was determined, and temporal chemical changes are postulated. Article enhanced by high quality photographs. Samples were unusually well-preserved, and no evidence of pathology was found.

1443 Céspedes Gutiérrez, Gerardo and Víctor Hugo Villegas A. Conceptos quirúrgicos: patología ósea y dentaria en cráneos precolombinos de Bolivia. Prólogo de Carlos Ponce Sanginés. La Paz, Ministerio de Educación, Instituto Boliviano de Cultura, 1976. 105 p., bibl., illus., plates, tables.

Brief but interesting analysis of skeletal remains of precolumbian populations from

Bolivia. Statistics are simple, bibliography is sparse, and photos are of medium quality, but authors still accomplish a great deal. Cranial and dental pathologies receive detailed coverage, based on examination of 418 specimens.

1444 Cordero Miranda, Gregorio; Víctor Hugo Villegas; and Gerardo Céspedes Gutiérrez. Superstición popular que la radiografía aclara en cráneos precolombinos. La Paz, Instituto Nacional de Arqueología [and] Instituto Boliviano de Cultura, 1975. 8 p., plates (Publicación del Instituto Nacional de Arqueología, 13)

Brief osteological and dental analysis of 50 precolumbian crania from Bolivia, Peru, Colombia, Ecuador and Chile. Mummified remains are studied radiographically. Coins discovered in the mouths of several of the specimens had been placed there by more modern peoples.

1445 Dobkin de Ríos, Marlene. Plant hallucinogens, out-of-body experiences and New World monumental earthworks (in Du Toit, B. M. ed. Drugs, rituals and altered states of consciousness. Rotterdam, Netherlands, A.A. Balkema, 1977, p. 237–249, bibl.)

Many prehistoric New World Indian groups utilized a wide variety of hallucinogenic plants, and author attempts to assess the influence of the psychotropic materials on the construction and art motifs of mounds and other earthworks. Archaeological data cited on the magicoreligious activities of the Olmec (Mexico), Nazca (Peru), and Adena/Hopewell (US).

1446 ———. Plant hallucinogens and the religion of the Mochica: an ancient Peruvian people (SEB/EB, 31:2, April/June 1977, p. 189–203, bibl., illus., tables)

Analysis of hallucinogenic plant usage in prehistoric Peruvian Indian population. Archaeological data suggest the ancient consumption of plant hallucinogens to achieve contact with the supernatural. Findings compared with patterns of drug plant use in modern Peruvian populations.

1447 Donnan, Christopher B. and Carol J. Mackey. Ancient burial patterns of the Moche Valley, Peru. Austin, Tex., Univ. of Texas Press, 1978. 424 p., bibl., illus., tables.

Detailed descriptive study of 103 burial tombs from prehistoric Peru. Data included

on fossil remains, artifacts and grave goods, associated game, tomb structure, and chronology. For archaeologist's comment, see item **789.**

1448 Dricot, J.M. Distances biologiques de populations péruviennes préhispaniques (IFEA/B, 6:3/4, 1977, p. 63–84, bibl., tables)

Biological distances among 10 prehispanic Peruvian populations representing four separate time periods are estimated from the statistical analysis of 14 cranial measurements. Geographic distance and altitude were not significantly correlated with observed biological relationships of populations, probably because of continuous migration since prehistoric times. Sexual differences are noted.

1449 Elzay, Richard P. and others. A comparative study on the dental health status of five precolumbian Peruvian cultures (AJPA, 46:1, Jan. 1977, p. 135–140, bibl., tables)

Skeletal remains of 101 individuals from five prehistoric Peruvian culture groups surveyed for dental pathologies. Significant differences found in caries, missing teeth, attrition, and osteitis. Variant patterns probably due to environmental and dietary diversity.

1450 Gerszten, Enrique and others. Diaphragmatic hernia of the stomach in a Peruvian mummy (Bulletin of the New York Academy of Medicine [N.Y.] 52:5, June 1976, p. 601–604, bibl., plates)

Case of herniated diaphragm presented for ancient Peruvian mummy. Report is brief and descriptive, with no discussion of possible etiology, comparison with other known examples, or evolutionary implications.

1451 Harner, Michael. The ecological basis for Aztec sacrifice (AAA/AE, 4:1, Feb. 1977, p. 117–135, bibl.)

Ancient Aztec sacrificial activities in Central America considered in terms of possible influence of population pressures and demography, religious beliefs, and nutritional factors. Evidence of cannibalism and nutritional stress indicates a possible functional aspect of the common practice. Many ethnohistorical and archaeological sources are consulted.

1452 ———. The enigma of Aztec sacrifice (AMNH/NH, 86:4, April 1977, p. 47–51, bibl., map, plates)

Archaeological and ethnohistorical evidence consulted to investigate possible functional aspects of ancient Aztec sacrifice. Anthropologists have traditionally theorized that the numerous sacrifices represent appeasement to the spiritual world. Author cites indications, however, that cannibalism may have added economic and nutritional dimensions to the practice—namely the frequent mention of cannibalism by early chroniclers and the notable deficiency of protein and fat in native diets.

1453 **Heyerdahl, Thor.** Early man and the ocean. Garden City, N.Y., Anchor Press, 1978. 456 p., bibl., maps, tables.

Possible prehistoric transoceanic migrations reconstructed, based upon author's research and exploration in Mexico, Central America and South America. Archaeological evidence suggests strong possibility of extensive precolumbian culture contact between Eastern and Western Hemispheres.

1454 **Lagunas Rodríguez, Zaíd; Carlos Serrano Sánchez;** and **Sergio López Alonso.** Enterramientos humanos de la zona arqueológica de Cholula, Puebla. Prólogo de Arturo Romano. México, Instituto Nacional de Antropología e Historia (INAH), Depto. de Antropología Física, 1976. 130 p., illus., map, plates, tables (Col. Científica: antropología física, 44)

Well-illustrated account of previously unpublished, prehistoric fossil remains excavated between 1967 and 1970 from Cholula site in state of Puebla, Mex. The several hundred burials represent a time span of approximately 2,000 years. Corpse preparation, artifacts, and associated grave goods are all carefully described.

1455 **Munizaga, Juan R.** Paleoindio en Sudamérica: restos óseos humanos de las Cuevas de Palli Aike y Cerro Sota, Provincia de Magallanes, Chile (in Niemeyer F., Hans ed. Homenaje al Dr. Gustavo le Paige, S.J. Santiago, Univ. del Norte, 1976, p. 19–30, bibl., plates, tables)

Descriptive study of series of human remains over 8,600 years old from cave sites in Chile. Morphological variation examined in the small sample (seven individuals). Speci-

mens are compared with other Paleo-Indian populations from South America.

1456 ——— and others. Cholelithiasis and cholecystitis in precolumbian Chileans (AJPA, 48:2, Feb. 1978, p. 209–212, bibl., plates)

Two cases of acute gallbladder disease documented among sample of 75 mummies from prehistoric Chile. Possible roles of diet and environment are mentioned.

1457 ——— and others. Diaphragmatic hernia associated with strangulation of the small bowel in an Atacameña mummy (AJPA, 48:1, Jan. 1978, p. 17–20, bibl., plates)

Two cases of herniated diaphragms detected in sample of 200 mummies from prehistoric Chile. Authors believe the abnormalities were congenital.

1458 **Rosel Sáez, Emilio José.** Fuentes bibliográficas para el estudio de la medicina en el Nuevo Mundo antes del descubrimiento: medicina precolombina. Zaragoza, Mex., Univ. de Zaragoza, Facultad de Medicina, Cátedra de Historia de la Medicina, 1975. 50 p.

Alphabetically arranged bibliography on medical systems in prehistoric and precolumbian populations in Latin America. More than 400 references in four languages on early and recent research on wide range of topics—diseases in ancient American populations, healing and surgical practices, instruments and paraphernalia, drug plants, etc.

Santos Filho, Lycurgo de Castro. História geral da medicina brasileira. See HLAS 40:4016.

1459 **Sawyer, Danny R.** and others. The mylohyoid bridge of precolumbian Peruvians (AJPA, 48:1, Jan. 1978, p. 9–16, bibl., plates, tables)

Frequency of occurrence of the mylohyoid bridge, a discretely inherited cranial trait, presented for sample of 122 precolumbian Peruvians. Age and sex differences are noted for this potentially significant genetic marker.

1460 **Sharon, Douglas** and **Christopher B. Donnan.** The magic cactus: ethnoarchaeological continuity in Peru (AIA/A, 30:6, Nov. 1977, p. 374–381, bibl., map, plates)

Analysis of ritual and medicinal use of San Pedro cactus (Trichocereus pachanoi) from prehistoric times through the present in Peru. Continuous utilization of the hallucinogenic cactus is traced over 3,000 years. Methods of preparation and consumption compared in ancient and modern populations. Artistic motifs on precolumbian Peruvian artifacts provide clues regarding usage patterns and importance of San Pedro cactus in Peruvian ethnohistory.

1461 Trinkaus, Erik. The Alto Salaverry child: a case of anemia from the Peruvian preceramic (AJPA, 46:1, Jan. 1977, p. 25–28, bibl., plates)

Juvenile skeleton from Peruvian archaeological site is described, and osteological evidence suggests the possibility of anemia. This represents the earliest evidence of anemia in Peru.

POPULATION STUDIES: BIODEMOGRAPHY

1462 Araujo, A.M. de and F.M. Salzano. Congenital malformations, twinning, and associated variables in a Brazilian population (IGM/AGMG, 24:1/2, 1975, p. 31–39, bibl., tables)

Incidence of congenital malformations and twinning reported for sample of 6,052 newborns from Brazil. Major malformations observed in 1.3 percent, while minor defects were exhibited by an additional 2.0 percent. Demographic characteristics of parents of twins and children with abnormalities are described.

Asociación Colombiana para el Estudio de la Población (ACEP), *Bogotá*. La población de Colombia. See item **5489.**

1463 Augusto Costa, Manoel. Fecundidade e mortalidade no Brasil entre 1960/70: estimativas para microregiões (IPEA/PPE, 7:2, agosto 1977, p. 261–290, tables)

Demographic investigation of fertility and mortality in Brazil, featuring urban-rural comparisons, national life tables, and long-term predictions of population size. Paper unfortunately lacks references to published literature or data from other such studies.

1464 Bailey, Jerald. La encuesta básica de profamilia: un estudio de fecundidad y

anticoncepción en una zona rural de Colombia (ACEP/EP, 2:4, abril 1977, p. 32–58, bibl., tables)

Detailed and thoroughly documented investigation of the interrelationship of changing fertility configurations and contraception in rural Colombia. Work is enhanced by the construction of population pyramids and the use of 21 tables containing abundant statistical data. For sociologist's comment, see item **9205.**

1465 Balakrishnan, T.R. Effects of child mortality on subsequent fertility of women in some rural and semi-urban areas of certain Latin American countries (LSE/PS, 32:1, March 1978, p. 135–145, tables)

Relationships between various fertility and childhood mortality parameters explored with data previously collected in Costa Rica, Colombia, Mexico, and Peru. Statistical analysis indicated that child loss is significantly associated with higher subsequent fertility at all parity levels in all four countries. Maternal age and economic status affected results.

1466 Baldwin, Wendy. Modernismo y fecundidad en Colombia. Revisión técnico de la versión en español: Enrique Pérez. Bogotá, Asociación Colombiana de Facultades de Medicina (ASCOFAME), División de Medicina Social y Población, 1975. 69 p., bibl., tables (Encuesta nacional de fecundidad, 7)

Demographic analysis of biosocial factors affecting fertility in Colombia punctuated by ample tabular data. Changing patterns of economy, sexual behaviors, and contraceptive usage have helped curb the exceptionally high reproductive rates that previously characterized the country. Other consequences of "modernization" on fertility and population control are discussed.

Bamberger, Michael; Mara del Negro; and George Gamble. Employment and contraceptive practice in selected barrios of Caracas. See item **9194.**

1467 Belcher, John C. Ecological factors and the demographic response (AU/P, 38:1, March 1977, p. 65–72, bibl.)

Ethnohistorical review of role of migration in the demographic evolution and ecological adaptation of populations of the Dominican Republic. Effects of interbreeding and hybridization on racial composition of country are discussed in nonquantified terms.

————; Kelly W. Crader; and Pablo B. Vázquez-Calcerrada. Style of life, social class and fertility in the rural Dominican Republic. See item 9138.

Bordes, Ary and Andrea Couture. For the people, for a change: bringing health to the families of Haiti. See item 1009.

Brackett, James W. Family planning in four Latin American countries: knowledge, use, and unmet needs: some findings from the World Fertility Survey. See item 9010.

Brody, Eugene B.; Frank Ottey; and Janet La Granade. Couple communication in the contraceptive decision making of Jamaican women. See item 9140.

————; ————; and ————. Fertility-related behavior in Jamaica. See item 9141.

Brzezinski, Steven. Church versus state: family planning in Colombia, 1966–1972. See item 7273.

Carvajal, M.J. David T. Geithman; and Lydia B. Neuhauser. The Costa Rican Family Planning Program. See item 9109.

Carvalho, José Alberto Magno de. Regional trends in fertility and mortality in Brazil. See item 9311.

1468 ———— and Charles Howard Wood. Renda e concentração da mortalidade no Brasil (IPE/EE, 7:1, jan./abril 1977, p. 107–130, bibl., tables)
Study of mortality in recent Brazilian populations, employing survey and census data. Mortality varies sharply by ethnic background and place of residence, but evidence is inconclusive. Average age at death and life expectancy are calculated.

1469 Colombia. Comité de Trabajo para el Estudio del Impacto de la Planificación Familiar sobre la Estructura Demográfica, Económica y Social de Colombia. Descenso de la fecundidad y planificación familiar en Colombia, 1964–1975. Prólogo de Guillermo López-Escobar y Juan B. Londoño. Bogotá, 1977. 70 p., bibls., tables.
Government advisory committee report on effects of ongoing family planning programs upon demographic and socioeco-

nomic structure of Colombia's national population. Fertility decline in the decade 1964–75 has brought new and unique cultural consequences in a country previously characterized by high fertility. The determinants and influencing factors in Colombia's fertility decline are sorted out and scrutinized.

1470 Cosminsky, Sheila. Childbirth and midwifery on a Guatemalan finca (Medical Anthropology [Redgrave, Pleasantville, N.Y.] 1:3, Summer 1977, p. 69–104, bibl., plates, tables)
Biological processes and behavioral customs related to childbirth examined in small Guatemalan plantation population. Special attention devoted to procedures of midwife and changing health-related activities due to rapid diffusion of "Western" medicine. Case studies of midwifery are featured.

1471 Davies, Peter J. and Walter Rodríguez. Distribución de anticonceptivos orales basada en la comunidad en Rio Grande do Norte, nordeste del Brasil (ACEP/EP, 1:7, julio 1976, p. 420–430, tables)
Historical account of ongoing program of oral contraceptive distribution in well-defined northeast Brazilian community. Social and political aspects of the work, organization of the program, birth control education, medical supervision, and results are all described.

1472 Denevan, William M. ed. The native population of the Americas in 1492. Madison, Univ. of Wisconsin Press, 1976. 353 p., bibl., illus., tables.
Eighteen essays devoted to historical demography of New World with special emphasis on impact of Spanish contact upon changes in size and distribution of various populations (for historian's comment, see HLAS 40:2279). Controversy surrounds reconstructions of population numbers in 1492 and subsequent years, especially in Central America and the Caribbean, and widely contrasting estimates and theories are presented. The more important chapters include the following: Woodrow Borah "The Historical Demography of Aboriginal and Colonial America: An Attempt at Perspective" p. 13–34. Angel Rosenblat "The Population of Hispaniola at the Time of Columbus" p. 43–66. David R. Radell "The Indian Slave Trade and Population of Nicaragua during the Sixteenth

Century" p. 67–76. William T. Sanders "The Population of the Central Mexican Symbiotic Region, the Basin of Mexico, and the Teotihuacan Valley in the Sixteenth Century" p. 85–150. Jane Pyle "A Reexamination of Aboriginal Population Estimates for Argentina" p. 181–204. William M. Denevan "The Aboriginal Population of Amazonia" p. 205–234.

1473 De Vany, Arthur and Nicolás Sánchez. Property rights, uncertainty and fertility: an analysis of the effect of land reform on fertility in rural Mexico (CAUK/WA, 4:113, 1977, p. 741–764, tables)

Institutional structure of Mexico's recent land reform program found to encourage high fertility because children are considered important economic assets. Author argues that changing land rights might therefore act to reduce fertility. Relationship of mortality parameters to fertility trends is emphasized. Report is basically a theoretical and empirical exercise without the benefit of original or published data.

1474 Dominican Republic. Secretaría de Estado de Salud Pública y Asistencia Social. Consejo Nacional de Población y Familia (CONAPOFA). Encuesta nacional de fecundidad: informe general. Prefacio de Luis González Fabra. Santo Domingo, 1976. 611 p., tables.

Results of nationwide research on fertility and related parameters in Dominican Republic. Following review of recent population trends, authors thoroughly describe questionnaires, census, and methods utilized in investigation. Numerous variables contributing to fertility differences are examined, including age at marriage, divorce, number of spouses, use of contraceptives, and attitudes regarding ideal family size.

Ebanks, G. Edward; P.M. George; and Charles E. Nobbe. Fertility and number of partnerships in Barbados. See item **9149.**

1475 Edmonston, Barry and Frank William Oechsli. Fertility decline and socioeconomic change in Venezuela (UM/JIAS, 19:3, August 1977, p. 369–392, bibl., tables)

Natality has declined in Venezuela since the early 1960s, accompanied by progressive socioeconomic development. Excellent tabular materials illustrate this trend and help identify regional geographic variations.

Increasing migration rates have contributed to fertility reductions. Future population projections are included. For sociologist's comment, see item **9020.**

1476 ——— **and Jorge Sapoznikow.** Measuring fertility in Latin America (IASI/E, 30:114, julio 1976, p. 68–78, tables)

"Synthesis" article on subject of high fertility in Latin America. Authors consider availability and reliability of data sources, as well as problems in sampling and formulating estimates. Quality of fertility data regarding Latin American populations is very uneven at present.

Encuentro Nacional sobre la Investigación Demográfica en la República Dominicana, *Santa Domingo, 1977.* La investigación demográfica en la República Dominicana: una evaluación. See item **9151.**

1477 Freire-Maia, N. and N. Takehara. Inbreeding effect on precocious mortality in Japanese communities of Brazil (UCGL/AHG, 41:1, July 1977, p. 99–110, bibl., tables)

Possible relationship between inbreeding and early mortality found in three endogamous Japanese communities in Brazil. The more inbred populations showed higher rates of prenatal mortality, stillbirths, infant mortality, and childbirth death. Inbreeding loads estimated with statistical techniques.

1478 García, Brígida and others. Revisión crítica de los estudios de fecundidad en América Latina. Presentación de Susana Lerner y Brígida García. Introducción de Elza Berquó. B.A., Grupo de Trabajo sobre el Proceso de Reproducción de la Población, Comisión de Población y Desarrollo, [and] Consejo Latinoamericano de Ciencias Sociales (CLACSO), 1974. 150 p., tables (Reproducción de la población y desarrollo, 1. Serie población)

Collection of seven articles resulting from conference on fertility and reproductive behaviors in various Latin American populations. Several methodological innovations are offered in a number of the papers.

1479 Giraldo Samper, Diego. Migración interna y salud en Colombia. Prólogo de Gilda Echeverría Alarcón. Bogotá, Asociación Colombiana de Facultades de Medicina (AS-COFAME), División de Medicina Social y Población, 1976. 171 p., fold. table, tables.

Effective and well-executed bio-demographic study of population movement and its multiple medical consequences in Colombia. Abundant demographic data provided on migrants as well as general national population.

González Navarro, Moisés. Población y sociedad en México: 1900–1970. See item **9079.**

1480 Gray, Elmer and J. Bortolozzi. Studies of the human sex ratio and factors influencing family size in Botucatu, Brazil (Journal of Heredity [American Genetic Assn., Washington] 68:4, July/Aug. 1977, p. 241–244, bibl., table)

Study of possible correlation between population sex ratio, mate selection, and fertility in Brazil. Sex ratio found to be identical to that in the US and falls near the middle of the range established for human populations.

1481 Halberstein, Robert A. Fertility in two urban Mexican-American populations (Urban Anthropology [State Univ. of New York, Dept. of Anthropology, Brockport, N.Y.] 5:4, 1976, p. 335–350, bibl., illus., tables)

Fertility levels in Mexican-Americans of Kansas City metropolitan area discovered to be notably lower than national averages for Mexican-Americans, and various explanatory theories are offered. The reduced fertility may be partly due to certain unique features of demographic structure and mate selection. Data compared with Mexican, US, and other Mexican-American populations.

1482 Hern, Warren M. High fertility in a Peruvian Amazon Indian village (Human Ecology [Plenum, N.Y.] 5:4, Dec. 1977, p. 355–368, bibl., tables)

Fertility studied in well-defined population from the Amazon jungle in Peru that is undergoing rapid acculturation. High fertility found to be the result of sizeable natality rates, early marriage, brief birth intervals, and diminishing infant mortality, with the latter related to the introduction of improved ("Western") medical care.

1483 Hill, K.; H. Behm; and A. Soliz. La situación de la mortalidad en Bolivia. La Paz, Presidencia de la República, Ministerio de Planeamiento y Coordinación, Instituto Nacional de Estadística, Centro Latinoamericano de Demografía, 1976. 39 p., bibl., tables.

Descriptive report on demographic aspects of mortality in Bolivia based mainly upon census data. Life tables are constructed, and sex, age, and regional differences in mortality are quantified. Substantial space devoted to methodological considerations, but monograph lacks table of contents and sufficient comparative reference citations.

1484 International Population Conference (Congrès International de la Population), *Mexico, 1977.* International Population Conference (Congrès International de la Population): Mexico, 1977. v. 3. Liège, Belgium, International Union for the Scientific Study of Population (IUSSP), 1977. 516 p., bibls., illus., tables.

Collection of 88 symposium papers dealing with population problems in Latin America and elsewhere. Topics include fertility, population growth, adult and childhood mortality, mate selection, migration, nutrition, urbanization, population genetics, energy conservation, and population policies.

1485 Kahley, William J. and R.T. Gillaspy. An economic model of contraceptive choice: analysis of family planning acceptors in Bogotá (Social Biology [Society for the Study of Social Biology, N.Y.] 24:2, Summer 1977, p. 135–143, bibl., tables)

Questionnaire data consulted to determine factors involved in choice of type of contraceptive (pill or IUD) by Bogotá women. Income, education level, parity, and age found to be significantly associated with choice of contraceptive.

1486 Lasker, Gabriel W. Increments through migration to the coefficient of relationship between communities estimated by isonymy (WSU/HB, 50:3, Sept. 1978, p. 235–240, bibl., table)

Genetic relationships among five Peruvian populations estimated by isonymy. Role of migration is assessed. Use of actual data indicates slight correction factors needed when employing isonymy data.

1487 Lazo, B. and others. Inbreeding and immigration in urban and rural zones of Chile, with an endogamy index (Social Biology [Society for the Study of Social Biology, N.Y.] 25:3, Fall 1978, p. 228–234, bibl., tables)

Breeding and migration patterns are described for urban and rural areas of Chile, based upon religious documents and vital statistics records dating from 1865. Populations are generally endogamous, more so in the rural sample.

1488 Malina, Robert M. and J.H. Himes.
Differential age effects in seasonal variation of mortality in a rural Zapotec-speaking *municipio*, 1945–1970 (WSU/HB, 49:3, Sept. 1977, p. 415–428, bibl., tables)

Seasonal variation in mortality reconstructed from vital registers pertaining to rural Mexican Indian community. Mortality rates higher during rainy months in children age 1–4, but infants (under one year of age) showed no season variation in mortality.

1489 ——— and ———. Seasonality of births in a rural Zapotec *municipio*, 1945–1970 (WSU/HB, 49:2, May 1977, p. 125–137, bibl., map, tables)

Seasonal distribution of births reported for rural Mexican community over 26-year period. Higher birth rates discovered during rainy season, and possible cultural explanations are offered.

1490 Mariscal, José D.O. and others. Consideraciones biopsicosociales de mujeres que solicitan esterilización (Ginecología y Obstetricia de México [Federación Mexicana de Asociaciones de Ginecología y Obstetricia, México] 41[32]:243, enero 1977, p. 15–21, bibl., tables)

Research on 252 Mexican women who requested tubal sterilization. Attendant biomedical, psychological, social, and economic variables are capably handled. Increased education is recommended.

1491 Mauldin, W. Parker. Tendencias en la fecundidad: 1950–1975 (ACEP/EP, 1:2, 1976, p. 387–398, tables)

World population increased by 60 percent during 1950–75, and author compares various developing and industrialized countries with regard to fertility and population growth. South and Central American countries show slight fertility reductions, mainly due to increased usage of contraceptives. Data provided on 18 Latin American and Caribbean nations.

Miller, Frank C. and Rolf Sartorius. Population policy and public goods. See item **944.**

1492 Müller, María S. La mortalidad en Buenos Aires entre 1855 y 1960. Prólogo de Jorge L. Somoza. B.A., Instituto Torcuato di Tella, Centro de Investigaciones Sociales, Editorial del Instituto [and] Centro Latinoamericano de Demografía, 1974. 141 p., bibl., tables (Programa de actividades demográficas, Serie naranja: sociología)

Multifaceted research on temporal patterns of mortality in B.A. Death rates manifest alternate periods of stability and rapid change between 1855 and 1960. Mortality found to vary by age, sex, place of birth, and disease. Considerable portion of monograph (64 p.) consists of statistical and graphic appendices. Excellent charts and tables are interspersed throughout the text. For sociologist's comment, see item **9276.**

1493 Onaka, Alvin T. and others. Reproductive time lost through marital dissolution in metropolitan Latin America (Social Biology [Society for the Study of Social Biology, N.Y.] 24:2, Summer 1977, p. 100–116, bibl., tables)

Survey data from six Latin American metropolitan areas (B.A., Mexico City, Caracas, Bogotá, Rio, and San José) examined to measure effects of marital dissolution upon fertility. More reproductive time is lost through dissolution of consensual rather than legal unions.

1494 Pérez Diez, A.A. and F.M. Salzano.
Evolutionary implications of the ethnography and demography of Ayoreo Indians (Journal of Human Evolution [Academic Press, London] 7:3, March 1978, p. 253–268, bibl., tables)

Demographic characteristics described for relatively unacculturated Ayoreo Indians of Bolivia and Paraguay. Fertility, mortality, and mate selection patterns are quantified, and their evolutionary implications are discussed. Vital statistics reveal, for example, that a high opportunity exists for the action of natural selection.

1495 Pinto-Cisternas J. and others. Some determinants of mating structure in a rural zone of Chile, 1810–1959 (Social Biology [Society for the Study of Social Biology, N.Y.] 24:3, Fall 1977, p. 233–244, bibl., tables)

Mate selection patterns determined for rural communities of Chile from 7,671 marriage certificates. Level of consanguinity has changed over the years, due to demographic and cultural variables. Mating structure also influenced by celibacy, widowhood, and illegitimacy.

1496 Potter, Joseph E. and others. El rápido descenso de la fecundidad (ACEP/EP, 2:1, Jan. 1977, p. 35–51, bibl., illus., tables)

Recent census data cited indicating a gradual decline in fertility in Colombia which began in 1964. Urbanization and contraceptive usage are inversely correlated with fertility levels throughout the country. Family planning programs have generally been successful in lowering fertility in Colombia. For sociologist's comment, see item **9219.**

1497 Pourchet, Maria J. El control de la natalidad entre los indios brasileños (III/AI, 37:2, abril/junio 1977, p. 337–351, bibl., tables)

Investigation of use of plants as contraceptives among the Kaingang Indians of Brazil. Some of the medicinals act as abortifacients and some prevent pregnancy. Natality rates are low in this traditionally hunting-gathering population.

1498 Prada, Elena and **Jerald Bailey.** Tendencias de la fecundidad en Colombia: "algo importante ha sucedido" (UA/TA, 26, abril/junio 1977, p. 19–24, graphs)

Speculations on possible causes of unexpected fertility decline in Colombia in recent years. Data cited suggest family planning and contraceptive usage have been successful in reducing natality rates.

Presser, Harriet B. Sterilization and fertility decline in Puerto Rico. See item **9181.**

1499 Reining, Priscilla and others. Village women, their changing lives and fertility: studies in Kenya, Mexico and the Phillippines. Washington, American Association for the Advancement of Sciences (AAAS), 1977. 273 p., bibl., tables.

Large computerized investigation of changing trends in "traditional" village population from three geographically diversified countries. The Mexican groups are from an area northwest of Mexico City. Methodology includes life histories, censuses, and socioeconomic surveys. Life tables and population pyramids are constructed and compared through historical periods. Case studies of extremely fertile and less reproductive women are presented.

Rivarola, Domingo M. and others. La población del Paraguay. See item **9289.**

1500 Roberts, George W. and **Sonja A. Sinclair.** Women in Jamaica: patterns of reproduction and family. Millwood, N.Y., KTO Press, 1978. 346 p., bibl., illus., tables.

Ambitious but often diffuse and repetitious exposition on family structure and fertility in Jamaica. Menarche, mate selection, birth control, achieved fertility, reproductive wastage, childhood mortality, and household composition are all quantified with simple statistics. Appendixed are case studies, sample survey questionnaires, and raw data. For sociologist's comment, see item **9184.**

Rojo, Alejandro. Las villas de emergencia. See item **9281.**

1501 Sainz, Santiago G. Investigación sobre el aborto en América Latina (ACEP/EP, 1:8, Aug. 1976, p. 439–449, bibl., tables)

Investigation of induced abortion in nine Latin American countries including discussions of incidence, different types and methods, attitudes, and outcomes. Elaboration of abortion education throughout region is recommended.

Samper, Diego Giraldo. Migración interna y salud en Colombia. See item **9220.**

1502 Simos, Bertha G. and **M. Kohls.** Migration, relocation, and intergenerational relations: Jews of Quito, Ecuador (The Gerontologist [Gerontological Society, St. Louis, Mo.] 15:3, June 1975, p. 206–211, bibl.)

Demographic analysis of aging in Jewish community (population = 800) of urban Quito, Ecua. (population = 409,000). Health, social, and psychological problems associated with aging are identified. Jewish population of Quito has sharply decimated since World War II, partly because of continuous emigration.

1503 Spinetti, Patrizia and **Erasmo Ramírez.** La Fría: aspectos demográficos y desalud. Mérida, Ven., Univ. de los Andes, Facultad de Economía, Instituto de Investigaciones Económicas, 1977. 102 p., bibl., tables.

Assemblage of demographic facts and statistics on populations in Venezuela, with emphasis upon fertility, mortality, migration patterns, population structure and growth, and public health. Future population projections are estimated.

1504 Taveres-Neto, José and E.S. Azevedo.
Racial origin and historical aspects of family names in Bahia, Brazil (WSU/HB, 49:3, Sept. 1977, p. 287–299, bibl., tables)

Surnames of 6,002 individuals from Brazil studied with respect to origins and racial history. Temporal study of names revealed influence of social and religious customs, historical events, and interbreeding and admixture with outside groups.

Universidad de La Habana. Instituto de Economía. Centro de Estudios Demográficos (CEDEM). La población de Cuba. See item **3083**.

1505 Universidad Nacional Pedro Henríquez Ureña (UNPHU), *Santo Domingo.*
Centro de Investigaciones. Unidad de Estudios Sociales. Estudio del aborto en 200 mujeres en la República Dominicana: recomendaciones para la educación en planificación familiar. Santo Domingo, 1975. 176 p., bibl., tables.

In-depth investigation of spontaneous and induced abortion in carefully selected and representative sample of 200 women in the Dominican Republic. Causes, results, and demographic aspects of abortion meticulously described in numerous tables, graphs, and charts. Author provides operational definitions of key terms, a discussion of methodological shortcomings, and practical recommendations for the future.

1506 Wasserstrom, Robert. Population growth and economic development in Chiapas, 1524–1975 (Human Ecology [Plenum, N.Y.] 6:2, June 1978, p. 127–143, bibl., illus., tables)

Employing historical and demographic evidence, author demonstrates that the recent destruction of lands and forests in state of Chiapas, Mex., is the direct result of development of commercial agriculture more so than overpopulation. Useful statistics on population size change are included.

1507 Wills Franco, Margarita. Diferencias regionales de la fecundidad en Colombia. Bogotá, Asociación Colombiana de Facultades de Medicina (ASCOFAME), División de Medicina Social y Población, 1976. 106 p., map, tables.

In-depth investigation of fertility and fecundity in Colombia. Following a cultural anthropological survey of different ethnic and linguistic groups, the fertility of 2,097 women is documented in terms of geography, climate, family structure, and different attitudes toward childbirth and ideal family size. For sociologist's comment, see item **9224**.

1508 Zambrano Lupi, Jorge H. Algunas consideraciones sobre el proceso de urbanización y la fecundidad en el estado Trujillo. Mérida, Ven., Univ. de los Andes, Facultad de Ciencias Forestales, Instituto de Geografía y Conservación de Recursos Naturales, 1975. 98 p., bibl., fold. tables, tables.

Outstanding statistical case study of relationship of urbanization and fertility in a large state in Venezuela. Following an operational definition of "urban" applicable to the study area, data are presented indicating that urbanization is statistically associated with fertility reduction.

POPULATION STUDIES: GENETICS

1509 Ahern, E. and others. Gamma chain variants in Jamaican newborns (Hemoglobin [Marcel Dekker Journals, N.Y.] 1:2, 1977, p. 153–169, bibl., tables)

15,661 cord blood samples from Jamaican newborns examined electrophoretically for abnormal hemoglobins. Sixteen variants were detected, and their biochemical and hematological characteristics are described.

1510 Baume, Robert M. and **Michael H. Crawford.** Discrete dental traits in four Tlaxcaltecan Mexican populations (AJPA, 49:3, Sept. 1978, p. 351–360, bibl., illus., map, tables)

Ten discrete dental characteristics studied in 700 dental casts taken from four Mexican Indian populations of known ethnohistory. Statistically significant morphological differences reflect population splintering from parental gene pool. Genetic distances are calculated, and the influence of Spanish and African admixture is estimated from the data.

1511 Bosch, N.B. de and others. An abnormal fibrinogen in a Venezuelan family (Thrombosis Research [Pergamon Press, Elmsford, N.Y.] 10:3, 1977, p. 253–265, bibl., tables)

An abnormal fibrinogen, "Caracas," reported for a Venezuelan family. Genetics and biochemical aspects of the variant protein are discussed. Molecular and hematological data are provided.

1512 Callegari Jacques, Sidia M. and others. Palmar dermatoglyphic patterns in twins (HH, 27:6, 1977, p. 437–443, bibl., tables)

Heritability of various palmar dermatoglyphic patterns estimated in series of 49 MZ and 51 DZ twins from Porto Alegre, Brazil. Spearman's rank correlation and analysis of variance tests suggest differential roles of genetics in the development of the different dermatoglyphic traits.

1513 Chakraborty, Ranajit. Cultural, language, and geographic correlates of genetic variability in Andean highland Indians (NWJS, 264:5584, Nov. 1976, p. 305–352, bibl., tables)

Data from Chilean populations suggest that genetic distances correlate best with geographic distances compared with cultural or linguistic distances. Seven different highland Indian tribes are examined with respect to seven serological-genetic markers.

1514 Chautard-Freire-Maia, E.A. Probable assignment of the serum cholinesterase (E_1) and transferrin (Tf) loci to chromosome 1 in man (HH, 27:2, 1977, p. 134–142, bibl., tables)

Results of new gene mapping work based mainly upon data from Brazilian populations. Assignment of loci for serum cholinesterase and transferrin to chromosome 1 is proposed, based upon their apparent close linkage with each other and with the Rh locus which has already been confirmed for chromosome 1.

1515 Crawford, Michael H. Population dynamics of Tlaxcala, Mexico: the effects of gene flow, selection, and geography on the distribution of gene frequencies (*in* Meier, Robert J., C. Otten; and F. Abdul-Hameed *eds.* Evolutionary models and studies in human diversity. The Hague, Mouton, 1978, p. 215–225, bibl., tables)

Summary paper which outlines several quantitative attempts to reconstruct recent evolutionary events in Central Mexico. Using historical, demographic, and gene frequency data, author charts patterns of Spanish gene

flow and hybridization which commenced some four and a half centuries ago. Genetic distances and admixture estimates are derived from five separate statistical methods applied to 15 genetic loci.

1516 Cruz-Coke, R. Epidemiología genética de las malformaciones congénitas en Chile (SMS/RMC, 105:4, 1977, p. 261–264, bibl., tables)

Statistical analysis of congenital malformation epidemiology in Chile. Morbidity and mortality records reviewed for Santiago hospitals. Malformations of the locomotor system were the most frequent, while those affecting the nervous system were the most lethal in the samples studied. Congenital hip dysplasia found to be an especially prevalent condition in Chile.

1517 Díaz, J.W. and **A.N. Cheredeev.** Distribution of HLA antigens in a Cuban population (Tissue Antigens [Copenhagen] 9:2, 1977, p. 71–79, bibl., tables)

HLA system studied in 160 blood samples of Cubans representing "white, black, and mixed" racial groups. Statistically significant differences found in genotypic and phenotypic frequencies found across the ethnic groups. Genetic distances are calculated, including comparisons with contemporary Spanish populations.

1518 Ebeli-Struijk, Alida C. and others. The distribution of esterase D variants in different ethnic groups (Human Genetics [Excerpta Medica Foundation, Amsterdam] 34:3, 1976, p. 299–306, bibl., tables)

General review of geographic and ethnic variation in gene frequencies and distributions of the multiple forms of esterase D (ESD), a polymorphic red blood cell enzyme. Nine South American Indian populations are included in the investigation, which involves both original and previously published data. Statistically significant differences discovered across different ethnic groups in the distribution of ESD alleles.

1519 Escobar, Víctor and others. The dentition of the Queckchi Indians: anthropological aspects (AJPA, 47:3, Nov. 1977, p. 443–452, bibl., tables)

Frequency of occurrence of nine discrete dental traits summarized for sample of 540 Queckchi Indians of Guatemala. Effects of admixture are estimated. Large amounts of published material drawn together in comparative table.

1520 Ferrell, Robert E. and others. The Aymara of western Bolivia: pt. 4, Gene frequencies for eight blood groups and 19 protein and erythocyte enzyme systems (ASHG/J, 30:5, Sept. 1978, p. 539–549, bibl., plates, tables)

Electrophoresis used to depict level of polymorphisms at 27 genetic loci determining blood characteristics of 429 Aymara Indians of Bolivia. Extensive intragroup genetic variation reported. Rare biochemical variants are described.

1521 ―― and others. The blacks of Panama: their genetic diversity as assessed of 15 inherited biochemical systems (AJPA, 48:3, March 1978, p. 269–278, bibl., map, plates, tables)

777 Panamanian blacks of African ancestry investigated with respect to 15 biochemical polymorphisms, including hemoglobin, serum proteins, and red cell enzymes. Diversity within and across village and linguistic groups shown with allele frequency tabulations, and genetic distances are calculated. Rare variants are described.

1522 Freire-Maia, N. and others. Genetic investigation in a northern Brazilian island: pt. 1, Population structure; pt. 2, Random drift (HH, 28:5, 1978, p. 386–396, bibl., map, tables; 28:6, 1978, p. 401–410, bibl., illus., tables)

Pt. 1 of this study reports on descriptive research on population structure of small (307) Brazilian island. Effective population size is low, but island is not isolated and inbreeding is avoided through migration and mate selection. As a result, inbreeding coefficient (0.0015) is about five to nine times lower than that expected statistically. Coefficient of kinship estimated as 0.01. Pt. 2 consists of genealogical, clinical, and histological data presented on a number of genetic anomalies of this small (307) Brazilian island. Distribution of albinism, brachydactyly, and achondroplasia suggested recent action of genetic drift. Index of isolation is calculated.

1523 ―― and others. Random genetic drift in the population of a Brazilian island (UC/CA, 18:2, June 1977, p. 353)

Brief preliminary report on evidence of genetic drift on small (307) island of Brazil.

Effective population size and migration rates are provided, along with fertility and mortality data. Unusually large number of albinos suggests action of genetic drift.

1524 Frisancho, A. Roberto and others. Taste sensitivity to phenylthiourea (PTC), tongue rolling, and hand clasping among Peruvian and other native American populations (WSU/HB, 49:2, May 1977, p. 155–163, bibl., tables)

Various genetic characteristics recorded for over 1,000 Quechua Indians and 850 mestizos from Peru. Similarities and differences among samples reflect environmental and genetic diversity across groups.

1525 Gallango, M.L. and **R. Suinaga.** Uridine monophosphate kinase polymorphism in two Venezuelan populations (ASHG/J, 30:2, March 1978, p. 215–218, bibl., plate, table)

Brief report on variation in red blood cell enzyme UMPK in Warao Indians and mestizos of Venezuela. Three different UMPK phenotypes distinguished in 510 blood samples, and their electrophoretic characteristics are described.

1526 Garay, Alfonso L. de; Lourdes Cobo de Gallegos; and James E. Bowman. Relaciones familiares en el pedigree de los lancandones de México (INAH/A, 5:53, 1974/1975, p. 271–285, plates, tables)

Pedigree analysis of the relatively isolated and genetically unique Lacandon Indians of Chiapas state, Mex. Numerous genetic markers, including blood groups and PTC taste sensitivity, are compared with other populations, and authors present several interesting cases of the effects of consanguinity upon human biology.

1527 Garcia, Marileila Varella. Blood groups and dermatoglyphics in a Brazilian population of Arabian origin (SBPC/CC, 29:7, julho 1977, p. 826–829, bibl., tables)

Gene frequencies of ABO and Rh blood group systems and dermatoglyphic traits presented for sample of 316 "unmixed" individuals of Arabian ancestry residing in Brazilian community. Results suggest increasing admixture and selective gene flow into the ethnic enclave.

1528 Gershowitz, Henry and **J.V. Neel.** The immunoglobin allotypes (Gm and Km) of 12 Indian tribes of Central and South America (AJPA, 49:3, Sept. 1978, p. 289–302, bibl., maps, tables)

Immunoglobin polymorphisms presented for 12 Indian tribes from Central and South America. Gene frequency data used to check previous theories of ancient peopling of South American continent and supposed recent patterns of gene flow.

1529 Go, R.C.P. and others. Association and linkage between genetic markers and morphological and behavioral attributes in dizygotic twins (Social Biology [Society for the Study of Social Biology, N.Y.] 24:1, Spring 1977, p. 62–68, bibl., tables)

Fifty-one same-sex dizygotic twin pairs from Brazil studied to establish possible association of 49 quantitative traits with seven genetic markers of the blood. Some significant correlations found, and authors postulate that social or physical environment may affect the linked traits simultaneously. Results may be also due to pleiotropy or epistasis.

1530 Goedde, H.W. and others. Genetic studies in Ecuador: acetylator phenotypes, red cell enzyme and serum protein polymorphisms of Shuara Indians (AJPA, 47:3, Nov. 1977, p. 419–426, bibl., maps, tables)

Population genetics of several enzyme and protein polymorphisms presented for Ecuadorian Indian group. Findings (based on 90 blood samples) compared with other populations.

1531 Hauptmann, G. and others. Bf polymorphism: another variant (Human Genetics [Excerpta Medica Foundation, Amsterdam] 36:1, 1977, p. 109–111, bibl., illus.)

Previously undescribed genetic variant in the polymorphic Bf protein system found in serum of three individuals from isolated communities of Brazilian Indians. New variant probably represents another allele at the Bf locus.

1532 Hutz, Mara H. and others. Three rare G-6-PD variants from Porto Alegre, Brazil (Human Genetics [Excerpta Medica Foundation, Amsterdam] 39:2, 1977, p. 191–197, bibl., plates, tables)

Three rare G-6-PD variants detected in electrophoretic screening of 772 children and their mothers in Porto Alegre, Brazil.

Characteristics of the three rare phenotypes are presented. Allele frequencies are estimated.

1533 Marques, M. and J. Marques. Dermatoglyphics and color blindness (IGM/AGMG, 26:3/4, 1977, p. 291–292, bibl., tables)

Dermatoglyphic analysis of all members of four Brazilian families containing color-blind members. Data did not show any significant differences from patterns seen in control subjects.

1534 Murillo, Federico and others. The Chipaya of Bolivia: determatoglyphics and ethnic relationships (AJPA, 46:1, Jan. 1977, p. 45–50, bibl., map, tables)

Data on 15 dermatoglyphic traits compiled from sample of 141 Chipaya Indians of Bolivia. Biological relationships with surrounding groups are estimated through genetic distance measures involving biochemical polymorphisms. Phylogenetic relationships based on the different data sets are compared with linguistic and geographic distances.

1535 Neel, James V. Application of multiple variable analysis to questions of Amerindian relationships (AI/I, 1:3, sept./oct. 1976, p. 147–155, tables)

Origins and biological relationships of Central and South American Indian populations traced through comparisons of genetic markers in some 50 "unmixed" tribes. Role of differential and selective migration in observed genetic affiliations is assessed. Paper represents theoretical synthesis of a tremendous amount of diverse data obtained over the past several years.

1536 ———. Rare variants, private polymorphisms, and locus heterozygosity in Amerindian populations (ASHG/J, 30:5, Sept. 1978, p. 465–490, bibl., map, tables)

Theoretical discussion of gene frequency distribution and variation in 21 tribes of South American Indians. Data consists of results of 21,103 electrophoretic typings and statistical analyses of variability at 28 genetic loci. Eleven "private" polymorphisms explained in evolutionary terms.

1537 ——— and E.A. Thompson. Founder effect and number of private polymorphisms observed in Amerindian tribes (NAS/P, 75:4, April 1978, p. 1904–1908, bibl., tables)

Twenty-eight genetic loci (polymorphic protein systems) studied in 12 Indian populations from Central and South America. Frequency and distribution of rare electrophoretic variants suggest the possibility of the founder effect in at least eight different cases.

1538 —— and others. Genetic studies of the Macushi and Wapishana Indians: pt. 1, Rare genetic variants and "private polymorphism" of Esterase A; pt. 2, Data on 12 genetic polymorphisms of the red-cell and serum proteins: gene flow between the tribes (Human Genetics [Excerpta Medica Foundation, Amsterdam] 36:1, 1977, p. 81–107, bibl., tables; 36:2, 1977, p. 207–219, bibl., tables)

Pt. 1 of this two-part study is a genetic, statistical, and microevolutionary analysis of polymorphisms and rare variants in 1,132 Amerindians from northern Brazil and southern Guyana. Twenty-five genetic systems are studied, including red cell enzymes, blood groups, and serum proteins. Previously undetected variants and intratribal variations are described. Pt. 2 reports on blood samples of 1,132 Amerindians from 14 villages in northern Brazil and southern Guyana analyzed with respect to 12 polymorphic genetic systems. Probable pattern of gene flow and population inbreeding constructed from gene frequency data and checked with linguistic and cultural information especially pertaining to mate selection customs.

1539 Palomino, Hernán and others. Dental morphology and population diversity (WSU/HB, 49:1, Feb. 1977, p. 61–70, bibl., tables)

Values of dental criteria in assessing genetic differences among populations investigated through previously collected data from seven Yanomama Indian villages in Brazil and Venezuela. Variation within and across populations is described. Sanghvi's distance measure used to construct dendrogram illustrating phylogenetic relationships of several new world populations based upon dental characteristics.

1540 Rothhammer, Francisco and others. A collation of marker gene and dermatoglyphic diversity at various levels of population differentiation (AJPA, 46:1, Jan. 1977, p. 51–60, bibl., tables)

Relative accuracy and value of dermatoglyphic traits in assessing population affinities tested by comparing data with biochemical genetic polymorphisms in eight South American Indian groups. Degree of congruence between dermatoglyphic and genetic marker data varied by population size, structure, and level of evolutionary differentiation.

1541 Roychoudhury, A.K. Gene differentiation in three tribes of American Indians (HH, 27:5, 1977, p. 389–392, bibl., tables)

Degree of genetic microdifferentiation estimated in subpopulations of Papago (US), Makiritare (Venezuela), and Yanomama (Brazil) Indians, based upon 11 blood group loci and two serum protein systems. Largest proportion of genetic differences discovered within, rather than across, the subpopulations.

1542 ——. Genetic distance between the American Indians and the three major races of man (HH, 28:5, p. 380–385, bibl., tables)

Gene frequencies and distributions of 26 loci reviewed for Amerindians and compared with those in "Caucasoids," "Negroids," and "Mongoloids." Results support theory of close evolutionary relationship of native Asian and New World peoples. Author estimates possible divergence dates of Amerindian groups and other "major races" of mankind. Published data are consulted on populations from Mexico, Venezuela, Peru, and Brazil.

1543 Salzano, Francisco M. Population structure and genetic variability in South American Indians (AI/I, 1:3, sept./oct. 1976, p. 155–158, tables)

Evolutionary origins of South American Indians addressed in theoretical overview of biodemographic and genetic information previously collected on over 12,000 individuals representing 17 different tribes. Extensive intratribal variability marks these groups, and the data suggest substantial gene flow and hybridization among linguistically distinctive populations.

1544 —— and others. Intra- and intertribal genetic variation within a linguistic group: the Ge-speaking Indians of Brazil (AJPA, 47:2, Sept. 1977, p. 337–348, bibl., map, tables)

Diversity in blood groups, serum proteins, and enzymes evaluated in 562 individuals from four villages of two separate tribes. Results compared with previously investigated populations from surrounding regions. Communities representing Ge linguistic group exhibited unusually low levels of internal variation in the polymorphic systems.

1545 ——— and others. Unusual blood genetic characteristics among the Ayoreo Indians of Bolivia and Paraguay (WSU/HB, 50:2, May 1978, p. 121–136, bibl., table)

Thirty-three serological and one salivary protein polymorphisms were examined in 363 Ayoreo Indians from three localities in southern South America. Populations found to be generally unacculturated, intratribally exogamous, and relatively undifferentiated in allelic frequencies. Numerous rare and unusual genetic characteristics are described, and genetic distances are calculated with 21 other Latin American Indian populations.

1546 Schanfield, M.S. and others. The distribution of immunoglobin allotypes in two Tlaxcaltecan populations (Annals of Human Biology [Taylor and Francis Publishers, London] 5:6, 1978, p. 577–590, bibl., tables)

Immunoglobin polymorphisms tabulated for 747 blood specimens collected in two migrant Mexican Indian populations. Gene frequencies are calculated, and populations are compared with other Mesoamerican native groups. Degree of Caucasian and African admixture estimated with statistical techniques. Unusual immunoglobin variants are reported.

1547 Serrano, Carlos. Distribución de los grupos sanguíneos sistemas ABO y Rh en un contigente militar mexicano (UNAM/AA, 14, 1977, p. 373–380, bibl., tables)

ABO and Rh blood group antigens examined in sample of 1,305 military personnel from Mexico City. Gene frequency distributions interpreted in light of evidence on different levels of European admixture among tested subjects.

1548 Smouse, P.E. and **J.V. Neel.** Multivariate analysis of genetic disequilibrium in the Yanomama (Genetics [Genetics, Inc. and Univ. of Texas, Austin] 85:4, April 1977, p. 733–752, bibl., illus., tables)

Gene frequencies examined for eight codominant loci in 50 Yanomama Indian villages from South America. 32 of the

populations departed widely from what would be predicted as genetic equilibrium. Several unusual genetic distributions are probably the result of past fissioning of previously related populations.

1549 ——— and **R.H. Ward.** A comparison of the genetic infrastructure of the Ye'cuana and the Yanomama: a likelihood analysis of genotypic variation among populations (Genetics [Genetics, Inc. and Univ. of Texas, Austin] 88:3, March 1978, p. 611–631, bibl., tables)

New method is developed for measuring and testing population differences in genetic structure using Ye'cuana (Makiritare) and Yanomama gene frequency distributions as example cases. Variations at 11 polymorphic loci interpreted in light of demographic, cultural, and historic features of the tribes.

1550 Spielman, Richard S. and others. Inbreeding estimation from population data: models, procedures, and implications (Genetics [Genetics, Inc. and Univ. of Texas, Austin] 85:2, Feb. 1977, p. 355–371, bibl., tables)

Four different estimation procedures for models of population structure are compared and tested with actual data on nine codominant allele pairs in 47 villages of Yanomama Indians of South America. Historical information on mate selection and computer simulation studies indicate that inbreeding coefficients are probably underestimated by most statistical predictors.

1551 Tanis, Robert J. and others. Two more "private" polymorphisms of Amerindian tribes: LDH^b GUA-1 and ACP1 GUA-1 in the Guaymi in Panama (ASHG/J, 29:5, Sept. 1977, p. 419–430, bibl., plates, tables)

Electrophoretic survey of 25 polymorphic proteins of blood sera and erythrocytes for existence of genetic variants among the Guaymi Indians of Panama. 493 serum and 484 whole blood samples were tested. Fifteen of 25 systems found to be monomorphic. Several "private" alleles were detected.

1552 Taveres-Neto, José and **E.S. Azevedo.** Family names and ABO blood group frequencies in a mixed population of Bahia, Brazil (WSU/HB, 50:3, Sept. 1978, p. 361–367, bibl., tables)

Relationship of ABO allelic frequencies and family names investigated in sample of 3,602 blood donors from a hybridized Brazilian population. Data suggest that family names are more of an indicator of biological affiliation than ABO blood types.

1553 Tchen, Paul and others. A genetic study of two French Guiana Amerindian populations: pt. 1, Serum proteins and red-cell enzymes; pt. 2, Rare electrophoretic variants (Human Genetics [Excerpta Medica Foundation, Amsterdam] 45:3, 1978, p. 305–326, bibl., illus., maps, plates, tables)

Pt. 1 of this two-part study (published in one issue) describes phenotypic and genotypic frequencies presented for 20 polymorphic serum and red blood cell proteins in blood samples from nearly 100 percent of the Wayampi and Emerillon Indians of French Guiana. Genetic characteristics of these relatively unacculturated tropical forest populations are compared with other New World native groups. Pt. 2 notes serum and erythrocytic proteins and enzymes studies in Wayampi and Emerillon Indians of French Guiana. Rare electrophoretic variants discovered in five genetic systems. Similar isozymes have been identified in other Amerindian populations.

1554 —— and others. Histocompatibility antigens in two American Indian tribes of French Guyana (Tissue Antigens [Copenhagen] 11:3, 1978, p. 315–319, bibl., tables)

Two South American Indian groups are typed for polymorphic HLA antigens. Related individuals whose genealogies were known were chosen in order to study the mode of inheritance of the variants. Results compared with other Latin American populations, and the effects of drift and gene flow are postulated.

1555 Thompson, E.A. and **J.V. Neel.** Probability of founder effect in a tribal population (NAS/P, 75:3, March 1978, p. 1442–1445, bibl., tables)

Possible cases of genetic drift through the founder effect studied in 12 different Indian populations from Central and South America. By looking at examples of "private" alleles in these relatively isolated groups, eight possible examples of the founder principle are discussed.

1556 Tiburcio, V. and others. Gene frequencies and racial intermixture in a mestizo population from Mexico City (Annals of Human Biology [Taylor and Francis Publishers, London] 5:2, March 1978, p. 131–138, bibl., tables)

Red cell and serum proteins and enzymes analyzed in blood specimens from 460 mestizos in Mexico City. Degree of admixture estimated from gene frequencies of polymorphisms. Data confirm that European contribution to present gene pool has been substantial, and there has also been a small amount of gene flow from native African populations.

1557 Tondo, C.V. Asymmetric tetramer in a second occurrence of hemoglobin Porto Alegre (Hemoglobin [Marcel Dekker Journals, N.Y.C.] 1:2, 1977, p. 195–210, bibl., tables)

Genetic and molecular analysis of abnormal hemoglobin Porto Alegre discovered in a second Brazilian family. Structural hemoglobin change traced to Beta chain mutation. Hemoglobin Porto Alegre exhibits higher oxygen affinity than normal hemoglobin.

1558 Valenzuela, Carlos Y. and **Z. Harb.** Socioeconomic assortative mating in Santiago, Chile: a demonstration using stochastic matrices of mother-child relationships applied to ABO blood groups (Social Biology [Society for the Study of Social Biology, N.Y.] 24:3, Fall 1977, p. 225–233, bibl., tables)

ABO gene frequency data suggested assortative mating by socioeconomic status in two populations of Santiago, Chile. Significant differences found in gene distributions across the two sub-populations of distinct socioeconomic status.

1559 Van der Does, J.A. and others. A rare PGM1 variant in Chilean Aymara Indians (Human Genetics [Excerpta Medica Foundation, Amsterdam] 45:3, 1978, p. 327–329, bibl., illus.)

Nineteen genetic markers were typed for blood samples of 102 Aymara Indians from small population in Chile. Rare PGM isozymes reported.

1560 Vergnes, H. and others. Serum and red cell enzyme polymorphisms in six Amerindian tribes (Annals of Human Biology

[Taylor and Francis Publishers, London] 3:6, Nov. 1976, p. 577–585, bibl., tables)

Genetic polymorphisms in the blood of members of six tribes of Central and South American Indians are presented. Observed measurements are compared with several other Latin American populations.

HUMAN ADAPTATION AND VARIATION

1561 **Arias C., Sergio.** Etiología múltiple del enanismo entre los indios yukpa (irapa) de la Sierra de Perija llamados "pigmoides" (VMJ/BIV, 17:13, enero/dic. 1976, p. 49–72, bibl., plates)

In-depth examination of evidence regarding dwarfism among the Yukpa (Irapa) Indians from Venezuela. Both achondrodystrophic (achondroplastic) and glandular dwarfism display high incidence in this relatively inbred population. Author discourages the use of the terms "Pygmy" or "Pygmoid" to describe these individuals.

1562 **Baker, Paul T.** Research strategies in population biology and environmental stress (in Giles, Eugene and J.S. Friedlaender eds. The measure of man: methodologies in biological anthropology. Cambridge, Mass., Harvard Univ., Peabody Museum Press, 1976, p. 230–259, bibl., illus., tables)

Colorful chapter on methodology in studies of human adaptation featuring extensive data and description regarding high altitude Peruvians. Advantages and pitfalls of various approaches to the study of environmental stresses are perceptively outlined.

1563 **Barac-Neito, M.** and others. Aerobic work capacity in chronically undernourished adult males (Journal of Applied Physiology [The American Physiological Society, Washington] 44:2, Feb. 1978, p. 209–215, bibl., tables)

Work capacity, measured by oxygen consumption and endurance in specified tasks, was investigated in 49 adult males undergoing nutritional recuperation in a rural population of Colombia. Work capacity was significantly reduced in cases of severe malnutrition, and authors study abnormal aspects of hemoglobin, albumin, and other characteristics of the blood.

1564 **Beall, Cynthia M.** and others. The effects of high altitude on adolescent growth in southern Peruvian Amerindians (WSU/HB, 49:2, May 1977, p. 109–124, bibl., tables)

Effects of altitude on growth in height, weight, and chest dimensions explored in 576 individuals age 6–25 representing Indian populations from southern Peru. Altitude tends to depress growth in height and weight, but thoracic development is not similarly affected, indicating genetic independence of this characteristic.

1565 **Boggio, J.M. Falen.** La fonction surrenale pendant l'adaptation aux hauts plateaus (IFEA/B, 6:3/4, 1977, p. 123–127, bibl., table)

Adrenal gland activity monitored in 12 normal males native to sea level who were rapidly transported to 3,220 m. (9,660 ft.) in the Peruvian Andes. Observed increase in steroid production interpreted as an adaptation to the stress of hypoxia.

1566 **Brody, Jerome S.** and others. Lung elasticity and airway dynamics in Peruvian natives to high altitude (Journal of Applied Physiology [American Physiological Society, Washington] 42:2, Feb. 1977, p. 245–251, bibl., tables)

Differential roles of genetics and environment in formation of large lung sizes characteristic of high altitude people analyzed in highland and lowland populations of Peru. Various lines of physiological evidence lead to the controversial conclusion that the enlarged lungs primarily "result from postnatal hypoxic stimulation of lung growth."

1567 **Dennis, R.L.H.** and others. The digital and palmar dermatoglyphics of the Brazilian Mato Grosso Indians (WSU/HB, 50:3, Sept. 1978, p. 325–342, bibl., tables)

Technical review of dermatoglyphic traits in 405 Indians representing 10 tribes from Mato Grosso region in Brazil. Observed patterns compared with other South American native groups.

1568 **Díaz, Biffret** and others. The multinational Andean genetic and health program: pt. 2, Disease and disability among the Aymara (PAHO/B, 12:3, 1978, p. 219–235, bibl., plates, tables)

Interdisciplinary research on adaptation

and health in Aymara Indian population of high altitude Arica, Chile. Results of medical exams of 2,096 highland and coastal residents from 12 separate communities are compared. Clinical, genetic, and survey data employed to clarify the effects of altitude on cardiovascular, hematological, renal, respiratory, digestive, dermatologic, and other diseases.

1569 Díaz Sánchez, María Elena. Estudio osteológico y osteométrico del húmero en chinos de Cuba (Antropología y Prehistoria [Univ. de La Habana, Escuela de Ciencias Biológicas] 9:5, March 1976, p. 3–30, bibl., illus., plates, tables)

Descriptive research on metrical characteristics of 102 humerus bones from recent Chinese population of Cuba. Statistical analyses conducted on 18 separate measurements, and various osteological pathologies are reported.

1570 Fuchs, Andrew. Coca chewing and high altitude stress: possible effects of coca alkaloids on erythropoiesis (UC/CA, 19:2, June 1978, p. 277–290, bibl., tables)

Highlanders from Andes mountains in South America often report that coca chewing helps relieve cold, pain, and fatigue. Author's review of physiological data suggests coca alkaloids may also be adaptive during hypoxic stress by slightly inhibiting red blood cell production, thus reducing the possibility of pronounced polycythemia. Theory draws mixed reaction from commentators.

1571 García-Palmieri, Mario R. and others. Nutrient intake and serum lipids in urban and rural Puerto Rican men (ASCN/J, 30:12, 1977, p. 2092–2100, bibl., tables)

Dietary data collected on 8,254 men from Puerto Rico. Statistically significant rural-urban differences found in serum lipids (especially cholesterol and triglycerides), body weight, and nutrient intake. Numerous biomedical and dietary differences are described.

1572 Haas, Jere D.; Paul T. Baker; and Edward E. Hunt, Jr. The effects of high altitude on body size and composition of the newborn infant in southern Peru (WSU/HB, 49:4, Dec. 1977, p. 611–628, bibl., tables)

Effects of altitude on fetal growth explored in comparison of small sample (N = 72) of infants from highland and lowland populations of southern Peru. Measures of body size, body composition, and skeletal development are all significantly reduced at high altitude. Data suggest fetal growth at high altitude is depressed most during the final trimester of gestation.

1573 Hoff, Charles and **Ralph Garruto.** Differentials in resting heart rates and blood pressures between a high and low altitude sample of southern Peruvian Quechua (ZMA, 63:3, Dez. 1977, p. 275–285, bibl., tables)

Possible effects of altitude upon heart rate, blood pressure, and other cardiovascular characteristics examined in genetically-related high and low altitude Quechua Indian populations of southern Peru. Significant differences discovered between highland and lowland groups, probably due to both genetic and environmental factors.

1574 Jacobson, A. and others. The craniofacial pattern of the Lengua Indians of Paraguay (AJPA, 47:3, Nov. 1977, p. 467–472, bibl., plates, tables)

Cephalometric headfilms taken of 60 Lengua Indians from Paraguay and compared with 48 South African Caucasians. Significant differences found in degree of prognathism, dental position, and other traits, but small sample sizes prevent firm conclusions.

1575 Jaén, María Teresa; Carlos Serrano; and Juan Comas. Data antropométrica de algunas poblaciones indígenas mexicanas: aztecas, otomís, tarascos, coras, huicholes. México, UNAM, Instituto de Investigaciones Antropológicas, 1976. 112 p., fold. tables, map, plates, tables (Cuadernos. Serie antropológicas, 28)

Anthropometric descriptions and comparisons of 680 Mexicans representing five separate Indian groups from five different states. Fifty body measurements and 16 indices are employed. Each population is characterized by distinctive anthropometric patterns. Relatively restricted ranges of variability were found in many metrical traits. Volume features 75 p. of raw data compiled in tabular form.

1576 Klayman, Jane E. and others. Digital and palmar dermatoglyphic patterns in two Peruvian Quechua populations (WSU/HB, 49:3, Sept. 1977, p. 363–374, bibl., tables)

Dermatoglyphic traits analyzed in sample of 678 Quechua Indians from Peru.

Sub-population evolutionary differentiation demonstrated in both dermatoglyphic and serological data. Several unusual characteristics are detailed.

1577 Lasker, Gabriel W. and Raynor Thomas. The relationship between size and shape of the human head and reproductive fitness (Studies in Physical Anthropology [Polish Academy of Sciences, Warsaw] 4, 1978, p. 3–9, bibl., tables)

Statistically significant association discovered between reproductive fitness and head shape among 480 Mexican adults. Individuals with relatively long heads and low cephalic index values exhibited higher fertility, as measured by number of liveborn children, fecundity, parents' achieved reproduction, and number of surviving siblings. Age and sex variations are noted.

1578 Less, Francis C. and P.J. Byard. Skin colorimetry in Belize: pt. 1, Conversion formulae (AJPA, 48:4, May 1978, p. 515–522, bibl., tables)

Skin color readings taken for 308 black Caribs and 175 Creoles from Belize using two different types of portable reflectometers. Multiple regression equations utilized to test compatibility of methods.

1579 McMurray, David N. and others. Effect of moderate malnutrition on concentrations of immunoglobins and enzymes in tears and saliva of young Colombian children (ASCN/J, 30:12, Dec. 1977, p. 1944–1948, bibl., tables)

Relationship of nutritional status and biological characteristics of sera, tears, and saliva examined in 71 Colombian children. Unusual immunoglobin and enzyme concentrations discovered in subjects diagnosed as malnourished.

1580 Marcellino, A.J. and others. Size and shape differences among six South American Indian tribes (Annals of Human Biology [Taylor and Francis Publishers, London] 5:1, Jan. 1978, p. 69–74, bibl., tables)

Seventeen villages representing six South American Indian tribes compared in height and face and head measurements. Morphological distances estimated using D^2 method. Morphological distances correlated well with degree of linguistic differentiation but not with geographic distances among tribes.

1581 Matznetter, Thusnelda. Mittelphalangalhaar bei Michpopulationen an der Brasilkuste (AGW/M, 107, 1977, p. 115–129, bibl., tables)

Mid-digital hair, skin color, and other morphological traits compared among 802 individuals from two Brazilian towns. Study populations differed significantly in amount of European and African admixture. Remarkably high degree of sexual dimorphism discovered in both groups.

1582 Mueller, William H. and others. A multinational Andean genetic and health program: growth and development in an hypoxic environment (Annals of Human Biology [Taylor and Francis Publishers, London] 5:4, July 1978, p. 329–352, bibl., tables)

Multidisciplinary study of health, disease, growth and adaptation of Aymara Indians of high-altitude Chile. Effects of age and ethnic background are assessed in 1,047 children and adults. Highland natives found to be shorter, lighter, and leaner than in sea level controls. Chests were significantly larger and rounder, however, in the high altitude residents.

1583 Neel, James V. and others. Man in the tropics: the Yanomama Indians (*in* Harrison, G.A. *ed.* Population structure and human variation. N.Y., Cambridge Univ. Press, 1977, p. 109–142, bibl., maps, tables)

General account of highlights and key results of multidisciplinary biocultural investigation of population structure and human evolution in relatively isolated Yanomama Indians of Brazil and Venezuela. More than 100 published studies on this group are reviewed, covering linguistics, demography, mating patterns, morphology, genetic markers and genetic distances, physiological adaptation, immunology, diet, and disease.

1584 Oliveira, Maria P. and E.S. Azevedo. Racial differences in anthropometric traits in school children of Bahia, Brazil (AJPA, 46:3, May 1977, p. 471–475, bibl., tables)

Anthropometric measurements collected from 2,444 Brazilian school children age 4–16. Height and weight did not seem to be correlated with genetic-ethnohistorical background, although some limb proportions were associated with degree of black admixture. Racial categories are highly subjective and are mainly based on skin color.

1585 Palomino, Hernán. The Aymara of western Bolivia: pt. 3, Occlusion, pathology, and characteristics of the dentition (Journal of Dental Research [International Association for Dental Research, St. Louis, Mo.] 57:3, March 1978, p. 459–467, bibl., tables)

Results of dental examinations of 429 individuals of all ages from highland communities of Bolivia. Age, sex, ethnic, and geographic differences observed in dental caries and diseases, malocclusion, morphological structures, and various pathologies and anomalies. Findings compared with other Latin American Indian populations. For pt. 2 of this study, see item **1586**.

1586 ────── and others. The Aymara of western Bolivia: pt. 2, Maxillofacial and dental arch variation (AJPA, 49:2, Aug. 1978, p. 157–166, bibl., tables)

Dimensions of face, maxilla, and dental arch presented for Aymara tribe of Bolivia. Age and sex variations are noted. Racial and populational differences are also provided. For pt. 3 of this study, see item **1585**.

1587 Parra, A. and others. Changes in hemoglobin and haematocrit values in children aged 6 to 13 1/2 years in Mexico City (Annals of Human Biology [Taylor and Francis Publishers, London] 3:6, Nov. 1976, p. 543–548, bibl., tables)

Hemoglobin levels and haematocrit values presented for 523 boys and 350 girls aged 6–13 1/2 from Mexico City. Significant age and sex differences are reported and effects of body build are taken into account.

1588 Rosa, Manuel de la. Dental caries and socioeconomic status in Mexican children (Journal of Dental Research [International Association for Dental Research, St. Louis, Mo.] 57:3, March 1978, p. 453–457, bibl., tables)

Dental examinations made on 2,445 children age 6–15 from Monterrey, Mex. Higher socioeconomic statuses associated with better dental care patterns and lower incidence of caries. Problems exist, however, in imprecise definition of socioeconomic categories.

1589 Salzano, F.M. and **D.C. Roa.** Path analysis of aptitude, personality, and achievement scores in Brazilian twins (Behavior Genetics [Greenwood Periodicals, West-port, Conn.] 6:4, Oct. 1976, p. 461–466, bibl., tables)

Aptitude and achievement tests administered to 45 monozygotic and 46 same-sex dizygotic twin pairs from Brazil. Heritability of test performance estimated from sample comparisons as greater than 50 percent.

1590 Schull, William J. and **Francisco Roth-hammer.** A multinational Andean genetic and health programme: a study of adaptation to the hypoxia of altitude (in Weiner, J.S. ed. Physiological variation and its genetic basis. London, Taylor and Francis, 1977, p. 139–169, bibl., map, tables)

Outstanding review of research on high altitude adaptation in South American populations. New data from Aymara Indian populations of highland Chile are included. Relative contributions of genetics and environments to human adaptation to high altitude hypoxia are appraised. The physiological and biochemical characteristics of 2,096 high altitude residents are presented.

1591 Spurgeon, John H. and others. Body size and form of children of predominantly black ancestry living in West and Central Africa, North and South America, and the West Indies (Annals of Human Biology [Taylor and Francis Publishes, London] 5:3, May 1978, p. 229–246, bibl., tables)

Anthropometric comparison of black children from various locations including nine Latin American and Caribbean countries. Age changes and group differences reported for several measurements and indices. Socioeconomic variations did not significantly affect results.

1592 Spurr, G.H. and others. Energy expenditure, productivity, and physical work capacity of surgarcane loaders (ASCN/J, 30:10, Oct. 1977, p. 1740–1746, bibl., tables)

Physiology and work capacity of 28 Colombian sugarcane loaders investigated during actual labor and in lab tests. Energy expenditure was related to oxygen consumption and heart rate, which in turn were affected by amount of body fat, physical fitness, and less so by age.

1593 Stinson, Sara and **A.R. Frisancho.** Body proportions of highland and lowland Peruvian Quechua children (WSU/HB, 50:1, Feb. 1978, p. 57–68, bibl., tables)

Comparison of 242 lowland and 294

highland Quechua Indian children ages 7–19 with regard to height, weight, limb proportions, and other features of body dimensions. Observed differences seemed to correlate better with differences in altitude and temperature than with differences in nutritional status.

1594 Valenzuela, Carlos Y. and others. Sex dimorphism in adult stature in four Chilean populations (Annals of Human Biology [Taylor and Francis Publishers, London] 5:6, Nov. 1978, p. 533–538, bibl., tables)

Degree of sexual dimorphism in adult stature compared in four Chilean populations which show distinctive differences in biochemical genetic markers. Statistically significant association discovered between sexual dimorphism and amount of admixture with Spanish and other outside groups.

1595 Watson, Ronald R. and others. Pancreatic and salivary amylase activity in undernourished Colombian children (ASCN/J, 30:4, April 1977, p. 599–604, bibl., tables)

Activity of the enzyme amylase monitored in undernourished children from Colombia. Relative increase in pancreatic amylase and relative decrease in amylase activity in serum, tears, and saliva were characteristic of the sample.

HUMAN DEVELOPMENT

Alves, Edgard Luiz G. Nivel alimentar, renda e educação. See item **3433.**

1596 Barac-Nieto, M. and others. Body composition in chronic undernutrition (ASCN/J, 31:1, Jan. 1978, p. 23–40, bibl., tables)

Forty-nine undernourished adult males from rural Colombia were clinically screened and examined with respect to anthropometric measurements, biochemistry, metabolism, and hematology. Up to 29 percent reduction in body cell mass and fat deposits were associated with undernutrition. Decreases in serum albumin concentration were closely related to deficits in muscle mass.

Beet, Chris de and **Miriam Sterman.** Male absenteeism and nutrition: factors affecting fertility in Matawai Bush Negro society. See item **1005.**

1597 Black, F.L. and others. Nutritional status of Brazilian Kayapo Indians (WSU/HB, 49:2, May 1977, p. 139–153, bibl., tables)

Diet and nutrition researched in two relatively unacculturated groups from Brazil. Anthropometric measurements and hair-root diameters compared to US norms. Serum albumin levels also quantified. Nutritional status of populations diagnosed as relatively favorable.

1598 Bogin, Barry A. Seasonal pattern in the rate of growth in height of children living in Guatemala (AJPA, 49:2, Aug. 1978, p. 205–210, bibl., tables)

Seasonal patterns in stature increase monitored in 164 school children from Guatemala City. Pre- and post-adolescent children found to follow seasonal pattern of growth, while adolescent children did not. Possible environmental influences are discussed.

1599 Brazil. Fundação Instituto Brasileiro de Geografia e Estatística (IBGE). Estudo nacional da despesa familiar. t. 1, Dados preliminares, consumo alimentar, antropometria; pt. 1, Região 1, Estado do Rio de Janeiro [and] Região 3, Paraná, Santa Catarina, Rio Grande do Sul; pt. 2, Região V, Maranhão, Piauí, Ceará, Rio Grande do Norte, Paraíba, Pernambuco, Alagoas, Sergipe e Bahia; pt. 3, Região 2, São Paulo [and] Região 4, Minas Gerais e Espírito Santo; pt. 4, Região 6, Distrito Federal [and] Região 7, Rodônia, Acre, Amazonas, Roraima, Pará Amapá, Goiás e Mato Grosso. t. 2, Despesas das famílias; pt. 1, Região 3; pt. 2, Região 1; pt. 3, Região 5. Rio, 1977/1978. 1 v. in 7 pts. (110, 72, 110, 85, 99, 85, 113 p.) tables.

Extremely thorough and comprehensive dietary and nutritional research in Brazil, with coverage of nearly each state and region. Consists of one volume in seven parts, each containing a detailed breakdown of all major food items into principal nutrient components. Protein, calorie, and carbohydrate content of foodstuffs evaluated in terms of economic and biomedical considerations.

———. **Ministério da Previdência e Assistência Social. Fundação Legião Brasileira de Asistência. Departamento de Serviço Social.** Unidades de Reeducação alimentar do pré-escolar: estudo para sua implantação; treinamento de pessoal para as URAPES. See item **4608**.

1600 Caicedo, Elizabeth and **Luz Helena Hoyos de Arbeláez.** Impacto de una redistribución del ingreso sobre la nutrición humana. Bogotá, Univ. de los Andes, Facultad de Economía, Centro de Estudios sobre Desarrollo Económico (CEDE), 1977. 164 p., bibl., tables (Documento, 042)

Relationship of nutrition and economic development reported for Chile, Colombia, and other Latin American countries. Consumption patterns are tabulated, and diets are evaluated in terms of constituent calories and proteins.

Campos Sevilla, Marcia J. Investigación sobre el desarrollo de la niñez en México: informe psicológico. See item **9063**.

1601 Castillo, José del. Notas para la investigación de las creencias y hábitos alimentarios dominicanos (Ciencia [Univ. Autónoma de Santo Domingo, Dirección de Investigaciones Científicas] 3:2, abril/junio 1976, p. 97–114, illus., tables)

Survey of dietary habits and associated attitudes and beliefs in the Dominican Republic. Study features questionnaire results (e.g., "What did your family eat yesterday?") and relatively complete inventories of foods reportedly ingested by informants.

1602 Condon-Paoloni, Deanne and others. Morbidity and growth of infants and young children in a rural Mexican village (APHA/J, 67:7, July 1977, p. 651–656, bibl., tables)

Relationship between morbidity and growth explored in sample of 276 infants and children in a rural Mexican population. While episodes of diarrhea appeared to impede incremental gains in height and weight, respiratory infections did not have the same effect.

1603 Cusminsky, Marcos and **Lilia Chaves de Azcona.** Estudio longitudinal del crecimiento del niño de 0–1 año de un área del partido de La Plata. La Plata, Arg., Comisión de Investigaciones Científicas (CIC), 1974. 29 p., bibl., tables (Informes, 5)

Large-scale investigation of growth and development of Argentine children utilizing approaches and methods of physical anthropology. Results compared with other Latin American populations. Numerous anthropometric indices are calculated and statistically analyzed.

1604 Dewalt, Kathleen M. and **G.H. Pelto.** Food use and household ecology in a Mexican community (in Fitzgerald, Thomas K. ed. Nutrition and anthropology in action. Assen, The Netherlands, Van Gorcum, 1976, p. 79–93, bibl., tables)

Food use, diet, nutrition, and health maintenance studied in agriculturally-based community in state of Mexico that is undergoing modernization and economic growth. Authors' findings and recommendations regarding possible modifications in consumption patterns might be questioned because of small sample size of informants.

1605 Faulhaber, Johanna and **María Villanueva.** Investigación longitudinal del crecimiento, en un grupo de niños caracterizado por su ambiente socioeconómico, su alimentación y su patología. México, Secretaría de Educación Pública (SEP), Instituto Nacional de Antropología e Historia, Depto. de Antropología Física, 1976. 310 p., bibl., plates, tables (Col. Científica: antropología física, 26)

Large-scale growth study in Mexico involving longitudinal data collected between 1957 and 1974. Evidence includes anthropometric measurements, radiographs, clinical examinations, and dietary evaluations. Special emphasis focused upon nutritional diseases and their effects on growth. Statistical analysis of data is featured.

1606 Fiallo Billini, Alberto E. Antropometría nutriológica del niño y el adolescente dominicano según el nivel socioeconómico. San Pedro de Macorís, R.D., Univ. Central de Este (UCE), 1977. 118 p., bibl, illus., tables (Serie científica, 6)

Growth and development, as measured by height, weight and four anthropometric characteristics, reported for 2,395 children from Dominican Republic. Significant age, sex, and socioeconomic differences discovered in tricep skinfolds, upper arm muscle circumference, and ponderal index.

1607 Freeman, Howard E. and others. Relations between nutrition and cognition in rural Guatemala (APHA/J, 67:3, March 1977, p. 233–239, bibl., tables)

Nutritional status of young children from four rural Guatemalan villages demonstrated to be strongly associated with cognitive abilities as measured by standarized tests. Children receiving high-calorie food supplements consistently scored highest in tests of cognitive performance.

1608 Frisancho, A. Roberto and others.
Influence of maternal nutritional status on prenatal growth in a Peruvian urban population (AJPA, 46:2, March 1977, p. 265–274, bibl., tables)

Anthropometric measurements made on 4,952 mothers and their newborns in Lima, Peru. Mother-child relationships tabulated by height, weight, fat, and muscle. Factors contributing to variations in infantile dimensions are discussed.

1609 Hakim, Peter and **Giorgio Solimano.**
Development, reform, and malnutrition in Chile. Cambridge, Mass., The MIT Press, 1978. 91 p, bibl., tables (International nutrition policy series, 4)

Well-documented account of changing nutrition in Chile with emphasis on politics of nutritional improvement policy formation. Historical trends in food consumption and nutritional standards addressed in brief introductory chapter. Remainder of volume deals with problems of economic development and government-sponsored nutritional programs.

1610 Himes, John H. and **W.H. Mueller.**
Aging and secular change in adult stature in rural Colombia (AJPA, 46:2, March 1977, p. 275–280, bibl., tables)

Age-changes in stature reported for 634 individuals age 22–81 from rural Colombia. Stature changes estimated by multiple regression.

1611 Honduras. Consejo Superior de Planificación Económica (CONSUPLANE). **Secretaría Técnica. Sistema de Análisis y Planificación de la Alimentación y Nutrición** (SAPLAN). Evaluación de las áreas prioritarias del problema nutricional de Honduras y sus posibles soluciones. Tegucigalpa, 1976. 495 p., fold. maps, fold. table, maps, tables.

Comprehensive and elaborate treatment of current nutritional status of Honduras national population. Dietary surveys revealed regional variations in nutritional deficiencies. Possible relationship of observed nutritional problems to several medical disorders is explored. Dietary and nutritional improvements are recommended.

1612 Jacovella, Bruno J. Alimentación (in Cultura Nacional. B.A., Ediciones Crisol, 1976, p. 347–361)

Extremely brief narrative concerning current picture of nutrition and dietary customs in Argentina. Possible effects of advertising and TV on consumption patterns are discussed. Projections for the future are provided. Article lacks references to published literature.

1613 Jansen, R. and others. Effect of income and geographic region on the nutritional value of diets in Brazil (ASCN/J, 30:6, June 1977, p. 955–964, bibl., tables)

Regional differences in diet and nutrient intake studies in Brazil. Significant variations found by geography and urbanization, but income level has only a minor influence on dietary quality.

1614 Jornadas Peruanas de Bromatología y Nutrición, IV, Lima, 1973. Actas. Prefacio de Carlos Payva C. Lima, n.p., 1975. 371 p., tables.

Consists of 54 edited papers on relationship of nutrition and disease in Peru stemming from national symposia. The relatively brief research reports concern a number of different topics including dietary customs, infectious disease susceptibility and nutrition, drug use (including alcohol) and nutritional status, laboratory methods in nutritional assessment, synthetic foodstuffs, and subpopulational differences in growth of children.

1615 Lejarraga, H. and others. Age of onset of puberty in urban Argentinian children (Annals of Human Biology [Taylor and Francis Publishers, London] 3:4, July 1976, p. 379–381, bibl., tables)

Timing of pubertal events summarized for children from city of La Plata, Arg. Breast and pubic hair development examined in sample of 504 females, while genital development monitored in 498 boys.

1616 Lowry, M.F. and others. Heights and weights of Jamaican children with homozygous sickle cell disease (WSU/HB, 49:3, Sept. 1977, p. 429–436, bibl., tables)

Ninety-nine Jamaican children age 2–13 with homozygous sickle cell anemia (SS) compared with Jamaican standards regarding childhood growth. SS children weighed less than other comparably aged Jamaicans, but height was not significantly different. No clear-cut relationships discovered between anthropometric measurements and hematologic and serologic findings.

1617 ——— and others. Skeletal development of Jamaican children with homozygous sickle cell disease (WSU/HB, 50:2, May 1978, p. 115–119, bibl., tables)

Hand-wrist radiographs of 120 Jamaican children age 2–13 with homozygous sickle cell anemia ("SS" genotype) compared with 665 controls with normal hemoglobin ("AA"). "SS" subjects showed delayed skeletal maturation in both sexes and in almost all ages.

1618 Lutz, Martín. La malnutrición en América Latina: sus causas y posibles soluciones (OAS/CI, 18:1, enero/marco 1977, p. 2–7, bibl.)

Protein-calories malnutrition, a serious public health problem throughout Latin America, affects large segments of local populations, especially younger people. Author cites numerous contributing cultural and economic factors. Various practical solutions are offered.

1619 Majia, N.N. and others. Vitamin A deficiency and anemia in Central American children (ASCN/J, 30:7, July 1977, p. 1175–1184, bibl., tables)

Possible link between vitamin A deficiency and anemia explored through analysis of six dietary surveys in Central America. Correlations found between several biochemical indicators of nutritional status, including serum iron, plasma retinol, transferrin concentration, hemoglobin, anemia, and dietary deficiency.

1620 Malina, Robert M. and **J.H. Himes.** Patterns of childhood mortality and growth status in a rural Zapotec community (Annals of Human Biology [Taylor and Francis Publishers, London] 5:6, Nov. 1978, p. 517–531, bibl., tables)

Rural Indian community of Oaxaca, Mex., investigated with respect to infant and childhood mortality and growth status of 143 children age 5–14. Mortality especially severe in ages 0–4, probably due to chronic malnutrition and disease. Results compared with US data.

1621 ——— and others. Age of menarche in Oaxaca, Mexico schoolgirls, with comparative data for other areas of Mexico (Annals of Human Biology [Taylor and Francis Publishers, London] 4:6, Nov. 1977, p. 551–558, bibl., tables)

Menarcheal ages recorded for girls from state of Oaxaca, Mex., are compared with several rural and urban populations from Mexico. Earlier menarche generally found in urban samples.

1622 ——— and others. Skeletal maturity of the hand and wrist in Oaxaca school children (Annals of Human Biology [Taylor and Francis Publishers, London] 3:3, May 1976, p. 211–219, bibl., tables)

Skeletal maturity assessed with hand-wrist radiographs of 394 children aged 5–18 from city of Oaxaca, Mex. Relatively delayed maturity observed in sample interpreted in terms of socioeconomic background and nutritional histories.

Manning, Diana H. Society and food: the Third World. See *HLAS 40:2197.*

1623 Martorell, Renaldo and others. Sibling similarities in number of ossification centers of the hand and wrist in a malnourished population (WSU/HB, 50:1, Feb. 1978, p. 73–81, bibl., tables)

Sibling correlations described for hand-wrist ossification centers in sample of chronically malnourished Guatemalan children age 1–7. Findings compared with results from US.

1624 Mata, Leonardo J. The children of Santa María Cauqué: a prospective field study of health and growth. Cambridge, Mass., the MIT Press, 1978. 395 p., bibl., plates, tables (International nutrition policy series, 2)

Unusually thorough treatment of complex interactions of fertility, child growth, disease, and nutrition in Guatemalan highland community. Separate chapters deal with fetal development, infant mortality, childhood growth and development, dietary habits and malnutrition, the demographic effects of various diseases, and predictions of future trends. Methodological procedures are carefully outlined.

1625 ——— and others. Antenatal events and postnatal growth and survival of children in a rural Guatemalan village (Annals of Human Biology [Taylor and Francis Publishers, London] 3:4, July 1976, p. 303–315, bibl., tables)

Fertility and childhood mortality described for rural Guatemalan population. Outcomes of 458 pregnancies, analyzed with respect to following factors: mother's age and anthropometric characteristics, infection, diet and nutrition, birth weight, antenatal and postnatal growth, and childhood survival.

1626 ——— and others. Effect of infection on food intake and the nutritional state: perspectives as viewed from the village (ASCN/J, 30:8, Aug. 1977, p. 1215–1227, bibl., tables)

Study of effects of infection on nutrition, gestation, and growth in rural Guatemalan population. High maternal morbidity and childhood infection were found. Infectious disease shown to suppress growth, development, nutritional state, and adult height and weight. Dietary analysis revealed extremely low caloric intake.

1627 Messer, Ellen. The evolution of vegetarian diet in a modernizing Mexican community (in Fitzgerald, Thomas K. ed. Nutrition and anthropology in action. Assen, The Netherlands, Van Gorcum, 1976, p. 117–124, bibl.)

Effects of modernization on traditional diets examined in small agricultural population in Oaxaca, Mex. Diet is largely vegetarian, based mainly upon maize, beans, and greens. Food customs and nutritional "rules" are changing through modernization and the increasing availability of packaged foods such as cakes, crackers, soft drinks, candies, etc. Future prospects are discussed.

Monckeberg Barros, Fernando. Jaque al subdesarrollo. See item 3231.

1628 ——— and Sergio Valiente B. eds. Antecedentes y acciones para una política nacional de alimentación y nutrición de Chile. Santiago, Consejo Nacional para la Alimentación y Nutrición (CONPAN) [and] Univ. de Chile, Instituto de Nutrición y Tecnología de los Alimentos (INTA), 1976. 145 p., bibl., tables.

General overview of nutritional situation in Chile featuring nutrient analysis of typical diets. Effects of diet on biological characteristics of children and adults demon-strated with available evidence. Practical problems of implementation of national policies are discussed.

1629 Mueller, William H. Sibling correlations in growth and adult morphology in a rural Colombian population (Annals of Human Biology [Taylor and Francis Publishers, London] 4:2, March 1977, p. 133–142, bibl., tables)

Body measurement correlations investigated in 207 pairs of school-aged siblings from a mestizo agricultural community from the Andes mountains of Colombia. Genetics, sex, age, disease, and nutrition all contributed to the variations discovered in the morphological measurements.

1630 ——— and M. Titcomb. Genetic and environmental determinants of growth of school-aged children in a rural Colombian population (Annals of Human Biology [Taylor and Francis Publishers, London] 4:1, Jan. 1977, p. 1–15, bibl., tables)

Parent-child correlations and heritability estimates presented for several body measurements in a sample of 403 families from a rural Colombian population. Chronic malnutrition considerably impeded growth in the community.

1631 Plail, Roger O. and J.M.S. Young. A nutritional, haematological and sociological study of a group of Chilean children under the age of five years (Journal of Biosocial Science [Blackwell Scientific Publications, Oxford, UK] 9:3, July 1977, p. 353–369, bibl., map, tables)

Clinical and demographic study of nutrition in 108 young Chilean children and members of their immediate families. 43.9 percent were diagnosed as having some degree of undernutrition or malnutrition. 46.1 percent of the children were classified as iron-deficient anemics. Recommendations are offered for possible improvements.

1632 Russell, Marcia. The relationship of family size and spacing to the growth of preschool Mayan children in Guatemala (APHA/J, 66:12, Dec. 1976, p. 1165–1172, bibl., tables)

Growth of 643 Mayan children ages 0–5 from highland Guatemala investigated through health records. Influence of family size and birth intervals studied statistically, and the tallest children were discovered in the largest and the smallest families. Birth intervals were positively correlated with height.

1633 Venezuela. Consejo Nacional de Investigaciones Científicas y Tecnológicas (CONICIT). Instituto Nacional de Nutrición (INN). Requerimientos de energía y de nutrientes de la población venezolana. Caracas, 1976. 38 p., bibl., tables (Serie de cuadernos azules, 38)

Government-sponsored survey of nutritional status and problems in Venezuela with special emphasis upon estimated average energy requirements and the adequacy of available nutrients. Extensive nutritional and anthropological data tabulated for national population.

1634 Ward, John O. and Agamenon Tavares de Almeida. Nutrição, renda e tamanho da família: um exame da situação nutricional em Canindé, Ceará (BNB/REN, 8:1, jan./março 1977, p. 77–94, bibl., tables)

Nutritional investigation on familial and individual level in northeast Brazil community. Elaborate statistical techniques employed to measure effects of substandard nutritional status upon general health, physical and mental development of children, productivity of workers, life expectancy, etc. Diets mainly found to be deficient in both protein and calories.

1635 Winikoff, Beverly ed. Nutrition and national policy. Cambridge, MIT Press, 1978. 580 p., bibl., maps, tables.

Collection of 20 papers on economic and political aspects of changing nutrition and dietary patterns in 11 "developing" nations including Chile, Colombia, Panama, Jamaica, and the US. Relationship of nutrition to climate, health, and culture is major theme.

EPIDEMIOLOGICAL ANTHROPOLOGY

Aho, William R. and Kimlan Minott. Creole and doctor medicine: folk beliefs, practices, and orientations to modern medicine in a rural and an industrial suburban setting in Trinidad and Tobago, The West Indies. See item **994**.

1636 Araújo, Alceu Maynard. Medicina rústica. 2. ed. São Paulo, Companhia Editora Nacional *em convênio com o* Minis-

terío da Educação e Cultura, Instituto Nacional do Livro, Brasília, 1977. 301 p. (Brasiliana, 300)

Thorough and lively account of traditional medical practices in rural Brazil. While reference citations are generally insufficient, monograph is bolstered considerably by firsthand informant reports on healing activities and medicinal preparation.

1637 Arenas, P. and R. Moreno Azorero. Plants of common use in Paraguayan folk medicine for regulating fertility (SEB/EB, 31:3, July/Sept. 1977, p. 298–301, bibl., table)

Brief descriptive report of herbal preparations for contraception and/or abortion in rural Paraguay. Data obtained from interviews with healers, vendors of medicinal plants, and 223 government-sponsored obstetricians. Fourteen separate recipes made from 33 plants are tabulated and discussed in detail.

1638 ——— and ———. Plants used as means of abortion, contraception, sterilization, and fecundation by Paraguayan indigenous peoples (SEB/EB, 31:3, July/Sept. 1977, p. 302–306, bibl., map)

Research on medicinal plants used to regulate fertility among Indian populations from Paraguay. Information gathered on 22 plants employed by 10 different ethnic groups. Method of preparation and consumption for each plant are briefly described.

1639 Bandoni, A.L. and others. Survey of Argentine medicinal plants—folklore and phytochemical screening (SEB/EB, 30:2, April/June 1976, p. 161–185, bibl., tables)

Simple listing without commentary of some of the 700 indigenous medicinal plant species of Argentina. Preparation methods, medical applications, and chemical components of plants are described.

1640 Bina, José Carlos and others. Greater resistance to development of severe schistosomiasis in Brazilian Negroes (WSU/HB, 50:1, Feb. 1978, p. 41–49, bibl., tables)

Racial differences in susceptibility to schistosomiasis studied in three populations in Brazil. Although "whites," mulattoes, and blacks exhibited similar infection rates, the black sample displayed greater resistance to the development of several complications arising from the parasite. Possible biological and genetic factors are summarized.

1641 Brewer-Carias, Charles and J.A. Steyermark. Hallucinogenic snuff drugs of the Yanomama Caburiwe-Teri in the Cauaburi River, Brazil (SEB/EB, 30:1, Jan./March 1976, p. 57–66, bibl., maps, plates)

Descriptive study of use of hallucinogen by small Brazilian Indian population. Biological and behavioral aspects are outlined.

1642 Carcavallo, Rodolfo U. and Ana Rosa Plencovich. Los ecólogos de la salud. Caracas, Monte Avila Editores, 1975. 158 p., bibl., tables (Col. Letra viva)

Basic text and primer manual on epidemiology and public health with the majority of research examples drawn from studies of Latin American populations. Ample statistical techniques are introduced, but bibliography and in-text citations are sparse and incomplete.

1643 Carniero, Robert L. Recent observations on shamanism and witchcraft among the Kuikuru Indians of Central Brazil (NYAS/A, 293, July 1977, p. 215–228, bibl.)

Narrative account of important roles of shamanism, witchcraft, and herbalism in curing among the Kuikuru Indians of Brazil. Article consists of patchwork collection of various healing instances and longitudinal case studies.

1644 Colombia. Ministerio de Educación Nacional. Instituto Colombiano para el Fomento de la Educación Superior (ICFES). **División de Documentación y Fomento Bibliotecario.** Catálogo de tesis de la región central: ciencias biomédicas. Introducción de José Arias Ordoñez. Bogotá, 1976. 384 p.

Bibliography of biomedical publications dealing with Latin American populations. The 5,000 items are arranged by author, topic, and "key words."

Colson, Audrey Butt. Binary opposition and the treatment of sickness among the Akawaio. See item **1013.**

1645 Conly, Gladys N. The impact of malaria on economic development: a case study. Foreword by Héctor R. Acuña. Washington, World Health Organization (WHO), Pan American Health Organization (PAHO), Pan American Sanitary Bureau, 1975. 117 p., map, plates, tables (Scientific publication, 297)

Tightly organized case study of natural history of malaria in tropical Paraguay. Relationships discovered between widespread presence of malaria and several demographic and economic features of sample populations. Monograph includes questionnaire forms, raw data, and impressive graphics.

1646 Cosminsky, Sheila. Alimento and fresco: nutritional concepts and their implications for health care (SAA/HO, 36:2, Summer 1977, p. 203–207, bibl.)

Changing health and nutritional beliefs documented for rural highland Guatemalan village experiencing acculturation and extended contact with "Western" medical care and health maintenance concepts.

1647 Craig, Richard B. La campaña permanente: Mexico's anti-drug campaign (UM/JIAS, 20:2, May 1978, p. 107–131, bibl., tables)

Historical assessment of drug problems in Mexico and the government-sponsored efforts to counteract them beginning in 1948. Changing directions in drug abuse and associated attitudes are cited. Collaborative US-Mexico policies are outlined.

1648 Cuba Review. Cuba Resource Center (CRC). Vol. 8, No. 1, March 1978–. N.Y.

Special issue devoted to changing trends in health care in Cuba. Epidemiological problems are identified, and preventative measures are described, including primary health care in the community, hospital care, infant care, and long-range health planning.

1649 Cupertino, Fausto. População e saúde pública no Brasil: povo pobre é povo doente. Rio, Editora Civilização Brasileira, 1976. 110 p., tables (Col. Realidad brasileira, 2)

Demographically oriented exposition of epidemiological patterns in Brazil written for general reader as well as specialist. Many useful demographic characteristics of country constructed from study of government documents. Fertility, mortality, morbidity, migration, mate selection, population structure, and household composition are all reviewed within geographic and ethnohistorical framework. Particular attention directed to changing causes of death in Brazil.

1650 Dobkin de Ríos, Marlene. Una teoría transcultural del uso de los alucinógenos de origen vegetal (III/AI, 37:2, April/June 1977, p. 291–304, bibl., tables)

Theoretical exploration of cultural factors influencing hallucinogen usage in different societies. Common themes are demonstrated with published data on Latin American populations.

1651 Falomir, Carlos N. Panorama epidemiológico del pediatra en Chihuahua (MANM/G, 112:4, Oct. 1976, p. 315–327, bibl., illus., tables)

Review of basic public health parameters in state of Chihuahua, Mex. Infantile morbidity and mortality are serious problems, and their likelihood is significantly influenced by socioeconomic status, nutritional state, hygienic and sanitary conditions, and quality of diagnostic work.

1652 Ginzbarg, Steven. Plantas medicinales de los indios bribris y cabécar (III/AI, 37:2, abril/junio 1977, p. 368–398, bibl., tables)

Listing of large number of medicinal plants utilized by Indian groups undergoing rapid acculturation in Costa Rica. Usage patterns and claimed curative powers are outlined.

1653 *Guatemala Indígena.* Instituto Indigenista Nacional. Vol. 12, Nos. 1/2, 1977–. Guatemala.

Special issue devoted to "science and folklore" in medical systems found in Guatemala. Popular and "folk" concepts of healing, reproduction, death, and other biological phenomena are changing due to recent development of "modern" medicine in the country. Issue consists of five tightly structured and problem-oriented field studies.

1654 Halberstein, Robert A. and **Ashley B. Saunders.** Traditional medical practices and medicinal plant usage on a Bahamian island (Culture, Medicine and Psychiatry [D. Reidel, Dordrecht, The Netherlands] 2:3, Sept. 1978, p. 177–203, bibl., maps, tables)

Field study of native medical system and health-related activities in indigenous population of small (1,450) island in the Bahamas. Health survey administered to 83 percent of population, and procedures of healing specialists and herbalists are described. The 25 most common local medicinal plants were collected and analyzed, and the results suggest that their chemical components have

numerous curative properties which are effective against several diseases as claimed. Authors discuss impact of relatively recent exposure to "Westernized" health care and "modern" prescription medications.

1655 Herrou Baigorri, José. Una política humanista en salud: problemática sanitaria argentina, 1976–1977. B.A., Ediciones Nueva Senda, 1977. 141 p., tables.

Broad survey of public health problems and recent advances in health care in Argentina. Private and public health care systems are described. Value of work is depreciated by absence of bibliography or other references to comparable literature.

1656 Koss, Joan D. Social process, healing, and self-defeat among Puerto Rican spiritists (AAA/AE, 4:3, Aug. 1977, p. 453–469, bibl.)

Paper focuses on Puerto Rican healers and structure of healing spirit cults in N.Y. and San Juan, P.R. Mediums exert positive therapeutic influence on their clients, especially those subjects with personal psychological adjustment problems accompanying common illnesses.

1657 León, Luis A. Salud y medicina en los grupos aborígenes del Oriente Ecuatoriano (III/AI, 37:2, abril/junio 1977, p. 399–424, bibl., tables)

Comprehensive article on multiple facets of health and health care in eastern Ecuador. Following topics are covered: regional geography and demography, sanitation, drinking water, diet and nutrition, traditional medical systems, and disease epidemiology. Uses of herbal medicines and plant hallucinogens are described.

Lieberman, Dena and **William W. Dressler.** Bilingualism and cognition of St. Lucian disease terms. See item **1055.**

1658 Livingston, Mario and **Dagmar Raczynski.** Salud pública y bienestar social. Con colaboraciones de José Pablo Arellano and others. Prólogo de Alejandro Foxley. Santiago, Univ. Católica de Chile, Centro de Estudios de Planificación Nacional (CEPLAN) [and] Univ. of Sussex, The Institute of Development Studies, U.K., 1976. 332 p., tables.

Loose compilation of 11 chapters by different authors reviewing disparate epidemiological and public health problems in Chile. Both broad literature surveys and particular research results are presented. The more important articles include the following: Fernando Rodríguez "Estructura y Características del Sector Salud en Chile" p. 65–82. Adela Legarreta "Factores Condicionantes de la Mortalidad en la Niñez" p. 219–232. Giorgio Solimano and Fernando Monckeberg "Desigualdades Alimentarias y Estado de Salud de la Población" p. 233–250. Horacio Boccardo and German Corey "Medio Ambiente: Efectos sobre la Salud" p. 251–290.

1659 Marzochi, Mauro Celio de A. and others. Carcinogênese hepática no norte do Paraná e uso indiscriminado de defensivos agrícolas: introdução a um programa de pesquisa (SBPC/CC, 28:8, agosto 1976, p. 893–901, bibl., tables)

Preliminary report on research concerning possible influence of organochloride pesticides on the etiology and epidemiology of primary hepatic tumors in northern Parana state, Brazil. Data suggest a positive correlation between insecticide usage and tumor incidence in the area.

1660 Mello, Carlos Gentile de. Saúde e assistência médica no Brasil. São Paulo, Centro Brasileiro de Estudos de Saúde (CEBES) *co-edição com a* Editora da Humanismo, Ciência e Tecnologia (HUCITEC), 1977. 269 p., tables (Col. Saúde em debate, 1)

Broad-spectrum survey of basic health problems and growth of modern medicine in Brazil. Contemporary facilities for treatment, prevention, and medical education are outlined. Rapid development of health "sector" has had widespread economic results.

1661 Molina, Aldo O. and **O.J. Serra.** La asistencia médico-sanitaria en las poblaciones indígenas (III/AI, 37:1, enero/marzo 1977, p. 179–183)

Brief summary of health and sanitation problems among 143 Brazilian Indian populations. Epidemiological conditions are described in relation to demographic factors such as population size, density, and breeding isolation. Problems in delivery of "modern" medical care to remote villages are discussed.

1662 Orellana, Sandra L. Aboriginal medicine in highland Guatemala (Medical Anthropology [Redgrave, Pleasantville, N.Y.]

1:1, Winter 1977, p. 113–156, bibl., maps, tables)

Traditional medical practices and use of herbal medicines in highland Guatemala are explored in literature of chroniclers and priests from 16th through 18th centuries. Many pre-contact procedures and medicinal substances have persisted to the present, although Spanish influence has been substantial.

1663 Pacheco, Mário Victor de Assis. A máfia dos remédios. Rio, Civilização Brasileira, 1978. 153 p., tables (Col. Retratos do Brasil, 113)

Closeup view of modern medical and pharmacological problems in urban Brazil. Spread of "Western" synthetic drugs and nutritional supplements charted and their economic and political aspects are noted. Medications commonly used in Brazil are analyzed, categorized and described chemically.

1664 Philippe, Jeanne. Bilinguisme, syncretisme religieux dans la vocabulaire des troubles mentaux en Haiti (IFH/C, 132, déc. 1976/jan. 1977, p. 45–58, bibl.)

Ambitious but awkward attempt to sort out the influence of bilingualism and religious syncretism upon the perception and exprience of mental disorders in Haiti. Without quantification, the author discusses this question with reference to perceptual problems, affective and emotional disorders, and troubles with memory, cognition, or conduct.

1665 Prance, Ghillean T.; D.G. Campbell; and **B.W. Nelson.** The ethnobotany of the Paumarí Indians (SEB/EB, 31:2, abril/junio 1977, p. 129–139, bibl., plates, tables)

Survey of indigenous botanical resources exploited by Paumarí Indians of Brazilian Amazon. Numerous plants described which are utilized as foods, beverages, medications, narcotic snuffs, abortifacients, poisons, and for other adaptive biosocial purposes.

1666 Ramírez, Ignacio and others. La profilaxis del cretinismo endémico en las sierras del Ecuador (III/AI, 37:4, oct./dic. 1977, p. 1057–1071, tables)

Hyperthyroidism and goiter in highland Ecuador is discussed in epidemiological terms. Utilization of iodine supplement has helped to offset the traditionally iodine-deficient diet in these areas during the mid-1960s, as ascertained by comparisons with control samples.

1667 *Revista Mexicana de Ciencias Políticas y Sociales.* UNAM, Facultad de Ciencias Políticas y Sociales. Año 22, No. 84, Nueva Epoca, abril/junio 1976–. México.

Entire issue devoted to community ("public") medicine in modern Mexico. Compendium includes seven research reports and three annotated bibliographies on epidemiology and social medicine. Two of the articles are especially useful: José C. Escuder "Desnutrición en América Latina: su Magnitud" p. 83–130. Hesio de Albuquerque Cordeiro and others "Los Determinantes de la Producción y Distribución de Enfermedad," p 159–182.

1668 Rubel, Arthur J. and **J. Gettelfinger-Krejci.** The use of hallucinogenic mushrooms for diagnostic purposes among some highland Chinantecs (SEB/EB, 30:3, July/Sept. 1976, p. 235–248, bibl., map)

Ingestion of hallucinogenic mushrooms (genus = *Psilocybe*) is tied to healing in some Indian populations of Oaxaca. Author notes usual circumstances surrounding usage patterns. Drug may be taken by both patient and healer for diagnostic and treatment purposes.

1669 Sandstrom, Alan R. The image of disease: medical practices of Nahua Indians of the Huasteca. Columbia, Univ. of Missouri, Dept. of Anthropology, 1978. 60 p., bibl., illus., tables (Monographs in anthropology, 3)

General descriptive research on traditional medical customs and procedures among Nahua Indians of Mexico. Monograph contains useful information, but suffers from confusing terminology, sparse bibliography, and poor quality illustrations.

1670 Simeon, George. Illness and curing in a Guatemalan village: a study of ethnomedicine. Honolulu, Univ. of Hawaii, School of Public Health, 1977. 104 p., bibl., map, tables.

Unusual field study of reported illnesses and treatments of Mayan population in Guatemala. Various herbal remedies are described, and substantial space is devoted to subject of witchcraft. Author's questionable methodologies, however, detract from overall value of study.

Stein, William W. Modernización y retroceso del mito: diagnosis por medio de la magia y curación en el pueblo de Vicos, Perú. See item **1321**.

1671 Wong, Wesley. Some folk medicinal plants from Trinidad (SEB/EB, 30:2, April/June 1976, p. 103–152, bibl., tables)

One hundred eighty six medicinal plants used in traditional medical activities on Trinidad are tabulated, including applications and chemical constituents. Common and taxonomic names are provided. Over 900 individual recipes and remedies made from these plants were elicited from informants, but author does not consider them in his skimpy discussion section.

1672 Woods, Clyde M. Alternative curing strategies in a changing medical situation (Medical Anthropology [Redgrave, Pleasantville, N.Y.] 1:3, Summer 1977, p. 25–54, bibl., tables)

Statistical analysis of changing patterns of healing and health maintenance in Mayan population undergoing acculturation in highland Guatemala. Three alternative medical systems are available to residents, and curing strategies represent a heterogeneous composite of elements drawn from each. Demographic variables significantly influence medical resource utilization.

Young, James C. Illness categories and action strategies in a Tarascan town. See item **990**.

JOURNAL ABBREVIATIONS
ANTHROPOLOGY

AAA/AA American Anthropologist. American Anthropological Association. Washington.

AAA/AE American Ethnologist. American Anthropological Association. Washington.

AAAS/S Science. American Association for the Advancement of Science. Washington.

ACEP/EP Estudios de Población. Asociación Colombiana para el Estudio de la Población. Bogotá.

AESC Annales: Économies, Sociétés, Civilisations. Centre National de la Recherche Scientifique *avec le concours de la* VI^E Section de l'École Pratique des Hautes Études. Paris.

AFS/JAF Journal of American Folklore. American Folklore Society. Austin, Tex.

AGHCR/A Anales de la Academia de Geografía e Historia de Costa Rica. San José.

AGW/M Mitteilungen der Anthropologischen Gesellschaft in Wien. Wien.

AI Art International. Zurich, Switzerland.

AI/A Anthropos. Anthropos-Institut. Psoieux, Switzerland.

AI/I Interciencia. Asociación Interciencia. Caracas.

AIA/A Archaeology. Archaeological Institute of America. N.Y.

AJPA American Journal of Physical Anthropology. American Association of Physical Anthropologists [and] The Wistar Institute of Anatomy and Biology. Philadelphia, Pa.

AMNH/NH Natural History. American Museum of Natural History. N.Y.

APHA/J American Journal of Public Health and the Nation's Health. The American Public Health Association. Albany, N.Y.

APS/P Proceedings of the American Philosophical Society. Philadelphia, Pa.

ARMEX Artes de México. Revista bimestral. México.

ASCN/J American Journal of Clinical Nutrition. American Society for Clinical Nutrition. N.Y.

ASHG/J American Journal of Human Genetics. The American Society for Human Genetics. Baltimore, Md.

AU/P Phylon. Atlanta Univ. Atlanta, Ga.

BBAA B.B.A.A. Boletín Bibliográfico de Antropología Americana. Instituto Panamericano de Geografía e Historia, Comisión de Historia. México.

BJS British Journal of Sociology. London School of Economics and Political Science. London.

BNB/REN Revista Econômica do Nordeste. Banco de Nordeste do Brasil, Depto. de Estudos do Nordeste. Fortaleza, Brazil.

BNBD Boletín Nicaragüense de Bibliografía y Documentación. Banco Central de Nicaragua Biblioteca. Managua.

BNJM/R Revista de la Biblioteca Nacional José Martí. La Habana.

CAAAP/AP Amazonía Peruana. Centro Amazónico de Antropología y Aplicación Práctica, Depto. de Documentación y Publicaciones. Lima.

CAE/AEQ Anthropology and Education Quarterly. Council on Anthropology and Education. Washington.

CAUK/WA Weltwirtschaftliches Archiv. Zeitschrift des Instituts für Weltwirtschaft an der Christians-Albrechts-Univ. Kiel. Kiel, FRG.

CCE/CHA Cuadernos de Historia y Arqueología. Casa de la Cultura Ecuatoriana, Núcleo del Guayas. Guayaquil, Ecua.

CCE/RA Revista de Antropología. Casa de la Cultura Ecuatoriana, Núcleo del Azuay. Cuenca, Ecua.

CDAL Cahiers des Amériques Latines. Paris.

CEDLA/B Boletín de Estudios Latinoamericanos. Centro de Estudios y Documentación Latinoamericanos. Amsterdam.

CEM/ECM Estudios de Cultura Maya. Univ. Nacional Autónoma de México, Centro de Estudios Mayas. México.

CIF/FA Folklore Americano. Organización de los Estados Americanos, Instituto Panamericano de Geografía e Historia, Comisión de Historia, Comité Interamericano de Folklore. Lima. *See* IPGH/FA.

CM/DE Demografía y Economía. El Colegio de México. México.

CNRS/ASR Archives de Sociologie des Religions. Center Nationale de la Recherche Scientifique. Paris.

CSSH Comparative Studies in Society and History. An international quarterly. Society for the Comparative Study of Society and History. The Hague.

CUA/AQ Anthropological Quarterly. Catholic Univ. of America, Catholic Anthropological Conference. Washington.

DGV/ZE Zeitschrift für Ethnologie. Deutschen Gesellschaft für Völkerkunde. Braunschweig, FRG.

EJ Explorers Journal. N.Y.

EM/A Årstryck. Etnografiska Museum. Göteborg, Sweden.

FAIC/CPPT Comunicaciones Proyecto Puebla-Tlaxcala. Fundación Alemana para la Investigación Científica. Puebla, Mex.

FDD/NED Notes et Études Documentaires. Direction de la Documentation. Paris.

FSCN/A Antropológica. Fundación La Salle de Ciencias Naturales, Instituto Caribe de Antropología y Sociología. Caracas.

GV/GR Geologische Rundschau. Internationale Zeitschrift für Geologie. Geologische Vereinigung. Ferdinand Enke Verlag. Stuttgart, FRG.

HH Human Heredity. Basel, Switzerland.

IAA Ibero-Amerikanisches Archiv. Ibero-Amerikanisches Institut. Berlin, FRG.

IAI/I Indiana. Beiträge zur Volker-und Sprachenkunde, Archäologie und Anthropologie des Indianischen Amerika. Ibero-Amerikanisches Institut. Berlin, FRG.

IAS/ÑP Ñawpa Pacha. Institute of Andean Studies. Berkeley, Calif.

IASI/E Estadística. Journal of the Inter-American Statistical Institute. Washington.

ICA/RCA Revista Colombiana de Antropología. Ministerio de Educación Nacional, Instituto Colombiano de Antropología. Bogotá.

ICC/T Thesaurus. Boletín del Instituto Caro y Cuervo. Bogotá.

ICP/R Revista del Instituto de Cultura Puertorriqueña. San Juan.

IFEA/B Bulletin de l'Institut Français d'Études Andines. Lima.

IFH/C Conjonction. Institut Français d'Haïti. Port-au-Prince.

IGFO/RI Revista de Indias. Instituto Gonzalo Fernández de Oviedo [and] Consejo Superior de Investigaciones Científicas. Madrid.

IGM/AGMG Acta Geneticae Medicae et Gemellologiae. Instituto Gregorio Mendel. Roma.

IGM/U L'Universo. Rivista bimestrale dell'Istituto Geografico Militare. Firenze, Italy.

IHGSP/R Revista do Instituto Histórico e Geográfico de São Paulo. São Paulo.

IIE/A Anales del Instituto de Investigaciones Estéticas. Univ. Nacional Autónoma de México. México.

III/AI América Indígena. Instituto Indigenista Interamericano. México.

IJSP International Journal of Social Psychiatry. London.

INAH/A Anales del Instituto Nacional de Antropología e Historia. Secretaría de Educación Pública. México.

INAH/B Boletín del Instituto Nacional de Antropología e Historia. Secretaría de Educación Pública. México.

INC/RNC Revista Nacional de Cultura. Instituto Nacional de Cultura. Panama.

IPA/AP Allpanchis Phuturinqa. Univ. de San Antonio de Abad, Seminario de Antropología Instituto de Pastoral Andina. Cuzco, Peru.

IPE/EE Estudos Econômicos. Univ. de São Paulo, Instituto de Pesquisas Econômicas. São Paulo.

IPEA/PPE Pesquisa e Planejamento Econômico. Instituto de Planejamento Econômico e Social. Rio.

IPGH/FA Folklore Americano. Instituto Panamericano de Geografía e Historia, Comisión de Historia, Comité de Folklore. México.

IU/AL Anthropological Linguistics. A publication of the Archives of the Languages of the World. Indiana Univ., Anthropology Dept. Bloomington.

IU/IJAL International Journal of American Linguistics. Indiana Univ. *under the auspices of* Linguistic Society of America, American Anthropological Association *with the cooperation of the* Joint Committee on American Native Languages. Waverly Press, Inc. Baltimore, Md.

JDA The Journal of Developing Areas. Western Illinois Univ. Press. Macomb.

JPS The Journal of Peasant Studies. Frank Cass & Co. London.

KITLV/B Bijdragen tot de Taal-, Land- en Volkenkunde. Koninklijk Instituut voor

Taal-, Land-, en Volkenkunde. Leiden, The Netherlands.

LARR Latin American Research Review. Univ. of North Carolina Press *for the* Latin American Studies Association. Chapel Hill.

LING Linguistics. An international review. Mouton. The Hague.

LNB/L Lotería. Lotería Nacional de Beneficencia. Panamá.

LSE/PS Population Studies. London School of Economics, The Population Investigation Committee. London.

MANM/G Gaceta Médica de México. Academia Nacional de Medicina. México.

MEMDA/E Etnía. Museo Etnográfico Municipal Dámaso Arce. Municipalidad de Olavarría, Provincia de Buenos Aires, Arg.

MH/OM Objets et Mondes. Musée de l'Homme. Paris.

MHD/B Boletín del Museo del Hombre Dominicano. Santo Domingo.

MLV/T Tribus. Veröffentlichungen des Linden-Museums. Museum für Länder- und Völkerkunde. Stuttgart, FRG.

MNAA/A Arqueológicas. Museo Nacional de Antropología y Arqueología, Instituto Nacional de Cultura. Lima.

MNCR/A Vínculos. Revista de antropología. Museo Nacional de Costa Rica. San José.

MNDJG/A Anales del Museo Nacional David J. Guzmán. San Salvador.

MP/R Revista do Museu Paulista. São Paulo.

MPEG/B Boletim do Museu Paraense Emílio Goeldi. Nova série: antropologia. Conselho Nacional de Desenvolvimento Científico e Tecnológico, Instituto Nacional de Pesquisas da Amazônia. Belém, Brazil.

MV/BA Baessler-Archiv. Museums für Völkerkunde. Berlin, FRG.

MVW/AV Archiv für Völkerkunde. Museum für Völkerkunde in Wien und von Verein Freunde der Völkerkunde. Wien.

NAS/P Proceedings of the National Academy of Sciences. Washington.

NWIG Nieuwe West-Indische Gids. Martinus Nijhoff. The Hague.

NWJS Nature. A weekly journal of science. Macmillan & Co. London.

NYAS/A Annals of the New York Academy of Sciences. N.Y.

OAS/CI Ciencia Interamericana. Organization of American States, Dept. of Scientific Affairs. Washington.

OLI/ZLW Zeitschrift für Lateinamerika Wien. Österreichisches Lateinamerika-Institut. Wein.

PAHO/B Bulletin of the Pan American Health Organization. Washington.

PEMN/R Revista del Museo Nacional. Casa de la Cultura del Perú, Museo Nacional de la Cultura Peruana. Lima.

PMK Paideuma. Mitteilungen Zur Kulturkunde. Deutsche Gesellschaft für kulturmorphologie von Frobenius Institut au der Johann Wolfgang Goethe—Universität. Wiesbaden, FRG.

PU/PPA Philosophy and Public Affairs. Princeton Univ. Press. Princeton, N.J.

PUCIRA/BSA Boletín del Seminario de Arqueología. Pontificia Univ. Católica del Perú, Instituto Riva Agüero. Lima.

RAI/M Man. A monthly record of anthropological science. The Royal Anthropological Institute. London.

RRI Revista/Review Interamericana. Univ. Interamericana. San Germán, P.R.

SA/J Journal de la Société des Américanistes. Paris.

SAA/AA American Antiquity. The Society for American Archaeology. Menasha, Wis.

SAA/HO Human Organization. Society for Applied Anthropology. N.Y.

SAA/R Relaciones de la Sociedad Argentina de Antropología. B.A.

SAIS/AIQ American Indian Quarterly. Southwestern American Indian Society [and the] Fort Worth Museum of Science and History. Hurst, Tex.

SBPC/CC Ciência e Cultura. Sociedade Brasileira para o Progresso da Ciência. São Paulo.

SBPL/RBL Revista Brasileira de Lingüística. Sociedade Brasileira para Professores de Lingüística. São Paulo.

SEB/EB Economic Botany. Devoted to applied botany and plant utilization. New Botanical Garden *for the* Society for Economic Botany. N.Y.

SEM/E Ethnos. Statens Etnografiska Museum. Stockholm.

SGL/B Boletín de la Sociedad Geográfica de Lima. Lima.

SJUG Saeculum. Jahrbuch für Universalgeschichte. München, FRG.

SM/M The Masterkey. Southwest Museum. Los Angeles, Calif.

SMA/RMEA Revista Mexicana de Estudios Antropológicos. Sociedad Mexicana de Antropología. México.

SMS/RMC Revista Médica de Chile. Sociedad Médica de Santiago. Santiago.

SOCIOL Sociologus. Zeitschrift für empirische Soziologie, sozialpsychologische und ethnologische Forschung (A journal for empirical sociology, social psychology and ethnic research). Berlin, FRG.

SP/DC Development and Change. Sage Publications. Beverly Hills, Calif.

SSA/B Bulletin. Société Suisse des Américanistes. Geneva.

UA Urban Anthropology. State Univ. of New York, Dept. of Anthropology. Brockport.

UA/TA Temas Administrativos. Univ. de Antioquia, Escuela de Administración y Finanzas e Instituto Tecnológico, Centro de Investigaciones. Medellín, Colombia.

UA/U Universidad. Univ. de Antioquia. Medellín, Colombia.

UAEM/H Histórica. Univ. Autónoma del Estado de México, Instituto de Investigaciones Históricas. México.

UC/A Anales de la Universidad de Cuenca. Cuenca, Ecua.

UC/CA Current Anthropology. Univ. of Chicago. Chicago, Ill.

UC/EDCC Economic Development and Cultural Change. Univ. of Chicago, Research

Center in Economic Development and Cultural Change. Chicago, Ill.

UCAB/M Montalbán. Univ. Católica Andrés Bello. Facultad de Humanidades y Educación, Institutos Humanísticos de Investigación. Caracas.

UCC/NG Norte Grande. Revista de estudios integrados referentes a comunidades humanas del Norte Grande de Chile, en una perspectiva geográfica e histórico-cultural. Univ. Católica de Chile, Instituto de Geografía, Depto. de Geografía de Chile, Taller Norte Grande. Santiago.

UCGL/AHG Annals of Human Genetics (Annals of Eugenics). Univ. College, Galton Laboratory. London.

UCLA/JLAL Journal of Latin American Lore. Univ. of California, Latin American Center. Los Angeles.

UCNSA/SA Suplemento Antropológico. Univ. Católica de Nuestra Señora de la Asunción, Centro de Estudios Antropológicos. Asunción.

UEN/LS Lateinamerika Studien. Univ. Erlangen-Nürnberg, Sektion Lateinamerika. Nürnberg, FRG.

UFP/CA Cadernos de Arqueologia. Univ. Federal do Paraná, Museu de Arqueologia e Artes Populares. Paranaguá, Brazil.

UFP/EB Estudos Brasileiros. Univ. Federal do Paraná, Setor de Ciências Humanas, Centro de Estudos Brasileiros. Curitiba, Brazil.

ULB/RIS Revue de l'Institut de Sociologie. Univ. Libre de Bruxelles. Bruxelles.

UM/JIAS Journal of Inter-American Studies and World Affairs. Univ. of Miami Press *for the* Center for Advanced International Studies. Coral Gables, Fla.

UNAM/AA Anales de Antropología. Univ. Nacional Autónoma de México, Instituto de Investigaciones Históricas. México.

UNAM/AL Anuario de Letras. Univ. Nacional Autónoma de México, Facultad de Filosofía y Letras. México.

UNAM/RMS Revista Mexicana de Sociología. Univ. Nacional Autónoma de México, Instituto de Investigaciones Sociales. México.

UNC/ED El Dorado. Univ. of Northern Colorado, Museum of Anthropology. Greeley, Colorado.

UNC/K Katunob. Univ. of Northern Colorado, Museum of Anthropology. Greeley, Colorado.

UNCIA/HC Hombre y Cultura. Univ. Nacional, Centro de Investigaciones Antropológicas. Panamá. See also UP/HC.

UNM/JAR Journal of Anthropological Research. Univ. of New Mexico, Dept. of Anthropology, Albuquerque, N. Mex.

UNT/H Humanitas. Univ. Nacional de Tucumán, Facultad de Filosofía y Letras. Tucumán, Arg.

UP/E Ethnology. Univ. of Pittsburgh. Pittsburgh, Pa.

UP/EA Estudios Andinos. Univ. of Pittsburgh, Latin American Studies Center. Pittsburgh, Pa.

UP/HC See UNCIA/HC.

UP/PSN Peasant Studies Newsletter. Univ. of Pittsburgh, Dept. of History. Pittsburgh, Pa. See also UP/PS.

UPR/CS Caribbean Studies. Univ. of Puerto Rico, Institute of Caribbean Studies. Río Piedras.

USMLA/LA La Antigua. Univ. de Santa María La Antigua, Oficina de Humanidades. Panamá.

UTIEH/C Caravelle. Cahiers du monde hispanique et luso-brésilien. Univ. de Toulouse, Institut d'Études Hispaniques, His-

pano-Americaines et Luso-Brésiliennes. Toulouse, France.

UWI/CQ Caribbean Quarterly. Univ. of the West Indies. Mona, Jam.

UWI/SES Social and Economic Studies. Univ. of the West Indies, Institute of Social and Economic Research. Mona, Jam.

UY/R Revista de la Universidad de Yucatán. Mérida, Mex.

UZ/R Revista de la Universidad del Zulia. Maracaibo, Ven.

VANH/B Boletín de la Academia Nacional de la Historia. Caracas.

VMJ/BIV Boletín Indigenista Venezolano. Ministerio de Justicia, Comisión Indigenista. Caracas.

VOZES Vozes. Revista de cultura. Editora Vozes. Petrópolis, Brazil.

WRU/JMF Journal of Marriage and the Family. Western Reserve Univ. Cleveland, Ohio.

WSU/HB Human Biology. Official publication of the Human Biology Council. Wayne State Univ., School of Medicine. Detroit, Mich.

YAXKIN Yaxkin. Instituto Hondureño de Antropología e Historia. Tegucigalpa.

ZMA Zeitschrift für Morphologie und Anthropologie. E. Nägele. Stuttgart, FRG.

ZMR Zeitschrift für Missionswissenschaft und Religionswissenschaft. Lucerne, Switzerland.

ECONOMICS

GENERAL

JOHN M. HUNTER, *Director, Latin American Studies Center, Michigan State University*

THIS BIENNIUM, LIKE ITS PREDECESSOR, saw an increase in the quantity of economic literature concerning Latin America, an improvement in its quality, and an expansion of the flow from Latin American sources. It is my intent below to note some of the highlights and to point out some of the more useful items—with apologies to authors of many interesting works which had to be excluded because of space limitations.

"Dependency," in a sense, has run full course. As a theory(ies), it now is attacked from the Left which seeks a more general (and more truly Marxist) explanation of reality. Jorge G. Castañeda and Enrique Hett (item **2777**), Liliana de Riz (item **2887**) and papers of the XLI International Congress of Americanists, as selected by Roger Bartra and Pierre Vilar, take this approach. Rhys Jenkins, on the other hand, fleshes out knowledge of dependency in a case study of the automotive industry in Argentina, Chile, and Mexico (item **2843**).

Three serials of particular merit came to our attention. *Revista de la CEPAL* appears semi-annually in Spanish and in English and permits more latitude in speculation and opinion than the older, more formal *Boletín. Cuadernos de la CEPAL* (item **2790**) is a relatively new monographic series with apparently several issues per year. *Estudios Rurales Latinoamericanos* (item **2804**) appeared first in Jan. 1978, and is to appear three times annually. It set high standards for itself with its first issue.

The Asociación Latinoamericana de Instituciones Financieras de Desarrollo (ALIDE) is publishing some excellent material in its area. See, for example, Tulio Andrea (item **2755**), Alberto Cerrolaza A. (item **2781**), Jorge Mustaffá and Alberto Varillas (item **2866**) and even the Reunión Ordinaria de la Asamblea General de ALIDE (item **2884**).

Two bibliographies merit mention. Elizabeth Ferris' selected bibliography on the Andean Pact emphasizes Spanish-language sources (item **2810**). André Gunder Frank in "Dependence is Dead! Long Live . . . " (item **2817**) classifies his critics, responds to them, and provides a considerable bibliography of pro-con works on Frank.

Two books concern the New World Order: Jagdish Bhagwati (item **2766**) edited a volume without area focus; and Joseph Grunwald (item **2828**), one which focuses on Latin America and the changing world economy.

Adolfo Figueroa (item **2814**) and Solon Barraclough (item **2760**) treated the agricultural sector, the former dealing particularly with agrarian reform and the latter with the more general crisis in agriculture. With respect to mineral production, Markos Mamalakis (item **2857**) has an excellent review article of six books dealing with mineral exploitation—largely regarding Latin America. Marian Radetski examines private and social costs and benefits from four parties' points of view in response to the question as to where LDC's mineral production should be processed (item **2881**).

Several important research activities came to published fruition in the period and are remarkable. Jorge Macon and José Merino Mañon's study, commissioned by the IDB, of the use of betterment levies in Latin America is a case in point. An ECIEL study of considerable duration on family income and spending appears in Philip Musgroves' volume (item **2865**). Associated with that is William Cline's (item **2784**) report in *Ensayos ECIEL* dealing with income distribution and development.

Three very different works in the (broadly defined) labor area require mention. Carmelo Mesa-Lago's *Social Security in Latin America* (item **2862**) is a pioneer and important work. Norberto García and Leonard Dudley's (item **2821**) projections to the year 2000 of employment, income, and distributional effects of technical change are provocative. The *Sector informal: funcionamiento y políticas* (item **2908**) prepared by the Programa Regional del Empleo para América Latina y el Caribe (PREALC) is an important examination of a large segment of the labor force.

2751 Agmon, Tamir and **Charles P. Kindleberger** eds. Multinationals from small countries. Cambridge, Mass., The MIT Press, 1977. 224 p., bibl.

Papers and a few commentaries from a 1976 MIT conference on the economics (not the politics) of small-country (defined in practice to be "relatively weak") corporations operating in nations other than those they regard as "home." Issues discussed are vertical integration, avoidance of bilateral monopoly scale, soft-ware. Papers, including one by Carlos Díaz Alejandro on Latin America, discuss Switzerland, Sweden, France, and Australia.

2752 Agüero Negrete, Max. El Pacto Andino y sus beneficios (CPU/ES, 10, dic. 1976, p. 55–73)

Author provides a competent review of thought on economic integration and then measures the Andean Group against these standards (see also items **2812** and **2923**).

Alejo, Francisco Javier and **Héctor Hurtado.** El SELA: un mecanismo para la acción. See item **8502**.

2753 Alvarez García, Marcos. Le Pacte Andin: un processus positif d'intégration en Amérique Latine (ULB/RIS, 3/4, 1975, p. 415–436, tables)

A competent review of the antecedents and experience of the Andean Group.

2754 Amin, Samir. El desarrollo desigual: o capitalismo periférico. Medellín, Colombia, Editora Ciencia Marxista, 1976? 290 p., bibl.

Descriptive development of the theory of the periphery and unequal development. Broad in scope, only incidentally deals with Latin America.

2755 Andrea, Tulio de and others. La banca de desarrollo en América Latina. t. 1, Políticas operativas; t. 2, v. 1/2, Fuentes de financiamiento; t. 3, Políticas operativas [and] fuentes de financiamiento: informe, análisis, principales, conclusiones y recomendación. Lima, Asociación Latinoamericana de Instituciones Financieras de Desarrollo (ALIDE), 1974. 3 v. in 4 pts. (454, 397, 674, 215 p.) fold. tables, tables.

The result and basis of a 1973 seminar in Venezuela. Encompasses 23 countries (including Puerto Rico) and is based on visits, interviews, documents. The extensive material reports by country, multinational institution, and also synthesizes. Although now somewhat dated, an extremely useful compendium. See also item **2866**.

Arriagada, Irma. Las mujeres pobres latinoamericanas: un esbozo de tipología. See item **9005**.

2756 Assael, Héctor and **Arturo Núñez del Pardo.** La inflación reciente en América Latina (BCV/REL, 13:50, 1977, p. 9–78, tables)

Latin America suffers a "new" inflation, and this study is concerned with its external causes and the mechanism for internalizing the imported inflation. Policy implications are finally considered. Deals particularly with Bolivia, Brazil, Colombia, Costa Rica, Ecuador, Uruguay. A somewhat shorter version appears in *El Trimestre Eco-*

nómico (México, 43:172, oct./dic. 1976, p. 969–1002, tables).

2757 Astori, Danilo. La industrialización en América Latina: algunas características fundamentales. Montevideo, Editorial la Academia, 1977. 82 p. (mimeo)
A careful study of the economy of Latin America in its dependency based on standard sources. A new economic world order is required.

2758 Bach, Luis. El Pacto Andino y la integración latinoamericana. B.A., Tierra Nueva, 1976. 124 p., tables (Col. Proceso, 9)
Analysis of integration to help overcome dependency, worsening terms of trade. Considerable bibliography, documents, and data.

2759 Barandiarán, Edgardo and Fernando Ossa. The design of balance-of-payments policies for the Andean countries: a progress report. Santiago, Univ. Católica de Chile, Instituto de Economía, 1976. 62 p., bibl.
A progress report on a larger project involving harmonization of macro policies of regional blocs in an interdependent world. Examines the complications of several balance of payments and exchange rates as well as the determination of regional objectives.

2760 Barraclough, Solon. Perspectivas de la crisis agrícola en América Latina (CLACSO/ERL, 1:1, enero/abril 1978, p. 33–57, bibl.)
A thoughtful piece looks at agriculture in the long run and evaluates its capacity to supply more and better food per capita. The greatest barrier is the social and economic organization supported by the capitalistic neo-colonial world. Great change depends on profound organizational changes which may not occur soon; in the meantime, there are marginal steps to be taken. The English version appears in *World Development* (Oxford, U.K., 5:5/7, May/July 1977, p. 459–476).

2761 Barrantes, Salvador; Cristian Gillen; and Nora Velarde. Los imperios financieros y el modo capitalista de producción como dominante a nivel mundial. Lima, Editorial Horizonte, 1975. 126 p., tables (Serie realidad peruana)
An abstract, Marxist exploration of the development of the capitalist, dominant world.

2762 Bartra, Roger and Pierre Vilar *eds.* Modos de producción en América Latina. Lima, Delva Editores, 1976. 107 p.
Includes a number of papers presented at the International Congress of Americanists, Mexico, 1974. The editors selected these studies because they depart from erroneous dependency theory, share a return to Marxism and thereby sharpen its tools for the analysis of Latin American reality. These papers were originally published in *Historia y Sociedad* (Mexico, 5, 1975). [Ed.]

2763 Bergalli Campomar, Olga. Los mecanismos y el funcionamiento de la integración económica en América Latina. B.A., Banco Interamericano de Desarrollo, Instituto para la Integración de América Latina (BID/INTAL), 1974. 170 p.
A text to be used in national schools for customs officials. Particularly interesting since it uses a "programmed learning" mode.

2764 Berger, Frederick E. Las políticas de endeudamiento y reservas en los países de menor desarrollo (UCC/CE, 13:39, agosto 1976, p. 3–26, bibl.)
Seeks to analyze the financing of external disequilibria as an alternative means of adjustment to them. Involves the concept of equilibrium role of exchange and reserve debt policy. Extends previous models particularly with an inclusion of risk and uncertainty with respect to financial decisions.

2765 Betancourt, Roger R. The dynamics of inflation in Latin America: comment (AEA/AER, 66:4, Sept. 1976, p. 688–691)
Comments on Vogel's work (see *HLAS* 37:4238) together with Edmund J. Sheehey (see item **2911**). For Vogel's reply to both critics, see item **2931**).

2766 Bhagwati, Jagdish N. The new international economic order: the North-South debate. Cambridge, Mass., The MIT Press, 1977. 390 p., tables (MIT bicentennial studies)
An extremely interesting volume resulting from an MIT workshop which sought to get outstanding economists to concentrate attention on the specific "demands" as components of a new world order. Topics include: debt relief, SDR's, oceans as a revenue source, taxing the brain drain, grain stocks, and many others. Closes with panel discussion on the new order. Applicable in general

to Latin America but does not concentrate thereon.

2767 Blejer, M.I. and A.C. Porzecanski *comps.* Economía monetaria: selección de textos. México, Centro de Estudios Monetarios Latinoamericanos (CEMLA), 1977. 290 p., tables.

An excellent collection of previously published essays largely on world-wide inflation and the international monetary mechanism. A few articles (e.g., Sjaastad, Fishlow) related particularly to Latin America. Most are general.

2768 Boloña Behr, Carlos. Una interpretación matemática del Modelo Sunkel sobre el subdesarrollo latinoamericano. Lima, Univ. del Pacífico, Centro de Investigación, 1975. 55 p. (Serie de ensayos, 11)

Actually two basic models: colonial and "liberal," with an attempt also to "dynamize" the former.

2769 Borisov, Eugenio Filippovich and others. Diccionario de economía política. Bogotá, Ediciones Suramérica, 1977. 250 p.

A frankly Marxist dictionary—and a good deal more than just simple biography and definition.

2770 Brittain, W.H. Bruce. Developing countries' external debt and the private banks (BNL/QR, 123, dic. 1977, p. 365–380, tables)

Examines the rapid build-up since 1973 of borrowing from private banks by developing countries. Seeks to explain the deficits and to anticipate the future and the risks the private banks face.

2771 Brodovich, Boris and others. Estructura económica en América Latina. Bogotá, Ediciones Suramérica, 1976. 123 p.

Six articles by Soviet economists which appeared in *América Latina*. They treat of the capitalist crisis and its effects, models of development, agrarian transformation, the scientific-technical revolution, historical development. This growing body of literature is of some considerable importance.

Cardoso, Fernando Henrique. The consumption of dependency theory in the United States. See item **7007**.

2771a ———. Las contradicciones del desarrollo asociado. Lima, Univ. Católica del Perú, Programa Académico de CCSS, n.d.

37 l., tables (Taller de estudios políticos)

A short provocative essay questioning some myths about economic development in Latin America. [M. Mamalakis]

2772 ———. The originality of a copy: CEPAL and the idea of development (CEPAL/R, 2, 1977, p. 7–40)

A generally favorable assessment of ECLA's contribution to matters of policy and particularly interesting is author's evaluation of it as a contributor to the economics of its time.

2773 ——— and **Enzo Faletto.** Dependency and development in Latin America. Translated by Marjory Mattingly Urquidi. Berkeley, Univ. of California Press, 1978. 227 p.

Translation of the authors' well-known study *Dependencia y desarrollo en América Latina: un ensayo de interpretación sociológica* (México, Siglo XXI Editores, 1969, 166 p.). Includes 10-year update described in item **2774**. Originally done in the 1960s, book views development/dependency in history as a broad, inseparable whole.

2774 ——— and ———. Post-scriptum a *Dependencia y desarrollo en América Latina.* B.A., Centro de Estudios de Estado y Sociedad (CEDES), 1976. 38 p. (Documentos CEDES/CLASCO, 6)

A new chapter to the first ed. of the authors' well-known study described in item **2773**. This additional chapter, a 10-year historical update, deals primarily with the political-historical struggle between classes on the one hand and with an evolution of economic-political structures of internal and external domination on the other.

2775 Carraud, Michel. Nature et portée de l'Accord d'Intégration Sous-Régionale Andine (FDD/NED [Problèmes d'Amérique Latine, 45] 4421/4423, 21 oct. 1977, p. 53–72, bibl., tables)

A review of the genesis and performance of the Andean Accord. There is incidental comparison with integration in Europe.

2776 Carreras, Charles. An early venture in trade promotion: the NAM's Caracas Center, 1895–1901 (IAMEA, 31:1, Summer 1977, p. 51–64)

The NAM experimented briefly with a "sample warehouse" in Caracas in the late 1890s in an effort to expand trade. This is an interesting historical footnote recounting that experience.

2777 Castañeda, Jorge G. and **Enrique Hett.** El economismo dependentista. México, Siglo XXI Editores, 1978. 191 p. (Economía y demografía)

Authors attack "dependentistas" as having an ideology for a theory and arguing circularly. Tentatively, they present their own Leninist-Marxist explanation of reality.

Castelo, Julio. The insurance market in Latin America, Portugal, and Spain. See *HLAS 40:2147.*

2778 Centro Latinamericano de Economía Humana, *Montevideo.* Desarrollo latinoamericano: de la raíz al desafío. Montevideo, 1977. 78 p.

Three articles: Walter Cancela's "Historical Evolution;" Luis A. Faroppa's "The Nature of the Challenge;" and Alfredo Echegaray's "Economic Integration." Concludes with portions of a paper produced by an *El Foro* task force in Mexico.

2779 ———, ———. El nuevo orden internacional: dimensiones de un debate histórico. Montevideo, 1977. 77 p.

Good quality papers presented to 1976 seminar on this topic.

2780 *CEPAL Review.* United Nations. Economic Commission for Latin America. Second half of 1976– . Santiago.

An important relatively new journal which permits ECLA to publish a variety of signed articles which can be and are a good deal more speculative and/or tentative than official ECLA documents. Articles have wide range. The Spanish ed. appears in June and Dec. apparently beginning in 1976. An English version follows this by about three months.

2781 Cerrolaza Asenjo, Alberto. Recursos financieros para el desarrollo latinoamericano. Madrid, Asociación Latinoamericana de Instituciones Financieras de Desarrollo (ALIDE) [and] Instituto de Crédito Oficial de España, 1976. 431 p., tables.

A very substantial document emanating from the I Extraordinary General Assembly of ALIDE, held in Madrid, 1975, on the general theme of the mobilization of external and internal developmental resources in view of the new world order. Two major general essays dominate, but a series of shorter pieces on specific topics are also of interest.

2782 Chayanov, A.V. On the theory of noncapitalist ecnomic systems (*in* Halperin, Rhoda and James Dow *eds.* Peasant livelihood: studies in economic anthropology and cultural ecology. N.Y., St. Martin's Press, 1977, p. 257–268)

Modern Western economics is held inapplicable to peasant production since the notions of wages, profits, exchange, are inapplicable. There is nonetheless a kind of equilibrium proposed between "family demand satisfaction and the drudgery of labor itself."

2783 Chonchol, Jacques. Acelerar el crecimiento agrícola en los países subdesarrollados: única respuesta a la crisis alimentaria mundial (FCE/TE, 43:172, oct./dic. 1976, p. 1051–1075)

Meeting the challenges of world food shortages requires a new development strategy—pro-agriculture rather than pro-industrialization. Discusses strategy and problems including the roles of the presently industrialized.

2784 Cline, William. Distribución de ingreso y desarrollo económico: un resumen y algunas pruebas para ciudades seleccionadas de América Latina (ECIEL, 4, 1977, p. 1–43, bibl.)

An important and careful study of income distribution with data from Asunción, Bogotá, Lima, Quito, Caracas. After review of the literature, uses data to test set of hypotheses. Related to ECIEL study on consumption (see item **2865**).

2785 Clinton, Richard L. The never-to-be-developed countries of Latin America (BAS/SPA, 33:8, Oct. 1977, p. 19–26, bibl., plates, tables)

Author believes the traditional view of development (increasing GNP) is flawed in the first place and, in the second place, the world cannot afford in energy and materials all nations achieving "developed" status.

Colard, Daniel. Vers l'établissement d'un Nouvel Ordre Économique International. See item **8516**.

2786 Conferencia de Ministerios de Trabajo de los Países del Grupo Andino, *III, Lima, 1975.* Los Ministerios de Trabajo de los Países del Grupo Andino: descripción orgánica-funcional. Lima, Ministerio de Trabajo del Perú [and] Centro Interamericano de Administración del Trabajo, 1975. 239 p.

A description of the various ministries of labor as a part of labor legislation and social security related to harmonization of socio-labor policy in the Andean Group.

2787 Conferencia sobre Cooperación Económica entre Países en Desarrollo, *México, 1976.* Declaraciones, resoluciones, recomendaciones y decisiones adoptadas en el sistema de las Naciones Unidas y otros foros interregionales relacionados con la cooperación económica entre países en desarrollo. México, 1976. 3 v. (751 l.) (Continuous pagination)(UN Doc. 77/COOP/CMEX/S. Ref. 1 13 Sept. 1976)

Three volumes in preparation for the 1976 Mexican conference. A rare collection of documentation. Includes resolutions of the General Assembly, ECOSOC, UNCTAD, UNIDO, UNDP, Group of 77, Unallied Countries, Raw Materials Producers, etc.

2788 ———, ———. Informe de la conferencia sobre cooperación económica entre países en desarrollo. v. 1, Decisiones de la conferencia y resumen de las deliberaciones. México, 1976. 1 v. (Various pagings) (UN doc. no. 77/COOP/MEX/12)

Vol. 1 is an account of the conference decisions and a review of its deliberations (and 10 appendices). Agreements are reported in following areas: commerce, production, infrastructure, services; money and finance; science and technical cooperation; and worldwide agreements to facilitate economic cooperation. Additional four volumes will provide background and working papers in support of decisions of vol. 1. Much of the meat will be found here but the edition is limited and the organization haphazard.

Cortés Conde, Roberto and **Stanley J. Stein** eds. Latin America: a guide to economic history, 1830–1930. See *HLAS 40:2386.*

2789 *Coyuntura Económica Andina.* Univ. de Chile, Depto. de Economía, Santiago [and] Fundación para la Educación Superior y el Desarrollo, Bogotá [and] Fundación para la Educación y el Desarrollo, Quito. No. 1, 1976–. Santiago.

An homogenized statistical abstract and review of the economics for each of the Andean countries. I do not know if, in fact, it has become semi-annual as its format suggests is the intent.

2790 *Cuadernos de la CEPAL.* Naciones Unidas. Comisión Económica para América Latina. No. 13 [through] No. 18, 1977–. Santiago.

Serial publication issued by ECLA or CEPAL which reports the organization's views on development and other relevant matters. No. 13 describes ECLA's views on import substitution; No. 14 includes excerpts from Raúl Prebisch's writings in 1949, 1954, 1961, 1963; No. 15 consists of a UN document prepared for a conference on water resources which surveys needs, policies, alternatives; No. 16, discusses social change as part of the development process (e.g., urbanization, rural life, marginalization, education, employment, etc.); No. 17 reviews Latin American development as a function of its international economic relations; and No. 18 turns to history in order to explain distribution of resources and its social consequences and includes some interesting case sketches and a discussion of the effects of urbanization and industrialization.

2791 Cueva, Agustín. El desarrollo del capitalismo en América Latina: ensayo de interpretación histórica. México, Siglo XXI Editores, 1977. 238 p.

A serious effort to describe the evolution of the Latin American economies from pre-colonial days—a considerable task. Oligarchic dependencies resulted—full of inconsistencies leading to the present crisis.

2792 Currie, Lauchlin. The objectives of development (WD, 6:1, Jan. 1978, p. 1–10)

This generally neglected author in development economics traces his own thinking from the New Deal through Operation Colombia and later writings especially with respect to "growth economics" and the meaning (and hence strategies) of development.

2793 D'Ascoli, Carlos. Los instrumentos de la política comercial. Caracas, Univ. Central de Venezuela (UCV), Facultad de Ciencias Económicas y Sociales, 1973. 365 p.

Essentially a text. Four-fifths examines international agreements beginning with Havana, GATT, etc. Is inclusive and provides good summaries.

2794 Davis, L. Harlan. Appropriate technology: an explanation and interpretation of its role in Latin America (IAMEA, 32:1, Summer 1978, p. 51–66, table)

Discusses meaning of "appropriate" when applied to technology and examines questions: if it is so appropriate why is it not more used? In part, it is not so "appropriate" as assumed.

Davis, Stanley M. and **Louis Wolf Goodman** *eds.* Workers and managers in Latin America. See item **9017**.

Delacroix, Jacques and **Charles Ragin.** Modernizing institutions, mobilization, and Third World development: a cross-national study. See item **9018**.

2795 Delgado de Puppo, Teresita. Empresa multinacional: una moderna estrategia de marketing o un nuevo desafío a la administración. Montevideo, Univ. de la República, Facultad de Ciencias Económicas y de Administración, Instituto de Administración, 1976. 82 p., bibl., illus. (Cuaderno, 71)

Examines the multinational as an administrative challenge and deals with it primarily in the marketing area.

2796 Den Boer, Cees. Centro y periferia: la fundación teórica en Prebisch (CEDLA/B, 12, junio 1972, p. 21–30)

Seeks to "model" Prebisch's 1950 report to test the validity of the attempt to explain the differences in income between nations. Finds that the theoretical structure fails but that there is nonetheless much of value in Prebisch.

2797 Diamand, Marcelo. Las empresas conjuntas latinoamericanas: coincidencias y conflictos de intereses. B.A., Banco Interamericano de Desarrollo, Instituto para la Integración de América Latina (BID/INTAL), 1976? 32 p. (Estudios INTAL, 16)

Restricted to binational, manufacturing cases. Analysis in terms of the firm exporting technology and/or capital, its country of origin, the importing firm, and its country. Makes recommendations for reducing conflicts.

2798 Díaz-Alejandro, Carlos F. International markets for LDCs: the old and the new (AEA/AER, 68:2, May 1978, p. 264–269, bibl.)

Seeks to convince that international markets and arrangements are not as efficient, competitive and liberal as they might be. Trade characteristics of the NIEO are largely understandable.

2799 Durán, Hermán and **Hubert Drouvot.** Y-a-t-il une place pour les moyennes et petites industries françaises en Amérique Latine? (FDD/NED [Problèmes d'Amérique Latine, 46] 4443/4445, 12 déc. 1975, p. 70–84, tables)

An interesting effort to answer the title's question in general and with inadequate data. Describes circumstances in which small-medium foreign firms may be successful.

2800 *Economundo.* Informe de la economía internacional. Secretaría de Hacienda y Crédito Público. No. 24, junio 1977– . México.

A monthly (?) publication with a different economic theme each issue. About half the issue consists of reprinted articles from *The Economist, Wall Street Journal,* etc. The remainder reports graphically on a variety of international economic data.

2801 Elías, Víctor Jorge. Sources of economic growth in Latin American countries (The Review of Economics and Statistics [Harvard Univ., Cambridge, Mass.] 60:3, Aug. 1978, p. 362–370)

Econometric study of growth determinants in Argentina, Brazil, Chile, Colombia, Mexico, Peru, Venezuela (1940–74). Most of increases in output—labor ratios are explained by increases in capital—labor ratio.

2802 La empresa latinoamericana en la próxima década. B.A., Consejo Interamericano de Comercio y Producción (CICYP), Sección Argentina, 1976. 271 p.

Proceedings of a seminar in B.A., May 1975. Excellent panel of speakers on topics such as: relations with the state, as tool of growth, energy problems, the world food problem, social responsibilities.

2803 Encuentro Latinoamericano sobre Desarrollo en América Latina, *Panamá, 1975.* Desarrollo integral de América Latina. t. 1, Objectivos y realizaciones; t. 2, Criterios y estrategias. Bogotá, Consejo Episcopal Latinoamericano (CELAM), 1976. 2 v. (162, 142 p.) (Documento CELAM, 24)

Series of formal papers considered by the Council of Bishops in Panama, 1975. Vol.

1 consists largely of country reports (19 were represented) on various topics related to the role of the Church and development (in a broad sense). Vol. 2 is a series of papers on a variety of topics. Among them is a consideration of the ethical content of ECLA's policies.

2804 *Estudios Rurales Latinoamericanos.*
Consejo Latinoamericano de Ciencias Sociales (CLASCO), Comisión de Estudios Rurales. Vol. 1, No. 1, enero/abril 1978–. Bogotá.
A new journal to appear three times per year. The first issue is Jan./April 1978. It is well presented and has a survey article on studies of the campesino (Archetti), small farmer organizations in Colombia (Bagley and Botero), agrarian reform and capital accumulations in Peru (Valderrama), cacao export in Ecuador (Chiriboga), the agricultural crisis (Barraclough) as well as service sections.

2805 *Estudos CEBRAP.* Centro Brasileiro de Análise e Planejamento [and] Editora Brasiliense. No. 18, out./dez. 1976 [through] No. 21, julho/set. 1977–. São Paulo.
A serious journal. The issue examined included a 1977 piece of Hirschman and several apparently original articles, two related to Brazilian urbanization, one by A. Pinto on CEPAL, and another on Max Weber and the Russian Revolution.

2806 Fajnzylber, Fernando. Las empresas transnacionales y el "collective self-reliance" (FCE/TE, 43:172, oct./dic. 1976, p. 879–921)
"Collective self-reliance" is characterized as: 1) weakening relations with developed countries, 2) strengthening relations with other developing countries, 3) mobilizing domestic potentialities; and 4) satisfying of basic necessities for most of the people. Article deals with the dynamics of moving from current situation to a new one and describes the role of the transnational firm and governmental strategies that will be required in seeking the new state.

2807 Faro, José Salvador. Nova Ordem Econômica Internacional: ilusões e realidades (SBPC/CC, 29:2, fev. 1977, p. 129–142)
Traces relationships since World War II which have led to present crisis in bipolar relationship. Notes considerable progress in managing international political matters, but

the lag in successes in managing international economic problems threatens even the former.

2808 Federación Latinoamericana de Bancos, *Bogotá.* Financiación y prefinanciación del comercio exterior latinoamericano. Bogotá, 1974. 214 p.
Country-by-country response to questionnaire regarding agencies, amounts, conditions, country discriminations, publications concerned with export finance. Highly specialized. Somewhat dated.

2809 Ferrer, Aldo. Latin America and the world economy (UM/JIAS, 20:3, Aug. 1978, p. 321–337)
Latin American economies are, for a number of reasons, increasingly autonomous. Their current external debts, increasingly privately held, are of considerable concern. The ability of the industrialized world, particularly the US, to solve its own problems is of critical importance to Latin America.

2810 Ferris, Elizabeth G. The Andean Pact: a selected bibliography (LARR, 13:3, 1978, p. 108–124)
Emphasis is on Spanish-language sources in four sections: background studies, general studies of the Andean Pact, studies of specific programs, studies of a single member nation's experience in the Pact. Contains about 375 items and notes on general sources.

2811 Ffrench-Davis, Ricardo. The Andean Pact: a model of economic integration for developing countries (WD, 5:1/2, Jan./Feb. 1977, p. 137–153, bibl., tables)
An entirely competent review of the Andean Pact—origins, justifications, objectives, provisions, successes, weaknesses.

2812 ———. Evolución reciente del Pacto Andino (CPU/ES, 10, dic. 1976, p. 38–54)
Up-dates events to Oct. 1976; examines behavior of non-traditional exports, particularly of Chile; a final section examines decisions of the Group after Chile's withdrawal. In spite of all difficulties the experiment continues to progress (see also items **2752** and **2923**).

2813 ———. Instrumentos no arancelarios en las políticas de comercio exterior. Santiago, Corporación de Investigaciones Económicas para Latinoamérica (CIEPLAN),

1977. 55 p. (Estudios CIEPLAN, 12)

Analyzes various instruments for modifying foreign trade. Generally standard textbook-like treatment but broad enough to include such matters as income redistribution effects.

2814 Figueroa, Adolfo. Agrarian reform in Latin America: a framework and an instrument of rural development (WD, 5:1/2, Jan./Feb. 1977, p. 155–168, bibl., tables)

Excellent piece on land reform. Shows land reform alone cannot do much to modify income distribution, increase efficiency, increase savings. Requires complementary set of policies *outside* agriculture to improve the poorest-of-the-poor agricultural subsector.

2815 Fortner, Robert S. Strategies for self-immolation: the Third World and the transfer of advanced technologies (IAMEA, 31:1, Summer 1977, p. 25–50, tables)

Self-immolation for the LDC's consists of giving up control of technological inputs by lack of adequate controls of MNC's and by adhering to international agreements on patents, licensing, etc.

2816 Foxley, Alejandro and **Oscar Muñoz.** Políticas de empleo en economías heterogéneas. Santiago, Corporación de Investigaciones Económicas para Latinoamerica (CIEPLAN), 1976. 37 p., bibl. (Estudios CIEPLAN, 1)

Traditional theory and policy are not much help in the face of long-term unemployment in less developed countries. Dualism "theory" was recognition of this, but several strata exist (this is what the "heterogeneity" consists of). Policies vary among strata.

2817 Frank, André Gunder. Dependence is dead, long live dependence and the class struggle: an answer to critics (WD, 5:4, April 1977, p. 355–370, bibl.)

It has become a full-time task to keep up with the pros and cons (particularly the cons) of André Gunder Frank. This is an extraordinary, not entirely comprehensible, piece in answer to critics of the right, old left, new left and miscellaneous. Five pages of bibliography on the polemic.

2818 ———. La inversión extranjera en el subdesarrollo latinoamericano. Lima, Editorial Causachun, 1976. 44 p. (Col. Cuadernos. Serie ideología y política, 1)

Foreign investment contributes to un-

derdevelopment rather than being helpful. Small pamphlet. Not much new or unexpected.

2819 Furtado, Celso. A economia latinoamericana: formação histórica e problemas contemporâneos. 2. ed. rev. São Paulo, Companhia Editora Nacional, 1976. 339 p., tables.

A new and rewritten edition of the 1969 work. An important, integrated look at the economy of Latin America with some special emphasis on external markets, regional cooperation, the agricultural sector. English translation by Suzette Macedo: *Economic development of Latin America* (Cambridge, U.K., Cambridge Univ. Press, 1976, 317 p.).

2820 García, Antonio. Cooperación agraria y estrategias de desarrollo. México, Siglo XXI Editores, 1976. 291 p.

An important look at cooperativism in the US, the socialist world, and the "Third" World. Roughly two-thirds of the volume examines the history and possible role of cooperativism in the development of Latin America.

2821 García, Norberto E. and **Leonard Dudley.** Tecnología, subempleo y pobreza en América Latina: perfiles a largo plazo (FCE/TE, 44:173, enero/marzo 1977, p. 169–198, bibl., tables)

Utilizes modified ECLA Model (1974) to project to the year 2000 the employment, income, distributional effects of technical change. Two policy sets are compared with a basic projection. Provocative.

2822 García Martínez, Luis. Teoría de la dependencia. B.A., Emecé Editores, 1976. 185 p.

An introduction for the general reader. Some data, some bibliography.

Gatemi, Nasrollah S.; Gail W. Williams; and **Thibault de Saint-Phalle.** Multinational corporations: the problems and the prospects. See *HLAS 40:2389.*

2823 George, Robert; Eldon Reiling; and **Anthony Scaperlanda.** Short-run trade effects of the LAFTA (KYKLOS, 30:4, 1977, p. 618–636, bibl, tables)

Econometric study with three principal findings: 1) LAFTA expanded trade but most of it was diverted trade; 2) initial concern over benefits to the least-developed was not warranted; and 3) the importance of the foreign exchange constraint was confirmed.

2824 González García, Leovigildo. Cronodinámica de la crisis monetaria internacional: 1971–1972, crisis del dólar. Asunción, Imprenta Comuneros, 1974 (i.e. 1977). 211 p. (Problemática monetaria, 2)

A sort of diary of the dollar crisis 1971–72 with chronological account of and commentary on world monetary events.

2825 González Montero, Jesús and others. La planificación del desarrollo agropecuario: un enfoque para América Latina. v. 1. México, Siglo XXI Editores, 1977. 334 p., tables (Textos del Instituto Latinoamericano de Planificación Económica y Social)

An introductory text (not necessarily for the classroom) on an important topic. Two general sections: general concepts, the diagnosis. It purports to cover Latin America and is general and organizationally oriented as opposed to empirical and descriptive of present planning.

2826 Graciarena, Jorge. Types of income concentration and political styles in Latin America (CEPAL/R, 2, 1976, p. 203–236)

Relates income distribution to that of power distribution. Concludes more egalitarian distribution awaits higher degrees of real democracy and broader diversions of power.

2827 Grunwald, Joseph. Los recursos de la América Latina en la economía mundial: cobre y mineral de hierro (FCE/TE, 44:173, enero/marzo 1977, p. 117–142, table)

Considers the expansion of copper and iron exploitation in particular as financial complements for industrialization. Policies are expected by Latin American countries to increase their control over their own resources and to increase their share of the return from exploitation.

2828 ——— ed. Latin America and world economy: a changing international order. Beverly Hills, Calif., Sage Publications *sponsored by the* Center for Inter-American Relations, 1978. 323 p., tables (Latin American international affairs series, 2)

The second in a series of the Center for Inter-American Relations. A collection of new essays from well-known authors on the changing world economy and Latin America's role in it. Sections concern: economic rela-

tions with industrial countries; Mexico and Brazil as large nations and leaders; regional integration; financing development and the multinational corporation.

2829 Guzmán Ferrer, Martín Luis. La inflación y el desarrollo en la América Latina. México, UNAM, Escuela Nacional de Economía, 1976. 653 p., bibl., tables.

A very thorough undertaking. Major subdivisions include consideration of the monetarist-structuralist confrontation with some special attention to income distribution and economic policy, including a number of country case studies. Well documented.

2830 Hanson, Simon G. Questionable payments?: notes on business practices in Latin America (IAMEA, 31:2, Autumn 1977, p. 25–40)

Concludes that solution to questionable payments practices finally rests with host governments and that efforts of the US to impose ethics on US firms in this matter will simply reduce competitiveness abroad.

2831 Hosono, Akio. Industrialización y empleo: experiencia en Asia y estrategia para América Latina (CEPAL/R, 2, 1976, p. 115–160, tables)

About two-thirds covers Japanese and Chinese developmental policies. The remaining portion relates these to Latin America. Emphasis is on policy to utilize "surplus" labor both in the cities and rural areas.

2832 Iglesias, Enrique and others. Perspectivas económicas. Washington, United States Information Service, 1971. 127 p.

Consists of articles by Enrique Iglesias, John Galbraith, Werner Baer, Raymond Vernon, Lester Pearson, etc. Most were published elsewhere. Most attend to development, capital, corporations in Latin America. Apparently translated from *Facetas* in their entirety. Useful collection.

2833 Inter-American Development Bank (IDB), *Buenos Aires*. **Instituto para la Integración de América Latina** (INTAL). Análisis de los márgenes de preferencia y el comercio intrazonal en el marco de la Asociación Latinoamericana de Libre Comercio. B.A., 1974. 79 p., tables (Estudios, 9)

A first approximation in econometric estimation of the effects of preference margins on intrazonal trade taking into account other variables as well, viz. over-and-under evaluation of exchange rates. Methodologically interesting.

2834 ———, ———. ———. Expansión y diversificación del comercio exterior de los países de ALALC: 1953–1969. B.A., 1974. 192 p., tables (Estudios, 11)

To p. 50, analysis of various levels (countries, type of countries, products, destinations) of LAFTA (i.e. ALALC) country exports. The remaining pages are raw data by commodity and country.

2835 ———, ———. ———. Proyectos conjuntos y empresas conjuntas en la integración económica de América Latina. B.A., 1974. 258 p. (Estudios, 13)

A very short study of means to stimulate "joint ventures." Three appendices bring together in summary form country legislation with respect to foreign investment; juridical treatment of foreign and domestic capital; law pertaining to LAFTA nations abroad. Other appendices are less interesting.

2836 ———, ———. ———. Régimen de las inversiones extranjeras en los países de la ALALC: textos legales y procedimientos administrativos. B.A., 1975. 370 p., tables.

Includes decrees, etc., forms, by country. A useful but highly specialized compendium.

2837 ———, *Washington.* A new partnership for development: the participation of the nonregional member countries in the Inter-American Development Bank. Washington, 1978. 22 p., tables.

In 1976–77, 15 non-regional members joined the IDB. Latin America's exports to them averaged 10.3 billion annually and imports from them averaged 13.1 billion. This pamphlet describes and discusses this important change in the structure of the institution.

2838 **Inter-American Foundation (IAF),** *Washington.* They know how . . . : an experiment in development assistance. Washington, 1976. 159 p., plates, tables.

A refreshing self-assessment of the Inter-American Foundation's first five imaginative years. Particular attention is called to the chapter "The Foundation as a Learner."

2839 **Istituto Italo-Latino Americano,** *Roma.* **Istituto per la Cooperazione Universitaria.** America Latina: il fattore edu-

cativo nell'integrazione. Milano, Italy, L.U. Japadre Editore, 1970. 171 p.

Results of a seminar in 1969. Pays particular attention to the Andean group.

2840 **Iyoha, Milton Ame.** Inflation and "openness" in less developed economies: a cross-country analysis (UC/EDCC, 22:1, Oct. 1973, p. 31–37)

Negative correlation between "openness" and roles of inflation suggest that balance of payments adjustments may absorb inflationary pressures. Policy implications relate to import substitution and export promotion. See also author's response to comment by Kirkpatrick and Nixson in *Economic Development and Cultural Change* (Chicago, 26:1, Oct. 1977, p. 147–155).

Jaguaribe, Hélio. Dependency and autonomy in Latin America. See item **7033.**

2841 **Jain, Shail.** Size distribution of income: a compilation of data. Washington, World Bank, 1975. 137 p., tables.

A short introduction describes method and weakness. The remainder is tables with comparable data for 81 countries and notes concerning data sources. Critical publication for those interested empirically in distribution.

2842 **Janvry, Alain de** and **Carlos Garramón.** The dynamics of rural poverty in Latin America (JPS, 4:3, April 1977, p. 206–216)

A complex argument in Marxist terms regarding the exploitation of subsistence agriculture on the "ultimate embodiment of the contradictions that derive from the process of accumulation in the centre-periphery binomial."

2843 **Jenkins, Rhys Owen.** Dependent industrialization in Latin America: the automotive industry in Argentina, Chile and Mexico. N.Y., Praeger, 1977. 298 p., bibl., tables (Praeger special studies in international economics and development)

A welcome addition to dependency literature—a careful industry study to flesh out theoretical structures. Shows the development of the Latin American automotive industry as conditioned by the international industry of which it is a part.

2844 **Jiménez, Roberto.** América Latina y el mundo desarrollado: bibliografía comentada sobre relaciones de dependencia.

Bogotá, Centro de Estudios para el Desarrollo e Integración de América Latina, 1977. 315 p.

Pt. 1 covers genesis and critique of dependency theory which the author now regards as passé. Pt. 2 (p. 103–315) is an occasionally annotated bibliography organized by theme. About 1000 items, about 10 percent annotated.

2845 Junta del Acuerdo de Cartagena, *Lima.* Programa de liberación: 1977–1978. Lima, 1978? 2 v. (692 p.) (Continuous pagination)

Highly specialized lists of products and their treatment by Andean group. Critical information for some but deadly in this form for most.

2846 Kádár, Béla. Las principales tendencias del desarrollo de las fuerzas productivas de América Latina. Budapest, Hungarian Academy of Sciences, Institute for World Economics, 1977. 82 p., tables (Studies on developing countries, 91)

Also includes L.L. Klochkovsky's "Prognóstico del Desarrollo Económico de los Países de América Latina en el Período hasta 1980." Both pieces by Kádár and Klochkowsky stem from an Annual Meeting on Development in Latin America held by the Science Academies of Socialist Countries. Kádár sees changes in external forces contributing to growth potential.

2847 Kamarck, Andrew M. The tropics and economic development: a provocative inquiry into the poverty of nations. With a foreword by Paul Streeten. Baltimore, Md., The Johns Hopkins Univ. Press *for the* World Bank, 1976. 113 p., bibl., maps (A World Bank publication)

The tropics, compared to temperate zones, hinder agriculture, handicap mineral exploitation, and make people less vigorous. The effects make technology transfer difficult and call for special research efforts.

2848 Khalatbari, Parvis. Demografía en países dependientes. Tunja, Colombia, Univ. Pedagógica y Tecnológica de Colombia, Secretaría de Investigaciones y Extensión Universitaria [and] Ediciones La Rana y El Aguila, 1976. 259 p. (Col. Nueva universidad, 11)

Five essays translated from German. Marxist treatment of demographic problems in dependent countries.

2849 Kirkpatrick, C.H. and F. I. Nixson. Inflation and "openness" in less developed economies: a cross-country analysis; comment (UC/EDCC, 26:1, Oct. 1977, p. 147–152)

Criticism and alternative explanation for regression results. Also see item **2840.**

2850 Kleiman, Ephraim. Cultural ties and trade: Spain's role in Latin America (KYKLOS, 31:2, 1978, p. 275–290, tables)

Tests hypothesis that close cultural ties (e.g., a common language) are positive factors in trade creation. Data do not support this as between Spain and Spanish-speaking Latin America. For political scientist's comment, see item **8552.**

2851 Klochkovsky, L. The multinationals in Latin America (IA, 10, Oct. 1977, p. 46–54)

Dependency increases and changes in character. Enclaves have become deep penetration. The struggle for independence goes on.

2852 Krieger Mytelka, Lynn. Licensing and technology dependence in the Andean group (WD, 6:4, April 1978, p. 447–459, bibl., illus., table)

Questions the policy of divestment as a solution to the problem of technological dependence within the Andean group on the grounds that state controlled and mixed firms are no less dependent than are foreign firms. [A. Berry]

2853 Kusnetzoff, Fernando. Spatial planning and development in Latin America: the critical approach (UM/JIAS, 19:3, Aug. 1977, p. 429–444, bibl.)

An interesting review of a series of publications by SIAP (Inter-American Planning Society). Concerns largely regional and particularly urban planning.

2854 Latin American Free Trade Association (LAFTA), *Montevideo.* Análisis de los sistemas bancarios de los países de la ALALC y de la República Dominicana: anexo a la *Guía bancaria.* Montevideo, Asociación Latinoamericano de Libre Comercio (ALALC), 1976. 131 p., tables.

More than an "anexo." Specialized. Integrates analysis of deposits, loans, amounts, etc., and has risk statement data (p. 48–59).

2855 Macon, Jorge and **José Merino Mañón.**
Financing urban and rural development through betterment levies: the Latin American experience. N.Y., Praeger, 1977. 146 p., bibl., map, tables (Praeger special studies in international politics and government)

An IDB commissioned study on betterment levies (special assessments) as fiscal devices in Latin America. Principal parts are: 1) the conceptual framework; 2) country experience; and 3) conclusions and recommendations. An important study of a useful public finance instrument. Also available in Spanish as *Contribución de mejoras en América Latina* (México, Fondo de Cultura Económica, 1976).

2856 Magariños, Gustavo. Perspectivas históricas e atuais de ALALC (BNB/REN, 9:1, jan./março 1978, p. 37–57)
Traces history and development of LAFTA, its problems, and rather gloomy future.

2857 Mamalakis, Markos J. Minerals, multinationals and foreign investment in Latin America: review article (JLAS, 9, pt. 2, Nov. 1977, p. 315–336)
Studies six books dealing with mineral exploitation (largely in Latin America) and does an excellent job of synthesizing them into the beginnings of an understanding of the issues and analysis of mineral exploration, exploitation, and distribution across national boundaries.

Manning, Diana H. Society and food: the Third World. See *HLAS 40:2197.*

2858 Massad, Carlos and **Roberto Zahler.**
Dos estudios sobre endeudamiento externo. Santiago, Comisión Económica para América Latina (CEPAL), 1977. 63 p., tables (Cuadernos de la CEPAL)
The first study concerns the size of the debt and considers options for treating it. The second disputes conventional wisdom that inflation (world) favors the debtor (national, Third World).

2859 Maza Zavala, Domingo Felipe. Evaluación crítica de la enseñanza de la economía en América Latina. Caracas, Univ. Central de Venezuela, Facultad de Ciencias Económicas y Sociales, División de Publicaciones, 1974. 31 p., tables.
A general and philosophic treatment of an important subject. Does not distinguish

between economics and business administration.

2860 Mehmet, Ozay. Conflicting development objectives and factor pricing in LDC's (IEI/EI, 29:1/2, feb./maggio 1976, p. 100–109, tables)
Examines proposition that resource shadow-pricing based on *social* benefit-cost considerations can contribute significantly to employment creation.

2861 Meller, Patricio; Soledad Léniz; and **Carlos Swinburn.** Comparaciones internacionales de concentración industrial en América Latina (ECIEL, 3, agosto 1976, p. 27–65, tables)
A pioneering study of industrial concentration. Its principal value will be as a benchmark since all census data came from the 1960s. The international *comparative* aspects in this area seem less important than the internal, national aspects. Clear in methodology with a good deal of valuable data.

2862 Mesa-Lago, Carmelo. Social security in Latin America: pressure groups, stratification, and inequality. Pittsburgh, Pa., Univ. of Pittsburgh Press, 1978. 351 p., tables (Pitt Latin American series)
A very important study of social security systems in Chile, Uruguay, Peru, Argentina, and Mexico. Sub-title notes special emphases. Detailed statistics support the conclusions and are valuable for themselves.

2863 Mizuno, Hajime. Colaboración económica entre América Latina y Japón (CEPAC/REP, 7, dic. 1973, p. 59–67, tables)
Recounts recent changes in trade, private investment, public assistance and the reasons therefore. There is no disaggregation by country.

2864 Montiel Ortega, Leonardo. Antes del año 2000. Caracas?, Editorial Antillas, 1976? 164 p., bibl., tables.
View of the future centers on three problems: overpopulation, deficit of world's resources, increasing contamination of the environment. He thinks these will require of us a new set of intradependent relationships.

Moxon, Richard W. Harmonization of foreign investment laws among developing countries: an interpretation of the Andean Group experience. See item **8847.**

2865 Musgrove, Philip. Consumer behavior in Latin America: income and spending of families in ten Andean cities. Foreword by Bruce K. MacLaury. Washington, The Brookings Institution, 1978. 365 p., tables (An ECIEL study)

Reports ECIEL research spanning a decade with household studies in five countries (Andean Pact except Bolivia). Important for its coverage and depth. Distribution, determinants of income, its distribution, are major topics.

2866 Mustaffá, Jorge and **Alberto Varillas.** Capacitación de personal en la Banca de Fomento. Lima, Asociación Latinoamericana de Instituciones Financieras de Desarrollo (ALIDE), 1976. 2 v. (119, 463 p.) tables.

Results of a survey of training programs and facilities for personnel in development banks in Latin America. Vol. 1, summarizes these results, and vol. 2 describes individual programs—in and out of the banks—in detail. See also item **2755.**

2867 Mytelka, Lynn K. Regulating direct foreign investment and technology transfer in the Andean group (JPR, 14:2, 1977, p. 155–184, bibl., tables)

A thorough survey of the background and five years of implementation of Decision 24. Found to be less radical than anticipated but useful in sensitizing governments to the need to regulate technology transfer. Considerable bibliography.

2868 Nash, Manning ed. Essays on economic development and cultural change in honor of Bert F. Hoselitz. Chicago, Ill., Univ. of Chicago Press, 1977. 448 p. (Economic development and cultural change, 25)

Covers a broad spectrum of development topics by group of distinguished contributors, including selected publications by Hoselitz (p. 449–460). Not directly related to Latin America, but not to be missed.

2869 Olcese Fernández, Jorge. La integración financiera para el Grupo Sub-Regional Andino. Lima, Asociación Latinoamericana de Instituciones Financieras de Desarrollo (ALIDE), 1975. 120 p., bibl., tables.

An ALIDE prize-winner. Examines the mechanisms and barriers to modest financial integration of the Andean Group, looking especially to mobilizing capital for development.

2870 Orrego Vicuña, Francisco. Cambio y estabilidad en la integración económica el marco conceptual y la experiencia del Grupo Andino. Santiago, Univ. de Chile, Instituto de Estudios Internacionales, 1976. 42 l. (Serie de publicaciones especiales, 13)

An examination of the processes of decision-making in the Andean Group.

2871 Painéis internacionais sobre desen-volvimento socioeconômico. Rio, Banco Nacional de Desenvolvimento Econômico [and] APEC Editora, 1974. 376 p., tables.

A conference on socio-economic development on the occasion of the 21st anniversary of the founding of the National Development Bank of Brazil. The format is that of principal papers and usually three commentators. Some of the principal papers are by: Chenery, Bernard, Simonsen, Baer, Massad, Prebisch, Silvert, Myint, Myrdal.

2872 Parkinson, F. International economic integration in Latin America and the Caribbean: a survey (LIWA/YWA, 31, 1977, p. 236–256)

Packed with comparative (LAFTA, CACM, CARICOM, Andean Group) and descriptive information. An excellent and convenient source for initial information. For political scientist's comment, see item **8746.**

2873 Peñaranda C., César. Integración andina: dimensionamiento del mercado subregional y distribución de ingresos (ECIEL, 3, agosto 1976, p. 1–26, bibl., tables)

Since one of the purposes of integration is to gain access to larger markets, article seeks to put some dimensions into Andean Pact "market." Considers demographic data, per capita income, income distribution, budget data. Very useful.

2874 Petras, James. Latin American agro-transformation from above and outside and its social and political implications (Journal of the Hellenic Diaspora [Pella Pub. Co., N.Y.] 4:4, Winter 1978, p. 29–48, tables)

Conventional "wisdom" on the agrarian "problem's" solution, i.e., redistribution of land and increased services is inadequate. Major changes in the agrarian sector are the growth of capital-intensive backward and forward linkages of foreign agro-business which will exploit the worker of the land no matter how it is distributed.

2875 **Porzecanski, Arturo C.** *comp.* Política fiscal en América Latina: selección de textos. México, Centro de Estudios Monetarios Latinoamericanos (CEMLA), 1977. 558 p., tables.

A useful compilation (with some editing) of pieces appearing 1970–76 built around five themes: description, taxation, public expenditures, incidence and effects of fiscal activity, taxation under inflation. Very commendable work.

2876 **Powelson, John P.** The balance sheet on multinational corporations in less developed countries (UCL/CD, 9:3, 1977, p. 413–432, bibl., tables)

Examines each of 13 major criticisms of multinationals and renders "guilty" "not guilty" and judgements in between on basis of analysis and data. Extensive bibliography.

2877 ———. The strange persistence of the "terms of trade" (IAMEA, 30:4, Spring 1977, p. 17–28, bibl., tables)

Notes persistent use of "terms of trade" argument, its origin. Examines post World War II data and fails to find empirical evidence that the terms of trade have systematically or any other way shifted against the Third World.

2878 **Prats, Raymond.** Une économie marginale, périphérique et dominée (CDAL, 13/14, 1976, p. 153–188, tables)

Discusses evaluation of economies of Latin America and in particular the economic-political relations with the US—evolution into SELA as an institutional effort to solve some of the new international order problems with the US. Suggests the US may find it hard to live with SELA.

2879 **Prebisch, Raúl.** Desarrollo y político comercial internacional (PPO, 22:88, agosto 1976, p. 443–472)

Touches on many points: character of Latin American exports, deficiencies of market forces, frustrations of integration. One of the author's interesting ideas is the formation of Latin American multinationals (in part since MNC's are powerful forces for integration).

2880 **Rachadell, Manuel.** Un modelo latinoamericano de administración para el desarrollo. Caracas, Centro de Información, Documentación y Análisis Latinoamericano (CIDAL), 1976? 35 p.

Planning has been a marginal activity among Latin American governments and requires a profound transformation if the complex tasks of development are to be carried out. Presents an administrative "model" which contains his recommendations for change.

2881 **Radetzki, Marian.** Where should developing countries' minerals be processed?: the country view versus the multinational company view (WD, 5:4, April 1977, p. 325–334, tables)

Four parties involved in private and social cost-benefit considerations: the company, the exporting nation, the user nation, the world community. Examines the situation with respect to each. Useful article.

2882 **Remmer, Karen L.** Evaluating the policy impact of military regimes in Latin America (LARR, 13:2, 1978, p. 39–54, bibl., table)

Concerned about fascinating questions as to whether military regimes have different development policies (and different successes). Prime concern is how research might be organized to begin to answer this question. The few studies which exist are flawed and inconclusive. For political scientist's comment, see item **7066**.

2883 **Retchkiman K., Benjamín.** Aspectos estructurales de la economía pública. México, UNAM, Instituto de Investigaciones Económicas, Dirección General de Publicaciones, 1975. 410 p., bibl. (Textos universitarios)

A companion and following volume to *Introducción al estudio de la economía pública* (1972). A text. Deals with federalism, the economics of social security, problems and techniques of international fiscal harmonization, state enterprises, and fiscal policy.

2884 **Reunión Ordinaria de la Asamblea General de la Asociación Latinoamericana de Instituciones Financieras de Desarrollo** (ALIDE), *VI, Lima, 1976.* Anales: recursos financieros adicionales para el desarrollo. Lima, ALIDE [and] Corporación Financiera de Desarrollo (COFIDE), 1977. 447 p., tables.

Beyond the usual material recording convention events, Sec. 3 contains some specific country reports on their experiences which will be of interest to some readers.

2885 *Revista FELABAN.* Federación Latinoamericana de Bancos. No. 28, dic. 1977–. Bogotá.

Tends to be highly specialized but does carry general articles (e.g. one on international reserves and exchange policy in this number). Will be of interest to banking specialists.

2886 Richardson, Neil R. Political compliance and U.S. trade dominance (APSA/R, 70:4, Dec. 1976, p. 1098–1109, tables)

Investigates the relationship between export dependence and political compliance with US positions on international issues.

2887 Riz, Liliana de. Formas de estado y desarrollo del capitalismo en América Latina (UNAM/RMS, 39:2, abril/junio 1977, p. 427–441)

Political essay on the forms of the state and the need to shift analysis away from current dependency theory to a more Marxist orientation.

2888 Robinson, Richard D. National control of foreign business entry: a survey of fifteen countries. N.Y., Praeger, 1976. 508 p., bibl., tables (Praeger special studies in international economics and development)

Includes Mexico, Brazil, Andean Group. There is a great deal of detail here related to flows, entry control, etc. for each country; but the study is brought together in examination of the data in light of 10 hypotheses tested.

2889 Rodríguez, Octavio. On the conception of the centre-periphery system (CEPAL/R, 1, 1977, p. 195–239, bibl., tables)

An excellent review of the intellectual evolution of ECLA, its critics, and shortcomings. Very useful bibliography.

2890 Rodríguez, Ricardo. Arancel externo común e inversión sectorial en el Pacto Andino: un análisis micro-económico. Santiago, Univ. Católica de Chile, Instituto de Economía, 1976. 35 p. (Documento de trabajo, 48)

Mathematical models for estimating net benefits of a common external tariff.

2891 Rodríguez Azuero, Sergio. Contratos bancarios: su significación en América Latina. Bogotá, Biblioteca FELEBAN, 1977. 696 p.

Encyclopedic account of commercial banking law throughout Latin America. Particular subject chapters are followed by appendixes providing details by countries. Highly specialized.

2892 Rolando, Eduardo. Cooperación económica y financiamiento de los exportaciones en América Latina. Caracas, Banco Central de Venezuela (BCV), 1977. 150 p. (Col. De estudios económicos, 4)

A competent review of cooperative ventures in Latin America with particular attention to export finance. Some country cases are presented.

2893 Rollins, Charles. Population and the labour force in Latin America: some simulation exercises (CEPAL/R, 1, 1977, p. 127–193, tables)

Simulation exercises for Argentina, Brazil, Venezuela, El Salvador. Basic concern is for 1970–2000 but also extrapolates population for 1970–2070 under varying assumptions. Even under extreme assumptions of rapid fall infertility rates to zero growth level in 1995, this labor force grows rapidly in 1970s and 1980s. Projections given in considerable detail.

2894 Romanova, Z. and others. Imperialismo y dependencia en América Latina. Bogotá, Ediciones Suramérica, 1976. 166 p., tables.

A collection of articles by Soviet specialists on Latin America. Pieces have previously appeared in USSR journal *América Latina*.

2895 Roschke, Thomas E. The GATT: problems and prospects (GWU/JILE, 12:1, 1977, p. 85–103)

The GATT has declined in respect and adherence for a variety of reasons. Inflexibility of its rules and the difficulty of changing them is a cause. As the new world situation is faced, this inflexibility may cost the GATT dearly.

2896 Rosenberg, Emily S. The exercise of emergency controls over foreign commerce: economic pressure on Latin America (IAMEA, 31:4, Spring 1978, p. 81–96)

Discusses growth of power of Executive with passage of Trading with the Enemy Act of 1917. Cites several World War I cases where this power was used for ends unrelated to the war effort (e.g., Ecuadorean cacao quota being withheld until interest payments on railroad bonds were resumed). These powers remain today.

2897 Rothstein, Robert L. Politics and policy-making in the Third World: does a reform strategy make sense? (WD, 48:8, Aug. 1976, p. 695–708)

Argues that there is a substantial group of LDC's where incremental change is both possible and probably a desirable alternative to revolution. Discusses the contribution of planning and plans to such incremental changes. Very useful article.

2898 Rúa Bejarano, Dulfredo. El problema agrario en América Latina o el fracaso de las reformas agrarias Made in USA (UC/A, 33, abril 1978, p. 21–56)

As title suggests, agrarian reforms à la Alliance for Progress have failed—as was to be expected. Only real hope is profound redistribution of presently held power via socialist revolution.

2899 Russell Tribunal, *Roma.* Le multinazionali in America Latina. Roma, Coines Edizioni, 1976. 269 p.

El volumen recopila estudios relativos a la actuación de las multinacionales en América Latina. De interés son los siguientes tres estudios: 1) Grupo de Trabajo de la Univ. de Grenoble "Características Generales de la Dominación Imperialista en América Latina;" 2) J. Arrat "La Nacionalización del Cobre Chileno;" y 3) A. López "El Rol de las Empresas Multinacionales en Argentina." [M. Carmagnani]

2900 Ruttan, Vernon W. The Green Revolution: seven generalizations (SID/IDR, 19:4, 1977, p. 16–23, bibl.)

An excellent review/summary article and bibliography. Not restricted to Latin America.

2901 Salazar Carrillo, Jorge. Prices and purchasing power parities in Latin America: 1960–1972. Washington, OAS *for the* ECIEL Program, Brookings Institution, 1978. 1 v. (Various pagings) tables.

An important research effort well described by the title. Key data are 150,000 price items from LAFTA countries' capital cities in May 1968. Permits a number of useful and interesting comparisons: purchasing power parities with exchange rates, relative levels of real income. Data are variously disaggrega-

ted, extrapolated to 1972 and compared to other related findings.

2902 Salinas Sánchez, Javier. La estructura agraria como obstáculo al desarrollo económico de América Latina (IEAS/R, 97:25, oct./dic. 1976, p. 81–116, tables)

A synthesis of general thinking on the agricultural sector in development and then on the performance and prospects of that sector in Latin America.

2903 Samaniego, Carlos and **Bernardo Sorj.** Articulaciones de modos de producción y campesinado en América Latina. Lima, Univ. Nacional Agraria La Molina, Centro de Investigaciones Socio-Económicas (CISE), 1976. 28 p.

An introduction to the study of Latin American peasantry. Develops a typology and proceeds with analysis found there.

2904 Sánchez, Javier Salinas. Hipótesis estructuralista del sistema económico transnacional (IDES/DE, 17:66, julio/set. 1977, p. 211–252, tables)

A systematic, useful study of the explanations of Latin American growth and barriers to it.

2905 Scapini, Juan Carlos and others. Capitalismo e sottosviluppo nell'America Latina. Milano, Italia, Franco Angeli Editore, 1977. 180 p., bibl.

Los diferentes estudios se articulan en torno a la problemática del subdesarrollo económico latinoamericano y a las diferentes teorías sobre el mismo. De contenido más concreto son los estudios de Saba *Oligopolio e sottosviluppo: l'esperienza delle cooperative industriali in Venezuela* y de Imbriani *Un'analisi empirica dell'inflazione nei paesi dell'America latina.* [M. Carmagnani]

2906 Schuldt Lange, Juergen. Los efectos "adaptación" e "innovación" en la producción de los países tecnológicamente dependentes. Lima, Univ. del Pacífico, Centro de Investigación, 1973. 17 p. (Serie ensayos, 1)

A competent geometric treatment of the partial case.

2907 Secretaría Ejecutiva Permanente del Convenio Andrés Bello (SECAB), *Bogotá.* Tratados internacionales de integración de los países andinos. Bogotá, 1974. 113 p.

A collection of documents not easily

found in one location: Cartagena Agreement; consensus of Lima; Constitution of the Andean Development Corporation; Integration of Education; and Scientific and Cultural Matters; Cooperation on Matters of Health; Labor and Social Integration.

2908 Sector informal: funcionamiento y políticas. Prólogo de Víctor E. Tokman. Santiago, Oficina Internacional del Trabajo (OIT), Programa Regional del Empleo para América Latina y el Caribe (PREALC), 1978. 369 p., bibl., tables.

An important examination of a critical portion of the labor market in Latin America—the urban, informal sector. Treats the matter on various levels: theory, methodology of research, case studies by cities and by activities, and policy.

2909 Seminario Latinoamericano de Administración Regional, *Caracas, 1975.* Administración regional en América Latina. B.A., Centro Latinoamericano de Administración para el Desarrollo [and] Sociedad Interamericana de Planificación (SIAP), 1976. 328 p.

Basic documents on papers at Caracas seminar in 1975 with representatives of 20 countries in attendance. Seeks to present an integrated treatment of "regional" administration. Does not treat particularly of international integration (e.g., Andean Pact) a regional group. Region may be either intra- or international.

Seminario sobre Problemas del Empleo en América Latina, *La Plata, Arg., 1975.* El empleo en América Latina: problemas económicos, sociales y políticos. See item **9283**.

2910 Serrano Parra, Guido. Algunas reflexiones sobre el poder negociador de los países importadores de tecnología. Santiago, Univ. de Chile, Instituto de Estudios Internacionales, 1976. 18 l. (Serie de publicaciones especiales, 14)

Analyzes the bargaining powers of technology-recipient countries, thought to be very little. More has been learned through experience about this and the key element for recipients is that the transmitters are frequently very concerned with market expansion.

2911 Sheehey, Edmund J. The dynamics of inflation in Latin America: comment (AEA/AER, 66:4, Sept. 1976, p. 692–694)

Comment on Vogel's work (see *HLAS* 37:4238) together with Roger R. Betancourt (see item **2765**). For Vogel's reply to both critics, see item **2931**.

2912 Sloan, John W. Dependency theory and Latin American development: another key fails to open the door (IAMEA, 31:3, Winter 1977, p. 21–40)

Reviews facets of dependency theory in several variations and criticizes its failures to provide the single explanation some of its proponents expect from it.

Soberón A., Luis. Las operaciones del capital extranjero en el contexto de su desarrollo global: el caso de W.R. Grace & Co. See item **8891**.

Solari, Aldo E. *comp.* Poder y desarrollo: América Latina. See item **9046**.

2913 Soles, Roger E. Rural credit in Latin America (Foundation News [Inter-American Foundation, Arlington, Va.] 19:5, Sept./Oct. 1978, p. 26–30, 38)

Recounts the experience of the Inter-American Foundation in increasing credit to the rural poor and points out principles involved which can be used by others.

Souza, João Crisóstomo de. Teorias do subdesenvolvimento e compreensão crítica da sociedade brasileira. See item **9402**.

2914 Squire, Lyn and Herman G. van der Tak. Economic analysis of projects. Baltimore, Md., The Johns Hopkins Univ. Press *for the* World Bank, 1975. 153 p., bibl.

Development of a rationale and methodology for project appraisal. Pt. 1 examines cost-benefit analysis. A lengthier Pt. 2 discusses shadow-pricing to deal with systematic bias against investment expenditure. Not Latin America-specific, but certainly of general relevance.

2915 Stansfield, D.E.; B.H. Slicher van Bath; and A.C. van Oss *eds.* Dependency and Latin America: a workshop. Amsterdam, Center for Latin American Research and Documentation, 1974. 301 p.

Consists of 16 separate pieces covering a wide variety of topics. Many seek to tie dependency to some other concept—e.g., internal migration, growth pole concept.

Street, James H. The internal frontier and technological progress in Latin America. See *HLAS 40:2410.*

2916 ———. Latin American adjustments to the OPEC crisis and the world recession (UT/SSQ, 59:1, June 1978, p. 60–76, bibl.)

An excellent review of impact, reaction, effects, and adjustment to oil price increases to producers in Latin America and 19 importers.

2917 Sunkel, Osvaldo. La dependencia y la heterogeneidad estructural (FCE/TE, 45 [1]:177, enero/marzo 1978, p. 3–20, tables)

Criticizes conventional economics and views of development. Proposes, in rough, a new schema—concentrating dependency, internal heterogeneity and a good deal of disaggregation. Utilizes Leontief-like input-output matrices.

2918 Svedberg, Peter. Foreign investment and trade policies in an international economy with transnational corporations: a theoretical and empirical study with references to Latin America. Stockholm, The Author, 1977. 164 p., bibl., tables.

Primarily an analytical work examining policy issues for small developing countries dealing with monopolistic transnational firms. Particular questions: Are there special reasons to impose tariffs; Are there rationales to encourage such firms to produce domestically rather than to export from the home-office (or others) country? Latin America data are examined against the findings.

2919 Symposium on the Use of Socio-economic Investment Criteria in Project Evaluation, *Washington, 1973.* Social and economic dimensions of project evaluation. Edited by Hugh Schwartz and Richard Berney. Washington, Inter-American Development Bank, 1977. 338 p., tables.

A useful three-stage report of a 1973 symposium on the title-topic. Stage 1 is a summary; stage 2 summarizes papers and discussion of them; stage 3 publishes papers in full. Discussions center on UNIDO *Guidelines* and the Little-Mirrlees *Manual* both of which seek to apply socio-economic criteria in project evaluation. Discussion of practical and theoretical problems is particularly revealing.

2920 Thebaud, Schiller. L'evaluation des transferts technologiques en Amérique Latine (FDD/NED [Problèmes d'Amérique Latine, 46] 4443/4445, 12 déc. 1975, p. 17–32, bibl., tables)

Defines technological-transfer, examines ways in which transfer occurs. Seeks measures of explicit costs and, further, some restrictive practices associated with it.

2921 Theberge, James D. and **Roger W. Fontaine.** Latin America: struggle for progress. Lexington, Mass., Lexington Books, 1977. 205 p., bibl., map (Critical choices for Americans, 14)

Vol. 14 in series of "Choices for Americans." Very clearly pointed to policy options and their implications. Focuses on specific problems and specific countries. An appendix (p. 145–193) deals exclusively with Venezuela. Conclusions for the area's progress and US relations with it in the next 10 years are not optimistic. For political scientist's comment, see item **8602.**

2922 *Tiers Monde.* Problèmes des pays sous-développés. Univ. de Paris, Institut d'Etude du Développement Economique et Social. Vol. 17, No. 68, oct./déc. 1976–. Paris.

This particular issue entitled "L'Amérique Latine après Cinquante Ans d'Industrialization" was edited by Pedro Calil Padis. Valuable examination of aspects of the experience of industrialization through 50 years in seven articles—roughly 200 p.

2923 Tironi B., Ernesto. La decisión 24 sobre capitales extranjeros en el Grupo Andino (CPU/ES, 10, dic. 1976, p. 84–99, bibl.)

Reviews the origins and intent of Decisión 24, its specific provisions and the economic rationality therefore, and finally its effects (see also items **2752** and **2812**).

2924 Turner, Frederick C. The rush to the cities in Latin America (AI/I, 2:1, enero/feb. 1977, p. 31–41, tables)

Examines causes of urban in-migration and its effects. Proposes six governmental policies to ameliorate the devastating movement of people.

2925 Unikel, Luis and **Andrés Necochea** *comp.* Desarrollo urbano y regional en América Latina: problemas políticos. México, Fondo de Cultura Económica, 1975. 732 p., tables (Lecturas, 15)

A reader of previously published pieces on urban and regional development. Criteria for selection emphasized material with indigenous content and orientation. Valuable material conveniently available.

2926 United Nations. Comisión Económica para América Latina (CEPAL). Políticas de promoción de exportaciones. Santiago, 1977. 2 v. (99, 93 p.) tables (CEPAL, 1046)

Results of ECLA/UNDP/IBRD seminar, 1976. Vol. 1, presents summaries of papers and comments thereon on: 1) Latin American exports; 2) exporting in developing countries; 3) country studies—Latin America; 4) country studies—other than Latin America. Vol. 2, consists of two pieces published in full: Angel Monti on manufacturing exports in the Latin American experience and Barend A. de Vries on exports in the changing world scenario.

2927 ———. ———. División Agrícola Conjunta. 25 [i.e. Veinticinco] años en la agricultura de América Latina: rasgos principales, 1950–1975. Santiago, 1978. 95 p., fold. tables, tables (Cuadernos de la CEPAL, 21)

An excellent review both for its text and assembled data. Organized around: role, production and supply, agricultural in the external sector, productive resources, basic institutional aspects.

2928 ———. Instituto Latinoamericano de Planificación Económica y Social. División de Desarrollo Social. Ensayos sobre planificación regional del desarrollo. México, Siglo XXI Editores, 1976. 570 p., tables (Textos de economía y demografía)

A substantial "reader" with chapters on regional spacial structures, strategies of regional development, program elaboration, implementation and administration, evaluation. Includes some cases. Puts in one place and in a useful language considerable valuable material.

2929 Vicuña Izquierdo, Leonardo. América Latina: algunos aspectos de su crisis económica. Guayaquil, Ecua., Univ. de Guayaquil, Depto. de Publicaciones, 1973. 130 p.

A great many tables and relatively little text. Surveys Latin American economies and treats particularly three problems (of the "crisis"): agricultural sector, foreign investment, export sector.

2930 Vilas, Carlos María and Oscar Silva. Las empresas multinacionales. B.A., Crisis, 1975. 80 p., tables.

Describes how national monopolies, extending beyond national boundaries, benefit capital exporters and damage importers.

2931 Vogel, Robert C. The dynamics of inflation in Latin America: reply (AEA/AER, 66:4, Sept. 1976, p. 695–698)

Reply by Vogel to comments by Betancourt (item **2765**) and Sheehey (item **2911**) of Vogel's basic article annotated in *HLAS 37:4238*. Discussions center on econometric interpretations.

2932 Vries, Barend A. de. Exports in the new world environment: the case of Latin America (CEPAL/R, 1, 1977, p. 93–126, tables)

Exports grew substantially 1968–73, considerably enhancing economies of Latin America. Article looks at developments 1971–75 and expected role of exports in next five–10 years. Projections are made then factors considered which will make possible realization of those projections. This article also appears in *Weltwirschaftliches Archiv* (Kiel, FRG, 113:2, 1977, p. 353–379).

2933 Weisskoff, Richard and Adolfo Figueroa. Examen de las pirámides sociales: un estudio comparativo de la distribución del ingreso en la América Latina (FCE/TE, 44[4]:176, oct./dic. 1977, p. 887–946, bibl., tables)

See *HLAS 39:2961* for comment on a slightly different version—and in English.

2934 Wells, Louis T., Jr. La internacionalización de firmas de los países en desarrollo (INTAL/IL, 2:14, junio 1977, p. 24–35)

There is some flow of direct capital investment from developing country to developing country. Explores in a tentative way the reasons therefore and an evaluation of same. Little is known about this phenomenon.

2935 Wilkie, James W. *ed.* Money and politics in Latin America. Los Angeles, Univ. of California, Latin American Center, 1977. 91 p., bibl., tables (Statistical abstract of Latin America, supplement 7)

A series worth knowing about as supplements to UCLA's annual *Statistical*

Abstract of Latin America. The purpose of the series is to give depth and analysis to the data provided in the abstract series. This volume includes three main articles: democratic vs. dictatorial budgeting (Cuba, Venezuela, Mexico); expenditures and personalism in Mexico; and post-Perón financing of corporate development. The approach, as announced, is heavily empirical.

2936 Wionczek, Miguel S. Latin American growth, trade and cooperation (FFES/V, 68, juni 1977, p. 107–118, bibl.)

A good summary review of Latin American development strategy and its problems and successes since World War II.

2937 ———. La transferencia de tecnología contemplada como proceso social (A transferência de tecnologia contemplada como processo social; Technology transfer viewed as a social process) (AI/I, 2:5, sept./oct. 1977, p. 262–263)

An editorial calling for a policy for LDC research and development which will help the evaluation of private company technology transfers and alternatives.

2938 ——— comp. Política tecnológica y desarrollo socioeconómico. Antología. México, Secretaría de Relaciones Exteriores, 1975. 293 p., tables (Cuestiones internacionales contemporáneas, 7)

Anthology of previously published pieces on technological transfer with the particular theme of examining policies to strengthen the autonomy of the receiving countries. Four principal sections: 1) general problems of technological dependency; 2) requisites for the development of an indigenous technology; 3) theoretical considerations in importing advanced technology; and 4) policy case studies of Mexico, Brazil, Andean Group, Japan, Poland.

2939 World Bank, *Washington.* World development report. N.Y., Oxford Univ. Press, 1978. 121 p., tables.

The first of an anticipated series of annual reports. It seeks first to examine a number of fundamental development issues and to explore their relationship to trends in the world economy. Separate chapters deal with "International Policy Issues," "Prospects for Growth and Alleviation of Poverty," "Development Priorities in Middle-Income Developing Countries." Of considerable additional value is the statistical appendix of 18 tables and their accompanying technical notes.

2940 *World Development.* Pergamon Press. Vol. 5, Nos. 1/2, Jan./Feb. 1977–. Oxford, U.K.

An increasingly important journal. This particular issue, edited by Werner Baer and Larry Samuelson, consists of an examination (in nine articles) of the effectiveness and problems of import substitution. Most are country studies.

2941 Zapata, Francisco. Enclaves y sistemas de relaciones industriales en América Latina (UNAM/RMS, 39:2, abril/junio 1977, p. 719–731, tables, bibl.)

Describes various types of enclaves and the characteristics associated with them.

2942 Zuvekas, Clarence, Jr. Income distribution in Latin America: a survey of recent research. Milwaukee, Univ. of Wisconsin, Center for Latin America *in cooperation with* North Central Council of Latin Americanists, 1975. 36 p., bibl., tables (Center essay series, 6)

A useful (note publication date) review of theoretical discussion, empirical studies, and policy matters since 1965.

MEXICO

ROBERT L. BENNETT, *Associate Professor of Economics, University of Maryland*

ALTHOUGH EACH OF THE SELECTIONS reviewed in this section has considerable merit, several studies are worthy of the special attention of all serious students of Mexico's economy. Easily the most important study is the monumental work on urban development by Unikel and others (item **2975**) which not only covers a broad historical period and the entire country, but also manages to be interdisciplinary. It reports on a very large research project in an obviously coordinated and readable manner—unfortunately a rare type of work. An understanding of Mexico's recent balance of payments problems is improved considerably by Villarreal's *El desequilibrio externo en la industrialización de México: 1929–1975* (item **2977**) and by Green's *El endeudamiento público externo de México: 1940–1973* (item **2959**). One should also be sure to read Villa's *Nacional Financiera* (item **2976**) for a comprehensive, scholarly description of the history of that important Mexican development institution. Finally, Fernández's *Renovación agraria* (item **2955**) provides us with that eminent scholar's reflections on Mexican agriculture—particularly his recommendations for reform.

Nacional Financiera's *Statistics on the Mexican Economy* (item **2968**) is a very convenient compendium of historical-statistical material which should prove quite useful to English-speaking students.

In this section the reviewer has not included separately several recurring publications which may be of great interest to the researcher. Statistical data are available in the current editions of Banco de México's annual *Asamblea General de Accionistas*; Nacional Financiera's annual *Informe Anual* and bi-weekly *El Mercado de Valores*; Banco Nacional de Comercio Exterior's annual *Comercio Exterior de México* and monthly *Comercio Exterior*; Secretaría de Industria y Comercio's *Anuario de Estadística*; and Banco Nacional de México's quarterly *Review of the Economic Situation of Mexico*. The most comprehensive bibliographical information is found in Banco de México's annual *Bibliografía Económica de México* and bi-monthly *Boletín Bibliográfico*.

2943 Aguilar Monteverde, Alonso and **Fernando Carmona.** México: riqueza y misera. Dos ensayos. 9. ed. México, Editorial Nuestro Tiempo, 1976. 270 p., tables (Col. Los grandes problemas nacionales)

Two essays orginally presented more than a decade ago (first ed. published in 1967) as a militantly leftist critique of Mexico's socio-economic system. Well worth a serious student's attention.

2944 Aguilera Gómez, Manuel. La desnacionalización de la economía mexicana. México, Fondo de Cultura Económica (FCE), 1975. 155 p., tables (Archivo del Fondo, 47)

This book makes the case forcefully that foreign investment and decision making for Mexican industry has largely impeded the development process. The author further concludes that the industries involved are those which could have provided the major impetus for modernization.

———. El eterno problema de la tierra en México. See *HLAS 40:2682*.

2944a Anaya, Pedro. Los problemas del campo. México, Editorial Jus, 1976. 223 p., bibl.

A useful primer on Mexican agrarian

questions without scholarly pretense, this is chiefly a work for the layman. [P.F. Hernández]

2945 Aspra, L. Antonio. Import substitution in Mexico: past and present (WD, 5:1/2, Jan./Feb. 1977, p. 111–123, bibl., tables)

After a brief analysis of Mexico's history of import substitution as an industrialization policy, the author discusses and recommends further export promotion.

Ballé, Catherine. Industrialisation et développment au Mexique: la création du complexe sidérurgique Las Truchas. See *HLAS 40:2686*.

2945a Bassols Batalla, Angel and **Gloria González Salazar.** Acerca de la colonización en México y del Plan Chontalpa. México, UNAM, 1973. 140 p., bibl., map, tables.

Modest, early account of Tabasco's Chontalpa Development Plan. Contains considerable research and information of a scholarly nature. An economist and a geographer, the authors make a good combination and have a keen sense for historical and social issues. [P.F. Hernández]

Benjamin, Thomas. International Harvester and the henequen marketing system in Yucatan, 1898–1915: a new perspective. See item **8612.**

2946 Blejer, Mario I. Dinero, precios y la balanza de pagos: la experiencia de México, 1950–1973. México, Centro de Estudios Monetarios Latinoamericanos, 1977. 105 p., bibl., tables.

Johnson's monetary approach to the balance of payments is applied to Mexico's experience under fixed exchange rates. An excellent quantitative study of the adjustment process between equilibria which received the Premio Rodrigo Gómez in 1976.

2947 Brasdefer, Gloria and others. Las empresas públicas en México: su importancia en el sector industrial y comercial; bases jurídicas de su acción. Coordinación de Alejandro Carrillo Castro. Presentación de Andrés Caso. México, Instituto Nacional de Administración Pública (INAP), 1976. 255 p., fold. tables, tables.

A description of Mexico's public enterprises from the historical, economic, and legal perspectives. Considerably more attention is given to the legal perspective than to the others.

2948 Clavijo, Fernando. Desarrollo y perspectivas de la economía mexicana en el corto plazo: un modelo econométrico trimestral (FCE/TE, 43:172, oct./dic. 1976, p. 845–877, bibl., tables)

Presentation of a quarterly econometric model for evaluating short-run effects of policies in Mexico. Results of some simulation experiments with alternative policies are reported.

2949 ——— and Octavio Gómez. El desequilibrio externo y la devaluación en la economía mexicana (FCE/TE, 44:173, enero/marzo 1977, p. 3–31, bibl., tables)

After a good econometric analysis of the recent data, the authors conclude that devaluation alone is not a sufficient policy for correcting Mexico's disequilibrium in the current account of the balance of payments. They recommend more attention to export promotion that would shift the demand curve.

2950 ———; Wistano Sáenz; and Philippe Scheuer. ¿A qué modelo de industrialización corresponden las exportaciones

mexicanas? (FCE/TE, 45[1]:177, enero/marzo 1978, p. 109–135, bibl., tables)

Thoughtful discussion and analysis of Mexico's export policy of the last two decades. The authors question substantial aspects of the current "export substitution" policies as well as the tendency to rely on petroleum exports for future relief of balance of payments problems.

2951 Clement, Norris and **Louis Green.** The political economy of devaluation in Mexico (IAMEA, 32:3, Winter 1978, p. 47–75, bibl., tables)

This study sees the 1976 devaluation of the peso relative to the dollar as a short-run measure necessary to prevent serious dislocation, but insufficient to promote long-run growth. More equality in the distribution of income and other structural changes are required for substantial further development.

2952 Cummings, Ronald G. Interbasin water transfers: a case study in Mexico. Baltimore, Md., Resources for the Future, 1974. 114 p., bibl., tables.

A cost-benefit analysis of a project for transferring water from one to another basin in Northwest Mexico. Originally study was for Mexico's Water Resources Ministry and used advanced methodology for decision making.

Delli Sante, Angela. La intervención ideológica de la empresa transnacional en países dependientes: el caso de México. See item **8617.**

Dillman, C.D. Maquiladoras in Mexico's northern border communities and the border industrialization program. See item **5343.**

2953 Fairchild, Loretta G. Performance and technology of United States and national firms in Mexico (JDS, 14:1, Oct. 1977, p. 14–34, bibl., tables)

Interesting study of paired firms in Monterrey, Mex.—one with foreign and one domestic ownership. Author finds Mexican ownership no disability in terms of profitability, growth and export performance.

2954 Feder, Ernest. El imperialismo fresa: una investigación sobre los mecanismos de dependencia de la agricultura mexicana. México, Editorial Campesina, 1977. 207 p., tables.

A very interesting study of the development and practice of foreign capitalist domination of Mexican agriculture using the strawberry industry as an example.

2955 Fernández y Fernández, Ramón. Renovación agraria. Chapingo, Mex., Secretaría de Agricultura y Ganadería, Colegio de Postgraduados, Centro de Economía Agrícola, 1977. 112 p., bibl.

This major authority on Mexican agriculture outlines the major alternatives for altering the land tenure and cultivation system to produce more acceptable results than at present. A comprehensive set of recommendations for reform of Mexico's agrarian reform is then discussed.

2955a Foxley, Alejandro; Eduardo Aninat; and **José Pablo Arellano.** Redistribución del patrimonio y erradicación de la pobreza (FCE/TE, 45[2]:178, abril/junio 1978, p. 247–296, tables)

Authors use case of Mexico to advance their thesis that an adequate combination of incentives and controls can foster the development of a nationalized industry and contribute towards the eradication of poverty. [P.F. Hernández]

Garza, Gustavo and **Martha Schteingart.** Mexico City: the emerging megalopolis. See item **9076**.

2956 Gollás, Manuel. Estructura y causas de la concentración industrial en México (FCE/TE, 45[2]:178, abril/junio 1978, p. 325–356, tables)

An analysis of the effects of size of the market and economics of scale on industrial concentration in Mexico. The author finds rather strong evidence of these two factors being significantly of Mexican industrial concentration in recent years.

2957 Gómez, Marta R. El crédito agrícola en México: estudio sobre su establecimiento y análisis de su funcionamiento hasta 1931; bases para su reorganización de acuerdo con el estado actual del Banco Nacional de Crédito Agrícola. Chapingo, Mex., Escuela Nacional de Agricultura, Colegio de Postgraduados, 1976. 150 p.

A history of Mexican agricultural credit institutions and laws prior to 1931 by a distinguished participant in shaping the present structure. Sixth in a series of studies published posthumously.

2958 Gómez Oliver, Antonio. La inflación interna y las causas de la devaluación del peso mexicano (BCV/REL, 13:50, 1977, p. 301–340, tables)

The author attempts to determine empirically the relative importance of events in the US and Mexican monetary policy in explaining Mexico's inflation and balance of payments deficits in recent years.

Grayson, George W. Mexico and the United States: the natural gas controversy. See item **8627**.

2959 Green, Rosario. El endeudamiento público externo de México: 1940–1973. México, El Colegio de México, 1976. 231 p., tables (Col. Centro de Estudios Internacionales, 15)

A comprehensive treatment of Mexico's public foreign debt (both from private and public sources) in the period largely from World War II through 1973. A very thorough and thoughtful treatment of the subject. Somewhat sketchy treatment of post-1973 when debt increased dramatically.

2960 Gribomont, C. and **M. Rimez.** La política económica del gobierno de Luis Echeverría, 1971–1976: un primer ensayo de interpretación (FCE/TE, 44[4]:176, oct./dic. 1977, p. 771–835, bibl., tables)

A primarily Marxist critique of the economic policies of 1971–76. The author sees the Mexican ruling group and bourgeoisie moving closer to socialist ideas in order to prevent political unrest while continuing economic domination of the masses.

Griffin, Keith B. The political economy of agrarian change: an essay on the green revolution. See item **3097**.

Grindle, Merilee S. Bureaucrats, politicians, and peasants in Mexico: a case study in public policy. See *HLAS 40:2719*.

2961 Gutiérrez Santos, Luis E. and **Michael G. Webb.** Comentarios sobre la evaluación de proyectos con referencia al sector energético mexicano (FCE/TE, 44[2]:174, abril/junio 1977, p. 371–388, tables)

A thoughtful discussion of some important considerations for project evaluation in the energy sector.

Hewitt de Alcántara, Cynthia. Modernizing Mexican agriculture: socioeconomic implications of technological change, 1940–1970. See item **5351**.

2962 Ibarra, David; Ifigenia M. de Navarrete; Leopoldo Solís M.; and Víctor L. Urquidi. El perfil de México en 1980. 7. ed. v. 1. México, Siglo XXI Editores, 1976. 199 p., tables.

Four distinguished Mexican authors combine their talents to produce a projection of Mexico's economic and demographic characteristics for 1980. A wealth of statistical information is provided and used in the projections.

Jenkins, Rhys Owen. Dependent industrialization in Latin America: the automotive industry in Argentina, Chile and Mexico. See item **2843**.

Johnson, Kirsten. Disintegration of a traditional resource-use complex: the Otomí of the Mezquital Valley, Hidalgo, Mexico. See item **5352**.

2963 Keesing, Donald B. Employment and lack of employment in Mexico: 1900–70 (in Wilkie, James W. and Kenneth Ruddle eds. Quantitative Latin American studies, methods and findings: statistical abstract of Latin America. Los Angeles, UCLA, Latin American Center Publications, 1977, p. 3–21,bibl., tables [Supplement, 6])

An excellent historical quantitative study finding unemployment primarily among females and due to technological displacement and discrimination.

2964 Ladenson, Mark L. ¿Una trampa de liquidez de divisas para México? (FCE/TE, 44[2]: 174, abril/junio 1977, p. 363–370, tables)

An econometric study supporting the Brothers and Solís theory of a foreign exchange liquidity trap of importance for Mexican monetary policy. There has been rather a long lag between this research and its publication in Spanish.

2965 Looney, Robert E. Mexico's economy: a policy analysis with forecasts to 1990. Boulder, Colo., Westview Press, 1978. 250 p., bibl., tables (Westview special studies on Latin America)

Good English language description of recent Mexican economic development and current problems.

2966 Méndez Villarreal, Sofía. La relación capital-producto en la economía mexicana. México, El Colegio de México, Centro de Estudios Económicos y Demográficos, 1974. 140 p., tables (Jornadas, 76)

A very good quantitative study of the capital-output ratio for the Mexican economy and its major sub-sectors. A brief review of the relevant theoretical problems is included. Major emphasis is on explaining the long-run decline in the ratio.

2967 Nacional Financiera, S.A., *México.* México: una estrategia para desarrollar la industria de bienes de capital. México, 1977. 490 p., tables.

A comprehensive study of both the demand and supply sides of the Mexican capital goods market—the past and present states as well as rather detailed plans and policy prescriptions for its future development. A wealth of statistical material is analyzed and presented.

2968 ——, ——. Statistics on the Mexican economy. Mexico, 1977. 452 p., tables.

This is the most comprehensive set of data on the Mexican economy that is currently available in English. The time series are post-World War II in most cases, but are long enough to get a rather comprehensive picture of Mexico's development and current situation.

NACLA's Latin America & Empire Report. See item **8636**.

2969 Peña, Sergio de la. La formación del capitalismo en México. México, Siglo XXI Editores, 1975. 245 p., tables (Economía y demografía)

An historical study of the development of capitalism in Mexico during the 1521–1910 period. More historical-social analysis than strictly economic analysis of the period.

Peters, J. Irwin. The new industrial property laws in Mexico and Brazil: implications for MNCs. See item **3501**.

Rengert, Arlene C. and **George F. Rengert.** Does out-migration hinder agricultural development? a view from rural Mexico. See item **5366**.

2970 Reynolds, Clark W. Por qué el "desarrollo estabilizador" de México fue en realidad desestabilizador, con algunas implicaciones para el futuro (FCE/TE, 44[4]:176, oct./dic. 1977, p. 997–1023, bibl., tables)

An evaluation of Mexican development policy over the past decade or two in which the author traces the roots of recent instability to the stable development period of the 1960s.

Rodríguez Araujo, Octavio. Una reforma política en Mexico. See *HLAS 40:2766.*

2971 Solís M., Leopoldo. Planes de desarrollo económico y social en México. México, Secretaría de Educación Pública (SEP), Dirección General de Divulgación, 1975. 197 p., tables (SepSetentas, 215)

This book includes a careful description and evaluation of each of the six-year development plans for Mexico since the 1930s. Must reading for an understanding of the planning of Mexico's social and economic development.

2972 Stavenhagen, Rodolfo and others. Neolatifundismo y explotación: de Emiliano Zapata a Anderson, Clayton & Co. 4. ed. México, Editorial Nuestro Tiempo, 1975. 217 p., tables (Col. Los grandes problemas nacionales)

Four essays by distinguished Mexican authors on various aspects of structural problems in Mexican agriculture. The essays are highly critical of current policies (first ed. published in 1968).

2973 Stern, Claudio. Las regiones de México y sus niveles de desarrollo socioecónomico. México, El Colegio de México, Centro de Estudios Sociológicos, 1973. 154 p., fold. tables, maps, tables (Jornadas, 72)

A basically quantitative study in which an index of socioeconomic development is devised and applied to rank Mexico's regions. The index weighs urbanization rather heavily.

2974 Stewart, John R., Jr. Potential effects of income redistribution on economic growth: an expanded estimating procedure applied to Mexico (UC/EDCC, 26:3, April 1978, p. 467–485, tables)

Excellent statistical study of the effect of income redistribution on economic development in Mexico. The author predicts relatively modest increases in the growth rate due to more equal distribution of income.

2975 Unikel, Luis; Cresconcio Ruiz Chiapetto; and **Gustavo Garza Villarreal.** El desarrollo urbano de México: diagnóstico de implicaciones futuras. México, El Colegio de México, Centro de Estudios Económicos y Demográficos, 1976. 466 p., bibl., fold. map, maps, tables.

Results of a long-term study of Mexico's urbanization. Interdisciplinary in approach and extraordinarily comprehensive in coverage over time and space. Also complete in descriptive, analytical and projection sections.

United States. Library of Congress. Congressional Research Service. Mexico's oil and gas policy: an analysis. See item **8654.**

2976 Villa M., Rosa Olivia. Nacional Financiera: banco de fomento del desarrollo económico de México. Presentación de Gustavo Romero Kolbeck. México, Nacional Financiera, 1976. 239 p., bibl., tables.

This comprehensive history of Mexico's premier development bank was commisioned by the bank but written by an independent observer. Must reading for students of Mexico's economic development and a generally balanced treatment of the subject.

2977 Villarreal, René. El desequilibrio externo en la industrialización de México, 1929–1975: enfoque estructuralista. México, Fondo de Cultura Económica (FCE), 1976. 280 p., bibl., tables.

Originally a doctoral dissertation at Yale, this important study analyzes from a structuralist viewpoint Mexico's import substituting industrialization and its balance of payments problems. The major recommendation is substitution of manufactured for primary exports.

2978 ——— and **Rocío R. de Villarreal.** Las empresas públicas como instrumento de política económica en México (FCE/TE, 45[2]:178, abril/junio 1978, p. 213–245, tables)

Good description and analysis of the role of government enterprises in Mexican development during the last 30 years. Some recommendations for change are offered.

2979 Walton, John. Elites and economic development: comparative studies on the political economy of Latin American cities. Austin, Univ. of Texas, Institute of Latin

American Studies, 1977. 257 p., bibl., tables (Latin American monographs series, 41)
    Studies elites and development in Guadalajara, Monterrey, Cali, Medellín. The

effort is to identify and characterize the elites, examine development in that context testing various hypotheses on the matter. [J.M. Hunter]

CENTRAL AMERICA AND THE WEST INDIES (except Cuba and Puerto Rico)

MARION HAMILTON GILLIM, *Distinguished Professor of Economics, Eastern Kentucky University*

IN A REVIEW OF PUBLICATIONS FROM many different countries, one is bound to find reference to any topic. Still, there are a few which invariably command attention. Most of the items included in this biennial review of the period 1976–78, appear to relate directly or indirectly to two regional organizations, the CARICOM and CACM. Four major issues in the disparate writings are 1) the degree of success or failure of these common markets; 2) inflation; 3) energy; and 4) agriculture.

An important volume on the main issues of integration appeared in 1978 for each region. They are William R. Cline and Enrique Delgado, eds., *Economic integration in Central America* (item **2988**) and a World Bank country economic report edited by Sidney E. Chernick *The Commonwealth Caribbean: the integration experience* (item **3026**). While the subjects covered are not identical, both works contain sections on employment, the allocation of the gains of integration among members, agriculture, and industry. The Brookings volume includes a valuable 30-page evaluation of writing in the field as Appendix B and entitled "A Survey of Literature on Economic Development in the Central American Common Market."

Both common markets have experienced similar crisis arising from the dissatisfaction of some members with their shares of the benefits of integration. In 1970 Honduras, while retaining other affiliations with the CACM, abandoned the free-trade system within the region. Although the immediate cause appeared to be the brief war with El Salvador over migration, the more basic cause probably lies in the Honduran balance-of-payments problems which are perceived as evidence that she was furnishing a market for the import substitution enjoyed by the rest of the members (see item **2988**, p. 36–121). A similar crisis arose in the CARICOM in early 1978 when Jamaica and Guyana restricted their imports from other members. Jamaica attributed the action to the inequitable distribution of the benefits of integration and specifically to her increasingly negative balance of trade with Trinidad-and-Tobago (items **3026** and **3040**).

Central America seems to be increasingly optimistic. The CACM is making plans for restructuring the regional organization toward closer integration and better sharing of its benefits (item **2988**). Honduras and El Salvador have agreed to mediation to their dispute and the mediator, Dr. Bustamente y Rivero of Peru, on a visit to Honduras reported that mediation was in progress (see *Carta Informativa*, No. 210, April 1979, p. 2). Costa Rica, too, had been dissatisfied with the benefits of integration, but in Feb. 1979, the Vice President of that country affirmed that Costa Rica would remain a member of the CACM (see also *Carta Informativa*, No. 209, March 1979, p. 1).

Since 1974, CARICOM has been attempting to strengthen its institutions towards closer integration. But Jamaica's recent economic problems may be more difficult to solve than those of Central America in the early 1970s in that Jamaica's may have been brought about by forces from outside the region, namely petroleum prices and inflation in the developed countries (item **3026**).

Inflation in both areas is blamed in part on the rising prices of imports (item **2994**). The resulting hardship is increased by the failure of export prices to rise proportionately. A number of estimates of national income have required adjustment because of inflation (items **3011** and **3020**). Some easing of the problem may result from the EEC's Lomé Convention of 1975 granting preferential treatment to the Caribbean, along with African and Pacific countries, and the US' publication of an executive order in 1975 which lists Central American products that are to be admitted free of duty (items **2986**, **3022**, and **3026–3027**).

Like other parts of the world, these two regions find the rising price of petroleum the most alarming of the increases in import prices. Trinidad-and-Tobago appears to be the one exception in that it both refines and produces oil for export (item **3036**). For the other countries, the higher price of petroleum raises the cost of energy which is seen as essential to their industrial and agricultural development. Their resulting anxiety is evident from the increase in the number of publications which address the problem of searching for other energy sources. These range from conventional hydroelectric power in countries with appropriate water resources to more unusual proposals for the harnessing of geothermal power in volcanic regions (items **2987**, **2995**, **2998**, **3018** and **3037–3038**).

This biennium much has been written on both regions. Improvements are being sought in farm productivity, diversification of crops, and standards of living in rural areas, all of which will promote self-sufficiency in food and reduce the migration from the country to the city (items **2989**, **3012**, **3016**, and **3024–3025**). Among the names tried are the redistribution of land holdings, cooperatives, *asentamientos*, and education for rural life. Strong Honduran efforts towards agrarian reform have met stiff opposition, but the program of education for the rural population appears active (items **2990**, **2994**, **3000** and **3017**). A series of publications has been issued from Honduras with the identification PROCCARA (i.e., Programa de Capacitación Campesina para la Reforma Agraria or Program of Rural Training for Agrarian Reform). The program was organized in 1973 by the Honduran National Agrarian Institute with the US Food and Agriculture Organization and the UN Program for Development (items **2999**, **3002** and **3009**).

In Central America, bananas are the crop attracting the most interest in recent years. Costa Rica, Guatemala, Honduras, and Panama have joined with Colombia in the Union of Banana Exporting Countries raising the question of whether a banana cartel might be feasible (items **2984**, **2995**, **2997** and **3004**). In 1975 by Decree-Law No. 253 Honduras ended the concessions to the two US banana companies, and in Decree-Law No. 270 she set up the Honduran Banana Corporation (item **2997**). Litvak and Maule in an article entitled "Transnational Corporations and Vertical Integration: The Banana Case" provide information useful to the banana-producing countries on the importance of access to ripening the marketing facilities (item **3005**).

CENTRAL AMERICA

2980 Alvarenga, Ivo P. Temas de derecho
agrario y reforma agraria. San José, Editorial Universitaria Centro Americana (EDUCA), 1977. 294 p., bibl., tables (Col. Aula)

An examination of the content of agricultural law and the law of agricultural reform. Selected papers presented at international seminars and a projected statue for agricultural reform for El Salvador.

2981 Astorga Lira, Enrique. Estructura
agraria en el valle de Sula. 2. ed. rev. Tegucigalpa, Instituto Nacional Agrario (INA), 1975. 85 p., tables.

A survey of production and labor of "asentamientos" (worker-run farms following the Decree Law No. 8, 1973), cooperatives, and small individual producers.

2982 Banco Central de Honduras, *Tegu-*
cigalpa. Objeto, organización y gestión del Banco Central de Honduras. Tegucigalpa, 1978. 17 p., tables.

Useful, brief presentation of the Honduran Central Bank's goals, tools of monetary policy, activities, and organization.

2983 ——, ——. Departamento de Es-
tudios Económicos. Cuentas nacionales de Honduras: 1960–1975. Tegucigalpa, 1977. 46 p., map, tables.

Data in both current and constant monetary units. Includes 17 p. of methodological notes.

Barlett, Peggy F. Labor efficiency and the mechanism of agricultural evolution. See item **9103**.

Bataillon, Claude and **Ivon Lebot.** Migración interna y empleo agrícola temporal en Guatemala. See item **9105**.

Bernsten, Richard H. and **Robert W. Herdt.** Towards an understanding of *milpa* agriculture: the Belize case. See item **5308**.

2984 Buse, Rueben C. and **L. Emil Kreider.**
The elasticity of demand for bananas (IAMEA, 32:1, Summer 1978, p. 33–50, tables)

Theoretical study of banana markets to determine the effect on the receipts of the banana producers of a change in the market price of the fruit. The ultimate goal is to find a measure for the evaluation of the benefits of a producers' cartel in bananas. Coefficients of price elasticity of demand, price flexibility coefficients, and consumption ratios for other fruits are used (see also item **3004**). This article would make a helpful example for a class in applied Economics.

2985 *Carta Económica.* Banco Nacional de
Panamá. Asesoría Económica y de Planificación. Año 7, No. 1, enero 1977–. Panamá.

This issue of the Bank's review (p. 4) describes briefly a treaty freeing from duty Panamanian goods entering Guatemala and reducing Panamanian tariffs on Guatemalan goods. This treaty, if successful, may serve as a model for other countries wanting to increase reciprocal trade.

2986 *Carta Informativa.* Secretaría Perma-
nente del Tratado General de Integración Económica Centroamericana (SIECA). No. 175, mayo 1976–. Guatemala.

This number announces the reprinting of two important publications of SIECA: 1) "Analysis of the present condition of the Central American textile industry and the possibility that it can replace imports and produce exports to third countries;" 2) A popular edition of the *Projected Treaty for Central American Economic and Social Community* as prepared by the High Level Committee for Restructuring the Common Market and sent to each government on 23 March 1976.

2987 ——. ——. No. 184, feb. 1977
[through] No. 191, sept. 1977–. Guatemala.

Monthly serial which publishes valuable information on SIECA. The issues reviewed are: No. 184 (feb. 1977, p. 2–4) describes the five-vol. study prepared by SIECA's Committee of Five entitled "Regional Cooperation and Central American Trade in Agricultural Products" (also known as INTAGRO). No. 185 (marzo 1977, p. 1–10) reproduces the text of the statement by the Honduran Council of Private Business regarding the projected Treaty for a Central American Economic and Social Community. No. 186 (abril 1977, p. 17–19) includes Resolution No. 167 issued by ECLA's Economic Cooperation Committee and designed to strengthen Central American integration. No. 187 (mayo 1977, p. 1–4) describes visit which officials of ECLA, UNCTAD, and the Andean Common Market paid SIECA. No. 188 (junio 1977, p. 11–23) reproduces the document submitted by the five Central American republics to the IDB stating their development priorities by economic sector. No. 190 (agosto 1977, p. 10) reports the signing of a Central American Agreement on Fiscal Incentives by the Ministers of Economy of Guatemala, El Salvador, Nicaragua, and Costa Rica. No. 191 (sept. 1977, p. 1–2) reports on the signing of another agreement of cooperation for the study of regional integration by SIECA and the Confederation of Central American Universities.

Carvajal, Manuel J. ed. Políticas de crecimiento urbano: la experiencia de Costa Rica. See item **7153**.

2988 Cline, William R. and **Enrique Delgado** eds. Economic integration in Central America: a study sponsored jointly by the Brookings Institution and the Secretariat of Economic Integration of Central America (SIECA). Foreword by Bruce K. MacLaury. Washington, The Brookings Institution, 1978. 712 p., tables.

An important book for the economist's library. Consists of collection of writings by a number of contributors on costs and benefits, employment, incomes, comparative advantage, agriculture, and economic development. Useful not only for information about the Common Market but also as a source of valuable illustrations of the methods employed and their applications in a study of common markets in general.

2989 Cohen Orantes, Isaac and **Gert Rosenthal.** Reflections on the conceptual framework of Central American economic integration (CEPAL/R, 3, 1. semester 1977, p. 21–57)

Important article both because of its content and because of the positions of the authors (G. Rosenthal, Director, and I. Cohen, staff member of CEPAL's Mexican office). They examine three approaches to economic integration, their application in Central America, and the causes of the present "crisis" or failure of the CACM to meet earlier expectations. They offer detailed suggestions for improvement. The divergent comments are valuable and interesting. The comments of Laura Beautell and Albert O. Hirschman follow the authors' paper.

Conte-Porras, J. Referencias históricas sobre el crédito, la banca y la moneda panameña. See *HLAS 40:2865*.

2990 Demyk, Michel. Le dévelopment coopératif au Guatemala (IFC/REC, 192:2, 2. trimestre 1978, p. 121–141, tables)
Growth of Guatemalan cooperatives with both political and economic difficulties.

2991 Demyk, Noëlle. L'integration centroaméricaine: problèmes et perspectives (FDD/NED [Problèmes d'Amérique Latine, 47] 4457, fev. 1978, p. 70–102, tables)
An historical evaluation of the goals and agreements of the CACM through the period 1960–76. The topics discussed include balance of payments problems, industrialization, and the background and effects of the withdrawal of Honduras. Among the sources cited by the author is SIECA's 11-vol. work (see *HLAS 39:3046*).

DeWitt, R. Peter, Jr. The Inter-American Development Bank and political influence with special reference to Costa Rica. See items **7155** and **8665**.

2992 Facio B., Rodrigo. Estudio sobre economía costarricense. 2. ed. Introducción de Federico Vargas Peralta. San José, Editorial Costa Rica, 1975. 424 p., bibl., plate, tables (Obras de Rodrigo Facio, 1)
For first ed. published 1972, see *HLAS 37:4382*.

2993 Funke, Klaus. Multinationale Konzerne und "modernisierende" Militärs in Honduras (BESPL, 1:5, Mai/Juni 1976, p. 14–22)
Brief overview of the Honduran military establishment's interest in modernizing the economic infrastructure in this Central American country. Funke perceives these efforts as somewhat similar to those of the Peruvian military. [G.M. Dorn]

2994 González del Valle, Jorge and **Miguel Angel Porras.** La reciente experiencia inflacionaria de Guatemala (BCV/REL, 13:50, 1977, p. 147–195, tables)
An examination of the Guatemalan inflation from 1972–76, its effects and the corrections attempted under the headings of prices, aggregate demand and supply, balance of payments, public finance and monetary policy with tentative conclusions regarding the

causes, particularly whether external or internal.

2995 Gordon, Michael W. Developed, developing and dependent nations: Central American development in a new economic realignment (GWU/JILE, 2:1, 1976, p. 1–33)

Examines the six Central American countries as "dependent" nations in their relation to each other, to the US, and to the "developing" Latin American nations—particularly Venezuela and Mexico. Specific topics include nationalization of foreign investment, a potential banana cartel, the strengthening of the CACM, and effects of the increased costs of oil imports.

2996 Gorostiaga, Xabier. Los banqueros del imperio: el papel de los centros financieros internacionales en las países subdesarrollados. San José, Editorial Universitaria Centro Americana (EDUCA), 1978. 113 p., bibl., tables (Col. Depto. Ecuménico de Investigaciones)

General presentation of the subject with a detailed analysis of Panama as a model of the functioning and effects of an international financial center in an underdeveloped country. Topics of interest include paper companies, inflation, growth, and sensitivity to outside economic forces. The author ends with his conclusions and proposals for further research.

2997 Honduras. Banco Central. La nueva política bananera de Honduras, 1903–1975. Tegucigalpa, Secretaría de Cultura, Turismo e Información, 1975? 182 p., plate.

Highly useful volume in that it brings together in one place the laws relating to concessions to two US banana companies, (Standard Fruit and Tela Railroad) from the first one in 1903 to Decree Law No. 253 of 15 Aug. 1975 ending the special concessions, and Decree Law No. 270 of 3 Oct. 1975 setting up the Honduran Banana Corporation. This is the first of a planned series of publications to provide information to the public on economic problems and designed to promote general interest in their solution.

2998 ———. **Consejo Asesor de la Jefatura de Estado. Comisión Económica Social.** Problema de los energéticos en Honduras: diagnóstico y política. Tegucigalpa, 1977. 1 v. (Various pagings) tables.

General description of the international petroleum situation as seen from Honduras, a diagnosis of Honduran power supplies and needs for development, and urgent policy recommendations including those for energy conservation and expansion of existing and already planned hydroelectric power facilities.

2999 ———. **Consejo Hondureño de la Empresa Privada** (COHEP). Honduras: debates sobre reforma agraria. Tegucigalpa, Instituto Nacional Agrario (INA), 1975? 81 p. (Programa de Capacitación Campesina para la Reforma Agraria [PROCCARA]. Programa de ediciones y divulgación, 77)

Describes objections of the organizations representing private enterprise, the meat packers, and the farmers and cattle raisers (Consejo Hondureño de la Empresa Privada, COHEP; Asociación Nacional de Empacadoras de Carne, ANEC; Federación Nacional de Agricultores y Ganaderos de Honduras, FENAGH), and the justification expressed by the National Agrarian Institute of Honduras (Instituto Nacional Agrario, INA).

3000 ———. **Consejo Superior de Planificación Económica** (CONSUPLANE). **Secretaría Técnica.** Plan Nacional de Desarrollo, 1974–1978: síntesis. Tegucigalpa, 1976. 110 p., tables.

Useful, abbreviated version of the National Plan for Development. Recognizing the great importance of agriculture and cattle raising in Honduras, the plan includes a section on agrarian reform. The Decree Law of Agrarian Reform, No. 170, was issued 30 Dec. 1974.

3001 ———. **Ministerio de Economía. Dirección General de Estadística y Censos.** Comercio exterior de Honduras: exportación 1976. Tegucigalpa, 1977. 171 p., tables.

Especially interesting for the time series of foreign trade over the period before, during, and after Honduran participation in free trade within the CACM.

3002 ———. **Programa de Capacitación Campesina para la Reforma Agraria** (PROCCARA). Plan Nacional de Reforma Agraria: curso intensivo de capacitación de técnicos en desarrollo agrario. Tegucigalpa, PROCCARA, Programa de Ediciones y Divulgación, n.d. 32 l., table.

Describes the structure of Honduran agriculture and includes a model for a law of agrarian reform which would include among other provisions a redistribution of part of the land. Indemnization would equal the amount which the owners had declared for property tax assessment.

3003 *Indicadores Económicos*. Banco Central de Nicaragua. Depto. de Estudios Económicos. Vol. 2, No. 2, junio 1976–. Managua.

Tabular presentation of time series (1960–75 or into 1976), of data prepared by a number of Nicaraguan agencies on labor, prices, national income, money and banking, public finance, foreign trade and domestic production.

3004 Kreider, L. Emil. Banana cartel?: trends, conditions, and institutional developments in the banana market (IAMEA, 31:2, Autumn 1977, p. 3–24, tables)

Discouraging analysis of the feasibility of a banana cartel including, besides the elasticity of demand, an examination of the importance of bananas in the producing countries' foreign trade, the labor-intensive quality of the industry, and political differences among the exporting countries.

3005 Litvak, Isaiah A. and **Christopher J. Maule.** Transnational corporations and vertical integration: the banana case (JWTL, 11:6, Nov/Dec. 1977, p. 537–549, tables)

Examines how three US transnational banana enterprises market bananas in the US and compares their performance in this regard with their operation in the EEC.

3006 López, Lorenzo. Estadística general de la República de El Salvador. 3. ed. San Salvador, Ministerio de Educación, Dirección de Publicaciones, 1974. 198 p., tables.

A wealth of information on mid-19th-century conditions. Contains by subdivisions of depts. the number of persons by sex, marital status, age, and occupation; and information on geography, crops, houses, illnesses, history, education, the church, customs and the celebration of holidays.

3007 Maldonado M., José Mario. Reforma agraria: factores limitantes en el proceso. Tegucigalpa, Instituto Nacional Agrario (INA), Oficina de Divulgación, 1975. 13 l., plates (Col. Cambios, 1)

Author anticipates a delay in the application of Decree Law No. 170 for Agrarian Reform and attributes it to a lack of social awareness on the part of the majority of Hondurans.

3008 Nicaragua. Banco Central. Departamento de Estudios Económicos (DEE). Presentación de avances sobre el estudio de actitudes en la actividad algodonera. Managua, 1976. 1 v. (Various pagings) tables (DEE-UEE Doc., 1)

Sample survey for forecasting cotton production by depts. in the crop year 1976–77. Appendix contains questionnaire used to assess the expectations of producers. It reports on yields: costs of production, including fertilizers and insecticides; areas in production, owned and rented; and methods of financing and marketing.

3009 Organization of American States. Comité Interamericano de Desarrollo Agrícola (CIAD). **Misión Conjunta de Programación para Centroamérica.** Tenencia de la tierra y desarrollo rural en Centroamérica. Prefacio de Thomas F. Carroll. Tegucigalpa, Programa de Capacitación Campesina para la Reforma Agraria (PROCCARA, 82)

Emphasizes the relationship among systems of land-holding and economic development in Central America and support for efforts to raise the incomes of the rural population and to promote the free movement of workers throughout the CACM.

3010 Panama. Dirección de Estadística y Censo. Estadística panameña: indicadores económicos y sociales, años 1975 y 1976. Panamá, 1977. 21 p., tables (Sección Oll)

3011 ——. ——. Estadística panameña: situación económica, cuentas nacionales, años 1974 a 1976. Panamá, 1977. 34 p., tables (Sección 342)

Introductory statement calls attention to revisions of the national income estimates 1974 and 1975 and in the preliminary estimates for 1976, made necessary by inflation.

3012 Peek, Peter and **Pedro Antolinez.** Migration and the urban labour market: the case of San Salvador (WD, 5:4, April 1977, p. 291–302, tables)

Employment, wages, and labor mobility of migrants into San Salvador from other cities and from rural areas, a comparison of them with urban natives, and a test of discrimination against the rural migrants. Uses data from 1974 labor force survey.

3013 Programa Regional del Empleo para América Latina y el Caribe (PREALC), *Santiago.* Situación y perspectivas del empleo en El Salvador. t. 1/2. Prólogo de Víctor E. Tokman. Santiago, Organización Internacional del Trabajo (OIT), 1977. 2 v. (453, 143 p.) tables.

Detailed presentation of the facts of employment and incomes with recommendations for improvement based on a labor force survey in the metropolitan area of El Salvador and the visit of an ILO mission in 1974.

3014 Salazar-Carrillo, Jorge. Metodología sobre medidas de políticas económica en Centroamérica y sus efectos sobre los precios (BCV/REL, 14:55, 1979, p. 101–151, tables)

On the basis of ECIEL and SIECA studies, the author delineates a methodology for measuring the impact which economic policies such as indirect taxes and import duties have on prices. He examines this phenomenon in the context of the Central American Common Market. [Roberto Correia Lima]

3015 Sandoval Corea, Rigoberto. Reforma agraria: disertación ante el Consejo Superior de la Defensa. Tegucigalpa, Instituto Nacional Agrario (INA), Oficina de Divulgación, 1976. 26 1., plates (Col. Cambios, 8)

The Executive Director of the National Agrarian Institute explains the provisions of Decree Law No. 170 for Agrarian Reform, presents arguments pro and con, its implementation, and strongly defends the position for reform.

3016 Tenencia de la tierra y desarrollo rural en Centroamerica. 2. ed. San José, C.R., Editorial Univ. Centroamericana (EDUCA), 1976. 199 p., tables (Col. Seis. Serie mayor)

Evaluation of rural programs in each of the five CACM countries designed to assist in devising a solution to social problems with attention to the holding and use of land, technical assistance, productivity, employment, income, and the role of the Common Market in agriculture. This study was sponsored by the OAS as well as by CEPAL, FAO, OIT, IICA and SIECA.

3017 Universidad Nacional Autónoma de Honduras, *Tegucigalpa.* **Departamento de Ciencias Sociales.** Lecturas sobre realidad nacional. Tegucigalpa, 1977? 145 p., tables.

Six readings compiled by the Social Science Dept. on underdevelopment, the banana region, agricultural land holdings, rural social classes, US investments, and industrial concentration in Honduras, with data into the 1970s.

3018 Valle, Alfredo del. En torno de una empresa geotérmica centroamericana (INTAL/IL, 2:10, enero:feb. 1977, p. 29–37, tables)

Describes proposal for the development of geothermal energy in the isthmus by an enterprise combining electrical power plants, possibly in two or more countries. Article contains helpful references to studies and tests already made toward the harnessing of this source of energy.

3019 Wilford, D. Sykes and **Walton T. Wilford.** On revenue performance and revenue-income stability in the Third World (UC/EDCC, 26:3, April 1978, p. 505–523, tables)

Consists of an application, using data from El Salvador, of a revenue-income elasticity coefficient as a measure of the response of revenues to the demand for capital expenditures and to changes in GDP.

WEST INDIES
(except Cuba and Puerto Rico)

3020 Banco Central de la República Dominicana, *Santo Domingo.* **Departamento de Estudios Económicos.** Cuentas nacionales: producto nacional bruto, 1970–1976. Santo Domingo, 1977. 195 p., tables.

This publication presents the real national income statistics in monetary units of 1970 instead of 1962 and changes some series to conform with revisions in national statistics. The data are preceded by a section giving the definitions and formulas used. Revises, enlarges, and brings through 1976 the 1970–75 ed.

3021 Berleant-Schiller, Riva. The social and economic role of cattle in Barbuda (AGS/GR, 67:3, July 1977, p. 299–309)

Offers an explanation of the unusual

system of raising small-scale cattle on the open range and the communal ownership of that range; and analyzes the effects of the practice on the economy of this small island.

3022 *Bulletin de la Sécretarie d'Etat des Finances et des Affaires Economiques.* Direction des Affaires Economiques, Division Etudes et Statistiques. No. 10, mars 1977–. Port-au-Prince.

This Haitian statistical bulletin is distinct in providing three pages on UNCTAD and a System of Generalized Preferences favoring the exports of developing countries. Reference is made to the list of products admitted free of duty into the US since 1976 and to those receiving preference in the EEC.

3023 Caribbean Community (CARICOM), *Georgetown.* **Secretariat.** A digest of trade statistics of Caribbean Community member states. Foreword by Alister McIntyre. Georgetown, 1976. 124 p., fold. tables, tables.

Important publication in that it is the initial presentation of statistics of intra-Caricom trade (1960–74) which are essential to an evaluation of the achievements of the Common Market.

3024 Carlson, Beverly; William Duncan; and **Preston Brown** *eds.* Procedural history: Dominican Republic cost of production survey. Washington, U.S. Agency for International Development, Sector Analysis Division, 1977. 185 p., tables (Dominican Republic agricultural sector analysis series. Methodological working document, 2)

This working document is one of a number made available in connection with a survey of the agricultural sector using 1800 farms. The methodology presented includes the sample design, questionnaire, training collection and processing of the data.

3025 Carvajal, M.J. and **David T. Geithman.** Migration flows and economic conditions in the Dominican Republic (UW/LE, 52:2, May 1976, p. 207–220, tables)

Authors have used migration estimates to find whether people migrate to improve their economic condition and whether, in fact, migration reduces the regional economic differences. They present their method of statistical estimation and their model of migration.

3026 Chernick, Sidney E. *ed.* The Commonwealth Caribbean: the integration experience. Foreword by Hollis Chenery. Baltimore, Md., The Johns Hopkins Univ. Press, 1978. 521 p., tables (A World Bank country economic report)

Report on a mission sent to the Commonwealth Caribbean by the World Bank covers 12 countries of the CARICOM taken as a unit. It analyzes problems related to trade, money, public finances, population, employment, transport, agriculture, tourism, and industry. This work is valuable not only for its statement of conditions in the region, the identification of issues, and its recommendations, but it is also worthwhile for the statistical appendix of 275 p.

3027 Demas, William G. The Caribbean and the new international economic order (UM/JIAS, 20:3, Aug. 1978, p. 229–263, tables)

Valuable article of broad coverage which views the Caribbean as a unit and analyzes its development problems, possible strategies to correct them, and its interest in sharing in the benefits of a New International Economic Order. For political scientist's comment, see item **8723.**

3028 ———. Essays on Caribbean integration and development. With an introduction by Alister McIntyre. Kingston, Univ. of the West Indies, Institute of Social and Economic Research (ISER), 1976. 159 p., bibl.

Two reasons why this study is valuable: 1) the author is an economist of the region who addresses a non-specialist audience; and 2) the study reveals important changes in economic thought on integration over the 15-year period prior to publication as applied to the West Indies.

3029 Dominican Republic. Academia de Ciencias de la República Dominicana. Fondo para el Avance de las Ciencias Sociales. Comisión de Economía. Economía dominicana: 1975. Santo Domingo, 1976. 305 p., tables.

Useful, comprehensive publication designed to be the first of a series of annual surveys of the economy by a private, non-profit institution founded in 1974 to promote scientific research. In this initial monograph, the Economic Committee describes conditions in one year and offers proposals for economic policy.

3030 **Dundas, Carl W.** Las empresas conjuntas en la comunidad del Caribe (INTAL:IL, 2:19, nov. 1977, p. 16–22)

Reports, as of the date of the article, on the organization of business associations of mixed ownership in a variety of fields including shipping, banking, agriculture, commerce, mining, and tourism, some unincorporated and others incorporated, some regional, some transnationals, others merely national, some owned by the public sector and others combining public and private capital.

3031 *Economie et Développement.* Secrétarie d'Etat des Finances et des Affaires Economique, Unité de Programmation. Vol. 1, No. 1, oct. 1977 [through] Vol. 1, No. 4, juillet/sept. 1978–. Port-au-Prince.

New Haitian quarterly bulletin on economy and public finances and their relation to planning for development. Subjects covered the first year were: the general system of tariff preferences, Haiti's application for admission to CARICOM, effects of rapid population growth, US AID (1973–78); the food problem; coffee; cotton; sugar; bananas; etc.

3032 **Haiti. Institut Haitien de Statistique. Département des Finances et des Affaires Economiques.** Guide économique de la Republique d'Haiti. Port-au-Prince, 1977. 667 p., fold. tables, maps, plate, tables.

Copious source of information on Haiti, more varied than the title suggests. First section in outline and tabular form concerns the country's history, geography, money, government organization, and culture (e.g., a listing of leading authors, musicians, painters, and sculptors. The second and major part consists of statistical tables, mostly time series, including the major economic series and, in addition, other series on climate, education, and attendance at movies and museums. There follows a directory of businesses, hotels, and banks and other useful current data.

3033 **Honorat, Jean Jacques.** Information and economic development (*in* Caribbean-American perspectives. Washington, Phelps-Stokes Fund, 1978, p. 79–88, tables)

Emphasizes planning for development requiring the collection of information as to Haiti's agricultural, mineral, and energy resources; nutritional, medical, and educational needs; and financial, technological and labor means of meeting the needs.

3034 **Jamaica. Department of Statistics.** Production statistics: 1977. Preface by C.P. McFarlane. Kingston, Jam., 1978? 75 p., tables.

Those concerned with the declining rate of growth during several years preceding 1978 will be interested in the time series given here for the decade 1968–77 by products for the agricultural, mining, manufacturing, and electrical industries.

Lacombe, Robert. La République d'Haiti. See *HLAS 40:126.*

3035 **McLure, Charles E., Jr.** and **Wayne R. Thirsk.** The inequity of taxing inequity: a plea for reduced sumptuary taxes in developing countries (UC/EDCC, 26:3, April 1978, p. 487–503, tables)

A paper of general applicability with examples drawn from Jamaica. Discusses the theory of the taxation of alcohol and tobacco; empirical evidence in the form of income, expenditure, and price elasticities; and recommendations.

NACLA: Report on the Americas. See item **8744.**

3036 *NACLA's Latin America and Empire Report.* North American Congress on Latin America (NACLA). Vol. 10, No. 8, Oct. 1976–. N.Y.

The situation of the oil industry in the Caribbean, followed by a section dealing specifically with Trinidad-and-Tobago as both a refining and producing nation with special attention to the roles of the government and the oil workers.

3037 **Organization of American States. General Secretariat. Department of Scientific Affairs. Regional Scientific and Technological Development Program.** Survey of science and technology development needs in Barbados. Washington, 1977. 132 p., bibls., maps, tables (Studies on scientific and technological development, 30)

Consists of 12 papers. The introductory article by David Jalife, OAS Consultant, offers an overall view of the needs of Barbados. Other papers are by specialists in agriculture, the food industry, marine resources, energy resources (solar), and environmental conservation.

3038 **Pierre-Louis, Fritz.** Sources d'énergie en Haïti (IFH/C, 129, mai 1976, p. 7–21)

Discusses causes of the world energy crisis and the extent of Haiti's possible sources of energy including lignite, bagasse (the residue from sugar cane), petroleum, hydroelectric power, geothermal power, and the wind.

3039 Ramlogan, Parmeshwar. Aspectos de la banca comercial en El Caribe: Trinidad y Tobago, Jamaica, Guyana y Barbados. México, Centro de Estudios Monetarios Latinoamericanos (CEMLA), 1977. 43 p., bibl., tables (Col. Monografías, 37)

For the period 1966–74, the author finds much similarity among these four countries. He examines aspects such as the importance of commercial banking among financial institutions, the extent of branch banking, the existence of a few relatively large banks, the degree of foreign ownership and its control as well as the liquidity of assets and where they are held.

3040 Ramsaran, Ramesh. CARICOM: the integration process in crisis (JWTL, 12:3, May/June 1978, p. 208–217, illus.)

Examines the crisis brought on by the decisions of Jamaica and Guyana to restrict their imports from both within and without the CARICOM. Immediate causes of their decisions are balance-of-payment problems and Trinidad-and-Tobago's unique position as an exporter of oil.

3041 Santana, Santiago. Actualidad y perspectivas en la economía dominicana: 1970–1980. Santo Domingo, Editora Alfa y Omega, 1977. 231 p., tables.

Examines changes in the economy (1970–76) broken down into the external, the fiscal and the monetary sectors; and includes a forecast for the years 1977, 1978 through 1980. Appendix to each chapter provides a collection of useful statistics.

Sharpe, Kenneth. El campesino de la sierra: el problema de vivir. See item **9186**.

3042 *Social and Economic Studies*. Univ. of the West Indies, Institute of Social and Economic Research. Vol. 26, No. 4, Dec. 1977–. Kingston.

This issue entirely devoted to public finance in the Caribbean is particularly interesting. Includes two articles on the region as a whole, and one on each of the following: Barbados, Trinidad-and-Tobago, Jamaica, the Bahamas, Surinam, the Virgin Islands, and the Associated States.

3043 United Nations. División Industrial (ONUDI). Estudio industrial sobre la República Dominicana (Ciencia [Univ. Autónoma de Santo Domingo, Dirección de Investigaciones Científicas, Santo Domingo] 3:2, abril/junio 1976, p. 11–76, illus., tables)

Recommendations and results of an examination of the development of the manufacturing sector conducted by a group of experts sent by the UN. The data used were national statistics and information from interviews with persons in business and government. Attention was given to investment, prices and foreign trade. Industries include agro-business, textiles, and construction.

3044 Werleigh, Georges. Essai d'analyse de nos réalités économiques (IFH/C, 136/137, fév. 1978, p. 5–26, bibl., tables)

Author has a pessimistic view of Haiti's emerging from underdevelopment through international assitance. He attributes this to the country's situation of inadequate production, inequitable distribution of wealth, and rapidly growing urban population.

3045 Young, Ruth C. The structural context of the Caribbean tourist industry: a comparative study (UC/EDCC, 25:4, July 1977, p. 657–672, tables)

Tests statistically the hypothesis that the tourist industry evolves in a plantation-type society in order to exhibit characteristics similar to those of the pre-tourist society.

Cuba

JORGE F. PEREZ LOPEZ, *Bureau of International Labor Affairs, United States Department of Labor*

IN THE LAST TWO YEARS CUBA HAS BEEN ENGAGED in an uphill fight to adjust to the severe shocks which jolted the world economy in the early 1970s. Sugar world-market prices in 1977 and 1978 stood at about one-seventh of the record levels reached in Nov. 1974 and close to production costs. The fall in the sugar world-market price weakened Cuba's capacity to import from hard-currency areas and led to the adoption of an economic austerity program: economic growth projections were moderated, imports of consumer goods were curtailed and purchases of capital goods for industrialization were either canceled or postponed. Because of the stagnation of prices for Cuba's principal export product, the emphasis was shifted to attaining growth through increases in economic efficiency and productivity. To this end, a new economic management and planning system (items **3057** and **3074**), which grants limited autonomy to enterprises and reintroduces material incentives and traditional economic instruments, such as cost accounting and price policy, was promulgated in Dec. 1975 and implemented beginning in 1977.

There are two noticeable trends in the availability of materials published in Cuba about its economy. The increasing number of economics textbooks suggest a growing emphasis on the teaching of economics designed presumably to train cadres in the implementation of a new economic management and planning system. For the first time, one finds important general textbooks, some written by Cuban economists, which address Cuban economic problems and institutions. Two outstanding examples are a three-volume set entitled *Manual de economía política del socialismo* (item **3068**) written by a Soviet professor of economics who was assisted by six Cuban economists and *Planificación económica* (item **3052**) authored by a group of Cuban economic planning instructors. A negative trend is the relative decrease in the number of articles about the Cuban economy in the leading journal *Economía y Desarrollo*. When the Economics Institute at the Univ. of Havana which edits the journal was reorganized in mid-1977, editorial policy noticeably changed. The emphasis in the recent issues (corresponding to late 1977 and 1978) has been on articles dealing with theoretical discussions of Marxism-Leninism; applications of sophisticated mathematical techniques to management and information problems; translations of articles from Soviet and Eastern European journals dealing with management and planning systems in those countries; and reports about the economies of COMECON members.

The publication of statistical data, a trend which began in the early 1970s, is still apparent. JUCEPLAN continues to publish and expand its statistical yearbooks (item **3053**) and to generate partial reports of the 1970 census (item **3054**). Other recently-published volumes rich in statistical data refer to public health (item **3055**) and demography (item **3083**). Also of interest are special studies of US economic influence in Cuba prior to the Revolution (item **3073**); international aspects of the Cuban sugar industry (item **3080**); residential construction (item **3059**); and economic costs of water pollution (item **3061**).

With reference to the economic literature published abroad, the most significant piece is a comprehensive study of the Cuban socioeconomic development model carried out by CEPAL (items **3056** and **3082**). This is the first attempt by CEPAL to analyze the Cuban economy since its controversial report published in 1963. Other works of significance are an analysis of sugar policies (item **3047**); a compilation of essays (items **3064–3066, 3072** and **3075**) dealing with Cuban international relations; and two articles which examine the applicability of the Cuban development model to other developing countries, one published in the US (item **3075**), and another in the USSR (item **3084**). Finally, economic problems and policies during the first years of the Revolution are discussed in a book which contains two essays by Carlos Rafael Rodríguez (item **3077**) and in a collection of papers written in 1959–62 by the Mexican economist Juan Noyola (item **3067**).

Baloyra, Enrique A. Democratic versus dictatorial budgeting: the case of Cuba with reference to Venezuela and Mexico. See item **7185**.

3046 Barkin, David. Cuba: evolución de las relaciones entre el campo y la ciudad (BNCE/CE, 28:2, feb. 1978, p. 135–143)

Discusses spatial aspects of Cuban development policy. Maintains that after Cuba settled on a growth strategy emphasizing the agricultural sector, a deliberate policy was adopted to discourage rural migration to the cities and to establish new towns in agricultural areas and new industrial plants across the country. Some successful Cuban regional development measures are discussed: greenbelts around major cities aimed at growing vegetables and fruits; secondary schools in the country-side which utilize student labor for agricultural work; "microbrigades" composed of workers relieved of their normal duties and charged with building housing for workers in their work center. However, in Dec. 1978, it was announced that, because of gross inefficiency, the construction microbrigades would be disbanded.

3047 Brunner, Heinrich. Cuban sugar policy from 1963 to 1970. Pittsburgh, Pa., The Univ. of Pittsburgh Press, 1977. 163 p., bibl., tables.

Analyzes Cuban sugar policy during the period leading to and including the proposed 10 million ton sugar crop of 1970. Chap. 2 is an interesting attempt to reconstruct output directives of the 1965–70 prospective sugar plan (the plan was never made public). Chap. 3 evaluates the outcome of each of the zafras 1964–70 with reference to sugar production, number of workers, acreage, yield, foreign trade, etc., with special emphasis on the 1970 zafra and the reasons why it failed to reach planned output levels.

3048 Castro Tato, Manuel. Apuntes sobre la productividad y la evaluación de inversiones (UH/ED, 38, nov./dic. 1976, p. 154–173, table)

In a socialist economy, characterized by full employment, productivity increases are a prerequisite for economic growth, i.e.,the productivity of new investments must exceed the average productivity of existing ones. Thus, productivity considerations should enter into the evaluation of investment deci-

sions. The author presents and discusses different formulations of the general concept of productivity which may be applied to the evaluation of productive investments in Cuba.

3049 Las construcciones básicas en el período 1971–1975 (UH/ED, 39, enero/feb. 1977, p. 198–205)

Reviews accomplishments during 1971–75 in the construction of industrial, agricultural, educational and residential facilities and in the production of construction materials.

3050 Cuba. Comité Estatal de Estadísticas. La economía cubana en el año 1975 (UH/ED, 38, nov./dic. 1976, p. 212–223)

Brief summary of the salient accomplishments of the Cuban economy in 1975. Data included refer to global indicators, output in the main sectors of the economy, education, culture, public health, etc. This study was also released as a mimeographed pamphlet entitled *La economía cubana: 1975* (La Habana, n.d., 6 p.).

3051 ——. ——. La economía cubana en el año 1976 (UH/ED, 41, mayo/junio 1976, p. 193–196)

Brief overview of the economy in 1976 using the same format as item **3050**.

3052 ——. Institutos Técnicos de Economía. Colectivo de Profesores de la Cátedra de Planificación Económica. Planificación económica: pt. 1. 2. ed. La Habana, Editorial Pueblo y Educación, 1976. 83 p.

Vol. 1 of textbook written by a group of economic planning instructors associated with the Technical Institutes for Economics. Authors indicate in the prologue that they were motivated to write the book by the lack of an appropriate textbook in their discipline. Although designed to serve as an introductory text on the concepts of economic central planning, the book provides a useful description of how Cuba's economic planning system operates.

3053 ——. Junta Central de Planificación. Dirección Central de Estadística. Anuario estadístico de Cuba 1974. La Habana, 1976. 301 p.

Statistical yearbook which follows the general format of two earlier volumes (see *HLAS 39:3110–3111*). Contains over 200 tables, generally covering the period 1962–74, divided into 16 sections: 1) territory and climate; 2) population; 3) global indicators; 4) labor force; 5) agriculture; 6) fishing; 7) industry; 8) construction; 9) transportation; 10) communications; 11) domestic commerce; 12) foreign commerce; 13) education; 14) cultural activities; 15) public health; and 16) sports and recreation. The sections on construction and education have been changed substantially from previous issues and the data on fishing are presented for the first time in a new section. Has subject index. An English translation of the titles of tables is available as a mimeographed attachment.

3054 ――――. ――――. ――――. **Departamento de Demografía.** La situación de la vivienda en Cuba en 1970 y su evolución perspectiva. La Habana, Instituto Cubano del Libro, Editorial Orbe, 1976. 78 p.

Partial report of the National Population and Housing Census of 1970 dealing with housing aspects (for a previously released report of the census dealing with population density and urbanization, see *HLAS 39:3112*). Includes chapters on the housing situation in 1970, the distribution of housing units by type, age, type of construction materials used, number of rooms, availability of utilities and appliances. Other chapters compare results of the 1970 and 1953 census and project housing needs through 1985.

3055 ――――. **Ministerio de Salud Pública.** Cuba: la salud en la Revolución. La Habana, Instituto Cubano del Libro, Editorial Orbe, 1975. 175 p.

Describes the Cuban national health care system with emphasis on preventive health care services and on the modes of delivering services to workers and to the agricultural population. Presents data on health care facilities, medical equipment and personnel in 1974 and compares them with existing conditions in 1958. Contains several tables on health-related statistics generally covering the period 1958–74.

3056 Cuba: politica económica bajo la Revolución (Economía de America Latina [Centro de Investigación y Docencia Económicas, México] 1, sept. 1978, p. 135–155, tables)

Very useful summary of sections dealing with economic matters from lengthy

CEPAL report evaluating economic and social aspects of the Cuban development model (see item **3082**).

3057 **Domenech, Nieves** and **Armando López Coll.** Sistema de planificación y dirección de la economía (UH/ED, 40, marzo/abril 1977, p. 82–107)

Discusses background and theoretical basis for Cuba's Economic Management and Planning System. Also discusses aspects of the system's implementation process and its implications for the Cuban economy.

3058 **Domínguez, Jorge I.** Cuba: order and revolution. Cambridge, Mass., Harvard Univ., Belknap Press, 1978. 683 p., bibl., tables.

Although the author indicates in the preface that his book is about "the politics and government of twentieth-century Cuba," his frequent references to economic matters make this study worthwhile reading for students of Cuban economics. Some of the economic issues touched upon are revolutionary Cuba's international economic relations (p. 137–165); economic growth and social welfare policies (p. 173–190); income distribution (p. 227–229); organized labor (p. 271–279); participation of the armed forces in the economy (p. 383–390); central planning (p. 417–420); and the agricultural sector (p. 423–463).

3059 **Fernández Núñez, José Manuel.** La vivienda en Cuba. La Habana, Instituto Cubano del Libro, Editorial Arte y Literatura, 1976. 165 p.

Describes housing conditions and assesses developments of the housing construction industry in Cuba prior to and after the Revolution. Analyzes in some detail government housing construction policies and accomplishments from 1959–75.

Fitzgerald, Frank T. A critique of the "Sovietization of Cuba" thesis. See item **7197**.

3060 **Grobart, Fabio.** Elementos para la elaboración de una política científico-técnica nacional (UH/ED, 38, nov./dic. 1976, p. 63–117, tables)

Discusses role of technological progress in Cuban economic development. Summarizes the process of determining Cuban national scientific-technical policy and identifies the critical variables which enter into the analysis.

3061 Liovin, Anatoli. Aspectos económicos de la protección de los recursos hidráulicos en Cuba (UH/ED, 42, julio/agosto 1977, p. 44–69, tables)

Discusses the serious and growing problem of water pollution in Cuba and its negative impact on the environment, public health, recreational areas and fishing resources. Concludes that the most serious water polluters are industrial plants. Author anticipates a worsening of the situation if additional ones (e.g., refineries, tanneries, plants for processing nickel, chemicals, cellulose, etc.) are built without heavy investments in water pollution control systems.

3062 Losman, Donald. The economic embargo of Cuba: an economic appraisal (UPR/CS, 14:3, Oct. 1974, p. 95–119, tables)

Concludes that the US economic embargo damaged the Cuban economy even if a reliable estimate of the extent of the injury is virtually impossible to make. Three factors account for the damage: 1) embargo-induced deterioration of capital stock; 2) additional input costs associated with transporting goods longer distances; and 3) problems of quality and substitutability of the new goods for goods (particularly inputs) they replaced. The embargo costs continue to this date, although they have been shifted partially to Cuba's socialist trading partners in the form of subsidies.

3063 Marrero y Artiles, Leví. Cuba: economía y sociedad. v. 3, El siglo XVII: pt. 1; v. 4, El siglo XVII: pt. 2; v. 5, El siglo XVII: pt. 3. Madrid, Editorial Playor, 1975/1976. 3 v. (309, 288, 227 p.)

These three new volumes are part of a multi-volume series on Cuban economic history begun by the author in 1972 (for v. 1, see *HLAS 37:4421*; for v. 2, *HLAS 39:3123*). Each of the volumes covers certain aspects of Cuban economic history during the 17th century. Vol. 3 studies population, land tenure and the development of copper mining (for historian's comment on this volume, see *HLAS 40:2970*); vol. 4 deals with the development of the sugar and tobacco industries, shipbuilding, foreign trade and smuggling, public finance, money, prices and salaries; and vol. 5 deals with social classes, the role of the Church, slavery and a general description of life in Cuba during the period. Volumes

contain many illustrations, maps, tables and a subject index.

3064 Mesa-Lago, Carmelo. The economics of U.S.-Cuban rapprochement (*in* Blasier, Cole and Carmelo Mesa-Lago *eds.* Cuba in the world. [see item **8713**] p. 199–224)

Explores economic issues which might be of significance in the resumption of US-Cuban relations. Author analizes export potential and import needs of the Cuban economy over the next few years and presents a very interesting section on Cuba's foreign debt. For political scientist's comment, see item **7211b**.

3065 ———. The economy and international economic relations (*in* Blasier, Cole and Carmelo Mesa-Lago. Cuba in the world. [see item **8713**] p. 169–198)

In this well-documented essay author analyzes current and planned capacity of the Cuban economy in order to anticipate and predict its future performance and changes in foreign trade through 1980. Contains nine tables on economic performance and foreign trade based on the most current Cuban official statistical yearbook. For political scientist's comment, see item **7211a**.

3066 Moran, Theodore H. The international political economy of Cuban nickel development (UP/CSEC, 7:2, July 1977, p. 145–165, tables)

Analyzes the Cuban nickel industry and assesses its mid-term prospects in the context of conditions in the world nickel market. Concludes that despite extensive nickel deposits and ambitious production plans, development of the Cuban nickel industry largely depends on access to the kind of Western technology that only a handful of multinational corporations can furnish. This article was also published as Chap. 12 in Cole Blasier and Carmelo Mesa-Lago *eds. Cuba in the World* (see item **8713**, p. 257–272).

3067 Noyola, Juan F. La economía cubana en los primeros años de la Revolución y otros ensayos. México, Siglo XXI Editores, 1978. 279 p.

Collection of eight essays about the Cuban economy based on writings and conferences by the author during 1959–62. Noyola, a Mexican-born and trained economist, occupied a prominent position on the Cuban Central Planning Board from 1960 until his accidental death in Nov. 1962. Of particular interest are the essays "Posibilidades Mediatas e Inmediatas de la Economía Cubana" and "Aspectos Económicos de la Revolución Cubana." The majority of the eight essays have been previously published in Cuban journals.

3068 Oleinik, Ivan. Manual de economía política del socialismo. vols. 1/3. La Habana, Instituto Cubano del Libro, Editorial de Ciencias Sociales, 1977. 3 v. (357, 285, 238 p.)

Textbook on the political economy of socialism which shows, for the first time, the specific application of Marxist-Leninist thought to the process of building a socialist society in Cuba. Oleinik, a Professor of Political Economy at the Academy of Social Sciences, adjunct to the Central Committee of the Communist Party of the Soviet Union, was assisted in this work by a group of six Cuban economists. Their primary responsibility was to use Cuban examples and brief case studies to illustrate the Marxist-Leninist general principles of the text. This work is destined to become the basic textbook for the teaching of economics in Cuba. It is, therefore, doubly important because of its actual content as theory and its eventual influence as teaching tool.

3069 Partido Comunista de Cuba. Comité Central. Departamento de Orientación Revolucionaria. DPA: división político-administrativa. La Habana, 1976. 40 p., maps, tables.

Very useful booklet which offers background information on the new politico-adminstrative division of Cuba and summary data for each of the new 14 provinces: maps, population, population density and labor force. Detailed maps on the new provinces are essential for those trying to compare data based on the new and old divisions.

3070 Pérez-López, Jorge F. The Cuban nuclear power program (UP/CSEC, 9:1, Jan. 1979, p. 1–42)

Description of the proposed Cuban nuclear power program based on published information available to the general public. Notes that the use of nuclear power for generating electricity is economically sound given

Cuba's inadequate domestic energy resources and growing dependence on imported petroleum. Concludes, however, that nuclear power invariably raises problems of a graver nature, such as the safety of nuclear power plants, possible diversion of irradiated fuel for the manufacture of nuclear weapons, etc.

3071 ———. An index of Cuban industrial output, 1930–58 (in Wilkie, James W. and Kenneth Ruddle eds. Quantitative Latin American studies, methods and findings: statistical abstract of Latin America. Los Angeles, Calif., UCLA, Latin American Center Publications, 1977, p. 37–72, bibl., tables [Suplement, 6])

Constructs a fixed-weight industrial production index, carefully noting methodology, for the period 1930–58. Careful evaluation of sources and compares with some other indexes. Can serve as a basis for comparisons with post-revolutionary production [J.M. Hunter]

3072 ———. Sugar and petroleum in Cuban-Soviet terms of trade (in Blasier, Cole and Carmelo Mesa-Lago eds. Cuba in the world. [see item 8713] p. 273–296)

Analyzes Cuban-Soviet terms of trade with reference to sugar-petroleum exchanges during 1960–76. Concludes that for 1960–74, the terms were generally favorable to Cuba. As prices of Soviet crude petroleum exports began to rise substantially in 1975, the relation turned against Cuba, although the terms of exchange are extremely favorable to Cuba compared with world market price levels for sugar and petroleum. For the remainder of the 1970s, however, the prospects are for petroleum import prices to continue to rise faster than sugar export prices to the detriment of the Cuban economy.

3073 Pino Santos, Oscar. El asalto a Cuba por la oligarquía financiera yanqui. La Habana, Casa de las Américas, 1973. 234 p.

Collection of five essays dealing with the influence of US corporations and their control of the Cuban economy from 1898 to 1958. Author's research relies heavily on documents generated by the corporations themselves (e.g., annual reports, financial statements, reports to the New York Stock Exchange, correspondence between corporate representatives in Cuba and headquarters, etc.) obtained for the author by a team of

American collaborators. Study is disappointing in that it deals almost exclusively with the sugar industry (a sector in which US influence has already received much attention) and fails to investigate sectors that are virtually untouched by researchers, e.g., mining, utilities, financial services, banking, etc. For author's more recent work on the same subject, see *HLAS 40:3061*.

3074 Resolución sobre el Sistema de Dirección y Planificación de la Economía (UH/ED, 36, julio/agosto 1976, p. 125–139)

Resolution adopted at the I Congress of the Cuban Communist Party in Dec. 1975 (see item **7193** and *HLAS 39:7204*). The Economic Management and Planning System, implemented experimentally in selected economic sectors beginning in 1978, continues to rely on central planning but grants substantial autonomy to enterprises to manage their resources. This new economic management also sets up a system of monetary transfers among enterprises and an economic information system, reestablishes the use of credit and enhances the role of prices.

3075 **Ritter, Archibald R.M.** The transferability of Cuba's revolutionary development models (*in* Blasier, Cole and Carmelo Mesa-Lago *eds*. Cuba in the world. [see item **8713**] p. 313–334)

Selects two Cuban socioeconomic development models (a "basic dynamic model" consisting of a sequence of goal priorities pertaining to redistribution and growth typical of the 1960s and the "emerging model of the 1970s" emphasizing central planning, growth, development of export-oriented industries and increased dependence on the Soviet bloc) and examines their transferability to other developing countries. Results suggest that because of differences among developing countries in resource base, institutions and problems, it is impossible to find a single model and optimal set of strategies to fit all times and places. Nonetheless, developing countries can gain useful insights by analyzing the two Cuban models and may adopt some components or sub-components. An earlier version of this study appeared in *Cuban Studies/Estudios Cubanos* (7:2, July 1977, p. 183–204).

3076 **Roca, Sergio.** Cuban economic policy in the 1970s: the trodden paths (RU/SCID, 12:1, Spring 1977, p. 86–114)

Cuban experimentation with a "moral economy" in the 1960s led to dismal economic performance. In the 1970's, a new economic pragmatism brought drastic policy changes. The author traces the emerging dominance of this new economic policy in three major areas: 1) decentralization of planning and management; 2) utilization of traditional economic instruments (e.g., cost accounting, price policy); and 3) material incentives.

3077 **Rodríguez, Carlos Rafael.** Cuba en el tránsito al socialismo: 1959–1973. Lenín y la cuestión colonial. Mexico, Siglo XXI Editores, 1978. 233 p.

The first essay is an important contribution to the study of Cuban political and economic policies in the critical years 1959–63. According to the author, this essay is based on a series of lectures delivered at Havana Univ. in the 1960s. The lectures' notes originally limited to circulation in Cuban academic circles, are made public for the first time. Of particular interest are Rodríguez's interpretations of economic development and the nature of social classes in Cuba during the 1950s as well as of economic policies instituted by the Revolution in the early years. The book includes an appendix on the transformation of agriculture from capitalism to socialism. The second essay entitled "Lenín y la Cuestión Colonial," was published earlier in the journal *Casa de las Américas*.

3078 **Seers, Dudley.** Cuba (*in* Chenery, Hollis and others. Redistribution with growth. London, Oxford Univ. Press, 1974, p. 262–268)

Brief note on income distribution policies in revolutionary Cuba is included as an appendix in a book analyzing policies to improve income distribution in the developing countries in the context of economic growth. Author gives Cuba very high grades on achieving equitable income distribution but raises some questions on whether or not drastic redistribution policies, such as those implemented in Cuba, may interfere with economic growth.

3079 **Sheinin, Eduard.** Vínculos internacionales de la economía cubana (URSS/AL, 1, 1979, p. 100–112, table)

Soviet survey of Cuban economic relations with COMECON, capitalist and Third World nations in the 1970s. Emphasis is on Cuban relations with individual Eastern European COMECON members and with the USSR.

3080 Silva León, Arnaldo. Cuba y el mercado internacional azucarero. 2. ed. La Habana, Instituto Cubano del Libro, Editorial de Ciencias Sociales, 1975. 183 p.

Informative study of international aspects of the Cuban sugar industry from World War I to 1973. Author discusses significant developments in the world sugar market and their impact on the Cuban sugar industry. Of particular interest are chapters on the unsuccessful Cuban attempts to negotiate a world sugar agreement to stabilize prices in the 1920s and the special commercial relationship between Cuba and the US as a result of reciprocity agreements and the US sugar import quota programs after World War II. The last chapter deals with the Cuban sugar industry after the Revolution and up to the proposed 1973 International Sugar Agreement.

3081 Torres Verde, Félix. El pensamiento económico de Raúl Cepero Bonilla (UH/ED, 41, mayo/junio 1977, p. 85–119, tables)

Analysis of the economic thought of Cepero Bonilla, who served as Minister of Commerce and President of the Cuban National Bank under the revolutionary government until his accidental death in 1962, based on his writings in popular magazines and newspapers in the late 1950s and early 1960s. Essay deals primarily with Cepero Bonilla's thought on the Cuban sugar industry and international sugar agreements, compensatory finance, industrialization, agricultural policy and operation of a central bank and of state-supported credit institutions. The essay has also been released as a paperback book titled *El pensamiento económico de Raúl Cepero Bonilla* (La Habana, Editorial de Ciencias Sociales, 1977, 63 p.).

3082 United Nations. Consejo Económico y Social. Comisión Económica para América Latina (CEPAL). Apreciaciones sobre el estilo de desarrollo y sobre las principales políticas sociales en Cuba. México, 1978. 221 p. tables(CEPAL/MEX/77/22/Rev.3)

Ambitious study describes and attempts to evaluate economic and social

policies of the Cuban revolutionary development model. Based primarily on published official and unofficial materials and on several field visits. Chapter on economic policies emphasizes problems and accomplishments in the productive sectors and in foreign trade, consumption, distribution and prices and employment policies. Chapter on social policies deals with education, culture, sports, public health, social security and housing. Contains 48 tables prepared primarily using data from official statistical yearbooks.

3083 Universidad de La Habana. Instituto de Economía. Centro de Estudios Demográficos (CEDEM). La población de Cuba. La Habana, Instituto Cubano del Libro, Editorial de Ciencias Sociales, 1976. 236 p., maps, tables (Demografía)

Collection of ten essays on Cuban demography written by members of the Centro de Estudios Demográficos associated with Havana Univ. Essays deal with aspects of Cuban demography such as fertility, mortality, population growth, international migrations, composition of the population, internal migrations, labor force, population projections, etc.

3084 Volkov, Serguei. Acerca de la elección de la estructura de la economía nacional: la experiencia de Cuba (URSS/AL, 2, 1977, p. 55–72)

Soviet author reviews Cuban economic development strategies since 1959. Infers from the Cuban experience that substantive structural changes, such as the eradication of monocultivation, an objective of the early 1960s' policies cannot be undertaken in the short run. In fact, under socialist development, it may not be desirable to do away with monocultivation since specialization may become the engine of balanced economic growth. Suggests that the key to the development of Third World nations is the adoption of socialist principles and of the international division of labor and cooperation with the socialist countries.

3084a Werrett, Rosemary. Cuba at the turning point. N.Y., Business International Corporation, 1977. 142 p.

Although written primarily as a manual of foreign businessmen on how to do business with Cuba, it provides a very readable guide to the organization, accomplishments and future courses of the Cuban economy. Chapters assessing the state of the economy, on principal export products and on the experiences of Western corporations in commercial contacts with Cuba, are particularly interesting.

SPANISH SOUTH AMERICA
Colombia, Ecuador, and the Guianas

R. ALBERT BERRY, *Professor of Economics, University of Toronto*

TWO ASPECTS OF THE COLOMBIAN ECONOMY which are receiving increasing attention are foreign investment and technological dependence. Among the critical evaluations, the most complete is the one by Matter (item **3105**). Armendariz's view is stronger (item **3086**) while Junguito (item **3099**) undertakes a careful empirical analysis of the balance-of-payments effect and Fleet discusses aspects of the negotiation process (item **3092**). The symposium held by the Asociación Bancaria on the question of foreign indebtedness presented valuable and balanced views on the issue of technological dependence (item **3119**). This new focus might be interpreted as the result on the one hand of increased trade and foreign investment and, on the other, of relatively less concern with problems of growth given the impressive performance of the economy over more than a decade. Moreover, the concerns of these authors are reflected to a certain extent in government policy as is evident from the nationalization of foreign banks (item **3088**).

Marxist and dependency theorists have participated in the above literature and have also evolved interpretations of the development process as a whole as, for example, in Kalmanovitz's work (item **3101**) or in studies of the economic-power structure and monopoly characteristics of the sytem (items **3106** and **3118**).

Current additions to the literature also include two especially complete discussions of the development of the industrial sector by Poveda (item **3109**) and Wogart (item **3121**), and one on agriculture by Kalmanovitz (item **3100**). Ramírez's analysis of technological change in electricity generation is notably sophisticated (item **3110**) and Rivas' look at the cattle industry fills a serious information gap (item **3115**). Salazar de Fals raises the important specter of expulsion of small, independent farmers in the face of the expansion of capitalist agriculture (item **3115**) and Reyes' attacks the continuing social and economic costs of the latifundio system (item **3112**).

As would be expected, considerable attention remains focused on the problems of inflation. Musalem's analysis (item **3107**) is the most thorough but items **3087**, **3098**, and **3120** also contribute to the overall discussion while Pombo concentrates on an important product of inflation, the extra-bank credit market (item **3108**).

As Colombia becomes more urbanized, attention to problems associated with this process has increased. The two papers by Gilbert discuss urban planning and strategies in the post-war periods (items **3095** and **3096**); Losada Lora examines the unregulated urban land-market (item **3104**); and Revéis Roldán and others open an important area of research by analyzing the types and sources of information used in certain urban-policy discussions (item **3111**).

Other studies of special interest are those by Fields on education and mobility (item **3091**) and by Losada Lora on the political side of decentralized financial institutions (item **3103**).

As usual, the literature on Ecuador remains limited. There are, however, two useful items, one piece by Bromley which reviews the country's planning process (item **3122**) and Vega and Báez's review of the nation's development in the post-war period (item **3124**).

No worthwhile works on the economies of Guyana, Surinam or French Guiana have come to the attention of this reviewer. There is however, a French Government publication reviewed in the Bibliography and General Works section of this volume which contains a good general overview of the economy of French Guiana (see item **149**).

COLOMBIA

3085 Alfonso Díaz, Jorge. La política comercial colombiana y el GATT. Bogotá, Asociación Nacional de Instituciones Financieras, 1977. 202 p., bibl., tables (Biblioteca ANIF de economía)

Detailed review of the implications for Colombia of full membership in GATT, as compared to non membership or provisional membership. Favors the first alternative.

3086 Armendariz, Amadeo and **Teodosio Varela** eds. Imperialismo y dependencia económica en Colombia. Bogotá, Ediciones Armadillo, 1977. 170 p., tables (Biblioteca marxista colombiana, 2)

Marxist interpretations of foreign investment in Colombia, technology transfer from abroad, capital flight, foreign aid, and related topics.

3087 Asociación Nacional de Entidades Financieras, Bogotá. Dinero, precios, salarios. Bogotá, Ediciones Tercer Mundo, 1975. 151 p., bibl., tables (Biblioteca ANIF de economía)

A set of analyses of the inflationary process in Colombia and its causes.

3088 Boyce, James Edward and **François J. Lombard**. Colombia's treatment of foreign banks: a precedent setting case? Washington, American Enterprise Institute for Public Policy Research, 1976. 56 p., tables (Foreign affairs study, 36)

A review of the history of foreign banking in Colombia, leading up to a discussion of Decree 295 of 1975 whereby foreign banks were nationalized, including the reasons for this step.

3089 Camacho Roldán, Salvador. Escritos sobre economía y política. Selección, notas y prólogo de Jesús Antonio Bejarano. Bogotá, Instituto Colombiano de Cultura, Sub-

dirección de Comunicaciones Culturales, 1976. 268 p., bibl., tables (Biblioteca básica colombiana)

Writings on a variety of economic and political issues by one of Colombia's noted 19th-century writers.

Colombia. Instituto Geográfico Agustín Codazzi. Estudio social aplicado de la Alta y Media Guajira. See item **9209**.

3090 Dependencia y desarrollo. Bogotá, Asociación Nacional de Instituciones Financieras (ANIF), 1978. 215 p., tables (Biblioteca ANIF de economía)

Includes some useful essays on the nature and effects of foreign investment in Colombia.

3091 Fields, Gary S. Educación y movilidad económica en Colombia. Bogotá, Univ. de los Andes, Facultad de Economía, Centro de Estudios sobre Desarrollo Económico, 1977. 50 p., bibl., tables (Documento, 041)

Argues, on the basis of intergenerational data, that education is a vehicle for considerable upward mobility in Colombia.

3092 Fleet, Michael. Host country multinational relations in the Colombian automobile industry (IAMEA, 32:1, Summer 1978, p. 3–32)

Revealing review of the evolution of government multinational negotiations, emphasizing the lack of continuity on the government's side and its implications.

3093 Fundación Friedrich Naumann, Bogotá. Comercialización de comestibles en el Grupo Andino. Bogotá, 1975. 376 p., tables.

A series of essays on agrarian sectors and their possible roles in economic integration. Organized by country "positions" or "presentations." Nearly half is devoted to analyses of Colombia. [J.M. Hunter]

3094 Fundación para el Fomento de la Investigación Científica y Tecnológica (FICITEC), *Bogotá*. Empresarios colombianos: un nuevo contexto de desarrollo. Presentación de Misael Pastrana Borrero. Bogotá, 1976. 158 p., bibl., tables.

An attempt to organize a framework for the analysis of the entrepreneur and his role in development, based on a review of literature and a detailed look at a few Colombian cases.

Gauhan, Timothy O'Dea. Housing and the urban poor: the case of Bogotá, Colombia. See item **7282.**

3095 Gilbert, Alan. Bogotá: politics, planning and the crisis of lost opportunities (*in* Cornelius, Wayne A. and Robert V. Kemper *eds*. Metropolitan Latin America: the challenge and the response [see item **9016**] p. 87–126, bibl., illus., tables)

Discusses the problems of effective planning in Bogotá, with special reference to the recent "cities-within-the-city" approach and to the politics of urban planning.

3096 ———. Urban and regional development programs in Colombia since 1951 (*in* Cornelius, Wayne A. and Felicity M. Trueblood *eds*. Urbanization and inequality [see *HLAS 39:9016*] p. 241–275, bibl., maps, tables)

Observes that the regional decentralization programs of two recent Colombian governments have been too weak to achieve much effect; this may in part reflect the underdeveloped state of ideas on regional development.

3097 Griffin, Keith B. The political economy of agrarian change: an essay on the green revolution. Cambridge, Mass., Harvard Univ. Press, 1974. 265 p., tables.

An essay on technical change in Asia and Latin America (Colombia, Mexico) which argues most of the benefits accrue mostly to prosperous people and prosperous regions, and, further, to urban industrialization. This occurs through biased technical change, market imperfections, government policy. [J.M. Hunter]

Grimes, Orville F., Jr. and Gill C. Lim. Employment, land values and the residential choice of low-income households: the case of Bogotá, Colombia. See item **9214.**

Guhl, Ernesto. Colombia: bosquejo de su geografía tropical. See item **5502.**

3098 Harf, Morris. Algunas determinantes de la inflación reciente en Colombia: 1971–1976 (BCV/REL, 13:50, 1977, p. 79–146, tables)

A review of the role of a number of possible sources of the bout of inflation suffered by Colombia since the early 1970s.

Instituto de Estudios Colombianos (IEC), *Bogotá*. Los llanos orientales de Colombia: estudio descriptivo. See item **5506.**

3099 Junguito, Nohra de. Efecto de la inversión extranjera sobre la balanza de pagos en Colombia. Bogotá, Univ. de los Andes, Facultad de Economía, Centro de Estudios sobre Desarrollo Económico, 1974. 71 p., bibl., tables (Documento CEDE, 015)

Careful estimate of the effects of foreign investment on the balance of payments, with an analysis of the effect on it of the Foreign Investment Decree of 1971.

3100 Kalmanovitz, Salomón. Desarrollo de la agricultura en Colombia. Bogotá, Editorial La Carreta, 1978. 360 p., tables (Libros de la carreta)

The most complete look at trends in agricultural output and incomes to date, including detailed statistics on individual products, wages, etc.

3101 ———. Ensayos sobre el desarrollo del capitalismo dependiente. Bogotá, Editorial Pluma, 1977. 216 p., tables.

Interpretations of the postwar evolution of Colombia's economy in Marxist-Leninist terms, criticizing various lines of thought and attempting to interpret Marxian thought in the Colombian context.

3102 López Arias, César Augusto. Empresas multinacionales. Bogotá, Ediciones Tercer Mundo, 1977. 195 p., bibl. (Col. Universidad y pueblo, 17)

Considerable data on the Colombian case. Well documented. Distinctly "anti." [J.M. Hunter]

3103 Losada Lora, Rodrigo. Los institutos descentralizados de carácter financiero: aspectos políticos del caso colombiano. Bogotá, Fundación para la Educación Superior y el Desarrollo (FEDESARROLLO), 1973. 26 p.

Discussion of the role of decentralized

agencies in Colombia, an increasingly important phenomenon. Focuses on the reasons for their growth and the nature of political influences on them.

3104 ——— and **Hernando Gómez Buendía.** La tierra en el mercado pirata de Bogotá. Bogotá, Fundación para la Educación Superior y el Desarrollo (FEDESARROLLO), 1976. 224 p., maps, tables.

A detailed study of the important phenomenon of illegal housing in Bogotá and the functioning of the land market on which this housing is constructed.

3105 Matter, Konrad. Inversiones extranjeras en la economía colombiana. Traducción de Luis Bernardo Flórez E. Presentación de Alvaro Tirado Mejía. Medellín, Colombia, Ediciones Hombre Nuevo, 1977. 407 p., bibl., tables (Serie sobre historia de Colombia, 3)

A study of the effects of foreign investment in Colombia, looking at the balance-of-payments effect, indirect benefits, etc. Reaches a generally negative conclusion.

3106 Melo, Héctor and **Ivan López B.** El imperio clandestino del café. Bogotá, Editorial Latina, 1976. 195 p., tables.

Studies the power of the Federación Nacional de Cafeteros through the delegation of unusual powers and privileges by the government to it and relates this to the uneven distribution of the economic benefits from the coffee industry.

3107 Musalem, Alberto Roque. Dinero, inflación y balanza de pagos: la experiencia de Colombia en la post-guerra. Bogotá, Banco de la República, 1971. 189 p., bibl., tables.

A sophisticated monetarist interpretation of price and balance of payments developments.

3108 Pombo Holguín, Joaquín de. Algunos aspectos del mercado libre de dinero en Colombia. Bogotá, Fundación para la Educación Superior y el Desarrollo (FEDESARROLLO), 1973. 68 p., tables.

Describes the extra bank credit market and attributes it to the low real rate of interest in the organized market.

3109 Poveda Ramos, Gabriel. Políticas económicas, desarrollo industrial y tecnología en Colombia: 1925–1975. Bogotá, Ministerio de Educación Nacional, Fondo Colombiano de Investigaciones Científicas y Proyectos Especiales Francisco José de Caldas (COLCIENCIAS), 1976. 163 p., bibl., fold. tables, tables (Serie proyecto de mecanismos e instrumentos)

A detailed history of Colombia's industrial sector, of public policy towards it and of key technological innovations during 1925–75. In the latter two respects, the most complete study available.

3110 Ramírez Gómez, Manuel. Cambio tecnológico en la industria de energía eléctrica en Colombia (UCC/CE, 11:32, enero 1974, p. 43–74, bibl., tables)

Useful analysis of the process of technological change in the thermal generation of electricity. Finds that the improvements are embodied in imported equipment but that in the process of repairing it, modifications towards greater use of labor are effected.

3111 Revéiz Roldán, Edgar and others. Poder e información: el proceso decisorio en tres casos de política regional y urbana en Colombia. Bogotá, Univ. de Los Andes, Facultad de Economía, Centro de Estudios sobre Desarrollo Económico (CEDE) *con la colaboración* del Depto. de Ciencia Política *y de la* Facultad de Ingeniería, 1977. 425 p., bibl., fold. tables, illus., tables.

The first in-depth study of how information at the disposal of various interested groups affects the public decision-making process, based on three case studies.

3112 Reyes Posada, Alejandro. Latifundio y poder político: la hacienda ganadera en Sucre. Bogotá, Editorial CINEP (Centro de Investigación y Educación Popular), 1978. 183 p., bibl., tables (Serie Colombia agraria, 2)

A history of the latifundio in Colombia, its political place in the system and the recent conflict with the pressures for agrarian reform.

3113 Rivas Ríos, Libardo. Some aspects of the cattle industry on the North Coast Plains of Colombia. Foreword by Per Pinstrup-Andersen. Cali, Colombia, Centro Internacional de Agricultura Tropical (CIAT), 1974. 142 p., bibl., maps, tables (Technical bulletin, 3)

Useful contribution to the limited information on the cattle industry, based on survey data. Identifies problems whose resolution could make the industry more productive.

3114 Rosenberg, Terry J. Individual and regional influences on the employment of Colombian women (WRU/JMF, 38:2, May 1976, p. 339–353, bibl., map, tables)

Argues, on the basis of regional comparisons of female labour force participation, that local sex-role ideologies play a major role (relative to economic and demographic factors) in determining female participation rates.

3115 Salazar de Fals, María Cristina. La expansión del capitalismo en el campo: sus consecuencias en la zona cafetera, Colombia y el Departamento del Tolima. Bogotá, Oficina de Investigaciones Socioeconómicas y Legales (OFISEL), 1973. 1 v. (Various pagings) bibl., tables (Documentos, 1)

Argues that the expansion of capitalist agriculture in Tolima has led recently to the expulsion of small producers and their conversion into a rural proletariat.

3116 Seminario de Economía Colombiana, *II, Bogotá, 1976.* Controversias sobre economía colombiana. Introducción de Rodrigo Manrique M. Bogotá, Univ. Externado de Colombia, 1976. 308 p., tables.

A set of essays on a variety of topics including inflation, urban growth and education.

3117 Seminario Nacional de Desarrollo Rural, *I, Bogotá, 1976.* El agro en el desarrollo histórico colombiano: ensayos de economía política. Presentación de Francisco Leal Buitrago. Bogotá, Editorial Punta de Lanza [and] Univ. de Los Andes, Depto. de Ciencia Política, 1977. 379 p., bibl., fold. tables, tables.

Essays presented as a symposium which discuss a wide range of issues in the political economy of Colombian agriculture, e.g. the effects of La Violencia on agriculture, the applicability of wage legislation in agriculture.

3118 Silva Colmenares, Julio. Los verdaderos dueños del país: oligarquía y monopolios en Colombia. Bogotá, Fondo Editorial Suramérica, 1977. 343 p., tables.

A detailed review by sector or indus-

try of the major firms and their characteristics, with a view of understanding the power structure in the economy.

3119 Simposio sobre Financiamiento Externo, *I, Medellín, Colombia, 1977.* Financiamiento externo: 1977. Bogotá, Banco de la República [and] Asociación Bancaria de Colombia, 1977. 393 p., tables.

Papers on a number of aspects of foreign indebtedness in Colombia and its relation to development.

3120 Simposio sobre Mercado de Capitales, *III, Medellín, Colombia, 1974.* El mercado de capitales en Colombia: 1974. Prefacio de Oscar Alviar y Jorge Marmorek. Bogotá, Banco de la República [and] Asociación Bancaria de Colombia (ABC), 1975. 238 p., map, tables.

Second in a useful series of published symposia on the capital market in Colombia. Papers on monetary policy, development banks, the effects of the foreign sector on economic policy.

Thomas, Larry P. The Colombian Supreme Court decision on the Andean Foreign Investment Code and its implications for the Law of Treaties. See item **8895.**

Walton, John. Elites and economic development: comparative studies on the political economy of Latin America cities. See item **2979.**

3121 Wogart, Jan Peter. Industrialization in Colombia: policies, patterns, perspectives. Tübingen, FGR, Univ. Kiel, Institut für Weltwirtschaft, 1978. 176 p., bibl., tables (Kieler studien, 153)

Informative review of the industrialization process, through the import substitution stage to the more export oriented development of recent years.

ECUADOR

3122 Bromley, R.J. Development and planning in Ecuador. London, Latin American Publications Fund [and] Univ. of Sussex, Centre for Development Studies, Sussex, U.K., 1977. 116 p., bibl., maps, tables.

Major review of economic conditions in Ecuador, focusing on dependence on developed countries, unequal income distribution and relatively little serious planning. Argues that recent oil based growth has brought little "development" in the sense of spread effects to the population as a whole.

Ecuador. Instituto Ecuatoriano de Reforma Agraria y Colonización (IERAC). La regionalización para la reforma agraria. See item 5826.

Guerrero, Andrés. Renta diferencial y vías de disolución de la hacienda precapitalista en el Ecuador. See item 9225.

3123 Inotai, András. The possibilities and limits of a balanced and harmonious development in the Andean integration. Budapest, The Hungarian Academy of Sciences, Institute of World Economics, 1975. 64 p., tables (Studies on developing countries, 80)

Examines the potential for harmonious, balanced growth between nations as sought by the Andean group—particularly for Bolivia, Ecuador. Is skeptical. [J. M. Hunter]

3124 Vega Moreno, Néstor and Gonzalo Báez D. Panorama de la situación económica del Ecuador en 1976. Quito, Ediciones Nueva Asociación de Empresarios (NADE), 1977. 52 p., tables.

Reviews development over 1950–76 in Ecuador and current problems and prospects.

Villacres Moscoso, Jorge W. Geoeconomía internacional del estado ecuatoriano. See item 8905.

Zuvekas, Clarence, Jr. Agrarian reform in Ecuador's Guayas River Basin. See item 5539.

GUYANA

Barnett, D. and P.A. Della Valle. An analysis of sugar production in a changing political environment. See item 7255.

Vining, James W. Presettlement planning in Guyana. See item 5541.

Venezuela

JORGE SALAZAR-CARRILLO, *Advisor and Technical Coordinator, Estudios Conjuntos sobre Integración Económica Latinoamericana (ECIEL), The Brookings Institution with the assistance of the ECIEL staff*

IN 1977 AND 1978 VENEZUELA CONTINUED to benefit from the boom generated by the rise in oil prices. Nevertheless, its economy displayed symptoms characteristic of the OPEC countries, despite the fact that Venezuela is the more developed member of the organization. Among these symptoms are the phenomenon of oil expansion overrunning the country's absorptive capacity with the result that a large proportion of the injection of funds is either recycled or squandered. Moreover, even funds effectively absorbed in projects which increase productive capacity are also hampered by lags in incrementing output. This, in turn, drastically diminished the foreign exchange surplus of the OPEC countries on a current account basis.

The same lag is observable in the economic literature. The expansive trend noted in volumes 37 and 39 of the *Handbook*, and corresponding to publications of the 1973–76 period, has lost much of its momentum. Perhaps, as with the country's economy, some of the investments in infrastructure, equipment, and human resources which began in 1975 will bear fruit in research and publications to appear in the 1979–81 period.

Another reason for the paucity of rigorous economic research reported in this volume is the late receipt of Venezuelan materials at the Library of Congress, a problem which prevents determination of trends. Moreover, the serious cutback in publications announced by the prestigious Venezuelan publishing house, Monteávila Editores, is an additional cause for concern. Monteávila was one of the few independent publishers of serious economic studies. Despite the country's economic bonanza, it appears as if Monteávila is cutting back because of "financial woes." As a result, the burden of publishing has now fallen on institutions that were referred to in volumes 37 and 39 of the *Handbook*. Strong support was provided by the Central Bank of Venezuela and the economic departments of the Univ. Central de Venezuela. Other institutions have played a less important but commendable publishing role: the Ministry of Finance; CORDIPLAN (the Planning Office); the Ministry of Energy and Mines; the Catholic Univ. Andrés Bello; and the Univ. de los Andes in Mérida. After the demise of *Economía y Ciencias Sociales* and the aborted birth of *Nueva Ciencia*, both issued by the Economics Faculty of the Univ. Central, one welcomed the rebirth of the *Revista de Hacienda*, edited by the Finance Ministry. The Central Bank's *Revista de Economía Latinoamericana* has maintained the standards which make it the best economic periodical in Venezuela. It should be noted that this journal devotes a substantial (albeit smaller) portion to articles on Latin American economic conditions. One would welcome additional periodicals and it appears as if the Central Bank is planning to reissue a journal which was discontinued sometime ago.

As to the topics of works annotated below, not surprisingly the oil question has regained importance. Other themes concern inflation, monetary management, macroeconomic policies, and foreign and domestic investment. A change is also evident at the Univ. Central where there is a less ideological and more research-oriented approach in the examination of the structure of the economy. Otherwise, there is much continuity with the mid-1970s in the choice of themes. The overall quality improvement noted in 1973–76 seems to have leveled off in the 1977–78 period.

To conclude, I would like to express my gratitude to the researchers who aided in covering the now vast Venezuelan economic literature: Roberto Correia Lima, Germinal Domínguez, Doreen Ellen Metzner and Angela Pinto. Their initials appear after their annotations; the rest were written by the author.

3125 Acosta-Hermoso, Eduardo Arturo. Petroquímica: ¿desastre o realidad? Caracas, Editorial Binev, 1977. 218 p., bibl., tables.

History of the process of creating and developing the petrochemical industry of Venezuela; the vicissitudes and alternatives that had to be faced. It reveals also the mistakes made, and what was not accomplished due to political and partisan compromises. [G.D.]

3126 Alezones, Ricardo. Reforma agraria: recursos y niveles de ingreso. Caracas, Univ. Central de Venezuela, Centro de Estudios del Desarrollo (CENDES), n.d. 157 p., tables (Serie 1. Documentos de trabajo, 22)

Attempts to show how the economic results obtained by the beneficiaries of the Venezuelan agrarian reform were related to the availability of the different means of production, and the way those resources were combined and utilized. [R.L.L.]

3127 Aranda, Sergio. La economía venezolana: una interpretación de su modo

de funcionamiento. Bogotá, Siglo XXI Editores, 1977. 294 p., bibl., tables.

Analysis of the Venezuelan economy from the 1920s to the present which describes the policies and economic factors which determined its performance and historical evolution. Author also examines the place of Venezuela in the world economy and defines the new period which began in 1974. Contains 112 statistical tables. [R.P.]

3128 Asociación Pro-Venezuela, Caracas. Denuncia y comercio exterior: la denuncia del Tratado con los Estados Unidos y el comercio exterior venezolano. Caracas, 1972. 270 p., tables.

Analysis of the problems which Venezuela, as an underdeveloped country, had to face in its dealing with foreign markets. According to the author, these problems became more evident after the denunciation of the commercial treaty with the US. [A.P.]

3129 Azpúrua Q., Pedro Pablo. 25 [i.e. Veinticinco] de 35. Presentación de Francisco G. Aguerrevere and Juan José Bolinaga I. Caracas, Editorial Latina, 1975. 408 p., tables.

A selection of the author's speeches, essays and papers written during the last 25 years. They deal with the administration of aqueducts, urbanism, investment of public funds and the utilization of hydraulic resources in Venezuela. [A.P.]

3130 —— and **Cecilia Sosa de Mendoza.** Venezuela: bases de una política hidráulica. Caracas, Editorial Latina, 1972. 136 p., tables.

Prepared by the technicians of Venezuela's Water Resources National Planning Commission, known as COPLANARH (its Spanish acronym), as a justification of a water resources law. This joint undertaking was led by Pedro Pablo Azpurua, who has had a long experience in water resources planning, and has written numerous books and articles on the subject. It illustrates the use of water resources planning and management principles. Includes English summary.

Badari, V.S. Disaggregation of urban populations into modern and traditional categories: a methodological note and application of Venezuela. See item **5565.**

3131 Banco Central de Venezuela (BCV), *Caracas.* Informe económico: 1975. 1 v. (Various pagings) tables.

This yearly publication constitutes the economic report of the Central Bank of Venezuela. It consists of an overview of the country's economic performance in 1975, in comparison with the previous year; an analysis of the financial and real aspects of this performance, emphasizing price movements, government functions and international economic relations. Includes a statistical annex covering the 1971–75 period, and a synthesis of economic legislation.

3132 ——, ——. Memoria especial: correspondiente al período 1971–1975. Presentación de Benito Raúl Losada. Caracas, 1975? 305 p., tables.

A comprehensive synthesis of Venezuela's economic development process which appraises economic and financial facts throughout successive annual reports (1971–75). [R.P.]

3133 ——, ——. Metodología de las cuentas nacionales de Venezuela: ver-

sión resumida. Caracas, 1976. 259 p.

An interesting report which describes the most important aspects of the methodology currently in use by Venezuela's Central Bank for the preparation of national accounts, adapted to the new system proposed by the UN. Also discusses methods, calculations and problems which arise in the attempt to apply standardized models to developing countries. [R.P.]

Betancourt, Rómulo. Venezuela's oil. See item **8773.**

3134 Boscán de Ruesta, Isabel. El "holding" en la organización del sector económico público. Presentación de Eduardo Ramírez López. Caracas, Procuraduría General de la República, 1975. 67 p., bibl., table (Col. de estudios especiales, 1)

Description of the holding as an organizational instrument of the public sector, and its perspectives in Venezuela. Includes an analysis of the structure and function of holdings in the public sector, how they work, and what are the necessary conditions for their operation, as well as their contribution to entrepreneurship in the public sector. [A.P.]

3135 Campbell, Pedro. En torno a la industrialización de los recursos naturales tomando como caso ejemplar el petróleo (NSO, 14, sept./oct. 1974, p. 12–23, tables)

A rather confusing attempt to combine various ecological and developmental strands related to non-renewable resources in order to present a plea for rationality, emphasizing human resources in planning the future growth of the nations of the world.

3136 Casas González, Antonio. Venezuela: una economía en transformación. Caracas, Oficina Central de Coordinación y Planificación (CORDIPLAN), 1972? 30 p.

Brief description of Venezuelan economic and social policies discusses considerations about more rational and effective planning for the country's development. [A.P.]

3137 Chaves Vargas, Luis Fernando. Proceso y patrón espacial de la urbanización en Venezuela durante el período 1961–1971. Mérida, Ven., Univ. de Los Andes, Facultad de Ciencias Forestales, Instituto de Geografía y Conservación de Recursos Naturales, 1974. 69 p., bibl., fold. maps, fold. tables, maps, tables.

In the Venezuelan university system it is customary for a professor to prepare research essays when opting for a higher rank. This research on Venezuelan urbanization in the 1960s was prepared in that context at the Univ. of Los Andes.

3138 5 [i.e. Cinco] años de cambio: pacificación y desarrollo en el gobierno de Rafael Caldera, 1969–1974. Caracas, Gráficas Armitano, 1975. 325 p., colored plates, facsim., plates, tables.

A panegyric of the Christian Democratic administration of President Caldera during the 1969–74 period. Its stated purpose is to provide a succinct view of the development of the country during his administration. It also includes Caldera's last two presidential messages.

3139 Corporación Venezolana de Guayana (CVG), *Caracas*. Informe anual: 1975. Caracas, 1975? 260 p., colored illus., colored plates, illus., maps, plates, tables.

This study deals with the CVG group annual report. The CVG is a multi-sectoral industrial conglomerate which, by the end of 1975, had achieved second place in Venezuela's economic life, i.e. 4.55 percent of the gross domestic product, second only to the oil industry. [R.P.]

3140 *Cuadernos de la C.V.F.* Corporación Venezolana de Fomento. No. 1, 1974–. Caracas.

An issue of one of the oldest economic periodicals of Venezuela. It has articles on natural resources and industry. The authors are technicians of the CVF (Corporación Venezolana de Fomento or Venezuelan Development Corporation). The contributions are descriptive.

3141 Dufumier, Marc. L'agriculture au Venezuela (FDD/NED [Problèmes d'Amérique Latine, 47] 4457, fév. 1978, p. 113–128, tables)

Historical analysis of the development and crisis of the Venezuelan agrarian sector; its colonial background, the intervention of the state, particularly the Agrarian Reform Law as well as the capitalistic development of the country's agriculture, and its more recent manifestation: agro-industrial integration. [G.D.]

3142 *Economía y Ciencias Sociales.* Univ. Central de Venezuela. Facultad de Cien-

cias Económicas y Sociales. Año 16, Nos. 3/4, junio/dic. 1974–. Caracas.

Special issue devoted to discussing an econometric model for measuring change in the social sciences. Author examines the formulation and application of this econometric model and compares this approach with that of historical materialism. Regards both as equally valid gauges for estimating the development of a society. [G.D.]

Eidt, Robert C. Agrarian reform and the growth of new rural settlements in Venezuela. See item **5571.**

3143 Flores Díaz, Max. Sentido y proyección de la política económica gubernamental (UCV/NC, 1:1, enero/abril 1975, p. 227–251)

Article based on a presentation given at the Univ. Central de Venezuela which analyzes the economic policies of the initial period of the Carlos Andrés Pérez Administration. Author questions the possibilities of attaining the stated goals and places the policies in the context of the basic socioeconomic characteristics of Venezuelan society. After considering the economy's major problems, author concludes that even though the policies have been numerous, implementation has been deficient.

3144 Fondo de Inversiones de Venezuela (FIV), *Caracas.* Memoria anual: 1975. Caracas, 1976. 136 p., tables.

Consists of annual report of activities of the FIV (Venezuela's Investment Fund). Includes profit and loss and balance statements, as well as other supporting documents. A statement of financial programming for 1975–80 is also part of the report. This agency was created by Venezuela for medium and long-term investment of its windfall gains from the increase in the price of oil.

3145 González-Gorrondona, José Joaquín. Una estrategia para el desarrollo económica y social de Venezuela. Caracas, Impresos Garamond, 1975. 147 p., bibl., tables.

Examines traces that are characteristic of the Venezuelan economy, as well as complex problems that must be overcome for it to achieve a faster growth rate. [R.C.L.]

3146 González Naranjo, Carlos. La inflación reciente en Venezuela (BCV/REL, 13:50, 1977, p. 273–299, tables)

Study seeks to find an explanation for the low rate of inflation in Venezuela prior to 1973, and to the high rate of change of prices after that date. For this purpose the preceding period should be subdivided into post-war years and 1960s.

3147 Hernández D., Carlos and **Oswaldo Rodríguez L.** Las reservas internacionales en divisas del Banco Central de Venezuela. Caracas, Banco Central de Venezuela, 1977. 53 p., bibl., tables (Col. Ernesto Peltzer)

Methodological essay attempts to determine what share of shortrun reserves should be kept in perfectly liquid form (bills and current deposits). Econometrics is used in the estimation of reserve levels and composition. This monograph was awarded the Peltzer prize.

3148 La inflación: un problema de nuestra época. Caracas, Asociación Pro-Venezuela, 1975. 169 p., tables.

Study, sponsored by the Pro-Venezuela Assn. and covering period 1972 through the oil crisis, consists of a great number of ideas and proposals on the nature and control of inflation. Among the subjects analyzed are: foreign trade and its inflationary projections; monetary inflation and forms of propagation; countervailing factors; mechanisms of international economic policy; mechanisms of domestic economic policy; etc. Study also examines traditional measures of economic policy designed to combat inflation (e.g., reduction of effective demands via unemployment; limitations on public spending; monetary controls, etc.). Includes 56 statistical charts. [R.P.]

3149 Izard, Miguel and others. Política y economía en Venezuela: 1810–1976. Presentación de Alfredo Boulton. Caracas, Fundación John Boulton, 1976. 292 p., bibls., tables.

Consists of a compilation of essays written since the independence of Venezuela and arranged in chronological order. They examine the interplay of economic and political strands in the history of the country. The authors are mostly historians, some Venezuelans, some Americans. Only the last chapter is written by a well-known economist and public figure, J.A. Mayobre.

3150 Jongking, Fred. Informe sobre la investigación de la gran y mediana industria manufacturera en Venezuela; la participación nacional y extranjera en la industria: resultados parciales y preliminares. Caracas, Instituto de Estudios Superiores de Administración (IESA), 1977. 13 l., tables.

Study of industrial development in Venezuela which analyzes and compares national and foreign participation in the country's industrialization process. [A.P.]

3151 Kobrin, Stephen J. and **Donald R. Lessard.** Large scale direct OPEC investment in industrialized countries and the theory of foreign direct investment: a contradiction? (CAUK/WA, 112:4, 1976, p. 660–673, table)

The accumulation of wealth by oil exporting countries has given rise to the recycling of these assets throughout the world. The author discusses the theory and evidence of this phenomenon and concludes that such capital flows will favor portfolio rather than direct investment. The exception to this will be countries where opportunities for portfolio investment do not exist.

3152 Lange S., Augusto. Cooperación Financiera Internacional de Venezuela (BCV/REL, 13:51, 1978, p. 35–78, tables)

Comprehensive survey of the various schemes of financial cooperation in which Venezuela is involved. Some of these concern the country's participation in LAFTA and the Andean group. Others arise from the massive reserves accumulated since the oil price rise in 1973. Funds flowed into international institutions, regional organizations and/or particular countries, chiefly in Central America and the Caribbean.

3153 Losada Aldana, Ramón. La tierra venezolana en la dialéctica del subdesarrollo. t. 1. Caracas, Univ. Central de Venezuela, Facultad de Ciencias Económicas y Sociales, División de Publicaciones, 1976. 262 p., tables.

Intensive study of the agricultural problems of underdeveloped countries focuses on Venezuela and its agrarian reform. This book is the translation of a Ph.D. thesis presented at the Univ. of Paris in 1971 under the title Venezuela: terre et société. [R.C.L.]

Mamalakis, Markos. The new international economic order. See item **8839.**

3154 Marin Salazar, Jesús. Participación de la Corporación Venezolana de Fomento en el desarrollo agroindustrial de Venezuela. Caracas, Corporación Venezolana de Fomento (CVF), 1976. 32 p., plates, tables.

Consists of a synopsis of the contributions of this development corporation to the agroindustrial development of the country in the 1958–73 period. During these years, CVF's lending was heavily concentrated in the sugar industry, with rice and cotton as distant seconds. Also includes an outline of the corporation's 1975–79 economic program.

3155 Martínez, Aníbal R. Gumersindo Torres. Caracas, Presidencia de la República, 1975. 239 p., plates.

A biography of Gumersindo Torres, the first political leader who attempted to regulate the first exploitation of Venezuelan petroleum. [R.C.L.]

3156 Martínez Infante, Angel B. El presupuesto empresarial: condiciones para la instalación de un sistema presupuestario. 3. ed. Caracas, Univ. Central de Venezuela, Facultad de Ciencias Económicas y Sociales, División de Publicaciones, 1976. 67 p., bibl., tables (Col. Esquema)

Short essay examines the requirements and basic elements for operation of an efficient budgeting system in private firms. Author reviews purposes of such a system with regard to planning, coordination and control. The treatment seems somewhat dated and superficial.

Martz, John D. Policy-making and the quest for consensus: nationalizing Venezuelan petroleum. See item **7625**.

3157 Mata Mollejas, Luis. Decisión e inversión: ocho temas fundamentales para la toma de decisiones en la actividad económica. Prólogo de Carlos Acedo Mendoza. Caracas, Equinoccio, Editorial de la Univ. Simón Bolívar, 1977. 231 p., tables (Col. Parametros)

University undergraduate-level textbook which attempts to establish a quantitative analysis of the decision-making process involved in foreign investment and its inherent difficulties, risks and uncertainties. Author presents an entire process of calculation and evaluation for potential investors faced with two or more alternatives. [D.E.M.]

3158 ———. La revolución petrolera y la política venezolana (BCV/REL, 13:49, 1977, p. 91–114)

Analysis of the 1973–74 "oil revolution" and the world's political and economic system. The use of oil supply as a trump card in international relations by oil-exporting nations is discussed, as well as the inability of the major western oil-importing nations (US and EEC countries) to formulate a common strategy in dealing with OPEC. It is seen that both the USSR and the US have reaped certain economic benefits from the OPEC revolution. Several suggestions are put forth for the formulation of a Venezuelan oil-exportation policy, principally the establishment and strengthening of the necessary domestic intelligence centers, in order to prevent the marginalization of Venezuela in the development of an international oil policy. [D.E.M.]

3159 Maza Zavala, Domingo Felipe. Análisis macroeconómico. Caracas, Univ. Central de Venezuela, 1976. 606 p., bibl., tables (Ediciones de la biblioteca, 29. Col. Ciencias sociales, 11)

Introductory book on macroeconomic theory, with special interest on the theories of consumption, investment, income distribution and balance of payments. Includes an essay on the capital-product relation, and a summary of the major macroeconomic theories in the history of economic thought. [R.C.L.]

3160 Mendoza, Rafael Martínez. Breves consideraciones sobre el sistema tributario de Venezuela (ACPS/B, 36:71, oct./dic. 1977, p. 197–265, tables)

Reproduction of a speech delivered by a Venezuelan fiscalist to the Academy of Political and Social Sciences, in the late 1910s. Supports the tax changes undertaken by the Gómez Administration. It recommends several changes in tariff laws, and makes interesting and illustrative reading, on how these matters were analyzed at the time.

3161 Nueva Ciencia. Univ. Central de Venezuela, Facultad de Economía, Instituto de Investigaciones. Año 1, No. 1, enero/abril 1975–. Caracas.

First issue of new serial published by the Univ. Central's Institute of Economic and Social Research and designed to present the institute's collective thought as did its defunct predecessor *Economía y Ciencias Sociales*. However, most of the articles in this issue are based on lectures given at the institute and have already appeared elsewhere and been reviewed in previous *HLAS*.

3162 ———. ———. Año 2, No. 2, marzo 1977–. Caracas.

Second and apparently last (?) issue of this serial (see item **3161**) which in three years managed to publish only two numbers. The ideological style characteristic of the writings of past members of the institute continues to dominate the work of current contributors to this second issue.

3163 Panorama de la economía venezolana en: el primer trimestre de 1976; el segundo trimestre de 1976; el tercer trimestre de 1976; el período enero/junio de 1977 (BCV/REL, 12:46, 1976, p. 7–38, tables; 12:47, 1977, p. 7–36, tables; 12:48, 1977, p. 7–34, tables; 13:51, 1978, p. 7–34, tables)

Each issue of the *Revista de la Economía Latinoamericana* (see item **3166**), published by the Central Bank of Venezuela, publishes these quarterly assessments ("panoramas") of the country's economy. The above title refers to four different issues of the magazine. The evaluation of the first quarter of 1976 concludes that the economy continued to expand although at a lower rate given the decrease in oil exports. The analysis of the second quarter of 1977 is chiefly devoted to monetary, fiscal, financial and balance-of-payment indicators. The assessment of the third quarter of 1976 detects some trouble signs in the expansive cycle, especially in the money-market and balance-of-payment areas. The evaluation of the months of Jan./June of 1977 notes a continuation of the expansive performance of the oil economy, that began after the large oil price increase in 1973. These quarterly assessments are useful for those interested in the short-run macroeconomic performance of the Venezuelan economy. For more on this excellent economic journal, see item **3166**.

3164 Pérez Alfonzo, Juan Pablo. Hundiéndonos en el excremento del diablo. Prólogo de Francisco Mieres. Illustraciones de Regulo Pérez. 2. ed. Caracas, Editorial Lisbona, 1976. 375 p., illus., plates, tables (Col. Venezuela contemporánea)

The author criticizes Venezuela's official policy on petroleum and other related matters, as well as its participation in OPEC. He also makes an evaluation of the effects the energy crisis has had in the western world. [A.P.]

Petras, James F.; Morris Morley; and **Steven Smith.** The nationalization of Venezuelan oil. See item **8855**.

3165 Rangel, Domingo Alberto. Capital y desarrollo. t. 2, El rey petróleo. 2. ed. Caracas, Univ. Central de Venezuela, Facultad de Ciencias Económicas y Sociales, División de Publicaciones, 1977. 417 p., tables (Col. Libros)

First ed. published 1970. This analysis of Venezuela's social and economic patterns in the period between the two World Wars examines the importance of petroleum in the country's economic growth. [A.P.]

3166 *Revista de Economía Latinoamericana.* Banco Central de Venezuela. Año 14, No. 55, 1979–. Caracas.

A recent issue of perhaps the best economic journal published in Venezuela. It usually includes an initial article which summarizes the short-run macroeconomic performance of the Venezuelan economy (see item **3163**). This journal also publishes worthwhile contributions on Latin America and relevant international economic affairs. Another useful economic journal for Venezuela is *Revista de Hacienda* (see item **3167**).

3167 *Revista de Hacienda.* Ministerio de Hacienda. Año 40, No. 67, abril/junio 1977 [and] Año 41, No. 72, julio/sept. 1978–. Caracas.

Like *Revista de Economía Latinoamericana* (see item **3166**) this is another excellent economic journal put out by an official Venezuelan agency, in this case, the Ministry of Finance. Suspended for eight years, the journal resumes publication with issue No. 67 and some measure of success. No. 67 consists of four articles which discuss the fiscal and financial contributions of oil in light of nationalization of the industry and the increasing importance of OPEC. The only contribution by a non-Venezuelan is N. Kaldor's piece on the subject of fiscal reform. No. 72 includes valuable contributions by specialists from both the Ministry of Finance and the Central Bank of Venezuela.

3168 Rico López, Darío. Análisis de estados financieros: banca comercial. Caracas, Univ. Central de Venezuela, Facultad de Ciencias Económicas y Sociales, División de Publicaciones, 1976. 80 p., bibl., tables (Col. Esquema)

Monograph analyzes the financial statements of the commercial banking sector, in terms of various indicators. It describes the activities of these banks in Venezuela, and explains their financial statements. The word "analysis" in the title refers to Venezuelan conditions.

3169 Rodríguez, Policarpo. Petróleo en Venezuela ayer y hoy. Prólogo de D.F. Maza Zavala. Caracas, Univ. Central de Venezuela, Facultad de Ciencias Económicas y Sociales, División de Publicaciones, 1977. 163 p., bibl., tables (Col. Libros)

Interesting study which analyzes both the performance and growth of the Venezuelan economy while under the influence of the foreign exploitation of domestic oil. It carefully examines aspects such as: the process of concession and nationalization; returned benefits and oil surpluses; the petroleum model of the Venezuelan economy; the real absorption of recent petroleum surpluses; and finally, the objectives and goals of nationalization. [R.P.]

3170 Rodríguez Campos, Manuel. Venezuela, 1902: la crisis fiscal y el bloqueo; perfil de una soberanía vulnerada. Caracas, Univ. Central de Venezuela, Facultad de Humanidades y Educación, 1977. 453 p., bibl., facsim., tables.

A study of the circumstances that caused Venezuela's involvement in the conflict of 1902 when the country became the focus of a jurisdictional (i.e. areas-of-influence) confrontation between European powers and the US. The author questions the assumption made at the time that nationalism was the chief motivation of Cipriano Castro. [R.C.L.]

3171 Salazar-Carrillo, Jorge. Comparaciones de valor y tipos de cambio de paridad en América Latina (BCV/REL, 11:45, 1976, p. 93–155, tables)

An ECIEL study whose author enhances the utilization of parity exchange rates in international value comparisons. A Latin American study illustrates this. For author's monograph on this subject, see item **2901**. [R.C.L.]

3172 ———. Oil in the economic development of Venezuela. N.Y., Praeger, 1976. 215 p., bibl., tables.

Uses a detailed analysis of the role of oil exports in Venezuelan development to question the proposition that primary exports cannot be relied upon to foster a successful overall growth process because their expansion cannot be transferred to other sectors. [R. Albert Berry]

3173 Schmink, Marianne. El desarrollo dependiente y la división del trabajo por sexo: Venezuela (UNAM/RMS, 39:4, oct./dic. 1977, p. 1193–1226, bibl., tables)

Within the framework of the dependency model, this interesting article examines the structure of female employment in Venezuela. As a data base it uses the censuses of 1950 and 1970. Concludes that dependent economies which follow the capitalist mode, produce a concentration of female employment in the services sector when they expand. This limits employment opportunities for women and allow their greater exploitation and discrimination. For sociologist's comment, see item **9201**.

3174 Silva, Carlos Rafael. La economía venezolana y sus instituciones financieras (BCV/REL, 11:44, 1974, p. 39–56)

Article based on a lecture delivered at the inaugural session of a seminar conducted in Caracas for British citizens. It covers the most salient characteristics of the Venezuelan economy and its financial structure. The author is the former manager and present president of the Central Bank of Venezuela.

3175 ———. Las relaciones económico-financieras de Venezuela con América Latina (BCV/REL, 10:40, 1974, p. 41–58)

A brief examination of the Venezuelan economic conditions, vis-à-vis Latin America as a whole, followed by a review of the economic relations among the Latin American countries, especially Venezuela's. The major conclusion is that a strengthening of the region's financial cooperation is required for the expansion of intra-regional trade.

3176 Silva Michelena, Héctor. Proceso y crisis de la economía nacional: 1960–1973 (UCV/NC, 1:1, enero/abril 1975, p. 105–129, tables)

Examines the main trends of the Venezuelan economy during the period in question. The author, a believer in the ideologies of dependency and accumulation, applies them to the Venezuelan case in order to seek explanations. His most interesting conclusion is that the process of industrialization initiated in the late 1950s has *not* freed Venezuela of the overbearing influence of oil.

3177 Sullivan, William M. and **Winfield J. Burggraaf** *comps.* El petróleo en Venezuela: una bibliografía. Caracas, Ediciones Centauro, 1977. 229 p. (Col. Manuel Segundo Sánchez)

This extensive bibliography on Venezuelan petroleum includes official publications, books, magazines, pamphlets, essays and thesis on this subject. [R.C.L.]

3178 Tovar, Ramón A. Venezuela: país subdesarrollado. 5. ed. Caracas, Univ. Central de Venezuela, 1976. 223 p., maps, tables (Col. Avance, 6)

Third ed. of collection of essays written in 1962 concerning the structural phenomenon of underdevelopment seen from a geographical perspective. [R.C.L.]

3179 Truitt, Nancy S. and **David H. Blake.** Opinion leaders and private investment: an attitude survey in Chile and Venezuela. N.Y., Fund for Multinational Management Education, 1976. 125 p., tables.

Foreign investment is generally deprecated by leaders as making too much profit (also other reasons) yet they badly over-estimate these profits. Authors call for new approach in public affairs. [J.M. Hunter]

3180 Universidad Central de Venezuela, *Caracas.* **Centro de Estudios del Desarrollo** (CENDES). La reforma agraria en Venezuela. v. 2, El proceso de dotación de tierras; v. 4, Datos económicos de la encuesta nacional de beneficiarios; v. 5, Datos sociales de la encuesta nacional de beneficiarios; v. 6, Metodología de la encuesta nacional de beneficiarios de la reforma agraria; v. 7, Seis trabajos sobre reforma agraria; v. 8, Los campesinos venezolanos, organización política, liderazgo y economía; v. 9, Cooperativas campesinas y cambio en Venezuela: 2 estudios de casos. Caracas, 1969/1970. 7 v. (Various pagings) bibls., tables (Estudio CENDES/CIDA. Documentos de trabajo, 1:6, 8, 9, 10, 11, 15, 16)

Preliminary version of a very large study about the results of the agrarian reform

in Venezuela, undertaken by CENDES, the Development Center of the Central Univ. of Venezuela, in collaboration with several government agencies, and with CIDA (the Interamerican Committee for Agricultural Development). Vol. 1 and 3 were not received at the Library of Congress.

3181 ———, ———. **Facultad de Ciencias Económicas y Sociales. Instituto de Investigaciones Económicas y Sociales.** La dependencia de Venezuela: bases teóricas y metodológicas. v. 1, Introducción. Caracas, 1975. 283 p., tables.

Multi and interdisciplinary collective work of exploration, analysis and diagnosis of the social and economic reality of Venezuela. Study attempts to determine the causes of the external and internal dependency of Venezuela. [G.D.]

3182 Universidad de los Andes, *Mérida, Venezuela.* **Instituto de Investigaciones Económicas.** Informe económico, 1973–1974: anexo estadístico. Mérida, Ven., 1976. 187 p., tables.

The Economic Research Institute of the Univ. of the Andes in Venezuela, prepares the basic estimates of economic activity of the country's Andean region. Principally these are estimates of the Gross Regional Product and the price index for that part of Venezuela. These and other statistics are presented in this compendium.

3183 Urdaneta, Lourdes. Distribución del ingreso análisis del caso venezolano. Caracas, Banco Central de Venezuela, 1977. 382 p., bibl., tables (Col. De estudios económicos, 5)

Author examines the general problems involved in measuring income with specific reference to Venezuelan conditions instead of taking into consideration per-capita income, he studies income distribution among the different social groups in the country. [R.C.L.]

3184 Venegas Filardo, Pascual. Siete ensayos sobre economía de Venezuela. Caracas, Monte Avila Editores, 1970. 141 p., plates, tables (Col. Temas venezolanos)

Seven essays about Venezuelan economic and social problems. Author perceives the economic geography of Venezuela as the determinant factor in the country's uneven deomographic distribution and analyzes attempts to correct it. [R.C.L.]

3185 Venezuela. Instituto de Comercio Exterior. Venezuela y el Pacto Andino. Presentación de Leopoldo Díaz Bruzual. Prólogo de Julio Sosa Rodríguez. Caracas, 1974. 378 p., bibl., table (Información Documental de América Latina [INDAL], 10)

This is a chronological compilation of the principal official documents generated since the "Declaration of Bogota" in 1966 up to 1973, the year of the signing of the "Consensus of Lima." The documents explain the pre-integrative process, in relation to both the official sector and public opinion. Some official Venezuelan documents concern subregional integration, the public and private sectors, and the Venezuelan national forum. Also includes essays on Latin American integration. [R.P.]

3186 ———. **Ministerio de Energía y Minas. Dirección General Sectorial de Hidrocarburos. Dirección de Planificación y Economía de Hidrocarburos. Departamento de Estadística.** Apéndice estadístico. Caracas, 1978. 1 v. (Various pagings) tables.

The Statistical Appendix of the Annual Report of the Ministry of Energy and Mines is distributed by itself, as it contains probably the most useful compilation of oil statistics produced in Venezuela. The period covered by this publication usually spans a 10-year period, in this case 1967–77.

3187 ———. ———. ———. ———. ———.
Datos generales de la industria petrolera 1977. Caracas, 1978. 39 p., tables.

Summary of the principal data relating to oil in Venezuela, for the last two years, and 10 years ago. Also reviews fundamental pieces of legislation affecting the Venezuelan petroleum industry.

3188 ———. **Ministry of Finance. Superintendency of Foreign Investment.** Legal regime of foreign investment and transfer of technology in Venezuela. Foreword by Rafael Soto Alvarez. Caracas, n.d. 101 p.

Study presents the body of legal norms which regulates foreign investment and technology transfer in Venezuela as well as a discussion of Venezuela's overall strategy for their application and the creation of a favorable environment for foreign investment

secured by stable, legal and political systems. Study also examines in depth measures of control over re-exportation of capital, transformation of foreign companies, utilization of foreign and domestic credit, importation of technology and use and exploitation of patents and trademarks. [D.E.M.]

3189 ———. **Oficina Central de Coordinación y Planificación** (CORDIPLAN). El sistema de planificación en Venezuela. Caracas, 1973. 59 l., map, table.

A description of the principal elements of the planning mechanism in Venezuela, and of its functions and methods. Study justifies and highlights the regional approach followed in this country and evaluates the future of planning in Venezuela.

3190 ———. **Presidencia de la República. Consejo Nacional de Recursos Humanos.** Informe sobre la situación general y perspectiva de los recursos humanos. Caracas, 1977. 661 p., tables.

This is an attempt to provide information needed for the formulation of an integral development policy. The study details the availability and requirements of human resources in the three sectors of the Venezuelan economy as well as in the complex social sector. Special attention is devoted to an analysis of the gap which exists between the surplus of financial resources available for investment in the public and private sectors and the scarcity of qualifications among available human resources. [G.D.]

3191 Viloria R., Oscar. Sobre el origen de la política de sustitución de importaciones en el proceso de industrialización de Venezuela (UCV/NC, 1 : 1, enero/abril 1975, p. 131–135)

A note attributes the import-substituting-industrialization of Venezuela in the 1960s to the difficult economic conditions of the country, Latin American stagnation, and the evolution of world capita.

3192 Vivas Terán, Abdón. Necesidad de definir la estructura macro-económica de la sociedad comunitaria. Caracas, Centro de Información, Documentación y Análisis Latinoamericano (CIDAL), n.d. 31 p. (Entrega, 24)

A young and dynamic leader of the Christian Democratic Party of Venezuela presents his ideas on "communitarian socialism." His example is the Yugoslavian model of workers' socialism wherein all property is in the hands of the working class. He regards the Yugoslav model as sound and practical and defends it from its critics.

Chile and Peru

MARKOS MAMALAKIS, *Professor of Economics, University of Wisconsin-Milwaukee*

AFTER REVIEWING THE LITERATURE on the economic history of Chile up to 1973, the year of the coup, one notices an uncomfortable, almost involuntary consensus which attempts to explain events in a multi-faceted and multi-dimensional fashion. In contrast, published interpretations of economic events between 1973 and 1979, the years of military rule, remain highly polarized with one group talking about an "economic miracle" while its opposite perceives the post-Allende era as a social, economic and, above all, political failure. With regard to economic trends since 1973, it is still too early to offer an objective, balanced and comprehensive verdict.

The following selection criteria have been applied to the compilation of this bibliography: materials were included if they contributed to our understanding of the long-term evolution of the Chilean economy or if they provided solid, though partial, blocks for building the edifice of Chilean economic history since 1973. There are three valuable and major recent monographs which supplement the economic history of Chile by Mamalakis reviewed in the preceding social-sciences volume (see *HLAS 39:3396*); Alexander's study of the political and economic history of the country since 1930 (item **3194**); Kirsch's work on the industrialization process before 1930; and, finally, the first volume of Mamalakis' *Historical statistics of Chile* (item **3229**).

In Chile the major publishers of research studies as well as statistical and institutional compendia are the government (especially since 1975), academia, and the private sector. The flurry of government publications (e.g., by the ministries of agriculture, internal revenue and mining, public agencies such as the Central Bank, CORFO or Chile's Development Corporation, oil and copper agencies, etc.) are due to the government's desire to promote private enterprise and initiative while guiding and stimulating private investment and promoting exports. Indeed, the most prolific publisher of studies and documents remains ODEPLAN, the Planning Office of the Presidency of the Republic. Among academic publishers the leaders are the University of Chile and the Catholic University of Chile which have issued research on macro-, sectoral-, and micro-economic events and trends during the eras of Frei, Allende and the Military Junta. CIEPLAN (Corporation of Economic Research for Latin America) has also played a leading role in generating high-quality studies. The private sector also issues a number of valuable publications which, although not cited in the ensuing bibliography, are deserving of mention. Important sources of basic data are newspapers, magazines, and the publications of certain societies such as the agricultural and industrial which have subjected economic events, between 1973–79, to subtle but intensive scrutiny. And finally, one should note the major flow of articles and books by non-Chileans, particularly North American and European scholars, whose works cover a wide spectrum of topics and offer a variety of views.

There is at present a notable difference between topics of economic research in Peru and Chile. Favorite subjects of academic scrutiny or government study in Chile are price stabilization, export promotion, private enterprise, unemployment, low investment, free trade and distribution of income, all of which constitute the ingredients of the *"social market system"* of the 1973–79 period. In Peru, on the other hand, the following are favored areas of investigation: government intervention, labor participation, labor-managed enterprises, foreign debt, dualism and stagnation, all of which shape the "market *social* system" criticized as an inadequate engine for sustained growth by both Right and Left. Thorp and Bertram's major study of growth and change (or lack of it) in the Peruvian economy between 1890 and 1977 fills some significant gaps in our understanding of the country's history (item **3292**).

Principal publishers of economic research on Peru are the government and the universities. Their works, however, reveal conflicting types of ideologies and a pervasive malaise about the past, present, and anticipated future course of events.

To conclude, one should note that there are a number of research topics which are neglected by economists writing about north Chile and Peru, i.e., the deteriorating quality of life in the central cities; environment and pollution; preconditions versus determinants of economic growth; types and nature of export-led growth (integration of macro-economic, trade-and-development approaches); and the multiple linkages between income distribution and economic development.

CHILE

3193 Albuquerque W., María Beatriz de. La agricultura chilena: ¿modernización capitalista o regressión a formas tradicionales? (LI/IA, 6:2, dec. 1976, p. 11–31, tables)
A highly informative examination of agrarian reform in Chile since 1973.

3194 Alexander, Robert Jackson. The tragedy of Chile. Westport, Conn., Greenwood Press, 1978. 509 p., bibl. (Contributions in political science, 8)
This is a solid, comprehensive and objective examination of the forces that led to the rise and fall of Salvador Allende. An analysis of Chilean political and economic history from 1930 to 1977.

3195 Barlow, B.H. Some basic problems of the agrarian reform in Chile (CH, 3:5/6, 1978, p. 53–77, tables)
The transformation in land ownership patterns in Chile did not bring along the other changes advocated by the Allende government.

Bauer, Arnold and **Ann Hagerman Johnson.** Land and labour in rural Chile: 1850–1935. See *HLAS 40:3612*.

Borsdorf, Axel. Städtische strukturen und entwicklungsprozesse in Lateinamerika. See item **5462**.

3196 Chile. Junta de Gobierno. Oficina de Planificación Nacional (ODEPLAN). Areas posibles de interés para inversionistas extranjeros. Santiago, 1976. 1 v. (Unpaged) tables.
A detailed panorama of areas for potential foreign investment developed by the Military Junta.

3197 ——. ——. ——. Balances económicos de Chile: 1960–1970. Presentación de Gonzalo Martner G. Santiago, Editorial Universitaria, 1973. 260 p., tables (Serie 4:2)
A valuable collection of tables with data for the 1960–70 period.

3198 ——. ——. ——. Chile: el desafío (Chile: the challenge). Santiago, 1976. 80 p., colored plates (Serie Auriga)
A presentation (in Spanish and English) of private capitalist development in Chile under the Military Junta.

3199 ——. ——. ——. Cuentas nacionales de Chile: 1960–1975. Santiago, 1976? 92 l., tables.
A complete set of Chile's national accounts between 1960–75.

3200 ——. ——. ——. Eficiencia económica para el desarrollo social: plan nacional indicativo de desarrollo, 1976–1981. Prólogo de Roberto T. Kelly V. Santiago, 1976? 65 p., tables.

The development strategy of Chile's Military Junta.

3201 ———. ———. ———. Estrategia nacional de desarrollo económico y social: políticas de Largo Plazo. Santiago, 1977. 162 p.

A detailed presentation of the social and economic ideology of Chile's Military Junta.

3202 ———. ———. ———. Informe económico: octubre 1976. Santiago, 1976. 64 l., tables.

Semi-annual economic report presenting the governmental views on economic problems and policies.

3203 ———. ———. ———. Informe social: primer semestre 1976. Santiago, 1976. 64 l., tables.

A semi-annual report on the social policies of the government during 1976.

3204 ———. ———. ———. **Subdirección Regional.** Indicadores regionales. Santiago, 1975. 50 l., tables.

A comprehensive statistical picture of Chile's regional indicators.

3205 ———. **Ministerio de Agricultura. Oficina de Planificación Agrícola** (ODEPA). Exportaciones agropecuarias chilenas: antecedentes y mercados. Introducción de Rodrigo Mujica Ateaga. Santiago, 1975. 428 p., fold. tables, tables.

As part of its export promotion policy, the government has put together here a detailed compendium of markets and prices for non-traditional agricultural products.

3206 Chonchol, Jacques. El sistema burocrático: instrumento y obstáculo en el proceso de reforma agraria chilena (CDAL, 15, 1977, p. 87–100)

Jacques Chonchol, who should know, considers the Chilean bureaucracy as the main obstacle in formulating an efficient land-reform program. For political scientist's comment, see item **7390.**

3207 Cifuentes, Malva. Testing WIP development concepts: Chile before and after the coup. Oslo, Univ. of Oslo, 1976. 55 p., tables (World indicators program, 11. Papers, 38)

This document, written by a political exile, contains one of the earliest critiques of economic policies in Chile since 1973.

3208 Coeymans, Juan Eduardo. Estimación del tipo de cambio de libre comercio para la economía chilena en un contexto de equilibrio general. Santiago, Univ. Católica de Chile, Instituto de Economía, n.d. 48 l., bibl., table (Documento de trabajo, 51)

A general equilibrium model is used to estimate a free trade foreign exchange price for Chile.

3209 *Comentarios sobre la Situación Económica.* Univ. de Chile, Facultad de Ciencias Económicas y Administrativas, Depto. de Economía. No. 42, 2. semestre 1976 [and] No. 52, 2. semestre 1977–. Santiago.

Issue No. 42 consists of examinations by leading Chilean economists of fiscal, financial, employment, investment, and other economic trends for the second semester of 1976. In issue No. 52 12 economists provide a panoramic, short-to-medium-term analysis of the cyclical position of Chile in the second semester of 1977.

3210 Corbo, Vittorio and **Patricio Meller.** Sustitución de importaciones, promoción de exportaciones y empleo: el caso chileno. Santiago, Corporación de Investigaciones Económicas para Latinoamérica (CIEPLAN), 1977. 48 p., tables (Estudios CIEPLAN, 15)

Corbo and Meller compare in this careful study the impact on employment in Chile during 1966–68 of export promotion and import substitution policies for manufacturing products.

3211 Cortázar, René and **Ramón Downey.** Efectos redistributivos de la reforma agraria (FCE/TE, 44[3]:175, julio/sept. 1977, p. 685–713, tables)

President Frei's agrarian reform program is given high marks as a political alternative and redistributive instrument.

Couyoumdjian, Ricardo. El mercado del salitre durante la Primera Guerra Mundial y la post-guerra, 1914–1921: notas para su estudio. See *HLAS 40:3625.*

3212 DIREXPO: directorio de la exportación chilena (DIREXPO: export directory of Chile): 1975–1976. Prólogo de José Toribio Merino Castro. Santiago, Turina, 1976. 312 p., maps, plates, tables.

This is a comprehensive export directory of Chile.

3213 Edwards, Sebastián. El efecto de un arancel externo común en la balanza de pagos y en el tipo de cambio: el caso de Chile y el Pacto Andino (FCE/TE, 44[3]:175, julio/sept. 1977, p. 665–684, tables)

An economic model is used to measure the effect of a common external duty within the Andean Pact on the composition of Chile's foreign trade.

3214 Epstein, Edward C. Anti-inflation policies in Argentina and Chile: or, who pays the cost (CPS, 11:2, July 1978, p. 211–230, bibl., tables)

This article hypothesizes that the groups who pay the price for the control of inflation are those without adequate representation in the government of the day.

3215 Escuela de Negocios de Valparaíso, Chile. The Chilean economy under the Popular Unity government: the Chilean way to Marxist socialism. Valparaíso, Chile, Fundación Adolfo Ibáñez, 1974. 80 l., colored plates, tables.

An interpretation of events during the Allende era by supporters of the Military Junta.

Espinosa, Juan Guillermo. The experience of worker participation in the management of industrial firms: the case of the social ownership area in Chile, 1970–1973. See item 9245.

Ffrench-Davis, Ricardo. La importancia del cobre en la economía chilena: antecedentes históricos. See HLAS 40:3632.

3216 ——— and José Piñera Echenique. Promoción de exportaciones y desarrollo nacional. Santiago, Corporación de Investigaciones Económicas para Latinoamérica (CIEPLAN), 1976. 42 p. (Estudios CIEPLAN, 2)

A short essay on formulating an export-promotion strategy and warning against excessive and inefficient export promotion.

3217 Figuerola, Marcelo and Alvaro Vial. Los efectos del desarrollo del mercado financiero sobre la política monetaria: el caso chileno (UC/EE, 6:2, 1975, p. 105–130, tables)

An examination of the relation between the evolution of Chile's financial markets and monetary policy since 1973.

3218 Foxley, Alejandro; Eduardo Aninat; and José Pablo Arellano. Chile: the role of asset redistribution in poverty-focused development strategies (WD, 5:1/2, Jan./Feb. 1977, p. 69–88, tables)

This essay examines the role and efficiency of asset redistribution in removing poverty and improving the distribution of income. For Spanish version of this study, see item 3220.

3219 ———; ———; and ———. Política fiscal como instrumento redistributivo: la experiencia chilena. Santiago, Corporación de Investigaciones Económicas para Latinoamérica (CIEPLAN), 1977. 42 p., tables (Estudios CIEPLAN, 14)

This is a systematic and highly informative examination of selected aspects of fiscal policy as a redistributive device during part of the Frei years.

3220 ———; ———; and ———. Redistribución del patrimonio y erradicación de la pobreza. Santiago, Corporación de Investigaciones Económicas para Latinoamericana (CIEPLAN), 1976. 70 p., tables (Estudios CIEPLAN, 3)

Examines the period 1965–73 in Chile and efforts there to redistribute income through nationalization of industry and agrarian reform. Thoughtful and careful analysis. For Spanish version of this study, see item 3218. [J.M. Hunter]

Grunwald, Joseph. Los recursos de la América Latina en la economía mundial: cobre y mineral de hierro. See item 2827.

3221 Harberger, Arnold. Cuatro momentos de la economía chilena. Santiago, Fundación de Estudios Económicos BHC, 1976. 147 p.

Harberger makes some general remarks about economic policy during 1974 and 1975.

3222 Jeanneret, Teresa; Leopoldo Moraga; and Lorraine Ruffing. Las experiencias autogestionarias chilenas. Santiago, Univ. de Chile, Facultad de Ciencias Económicas y Administrativas, Depto. de Economía, 1976? 164 p., tables (Publicación, 29)

This is a very informative and objective examination of Chile's labor-managed enterprises between 1969 and 1973 by three highly qualified scholars.

Jenkins, Rhys Owen. Dependent industrialization in Latin America: the automotive industry in Argentina, Chile and Mexico. See item **2843.**

3223 Kay, Cristóbal. Agrarian reform and the transition to socialism in Chile: 1970–1973 (JPS, 2:4, July 1975, p. 418–445, bibl.)

A critical review of Allende's land reform program. For political scientist's comment, see item **7416.**

3224 ———. Tipos de reforma agraria y sus contradicciones: el caso de Chile (UNAM/RMS, 39:3, julio/sept. 1977, p. 857–872, table)

Kay argues that the internal contradictions of Chilean democracy and of the agrarian reform itself led to the failure of the latter.

3225 Kirsch, Henry W. Industrial development in traditional society: the conflict of entrepreneurship and modernization in Chile. Gainesville, Univ. Presses of Florida, 1977. 210 p., bibl., tables (Latin American monographs. Second series, 21)

A major contribution to the understanding of industrialization in Chile before 1930.

3226 Landsberger, Henry A. and **Tim McDaniel.** Hypermobilization in Chile: 1970–1973 (PUCIS/WP, 28:4, July 1976, p. 502–541)

An excellent essay describing the process and effects of hypermobilization in Chile during the Allende era. For political scientist's comment, see item **7420.**

3227 Lavados, Hugo. Empresas multinacionales, mercados externos y políticas económicas en la industria del cobre en Chile (CPU/ES, 12:2, 1977, p. 9–32, tables)

A balanced and thorough analysis of the impact of economic policies and multinational corporations upon the development of the copper sector.

Leuchter, W. Zur Rolle der staatlichen Investitionspolitik im Rahmen der Strategie und Taktik der herrschenden Klassen Chiles in den fünfziger und sechziger Jahren. See item **7422.**

3228 Lira, Ricardo. Precios implicitos de características de viviendas en Santiago (UCC/CE, 15:44, abril 1978, p. 67–90, bibl., tables)

A provocative econometric study of the housing sector in Santiago.

3229 Mamalakis, Markos. *comp.* Historical statistics of Chile: national accounts. Westport, Conn., Greenwood Press, 1978. 262 p., bibl.

The most comprehensive and up-to-date presentation of the national accounts of Chile between 1940 and 1977. It also includes an extensive methodology.

3230 Martín M., María Loreto. Análisis de la oferta monetaria en Chile: 1956–1970. Santiago, Univ. Católica de Chile, Instituto de Economía, 1975. 64 l., bibl., tables (Documento de trabajo, 35)

This short essay examines the monetary supply in Chile during 1956–70.

Molina Silva, Sergio. El proceso de cambio en Chile: la experiencia, 1965–1970. See *HLAS 40:3650.*

3231 Monckeberg Barros, Fernando. Jaque al subdesarrollo. 4. ed. corregida y aumentada. Santiago, Editora National Gabriela Mistral, 1976. 234 p., bibl., tables (Pensamiento contemporáneo)

Scholarly work dealing particularly with Chile and with nutrition. Gives attention to the critical nature of human resources and the vicious circle—poverty, malnutrition, low productivity, poverty. A general treatise on development with emphasis as indicated. [J.M. Hunter]

3232 ——— and others. Agroindustria y desarrollo. t. 1. Santiago, Univ. de Chile, Facultad de Ciencias Económicas y Administrativas, Depto. de Economía, 1975 [i.e. 1976]. 239 p., tables.

These are the proceedings of a conference on Chilean agroindustry held in Santiago in 1975. This volume is of special interest because it deals also with issues rarely examined by economists such as the cost of protein production and organic garbage.

3233 Muñoz Gomá, Oscar and **Ana María Arriagada.** Orígenes políticos y económicos del estado empresarial en Chile. Santiago, Corporación de Investigaciones Económicas para Latinoamérica (CIEPLAN), 1977. 53 p., tables (Estudios CIEPLAN, 16)

This essay examines the entrepreneurial role of the state in Chile and its economic and political foundations from a historical perspective.

3234 *NACLA's Latin America & Empire Report.* North American Congress on Latin America. Vol. 10, No. 9, Nov. 1976–. N.Y.

Issue entitled "Chile: Recycling the Capitalist Crisis" consists of detailed Marxist review of events in Chile between 1969 and 1975.

3235 Opazo D., Hernán. Efectos de la política cambiaria sobre la distribución del ingreso en el período 1971-primer semestre 1973. Santiago, Univ. Católica de Chile, Instituto de Economía, 1974. 85 l., bibl., tables (Documento de trabajo, 30)

An examination of the relationship between foreign exchange policy and income distribution during 1971–74.

3236 Plan de recuperación económica. Santiago, Editora Nacional Gabriela Mistral, n.d. 78 p., illus.

A pictorial and easy-to-understand description of the economic recovery plan during the Military Junta government.

3237 Raczynski, Dagmar. El sector informal urbano: controversias e interrogantes. Santiago, Corporación de Investigaciones Económicas para Latinoamérica (CIEPLAN), 1977. 56 p., bibl., table (Estudios CIEPLAN, 13)

An attempt to clarify the highly ambiguous concept of the urban informal sector.

3238 Rochac, Alfonso. La socialización de la banca en Chile. San Salvador, n.p. 1976? 193 l., facsims., tables.

A highly informative and detailed review of the socialization of Chilean banking under Allende.

Stallings, Barbara. Class conflict and economic development in Chile: 1958–1973. See item **7446**.

Steenland, Kyle. Agrarian reform under Allende: peasant revolt in the south. See item **7447**.

3239 Stemplowski, Ryszard. Chile y las compañías petroleras, 1931–1932: contribución al estudio del entrelazamiento

dominación-dependencia (IAA, 4:1, 1978, p. 1–19, bibl.)

An examination of the petroleum companies in Chile during 1931–32 within a dependency framework.

Truitt, Nancy S. and **David H. Blake.** Opinion leaders and private investment: an attitude survey in Chile and Venezuela. See item **3179**.

3240 Universidad Católica de Chile, *Santiago.* **Programa de Postgrado en Economía Agraria.** Chile: agricultural sector overview, 1964–1974. Santiago, 1976. 1 v. (Various pagings) bibl., tables.

This is a major study of Chile's agricultural sector between 1964 and 1974. Covering almost every aspect of agriculture, it contains valuable statistical and institutional information.

3241 Universidad de Chile, *Santiago.* **Facultad de Ciencias Económicas y Administrativas. Departamento de Economía.** La reforma tributaria: sus efectos económicos, 1975. Prólogo de Andrés Sanfuentes Vergara. Introducción de José F. Guzmán. Santiago, 1975. 1 v. (Various pagings) tables (Publicación, 25)

In these proceedings of a 1975 conference on economic effects of fiscal reform, the reader will find a systematic theoretical, empirical and institutional examination of fiscal issues confronting Chile in 1975.

3242 Valdés, Alberto. Protección a la industria de fertilizantes y su efecto en la producción agrícola y en el ahorro de divisas: el caso del salitre (UCC/CE, 13:39, agosto 1976, p. 93–108, bibl., tables)

An excellent essay demonstrating the inhibitive effects of excessive protection of nitrate on agricultural development and the balance of payments.

PERU

3243 Alberti, Giorgio; Jorge Santistevan; and **Luis Pasara.** Estado y clase: la comunidad industrial en el Perú. Lima, Instituto de Estudios Peruanos (IEP), 1977. 38 p. (Perú problema, 16)

Some idiosyncratic elements of Peru's economic, social and political structure are explored by analyzing the interactions between the state, the industrial bourgeoisie and the urban proletariat. For sociologist's comment, see item **9229**.

3244 Ballantyne, Janet Campbell. The political economy of Peruvian gran minería. Ithaca, N.Y., Cornell Univ., Latin American Studies Program, 1976. 336 p., tables (Latin American studies program dissertation series, 60)

A highly informative examination of Peru's large scale mining sector between 1950 and 1973.

3245 Bertram, Geoffrey. Modernización y cambio en la industria lanera en el sur del Perú, 1919–1930: un caso frustrado de desarrollo (UP/A, 3:6, 1977, p. 3–22, tables)

A description of the aborted development of the wool industry of southern Peru during 1919–30. For historian's comment, see *HLAS 40:3489.*

3246 Boloña Behr, Carlos. La aplicación de un modelo econométrico a la economía peruana: un ejercicio metodológico. Lima, Univ. del Pacífico, Centro de Investigación (CIUP), 1976. 234 l., tables (Serie: Documento de trabajo, 3)

An econometric model of the Peruvian economy.

3247 ———. Las importaciones del estado: aspectos teóricos y el caso peruano, 1971–1976 (UP/A, 4:8, 1978, p. 99–141, tables)

An examination of the commercialization of imports by the Peruvian government during 1971–76.

3248 ———; Jorge Campos Rivera; and **Raúl Musso Vento.** Las importaciones del sector público en el Perú: 1971–1974. Lima, Univ. del Pacífico, Centro de Investigación (CIUP), 1977. 160 l., bibl., tables (Trabajo de investigación, 5)

A detailed statistical examination of the imports of Peru's public sector between 1971 and 1974.

3249 Bonilla, Heraclio. La emergencia del control norteamericano sobre la economía peruana: 1850–1930 (IDES/DE, 64:16, enero/marzo 1977, p. 581–600, tables)

Bonilla traces the gradual rise of North American hegemony over the Peruvian econ-

omy between 1850 and 1930. For historian's comment, see *HLAS 40:3495.*

3250 Burneo, José; Adolfo Ciudac; and **Luis Pásara.** Empleo y estabilidad laboral. Lima, Centro de Estudios y Promoción del Desarrollo (DESCO), Area Laboral, 1976. 204 p., tables (Serie praxis, 6)

This is an informative, multifaceted examination of employment stability and instability in Peru between 1970 and 1975.

3251 Cabieses Cubas, Hugo. Comunidad laboral y capitalismo: alcances y límites. Lima, Centro de Estudios y Promoción del Desarrollo (DESCO), 1976. 159 p., fold. tables, tables.

Based on extensive statistical data, this major study traces the evolution of labor communities in Peru and their economic impact, especially on workers.

3252 Drassinower Katz, Samuel. Realismo industrial. Prólogo de Marco Fernández Baca. Lima, Librería Editorial Minerva-Miraflores, 1977. 295 p.

A Peruvian businessman and entrepreneur examines industrial development in a collection of articles.

3253 *Economía.* Pontificia Univ. Católica del Perú, Depto. de Economía. Vol. 1, No. 1, dic. 1977–. Lima.

This promising inaugural volume of *Economía* contains informative and balanced articles, analyses, debates and reviews of books dealing with Peru.

3254 Esculies Larrabure, Oscar; Marcial Rubio Correa; and **Verónica González del Castillo.** Comercialización de alimentos: quiénes ganan, quiénes pagan, quiénes pierden. Lima, Centro de Estudios y Promoción del Desarrollo (DESCO), 1977. 190 p., bibl., fold. table, tables (Praxis, 8)

The trade of agricultural products is thoroughly examined in this document.

3255 Estado y política agraria: 4 ensayos. Lima, Centro de Estudios y Promoción del Desarrollo (DESCO), 1977. 351 p., tables.

Four essays dealing with various unresolved issues of agrarian reform in Peru. For historian's comment, see *HLAS 40:3512.*

3256 Fernández Pereda, Víctor M. Situación de la agricultura, la planificación agraria y la participación campesina en el

Perú: críticas y perspectivas. Lima, Univ. Nacional Agraria la Molina, Centro de Investigaciones Socio-Economicas (CISE), 1976? 67 l., tables.

A discussion of the role of planning and participation of farmers in agricultural development in Peru.

3257 Flores Sáenz, Otto. Tecnología agrícola u estructura de exportación peruana. Lima, Univ. Nacional Agraria La Molina, Centro de Investigaciones Socio-Económicas (CISE), 1976? 52 l., bibl., tables.

An examination of Peru's agricultural export sector as it relates to agricultural technology.

3258 Freyre J., Iris. Exportaciones e industria en el Perú: el caso de Grace y Paramonga. Lima, Pontificia Univ. Católica del Perú, Depto. de Ciencias Sociales, Areas de Sociología, 1976. 60 l., tables (Publicaciones Centro de Investigaciones Sociales, Económicas, Políticas y Antropológicas [CISEPA]. Serie: Publicaciones previas, 15)

An examination of foreign investment in Peru's sugar sector and its impact on the growth of Peru.

3259 Garrido Lecca Alvarez Calderón, Guillermo. La represión financiera en el Perú. Lima, Escuela de Administración de Negocios para Graduados (ESAN), 1977. 100 p., bibl., tables.

The pivotal role of the financial sector is demonstrated and the validity of dualistic, labor surplus models to Peru is questioned.

3260 ——— and Gerald T. O'Mara. Eficiencia del mercado de capitales peruano. Lima, Escuela de Administración de Negocios para Graduados (ESAN), Depto. de Investigación, 1975. 49 l., tables (Serie: Documento de trabajo, 6)

An analysis of the efficiency of the allocation of resources by the Peruvian financial sector.

3261 Gonzáles Mayorca, Grimaldo. Cooperativismo y revolución. t. 1/2. Presentación de José Martínez Gea. Lima, Banco Nacional de las Cooperativas del Perú (BANCOOP), 1976. 2 v. (352, 429 p.)

An excellent, multifaceted collection of articles, speeches and related documents on Peru's cooperativism.

3262 González Vigil, Fernando and Carlos Parodi Zevallos. Los grupos financieros internacionales y el sistema financiero nacional: los casos de los proyectos mineros y siderúrgicos en el Perú, 1968–74. Lima, Univ. del Pacífico, Centro de Investigación (CIUP), 1975. 85 l., tables (Trabajos de investigación, 3)

An examination of international and national financial system as regards the mining and iron and steel industry.

3263 Granda Alva, Germán. El sector público peruano y su política de financiamiento en el período 1950–1967. Lima, Univ. del Pacífico, Centro de Investigación (CIUP), 1974. 25 l., tables (Serie ensayos, 6)

A brief examination of Peru's public sector during 1950–67 from a dependency perspective. It emphasizes financial aspects.

3264 Investigación tecnológica industrial en el Perú: análisis y comentarios. Lima, Instituto de Investigación Tecnológica Industrial y de Normas Técnicas (ITINTEC), 1975? 149 p., tables (Serie política tecnológica, 4)

Various authors discuss the role of technological progress in Peruvian development.

3265 Kuczynski, Pedro-Pablo. Peruvian democracy under economic stress: an account of the Belaúnde Administration, 1963–1968. Princeton, N.J., Princeton Univ. Press, 1977. 308 p., bibl., map, tables.

A detailed and first-rate treatment of economic policies in Peru during the Belaúnde era. For political scientist's comment, see item **7338**.

3266 Linares Salas, Agapito. Estudio para reducir las importaciones de trigo en el Perú. Lima, Univ. Nacional Agraria la Molina, Centro de Investigaciones Socio-Económicas (CISE), 1976. 87 l., bibl., map, tables.

An examination of Peru's wheat market and of the possibilities of reducing wheat imports.

3267 López Soria, José Ignacio. El modo de producción en el Perú y otros ensayos. Lima, Mosca Azul Editores, 1977. 152 p.

A socio-economic explanation of Peru's economic development.

3268 Magni, Roberto. Autogestione e sottosviluppo: il caso del Perú. Roma,

Coines Edizioni, 1975. 211 p., bibl.

Optimo análisis de las características y de los límites del proceso de participación popular desarrollado por los militares peruanos. El análisis trata en especial de mostrar las características de la autogestión y de la comunidad industrial. [M. Carmagnani]

3269 Maletta, Héctor. El subempleo en el Perú: una visión crítica (UP/A, 4:8, 1978, p. 3–48, bibl., tables)

A critical theoretical and empirical review of underdevelopment in Peru.

3270 Malpica Silva Santisteban, Carlos. El desarrollismo en el Perú: década de esperanzas y fracasos, 1961–1971. Lima, Editorial Horizonte, 1975. 159 p., fold. tables, tables (Serie realidad peruana)

A critical examination of Peruvian economic development between 1961 and 1971.

3271 ———. El mito de la ayuda exterior. 3. ed. Lima, Ediciones Ensayos Sociales, 1977? 251 p., tables.

The impact of "foreign aid" defined very broadly is examined in detail.

3272 Ortiz de Zevallos M., Felipe. Evaluación de proyectos en el Perú: comentarios y reflexiones. Presentación de Luis Paredes Stagnaro. Lima, Univ. del Pacífico, Depto. de Economía, 1977. 123 p., tables.

A panoramic examination of project evaluation issues in Peru.

3273 Pennano, Guido. Economía política del caucho en el Perú: una aproximación bibliográfica (UP/A, 4:8, 1978, p. 151–167, bibl.)

A short essay and a long bibliography on Peru's rubber export sector.

3274 Peru. Banco Central de Reserva. Cuentas nacionales del Perú: 1960–1974. Lima, 1976. 44 p., tables.

Peru's national accounts between 1960 and 1974.

3275 ———. ———. El desarrollo económico y financiero del Perú: 1968–1973. Lima, 1974. 295 p., tables.

A systematic review of financial and economic development of Peru during 1968–73.

3276 ———. ———. Departamento de Análisis Externo. División de Estudios Económicos. Estudio económico del comercio exterior del Perú con los países del grupo sub-regional andino: 1960–1969. Lima, 1970. 95 p., fold. tables, map, tables.

A detailed report of Peru's trade with Andean countries during 1960–69.

3277 ———. ———. Oficina de Asesoría Legal. Instituciones financieras de desarrollo en el Perú. Lima, 1976. 52 l. (Documento de trabajo)

A highly informative analysis of Peru's financial institutions and their contributions to development.

3278 ———. Ministerio de Alimentación. Dirección General de Comercialización. Plan de desarrollo del sector alimentación, 1977–1978: problemática y perspectivas de la comercialización de los principales productos; agrícolas, pecuarios e hidrobiológicos, industriales, alimenticios. Lima, 1976. 1 v. (Various pagings) tables.

A governmental report on background and planning of Peru's food sector.

3279 ———. Ministerio de Energía y Minas. Oficina Sectorial de Planificación. Plan bienal de desarrollo, 1973–1974: minería, hidrocarburos, electricidad. Lima, 1973. 142 p., maps, tables.

A detailed presentation of the biennial mining, oil and electricity plan for 1973–74.

3280 ———. Ministerio de Industria y Turismo. Oficina de Estadística. Evolución industrial manufacturera peruana: 1971–1972. Presentación de Jaime Robles Guillen. Lima, Banco Industrial del Perú, 1974? 217 p., tables.

A detailed report on the Peruvian manufacturing sector during 1971 and 1972.

3281 ———. Presidencia. Instituto Nacional de Planificación (ODEPLAN). Plan Nacional de Desarrollo: 1975–1978. Aprobado por Decreto Supremo No. 009–75–OM del 2 de junio de 1975. Lima, 1975. 163 p., tables.

A detailed presentation of Peru's development plan between 1975 and 1978.

3282 Petróleos del Perú (PETROPERU), *Lima*. Peruvian petroleum: present and future. Lima, 1975. 1 v. (Unpaged) maps, plate, tables.

A comprehensive essay of Peru's petroleum sector.

3283 Portocarrero, Felipe. El gobierno militar y el imperialista. Lima, Perugraph Editores, 1976. 34 p., tables (Cuadernos de sociedad y política, 1)

A Marxist review of the relationship between the Peruvian state and foreign capital.

3284 Propiedad social: polemicas. Lima, Centro de Estudios y Promoción de Desarrollo (DESCO), 1975. 296 p.

A compilation of research papers discussing "social property" in Peru.

3285 Reynolds, Clark W. Reforma social y dueda exterior: el dilema peruano (FCE/TE, 45[3]:179, julio/sept. 1978, p. 643–668, bibl., tables)

An examination of the different roles that foreign debt-credits have played in Peru and how social reform could improve their performance.

3286 Sagasti, Francisco R. El financiamiento industrial como instrumento de política tecnológica: un caso-estudio peruano (FCE/TE, 45[2]:178, april/junio 1978, p. 401–441, tables)

Sagasti examines and evaluates the actual and potential role of industrial credit (institutions) as an instrument of technological progress in Peru.

3287 ———. Tecnología, planificación y desarrollo autónomo. Presentación de José Matos Mar. Lima, Instituto de Estudios Peruanos (IEP), 1977. 158 p., tables (Serie Análisis económico, 3)

Examines the role of technology in eliminating underdevelopment and proposes various solutions.

3288 Schirmer, Ute. Reforma agraria y cooperativismo en el Perú (UNAM/RMS, 39:3, julio/sept. 1977, p. 799–856, bibl., tables)

A review of agrarian reform in Peru. Although some problems were solved and progress was made, many new problems were created and many old ones remained unresolved.

3289 Scott, C.D. Peasants, proletarianization and the articulation of modes of production: the case of sugar cane cutters in northern Peru, 1940–69 (JPS, 3:3, April 1976, p. 321–342, bibl., map)

Scott finds that the articulation of modes of production framework is more useful in analyzing the evolution of the labor market for sugar cane cutters than the Lewis model of dualism.

3290 Seminario Andino, Quito, 1975. Docencia, investigación y extensión sobre integración andina en las universidades del área. Edited by Manfred Wilhelmy von Wolff. Santiago, Corporación de Promoción Universitaria (CPU), 1976. 195 p., tables (Publicación, 37)

A review of courses, research and extension activities on the Andean Pact.

3291 Thorp, Rosemary. The post-import-substitution era: the case of Peru (WD, 5:1/2, Jan./Feb. 1977, p. 125–136, bibl., tables)

Both the pre-1968 import-substitution and the post 1968 export promotion strategies are considered as failures. More public investment and state role are viewed as the needed remedy.

3292 ——— and **Geoffrey Bertram.** Peru, 1890–1977: growth and policy in an open economy. London, MacMillan Press, 1978. 475 p., bibl., tables.

This is a major historical, empirical and analytical examination of economic growth and change in Peru between 1890 and 1977. It also attempts to explain the persistent poverty in Peru.

3293 Valderrama, Mariano. Reforma agraria y acumulación capitalista en el Perú: el modelo, sus límites y sus contradicciones (CLACSO/ERL, 1:1, enero/abril 1978, p. 97–110)

This short article argues that Peruvian agrarian reform has maintained, not changed, unequal capitalist development.

3294 ———. 7 [i.e. Siete] años de reforma agraria peruana: 1969–1976. Lima, Pontificia Univ. Católica de Perú, Fondo Editorial, 1976. 632 p., fold. table, tables.

A rather comprehensive examination of agrarian reform in Peru between 1969 and 1976. For historian's comment, see *HLAS 40:3565.*

3295 Vargas Haya, Héctor. Contrabando. 2. ed. Lima, Enrique Delgado Valenzuela, 1976. 296 p., facsims., illus., tables.

A fascinating exposé of smuggling in Peru.

3296 Williams, Lynden S. Land use intensity and farm size in highland Cuzco, Peru (JDA, 11:2, Jan. 1977, p. 185–204, maps, tables)

An inverse relationship is found to exist between farm size and land use intensity in highland Cuzco, Peru. For geographer's comment, see item **5558**.

Bolivia, Paraguay, and Uruguay

MICHAEL L. COOK, *Assistant Professor of Agricultural Economics, Texas A&M University*

THIS REVIEW OF RECENT ECONOMIC RESEARCH on Uruguay, Paraguay, and Bolivia reveals a number of trends: 1) most of the research is non-controversial and apolitical; 2) the intensification of data gathering in all three countries has resulted in a number of statistical and descriptive studies of noted sophistication; 3) the chief means of publication for such works are not journals, but government documents and monographs; 4) Uruguay's swing from an "economie dirigée" to a more price-oriented system has led to numerous publications which attempt to justify this policy change; 5) the scarcity and irregularity of Paraguayan economic literature still hinder research in the field; and 6) government-planning studies for the agricultural and non-renewable resource sectors continue to dominate the economic literature on Bolivia.

Of the 70 plus works annotated in this section, there was only one that was "anti-regime" in tone, Leiva's study of underdevelopment (item **3324**). While most authors supported the armed forces in power, the few who disagreed with military policy did so politely or by couching their objections in technical, non-controversial language. The absence of critical literature, characteristic of Paraguay and Bolivia, is a relatively new phenomenon in Uruguay, a country with a long tradition of political criticism.

The increasing complexity of the economic environment in these three countries requires much compilation of data. And although all three appear to be developing good macroeconomic data files, only Uruguay's COMCORDE has made significant progress at the microeconomic level. Scholarly research in the field is suffering in all three nations because of the scarcity of data analysis which is largely due to the lack of investigators. Why so few individuals are engaged in economic research can be attributed to political constraints, low academic salaries, and to the low level of university funding allocated to economic research.

There is no institution in the region that acts as a catalyst for interchanges on economic theory, policy, or methodology. This institutional vacuum and the absence of economic journals inhibits professional dialogue on economic performance and the factors which influence it. Because of the lack of national or regional journals, the only research to be published is either government-sponsored (thus invariably government-oriented) or on popular subjects for the mass market. Neither the government nor the popular press are adequate vehicles for informed dialogue among economic researchers and policy-makers.

Themes that dominate Uruguayan publications include the National Development Plan, 1973–77 (item **3362**) and agricultural topics. Other works concentrate on economic history and miscellaneous micro and macroeconomic areas. Even though the publications of the National Development Plan are descriptive or legalistic in nature one should recognize their significance for the economic history of Uruguay and recommend the perusal of Development Plan material. An examination of the book by Harvard-trained Végh Villegas allows the researcher to gain an understanding of the theoretical underpinnings of the new policies (item **3363**). Végh Villegas was the major economic policy-maker during the implementation period of the Development Plan.

The number of empirical studies being completed on Uruguay's agricultural sector is largely due to the return of foreign-trained agricultural economists to the country. The DINACOSE compendium is representative of this improvement in output (item **3360**). However, no articles have addressed the economic adjustment and welfare problems that recent radical structural changes were expected to induce. It is hoped that the next *HLAS* volume will include a plethora of titles on these subjects.

In Bolivia, agricultural researchers produced the largest number of works. Most of them were related to resource-allocation policy and food-demand estimation projects under the guidance of USAID. Mineral economics researchers authored a number of outstanding pieces. Of particular interest and quality were Gilles' compendium of articles on the tax structure in the Bolivian mining sector (item **3309**) and Fernández Solís' article on the economic history of petroleum in Bolivia (item **3308**). Several unrelated but well-conceived studies on Bolivia were published in the *Journal of Developing Areas.* Of these, the article by Gómez on the failure to generate surplus revenues before and after the 1952 Revolution will be of particular interest to those evaluating the economic dynamics of Third World change.

Economic research in Paraguay continues to depend on individual initiative, is invariably sparce and sporadic or unrelated to previous work. The highlight of the literature under review was Miranda's objective and balanced analysis of foreign investment in Paraguay (item **3325**). The study evaluates the costs and benefits of foreign-capital ownership utilizing an implied multiple-objective function.

To conclude, one must recognize that the state of economic research in these three struggling River Plate Basin countries is lamentable. The lack of coordination, direction, and openness are characteristics of a permanent condition that are seldom challenged except for intermittent flashes of genius.

BOLIVIA

3297 Asociación de Consultores, Ltda., *Santa Cruz, Bol.* Diagnóstico agropecuario de Santa Cruz. t. 1, Aspectos generales; t. 2, Sector agrícola; t. 3, Sector pecuario; t. 4, Anexo estadístico. Santa Cruz, Bol., 1975. 4 v. (82, 313, 185, 82 p.) inserted map, tables.

A detailed four-volume analysis of the agricultural sector of Santa Cruz, Bol. Provides a micro view of commodity subsectors and production organization in this important region.

Bolivia. Comité Nacional del Sesquicentenario de la República. Monografía de Bolivia. See *HLAS 40:3580.*

3298 ———. Consejo Nacional de Reforma Agraria. Departamento de Estadística. El proceso de reforma agraria en cifras. Introducción de Jorge García Ramos. La Paz, 1975. 163 p., tables.

Vol. 2 of Bolivian agrarian reform program statistics. Aggregated and disaggregated tables. No text.

3299 ———. ———. Dirección de Planificación. Departamento Agrotécnico. Departamento Socio-Económico. Estudio socioeconómico y agropecuario: Departamento del Beni. Presentación de Casto Arteaga Balderrama. La Paz, 1976. 539 p., fold. maps, maps, tables.

Socio-economic description of agricultural sector in Beni. Data is extensive but of 1973 vintage.

3300 ———. **Ministerio de Asuntos Campesinos y Agropecuarios. Oficina de Estudios Económicos y Estadísticos. División de Estadísticas.** Estadísticas agropecuarias: 1961–1975. Presentación de Alberto Natusch Busch. La Paz, 1976. 81 p., tables (Boletín, 2)

Consists of 15 years of data on crop area planted and crop production for 59 commodities. Some production figures for livestock.

3301 ———. **Ministerio de Industria, Comercio y Turismo.** Informe de labores: agosto 1971–mayo 1975. La Paz, 1975. 127 p., tables.

A review of investments in and progress of national development projects during the period 1971–75. Numerous tables.

3302 ———. **Ministerio de Minería y Metalurgia.** Bolivia: minera en números. La Paz, 1975. 152 p., tables.

Excellent source of data on mineral export volume and value, destination of exports, exporting firm volume for the period 1965–74. Also reviews contents of the International Tin Agreement.

3303 ———. **Ministerio de Planeamiento y Coordinación.** Informe anual al CEP-CIES. La Paz, 1975. 1 v. (Various pagings) maps, tables.

A descriptive evaluation of the Bolivian economic situation as seen by the administration in 1975. No economic analysis included. Detailed tables and data.

3304 ———. ———. Plan de desarrollo económico y social: inventario de proyectos con requerimientos de financiamiento externo, 1977–1978. La Paz, 1976. 301 p., tables.

An annotated listing of planned development projects as of 1977 and their estimated costs.

3305 ———. ———. Plan de desarrollo económico y social, 1976–1980: resumen. La Paz, 1976. 333 p., fold. tables, tables.

A summary of the 1976–80 Bolivian National Development Plan. Very detailed government agency organization charts and tables.

3306 ———. ———. Plan nacional de desarrollo económico y social: 1976–

1980. t. 3/4. La Paz, 1976. 2 v. (401, 265 p.) tables.

For vols. 1/2, see *HLAS 39:3360.* These vols. 3/4 cover the urban, sanitation, education, health, social security and nutrition sectors. Valuable statistics.

———. ———. Sector industrias. See item **5759.**

3307 ———. ———. **Instituto Nacional de Estadística.** Estadísticas industriales: años 1972–1973. Presentación de Jorge Félix Ballivián Valdés. La Paz, 1972. 278 p., map, tables.

Continuation of industrial statistical series for 1972 and 1973. Production, sales, employment, salaries and wages, by product class.

3308 Fernández Solís, Jorge. Tema: el petróleo. La Paz, Los Amigos del Libro, 1976. 279 p., illus., plates.

Comprehensive legal and economic history of the petroleum industry in Bolivia from 1825 to the present. Good data and well documented.

3309 Gillis, Malcolm and others. Taxation and mining: nonfuel minerals in Bolivia and other countries. Cambridge, Mass., Ballinger, 1978. 358 p., bibl., tables.

Consists of nine well-coordinated articles with the tax structure of Bolivian mining as the central focus. Comprehensive chapter on comparative mining taxes covering 17 countries' tax structures. Other chapters range from descriptive to analytical.

3310 Gómez, Walter. Bolivia: problems of a pre- and post-revolutionary export economy (JDA, 10:4, July 1976, p. 461–484, map, tables)

Insightful explanation as to why the "surplus" that might have been extracted from the mining sector and applied to domestic development was lost both before and after the 1952 revolution.

3311 González M., René. Informativo económico de Bolivia. 2. ed. La Paz, Los Amigos del Libro, 1977. 188 p., tables.

Very superficial description of the major sectors constituting the Bolivian economy.

Inotai, András. The possibilities and limits of a balanced and harmonious development in the Andean integration. See item **3123.**

3312 Linares Arraya, Adolfo. La realidad económica y social de Bolivia: memorandum. Introducción por Mariano Baptista Gumucio. La Paz, Editorial Los Amigos del Libro, 1974. 99 p. (Mini Col. Un siglo y medio)

A series of essays stressing the importance of a balanced approach to development, e.g., that agriculture should receive attention as well as the mining, manufacturing, and energy sectors.

3313 Madsen, Albert G. Evaluación de responsabilidades legales y funcionales de entidades públicas para actividades de mercadeo agrícola en Bolivia. With the assistance of Freddy Arteaga H. La Paz, Consortium for International Development (CID), 1977. 67 p., bibl. (Working paper [Documento de trabajo], 004/77)

A comprehensive description of the functions of public institutions involved in agricultural commodity and product marketing. Table 1 provides an excellent one-page review of the article.

3314 Mantilla, Julio and Allen D. LeBaron. Estimaciones de demanda para productos escogidos de origen agropecuario en Bolivia: 1980–1985. La Paz, Ministerio de Asuntos Campesinos y Agropecuarios, Oficina de Planificación Sectorial, 1977. 50 p., tables.

Price and income elasticity estimates for numerous Bolivian food products. Demand estimated for the period 1980–85.

3315 Mounier, Alain. Formes initiales de l'industrialisation bolivienne (FDD/NED [Problèmes d'Amérique Latine, 46] 4443/4445, 12 déc. 1975, p. 50–60, tables)

A brief economic history of Bolivia's mineral export dependence and the 1960s thrust into an industrial development program.

3316 Pinell Siles, Armando. Características de la población económicamente activa de Bolivia: análisis de algunos resultados de la encuesta demográfica nacional de 1975. La Paz, Ministerio de Planeamiento y Coordinación, Instituto Nacional de Estadística, 1976. 35 p., tables.

Summary of 1975 National Demographic survey. Concentrates on the characteristics of the economically active population of Bolivia. Nationally aggregated tables.

Schoop, Wolfgang. Industrialization and regional planning in Bolivia. See item **5452.**

3317 Smith, Stephen M. Labor exploitation on pre-1952 haciendas in the lower valley of Cochabamba, Bolivia (JDA, 11:2, Jan. 1977, p. 227–244, tables)

More historical than analytical summary of peasant labor exploitation in the region where Bolivia's militant peasant movement originated.

3318 Urquidi, Arturo. Temas de reforma agraria. Prefacio por Alipio Valencia Vega. La Paz, Librería Editorial Juventud, 1976. 120 p., bibl.

Three critical essays on the Agrarian Reform Law of 1953 and proposed amendments authored by one of the formulators of the original legislation.

3319 Villavicencio Chumacero, Ismael. Esquema histórico, económico y social de la empresa minera Catavi: en el vigésimo aniversario de la nacionalización de las minas. 2. ed. Cochabamba, Bol., Editorial Serrano, 1976. 171 p., plates.

A socio-economic case study description of technological, geographic, management, labor and legal problems confronted by a Bolivian mining company.

3320 Whitaker, Morris D. and E. Boyd Wennergren. Common-property rangeland and induced neighborhood effects: resource misallocation in Bolivian agriculture. La Paz, Consortium for International Development (CID), 1976. 35 p., bibl., table (Technical report, 001/76)

Concludes that immediate reforms need to be implemented to prevent destruction of a significant proportion of the arable lands of Bolivia's traditional production areas. A number of alternatives are suggested based on economic models.

3321 Zuvekas, Clarence, Jr. Unemployment and underemployment in Bolivian agriculture: a critical survey of the literature. Washington, U.S. Agency for International Development, Bureau for Latin America, Rural Development Division, 1977. 70 p., bibl., map, tables (Working document series: Bolivia. General working document, 3)

A well documented critical review of the rural unemployment, internal and external migration, wage rates, and government employment policy literature related to the nonurban sector of Bolivia.

PARAGUAY

3322 Frutos, Juan Manuel. De la reforma agraria al bienestar rural, y otros documentos concernientes a la marcha de la reforma agraria. Prólogo de Mario Halley Mora. Asunción, Instituto de Bienestar Rural, n.d. 177 p., maps, tables.

Papers delivered at the V Reunión Interamericana de Ejecutivos de la Reforma Agraria, Asunción (no date given). They consist of a detailed description of the history, objectives, and implementation of the Paraguayan agrarian reform program by the first President of the Instituto de Reforma Agraria. Some noncontroversial opinions given by an international panel of experts on agrarian reform. Tables and maps are informative. None of the papers address the hard questions that need to be confronted in this policy area.

3323 González García, Leovigildo. Problemática monetaria. t. 1, Elementos de economía. Asunción, Imprenta Comuneros, 1972. 321 p., bibl., tables.

The first of a three volume set on international monetary history, policy, and strategies. Pt. 1 is a review of the 20th-century international monetary system. Pt. 2 reviews in detail the 1968–69 European monetary crisis. Pt. 3 introduces the concept of Special Drawing Rights. The brief section on the Paraguayan monetary policy during this period is of specific interest.

3324 Leiva, Ramón. Paraguay, subdesarrollo: sugerencias para un programa de liberación nacional. Presentación de Arturo Acosta Mena. B.A., Artes Gráficas Negri, 1975. 309 p., maps, tables.

An impassioned call by an exiled thinker for Paraguay to follow a more autonomous development strategy. An extensive documentation of the history of Paraguay's economic "dependencia" precedes final section on the limitations of Brazil's development as a model of neocapitalism. Author also expresses concern about Brazil's expansionist ambitions.

3325 Miranda, Anibal. Efecto de las inversiones extranjeras en la economía paraguaya (UCNSA/EP, 4:1, dic. 1976, p. 129–160, tables)

Refreshingly objective study of the effects of foreign investment on the economy of Paraguay. Concludes that foreign investment has brought both costs and benefits to a number of economic sectors. Suggests that more attention be given to equity performance measures when approving foreign investment ventures in Paraguay.

3326 Paraguay. Ministerio de Agricultura y Ganadería. Proyecto de educación agropecuaria. Asunción, Banco Interamericano de Desarrollo (BID) [and] Instituto Interamericano de Ciencias Agrícolas (IICA), 1977. 5 v. (Various pagings) fold. tables, tables.

A five-volume project outline for increasing the number of domestically trained agricultural technicians. An in-depth look at the agricultural education system in Paraguay. Some comprehensive tables of the general Paraguayan economy.

3327 ———. Ministerio de Hacienda. Dirección General de Presupuesto. Presupuesto general de la nación: administración central, ejercicio fiscal. Asunción, 1977. 622 p., tables.

No time series figures and no actual versus proposed budget comparisons.

3328 *Quarterly Economic Review: Uruguay, Paraguay.* The Economist Intelligence Unit (EIU). No. 1, 1973 [through] No. 4, 1976–. London.

The Economist Intelligence Unit of London publishes 70 *Quarterly Economic Reviews* which cover 150 countries. One of these 70 is devoted to covering both Uruguay and Paraguay (i.e., No. 1, 1973; No. 2, 1973; No. 3, 1973; No. 4, 1973, etc.). Moreover, each year an *Annual Supplement* is also published (e.g., *Quarterly Economic Review: Uruguay, Paraguay—Annual Supplement 1973; Quarterly Economic Review: Uruguay, Paraguay—Annual Supplement 1974*, etc.). The former or regular quarterly issues provide excellent introductory material and objective description of the countries' political, agricultural, foreign trade and payments, and general economic events on a quarterly basis. The latter or annual supplements are more detailed and comprehensive and include numerous tables on government, employment, population, currency, national income, agriculture, mining, fuel use, manufacturing, transport and communications, finance, foreign trade and payments, and trade/exchange regulations. The supplements provide an excellent overall view of Paraguay's economy for the given years.

Rivarola, Domingo M. and **José N. Morinigo.** La vivienda en el Paraguay: sus condicionantes socio-económicos. See item **9288.**

—— and others. La población del Paraguay. See item **9289.**

3329 Viedma, Pablo Franco ed. Album conmemorativo de la estabilidad monetaria en el Paraguay. Asunción, n.p., 1977. 90 p., facsim., illus., plates, tables.

Several informative and conceptual articles by Central Bank economists on the recent history (1967–77) of monetary policy of Paraguay. Little data, few tables.

URUGUAY

3330 Anichini, Juan José; Jorge Caumont; and **Larry Sjaastad.** La política comercial y la protección en el Uruguay. Montevideo, Banco Central del Uruguay, Secretaría General, 1977. 211 p., fold. tables, tables.

Excellent review of the economic and political roots of an import-substitution policy that has created significant resource allocation distortions. Concludes that a modified move toward free trade is the only solution for Uruguay's economic sector to return to a dynamic force. Some empirical estimates of costs of protection.

3331 Astori, Danilo; Ricardo Zerbino; Juan Rodríguez López; and **Alberto Tisnes.** Inversión extranjera y desarrollo económico. Montevideo, Fundación de Cultura Universitaria [and] Colegio de Doctores en Ciencias Económicas y Contadores del Uruguay, 1975. 109 p.

Four papers by Uruguayan economists responding to the enactment of the 1974 Law No. 14.179 allowing for increased foreign investment in Uruguay. Also includes well-thought-out opposing opinions with good history of previous foreign investment activity in this staunchly independent republic.

3332 Azzarini, Mario and others. Relevamiento básico de la producción ovina

en el Uruguay: 1972/1973. Montevideo, Secretariado Uruguayo de la Lana, 1975. 47 p., map, tables.

Very professional presentation of the production and marketing system of Uruguay's most important product: sheep-wool. Excellent but dated tables.

3333 Bolsa de Valores, *Montevideo.* **Asesoria Estadística.** Análisis estadístico de 50 años de Bolsa: 1925–1975. t. 1/2. Montevideo, 1976. 2 v. (68, 75 p.) bibl., fold. tables, tables.

Excellent data base for 50 years of prices and finance variables.

3334 ——, ——. Valores de renta variable: rentabilidad bruta del inversionista en Bolsa. t. 1, Sectores: metálicos, caucho y químicos; período 1972–1976; t. 2, Sectores: bebidas, papel, y minerales no metálicos; período 1972–1976; t. 3, Sectores: financiero, alimentación y textil; período 1972–1976. Montevideo, 1977? 3 v. (24, 25, 24 p.) tables.

A detailed graphical description of the Uruguayan stock market performance in selected industries during the period of 1972–1976. Detailed set of data presented in tables.

3335 Centro Latinoamericano de Economía Humana, *Montevideo.* Cuenca del Plata. Montevideo, 1977. 99 p., map.

Series of thoughtful essays of the Plata Basin and its possible development. Some emphasis on Uruguay. [J.M. Hunter]

3336 ——, ——. El proceso de integración en América Latina. Montevideo, 1976. 94 p., bibl.

A series of papers, delivered at a 1975 conference, on integration particularly with regard to Uruguay. Contributors include officials of INTAL. [J.M. Hunter]

3337 Comisión Coordinadora para el Desarrollo Económico (COMCORDE), *Montevido.* **Secretaría Técnica.** Aspectos de la evolución económica del Uruguay: 1972–1976. Montevideo, 1977. 110 p., tables.

A descriptive evaluation of the macroeconomic policies adopted and the resulting performance for each of the five years presented. Study details the indecisiveness of the policies during the first two years of the National Development Plan. Important introductory material for researcher interested in the economics of a country suffering through severe political uncertainty.

3338 ——, ——. ——. COMCORDE: estatutos y documentos principales. Montevideo, 1977. 44 p.

The legal statutes and constitution of COMCORDE, an Uruguayan economic research and information service organization, is presented. Their most recent publications and members are also listed.

3339 ——, ——. ——. Evolución de los precios relativos a una selección de productos de primera necesidad: período 1955–1977. Montevideo, 1977. 8 p., fold. tables, tables.

Detailed price statistics for major consumer goods. Updates publication annotated in *HLAS 39:3477.*

3340 ——, ——. ——. Guía de los esquemas de financiamiento disponibles en el Uruguay. Montevideo, 1977. 174 p., tables.

A technical description of debt capital acquisition methods for the industrial, agricultural, fishing, commercial, hotel and export sectors in Uruguay.

3341 ——, ——. ——. La indústria alimentaria en el Uruguay: elementos para un análisis de la rama de procesamiento de frutos y hortalizas. Montevideo, 1976. 74 p., tables.

This feasibility study of the fruit-processing industry in Uruguay is important because of the trade and cost-data presented in the appendices.

3342 ——, ——. ——. La indústria de la construcción y la economía nacional: 1970–1975. Montevideo, 1976. 1 v. (Various pagings) tables.

Data filled description of Uruguay's construction industry and the role it plays in the national economy.

3343 Echeverría Leunda, Jorge. Proyecto Salto Grande: aspectos económicos y financieros. Montevideo, Academia Nacional de Economía, 1976? 34 l., tables.

A general description of the costs and benefits of a major hydroelectric project being constructed through cooperative efforts of Uruguay, Argentina and a number of international creditors. No rigorous economic analysis but a brief, well written summary of a major project that has been in development for more than 20 years and is vitally important to the future development of Uruguay's energy sector.

3344 *Encuesta de Hogares.* República Oriental del Uruguay, Ministerio de Economía y Finanzas, Dirección General de Estadística y Censos. Año 8, Tomo 11, enero/junio 1976–. Montevideo.

Issue entitled "Ocupación Desocupación" consists of 43 tables of unemployment-employment data collected from a well designed sample covering the period Jan./June 1976.

Faraone, Roque. Introducción a la historia económica del Uruguay: 1825–1973. See *HLAS 40:3934.*

3345 Germany. Bunesstelle für Aussenhandels-information. Uruguay: wirtschaftliche entwicklung, 1976. Köln, FRG, 1977. 24 p., tables.

Succinct and broad overview of the Uruguayan economy from 1974 through 1976.

3346 Horta Berro, Roberto. La encuesta industrial mensual: análisis de los resultados, marzo 1973–junio 1976. Montevideo, Comisión Coordinadora para el Desarrollo Económico (COMCORDE), Secretaría Técnica, 1976. 56 p., fold. tables, tables.

A sample of 150 industrial firms who report monthly on production, sales and employment changes related to their firms and industries. Both quantitative and qualitative results indicate the obvious high degree of uncertainty that existed during the 1973–1976 period.

3347 Inter-American Development Bank. Instituto para la Integración de América Latina (INTAL). Estrategias para incrementar el comercio entre los países miembros de URUPABOL. B.A., 1974. 150 p., tables (Estudios, 10)

An IDB study on the feasibility of increasing trade between Uruguay, Paraguay, and Bolivia. Generates lists of potential export and import products and commodities. Some good trade data relevant to commerce between these three River Plate Basin countries.

3348 Jacob, Raúl. El Uruguay en la crisis de 1929: algunos indicadores económicos.

Montevideo, Fundación de Cultura Universitaria (FCU), 1977. 92 p., tables.

Consists of 90-plus pages of well organized data relevant to the 10-year period preceding and following the 1929 economic crisis in Uruguay.

3349 Lerin, François and **Cristina Torres.**
La politique économique du gouvernement uruguayan (FDD/NED [Problèmes d'Amérique Latine, 49] 4485/4486, 6 nov. 1978, p. 59–84, tables)

History of the abrogation of Uruguay's National Development Plan (CIDE, 1964–74) by the new military leaders, and a description of the implementation of a more price-oriented National Plan (1973–77). Not economically rigorous but historically an important piece.

3350 Pereyra, Arturo and others. Regionalización: un aporte al estudio del caso uruguayo. Montevideo, Centro Latinoamericano de Economía Humana, 1977. 78 p., bibls., maps, tables.

A compendium of five articles on the subdiscipline of spatial economics in Uruguay. Topics cover geographic, political, administrative, historical and regional development. Several of the authors offer particularly stimulating concepts for those interested in the future development of Uruguay.

3351 Petit de Prego, María. Etapes d'un processus économique: de l'expansion a la crise (FDD/NED [Problèmes d'Amérique Latine, 49] 4485/4486, 6 nov. 1978, p. 107–136, bibl., tables)

Descriptive analysis of the economic development of Uruguay during the 20th century. Develops various hypotheses as to why the 1973 coup took place. Good tables.

3352 Price, Waterhouse, Peat & Co., *Montevideo!* Guía para inversiones en el Uruguay. Montevideo, Comisión Coordinadora para el Desarrollo Económico (COMCORDE), Secretaría Técnica, 1976. 55 p., tables.

Necessary reading for researcher who is interested in Uruguay's new (1973) foreign investment laws, (incorporation, credit, taxes, and social contributions).

3353 Prost, Gérard. Ganados sin hombres ou la latifundium en Uruguay résiste au temps (UTIEH/C, 28, 1977, p. 105–122)

Interesting hypotheses on how latifundia resist change over time in Uruguay. Especially important socio-economic analysis since the latifundista has dominated much of the political and economic scene in Uruguay over last two centuries.

3354 Quagliotti de Bellis, Bernardo; Leonel Falco Frommel; Oscar W. Paris; and **Oscar Abadie Aicardi.** Cuenca del Tacuarembó: Plan de Desarrollo: informe preliminar. Montevideo, n.p., 1976. 64 l., maps, tables.

A descriptive evaluation of the geo-socio-economic variables affecting the geopolitical development of the Brazilian-Uruguayan frontier. No original data presented. Organized section of secondary data is unique.

3355 *Quarterly Economic Review: Uruguay, Paraguay.* The Economist Intelligence Unit (EIU). No. 1, 1973 [through] No. 4, 1976–. London.

The Economist Intelligence Unit of London publishes 70 *Quarterly Economist Reviews* which cover 150 countries. One of these 70 is devoted to covering *both* Uruguay and Paraguay (i.e., No. 1, 1973; No. 2, 1973; No. 3, 1973; No. 4, 1973; etc.). Moreover, each year an *Annual Supplement* is also published (e.g., *Quarterly Economic Review: Uruguay, Paraguay—Annual Supplement 1973; Quarterly Economic Review: Uruguay, Paraguay—Annual Supplement 1974,* etc.). The former or regular quarterly issues provide excellent introductory material and objective description of the countries' political, agricultural, foreign trade and payments, and general economic events on a quarterly basis. The latter or annual supplements are more detailed and comprehensive and include numerous tables on government, employment, population, currency, national income, agriculture, mining, fuel use, manufacturing, transport and communications, finance, foreign trade and payments, and trade/exchange regulations. The supplements provide an excellent overall view of Uruguay's economy for the given years.

3356 Ricaldoni, América Pablo; José Enrique Santías; and **Lindor Silva.** El régimen de promoción industrial: análisis del régimen de la Ley No. 14.178 y sus vinculaciones con el de inversiones extranjeras. Montevideo, Fundación de Cultura Universitaria, 1975. 183 p., tables.

An explanation of the "Industrial Promotion Law" and "Foreign Investment Law" adopted by the military regime in 1973. Detailed legal treatment outlining the policy of "freeing" foreign investment and resource allocation. No analysis on data. Description of new policies.

3357 Seminario sobre Mercado de Capitales en el Uruguay, *Montevideo, 1973.* Seminario: mercado de capitales en el Uruguay, Montevideo, diciembre de 1973. t. 1/2. Montevideo, Banco Central del Uruguay, Asesoría Económica y Estudios, 1974. 2 v. (702 p.) (Continuous pagination) fold. tables, tables.

Two volumes containing 14 papers given at a special capital markets seminar sponsored by the OAS and the Banco Central del Uruguay. Topics range from detailed studies of the Uruguayan capital markets to an overview of Development Banks in Latin America. Most articles are well documented and provide an excellent data base.

3358 Universidad de la República, *Montevideo.* **Facultad de Ciencias Económicas y de Administración. Instituto de Estadística.** Uruguay: estadísticas básicas. Montevideo, 1975? 215 p., tables.

End product, income, population, prices and financial data on the agricultural, industrial, service and public sectors is presented in a well documented fashion.

3359 Uruguay. Ministerio de Agricultura y Pesca (MAP). **Dirección de Investigaciones Económicas Agropecuarias** (DIEA). **Sub-Dirección de Estudios Econométricos.** Información histórica de precios agrícolas. 2. ed. rev. y actualizada. Montevideo, 1976. 71 p., tables (Serie informativa, 5)

Evaluation of trends in Uruguayan grain and oil-seed prices over the past 15 years. Some average profitability estimates for production enterprises are also made. Data is well presented.

3360 ——. ——. Dirección Nacional de Contralor de Semovientes, Frutos del País, Marcas y Señales (DI.NA.CO.SE.). Investigaciones sobre la problemática agropecuaria actual. Montevideo, Editorial Hemisferio Sur, 1976. 287 p., bibl., map, tables.

Well edited compendium addressing the optimal allocation of resources by individual firms involved in the livestock sector.

Excellent data analyzed with intermediate level econometric techniques.

3361 ——. Ministerio de Ganadería y Agricultura. Oficina de Programación y Política Agropecuaria. Plan de Desarrollo Agropecuario. t. 1, Lineamientos de política agropecuaria; t. 2, Período 1973–1977. Montevideo, 1973. 2 v. (299 p.) (Continuous pagination) maps, tables.

Obligatory reading for researchers interested in understanding the agricultural policy (price, subsidy and tax) of Uruguay. Also includes commodity specific policies. Not a good data source but excellent description of agricultural policy.

3362 ——. Presidencia. Oficina de Planeamiento y Presupuesto. Plan Nacional de Desarrollo: 1973–1977. t. 1/2. Montevideo, 1977. 2 v. (667, 561 p.) fold. tables, tables.

Imperative for researchers interested in understanding recent developments in Uruguay to at least peruse this detailed National Plan of Development. The first two chapters espouse the military regime's socio-economic philosophy and objectives. These chapters are followed by the Investment, Industrial, and Agricultural Plans. Detailed tables.

3363 Végh Villegas, Alejandro. Economía política: teoría y acción. Montevideo, Ediciones Polo, 1977. 123 p., tables.

A summary of the theoretical underpinnings of policies (move to a more market oriented price system) adopted during the restructuring of the Uruguayan economy. Author was the main economic policy maker during this 1973–77 period. Book also includes a collection of author's speeches presented during this period.

3364 Wolf, Bernard van der. La programación monetario-financiera en el Uruguay: 1955–1970. Santiago, Instituto Latinoamericano de Planificación Económica y Social (ILPES), 1974. 130 p., fold. tables, tables (Cuadernos del ILPES. Serie 2:22. Anticipos de investigación)

A respectable qualitative and quantitative analysis of Uruguayan monetary policy from 1955–70. Concludes that some of Uruguay's current problems result from lack of coordination between monetary and other macroeconomic policy tools.

Argentina

JAN PETER WOGART, *Economist, World Bank*

ALTHOUGH RELATIVELY FEW BOOKS HAVE BEEN published on the Argentine economy during 1976-1978, the titles selected below reveal the surprising depth and breadth of current economic research. To a large extent, this is due to the excellent articles published in economic journals such as: *Desarrollo Económico, Ensayos Económicos,* and *Estudios,* the latter a new publication of the Instituto de Estudios Económicos de la Realidad Argentina (IEERA) in Córdoba. In addition, the many problems related to Argentina's high and persistent inflation have attracted the attention of outside observers (items **3377, 3383, 3425**).

Whereas current macro-economic policies are discussed as heatedly as ever in the large and relatively sophisticated daily and weekly newspapers and magazines, academic analysis concentrates on major policies and their significance for economic development in the last 30 years; for this period sufficient data has been gathered and some perspective has been gained (items **3378, 3380, 3384–3385, 3387–3389, 3391, 3402, 3404, 3407–3409** and **3412**).

Nevertheless, there are several contributions concerned with immediate policy problems. In the case of the external tariff reform which is currently implemented, Berlinski's study on effective protection stands out not only because of the controversy and policy action it led to, but also as an example of solid craftsmanship in economic analysis (item **3376**). Although another contribution elaborates on the topic of effective protection (item **3426**), economists have not done full justice to the imminent need to analyze the transformation problems which industry will face, once the tariff structure is substantially lowered.

In the case of the monetary reform, implemented in 1977, several attempts have been undertaken to analyze its major characteristics and to measure its impact on the real and the monetary sector (items **3365, 3371–3372** and **3414**). These essays do not restrict themselves to criticism, but propose additional measures to avoid new distortions and to streamline monetary control.

With respect to sector work, valuable empirical investigations in the energy sector have concentrated on issues of pricing, as well as on demand-and-supply forecasts (items **3395–3396** and **3427**). In industry, problems of concentration and technology transfer have attracted some attention. In that context, a study by Schvarzer on the relationship between the development of the largest enterprises and an emerging industrial strategy is interesting (item **3420**). Finally, an excellent study on the agricultural sector by Recca and Verstraeten attempts not to measure the major factors of production in the past and to evaluate their potential role in the future (item **3413**).

Although most publications are currently coming from research institutions rather than universities, the papers presented at the annual meetings of the Argentine Economic Assn. reflect some important research activities at such universities as Tucumán, La Plata, Córdoba, Buenos Aires and Mendoza. These papers are not included here, since most of them were presented in preliminary form for discussion only. The topics chosen and the type of analysis indicate, however, that we can expect additional quality economic work from Argentina in the years to come. This trend will be strengthened by studies emerging from newly-founded institutions, such as the above mentioned IEERA in Córdoba and the B.A. Institute for Macroeconomic Studies (CEMA).

Alén Lascano, Luis. Desarrollo histórico socioeconómico de la Provincia de Santiago del Estero. See *HLAS 40:3678*.

3365 Argentina. Banco Central. Sector Programación Financiera. La reforma del sistema financiero en la República Argentina. B.A., 1977. 55 p. (Discussion paper, 14)

Discusses in detail rationale and mechanism of monetary reform, but points out that these measures only constitute the basis for a freer and hopefully more efficient development of Argentina's monetary system. This paper was originally delivered at the Reunión de Bancos Centrales del Continente Americano, held in Bariloche, Arg., 1977. As of Aug. 1977, the conference papers were still not published.

3366 ――――. Consejo Federal de Inversiones. La región árida: esquema de su realidad y programa de desarrollo. B.A., 1975. 83 p., table (Serie Bases regionales, 3)

Brief sketch on the arid regions of Argentina, which occupy more than half of the territory and include the poorest provinces of the northwest.

3367 ――――. ――――. Región Comahue: esquema de su realidad y perspectiva. B.A., 1975. 89 p., maps (Serie Bases regionales, 2)

Regional study of the area southwest of Argentina's capital, including the provinces of Neuquén, Río Negro, La Pampa, and a small part of Buenos Aires prov. After brief economic background description study concentrates on feasible projects of agroindustrial character which should stimulate development in that potentially rich but underutilized portion of the country.

3368 ――――. Ministerio de Economía. Fifteen months of Argentine economic development: April 1976–June 1977 (Quinze mois d'évolution economique argentine: avril 1976–juin 1977). B.A., 1977. 66 p., tables.

Account by the Ministry of Economy of the stabilization program and its result during the first 15 months in office. As it turned out the 15 following months were charac-

terized by a substantial number of new difficulties not expected in mid 1977.

3369 ――――. ――――. Ministry of Economy of the Nation: one year of Argentine economic development, 1976–1977. B.A., 1977? 52 p., tables.

Summary of the economic policies designed and implemented by the military government in March–April 1976. Besides the speeches of the President and the Economic Minister, volume contains an analysis of the problems facing the nation in early 1976, the adopted emergency measures and an outlook for 1976. Valuable background material for work on Argentina's latest stabilization effort.

3370 Arnaudo, Aldo A. Economías de operación y economías de escala en el sistema bancario comercial argentino: 1960–72 (BCRA/EE, 2, 1977, p. 41–66)

Study of unit costs of various banking institutions reveals that average costs differ significantly, with provincial banks at the top. In all cases, however, there is little evidence of scale economies, a characteristic one should have expected at least in the large metropolitan banks.

3371 ――――. El nuevo régimen financiero argentino: una perspectiva (IEERAL/E, 1:5, sept./oct. 1978, p. 203–211)

Brief critical essay concentrating on three major aspects of monetary policy in 1977/78: the freeing of interest rates, legal changes in the monetary system and their impact on the efficiency of the financial sector, and the control mechanism of the Central Bank.

3372 ――――; Domingo F. Cavallo; and Aldo R. Dadone. Evaluación de la eficacia del actual régimen financiero argentino (IEERAL/E, 1:2, marzo/abril 1978, p. 50–58)

Analysis of the financial sector and policy proposal for its transformation into an efficient mediator. Article includes an additional analysis of possible ways in which the Central Bank can control the money supply and use open market policies more actively.

3373 Ayres, Robert L. The Social Pact as anti-inflationary policy: the Argentine experience since 1973 (PUCIS/WP, 28:4, July 1976, p. 473–501)

Although admitting that the Social Pact did not solve any of the economic problems Argentina faced in the early 1970s, the author argues that this type of action may have some value for future short-term political decision-making. It provided the government with room to maneuver in an unstable environment.

3374 Bajraj, Reynaldo F. La inflación Argentina en los años sesenta (BCV/REL, 13:50, 1977, p. 197–272, tables)

Lengthy study on Argentina's inflation between 1970 and 1975, analyzing both, the real and monetary factors contributing to the accelerating rate of inflation. Author puts major emphasis on the role of imported inflation and the fight for increasing income shares, which became particularly serious after 1973.

3375 Balán, Jorge. Una cuestión regional en la Argentina: burguesías provinciales y el mercado nacional en el desarrollo agroexportador. B.A., Centro de Estudios de Estado y Sociedad, 1977? 53 p., bibl. (Estudios sociales, 8)

Socio-economic analysis of the creation of two "agro-burgeois" societies in the interior of Argentina during the late 19th century, exemplified by the sugar-dominated economy of Tucumán and the wine-growing region of Mendoza. Emphasis is put on the origin of their power, their relation to the central government authorities, and the participation of foreign capital in production, transport, and marketing.

3376 Berlinski, Julio. La protección arancelaria de actividades seleccionadas de la industria manufacturera argentina. B.A., Ministerio de Economía, 1977. 44 p., tables.

Crucial study on effective protection of manufacturing, based on sample survey of 140 firms in early 1977, concludes that the basic problem is less the relatively high average level, which turned out to be close to 40 percent, but the enormous spread of effective protection among major industrial branches. Study served as a basic input for government's liberalization strategy in 1977–78.

3377 Blejer, Mario I. Money and the nominal interest rate in an inflationary economy: an empirical test (JPE, 86:3, 1978, p. 529–534)

While theoretically the liquidity and credit effects should lower the rate of interest in times of money-supply increase, higher inflationary expectations work in the opposite direction. The empirical test of Argentina's recent experience confirms the importance of inflationary expectations.

3378 Brodersohn, Mario S. Conflictos entre los objetivos de política económica de corto plazo en la economía argentina. B.A., Instituto Torcuato Di Tella, Centro de Investigaciones Económicas, 1977. 37 p., bibl., tables (Documento de trabajo, 77)

Survey of Argentine economic policy since 1950 pointing towards the inconsistencies of policymakers and their plans. This is followed by impact analysis in major sectors. Recommendations for more coherent policies put special emphasis on income distribution aspects. This same study was also published as an article in *Revista de Economía Latinoamericana* (Banco Central de Venezuela, Caracas, 13:49, 1977, p. 115–152).

3379 Cafasso, José and **Enrique Recchi.** Economía energética argentina: los esclavos mecánicos. Prólogo de Juan Sábato. B.A., Editorial Don Bosco, 1976. 421 p., bibls., illus., tables.

Richly documented and illustrated study of Argentina's energy sector, concentrating mainly on sources and factors of supply.

3380 Cavallo, Domingo F. Los efectos recessivos e inflacionarios de las políticas monetaristas de estabilización (BCRA/EE, 4, dic. 1977, p. 107–148)

Synthesis of doctoral dissertation analyzing the recessionary and inflationary effects of monetary stabilization programs both, in a theoretical model and with empirical data from Argentina. Since "stagflation" has led to economic and political instability, author proposes using strong income policy, including price controls, at the beginning of stabilization efforts.

3381 ———— and Jorge H. Alfonso. Un examen global del sistema tributario argentino en 1977 (IEERAL/E, 1:1, enero/feb. 1978, p. 3–18)

Global survey of Argentine tax system in 1977 finds that, although tax burden has increased considerably, deficit financing was still too large to follow a price stabilization policy in 1977. Authors further maintain that tax system and legislation required immediate corrections in order to avoid additional distortions in the productive structure of the economy.

3382 ———; **Héctor E. Montero; and Dante A. Olivieri.** Distribución de recursos fiscales nacionales entre provincias y municipalidades: una evaluación sobre la equidad en los criterios de reparto (IEERAL/E, 1:1, enero/feb. 1978, p. 19–31)

Study on fiscal federalism points toward the privileged position of B.A. city, which is found to be heavily subsidized by the major provinces of the country.

Cervera, Felipe Justo. Sociología de la dependencia interna. See item **9260**.

3383 **Chu, Ke-Young and Andrew Feltenstein.** Relative price distortions and inflation: the case of Argentina, 1963–1976 (IMF/SP, 25:3, Sept. 1978, p. 452–493)

Good study of the self-generating mechanism of Argentina's inflation, resulting from structural distortions of relative prices. Since most of these distortions were created by price controls, those measures which were primarily designed to control inflation did contribute to persistent price increases several years later. A simulation exercise using quarterly data between 1967 and 1976 confirms the authors' hypothesis.

3384 **Dagum, Camilo.** El modelo log-logístico y la distribución del ingreso en la Argentina (FCE/TE, 44[4]:176, oct./dic. 1977, p. 837–864, bibl., tables)

Income distribution study for three selective years (1953, 1959, 1961) shows slight increase in concentration (Gini coefficient rises from .44 to .49 and reaches .46 in last year) during post-Perón era. Comparison with US and Canada demonstrates that Argentina's income distribution was somewhat more unequal than two highly industrialized countries but far better than all other Latin American countries during the 1950s and early 1960s.

3385 **Eiteman, David K.** Financing Argentine industrial corporate development in the aftermath of the first Perón period (in Wilkie, James W. ed. Money and politics in Latin America [see item **2935**] p. 41–91, tables)

Detailed analysis by FIEL of industrial corporate financing in the late 1950s and early 1960s, based on a sample survey of 50 largest industrial corporations. Results are significantly influenced by macro-policies, but consistent trends of substantial auto-financing—through retained earnings and use of funds for working capital rather than for fixed investment—provide a good insight of industrial financing.

Epstein, Edward C. Anti-inflation policies in Argentina and Chile: or, who pays the cost. See item **3214**.

3386 **Feldman, Ernesto.** Comportamiento de la demanda de bienes durables en un período de alta inflación: Argentina, 1974–1975 (BCRA/EE, 2, junio 1977, p. 67–98)

Interesting study explaining that the high demand for durable consumer goods in 1974–75 was not only a function of relatively high real wages but more importantly due to the relatively low prices of these goods, the rapidly declining value of monetary assets, and the all-important inflationary expectations.

3387 **Ferrer, Aldo.** Crisis y alternativas de la política económica argentina. B.A., Fondo de Cultura Económica, 1977. 123 p.

Following the successful style of analysis used in his book on the Argentine economy, which summarized the economic history of that country until World War II (see HLAS 37:4716), Ferrer now presents a brief examination of the major economic policies shaping the post-war economy. Since the constant shift between populism and liberalism has led to increasing instability and slow growth, author outlines an alternative course of action and sketches the major elements of such a strategy.

3388 ———. La economía política del peronismo (FCE/TE, 44:173, enero/marzo 1977, p. 73–115)

Analysis of peronist economic policies during two post-war periods finds that constraints in the public sector and in the balance of payments made an adverse effect on the viability of these policies unviable for a prolonged period of time.

3389 ——— and others. La economía argentina. B.A., Editorial de Belgrano, 1977. 266 p. (Cátedra del pensamiento argentino)

Transcript of 1977 conference focussing on major issues of current economic policy: monetary management and fiscal policy, international finance and foreign investment, public enterprise, basic industries and the role of technology in the economy.

3390 Flichman, Guillermo. La renta del suelo y el desarrollo agrario argentino. México, Siglo XXI Editores, 1977. 241 p., tables.

Essay on rent and quasi-rent in agricultural sector attempts to explain stagnation of Pampean output within the framework of Marxian analysis.

3391 Fogarty, John P. Difusión de tecnología en área de asentamiento reciente: el caso de Australia y de la Argentina (IDES/DE, 17:65, abril/junio 1977, p. 133–142)

Brief comparative analysis of major factors accounting for distinct development patterns of Argentina and Australia. The latter country's need to stimulate stagnant agricultural output in the late 19th century required large-scale government involvement in agricultural research and development, an involvement which has taken place in Argentina only since the mid-1950s.

3392 Frediani, Ramón; Carlos E. Sandrini; and Carlos P. Scaro. Comparación internacional de precios de productos siderúrgicos (IEERAL/E, 1:5, sept./oct. 1978, p. 167–186)

In early 1978, Argentina's steel prices averaged about 20 percent more than prices charged for the same products in major industrial countries. Once shipping and higher transport costs were accounted for that difference shrank to about 14 percent. More interesting than this spot comparison is the finding that the price difference increased with higher degree of production and value added. This would point either to relatively higher inefficiency or higher degree of monopoly power of the producers.

3393 ——; ——; and Juan Tomasetti. Algunas causas de los elevados aportes previsionales en Argentina (IEERAL/E, 1:2, marzo/abril 1978, p. 73–87)

Study of the social security system examines problems of financing, evasion, services rendered, and costs. Maintains that if the contributions of the private sector would not be transferred to public sector employees, labor costs could be reduced by six percent, or at least better services could be introduced in the case of accidents and sickness. This in turn would require a reduction in the evasion of social security payments.

3394 Freyssinet, Jacques. L'effet des enterprises multinationales sur l'emploi en Amérique Latine (FDD/NED [Problèmes d'Amérique Latine, 46] 4443/4445, 12 déc. 1975, p. 5–16, tables)

Employment data for national and multinational firms was found to be inadequate. Thus, data had to be especially developed. Firms contribute more to production than to employment and have high capital-to-labor ratios. Considers other elements, e.g., training. A case study: Argentine vehicle manufacturing. [J.M. Hunter]

Frigerio, Rogelio. La crisis argentina: sus causas, los responsables, sus soluciones. See item **7479.**

3395 Givogri, Carlos A. and Alfred A. Visintini. Las proyecciones de la demanda de energía en Argentina (IEERAL/E, 1:2, marzo/abril 1978, p. 59–71)

Projection of energy demand in Argentina until 1985 uses three alternative assumptions of growth of GDP. In comparing their own results with a recent government study, authors find that while growth of electricity consumption is projected as growing at very similar rates, estimates of other energy consumptions differ widely. Authors attribute these differences to income elasticities assumed to be much lower by the government authorities.

3396 —— and Juan Carlos Kusnir. Análisis comparativa de las tarifas de las principales empresas eléctricas argentinas (IEERAL/E, 1:3, abril/mayo 1978, p. 102–121)

Analysis of electric power tariffs, criticizing the regional discrimination in favor of large industrial consumers in B.A. Differential price structure is not based on cost differentials but is a consequence of the lack of coordination and uniform policies in the sector. International comparisons show that Argentina's electricity rates are substantially above the rates of other Latin American countries and are also higher than most rates charged in industrialized countries.

3397 Goetz, Arturo Luis. Concentración y desconcentración en la industria argentina desde la década de 1930 a la de 1960 (IDES/DE, 15:60, enero/marzo 1976, p. 507–548, tables)

Detailed study of the concentration of Argentine industry in the 1950s and 1960s. Major findings are that the large industries of national origin declined in importance while concentration increased among the new and dynamic industries dominated by foreign enterprise.

3398 Guerberoff, Simón L. Un análisis de la performance del segmento industrial estable y su impacto en el modelo de crecimiento económico argentino: 1949–1967 (IDES/DE, 64:16, enero/marzo 1977, p. 467–504, tables)

Study based on doctoral dissertation. Author offers interesting analysis of the relationship between output, productivity changes, factor shares, and balance-of-payments in Argentina's "stable" industrial sector (i.e., that part of manufacturing, which was not characterized by rapid import substitution during the 1950s and 1960s). Although author's conclusions are pessimistic with respect to raising real wages, his comparative analysis of domestic and foreign enterprises shows that the latter performed better by increasing both worker productivity and income.

Jenkins, Rhys Owen. Dependent industrialization in Latin America: the automotive industry in Argentina, Chile and Mexico. See item **2843.**

3399 Katz, Jorge. Precios de transferencia, rentabilidad y esfuerzos de investigación y desarrollo: un estudio de casos en el mercado farmacéutico (IDES/DE, 16:62, julio/sept. 1976, p. 281–291)

This article is part of Katz's larger study of technological progress and adaptation in various industries. Author uses the pharmaceutical market as a case to demonstrate, with the help of transfer pricing analysis, the less than beneficial impact of multinational investment in developing countries.

3400 Krieger, Mario and Norma Prieto. Comercio exterior, sustitución de importaciones y tecnología en la industria farmacéutica argentina (IDES/DE, 17:66, julio/sept. 1977, p. 179–210, tables)

Critical study of the pharmaceutical industry, with special emphasis on technology. Proposes an outward reorientation of this subsector.

3401 Lascano, Marcelo Ramón. El crecimiento económico: condición de la estabilidad monetaria en la Argentina: 1900–1968. 2. ed. B.A., EUDEBA, 1977. 151 p., bibl., tables (Temas de EUDEBA/Economía)

Historical essay on the interrelationship between growth and inflation, stressing the recurrent problem of "stagflation." Author concludes with policy proposal favoring aggressive demand management to stimulate output.

Lindenboim, Javier. El empresariado industrial argentino y sus organizaciones gremiales entre 1930 y 1946. See *HLAS 40:3798.*

3402 Llosa, Hernán P. La política económica argentina en el período: 1967–1970 (UNLP/E, 22:2/3, mayo/dic. 1976, p. 173–200, tables)

Author reviews the Krieger-Vasena stabilization program (1967–70) and offers some advice for improving economic policy-making in the future. And yet, after looking at the statistics of the appendix tables (e.g., a rapidly declining rate of inflation, increasing growth, slight improvement of the wage-earners' share, lower unemployment, etc.) one cannot help but wonder why Argentina opted to change its economic team one more time.

3403 Machinea, José Luis and Julio Rotemberg. Estimación de la función de importaciones de mercancías (BCRA/EE, 3, sept. 1977, p. 5–50)

Authors estimate import-function by using industrial output and external monetary assets as major explanatory variables. They also introduce the rate of interest reflecting the opportunity costs of import hoarding and the differences between official and parallel rates of exchange, which serve as a proxy for speculative imports. Authors' results show that the import elasticity with respect to income is 1.5 or substantially above estimates which do not consider the peculiar speculative factors.

3404 Marshall, Adriana. Inmigración, demanda de fuerza de trabajo y estructura ocupacional en el área metropolitana argentina (IDES/DE, 17:65, abril/junio 1977, p. 3–37, tables)

Descriptive essay examines the relation between demand for labor and inflow of immigrants in Argentina's capital city. Author shows that the continuous inflow of people from other Latin American countries during the last two decades has provided industry, particularly construction, with an elastic labor supply which facilitated expansion and growth without raising labor costs.

3405 Montuschi, Luisa. Efectos redistributivos de la inflación en el sector manufacturero argentino (UNLP/E, 22:2/3, mayo/dic. 1976, p. 201–219, tables)

Empirical test of the Keynes-Fisher effect fails to find evidence that the real assets of industrial enterprises benefited from the inflationary process, which allegedly increases the income and wealth of net debtors.

Nicolau, Juan Carlos. Industria argentina y aduana: 1835–1854. See *HLAS 40:3822.*

Oliver, Juan Pablo. El verdadero Alberdi: génesis del liberalismo económico argentino. See *HLAS 40:3824.*

3406 Olivera, Julio H.G. Autonomía y heteronomía monetarias (BCRA/EE, 4, dec. 1977, p. 185–196)

Theoretical study attempts to show that the classical statement of fixing either the exchange rate on the money supply is not necessarily true, since under special circumstances it is possible to control the money supply, even under a fixed exchange rate.

3407 Pablo, Juan Carlos de. Un análisis sectorial de la distribución funcional del ingreso (IDES/DE, 64:16, enero/marzo 1977, p. 555–569, tables)

Concise analysis of functional income distribution which warns against accepting the wage share data published by the Central Bank on face value. Author analyzes problems such as: retired among the dependent population, the deflation of various price and wage series, and the partial information available on the total wage bill.

3408 ———. Beyond import substitution: the case of Argentina (WD, 5:1/2, Jan./Feb. 1977, p. 7–17, bibl., tables)

Brief and brilliant piece by one of Argentina's brightest economists who analyzes the structural problems created by import substitution policies. Author suggests how to stimulate exports without adversely affecting the domestic economy.

3409 ——— *ed.* Los economistas y la economía argentina opinan: R.T. Alemann, A.C. Alsogaray, A.A. Arnaudo, A.M.P. Canitrot, R.E. Cuello, M. Diamand, G. Di Tella, A. Ferrer, R.J. Frigerio, J.M. Katz, F. Pinedo. B.A., Ediciones Machi, 1977. 250 p.

Interviews with 12 well-known Argentine economists and economic policymakers. Topics range from possible solutions to the problems of the country's development to the future of the world economy. Despite the diversity of opinions expressed, the volume offers few new insights. This may be due to the lack of imagination characteristic of economists or to the fact that the problems of Argentina's development lie beyond the reach of economic explanations.

3410 Parino, Gustavo A. and **José M. Cartas.** Evolución del precio real de las divisas entre 1967 e 1978 (IEERAL/E, 1:4, julio/agosto 1978, p. 139–153)

Simple study of changes in the real exchange rate—defined as the nominal exchange rate deflated by the relative price index of Argentina and its major trading partners—demonstrates substantial fluctuations with peaks in 1967, 1972, and 1976. Authors are concerned about the deterioration of the real exchange rate in 1977–78 and doubt if slow devaluation policy can contribute significantly to internal price stabilization.

3411 Petrei, Humberto A.; Domingo F. Cavallo; and Héctor Nazareno. La base del impuesto a las ganancias y la inflación (IEERAL/E, 1:2, abril/mayo 1978, p. 91–102)

This discussion of inflation, accounting, and the corporate income tax in Argentina, leads authors to formulate a number of tax policy measures that should apply to business profits inflationary economy.

3412 Randall, Laura. An economic history of Argentina in the twentieth century. N.Y., Columbia Univ. Press, 1978. 322 p., bibl., tables.

Interesting account of Argentine economic history in the last 70 years. Author attributes the failure in overall economic development to the country's domestic policies. Although future research may corroborate this thesis, the author's empirical evidence and her method of presentation do not give

justice to such a broad and demanding topic.
For historian's comment, see *HLAS 40:2440.*

3413 Reca, Lucio G. and Juan Verstraeten.
La formación del producto agropecuario
argentino: antecedentes y posibilidades
(IDES/DE, 17:67, oct./dic. 1977, p. 371–389,
bibl., tables)
This production study of Argentina's
agricultural sector during 1950–75 emphasizes the importance of the factor land vis-à-
vis other inputs. However, if present trends
continue, new estimates must be undertaken
in order to test the role of technology in
changing agricultural output more rigorously.

3414 Rivera, José María. Argentina, programa económico y política financiera:
1976–1978 (IAEERI/E, 52/53, mayo/agosto
1978, p. 50–62)
Critical evaluation of the stabilization
strategy carried out by the Videla government's economic team. After examining the
underlying philosophy, implementation, and
results of monetary policies, author notes the
short-run adverse effects but fails to consider
the long-run implications of the 1976–78 economic program.

3415 Roggero, María A. Urbanización, industrialización y crecimiento del sector
servicios en América Latina. B.A., Ediciones
Nueva Visión, 1976. 136 p., bibl., tables (Col.
Fichas)
Analysis of occupational distribution
and its history, particularly in Argentina. Considers CEPAL's emphasis on industry as
labor-absorber to have been in error. Considerable emphasis on education. [J.M. Hunter]

3416 Romero, Luis Alberto. Los efectos de
la promoción industrial en una región
atrasada: Chaco y Formoso, 1954–1972 (Revista Interamericana de Planificación [Bogotá]
11, 1977, p. 5–32)
This essay, part of a larger study on
urbanization policies in Argentina, examines
the major causes of backwardness in two
northern provinces, Chaco and Formosa. Neither agriculture nor recent attempts at industrialization seem to have had an impact on
economic development.

3417 Salama, Elías. Estimaciones econo-
métricas de los rezagos fiscales
(BCRA/EE, 2, junio 1977, p. 25–40)
Short empirical investigation of the relation between inflation and fiscal revenues

continues previous work undertaken by
Olivera and Dutton. In this case, however,
author uses different data than Dutton in
order to reach the same results, i.e., lags in tax
collection play an ever increasing role in an
accelerating inflation.

3418 Schroeder, Norberto. Radiación de
capitales extranjeros: la experiencia argentina, 1954–1972 (UNLP/E, 22:1, en-
ero/abril 1976, p. 99–117, tables)
In this analysis of foreign investment,
the author is concerned that American capital
concentrated in B.A. produced goods such as
automobiles, chemicals, petrochemicals, and
metal products.

3419 Schvarzer, Jorge. Las empresas industriales más grandes de la Argentina: una
evaluación (IDES/DE, 17:66, julio/sept. 1977,
p. 319–337, tables)
In this examination of the 100 largest
industrial enterprises in Argentina, author
finds that the giants are in food processing,
despite this subsector's declining share of the
GDP. Over 40 percent of these industries
were established before 1930 with national
participation exceeding 80 percent (if public
enterprises in industry are included).

3420 ———. Estrategia industrial y grandes
empresas: el caso argentino (IDES/DE,
71:18, oct./dic. 1978, p. 307–352)
After analyzing investment, output,
and export of major industrial enterprises in
Argentina between 1976–78, author concludes that current patterns reflect government policies which are designed to open up
the economy, stimulating enterprises which
have a comparative advantage, and restraining
those whose resource base or markets are
unlikely to expand in the future.

3421 Sercovich, Francisco Colman. Tecnología y control extranjeros de la
industria argentina. B.A., Siglo XXI Editores,
1975. 262 p., tables.
Book based on author's dissertation on
the role of technology in international trade
and its importance for multinational investment in Argentina.

3422 Sommer, Juan F. La deuda externa argentina entre 1972 y 1976 (BCRA/EE, 3,
sept. 1977, p. 52–99)
Thorough study of Argentina's external debt. Author notes the enormous increases which occurred in less than five years

in the early 1970s. Although expansion was swift in the public sector, the need for foreign exchange reserves became so acute in 1975 that in less than six months Argentina accumulated more than two billion dollars in short-term private debt, stimulated by special exchange-rate guarantees. The reduction and restructuring of that large debt became one of the most immediate tasks of the economic team which took over on April 1976.

3423 Steed, Leonardo Douglas and **Frida Johansen.** La estructura salarial en Argentina: un análisis del sector industrial (ECIEL, 3, agosto 1976, p. 127–151, tables)

Empirical study on industrial wages examines the differences among various skills and industries. The findings are in line with the results of similar studies in other countries. For a given job, the wage differential is substantial, depending on the growth of that industry as well as the capital and size of firm.

3424 Sturzenegger, Adolfo C. Un modelo multisectorial computable para la economía argentina: aspectos analíticos (UNLP/E, 22:1, enero/abril 1976, p. 65–89)

Analytical design of a general equilibrium, multi-sector model attempts to compute the impact of exogenous changes, such as international prices or exchange-rate policy, on sectoral output, exports, imports, relative prices and balance of payments.

3425 Tanzi, Vito. Inflation, real tax revenue, and the case of inflationary

finance: theory with an application to Argentina (IMF/SP, 25:3, Sept. 1978, p. 417–451)

Modern income-tax systems usually raise public revenues in inflationary times. However, in economies whose tax structures are regressive and where tax collection is slow and subject to considerable lags, the opposite is true. Author notes how this was particularly noticeable in Argentina during the last decade when tax collection slowed down as inflation accelerated.

3426 Tow, Fernando and **Juan L. Bour.** Esbozo de una estrategia para modificar racionalmente los aranceles. B.A., Fundación de Investigaciones Económicas Latinoamericanas (FIEL), 1978. 33 p.

In this survey of major issues concerning the tariff reform of 1977–78, authors recommend a whole package of policy measures within a global industrial strategy.

3427 Visintini, Alfredo. Comparación internacional de los precios de los derivados del petróleo (IEERAL/E, 1:4, julio/agosto 1979, p. 154–164)

Comparison of petroleum pricing in Argentina, Latin America, the US and Europe. Author shows that Argentine prices are on a par with other major producers in the region (US, Peru) but that they lie in between the low prices charged by exporting countries (Venezuela, Ecuador) and, the high world-market prices of European countries and the even higher prices of Argentina's neighbors: Brazil, Chile and Uruguay.

BRAZIL

PETER T. KNIGHT, *Economist, World Bank*
DENNIS J. MAHAR, *Economist, World Bank*

A LARGE PROPORTION OF THE LITERATURE reviewed was either directly or indirectly concerned with the new set of national and international economic realities initiated by the dramatic increase in petroleum prices in late 1973. With a decline in the average growth, a deterioration in the balance of payments, and a resurgence of inflation, it became evident to many that the 1968–73 Brazilian "economic miracle" was over. Compared with the boom years, constraints on achieving widely held goals (e.g., continued rapid growth, greater income equality, poverty redressal, and fuller development of human resources) and the possible trade-offs among them have been more clearly perceived. Interest has grown in distributional aspects of development. Alternative development strategies for the future, once discussed only by small groups of intellectuals, are now widely debated in the press and within government, universities, trade associations, unions, and political groupings. This new climate has encouraged attempts inside and outside government to evaluate what has been achieved in the development process to date, and what remains to be accomplished.

Brazilian economists have played an important role in the growing debate. While the Brazilian economics establishment quite expectedly attributed the economic problems of the mid-1970s mainly to exogenous factors such as the petroleum price hikes and recession in the industrialized nations, an important opposition viewpoint gives far more emphasis to intrinsic defects of the post-1964 development strategy itself. Among the most frequently cited of these defects are the strategy's relative neglect of agriculture (especially small-scale agriculture geared to domestic markets) and its seeming inability to significantly improve the material well-being of those at the lower end of the income distribution. Other characteristics of the strategy, such as its reliance on foreign capital and technology and the growth of state intervention in the economy (estatização), are also sharply criticized in the literature, even by establishment economists.

As first noted in HLAS 39 (p. 350), both the scope and quality of Brazilian economic research continue to improve. By and large, the most significant economic research is still being carried out by the institutions located in São Paulo, Rio and, to a lesser extent, in Brasília and Belo Horizonte. Of these institutions, the work of INPES (Instituto de Pesquisas, Instituto de Planejamento Econômico e Social, Secretaria de Planejamento, also known as INPES/IPEA) is probably the best of the best. INPES continues to make available to the public a wealth of economic research through its research report, monograph, and economic thought series, and its two journals (Pesquisa e Planejamento Econômico in Portuguese and Brazilian Economic Studies in English). This institution also produced an important document in 1977 which comprehensively analyzed the Brazilian economy and outlined some of the future policy options. Though originally intended for restricted circulation in the government, the INPES document became the subject of national debate when it was subsequently leaked to the press.

Other southern research institutions which rival the output of INPES in terms of quality (but not in terms of quantity) are 1) FIPE (Fundação Instituto de Pesquisas Econômicas) of the Univ. of São Paulo which published the high-quality journal Estudos Econômicos; 2) CEBRAP (Centro Brasileiro de Analise e Planejamento), the home-base of such distinguished opposition social scientists as Fernando Henrique Cardoso, Paul Singer, and Octavio Ianni; 3) the Univ. of Campinas; 4) the Getúlio Vargas Foundation (both in São Paulo and Rio), which publishes the well-known Revista Brasileira de Economia; 5) CEDEPLAR (Centro de Estudos Demográficos e Planejamento Regional) at the Federal Univ. of Minas Gerais in Belo Horizonte; 6) the Univ. of Brasília; and 7) IBMEC (Instituto Brasileiro de Mercado de Capitais) which publishes the journal Mercado de Capitais.

While the institutions mentioned above continue to dominate the national economic research scene, recently there have been significant improvements in the research capabilities of some northern and northeastern institutions, particularly the graduate economics program of the federal universities of Bahia, Ceará, Pernambuco, and Pará. This occurrence has no doubt been instrumental in promoting the marked intensification of research on regional socioeconomic problems. In this respect, the master's degree in economics and sociology program (CME-PIMES) of the Federal Univ. of Pernambuco and the Amazonian Studies Nucleus (NAEA) of the

Federal Univ. of Pará, respectively, have become important centers of thought on northeastern and Amazonian economic development.

In addition to the growing supply of highly-trained economists, Brazilian economic research has also benefitted from the superb information base developed by the FIBGE (Fundação Instituto Brasileiro de Estatística e Geografia). Significant new data sources produced by this institution include a national input-output matrix, a national household survey for 1976 (Pesquisa Nacional por Amostra de Domicillios or PNAD), and a national family expenditure study for 1974–75 (Estudo Nacional de Despesas Familiares or ENDEF) based on a sample of 50,000 families. This latter study is probably the most comprehensive and sophisticated of its kind ever carried out in Latin America and has already spawned considerable research on the nutritional status of the Brazilian population. Under the very capable direction of Dr. Isaac Kerstenetzky, FIBGE has also developed as a quality research institution in its own right.

After reviewing the economic literature of the past few years, one gets the definite impression that the Brazilian economics profession is well-equipped to face the problems and uncertainties of the 1980s. The recent debates on national economic policy have not only been more imaginative and lively than in the past, but more open as well. Judging from the spate of literature on economic history, moreover, it is evident that many Brazilians have wisely concluded that those who do not learn from the mistakes of the past are bound to repeat them.

3428 Afonso, Carlos A. and **Herbet de Souza.** O estado e o desenvolvimento capitalista no Brasil: a crise fiscal. Rio, Editora Paz e Terra, 1977. 133 p., tables (Col. Estudos brasileiros, 20)

Neo-Marxist approach to Brazilian public finance. Basic premise is that budget deficits (the "fiscal crisis") inevitably arise as a result of Monopoly Capital's reluctance to pay for the government services it needs for survival. Analysis is based on questionable statistical data and completely ignores the extensive research done on the Brazilian public sector in recent years.

3429 Almeida, Anna Luiza Ozorio de. Distribuição de renda e emprego em serviços. Rio, Instituto de Planejamento Econômico e Social, Instituto de Pesquisas (IPEA/INPES), 1976. 421 p., bibl., tables (Col. Relatório de pesquisa, 34)

A sophisticated analysis of the impact of postwar industrialization on the "informal" sector of urban labor markets. Principal finding is that large-scale industry using imported technology generates little demand for unskilled labor in the service sector. To improve the absorption of this type of labor and to enhance job security, the author argues for government subsidies to small- and medium-sized enterprises using "intermediate technology," and for the extension of social protection legislation to the informal service sector.

3430 Almeida, Wanderly J. Manso de. Abastecimento de água à população urbana: uma avaliação do PLANASA. Rio, Instituto de Planejamento Econômico e Social, Instituto de Pesquisas (IPEA/INPES), 1977. 155 p., tables (Relatório de pesquisa, 37)

Thorough and objective evaluation of the National Sanitation Plan (PLANASA) for urban water supply and sewerage, including its implementation by the National Housing Bank (BNH) and state sanitation companies through 1975. The best published work on the subject. Warns that installation of capacity will not assure its effective utilization by the poor.

3431 —— and **José Luiz Chautard.** FGTS: uma política de bem-estar social. Apresentação de Hamilton Carvalho Tolosa and Fernando A. Rezende da Silva. Rio, Instituto de Planejamento Econômico e Social, Instituto de Pesquisas (IPEA/INPES), 1976. 159 p., tables (Relatório de pesquisa, 30)

Excellent critical study of the Time-on-Job Guarantee Fund (FGTS or: Fundo de Garantia do Tempo de Serviço), which is financed by an eight percent payroll tax, and of its use by the National Housing Bank (BNH) for which the FGTS is the principal source of new funds. Points out the difficulties in reconciling the provision of low-income housing and urban infrastructure by BNH with those of promoting the welfare of workers through a forced savings program with limited withdrawal rights. Well-documented and certainly the best study on the BNH/FGTS system.

3432 Almonacid, Rubén D. and **Alfonso C. Pastore.** El tipo de cambio, la crisis del petróleo y la deuda externa de Brasil (UCC/CE, 14:43, dic. 1977, p. 109–127, tables)

Well-documented analysis of the Brazilian response to the petroleum crisis through 1976. Concludes that Brazil chose to return to the import substitution model. The authors argue that real devaluation is necessary both to stabilize the balance of payments and to maintain the long-run objective of a strategy based on free trade.

3433 Alves, Edgard Luiz G. Nivel alimentar, renda e educação (IPE/EE, 7:2, maio/agosto 1977, p. 111–146)

Based on a family budget survey conducted in São Paulo in 1971–72, this excellent study breaks the families surveyed into two groups: those with adequate diets (in terms of both calories and protein) and those with dietary deficiencies in one or both nutrients. Most of the analysis maintains this dichotomization while introducing other variables, such as family income per capita. In general, income is found to be the most fundamental factor in explaining dietary deficiencies. The basket of foods consumed by families with adequate and inadequate diets varies relatively little in its composition—the principal difference is in the quantity consumed. Education of the mothers was not found to be an important factor in explaining dietary sufficiency. On the average (between income groups) families with inadequate diets had one more member than those with adequate diets.

3434 Andrade, Manuel Correia de Oliveira. História econômica e administrativa do Brasil. São Paulo, Editora Atlas, 1976. 193 p., bibl., maps, plates.

An economic history of Brazil with a textbook format. Probably too elementary for all but the neophyte.

3435 Araújo, José Tavares de, Jr. *ed.* Difusão de inovações na indústria

brasileira: três estudos de caso. Vera Maria Candido Pereira and others. Rio, Instituto de Planejamento Econômico e Social, Instituto de Pesquisas (IPEA/INPES), 1976. 246 p., bibl., tables (Série monografia, 24)

Three interesting case studies of technological innovations: shuttleless looms in the textile industry, special presses in the paper industry, and dry kiln processing of portland cement. Diffusion of these innovations in Brazil is analyzed.

Atroshenko, A. Brazil: problems of development. See item **8766.**

3436 Bacha, Edmar Lisboa and **Roberto Mangabeira Unger.** Participação, salário, e voto: um projeto de democracia para o Brasil. Rio, Paz e Terra, 1978. 75 p.

This proposal for combining democratization of Brazil's political and economic systems was prepared by one of Brazil's best-known economists in collaboration with a political scientist. It is a major contribution to the debate on reorienting Brazilian society along more egalitarian and democratic lines. Among the reforms proposed are: income redistribution through fiscal reform, a negative income tax, and selective agrarian reform; gradual introduction of worker self-management in all enterprises with more than 100 employees, including state enterprises, with gradual elimination of the obligation to pay dividends to private shareholders; gradual introduction of a democratic planning system including National and Sectoral Planning Councils eventually to have a majority of members elected by self-managed and small enterprises but initially with a predominance of appointees of the Federal executive branch of government; establishment of a directly elected president and a unicameral legislature; and free development of unions in all areas of economic activity. Attacked by some as utopian, this proposal nevertheless has the merit of stimulating debate on the fundamental problems of economic and political organization.

3437 Baer, Werner; Pedro Pinchas Geiger; and **Paulo Roberto Haddad** *eds.* Dimensões do desenvolvimento brasileiro. Rio, Editora Campus, 1978. 396 p.

Collection of 12 articles on various aspects of recent Brazilian regional development. All of Brazil's macroregions are discussed, with an emphasis on policy considerations. Consistently high-quality analyses, most not previously available. An outstanding contribution to the literature.

3438 ———; **Richard Newfarmer;** and **Thomas Trebat.** On state capitalism in Brazil: some new issues and questions (IAMEA, 30:3, Winter 1976, p. 69–91, tables)

Reviews the evolution of state capitalism in Brazil and suggests areas for research. A provocative piece analyzing the diverse and sometimes contradictory functions of the Brazilian state's economic apparatus. Recommends more emphasis be placed on historical and institutional studies of the behavior of the state by economists working closely with other social scientists.

3439 ——— and others. Industrialização, urbanização e a persistência das desigualdades regionais do Brasil (IBGE/R, 38:2, abril/junho 1976, p. 3–99, bibl., maps, tables)

This well-documented study shows how industrialization and urbanization processes have given rise to problems of regional disparities and examines the dilemmas that these pose for political decision-makers seeking to reconcile national growth with regional equity. Contains extensive statistical tables of use to the researcher.

3440 Barat, Josef ed. Política de desenvolvimento urbano: aspectos metropolitanos e locais. Rio, Instituto de Planejamento Econômico e Social, Instituto de Pesquisas (IPEA/INPES), 1976. 334 p., tables (Monografia, 22)

A collection of papers on diverse aspects of urban development policy. Includes studies of underemployment and mobility of urban manpower (Hamilton Tolosa); components of urban, rural, and total demographic growth over the period 1960–70 (Manoel Costa); the dynamic potential of the service sector, a case study of Rio (João Paulo de Almeida Magalhães); and commercial centers and metropolitan decentralization, an examination of the Belo Horizonte case (James Hicks). Contains a useful introductory essay by Joseph Barat.

3441 Barros, José Roberto Mendonça de and **Douglas H. Graham.** The Brazilian economic miracle revisited: private and public sector initiative in a market economy (LARR, 13:2, 1978, p. 5–38, bibl., tables)

Well-written and comprehensive review of the role of Brazil's public sector, with good treatment of financial as well as productive activities. Concludes that despite the professed goals of strengthening the private sector and restructuring the market economy to promote that end, the growth of state enterprises in the industrial and infrastructure areas has increased relative to private sector activity. At the same time, the reform and expansion of the money and capital markets has been brought about largely through state initiative and the state dominates in mobilizing savings and allocating investment. Three elements stand out as the major explanatory factors producing this result: 1) rapid economic growth has always been a more important legitimating factor for post-1964 Brazilian governments than any restructuring of society to promote capitalist institutions or free market forces per se; 2) the technological and financial scale economies enjoyed by state enterprises merely confirm the historic weakness of the private sector in Brazil; and 3) the lack of any workable strategy to generate low-cost, long-run capitalization for private firms has become apparent in the recent attempts to reform the stock market and development investment banks for new underwritings.

3442 Benchimol, Samuel. Amazônia: um pouco-antes e alémdepois. Manaus, Brazil, Editora Umberto Calderaro, 1977. 841 p., illus., maps, tables (Col. Amazoniana, 1)

An eclectic work whose subject matter ranges from the author's experiences as a student in the US during the 1940s to scholarly discussions of development policy for Amazonia. Much useful information on the Brazilian Amazon for those who read closely. Among other things, it contains fascinating interviews with northeastern migrants drawn to Amazonia by the World War II rubber boom.

Beyna, Jean-Michel. Crise de l'énergie et développement régional au Brésil. See item **7515.**

3443 Blake, David H. and **Robert E. Driscoll.** The social and economic impacts of transnational corporations: case studies of the U.S. paper industry in Brazil. Foreword by Henry R. Geyelin. N.Y., Fund for Multinational Management Education, 1977. 133 p., tables.

Contains information about the social,

economic, political, and human impact of two US-owned pulp and paper companies operating in Brazil.

3444 Bonelli, Regis. Tecnologia e crescimento industrial: a experiência brasileira nos anos 60. Rio, Instituto de Planejamento Econômico e Social, Instituto de Pesquisas (IPEA/INPES), 1976. 227 p., bibl., tables (Monografia, 25)

A translation of the author's 1975 doctoral dissertation submitted to the Univ. of California, Berkeley. By applying a variant of the models developed by Kendrick, Denison, and others, an attempt is made to statistically explain the growth of Brazilian industry during the 1960s. The findings attest to the prime importance of imported industrial technology as a source of growth.

3445 Borges, João Gonsalves and Fábio Puccetti de Vasconcellos. Habitação para o desenvolvimento. Prefácio de José Eduardo de Oliveira Penna. Rio?, Edições Bloch, 1976? 254 p., bibl., tables.

One of the few works in Portuguese on the operations of the National Housing Bank (BNH) and the various housing finance schemes which it orients and controls. Written by two former BNH officials, the book benefits by insider familiarity with housing finance problems in its description and analysis. On the other hand, it is essentially sympathetic to the BNH system, suggesting only relatively limited reforms. The data and analysis are somewhat outdated, covering the period through 1973 or at most the first half of 1974, prior to the development of major innovations such as the PROFILURB sites-and-services program and the system of treasury-financed fiscal benefits for mortgage holders.

3446 Brazil. Ministério da Fazenda. Departamento de Administração. Divisão de Documentação. Indicador das publicações do Ministério da Fazenda: 1968–1974. Apresentação de Elyanna de Niemeyer Mesquita. Rio, 1975. 143 p. (Guias de biblioteconomia, documentação, informática e editoraçõa, 1)

Useful bibliographical reference for the researcher.

3447 ———. Ministério do Interior (MINTER). **Secretaria Geral. Secretaria de Planejamento e Operações.** As desigualdades regionais no Brasil e os incentivos fiscais. Brasília, 1976. 44 p., table (Publicação, 06///)

Contains socioeconomic descriptions of Brazil's macro-regions and a brief summary of the fiscal incentives legislation. Virtually no analysis.

3448 ———. ———. Superintendência do Desenvolvimento do Nordeste (SUDENE). **Departamento de Agricultura e Abastecimento** (DAA). Suprimento de gêneros alimentícios de Caruaru. Recife, 1973. 235 p., bibl., fold. maps, tables (Série estudos e pesquisas, 1)

Analysis of food consumption and supply in an important provincial city of Pernambuco, based on survey of 610 families. Contains calculations of income elasticity of demand for 99 food products, percentage composition of food budgets and food expenditures as percent of income by expenditure classes, and sources of food supply. Food products are given in natural units rather than calories or other nutrients. A quite sophisticated study with a wealth of detail.

3449 *Brazilian Economic Studies*. Instituto de Planejamento Econômico e Social, Instituto de Pesquisas (IPEA/INPES). No. 1, 1975–. Rio.

A first issue of a new IPEA series published in English and edited by Wanderly J. Manso de Almeida. A collection of seven essays by Brazilian and foreign economists based on research wholly or partially carried out at IPEA. Topics cover: general aspects of recent economic development, foreign trade policy, agricultural technology, vocational training, employment, and regional and urban development Econômico e Social, Instituto de Pesquisas contains six excellent articles on being done at IPEA.

3450 ———. ———, ———. No. 4, 1978–. Rio.

This number in the English language series published by the Instituto de Planejamento Econômico e Social, Instituto de Pesquisas contains six excellent articles on the Brazilian economy by Brazilian and foreign researchers and a review of William Tyler's book on Brazilian manufactured exports (see *HLAS 39:3696*). Each of these six articles merits citation in the current *HLAS*: Dionísio Dias Carneiro Neto's "Brazilian Economic Policy in the Mid-Seventies;" João Sayad's "Real Estate Investments and Financial Markets;" Hamilton C. Tolosa's "Dualism in the Urban Labor Market;" David Goodman's and

Daniel Oliveira's "Urban Unemployment in Brazil;" Marcelo de Paiva Abreu's "Brazilian Foreign Debt Policy, 1931–1943;" and Gervásio C. Rezende's "Production, Employment and Agrarian Structure in the Cacao Regions of Bahia."

Bret, Bernard. L'agriculture du Brésil: expansion agricole et crise agraire. See item **7520.**

3451 Buescu, Mircea. Guerra e desenvolvimento: a economia brasileira durante a Segunda Guerra Mundial. Prefácio do Edmundo de Macedo-Soares e Silva. Rio, Apec Editora, 1976. 170 p., bibl., tables.

A study of the impact of World War II on the Brazilian economy. Attempts to refute the "external shock" theory which holds that profound disturbances in international trade associated with wars and global depressions tend to accelerate the industrialization process. Author presents data which show substantial increases in both exports and imports, and only modest industrial growth, between 1939 and 1945 in support of his counter-thesis.

3452 Bulhões, Octavio Gouvêa de and others. Evolução do capitalismo no Brasil. Rio, Edições Bloch, 1976. 219 p., tables.

Discusses the role of profit in the capitalist system, both in theory and practice. Particularly useful for non-Brazilians are the chapters which describe the evolution and workings of the Brazilian capital market.

3453 Campal, Esteban F. La soja en Brasil: balance de un ciclo agrario explosivo (UTIEH/C, 28, 1977, p. 187–208 p., map, tables)

Critical analysis of the agricultural modernization process in southern Brazil, including its international impact as Brazilian farmers colonize neighboring Paraguay.

3454 Cardoso, Fernando Henrique and **Geraldo Muller.** Amazonia: expansão do capitalismo. São Paulo, Editora Brasiliense, 1977. 208 p.

Critical evaluation of recent development of the Amazon region by leading Brazilian social scientists. Basic theme is that frontier is being pre-empted by large domestic and multinational corporations assisted by the government through generous fiscal and credit incentives. Persuasively argued, though one-sided, thesis. Analysis based mainly on newspaper clippings which detracts somewhat

from its scholarly pretentions. A useful source for research on frontier development.

3455 Carneiro, Dionísio Dias ed. Brasil: dilemas da política econômica. Rio, Editora Campus, 1977. 193 p., bibl., tables (Contribuições en economia, 1)

A collection of eight essays on Brazil's current economic problems by some of the country's best young economists. Themes discussed include general macroeconomic policy, balance-of-payments considerations, inflation control, monetary policy, industrialization, income distribution, and agriculture.

3456 Carneiro Leão, Antonio Sérgio and **Elcio Giestas.** Matriz de investimentos do Brasil 1969 (IPE/EE, 7:2, 1977, p. 157–163, table)

Presents partial preliminary matrix of investments for Brazil in 1969, based on analysis of industrial products tax data. The matrix has as rows the capital goods producing industries and as columns 22 manufacturing industries, "others" and total gross fixed capital formation. Government and household demand for capital goods is not included, nor are household or government consumption, stock changes, or exports.

3457 Carone, Edgard. comp. O pensamento industrial no Brasil: 1880–1945. São Paulo, Difel Editorial, 1977. 582 p., bibl. (Corpo e alma do Brasil, 54)

Collection of historical documents on early Brazilian industrialization among the issues discussed are: free trade versus protectionism, government planning, economic nationalism, trade unionism and social protection legislation. An important source for economic historians.

3458 Carvalho, Getúlio ed. Multinacionais: os límites da soberania. Apresentação de Ana Maria B. Goffi Marquesini. Rio, Fundação Getúlio Vargas (FGV), Instituto de Documentação, 1977. 387 p., bibl., tables.

Collection of eight previously-published essays on the nature of multinational corporations and their roles in the developing world. Only two essays are directly concerned with Brazil, and only one of these (by Mario Simonsen) is written by a Brazilian. Of minimal interest to non-Brazilian readers.

3459 Cassuto, Alexander E. Monetary stability and inflation in Brazil (IEI/EI,

29:1/2, feb./maggio 1976, p. 161–175, bibl., tables)

Shows how the use of compensating balances, a technique banks use to circumvent usury laws during periods of rapid inflation, may induce shifts in the money supply function by changing the money multiplier. Develops a model which indicates that the demand for real cash balances was remarkably stable over the period 1952–72 when the economic reforms of 1964 are taken into account by a dummy variable.

3460 Chalout, Yves. Estado, acumulação e colonialismo interno: contradições Nordeste/Sudeste, 1960–1977. Petrópolis, Brazil, Editora Vozes, 1978. 152 p., tables, bibl.

Uses the concept of internal colonialism to focus on relations of dependence between Northeast and Southeast Brazil. Shows that the redistributive policies of the State, as they affect regional development, are not strong enough to counterbalance the concentrating effects of macroeconomic and sectoral policies. Consequently, the State, through various mechanisms (including legislation, government expenditures and transfers, loans, and fiscal incentives) accelerates the process of capital accumulation in the Southeast, especially in São Paulo. The State, the author concludes, defends the interests of the dominant classes, which are located in the Southeast, while preserving its own interests and accentuating the dependence of the Northeast on the Southeast and on the monopoly capital of national and transnational corporations. Well-documented study of general interest.

Cline, William R. Brazil's emerging international economic role. See item **8782**.

Coleção Nosso Brazil: Estudos Sociais. See item **5614**.

Colonização e desenvolvimento do norte do Paraná: depoimentos sobre a maior obra no gênero realizada por uma empresa privada, 24 de setembro de 1975. See item **5615**.

3461 Contador, Claudio Roberto. Os investidores institucionais no Brasil. With the assistance of Marco Antonio A. de Souza and others. Rio, Instituto Brasileiro de Mercado de Capitais (IBMEC), 1975. 174 p., bibl., tables.

A sophisticated analysis of the performance of institutional investors in Brazil.

Begins with a brief description of the principal types of institutional investors and the legislation governing them, then develops a model for evaluation of risk and return of portfolios. The empirical analysis concludes that the performance of mutual funds (both large and small) left much to be desired, both in the bull market ending in June 1971 and subsequently. The author suggests that the bad performance may be due to over-emphasis of portfolio managers on return with insufficient attention being paid to risk. Though impressive in terms of the techniques of analysis used, this work suffers from a lack of discussion of institutional factors affecting the performance of the mutual funds and the stockmarket in general.

3462 ———. A transferência do imposto de renda e incentivos fiscais no Brasil. Apresentação de Hamilton Tolosa and Fernando Rezende. Rio, Instituto de Planejamento Econômico e Social, Instituto de Pesquisas (IPEA/INPES), 1976. 178 p., bibl., tables (Relatório de pesquisa, 33)

This sophisticated study of the incidence of the Brazilian corporate income tax (IRPJ) includes a thorough review of the theoretical and empirical literature on the incidence of profits taxation as well as economic analysis of the relevant Brazilian legislation and econometric analysis which attempts to test various hypotheses about tax incidence. On the theoretical level the study shows that total or partial transfer of the IRPJ is compatible with neoclassical price theory. On the empirical plane, the results confirm the expectation that a high proportion if not all of the IRPJ is transferred to the final consumer. These findings have important consequences for fiscal policy, particularly the fiscal incentive system widely used in Brazil.

3463 Cupertino, Fausto. Raízes do atraso: país subdesenvolvido ou potência emergente? Rio, Editora Civilização Brasileira, 1977. 155 p. (Col. Realidade brasileira, 6)

A polemical interpretation of Brazilian economic history written in a semi-journalistic style. Argues that the country's development continues to be retarded by the latifundia and foreign influences inherited from colonial times. The author's credibility could have been improved by the use of a few more supporting statistics.

3464 Curitiba: uma experiência em planejamento urbano. v. 9, Circulação:
sistema viário básico; v. 10, Circulação: sistema integrado de transportes; v. 11, Circulação: terminais de trocas de meios de
transporte; v. 12, Circulação: transporte de
massa. Curitiba, Brazil, n.p., 1975. 4 v. (Unpaged) maps, plates.

Curitiba's experience in planning public and private transportation is well-known
by urban planners. In these publications those
interested may learn some of the details.
Largely descriptive, principally of interest to
urban planners.

3465 Dantas, Antonio. Desempenho econômico e tecnológico das empresas
brasileiras e multinacionais: 1970–1974
(IPE/EE, 7:2, 1977, p. 73–88, bibl., tables)

This study seeks to avoid some problems of earlier works which compared foreign
and domestic firms and were not able to isolate the influence of market structure or the
sector of economic activity on firm behavior.
Dantas' method was to select six subsectors
of manufacturing activity and then to select
multiple pairs of foreign and domestic firms of
the same size. Data were then collected
through questionnaires. The general conclusion is that it is not possible to reject or
confirm the hypothesis that foreign firms are
more dynamic and innovating than Brazilian
firms.

3466 Duque, Hélio M. As luta pela modernização da economia cafeeira: assim
agem as multinacionais. São Paulo, Editora
Alfa-Omega, 1976. 207 p., bibl., tables (Biblioteca alfa-omega de cultura universal. Série, 1.
Col. Esta América, 4)

Useful study presenting a Brazilian
view of the acrimonious soluble coffee dispute
between Brazil and the US.

3467 *Estudos Econômicos.* Univ. de São
Paulo (USP), Instituto de Pesquisas Eco-
nômicas (IPE). Vol. 6, No. 3, set./dez. 1976–.
São Paulo.

Issue distinguished by articles by O.E.
Reboucas, and W. Baer and P. Beckerman. Re-
bouças, employing a general equilibrium
model, measures the impact of government
economic policies on the impoverished Northeast region. Baer and Beckerman describe
and evaluate the Brazilian system of "monetary correction" (indexing) used to offset the
effects of inflation.

3468 Evans, Peter. Multinationals, state-
owned corporations, and the transformation of imperialism: a Brazilian case study
(UC/EDCC, 26:1, Oct. 1977, p. 43–64)

This insightful study examines the
development of the Brazilian petrochemical
industry through the mid 1970s with particular attention to the interactions between
domestic private capital, multinational corporations, and Brazilian state enterprises which
evolved into the "tripod" model of industrial
development. The "tripod," despite important
mutual interests between the three partners,
is seen by Evans as a tripartite structure erec-
ted to escape dealing with an underlying
logic that is dualistic (multinational corporations and state enterprises) in strictly economic or technical terms. He argues that the
contradiction between the necessity (for essentially political reasons) of including local
capital and the inability of local capital to
provide any special contribution would appear
to be an important source of instability in
the model over the longer run. Other potential
sources of instability include greater political democracy or stagnant or declining demand, all of which could push in the direction
of an explicitly state capitalist model.

**Ferraz, Francisco; Hélgio Trindade; Judson
de Cew; and Eduardo Aydos.** Perfil sócio-econômico das populações urbanas de baixas
rendas no Rio Grande do Sul. See item **9324.**

3469 Fields, Gary S. Who benefits from
economic development?: a reexamination of Brazilian growth in the 1960s
(AEA/AER, 67:4, Sept. 1977, p. 570–582, bibl.,
tables)

An important article on a controversial topic. Focusing on absolute rather than
relative poverty and drawing his own poverty
line, Fields argues that the poor did participate in Brazil's economic growth during the
1960s, in fact the incomes of the poor increased faster than those of the non-poor.
Thus the relative income gap between poor
and non-poor persons narrowed in terms of
ratios, but widened absolutely. And the very
rich got richer than before, both in absolute
and in relative terms. Fields concludes that
the real debate is about whether greater
weight should be given to the alleviation of
absolute poverty or to the narrowing of relative income inequality. He opts for the former.

Flynn, Peter. The Brazilian development model: the political dimension. See item 5625.

3470 Francisconi, Jorge Guilherme and **Maria Adélia Aparecida de Souza.** Política nacional de desenvolvimento urbano: estudos e proposições alternativas. Revisão de Marco Antônio Dias Pontes. Brasília, Instituto de Planejamento Econômico e Social, Instituto de Planejamento (IPEA/IPLAN), 1976. 214 p., maps, tables (Série estudos para o planejamento, 15)

Important and broad-ranging study which served as the basis for establishing the National Urban Policy Council, whose first head was Francisconi, one of the authors.

3471 Fuenzalida, Luis Arturo. Criação mais rápida de emprego e renda mediante e expansão e modernização de microempresas (BNB/REN, 7:2, abril/junho 1976, p. 253–283)

Reviews international experience with small scale enterprises, factors limiting their growth, and policies of technical and financial assistance to them. Contains an extensive bibliography.

3472 Fundação Getulio Vargas, Rio. Instituto Brasileiro de Economia. Centro de Estudos Agrícolas. Variações sazonais: 10 anos. Rio, 1977. 246 p., tables.

Detailed data on seasonal price variations for 21 agricultural products disaggregated by the principal producing states. Of interest to the specialist in agricultural marketing.

3473 Furtado, Milton Braga. Síntese da economia brasileira. Ribeirão Preto, Brazil, The Author, 1977. 300 p., bibl., tables.

A concise economic history of Brazil from the colonial period to the present. Reiterates the product cycle interpretation popularized by Celso Furtado. Contains few new insights.

3474 Galvêas, Ernane. Brasil: desenvolvimento e inflação. Prefácio de Octávio Gouvêa de Bulhões. Rio, Apec Editora, 1976. 167 p., tables.

Essentially a textbook on money and banking with a liberal dose of statistics on the Brazilian financial system as well as the author's personal views. Galvêas was President of the Central Bank of Brazil during the Medici administration.

3475 Goodman, D.E. Rural structure, surplus mobilization and modes of production in a peripheral region: the Brazilian Northeast (JPS, 5:1, Oct. 1977, p. 3–32, bibl., table)

In this study, Goodman examines alternative formulations of agricultural surplus mobilization and peasant economic integration in Northeast Brazil. The competing hypotheses are whether recent output growth has consolidated precapitalist modes of production or has been accompanied by the increasing penetration of capitalist relations of production. It is suggested that these models give incomplete specifications of rural social structure and posit a false dilemma between capitalist and precapitalist modes of production. The evidence available on land tenure, regional marketing systems, labor supply, and rural proletarianization for the period 1940–70 is reviewed in analyzing these issues. The coexistence and interaction of different production relations in the rural Northeast is emphasized. Clearly written and insightful analysis.

3476 Grossi, Maria das Graças. Minas Gerais: del estancamiento al boom: una réplica local del modelo brasileño (UNAM/RMS, 39:1, enero/marzo 1977, p. 251–267)

Examines the political and economic development of Minas Gerais, comparing and contrasting it with that of Brazil as a whole. The emphasis is on the late emergence of a stratum of technocrats which replaced the state political elite as the privileged interlocutor with the national level political and economic decision-making system. Like the "Brazilian Model," the "Minas Model" has meant intensification of the internationization of capital and markets. The major difference is summarized by the author's conclusion that in the case of Brazil, one can say that 1964 meant economic continuity and political rupture, while in Minas, political change preceded the process of industrial development (other than mining and steel). There has been a virtual rejection of alliance with the local bourgeoisie by the technocrats, who seek foreign investment as the principal motor of economic development.

Kacowicz, Mateus and others. Desenvolvimento e política urbana. See item 7551.

3477 Katzman, Martin T. Cities and frontiers in Brazil: regional dimensions of economic development. Cambridge, Mass., Harvard Univ. Press, 1977. 255 p., maps, tables.

An important study of regional and urban development in Brazil. Drawing heavily on his previously-published work, the author skillfully describes and analyzes the historical processes which have led to the present state of frontier development and urbanization. Though highly recommended as an overview, the reader would be wise to also consult the extensive literature on these topics now being produced in Brazil.

3478 ———. Paradoxes of Amazonian development in a resource starved world (JDA, 10:4, July 1976, p. 445–460)

Reviews the history of economic development in the Amazon from the rubber cycle to the Transamazon highway and recent large-scale mining and cattle ranching ventures. Concludes that administrative and technological obstacles to settling Amazonia as a food-producing region are not insuperable, but their solution presupposes a reorientation of development priorities toward "people prosperity." Unfortunately, in the view of the author, avoiding the delivery of capital and technical assistance to large numbers of people in favor of fomenting high-technology, capital-intensive enterprises follow the general thrust of Brazilian development planning.

3479 Kleiman, Ephraim. Correção monetária e indexação: experiência brasileira e experiência israelense (IPE/EE, 6:1, 1976, p. 113–157, tables)

Interesting discussion of indexation and comparison of the Brazilian and Israeli experiences. Notes that in Israel indexation was introduced first for equity reasons to protect labor income, while in Brazil it has been used basically for allocative reasons, to improve capital allocation and accumulation. Both Brazilian and Israeli experiences suggest that limiting indexation to certain population groups or to long-term financial instruments may in practice be impossible.

3480 Langoni, Carlos Geraldo. Income distribution and economic development in Brazil. Rio, Banco Nacional da Habitação (BNH), 1973? 34 p., tables.

Another installment in the ongoing debate on the distribution of income. The author, a major proponent of the "official" line, refutes the arguments of those who hold that the increase in income concentration observed between 1960–70 was a deliberate government goal, and that this concentration was instrumental in ensuring the success of the post-1964 economic model. While admitting that some concentration did occur in the 1960s, the author argues that this phenomenon was a consequence (not a cause) of major structural changes in labor markets occuring during the development process. Little new for those who have followed the debate.

3481 ———. A política econômica do desenvolvimento. Rio, Fundação Getúlio Vargas [and] Editora APEC, 1978. 125 p., tables.

In this collection of essays Langoni addresses the question of how to assure the long-term viability of the "Brazilian model" by integrating in a harmonious manner State action and private enterprise, thus conciliating economic efficiency, political stability, and social equilibrium. In his view the principal danger to be avoided is the excessive expansion of the State, which could alter the very basis of the Brazilian economic system. Chapters treat such diverse topics as wages, inequality, and social mobility; State, enterprise, and society; the presence of the State in capital markets; decentralization and development; the new Brazilian inflation, and the foreign sector since the petroleum crisis. A well-written series of essays by an articulate advocate of private enterprise and free competition.

Lima, Heitor Ferreira. História do pensamento econômico no Brasil. See *HLAS* 40:3992.

3482 ———. 3 [i.e. Três] industrialistas brasileiros: Maúa, Rui Barbosa, Roberto Simonsen. São Paulo, Editora Alfa-Omega, 1976. 197 p., tables (Biblioteca alfa-omega de ciências sociais. Série 1. Col. História, 12)

Presents biographical sketches of three of Brazil's most important historical figures. Emphasizes their roles in shaping the country's economic history. Contains appendix which reprints the following rare documents: "O Meio Circulante do Brasil" by Maúa; "A Notavel Conferencia do Dr. Ruy Barbosa" by

Barbosa; and "As Crises no Brasil" by Roberto Simonsen. A useful addition to the literature on the economic history of Brazil from the late 19th to the mid 20th centuries.

3483 Lopes, Juarez Rubens Brandão. Dévéloppement capitaliste et structure agraire au Brésil (ADST/SDT, 19:1, jan./mars 1977, p. 59–71)

Presents a Marxist analysis of political and economic development in the postwar period, with emphasis on the heterogeneous agrarian structure where purely capitalist agricultural enterprises, small family farms, and more primitive agrarian structures coexist with capitalist development in urban areas. The changing nature of class alliances in power before and after 1964, the appearance of a rural proletariat (especially in the southeast and south) and the unification of rural and urban labor markets are discussed.

3484 ———. Do latifúndio à empresa: unidad e diversidad do capitalismo no campo. São Paulo, Editora Brasiliense, 1976. 55 p., maps, tables (Caderno CEBRAP, 26)

Develops two typologies for studying the development of capitalism in agriculture. The first is based on modes of insertion of a particular region or production unit in the social division of labor of the country—essentially the degree to which it is involved in the market economy. The second is based on production relations (capitalist, latifundium, family farm producing for the market, and peasant subsistence farm). The system is then used to classify micro regions in an effort to facilitate analysis of rural development in Brazil. First stage of an ambitious research project being undertaken by CEBRAP.

3485 Lorenzo-Fernández, O.S. A evolução da economia brasileira. Prefácio de Roberto de Oliveira Campos. Rio, Zahar Editores, 1976. 332 p., tables (Biblioteca de ciências sociais: economia)

An economic history of Brazil from the colonial period to the mid-1970s. Approximately one-third of the book devoted to analyzing the post-1964 model. Historical phases are characterized in terms of the nature and locus of the decision-making process. An imaginative and well-researched work.

3486 Loureiro, Maria Rita Garcia. Parceria e capitalismo. Rio, Zahar Editores, 1977. 135 p., bibl., tables (Biblioteca de ciên-

cias sociais: sociologia e antropologia)

Fascinating detailed empirical study which seeks to answer the question of how and why capitalist rural enterprises use share-cropping. Based on a case study of a large farm in southern Goiás which produces basic food crops for the Rio de Janeiro and São Paulo markets. Author is informed by a good knowledge of the Marxist classics and recent works on the articulation of different modes of production. Using anthropological techniques and presenting considerable numerical data the author concludes that the adoption of share-cropping represents, for the entrepreneur-landowner, a rational procedure which attenuates the lowering of relative profitability or, in the limiting case, relative decapitalization which the agricultural enterprise suffers in the process of capital accumulation in the economy as a whole.

3487 Mahar, Dennis J. Frontier development policy in Brazil: a study of the Amazon experience. N.Y., Praeger Publishers, 1979. 208 p., bibl., tables.

This is probably the most complete and up-to-date study available on the economic development of Brazil's Amazon region and was originally published in Portuguese as: *Desenvolvimento econômico da Amazônia: um análise das políticas governamentais* (Rio, Instituto de Planejamento Econômico y Social, Instituto de Pesquisas [IPEA/INPES], 1978). Its focus is on regional development policies and their impact. The experience with fiscal incentives and other policy tools is carefully evaluated making extensive use of available published data and analyses, unpublished SUDAM and SUFRAMA data, interviews, and field visits. Mahar finds that despite recent successes in the fields of transport and communications which have reduced the region's traditional isolation, the Amazon still lacks a coherent and equilibrated development policy. Many of the problems analyzed are derived from the pursuit of conflicting and even mutually exclusive objectives by policymakers. Serious doubts are raised, for example, concerning the coherence of encouraging human occupation of the Amazon while at the same time attracting private developers through a system of subsidies to capital. The study concludes with recommendations whose basic theme is that promotion of the prosperity of the people who live in the region should get greater emphasis and that this need not be at the expense of current attempts to increase the region's aggregate output. [P.T.K.]

3488 Malan, Pedro S. and others. Política econômica externa e industrialização no Brasil: 1939–52. Rio, Instituto de Planejamento Econômico e Social, Instituto de Pesquisas (IPEA/INPES), 1977. 535 p., bibl., tables (Col. Relatório de pesquisa, 36)

Vol. 1 of a planned trilogy on the economic history of Brazil from 1939 to the present. Emphasis is placed on the relation among the external sector, domestic industrialization, inflation, and the economic role of the State. Characterized by high quality analysis based on comprehensive statistical data, some published for the first time. A major work on an important and underresearched period of Brazilian history.

Malloy, James M. Social insurance policy in Brazil: a study in the politics of inequality. See item **7556.**

———. Social security policy and the working class in twentieth-century Brazil. See item **7557.**

Martins, Carlos Estevam. Capitalismo de estado e modelo político no Brasil. See item **7559.**

3489 Martins, José de Souza. El café y la génesis de la industrialización en São Paulo (UNAM/RMS, 39:3, julio/sept. 1977, p. 781–797)

This article begins by noting Furtado's scanty treatment of the origins of industry in Brazil and particularly of the relations between industry and the coffee economy. The author argues that the principal industrial groups in São Paulo arose in the last quarter of the 19th century, largely by displacing small artesanal producers rather than by substituting imports. This is contrary to Warren Dean's thesis that the experience of businessmen who began as importers was a principal factor in industrialization. From about 1900, the author concludes, the industrial sector began to be vitally important for the public bureaucracy. Industry imposed itself in government decisions, as occurred in 1931 in the so-called socialization of the losses of the coffee owners. This benefitted industry, not just coffee growers, as is generally known.

3490 Medeiros, Paulo de Tarso. Diferenças geográficas no custo de vida: comparações entre as regiões Nordeste e Sudeste e as cidades do Rio de Janeiro e São Paulo (IBE/RBE, 31:2, abril/junio 1977, p. 353–370, tables)

A first attempt to look at regional differences in the cost of living, albeit only for food, housing, and urban transportation. Author believes it should be possible to make considerable progress on this front using the 1974–75 National Family Expenditure Survey (ENDEF). The subject is fraught with index number problems, but very important.

3491 Melo, Fernando B. Homen de and **Maria Helena G.P. Zockun.** Exportações agrícolas, balanço de pagamentos e abastecimento do mercado interno (IPE/EE, 7:2, 1977, p. 9–50, bibl., tables)

The main point of this long article is that the agricultural sector can play an important role in alleviating the balance-of-payments problems experienced by Brazil since 1973. The major policy instruments proposed are greater real devaluation of the exchange rate and exemption of agricultural exports from indirect taxation (the ICM). According to the authors, the principal constraint on adopting such policies is the possible impact on internal prices of foodstuffs which might be occasioned by greater incentives to exports, though the fact that many important foodstuffs are strictly "domestic goods" suggests that the impact might not be as strong as some fear. Furthermore, the general stimulus to the agricultural sector could expand rural employment and modernization in the medium to long term. The possible contradiction between employment and modernization is not explored.

3492 Miranda Neto, Manoel José de. O dilema da Amazonia. Petrópolis, Brazil, Editora Vozes, 1979. 224 p., bibl.

An economic history of the Amazon region. Approximately one-third of book devoted to general discussion of economic planning in developing countries. Remainder of book is comprehensive, if somewhat poorly organized, synthesis of previously-published work on the Amazon. Little originality except for the author's discussion of the region's traditional credit system known as "aviamento."

3493 Morley, Samuel A.; Milton Barbosa; and Maria Cristina Cicciamali de Souza. Evidências no mercado interno de trabalho durante um processo de rápido crescimento econômico (IPE/EE, 7:3, 1977, p. 61–102, bibl., tables)

Based on a survey of 82 São Paulo firms in industry, commerce, and services, this significant study examines the functioning of labor markets in Brazil. It finds that internal or segmented labor markets do exist in Brazilian industry, despite the absence of effective labor unions, and this fact has important implications for wage and salary differentials in conditions of rapid employment growth.

3494 Neuhaus, Paulo. História monetário do Brasil: 1900–45. Prefácio de Arnold Harberger. Rio, Instituto Brasileiro de Mercado de Capitais (IBMEC), 1975. 198 p., bibl., tables.

Based on the author's Univ. of Chicago Ph.D. dissertation, this is a high quality study and comes complete with a glowing preface by Arnold Harberger. Amply documented and readable text with insights into political as well as economic events.

3495 ——— and Uriel de Magalhães. Crédito ao consumidor: uma análise econômica. Rio, Instituto Brasileiro de Mercado de Capitais (IBMEC), 1976. 231 p., bibl., tables (Série estudos especiais, 2)

Reviews the evolution of credit, finance, and investment companies in Brazil since 1940, summarizes the literature on evaluation of risks for direct consumer credit and macroeconomic aspects of regulation affecting consumer credit, reviews international experience with consumer credit, and then applies all this information in a short analysis of the problems and outlook for the development of the consumer credit industry in Brazil. The authors suggest that the Brazilian financial system established in the mid 1960s is overly specialized by function and at times has been overregulated, though a period of liberalization began in 1975, and this is seen as healthy by the authors. They recommend further liberalization, creation of a centralized information bank on credit users, and the equivalent of a truth-in-lending act.

Osório, Carlos. Absorção dos migrantes na região metropolitana do Recife. See item **9369.**

3496 Paiva, Ruy Miller; Salomão Schattan: and Claus F. Trench de Freitas. Setor agrícola do Brasil: comportamento econômico, problemas e possibilidades. Apresentação de Rubens Araújo Dias. Rio, Univ. de São Paulo, 1976. 442 p., illus., maps, plates, tables.

Encyclopedic study of the agricultural sector commissioned for presentation to a congress of the International Assn. of Agricultural Economists held in São Paulo in 1973. Presents an overview of the principal problems of Brazilian agricultural development, government agricultural policies, and a description of the natural resources of five major geographical regions. Most data only through 1970 or 1971. Contains an exposition of Paiva's well-known model of the "self-control" mechanism limiting agricultural modernization. Otherwise, study tends towards the descriptive and is somewhat acritical. Many useful bibliographic references in footnotes.

Peláez, Carlos Manuel. The establishment of banking institutions in a backward economy: Brazil, 1800–1851. See *HLAS 40:4005*.

3497 Peláez, Carlos Manuel and Mircea Buescu *eds.* A moderna história econômica. Rio, Apec Editora, 1976. 259 p., tables.

A wide-ranging collection of 20 essays on Brazilian economic history by distinguished Brazilian scholars. Emphasis is on the Empire and First Republic. Includes contributions by Antonio Delfim Netto, Nicia Villela Luz, Warren Dean, Stanley Stein, and others. A fine sampling of the "new" economic history.

3498 ——— and Wilson Suzigan. História monetária do Brasil: análise da política, comportamento e instituições monetárias. Rio, Instituto de Planejamento Econômico e Social, Instituto de Pesquisas (IPEA/INPES), 1976. 487 p., fold. tables, tables (Monografia, 23)

Encyclopedic and well-documented monograph on Brazil's monetary history. Students of monetary affairs and Brazilian economic history will no doubt find it a useful reference.

3499 Penna, Júlio A. and Charles C. Mueller. Fronteira agrícola, tecnologia e margem intensiva: algumas reflexões sobre o papel desses fatores para o crescimento agrícola brasileiro (IPE/EE, 7:1, jan./abril 1977, p. 53–106, bibl., tables)

This study seeks to promote discussion of some relatively little-discussed aspects of Brazilian agricultural development. It suggests numerous areas for research related to the future expansion of agriculture. The basic division of the work is between the incorporation of new lands on the agricultural frontier and the intensification of land use within existing agricultural establishments. According to the Institute for Colonization and Land Reform (INCRA) there are some 80 million hectares of potentially productive but unused land within existing agricultural establishments. Both structuralist and purely economic explanations for behavior of owners of such "underutilized" land are examined, and it is suggested that purely economic motives (viewed in the context of portfolio selection theory) can explain much of the behavior observed. The authors suggest that more attention be given to intensification of land in non-frontier regions where transport and infrastructure costs are less than on the frontier.

3500 Pereira, Jesus Soares. Petróleo, energia elétrica, siderúrgia: a luta pela emancipação; um depoimento de . . . sobre a política de Vargas. Rio, Paz e Terra, 1975. 197 p., tables (Estudos brasileiros, 7)

Oral history probing the mind of a Brazilian central bureaucrat and intellectual, advocate of a strong nationalist energy policy, on energy situation in Brazil from 1930. [R.J. Barman]

3501 Peters, J. Irwin. The new industrial property laws in Mexico and Brazil: implications for MNCs (CJWB, 12:1, Spring 1977, p. 70–79, bibl., plate)

Warns that the industrial property laws (governing technology transfer) promulgated in 1976 in both Brazil and Mexico may serve as deterrents to, rather than promoters of, technology transfer since they ignore legitimate interests of the companies making the transfers. Concludes that while many of the provisions of the new laws are justified and workable, others are difficult if not impossible for corporations from developed countries to accept. Calls for both sides to judge the situation on a "businesslike basis" while aiming at mutual future benefits rather than remain-

ing preoccupied with recriminations about the past.

3502 Piauí, Francelino S. Cinco séculos de reportagem econômica: síntese histórica da economia brasileira. Prefácio de Alcides Ribeiro Soares. Apreciação crítica de Cândido Ferreira da Silva. Campinas, Brazil, The Author, 1976, 142 p., bibl.

A very brief economic history of Brazil written in a journalistic style. Discusses the various product cycles (e.g., sugar, cattle, coffee, minerals, rubber) and recent industrialization.

3503 Planejamento. Governo de Estado da Bahia, Secretaria do Planejamento, Ciência e Tecnologia. Vol. 4, No. 1, jan./março 1976–. Salvador, Brazil.

Of interest in this issue are articles on property and use of land in the northern periphery of the Reconcavo of Bahia Maria de Azevedo Brandao; triangularization of the 1971 preliminary input-output matrix for Brazil by Celestino da Silva; monoculture and urbanization in the cacao region of Bahia by Johannes Augel and Antonio Fernando Guerreiro de Freitas; and the growth crisis of Brazilian universities by Luiz Navarro de Britto. It is interesting to note that even in a little-known journal such as this one, one finds articles of fairly good quality.

3504 Queiroz, Maurício Vinhas de and others. Multinacionais: internacionalização e crise. São Paulo, Editora Brasiliense [and] Centro Brasileiro de Análise e Planejamento (CEBRAP), 1977. 86 p., bibls., tables (Caderno CEBRAP, 28)

This publication contains three separate articles: 1) Mauricio Vinhas de Queiroz and Peter Evans discuss relations between international and local capital in the Brazilian industrialization process. This article contains a wealth of interesting detail and is both original and well-written. It concludes that due to the fact that the gradual increase in foreign control has been balanced by a gradual incorporation of the elite of the national bourgeoisie into the community of international capital, what would have been relations of intense political struggle has become a delicate equilibrium of competition and collaboration. 2) Guido Mantega's piece has little new to offer. 3) Paulo Singer's examines the international division of labor and the MNCs.

This article is basically a rather long-winded review of the development of MNCs and economic theory dealing with international trade and investment, concluding with a kind of product-cycle-cum-Hecksher-Olhin-theory of MNC investment based on labor costs (and discipline) and technology. Political considerations also play a part, encouraging joint ventures with host country states.

3505 *Revista Brasileira de Economia.* Fundação Getúlio Vargas, Instituto Brasileiro de Economia. Vol. 31, No. 1, jan./março 1977–. Rio.

In July 1976 the Graduate School of Economics of the Getúlio Vargas Foundation held an international symposium to celebrate the 200th anniversary of the publication of Adam Smith's *Wealth of nations.* This number of RBE contains the papers presented in the symposium, which are not limited to discussions of Smith's classic itself, but includes applications of Smithian concepts to present day problems. Includes articles by Octavio Gouvêa de Bulhoes, Antonio Carlos Lemgruber, Elysio de Oliveira Belchior, José L. Carvalho and Cláudio L.S. Haddad, Carlos Augusto Crusius, Arnold C. Harberger, Adroaldo Moura da Silva, Antonio Maria da Silveira, José L. Carvalho, Cláudio R. Contador, Edy Luiz Kogut, Allan Meltzer, Paulo Neuhaus, Joao Syad, Roberto Fendt, Jr. and Julian M. Chacel.

3506 ——. ——, ——. Vol. 31, No. 3, julho/set. 1977–. Rio.

Contains articles on the Brazilian banking system (André Franco Montoro Filho); a cost-benefit study of coal mining in Rio Grande do Sul (Mariene B. Lehwing); taxation of real estate in Brazil (Raymond L. Richman); and an evaluation of Brazilian policy toward British investments in Brazil, 1870–1913 (Roberto Fendt).

3507 ——. ——, ——. Vol. 31, No. 4, out./dez. 1977–. Rio.

Special issue commemorating the 30th anniversary of the journal. Articles comment on trends in the various areas of economics, e.g., economic history, development, inflation, as revealed in past contributions to the journal. Contains interesting observations on the evolution of Brazilian economic thought in the postwar years.

3508 ——. ——, ——. Vol. 32, No. 1, jan./março 1978–. Rio.

This number includes an excellent article by Pedro Carvalho de Melo on the economics of slavery in Rio coffee production 1850–88 based on his Univ. of Chicago Ph.D. dissertation, a sophisticated analysis of Brazil's export promotion strategy 1950–74 by José L. Carvalho and Claudio Haddad, and a report by Marc Nerlov on an international meeting on population and development reviewing research in progress or recently completed in Brazil and elsewhere in Latin America. There are also several theoretical articles which do not treat Brazil explicitly.

3509 ——. ——, ——. Vol. 32, No. 2, abril/junho 1978–. Rio.

Special issue dedicated to the memory of the brilliant economist, Harry G. Johnson. Contains six highly technical articles on foreign trade and inflation plus a eulogy by Arnold C. Harberger.

3510 ——. ——, ——. Vol. 32, No. 4, out./dez. 1978–. Rio.

There are two articles of interest, particularly on the theoretical level, in this issue. The first, by Uriel de Magalhães, presents a formal theoretical model on the demand for health in which the demand for medical services is a derived demand. An empirical test is done based on family budget data from Rio and São Paulo. The second, by Ruben Almonacid, develops an aggregate supply function in which the existence of information costs is introduced.

3511 *Revista Brasileira de Mercado de Capitais.* Instituto Brasileiro de Mercado de Capitais (IBMEC). Vol. 2, No. 4, jan./abril 1976–. Rio.

Contains articles of interest on monetary correction, inflationary expectations, and the demand for financial assets by Claudio Contador and options for adjustment of Brazil's trade balance by Edy Luiz Kogut.

3512 ——. ——. Vol. 3, No. 9, set./dez. 1977–. Rio.

Contains articles of interest on determinants of the variance in the return on shares in the Brazilian stock market by Walter Ness, Jr.; the demand by banks for free reserves by Antonio Carlos Lemgruber; and concentration in the Brazilian commercial banking system by Jairo Simon da Fonseca and Antonio Zoratto Sanvicente.

3513 ———. ———. Vol. 4, No. 12, set./dez. 1978–. Rio.

Contains articles of interest on state development banks by Pedro Carvalho de Mello; the state enterprise in the capital market by Walter Ness; growth, economic cycles and inflation: a description of the Brazilian case by Claudio Roberto Contador; the indecisions of interventionism in Brazil since 1930: Brazil's exchange rate policy in the Vargas period by Beauclair M. de Oliveira; the market structure of brokerage firms by Miguel Dirceu Fonseca Tavares; and money and capital markets in developing countries, an argument in favor of planning by David Gill. The journal's improving quality reflects the growing number of economists with training in monetary and financial affairs working in Brazil.

3514 *Revista Econômica do Nordeste.*

Banco do Nordeste do Brasil (BNB), Depto. de Estudos Econômicos do Nordeste (ETENE). Vol. 6, No. 3, julho/set. 1975–. Fortaleza, Brazil.

Includes a study on regionalization in Piauí (Gerson Portela Lima), foreign trade promotion (Paulo Francisco Frota Soares), internal migration in the Salvador metropolitan region (Mary Garcia Castro), and the dairy industry in the Northeast (Francisco Alzir de Lima and others).

3515 ———. ———, ———. Vol. 7, No. 1, jan./março 1976–. Fortaleza, Brazil.

Contains interesting articles on migratory flows at the microregion level in the Northeast (Helio A. de Moura, Carmen Suzana Holder and Aidil Sampaio); regional export promotion (M. Cleide and Carlos Bernal); agroindustry and the growth of agriculture in the Northeast (Jose Almar Almeida Franco); and the potential demand for sorghum as a feedgrain in the Northeast (Teobaldo Campos Mesquidta, Paulo Roberto Silva and John H. Sanders, Jr.). The last is a particularly well done study.

3516 *Revista Pernambucana de Desenvolvimento.* Instituto de Desenvolvimento de Pernambuco (CONDEPE). Vol. 3, No. 1, jan./junho 1976–. Recife, Brazil.

Of interest to economists are the articles on "foreign" trade and inter-regional income movements, a study based on Pernambuco's "balance of payments" with the rest of Brazil (Olímpio de Arroxelas Galvão) and the integration of research and teaching in economics (Jorge Jatobá). There are other articles in the fields of urban and regional planning and geography.

Reynolds, Clark W. and **Robert T. Carpenter.** Housing finance in Brazil: towards a new distribution of wealth. See item **9386.**

Roche, Jean. A colonização alemã no Espírito Santo. See *HLAS 40:4163.*

3517 Sampaio, Yony D.S.B. Modelos de otimização na agricultura do Nordeste do Brasil com énfase em agricultura de consorciação em parceria (BNB/REN, 7:4, out./dez. 1976, p. 605–642, tables)

Excellent study which combines structural and institutional analysis (systems of sharecropping and joint cropping in the Northeast) with elegant modeling in the neoclassical tradition and the use of data collected in the SUDENE/World Bank research project on agriculture in the Northeast. Shows that sharecropping gives greater income to workers than direct capitalist production, and that labor scarcity is virtually a condition for sharecropping to persist. The end of sharecropping is likely to come from fear of labor legislation by landowners and the effects of government agricultural production incentives. Sampaio concludes that agricultural modernization in the Northeast has been income concentrating, basically because it has occurred without modification in the ownership patterns of land and capital, while incentives to the use of capital further concentrate land and capital ownership and discourage labor use.

3518 ——— and **José Ferreira.** Emprego e pobreza rural. Recife, Brazil, Univ. Federal de Pernambuco, 1977. 166 p.

Scholarly, and empirically well-founded, study of employment conditions in rural areas of Pernambuco state. Discusses, *inter alia,* the relation between farm size and labor absorption, and the factors causing rural-to-urban migration. Highly recommended for students of the rural Northeast.

3519 Sanders, John Houston, Jr. and **Antonio Dias de Hollanda.** Elaboração de nova tecnologia para os pequenos agricultores:

um estudo de caso na zona semi-árida do Nordeste Brasileiro (BNB/REN, 8:4, out./dez. 1977, p. 627–655, bibl.)

Applies a quadratic programming model taking into account risk and return to study the potential for adoption of various new technologies by small farmers in the semiarid regions of the Northeast. The model is also used to study traditional cropping patterns and technologies. A sophisticated study on an important topic.

—— and **Frederick L. Bein.** Desenvolvimento agrícola na fronteira brasileira: sul de Mato Grosso. See item **5696.**

3520 São Paulo (state), *Brazil*. **Secretaria de Economia e Planejamento. Coordenação de Ação Regional.** Handbook for the foreign investor in Brazil. 2. ed. rev. São Paulo, 1975. 192 p., bibl., tables.

Handy publication containing, in a well-organized form, the principal regulations governing foreign business activity in Brazil.

3521 Scandizzo, Pasquale L. and **Túlio Barbosa.** Substituição e produtividade de fatores na agricultura nordestina (IPEA/PPE, 7:2, agôsto 1977, p. 367–404, tables)

Production function analysis with various types of function and degrees of disaggregation (using survey data from the SUDENE/World Bank research project on Northeast agriculture) is used to investigate the existence of scale economies, the elasticity of substitution between labor and capital, the relation between wages and the marginal product of labor, and the marginal product of various non-labor inputs. Six regions and various crop production systems are considered. In general, unitary elasticity of substitution between labor and capital and few economies of scale were found. Disaggregation results in more variation in the findings. At the level of crops the existence of scale economies depends on the production system—except for rice, they are greater the greater the degree of specialization. Diversified farms in the Northeast appear to exist because of risk aversion rather than profit maximization. The authors suggest their findings be considered in making proposals for agrarian reform.

3522 Silva, Maria da Conceição. A dívida do setor público brasileiro: seu papel no financiamento dos investimentos públicos.

Rio, Instituto de Planejamento Econômico e Social, Instituto de Pesquisas (IPEA/INPES), 1976. 201 p., bibl., fold. table, tables (Relatório de pesquisa, 32)

This study of the Brazilian public debt analyzes its magnitude and structure as well as its role in financing government investments. The data presented cover the period through 1974. A pioneering study in a field of increasing importance as the management of the domestic debt along with that of the foreign debt becomes an important constraint on economic policy makers.

3523 Simonsen, Mário Henrique and **Roberto de Oliveira Campos.** A nova economia brasileira. 2. ed. Rio, Livraria José Olympio Editora, 1976. 257 p., tables.

Collection of 10 previously-published essays by two of Brazil's most influential economists. A benign assessment of the post-1964 economic model. Recommended as an introduction to the views of the policy-making Establishment.

3524 Simonsen, Roberto Cochrane and **Eugênio Gudin.** A controvérsia do planejamento na economia brasileira: coletânea da polêmica Simonsen e Gudin, desencadeada com as primeiras propostas formais de planejamento da economia brasileira ao final do Estado Novo. Introdução de Carlos von Doellinger. Rio, Instituto de Planejamento Econômico e Social, Instituto de Pesquisas (IPEA/INPES), 1977. 236 p., tables (Série pensamento econômico brasileiro, 3)

A collection of essays and reports written during the mid-1940s which documents the debates surrounding the first formal proposals of economic planning in Brazil. Simonsen, the eminent industrialist and intellectual, is the protagonist in these debates and argues for state-supported industrialization as the best means of freeing the country from poverty. Gudin, one of Brazil's greatest economists, forcefully takes the side of the free market. He calls for channelling more savings to the private sector, coupled with programs (such as vocational education), aimed at raising labor productivity. Required reading for students of Brazilian economic history.

Singer, Paul. O Brasil no contexto do capitalismo internacional: 1889–1930. See *HLAS 40:4173.*

3525 —— and others. Capital e trabalho no campo. Organizado por Jaime Pinsky. São Paulo, Editora HUCITEC, 1977. 146 p., bibl., tables (Col. Estudos brasileiros, 7)

A collection of Marxist analyses of the process of rural proletarianization in Brazil, with special emphasis on landless laborers (*trabalhadores volantes* or *boías frias*). Contains theoretical analysis and some reports of anthropological fieldwork. Uneven in quality, but contains useful insights.

Smith, Peter Seaborn. Brazilian oil: from myth to reality? See item **5701**.

3526 Suplicy, Eduardo Matarazzo. Os efeitos das minidesvalorizações na economia brasileira. Tradução de Cândido Bueno de Azevedo. Rio, Fundação Getúlio Vargas (FGV), Instituto de Documentação, 1976. 254 p., bibl., tables.

Portuguese version of the author's 1973 Michigan State Univ. Ph.D. dissertation. This econometric study concludes that the institution of the minidevaluation system in Brazil beginning in Aug. 1968 has had largely positive effects on growth and trade for the Brazilian economy by allowing a greater stability in the ratio of world to domestic prices for tradeable goods, thereby greatly reducing the foreign exchange risk implicit in foreign trade and capital movements. The author is currently an opposition deputy in the São Paulo state legislature.

Tourinho, Luiz Carlos Pereira. Distroções fisionômicas do Brasil. See item **5709**.

3527 Velloso, João Paulo dos Reis. Brasil: a solução positiva. São Paulo, Abril-Tec Editora, 1978. 238 p., bibl., tables.

Economic and political testament of Brazil's planning minister during the Medici and Geisel administrations. A professed admirer of Giscard d'Estaing, Velloso specifies his objective as a democratic society with a socially just market economy, which he calls neo-capitalist. By "positive solution" he means a gradualist, democratic, and pluralist approach "authentic" in that it is consistent with the cultural values of Brazilian society in the economic, social, and political realms. Looking both backward and forward in 1977, he evaluates favorably what has been achieved, advocates increased but gradualist redistribution with growth, and calls for no radical departures. Sometimes polemic but

particularly interesting are the chapters on the "positive solution," alternatives to the Brazilian model and the radical solution, and the group of five chapters on transformations and social progress. A view through rose-colored glasses, mixing statistics and philosophy, but worth reading.

3528 Versiani, Flávio Rabelo and **José Roberto Mendoça de Barros** eds. Formação econômica do Brasil: a experiência da industrialização. São Paulo, Edição Saraiva, 1977. 410 p., bibl., tables (Série ANPEC de leituras de economia)

A collection of 14 essays on the history of Brazilian industrialization by Brazilians and Brazilianists. Most contributions are reprinted from other published sources. Useful for didactic purposes. Among other things, contains the classic "Uma Política de Desenvolvimento Econômico para o Nordeste," a document prepared in the late 1950s and which continues to be one of the most trenchant analyses of the "Northeast problem" ever written.

3529 Villela, Annibal V. and **Wilson Suzigan.** Government policy and the economic growth of Brazil: 1889–1945. Rio, Instituto de Planejamento Econômico e Social, Instituto de Pesquisas (IPEA/INPES), 1977. 393 p., bibl., tables (Brazilian economic studies, 3)

This extensive study's objective is to analyze the trends in structural changes in the Brazilian economy in the period 1889–1945. The authors state that the extensive statistical series contained in the appendices are the most important contribution of the work, but caution that they are incomplete and should be used and interpreted with care. The principal conclusion of this monograph, which should be of great interest to economic historians, is that the restrictive policies and coffee-support programs followed up to 1945 failed to promote economic development. In fact, they impeded development during certain periods, being most detrimental in the years 1898–1902, 1925–26, and in 1930s. Why? Overdependence of the domestic economy of foreign trade was prolonged. Agricultural diversification was delayed. Industrial development proceeded in surges rather than occurring as a continuous process. Per capita income stagnated in the 1930s. And finally, regional concentration and the national allocation of manpower worsened. One is tempted to assert that this sounds like the definition of a dependent capitalist economy. For Portuguese version of this work, see *HLAS 38:4137*.

3530 Werneck, Dorothea F.F. Emprego e salários na indústria de construção. Rio, Instituto de Planejamento Econômico e Social, Instituto de Pesquisas (IPEA/INPES), 1978. 176 p., tables (Relatorio de pesquisa, 40)

Analyzes the rather extensive data available on wages and employment in the construction industry, which in 1973 directly employed roughly one third of all workers in the industrial sector. Examines data on geographical and skill differentials in wages. Solid research, but no particularly surprising findings from a theoretical or policy-making point of view.

3531 Whitaker, Morris D. and **G. Edward Schuh.** O mercado de trabalho industrial no Brasil e suas implicações para a absorção de mão-de-obra (IPEA/PPE, 7:2, agôsto 1977, p. 333–366, tables)

Econometric analysis of the industrial labor market in Brazil. Includes a review of the literature, formulation of a model, and presentation of results. Modern and traditional sectors of industry are distinguished. In general the price elasticity of demand for labor in the modern sector is estimated to be lower than in the traditional sector, but sufficiently high to suggest that policies which change the real price of labor will have a strong impact on employment. The study concludes that Brazilian development policy has had a strong anti-employment bias, but that if policies are altered, the employment problem can be greatly attenuated. The authors recommend changing the fiscal disincentive to labor use (like subsidized credit and taxes falling on wages) and expanding the formation of human capital through government financed education and training programs which reduce private costs of labor to employers and expand employment opportunities.

Wirth, John D. and **Robert L. Jones** eds. Manchester and São Paulo: problems in rapid urban growth. See item **9411**.

3532 Zockun, Maria Helena Garcia Pallares and others. A agricultura e a política comercial brasileira. São Paulo, Instituto de Pesquisas Econômica (IPE), 1976. 136 p., tables (Série monografias, 8)

A comprehensive monograph by a group of first-rate economists from the Univ. of São Paulo. Includes chapters on the history of Brazilian foreign trade policy, 1946–75; exchange rate and commercial policy, 1968–75; purchasing power parity theory, minidevaluations, and equilibrium in the trade account; the Brazilian system of export promotion, restrictions on agricultural exports, and a conclusion advocating increased agricultural export promotion to help achieve equilibrium in the trade account following the 1973 petroleum crisis. Among the findings are that the system of minidevaluations resulted in an overvalued exchange rate given unfavorable changes in the terms of trade since 1973 and that agricultural exports have been given unfavorable treatment compared with industrial exports.

JOURNAL ABBREVIATIONS
ECONOMICS

ACPS/B Boletín de la Academia de Ciencias Políticas y Sociales. Caracas.

ADST/SDT Sociologie du Travail. Association pour le Développement de la Sociologie Travail. Paris.

AEA/AER American Economic Review. American Economic Association. Evanston, Ill.

AGS/GR The Geographical Review. American Geographical Society. N.Y.

AI/I Interciencia. Asociación Interciencia. Caracas.

APSA/R American Political Science Review. American Political Science Association. Columbus, Ohio.

BAS/SPA Bulletin of the Atomic Scientists. Science and Public Affairs. Educational Foundation *for* Nuclear Science *with the cooperation of the* Adlai Stevenson Institute of International Affairs. Chicago, Ill.

BCRA/EE Ensayos Económicos. Banco Central de la República Argentina. B.A.

BCV/REL Revista de Economía Latinoamericana. Banco Central de Venezuela. Caracas.

BESPL Berichte zur Entwicklung in Spanien, Portugal, Lateinamerika. München, FRG.

BNB/REN Revista Econômica do Nordeste. Banco do Nordeste do Brasil, Depto. de Estudos Econômicos do Nordeste. Fortaleza.

BNCE/CE Comercio Exterior. Banco Nacional de Comercio Exterior. México.

BNL/QR Quarterly Review. Banca Nazionale del Lavoro. Rome.

CAUK/WA Weltwirtschaftliches Archiv. Zeitschrift des Instituts für Weltwirtschaft an der Christians-Albrechts-Univ. Kiel. Kiel, FRG.

CDAL Cahiers des Amériques Latines. Paris.

CEDLA/B Boletín de Estudios Latinoamericanos. Centro de Estudios y Documentación Latinoamericanos. Amsterdam.

CEPAC/REP Revista de Estudios del Pacífico. Consejo Coordinador Universitario de Valparaíso, Centro de Estudios del Pacífico. Valparaíso, Chile.

CEPAL/R CEPAL Review/Revista de la CEPAL. Naciones Unidas, Comisión Económica para América Latina. Santiago.

CH Cuadernos Hispanoamericanos. Instituto de Cultura Hispánica. Madrid.

CJWB Columbia Journal of World Business. Columbia Univ. N.Y.

CLACSO/ERL Estudios Rurales Latinoamericanos. Consejo Latinoamericano de Ciencias Sociales, Secretaría Ejecutiva y de la Comisión de Estudios Rurales. Bogotá.

CPS Comparative Political Studies. Northwestern Univ., Evanston, Ill. [and] Sage Publications. Beverly Hills, Calif.

CPU/ES Estudios Sociales. Corporación de Promoción Universitaria. Santiago.

ECIEL Ensayos ECIEL. Programa de Estudios Conjuntos sobre Integración Económica Latinoamericana, Brookings Institution. Washington.

FCE/TE El Trimestre Económico. Fondo de Cultura Económica. México.

FDD/NED Notes et Études Documentaires. Direction de la Documentation. Paris.

FFES/V Vierteljahresberichte. Probleme der entwicklungsländer. Forschungs-institut der Friedrich-Ebert-Stiftung. Hannover, FRG.

GWU/JILE Journal of International Law and Economics. George Washington Univ., The National Law Center. Washington.

IA International Affairs. A monthly journal of political analysis. Moskova.

IAA Ibero-Amerikanisches Archiv. Ibero-Amerikanisches Institut. Berlin, FRG.

IAMEA Inter-American Economic Affairs. Washington.

IBE/RBE Revista Brasileira de Economia. Fundação Getúlio Vargas, Instituto Brasileiro de Economia. Rio.

IBGE/R Revista Brasileiro de Geografia. Conselho Nacional de Geografia, Instituto Brasileiro de Geografia e Estatística. Rio.

IDES/DE Desarrollo Económico. Instituto de Desarrollo Económico y Social. B.A.

IEAS/R Revista de Estudios Agro-Sociales. Instituto de Estudios Agro-Sociales. Madrid.

IEERAL/E Estudios. Instituto de Estudios Económicos sobre la Realidad Argentina y Latinoamericana. Córdoba, Arg.

IEI/EI Economia Internazionale. Istituto di Economia Internazionale. Genova, Italy.

IFC/REC Revue des Études Coopératives. Institut Français de la Coopération. Paris.

IFH/C Conjonction. Institut Français d'Haïti. Port-au-Prince.

IMF/SP Staff Papers. International Monetary Fund. Washington.

INTAL/IL Integración Latinoamericana. Instituto para la Integración de América Latina. B.A.

IPE/EE Estudos Econômicos. Univ. de São Paulo, Instituto de Pesquisas Econômicas. São Paulo.

IPEA/PPE Pesquisa e Planejamento Econômico. Instituto de Planejamento Econômico e Social. Rio.

JDA The Journal of Developing Areas. Western Illinois Univ. Press. Macomb.

JDS The Journal of Development Studies. A quarterly journal devoted to economics, politics and social development. London.

JLAS Journal of Latin American Studies. Centers or institutes of Latin American studies at the universities of Cambridge, Glasgow, Liverpool, London and Oxford. Cambridge Univ. Press. London.

JPE Journal of Political Economy. Univ. of Chicago. Chicago, Ill.

JPR Journal of Peace Research. International Peace Research Institute. Universitetforlaget. Oslo.

JPS The Journal of Peasant Studies. Frank Cass & Co. London.

JWTL Journal of World Trade Law. Crans, Switzerland.

KYKLOS Kyklos. International review for social sciences. Basel, Switzerland.

LARR Latin American Research Review. Univ. of North Carolina Press *for the* Latin American Studies Association. Chapel Hill.

LI/IA Ibero-Americana. Research news and principal acquisitions of documentation on Latin America in Denmark, Finland, Norway and Sweden. Latinamerika Institutet. Stockholm.

LIWA/YWA The Yearbook of World Affairs. London Institute of World Affairs. London.

NSO Nueva Sociedad. Revista política y cultural. San José.

PPO Pensamiento Político. Cultura y ciencia política. México.

PUCIS/WP World Politics. A quarterly journal of international relations. Princeton Univ., Center of International Studies. Princeton, N.J.

RU/SCID Studies in Comparative International Development. Rutgers Univ. New Brunswick, N.J.

SBPC/CC Ciência e Cultura. Sociedade Brasileira para o Progresso da Ciência. São Paulo.

SID/IDR International Development Review. The Society for International Development. Washington.

UC/A Anales de la Universidad de Cuenca. Cuenca, Ecua.

UC/EDCC Economic Development and Cultural Change. Univ. of Chicago, Research Center in Economic Development and Cultural Change. Chicago, Ill.

UC/EE Estudios de Economía. Univ. de Chile, Facultad de Ciencias Económicas y Administrativas, Depto. de Economía. Santiago.

UCC/CE Cuadernos de Economía. Univ. Católica de Chile. Santiago.

UCL/CD Cultures et Développement. Revue internationale des sciences du développement. Univ. Catholique de Louvain avec le concours de la Fondation Universitaire de Belgique. Louvain, Belgium.

UCNSA/EP Estudios Paraguayos. Univ. Católica Nuestra Señora de la Asunción. Asunción.

UCV/NC Nueva Ciencia. Revista cuatrimestral. Univ. Central de Venezuela, Facultad de Economía, Instituto de Investigaciones. Caracas.

UH/ED Economía y desarrollo. Univ. de La Habana, Instituto de Economía. La Habana.

ULB/RIS Revue de l'Institut de Sociologie. Univ. Libre de Bruxelles. Bruxelles.

UM/JIAS Journal of Inter-American Studies and World Affairs. Univ. of Miami Press *for the* Center for Advanced International Studies. Coral Gables, Fla.

UNAM/RMS Revista Mexicana de Sociología. Univ. Nacional Autónoma de México, Instituto de Investigaciones Sociales. México.

UNLP/E Económica. Univ. Nacional de La Plata, Facultad de Ciencias Económicas, Instituto de Investigaciones Económicas. La Plata, Arg.

UP/A Apuntes. Univ. del Pacífico, Centro de Investigación. Lima.

UP/CSEC Cuban Studies/Estudios Cubanos. Univ. of Pittsburgh, Univ. Center for International Studies, Center for Latin American Studies. Pittsburgh, Pa.

UPR/CS Caribbean Studies. Univ. of Puerto Rico, Institute of Caribbean Studies. Río Piedras.

URSS/AL América Latina. Academia de Ciencias de la URSS [Unión de Repúblicas Soviéticas Socialistas]. Moscú.

UT/SSQ Social Science Quarterly. Univ. of Texas, Dept. of Government. Austin.

UTIEH/C Caravelle. Cahiers du monde hispanique et lusobrésilien. Univ. de Toulouse, Institute d'Études Hispaniques, Hispano-Americaines et Luso-Brésiliennes. Toulouse, France.

UW/LE Land Economics. A quarterly journal of planning, housing and public utilities. Univ. of Wisconsin. Madison.

WD World Development. Pergamon Press. Oxford, U.K.

WRU/JMF Journal of Marriage and the Family. Western Reserve Univ. Cleveland, Ohio.

EDUCATION

LATIN AMERICA (except Brazil)

GORDON C. RUSCOE, *Professor, School of Education, University of Louisville*
with the assistance of Candyce Leonard and Margaret Murchison, School of Education,
University of Louisville

IT IS USUALLY FOOLHARDY to attempt to give form to a collection of literature which is almost random in nature. But the materials reported here, like previous collections, invite some synthesizing remarks. These remarks might take the form of categorizing the materials by level of education considered or by type of research technique employed. And clearly this year's literature again contains a large quantity of writings on universities, their students, their reform, and their role in societal change (see in particular items **4366, 4413, 4476, 4511** and **4526**). Clearly, too, this year's literature again does *not* contain an overabundance of research rigorously argued, either on empirical or on logical grounds.

Nonetheless, a certain recurrent theme does emerge, if only in ill-defined outline. This concern may best be described as a continued uneasiness about the presumed links between education and society. The "failure" of formal education to live up to the expectations of those who require it to perform miracles of individual and national salvation has produced another crop of demands, throughout the world, for anything from outright abolition of schools to the more persistent tinkering with school organization and procedures. Latin America has not escaped these reactions. And it is precisely these reactions which give some sense to a portion of this year's materials.

Although the total elimination of schools has never been a popular notion among social reformers, alternatives to formal education continue to receive attention. These alternatives are not all of a piece, however. Some of the recommended changes would seem to function principally as additions to the existing system. TV-based instruction, for example, might supplement education already received (see for example items **4402** and **4485**). And even proposals for truly alternative, nonformal education (as for example items **4301** and **4593**) might well be viewed with some caution, for such nonformal efforts have a way of becoming programatized, organized and otherwise formalized.

Attempts to discover alternatives to the present educational system seek to remedy problems which, as Solari reminds us (item **4355**), are also addressed by those who recommend incremental changes in the existing system. Such recommendations usually involve tinkering, on a small or grand scale, with elements of existing schooling: expanding preschool education, improving post-graduate programs, or remedying the ills in-between. (Representative items would include **4319, 4473, 4490** and **4580**).

The promotion of adult education, whether by formal or by nonformal means, continues to be a focal point in examining school reform. Techniques of adult education range from fairly conventional methods (item 4549) to somewhat experimental instruction (items 4414 and 4423) to Freire-style literacy programs and proposals (items 4303, 4347, 4491, and 4532). Perhaps the most interesting of these expositions is that of Kozol (item 4466) who recounts the 1961 Cuban literary campaign. The extensive use of participants' recollections, coupled with Kozol's own observations, make the book a useful addition to our knowledge about Cuba. Wald's (item 4469) methodologically similar book on Cuban child-care provides an excellent companion piece.

Literature about Cuba continues to be—at least in our opinion—the most interesting new material on Latin America. In part, this interest is generated by the very nature of the social situation in Cuba. That is, the subject being examined is unique in relation to the rest of Latin America. Moreover, the writings themselves are often exciting: Castro's speeches (items 4457 and 4459), personal (item 4464) and professional (items 4462–4463 and 4467) accounts of aspects of Cuban education all suggest a certain dynamic quality to the society which is missing in writings about other parts of Latin America. It is unfortunate that the Kozol-Wald types of books— well-written, interesting, based on observation and on participants' narratives—are not more readily available for countries which seem *superficially* less enticing than Cuba.

To be sure, strong empirical studies of Argentine education are available, especially those under the auspices of CIE (Centro de Investigaciones Educativas) (see for example items 4381-4382 and 4387–4388). Careful historical and contemporary studies of Mexican and Venezuelan education also continue to appear (see for example items 4504, 4520–4521, 4524, 4574 and 4576). But these and similar writings do not seem to stimulate interest so strongly as do the materials on Cuba. Perhaps reports on the Cuban social experiment would be provocative, whatever one's particularly political leanings. In any case, such reports should be especially appealing to anyone seriously concerned about the ways in which school and society can be linked.

An understanding of the socialistic treatment of education in Castro's Cuba, moreover, may provide a useful perspective for evaluating current arguments about Latin American development. As Christiansen (item 4308) has pointed out, Latin America's underdevelopment is increasingly viewed as a result of its dependency within the international system. To break down this dependency would seem to call for radical interventions into the complex interaction of economic, political, social and educational factors which have led to the dependency.

Calls for radical action are, of course, by no means new (this year, see for example items 4337 and 4364). Nor is it uncommon to find those who trace the failure of educational programs to the lack of such action (item 4322). Even recent writings on Latin American research efforts seem more and more to stress the necessity of solid research as a major component of any effective strategy for breaking out of the cycle of dependency (see for example items 4362 and 4379). The growing data base for Latin American education can help to promote solid research in this area. One must now hope that advocates of specific educational reforms will use research to support their proposals for change or at least will sketch out alternative solutions and suggest the kinds of research necessary to select among these alternatives.

GENERAL

4301 Alberti, Giorgio and others. Educación y desarrollo rural (CYC, 4, 1975, p. 171–182, bibl.)

Arguing that rural education cannot simply be a part of national planning, authors call for rural development of which education will be one part.

Arriagada, Irma. Las mujeres pobres latinoamericanas: un esbozo de tipología. See item **9005**.

4302 Atcon, Rudolph P. La universidad latinoamericana: observaciones al informe de Jaime Jaramillo Uribe. Caracas, Congreso de la República, Comisión de Reforma Universitaria, 1971. 195 p.

Author argues that the socioeconomic development of a community is in direct relation to its educational development. The evidence for the argument, however, is scant.

4303 Barreiro, Julio; Julio de Santa Ana; Ricardo Cetrulo; and Vincent Gilbert. Conciencia y revolución: contribución al proceso de concientización del hombre en América Latina; ensayos sobre la pedagogía de Paulo Freire. B.A., Schapire Editor, 1974. 87 p.

Essays on the pedagogical method of Freire, providing various approaches which can be used in the midst of social transition and revolutionary change.

4304 Bauermeister, José J. Terapeutas de conducta como implementadores del modelo preventivo y de psicología comunal (UPR/RCS, 18:1/2, marzo/junio 1974, p. 57–82, tables)

Results of a seminar of Puerto Rican teachers who received special training designed to help them achieve better results with special children and to improve classroom situations. [P.F. Hernández]

4305 Bender, Lynn Darrell. Education and U.S. policy toward Latin America (RRI, 6:4, Winter 1976/1977, p. 481–484)

Author argues that educational assistance to Latin America is both needed and less threatening to independence than other kinds of assistance.

4306 *Boletín de Educación.* Publicación semestral. UNESCO, Oficina Regional de Educación. No. 19, enero/junio 1976–. Santiago.

Current issue devoted to report on 1976 meeting of ministers of education in Venezuela.

4307 Castellanos, Juan F.; Jesús Hidalgo; Juan José Huerta; and Ignacio Sosa. Examen de una década: sociedad y universidad, 1962–1971. Presentación de Efrén C. del Pozo. México, Unión de Universidades de América Latina (UDUAL), Secretaría General, 1976. 257 p., tables.

Detailed study of more than 85 percent of Latin American universities, stressing the relationship of university to the sociopolitical and economic structure and providing data on growth of enrollments and on relationship of enrollments to national needs.

4308 Christiansen, Jens. Teaching on Latin America: the dependency perspective (PCCLAS/P, 5, 1976, p. 95–100)

Brief outline of dependency argument of underdevelopment and its role in teaching about Latin America.

4309 Colombia. Ministerio de Educación Nacional. Los sistemas educativos de los países signatarios del Convenio Andrés Bello. Nota de presentación de Juan Jacobo Muñoz. Bogotá, 1974. 287 p., fold. table, table.

Examines each of the six national educational systems included in the Convenio, using whenever possible comparable categories. Good basic information.

4310 ———. ———. Instituto Colombiano para el Fomento de la Educación Superior (ICFES). **División de Documentación y Fomento Bibliotecario. Sección Biblioteca.** Análisis de los documentos presentados al Seminario Latinoamericano sobre Teleducación Universitaria. Bogotá, 1976. 1 v. (Various pagings) (Serie bibliográfica, 1:4)

Essentially a brief, annotated bibliography on TV instruction in higher education, with virtually no analysis.

4311 Consejo Episcopal Latinoamericano (CELAM), *Bogotá*. **Secretariado General.** Pastoral Educativa Latinoamericana: su compromiso con la evangelización y la justicia. Bogotá, 1977. 97 p., bibl. (Documento CELAM, 31)

Collection of essays from 1977 Pastoral Education conference in Bogotá, including an essay on education and justice.

Delacroix, Jacques and **Charles Ragin.** Modernizing institutions, mobilization, and Third World development: a cross—national study. See item **9018.**

4312 *Docencia.* Univ. Autónoma de Guadalajara. Comunidad Académica. Vol. 3, No. 3, 30 junio 1975 [through] Vol. 6, No. 6, 31 dic. 1977–. Guadalajara, Mex.

Contains articles on universities and on university teaching as well as information on current events.

4313 Douhourq, Carlos Alberto. Educación popular por televisión (CYC, 4, 1975, p. 129–170)

Lengthy discussion of experiment in community educational TV in which author reports some success in promoting community self—improvement.

4314 *La Educación.* Organización de los Estados Americanos (OEA), Secretaría General, Depto. de Asuntos Educativos. Año 19, Nos. 70/71, sept./dic. 1974 [through] Año 20, Nos. 72/74, 1977–. Washington.

Issues devoted to problems of Latin American youth, women and education, and adult education, as well as usual coverage of current educational developments and book reviews.

4315 *Educación U.P.B.* Univ. Pontificia Bolivariana. Vol. 1, No. 1, mayo 1977–. Medellín, Colombia.

A new education journal from Colombia which includes articles on university and general educational questions.

4316 Fernández, Juan. Mito y realidad de las universidades latinoamericanas (CAM, 36[215]:6, nov./dic. 1977, p. 56–78)

A rather standard account of the "crisis" of Latin American universities.

Figueroa, Peter M.E. and **Ganga Persuad** eds. Sociology of education: a Caribbean reader. See item **1023.**

4317 Frame, J. Davidson. Mainstream research in Latin America and the Caribbean (AI/I, 2:3, mayo/junio 1977, p. 143–148, bibl., tables)

Author argues that Latin American research is somewhat out of the mainstream of worldwide research, emphasizing as it does life sciences rather than physical sciences, but that problems of the area probably explain this emphasis.

4318 Freire, Paulo. Entrevista. Contra la escuela [by] Tomás Vasconi. La escuela en una sociedad de clases [by] Herbert Gintis. Lima, Centro de Publicaciones Educativas, TAREA, 1976. 153 p.

Interview with Freire covers various educational topics, including his reaction to criticism of him and his theories; examination of the school as an instrument for "reproducing society;" and a critical assessment of Illich's educational thought.

4319 Galán, Liliana and **Raquel Ruiz.** Administración de la educación (UNLP/CA, 17:46/48, enero/dic. 1975, p. 37–64, bibl.)

After briefly reviewing general principles of administration, authors urge more efficient management of education.

4320 Gómez, Juan M. La educación frente a las relaciones ecológicas (CEPAC/REP, 9, julio 1974, p. 63–78)

Call for an educational ideology of human solidarity and responsibility in order to promote proper use of natural resources.

4321 *Indice de Artículos sobre Educación y Adiestramiento.* Servicio Nacional ARMO. Vol. 4, No. 2, abril/junio 1976 [through] Vol. 5, No. 4, oct./dic. 1977–. México.

Unannotated entries, compiled from US and Latin American journals, on training and vocational education.

Kaplan, Marcos. La investigación latinoamericana en ciencias sociales. See item **9029.**

4322 La Belle, Thomas J. Goals and strategies of nonformal education in Latin America (CES/CER, 20:3, Oct. 1976, p. 328–345)

Whether viewed from dependency or from deprivation notions of development, author argues, nonformal education has largely failed because it has not been accompanied by socioeconomic changes necessary to reinforce it.

4323 ———. Nonformal education and social change in Latin America. Los Angeles, UCLA, Latin American Center Publications, 1976. 219 p., bibl., table (UCLA Latin American studies, 35)

Author explores in detail four major areas of nonformal education: development of technical/vocational skills, techniques of adult education and literacy, extension education, and community development and integration.

4324 Larrea, Julio. Las bases económicas de la educación en América Latina (CAM, 209:6, nov./dic. 1976, p. 7–23)

Conventional review of the economic problems of education and the need for increased expenditures for human resource development.

Latin American studies in Great Britain: an autobiographical fragment. See *HLAS 40:127*.

4325 Leite Lopes, J. A scientist's plea for human rights in South America (BAS/SPA, 32:10, Dec. 1976, p. 3)

The constraint on scientists' freedom under dictatorships should be an international concern, author argues.

4326 Lipp, Solomon. The university reform in Latin America: background and perspective (NS, 1:1/2, 1976, p. 106–119)

General historical review of the reform movement, stressing its origins and its links to larger social issues.

4327 Llerena Quevedo, J. Rogelio. Universidad y estudiante: naturaleza jurídica de la relación estudiantil; hacia un derecho universitario. Lima, Pontificia Univ. Católica del Perú, Fondo Editorial, 1976. 261 p., bibl.

Examination of legal issues related to university students' rights, focusing on the rights of the university as well. Complex argument, to say the least.

Lomnitz, Larissa. Conflict and mediation in a Latin American university. See *HLAS 40:2743*.

4328 Maza Zavala, D.F. Evaluación crítica de la enseñanza de la economía en América Latina. Caracas, Univ. Central de Venezuela, Facultad de Ciencias Económicas y Sociales, División de Publicaciones, 1974. 31 p., tables.

A very general attempt to identify the skills and knowledge appropriate to economists and to suggest curricula to develop these skills and knowledge. For economist's comment, see item **2859**.

4329 Meeting of the Inter–American Council for Education, Science, and Culture, *VII, San Salvador, 1976.* Seventh meeting of the Inter–American Council for Education, Science, and Culture: final report. Washington, OAS, General Secretariat, 1976. 151 p. (OAS official records, OEA/Ser.C/V.18)

Agenda and resolutions of the meeting.

Mörner, Magnus. El estudio actual de la historia latinoamericana. See *HLAS 40:2200*.

4330 Mraz, John. Light and sound: teaching Latin American history with media (PCCLAS/P, 5, 1976, p. 121–134)

Use of media—slides, tapes, music, films—as vehicle for teaching is explained, based on author's personal experience.

4331 Neglia, Erminio. The teaching of Latin American culture: a Spanish teacher's view and suggestions (NS, 2:3/4, 1977, p. 270–279, bibl.)

Spanish–language teacher who teaches Latin American culture urges the use of folklore and drama as part of curriculum.

4332 Oficina Internacional del Trabajo. Centro Interamericano de Investigación y Documentación sobre Formación Profesional (OIT/CINTERFOR). Estudio prospectivo sobre la formación profesional en América Latina y el Caribe. t. 1, Panorama de la región. Introducción de Julio Bergerie. Montevideo, 1975. 99 p., tables (Estudios y monografías, 17)

Current status of 15 institutions (e.g., INCE in Venezuela, SENAI in Brazil), based in part on questionnaire data.

4333 ———. ———. Formación profesional, educación y empleo: seminario efectuado en Córdoba, Argentina, 4–6 abril 1973; proyecto 085. Montevideo, CINTERFOR, 1973. 138 p., tables (Informes, 52)

General conference report plus papers on vocational education in the area.

4334 ———. ———. Orígenes de CINTERFOR. t. 1, Situación de la formación profesional en América Latina hacia 1960; t. 2, Contribución documental. Montevideo, 1974. 2 v. (122, 102 p.)

Vol. 1 is a reprint of an earlier ILO document which examines problems of manpower development; vol. 2 contains reprints of documents which support or further illustrate the ILO work.

4335 Organización Continental Latinoamericana de Estudiantes (OCLAE),

La Habana. Aniversario de la OCLAE. La Habana, 1976. 47 p.

In addition to OCLAE statues and resolutions, contains brief history of the "struggle" for academic freedom through university and democratization.

4336 Palacio Díaz, Alejandro del. Los residuos de la educación: ¿es la escuela la puerta de aceso a la dignidad y libertad o la institución donde se domestica y enajena al hombre? México, Editorial Diana, 1976. 159 p.

Author argues that education focuses on political and economic expediency rather than on individual integrity and growth.

4337 Parra Luzardo, Gastón. La universidad comprometida con su pueblo (UZ/R, 57, enero/dic. 1977, p. 38–44)

Typical call for Latin American universities to lead the way in promoting social change necessary to eliminate dependency.

4338 Peñalver, Luis M. Hispanoamérica requiere de un nuevo tipo de educación superior que le permita superar el subdesarrollo (UY/R, 18:108, nov./dic. 1976, p. 15–30)

Discussing the inability of Latin American universities to keep pace with changing times and need to utilize natural resources for national development, Venezuelan educational minister offers suggestions for change.

4339 Petty, Miguel. Problemática de la insuficiencia de los sistemas educativos en América Latina (Revista del Centro de Investigación y Acción Social [B.A.] 25:252, mayo 1976, p. 5–38, bibl., tables)

Main articles document discrepancies between educational goals and actual accomplishments throughout Latin America.

4340 Piñera Echenique, Sebastián. Segmentación en el mercado del trabajo y el retorno social de la educación (UCC/CE, 15:44, abril 1978, p. 27–65, bibl., tables)

Attempt to calculate rates of return on education when part of the labor force is employed in occupations for which salaries are set by law.

4341 *Resúmenes Analíticos en Educación.* Centro de Investigación y Desarrollo de la Educación (CIDE). Nos. 703/762, 2. trimestre, 1976; Nos. 763/822, 3. trimestre, 1976; Nos. 883/942, 1. trimestre, 1977; [and] Nos. 943/1003, 2. trimestre, 1977–. Santiago.

Well–annotated entries drawn from a wide variety of journals, national and international reports. Each issue is devoted to one or more specific topics such as education and poverty, economics of education and educational research.

4342 *Resúmenes de Formación Profesional.* Centro Interamericano de Investigación y Documentación sobre Formación Profesional (CINTERFOR). Vol. 2, Nos. 79/150, mayo/agosto 1976; Vol. 3, Nos. 76/151, set./dic. 1976, and Vol. 1, Nos. 1/81, enero/abril 1977–. Montevideo.

Annotated entries on professional training and development compiled from Latin American journals, documents and reports.

4343 Reunión de la Comisión de Cursos de Postgrado, *IV, Caracas, 1974.* Algunos sistemas educativos de postgrado: materiales para su estudio. Coordinación de Gustavo Díaz Solís. Caracas, Consejo Nacional de Investigaciones Científicas y Tecnológicos (CONICIT), Depto. de Educación, 1975. 390 p., bibl., tables.

A number of articles on post–graduate education in Europe, North America and Latin America, including Argentina, Brazil, Colombia, Chile and Peru.

4344 Reunión de Ministros de Educación de la Región Andina, *V, La Paz, 1974.* V [i.e. Quinta] Reunión de Ministros de Educación de la Región Andina: informe final. La Paz, Ministerio de Educación y Cultura, Dirección Nacional de Planificación Educativa, 1974? 153 p.

Contains the addresses delivered by the ministers and the resolutions passed as well as comments on current educational development in the region.

4345 *Revista del Instituto de Investigaciones Educativas.* Año 1, No. 1, mayo 1975 [through] Año 2, No. 9, nov. 1976–. B.A.

General education journal which covers such topics as Piagetian theory, sex education, educational policy and programmed instruction.

4346 Roche, Marcel. Productividad de la ciencia en América Latina (AI/I, 3:3, May/June 1978, p. 134–135)

Citing figures on the low rate of publishing among Latin American scientists, author urges more publications as evidence of commitment to the importance of science in the area's development.

4347 Ruiz Olabuenaga, José I. and others. Paulo Freire: concientización y andragogía. B.A., Editorial Paidos, 1975. 256 p., bibl. (Biblioteca del Ecuador contemporáneo. Serie menor, 199)

Authors examine Freire's concept of "educación liberadora" in terms of epistemology and social change.

4348 Scherz García, Luis *ed.* La universidad latinoamericana en la década del 80. pt. 2, Posibles estrategias de desarrollo. Santiago, Corporación de Promoción Universitaria (CPU), 1976. 289 p., tables (Publicación, 38)

Nine articles examine questions of university development and finance in countries such as Venezuela, Peru, Ecuador and Colombia.

Seminario Andino, *Quito, 1975.* Docencia, investigación y extensión sobre integración andina en las universidades del área. See item **3290.**

4349 Seminario Iberoamericano de Investigación Educativa, *Madrid, 1970.* Seminario Iberoamericano de Investigación Educativa del 23 al 31 de octubre de 1970: patrocinado por la Organización de Estados Americanos, en colaboración con el Centro Nacional de Investigaciones para el Desarrollo de la Educación y el Instituto de Cultura Hispánica. Presentación de Ricardo Diez Hochleitner. Madrid, Ministerio de Educación y Ciencia, Centro Nacional de Investigaciones para el Desarrollo de la Educación (CENIDE), 1972? 197 p., fold. tables, tables.

Collection of papers on the nature of educational research, with little reference to actual research completed.

4350 Seminario Metodológico sobre Ciencia y Tecnología, *II, Bogotá, 1972.* Visión latinoamericana sobre ciencia y tecnología en el desarrollo: Fondo Colombiano de Investigaciones Científicas y Proyectos Especiales Francisco José de Caldas (COLCIENCIAS). t. 1, 3. Presentación de Milciades Chaves. Bogotá, OEA, Programa Regional de Desarrollo Científico y Tecnológico, 1973. 2 v. (612, 289 p.) fold. tables, tables.

Extensive collection of reports on topics such as training and utilizing manpower,

migration of trained manpower, planning and policy making.

4351 Seminario sobre Curriculum, *Caracas, 1975.* Del diálogo a la acción. v. 1/2. Prólogo de Marta Arango de Nimnicht. Caracas, Ministerio de Educación, 1975. 2 v. (330, 282 p.) bibl., tables.

Conference papers examine the development of school curricula uniquely suited to Latin America and training teachers to use these curricula.

4352 Sergeeva, Zhanna Ivanovna. Izuchenie Latinskoi Ameriki v SShA (The study of Latin America in the U.S.). Moscow, n.p., 1975. 88 p.

Study issued by the Institute of Latin America of the Academy of Sciences of the USSR. Surveys American institutes that specialize in Latin American studies (sources of funds, themes of study, professional journals, etc.) Emphasizes "ideological purposes" of US activities. [R.V. Allen]

4353 Simposio sobre la Educación en América Latina, *I, Quito, 1973.* Simposio sobre la educación en América Latina: Quito, abril 15–20 de 1973. Introducción de E. Uzcátegui. Quito, Univ. Central del Ecuador, Editorial Universitaria, 1975. 330 p.

Selection of conference papers, including topics such as philosophy and sociology of education, the teaching of history, and development of research.

4354 Socías López, Juan. The future as science and Latin America (AI/I, 2:1, enero/feb. 1977, p. 20–24)

Author urges Latin American governments and universities to develop programs in future studies and to maintain these programs in a nonpolitical atmosphere.

4355 Solari, Aldo. Development and educational policy in Latin America (CEPAL/R, 3:1, 1977, p. 59–91)

Criticism of traditional education is warranted, author concludes, but expectations for nonformal and other "utopian" solutions are based on precisely the same questionable premises which underlie the defense of traditional education.

4356 Unión de Universidades de América Latina (UDUAL), *México.* **Secretaría General.** Historia de la Unión de Universidades de América Latina: a través de los informes de sus secretarios generales a los consejos ejecutivos (I a XX) y a las asambleas generales (I a VI). Edited by Efrén C. del Pozo. México, 1976. 391 p.

Collection of major addresses of the General Assembly and the Executive Council of UDUAL since its beginning in 1949.

4357 United Nations Educational, Scientific, and Cultural Organization (UNESCO), *Paris.* Oficina Regional de Educación para América Latina y el Caribe. Evolución reciente de la educación en América Latina. v. 4, Análisis regional: Colombia, Costa Rica, Cuba y Chile. México, Secretaría de Educación Pública (SEP), 1976. 163 p., tables (SepSetentas, 232)

A comparative study of Colombia, Costa Rica, Cuba and Chile which examines recent developments, including financial and out-of-school concerns.

4358 Universidad y cambio social en América Latina: jornadas educativas celebradas del 20 al 22 de octubre de 1975. México, Univ. Autónoma Metropolitana–Xochimilco, 1976. 114 p.

A collection of essays on the topic of social change and universities in which universities are urged to play a more active role in change.

4359 Urbina, René. Las enseñanzas del urbanismo en las Facultades de Arquitectura en Latinoamérica: ponencia de la Universidad de Chile elaborada en la época de Presidente Allende (UC/A, 33, abril 1978, p. 107–124, tables)

Author urges greater attention to the role of urban studies in architecture, citing as an example pre-coup plans at the Univ. of Chile.

4360 Vasconi B., Tomás Amadeo. Contra la escuela: borradores para una crítica marxista de la educación. 3. ed. Medellín, Colombia, Editorial La Pulga, 1976. 56 p. (Cuadernillos marxistas, 2)

Author argues that the school system is merely an instrument for capitalistic selection and training and that transformation of schooling to promote socioeconomic reform is necessary.

4361 Weinberg, Gregorio. On the history of Latin American scientific tradition (AI/I, 3:2, marzo/abril 1978, p. 72–78)

Author traces scientific developments in Latin America, stressing the rich tradition of science and technology in the continent.

4362 Witker V., Jorge. Universidad y dependencia científica y tecnológica en América Latina. México, UNAM, 1976. 87 p., bibl., tables (Comisión técnica de estudios y proyectos legislativos, 5)

Arguing that Latin American universities cannot foster scientific and technological progress without social, political and economic bases which science itself cannot generate, author calls for governmental assistance.

4363 Zanotti, Luis Jorge *ed.* Educación, ideología y política. B.A., Instituto de Investigaciones Educativas (IIE), 1975? 92 p., bibl. (Ediciones de la *Revista del Instituto de Investigaciones Educativas*)

A collection of articles, first appearing in the IIE's *Revista*, which focuses loosely on the issue of education and politics.

4364 Zea, Leopoldo. El problema de la educación en Latinoamérica (NS, 1:1/2, 1976, p. 120–129)

Arguing that the continuous search for educational reform has been a part of the search for politico–economic independence, Zea fears current elites have not learned to involve the masses in attempted changes.

ARGENTINA

4365 Aguerrondo, Inés. El centralismo en la educación primaria Argentina. Presentación de Miguel Petty. B.A., Centro de Investigaciones Educativas (CIE), 1976. 64 l., tables (Cuadernos, 15)

Historical and contemporary examination of the conflicting desires for centralization and decentralization within Argentine primary education and the mechanisms by which centralization continues to operate.

4366 Amadeo, Jaime. La reforma universitaria argentina, 1918–1928: la debilidad que perdura. B.A., Centro de Investigaciones Educativas, 1976. 60 l. (Cuadernos, 20)

Author considers the characteristics of the reform movement and the reasons why many of these characteristics persist in current attempts to change universities.

4367 ———. La universidad condicionada: la Universidad de Buenos Aires y su lugar en el proyecto político del siglo XIX. B.A., Centro de Investigaciones Educativas (CIE), 1976. 231 l., bibl., tables (Cuadernos, 18)

Examines role of graduates in promoting change within the university and society and concludes that the Univ. of Buenos Aires accommodated itself, by necessity, to political demands.

4368 **Argentina. Ministerio de Cultura y Educación. Subsecretaría de Asuntos Universitarios. Sector Estadística, Documentación e Imprenta.** Educación superior: universitaria—extrauniversitaria. B.A., 1975. 1 v. (Unpaged) maps.

Maps and addresses of all higher-education institutions in Argentina.

4369 **Aznares, Enrique.** La creación de la Facultad de Ciencias Médicas de Córdoba (JPHC/R, 6, 1977, p. 115–125)

Traces events during the mid–1800s which preceded the establishment of the medical faculty in 1878.

4370 **Babini, José.** La ciencia argentina (in Cultura nacional. B.A., Ediciones Crisol, 1976, p. 273–297)

Traces scientific developments, particularly in the 1800s and early 1900s. No citations or other documentation, however.

4371 **Buenos Aires** (prov.), *Arg.* **Ministerio de Educación. Instituto de Bibliografía.** Bibliografía argentina. v. 11, Educación. La Plata, Arg., 1976. 170 l.

A lengthy but unclearly organized bibliography which includes such items as journal articles and translated textbooks. Not very useful, lacking as it does a clear focus.

4372 **Cassano, Alberto E.** El sistema de promociones en la investigación y desarrollo en el marco de la Universidad Nacional del Litoral (UNL/U, 85, julio/dic. 1976, p. 139–149, tables)

Examines disparities in promotions and salaries between university teachers and university researchers and the reasons why these disparities continue to exist, despite the need to attract more personnel into research.

4373 **Escudé, Carlos.** Aspectos ocultos de la educación en la Argentina: políticas de inversión y productividad, 1900–1970. B.A.,

Editorial El Coloquio, 1975. 281 p., bibl., tables.

Extensive examination of primary and secondary education in which author argues that investments at these levels during the period examined have produced rather low pay-offs.

4374 Las estadísticas de la educación en la República Argentina (IASI/E, 30:114, julio 1976, p. 79–84, tables)

Brief description of the organization and operations of the Dept. of Statistics, Ministry of Education.

4375 **Gallart, María Antonia.** Marcos de análisis para la comprensión de la institución escolar. Presentación de Miguel Petty. B.A., Centro de Investigaciones Educativas (CIE), 1977. 116 l., bibl., table (Cuadernos, 22)

Focusing particularly on secondary schools, author presents three methods of examining schools (psychoanalytic, psychosocial, and bureaucratic) and applies some of the techniques of each.

4376 ——— and **Marta Coelho.** La escuela secundaria: la imbricación entre la tarea y el poder como límite a la innovación. Presentación de Miguel Petty. B.A., Centro de Investigaciones Educativas (CIE), 1977. 168 l., bibl., table (Cuadernos, 21)

Authors examine the internal organization of secondary schools and the effects of this organization on the introduction of innovation.

4377 **Guerrero, César H.** La escuela superior Paula Albarracin de Sarmiento en sus bodas de oro. San Juan, Arg., Asociación Amigos de la Casa Natal de Sarmiento, 1975. 109 p., plates.

History of the school from its founding in 1925.

4378 **Jornadas de Trabajo Realizadas en el C.I.E.,** *III, Buenos Aires, 1974?* Limitaciones y posibilidades de la investigación educativa actual. Presentación de Miguel Petty. B.A., Centro de Investigaciones Educativas (CIE), 1974? 131 l. (Cuadernos, 10)

Papers examine problems facing those in educational research, including unstable political situations, lack of financial resources, and lack of access to information.

Mignone, Emilio Fermín. Estudio de la realidad social argentina. See item **9272.**

4379 Oszlak, Oscar. Política y organización estatal de las actividades científico–técnicas en la Argentina: crítica de modelos y prescripciones corrientes. B.A., Centro de Estudios de Estado y Sociedad (CEDES), 1976. 62 p., tables.

Author argues that the quality of scientific–technical research and its relevance to production are problematic and that current thought is inadequate to solve the problems.

4380 Pardo, Esteban and Fernando Mateo. Argentina: educación y capitalismo dependientes; esbozos críticos para una investigación. B.A., Editorial Tiempo Contemporáneo, 1975. 251 p., tables (Col. Teoría y política)

Authors argue that education must be understood as an interaction between educational policy and capitalistic growth and that educational conflicts reflect larger societal conflicts.

4381 Petty, Miguel. Dinámica histórica del cambio educativo. B.A., Centro de Investigaciones Educativas (CIE), 1974. 24 l. (Cuadernos, 9)

Author argues that educational change has normally resulted from larger social changes and that, interestingly, one must be suspicious of proclaimed educational changes which are not accompanied by or preceded by wider social change. Work presented at the V Semana Académica de las Facultades de Filosofía y Teológia de la Univ. de Salvador, Aug. 1974.

4382 ——— and Ana Tobin. La deserción escolar en la provincia de Río Negro, Argentina. B.A., Centro de Investigaciones Educativas (CIE), 1973. 207 p., maps, tables (Cuadernos, 6)

Extensive study of school dropout in the province, relating this problem to socioeconomic status, distance of home from school, and other factors which influence dropout rates. Based in part on questionnaire data.

4383 ——— and Héctor Mignoli. Las desigualdades en los gastos nacionales y provinciales para educación primaria. B.A., Centro de Investigaciones Educativas (CIE), 1975? 66 p., tables (Cuadernos, 14)

Part of a larger study of Argentine education, the current work describes the relationship between finances and education, stressing inequalities of distribution.

4384 ———; Rodrigo Vera Godoy; and Ana Tobin. Hacia una alternativa de educación rural: estudio exploratorio. B.A., Centro de Investigaciones Educativas (CIE), 1976. 62 l. (Cuadernos, 19)

Authors argue, after examining rural education in a number of countries and considering the problems and objectives of this type of education, that the problem of alternatives is so massive that it requires further study.

4385 Rodríguez Feijóo, Nélida; María C. Richaud de Minzi; and Dorina Stefani. Estudio comparativo entre estudiantes argentinos y estadounidenses a través del test 16 PF de R. Cattell (SIP/RIP, 2:1, p. 23–26, bibl., table)

Comparison, using 180 Argentine students and several US samples, of results on a personality test. Conclusions are conflicting.

4386 Rodríguez Kauth, Angél. La inversión en investigación científica y tecnológica en Argentina durante 1975 (AI/I, 2:6, nov./dic. 1977, p. 360–365, bibl., tables)

National budget for research is low, author points out, and some funds are diverted to teaching while other funds are used for recurrent rather than capital expenses.

Rojo, Alejandro. Las villas de emergencia. See item **9281.**

4387 Sánchez Guerra, José and María A. Gallart. Proyecto piloto de profesores de tiempo completo en la enseñanza media. B.A., Centro de Investigaciones Educativas, n.d. 128 p., tables (Cuadernos, 11)

Attempts to establish full–time teaching staffs in secondary schools, author reports, have pleased both teachers and students but bureaucracy continues to hamper greater staff participation in decision–making.

Tedesco, Juan Carlos. Clases sociales y educación en la Argentina. See item **9284.**

4388 Tobin, Ana. Escuela rural productiva: descripción de experiencias. Presentación de Miguel Petty. B.A., Centro de Investigaciones Educativas (CIE), 1977. 136 l., tables (Cuadernos, 24)

Comparison of seven rural schools, each attempting to incorporate agricultural work into the school curriculum, and discussion of how changes of this type might lead to effective reform of rural education.

4389 ————. Permanencia del sistema educativo de nivel primario: sus intentos de reforma, 1880–1969. Presentación de Miguel Petty. B.A., Centro de Investigaciones Educativas (CIE), 1976. 92 1 (Cuadernos, 16)

Author examines 90 years of reform and concludes that reform has been successful only to the extent that it has been supported by general social reform.

4390 Vera Godoy, Rodrigo; Manuel Argumedo; and Elba Luna. Situación actual del perfeccionamiento docente en la Argentina. Con la colaboración de José Arocena and Catalina Schiuma. Presentación de Miguel Petty. B.A., Centro de Investigaciones Educativas (CIE), 1976. 247 l., tables (Cuadernos, 13)

Extensive study of teacher training, concentrating on the years from 1970 to 1974, from which the authors conclude that teaching has not improved significantly.

Wiñar, David L. Poder político y educación: el peronismo y la Comisión Nacional de Aprendizaje y Orientación Profesional. See item **7507**.

BOLIVIA

4391 Anaya A., Ricardo. Desarrollo y universidad. La Paz, Librería Editorial Juventud, 1975. 206 p.

Collection of speeches by Anaya, one of the principal leaders of university reform in the early 20th century at Univ. de Cochabamba. Topics discussed include social, political and economic issues as they relate to the university.

4392 Balderrama C., Teresa and Augusto del Castillo. Visión cuantitativa de la educación privada en Bolivia. Introducción de Hermann Artale. La Paz, Comisión Episcopal de Educación, Secretariado Nacional, 1976. 181 p., tables (Estudios educacionales, 4)

Wide–ranging study of private education from 1970 to 1974, based largely on questionnaire data. Little analysis, however.

4393 Bolivia. Presidencia. Comisión de Integración y Alternativas Educacionales (COMIR). Informe. Presentación de Miguel Bonifaz Ponce. La Paz, 1976. 192 p., tables.

Report includes both description of current formal and nonformal educational provisions and suggestions for future developments.

4394 Bonifaz Ponce, Miguel. La universidad en Bolivia: estudio crítico. La Paz, Empresa Editora Urquizo, 1975. 57 p., bibl.

Cursory review of the Bolivian university and its current problems.

4395 Cortés León, Eduardo. Mito y realidad de la educación boliviana. Cochabamba, Bol., Editorial Serrano, 1973. 227 p., bibl., facsim., plate, tables.

Building from the 1955 education code and subsequent changes, author decries current state of education, particularly in rural, provincial areas.

Font, Carlos. El movimiento estudiantil lucha y se reorganiza en Bolivia. See item **7372**.

4396 Guerra Mercado, Juan. La universidad boliviana en crisis. La Paz, Editorial los Amigos del Libro, 1975. 87 p., bibl. (Col. Un siglo y medio)

Author argues that the university crisis arises from the failure to introduce necessary university reform such as avoiding duplication of courses, promoting research, and unifying courses and programs across the country.

4397 Mendoza Britto, Guido; José Monje Rada; Gregorio Olivera Rojas; and Manuel Paz Soruco. Educación no formal en Bolivia. Prólogo de Waldo Bernal Pereira. La Paz, Ministerio de Educación y Cultura, Consejo de Racionalización Administrativa (CRA), 1975. 1 v. (Various pagings) fold. table, tables.

Extensive review of nonformal educational opportunities in Bolivia and recommendations for expanding and improving these opportunities.

4398 Morales, Juan Antonio and Armando Pinell–Siles. Determinantes y costos de la escolaridad en Bolivia. La Paz, Univ. Católica Boliviana, Instituto de Investigaciones Socioeconómicas (IIS), 1977. 304 p., bibl., tables (Documento de trabajo, 01/77)

Correlational analysis of questionnaire data reveals that school success depends on both school and home factors and that schooling does little to redistribute socioeconomic opportunities. Well worth reading.

4399 Rolón Anaya, Mario. La crisis universitaria. Oruro, Bol., Editorial Universitaria, 1975. 128 p., facsim., illus.

General discussion of historical development and current problems of university autonomy, with special reference to Bolivia.

4400 Seminario Nacional sobre Democratización de la Educación, I, La Paz, 1974. Democratización de la educación: documento final. Presentación de Gabriel Codina. La Paz, Asociación Boliviana de Educación Católica [and] Comisión Episcopal de Educación, Secretariado Nacional, 1975. 76 p., tables.

Final seminar report in which nontraditional solutions to persistent educational problems are promoted.

4401 Tamayo, Franz. Creación de la pedagogía nacional. v. 2. La Paz, Biblioteca del Sesquicentenario de la República, 1975. 226 p.

First printed in 1910, this collection of newspaper articles focuses on need to develop national education without depending on ideas and techniques from other countries.

4402 Tirado C., Nazario and Dulfredo Retamozo L. ERBOL: Escuelas Radiofónicas de Bolivia, una aproximación descriptiva. La Paz, Univ. Católica Boliviana, Depto. Ciencias de la Comunicación, 1977. 223 p., bibl., map, tables (Documentos de trabajo)

Description of the organization and objectives of ERBOL, including details on regions covered and on the process of educational TV instruction.

CHILE

4403 Cori, Osvaldo ed. Las ciencias naturales en Chile: visión crítica y perspectivas. Santiago, Corporación de Promoción Universitaria, 1976. 183 p. (Serie CPU, 36)

Examination of development and current status of research in and teaching of the natural sciences, including examples of successful programs.

4404 Cruz, Juan Manuel. Política educacional y distribución del ingreso en Chile (CPU/ES, 11:1, 1977, p. 38–62, bibl., tables)

Although recognizing limitations of data, author suggests that education is related to income but that educational policy does not necessarily promote income equality.

4405 Figueroa, Patricio and Lucrecia Roca. Bibliografía para la historia de la educación chilena. Santiago, Univ. de Chile, Facultad de Filosofía y Educación, Depto. de Educación, Comisión de Investigación, 1971. 161 p.

Unannotated bibliography with no cross–indexing. Impressive in length but not in organization.

4406 Mac-Hale, Tomás P. Imperativos de la universidad chilena. Santiago, Editorial Univ. Técnica del Estado, 1976. 22 p. (Documentos, 1)

Author briefly reviews student takeover as leftist movement and concludes that Marxist regime was a failure. Argues that Chile must now improve quality of higher education through scientific and technological research.

4407 Melville L., Tomás. El poder que otorga la educación (Stylo [Pontificia Univ. Católica de Chile, Temuco] 11:15, 1. semester 1976, p. 1–23, bibl.)

Author argues that power structure does not promote the education of Indian populations, despite an educational structure defined by law.

4408 Menanteau–Horta, Darío. Características sociales y económicas de los estudiantes de la Universidad Austral de Chile. Valdivia, Univ. Austral de Chile, Depto. de Sociología, 1976. 94 p., tables.

Extensive study of current students and their background as a prelude for the university to plan better to meet student needs.

4409 OCLAE. Revista mensual. Organización Continental Latinoamericana de Estudiantes. Año 10, Nos. 9/10, 1976–. La Habana.

Leftist accounts of university student activities and problems, several focusing on Chile.

4410 Padua, Jorge. Aspectos psicológicos del rendimiento escolar. México, El Colegio de México, Centro de Estudios Sociológicos (CES), 1974. 28 p., tables (Cuadernos del CES, 5)

Based on 1969 Chilean data, author argues that socioeconomic class affects school performance precisely because advantaged students have greater opportunities to develop their potential.

4411 *Resúmenes Analíticos en Educación.* Centro de Investigación y Desarrollo de la Educación (CIDE), Servicio de Documentación. Nos. 1185/1244, 2. trimestre 1978–. Santiago.

Summaries of recent research studies in education, with some emphasis on research involving technological innovations in adult education.

4412 Rothhammer, Francisco and **Elena Llop.** Amerindian descent and intellectual performance in Chilean university students (WSU/HB, 48:3, Sept. 1976, p. 455–464, bibl., tables)

Using sample of 63 Chilean university students, author finds that Amerindian descent is not an important variable in explaining intelligence and academic performance. For sociologist's comment, see item **9249.**

4413 Schiefelbein, Ernesto and **Noel McGinn** *eds.* El sistema escolar y el problema del ingreso a la universidad. Santiago, Corporación de Promoción Universitaria (CPU), 1975. 532 p., tables (Ediciones CPU, 35)

A good collection of both current and older research studies on the topic which, as the editors point out in their opening essay, continues to merit research and examination.

COLOMBIA

4414 Acero, Hernán D. Educación superior a distancia como un nuevo sistema de enseñanza. Bogotá, Ministerio de Educación Nacional, Instituto Colombiano para el Fomento de la Educación Superior (ICFES), 1976. 23 1. (Serie documentos de divulgación, 28)

General review of ideas on this form of adult education and report on several experimental programs currently being carried out.

4415 ———. Formación capacitación y entrenamiento de administradores univer-

sitarios. Bogotá, Ministerio de Educación Nacional, Instituto Colombiano para el Fomento de la Educación Superior (ICFES), 1976. 13 1., tables (Serie documentos de divulgación, 30)

Very brief "model" of good university administration.

4416 Alvarado A., Alberto and others. Estudio sobre formación y utilización de recursos humanos para el sector minero y energético. Presentación de Pedro J. Amaya Pulido. Bogotá, Ministerio de Educación Nacional, Subgerencia de Asuntos Científicos y Tecnológicos, División de Recursos Científicos y Tecnológicos [and] COLCIENCIAS, 1974. 50 1. (Fondo Colombiano de Investigaciones Científicas y Proyectos Especiales Francisco José de Caldas, 21)

Assessment of problems in coordinating supply and demand of human resources, in this case in mining and energy. Some questionnaire data included.

4417 Anzola Gómez, Gabriel. Sobre la universidad: aspectos académicos. Bogotá, Univ. Externado de Colombia, 1976. 206 p., bibl.

Explanation of the university system, its history and current operations, based in large measure on comments from prominent educators.

4418 Braun, Juan. Comunicación, educación no formal y desarrollo nacional: las radio–escuelas colombianas. Bogotá, Acción Cultural Popular, 1976. 174 p., bibl., tables (Serie educación fundamental integral, 1)

Survey study of five rural communities to determine if radio–schools would help to improve living conditions by educating the population. Evidence inconclusive.

4419 Caviedes, Sergio. Tecnología educativa y satélite educativo. Bogotá, Ediciones Suramérica, 1975. 100 p.

An examination of Skinnerian psychology, educational technology and their role in promoting educational and consequently national development.

4420 Colombia. Ministerio de Educación Nacional. Instituto Colombiano de Pedagogía (ICOLPE). Experiencias educativas en el medio rural colombiano. Introducción de Julio Ernesto Vera O. Bogotá, Centro Nacional de Documentación e Información Pedagógica (CENDIP), 1972. 51 p., fold. map, fold. tables, plates, tables (Serie divulgación, 2)

Three "case studies" of rural education, including aims and recent projects and accomplishments.

4421 ———. ———. ———. ICOLPE: funciones, programas, realizaciones, proyecciones. Presentación de Irene Jara de Solorzano. Bogotá, Centro Nacional de Documentación e Información Pedagógica (CENDIP), 1973. 81 p., fold. table, tables (Serie divulgación, 3)

Description of organization and programs of ICOLPE.

4422 ———. ———. ———. **Centro Nacional de Educación e Información Pedagógica** (CENDIP). Estudios sobre educación en Colombia: 1968–1973. Bogotá, 1974. 422 p. (Serie directorios, 2)

Catalogue of education research activities, including names and locations of researchers and summaries of research findings.

4423 ———. ———. **Instituto Colombiano para el Fomento de la Educación Superior** (ICFES). Universidad a distancia: una alternativa. Presentación de Pablo Oliveros Marmolejo. Bogotá, 1974. 1 v. (Various pagings) plates, tables (Tendencias de la educación superior en Colombia, 2)

Discusses promotion of higher education among adults via TV, radio, tutorials. Provides some basic statistics on education as well.

4424 ———. ———. ———. **División de Educación Tecnológica y Ocupacional. Sección Programación.** Aspectos metodológicos de la encuesta para determinar perfiles profesionales del egresado de la educación tecnológica. Bogotá, 1975. 1 v. (Various pagings) map, tables (Serie documentos de divulgación, 13B)

Report on questionnaire development to study human resource needs and supplies.

4425 ———. ———. ———. ———. ———.

Inventario de estudios de recursos humanos y su correlación con la educación tecnológica en Colombia. Bogotá, ICFES, División de Documentación y Fomento Bibliotecario, Biblioteca, 1974. 40 l., bibl., tables (Serie documentos de divulgación, 10)

Examines recent attempts to study and coordinate human resource production.

4426 **Correa Velásquez, Jairo.** Docencia universitaria por el sistema de módulos. Bogotá, Ministerio de Educación Nacional, Instituto Colombiano para el Fomento de la Educación Superior (ICFES), 1976. 37 l., bibl., illus. (Serie documentos de divulgación, 29)

Explanation of purposes and techniques of modular instructional programs and their potential use in Colombian higher education.

4427 **Crespo C., Virgilio** and **Beatriz Rodríguez de Crespo.** Iglesia, educación y lucha de clases en Colombia. Bogotá, Editorial América Latina, 1977. 206 p., bibl., tables.

Argues that the Church is unable to play a significant role in social and educational change because of its own internal conflicts.

Davis, Robert H. Education in New Granada: Lorenzo María Lleras and the Colegio del Espíritu Santo. See *HLAS 40:3422.*

4428 **Educación.** Bogotá, Fundación para la Nueva Democracia [and] Fundación Friedrich Naumann, 1975. 105 p., tables (Enfoques colombianos: temas latinoamericanos. Serie monografías, 3)

Essays on financing and developing rural education. Some statistics provided.

Fields, Gary S. Educación y movilidad económica en Colombia. See item **3091.**

4429 **Geist, Harold.** Comparación entre los intereses vocacionales en Colombia y Estados Unidos (RLP, 8:3, 1976, p. 411–416, bibl., tables)

Comparison of Colombian and US students' vocational interests reveals a number of similarities and few differences.

4430 **Gómez Duque, Luis Fernando.** La universidad posible. Bogotá, Ediciones de la Univ. Externado de Colombia, 1976. 171 p., bibl., illus.

Author examines the notion of interdisciplinary studies, their possible organization, their potential accomplishments, and their relationship to larger social issues of the country.

4431 **González, Guillermo Alberto.** La lucha por saber: una teoría sobre la educación colombiana. Prólogo de Luis Carlos Galán. Bogotá, Ediciones Tercer Mundo, 1978. 98 p. (Col. Tribuna libre)

An attempt to analyze the problem of illiteracy in Colombia and to set forth methods to improve the educational system in general.

4432 González Joves, Jaime. La oferta y la demanda de trabajadores con educación formal. Bogotá, Ministerio de Educación Nacional, Instituto Colombiano para el Fomento de la Educación Superior (ICFES), 1975. 80 p., bibl., tables (Serie documentos de divulgación, 27)

Essentially a review of literature in the field, with little direct reference to Colombia.

4433 Hincapié Quintero, Augusto. La universidad colombiana, fruto de nuestra idiosincracia (*in* El nuevo pensamiento colombiano. Bogotá, FEDELCO, 1977. p. 147–164)

Examines goals and methods of universities which fail to prepare students to meet either personal or social needs and argues that students are instructed in an Hellenic ideal but are unprepared to face the world of hunger and underdevelopment around them.

4434 Leyva D., Jorge and **Jorge Ortíz A.** ¿La universidad: cambiarla o cerrarla? Bogotá. Ediciones Tercer Mundo, 1976. 152 p., table.

Authors attempt to examine the nature and current problems of Colombian higher education, including academic programs, planning and finance.

4435 Medellín, Carlos. La universidad conflictiva entre otras cosas. Bogotá, Ediciones Univ. Externado de Colombia, 1976. 139 p.

Commemorative essays to mark the 90th anniversary of the Univ. Externado, focusing on the theory of and contributing factors to university conflict rather than specific issues and events.

4436 Molano Bravo, Alfredo. Economía y educación en 1850: algunas hipótesis sobre su relación. Bogotá, Oficina de Investigaciones Socioeconómicas y Legales (OFISEL), 1974. 75 p., bibl. (Documentos, 2)

Author argues that mid-1800 educational reforms are to be understood in terms

of the economic and social changes of the period.

4437 Montoya, Amanda; Juan María Hidalgo; and Ernestina Rojas de C. Indice colombiano de educación: 1905–1973. Introducción de Martha Valencia H. Bogotá, Ministerio de Educación Nacional, Instituto Colombiano para el Fomento de la Educación Superior (ICFES), División de Documentación y Fomento Bibliotecario, 1974. 299 p., bibl.

Bibliographic review of periodical publications referring to every aspect of Colombian education. Listings are by subject and by author.

4438 Parra Sandoval, Rodrigo. La expansión de la escolaridad en Colombia. Bogotá, Univ. de los Andes, Centro de Estudios sobre Desarrollo Económico (CEDE), Facultad de Economía, 1977. 77 p. (Documento, 0.37)

Using data as far back as 1920, author profiles growth of education, by level. Some insightful text accompanies the many tables.

4439 Pérez Piedrahita, Otto. Estructura y organización de la universidad colombiana. Bogotá, Instituto Colombiano para el Fomento de la Educación Superior (ICFES), n.d. 87 p., bibl., fold. tables (Serie universidad hoy, 3)

Two–part study, looking first at selection and retention of teaching and administrative personnel, and second at the organizations and committees charged with governing universities.

4440 Secretaría Ejecutiva Permanente del Convenio Andrés Bello (SECAB), *Bogotá.* Documentos. Bogotá, 1975. 3 v. (101, 30, 15 p.) tables.

Reports pertaining to implementation of the Andrés Bello Convention, which seeks educational and cultural integration among Bolivia, Colombia, Chile, Ecuador, Peru, and Venezuela. Some examples: Document No. 41, "Diagnosis y Evaluación Integral del Convenio Andrés Bello"; No. 42: "Normas Legales y Tabla de Equivalencias de Educación Primaria y Media del Area Andina"; and No. 47: "Aplicación de las Resoluciones de la Quinta Reunión de Ministros de Educación del Convenio Andrés Bello".

4441 Sepúlveda Niño, Saturnino. Maestros, estudiantes y lucha de clases. Bogotá, Ediciones Unidad, 1977? 106 p.

Marxist analysis of the educational system and student unrest as reflections of the socioeconomic system of the country, particularly stressing that socioeconomic existence determines the conscience of man.

4442 Silva, Juan José; Ernesto Toro; Antonio Valenzuela; and Washington Rojas. Educación de adultos: una experiencia comunitaria. Bogotá, Centro de Investigaciones Educativas (CIDE) [and] Asociación de Publicaciones Educativas, 1975. 124 p., tables (Col. Educación hoy, 12)

Report on a CIDE—sponsored study of six groups of adults who were asked to discuss education and its impact on their lives. Results of the study might be useful in developing curricula for adult education.

4443 Universidad Nacional de Colombia, Bogotá. Oficina de Planeación. Serie historica: 1967–1971. Bogotá, 1972? 107 l., map, tables.

Extensive data on enrollments, staff and budgets, but very little analysis.

4444 ————. ————. División de Programación Académica. Objectivos y políticas de la universidad: alternativas. Bogotá, 1974. 69 l., tables.

Provides objectives for virtually all aspects of university life aimed at improving the quality of education and promoting education to meet national needs. Also contains reprints of legislative and university documents addressing these objectives.

4445 Universidad Pedagógica y Tecnológica de Colombia, Tunja. Oficina de Investigaciones Socio–Económicas y Legales (OFISEL). Regionalización y educación primaria en áreas rurales de Boyacá. Tunja, Colombia, Univ. Pedagógica y Tecnológica, Secretaría de Investigaciones y Extensión Universitaria, Fondo Especial de Publicaciones, 1976. 191 p., fold. maps, tables (Ediciones la rana y el aguila)

Examination of primary education in the Dept. of Boyacá based in part on questionnaire data. Additional analysis would be useful.

4446 Universidad Pontificia Bolivariana, Medellín. Departamento de Planeación. Boletín estadístico: 1974. Presentación de Héctor Mejía Vélez. Medellín, Colombia, 1974. 51 l., tables.

Data on the university's enrollments, staff and budget. Very little analysis of the data, however.

COSTA RICA

4447 Azofeifa, Isaac Felipe. Don Mauro Fernández: teoría y práctica de su reforma educativa. San José, Editorial Fernández—Arce, 1975. 69 p., bibl., plates (Serie cuadernos pedagógicos, 2)

An exposition of the late 19th—century educational reforms of Costa Rica as set forth by Fernández, a key figure in these reforms.

4448 Barahona Jiménez, Luis. La Universidad de Costa Rica: 1940–1973. Presentación de Carlos Monge Alfaro. San José, Editorial Univ. de Costa Rica, 1976. 408 p., tables.

Analysis of the University's development in which historical documents are examined rather than merely reprinted. Citations are scarce, however.

4449 Costa Rica. Ministerio de Educación Pública. Dirección General de Planeamiento y Desarrollo Educativo. Nuclearización educativa. San José, 1976. 121 l., bibl., tables.

Report on two experimental programs in rural community—based education. Few conclusions are reported or even apparent.

4450 Facio, Rodrigo. Documentos universitarios. San José, Editorial Costa Rica, 1977. 200 p., tables (Obras de Rodrigo Facio, 3)

Collection of speeches, letters, articles and other works of Facio, attorney, economist and rector of the Univ. de Costa Rica. Topics range from ideological preferences to university objectives.

4451 Gamboa, Emma. Educación en una sociedad libre: fundamentos y ejemplario. San José, Editorial Costa Rica, 1976. 168 p.

Gamboa argues that democracy and education can reinforce each other and sets out some theoretical and practical thoughts on this relationship, with special reference to Costa Rica.

4452 González, Luis Felipe. Historia de la influencia extranjera en el desenvolvimento educacional y científico de Costa Rica. Prólogo de Constantino Lascaris. San José, Editorial Costa Rica, 1976. 296 p., plates (Biblioteca patria, 10)

Commemorative work for Costa Rica's 100th anniversary in which author examines that context in which education has developed and the effects of foreign ideas on this development.

CUBA

4453 Aguzzi, Luciano. Educazione e societa a Cuba. Milano, Italy, Gabriele Mazzota Editore, 1973. 368 p., bibl.

Sólido estudio analiza, en base a amplia documentación cubana e internacional, la organización de la educación en Cuba y sus implicaciones sociales y políticas. El estudio se divide en tres partes: 1) la política educacional de la revolución hasta 1963; 2) la organización de la educación básica, secundaria, universitaria y para adultos; y 3) los problemas sociales y políticos relacionados con la educación pública. [M. Carmagnani]

4454 Castro, Fidel. La educación. Prólogo de Juan Marinello. La Habana, Instituto Cubano del Libro, 1974. 233 p., facsim., plates.

Excerpts from Castro's writings and speeches are organized around a number of topics reflecting the basic theme that productivity in the future depends on educating and training the young now.

4455 Cuba. Ministerio de Educación (MINED). Viceministerio de Economía y Servicios Generales. Dirección de Producción de Medios de Enseñanza. Educación formal: Resolución Ministerial No. 304/76. La Habana, 1976? 38 p.

Socialistic guidelines, in the form of a ministerial resolution, for fostering intellectual, personal and social growth for the benefit of future generations.

4456 Durasevich, ÍÚriĭ Evgen'evich. Fundamentación de la preparación politécnica en la educación general. La Habana, Ministerio de Educación (MINED), Viceministerio de Economía y Servicios Generales, n.d. 47 p., tables.

Curricular and theoretical guidelines for the development of polytechnical training to meet the demands of a socialist society.

4457 Educación. Revista trimestral. Ministerio de Educación. Año 6, No. 21, abril/junio 1976–. La Habana.

In addition to articles on educational methods and theory, current issue includes Castro's speech of April 1976 to the Pioneers' Union and the Union of Communist Youth, in which he urges greater cooperation between the two organizations.

4458 ———. ———. ———. Año 6, No. 23, oct./dic. 1976–. La Habana.

Present number includes speech by Castro, marking 20th anniversary of the *Granma* landing, in which the growth of the school system is examined.

4459 ———. ———. ———. Año 7, No. 27, oct./dic. 1977–. La Habana.

Issue includes two of Castro's speeches of Sept. 1977, the first describing present and future growth of education, the second extolling sports participation and excellence as both a right and a duty of all Cubans.

4460 Eklund, Per. Appropriate technology for learning aids production: a case study of a Cuban project (UNESCO/IRE, 23:1, 1977, p. 132–137)

Report on Cuban project to produce science–learning aids in a factory which will also serve as a school for vocational students–cum–workers.

4461 Fernández Alvarez, José Ramón. Intervención del Ministro de Educación en el acto de fin de curso de la Escuela de Formación de Profesores de Marxismo–Leninismo, la Escuela Nacional de Cuadros del MINED y el Instituto Pedagógico de Educación Técnica y Profesional. La Habana, Ministerio de Educación (MINED), Viceministerio de Economía y Servicios Generales, 1976. 73 p.

Minister's speech in which he outlines the principles of communist education and their implications for school organization and teaching.

4462 Figueroa, Max; Abel Prieto; and Raúl Gutiérrez. The basic secondary school in the country: an educational innovation in Cuba. Paris, UNESCO Press, 1974. 47 p., tables (Experiments and innovations in education, 7)

Brief review of the *escuela al campo* program, its organization and its place within the school system. Authors stress particularly the ideological bases for the program.

4463 González Manet, Enrique. ¿Por qué y cómo cambia la educación en Cuba? (OCLAE, 2, 1977, p. 18–31, plates)

Author describes current changes, particularly those incorporated into the 1975 educational plan, and stresses the underlying belief in society as educator.

4464 Henríquez–Ureña, Camila. Entrevista (UH/U, 200, 1973, p. 85–190)

Interview with Dominican–born Cuban university educator, who summarizes current Cuban educational organization and philosophy (for more on her, see *HLAS* 40:3041).

4465 Herrera Hernández, Hermes. La realidad de la universidad en la Cuba de hoy (HU, 1:2, feb./abril 1975, p. 63–79)

Rector of the Univ. of Havana describes current organization, stressing the educative role of work for university students, elimination of discriminatory admissions policies, and the justification for the absence of university autonomy.

4466 Kozol, Jonathan. Children of the Revolution: a Yankee teacher in the Cuban schools. Preface by Paulo Freire. N.Y., Delacorte Press, 1978. 245 p., bibl., plates.

Using extensive interviews and observation, Kozol writes persuasively about the 1961 literacy campaign and subsequent educational achievements.

4467 Pérez, Lisandro. The demographic dimensions of the educational problem in socialist Cuba (UP/CSEC, 7:1, Jan. 1977, p. 33–57, bibl., tables)

Examines the growth of primary school enrollments as the result of both expansion of the system and as a response to increasing birth rates.

4468 Pérez Rojas, Niurka. El movimiento estudiantil universitario de 1934 a 1940. La Habana, Instituto Cubano del Libro, Editorial de Ciencias Sociales, 1975. 355 p., bibl., tables (Col. Nuestra historia)

Good discussion of the Cuban student movement, presenting political climate as well as specific events during the period covered. Thorough bibliography.

4469 Wald, Karen. Children of Che: child–care and education in Cuba. Foreword by Hal Z. Bennett. Palo Alto, Calif., Ramparts Press, 1978. 399 p., plates, tables.

Nicely balanced account of Cuban education, relying especially on children's own statements about schooling and childhood in a revolutionary society.

DOMINICAN REPUBLIC

4470 Brown–John, C. Lloyd. Higher education in the Dominican Republic: background and evaluation (NS, 2:3/4, 1977, p. 109–149, tables)

Extensive background information on education and a catalog of current problems. Many tables included.

4471 Castillo, José del. El sistema científico-tecnológico dominicano (Ciencia [Univ. Autónoma de Santo Domingo, Dirección de Investigaciones Científicas] 2:3, julio/sept. 1975, p. 55–75, bibl., illus., tables)

Based on 1972 data, author profiles scientific and technological research activities and urges a more dynamic national research policy.

4472 Congreso de Estudiantes de Educación, I, *Universidad Autónoma de Santo Domingo, 1976.* Educación, desarrollo, e ideología: ponencias, conclusiones y recomendaciones de . . . Prólogo de Víctor Hugo de Lancer Sánchez. Santo Domingo, Centro de Investigaciones Pedagógicas (CIPE), 1977. 99 p., tables (Biblioteca CIPE, 1)

Reports from first congress, including discussion of specific educational problems, recommendations for altering the present situation.

4473 Cordero Michel, Emilio; Antinoe Fiallo Billini; and Franklin Almeyda Rancier. La renovación académica del Colegio Universitario. Santo Domingo, Univ. Autónoma de Santo Domingo (UASD), 1976. 24 p., tables (Col. Conferencia, 32:203)

Arguing that education must prepare students to be active in Dominican life, authors propose revisions of the Colegio to promote national sentiment among those entering UASD.

4474 Fiallo Billini, José Antinoe. Estrategia alternativa para la reforma de la educación primaria. Santo Domingo, Univ. Autónoma de Santo Domingo (UASD), 1976. 23 p., bibl. (Col. Conferencia, 34:205)

Relying heavily on lengthy quotations author argues that a Marxist interpretation of education–and–work is necessary to promote educational reform. Argument is vague and rambling.

4475 ————. Nueva estrategia universitaria para la liberación nacional. Santo Domingo, Univ. Autónoma de Santo Domingo (UASD), 1976. 23 p., bibl. (Col. Conferencia, 33:204)

Call for extensive university reorganization, including production–oriented programs and extension services for the masses.

4476 García Godoy, Federico. La problemática universitaria latinoamericana y la Universidad Autónoma de Santo Domingo. Santo Domingo, Editora Cultural Dominicana, 1975. 288 p., table.

Dental School professor's personal account of student unrest at the Univ., including a discussion of actual events occurring within the School. Interesting reading.

4477 Mejía Ricart, Tirso. Origen, presente y perspectivas futuras de los centros universitarios regionales (Universo [Univ. Autónoma de Santo Domingo, Facultad de Humanidades] 4, julio/dic. 1973, p. 171–214, tables)

Review of successes and problems of regional centers established to make university education more accessible geographically and economically.

4478 Richardson, Felipe. Informe Richardson: opiniones críticas sobre la UASD. Santo Domingo, Editora Taller, 1977. 39 p. (Biblioteca taller, 79)

Chilean advisor criticizes the Santo Domingo Univ. and offers recommendations, particularly to raise level of education offered.

4479 Seminario sobre Educación y Cambio Social, *Santo Domingo, 1974.* Educación y cambio social en la República Dominicana: criterios para la reforma educativa en una sociedad en transición. Prólogo de Ramón Flores. Santo Domingo, Instituto Tecnológico de Santo Domingo (INTEC), 1974. 169 p., tables.

Detailed examination of Dominican Republic education and criticism of methods used and of the qualifications of teachers.

ECUADOR

4480 Ribadeneira, Edmundo M. La reforma universitaria. Quito, Univ. Central del Ecuador, Editorial Universitaria, 1975. 90 p., bibl.

A call to Ecuadorian university students and professors to recapture the ideals of the 1942 reform movement.

4481 United Nations Educational, Scientific and Cultural Organization (UNESCO), *Paris* and **United Nations Development Programme** (UNDP), *Paris.* The experimental world literary programme: a critical assessment. Preface by Amadou-Mahtar M'Bow and Rudolph A. Peterson. Paris, UNESCO Press, 1976. 198 p., bibl., tables.

Among other reports, a brief evaluation of Ecuador's efforts indicates failure was due principally to lack of funds and of true functional literacy programs.

4482 Uzcátegui García, Emilio. Medio siglo a través de mis gafas. Quito, n.p., 1975. 300 p., tables.

While disclaiming this as an autobiography, author recollects the events of his long and varied educational life. Excellent reading.

EL SALVADOR

4483 Campos, Camilo. Normas supremas. 5. ed. San Salvador, Ministerio de Educación, Dirección de Publicaciones, 1976. 155 p. (Biblioteca popular, 7)

First published in 1938, this collection of essays by a Salvadorean educator seeks to define the elements for a higher quality of life. Quixotic and vague.

4484 Escamilla, Manuel Luis. La reforma educativa salvadoreña. San Salvador, Ministerio de Educación, Dirección de Publicaciones, 1975. 204 p., bibl.

Explanation of the educational reform, including historical background, purposes and future hopes. Short on data.

4485 Mayo, John K.; Robert C. Hornik; and Emile G. McAnany. Educational reform with television: the El Salvador experience. Stanford, Calif., Stanford Univ. Press, 1976. 216 p., maps, plates, tables.

Authors examine the origins and development of Salvadorean educational TV and report on outcomes of research on the effectiveness of this program.

4486 Sánchez, Rogelio. Memoria de las labores del Ministerio de Educación: 1974–1975. Memoria de las labores del Ministerio de Educación: 1975–1976. Presentada a la Asamblea Legislativa por el Ministro del Ramo. San Salvador, Ministerio de Educación, 1975/1976. 2 v. (56, 246 p.) plates, tables.

Report on organization and development of Salvadorean education. A useful basic reference.

GUATEMALA

4487 Guatemala. Ministerio de Educación. Consejo Nacional de Planificación Económica. Plan nacional de educación ciencia y cultura: 1975/79. Guatemala, Editorial José de Pineda Ibarra, 1975. 174 p., fold. tables, map, tables.

Rather standard education plan, but interesting for its attempt to project the role of schools in changing traditional values to meet modern socioeconomic goals.

GUYANA

Anderson, W.W. and R.W. Grant. Political socialisation among adolescents in school: a comparative study of Barbados, Guyana and Trinidad. See item **996**.

4488 Field-Ridley, Shirley. Adult education in the new society (NHAC/K, 14, July 1976, p. 115–121)

Rambling discourse on the importance of adult education in Guyana.

4489 Macchus, M.K. A study of change in a plural society: the influence of political development on church control of schools in Guyana (UPR/CS, 14:3, Oct. 1974, p. 141–162)

Decline in church–controlled education is, author argues, attributable to democratizing political relationships among the groups comprising the "plural" society of Guyana.

HAITI

4490 Colimon, Marie Thérèse. Plaidoyer pour l'école maternelle populaire (IFH/C, 133, mars/avril 1977, p. 5–29, illus.)

Review of the aims and organization of preschool education and outline of problems facing Haitian preschool youngsters and their parents.

4491 Groupe de Recherches en Alphabétisation Liée au Développement (GREAL), Port–au–Prince. Alphabétisation 1978: une nouvelle orientation (IFH/C, 138, mai 1978, p. 37–75, illus.)

Report on experimental program incorporating newest adult literacy approaches—including Freire's philosophy, community action groups, and Creole and French as languages of instruction. Results have led to revisions of programs and to additional experiments.

4492 Herbinière Lebert, Suzanne. L'education préscolaire en pays francophone: l'apprentissage du française dans les pays francophones dont la langue maternelle n'est pas le français (IFH/C, 133, mars/avril 1977, p. 39–49, illus.)

Reviews problems of bilingualism and its effects on language instruction in pre–school education.

4493 Roy Fombrun, Odette. Sur l'éducation pré–scolaire (IFH/C, 135, oct. 1977, p. 101–110)

General suggestions for improving pre–school education in Haiti.

HONDURAS

4494 *Ediciones* Educación y Desarrollo. Comisión Nacional de Reforma de la Educación, Secretaría de Educación Pública. Nos. 4, 5, 9, 11, 13, 1975–. Tegucigalpa.

Monographic series consisting of documents prepared by the National Commission on Education and designed to assist educational reform. Includes such topics as the application of group dynamics techniques to education (No. 13), existing educational laws and needed revisions (No. 9), and techniques of social research (No. 11). Some examples: Ventura Ramos Alvarado "Educación, Reconstrucción y Cambio" and "Política Cultural de Honduras: Diagnóstico y Bases."

4495 Encuentro de la Comunidad Universitaria, I, *Tegucigalpa, 1974.* Primer encuentro de la comunidad universitaria: 12–16 noviembre, 1974, Tegucigalpa, Honduras. 2. ed. Tegucigalpa, Editorial Universitaria, 1977. 29 p., plates.

Pamphlet–like report on the 1974 meeting of university students, professors and staff to discuss the role of universities.

4496 Honduras. Secretaría de Educación Pública. Comisión Nacional de Reforma de la Educación. Sección de Investigación. Opciones requeridas para los institutos de ocho comunidades de acuerdo con las necesidades de éstas. Tegucigalpa, 1974. 123 p., tables.

Questionnaire study of adequacy of programs offered in vocational schools in terms of community needs. Interesting data which merit further analysis.

4497 Universidad Nacional Autónoma de Honduras, *Tegucigalpa.* **Departamento de Pedagogía y Ciencias de la Educación.** Investigación sobre la supervisión escolar en Honduras. Tegucigalpa, 1973. 137 p., tables.

Report based on interviewing supervisors as well as on historical and legal information. In general, the findings suggest that supervisors are not well–trained and are not always well–received in the school.

JAMAICA

4498 Foner, Nancy. Status and power in rural Jamaica: a study of educational and political change. Foreword by Raymond T. Smith. Edited by Lambros Comitas. N.Y., Columbia Univ., Teachers College Press, 1973. 172 p., bibl., map, tables.

Author argues that expended education not only affects political structure in general but also in rural communities, which are not, as sometimes thought, untouched by education.

MEXICO

4499 Aguilar Alcérreca, José and others. México y su ingeniería para el año

2000. Prólogo de Víctor Lomelí Delgado. México, Fondo de Cultura Económica, 1976. 86 p., tables (Archivo del fondo, 71)

Projections of needs in various engineering fields for the year 2000. Includes present development and steps to attain projected goals.

4500 Alcocer Andalón, Alberto. Historia de la Escuela de Medicina de la Universidad Autónoma de San Luis Potosí, S.L.P. (México), 1877–1977. México, Aconcagua Ediciones y Publicaciones, 1976. 109 p., facsims., plates (Biblioteca de historia potosina. Serie estudios, 16)

A history not only of the School of Medicine but also of the practice of medicine since Cortés.

4501 Beltrán, Enrique. Desarrollo histórico de la enseñanza de la biología en México (SMHN/R, 35, dic. 1974, p. 23–44)

Discussion of the teaching of the biological sciences in Mexico since the 16th century and a review of schools which currently include biology in their curricula.

4502 Bravo Ahuja, Víctor. La problemática educativa de México en el marco internacional. México, Secretaría de Educación Pública, 1974. 183 p., bibl., tables (SepSetentas, 161)

Brief analysis of the present educational system in which author proposes methods for educational development. Comparisons are made with the US, USSR, and other countries.

4503 —— and **José Antonio Carranza.** La obra educativa. Prólogo de Henrique González Casanova. México, Secretaría de Educación Pública, Dirección General de Divulgación, 1976. 211 p., bibl., map, tables (Serie SepSetentas)

Against backdrop of Mexico's development since 1810, authors examine official statements of educational policies and goals, particularly during the 1970–76 period.

4504 Britton, John A. Educación y radicalismo en México. v. 1, Los años de Bassols: 1931–1934; v. 2, Los años de Cárdenas: 1934–1940. México, Secretaría de Educación Pública (SEP), 1976. 2 v. (162, 173 p.) tables (SepSetentas, 287/288)

Well–documented study of the Secretaría, first from the point of view of Marxist radicalism and institutional development and second from the point of view of using schools as instruments of social change and the sometimes violent reactions against such change. From historian's comment, see *HLAS 40:2694*.

4505 Büttner, Elizabeth Holt. Analfabetismo y carencias de la educación en el Estado de Guerrero (UNAMCG/A, 14, 1974, p. 141–208, bibl., maps, tables)

Interesting examination of illiteracy, largely focusing on geographical distribution of illiteracy within the State of Guerrero.

Burke, Michael E. The University of Mexico and the Revolution: 1910–1940. See *HLAS 40:2695*.

Davis, Charles L. and **Kenneth M. Coleman.** Discontinuous educational experiences and political and religious non–conformity in authoritarian regimes: Mexico. See item **9070**.

4506 Gálvez A., Elioth; Rafael Villagómez V.; and Alfonso Valdez G. La población escolar de educación superior en México: licenciatura, 1970–75. México, Asociación Nacional de Universidades e Institutos de Enseñanza Superior (ANUIES), 1976. 234 p., maps, tables.

Data on first–year and total enrollments, by specialty, for 1970 and 1975. Data are broken down by state, but no analysis is included.

4507 Hodara, J. El intelectual científico mexicano: una tipología (AI/I, 3:1, enero/feb. 1978, p. 20–23, bibl.)

Viewing scientific intellectuals as researchers who also address social issues, author argues that such researchers in Mexico currently seek to blend search for autonomy of inquiry with careful public relations.

4508 Hurtado Márquez, Eugenio *comp.* La Universidad Autónoma, 1929–1944: documentos y textos legislativos. México, UNAM, 1976. 207 p. (Comisión técnica de estudios y proyectos legislativos, 4)

Largely reprints of official documents concerning UNAM, from 1929 through 1944, with very brief introductory essay.

4509 Jurado, Rogelio Luna. Los maestros y la democracia sindical (CP, 14, oct./dic. 1977, p. 73–103, tables)

Reviews teacher syndicalism in Chihuahua from 1972 to 1976, especially the problems of establishing and maintaining a democratic organization.

4510 Lee, James H. Church and State in Mexican higher education: 1821–1861 (BU/JCS, 20:1, Winter 1978, p. 57–72)

During period examined, author argues, relationships between Church and State were marked by both conflict and cooperation and Church seldom officially opposed much of educational reform.

4511 Lomnitz, Larissa. Conflict and mediation in a Latin American university (UM/JIAS, 19:3, Aug. 1977, p. 315–338, bibl.)

Author argues that UNAM faces conflict precisely because its functions include social reform and criticism and because it must constantly balance demands of its academic, professional and political constituents.

4512 Martínez Ovando, Angel. Educación y gobierno: crítica de los actual y sugestiones para el porvenir. México, Editorial Dopacio, 1976. 29 p.

Author views current educational difficulties as directly related to current capitalistic economic system.

4513 Mexico. Secretaría de Educación Pública (SEP). Subsecretaría de Planeación y Coordinación Educativa. 4 [i.e. Cuatro] años de labor educativa: 1970–1974. México, 1975. 136 p., plates.

Attractive presentation of educational developments at all levels. Probably more useful for public relations than for research.

4514 ———. ———. ———. Informes de labores: 1970–1976. México, 1976. 224 p., tables.

General review of educational development, including enrollment figures, recent legislation and attempts at reform.

4515 Oleynik Figueroa, Yaroslaw and **Arturo Unguez Tong.** El componente informático en los curricula universitarios (UAG/D, 3:2, abril 1975, p. 86–110, bibl.)

Authors urge greater attention be given to information sciences, both as a postgraduate major and as a minor in regular university programs.

4516 Panabière, Louis. La universidad: reforma e instituciones (UIA/C, 12:59, feb. 1977, p. 38–47, plates)

Comparative study of university reform in Mexico and France from which author concludes that state–university problems are institutional rather than political in nature.

4517 Pereznieto Castro, Leonel. Algunas consideraciones acerca de la reforma universitaria en la Universidad Nacional Autónoma de México. Prólogo de Ignacio Carrillo Prieto. México, UNAM, 1976. 118 p., bibl., tables (Comisión técnica de estudios y proyectos legislativos, 6)

Examines problems facing UNAM, emphasizing the need for planning to reduce discrepancies between university production and national needs.

4518 Pinto Mazal, Jorge comp. La autonomía universitaria. Antología. México, UNAM, Comisión Técnica de Legislación Universitaria, 1974. 291 p.

Collection of documents on university autonomy in Mexico, mostly concerning UNAM. Order of presentation confusing.

4519 Raby, David L. Educación y revolución social en México: 1921–1940. Traducción de Roberto Gómez Ciriza. México, Secretaría de Educación Pública, Dirección General de Divulgación, 1974. 254 p. (Serie SepSetentas)

Author examines the socialistic origins of rural education and argues that rural teachers played an important role in national politics as catalysts for social reform.

4520 ——. Ideology and state–building: the political function of rural education in Mexico, 1921–1935 (IAA, 4:1, 1978, p. 21–37, bibl.)

The regimes of Obregón and Calles, author argues, used rural education principally to mobilize the masses through revolutionary, nationalist culture taught in the schools.

4521 Ramírez Castañeda, Rafael. La escuela rural mexicana. Introducción de Gonzalo Aguirre Beltrán. México, Secretaría de Educación Pública (SEP), 1976. 214 p. (SepSetentas, 290)

A collection of writing of Ramírez, one of the principal founders of Mexican rural education. Includes history of this movement.

4522 Repetto Milán, Guillermo. Los exámenes de admisión en la escuela preparatoria (UY/R, 19:114, nov./dic. 1977, p. 84–89)

Very poor performance of students on the preparatory school's entrance examination leads author to suggest, inter alia, a general decline in students' verbal abilities.

4523 Revista de la Educación Superior. Publicación trimestral. Asociación Nacional de Universidades e Institutos de Enseñanza Superior. Vol. 5, No. 2:18, abril/junio 1976–. México.

Contains articles and current news on education.

4524 Robles, Martha. Educación y sociedad en la historia de México. México, Siglo XXI Editores, 1977. 262 p., bibl., tables.

A short but interesting history of education as a reflection of the shifting distribution of power in Mexican society.

4525 Rodríguez–Sala Gómezgil, María Luisa. Círculos y canales de comunicación en el dominio de la ciencia (UNAM/RMS, 39:4, oct./dic. 1977, p. 1363–1395)

Author argues that scientific research is often couched in a language which appeals only to the intellectual elite and that Mexico can develop diverse methods of communicating research to better meet the needs of all sectors of the country.

4526 Shapira, Yoram. México: the impact of the 1968 protest on Echeverría's reformism (UM/JIAS, 19:4, Nov. 1977, p. 557–580, bibl.)

Author argues that the 1968 student protests are casually connected to liberal reforms of the Echeverría government, despite the government's efforts to "delegitimatize" the protests. For historian's comment, see *HLAS 40:2774.*

4527 Toledo, Monteforte. Temas y problemas del cogobierno universitario (NS, 1:1/2, 1976, p. 148–157)

Author argues that cogovernment is a means of restructuring a university's power system and uses both historical and current data to support this argument, particularly focusing on student action at UNAM at 1968.

4528 Ulloa Ortiz, Manuel. El estado educador. México, Editorial Jus, 1976. 461 p., bibl.

Interesting examination of current

thought on educational rights in Mexico, which also includes reprints of a number of documents pertaining to educational and more broadly human rights.

4529 Valadés, Diego. La Universidad Nacional Autónoma de México: formación, estructura y funciones. México, UNAM, Comisión Técnica de Legislación Universitaria, 1974. 129 p., fold. tables, tables.

Rather general but informative picture of UNAM, including its history and current organization.

4530 Vallejo Sánchez, Russell Ramón. Apuntaciones de un maestro rural (UY/R, 20:115, enero/feb. 1978, p. 13–34)

Call by rural teacher to rekindle rural reform movement as a necessary part of national development.

Vaughan, Mary Kay. Education and class struggle in the Mexican Revolution. See *HLAS 40:2783.*

4531 Villegas, Abelardo. La ideología del movimiento estudiantil de México (NS, 1:1/2, 1976, p. 130–147)

Examines four interpretations of student activism: universities as agents of social change; students as seekers of less repressive academic environments; universities as too dependent on status quo to serve as social change agents; and students as immature adults.

NICARAGUA

4532 Macías Gómez, Edgard. Jordana pedagógica de San Rafael del Sur (Encuentro [Revista de la Univ. Centroamericana, Managua] 4, enero/feb. 1974, p. 53–61, tables)

Using Freire's ideas on teaching literacy, researchers uncovered key words used by rural Nicaraguans which might serve as the basis for improved literacy instruction.

PANAMA

4533 Domínguez Caballero, Diego. Servicio a la Universidad de Panamá (LNB/L, 263, enero 1978, p. 1–16)

Anecdotal, autobiographical reminiscences of a retiring philosophy professor.

4534 Núñez G., Carlos E. Recursos humanos profesionales y técnicos a 1980, en la Universidad de Panamá. Panamá, Univ. de Panamá, 1975. 153 p., fold. table, tables.

Attempt to relate university programs to economic needs and recommendations for deparmentalizing the university in order to promote this relationship.

4535 Rosas Quirós, Gaspar. Educación (USMLA/LA, 6:9, nov. 1977, p. 79–114, table)

Author traces development of education in the Province of Coclé (Panama) from 1643 to 1976.

PARAGUAY

4536 Brugada Guanes, Alejandro. Pedro Aguilera: su vida y sus obras. Prólogo de Fabio Rivas. Asunción, Casa América, 1976. 141 p., plates.

Eulogistic account of the life–and–works of Aguilera, an educator of Paraguay.

4537 Ferraro, Oscar. Datos y estudios sobre educación en el Paraguay. Presentación de Graziella Corvalán. Asunción, Centro Paraguayo de Estudios Sociológicos [and] Centro Paraguayo de Documentación Social, 1976. 71 p. (Serie bibliográfica)

An unannotated bibliography of some 400 items, ranging from books to newspaper articles. Some cross–indexing.

PERU

4538 Arestegui Moras, Miguel. Nuclearización educativa: teoría y practica. Lima, Talleres de Ital–Perú, 1976. 336 p., bibl., tables.

Extensive review of current Peruvian reforms, especially of community–based education, and includes descriptions of each of the educational zones of the country.

4539 Ballon Echegaray, Eduardo and others. Educación básica laboral: proceso a un proceso. Lima, Centro de Estudios y Promoción del Desarrollo (DESCO), 1978. 142 p., tables (Praxis, 9)

Basic labor education, enacted in 1972 as part of general reform and intended for adults, is described. The failures of this education are attributed to lack of political support.

4540 Bernales R., Enrique and others. El desarrollo de la educación en el Perú y la dominación interna. Lima, Pontificia Univ. Católica del Perú (PUC), Depto. de Ciencias Sociales, 1977. 55 p., fold. tables, tables.

Arguing that previous educational growth has failed to reduce inequalities of opportunity, authors suggest that current reforms might well help to reduce income disparities.

4541 Cáceres, Baldomero and others. La cultura en crisis: universidad. Lima, Pontificia Univ. Católica del Perú (PUC), Depto. de Ciencias Sociales, 1975. 58 l., tables.

Interviews with professors and experts on the problems of universities.

4542 Consejo Nacional de la Universidad Peruana, *Lima.* **Dirección de Planificación Universitaria. Oficina de Estadística e Informática.** Crecimiento cuantitativo de la población universitaria: años 1960–1974. Lima, 1975. 93 p., map, tables (Boletín estadístico, 7)

Data on university expansion, including enrollment by sex and specialization. Unfortunately, there is no accompanying analysis of the data. See item **4543.**

4543 ———. ———. ———. Graduados y titulados en la universidad peruana: década 1960–1969. Lima, 1972. 91 p., tables (Boletín estadístico, 6)

Data aplenty but no analysis. See item **4542.**

4544 Elogio y bibliografía de Rómulo Ferrero Rebagliati. Lima, Univ. del Pacífico, 1977. 58 p., plate.

Tribute to Ferrero, a founder of the Univ. del Pacífico. Bibliographical and biographical data are included.

4545 Encinas, José Antonio. La reforma universitaria en el Perú: 1930–1932. Lima, Ediciones 881, 1973. 252 p.

Former San Marcos Univ. Rector recounts, apparently from his own experiences and memory, the events and ideas of the 1930s reforms.

4546 Negrón Alonso, Luis and **Jaime Bonet Yepez.** El fenómeno educativo en el medio rural: zona de concentración de co-

munidades campesinas Cuzco. Lima, Instituto Nacional de Investigación y Desarrollo de la Educación Augusto Salazar Bondy, Sub–Dirección de Investigaciones Educacionales, Unidad de Investigación Curricular, 1976. 198 p., tables.

Extensive examination of rural education in which authors argue that progress has been slow, in part because of lack of coordination with other rural efforts such as agrarian reform.

4547 Peru. Ministerio de Educación. Instituto Nacional de Investigación y Desarrollo de la Educación Augusto Salazar Bondy (INIDE). Resúmenes: investigaciones, 1973–1975. Lima, 1976. 174 p.

Brief summaries of recent sociological, pedagogical, psychological and economic research on Peruvian education. Includes information on methods of research and conclusions reached.

4548 ———. ———. Oficina Sectorial de Planificación. Desarrollo de la educación peruana, 1973–1975: informe a la 3ª Reunión de la Conferencia Internacional de Educación, Ginebra, setiembre 1975. Lima, 1975? 86 l., fold. map, fold. tables, map, tables.

Short review of educational development, including new legislation, current reform and research, and financing.

4549 Picón, César. Tres temas de educación de adultos. Lima, Juan V. Barca Editorial, 1975? 146 p.

Author considers current developments in adult education throughout Latin America and examines in particular adult education in Peru.

4550 Salazar Bondy, Augusto. La educación del hombre nuevo: la reforma educativa peruana. B.A., Editorial Paidós, 1976. 180 p. (Biblioteca del educador contemporáneo. Serie menor, 201)

A general discussion of educational reform in Third World countries within the context of current Peruvian attempts to develop mass education.

4551 Universidad de San Cristóbal de Huamanga, *Ayacucho, Perú.* Universidad de San Cristóbal de Huamanga, 1677: libro jubilar de homenaje al tricentenario de su fundación, 3–VII–1977. Ayacucho, Perú,

1977. 270 p., colored plates, plates, tables.

Essentially an institutional history, including reprints of a number of documents pertaining to this history.

4552 Velásquez Castillo, Víctor Alcides. La pedagogía de la dinámica de grupos y el nuevo sistema de la educación peruana. Lima, n.p., 1976. 175 p., tables.

Author examines various ways in which groups can be used in education, relating these to current Peruvian attempts to reform education.

PUERTO RICO

4553 Negrón de Montilla, Aida. La americanización de Puerto Rico y el sistema de instrucción pública: 1900–1930. San Juan, Univ. de Puerto Rico, Editorial Universitaria, 1977. 290 p., bibl.

Author examines the americanization of Puerto Rican education through an analysis of the work of the Dept. of Instruction and the various education commissioners during the first 30 years of the century.

4554 Parker, Franklin and **Betty June Parker** eds. and comps. Education in Puerto Rico and of Puerto Ricans in the U.S.A.: abstracts of American doctoral dissertations. San Juan, P.R., Inter–American Univ. Press, 1978. 601 p., tables.

Bibliography of Puerto–Rican related dissertations, each entry well annotated. Indexing somewhat inadequate, however.

4555 Rodríquez Pacheco, Osvaldo ed. A land of hope in schools: a reader in the history of public educaton in Puerto Rico, 1940 to 1965. San Juan, P.R., Editorial Edil, 1976. 359 p., bibl., tables.

An evaluation of Puerto Rican education, its development, goals and problems. Includes addresses of various educators.

4556 Vélez Díaz, Angel. Texto Rápido Barranquilla y revisado: beta examinación en sujetos puertorriqueños (SIP/RIP, 2:1, p. 14–17, bibl.)

Using a sample of 31 subjects, author compares 2 intelligence tests and finds that the beta does not correlate well with educational level of the subjects.

URUGUAY

Centro Interamericano de Investigación y Documentación sobre Formación Profesional (CINTERFOR), *Montevideo*. Proyecto 079: participación del movimiento sindical en la formación profesional; seminario efectuado de Montevideo. See item **7008a**.

4557 Lombardi de Almirati, Olga and **Blanca Martínez Gil** comps. Bibliografía uruguaya sobre educación. Montevideo, Consejo Nacional de Educación, Consejo de Educación Primaria, Biblioteca Pedagógica Central, 1973. 50 l.

An unannotated but indexed collection of some 750 items dealing with Uruguayan education. Includes reports and unpublished documents.

4558 Pimienta, Juan comp. Centenario de la Ley de Educación Común. Idea: Matilde Grucci de Lamónaca and Ofelia Acosta de Montero López. Editor: Wilfredo Pérez. Prólogo: Rubén A. Bulla. Montevideo, Palacio Legislativo, Depto. de Publicaciones, 1977. 210 p., bibl., plates (Serie de temas nacionales, 1)

Tribute to José Pedro Varela and the Education Law of 1877, including biographical and historical background.

VENEZUELA

4559 Adam, Félix. Un modelo universitario operacional venezolano. Caracas, Univ. Nacional Experimental Simón Rodríguez, 1976. 22 p.

University's president outlines six premises which govern the institution, including the belief that the university must respond to national needs wherever and whenever they occur.

4560 Albornoz, Orlando. Higher education and the politics of development in Venezuela (UM/JIAS, 19:3, Aug. 1977, p. 291–314, bibl., tables)

Higher education has failed to produce human resources essential to development, author argues, and the failure in the public university sector is particularly noticeable. For political scientist's comment, see item **7613**.

4561 ———. Poder y liderazgo en la escuela primaria venezolana. Caracas, Instituto Societas, 1977. 315 p., bibl., tables.

Based in part on questionnaire data, study of the primary school as a social system and of the school director within that system.

4562 ———. Sociología de la educación. 3. ed. Caracas, Univ. Central de Venezuela, Ediciones de la Biblioteca, 1977. 266 p., tables (Col. Temas, 47)

Intended as a supplemental readings book, contains a number of essays on topics within sociology of education such as student opposition and university development.

4563 **Arnao de Uzcátegui, Dulce** and others. Diagnóstico de la actividad de investigación y desarrollo experimental que se realiza en el país. Prólogo de Marcel Roche. Caracas, Consejo Nacional de Investigaciones Científicas y Tecnológicas (CONICIT), Depto. de Sociología y Estadísticas, 1973. 259 p., tables.

Assessment of research potential and accomplishments, based in part on interview data. Analysis suggests need for continued growth of research efforts to promote national development.

4564 **Arnove, Robert F.** Students in politics (*in* Martz, John D. and David J. Myers *eds.* Venezuela: the democratic experience. N.Y., Praeger, 1977, p. 195–214)

Author examines the participation of students in Venezuelan political parties and the role of student organizations in promoting social change.

4565 **Baldirio, Ismenia R. de; Dríades Sanabria G.; and Jorge Nunes.** Dos análisis parciales de los resultados obtenidos en la aplicación del test de inteligencia de Kuhlmann–Anderson a una muestra de alumnos de educación primaria. Caracas, Ministerio de Educación, Dirección de Planeamiento, Depto. de Investigaciones Educacionales, Programa Nacional de Investigaciones Educacionales, 1974. 81 p., tables (Serie, 2. Análisis e interpretación de datos, 5)

Intelligence test data are analyzed, first, to examine distribution of scores, and second, to determine item difficulty. Interesting results.

4566 *Boletín de Legislación Educativa Venezolana.* Univ. del Zulia, Facultad de Humanidades y Educación, Centro de Documentación e Investigación Pedagógica (CEDIP). No. 1, 1976, [through] No. 2, 1977–. Maracaibo, Ven.

Listings of legislative actions taken on Venezuelan education between 1975 and 1977. Brief summary of each action not particularly helpful.

4567 **Caballero, Manuel.** Sobre autonomía, reforma y política en la Universidad Central de Venezuela: 1827–1958. Caracas, Univ. Central de Venezuela, Facultad de Humanidades y Educación, Escuela de Historia, 1974. 113 p. (Serie varia, 21)

Author argues that UCV has been constantly used by government and has had neither political nor economic autonomy.

4568 **Delgado Dugarte, Carlos.** Discurso impopular a la juventud. Caracas, Monte Avila Editores, 1974. 118 p. (Col. Temas venezolanos)

Author considers youthful resistance as normal, but argues that resistance which loses perspective and threatens the continuity of society represents a crisis.

4569 **Fundación para el Desarrollo de la Región Centro Occidental de Venezuela** (FUDECO), *Barquisimeto, Ven.* Investigación social y de educación no–formal: Proyecto Cumaripá, Estado Yaracuy. Barquisimeto, Ven., 1976. 1 v. (Various pagings) fold. table, illus., table (Serie de investigación social y educativa, 2)

Questionnaire study of six collective farms in Yaracuy in which participants are asked to identify the training necessary to improve farm efficiency.

4570 **Ganem Martínez, Jesús.** La universidad y el nuevo abogado por el desarrollo. Valencia, Ven., Univ. de Carabobo, Facultad de Derecho, 1977? 35 p.

A brief examination of current problems in legal eduation and some recommendations for solving these problems.

4571 **Godoy Castro, Roger.** Educación y recursos humanos en Venezuela: un aporte al estudio de los recursos humanos de nivel superior. Prólogo por J.F. Reyes Baena. Caracas, Univ. Central de Venezuela, Facultad de Ciencias Económicas y Sociales, 1976. 241 p., bibl., tables (Col. Libros)

Extensive examination of manpower

production in higher education, the likely needs for such manpower, and means to coordinate supply and demand.

4572 González Bogen, Américo. Salvar la universidad. Caracas, Editorial Arte, 1976. 93 p., facsims, illus.

An idealistic essay on what the Venezuelan university ought to be, coupled with a collection of letters and documents on problems confronting the medical school at UCV.

4573 Grooscors, Enrique, hijo. Pasión y acontecer de la instrucción en Carabobo. Valencia, Ven., Secretaría de Educación y Cultura, Ediciones del Ejecutivo del Estado Carabobo, 1975. 150 p.

Two–part study of education of Carabobo: history for the past two and a half centuries and biographies of outstanding educators. Necessarily brief treatment.

4574 Hanson, Mark. Decentralization and regionalization in the Ministry of Education: the case of Venezuela (UNESCO/IRE, 22:2, 1976, p. 155–176)

After four years of decentralization, author argues, changes are occurring despite resistance caused by real and feared redistribution of power.

4575 Leal, Ildefonso. 250 [i.e. Doscientos cincuenta] años de la fundación de la Real y Pontificia Universidad de Caracas: 1721–1971. Caracas, Universidad Central de Venezuela (UCV), Rectorado, 1971. 151 p., facsims., plates.

Chiefly facsimiles and plates.

4576 Lemmo, Angelina. La educación en Venezuela en 1870. 2. ed. Caracas, Univ. de Venezuela, Ediciones de la Facultad de Humanidades y Educación, 1976. 138 p., bibl., facsims., tables.

Second edition of study of public education, based largely on analysis of documents, many of which are reprinted with the study.

4577 Matute O., Oscar. Evaluación diagnóstico del sistema educación superior de la Región Centro Occidental de Venezuela: los egresados del sistema. Barquisimeto, Ven., Fundación para el desarrollo de la Región Centro Occidental de Venezuela (FUDECO), 1977. 105 p., tables (Serie de investigación social y educativa, 6)

Based on questionnaire–interview data from a sample of 168 graduates between

1969 and 1973, author examines relationship between job satisfaction and satisfaction with previous education. Well–done study.

4578 Mesa Redonda sobre Experiencias Venezolanas en Educación Pre–Escolar, *Caracas, 1974.* Mesa redonda sobre experiencias venezolanas en educación pre–escolar. Edición de Modesto Sánchez. Colaboradores: Lucy Ernst Contreras and others. Caracas, XIV Congreso Mundial de Educación Pre–Escolar, 1974. 1 v. (Various pagings) tables.

Pre–school education is examined in five separate papers, including one on the legal aspects of this level of education and one on the role of health education.

4579 Ocando Yamarte, Gilberto and **José Villalobos Paz.** La enseñanza de las relaciones públicas en Venezuela: análisis crítico. Maracaibo, Ven., Univ. del Zulia, 1975. 1 v. (Various pagings) fold. tables, tables.

Study of the teaching of public relations, based largely on examining documents in the field.

4580 Reunión de la Comisión de Cursos Postgrado, *IV, Caracas, 1974.* La educación de postgrado en Venezuela: situación actual. Caracas, Consejo Nacional de Investigaciones Científicas y Tecnológicas (CONICIT), Depto. de Educación, 1974. 230 p., bibl., tables.

Study of postgraduate education, in part based on interview data, which reveals lack of coordination and variable quality.

4581 Rivera, Beatriz. Estructura universitaria y educación. 2. ed. Caracas, Univ. Central de Venezuela, Ediciones de la Biblioteca, 1976. 103 p., bibl. (Col. Avance, 37)

Author argues that university reform must center on universities' central role in national development, both in teaching and in research.

4582 Rovar Díaz, Amneris. Educación y estructura social. 2. ed. Caracas, Univ. Central de Venezuela, Facultad de Ciencias Económicas, División de Publicaciones, 1977. 199 p., bibl., tables (Col. Libros)

Argues that educational planning is necessary to correct school's failure to prepare students adequately for current social and economic reality.

4583 Ruscoe, Gordon C. Educational policy in Venezuela (*in* Martz, John D. and

David J. Myers *eds.* Venezuela: the democratic experience. N.Y., Praeger, 1977, p. 255–282, tables)

Author examines the expansion of schooling in recent years and suggests that expansion has not answered the problems of quality, equality and underlying social reform.

4584 Saint Surin, Judit de. Situación de la educación pre–escolar en la Región Centro–Occidental de Venezuela. Barquisimeto, Ven., Fundación para el Desarrollo de la Región Centro Occidental de Venezuela (FUDECO), 1976. 37 p., bibl., tables (Serie de investigación social y educativa, 3)

Statistical presentation of preschool enrollments, teachers' qualifications and relationship between preschool and primary education.

4585 ———. Situación de la educación primaria en la Región Centro–Occidental de Venezuela. Barquisimeto, Ven., Fundación para el Desarrollo de la Región Centro Occidental de Venezuela (FUDECO), 1976. 163 p., bibl., tables (Serie de investigación social y educativa, 4)

Extensive data for the region (the states of Falcón, Lara, Portuguesa and Yaracuy), including enrollments, retention and petition, and pupil–teacher ratios.

4586 Seminario Nacional de Información Educativa y Ocupacional, *I, Caracas, 1974.* Primer seminario nacional de información educativa y ocupacional: mayo 22–23–24, 1974. Edición de Beatriz Rivera. Caracas, Univ. Central de Venezuela, Ediciones del Rectorado, 1974. 162 p.

Conference report, including papers on career educaton and recommendations for improving information in this area.

4587 Seminario sobre Curriculum, *Caracas, 1975.* Del diálogo a la acción: informe. v. 1/2. Prólogo de Marta Arango de Nimnicht. Caracas, Ministerio de Educación, 1975. 2 v. (330, 282 p.) bibl., tables.

Includes both general conference report and papers on topics such as curriculum evaluation and teacher training.

4588 Seminario sobre Investigación y Planificación de los Costos de la Educación, *II, Ciudad Guayana, Ven., 1973.* Los estudios de costos de la educación en Venezuela. Caracas, Ministerio de Educación,

Oficina Sectorial de Planificación y Presupuesto [and] Organización de los Estados Americanos (OEA), Programa Regional de Desarrollo Educativo, 1975. 607 p., bibls., tables.

Based on a reworking of documents from a 1973 seminar, present volume provides a comprehensive look at the costs of education and some of the results of educational expenditures.

4589 Silva, Carlos Rafael. Memoria y cuenta: 1976, que el Ministro de Educación presenta al Congreso Nacional de la República de Venezuela en sus sesiones de 1977. Caracas, Ministerio de Educación, 1977. 555 p., fold. tables, plates, tables.

Extensive presentation on the organization and development of Venezuelan education in 1976. Always a useful research tool.

4590 Universidad Central de Venezuela, *Caracas.* **Centro de Estudios del Desarrollo** (CENDES). Informe sobre las actividades del CENDES en 1975 y planes para 1976. Caracas, 1976. 115 p., tables (Serie 2)

Well–done report on CENDES activities, including detailed description of current center research in economic, social and education areas.

4591 ———. Dirección de Economía y Planeamiento. División de Planeamiento. Oficina de Planeamiento. La oferta de recursos humanos de nivel universitario en Venezuela: 1901–1970. Caracas, 1972. 51 p., tables.

Largely collection of statistics on graduates from professional degree programs of Venezuelan universities. Little explication of findings.

4592 Universidad Nacional Experimental Simón Rodríguez, *Caracas.* Filosofía y estructura de la Universidad Simón Rodríguez. Informe presentado al Consejo Nacional de Universidades, Barinas, mayo 1976. Caracas, 1976. 39 p., tables.

Brief profile of the University from its inception in 1974 to 1976.

4593 Urdaneta de Matute, Aminta. Una experiencia en capacitación campesina con elementos de educación no–formal: Empresa Campesina "La vigía," Distrito Jiménez, Estado Lara. Barquisimeto, Ven., Fundación para el Desarollo de la Región Centro Occidental de Venezuela (FUDECO), 1976. 76 p., illus., tables (Serie de investigación social y educativa, 5)

Rationale, organization and evaluation of non–formal training program for campesino leaders in agricultural businesses.

4594 Venezuela. Ministerio de Educación. Oficina Sectorial de Planificación y Presupuesto. Centro de Documentación. Lineamientos generales del V plan de la Nación: 1976–1980. Caracas, 1977. 11 l.

Extremely brief account of education's role in the 1976–80 national development plan.

4595 Oficina Central de Coordinación y Planificación. Dirección de Planificación Social y Cultural. Departamento de Recursos Humanos. Fundamentos teóricos y metodólogicos del proyecto de investigación y planificación de los recursos humanos en Venezuela. Caracas, 1974. 91 l.

Lays out both theoretical and methodological considerations necessary in planning human resource development, including problems of unplanned educational supply.

4596 ———. ———. ———. ———. Un modelo de simulación del sistema educativo venezolano: EDUC4L. Caracas, 1975. 90 l., tables.

Intriguing simulation model, with sample projections to 1985. What is now needed, of course, is some applications of the model.

WEST INDIES

4597 Bremner, Theodore A. Science education in the Caribbean: curricular and other concerns (*in* Singham, A.W. ed. The Commonwealth Caribbean into the seventies: proceedings of a conference held on 28–30 September, 1973, Howard University, Washington, D.C. Montreal, Canada, McGill Univ., Centre for Developing–Area Studies *in co–operation with* Howard Univ., Committee on Caribbean Studies, Washington, 1975, p. 170–178 [Occasional papers series, 10])

Author criticizes lack of science education and reports on plans of the Caribbean Institute of Science and Technology to help remedy this situation.

4598 *Journal of the Caribbean Society of Educational Administrators* (CARSEA). Univ. of the West Indies, School of Education. Vol. 1, No. 1, June 1976 [and] Vol. 1, No. 2, Nov. 1976–. Mona, Jam.

New journal devoted to research and opinion on effective administration for the development of education. Largely focuses on Jamaica.

4599 Preston, A.Z. Vice–Chancellor's report: 1976. Vice–Chancellor's report: 1977. Mona, Jam., Univ. of the West Indies, 1976/1977. 2 v. (56, 64 p.)

General review of university developments, including faculty activities, honors and grants.

BRAZIL

AGNES E. TOWARD, *Policy Analyst, Southwest Educational Development Laboratory, Austin, Texas*

4600 Alencar, Eunice; John F. Feldhusen; and Fred W. Widlack. Creativity training in elementary schools in Brazil (The Journal of Experimental Education [The Helen Dwight Reid Education Foundation, Washington] 44:4, Summer 1976, p. 23–27, bibl., tables)

Based on an experiment with 578 Brazilian fourth and fifth–graders in Brasília, the authors conclude that: "it seems likely that creativity training can be profitable for chil-

dren in underdeveloped countries" since gains in creative thinking ability were substantial despite conditions in the schools which might be expected to make children impervious to creativity training. Researchers used the Purdue Creative Thinking Program (PCTP) with and without reinforcement. Reinforcement appeared to have a decremental effect.

4601 Andrade, Antônio Ferreira de. Educação ou desatino? Belo Horizonte, Brazil, Serviço Nacional de Aprendizagem Industrial (SENAI), Depto. Regional de Minas Gerais, 1976. 85 p., bibl. (Assessoria de planejamento, 2)

An economist examining both economic and philosophical factors influencing formal and non–formal education, adopts an informal approach, stressing the need to accept and apply what is already known to present and future educational needs. Andrade, director of a research project on non–formal education programs in Latin America and the US finds that education continues to be largely intuitive. Despite sections on selection of investment strategies with graphs, and formulas, content is lightweight, questions are posed but not pursued. Uneven bibliography.

4602 Azevedo, José Carlos de. Omissão da universidade ou culpa da sociedade? (SBPC/CC, 29:4, abril 1977, p. 444–448)

In this reprint of a commentary first published in the newspaper *Folha de São Paulo*, the author, identified as Rector of the Univ. of Brasília, naval officer, and Ph.D. in physics from MIT analyzes educational and scientific policies since 1964. Azevedo questions the need for additional research centers outside of the universities, suggests that universities have been given additional tasks for which they are neither prepared nor properly compensated, and opposes the transformation of university extension activities into community action programs. After his nine-point critique the author moves on to discuss philosophical and administrative issues relevant to higher education.

4603 Barbosa, Ana Mae Tavares Bastos. Teoria e prática de educação artística. São Paulo, Editor Cultrix, 1976. 114 p., plates.

Barbosa earned a master's in art education in the US, now teaches in the School of Communications and Arts of the Univ. of São Paulo. She emphasizes art theory, rather than empirical experience, compares art education in the US and Brazil, and discusses art as process and as product, commenting on work by her students.

Barroso, Carmen Lúcia de Melo. A participação da mulher no desenvolvimento científico brasileiro. See item **9299.**

———. Porque tão poucas mulheres exercem atividades científicas? See item **9300.**

4604 Beltrami, Arnaldo. Comunicação constrói?: noções de comunicação social e educação. São Paulo, Shalom Livraria, 1976. 93 p., bibl., facsims., illus.

This is a short book to be used as a text on courses in communication. The author discusses: what is communication; modalities of communication; history of communication; relationships between social communication and education; and the practice of social communication. [J.F.B. Dasilva]

4605 *Boletim do CEPE.* Univ. para o Desenvolvimento do Estado de Santa Catarina (UDESC). Faculdade de Educação, Centro de Estudos e Pesquisas Educacionais. Ano 11, No. 49, março 1976–. Florianópolis, Brazil.

Modest publication from the educational research center with articles on pre–school education, attrition in primary schools, and educational freedom.

4606 Brasília (Distrito Federal), *Brazil.* **Secretaria de Educação e Cultura.** Plano de educação do Distrito Federal: 1976/79. Brasília, 1976. 67 p., tables.

Education plan in response to new legislation, covering primary, secondary, special, and supplementary education in the federal district. Projects identified include: qualitative improvement of instruction, pre–school education, maintenance, expansion and equipment of primary schools, special education, student aid, and library networks.

4607 Brazil. Ministério da Educação e Cultura. Departamento de Ensino Fundamental. Departamento de Documentação e Divulgação. Educação para o trabalho no ensino de 1°grau: convêncio PREMEN/DEF. Brasília, 1976. 54 p., bibl., tables (Série ensino fundamental, 16)

Format suggests a teacher's guide. Begins with historical summary of career education in Brazil education and includes chapters on objectives, methodology, evaluation, and resources.

4608 ———. **Ministério da Previdência e Assistência Social. Fundação Legião Brasileira de Assistência. Departamento de Serviço Social.** Unidades de reeducação alimentar do pré–escolar: estudo para sua implantação; treinamento de pessoal para as

URAPES. Rio, 1975. 31 p., tables (Documento de trabalho, 1)

Handbook for personnel working with nutrition programs for pre–school children. Includes guidelines for service units, sample forms for enrollments and record keeping, and charts with nutrition information.

4609 ——. **Serviço Nacional de Aprendizagem Industrial. Departamento Regional de Minas Gerais.** SENAI: o ensino de hoje para o futuro. Belo Horizonte, Brazil, 1976. 112 p., illus.

Account of the adaptation and approval (by the State Education Council of *Minas Gerais*) of SENAI courses of study as equivalent to the last four years of primary education (5, 6, 7, and 8 levels). Planning process for adapting SENAI programs to comply with Law 5.692 is summarized, followed by detailed descriptions (in terms of class hours) of various equivalency options. This change allows SENAI to accommodate students in three groups: a) 12–14 year–old students; b) 15–18 year–olds who did not complete primary studies; and c) over 18 year–old students.

Cadaval, Mauricio. Notas para um debate sobre mercado de trabalho e orientações no ensino da sociologia. See item **9307.**

4610 Carvalho, Vilma Cloris de. O ensino de neuranatomia no curso de medicina da Universidade Estadual de Campinas (SBPC/CC, 28:6, junho 1976, p. 641–644, bibl., tables)

The author describes how she prepared for, planned, and taught a Neuranatomy course for first–year medical students at the State Univ. of Campinas. She reports that her concern for combining good teaching methods with appropriate content appears justified by the results, since 96 percent of the students qualified for second year studies. She describes the course and the experience in some detail.

4611 Collet, Heloisa Gouvêa. Educação permanente: uma abordagem metodológica. Rio, Serviço Social do Comercio, Depto. Nacional, 1976. 111 p., bibl.

Extensive bibliography accompanies thorough overview of adult education or lifelong learning. Author interviewed specialists, staff members from SENAC, SENAI, appro-

priate department staff in the Ministry of Education and examined recent methodological developments in adult education in Europe. She identifies her point of departure as the UNESCO report *Aprender a ser* which represents a new educational strategy developed by the International Commission for the Development of Education. Among 18 conclusions she suggests that: mass media be used more, learners take charge of their own programs, groups be based on mutual interests, diplomas and degrees be less important than student motivation and self–assessments.

Ferreira, Gilda Pires. A biblioteca universitária em perspectiva sistêmatica. See *HLAS 40:46.*

4612 Freire, Paulo. Ação cultural para a liberdade e outras escritos. Rio, Paz e Terra, 1976. 149 p. (Col. O mundo hoje, 10)

Book of essays by the well–known pedagogue. Includes discussion of adult literarcy; peasants and their school–texts; education and agrarian reform; the role of social workers in social change; the meaning of cultural action and freedom; the process of political education; the meaning of humanism and its pedagogic implications; the educational role of the Church in Latin America; consciousness–raising; etc. [J.F.B. Dasilva]

4613 Garcia, Pedro Benjamin de Carvalho e Silva. Educação: modernização ou dependência? Rio, Francisco Alves, 1977. 136 p., bibl. (Série educação em questão)

Basic objective of the thesis of this revised manuscript was to devise a theoretical framework that might permit a better understanding (sociologically) of the transposition of educational values from one nation to another. In doing so, Garcia elected to work with the theories of modernization and dependency. He suggests that this effort may a) place education within the context of those two theories, b) establish a theoretical framework for a better understanding of transposition of educational values; c) attempt to understand the assimilation of such new measures within the larger social context; and d) suggest how to proceed from a theoretical framework to analysis of text. Theory of modernization and education is covered in first section, then dependency followed by Garcia's analysis of the *Plano Setorial de Edu-*

ção e Cultura (1975–79), in which he finds an inner tension he attributes to the adaptation and adjustment of a liberal and humanistic point of view to an authoritarian regime. Extensive notes follow each section.

4614 Geribello, Wanda Pompeu. Anísio Teixeira: análise e sistematização de sua obra. São Paulo, Editora Atlas, 1977. 211 p., bibl.

Geribello chooses to emphasize the personal, internal struggle between Teixeira's early religious training and convictions and the intellectual public–education administrator he became, stressing his role as that of selfless, dedicated public servant engaged in the struggle to provide education for all Brazilians and to develop the capacity for research and innovation. Her premises, as she defines them are: 1) Teixeira developed his philosophy through his research in eduational administration; 2) his adherence to Dewey's experimentalism was a way of compensating for Thomism's insufficiency in response to the realities of educational problems; 3) the greatest influence on his reformist, innovative policies was that of North American educators and philosophers (e.g. Dewey and Kilpatrick); and 4) theoretically, his work and thought were based on two propositions; redefinition of education within a school–society context and experimental epistomology as the source for developments in educational philosophy. That Anísio was dedicated brilliant educator and administrator becomes self–evident as his career is reviewed; that he participated in, provoked, and to some extent personified some of the major controversies in Brazilian education for over 40 years is much less apparent in Geribello's reverent recapitulation. Helpful, however, are her bibliography of Teixeira's writings (chronologically arranged, 1924–71), items (books, speeches, articles) about Teixeira, and supplementary items included "for a better understanding of the historical and educational context in which Teixeira lived and worked."

4615 Greer, Leslie. Teacher–training projects (English Language Teaching [London] 31:2, Jan. 1977. p. 89–96, illus.)

Examples (including graphics) of trainees' projects for the teaching of English at the Brazilian Society for English Culture are the basis of discussion in this article. The author writes from the point of view of a teacher–trainer, commenting on the introductory training course at the Society and emphasizing the variety and value of the individual projects developed by trainees.

Instituto de Acción Cultural, *Geneva.* Concientización y liberación. See item **9333.**

4616 Keller, Fred S. Recentes desenvolvimentos no ensino de ciência (SBPC/CC, 25:1, jan. 1973, p. 3–10, illus., tables)

A misleading title for this subjective presentation of one man's version of "individualized instruction" at the university level. Keller covers the usual ground of complaints about the level, quality, and efficiency of education, then reviews the history of tutors, monitors, and teaching–assistants while leading up to his Brasília Plan, an instructional method that relies on programmed learning, monitors, and mastery of units based on skill levels. Similar methods have been proposed and tested, before and since, however, the author suggests that this particular method will eliminate registration or enrollment problems, alter educational architecture and textbooks, and make learning more efficient.

Lobo, Roberto Jorge Haddock. Geografia do Brasil. See item **5659.**

Loureiro, Maria Amélia Salgado *comp.* História das universidades. See *HLAS* 40:3993.

4617 Martins, Waldemar Valle. Liberdade de ensino: reflexões a partir de uma situação no Brasil. São Paulo, Edições Loyola, 1976. 205 p.

Observations first written 13 years earlier, revised in 1975 by which time Martins could comment on several years' experience with the Law of Directives and Bases, passed in 1961. Of three sections (the debate over the Law, discussion of principles, and analysis of the role of the Catholic Church), the first provides a useful review of the struggle between public and private school interests while the others present lengthy arguments for public support of private schools. Includes extensive notes throughout and charts compare a) the bill and the education law and b) the education articles in the Constitutions of 1946 and 1967 and the Constitutional Amendment of 1969.

Medina, C.A. de and **M.L. Rodrigues de Almeida.** Hábitos de leitura: uma abordagem sociológica. See item **9348.**

—— and others. Condições socioculturais do relacionamento familiar na transformação da sociedade brasileira. See item **9349.**

—— and others. Estudo das condições de programas de aperfeiçoamento cultural num contexto de comunicação intergeracional. See item **9350.**

Mello, Syliva Leser de. Psicologia e profissão em São Paulo. See item **9352.**

4618 Minas Gerais (state), *Brazil.* **Secretaria de Estado da Educação.** Plano mineiro de educação: carta compromisso. Belo Horizonte, Brazil, 1976. 30 p.

Compact summary of educational goals and priorities for *Minas Gerais,* issued by the State's Secretary of Education. Emphasis on the productivity of the system, to be attained through "renewed, multifunctional" primary schools; ecological awareness; rural development; community–centered library networks; professionalization of secondary level instruction; control of higher education (to improve quality of institutions, coordination, and response to regional and state needs); increased attention to special education and early childhood education; and some reorganization of the state's education system.

Miranda, Glaura Vasques de. Participación de la mujer en la fuerza de trabajo de una sociedad en vía de desarrollo: el caso del Brasil. See item **9357.**

4619 Moreira, Manoel da Frota and **B.K. Wesley Copeland.** International cooperation in science: Brazil–U.S. chemistry program (AI/I, 1:3, sept./oct. 1976. p. 138–146, tables)

Report on six–year program to strengthen postgraduate research and teaching in chemistry. New programs established and research papers published are offered as evidence of success. [G.C. Ruscoe]

Mota, Mauro. Cara e c'roa: uma fase do Instituto Joaquim Nabuco de Pesquisas Sociais. See item **9361.**

4620 Movimento Brasileiro de Alfabetização (MOBRAL), *Rio.* Solete MOBRAL e leia Brasil: cinco anos de luta pela alfabetização. Rio, 1976? 64 p., plates.

This version of the Brazilian campaign to eradicate illiteracy, MOBRAL, includes some interesting statistics on primary, secondary, and higher education, describes the history and activities of MOBRAL and predicts an illiteracy rate of 10 percent (of population 15 or older) by 1980. Public relations effort with color illustrations and tables, contrasts and compares illiteracy statistics for north/south, urban/rural, male/female, by region. Of 100 enrolled in five–month course, 80 complete it, 40 become literate, at a cost of 110 cruzeiros per successful graduate. Criticism of program are acknowledged and rejected.

Oliveira, Nei Roberto da Silva. A juventude como status permanente. See item **9363.**

4621 Paupério, Artur Machado. Introdução ao estudo de problemas brasileiros: educação para a cidadania. São Paulo, Livraria Freitas Bastos, 1977. 150 p.

Consists of textbook, approved by National Commission on Morals and Civics (of which author is a member) for use at higher education level, in courses with the same title, "Study of Brazilian Problems." Author identified as nationally recognized writer, trained in law and political science, recently published a series on democratic theory, has written books and articles about law, government, and public issues since 1946. His three basic "suggestions for a program of study on Brazilian problems" are 1) philosophical bases of the Brazilian constitution; 2) the democratic principle and its philosophical–political assumptions", and 3) democracy, underdevelopment, and security.

4622 Pernambuco (state), *Brazil.* **Secretaria da Educação e Cultura.** Educação e cultura em Pernambuco. Recife, Brazil, 1975. 133 p., plates, tables.

Deluxe report on education in Pernambuco, illustrated with color photographs. Information on budget, grants, projects, cultural activities, teacher preparation, and future plans.

4623 Pinheiro Neto, Liberato Manoel. Prefeitura, comunidade e educação. Florianópolis, Brazil, Editora Lunardelli, 1976. 30 p.

Transfer of responsibility for primary

education from the state to the municipality is the subject of this work. Pinheiro, an administrator with the State Secretariat of Education in Santa Catarina, has devoted several years to the study of legislation and problems of state–municipal integration. He warns against a paternalistic approach to integration, stresses the geographical and cultural diversity of school clientele and analyzes the respective roles of the administrative hierarchy. Chapters on Means and Ends of Municipal Administration, Transfer of Services, Rural Education, Educational Planning, Resources.

4624 *Revista da Faculdade de Educação.* Univ. de São Paulo, Faculdade de Educação. Vol. 2, No. 2, dez. 1976–. São Paulo.

Another of the new journals from a university education dept. divided into sections devoted to articles, conferences and reports and documentation. Fermat, Piaget, and Dewey are the subjects of articles; of special interest is a report on the university's "advanced campus" in Marabá, Pará.

4625 **Rio Grande do Sul** (state), *Brazil.* **Secretaria da Educação e Cultura.** Configuração do desempenho dos profissionais em educação no Rio Grande do Sul, 1973: relatório de pesquisa. Porto Alegre, Brazil, Superintendência do Desenvolvimento da Região Sul (SUDESUL), 1974. 1 v. (Various pagings) tables.

Collaborative research report prepared by teams from the Secretariat of Education in Rio Grande do Sul and the Regional Development Superintendency, under a grant from the Ministry of the Interior. For evaluation and planning purposes, data was collected and analyzed over a six–year period to determine the effectiveness of professional activities and application of human resources.

4626 **Rocha e Silva, Mauricio.** Birth and development of experimental science in Brazil (AI/I, 1:4, nov./dic. 1976, p. 215–219)

Traces the development of empirical sciences and argues that Brazilian science is now ready to expand rapidly. [G.C. Ruscoe]

Rodrigues, José Honório. Os estudos brasileiros e os "Brasilianists." See *HLAS 40:4013.*

Saffioti, Heleieth I.B. Professionalização de sociólogos. See item **9393**.

4627 **Santos, Ely Souto dos.** Os proletários da cultura: uma análise socio–econômica entre o ser e o dever ser do professor. Porto Alegre, Gráfica Dom Bosco, 1975. 209 p., bibl., tables.

Santos takes her title from teachers' commentaries in which they refer to themselves as the "proletariat of culture." While idealizing the teacher "as he ought to be" (the entire first chapter is devoted to quotes from Hilton's *Goodbye Mr. Chips*), she nevertheless moves on to discuss teacher salaries (with ample quotes and figures from a variety of sources), deplores the impact of the technocrat who has turned the school into a factory, points out the lack of time and facilities, describes the pattern of teaching several schedules in different schools . . . in short embarks on the first–person critique of the teacher's situation in today's schools (much of it relevant to Brazilian secondary schools in Rio Grande do Sul). Among her conclusions: "Our instruction is deficient because it is democratic; in Brazil the major supporter of education is the teacher himself [due to low salaries]; extending semesters and exams without benefit to the instructional program interferes with other sectors of national life, such as recreation; salaries should not discriminate against the private school teacher." Of possible interest in her chapter called "Profile of the Teacher"—responses to questions about standard of living, family background, training, ethnicity, schedules, and attitudes, derived from her interviews with secondary teachers in Rio Grande do Sul.

4628 **São Paulo** (state), *Brazil.* **Centro de Recursos Humanos e Pesquisas Educacionais** (CERHUPE). Escolas de primeiro grau: levantamento do pessoal técnico–administrativo e docente da rede oficial do Estado de São Paulo. São Paulo, 1976. 220 p., maps, tables.

Analysis of data collected in state survey of educational resources for primary education. Includes technical, administrative, and instructional personnel; data organized by regions.

4629 ———. **Secretaria de Economia e Planejamento.** Sistema estadual de análise de dados estatísticos: aspectos do sistema de ensino de Estado de São Paulo. São Paulo, 1976. 55 p., bibl., tables (Série estudos e pesquisas, 2)

Analysis, based on data from 1963 to 1973, of indicators (access, survival, and system selectivity) to examine how state policies (assuring access to primary schools, guaranteeing all children a minimum of eight years of schooling and providing equal opportunities for higher education) have influenced the system. Methodology is described, sources are identified, and tables are provided. Major conclusion attributes a quantitative or qualitative transformation in large part to state policies.

Silva, Maria Beatriz Nizza da. Educação feminina e educação masculina no Brasil colonial. See *HLAS 40:4051.*

4630 Souza, Altamir. Apontamentos para a historia do Instituto de Educação do Para. Belém, The Author, 1972. 160 p., plates, tables.

A detailed history of the Education Institute's 100 years of teacher–training in Para. Photographs, statistics, correspondence, and reminiscences.

4631 Stein, Suzana Albornoz. Por uma educação libertadora. Petrópolis, Brazil, Editora Vozes, 1976. 108 p., bibl.

Presentation of attacks and defenses of schools as social institutions, analysis of inherent contradictions in education, and review of attempts to modify traditional schools (examples from Illich, Reimer, Goodman, Dennison, Hentig, and Neill). Frequent quotes from Lauro de Oliveira Lima and examples from Freire, but Albornoz adopts a populist position, notes that discussing liberation of learning is not "an ingenuous struggle against the school" but a defense of access to other ways of learning and a critique of the school as a bureaucratic monopoly.

4632 Távora, Virgílio. O Acordo Nuclear Brasil–Alemanha e a universidade. Fortaleza, Brazil, Univ. Federal do Ceará, 1977. 32 p., fold. tables.

Brief explanation and description of the agreement between Brazil and Germany and subsequent plans for development of nuclear energy in Brazil. Includes discussion of estimated time frame and projected personnel needs and how these will be met. Tables, diagrams, and text of the agreement are appendices.

4633 Universidade Federal da Paraíba, *Brazil.* **Sub–Reitoria para Assuntos Di-**

dáticos. A reforma universitária na UFPB: experiência de uma equipe. João Pessoa, Brazil, 1971. 51 p., tables.

Succinct report on re–organization of the university after the reform of the Univ. of Brasília established norms and administrative guidelines for federal institutions of higher education. Steps taken to revise procedures, strengthen structure, identify and define courses of study, and explain process are presented in sequence, accompanied by illustrations (charts, tables), providing the reader with a clear, concise description of the reform.

Weber, Silke. Formação escolar e funções profissionais do sociólogo. See item **9410.**

JOURNAL ABBREVIATIONS
EDUCATION

AI/I Interciencia. Asociación Interciencia. Caracas.

BAS/SPA Bulletin of the Atomic Scientists. Science and Public Affairs. Educational Foundation for Nuclear Science *with the cooperation of the* Adlai Stevenson Institute of International Affairs. Chicago, Ill.

BU/JCS A Journal of Church and State. Baylor Univ., S.W. Dawson Studies in Church and State. Waco, Tex.

CAM Cuadernos Americanos, México.

CEPAC/REP Revista de Estudios del Pacífico. Consejo Coordinador Universitario de Valparaíso, Centro de Estudios del Pacífico. Valparaíso, Chile.

CEPAL/R CEPAL Review/Revista de la CEPAL. Nacional Unidas, Comisión Económica para América Latina. Santiago.

CES/CER Comparative Education Review. Comparative Education Society. N.Y.

CP Cuadernos Políticos. Revista trimestral. Ediciones Era. México.

CPU/ES Estudios Sociales. Corporación de Promoción Universitaria. Santiago.

CYC Comunicación y Cultura. La comunicación masiva en el proceso político latinoamericano. Editorial Galerna. B.A. [and] Santiago.

HU Hojas Universitarias. Revista de la Fundación Univ. Central. Bogotá.

IAA Ibero-Amerikanisches Archiv. Ibero-Amerikanisches Institut. Berlin, FRG.

IASI/E Estadística. Journal of the Inter American Statistical Institute. Washington.

IFH/C Conjonction. Institut Français d'Haïti. Port-au-Prince.

JPHC/R Revista de la Junta Provincial de Historia de Córdoba. Archivo Histórico Monseñor P. Cabrera. Córdoba, Arg.

LNB/L Lotería. Lotería Nacional de Beneficencia. Panamá.

NHAC/K Kaie. National History and Arts Council of Guyana. Georgetown.

NS NS NorthSouth NordSud NorteSul. Canadian journal of Latin American Studies. Canadian Association of Latin American Studies. Univ. of Ottawa. Ottawa.

OCLAE OCLAE. Revista mensual de la Organización Continental Latinoamericana de Estudiantes. La Habana.

PCCLAS/P Proceedings of the Pacific Coast Council on Latin American Studies. Univ. of California. Los Angeles.

RLP Revista Latinoamericana de Psicología. Bogotá.

RRI Revista/Review Interamericana. Univ. Interamericana. San Germán, P.R.

SBPC/CC Ciência e Cultura. Sociedade Brasileira para o Progresso da Ciência. São Paulo.

SIP/RIP Revista Interamericana de Psicología (Interamerican Journal of Psychology). Sociedad Interamericana de Psicología (Interamerican Society of Psychology). De Paul Univ., Dept. of Psychology. Chicago, Ill.

SMHN/R Revista de la Sociedad Mexicana de Historia Natural. México.

UAG/D Docencia. Univ. Autónoma de Guadalajara. Guadalajara, Mex.

UC/A Anales de la Universidad de Cuenca. Cuenca, Ecua.

UCC/CE Cuadernos de Economía. Univ. Católica de Chile. Santiago.

UH/U Universidad de La Habana. La Habana.

UIA/C Comunidad. Revista de la U.I.A. Cuadernos de difusión cultural. Univ. Iberoamericana. México.

UM/JIAS Journal of Inter-American Studies and World Affairs. Univ. of Miami Press *for the* Center of Advanced International Studies. Coral Gables, Fla.

UNAM/RMS Revista Mexicana de Sociología. Univ. Nacional Autónoma de México, Instituto de Investigaciones Sociales. México.

UNAMCG/A Anuario de Geografía. Univ. Nacional Autónoma de México, Facultad de Filosofía y Letras. México.

UNESCO/IRE International Review of Education. United Nations Educational, Scientific and Cultural Organization, Institute for Education. Hamburg, FRG.

UNL/U Universidad. Univ. Nacional del Litoral. Sante Fe, Arg.

UNLP/CA Ciencias Administrativas. Univ. Nacional de La Plata, Facultad de Ciencias Económicas, Instituto de Investigaciones de Ciencias Administrativas. La Plata, Arg.

UP/CSEC Cuban Studies/Estudios Cubanos. Univ. of Pittsburgh, Univ. Center for International Studies, Center for Latin American Studies. Pittsburgh, Pa.

UPR/CS Caribbean Studies. Univ. of Puerto Rico, Instituto of Caribbean Studies. Río Piedras.

USMLA/LA La Antigua. Univ. de Santa María La Antigua, Oficina de Humanidades. Panamá.

UY/R Revista de la Universidad de Yucatán. Mérida, Mex.

UZ/R Revista de la Universidad del Zulia. Maracaibo, Ven.

WSU/HB Human Biology. Official publication of the Human Biology Council. Wayne State Univ., School of Medicine. Detroit, Mich.

GEOGRAPHY

GENERAL

CLINTON R. EDWARDS, *Professor of Geography, University of Wisconsin-Milwaukee*

THE CONCERN OF GEOGRAPHIC AND other scholars over environmental effects of man's actions and problems of effective and sustained use of environ-ments and natural resources continues to loom large in the Latin American context. Papers on individual cases are accompanied by efforts to assess the general situa-tion. The latter generally argue, some urgently, for the need to integrate environ-mental concerns and assessments with policies on economic development, popu-lation, and internal migration. Increasingly, much of the literature reflects the persuasion that Geography and related disciplines have much to offer in the analysis of environmental problems, especially those amenable to regional analysis. The older economic interest in "landscape change" is taking on a new light, but the insistence on attention to details of process will, we hope, not lessen because of the practical urgency with which some phenomena are being studied. Budowski (item **5253**), Dickinson (item **5260**), García (item **5265**) and Mabogunje (item **5270**) offer specific commentary on the relationships between "academic" and "ap-plied" geography.

Since Latin American capitals and other primate cities are among the fastest growing in the world, it is no surprise to find urban geography continuing as a strong field of research. A good barometer for this is the series of symposia on Latin American urbanization which have become a permanent fixture and are growing in breadth and depth of treatment of diverse urban topics. These range from con-tinuing interest in the large precolumbian population centers to modern problems of overpopulation and social disruption in cities. Cowell reports on the proceed-ings of the V Symposium (item **5257**).

Some years ago the comment was made in this section that general studies of widespread phenomena were becoming scarcer, in favor of more detailed studies on the scale of individual countries or smaller regions. It is fortunate, however, that in two aspects of physical geography, coastal landforms (item **5261**) and grasslands (item **5267**), this trend has been reversed. General articles about physical re-sources, such as marine fauna (item **5283**) and brackish water (item **5276**) also contribute to more global views of the relationship between man and environment.

Conservation is represented implicitly in many contributions, but is explicit in a relatively new context, that of the humid tropics, as exemplified by the proceed-ings of a symposium on Central America (item **5277**).

Three useful bibliographies have appeared recently, one on environmental studies (item **5266**), and two that will facilitate the use of data in historical studies (items **5282** and **5286**).

Diverse approaches to the historical geography of the New World continue in interesting contributions, including some persistent controversies such as that over

Juan de la Cosa's map (item **5259**), the name "America" (item **3268**), and the precolumbian transatlantic diffusion of cultures and culture traits (items **5256** and **5262**).

5251 Aldunate Phillips, Arturo. El amenazante: año 2000. Santiago, Joaquín Almendros Editor, 1975. 223 p., illus., map, plates, tables.

Concerned look into the future, emphasizing adverse effects of industrialization and wasteful use of resources, ecological disequilibrium, political factors, and other ills of our time that if not corrected will lead to a bleak future for man.

5252 Bähr, Jürgen. Neuere entwicklungstendenzen lateinamerikanischer grosstädte (GR, 28:4, 1976, p. 125–133, bibl., maps)

Includes interesting commentary on an "ideal plan" of a Latin American primate city.

5253 Budowski, Gerardo. La conservación del medio ambiente: ¿conflicto o instrumento para el desarrollo? (OAS/CI, 17:1, enero/marzo 1976, p. 2–8, plates)

Effective general statement of need for conservation, indicating true "development" must include conservative use of resources.

5254 Cardona G., Ramiro ed. América Latina: distribución espacial de la población. Bogotá, Corporación Centro Regional de Población, 1975. 544 p., tables.

Readings on urbanization and political factors as they relate to the distribution of population and to problems of overpopulation. Analysis of individual countries includes Venezuela, Peru, Mexico and Brazil.

5255 Cole, John P. Una introducción al estudio de métodos cuantitativos aplicables en geografía. México, UNAM, Instituto de Geografía, 1975. 93 p., bibl., maps, tables.

Introductory level text including elements of statistics, analytical techniques, and systems analysis.

5256 Comas, Juan. Simposio internacional sobre posibles relaciones transatlánticas precolombinas (UASD/R, 2:4, julio/dic. 1972, p. 41–45, bibl.)

Lists papers presented, with com-

mentary emphasizing "diffusion vs. independent invention" controversy. Also appears in *Anuario de Estudios Atlánticos* (Madrid/Las Palmas, 17, 1971).

5257 Cowell, Bainbridge, Jr. The Fifth Symposium on Urbanization in America: a report on the proceedings (LARR, 11:1, 1976, p. 187–194)

Good, brief reviews of papers on broad range of urban topics, from precolumbian settlements to modern urban social and economic problems.

5258 Crosson, Pierre R.; Ronald G. Cummings; and Kenneth D. Frederick eds. Selected water management issues in Latin American agriculture. Baltimore, Md., The Johns Hopkins Univ. Press for Resources for the Future, Washington, 1978. 190 p., bibl., tables.

General commentary on water management problems, need for improved water management, and policy matters is followed by case studies in Peru, Argentina, northwest Mexico, and Colombia.

5259 Davies, Arthur. The date of Juan de la Cosa's world map and its implications for American discovery (RGS/GJ, 142:1, March 1976, p. 111–116, bibl., map)

Actually an assemblage of maps, and not drawn by Juan de la Cosa, but created no later than 1501. Amerigo Vespucci may have aided in its construction, and may have taken it to Portugal, from which it was retrieved by la Cosa, its owner.

5260 Dickinson, Joshua C., III. An applied geographer in Latin America (AGS/GR, 67:2, April 1977, p. 232–234)

Personal commentary on geographer's role in development, with emphasis on environmental impact assessment in Latin America.

5261 Dolan, R.; B. Hayden; and M. Vincent. Classification of coastal landforms of the Americas (ZG, 22 [supplement band] 1975, p. 72–88, bibl., maps, tables)

"A new descriptive classification . . . based on lithology, topography, and shoreline type . . ." Applicable scale is 1:20,000,000. Relates various shoreline types to wave energy. Includes review of the literature and approaches to classification of shorelines.

5262 Dupuis, Jacques. Um problema de geografia medieval: difusão do milho e a travessia do Atlântico na época pré-colombiana (FFCLM/EH, 15, 1976, p. 63–73, bibl.)

Reviews the question of existence of maize in Europe, Asia and Africa in precolumbian times, without reaching conclusions.

5263 Edmonston, Barry. Latin American population: a changing phenomenon (Latin American Digest [Arizona State Univ., Tempe] 10:2, Winter 1976, p. 1–3, 8, tables)

Describes present population policies, with attempt to project future development.

5264 Gangas Geisse, Mónica. Dimensión geográfica de la urbanización en América Latina y Anglosajona. Santiago, Univ. Católica de Chile, Instituto de Geografía, 1976. 64 l., bibl., map, tables.

Compares urbanization and industrialization in Latin America and "Anglo-Saxon" America, with analysis of processes in Latin America.

5265 García G., Rigoberto. Otra geografía latinoamericana: algunas reflexiones críticas en torno a la metodología (LI/IA, 4:2, 1974, p. 30–42)

Argues that in Latin America, geographical works emphasize particular phenomena, providing scant possibilities of using them in general development strategies.

5266 Hernández de Caldas, Angela and **Fabiola Bohórquez de Briceño.** Bibliografía sobre medio ambiente. Bogotá, La Cámara de Comercio, 1977? 44 p.

Includes 292 references found in the "bibliotecas económicas" of Colombia; author and subject-geographical indexes.

5267 Kesel, Richard H. *ed.* Grasslands ecology: a symposium. Baton Rouge, Louisiana State Univ., School of Geoscience, 1975. 79 p., bibls., maps (Geoscience and man, 10)

Includes papers with Latin American content, e.g.: Lee M. Talbot and Richard H.

Kesel "The Tropical Savanna Ecosystem" and W. G. Smith and Judith A. Monte "The Wet Grasslands." Both are useful summaries of extent and character of grassy vegetation associations. Papers were delivered at symposium organized by Louisiana State Univ., Dept. of Geography and Anthropology, April 1972.

5268 Klemp, Egon. The naming of America (EJ, 55:2, June 1977, p. 68–69, maps)

Brief review of the roles of Vespucci, Waldseemuller, and Mercator in the attachment of "America" to the New World. Adapted from Klemp's *America in Maps* (N.Y., Holmes & Meier, 1976).

5269 Kohlhepp, Gerd. Der Beitrag Gottfried Pfeifers zur kulturgeographischen Latcinamerika-Forschung (GZ, 64:1, 1976, p. 1–12, bibl.)

Concise and informative commentary, with complete bibliography, on Pfcifer's work on Latin America, 1939–73. Brazil predominates, but there are contributions also from Mexico and Latin America in general, as well as Humboldt studies.

5270 Mabogunje, Akin L. Geography and the problems of the Third World (UN/ISSJ, 27:2, 1975, p. 288–302)

Commentary on the role and utility of geographical studies of the "Third World." As an academic subject, geography has "a duty to provide means of conceptualizing and analyzing problems such that options for a resolution can become clear to decision-makers." There is a need for re-formulating environmental problems, and for new analytical tools for the study of development.

5271 Méndez-Arrocha, Alberto. La integración energética de América Latina: trabajo complementario, tema VI; XIV Convención de UPADI (Unión Panamericana de Asociaciones de Ingenieros), Rio de Janeiro, octubre de 1976. With the collaboration of Carmen de Calderaro and others. Caracas, Colegio de Ingenieros de Venezuela, 1976. 290 p., bibl., maps, tables.

Reviews and analyzes economic condition and actual and potential energy situation, with objective of providing information for planning integration of energy sources and distribution at national and international levels.

5272 Ortiz Mena, Antonio. Development in Latin America: a view from the IDB. Washington, Inter-American Development Bank (IDB), 1975. 515 p.

Addresses and documents of IDB President, 1971–75. His "main theme has been the need to strengthen external financial and technical cooperation with the Latin American countries . . ."

5273 Peterson, Mendel. Reach for the New World. Photographs by David L. Arnold. Paintings by Richard Schlecht (NGS/NGM, 152:6, Dec. 1977, p. 724–767, plates)

Brief review of competition between Spain and other western European countries for trade and plunder in the colonial New World, as seen from evidence of underwater archaeology.

5274 Petrides, George A. The importation of wild ungulates into Latin America, with remarks on their environmental effects (Environmental Conservation [Elsevier Sequoia, Lausanne, Switzerland *with the collaboration of the* International Union for Conservation of Nature and Natural Resources and others *for the* Foundation of Environmental Conservation, Geneva] 2:1, Spring 1975, p. 47–52, bibl., table)

"Preliminary effort" to comment on both the dangers and benefits of the importation of exotic species. Guidelines for importation are needed, since full effects of successful escapes from captivity on the environment cannot be predicted.

5275 Population, environment and development: the Latin American experience (UNECLA/B, 19:1/2, 1975, p. 10–28)

Concludes that "environmental questions and economic growth ought not to be treated as mutually exclusive alternatives."

5276 Probstein, Ronald F. and **J. Manuel Alvarez R.** The role of desalting and brackish water resources in the arid regions of the Americas (AI/I, 1:1, May/June 1976, p. 17–25, bibl., illus., maps)

Recommends desalting of brackish rather than sea water, suggesting priorities and outlining various desalting techniques applicable to brackish water purification. Summaries in Spanish and Portuguese.

5277 *Revista de Biología Tropical.* Univ. de Costa Rica [and] Consejo Nacional de Investigaciones Científicas y Tecnológicas (CONICIT). Vol. 24, suplemento 1, junio/dic. 1976– . San José.

Symposium on ecology and conservation in the Central American isthmus arranged in 1975 by Charles F. Bennett and sponsored by the Organization of Tropical Studies and the Consejo Nacional de Investigaciones Científicas y Tecnológicas de Costa Rica, was attended by about 200 scientists and government officials from the US and Central American countries. Objective was to make government officials and policy makers more aware of the need for attention to environmental problems. Individual papers of particular interest to geographers are reviewed elsewhere in this section (see items **5279, 5299, 5303, 5306–5307** and **5312**).

5278 Richardson, Harry W. and **Margaret Richardson.** The relevance of growth center strategies to Latin America (CU/EG, 51:2, April 1975, p. 163–178, bibl.)

Experience with growth pole analysis is not yet sufficient for evaluation of its utility. However, it could be very useful if modified suitably for the Latin American context.

5279 Romero García, Alejandro. Plaguicidas en los agroecosistemas tropicales: evaluación del conocimiento actual del problema (UCR/RBT, 24 [suplemento 1] junio/dic. 1976, p. 69–78)

Describes role of pesticides in tropical agriculture, with commentary on the many problems caused by their use. Recommends continuing search for non-chemical means of pest control.

Rouse, John E. The criollo: Spanish cattle in the Americas. See *HLAS* 40:2226.

5280 Sánchez Albornoz, Nicolás. The population of Latin America: a history. Translated by W.A.R. Richardson. Berkeley, Univ. of California Press, 1974. 299 p., bibl., maps, tables.

Work in historical demography traces Latin America's population changes from precolumbian times to contemporary urbanization, concluding that by year 2000 there will be more Latin Americans than Europeans or Anglo-Americans, and that most of them will live in cities. For historians comment see *HLAS* 40:2114. [T. L. Martinson]

5281 Slater, Paul B. Nodal migration regions: pt. 1, Brazil; pt. 2, Mexico; pt. 3, Argentina (IASI/E, 31:117, agosto 1977, p. 180–188, tables)

The nodal regions are based on non-trivial dichotomies found using network flow algorithm. Groups of states form nodal in- and out-migration regions, with a nodal state in each. In-migration to regions, in-migration to nodes, and the ratios of these are shown in tables.

5282 Steele, Colin. English interpreters of the Iberian New World from Purchas to Stevens: a bibliographical study, 1603–1726. Oxford, UK, Dolphin Book, 1975. 206 p., bibl.

Useful for historical geographers. Detailed commentary on authors and translators, with bibliography of English translations of Spanish and Portuguese books on "Iberian New World" from 1603–1726. Includes index.

5283 Steinberg, Maynard A. Los recursos de la fauna marina en Latino América: sus posibles usos en la alimentación humana [Os recursos da fauna marinha na America Latina: seus posíveis usos a alimentação humana; Living marine resources in Latin America: thcir usc and potential for food] (AI/I, 2:6, nov./dic. 1977, p. 350–359, bibl., tables)

Points up the paradox of protein-calorie malnutrition in Latin American countries with abundant fish and other marine resources. Discusses means of inducing greater utilization through development of new fishery products and different processing of existing ones.

5284 Street, James H. Latin American energy resources and internal development (AI/I, 3:2, marzo/abril 1978, p. 87–92)

Describes effects of increase in energy costs in Latin America. Surveys various energy sources, suggesting that the most underutilized source is water power, and indicating the future importance of nuclear energy. Calls for increased research on a regional scale to find alternatives to continued use of petroleum fuels.

5285 Turner, Frederick C. The rush to the cities in Latin America (AAAS/S, 192:4243, 4 June 1976, p. 955–962, tables)

Subtitle is "Government Actions havc More Effect than is Generally Recognized." Suggests that most effective way to deal with overpopulation of primate cities may be to redirect internal migration to smaller cities, with inducements of employment and attractive living environments. The alternative may be increasing government control of internal movement and place of residence.

5286 Wilgus, Alva Curtis. Latin America in the nineteenth century: a selected bibliography of books of travel and description published in English. Metuchen, N.J., Scarecrow Press, 1973. 174 p.

Contains 1182 entries, with geographical index.

MIDDLE AMERICA
(Caribbean Islands, Central America, and Mexico)

TOM L. MARTINSON, *Professor of Geography, Ball State University*
GARY S. ELBOW, *Associate Professor of Geography, Texas Tech University*

HISTORICAL GEOGRAPHY DOMINATES the literature on Mexico in this edition of the *Handbook*, with many contributions coming from US and West German researchers. Of special interest are articles by Cross (item **5341**), Mathewson (item **5357**), and Turner (see *HLAS 39:512* and item **360**), which challenge established conceptions about the regions and period of which they write. Readers with an interest in the history of resource exploitation will be drawn to the April 1975 volume of *Journal of the West*, which is devoted exclusively to a series of articles on early mining in New Spain by Probert (item **5363**).

The relative paucity of items on contemporary agriculture is compensated in part by the appearance of a book by Hewitt de Alcántara (item **5351**) which may well become the landmark analysis of Mexican agriculture in the mid-20th century. Hewitt de Alcántara's work will bring to mind numerous possibilities for research on agriculture which could be undertaken by geographers, some of which will, hopefully, be pursued over the next few years.

The offerings of interest to urban and social geographers are highlighted by what is probably the most sophisticated and comprehensive treatment of Mexican urban growth to date (item **5372**). Despite increased production of theoretically-oriented work on such topics as migration, diffusion, and marketing behavior, there is still much room for application of theory developed in the US or Europe to the Mexican (or Latin American) situation, and there is a continuing need for cross-cultural studies of human spatial behavior, many of which could be carried out in Mexico or elsewhere in Latin America.

Mexican geographers produced several regional surveys focusing on natural resources and/or economic development. The most comprehensive of these studies (many of which were omitted from this bibliography because of space limitations) is by Tamayo and Beltrán (item **5367**). Such studies reflect the interest of Mexicans in the development of their own country and the need for information on resources and economic activities for planning purposes. A new journal, *Anales de Geografía* (item **5332**) which is devoted largely to publication of physical geographic inventories conducted by students and faculty at the Univ. Nacional Autónoma de México, reflects this concern with basic data collection.

The literature on Guatemala has, understandably, a decided orientation toward the disastrous earthquake of 4 Feb. 1976. However, the most noteworthy item on the country is a lengthy annotated bibliography on water resources produced under the auspices of the Instituto Geográfico Nacional (item **5324**). This work cites numerous government publications and other hard to locate sources and should prove to be of great utility for researchers.

In other Central American nations and in the Caribbean area, studies of population and agriculture dominate this year's selections. In many works, old ideas are challenged. In agriculture, Turner (see *HLAS 37 : 687*) has discovered new evidence to support the assertion that ancient Maya farming was quite sophisticated, while Young (item **5291**) uses components analysis to challenge the notion that plantation agriculture dominates national economies or societies in the Caribbean, and Hoy and Fisher (item **5289**) measure agricultural supply and demand to discover that Antigua, Barbados, and El Salvador may experience shortages in food. Population studies include one by Karush (item **5315**) that blames El Salvador's rapid population increase on economic factors, specifically poverty, economic dependency, and maldistribution of income.

Important aside from these works on population and agriculture is a good study by Porta Caldera (item **5329**) on the value of cadastral maps in reconstructing Managua and the appearance of a welcome new journal, the *Revista Geográfica de América Central* (item **5304**) that emphasizes applied geography.

CARIBBEAN
GENERAL

5287 Allsopp, W.H.L. Some fishery options for food supply increase in the Caribbean Atlantic (AI/I, 3:2, marzo/abril 1978, p. 93–98, map, plate, tables)

Develops opportunities for aquaculture in a region that has made little use of these resources.

Carvajal, Manuel J. *ed.* Políticas de crecimiento urbano: la experiencia de Costa Rica. See item **7153**.

5288 Grases, José. Introducción al estudio sobre los sismos destructores del Caribe (AI/I, 2:4, julio/agosto 1977, p. 222–230, maps, tables)

First step in a proposed compilation and synthesis of information on seismic activity along the Caribbean rim in order to develop guidelines for building construction.

5289 Hoy, Don Roger and James S. Fisher. Primary production and the measurement of agricultural potential in the Caribbean (PAIGH/G, 80, junio 1974, p. 71–87, bibl., maps, tables)

Uses climax vegetation as an indicator of agricultural potential to develop an index value for each country in the Caribbean rimlands. This rough measure indicates that demand for food exceeds supply in Antigua, Barbados, and El Salvador.

5290 Mattson, Peter H. *ed.* West Indies island arcs. Foreword by Rhodes W. Fairbridge. Stroudsburg, Pa., Dowden, Hutchinson & Ross, 1977. 382 p., bibl., maps, tables (Benchmark papers in geology, 33)

Compilation of 20 reprinted papers illustrating development of geologic knowledge about West Indies.

5291 Young, Ruth C. The structural context of Caribbean agriculture: a comparative study (JDA, 10:4, July 1976, p. 425–444, tables)

Plantation agriculture, viewed through components analysis, does not dominate the national economies nor maintain a rigid caste system of disenfranchised, unskilled agricultural labor by controlling repressive governments on the 18 Caribbean islands studied.

CUBA

5292 García Avila, Israel. Administración de fauna silvestre y reservas biológicas en la República de Cuba (SMHN/R, 35, dic. 1974, p. 175–179)

Relates location of Cuban "parks" and evolution of legislation affecting their flora and fauna.

5293 Provincia Santiago de Cuba: cuna de la Revolución. Santiago, Cuba, Editorial Oriente, 1977. 166 p., illus., maps, plates, tables.

Thumbnail sketch of this province contains data not readily available elsewhere as well as many regional maps.

DOMINICAN REPUBLIC

5294 Fuente García, Santiago de la. Geografía dominicana para bachillerato. With the collaboration of Ninón de Saleme and others. Santo Domingo, Editora Colegial Quisqueyana, 1976. 266 p., fold. map, fold. table, maps, plates, tables.

Good introductory text is encyclopedic in approach but contains data and maps not readily available elsewhere.

GRENADA

5295 Steele, Beverley A. Grenada: an island state; its history and its people (UWI/CQ, 20:1, March 1974, p. 5–43)

Examines historical trends, especially in population migration, to support the thesis that Grenada's culture is extremely diverse and cannot easily be identified as a plural society.

PUERTO RICO

5297 Navas, Gerardo *ed.* Geography and planning. Río Piedras, Univ. de Puerto Rico, Editorial Universitaria, 1977. 67 p., bibls. (Graduate School of Planning series, R-1)

Excellent statements on the interrelationships between geography and planning by several authors should be distributed to a wider audience.

5298 Picó, Rafael. The geography of Puerto Rico. Chicago, Ill., Aldine, 1974. 439 p., bibl., maps, plates, tables.

Valuable, detailed, and encyclopedic review of the geography of Puerto Rico, written from the point of view of a geographer-banker-development planner.

CENTRAL AMERICA
GENERAL

5299 Bennett, Charles F. Cultural diversity in Central America and Panama: its relationship to conservation and planning (UCR/RBT, 24 [suplemento 1] junio/dic. 1976, p. 5–12)

Different cultures have different needs with respect to resource use and conservation as well as to economic development. Cultural diversity needs more recognition as a resource. [C. Edwards]

5300 Golley, Frank B. and others. Mineral cycling in a tropical moist forest ecosystem. Athens, Univ. of Georgia Press, 1975. 248 p., bibl., plates, tables.

The paradox of a luxuriant forest and an infertile soil may be explained by its almost closed mineral cycle. Research for this finding was conducted in Panama.

5301 Grases, José. Sismicidad de la región asociada a la cadena volcánica centroamericana del Cuaternario. Caracas, Univ. Central de Venezuela (UCV) [and] Organization of American States, 1975. 106 p., bibl., fold. tables, tables.

Comprehensive study of vulcanism contains a critique of previous seismic observations, a general description of the area's tectonic history, and a discussion of the implications of seismic activity here.

5302 Lauer, Wilhelm. Nature process, ecological balance and cultural landscape in the tropics: Central America as an example (in Colloquium on Regional Inequalities of Development, Vitoria, Brazil [Espírito Santo] 1971. Proceedings of the Commission on Regional Aspects of Development of the International Geographical Union. v. 1, Methodology and case studies. Edited by Richard S.Thoman. Hayward, California State Univ., 1974, p. 473–500, bibl., maps)

Opening Central America's rain-forest would require great technical ability, capital, and knowledge of this different environment if its destruction is to be avoided.

5303 Parsons, James J. Forest to pasture: development or destruction? (UCR/RBT, 24 [suplemento 1] junio/dic. 1976, p. 121–138)

Removal of forest for the formation of pasture is a major landscape change in Central America and Panama, accounting for the nearly doubling of the area of planted pasture in the last 15 years. However, per capita consumption of beef has declined as exports have increased. African grasses dominate improved pastures. Ecologic effects of conversion of forest to pasture are largely unknown, and capability of the land to sustain such use is doubtful. [C. Edwards]

5304 *Revista Geográfica de América Central.* Univ. Nacional, Facultad de Ciencias de la Tierra y el Mar, Escuela de Geografía. No. 2, 1. semestre, 1975- . Heredia, C.R.

Welcome new journal with an editorial preference for applied studies balances scholarly contributions in physical and in social geography.

5305 Simposio Internacional sobre la Ecología de la Conservación y del Desarrollo en el Istmo Centroamericano. *Ciudad Universitaria Rodrigo Facio*, 1975. Simposio internacional sobre la ecología de la conservación y del desarrollo en el Istmo Centroamericano: Ciudad Universitaria Rodrigo Facio, 24, 25, 26 de febrero de 1975. Introducción de Jay M. Savage. Ciudad Universitaria Rodrigo Facio, C.R., Oficina de Publicaciones, 1976. 209 p., bibls., maps, plates, tables (*Revista de Biología Tropical*, 24:

Several short papers outline the extent of environmental change in Central America. Included are original contributions and maps by prominent geographers.

5306 Soria V., Jorge. Los sistemas de agricultura en el Istmo Centroamericano (UCR/RBT, 24 [suplemento 1] junio/dic. 1976, p. 57–68)

Principal systems are monoculture, multiple culture, associated culture, and combinations of these. Stresses need for detailed ecological, economic, and social study of small farmers. [C. Edwards]

5307 West, Robert C. Conservation of coastal marine environments (UCR/RBT, 24 [suplemento 1] junio/dic. 1976, p. 187–209)

Classifies intertidal zones of Central American coasts and describes ecosystems of some, emphasizing estuarine mangrove associations, which are important to nutrient supply of other life forms. Preservation of mangrove is related directly to maintenance of offshore fisheries. Cliffed and sand beach coastlines are also worthy of protection as tourist attractions and wildlife habitats. [C. Edwards]

BELIZE

5308 Bernsten, Richard H. and **Robert W. Herdt.** Towards an understanding of *milpa* agriculture: the Belize case (JDA, 2:3, April 1977, p. 373–392, tables)

Describes the agriculture of a sample of farmers from three Mayan Indian villages, including comments on technology, labor utilization, and marketing. Concludes with a series of low cost recommendations for improving the productivity of this form of agriculture.

COSTA RICA

5309 Costa Rica. Dirección General de Estadística y Censos (DGEC). **Centro Latinoamericano de Demografía** (CELADE). Costa Rica: evaluación del censo de 1973 y proyecciones de población por sexo y grupos de edades; años 1950 al 2000. San José, 1976. 105 p., tables.

New information on a lower growth rate and greater longevity necessitates a downward revision of population projections for Costa Rica for the year 2000.

5310 Cuevas C., Marco A. Características y posibilidades del crecimiento urbano de San José. San José, Ministerio de Obras Públicas y Transportes (MOPT) [and] Alan M. Voorhees y Associates (AMV), 1974. 1 v. (Various pagings) fold. map, tables (Estudio de transportes del área metropolitana de San José, informe técnico de trabajo, 16)

Basic socioeconomic data projected to 1990 indicate a great increase in population, income, employment, and other measures in San José, but planning must be careful.

5311 Dufour, Jules. Paramètres thermiques de l' air et du sol sous les tropiques hyperhumides meso-américains: le cas du Valle de Turrialba, Costa Rica (NS, 2:3/4, 1977, p. 51–64, bibl., tables)

Precise temperature data and recommendations on how they may be used to improve coffee production in the Turrialba Valley.

5312 Fournier O., Luis A. Efecto del urbanismo sobre el futuro desarrollo agrícola de Costa Rica (UCR/RBT, 24 [suplemento 1] junio/dic. 1976, p. 49–55)

Urban and transportation land uses must be planned not to impinge on productive agricultural land. Suggests selective land taxation system to preserve and encourage agriculture near urban centers. [C. Edwards]

5313 Holdridge, Leslie R. and **Luis J. Poveda A.** Arboles de Costa Rica. v. 1, Palmas, otras monocotiledónes arbóreas y árboles con hojas compuestas o lobuladas. San José, Centro Científico Tropical, 1975. 546 p., bibl., plates.

Excellent field identification guide by the distinguished ecologist.

EL SALVADOR

5314 Browning, David G. El Salvador: la tierra y el hombre. Traducción de Paloma Gastesi and Augusto Ramírez C. San Salvador, Ministerio de Educación, Dirección de Publicaciones, 1975. 482 p., bibl., maps, tables.

Extremely valuable book, now in Spanish translation, traces man-land relationships since precolumbian times. Original ed.: *El Salvador: landscape and society* (London, Oxford Univ. Press, 1971).

5315 Karush, Gerald. Tierra, población y pobreza: las raíces de la crisis demográfica en El Salvador (UJSC/ECA, 32:350, dic. 1977, p. 893–910, tables)

Poverty, economic dependency, and mal-distribution of income are the roots of El Salvador's current rapid population increase.

GUATEMALA

5316 Biechler, Michael J. The regionalization of coffee culture in Guatemala (PAIGH/G, 77, dic. 1972, p. 33–55, maps, tables)

Identifies three discrete coffee production regions and identifies their distinguishing characteristics.

5317 Driever, Steven L. and Don R. Hoy.
Periodic markets of southwestern Guatemala: a comparison of the spatial system in the 1930's and 1960's (PAIGH/G, 85, junio 1977, p. 133–147, illus., map, tables)

Study utilizes graph theory to determine that Guatemala's periodic marketing system has deteriorated significantly in the time period under study. Authors attribute this process to modernization, especially of transportation systems.

5318 Fiedler B., Günther. Das erdbeben von Guatemala vom 4. Februar 1976 (GV/GR, 66:2, 1977, p. 309–335, bibl., maps, plates, tables)

Describes Guatemalan earthquake of 4 Feb. 1976 in terms of plate tectonic theory. Article includes tables listing previous severe earthquakes in Guatemala (with Richter magnitudes for those in 20th century) and seismographic records from Guatemala City airport on the major quake and selected aftershocks.

5319 Glass, Roger I. and others. Earthquake injuries related to housing in a Guatemalan village (AAAS/S, 197:4204, 12 Aug. 1977, p. 638–643, bibl., illus., map, tables)

In depth interviews with earthquake survivors and examination of their houses in Santa María Cauqué indicate that all earthquake-related deaths in the village were caused by collapse of adobe houses. Residents of older adobe houses were 1.6 times more likely to have received a serious injury than residents of newer houses also of adobe. This paper has much information of potential interest for all geographers, social scientists, not just those working on disaster research.

5320 Kelsey, Vera and Lilly de Jongh Osborne. Four keys to Guatemala. Revised by Larry Handel. 2. rev. ed. N.Y., Funk & Wagnalls, 1978. 255 p., illus.

Most recent publication of the classic travel guide to Guatemala. Unfortunately, there appears to have been no revision of the basic text of the book, which was written in the late 1930s. Updating seems to apply only to information on hotels, motels, night spots, car rental agencies, and other tourist-oriented activities.

5321 Plafker, George. Tectonic aspects of the Guatemala earthquake of 4 February 1976 (AAAS/S, 193:4259, 24 Sept. 1976, p. 1201–1208, bibl., illus., maps, plates)

Relates occurrence of this earthquake to plate tectonic theory. Observations support the hypothesis that the Caribbean plate is breaking apart as it traverses Guatemala, causing shallow-focus earthquakes in highly populated areas where they pose a serious hazard.

5322 Rose, Susan O. The United Fruit Company in Tiquisate, Guatemala (in Conference of Latin Americanist Geographers, VII, El Paso, Tex., 1976. International aspects of development: geographical perspectives. Edited by Gary S. Elbow. v. 6. Muncie, Ind., CLAG Publications, 1977, p. 105–110, bibl., tables)

Interviews with a sample of residents of the agrarian reform colony Nueva Concepción indicate that those who were former employees of the United Fruit Company, which abandoned its holdings in the area in 1964, had higher literacy rates, earned higher incomes, and generally attained higher levels of socioeconomic well-being than did *parcelarios* who had never been employed by the Company. The article concludes that the Company acted as a positive agent for change among its former employees.

5323 Stadel, Christoph. Ciudad Guatemala: grundzüge seiner städtischen Entwicklung und Struktur (OLI/ZLW, 10, 1976, p. 21–26, bibl., tables)

Describes city's growth with comments on urban morphology, social differentiation, and rates of growth. Concludes with summary of government plans to control development of the capital city.

5324 Váldez Illescas, Raquel Yolanda. Bibliografía sobre el recurso agua en Guatemala. Presentación de Federico Hernández C. and Hugo Quan Ma. Guatemala, Univ. de San Carlos, Facultad de Humanidades, Facultad de Ingeniería [and] Ministerio de Comunicaciones y Obras Públicas, Instituto Geográfico Nacional, 1974. 321 p., bibl.

This work will be indispensable for anyone interested in any aspect of water resources in Guatemala. Includes exceptionally well-done and detailed annotations.

5325 Veblen, Thomas T. Forest preservation in the Western Highlands of Guatemala (AGS/GR, 68:4, Oct. 1978, p. 417–434, maps, plates, tables)

This work considers the anomalous persistence of forest in an area which currently maintains one of the highest population densities in all Central America. Forest preservation is explained as a product of communal ownership in closed, corporate communities and of local recognition of the importance of commercial forest products to the survival of independent Indian villages.

5326 ———. Native population decline in Totonicapán, Guatemala (AAG/A, 67:4, Dec. 1977, p. 484–499, maps, tables)

Well-documented analysis presents population estimates for seven dates between 1520 and 1892. Concludes that area may have been on the verge of demographic collapse at the time of conquest. Population declined by perhaps as much as 90 percent by late 17th century, largely as a result of Spanish-introduced diseases and disruption of native societies.

NICARAGUA

Lanuza, Alberto. Nicaragua: territorio y población, 1821–1875. See *HLAS 40:2894.*

5327 Loveland, Christine. Rural-urban dynamics: the Miskito coast of Nicaragua (UA, 2:2, Fall 1973, p. 182–193, bibl., tables)

The Rama Indians continue to live in rural areas surrounding Bluefields, and have a negative image of the city.

5328 Nicaragua. Empresa Nacional de Luz y Fuerza. División de Estudios Básicos. Análisis de frecuencia de crecidas para ríos de Nicaragua. Introducción de Roberto Araica Salas. Managua, 1976. 18 l., tables.

Compilation of flood data would be useful for physical geographers interested in natural hazards.

5329 Porta Caldera, Humberto. Aplicación del catastro en la reconstrucción de la capital de Nicaragua (PAIGH/RC, 26, junio 1974, p. 95–109, fold. maps, maps, plate, table)

Managua earthquake proves the value of cadastral maps as records of landholding.

5330 Seminario para el Establecimiento y Manejo del Parque Nacional Volcán y Laguna de Masaya, *Managua, 1975.* Plan maestro para el establecimiento y manejo del área del Volcán Masaya como Parque Nacional. [Edición preparada por] Jaime Incer Barquero y Claudio Gutiérrez Huete. Managua, Banco Central de Nicaragua, Programa de Desarrollo Turístico, 1975. 145 p., bibl., fold. map, maps, plates, tables.

Full description of the volcano and its surrounding area offer ample justification for its selection as a national park. Seminar was held 18–21 Feb. 1975.

PANAMA

5331 Gentry, Alwyn H. Botanical exploration of Cerro Tacarcuna (EJ, 55:1, March 1977, p. 40–45, map, plates)

First botanical expedition to the Cerro Tacarcuna in Panama. Approximately 20 percent of the species collected were new. [R. C. Eidt]

MEXICO

Ames, Charles R. Along the Mexican boundary—then and now. See *HLAS 40:2684.*

5332 *Anales de Geografía.* Univ. Nacional Autónoma de México, Facultad de Filosofía y Letras, Centro de Investigaciones Geográficas. Años 1/2, 1975/1976-. México.

First two issues of new annual publication of UNAM's Centro de Investigaciones Geográficas. Año 1 (1975) contains five articles: three deal with descriptive geomorphology of selected areas in Mexico, two describe physical base (soils and geomorphology) and progress made in irrigation in lowlands of Guerrero state. Año 2 (1976) consists of five articles: three of which comprise report of field study carried out by group of Mexican students on Clarión island (one of Revillagigedo group), fourth describes geology of Tehuantepec Isthmus and fifth, geologic history of Pantitlan fractures in Mexican Federal District.

Annual Meeting of the National Wildlife Federation, *XXXVI* [and] **North American Wildlife and Natural Resources Conference,** *XXXVII, Mexico, 1972.* Aspectos internacionales de los recursos renovables de México. See item **8611.**

5333 Bahre, Conrad J. and **David E. Bradbury.** Vegetation change along the Arizona-Sonora boundary (AAG/A, 68:2, June 1978, p. 145–165, maps, plates, tables)
Review of general land-use history of area leads into comparative study of vegetation on both sides of fenced boundary. Research, based in part on ground photography from 1892, 1969, and 1976, concludes that differences in grazing practices have caused greater depletion of desirable vegetation on Mexican side of the boundary than on US lands.

5334 Barkenbus, Jack N. The Trans-Peninsular Highway: a new era for Baja California (UM/JIAS, 16:3, Aug. 1974, p. 259–273, bibl., map)
Mexican government goals in constructing this highway were to promote tourism and further the integration of Baja California into the mainstream of national life. These goals may be incompatible as increased US tourism accentuates contrasts between US and Mexican life styles.

5335 Bassols Batalla, Angel. Recursos naturales de México: teoría, conocimiento y uso. 6. ed. aumentada. México, Editorial Nuestro Tiempo, 1976. 345 p., bibl., maps, tables (Col. Los grandes problemas nacionales)
Most recent ed. of book first published 1967. Contains some data through 1974 and into 1975. Offers no new insights into the Mexican resource situation and gives only passing attention to recently discovered petroleum reserves which will certainly alter Mexico's economy and position among world powers in the future.

Bennett, E. Fay. An afternoon of terror: the Sonoran earthquake of May 3, 1887. See *HLAS 40:2595.*

5336 *Boletín del Instituto de Geografía.* Univ. Nacional Autónoma de México (UNAM), Instituto de Geografía. Vol. 6, 1975- . México.
Contains series of nine articles on aspects of the physical geography of Mexico. Topics studied include: weather systems of the Gulf of Mexico; climate zones of Mexico City; aspects of the physical geography of eastern versant of Sierra Madre Oriental; humidity and vegetation in Baja California; climate/vegetation associations in the Tarascan Sierra; and landscape development on the Pueblo piedmont of Popocatépetl and Iztaccihuatl volcanoes.

5337 ———. ———, ———. Vol. 7, 1975- . México.
Collection of six articles. Topics include a historical study of Atlixco, Puebla; a description of the ex-hacienda Santa Cruz; development of tourism in Mexico; and a review of Aztec soil science.

5338 Brown, Lawrence A. and **Barry Lentnek.** Innovation diffusion in a developing economy: a mesoscale view (PAIGH/G, 82, junio 1975, p. 109–130, illus., maps, tables)
Theoretically oriented study of mesoscale diffusion within a single urban hinterland using the spread of dairying in Aguascalientes, Mexico as an empirical example by which to test a generalized model.

5339 Carrasco Puente, Rafael. Bibliografía del Istmo de Tehuantepec. t. 2. México, Comisión Coordinadora para el Desarrollo Integral del Istmo de Tehuantepec, 1976. 634 p., map, plates, tables (Monografías bibliográficas mexicanas, 2)
This bibliography, arranged by author, updates vol. 1 compiled in 1948. Some 1821 entries are annotated, others quoted extensively.

5340 Crosby, Harry. El Camino Real in Baja California: Loreto to San Diego (SDHS/J, 23:1, Winter 1977, p. 1–45, bibl., maps, plates)
Traces development of the colonial trail which once connected Mexico City with Alta California by way of Baja California. Includes many photographs, a series of 12 excellent detailed maps of the trail route (scale 1:280,000), and a translation into English of an original account of the road

building. This article will be of value to those with an interest in the development of transportation in Mexico.

5341 Cross, Harry E. Living standards in rural nineteenth century Mexico: Zacatecas, 1820–80 (JLAS, 10:1, May 1978, p. 1–19, tables)

Carefully reasoned study based on examination of the records of Hacienda Maguey, a medium-sized hacienda located near Zacatecas. Data indicate that conditions of hacienda peones were better than those suggested by generalized accounts of living conditions in 19th-century Mexico and that such generalizations may not be appropriate for much of northern Mexico.

5342 Davies, Shane; Richard Blood; and Melvin Albaum. The settlement pattern of newly-arrived migrants in Guadalajara (PAIGH/G, 77, dic. 1972, p. 114–121, bibl., maps)

Study applies factorial ecology to 1970 census data and finds discrepancies with earlier migration models. Guadalajara has not developed inner city slums, retaining instead a largely middle-class core. Notes importance of kinship ties in the selection of initial residential sites by migrants.

5343 Dillman, C.D. Maquiladoras in Mexico's northern border communities and the border industrialization program (TESG, 67:3, 1976, p. 138–150, bibl., maps, tables)

Analyzes progress of border industrialization program through 1974, describing and explaining growth of industrial employment in Mexican border cities, and commenting on possible future impact of the border industrialization program in Mexico.

5344 Ewald, Ursula. The von Thünen principle and agricultural zonation in colonial Mexico (Journal of Historical Geography [Academic Press, London] 3:2, April 1977, p. 123–133)

Author finds that the highly complex pattern of agricultural land uses which existed in colonial Mexico can be broken down into discrete units based on land-holding type (Indian traditional farming communities and haciendas) and location with relationship to markets. Broken down into smaller and simpler units, land use patterns exhibit a von Thünen type zonation.

5345 Fredrich, Barbara E. Urban dooryard gardens as indices of culture-ecologic conditions: an example from Mexicali, Baja California (in Conference of Latin Americanist Geographers, VII, El Paso, Tex., 1976. International aspects of development in Latin America: geographical perspectives. Edited by Gary S. Elbow. v. 6. Muncie, Ind., CLAG Publications, 1977, p. 29–43, bibl., maps, tables)

Species composition of dooryard gardens tends to reflect a variety of socio-economic conditions of gardeners, including length of residence in the community, degree of movement away from traditional values, and relative levels of income. Study of gardens provides useful data which can be collected in a convenient and non-controversial manner and provides an entré to revealing conversations which might otherwise be difficult to initiate.

5346 Frost, Melvin J. Mormon settlements in Mexico: a study in the hazards of foreign colonization (in Conference of Latin Americanist Geographers, VII, El Paso, Tex., 1976. International aspects of development: geographical perspectives. Edited by Gary S. Elbow. v. 6. Muncie, Ind., CLAG Publications, 1977, p. 85–96, bibl., map)

Author maintains that Mormon colonies in Mexico are successful, despite the fact that most have ceased to exist, because of the colonists' accomplishments in farming, education, and diffusion of the Mormon religion in Mexico.

5347 Gerhard, Peter. Continuity and change in Morelos, Mexico (AGS/GR, 65:3, July 1975, p. 335–363, maps)

One of the foremost historical geographers of Mexico traces the changes in political and ecclesiastical divisions since the Conquest. Contains several useful maps.

5348 Griffin, Ernst C. and Larry R. Ford. Tijuana: landscape of a culture hybrid (AGS/GR, 66:4, Oct. 1976, p. 435–447, maps, plates)

Delightful exploration of the landscape of a border town, this article documents the blending of Mexican and North American influences to create a unique urban ambience.

5348a Gutiérrez, Celedonio. San Juan Parangaricutiro: memorias de un campesino (INAH/A, 5:53, 1974/1975, p. 85–120, maps, plates)

First-hand account of eruption of Parícutin Volcano with much material on response of local people to eruption and its impact on them. Introductory comment by Mary Lee Nolan, a geographer who worked with Gutiérrez and transcribed his account for publication.

5349 Gutiérrez de MacGregor, María Teresa and **Carmen Valverde V.** Evolution of the urban population in the arid zones of Mexico: 1900–1970 (AGS/GR, 65:2, April 1975, p. 214–228, maps, tables)

The urban population of Mexico's arid and semi-arid zones has increased 12-fold in 70 years. This growth is attributed to a variety of causal factors.

5350 Hardy, Robert William Hale. Travels in the interior of Mexico in 1825, 1826, 1827, & 1828. Glorieta, N. Mex., Rio Grande Press, 1977. 558 p., music, plates (A Rio Grande classic)

This reprint of an 1829 travel diary by a commercial agent in Baja California is highly descriptive and will provide good contrast to contemporary travel accounts that accentuate food and accommodations.

5351 Hewitt de Alcántara, Cynthia. Modernizing Mexican agriculture: socioeconomic implications of technological change, 1940–1970. Preface by Andrew Pearse. Geneva, United Nations Research Institute for Social Development (UNRISD), 1976. 350 p., bibl., tables (UNRISD studies on the green revolution, 11. Report, 76.5)

Careful and well-documented study of the process of agricultural modernization in a country which, in many ways, has been a model for subsequent modernization programs. The main thesis is that private and government efforts at modernization (largely associated with the Rockefeller Foundation-sponsored crop improvement schemes gathered under the rubric of green revolution) have been directed toward creation of a capitalist-oriented commercial agricultural sector at the expense of subsistence or near subsistence producers.

5352 Johnson, Kirsten. Disintegration of a traditional resource-use complex: the Otomí of the Mezquital Valley, Hidalgo,

Mexico (CU/EG, 53:4, Oct. 1977, p. 364–367, bibl., illus.)

Describes decline of a once self-sustaining resource-use system under the impact of changing social and economic conditions by tracing the plight of an Indian family.

5353 Lauer, Wilhelm. The altitudinal belts of the vegetation in the central Mexican highlands and their climatic conditions (Arctic and Alpine Research [Univ. of Colorado, Institute of Arctic and Alpine Research, Boulder] 5:3 [pt. 2] 1973, p. A99-A113, bibl., maps, plates, tables)

Describes extra-tropical vegetation types in certain of the altitudinal belts of the eastern slopes of the Central Highlands and analyzes their relationship to extra-tropical climate elements, especially cool temperatures, caused by invasions of cool fronts (nortes) into the area in winter.

5354 Lentnek, Barry; S. Lieber; and I. Sheskin. Consumer behavior and urban spatial structure in Mexico (in Conference of Latin Americanist Geographers, V, Boca Raton, Fla., 1974. Latin America: search for geographic explanations. Edited by Robert J. Tata. v. 5. East Lansing, Mich., CLAG Publications, 1976, p. 57–64, bibl., illus., map, tables)

Authors analyze patterns of food shopping in Aguascalientes state, finding that the distance that shoppers will travel to make food purchases breaks sharply at three-km., the apparent point at which the advantage of public transportation overcomes the low cost of walking.

5355 López Rosado, Diego G. Los servicios públicos de la Ciudad de México. México, Editorial Porrúa, 1976. 307 p., bibl., fold. illus., fold. maps, fold. table, tables.

Detailed historical account of the development of public services in Mexico City from the pre-Conquest period to 1925. Contains many maps, the value of which is greatly reduced by poor cartography and reproduction. Nevertheless, there is much of potential value for students of the historical development of Mexico City.

5356 Malmstrom, Vincent H. Izapa: cultural hearth of the Olmecs? (in Meeting of the Association of American

Geographers, LXXII, N.Y., 1976. Proceedings. Edited by Michael P. Conzen. Washington, Assn. of American Geographers, 1976, v. 8, p. 32–35)

Presents circumstantial evidence in support of theory that Izapa was the place of origin for both the long and short count Mayan calendars and suggests that Izapans knew the use of lodestones for magnetic direction finding.

5357 Mathewson, Kent. Maya urban genesis reconsidered: trade and intensive agriculture as primary factors (Journal of Historical Geography [Academic Press, London] 3:3, July 1977, p. 203–215, bibl., map)

Brief but thorough review of literature on major trends in theory of Maya urbanization. Criticizes early attempts to portray Mayan civilization as non-urban and dependent upon swidden agriculture, pointing out that research over the past 20–30 years has uncovered evidence of true urbanization, high population densities, well-developed local trade patterns, and permanent intensive agriculture.

5358 Muría, José María. Historia de las divisiones territoriales de Jalisco. México, Secretaría de Educación Pública (SEP) [and] Instituto Nacional de Antropología e Historia (INAH), Centro Regional de Occidente, 1976. 219 p., maps, tables (Col. Científica: historia, 34)

Traces internal and external boundary changes from the founding of Nueva Galicia to the contemporary state of Jalisco. Contains data of interest for historical geographers and others but very little analysis is provided. The poor quality of the maps reduces overall value of study.

5359 North, Arthur Walbridge. Camp and camino in lower California: a record of the adventures of the author while exploring peninsular California, Mexico. Foreword by Robley D. Evans. Glorieta, N. Mex., Rio Grande Press, 1977. 346 p., bibl., col. plates, fold. map, illus., map, plates (A Rio Grande classic)

North, the first "tourist" in Baja California, writes glowingly of his experiences there in 1906, when pack mules and Indians provided the adventure. Reprint of 1910 ed.

5360 Nostrand, Richard L. The borderlands in perspective (*in* Conference of

Latin Americanist Geographers, VII, El Paso, Tex., 1976. International aspects of development in Latin America: geographical perspectives. Edited by Gary S. Elbow. v. 6. Muncie, Ind., CLAG Publications, 1977, p. 9–28, bibl., maps)

Well-reasoned elaboration of the varying perceptions of the US-Mexico borderland over time. Identifies six discrete perceptions of the region and discusses the events which led to or resulted from these real or imagined images.

5361 Pompa y Pompa, Antonio. Espejo de provincia: geografía del paisaje mexicano. México, Editorial Porrúa, 1975. 285 p.

Collection of essays characterizing various places in Mexico. This book will please readers with an appreciation for Hispanic-American literature, but contains little for those seeking hard facts about the country.

5362 Popp, Kilian and **Konrad Tyrakowski.** Der caserío Metepec, Atlixco: zur Entwicklung einer frühen Industriesiedlung in Mexiko (IAA, 3:3, 1977, p. 267–180, bibl., maps, plate)

Historical study of the impact of a large textile mill on a small community over a period of half a century. Will probably be of greater interest for economic historians than geographers.

5363 Probert, Alan. Silver quest: episodes of mining in New Spain (JW, 14:2, April 1975, p. 5–144, bibl., illus., maps)

Entire volume devoted to series of nine sketches by the same author, each dealing with an aspect of history of mining in Mexico. Several of the articles contain valuable information on mining technology and its development.

5364 Razo Zaragoza, José Luis. Guadalajara. Guadalajara, Mex., Univ. de Guadalajara, Instituto Jalisciense de Antropología e Historia, 1975. 302 p., maps, plates.

Description of major public buildings in Guadalajara on a street-by-street basis, with many maps and photos.

5365 Rees, Peter W. Origins of colonial transportation in Mexico (AGS/GR, 65:3, July 1975, p. 323–334, maps)

Interesting and well-reasoned analysis of the establishment of transportation -

routes between Mexico City and Vera Cruz. Concludes that the Spaniards ignored earlier Aztec trade routes in constructing an externally-oriented *camino real* which created a pattern that has persisted to the present.

5366 Rengert, Arlene C. and George F. Rengert. Does out-migration hinder agricultural development? a view from rural Mexico (*in* Conference of Latin Americanist Geographers, V, Boca Raton, Fla., 1974. Latin America: search for geographic explanations. Edited by Robert J. Tata. v. 5. East Lansing, Mich., CLAG Publications, 1976, p. 133–140, bibl., tables)

Findings from Ojuelos, Mexico contradict conclusions of earlier researchers regarding characteristics of rural outmigrants. In Ojuelos it appears that those individuals who are most likely to contribute to improving agricutural productivity remain in the rural community rather than migrating to the city.

5367 Tamayo, Jorge L. and Enrique Beltrán. Recursos naturales de la Cuenca del Papaloapan. México, Instituto Mexicano de Recursos Naturales Renovables (IMERNAR), 1977. 2 v. (878 p.) (Continuous pagination) col. fold. maps, illus., maps, plates, tables.

Collection of 19 essays on the physical and bio-geography, meteorology and climatology, non-renewable resources, agricultural population, and ecological aspects of the Papaloapan Basin as well as review of the activities of the Papaloapan Commission make this an invaluable survey of the physical and social environment of this famous region.

5368 Tata, Robert J. A space-potential interpretation of transportation efficiency in Northeast Mexico (PAIGH/G, 78, junio 1973, p. 35–53, maps, tables)

Comparison of existing transportation network with theoretically perfect system yields results which planners may utilize in setting priorities for transportation development.

5369 Tichy, Franz. Deutung von Orts- und Flurnetzen im Hochland von Mexiko als kultreligiöse Reliktformen altindianischer Besiedlung (UBGI/E, 28:3, sept. 1974, p. 194–207, bibl., maps, plate, tables)

Analysis of field and village networks in conjunction with measurement of the orientation of ruins yields evidence of four differently arranged and oriented rectangular systems. Three of these systems are interpreted as relict patterns developed by a religious cult of precolumbian origin. The fourth pattern is attributed to postconquest Christian activities.

5370 Trabulse, Elías. El problema de las longitudes geográficas en el México colonial (AI/I, 2:4, julio/agosto 1977, p. 202–206, bibl.)

Relates various attempts to determine the precise longitude of Mexico. Despite inadequate instrumentation and other problems, some of these measurements were remarkably accurate.

5371 Trautmann, Wolfgang. Ergebnisse der Wüstungsforschung in Tlaxcala, Mexiko (UBGI/E, 28:2, juni 1974, p. 115–124, bibl., maps, plates, table)

Historical study of settlement desertion of Tlaxcala. Finds that nearly all desertions occurred between 1539 and 1764, with 80 percent occurring between 1557–1627, the period of highest intensity. Most desertions occurred on the periphery of Tlaxcala or in locations removed from streams or lakes from which irrigation water could be obtained.

5372 Unikel, Luís; Crescencio Ruíz Chiapetto; and Gustavo Garza Villareal. El desarrollo urbano de México: diagnóstico e implicaciones futuras. México, El Colegio de México, Centro de Estudios Económicos y Demográficos, 1976. 466 p., bibl., fold. map, maps, tables.

Comprehensive analysis of the process of urbanization in Mexico, utilizing data from 1970 and previous censuses. This study, which contains projections of future trends in addition to analyses of past urban growth, is another example of the high quality of research produced by social scientists affiliated with the Colegio de Mexico.

United States. Library of Congress. Congressional Research Service. Mexico's oil and gas policy: an analysis. See item **8654.**

5373 Vita-Finzi, C. Quaternary alluvial deposits in the central plateau of Mexico (GV/GR, 66:1, Feb. 1977, p. 99–120, bibl., plates, tables)

Detailed analysis of alluvial deposits yields inferences regarding the paleo-climate of the area. Author concludes that his findings conflict with speculations postulating early man-induced soil erosion.

5374 Walton, Mylie K. The evolution and localization of *mezcal* and *tequila* in Mexico (PAIGH/G, 85, junio 1977, p. 113–132, maps, plates)

Traces the development and spread of the mezcal liquor industry in Mexico. Describes production techniques and identifies three generalized mezcal distilling regions.

5375 Wasserstrom, Robert F. La tierra y el trabajo agrícola en la Chiapas central: un análisis regional (UNAM/RMS, 39:3, julio/sept. 1977, p. 1041–1064, maps, tables)

Commercial agriculture is replacing indigenous agriculture among Indians as Chiapas enters Mexico's modern economy.

5376 Wenzens, Gerd. Junge Wandlungen in der Agrarlandschaft der Comarca Lagunera, Nordmexico (OGG/M, 116:1/2, 1974, p. 22–38, bibl., maps, tables)

This study of agricultural change suggests that the most significant developments in the region have occurred on privately owned lands, not on ejidos. Author attributes lack of progress on ejidos to attitudes of resistance on the part of ejidatarios.

5377 Williams, Aaron, Jr. The interpretation of rainfall patterns in Northern Yucatan utilizing meteorological satellite imagery (*in* Meeting of the Association of American Geographers, LXXII, N.Y., 1976. Proceedings. Edited by Michael P. Conzen. Washington, Assn. of American Geographers, 1976, v. 8, p. 15–19, bibl., maps)

Utilizes satellite imagery to explain occurrence of a rainfall anomaly in northeastern quadrant of peninsula. Higher than expected precipitation levels result from convergence of sea breezes from north and east.

SOUTH AMERICA
(except Brazil)

ROBERT C. EIDT, *Professor of Geography, University of Wisconsin-Milwaukee*

ITEMS DEALING WITH ARGENTINA, COLOMBIA, Chile and Venezuela made up almost three-quarters of the total reviewed for this *Handbook*. A notable decline in contributions from Peru and Venezuela, and an increase from Colombia and Uruguay should be mentioned.

In conformity with the usual distribution of topics in the *Handbook*, the subject of human geography far outweighed that of physical geography, suggesting continued economic pressures. In fact, fully 30 percent of all items dealt with economic geography. These observations are reflected even in the general part of this section. A departure from the norms of the past few years has come with a growing emphasis on urban topics. The article dealing with barrack settlements, or the "cinturones de misera," is important (item **5458**).

Of special general note is the meeting of the IX Consultative Assembly of the "Antarctic Club," held in London in 1977 (item **5397**). The Club is formed by members from countries which conduct independent scientific research in Antarctica. As of 1977, when Poland joined, there were 13 member nations. The scientific communities of the world support 750 people in Antarctica on a year-round basis; in summer the population expands to about 5,000. In 1973 natural gas was discovered under the Ross Sea; large oil deposits are also known to be present. Moreover, world food shortages have heightened interest in potential krill harvests south of 60 degrees latitude. FAO estimates suggest harvest possibilities equal to the present world marine catch. Of note is the fact that the Japanese already sell krill in the frozen form. The most immediate question that arises is whether exploitation of the resources of Antarctica should be controlled. Until a decision is reached, Club members have agreed to restrain activities. Because of the growing economic significance of the region in a period of world-wide food and energy shortages, we may expect more research to be forthcoming by the printing of volume 43 of the *Handbook*.

One other organization merits attention for its potential as a contributor to *Handbook* selections. It is CIAT, the Centro Internacional de Agricultural Tropical, which has its new headquarters at Apartado Aéreo 67–13, Cali, Colombia. CIAT already has outreach programs in Bolivia and Costa Rica, backed by a grant from the International Development Research Center of Canada. Emphasis is placed on internship training by doctoral students from various countries. Practical results of the program are reflected in the introduction of improved varieties of lowland rice in Colombia, and in the drafting of reports on land use in the lowland tropics (items **5500, 5506** and **5521**).

GENERAL

5378 Acosta Solís, Misael. Conferencias fitogeográficas. Quito, Instituto Panamericano de Geografía e Historia, 1977. 295 p., bibl., illus., maps, tables (Biblioteca Ecuador)

Ten lectures by author on plant geography in which evolution of phytogeography is discussed, major plant regions for the Americas are presented, and special analysis for Ecuador is given.

5379 ———. Ecología y fitoecología. Quito, Editorial Casa de la Cultura Ecuatoriana, 1977. 423 p., bibl., facsims., illus., maps, plates, tables.

First part of this book deals with basics of ecology; the second is a treatment of physical geographical factors which influence the distribution of vegetation. Special emphasis is made of the American tropics. Third part describes phytogeographical divisions of Ecuador. Includes lengthy bibliography.

5380 ———. Investigadores de la geografía y la naturaleza de América tropical: viajeros cronistas e investigadores con especial referencia al Ecuador. pt. 1. Quito, Instituto Panamericano de Geografía e Historia (IPGH), Sección Nacional del Ecuador, 1976. 201 p., illus., maps (Biblioteca Ecuador)

Resumé of scientific investigations of physical and human geographical types made in Latin America from the conquest to the present century. Special attention to Ecuador.

5381 Adams, John W. and **James R. Simpson.** Estimates of South American beef export multipliers (Growth and Change: A Journal of Regional Development [Univ. of Kentucky, College of Business Economics, Lexington] 8:4, Oct. 1977, p. 28–32, tables)

Author reports income and output multipliers from five common beef exports. Concludes that export of cooked/frozen or canned beef should be encouraged for increased profits.

5382 Bardy, Philippe; Michèle Cail; and **Romain Gaignard.** Recherches sur les types de colonisation agricole dans le basin moyen du Paraná: Argentine, Brésil, Paraguay (UTIEH/C, 28, 1977, p. 169–185, table)

Highly generalized article dealing with the opening of land in the colonization zone along the Alto Paraná River.

5383 Cruz Buenaventura, Jaime. Yacimientos de hierro en Colombia y depósitos de hierro en Sudamérica (COIGN/BG, 20:3, 1972, p. 59–89, maps, tables)

This article will be of much use to economic geographers and others interested in specific details about iron ore deposits in Colombia and South America. Types of mineralization, quality, reserves, and recommendations are given for each deposit.

5384 **Enger, Erich.** Die Rolle der Lebens-
haltung in der wirtschaftlichen Entwicklung verdeutlicht an der Unterschicht
der Andenländer (IAA, 1, 1975, p. 351–368,
bibl.)

Considers economic development only
from the point of view of production. The
individual as consumer and his psychology
are viewed as potential obstacles to development in the Andes.

5385 **Gloaguen, Philippe** and **Michel Du-
val.** Le guide du routard: Amérique du
Sud. 3. ed. Paris, Librairie Hachette, 1977.
192 p., illus., maps.

French travel guide to South America
with some comments on the Lesser Antilles
route of entry. Includes bus times for longer
trips overland and hotel tips.

5386 **Guevara Díaz, José Manuel.** La geografía regional, la región y la regionalización. Caracas, Univ. Central de Venezuela,
Facultad de Humanidades y Educación,
1977. 191 p., bibl., tables.

This book reviews the concept of the
region by discussing the ideas of Wittlesey,
Kayser, and Juilliard classes of regions, and
the application of quantification to regional
analysis.

5387 **Hannell, F.G.** Some features of the
heat island in an equatorial city
(SSAG/GA, 58A:1/2, 1976, p. 95–109, bibl.,
tables)

Heat islands in urban areas are different in a highland Andean tropical city
when compared with mid-latitude results.
Air drainage at night changes characteristics
but daytime winds do not. Albedo effects
are responsible.

5388 **Ilg, Karl.** Pioniere in Argentinien,
Chile, Paraguay und Venezuela: Durch
Bergwelt, Urwald und Steppe erwanderte
Volkskunde der deutschsprachigen Siedler.
Innsbruck, Australia, Tyrolia Verlag, 1976.
318 p., colored plates, illus., maps, tables.

Historical geographical treatment of
pioneer settlement by German-speaking
colonists in selected South American countries visited by the author. Informative
photographs and drawings, especially of
house types.

5389 **Martínez, Héctor.** El saqueo y la de-
strucción de los ecosistemas selváticos

(III/AI, 38:1, enero/marzo 1978, p. 125–150,
bibl., tables)

Rubber, wood, skins, live animals, and
migratory agriculture are among the destructive elements in the Peruvian Oriente—
probably the most exploited East Andean
area in South America. Criticism is made of
the weak response by governing officials to
this depredation of landscape.

5390 **Meisch, Lynn.** A traveler's guide to
El Dorado & the Inca empire: Colombia, Ecuador, Perú, Bolivia. San Francisco,
Calif., Headlands Press Book, 1977. 446 p.,
bibl., illus., maps, tables (Penguin hand-
books)

This book should be read by all graduate students and others who want the real
flavor of Andean life and who must travel on
restricted budgets.

5391 **Money, D.C.** South America. 6. ed.
London, Univ. Tutorial Press (UTP),
1976. 331 p., maps, plates, tables (Advanced
level geography series)

Up-dated version of a good introductory text to South American geography.

5392 **Pichler, H.; F.R. Stibane; and R.
Weyl.** Basischer Magmatismus und
Krustenbau im südlichen Mittelamerika,
Kolumbien und Ecuador (Basic igneous rocks
and their bearing to crustal evolution in
Central America, Colombia, and Ecuador)
(NJGP, 2, Feb. 1974, p. 102–126, bibl., tables)

Petrochemical and mineralogical tests
of Cretaceous basic igneous rocks show
oceanic origin. Ocean floor spreading has
been directed toward Central and South
America and is combined with down-pulling
of the former shelf region.

5393 **Rodríguez Arias, Julio C.** Geoadmi-
nistración. Mendoza, Arg., Consejo
Nacional de Investigaciones Científicas y
Técnicas (CONICET) [and] Univ. Nacional
de Cuyo, Centro de Estudios Interdici-
plinarios de Fronteras Argentinas (CEIFAR),
1975. 62 p., maps.

Author outlines new approach to managerial training by emphasizing principle
that public officials should be trained with
maps to understand the potentials of the
lands they serve. He calls this geoadministrative training, and notes that it is based on
law and geography.

5393a Schuurman, F.J. From resource frontier to periphery: agricultural colonization east of the Andes (TESG, 69, 1978, p.
95–104)
Review of official colonization activities in the tropical Andean countries. The
center-periphery model is used to demonstrate the progressive marginalization of
peasants and the accelerated exploitation of
the natural resources in the Amazon basin.

5394 Terán, Francisco. Geografía de los
países del Grupo Andino. Quito, Editorial Casa de la Cultura Ecuatoriana, 1975.
572 p., bibl., maps, tables.
Survey of salient human and physical
features of the Andean landscape. Encyclo-
paedic, few references.

5395 Velbinger, Martin. Südamerika:
1977/78. München, FRG, The Author,
1977. 672 p., illus., maps (Südamerika-
Reiseführer, 1)
One of the exceptionally good guides
from the point of view of practical travel
hints and ideas about what to observe on the
natural and cultural landscapes.

5396 Vietmeyer, Noel D. Incredible odyssey of a visionary Victorian peddler
(Smithsonian [Smithsonian Institution,
Washington] Aug. 1978, p. 91–102)
Little-known attempt at raising alpacas in Australia after illegal shipment of
the animals from Peru in the 1850s. Failure
of the plan after 12 years resulted in its
author's attempting to smuggle cinchona
seeds from Peru. The seeds were successfully
reproduced in Java and provided the world
with quinine.

5397 Wasserman, Ursula. The Antarctic
Treaty and natural resources (JWTL,
12:2, March/April 1978, p. 174–179)
As a result of continued discoveries in
Antarctica, such as natural gas found in
1973, various nations have consulted each
other by means of the IX consultative assembly (1977). Report of activities presented
herein with useful summary of the stand of
various members on Antarctic claims.

ARGENTINA

5398 Alves Carneiro, Carlos R. La solución del diferendo limítrofe entre

Mendoza y San Juan (JEHM/R, 1:8, 1975, p.
309–324, map, plates)
Antecedents of the territorial dispute
between Mendoza and San Juan are discussed
and recommendations made.

**5399 Argentina. Consejo Nacional de In-
vestigaciones Científicas y Técnicas
(CONICET) [and] Universidad Nacional de
Cuyo. Centro de Estudios Interdisciplinarios
de Fronteras Argentinas (CEIFAR).** Facilidades del tránsito terrestre entre Argentina y
Chile. Mendoza, Arg., 1974. 55 p., bibl.,
fold. map, maps, tables.
Transportation study which suggests
the integration of Argentine and Chilean
equipment and administration of cargo car-
riers across the Andes, and of cooperation in
oceanic shipping.

**5400 ———. Ministerio de Obras y Ser-
vicios Públicos [and] Ministerio de
Economía. Secretaría de Estado de Transporte y Obras Públicas.** Estudio preliminar
del transporte de la región metropolitana. t.
1/2. B.A., 1972/1973. 2 v. (325, 318 p.) maps,
tables.
Organization of transport system in
B.A. with colored maps of factors such as
generation of trips, time of journeys, inter-
change of trips by regions, daily capacity, etc.
Includes passenger and cargo transport of
surface type. Vol. 2 discusses economic factors and future demands.

**5401 ———. Secretaría de Estado de Agri-
cultura y Ganadería. Servicio Nacional
de Parques Nacionales.** Derrotero del Lago
Nahuel-Huapi. B.A., 1972. 61 p., plates.
Brief description of physical surroundings of Lake Nahuel Huapi, Arg., followed
by listing of small port facilities.

5402 Armani, Roberto. Trenel, un pueblo
de La Pampa: estudio histórico-
geográfico. Trenel, Arg., n.p., 1973. 54 p.,
bibl., facsims., maps, plates, tables.
Brief documentation of general settlement history and physical-economic conditions of Trenel, a small town in the
northernmost part of the Province of La
Pampa, Arg.

Arcocha, Carlos Enrique. Hidrocarburos
gaseosos: historia, régimen legal. See *HLAS
40:3686.*

5403 Auza, Néstor Tomás. La Patagonia mágica. B.A., Marymar Ediciones, 1977. 300 p., illus., plates (Col. Patagonia)

Description of historical incidents, Indians, landscapes, harvests, settlements, from early and recent publications dealing with Patagonia.

5404 Barrera V., Humberto. Los antiguos caminos entre Santiago de Chile y Mendoza (JEHM/R, 1:8, 1975, p. 189–210, plates, map)

A study of historical routes between Santiago and Mendoza and their significance. Indians, miners, and soldiers pioneered trans-Andean passages. For historian's comment see *HLAS 40:3610.*

5405 Bartolomé, Leopoldo J. Populismo y diferenciación social agraria: las ligas agrarias en Misiones, Argentina (UTIEH/C, 28, 1977, p. 141–168, bibl., tables)

Social-political analysis of the agrarian movement in the Province of Misiones, Arg. Describes mechanism of alliance of agricultural groups and consequences thereof. Partly based on data from the new Movimiento Agrario de Misiones, started in 1971. For political scientist's comment, see item **7465.**

5406 Belza, Juan E. En la Isla del Fuego. t. 3, Población. B.A., Instituto de Investigaciones Históricas Tierra del Fuego, 1977. 326 p., bibl., facsims., illus., maps, plates, tables.

Population analysis with statistics, and some economic analysis of Tierra del Fuego. Useful bibliography.

5407 *Boletín de Estudios Geográficos.* Univ. Nacional de Cuyo. Facultad de Filosofía y Letras. Instituto de Geografía. Vol. 18, No. 70/73, enero/dic. 1971–. Mendoza, Arg.

This bound copy of two volumes of the *Boletín* consists of contrasting studies of an urban region and its influence in a province (San Juan, Cuyo) and of a regional network of settlements. Both studies offer suggestions as to the need for planning and restructuring economic analysis.

5408 Buenos Aires (province), *Arg.* **Ministerio de Economía, Dirección de Recurso.** Distribución de la propiedad rural en la Provincia de Buenos Aires (UNLP/E, 22:1, enero/abril 1976, p. 91–97, tables)

Between 1958 and 1972 the number of rural land-holders decreased slightly for farms measuring 2,000 to 25,000 ha. Substantial increase in number of holders occurred only among farms measuring more than 25,000 ha.

5409 Calamaro, Eduardo S. Regiones culturales (*in* Cultura nacional. B.A., Ediciones Crisol, 1976, p. 117–137)

This article traces development of regionalism in Argentina stemming from the original influx of settlers from various quarters to the present tendency for amalgamation of cultural attributes everywhere.

5410 Chatwin, Bruce. In Patagonia. London, Jonathan Cape Ltd., 1977. 204 p., bibl., map, plates.

Detailed account of modern travels in Patagonia written in popular style. Mixed with historical events in which figures like Fitz Roy and Darwin play a role. For historian's comment, see *HLAS 40:3723.*

5411 Combetto de Bariffi, Argelia. Localización industrial en la conurbación de Buenos Aires. B.A., Instituto de Geografía R. Ardissone, Facultad de Filosofía y Letras, 1976. 33 p., bibl., maps, tables (Cuadernos de geografía, 2)

Model of industrial localization is presented which suggests a close relationship with communication lines in B.A. Only five industrial sectors demonstrate homogeneous distribution: shoe manufacturing, printing, and tobacco processing in the federal capital, and chemical industries, machinery, and non-metallic minerals in the outskirts.

5412 Corrientes (province), *Arg.* **Secretaría de Planeamiento.** Corrientes. 3. ed. Corrientes, Arg., 1975. 81 p., bibl., maps, tables.

Monograph depicting physical and human geography of the Province of Corrientes. Numerous maps of climate, population, roads, accompanying text, and bibliography included.

5413 Curutchet, Marta I. Kollmann. Eficiencia funcional de los Centros de Servicios. Prólogo de Roberto Combetto. B.A., Univ. Nacional de Buenos Aires, Facultad de Filosofía y Letras, Instituto de

Geografía R. Ardissone, 1976. 35 p., bibl., maps, illus., tables (Serie cuadernos de geografía, 1)

Resumé of a Master's degree thesis (Chicago) dealing with the effectiveness of service centers in B.A. As a result of the investigation, expected relationships between the city and its services were confirmed, and areas of expansion and decline mapped.

5414 Denis, Paul-Yves. Desarrollo turístico e integración en Neuquén, Argentina: un estudio de geografía aplicada (PAIGH/G, 80, junio 1974, p. 111–128, illus., maps, plates, tables)

Discusses future corridor of development from the area of the north of Patagonia and the southwest of the Province of Buenos Aires to present centers of progress (B.A. and Bahía Blanca) in the light of preventing urban problems.

5415 Doake, C.S.M. Land beneath Antarctic ice (GM, 48:11, Aug. 1976, p. 670–674, map, plates)

The British Antarctic Survey has drawn a profile of bedrock surfaces in the Antarctic by using airborne radar. The discovery of subterranean lakes has led to rejection of the idea of storing atomic waste in this region.

5416 Enríquez Gamón, Efraín. Itaipú: aguas que valen oro. B.A., Gráfica Guadalupe, 1975. 786 p., tables.

Data concerning the hydroelectric project on the Alto Paraná as seen by the Argentine press and political groups.

5417 Fabry, Julio R. San Francisco: la tierra prometida (JPHC/R, 5, 1977, p. 119–146, plate)

Colonization history of a settlement in Córdoba, Arg.

5418 Falkner, Thomas. A description of Patagonia and the adjoining parts of South America. With an introduction and notes by Arthur E.S. Neumann. N.Y., AMS Press, 1976. 168 p., bibl., fold. map.

Reprint of 1935 original English edition of classic study of Patagonia first published in 1774 (in Newark Public Library). It should be noted that Falkner's concept of Patagonia was not as broad as the modern version.

5419 Ferro, Emilio E.J. La Patagonia como la conocí. Palabras preliminares de Luis Petraglia. B.A., Ediciones Marymar, 1978. 447 p., plates (Col. Patagonia)

Historical-geographical study of Patagonia in which accounts of various colonies may be of use to settlement investigations.

5420 García Olivera, Luis A. Arboles evocativos. Prólogo de Carlos Enrique Urquía. B.A., Talleres Gráficos INDEX, 1974. 192 p., bibl., plates.

Historical treatment of facts concerning famous trees in the settlement of Argentina.

5421 García Pulido, José. Resistencia, ayer y hoy: a cien años de su colonización. 2. ed. corregida y aumentada. Prólogo de Hector Azzetti. Resistencia, Arg., Librería y Papelería Casa García, 1977. 129 p., plates.

Historical resumé of the development of the Chaco in Argentina.

5422 Giai, Andrés G. Vida de un naturalista en Misiones. Prólogo de Carlos Selva Andrade. B.A., Editorial Albatros, 1976. 171 p., illus.

First-hand account of wild life in Misiones Province, Arg., by a naturalist who lived in the selva four months. Descriptions of construction of shelter, hunting, and experiences with insects and animals accompany a vivid analysis of both old and new faunal species in this part of South America.

5423 Gioja, Rolando I. Sistemas regionales y proyecto nacional. Prólogo de Federico A. Daus. B.A., Editorial El Ateneo, 1977. 229 p., bibl., illus., maps, tables.

An attempt at regionalization of the Argentine landscape by means of gravity-model theory.

Goldberg, Marta B. La población negra y mulata de la ciudad Buenos Aires: 1810–1840. See *HLAS 40:3767.*

5424 Igarzábal, Antonio P. Rasgos morfológicos de Isla Decepción: Islas Shetland del Sur Antártida Argentina. B.A., Dirección Nacional del Antártico, 1974. 21 p., bibl., map, plates, table (Contribución del Instituto Antártico Argentino, 172)

Physical evolution of Deception Island is explained, as well as the glacial and periglacial features deriving from later periods.

5425 López Piacentini, Carlos P. Isla del Cerrito. Resistencia, Arg., Librería Casa García, 1976. 67 p., illus., maps, plates.

Describes one more place in Argentina being promoted by its tourist industry. Includes historical resumé of the role of this island near Corrientes and what part it played in relations among Paraguay, Brazil and Argentina.

5426 Manrique, Washington G. Argentina año 2000: epílogo para un mundo feliz. B.A., Ediciones Colombo, 1976. 199 p., illus., tables.

Politics and economics of development in Argentina are discussed with author's opinions regarding planning needs.

5427 Melli, Oscar Ricardo. Geografía del partido de Chacabuco. B.A., Talleres de COGTAL, 1975? 311 p., maps, plates, tables.

Encyclopedic presentation of physical and human geographical traits in a north-central part of the Province of Buenos Aires.

5428 Mercadier, Hélène and **Gilbert Mercadier.** Aux limites de l'oecumène: le ravitaillement de la ville de Río Gallegos, Patagonie du Sud (SGB/COM, 29:113, jan./mars 1976, p. 18–48, map, tables)

Río Gallegos has been supplied traditionally from Buenos Aires, but improving overland transportation suggests the development of closer supply centers.

5429 Núñez, Julio. Iviraretá: país de árboles. Posadas, Arg., Instituto Superior del Profesorado Antonio Ruiz de Montoya, Centro de Investigación y Promoción Científico-Cultural, 1975. 117 p., bibl., illus., map, plates (Scrie antropología, 1)

Useful regional study of Misiones Province, Arg., with bibliography. Discussion of physical and human geography from the period of yerba-mate exploitation. Special emphasis on lumbering activities.

5430 Ojeda, Hugo Edgardo. El complejo hidroeléctrico del Paraná medio y la Cuenca del Plata. B.A., Ediciones Nueva Senda, 1977. 76 p.

Polemical survey of regional agricultural activities in the La Plata Basin

5431 Olascoaga, Manuel J. Estudio topográfico de La Pampa y Río Negro. 2. ed. Prólogo de Juan Carlos Walter. B.A., EUDEBA, 1974. 519 p., maps (Col. EUDEBA lucha de fronteras con el indio)

Military reports written by army officer about 1930 detailing expeditions into the Río Negro area. Includes descriptions of landscape, physical and settlement geography and aspects of Patagonian colonization problems from entry of Spanish until the turn of the present century. Largely based on correspondence between government officials.

5432 Onelli, Clemente. Trepando los Andes. 3. ed. Prólogo de Julián Cáceres Freyre. B.A., Marymar Ediciones, 1977. 175 p., plates (Col. Patagonia)

Copy of first edition of this explorer's comments on Patagonia published in 1904. The flavor of life in Patagonia is well-presented, although life among Indians now seems remote.

5433 Organization of American States. Programa de Desarrollo Regional [and] **Programa de las Naciones Unidas para el Medio Ambiente.** Calidad ambiental y desarrollo de cuencas hidrográficas: un modelo para planificación y análisis integrados. Prefacio de Kirk P. Rodgers and Roberto Casañas. Washington, Organization of American States, 1978. 118 p., bibl., tables.

Methodological treatment of watershed planning with economic and ecological aspects, as well as example of environmental impact of the Río Bermejo. Four appendices deal with evaluation and organization of planning.

5434 Paolera, Carlos María della. Buenos Aires y sus problemas urbanos. Introducción y selección a cargo de Patricio H. Randle. B.A., OIKOS, Associación para la Promoción de los Estudios Territoriales y Ambientales, 1977. 146 p., plate.

An investigation of problems of B.A.'s urban environment and their solutions. Author supports concept of constant planning in the present and for the semi-distant future.

5435 Recchini de Lattes, Zulma and **Alfredo E. Lattes** comps. La población de Argentina. B.A., Ministerio de Economía,

Secretaría de Estado de Programación y Coordenación Económica, Instituto Nacional de Estadística y Censos, 1975. 212 p., bibl., maps, tables (Serie investigaciones demográficas, 1. Committee for International Coordination of National Research in Demography series)

Seven chapters analyze population growth, change in composition, redistribution, urbanization, labor, and future projections. Population of 30,000,000 by 1990 forecast.

5436 Salta (province), *Arg.* **Dirección General de Estadística e Investigaciones Económicas.** Ciudades, pueblos, caseríos y parajes de la Provincia de Salta. pt. 1. Salta, Arg., 1975. 85 p., illus., maps, table.

Evaluation of settlements by type and public services available in the Province of Salta, Arg.

5437 Schiesser, Fritz. Argentinien 1976: Bericht über eine Exkursion des Verbandes Deutscher Schulgeographen (GR, 28:11, Nov. 1976, p. 476–482)

Report on an excursion by the German School Teacher's Organization to various parts of Argentina.

5438 Shackleton, Ernest Henry; R.J. Storey; and R. Johnson. Prospect of the Falkland Islands (RGS/GJ, 143, pt. 1, March 1977, p. 1–13, maps)

Discusses possibilities for diversification of economic endeavors in the Falkland Islands as prospects for the wool industry decline.

5439 Steelstrang, Arturo. Informe de la Comisión Exploradora del Chaco. 2. ed. B.A., EUDEBA, 1977. 102 p., map (Col. Lucha de fronteras con el indio)

Account of the process of settlement in the Chaco following the establishment of governmental administration in 1874 during the presidency of Nicolás Avellaneda. Descriptive physical and human geography of the territory and attempts at colonization are outlined. Reprint of first ed. B.A., 1878.

5440 Strang, Ian J. Ravaged Falkland Islands (GM, 48:5, Feb. 1976, p. 297–304, maps, plates)

An unbalanced ecology has resulted from over-grazing in the Falkland Islands. Islands of the Jason group can no longer support sheep.

5441 Torres, María Irma. Ingeniero Guillermo Nicasio Juárez y los parajes del oeste de Formosa. Xilografías de Osvaldo Dubatti. Gráficos de Cristina Folino. B.A., Ediciones Tiempo de Hoy, 1975. 165 p., maps, plate, tables.

Attempt at reconstructing the settlement genesis of Formosa, Arg., by means of oral tradition analysis as well as other forms of field observation.

5442 Trelles, Rogelio A. Los profetas de la contaminación: nuestros problemas del medio ambiente y algunas medidas para su corrección. B.A., Editorial Crespillo, 1974. 267 p., illus., maps, tables.

Generalized discussion of hygienic problems of the atmosphere, water supplies, and soils of Argentina.

5443 United Nations Environment Programme (UNEP). Environmental quality and river basin development: a model for integrated analysis and planning. Washington, Organization for American States, 1978. 107 p., bibl., tables.

Model river basin planning program developed from a study of the Rio Bermejo basin in northern Argentina during 1970–75. Useful planning exercise for numerous river basin projects being studied in South America.

5444 Vaca Hernández, José María. Inquietudes y realidades antárticas: el continente de Gondwana. B.A., Ediciones Heraldo, 1977. 134 p., bibl., illus., maps, plates, tables.

Brief summary of theories of earth and moon formation, derivation of Gondwanaland, and the Argentine position regarding occupation of Antartica.

BOLIVIA

Bolivia. Comité Nacional del Sesquicentenario de la República. Monografía de Bolivia. See *HLAS 40:3580.*

5445 ———. Ministerio de Planeamiento y Coordinacíon. Instituto Nacional de Estadística. Estadísticas regionales. v. 2, Oruro, Bolivia. La Paz, 1978. 33 p., maps, tables.

Statistical presentation of climatic data, as well as political divisions and population, agricultural production, mining, industry, and transportation. Data from 1968 where available.

5446 ——. ——. ——. Resultados anticipados por muestreo: censo nacional de población y vivienda, 1976. La Paz, 1976. 77 p., map, tables.

Data from the population and housing census of 1976 are presented in table and graph form. Total population by Indian languages (Quechua and Aymara) and Spanish graphed.

5447 ——. ——. **Instituto Nacional de Preinversión.** Creación de nuevos centros urbanos (Creation of new urban centers). La Paz, 1977. 23 p.

The Bolivian Council of Ministers has decreed that the appropriate offices of the nation shall prepare for establishing two new urban centers for 100,000 people each in the Beni River area near the eastern Cordillera, and in the area equidistant between Santa Cruz and Trinidad.

5448 Botelho Gosálvez, Raul. El hombre y el paisaje de Bolivia. La Paz, Bol., Ministerio de Relaciones Exteriores y Culto, Dirección General de Asuntos Culturales, 1975. 283 p., illus. (Biblioteca del Sesquicentenario de la República, 1)

Descriptive passages about different aspects of Bolivian physical and human geography are presented from the writings of foreign visitors such as D'Orbigny, Keyserling, and Frank, and from the writings of Bolivians.

5448a Kashiwazaki, Hiroshi and **Tsuguyoshi Suzuki.** Emigration and re-migration of Okinawans settled in the lowlands of eastern Bolivia in relation to background characteristics of their place of origin (Human Ecology [Plenum, N.Y.] 6, 1977, p. 3–14)

Study of immigrant permanency rates in the Okinawan colonies of eastern Bolivia. Spearman's rank correlation technique is used to understand the type of settlers most likely to remain in the pioneering areas.

5449 Kyllmann, Gerhard. Das leben ein Märchen: ein Deutscher in Bolivien. Hamburg, FRG, Verlag Hanseatischer Merkur, 1975. 116 p., plates (Veröffentlichungen der Wirschaftsgeschichtlichen Forschungsstelle, 38)

Story of family life among foreigners who settled permanently in Bolivia around the turn of the century.

5450 Muñoz Reyes, Jorge. Geografía de Bolivia. La Paz, Academia Nacional de Ciencias de Bolivia, 1977. 478 p., bibl., maps, plates, tables.

New and detailed compendium of physical and human geographical characteristics of the country of Bolivia. Well illustrated by maps and photographs.

5451 Schmidt, Hans. Bolivien. 3. ed. München, FRG, Verlag Volk und Heimat, 1975. 107 p., bibl., fold. maps, plates, tables (Mai's weltführer, 8)

Third ed. of small travel book on Bolivia. Useful bibliography.

5452 Schoop, Wolfgang. Industrialization and regional planning in Bolivia. Amsterdam, Interuniversitair Centrum voor Studie en Documentatie van Latijns Amerika, 1978. 13 p.

Discussion of new law concerning regional development corporations, with special reference to Santa Cruz, and the five-year plan 1976–80. Maps of centers of planned industrial promotion in Bolivia, macrospatial development; bibliography.

Schuurman, F.J. From resource frontier to periphery: agricultural colonization east of the Andes. See item **5698.**

5453 South, Robert B. Coca in Bolivia (AGS/GR, 67/1, Jan. 1977, p. 22–33, map, plates)

National use of coca by chewers is declining in the face of international demand for cocaine.

5454 Stearman, Allyn MacLean. The highland migrant in lowland Bolivia: multiple resource migration and the horizontal archipelago (SAA/HO, 37:2, Summer 1978, p. 181–185)

John Murra's concept of vertical exploitation of environmental resources in the Andean highlands is employed to explain the multiple economic activities practiced by recent highland colonists in the Santa Cruz area of eastern Bolivia. [M. Hiraoka]

5455 Whitaker, Morris D. and **E. Boyd Wennergren.** Investment in access roads and spontaneous colonization: additional evidence from Bolivia (UW/LE, 52:1, Feb. 1976, p. 88–95, bibl., tables)

This paper supports the hypotheses that migrants to new areas exhibit rational economic behavior in marketing produce and that investment returns in newly opened landscapes that have good infrastructure are high compared to those from "directed" colonization projects in general.

CHILE

5456 *Anales de la Universidad del Norte.* Univ. del Norte. No. 9, 1975- . Antofagasta, Chile.

This issue contains an article which discusses distribution of heavy metals in igneous and sedimentary rocks in the north of Chile. Comments about the genesis of rock formations are made from the chemical investigation.

Argentina. Consejo Nacional de Investigaciones Científicas y Técnicas (CONICET) [and] Universidad Nacional de Cuyo. Centro de Estudios Interdisciplinarios de Fronteras Argentinas (CEIFAR). Facilidades del tránsito terrestre entre Argentina y Chile. See item **5399**.

5457 Bähr, Jürgen. Die chilenische Salpeterzone: die Niedergang eines Industriezweiges und seine bevölkerungsgeographischen Konsequenzen (GR, 28:7, Juli 1976, p. 282–289, bibl., map, tables)

Settlement geography in Atacama desert where numerous abandoned saltpeter mining relicts are preserved in the arid climate. Map of ghost-town type and analysis of current depopulation trends included.

5458 ———. Suburbanisierungsprozesse am Rande des Ballungsraumes Gross-Santiago, Chile (*in* Deutscher Geographentag. Verhandlungen. Wiesbaden, FRG, Franz Steiner Verlag, 1978, v. 41, p. 228–248, bibl., maps, tables)

One out of three Chileans lives in the capital city today. In 1930 it was one in every six. The tendency for growth is discussed along with the form of cell additions to the city which characterize expansion. With the first influx of migrants from outside, the existing dwellings in the city are important; only later, when job security is achieved, are the barracks settlements built

and offered as receiving points for new waves of migrants.

5459 ———. **Winfried Golte; and Wilhelm Lauer.** Verstädterung in Chile (IAA, 1, 1975, p. 3–38, bibl., maps, tables)

In 1970 the urban population of Latin America surpassed the rural population for the first time by a measurable amount. This phenomenon is examined for the capital and other regions of Chile. Imbalance is severe with regard to population and economy, as expected.

5460 Baker, M.C.W. Geochronology of upper tertiary volcanic activity in the Andes of north Chile (GV/GR, 66:2, 1977, p. 455–465, bibl., maps, tables)

Ignimbritic eruptions in the North of Chile are identified. If these are relatable to active plate subduction, the author states that age differences would imply that subduction is a sporadic process which affects the descending plate at different times and places.

Barrera V., Humberto. Los antiguos caminos entre Santiago de Chile y Mendoza. See item **5404** and *HLAS 40:3610*.

5461 Börgel O., Reinaldo. La regionalización física del territorio chileno y sus recursos naturales básicos. pt. 1, Geomorfología de Chile. Santiago, Univ. Católica de Chile, Depto. de Geografía Física y Recursos Naturales, Instituto de Geografía, 1975. 76 l. (Serie manuales universitarios científicos y técnicos, 1) (mimeo)

Five geomorphological regions of Chile are named, and the first, the Northern Pampean Desert and Pre-Altiplano Cordilleras, is described.

5462 Borsdorf, Axel. Städtische Strukturen und Entwicklungsprozesse in Lateinamerika (GR, 30:8, Aug. 1978, p. 309–313, bibl., illus., table)

Structural graphics of the socioeconomic processes of urban development based on experiences in Chile.

5463 Chile. Instituto Nacional de Estadísticas. Población: XIV censo de población y III de vivienda, 1970. v. 1, Total país; v. 2, Santiago. Santiago, 1977. 2 v. (157, 163 p.) fold. table, tables.

The National Institute of Statistics has prepared attractively bound summaries of the XIV National Census (1970) data on population in a series of 26 volumes. These deal with the nation as a whole and with the Province of Santiago. Urban and rural populations separated, as usual.

5464 ———. ———. Proyecciones de población por sexo y grupos de edad, 1970–2000: total país y sus regiones; cifras oficiales, junio 1975. Santiago, 1975. 59 p., tables.

Total population of Chile is estimated to reach 15,850,312 by the year 2000. Includes estimates for five-year periods of male and female population for the 12 regions of Chile and the principal metropolitan area.

5465 Chong Díaz, Guillermo. Contribution to the knowledge of the Domeyko Range in the Andes of northern Chile (GV/GR, 66:2, 1977, p. 374–404, bibl., fold map, fold. tables, map, table)

The pre-Andean Domeyko Range of northern Chile is described in this article. A basement of Paleozoic rocks and Triassic volcanics provides the pedestal over which the Andean Basin developed. Marine-continental episodes covered by volcanic, detrital, and saline deposits represent the Cretaceous to Pleistocene. Complex intrusive cycles and tensional phases mark the rest of the development.

5466 Cunill Grau, Pedro. La temprana sementera urbana chilena y los comienzos del deterioro ambiental (*in* Siete estudios: homenaje de la Facultad de Ciencias Humanas a Eugenio Pereira Salas. Santiago, Univ. de Chile, 1975, p. 59–80, maps)

Discussion of effects on the landscape caused by the rise of pre-urban nuclei in the Aconcagua valley and other places. Concludes that arboreal vegetation suffered especially, in what may have become an irreversible process. For historian's comment, see *HLAS 40:3248*.

5467 Expedición a Chile. v. 3. Santiago, Editora Nacional Gabriela Mistral, n.d. 244 p., colored illus., colored plates.

Expedition to southern Chilean Indian settlements and to the coastal desert. Comments on abandonment of indigenous way of life.

5468 Fischer Bernard, Charles L. Notas para una bibliografía sobre la Isla de Pascua: 1923–1972 (BBAA, 37:46, 1974/1975, p. 101–124, bibl.)

Bibliography on Easter Island contains 213 items of international coverage.

5469 Gúzman, Leonardo and **Italo Compodónico.** Mareas rojas en Chile (AI/I, 3:3, mayo/junio 1978, p. 144–149)

Discussion of the red sea phenomenon caused by plankton along the coast of Chile. The so-called *marea roja* can be green, yellow, black, or even white, and can cause health problems for settlers, recreation centers, and fishermen.

5470 Herrera, Pablo. Total utilización de los alimentos marinos en Chile (CEPAC/REP, 8, julio 1974, p. 55–61, tables)

Proposal for manufacturing fish pulp for human consumption in Chile.

5471 Jurgan, Hermann. Zur gliederung der Unterkreide-serien in der Provinz Atacama, Chile (GV/GR, 66:2, 1977, p. 404–434, bibl., maps, plates, tables)

Four marine formations of lower Cretaceous age are described for the Province of Atacama.

5472 Martinić Beros, Mateo. Actividad lobera y ballenera en litorales y aguas de Magallanes y Antártica, 1868–1916 (Revista de Estudios del Pacífico [Centro de Estudios del Pacífico, Valparaíso, Chile] 7, dic. 1973, p. 7–26)

Seal and whale hunting activities in southern South America between 1868 and 1916, as seen from the records of various companies.

5473 ———. Historia del Estrecho de Magallanes. Santiago, Editorial Andrés Bello, 1977. 261 p., bibl., fold. map, illus., maps, plates, tables.

Geographical and historical account of the Strait of Magellan and its role in the settlement of South America and other parts of the world. Cartography and shipping both considered.

5474 Parks, Loren L. Estimation of water production functions for evaluation of irrigation methods: a case study in Chile (AI/I, 3:2, marzo/abril 1978, p. 79–86, tables)

Certain moisture-related production data are quantified and it is shown that use of these figures can bring about sizeable economic gains in farm production. Application in Chile bears out assumptions.

5475 Paskoff, Roland. Aspects géomorphologiques de l'Ile de Pâques (AGF/B, 55:452, avril 1978, p. 147–157, bibl., illus., maps)

Geomorphology of Easter Island is discussed. No permanent stream exists on the island because of porous volcanic rocks. Sea level variations and wave action dominate morphological processes.

5476 Pérez D'A., Ernesto and **Renato Reyes B.** Las trigonias jurásicas de Chile y su valor cronoestratigráfico. Santiago, Instituto de Investigaciones Geológicas [and] Univ. de Chile, Depto. de Biología, Valparaíso, Chile, 1977. 58 p., maps, tables (Boletín, 30)

Trigoniidae (as diagnostic features) in Chilean Jurassic formations.

5477 Porteus, J. Douglas. Urban symbiosis: a study of company-town camp followers in the Atacama Desert (NS, 3:5/6, 1978, p. 210–221, map)

Settlement analysis of the so-called company town and its effects on the surrounding area. Scavenger settlements, *pirquineros* (hand miners who occupy abandoned company mines), food suppliers, and entertainment centers are mapped in an Atacama Desert Community.

5478 Quintanilla, Víctor G. La localización espacial de la contaminación en la Quinta Región (UCIG/IG, 23, 1976, p. 31–55, bibl., maps)

Discussion of principal point sources of contamination between 32–34° south latitude in Middle Chile. Coast, Marga-Marga basin, and south Aconcagua valley are most affected.

5479 Retamal, Marco A. and **L. Alejandro Yañez A.** Análisis cuali y cuantitativo de los fondos sublitorales blandos de la Bahía de Concepción, Chile (Gayana: Zoología [Univ. de Concepción, Instituto de Biología, Chile] 23, 1973, 47 p., illus., maps, tables)

Analysis of 900 specimens of *Crustacea* from the bottom of the Bay of Concepción. Nine different families have been identified.

5480 *Revista Geográfica de Chile.* Terra Australis. Instituto Geográfico Militar.

Comité Nacional de Geografía, Geodesia y Geofísica [and] Instituto Pan-Americano de Geografía e Historia. Sección Nacional. Nos. 23/24, 1972/1973-Santiago.

This issue contains four outstanding articles on physical geography dealing with glaciation, thermal springs, vulcanism, and origin of coastal ranges. Eight articles deal with human geography and methodology. An excellent study of small-scale farming in the Valle de Coyanco (near Concepción) is included.

5481 Rother, Klaus. Eine mittelchilenische Agrarlandschaft im Luftbild: der Sonderkulturbau von Péumo am Río Cachapoal (GEB/E, 106:4, 1975, p. 228–242, bibl., maps, plates)

Recent fruit production in middle Chilean Río Cachapoal Valley. Citrus, avocado, chirimoya and other types are being raised in a variety of ways by differing social strata from the agricultural population. Nicely tied-in with air photography.

5482 Routledge, Scoresby. The mystery of Easter Island: the story of an expedition. 2. ed. N.Y., AMS Press, 1978. 404 p., fold. maps, illus., maps, plates.

Reprint of the 1919 ed. of author's well-known account of her life on the island.

5483 Salinas Messina, Rolando. Desequilibrios en la distribución y en el crecimiento de la población del área metropolitana de Valparaíso (UCIG/IG, 23, 1976, p. 56–75, bibl., maps, tables)

Variations in population between 1952 and 1970 for 11 sectors of Valparaíso and Viña del Mar are analyzed.

5484 Santiago, Jacques. Urbanisation et sous-développement: Santiago du Chile (SGB/COM, 30:118, avril/juin 1977, p. 153–177, maps, tables)

Study of *poblaciones callampas* in Santiago de Chile, and their role since 1940 in the disequilibrium of economic functions within the city (e.g., transportation, social unrest, etc.). Period-growth of the city and its transport routes as well as other features are mapped. Based on 1972 statistics.

5485 Seminario Internacional sobre Preservación del Medio Ambiente Marino, *Santiago, 1975.* Preservación del medio ambiente marino: estudios. Editado por

Francisco Orrego Vicuña. Santiago, Editorial Univ. Técnica del Estado [and] Univ. de Chile, Instituto de Estudios Internacionales, 1976. 353 p., bibl., maps, tables (Col. Estudios internacionales)

Pt. 1 of this book is a discussion of equilibrium of the oceanic ecosystem; pt. 2 deals with petroleum and other factors that break the equilibrium; pt. 3 has case studies from which experience has been gained in dealing with oceanic problems; pts. 4/5 deal with national and international politics relating to marine problems.

5486 Varela, Juan and **Sonia Vogel.** Apéndice I: informe sedimentológico de la muestra men-corral P. (*in* Niemeyer F., Hans *ed*. Homenaje de Dr. Gustavo le Paige, S.J. Santiago, Univ. del Norte, 1976, p. 58–63, tables)

During the postglacial development between 11,000 and 9,500 BP, a supposedly colder period coincides with the genesis of a lacustrine terrace at the Laguna Meñiques, Chile.

Weischet, W. and **E. Schallhorn.** Altsiedelkerne und frühkolonialer Ausbau in der Bewässerungskulturlandschaft Zentralchiles. See *HLAS 40:3257.*

5487 Zeil, Werner. Relaciones entre la tectónica y el volcanismo cenozioco en la parte central de la Cordillera de los Andes (IAA, 1, 1975, p. 183–190, bibl., illus., maps)

Tectonic units in the central part of the Andes (12–24°S) and the relation between vulcanism and tectonics are tied to plate-tectonic theory.

COLOMBIA

5488 Adams, Mike. Trapped in a Colombian sierra (GM, 49:4, Jan. 1977, p. 250–254, map, plates)

Interesting detective work regarding presence of insect and bird species and hypothetical mountain range no longer present in northern South America.

5489 Asociación Colombiana para el Estudio de la Población (ACEP), *Bogotá.* La población de Colombia. Introducción de Ricardo Rueda y Miguel Angél González. Bogotá, 1974. 183 p., maps, tables (Committee for International Coordination of

National Research in Demography [CICRED] series)

Useful analysis of population growth and characteristics in Colombia. Includes mortality, fecundity, migrational, structural and labor categories. Future projections and economic and social implications of rapid growth are presented. Contrasting points of view regarding population growth are dealt with.

5490 Bogotá (city), *Colombia*. **Alcaldía Mayor. Departamento Administrativo de Planeación Distrital.** Desconcentración administrativa alcaldías menores. Prefacio de Patricio Samper Gnecco. Bogotá, 1972. 207 p., maps, tables.

It is predicted that Bogotá will reach a population of five million by 1980. Problems of administrative decentralization are discussed and models attempted.

5491 Brucher, Wolfgang von. Formen und Effizienz Staatlicher Agrarkolonisation in den Östlichen Regenwaldgebieten der Tropischen Andenländer (GZ, 65:1, 1977, p. 3–22, map)

Up-dating of colonization efforts in the eastern Andean region with conclusion that even partially-planned pioneer settlement is better than spontaneous settlement which wreaks havoc on the natural landscape.

Campo, Urbano. La urbanización en Colombia. See item **7274.**

5492 Cediel, Fabio. Investigación geológica en Colombia (ACCEFN/R, 14:55, dic. 1976, p. 49–53, bibl.)

Author traces development of geological investigations in Colombia since beginnings of the German Scientific Mission in the 1930s. Recommends much more attention to field investigation than has occurred recently.

5493 Christie, Keith H. Antioqueño colonization in western Colombia: a reappraisal (HAHR, 58:2, May 1978, p. 260–283, maps, tables)

Complexities of Antioqueño colonization in western Colombia have tended to mask the fact that inequalities of opportunity and of political influence were really present all along, contrary to what has been thought until recently. Thus, colonization of the Antioqueño frontier remains "epic," but not as distinctive as was once thought. Reexamination of similar frontiers may be necessary if this thesis is correct.

5494 Colombia. Departamento Administrativo Nacional de Estadística (DANE). Medellín en cifras: ciudad tricentenaria, 1675–1975. Bogotá, 1976. 312 p., colored map, colored plates, fold. maps, maps, plates, tables.

Statistical summary of economic nature and photographs illustrating historical growth of the city of Medellín on its tricentennial (1975).

5495 ——. ——. La vivienda en Colombia, 1973: resumen nacional por departamentos y 10 ciudades principales; XIV Censo Nacional de Población y III de Vivienda; muestra de avance. Bogotá, 1977. 204 p., tables.

Valuable statistics on population and housing in Colombia from the XIV national census (1973) and the III housing census. Condition of housing, type of housing, abandoned housing, etc., presented for departments, capital cities with over 30,000 dwellings, and the nation.

5496 ——. Instituto Geográfico Agustín Codazzi. Dirección de Estudios Geográficos. Monografía del Departamento de Risaralda. Bogotá, 1972. 102 p., bibl., maps, plates, tables.

Part of the departmental series of the Institute. Physical geography is discussed in the first 50 p., with emphasis on relief and climate, the latter augmented by precipitation and other records. Soils are given short shrift. Human geography stresses historical and urban factors, as well as economic activities. Brief bibliography.

5497 ——. ——. Subdirección Agrológica. Estudio detallado de suelos del Centro de Desarrollo Integrado Las Gaviotas: Comisaría del Vichada. Bogotá, 1974. 283 p., illus., inserted maps, tables (Boletín, 10:3)

Discussion of soil characteristics in a part of the Comisaría del Vichada, eastern Colombia, with land use capabilities. Preliminary to a project involving studies of rural occupational possibilities in the region.

5498 ——. ——. ——. Estudio general de suelos de los municipios de San Martín, Granada y Castilla la Nueva: Departamento del Meta. Bogotá, 1975. 303 p., maps, tables (Boletín, 11:6)

Part of a series of publications on soils of departments in Colombia. Contains detailed information on vegetation, topography, drainage, and climate in addition to soils. Bibliography and glossary both useful.

5499 Colonización. 2. ed. Bogotá, Fundación para la Nueva Democracia [and] Fundación Friedrich Naumann, 1976. 80 p., bibls., table (Enfoques colombianos: temas latinoamericanos. Serie monografías, 2)

This monograph is one in a series and analyzes the prospects for colonization of the tropical parts of Colombia. Careful attention is paid to soil traits and other physical landscape factors which influence settlement possibilities.

Cruz Buenaventura, Jaime. Yacimientos de hierro en Colombia y depósitos de hierro en Sudamérica. See item **5383**.

5500 Ecología: suelos del trópico. Bogotá, Fundación para la Nueva Democracia [and] Fundación Friedrich Naumann, 1976. 155 p., bibls., fold. maps, fold. tables, maps, tables (Enfoques colombianos: temas latinoamericanos. Serie monografías, 8)

This monograph has three items dealing with soils of the tropics: 1) a preliminary attempt at classification of humid lowland soils; 2) the influence of boron on the growth of conifers; and 3) ecological bases for soil use in the tropics.

5501 Eidt, Robert C. Detection and examination of anthrosols by phosphate analysis (AAAS/S, 197, 1977, p. 1327–1333)

Chemical analysis of soils showing relationship between types of phosphate and land-use varieties. Example from pre-columbian Chibcha settlement near Bogotá.

Gauhan, Timothy O'Dea. Housing and the urban poor: the case of Bogotá, Colombia. See item **7282**.

5502 Guhl, Ernesto. Colombia: bosquejo de su geografía tropical. t. 2. Bogotá, Instituto Colombiano de Cultura, Subdirección de Comunicaciones Culturales, 1976. 452 p., fold. maps, fold. tables, plates, tables (Biblioteca básica colombiana, 11)

This excellent portrayal of the status of integration between the physical and human landscapes of Colombia contains two major subdivisions: the population of Colombia, and the five major geographical regions of the country. The last parts of the book deal with particular aspects of the economic life of Colombia and its position in Latin America.

5503 ———. Estudios geográficos. Bogotá, Instituto Colombiano de Economía y Cultura (ICEC), 1972. 152 p., map, tables (Temas colombianos, 1)

Thoughtful essays by the dean of Colombian geographers which deal with a large variety of topics (e.g., theory and function of geography; the concept of mankind and its dominion of space; geo-ecology of the tropical mountains of the Americas and of the páramos of Bogotá; population problems of Colombia; a critique of a school atlas of Colombia; etc.).

Hernández de Caldas, Angela and **Fabiola Bohórquez de Briceño.** Bibliografía sobre medio ambiente. See item **5266.**

5504 Hettner, Alfred. Viajes por los Andes colombianos: 1882–1884. Primera versión castellana del alemán de Heinrich Henk. Prólogo de Ernesto Guhl. Bogotá, Banco de la República, 1976. 415 p., plate (Archivo de la economía nacional, 37)

In 1882 Hettner was invited to accompany the British ambassador to Bogotá. There followed a period of two years of excursions and investigations of both physical and human geographical characteristics of Colombia. This new edition includes Hettner's first impressions and analyses of his journeys and will attract more readers of this important pioneer of geographical methodology. Originally published in Stuttgart and entitled *Reisen in den columbianischen Anden,* the work presents a geography of Colombia's heartland which complements nicely author's other work on the Cordillera of Bogotá.

5505 Howarth, Stephen. Atrato canal revealed (GM, 49:7, April 1977, p. 420–423, map, plates, table)

Account of the rediscovery of the Raspadura canal linking Atlantic and Pacific oceans more than a century prior to the construction of the Panama Canal.

5506 Instituto de Estudios Colombianos (IEC), *Bogotá.* Los llanos orientales de Colombia: estudio descriptivo. Bogotá, 1975. 102 l., fold. map, maps, tables.

Concerns development planning in the Colombian *llanos* where one fourth of the country's land is inhabited by only one percent of its people. Study includes statistical analysis of economic factors such as agriculture, cattle-raising, transportation, marketing, etc. Discusses transportation and land tenure problems as well as lack of political impulse to settle the region. Introductory section includes resumé of physical geography and brief description of soils which do not seem to be a deterrent to productive use of land.

Kirby, John. Agricultural land use and the settlement of Amazonia. See item **5650.**

5507 Leal Correa, Tobías. Dabeiba de 1900 a 1910: antecedentes e historia de su fundación, conceptos, fundadores, creadores de su espiritualidad, propulsores de su riqueza y progreso, etc. pt. 1. Medellín, Colombia, Editorial Universo, 1975. 130 p., plates, tables.

Popularized account of the evolution of the city of Dabeiba, Colombia, with special attention to early residents.

5508 Londoño Paredes, Julio. Cuestiones de límites de Colombia. Bogotá?, Editorial Retina, 1976? 111 p., facsim., fold. maps (Col. Breviarios colombianos, 4)

Historical summary of the formation of boundaries with detailed maps. No bibliography.

5509 Martínez, Carlos. Bogotá: sinopsis sobre su evolución urbana. v. 1, 1536–1900. Bogotá, Escala Fondo Editorial, 1976. 162 p., bibl., fold. plate, illus., maps, plates, tables (Col. Historia: Bogotá, 2)

This is a detailed, historical-geographical summary with citations from the colonial and more modern literature describing the evolution of the city of Bogotá up to the turn of the present century. Maps are especially useful, as are data on development of barrios.

5510 Mohr, Bernhard. Bodennutzung, Ernährungsprobleme und Bevölkerungsdruck in Minifundienregionen der Ostkordillere Kolumbiens (*in* Deutscher Geographentag: Verhandlungen. Wiesbaden,

FRG, Franz Steiner Verlag, 1978, v. 41, p. 299–310, bibl., map, tables)

Minifundia agriculture examined from three places in the Colombian Andes: the páramo, tierra fría, and tierra templada. Recommendations for more mixed agriculture and better transportation facilities.

5511 Patiño, Aníbal E. Impacto ecológico: estudio sobre un caso en Colombia (III/ AI, 38:1, enero/marzo 1978, p. 151–164, table)

Contamination of the landscape by a mining enterprise in the Department of Cauca, Colombia, is examined. Water, air, soil, and plant life changes are assessed. Low pH in the area (two-to-three) is harmful to natural and human life and a plea is made for control.

5512 Pérez Sanín, Enrique. Perfil de Colombia. Bogotá, Asociación Colombiana para el Estudio de la Población (ACEP), 1976. 24 p., bibl., map, tables.

Informative booklet about current problems of demography in Colombia. Its urban population has spiraled from 39 percent in 1951 to 61 percent in 1975, a change which represents a complete reversal of conditions since 1950. Since more than half the rural families have less than three hectares of land, the attractions of city life is great. This has led to internal population movements that have been a major characteristic of human geography for many years. Author criticizes government's failure to alleviate the situation by creating new jobs or an adequate infrastructure in newly opened lands.

5513 Planificación de la Salud de Antioquia (PLANSAN), *Medellín, Colombia.* La población en Antioquia. v. 1, Evolución. v. 2, Proyecciones y tablas de vida. Medellín, Colombia, 1974/1975. 2 v. (71, 73 p.) bibls., tables (Publicación PLANSAN, 5/6)

This two-volume study of population in Antioquia encompasses a historical statement of population growth from the colonial period to present, and analysis of growth, migration, and distribution of population in the Department.

5514 Ramírez, J.E. and L.T. Aldrich *eds.* La transición océano-continente en el suroeste de Colombia (The ocean-continent

transition in SW-Colombia). Bogotá, Univ. Javeriana, Instituto Geofísico, 1977. 313 p., bibls., maps, plates, tables.

Consists of 12 articles on geology and geophysics of southwest Colombia. Sample topics: plate tectonics, mantle velocities, and refraction observations.

5515 Reunión de Trabajo sobre Políticas de Migración y Distribución de la Población en América Latina, *I, Sochagota, Colombia, 1973.* Colombia: distribución espacial de la población. Edición de Ramiro Cardona Gutiérrez. Bogotá, Corporación Centro Regional de Población (CCRP), 1976. 243 p., bibl., maps, tables.

Problems of rural-urban migration in Colombia continue to plague the country's economy and dim hopes for social improvement. This discussion centers around overall phenomena associated with overpopulation of the cities, such as the role of intermediary cities, level of education, and causes of migratory problems.

5516 Revista Geográfica. Univ. de Los Andes, Facultad de Ciencias Forestales, Instituto de Geografía y servación. Vol. 14, No. 1/2, enero/dic. 1973–. Mérida, Colombia.

This issue contains five articles treating general rural services and settlements, growth of population in Sogamoso, Colombia, and socioeconomic characteristics of urbanization of Venezuela.

5517 Salcedo Collante, Humberto. La verdad sobre la vía alterna al llano. Bogotá, Instituto Geográfico Agustín Codazzi, 1977. 71 p., facsims., maps, plates, tables.

Political discussion conducted in the Colombian Senate about the merits of marginal highway planning east of the Andes with some economic data of value to investigators.

5518 Sánchez de Sánchez, Ofelia. Bibliografía anotada de las tesis sobre ingeniería forestal presentadas en la Universidad Distrital Francisco José de Caldas. Prefacio de Angelia Hernández de Caldas. Bogotá, Corporación Nacional de Investigación y Fomento Forestal (CONIF), 1976. 66 p. (Serie de documentación, 1)

Bibliography of forestry engineering containing 144 items.

5519 Santa Marta, 1525–1975. Bogotá, Banco de la República, 1976? 1 v. (Unpaged) facsim., plates.

The first book of Fray Pedro de Aguado is reproduced here as worthy of reconsideration. Some of the facts presented are not in accord with those of better-known chroniclers.

5520 Schrimpff, Ernst. Räumliche Verteilung von Schwermetallniederschlägen, angezeigt durch Epiphyten im Cauca-Tal/Kolumbien - Zur Schwermetallbelastung eines tropischen Raumes (*in* Deutscher Geographentag: Verhandlungen. Wiesbaden, FRG, Franz Steiner Verlag, 1978, v. 41, p. 567)

Investigation of heavy metal concentration in the Cauca Valley, Colombia made by examination of Tillandsia accumulation. The highest values occur in the area of the Cali-Yumbo industrial region; the lowest in the north and south extremes of the Cauca Basin.

5521 Seminario sobre el Potencial para la Producción de Ganado de Carne en América Tropical, *Cali, Colombia, 1974.* El potencial para la producción de ganado de carne en América tropical. Cali, Colombia, Centro Internacional de Agricultura Tropical (CIAT), 1975. 307 p., bibls., tables.

Limitations of beef production and approaches for improvement are discussed by 20 participants and seven moderators in an effort to deal with the tropics of America. Attempt made to establish exchange of ideas by means of seminar technique and publication of results. Excellent bibliography.

5522 Simon, Arthur M.L. Marco teórico-práctico sobre la problemática del manejo ambiental en Colombia. Bogotá, Oficina de Investigaciones Socioeconómicas y Legales (OFISEL), 1974. 56 l., bibl., tables (Documentos, 3)

Author criticizes tendency to transfer methods of environmental management from one area to another that is different. He cites as an example how the land use classification system devised by the US Soil Conservation Service has been applied in Colombia where large regions have been classified as Class IV and VII. And yet these are precisely the regions that produce the largest share of Colombia's coffee. Study

presents a model which emphasizes the region as the object of study and in which the concept of region relates to human settlements.

5523 Sociedad Geográfica de Colombia, *Bogotá.* Indice por autores del *Boletín de la Sociedad Geográfica de Colombia* del No. 1 al No. 100: 1903–1973. Bogotá, Univ. de Bogotá Jorge Tadeo Lozano, 1974. 106 p.

Index of authors for the first 70 years of the *Boletín.*

5524 Velandia, Roberto. Ciudades históricas de Cundinamarca. v. 1, Funza, Mosquera, Madrid, Bojacá, Facatativá, Albán, Sasaima, Villeta, Utica, Guaduas; v. 2, Chía, Cota, Tenjo, Tabio, Cajicá, Zipaquirá, Nemocón, Cogua, Tausa, Sutatausa, Ubaté, Cucunubá, Lenguazaque, Guachetá, Fúquene, Susa, Simijaca; v. 3, Sopó, Tocancipá, Gachancipá; Suesca, Chocontá, Villapinzón, Sesquilé, Guatavita, Guasca, La Calera. Bogotá, Corporación de Turismo de Cundinamarca [and] Publicaciones Imprenta Departamental Antonio Nariño, 1972/1973. 3 v. (22, 35, 38 p.) plates.

Tourist guide to cities of historical interest in Colombia as listed.

5525 Williams, Lynden S. and **Ernst C. Griffin.** Rural and small town depopulation in Colombia (AGS/GR, 68:11, Jan. 1978, p. 13–30, maps, tables)

In spite of high birth rates, rural depopulation portends deep economic trouble in the major population zones of Colombia. Moreover, authors think that rural depopulation phenomenon constitutes a brain drain.

ECUADOR

Acosta Solís, Misael. Conferencias fitogeográficas. See item **5378**.

———. Ecología y fitoecología. See item **5379**.

———. Investigadores de la geografía y la naturaleza de América tropical: viajeros cronistas e investigadores con especial referencia al Ecuador. See item **5380**.

5527 Ballard, Robert D. Notes on a major oceanographic find (OCEANUS, 20:3,

Summer 1977, p. 35–44, illus., map, plates)
Describes discovery of marine life at depths of 2,700 m. in water warmed by molten lava in Galapagos rift.

5528 Blandín Landívar, Carlos. El clima y su características en el Ecuador. Quito, Instituto Panamericano de Geografía e Historia, 1976. 84 p., bibl., illus., tables (Biblioteca Ecuador)
Climatic types according to Koeppen and discussion of tropical climate and weather in Ecuador. Includes numerous rainfall and temperature charts for representative places.

5529 Boltovskoy, Esteban and **Elena Gualancañay.** Foraminíferos bentónicos actuales de Ecuador. v. 1, Provincia Esmeraldas. Guayaquil, Ecua., Instituto Oceanográfico de la Armada, 1975. 56 p., bibl., map, plates, tables.
Various species of foramanifera have been found offshore from Ecuador which have not been located elsewhere in South American waters.

5530 Deler, Jean Paul. El espacio nacional ecuatoriano: un modelo estructura geográfica (UC/A, 31:3/4, julio/dic. 1975, p. 89–121, bibl., illus.)
Geopolitical view of centrifugal forces in the national space of Ecuador.

5531 Germán Pascal, Remigio. Relación histórica del terremoto del 16 de agosto de 1868 en Imbabura e intervención heroica de García Moreno como Jefe Civil y Militar de la provincia. Ibarra, Ecua., Imprenta Municipal, 1972? 34 p., illus., plates.
Record of a famous earthquake in Ecuador (1868). National heroic action extolled.

Kirby, John. Agricultural land use and the settlement of Amazonia. See item **5650.**

5532 Larrea, Carlos Manuel. Cartografía ecuatoriana de los siglos XVI, XVII y XVIII. Quito, Ediciones Corporación de Estudios y Publicaciones (CEP), 1977. 177 p., maps.
Description of maps from the time of Waldseemüller to the Real Audiencia de Quito. Useful comments on origins and locations of maps, especially those pertaining to Ecuador.

5533 Lewin, Roger. Galápagos: the rise of optimism (NSCI, 79:1113, 27 July 1978, p. 261–263, plates)
Feral animals and growing tourism threaten the ecological balance in the archipelago. Cautious optimism resulting from a new program is reported.

5534 ———. Gentle giants of the Galapagos (NSCI, 79:1114, 3 Aug. 1978, p. 334–336, map, plates)
A new program for saving the giant tortoises of the Galápagos from extinction is discussed.

5535 Revista Geográfica. Instituto Panamericano de Geografía e Historia. Comisión de Geografía. No. 84, 1976- México.
This issue has 10 articles dealing with various aspects of geographical interest in Ecuador. Rural emigration, colonization, urban growth, and land use are representative topics.

5536 Snailham, Richard. The Sangay tragedy (GM, 50:2, Nov. 1977, p. 129–134, colored plates, map, plates)
The British Vulcan expedition to Sangay terminated in tragedy when the volcano erupted. Ecuadorian Sangay is a basic andesite which erupts more easily than the andesite of the central Andes.

5537 Thomsen, Moritz. The farm on the River of Emeralds. Boston, Mass., Houghton Mifflin, 1978. 329 p.
First-hand account of an American who returned to Ecuador's Rio Esmeraldas area to farm in the selva after a stint in the Peace Corps. Filled with authentic interpretations of the life of the poor.

5538 Wolf, Teodoro. Geografía y geología del Ecuador. Quito, Editorial Casa de la Cultura Ecuatoriana, 1975. 798 p., fold. maps, illus., plates, tables.
This new edition of Wolf's classic work is accompanied by various statements outlining the life of this illustrious 19th-century scientist, and by a lengthy supplement which brings the geomorphology, climatology, natural vegetation, mineralogical, and human aspects of Wolf's work up to date.

5539 Zuvekas, Clarence, Jr. Agrarian reform in Ecuador's Guayas River Basin (UW/LE, 52:3, August 1976, p. 314–329, bibl., tables)

A land-scale guaranty system for assisting cooperatives in the Guayas River Basin has not resulted in success, although it may have stimulated government sponsorship of a traditional agrarian reform program in the rice producing area.

GUYANA

5540 Guyana. Information Services. A portrait of Guyana. Photographs by Jonathan C. Wilins and others. Georgetown, Design & Graphics, 1976? 128 p., colored plates, maps, tables.

Pictorial presentation of tourist information about Guyana in honor of the 10th anniversary of independence.

5541 Vining, James W. Presettlement planning in Guyana (AGS/GR, 67:4, Oct. 1977, p. 469–480, maps, tables)

Discusses insufficient preplanning, overly large holding sizes since the 1950s, failure of dispersed settlement form, and other problems, all of which suggest what is needed in future considerations for economic success of land opening.

PARAGUAY

5542 Krier, Hubert and Gerhard Ponemunski. Paraguay: Herzland Südamerikas, Reiseführer mit Landeskunde. 2. ed. München, FRG, Volk und Heimat, 1977. 78 p., bibl., fold. map, plates, tables (Mai's weltfürer, 11)

Brief handbook for travellers in Paraguay. Statistics somewhat carelessly employed.

5543 Samaniego, Marcial. El Chaco paraguayo: conferencia pronunciada a los alumnos del Colegio Nacional de Guerra. Asunción, Imprenta Militar, 1976. 95 p., maps, tables.

Resumé of economic and settlement characteristics of the Paraguayan Chaco with emphasis on transportation facilities.

PERU

5544 Amazonia peruana. Lima, Editorial Ioppe, 1972. 160 p., fold. plates, maps, plates (Documental del Perú, 1. El reto geográfico y el hombre peruano, 2. Serie roja, 2)

Vol. 1 of a monographic series devoted to Peruvian geography. This volume on the Amazonian region of Peru contains economic information on the area's fishing, mining, agriculture and tourism. Color photographs.

5545 Capdevila, Raymond; François Mégard; Jorge Paredes; and Philippe Vidal. La batholite de San Ramón, Cordillère Orientale du Peróu central (GV/GR, 66:2, 1977, p. 434–446, bibl., map, tables)

The batholith found in the central region of the eastern cordillera of Peru is described. Coarse-grained to porphyritic granite extends over 90 km in this area. A Late Permian to Early Triassic age is assigned.

5546 Cardich, A.; L. Cardich; and D. Rank. Datierung der jungpleistozänen Vereisung Lauricocha in den peruanischen Anden (GV/GR, 66:2, 1977, p. 446–454, bibl., map, plates)

Old glacial advances stemming from the last Pleistocene glaciation are identified in the Raura mountain range of central Peru. Radiocarbon dating verifies the previously assumed age and identifies an interstadial period called the Aguamiro. Earlier glaciation was more extensive than the later episodes.

5547 Graig, Alan K. Placer gold in eastern Peru: the great strike of 1942 (PAIGH/G, 79, dic. 1973, p. 117–128, bibl., maps, table)

The gold rush of 1942 in eastern Peru resulted in 5,000 settlers arriving in the area. Difficulties of transport, removing alluvial overburden heavy with forest vegetation, and short-lived deposits brought downfall of settlement in the zone. However, ease for obtaining mining claims in Peru and increased world price of gold may bring about further attempts.

5548 Hastenrath, Stefan. Observations on soil frost phenomena in the Peruvian Andes (ZG, 21:3, Sept. 1977, p. 357–362, bibl., map, plates)

Rare observation of vegetated stone

stripe patterns at 4680 m. on south-facing slopes with conclusion that the formations may represent a change in climatic conditions.

5549 Jones, David R.W. Structure and infrastructural change in the Upper Amazon: their effects on international trade prospects (NS, 2:3/4, 1977, p. 39–50)

Factors like labor, credit, transportation, government policies, and market structure that influence economic changes in the Upper Amazon are identified. The interpretation is based primarily on data acquired in eastern Peru. [M. Hiraoka]

5550 Morisset, Jean. Puno: a geography of social and development ambivalence (NS, 2:3/4, 1977, p. 21–38)

Puno has become the center of attention for development studies of the Peruvian altiplano region. Poverty and complex Indian social strata demand solution to worsening conditions. Summary of aid programs and useful bibliography.

5551 Organization of American States. Instituto Panamericano de Geografía e Historia. Sección Nacional del Perú. Informe: 1973–1975. México, 1975? 29 p.

Notes on possible sources of information concerning economic development in Peru. Mostly obscure and poorly documented references.

5552 Orlove, Benjamin S. Integration through production: the use of zonation in Espinar (AAA/AE, 4:1, Feb. 1977, p. 84–101, bibl., maps)

Excessive attention has been paid to the distribution mechanisms in the study of human societies by ecological and economic anthropologists. This has been accomplished primarily by neglecting the production systems. By applying Murra's "verticality model" to Espinar, a community in the Southern part of the Dept. of Cuzco, Peru, the author attempts to demonstrate the central role of production as an integrative element of social organization. [M. Hiraoka]

5553 Ortiz, P. Dionisio. Las montañas del Apurimac, Mantaro y Ene. t. 2. Lima, Imprenta Editorial San Antonio, 1976. 778 p., maps, plates, tables.

Vol. 1 of this study (see *HLAS 39:5592*) consisted of economic data, explo-

ration, colonization, and government in the Montaña region. Vol. 2 is a continuation which includes an account of missionary work by the Franciscans in the region.

5554 Ponce de León, Jorge; José María de Romaña; Clive D. Page; and Tulio Cusmán eds. Peru, challenge and response: portrait of a resurgent nation. Lima, Publicaciones Continente, 1971. 188 p., plates, tables.

Popularized geography of Peru with outstanding color photography.

5555 Pozuzo: un paraíso en los Andes peruanos (MH, 353, agosto 1977, p. 28–32, plates)

Recounting and updating of settlement founded by German-speaking people during the last century in eastern Peru. Thirteen families remain which have not intermarried.

5556 San Roman, Jesús V. Pautas de asentamiento en la selva (Amazonia Peruana [Centro Amazónico de Antropología y Aplicación Práctica, Lima] 1:2, junio 1977, p. 29–52, bibl., illus., map)

Schuurman, F.J. From resource frontier to periphery: agricultural colonization east of the Andes. See item **5393a**.

5557 Skeldon, Ronald. The evolution of migration patterns during urbanization in Peru (AGS/GR, 67:4, Oct. 1977, p. 394–411, maps, tables)

Author argues that temporal and spatial patterns combine to form a definite structure of migration which varies predictably over space and time in conjunction with development of urbanism.

Vargas Haya, Héctor. Amazonia: ¿realidad o mito? See item **5713**.

Vietmeyer, Noel D. Incredible odyssey of a visionary Victorian peddler. See item **5396**.

5558 Williams, Lynden S. Land use intensity and farm size in highland Cuzco, Peru (JDA, 11:2, Jan. 1977, p. 185–204, maps, tables)

The explanation that culture traits are to blame for the dichotomy between large estates and intensively used subsistence plots masks the fact that land-use intensity varies throughout the range of farm sizes.

Relationships between land-use intensity and farm size are investigated.

URUGUAY

5559 Assef, Alberto E. Un proyecto en el alto Uruguay (IAEERI/E, 41/42, mayo/agosto 1976, p. 38–49, maps)
Geopolitical considerations make it advantageous for Uruguay to approve a proposed canal linking the Ibicui and Jacui rivers for a transport system across southern Brazil.

5560 Griffin, Ernst Clark. Causal factors influencing agricultural land use patterns in Uruguay (PAIGH/G, 80, junio 1974, p. 13–33, bibl., maps, tables)
In Uruguay soil fertility and market attraction are the dominant factors which explain the nation's agricultural structure. Other influential elements are climate, topography, transport, population, and taxation policies.

5561 Prost, Gérard. Structures agraires en Uruguay: l'example du Départment d'Artigas (SGB/COM, 30:118, avril/juin 1977, p. 178–192, maps, tables)
Status of land tenure in northern Uruguay is examined. It is not uncommon for one family to have several parcels of land in various areas, nor is it unusual for wealthy landowners to graze cattle on good soils.

Schinca, Milton A. Boulevar Sarandí: 250 años de Montevideo: anécdotas, gentes, sucesos. See *HLAS 40:3950.*

5562 Suárez Recaredo, Lebrato. La Coronilla: un gran puerto oceánico para el área platense (IAEERI/E, 42, sept./oct. 1976, p. 20–33)
Article which confirms that the dream of a deep water oceanic port at La Coronilla (316 km. from Montevideo) is still alive.

VENEZUELA

5563 Aguilera, Jesús Antonio. Las fronteras de Venezuela. Prólogo de María Azócar Silva. Caracas, Gráficas Continente, 1976. 105 p., bibl., maps.
Geopolitical considerations regarding the borders of Venezuela. Useful summary of the development of border problems with Guayana and the Dutch Antilles.

5564 Anduze, Pablo J. Bajo el signo de Mawari. Introducción de Martín Vegas. Caracas, Imprenta Nacional, n.d. 415 p., facsims., maps, plates.
Travel account of a 95-day journey into Amazonia for purposes of assessing Indian conditions. Detailed and captivating field notes with a series of photographs.

5565 Badari, V.S. Disaggregation of urban populations into modern and traditional categories: a methodological note and application of Venezuela (IASI/E, 30:114, julio 1976, p. 30–49, bibl., tables)
A methodology for disaggregation of the urban population into modern and traditional groups is proposed. As applied to Venezuela, the method indicates that about 26 percent of the urban male labor force is modern. Fertility differences exist between the modern and traditional groups.

5566 Badillo, Víctor M. and **Ludwig Schnee.** Clave de las familias de plantas superiores de Venezuela. Confeccionada sobre el original de Thonner. 5. ed. Maracay, Univ. Central de Venezuela, Facultad de Agronomía, 1972. 246 p. (Alcance, 18)
Key to the classification of flowering plants in Venezuela with glossary and index.

5567 Boscan F., Luis A.; Fausto Capote F.; and José Farías. Contaminación salina del Lago de Maracaibo: efectos en la calidad y aplicación de sus aguas (Boletín del Centro de Investigaciones Biológicas [Univ. del Zulia, Maracaibo, Ven.] 9, 1973, p. 1–37, bibl., map, tables)
Surface contamination of the Lago de Maracaibo is considered serious enough to call for immediate action to correct existing conditions.

5568 Conaway, Mary Ellen. Circular migration in Venezuelan frontier areas (ICEM/IM, 15:1, 1977, p. 35–42, bibl.)
Circular migration is seen as a pattern of recurrent movement at intervals during the lifetime of a migrant in fringe areas. Short-term and long term migrations are identified for the Orinoco River area.

5569 Cortina, Alfredo. Caracas: la ciudad que se nos fué. 3. ed. Caracas, Editorial Roble, 1976. 201 p., illus.

Impressions of Caracas at the turn of the century are given in fictitious accounts to recreate the atmosphere of former times. Useful as a model of one type of perception by which some traces of modern life can be explained. See also item **5577**.

Cunill Grau, Pedro. Cambios en el paisaje geográfico venezolano en la época de la emancipación. See item **3350**.

5570 Demyk, Noëlle. Aspects régionaux de l'agriculture venezuelienne (FDD/NED [Problèmes d'Amérique Latine, 47] 4457, fev. 1978, p. 103–110, map)
In 1971 some 21 percent of the active galley 44

population was engaged in agriculture in Venezuela. Nearly half the land farmed was in small holdings less than five hectares (1961). Regional problems are outlined and discussed.

5571 Eidt, Robert C. Agrarian reform and the growth of new rural settlements in Venezuela (UBGI/E, 29:2, June 1975, p. 118–133, maps)
Writer surveys a number of major land use reform programs from earlier times, and shows why all fell short of original hopes. He then turns to current land reform policy and demonstrates that there has been, within the past 25 years, a major turnaround in traditional Latin American social, economic and agricultural patterns, as well as some notable progress toward resolution of the migration to cities so common elsewhere. [P.B. Taylor, Jr.]

5572 Grabert, Hellmut. Die Insalberg-Landschrift des Roraima in Venezolanisch-Guyana (GEB/E, 107:1, 1976, p. 57–69, bibl., map, plates)
The Roraima mountains in Venezuela have been scientifically investigated only since the 1950s. This addition to geomorphological explanation is useful for an overview of facts and literature.

5573 Jones, Richard C. Myth maps and migration in Venezuela (CU/EG, 54:1, Jan. 1978, p. 75–91, illus., tables)
Popular conception of economic potential in different regions of Venezuela do not coincide with the facts. It may be that misperceptions can be attributed to newspaper images. Such research helps explain in

part the rural-urban migration phenomenon, according to the author.

5574 León A., Rafael de and **Alberto J. Rodríguez Díaz.** El Orinoco aprovechado y recorrido. Presentación de Argenis Gamboa and Arnoldo José Gabaldón. Caracas, Ministerio de Obras Públicas (MOP) [and] Corporación Venezolana de Guayana (CVG), 1976. 214 p., bibl., illus., maps, plates, tables.
Past, present, and future developments in the Orinoco Delta region are discussed in a continental and local context in semi-popularized fashion.

5575 Memoria. Sociedad de Ciencias Naturales La Salle. t. 35, no. 101, mayo/agosto 1975–. Caracas.
This issue has two articles of interest to geographers and other geoscientists. The first contains hydrological information with climatic and chemical data on the Laguna de la Restinga (Margarita Island), the second is an analysis from field studies of the dry season effects on the biology of caimanes. Also includes practical information on savanna conditions of value to earth scientists.

5576 Nweihed, Kaldone G. La delimitación marítima al noroeste del Golfo de Venezuela. Caracas, Univ. Simón Bolívar, Instituto de Tecnología y Ciencias Marinas (INTECMAR), 1975. 124 p., bibl., maps.
Historical and analytical discussion of boundary problems between Venezuela and Colombia offshore from the Gulf of Venezuela. Colombia suspended negotiations in 1973.

5577 Pinedo N., Angel G. Memorias de un viajero. Caracas, Gráficas Armitano, 1976. 185 p., illus., plates.
Well-written series of accounts of life in Caracas around the turn of the century. Facilitates documentation of change and supplies understanding of evolution of urban structure. See also item **5569**.

Les problèmes agraires au Venezuela. See item **7631**.

5578 Ruddle, Kenneth and **Ray Chesterfield.** Education for traditional food procurement in the Orinoco Delta. Berkeley, Univ. of California Press, 1977. 172 p., bibl., maps, plates, tables (Ibero-americana, 53)
Well-done study of the livelihood pat-

terns of family life on the Island of Guara in the Orinoco Delta, Ven. Detailed explanations of preparation of children for various tasks in life, including farming, fishing, animal husbandry, and marketing. Intimate man-land relationships derived from field study.

5579 Salazar-Quijada, Adolfo. La toponimía en Venezuela. Caracas, Univ. Central de Venezuela, 1975. 313 p., bibl., maps, tables.

Consists of definition, categories, and symbolization of names discussed in methodological form. Also reports on toponimic studies underway in Latin America, with emphasis on Venezuela.

5580 Schauensee, Rodolphe Meyer de. A guide to the birds of Venezuela. Foreword by Ruth Patrick. Princeton, N.J., Princeton Univ. Press, 1978. 424 p., bibl., illus., maps, plates.

The introduction to this reference manual describes briefly the physical conditions in Venezuela. Color drawings of birds and English-Spanish names make it a useful field guide.

5581 Schubert, Carlos. Evidence of former glaciation in the Sierra de Perijá, western Venezuela (UBGI/E, 30:3, Sept. 1976, p. 222–224, bibl., map)

First report on glaciation in the Sierra de Perijá indicates morainic and other features similar to those in the Sierra de Mérida.

5582 ———. Investigaciones geológicas en los Andes de Venezuela (IAA, 3:3, 1977, p. 295–309, bibl., map, tables)

Discussion of types of geologic analysis in Venezuelan Andes and lengthy bibliography.

5583 ———. Neotectonic research in Venezuela: objectives and results (AI/I, 1:3,

sept./oct. 1976, p. 159–169, bibl., maps)

Radio carbon and thorium/uranium dating applied to Venezuela show that the coast is rising at the rate of 0.03 to 0.06 cm/year.

5584 Terra. Univ. Central de Venezuela, Facultad de Humanidades y Educación, Area de Geografía. Año 2, No. 3, sept./oct. 1978- . Caracas.

Issue contains articles about Venezuela by M.A. Vila (territorial organization), and C. Muñoz and G. Wettstein (agricultural changes in the Venezuelan Andes).

5585 Van Niekerk, Arnold E. La urbanización en Venezuela (IAA, 2:4, 1976, p. 319–337, bibl., tables)

The problem of marginal population in an urban environment does not increase with population increase in the city per se, but is much more complex. This article establishes a ranking of cities according to level of development and socio-urban traits.

5586 Venezuela. Ministerio de Fomento. Dirección General de Estadística y Censos Nacionales (DGECN). Proyección de la población de Venezuela. t. 1, Total nacional: por edad, sexo, urbano, rural, entidades federales y fuerza de trabajo. Presentación de Jorge García Duque. Caracas, 1975. 187 p., tables.

General population projections to the year 2000 by characteristics and by states.

5587 Zawiska, Leszek M. Colonización agrícola en Venezuela (FJB/BH, 37, enero 1975, p. 1–47, tables)

Brief resumé of attempts at colonization of rural areas in Venezuela since time of the conquest.

BRAZIL

MARIO HIRAOKA, *Visiting Researcher, Special Research Project on Latin America, University of Tsukuba, Ibaraki, Japan*

IN *HLAS 39* WE NOTED THAT CERTAIN THEMES dominated much of the literature. The trend continues in this volume with many studies on unchecked urbanization, attendant environmental problems, and development activities in the

Amazon region. The rapid urbanization and resulting social and economic problems are the subject of study by social scientists, including geographers. Attention has been paid to aspects like mass transport (item **5596**), population projections and regional changes (items **5606–5607, 5616** and **5677**), and changing urban patterns (items **5620, 5623, 5658,** and **5705**) in large metropolises such as São Paulo, Rio, and Belo Horizonte. Population growth and concentration in a few areas as well as the phenomenal industrial expansion of Brazil are perceived as the causes of deteriorating environments which threaten the quality of life in the country. Concurrently, information on environmental conservation attempts carried out in the developed countries have been disseminated and an environmental ethic appears to be taking root in Brazil. This is reflected in the proliferation of journals and books that emphasize environmental improvement (items **5635, 5638, 5661** and **5708**).

The preference of scholars for certain themes also applies to regions, two of which take precedence as subjects of study: the vast rain-forest area of sparsely occupied Amazonia, and the climatically marginal, relatively over-populated, and poverty-stricken Northeast.

Literature on Amazonia can be divided broadly into two categories: governmental ones which tend to promote the development potentials of the region (items **5591, 5605, 5684, 5690** and **5718**), and the scientific community that tends to disfavor the rapid and uncontrolled opening of the hylaea (items **5601, 5610, 5626, 5636, 5641, 5650, 5652, 5653–5654, 5674, 5702, 5712** and **5716**). Major concerns in the Northeast are the rural problems created by the polarization of holdings somewhat attenuated by the demographic growth in the *zona da mata*, and the plight of farmers in the drought-stricken *sertão* (items **5592, 5613, 5655, 5666, 5672, 5677** and **5720**).

There are certain works which deserve special mention among those selected for this volume: The Fundação Instituto Brasileiro de Geografia e Estatística (I.B.G.E.) has published a new (1977) five-volume edition of the well-known *Geografia do Brasil* (item **5629**). Most of the statistical information and the maps have been revised, and new textual material added. Knowledge of less studied regions of Brazil, North and Central West, has been greatly improved as a result of new data and analysis. The *Coleção Nosso Brasil: estudos sociais*, a series of 22 volumes, has been written by people like Oscar Mendes, Jarbas Passarinho, and Leandro Tocantins to provide an easy geographical synthesis of the nation (item **5614**). Mario Lacerda de Melo's study of *zona da mata*'s socioeconomic problems, especially those related to the sugar-cane producing areas, provide an added dimension in understanding the Northeast (item **5672**). Similarly, Hilgard O'Reilly Sternberg's perceptive and well-balanced study of man and land in Amazônia (item **5702**) serves as a timely addition to our knowledge of this increasingly important region.

Unlike their colleagues in archaeology, Japanese geographers had shown until recently only a limited interest in Latin America (see *HLAS 40:86*). However, as was noted in *HLAS 39*, a group of geographers at the Tokyo Kyoiku Univ. (presently Univ. of Tsukuba) led by Ichikawa, Machida, and Yamamoto began, in the late 1960s, to conduct field investigations in Brazil, especially in the Northeast. Some of the results of their research are included in this volume (items **5662** and **5720**), as well as in the preceding volume (see *HLAS 39:5789–5790*). It is expected that by late 1979, another research team will be on its way to the Northeast and the *cerrado* area. A Special Research Project on Latin America has been funded by the government and established at the Univ. of Tsukuba under the direction of Professor

Ichikawa. This is the first major center of its kind in Japan, with programs that include foreign investigators, publications (item **5711**), and symposia. The first inter-disciplinary meeting of Latin Americanists entitled "Latin American Environment and Development" was held at Tsukuba between 31 Jan. and 1 Feb. 1979.

Periodicals of interest to geographers continue to appear: *Interciência*, a journal published in Caracas, includes articles related to man-environment relations. For example, the July-Aug. 1978 issue was devoted entirely to the Amazon basin ecosystems. The *North/South Canadian Journal of Latin American Studies* promises to be another publication of importance to geographers, particularly in view of its inter-disciplinary nature. Finally, *Estudos Brasileiros*, first published in Curitiba in 1976, brings us regional and topical coverage of Brazil. Although multi-disciplinary in focus, many of the essays treat topics related to man and the environment (see item **5709**).

5588 Alegre, Marcos and others. Aspectos quantitativos do fato urbano no Brasil: 1960–1970 (BDG, 4/6, 1972/1974, p. 83–281, maps, tables)

Survey of Brazilian urbanization based primarily on the 1960 and 1970 censuses. Lengthy description of changes are presented; however, analysis of statistical materials is almost totally lacking.

5589 Allen, Elizabeth. New settlement in the Upper Amazon Basin (Bank of London and South America Review [Lloyds Bank Group Publication, London] 9:11, Nov. 1975, p. 622–628)

Summary of settlement activities in the Upper Amazon Basin. It is argued that financial and technical assistances by Andean governments should be directed to spontaneous settlers. Dispersed settlements should be avoided to conserve the existing resources for the future.

5590 Alvim, P. de T. Perspectivas de produção agrícola na região amazonica (AI/I, 3:4, julio/agosto 1978, p. 243–251)

Low fertility of soils in Amazonia has been one of the major deterrents for the development of the region. Considering the high cost of fertilizers and the presently available technology, three alternatives are offered: a) utilization of inherently fertile soils, e.g., várzea; b) ranching in appropriate terrain, e.g., level forested land, and natural grasslands; and c) self-sustaining systems, e.g., improved shifting cultivation.

5591 Amazonas (state), *Brazil.* **Superintendência do Desenvolvimento da Amazônia** (SUDAM). **Banco da Amazônia** (BASA). **Superintendência da Zona Franca de Manaus** (SUFRAMA). Isto é Amazônia. Manaus, Brazil, n.d. 48 p., plates, tables.

Booklet describing the three major government development agencies in Amazônia: SUDAM, BASA, AND SUFRAMA.

5592 Andrade, Manuel Correia de Oliveira. Espaço, polarização e desenvolvimento: a teoria dos pólos de desenvolvimento e a realidade nordestina. 4. ed., revista e atualizada. Prefácio de Fernando de Oliveira Mota. São Paulo, Editorial Grijalbo, 1977. 135 p., bibl., tables.

Short, regional planning text which emphasizes the genesis of spatial inequality in the Northeast. François Perroux's theoretical constructs are employed in the study. For comment on first ed. of this work (1967), see *HLAS 31:3907*.

5593 ———. O planejamento regional e o problema agrário no Brasil. São Paulo, Editôra de Humanismo, Ciencia e Tecnologia (HUCITEC), 1976. 180 p. (Col. Estudos brasileiros, 4)

Discusses two themes: spatial inequality in economic development, and processes of modernization of traditional agrarian sectors. The topics are illustrated with eight essays, originally published between 1973–75.

5594 Azevedo, Aroldo de. Geografia do Brasil: bases físicas, vida humana e vida econômica. 7. ed. rev. e atualizada. São Paulo, Companhia Editora Nacional, 1976. 325 p., bibl., maps, tables.

The present edition, intended primarily for secondary school students, continues to follow the time-tested didactic presentation technique, i.e., the cultural section follows the bio-physical one. The value of the text lies primarily in the updated information and the useful reference section appended to the end of chapters.

5595 Bahia (state), *Brazil.* **Secretaria das Minas e Energia.** Bibliografia comentada da geologia da Bahia: 1817–1975. Salvador, Brazil, 1976. 579 p.

An annotated geological bibliography of Bahia.

5596 Barat, Josef. Estrutura metropolitana e sistema de transportes: estudo do caso do Rio de Janeiro. Rio, Instituto de Planejamento Econômico e Social (IPEA) [and] Instituto de Pesquisas (INPES), 1975. 292 p., bibl., tables (Série monográfica, 20)

Analysis of modes of intra-urban transportation in Rio. A review of theories concerning the distribution of various transport modalities in metropolitan areas is followed by a study of distinctive forms of transportation currently existing in Rio. The costs and demands for each type of transportation are quantified, and these data are analyzed to understand the problem of equilibrium between mass and personal transportation.

5597 Barbosa, José Maria de Azevedo. Santa Maria de Belém do Grão-Pará: o nome da capital paraense. Prefácio de Arthur Cezar Ferreira Reis. Belém, Brazil, Imprensa Oficial, 1977. 92 p., bibl., facsims., plates.

Attempts to clarify the arguments concerning the toponimy Santa Maria de Belém do Pará, present-day Belém.

5598 Barreiros, Eduardo Canabrava. D. Pedro: jornada a Minas Gerais em 1822. Prefácio de Pedro Calmon. Rio, Livraria José Olympio Editora, 1973. 138 p., facsims., illus., maps, plates, tables (Col. Documentos brasileiros, 161)

Description of the colonial highway between Rio and Ouro Preto. The skillful use of historical sources, old photographs, and maps provide a vivid portrait of land and society along the road during the early 19th century.

5599 Bastos, Wilson de Lima. Do caminho novo dos campos gerais à atual BR-135. Juiz de Fora, Brazil, Univ. Federal de Juiz de Fora, 1975. 82 p., bibl., tables.

Describes the evolution of the high-

way that links Rio to the former gold mining region of Minas Gerais by noting the changes that have occurred since the colonial period.

5600 Batista, Djalma. O complexo da Amazônia: análise do processo de desenvolvimento. Prefácio de Arthur Cezar Ferreira Reis. Ilustrações de Israel Cysneiros, Percy Lau e Renato Silva. Rio, Conquista, 1976. 292 p., bibls., illus., tables (Temas brasileiros, 20)

Sketches of various aspects of Amazônia, ranging from diets, diseases, and floral exploitation to colonization, free trade zone of Manaus, Transamazon highway, and the RADAM project. The main thrusts in these brief descriptions are: the conservation of the Amazonian environment, and the development of an appropriate agricultural technology for the region.

5601 Becker, Bertha K. A propósito de um modêlo de ocupação racional da Amazônia (IBGE/R, 38:1, jan./março 1976, p. 137–141)

Proposal of a development model for Amazônia. The model envisages two goals: maintenance of environmental equilibrium, and development of an economic plan intended to benefit mainly the local inhabitants.

5602 Beretta, Pier Luigi. Contributo per una bibliografia geográfica del Rio Grande do Sul, Brasile (IAA, 3:1, 1977, p. 53–83)

A geographical bibliography of Rio Grande do Sul state. This work should be of interest especially to agricultural and settlement geographers.

5603 ———. Notas sôbre a ocupação rural na antiga area de colonização italiana no Rio Grande do Sul (DRG/BG, 20:18, jan./dez. 1975, p. 62–79)

The evolution of rural dwelling forms among Italian colonists of Rio Grande do Sul is traced and the changes are explained. The role of chapels as an integral part of the colonies, and their importance as foci of group settlement growth are also briefly discussed.

Beyna, Jean-Michel. Crise de l'énergie et développement régional au Brésil. See item **7515.**

5604 Brazil. Ministério da Agricultura. Secretaria Geral. Coordenação de Informação Rural. Bibliografia do café. v. 1, Projeto PNUD/FAO/BRA/72/020, Sistema Nacional de Informação e Documentação Agrícola. Apresentação de Alysson Paulinelli. Introdução de Francisco Décio Stortini and Jaime Robredo. Brasília, 1975. 169 p. (DOC/TEC/75/004)

A partial bibliography on coffee with 521 entries, based on the holdings of the Biblioteca Central do Ministério de Agricultura.

5605 ———. Ministério do Interior (MINTER). **Secretaria Geral. Secretaria de Planejamento e Operações.** Programa de pólos agropecuários e agrominerais da Amazônia: POLAMAZÔNIA. Brasília, 1976. 40 p., map, tables.

Explanation of the POLAMAZÔNIA, a program created by Decree No. 74,607, on 25 Sept. 1974, which established 15 agricultural and mining centers in Amazônia.

5606 ———. ———. Superintendência do Desenvolvimento do Nordeste (SUDENE). **Assessoria Técnica. Divisão de Análise Econômica. Setor de Demografia.** Projeções da população do Nordeste brasileiro: 1975–1990. Recife, Brazil, 1972. 149 p., bibl., tables.

Population projections for the Northeast to 1990. The projections are based on the census data covering the period 1940–70. Following a short methodological section, the bulk of the volume consists of statistical tables, where demographic variables like morality, natality, and migrations are summarized.

Bret, Bernard. L'agriculture du Brésil: expansion agricole et crise agraire. See item 7520.

5607 ———. Faits de population et types d'organisation régionale dans le Sud du Brésil (SGB/COM, 29:115, juillet/sept. 1976, p. 225–250, bibl., maps, tables)

Demographic growth of the emerging spatial patterns of Southern Brazil (Paraná, Santa Catarina, and Rio Grande do Sul) are described. Topics such as urbanization, land-use changes, and cropping patterns are discussed.

5608 Burton, Richard Francis. Viagem do Rio de Janeiro a Morro Velho. Prefácio, 1868, de Isabel Burton. Apresentação e notas de Mário Guimarães Ferri. Tradução de David Jardim Júnior. São Paulo, Livraria Itatiaia Editora [and] Editora da Univ. de São Paulo, 1976. 366 p., tables (Col. Reconquista do Brasil, 36)

A mid-19th century description of the gold mining district of southeast Minas Gerais, e.g., Ouro Preto, Mariana, Congonhas do Campo, and São João del Rei by a British explorer and diplomat. Details like environmental changes brought about by the gold boom and the economic changes that followed the mining activities, alternates with interesting descriptions of the region's people and lands. Title of English original: *Explorations of the highlands of the Brazil, with a full account of the gold and diamond mines* (London, Tinsley Brothers, 1869).

5609 Câmara, Antônio Alves. Ensaio sobre as construções navais indígenas do Brasil. Prefácio de Alves Câmara Júnior. 3. ed. São Paulo, Companhia Editora Nacional *em convenio com o* Ministério da Educação de Cultura (MEC), Instituto Nacional do Livro (INL), Brasília, 1976. 174 p., illus., tables (Col. Brasiliana, 92)

Description of aboriginal water crafts of Brazil. Originally published in 1888, the depiction of various native vessels like *jangadas* and canoes is outstanding.

5610 Cardoso, Fernando Henrique and Geraldo Müller. Amazônia: expansão do capitalismo. Revisão ortográfica de Maria Luíza Alvarenga Correa and Vera Lúcia Emídio. São Paulo, Editora Brasiliense, 1977. 205 p., maps, tables.

An attempt to demonstrate the role of capitalism in the destruction of Amazônia. The instruments used by the state to secure the conditions necessary for the settlement and economic expansion of the region are analyzed.

5611 Carvalho, Carlos Gomes de. A natureza pede socorro: um enfoque ecológico a fauna e a flora. Goiânia, Brazil, Editora Oriente, 1976. 196 p., bibl., plates.

An alarmist's view of the deterioration of Brazilian flora and fauna. The subjective assessment of topics, as well as the generalized nature of the statements serve to provide only a partial view of the environmental problems.

5612 —— *ed.* and *comp.* As fabulosas
aguas quentes de Caldas Novas. Antologia. 3. ed. rev. Goiânia, Brazil, Editora
Oriente, 1975. 146 p., tables.

Anthology about the thermal springs
located at the foot of Serra de Caldas, Goiás
state. Includes articles from various sources
such as government-agency reports and descriptions by naturalists like Augustin de
Saint-Hilaire (see also item **5693**).

5613 Carvalho Filho, Joaquim Ignácio de.
O Rio Grande do Norte em visão
prospectiva. Apresentação de Raimundo
Nonato. Natal, Brazil, Fundação José Augusto, 1976. 194 p., fold. table, maps, tables.

Number of essays relating to the early
20th-century Rio Grande do Norte. The
personal observations provide valuable information about man's constant struggle with
the semi-arid *sertão*.

5614 *Coleção Nosso* Brasil: Estudos So-
ciais. Rio, Bloch Educação, 1976- .
Monographic series consisting of vol-
umes on the states of Brazil, their land,
people, history, and social and economic
features. These syntheses provide excellent
background for each Brazilian state, e.g.:
André de Figueiredo *Estado de Paraíba*
(80 p.)
Ivo Lêdo *Estado de Alagaos* (95 p.)
Herculano Gomes Mathis *Estado do
Rio de Janeiro* (71 p.)
Oscar Mendes *Estados de Minas
Gerais* (78 p.)
Jarbas Gonçalves Passarinho *Estado do
Pará* (96 p.)
Marcos Konder Reis *Estado de Santa
Catarina* (87 p.)
Leandro Tocantins *Estado do Acre* (64
p.).

5615 Colonização e desenvolvimento do
norte do Paraná: depoimentos sobre a
maior obra no gênero realizada por uma
empresa privada, 24 de setembro de 1975.
São Paulo, Companhia Melhoramentos Norte
do Paraná, 1975. 295 p., plates, tables.

History of a land company, the Company Melhoramentos Norte do Paraná. In a
country where short-term, speculative investments have taken precedents, the long-
range development of a pioneering region,
especially by a private enterprise, is considered to be an anomaly in Brazil. The
company has been successful not only in

carrying out most of its original goals, but
also in opening the region to family farmers.
As such, the book may provide valuable
insights to regional planners.

5616 Costa, Rubens Vaz da. Perspectivas
demográficas do Brasil (SESC/PB,
15:167, julho 1977, p. 2–13, tables)
Causes and possible effects of rapid
demographic growth in the country are analyzed. Government inattention to family
planning is criticized.

5617 Cunha, Euclides da. Um paraíso per-
dido: reunião dos ensaios amazônicos.
Seleção e coordenação de Hildon Rocha.
Introduçâo de Arthur Cézar Ferreira Reis.
Petrópolis, Brazil, Editora Vozes *em convênio
com o* Ministério da Educação e Cultura
(MEC), Instituto Nacional do Livro (INL),
Brasília, 1976. 327 p. (Col. Dimensões do
Brasil, 1)

Turn-of-the-century description and
interpretation of man and land in the rubber-
gathering region between the Madeira and
Javarí rivers. The author, who wrote the
Rebellion in the backlands, offers a penetrating essay about a society dominated by
gum elastic.

5618 Denevan, William M. The aboriginal
population of Amazonia (*in* Denevan,
William M. *ed.* The native population of
the Americas in 1492 [see *HLAS 40:2279*] p.
205–234)

Updated version of paper first published in 1970. The aboriginal population of
Amazonia is estimated by studying the natives' techniques of resource utilization and
their relations with each of the five main
ecological regions: the floodplain, coast, lowland savanna, upland forest, and upland
savanna. The habitat-density method employed in the analysis yields an approximate
population of 6,800,000 for the region.

5619 *Documentação Amazônica: catálogo coletivo.* Superintendência do
Desenvolvimento da Amazônia (SUDAM).
Rede de Bibliotecas da Amazônia (REBAM).
Vol. 1, No. 1, jan./abril 1974- . Belém, Brazil.
This 543 p. bibliography with 650
entries is the first volume of an on-going
project begun by the Superintendência do
Desenvolvimento da Amazônia (SUDAM) to
catalog materials being received by the major public libraries in the region.

5620 Duarte, Haidine da Silva Barros. A cidade do Rio de Janeiro: descentralização das atividades terciárias; os centros funcionais (IBGE/R, 36:1, jan./março 1974, p. 53–98, bibl., maps, tables)

Explanation of Rio's urban space based on a series of functional centers.

5621 Duarte, José de Côrtes. O fogo e o boi. Belo Horizonte, Brazil, Editora Comunicação, 1976? 75 p., plates.

Timely series of essays concerning the environmental changes occurring in the Jequitinhonha Valley. The vignettes describe the process of conversion of tropical forests to grasslands, and their effects on ecological balance. The system, well known in the American tropics, has been one of the principal means of drastically changing the face of Brazil since the colonial period.

5622 Faé, Walter José. Italianos no Rio Grande do Sul: 1875–1975. Americana, Brazil, Edições Focam, 1975. 228 p., bibl.

Synthesis of Italian immigration and colonization in Rio Grande do Sul, including vignettes of urban centers and outstanding Italian-Brazilians of the region.

5623 Ferraz, José Carlos de Figueiredo. São Paulo e seu futuro: antes que seja tarde demais. Prefácio de Diogo Lordello de Mello. Rio, Instituto Brasileiro de Administração Municipal (IBAM), 1976. 90 p., bibl., tables.

Impassionate plea by a former mayor to decelerate the growth of Greater São Paulo. The problems outlined are infrastructural (e.g., transportation, housing, and education) as well as social, such as the increasing marginalization of the poor.

5624 Ferraz, Paulo Malta. Pequena história da colonização de Blumenau. Blumenaus, Brazil, Fundação Casa Dr. Blumenau, 1976. 87 p., plates (Publicação, 16)

Historical sketch of the German colony of Blumenau, in the state of Santa Catarina.

5625 Flynn, Peter. The Brazilian development model: the political dimension (RIIA/WT, 29:11, Nov. 1973, p. 481–494)

Brief review of the Brazilian development model and its inherent weaknesses, e.g., unequal income distribution, heavy re-

liance on foreign investments, and suppression of nationalism.

5626 Foucher, Michel. Actualités amazoniennes(AGF/B, 54:441/442, mars/avril 1977, p. 125–132)

Government-assisted occupation of Amazônia by family farmers has changed from active promotion and settlement to the simple task of recognizing the areas settled by squatters. In contrast, the development of the region by large, agropastoral enterprises has been actively promoted.

5627 Freire, Lucy A. da; Maria Therezinha de S. Soares; and Marlene P.V. Teixeira. Organização espacial da agricultura no estado do Rio de Janeiro (IBGE/R, 39:2, abril/junho 1977, p. 41–98)

Three methods, i.e., crop diversification index, agricultural regionalization technique, and von Thunen's model are employed to understand the spatial organization of agriculture in the state of Rio.

5628 Freyre, Gilberto; Renato Campos; Gleide Guimarães Carneiro; and Alberto Cunha Melo eds. Trópico & pesca, sexo, universidade, profilaxia, algodão, madeira, política internacional, arqueologia, pecuária. Recife, Brazil, Univ. Federal de Pernambuco, Seminário de Tropicologia, 1976. 2 v. (662 p.) (Continuous pagination)

Bulk of these two volumes consists of discussion and papers read at the seminars on tropicology held during 1969 at the Federal Univ. of Pernambuco. Topics of interest to geographers include fisheries (Vol. 1) and cotton and livestock in the tropics (Vol. 2).

5629 Fundação Instituto Brasileiro de Geografia e Estatística (IBGE), Rio. **Diretoria Técnica. Superintendência de Estudos Geográficos e Sócio-Econômicos. Departamento de Geografia.** Geografia do Brasil. v. 1, Região Norte; v. 2, Região Nordeste; v. 3, Região Sudeste; v. 4, Região Centro-Oeste; v. 5, Região Sul. Prefácio de Isaac Kerstenetzky. Apresentações de Marília Velloso Galvão. Rio, 1977. 5 v. (466, 454, 667, 364, 534 p.) bibls., maps, plates, tables.

These five volumes offer comprehensive geographical coverage of the five Brazilian macro-regions. Each volume is devoted to a region and begins with a bio-physical section where geomorphic, climatic, floristic, and hydrographic characteristics are depicted. This is followed by a demographic-economic section that includes topics like population dynamics, transportation, agriculture, manufacturing, and urban systems. The books serve as useful reference and also provide background basic to the study of the country.

5630 Fundação João Pinheiro, *Belo Horizonte, Brazil.* **Centro de Recursos Naturais.** Levantamento de reconhecimento de solos, da aptidão agropastoril, das formações vegetais e do uso da terra em área do Território Federal de Rondônia. Apresentação de José Israel Vargas. Belo Horizonte, Brazil, 1975. 171 p., bibl., fold. tables, maps, plates, tables.

Field survey and photo-interpretation results of a 17,000 km² area in Southeast Rondônia territory. The bio-physical elements of the study area are analyzed to produce land-use capability maps.

5631 Gardner, George. Travels in the interior of Brazil, principally through the northern provinces, and the gold and diamond districts, during the years 1836–1841. Reprint ed. Boston, Longwood Press, 1977. 562 p., map.

Reprint of 1846 ed. published by Reeve Brothers, London. Description of author's travels from Rio to the Northeast and Central Brazil, including Bahía, Pernambuco, Ceará, Piauí, and Mato Grosso during the early 19th century. The minute accounts of man and nature should be most valuable for those who wish to learn about past man-environment relations.

5632 Geiger, Pedro Pinchas; María Salette Ney da Motta Lima; and **Mariam Emile Abi Abib.** Distribuição de atividades agropastorais em torno da metropole de São Paulo (PAIGH/G, 80, junio 1974, p. 35–70, tables)

The von Thunen's model is tested in Southern Brazil, with São Paulo as its epicenter. It is found that the results generally conform to the model. Possibilities for application of the model, e.g., freight rates, transportation planning, and future land use are contemplated.

5633 Görgen, Hermann Matthias. Brasil. Tradução de José Wisniewski Filho. Rio, Presença Edições *em convênio com o*

Ministério da Educação e Cultura (MEC), Instituto Nacional do Livro (INL), 1977. 94 p., bibl., plates, tables.

Summary of Brazilian land, history, and culture as viewed by a German. This little encyclopedia may be of use as an introduction to the country. German original: *Brasilien* (Nuremberg, FRG, Glock & Lutz, 1971).

5634 Goldemberg, J. Brazil: energy options and current outlook (AAAS/S, 200, 14 April 1978, p. 158–164)

Main sources of energy in Brazil are reviewed; then, possible solutions for an eventual energy independence are discussed, e.g., the biomass program, hydroelectric projects, and the solar and nuclear energies.

5635 Gomes, José de Melo. A economia da proteção ambiental (SBPC/CC, 29:4, abril 1977, p. 407–409)

It is suggested that environmental conservation in Brazil should not be viewed solely from an economic perspective. It is further believed that the country should develop environmental protection technology and ethics of its own, tailored to suit the local conditions.

5636 Goodland, R.; H.S. Irwin; and **G. Tillman.** Ecological development for Amazonia (SBPC/CC, 30:3, março 1978, p. 275–289, illus., tables)

Regards current agricultural activities practiced in Amazonia as irrational. A sustained-yield farming system based on tree cultivation is proposed as the ideal solution.

5637 Grupo de Estudos de Regionalização-IBGE: proposição metodológica para revisão da divisão do Brasil em regiões funcionais urbanas (IBGE/R, 38:2, abril/junho 1976, p. 100–129, bibl., tables)

Updating of the "functional urban regions" regionalization model first proposed in 1972 by the Instituto Brasileiro de Geografía e Estatística (IBGE).

5638 Guerra, Antônio Teixeira. Recursos naturais do Brasil. 2. ed. revista e atualizada. Rio, Fundação Instituto Brasileiro de Geografia e Estatística (IBGE), Diretoria de Divulgação, 1976. 220 p., bibl., illus., maps, plates, tables (Biblioteca geográfica brasileira, 25. Série A: livros)

Introductory text on the conservation of natural resources in Brazil. The extensive bibliography and a section treating the environmental conservation activities in the country are of special interest.

5639 Guidugli, Odeibler Santo. Reflexões a propósito da geografia histórica (FFCLM/EH, 15, 1976, p. 103–122, bibl.)

An explanation of the field of historical geography, including its development in both the US and Europe.

5640 Gusmão, Rivaldo Pinto. Estudo da organização agrária da região sul através da uma análise fatorial (IBGE/R, 36:1, jan./março 1974, p. 33–52, bibl., maps, tables)

Differences in the socioeconomic organization of agriculture in Southern Brazil are investigated by applying the factor analysis. The study identifies 21 functional micro-regions in the area.

5641 Herrera, R. and others. Amazon ecosystems: their structure and functioning with particular emphasis on nutrients (AI/I, 3:4, July/Aug. 1978, p. 223–232)

Recent studies concerning nutrient conserving mechanisms in the rainforest are discussed, following an explanation of elements that characterize the Amazon ecosystems.

5642 Honorato, Manoel da Costa. Dicionário topográfico, estatístico e histórico da província de Pernambuco. Estudo introdutório de José Antônio Gonsalves de Mello. 2. ed. Recife, Brazil, Governo do Estado de Pernambuco, Secretaria de Educação e Cultura, 1976. 150., tables (Col. Pernambucana)

This toponimic and statistical dictionary of the late 19th-century Pernambuco may be of potential value to historical geographers. Details about site and situation of settlements, land use, and other socioeconomic information comprise the bulk of the book.

5643 Irmler, Ulrich. Matas de inundação da Amazônia Central em comparação entre águas brancas e pretas (SBPC/CC, 30:7, julho 1978, p. 813–821, bibl., tables)

The inundation forests of Central Amazônia, igapó and várzea are differentiated according to their aquatic soil invertebrates. The biological differences in the two forests derive from the distinctive ways of nutrient

cycling. In the black water (igapó), the forests serve as the source of nutrients, while in the white water (várzea), the vegetation takes up nutrients from the water-borne sediments.

5644 Itaipú (power plant), Brazil. Foz de Iguaçú: plano de desenvolvimento urbano. Curitiba, Brazil, Itaipú Binacional [and] Univ. Federal do Paraná, 1974. 478 p., maps, tables.

Varied social and economic information are collated for the border city of Foz de Iguaçú, Paraná, and guidelines for its growth are outlined in the present document.

5645 Joffily, Irenêo Ceciliano Pereira. Notas sôbre a Parahyba. Prefácio de Capistrano de Abreu. Apresentação e observações de Geraldo Irenêo Joffily. Brasília, Tesaurus Editôra, 1977. 2 v. in 1 (449 p.) plates, tables.

Late 19th-century account of man and land in Paraíba (reprint of 1892 ed). The detailed descriptions of the environment, economy, society, and settlements may be of special interest to historical geographers. First ed. of this work was based on crônicas published in newspapers of Paraiba and Pernambuco in the 1880s.

5646 Journaux, André. Eboulements, ravinements et mouvements de masse dans la Serra do Mar, Brésil (AGF/B, 55:450/451, fév./mars 1978, p. 75–81, illus.)

The tropical rainforest-covered Serra do Mar escarpments between Rio and Tubarão in Santa Catarina have been the scene of mass soil movements since 1966. Three major phenomena are pointed out: rock falls, fan ravining, and landslides. The accelerated denudation processes are believed to be mainly man-induced.

Kacowicz, Mateus and others. Desenvolvimento e política urbana. See item **7551.**

5648 Katzman, Martin T. Colonization as an approach to regional development: Northern Paraná, Brazil (UC/EDCC, 26:4, July 1978, p. 709–724)

The experience of Companhia de Terras Norte do Paraná, a private colonization project in Northern Paraná, is reviewed. The project is seen as a planning and economic success to those who devised it, but failed to create a middle-class society as originally envisaged. The implications of such experiences for future colonization efforts are described.

5649 Kerr, Warwick Estevam. Considerações sobre a situação florestal brasileira (SBPC/CC, 29:3, março 1977, p. 269–273)

A plea for the conservation of Brazilian flora presented to the Federal Senate by the author on 2 June 1976. Effects of indiscriminate deforestation and possible solutions for arresting the rapid floral destruction are also discussed.

5650 Kirby, John. Agricultural land use and the settlement of Amazonia (Pacific Viewpoint [Victoria Univ. of Wellington, Dept. of Geography, Wellington, New Zealand] 17:2, 1976, p. 105–132)

Review of new land settlement activities in three areas of Amazônia: Transamazon highway of Brazil, Northeast Ecuador, and Caquetá of Colombia. Agricultural success is seen primarily from an ecological viewpoint.

5651 Klein, Roberto M. Southern Brazilian phytogeographic features and the probable influence of Upper Quaternary climatic changes in the floristic distribution (UFP/BPG, 33, 1975, p. 67–88)

An explanation is offered for the current lack of correspondence between climate and vegetation in Southern Brazil. The incongruity is attributed to the four climatic fluctuations that occurred during the Quaternary period.

5652 Kleinpennig, J.M.G. A further evaluation of the policy of integration of the Amazon region: 1974–1976 (TESG, 69, 1978, p. 78–84)

Summary of economic development and integration activities in Amazonia since 1974. Changes in government planning, stressing development through agribusinesses and multinationals are emphasized.

5653 Kohlhepp, Von Gerd. Erschliessung und wirtschaftliche Inwertsetzung Amazoniens Enwicklungstrategien brasilienischer Planungspolitik und privater unternehmen (GR, 30:1, jan. 1978, p. 14–20)

Evaluation of government-planned development attempts in Amazonia since

1970. The region is developing in an unbalanced way: large private enterprises have been favored over family farmers for agricultural concessions. A similar trend is also visible for exploitation of flora and mineral resources.

5654 ———. Planung und heutige situation staatlicher kleinbäuerlicher kolonisationsporjekte an der Transamazônica (Planning and actual situation of state-controlled small-scale colonization projects along the Transamazônica) (GZ, 64:3, 1976, p. 171–211, bibl., maps, plates, tables)

This evaluation of agricultural development attempts in the Brazilian Amazonia by the government since 1970 reveals that the programs have failed to solve the serious socioeconomic problems of coastal regions, especially the Northeast.

5655 Kruger, Hans-Jurgen. Migration, landliche Ubervolkerung und kolonisation in Norosten Brasiliens (GR, 30:1, Jan. 1978, p. 14–20)

Effects of relative overpopulation in rural Northeast Brazil are summarized. Government programs to stabilize rural exodus, e.g., colonization and irrigation projects are described and analyzed.

5656 Le Lannou, Maurice and **Nice Lecocq-Muller.** Le nouveau Brésil. Paris, Librairie Armand Colin, 1976. 248 p. bibls., maps (Col. U prisme, 54)

This is a regional geography text of Brazil. The organization of the book follows a traditional format, i.e., the chapters on the physical elements and historical-spatial changes are followed by regional analysis. The major emphasis is on current economic developments and their consequences.

Leonardos, Othon Henry. Geociências no Brasil: contribuição germânica. See *HLAS 40:3991.*

5657 Libault, André. Geocartografia. Prefácio de Aziz Nacib Ad'Sáber. São Paulo, Companhia Editora Nacional [and] Editora da Univ. de São Paulo, 1975. 388 p., maps, tables (Biblioteca universitária. Série 6: geografia e história, 1)

Cartography textbook written by the author during his stay in Brazil (1962–73). The clear and concise explanations, coupled with materials ranging from basic to advanced, serve to make the book an ideal text for beginning and advanced students.

5658 Lindgren, C. Ernesto S.; Elane Frossard Barbosa; and Roberto Tavares Petterle. Hierarquia de centros na cidade do Rio de Janeiro (IBGE/R, 38:1, jan./março 1976, p. 83–123, bibl., maps, tables)

Study of the hierarchy of urban sectors nested within a city. The idea is to understand the morphology of cities. The concept is tested, using as example the city of Rio.

5659 Lobo, Roberto Jorge Haddock. Geografia do Brasil. 9. ed. São Paulo, Editora Atlas, 1976. 226 p., maps, plates, tables.

Middle school geography textbook. The present edition provides the basis for evaluating the changes occurring in the geography curriculum taught at the lower grades.

5660 Lopes, J. Leite. Atoms in the developing nations (BAS/SPA, 34:3, April 1978, p. 31–34)

The atomic energy policy development in Brazil and the future role of nuclear energy in the country are reviewed.

5661 Lutzenberger, José A. Fim do futuro?: manifesto ecológico brasileiro. Porto Alegre, Brazil, Editora Movimento, 1976. 96 p., bibls. (Col. Documentos, 12)

A sensitive synthesis of present-day environmental problems in Brazil. The monograph is divided into two parts. Examples of current ecological destruction are provided in the first part, while possible solutions are offered in the latter section.

5662 Machida, Tadashi; Masao Inokuchi; and Eiji Matsumoto. A study of débris movement on the low-relief land around Patos, Paraíba, Northeastern Brazil (Tokyo Geography Papers [Kyoiku Univ., Dept. of Geography, Tokyo] 20, 31 March 1976, p. 83–98)

From a geomorphologic study conducted in a small area around Patos, in the state of Paraíba, the authors conclude that the key for understanding the development of local landforms lies in the *riacho*, or small intermittent streams, as well as in the characteristics of the weathered materials.

5663 Madeira, Luiz Sérgio. Geografia contemporânea. Rio, Editora Rio *em convênio com as* Faculdades Integradas Estácio da Sá, 1976. 102 p., bibl., maps (Col. Fundamentos de estudos sociais, 4)

A summarized, descriptive world regional geography text for secondary school students. One third of the book is devoted to explain the regional patterns of Brazil.

5664 Maia, Jerônimo Vingt-un Rosado and Antônio Campos e Silva. Louis Jacques Brunet: naturalista viajante. v. 1. Natal, Brazil, Artes Gráficas da Companhia Editora do Rio Grande do Norte (CERN), 1973. 338 p., map, plates (Col. Mossoroense, 30. Série C)

Poorly organized collection of data, including correspondence and technical reports, of a French naturalist working in Northeast Brazil from the late 1850s. [R. & J. Barman]

5665 Manfroi, Olívio. A colonização italiana no Rio Grande do Sul: implicações econômicas, políticas e culturais. Prefácio de Itálico Marcon. Porto Alegre, Brazil, Gráfica Editora Fotogravura do Sul (GRAFOSUL) *em co-edição com o* Secretaria de Educação e Cultura (SEC), Depto. de Assuntos Culturais (DAC), Instituto Estadual do Livro (IEL), 1975. 218 p., bibl., tables (Série Biênio da colonização e imigração, 7)

An attempt to analyze the "socio-cultural behavior of the Italian immigrants within the economic, political, and cultural contexts of Brazil." The first part includes the Italian immigrants within the Brazilian economic and political framework. The second is an analysis of the socio-cultural aspects, e.g., migration and the initial psychological shock, how the cultural homogeneity of the colonists was a reaction to the physical isolation and, finally, the search for a cultural identity through religion.

5666 Marcelo de Albuquerque Lima, Dalmo and John Houston Sanders, Jr. Seleção e avaliação de nova tecnologia para os pequenos agriculturas do Sertão Central do Ceará (BNB/REN, 9:1, jan./março, p. 99–118, bibl., tables)

Hayami and Ruitan's theory of induced innovation is tested among small farmers in the *município* of Canindé, Ceará. It is believed that, among the new technologies to be introduced in the region, animal drafted cultivators would bring the greatest results in increasing farm productivity.

5667 Margolis, Maxine. Historical perspectives on frontier agriculture as an adaptive strategy (AAA/AE, 4:1, Feb. 1977, p. 42–64, bibl.)

Examination of ecological and economic factors responsible for environmental degradation in frontier agricultural situations, where export-oriented crops are cultivated. The coffee planters of Southern Brazil and the cotton farmers of the Southern US are compared. An effort is made to demonstrate that the colonists' attitudes toward the land are analogous to the "fugitive strategies" of some non-human species.

5668 McDowell, Bart. Brazil's golden beachhead (NGS/NGM, 153:2, Feb. 1978, p. 246–277, colored plates)

Generalized description of man, land, and culture in the area between Rio and Paraná.

5669 McIntyre, Loren. Brazil's wild frontier: treasure chest or Pandora's box? (NGS/NGM, 152:5, Nov. 1977, p. 684–719, map, plates)

Pictorial description of current developments in the Brazilian Amazon.

5670 Megale, Januario Francisco. Geografia agrária: objeto e método (SBPC/CC, 28:10, out. 1976, p. 1139–1145, bibl.)

The scope and methods of agricultural geography as seen by a Brazilian geographer are outlined. The increasing concern toward urban and industrial location studies in recent years employing quantitative techniques and mathematical models has relegated agricultural geography to a secondary position. This is reflected in the largely qualitative studies being carried out in the rural studies.

5671 Melgaço, Augusto Leverger, *barão de.* Vias de comunicação de Matto-Grosso. Cuiabá, Brazil, Edições Universidade Federal de Mato Grosso (UFMT) [and] Secretaria de Educação e Cultura, 1975. 70 p., illus., tables (Col. Ciclo das águas, 11. Série: Leverger)

Republication of the 1905 ed. that describes the main waterways of Mato Grosso

as avenues of fluvial communication and transportation. Written in the latter part of the 19th century, the book provides interesting glimpses of the means of communication of the period, as well as the riverine settlements.

5672 Melo, Mário Lacerda de. O açúcar e o homem: problemas sociais e econômicos do Nordeste canavieiro. Recife, Brazil, Ministro da Educação e Cultura (MEC), Instituto Joaquim Nabuco e Pesquisas Sociais, 1975. 304 p., bibl., maps, tables (Série estudos e pesquisas, 4)

A comprehensive, socioeconomic analysis of the *zona da mata*, the sugar cane region of Northeast Brazil. Topics such as, land tenure, evolution of agricultural systems, demographic problems, and the role of the government in the sugar cane industry are reviewed from a multi-disciplinary viewpoint.

5673 Miranda Neto, Manoel José de. Marajó: desafio da Amazônia, aspectos da reação a modelos exógenos de desenvolvimento. Rio, Distribuidora Record, 1976. 178 p., bibl., tables.

A well-written summary of the Marajó Island at the estuary of the Amazon. Descriptions of the environment, historical evolution, and current socioeconomic conditions, coupled with a short, but useful bibliography serve to provide a good introduction to the island.

5674 Moreira, Eidorfe. Os Igapós e seu aproveitamento. Apresentação de José Marcelino Monteiro da Costa. Belém, Brazil, Univ. Federal do Pará, Núcleo de Altos Estudos Amazônicos (NAEA), 1976. 109 p., illus. (Cadernos NAEA, 2)

Classification and explanation of *igapós*, the backswamps and the low-lying terrain found along the Amazon and its tributaries that are subjected to periodic inundations. The ecology of the *igapós* is described, along with possible uses of this riverine land.

5675 Moreira, José Roberto; Gil Eduardo Serra; and José Goldemberg. Alcool: um novo meio de gerar electricidade (SBPC/CC, 30:7, julho 1978, p. 822–829, tables)

A review of existing production techniques of sugar-cane alcohol indicates that considerable amount of potential energy goes unused. Based on existing technology and cost/benefit analysis, the authors offer valuable suggestions for increasing domestic power generation through a more rational use of the sugar cane biomass.

5676 Morton, F.W.O. The royal timber in late colonial Bahia (HAHR, 58:1, Feb. 1978, p. 41–61)

Floral conservation attempts in southern Bahia during the late colonial period are reviewed. The methods of timber exploitation during the period serves to illustrate how the current "development versus conservation" theme was already being manifested.

5677 Moura, Hélio Augusto de and **José Olímpio Marques Coelho.** Migrações para as grandes cidades do Nordeste: intensidade e características demográficas. Fortaleza, Brazil, Banco do Nordeste do Brasil, 1975. 112 p., bibl., tables (Estudos econômicos e sociais, 1)

Preliminary and descriptive study of internal migrations based on the demographic census of 1970. Two major aspects are investigated: delineation of main migration routes to understand the places of origin and destination, and identification of migration currents to verify the demographic, social, and economic aspects for the movements.

5678 Müller, Jürg. Japaner in Brasilien: die Stellung und Bedeutung der Einwanderer japanischer Herkunft im Brasilien unserer Tage (GH, 30:2, 1975, p. 67–70)

Summary of Japanese immigration and settlement in Brazil based primarily on secondary sources.

5679 Muraiama, Shisuto José and **Noriyoshi Sakamoto.** O fantástico kiri: instruções práticas sobre seu cultivo. São Paulo, Livraria Nobel, 1976. 69 p., bibl., plates, tables.

A manual for the cultivation of *kiri (Paulownia spp.)*, a cultivar recently introduced to Brazil from Southeast Asia and used primarily for reforestation in Southeast Brazil.

5680 Nogueira, Dyrceu Araújo. Política de transportes no Brasil (MEC/C, 6:22, julho/set. 1976, p. 40–45, plates)

Generalized statements on transportation needs and planning in Brazil.

5681 Nomura, Hitoshi. Desenvolvimento atual e perspectivas futuras da piscicultura intensiva e extensiva no Estado de São Paulo (SBPC/CC, 28:10, out. 1976, p. 1097–1107, bibl.)

Description of the modalities of fish culture and its prospects in the state of São Paulo. The increasing interest in pisciculture is rapidly increasing in view of the expanding markets and the need for inexpensive protein sources.

5682 Oliveira, Lejeune P.H. de and **Luiza Krau.** Estudos aplicados à recuperação biológica da Bahía de Guanabara (IOC/M, 74:2, 1976, p. 99–145, bibl., maps, plates, tables)

Ecological study of an inlet in the Guanabara Bay to ascertain the degree of biological changes resulting from the rapid increase of pollutants in the environment.

5683 Paraná (state), *Brazil.* **Coordenação da Região Metropolitana de Curitiba** (COMEC). Região metropolitana de Curitiba: demografia, projeções. Curitiba, Brazil, 1970. 51 l., maps, tables.

The metropolitan population of Curitiba is projected for the period 1970–90, according to the population of each of the homogeneous regions devised by the *Plano de Obras Adequado a Tipologia Urbana.* Historical tendencies, demographic density, and economic behavior were some of the variables included in the design of the homogeneous micro-regions.

5684 Passos, Djalma. Ocupação da Amazônia e outros problemas. Manaus?, Brazil, Edições, Madrugada, 1974? 189 p., tables.

Collection of speeches by the author relating to the development of Amazonia. The optimism evident in these essays were typical of the government in the early years of this decade.

5685 Pebayle, Raymond. Os difíceis encontros de duas sociedades rurais (DRG/BG, 20:18, jan./dez. 1975, p. 3–22)

Contacts and their effects between two formerly distinctive agrarian societies in Rio Grande do Sul, the Luso-Brazilian ranchers of the grasslands and the Italian and

German colonists of the forested Serra Geral escarpments, are studied and interpreted.

5686 Peluso Júnior, Victor Antônio. Problemas demográficos: avaliação e prospectiva do fenômeno urbano em Santa Catarina. Florianópolis, Brazil, Associação dos Diplomados da Escola Superior de Guerra, 1974. 26 p., tables.

Summary of causes and consequences of accelerated urbanization in the state of Santa Catarina. Aside from the statistical tables, the descriptions are sketchy and of little value.

5687 Pereira, Potyara A.P. Burocracia e planejamento regional na Amazônia (UMG/RBEP, 46, jan. 1978, p. 127–157)

Study which evaluates the center-periphery thesis by taking as an example a regional development agency, the SUDAM. The proposed generalities lack substantiation and much of the argument consists of rhetoric. For political scientist's comment, see item **7570.**

5688 Pernambuco (state), *Brazil.* **Universidade Federal. Seminario de Tropicologia.** Contribuição paulista à tropicologia: trabalhos apresentados. Apresentação de Gilberto Freyre. Prefácio de J.V. Freitas Marcondes. São Paulo, Livraria Pioneira Editora, 1974. 204 p., tables (Biblioteca pioneira de estudos brasileiros)

Eight papers selected from the Seminar of Tropicology held at the Federal Univ. of Pernambuco are included in the volume. The on-going seminars, begun in 1966, take place eight to ten times a year under the direction of Gilberto Freyre. Most of the papers read at the conference are published by the university press. Topics in the present volume include work and leisure, architecture, clothing, language and literature, and graduate studies in the tropics.

5689 Pinto, Hilton Silveira and **Rogério Remo Alfonsi.** Mapeamento ecológico por computador (SBPC/CC, 28:10, out. 1976, p. 1108–1113, bibl., illus.)

The importance of dynamic cartography is pointed out for a number of ecological studies. Among the various computer programs, the SYMAP system seems to be the most promising. As an illustration, the system is used to estimate the areas of coffee cultivation affected by the frosts of July 1975.

5690 Pontes, Rosa de Oliveira. Zona Franca: fator de desenvolvimento para a Amazônia Ocidental. Brasília, Ministério do Interior (MINTER), Gabinete do Ministro, Coordenadoria de Comunicação Social, 1977. 37 p., bibl., tables.

Timely synthesis of the duty-free zone of Manaus. Topics such as tourism, demographic changes, and industrial development, evolving as part of the governmental efforts to develop western Amazonia are outlined.

5691 Reis, Maurício Rangel. O Nordeste e o II PND. Brasília, Ministério do Interior (MINTER), Gabinete do Ministro, Coordenadoria de Comunicação Social, 1975. 24 p., tables.

Summary of government activities to be conducted in the Northeast during the 1975–79 period (PND II stands for National Development Plan II).

5692 Resor, Randolph R. Rubber in Brazil: dominance and collapse, 1876–1945 (HU/BHR, 51:3, Autumn 1977, p. 341–366)

The "boom and bust" of wild rubber in Amazonia is reviewed, with interesting economic details as to why Brazilian producers were unable to compete with Southeast Asian plantations.

Roche, Jean. A colonização alemã no Espírito Santo. See *HLAS 40:4163.*

5693 Saint-Hilaire, Augustin François César Prouvençal de. Viagem á província de Goiás. Tradução de Regina Regis Junqueira. Apresentação de Mário Guimarães Ferri. São Paulo, Editora da Univ. de São Paulo [and] Livraria Itatiaia Editora, 1975. 158 p., plate, tables (Col. Reconquista do Brasil, 8)

One of the projected eight volumes of the reedition of this classic originally published in Paris between 1947–48 and consisting of the French naturalist's accounts and descriptions of his voyages through central and south Brazil in 1816–22. Saint Hilaire was one of the most perceptive foreign observers to write not just about nature but on the social structure of Brazil as well. These volumes should be required reading for all

Brazilianists interested in the geography and history of the country. Includes good indexes. See also items **5612** and **5694**.

5694 ———. Viagem pelas provincias do Rio de Janeiro e Minas Gerais. Tradução de Vivaldi Moreira. Belo Horizonte, Brazil, Editora da Univ. de São Paulo [and] Livraria Itatiaia Editora, 1975. 378 p. (Col. Reconquista do Brasil, 4)

Like item **5693**, this is another volume of Saint Hilaire's superb descriptions of Brazil in the late 1810s and early 1820s. This volume indicates his account of the land and people of the provinces of Rio and Minas Gerais. See also item **5612**.

5695 **Saito, Hiroshi.** The integration and participation of the Japanese and their descendants in Brazilian society (ICEM/IM, 14:3, 1976, p. 183–199, bibl., tables)

Skillful interpretation of the integration process of Japanese and their descendants into Brazilian society. Following a long period or predominantly rural distribution, and therefore of limited opportunities for participation in the larger society, the Japanese are now rapidly joining the mainstream through increased urbanward migration and opportunities for social and economic advancement.

5696 **Sanders, John H.** and **Frederick L. Bein.** Desenvolvimento agrícola na fronteira brasileira: sul de Mato Grosso (IPE/EE, 6:2, 1976, p. 85–112, bibl., tables)

Growth in agricultural output in the post World War II period has been accomplished primarily through increases in the factors of production, labor and land. Studies of two areas in southern Mato Grosso reveal that increase in production along the frontier region has been aided by infra-structural developments and diffusion of new ideas and techniques introduced by recent settlers.

5697 **Santos, Joaquim Felício dos.** Memórias do Distrito Diamantino da Comarca do Serro Frio, Província de Minas Gerais. Apresentação de Mário Guimarães Ferri. Prefácio e bibliografias de Alexandre Eulálio. Notas de Nazaré Meneses e José Teixeira Neves. 4. ed. São Paulo, Editôra da Univ. de São Paulo [and] Livraria Itatiaia Editôra, 1976. 338 p., bibl. (Col. Reconquista do Brasil, 26)

Chronicles of activities in the mining district of southeast Minas Gerais, especially Diamantina, during the 18th and early 19th centuries. Describes economic, political, and social conditions of the region and offers numerous details on subjects such as mining techniques and agricultural methods (see also item **5608**). First ed. was published 1868 in Rio.

5699 **Silva, Darcy da.** A castanha do Pará como fator inicial de desenvolvimento de Marabá: perspectivas atuais. São Paulo, Univ. de São Paulo, Instituto de Geografia, 1973. 36 p., bibl., tables (Geografia econômica, 12)

Study illustrates the transition from an exploitative economy (gathering of Brazil nut) to a commercial one (cattle-ranching) which results from the construction of highways as exemplified by the region around Marabá, in southern Pará state. The construction of two major highways, the Belém-Brasília and the Transamazon have brought about not only changes in land use, but also a decline of river settlements.

5700 **Siqueira, Moema Miranda de.** O papel da função administrativa na evolução urbana de Belo Horizonte (UMG/RBEP, 44, jan. 1977, p. 103–138, tables)

Historical analysis of Belo Horizonte reveal that, among various functions performed by the city, the administrative ones were primarily responsible for its development.

5701 **Smith, Peter Seaborn.** Brazilian oil: from myth to reality? (IAMEA, 30:4, 1977, p. 45–61)

Discussion of perception and reality of oil production in Brazil. A review of the country's oil exploitation history shows that despite the large investments in sedimentary basins and the continental shelf, the results have been short of expectations.

5702 **Sternberg, Hilgard O'Reilly.** The Amazon river of Brazil. Wiesbaden, FRG, Franz Steiner Verlag, 1975. 74 p., bibl., maps, plates (Erdkundliches wissen. Schriftenfolge für forschung und praxis, 40)

This monograph states that it consists of "information and reflects on the Amazon River of Brazil [and that it] has no pretensions of being a structured and exhaustive study." Nevertheless, the well-written text with its numerous photographs, maps, and other visual aids provides not only an excellent idea of Amazonia but also offers valuable insights and perspectives of the region's ecology.

5703 Sylos, Honório de. São Paulo e seus caminhos. São Paulo, Editora McGraw-Hill do Brasil, 1976. 119 p., facsims., maps, plates, tables.

Journalist's interpretation of the societal changes in the state of São Paulo since the colonial period. Although personal at times, the account enables the reader to acquire a synthesis of the state's economic, historic, and political changes.

5704 Tarifa, José Roberto and others. A gênese dos episódios meteorológicos de julho de 1975 e a variação espacial dos danos causados pelas geadas á cafeicultura no estado de São Paulo (SBPC/CC, 29:12, dez. 1977, p. 1362–1374, maps, tables)

The article attempts to explain three aspects of the widespread frost damage that occurred to coffee plantations of São Paulo state in July 1975: a) the spatial variations of damages; b) the causes of such variations; and c) the genesis and forms of frost occurrences. The authors determine that about 70 percent of the variations in temperature were associated with the position and intensity of continental polar anticyclones.

5705 Teixeira, Marlene P.V. Padrões de ligações e sistema urbano: uma análise aplicada aos estados da Guanabara e Rio de Janeiro (IBGE/R, 37:3, julho/set. 1975, p. 16–55, tables)

Elaboration of a geographic model to explain the relationships between a regional center and its areas of influence. The model is applied to the state of Rio.

5706 Thery, Hervé. Pourquoi l'Amazonie?: presentation d'une recherche et d'un espace (AGF/B, 54:441/442, mars/abril 1977, p. 109–116, map)

Despite its long economic and settlement history, Amazônia has been a very poorly understood region. A realistic understanding of the region can be derived only from studying it within a national context.

5707 Tigre, Carlos Bastos. Porque reflorestamento no polígono das sêcas. Prefácio de José Lins Albuquerque. Fortaleza,

Brazil, Ministério do Interior, Depto. Nacional de Obras Contra as Seças (DNOCS), 1970. 146 p., bibl., tables.

Author emphasizes the importance of reforestation in the semiarid Northeast as an instrument for restoring ecological balance and for effecting economic change. Causes of present-day desertification, the root of most rural problems in the so-called "Drought Polygon" are also discussed.

5708 Tommasi, Luiz Roberto. A degradação do meio ambiente. São Paulo, Livraria Nobel, 1976. 169 p., bibl., maps, plates, tables.

Introductory text on environmental conservation geared primarily to the layman and secondary students. Standard topics like air pollution, aerosols, solid wastes, and the eutrophication of water are treated.

5709 Tourinho, Luiz Carlos Pereira. Distorções fisionômicas do Brasil (UFP/EB, 1:1, 1976, p. 53–75, tables)

Increasing economic disparities between the South and Brazil's other regions tend to erode national unity. Recent attempts to correct these areal imbalances, however, have failed. Concentrated infusion of economic aid into small areas seems a possible solution.

Trias, Rolando A. Laguarda. Rio de Janeiro: historia de sus denominaciones. See *HLAS 40:4054.*

5710 Tricart, Jean L.F. Tipos de planícies aluviais e de leitos fluviais na Amazônia brasileira (IBGE/R, 39:2, abril/junho 1977, p. 3–39)

Study describes geomorphologic characteristics of the Brazilian Amazonia, especially along rivers. Three factors are believed to have determined the current morphogenesis: the structural and tectonic history, climatic oscillations, and sea level changes.

5711 Tsukuba Daigaku. Latin America Tokubetsu Kenkyu Project. Jumbi linkai. Burajiru to Nippon. Sakura-mura, Ibaraki, Japan, Univ. of Tsukuba, 1978. 88 p.

This short monograph includes topics such as, the status of Japanese-Brazilians in a multi-racial and multi-cultural society, implantation of Japanese businesses and their perception by the Brazilians, current agricultural problems, and urbanization and environmental problems.

5712 Van Wambeke, A. Properties and potentials of soils in the Amazon Basin (IA/I, 3:4, July/Aug. 1978, p. 233–242)

Similarities as well as differences of soils in Amazonia are explained in general terms. Then, development alternatives are offered which include: agricultural intensification through soil modification, extensive cultivation by adoption of shifting cultivation systems, and crop adaptation to suit local conditions.

5713 Vargas Haya, Héctor. Amazonia: ¿realidad o mito? Prólogo de Enrique Rivero Vélez. Lima, Gráfica Inclán, 1977. 206 p., map, plates.

General review of current developments in the Amazon basin and suggestions for an economic and political integration of the region.

5714 Vetter, David M. and **Ana Maria Brasileiro.** Toward a development strategy for Grande Rio de Janeiro (*in* Cornelius, Wayne E. and Robert V. Kemper *eds.* Metropolitan Latin America: the challenge and the response [see item **9016**] p. 259–278, bibl., illus.)

Survey of the causes and effects of Greater Rio's growth, and the governmental responses to it.

5715 Viagnoni, Lida. La rete urbana del Nordeste del Brasile (SSG/RGI, 85:1, marzo 1978, p. 56–67, map, tables)

The rapid urbanization that has occurred in the Northeast has been spatially confined to a 200 km zone along the coast. Within this belt, the fastest growth has taken place in the administrative or commercial/port cities such as Recife, Salvador, and Fortaleza. These places completely dominate the social, economic, and political life of the region.

5716 von Kanel, Alfred. Ergebnisse und Probleme bei der Erschliung der brasilianischen Grobregion Amazonien

(GGDDR/GB, 85[22]:4, 1977, p. 241–257, maps, tables)

Summary of current developments in Amazonia and their possible socioeconomic and environmental outcomes.

5717 Williams, Richard. Uma provável cratera meteorítica no norte de Goiás (SBPC/CC, 28:8, agosto 1976, p. 861–863, map, plates)

On the basis of scientific data, geologic history, and energy balance calculations, author concludes that the Serra da Cangalha in Northeast Goiás emerged from the impact of a meteorite.

5718 Wozniewicz, Wenceslau Dyminski. The Amazonian highway system (*in* Wagley, Charles *ed.* Man in the Amazon [and *HLAS 37:523*] p. 21–314, map, tables)

Lengthy, semi-technical paper describing the highways being built in the Brazilian Amazon. Unfortunately, study does not include maps.

5719 Xavier, Carlos. Plantas indiáticas no Brasil (IHGB/R, 314, jan./março 1977, p. 45–50)

Describes attempts by the Portuguese monarchs of the 18th century to introduce East Asian specialty crops in Brazil, e.g., clove, cinnamon, nutmeg, ginger, and black-pepper. Based on materials from the Arquivo Histórico de Goa.

5720 Yamamoto, Shozo and **Mario Hiraoka.** Three farm types in the Patos basin of the inland Paraiba state, Brazilian Northeast (Geographical Review of Japan [Association of Japanese Geographers, Tokyo] 50:9, 1977, p. 511–529)

Three types of farms, the *fazenda*, the *sitio*, and the *vazante* are found in the semi-arid *sertão* of northeast Brazil. The case study of Patos basin, Paraíba, reveals that these distinctive agricultural units developed as a result of both the socioeconomic and environmental conditions peculiar to the region.

CARTOGRAPHY

ANDREW M. MODELSKI, *Bibliographer, Geography and Map Division, Library of Congress*

SINCE THE ESTABLISHMENT OF A SEPARATE cartography section in the *Handbook*, some 10 years ago, the basic working concepts and goals for selection discussed in previous essays has remained unchanged. Contributing to this uniformity over the years has been the fact that the editors for the section have been members of the staff of the Geography and Map Division of the Library of Congress. The continued use of the Division's current cartographic accessions as the major source has helped in establishing a more uniform criteria for selection of items to be included in the section.

It requires a listing of approximately 10 percent of the Library's two-year cartography accessions to provide an adequate spectrum of the most important works in Latin America's sociocultural environment. In this reporting period the Library acquired and cataloged over 2,500 maps and atlases of the countries of Latin America.

The trend continues in increased cartographic production in Argentina, Brazil, Chile, Colombia, Mexico, Peru, and Venezuela, and increases have also been noted in Bolivia, Ecuador, Guatemala, and Panama. Noteworthy maps and atlases for this reporting period include a 29-sheet set of large scale geology maps of Venezuela (1976, item **5916**), a railroad atlas of Latin America (1977, item **5721**), a physical atlas of Chile (1978, item **5801**), a coffee atlas of Colombia (1976, item **5815**), a highly technical physical environment atlas of Ecuador (1977, item **5828**), a climatic atlas of Brazil's Estado da Bahia (1977, item **5777**), and a facsimile atlas of early maps and documents of Venezuela's Federal District (1977, item **5909**).

For the first time in 20 years the International Cartographic Association (ICA) held its biannual international conference on cartography at the Univ. of Maryland, College Park, Maryland, from 26 July through 2 Aug. 1978. This conference brought together top scholars and experts in the field from academic departments, government bureaus, and from private industry. For this meeting there were 754 delegates and observers from national committees and other organizations representing some 60 nations including all the nations of Latin America.

The Conference program and exhibits focused on five themes which included automation in cartography, with special reference to the new user, digitizing and editing, output systems, data bases and technological exchange; map perception and design with special reference to map reading, color, symbolism, tactual mapping, and statistics; cartography in the developing nations of the world; remote sensing with special reference to Landsat status, future plans, application in aeronautical charting, and land cover and condition; and oceanic and coastal cartography with special reference to boundary demarcation, remote sensing, positional data, and automated chartmaking.

In addition to 12 plenary sessions, at which simultaneous translation in English, French and Spanish was provided, there were meetings of the ICA Commissions and Working Groups, and a poster session where cartographers displayed maps, graphs, diagrams and data related to their current research in cartography.

The US Organizing Committee arranged a program of exhibits to harmonize with the above five themes of the Conference. A variety of technical tours enabled participants to visit cartographic facilities in the Washington, D.C. area.

All the many maps and atlases displayed at this important conference were presented to the Library of Congress for its permanent collections. Some of them are represented in the present listing. Other items pertaining to Latin America will appear in the next *Handbook* volume listing maps. Information on specific exhibit items is available from the Geography and Map Division's Reference and Bibliography Section, Library of Congress, Alexandria, Virginia 22304.

GENERAL

5721 Asociación Latinoamericana de Ferrocarriles, *Buenos Aires.* Atlas ferroviario latinoamericano. B.A., 1977. 40 p., colored maps.

Railroad atlas of Latin America.

Nemby, Eric. The Rand McNally world atlas of exploration. See *HLAS 40:2308.*

5722 Ti t' u ch'u pan she. La-ting Mei-chou. Ti l pan. Peking, Hsin hua shu tien Pei-ching fa hsing so fa hsing, 1974. Colored. 99 x 98 cm. Scale 1:10,000,000.

Chinese school wall map of Latin America. Relief shown by gradient tints and spot heights. Depths shown by gradient tints. Chinese. Cover title also in P'ing yin. Includes location map.

5723 Union of Soviet Socialist Republics. Glavnoe Upravlenie Geodezii i Kartografii. Latinskaia Amerika, ekonomicheskaia uchebnaia karta. Edited by V.S. Chudinova. Moscow, 1976. Colored. 131 x 110 cm. on 2 sheets 70 x 115 cm. Scale 1:8,000,000.

Soviet school map of Latin America showing economic conditions.

CARIBBEAN

5724 Map of the Cayman Islands, British West Indies. n.p., n.p., 1976? 3 colored maps on sheet 41 x 52 cm. Scale ca. 1:67,500 and 1:150,000.

Issued with the *Cayman Islands holiday guide 1976*, a Nor'wester publication. Includes indexed road map of George Town and map of airline routes to Cayman Islands.

5725 Société Nouvelle Pétrole et Affretements, *Paris.* Fretoil: Caribbean area. Paris, Fretoil Tanker and Oil Brokers, 1975.

Photocopy. On sheet 76 x 101 cm.

Legend in English and French. Includes explanatory note, distance list, and inset of "Maracaibo Lake." Petroleum shipping terminals.

5726 United States. Central Intelligence Agency. Caribbean America. Washington, 1976. Colored. 66 x 87 cm. Scale ca. 1:6,000,000.

General map with relief shown by shading and spot heights.

CENTRAL AMERICA

5727 Barrenechea MLA (firm), *Rio.* América Central. Rio, J. Paulini, 1976. Colored. 84 x 122 cm. Scale 1:3,000,000.

General map of the West Indies with an inset of Central America.

5728 Union of Soviet Socialist Republics. Glavnoe Upravlenie Geodezii i Kartografii. TSentral naîa Amerika i Vest Indiîa. Edited by A. Monkhe Barredo and T.G. Novikova. Technical editing by A.S. Tikhomirova and A.V. Katen. 3. ed. Moscow, 1977. Colored. 66 x 86 cm. Scale 1:5,000,000.

Russian school map of Central America and Caribbean showing ethnology and economic conditions.

5729 United States. Central Intelligence Agency. Middle America. Washington, 1977. Colored. 84 x 107 cm. Scale 1:5,750,000.

Clear general outline map.

SOUTH AMERICA

5730 Denoyer-Geppert (firm), *Chicago, Ill.* Amrīka āl-Janūbiyah al-siyāsīyah. Chicago, Ill., 1978. Colored. 127 x 106 cm. Scale 1:7,250,000.

School wall map in Arabic. Shows Central America, South America, and Caribbean area. Includes location map and inset.

5731 John Bartholomew and Son (firm), *Edinburgh, Ind.* South America. Edinburgh, Ind., 1975. Colored. 86 x 61 cm. (Bartholomew world travel series) Scale 1:10,000,000.

General map of South America. Relief shown by gradient tints and spot heights. Depths shown by gradient tints. Includes inset of Galapagos Islands.

5732 Rowe, John Howland. Indian tribes of South America. Berkeley, Calif., The Author, 1974. 56 x 39 cm. Scale ca. 1:14,000,000.

Detailed Indian tribe map with index to 216 tribes.

5733 United Nations, *New York.* South America: international river basins, including section of rivers/lakes forming international boundaries. N.Y., 1977. 33 x 25 cm. Scale ca. 1:25,000,000.

Map indicating international rivers lakes and watersheds.

ARGENTINA

5734 Argentina. Instituto Geográfico Militar. Atlas de la República Argentina. B.A., 1976. 28 p., colored illus., maps. 29 x 40 cm.

General atlas of Argentina.

5735 ——. ——. República Argentina. B.A., 1975. Colored. 163 x 101 cm. on 2 sheets 89 x 107 cm. Scale 1:2,500,000.

Detailed general map. Relief shown by gradient tints, shading, and spot heights. Depths shown by gradient tints. Insets: Territorio Nacional de la Tierra del Fuego, Antártida e Islas del Atlántico Sur. Buenos Aires y alrededores. División política.

5736 ——. Servicio de Hidrografía Naval. Sección de Oceanografía. Carta batimétrica, Atlántico sur occidental. Cartógrafos: Miguel A. Curci and María T. Maza. B.A., 1976. Colored. Scale 1:5,000,000.

Bathymetric chart of the continental shelf.

5737 ——. Yacimientos Petrolíferos Fiscales. Departamento Difusión y
Ceremonial. Sector Prensa y Publicaciones. República Argentina, mapa petrolero. Esmeralda, Arg., 1975. 5 colored maps 40 x 26 cm. Scale ca. 1:9,000,000.

Oil and gas maps indicating pipe lines.

5738 Automóvil Club Argentino, *Buenos Aires.* República Argentina: red caminera principal. Dibujó: Juan C. Corso. B.A., 1977. Colored. 97 x 58 cm. fold. to 21 x 11 cm. (Publicación, 654) Scale 1:4,000,000.

Relief shown by shading. Published jointly with Ford Motor Argentina S.A. Includes three insets. Index, text, map of "Esquemas de Distancias," map showing distances from B.A. (colored illus.) directories of Automóvil Club Argentino's lodgings, recreational facilities, and automobile service stations, and directory of Ford Motor Argentina S.A. Distributors on verso.

5739 Bustos, R. Carte géomorphologique de la région de l'Aconcagua, haut Río Mendoza-Andes de Mendoza, Rep. Argentine. Bordeaux, France, Univ. de Bordeaux, Institut de Géographie, 1977. Colored. 93 x 82 cm. on 4 sheets 56 x 44 cm. and 42 x 44 cm. Scale ca. 1:500,000.

Geomorphological map of Aconcagua region.

5740 Editorial Filcar (firm), *Buenos Aires.* Zona Atlántica planos: San Clemente del Tuyu, Las Toninas, Santa Teresita, Mar del Tuyu, La Lucila del Mar, San Bernardo, Mar de Ajó, Pinamar, Ostende, Valeria del Mar, Villa Gesell, Santa Clara del Mar. B.A., 1976. 11 colored maps on sheet 59 x 81 cm.

Eleven Atlantic beach cities south of the La Plata R.

5741 Labrecque, John and **Philip D. Rabinowitz.** Magnetic anomalies, Argentine continental margin, Argentine Basin, North Scotia Ridge, Falkland Plateau. Illustrated by Virginia Rippon. Tulsa, Okla., American Association of Petroleum Geologists, 1977. bibl., 85 x 117 cm.

Compiled under the sponsorship of the NSF Office for the International Decade of Ocean Exploration. Includes text, list of compiled magnetics data and two profiles. Has bibliography.

5742 Nuevo atlas geográfico de la Argentina. B.A., Ediciones Mundo Técnico, 1976. 24 p., colored maps. 36 cm.

General and historical atlas.

5743 **Peuser (Jacobo) Ltda.** (firm), *Buenos Aires.* Guía Peuser de turismo, Argentina y Uruguay. n.p., Editorial Circulación Latino-Americana, 1977. 23 colored maps on 2 sheets 82 x 59 cm. and 65 x 48 cm.

Tourist map of Argentina and Uruguay. Includes inset with index to embassies. Accompanied by the text (162 p., maps).

5744 **Rabinowitz, Philip D.** Free-air gravity anomalies, Argentine continental margin, Argentine Basin, North Scotia Ridge, Falkland Plateau. Illustrated by Virginia Rippon. Tulsa, Okla., American Association of Petroleum Geologists, 1977. bibl., colored. 86 x 118 cm.

Compiled under the sponsorship of the National Science Foundation Office for the International Decade of Ocean Exploration. Includes text, table of "Instruments and Navigation," for profiles, and map of "Study Area, Offshore Argentina, Showing locations of profiles . . ." Bibliography.

5745 ——— and others. Bathymetric chart, Argentine continental margin, Argentine Basin, North Scotia Ridge, Falkland Plateau. Illustrated by Virginia Rippon. Tulsa, Okla., American Association of Petroleum Geologists, 1978. bibl., colored. 86 x 117 cm. Scale not given.

Depths shown by contours, gradient tints, and soundings. Includes text, map, and bathymetric profiles. Has bibliography.

REGIONS, STATES, AND CITIES

5746 **Argentina. Consejo Federal de Inversiones.** Mapa geológico de la Provincia de Buenos Aires: programa para la planificación del uso de los recursos naturales. B.A., 1975. bibl., Colored. 58 x 42 cm. Scale ca. 1:2,000,000.

Includes location map. Accompanied by sheet of stratigraphic table and text. 61 p. colored map. Bibliography in accompanying text.

5747 **Automóvil Club Argentino,** *Buenos Aires.* **División Cartografía.** Buenos Aires, carta vial de zona, República Argentina. Dibujos: Nélida M. de Lechners. Colored. 82 x 69 cm. (Publicación, 660) Scale ca. 1:1,100,000.

Relief shown by shading and spot

heights. Includes inset of B.A. region and location map. Index, text, four local route maps, and indexed map of La Plata on verso.

5748 **Bregna** (firm), *Buenos Aires.* Guía de Buenos Aires. Nuevo plano de la Ciudad de Buenos Aires. Cartographers: Alberto J. Brú and Jorge F. Valls. B.A., 1978. Colored. 79 x 64 cm. Scale ca. 1:37,000.

General city map showing subways in inset.

5749 **Buenos Aires** (city), *Arg.* Red de los subterráneos de Buenos Aires. B.A., n.p., 1978. Colored. 64 x 44 cm.

Good subway map. No publisher or printer information.

5750 **Editorial Filcar** (firm), *Buenos Aires.* **Departamento Cartografía.** Alrededores de Buenos Aires. B.A., 1977. Colored. 84 x 115 cm. Scale 1:100,000.

Detailed general map of the city and vicinity.

5751 **Río Negro** (province), *Arg.* **Secretaría de Turismo.** Mapa de la provincia de Río Negro. Viedma, Arg., 1976. Colored. 52 x 77 cm. Scale ca. 1:1,200,000.

Good general map of the province.

5752 **Ruthsatz, Barbara.** Mapa de vegetación: area noreste de la Provincia de Jujuy, Argentina. n.p., n.p., 1976. 2 colored 55 x 94 cm. Scale 1:50,000.

Detailed vegetation map of the province. No place or publisher given.

BAHAMAS

5753 **Arrow Publishing Co.** (firm), *Newton Upper Falls, Mass.* Visitors & residents approved maps: Nassau, Freeport, Bahama family islands; including large scale map of the downtown shopping area, Nassau and vicinity, New Providence, Cable Beach, Bahama Islands, Freeport. Newton Upper Falls, Mass., 1977. 7 colored maps on sheet 104 x 68 cm.

Detailed tourist map. Includes indexes, text, colored illustrations, plan of "Nassau International Airport," and 19 plans of shopping centers.

BELIZE

5754 United Kingdom. Great Britain. Directorate of Overseas Surveys. Belize River valley agricultural survey. Tolworth, U.K., Overseas Development Administration, Land Resources Division, 1973. 5 colored maps. 36 x 46 cm. and 58 x 56 cm. (DOS 3145A, 3144B, and 3144A) Scale 1:100,000 and 1:250,000.

Title taken from the first map. Relief shown by spot heights on some sheets. This map accompanies Land Resource study: "The agricultural development potential of the Belize Valley" by R.N. Jenkins and others. Some sheets include boundary diagrams and sheet indexes. Shows landforms, agriculture, and land use.

BOLIVIA

5755 Bolivia. Corporación Minera de Bolivia (COMIBOL). Departamento de Propiedades Mineras. Mapa general demonstrativo de los yacimientos minerales de COMIBOL. La Paz, 1975. Colored. 70 x 53 cm. Scale 1:1,500,000.

Mines and mineral resources. Relief shown by spot heights. Shows southwestern Bolivia. Includes distance list.

5756 ———. Instituto Boliviano de Turismo. Plano turístico de la ciudad de La Paz. La Paz, 1977. 19 x 29 cm.

5757 ———. Ministerio de Planeamiento y Coordinación. Exploración y prospección mineralógica. La Paz, 1976. 98 x 76 cm.

Shows situations of mineral exploration and prospecting in 1975 and 1980.

5758 ———. ———. Sector agropecuario. La Paz, 1976. 97 x 79 cm.

Shows situations of agriculture, cattle, and forestry in 1975 and 1980.

5759 ———. ———. Sector industrias. La Paz, 1976. 98 x 76 cm.

Shows situation of industries in 1975 and 1980.

5760 ———. ———. Instituto Nacional de Estadística y Censos. División de Cartografía. Mapa de Bolivia: Depto. Beni. Di-

bujos de R. Bernal A. La Paz, 1975. 82 x 86 cm. Scale 1:1,000,000.

General map of Bolivia.

5761 Holdridge, Leslie R. Mapa ecológico de Bolivia. Con la colaboración de la Organización de los Estados Americanos. Levantaron: Joseph Tosi and others. Mapa base, separación de colores e impresión: Instituto Geográfico Militar. La Paz, Ministerio de Asuntos Campesinos y Agropecuarios, División de Suelos, Riegos e Ingeniería, 1975. Colored. 177 x 147 cm. on 9 sheets 70 x 55 cm. or smaller fold. in cover 29 x 22 cm. Scale 1:1,000,000.

Includes insets of "Mapa de Regiones" and "Mapa de Vegetación," diagrams of "Perfil Longitudinal," "Regiones Latitudinales," and "Pisos Altitudinales," location map, and index map. Accompanied by text by Orlando Unzueta, 312 p. and 6 p. illus., maps (part colored).

5762 International Bank for Reconstruction and Development, *Washington.* Bolivia, power systems. Washington, 1976. Colored. 25 x 23 cm. Scale ca. 1:6,000,000.

Shows power plants and transmission lines. Includes location map (publication no. is IBRD-1034OR3).

5763 United Kingdom. Great Britain. Directorate of Overseas Surveys. Mapa de los sistemas de tierras, Bolivia. La Paz, Instituto Geográfico Militar de Bolivia, 1974. Colored. 97 x 79 cm. (Its DOS, 3186) Scale 1:1,750,000.

Land use map. Relief shown by contours. "Impreso para el Instituto Geográfico Militar de Bolivia por el Ordnance Survey, Inglaterra." Includes location map.

BRAZIL

5764 Brazil. Departmento Nacional de Estradas de Rodagem. Diretoria de Planejamento. Grupo de Trabalho de Projectos Cartográficos. Mapa rodoviário . . . Brasília, 1975. Colored. 60 x 50 cm. and 50 x 60 cm.

Clear and detailed road maps of the states and territories of Brazil. Geographic coverage complete in 27 sheets. Includes index map. Most sheets are dated 1976.

5765 ———. **Ministério do Interior.** Programas especiais de desenvolvimento regional. Brasília, 1976? Colored. 50 x 62 cm.
Regional planning map.

5766 ———. **Petróleos Brasileiros** (PE-TROBRAS). Petrobrás. Brasília, Editora Gráfica Barbero, 1977? Colored. 102 x 73 cm. No scale given.
Petroleum map of Brazil.

5767 ———. **Rede Ferroviára Federal. Diretoria de Planejamento.** Mapa das linhas: sistema ferroviário nacional. Rio, Ministério dos Transportes, 1976. 19 l., colored maps. 32 x 41 cm.
Atlas of railroad network.

5768 **Fundação Instituto Brasileiro de Geografia e Estatística** (IBGE), *Rio.* **Diretoria de Geodésia e Cartografia. Superintendência de Cartografia** (SUCAR). República Federativa do Brasil. Brasília, 1978. Colored. 31 x 36 cm. Scale ca. 1:17,500,000.
Good general map showing state boundaries and the drainage and transportation networks.

5769 **Polimapas Editora Ltda.** (firm), *São Paulo.* República Federativa do Brasil, regiões sudeste e sul; rodoviário-político-regional-turístico. Desenhado por José Nonoya Filho, Natanael Alves da Silva, Manuel Salvador da Silva. São Paulo, 1977. Colored. 96 x 82 cm. Scale: 1:2,500,000.
Detailed general road and tourist map. Includes distance charts. Index on verso.

5770 **Ribeiro, José** and others. Esboço de um atlas lingüístico de Minas Gerais. Brasília, Ministério da Educação e Cultura, 1977. 1 v. (244 p.) maps, 30 cm.
Vol. 1 of a linguistic atlas of the state of Minas Gerais, Brazil.

5771 **Sociedade Comercial e Representações Gráficas,** *Curitiba, Brazil.* Brasil. Curitiba, Brazil, 1977. Colored. 102 x 97 cm. Scale 1:4,500,000.
Detailed general map.

5772 **United States. Central Intelligence Agency.** Brazil. Washington, 1977. Colored. 39 x 45 cm. Scale 1:11,800,000.
Relief shown by shading and spot heights. Includes comparative location map, distance map, and subject maps of "Popula-

tion, Administrative Divisions, and Economic Regions," "Natural Vegetation," "Land Use," "Temperature and Precipitation," and "Economic Activity" in margin.

REGIONS, STATES, AND CITIES

5773 **Brazil. Superintendência do Desenvolvimento da Amazônia** (SUDAM). Engeria. Brasília, 1976? Colored. 14 x 20 cm.
Electric power plants and transmission lines in Amazon Valley.

5774 ———. ———. Zona nordeste da Amazônia legal. Brasília, 1976? Colored. 53 x 76 cm. Scale 1:5,000,000.
Regional planning for Amazon Valley.

5775 ———. ———. Telecomunicações. Brasília, 1976? Colored. 14 x 20 cm.
Shows telecommunication network in Amazon Valley.

5776 **Costa, Manoel Teixeira da** and **Antônio Wilson Romano.** Mapa geológico do Estado de Minas Gerais. Elaboração cartográfica: Geocarta S.A. Belo Horizonte, Brazil, Secretaria do Planejamento e Coordenação Geral, 1976. Colored. 100 x 121 cm. Scale 1:1,000,000.
Detailed geological map.

5777 **Fundação Centro de Planejamento da Bahía. Coordenação de Recursos Naturais.** Atlas climatológico do Estado da Bahia: potencial agroclimático do Estado da Bahia. Salvador, Brazil, 1977. 46 l., maps, plates, 49 cm.
Climate atlas of state of Bahia.

5778 **Fundação Instituto Brasileiro de Geografia e Estatística** (IBGE), *Rio.* **Directoria de Geodésia e Cartografia. Superintendência de Cartografia** (SUCAR). Cartaguia de Brasília. Brasília, 1976. Colored. 70 x 73 cm.
Includes three insets and descriptive note. Colored illustrations, text, 10 graphs, location map, map of Eixo Monumental and indexed map of Plano Rodoviário do Distrito Federal on verso.

5779 **Fundação João Pinheiro,** *Belo Horizonte, Brazil.* **Centro de Recursos Naturais.** Aptidão agropastoril, sistema de manejo desenvolvido sem irrigação. Porto Velho, Brazil, Superintendência do De-

senvolvimento da Região Centro-Oeste (SUDECO), 1975. Colored. 75 x 114 cm. Scale 1:250,000.
Irrigation map of central west region of Rondônia. Includes location map.

5780 ——. ——. ——. Reconhecimento de solos. Porto Velho, Brazil, Superintendência do Desenvolvimento da Região Centro-Oeste (SUDECO), 1975. Colored. 75 x 114 cm. Scale 1:250,000.
Detailed soils map of central west region of Rondônia. Includes location map.

5781 **Furnas Centrais Elétricas** (firm), *Rio*. Furnas Centrais Eletricas SA, subsidiary of Eletrobrás. Rio, 1976. Colored. 46 x 63 cm. Scale ca. 1:3,000,000.
Map of the FURNAS power distribution area of Brazil. Shows electric power plants and distribution. Includes inset of "Regional Companies of Eletrobrás." Text, statistical data, distance chart, map of "Furnas System," and colored illustration on verso. FURNAS is responsible for the supply of electric power to a vast area of Central-West and Southeast Brazil comprising the states of Rio, São Paulo, Minas Gerais, Espirito Santo, Distrito Federal and part of Goiás and Mato Grosso, where most of Brazil's population is concentrated, generating 66 percent of the nation's internal product.

5782 **Lima, Ivan Fernandes.** Diagrama hidro-orográfico. Desenho original: Fernando Porto e Sérgio Acioly da Silva. Desenho final: Pepito Marques. Cartografia: Depto. Cartográfica Abril. Maceio, Brazil, Secretaría de Planejamento, 1976? Colored. 68 x 88 cm. Scale 1:400,000.
Physical map. Relief shown by shading. Base map: Estado de Alagoas, plano de ação 1976/79. Includes coat of arms and index to mountains.

5783 ——. Estado de Alagoas, plano de ação 1976–79. Desenho original: Fernando Porto. Cartografia: Depto. Cartográfico Abril. Maceió, Brazil, Secretaría de Planejamento, 1976. Colored. 68 x 89 cm. Scale 1:400,000.
Regional and economic planning map. Includes coat of arms and inset of "Mapa Econômico do Estado de Alagoas."

5784 **Minas Gerais** (state), *Brazil*. **Secretaria de Planejamento e Coordenação Geral.** Estado de Minas Gerais, cartograma.

Belo Horizonte, Brazil, 1976. Colored. 50 x 61 cm. Scale 1:2,000,000.
Good administrative map showing district boundaries.

5785 **Moreno, José Alberto** and **Miron Zaions.** Diagrama morfológico. Perifs geológicos: Nelson Amoretti Lisboa e Darcy de Souza Picada. Porto Alegre, Brazil, Central de Comandos Mecanizados de Apoio a Agricultura, Unidade de Geografia e Cartografia, 1975. Colored. 70 x 99 cm. Scale ca. 1:750,000.
Geomorphologic map of the state of Rio Grande do Sul.

5786 **Pacheco, J.B.** Estado do Maranhão. São Paulo, Polimapas Editora, 1976. Colored. 103 x 79 cm. Scale 1:1,000,000.
Good general map of the state.

5787 **Paraná** (state), *Brazil*. **Sistema Estadual de Planejamento.** Mapa do Estado do Paraná, associação dos municípios. Curitiba, Brazil, 1977. Colored. 32 x 41 cm. Scale ca. 1:1,950,000.
Administrative and political divisions in the state of Paraná.

5788 **Pernambuco** (state), *Brazil*. **Secretaria de Transportes e Comunicações. Departamento de Estradas de Rodagem.** Mapa rodoviário. Recife, Brazil, 1977? Colored. 28 x 77 cm. Scale 1:1,000,000.
Relief shown by shading. Index and two maps on verso. Text in cover.

5789 **Polimapas Editora Ltda.** (firm), *São Paulo*. Mapa polivisual da Região Nordeste do Brasil. Desenho de: José Nonoya Filho, Manuel Salvador da Silva e Natanael Alves da Silva. São Paulo, 1975. Colored. 106 x 78 cm. Scale 1:2,500,000.
Good general map.

5790 ——. ——. Planta polivisual de Cidade de Manaus. São Paulo, 1979. Colored. 84 x 109 cm.
Detailed street plan of city with names of subdivisions.

5791 ——. ——. ——. São Paulo: político, regional, escolar, polivisual. Desenho de : José Nonoya Filho, Natanael Alves da Silva, Manuel Salvador da Silva. São Paulo, 1977. Colored. 81 x 108 cm. Scale 1:1,000,000.
Detailed general state map.

5792 **Quatro Rodas** (firm), *Porto Alegre, Brazil.* **Departamento Cartográfico.** Porto Alegre. Porto Alegre, Brazil, Empresa Portoalegrense de Turismo (EPATUR), 1976? Colored. 76 x 88 cm.

Detailed tourist map of the city. Relief shown by shading and spot heights. Notable buildings and monuments shown by drawings. Indexed for points of interest. Published jointly with Prefeitura Municipal de Porto Alegre, Depto. de Turismo e Divulgação (COMTUR).

CHILE

5793 **Chile. Dirección de Vialidad. Departamento de Estudios. Sección Planificación.** Carta caminera. Santiago, 1976. 6 col. maps. 86 x 68 cm.

Detailed road maps. Relief shown by spot heights. Includes index map. Some sheets include insets. Distance charts on verso.

5794 ———. **Empresa Nacional de Electricidad** (ENDESA). **Oficina de Información y Control de Resultados de Explotación.** Chile: sistemas eléctricos primarios, segunda e quinta zona eléctrica. Santiago, 1976. Colored. 75 x 16 cm.

Map of electric power plants and power distribution in Chile by ENDESA.

5795 ———. **Instituto de Investigaciones Geológicas.** Carta geológica de Chile. Santiago, 1977. bibl., colored 74 x 109 cm. fold. in cover 24 x 13 cm. Scale 1:100,000.

Relief shown by contours and spot heights. Includes cross sections, list of "Localidades Fosilíferas," fault map, sheet index, and location map. Each sheet accompanied by text. Bibliography in accompanying text.

5796 ———. **Instituto Geográfico Militar.** Mapa de Chile. Santiago, 1977. Colored. 123 x 87 cm. Scale 1:2,000,000.

Relief shown by gradient tints, shading, and spot heights. Includes coats of arms, eight insets, chart showing organization of administrative and government system, table of "Chile: sus Regiones, Provincias y Capitales," and distance chart.

5797 ———. **Instituto Nacional de Estadísticas. Departmento de Geografía y Censos.** Mapa esquemático de Chile. Dibu-

jante: José Tortella Latorre. Santiago, 1976. 110 x 78 cm. Scale 1:3,000,000.

Shows new administrative divisions. Includes location map, inset of "Provincia antártica Chilena," five other insets and indexes.

5798 ———. **Ministerio de la Vivienda y Urbanismo. Dirección de Planificación del Desarrollo Urbano. Departamento Area Metropolitana.** Plan intercomunal de Santiago (Plan Director del Area Metropolitana). Diseñadoras: M. Norma Guajardo e Ivonne Moriamez. Santiago, 1976. Colored. 88 x 74 cm. Scale ca. 1:40,000.

Urban land use and city planning map. Relief shown by form lines and spot heights. "La actualización de este plano se realizó incluyendo las modificaciones aprobadas por . . . al 30 de marzo de 1976."

5799 **Geoplan** (firm), *Santiago.* Mapa de Chile. Santiago, Editorial Lord Cochrane, 1976. Colored. 247 x 40 cm. on 9 sheets 36 x 40 cm. or smaller. Scale 1:2,000,000.

Good general map. Relief shown by gradient tints and spot heights. Depths shown by gradient tints and soundings. "Actualizado con los Límites Provinciales y Regionales de Acuerdo a los Decretos No. 575 de Julio de 1974, No. 1230 de Octubre de 1975 y No. 1317 de Diciembre de 1975."

5800 ———, ———. Mapa de Chile. Santiago, Editorial Lord Cochrane, 1977. Colored. 77 x 120 cm. Scale 1:2,000,000.

Relief shown by gradient tints and spot heights. Depths shown by contours and gradient tints. Includes insets showing political divisions and of Territorio Chileno Antártico and five other insets. Map No. (No. de Inscripción) 46178-24/1/77.

5801 **León Ribera, G.** and **Paulina L. Ponce.** Atlas de Chile 78: regionalizado. Santiago, Editorial Lord Cochrane, 1978. 61 p., 24 cm.

Atlas of physical and general geography maps of the state of Chile.

5802 **Schmidt Walters, Rudy** and **Patricio Valdés Sagrista.** Atlas, Chile y sus nuevas provincias. Santiago, Publicaciones Didácticas, 1976. 34 p., colored illus., colored maps, 27 cm.

General atlas of Chile.

COLOMBIA

5803 Arango Cálad, Jorge L.; T. Kassem Bustamante: and H. Duque Caro. Mapa geológico de Colombia. Elaboración cartográfica y edición: Ingeominas. Bogotá, Instituto Nacional de Investigaciones Geológico-Mineras, 1976. Colored. 131 x 94 cm. Scale 1:1,500,000.

Geological map. Relief shown by contours and spot heights. Depths shown by contours. Includes four insets and location map.

5804 Barrero Lozano, Darío and Taissir Kassem. Mapa metalógenico de Colombia. Metallogenic map of Colombia. Bogotá, Instituto Nacional de Investigaciones Geológico-Mineras, 1976. Colored. 45 x 31 cm. Scale 1:5,000,000.

Map of ore deposits. Insets: San Andrés; Providencia y Santa Catalina; Malpelo.

5805 Cartur (firm), *Bogotá.* Departamento de Cundinamarca. Bogotá, 1976. Colored. 49 x 43 cm. Scale 1:500,000.

Relief shown by contours. Shows climate by color. Includes location map, coat of arms, text, statistical data, map of "Bogotá," and indexed map of "Regiones Naturales."

5806 ———, ———. República de Colombia, mapa físico. Bogotá, 1975. Colored. 95 x 68 cm. Scale 1:2,000,000.

General physical map. Relief shown by gradient tints, contours, and spot heights. Includes text, location map, two insets, and table of "Principales Alturas."

5807 ———. ———. República de Colombia, mapa vial. Bogotá, 1977. Colored. 72 x 54 cm. Scale 1:2,000,000.

Good road map. Relief shown by spot heights. Includes index, text, and five insets. Maps of "Barranquilla," "Cartagena," "Medellín," and "Cali," and indexed map of "Bogotá" on verso.

5808 Cediel M., Fabio; Guillermo Ujueta; and Carlos Cáceres. Mapa geológico de Colombia. Diagramación: Clara F. de Cediel. Dibujo y Grabado: Arturo Ujueta L. Bogotá, Ediciones Geotec, 1976. bibl., colored. 136 x 95 cm. Scale 1:1,000,000.

Geological map. Includes six insets, location map, and table of "Estratigrafía."

Accompanied by text (23 p). Bibliography in accompanying text.

5809 Colombia. División de Conservación de Carreteras. Mapa vial del Departamento de Norte de Santander. Bogotá, 1977? 71 x 60 cm. Scale ca. 1:500,000.

One of a series of good road maps of the Departments of Colombia.

5810 ———. **Instituto Geográfico Agustín Codazzi.** Atlas básico de Colombia. Bogotá, 1978. 141 p., 34 cm.

Good general atlas including physical, cultural, and economic maps, and maps of departments and cities.

5811 ———. ———. República de Colombia, mapa vial y artesanal. Bogotá, 1976. Colored. 98 x 65 cm. Scale 1:1,500,000.

Excellent road map. Relief shown by shading and spot heights. Published jointly with Banco de Colombia and Artesanías de Colombia S.A. Shows regions of artistic (crafts) production and locations of artistic classifications and varieties of regional crafts. Includes five insets, location map, and distance chart.

5812 ———. ———. **Subdirección Cartográfica.** Plano de la ciudad de Bogotá. Bogotá, 1976. 69 x 99 cm. Scale 1:25,000.

One of a series of excellent city plans. Relief shown by contours. Oriented with north toward the lower left. Text, indexes, and maps of "Bogotá y sus Alrededores" and "Ciudad de Bogotá, Zona del Centro" on verso.

5813 ———. ———. República de Colombia, mapa físico político. Bogotá, 1976. 131 x 94 cm. Scale 1:1,500,000.

General map with relief shown by contours and spot heights. Depths shown by contours. Includes four insets and location map.

5814 ———. **Instituto Nacional de los Recursos Naturales Renovables y del Ambiente.** Mapa general de erosión. Bogotá, 1976. Colored. 140 x 93 cm. Scale 1:1,000,000.

Cover title: "La Erosión de Tierras en Colombia con Mapa de Procesos Dinámicos;" "Proyección conforme de Gauss." Includes five insets. Accompanied by text (56 p.).

5815 **Federación Nacional de Cafeteros de Colombia,** *Bogotá.* **División de Investigaciones Económicas.** Atlas cafetero de Colombia. Bogotá, 1976. 187 p., bibl., colored illus., colored maps, 42 cm.

Coffee atlas based on research of the 1970 Coffee Census. Includes bibliographical references and index.

5816 **Ramírez, Jesús Emilio.** Mapa de riesgo sísmico. Preparación: Gabriel Estrada Uribe. Bogotá, The Author, 1977. Colored. 41 x 29 cm. Scale 1:5,000,000.

Earthquake map of Colombia. Insets: San Andrés; Providencia; Malpelo; Estaciones Sismológicas. Accompanied by: "Explicación al Mapa de Riesgo Sísmico." (4 p., 22 cm).

COSTA RICA

5817 **Costa Rica. Instituto Costarricense de Turismo. Departamento de Promoción.** Mapas de Costa Rica y San José. San José, 1975. Colored. 43 x 55 cm. Scale 1:800,000.

Tourist map with relief shown by spot heights. Includes distance chart, two insets, map of highway and airline routes, and text. Indexed map of "Ciudad de San José" on verso.

5818 ———. **Instituto Nacional de Aprendizaje.** Mapa de carreteras: educación y seguridad vial. San José, 1976. Colored. 37 x 40 cm. Scale 1:1,000,000.

Good general road map with distance chart on verso.

5819 ———. **Ministerio de Transportes. Instituto Geográfico Nacional.** Costa Rica, mapa físico-político. En colaboración con el Servicio Geodésico Interamericano. San José, 1977. Colored. 75 x 80 cm. Scale 1:500,000.

Good general map made in colaboration with the Inter-American Geodetic Survey. Shows relief by contours, gradient tints, and spot heights. Depths shown by contours and gradient tints. "Compilado con los Mapas de Costa Rica, Escala 1:50,000 y por Métodos Planimétricos." Insets: Isla del Coco and Zona central.

CUBA

5820 **Asociación Cubana de las Naciones Unidas,** *New York.* Nueva división político-administrativa de Cuba. La Habana, 1976? Photocopy. 21 x 27 cm. "Boletín ACNU."

Outline map of Cuba showing new administrative divisions. Source of map: *Boletín de la Asociación Cubana de las Naciones Unidas* (1976).

5821 **Lesassier, Miguel.** Mapa histórico de Cuba. Miami, Fla., n.p., 1977. Colored. 66 x 122 cm.

Historical map showing landings and invasions between 1826 and 1898.

5822 **Union of Soviet Socialist Republics. Glavnoe Upravlenie Geodezii i Kartografii.** Kuba, uchebnaia karta. Moscow, 1977. 2 maps: colored; 47 x 112 cm. on sheet 92 x 118 cm.

Relief shown by shading, gradient tints, and spot heights on physical map. Depths shown by gradient tints and soundings on physical map. In Russian.

5823 **United States. Central Intelligence Agency.** Cuba. Washington, 1977. Colored. 22 x 53 cm. Scale 1:2,450,000.

Relief shown by shading and spot heights. Includes comparative area map, location map, and subject maps of "Economic activity," "Sugar," "Population," and "Land Utilization."

DOMINICAN REPUBLIC

5824 **General Drafting Co., Inc.** (firm), *New York.* La República Dominicana. N.Y., Dominican Tourist Information Center, 1977. Colored. 42 x 60 cm. Scale 1:672,000.

Good road map. Relief shown by spot heights. Includes distance chart, indexes, "Taxi and Car Rental Information," and colored illustrations. On verso, with indexes: Santo Domingo and Santiago de los Caballeros.

5825 **Rand McNally and Co.** (firm), *Chicago, Ill.* República Dominicana. Chicago, Ill., Texaco, 1976. Colored. 37 x 59 cm. Scale ca. 1:700,000.

Detailed general road map. Spanish and English. Relief shown by shading and spot heights. Includes distance chart, location map, and indexes. Indexed maps of "Santiago" and "Santo Domingo," text, and colored illustrations on verso.

ECUADOR

5826 Ecuador. Instituto Ecuatoriano de Reforma Agraria y Colonización (IERAC). La regionalización para la reforma agraria. Quito, 1976. 23 l., colored maps, 31 x 42 cm.

Agricultural reform atlas of Ecuador.

5827 ———. ———. Departamento de Ingeniería. Areas de intervención en reforma agraria y colonización. Compilación: Gualberto Cortés Q. Revisó: Alfonso Orejuela. Quito, 1977. Colored. 43 x 57 cm. Scale 1:2,000,000.

Map showing agricultural regions and land reform.

5828 ———. Instituto Geográfico Militar. Atlas geográfico de la República del Ecuador. Quito, 1977. colored maps, 48 x 65 cm. Scale of principal maps 1:2,000,000.

Atlas published on 50th anniversary of Ecuador's Instituto Geográfico Militar. Includes highly technical maps, e.g. ecological, geological and soils maps. Also includes world maps.

5829 ———. ———. Mapa básico regional de la cuenca del Río Guayas, Península de Santa Elena y regiones contiguas. Quito, 1977. Colored. 132 x 124 cm. (Serie, J521) Scale 1:250,000.

Detailed regional map of the Guayas Valley and Santa Elena peninsula in western Ecuador.

5830 ———. ———. Plano de la Ciudad de San Francisco de Quito. Quito, 1977. Colored map on 2 sheets 46 x 49 cm. Scale 1:15,000.

Cover title: *Plano guía de la ciudad de Quito.* Printed on both sides of sheets. Relief shown by contours and shading. Includes index and indexed insets of "División Política de la Ciudad de Quito 1977." Accompanied by index (36 p.).

5831 ———. ———. Plano guía de líneas de colectivos y buses de servicio urbano de la ciudad de Quito. Quito, 1976. 5 colored maps on 3 sheets 29 x 82 cm. Scale 1:25,000 and ca. 1:500,000.

Good transportation map of city showing motor-bus lines.

5832 ———. Ministerio de Obras Públicas. Dirección General de Obras Públicas. Red de carreteras principales y secundarias. 2. ed. Quito, 1976. Colored. 43 x 57 cm. Scale 1:2,000,000.

"Mapa de Carreteras y Telecomunicaciones." Relief shown by spot heights. Includes location map, location map of Galápagos, inset of Provincia de Galápagos, Archipiélago Colón (Territorio Insular) and profile of "Principales Volcanes." Distance chart, map of "Telecomunicaciones Principales," and colored illustrations on verso.

5833 Sampedro V., Francisco. Atlas geográfico del Ecuador "SAM": con las básicas nociones históricas de la nacionalidad. Quito, Ministerio de Relaciones Exteriores [and] Instituto Geográfico Militar, 1975/1976. 71 p., colored maps, illus.; 22 x 31 cm.

Historical atlas of Ecuador.

EL SALVADOR

5834 El Salvador. Centro de Investigaciones Geotécnicas. Mapa geológico preliminar de la República de El Salvador. San Salvador, 1973. Colored. 33 x 61 cm. Scale ca. 1:650,000.

Geological map including major faults and volcanoes in El Salvador.

5835 ———. Instituto Geográfico Nacional Ingeniero Pablo Arnoldo Guzmán. República de El Salvador. San Salvador, 1977? Colored. 43 x 61 cm. Scale 1:450,000.

Road map with relief shown pictorially and by spot heights. Includes index, distance chart, and colored illustrations. Maps of "San Salvador y Alrededores," "San Miguel," and "Santa Ana," text, and colored illustrations on verso.

5836 ———. Servicio Hidrológico. Cuenca hidrográfica del Río Grande de San Miguel. San Salvador, 1976. Colored. 99 x 74 cm. Scale 1:100,000.

Hydrological map with relief shown

by contours and spot heights. Includes text, statistical data, diagrams and insets of "Perfil Esquemático del Río Grande de San Miguel," "Caudales Estacionales, Período 1969–1975," and "Altimetría de la Cuenca del Río Grande de San Miguel."

GUATEMALA

5837 Empresa Portuaria Nacional Santo Tomás de Castilla, *Guatemala.* Plan urbanístico ciudad portuaria. Santo Tomás de Castilla?, Guatemala, 1976? 78 x 102 cm.

Cadastral map with relief shown by form lines.

5838 Guatemala. Instituto Geográfico Nacional. Ciudad de Guatemala. Guatemala, 1977. Colored. 61 x 51 cm. Scale 1:25,000.

Detailed city plan.

5839 ———. ———. Mapa escolar de la República de Guatemala. Guatemala, 1976. Colored. 111 x 106 cm. Scale 1:500,000.

Relief shown by shading. Includes tables of "Municipios de la República de Guatemala" and "Símbolos Patrios," inset of "Ejemplos de Accidentes Geográficos en Perspectiva," and relief profile of "Principales Volcanes de Guatemala."

5840 ———. ———. Mapa hipsométrico de la República de Guatemala. 6. ed. Guatemala, 1977. Colored. 111 x 109 cm. Scale 1:500,000.

Detailed general physical map indicating administrative divisions and roads. Relief shown by gradient tints. Includes colored illustrations, index, table of "Posición Geográfica de las Cabeceras Departamentales de la República," and chart of "Elevación de los Principales Volcanes de la República."

5841 ———. Instituto Nacional de Sismología, Vulcanología, Meteorología e Hidrología (INSIVUMEH). **Departamento de Sistemas Geofísicos.** Carta isogónica de la República de Guatemala para 1978–79. Guatemala, 1978. Colored. 111 x 109 cm. Scale 1:500,000.

Terrestrial magnetism map using the fifth ed. of "Mapa Hipsométrico" (see *HLAS* 39.5930) and overprinted to show isogonic lines and magnetic stations.

GUYANA

5842 United Kingdom. Great Britain. Directorate of Overseas Surveys. Guyana 1:200,000 (approximately). Georgetown, Guyana Govt., 1973. Colored. 67 x 59 cm. (DOS, 1182) Scale 1:200,000.

Very detailed geologic maps. Relief shown by spot heights on some sheets. "Geology is based on the interpretation of 1:60,000 aerial photographs (flown by the Royal Air Force, 1962) and reconnaissance field checking by Jevan P. Berrangé (1966–1971), Photogeological Unit, Institute of Geological Sciences, London and on maps and reports of the Geological Survey Department, Guyana; under a Technical Assistance Programme sponsored by the Overseas Development Administration, Foreign and Commonwealth Office, London, in collaboration with the Geological Survey Department, Guyana."

HAITI

5843 Rand McNally and Co. (firm), *Chicago, Ill.* Haiti. Chicago, Ill., Texaco, 1975. Colored. 44 x 61 cm. Scale ca. 1:700,000.

General road map. Relief shown by hachures. French and English. Includes inset of Port-au-Prince with index. On verso map of West Indies.

5844 United Nations, *New York.* **Special Fund.** Plaine des Gonaïves. Firenze, Italy, Litografia Artistica Cartografica, 1975? 5 colored maps on sheet 75 x 105 cm. Scale 1:50,000.

Soils and hydrology map with relief shown by contours and spot heights. Includes four stratigraphic sections. Contents: Planche No. 1 "Carte Piézométrique;" Planche No. 2 "Carte des Isobathes;" Planche No. 3 "Cartes des Isopaques;" etc.

HONDURAS

5845 Honduras. Consejo Superior de Planificación Económica. Unidad de Programación Regional. Honduras: regiones de planificación. Tegucigalpa, 1975. 48 x 70 cm. Scale 1:1,000,000.

Regional planning map including inset and index.

5846 ———. **Instituto Geográfico Nacional.** Mapa general: República de Honduras. Tegucigalpa, 1977. Colored. 45 x 71 cm. Scale 1 : 1,000,000.

Good general map showing first order administrative divisions.

5847 ———. **Instituto Hondureño de Turismo.** Honduras, Central America—Honduras, America Central. Tegucigalpa, 1978. Colored. 55 x 86 cm.

Pictorial map. Includes two insets, colored illustrations, distance chart, and index. Text and colored illustrations on verso. Also on verso, with indexes: La Ceiba; San Pedro Sula; Tegucigalpa.

MEXICO

5848 **Asociación Nacional Automovilística,** *México.* Carta geográfica de México. 8. ed. México, 1977. Colored. 84 x 116 cm. Scale ca. 1 : 2,550,000.

Detailed road map. Includes inset of Mexico City region. Distance chart in accompanying index. Accompanied by: Carta Geográfica de México: Indice General de Poblaciones y Pueblos (64 p.; 17 cm.).

5849 **Encinas, Carlos.** Carreteras de México (Road map of Mexico). 4. ed. México, Asociación Nacional Automovilística (ANA), 1977. Colored. 51 x 80 cm. fold. to 26 x 10 cm. Scale ca. 1 : 2,750,000.

Includes distance chart, tables of road signs, advertisements, and insets of Mexico City region, Guadalajara, Monterrey, Puebla, and Acapulco.

5850 **García de Miranda, Enriqueta.** Atlas: nuevo atlas Porrúa de la República Mexicana. México, Editorial Porrúa, 1977. 197 p., colored maps, 35 cm.

Includes historical maps; monographs and maps of federal entities; thematic maps; and index.

5851 **Guía Roji, S.A.** (firm), *Mexico.* México, mapa turística—Mexico tourist map. México, 1977? Colored. 42 x 65 cm.

Includes distance chart, index, and inset of Mexico City region. Tourist information and map of Mexico showing distances and time on verso.

5852 **López Ramos, Ernesto.** Carta geológica de la República Mexicana. Com-

pilada con la colaboración de Santiago Hernández Sánchez Mejorada. Grabado y Dibujo: Luis Burgos, Jorge Becerril Munciño and others. 4. ed. México?, Comité de la Carta Geológica de México, 1976. Colored. 114 x 158 cm. Scale 1 : 2,000,000.

Detailed geologic map with depths shown by gradient tints. Includes inset of "Archipielago Revillagigedo."

5853 **Mexico. Comisión de Estudios del Territorio Nacional** (CETENAL). Estados Unidos Mexicanos, zona económica exclusiva. México, 1976. 58 x 79 cm. Scale 1 : 5,000,000.

Economic policy map showing boundaries of territorial waters. Tables of coordinates on verso.

5854 ———. **Comisión de Fomento Minero.** Principales centros mineros productores de oro, plata, plomo, cobre y zinc, con datos de producción de 1976. México, 1977. Colored. 31 x 45 cm.

Mines and mineral resources. "Producción por Municipios durante los Años de 1975 y 1976" on verso. Accompanied by: "Producción por Municipios durante los Años de 1975 y 1976" (p. 2–3; 47 cm.).

5855 ———. **Comisión Federal de Electricidad. Centro Nacional de Control de Energía.** Sistema eléctrico nacional, principales instalaciones, México 1977. Elaboró: Antonio San Román. Revisó: Sergio Guerrero A. México, 1977. Colored on sheet 83 x 119 cm.

Shows power plants and electric power distribution.

5856 ———. **Dirección General de Programación.** Mexican Republic. Beverly Hills, Calif., Mexican National Tourist Council, 1975. Colored. 46 x 60 cm.

New tourist map with distance chart and text. Folded title: Mexico, New Resorts, Baja Peninsula, Western Coast, Central Coast, Southern Coast, Mexico's Caribbean, Gulf of Mexico. Insets: Mazatlán, Acapulco, Monterrey, Mexico City, Guadalajara.

5857 ———. **Dirección General del Inventario Nacional Forestal.** República Mexicana: mapa de tipos de vegetación y uso suelo. México, 1975. 4 maps, 66 x 67 cm. or smaller. Scale ca. 1 : 2,000,000.

Four maps showing soils and vegetation.

5858 ———. Secretaría de Agricultura y Recursos Hidráulicos. Dirección de Agrología. Mapa general de la República Mexicana. Colaboradores: Gaudencio Flores Mata; Fernando Angeles Castillo; César Moreno Moreno; Rafael Ocegueda Armenta; Fidel Galicia Santamaría; Jesús Fajardo Valadez y Honorio Herrera Montes. México, 1977. Colored. 103 x 152 cm. Scale 1:2,000,000.

Good general physical map with relief shown by gradient tints. Inset: I Guadalupe.

5859 ———. Secretaría de Comunicaciones y Transportes. Carreteras de México. México, 1976. 24 p., colored illus., colored maps, 18 x 26 cm.

Highway atlas of Mexico.

5860 ———. Secretaría de Obras Públicas. Mapa turístico de carreteras. Tourist road map. 8. ed. México, 1976. Colored. 67 x 87 cm. Scale 1:3,500,000.

Folded title: "Mexico, Mapa Turístico de Carreteras." Tourist road map. Relief shown by shading. Includes index, distance chart, diagram of "Approximate driving time," and inset of Mexico City region. Tourist information on verso. On verso, with indexes; Mexico, Centro de la ciudad de México; Monterrey; Acapulco; Puerto Vallarta; Guadalajara; Quintana Roo turístico.

5861 ———. Secretaría de Recursos Hidráulicos. Obras de riego. México, 1975. Colored. 43 x 65 cm. Scale ca. 1:5,000,000.

Shows water resources development, irrigation and water reservoirs. Tables of statistical data on verso.

5862 Pintado Reyes, Carlos and Roberto Beltrán Frías. Atlas de México. Ciudad López Mateo, Mex., Editorial Mapas de México, 1978. 32 l., col. maps; 47 x 65 cm.

Road atlas of Mexico.

5863 Union of Soviet Socialist Republics. Glavnoe Upravlenie Geodezii i Kartografii. Meksika. Moscow, 1977. Colored. 56 x 80 cm. Scale 1:4,000,000

Russian map. Cover title: "Meksika: Spravochnaîâ Karta." Relief shown by shading, gradient tints, and spot heights. Depths shown by gradient tints and soundings. Inset map shows economic conditions.

STATES AND REGIONS

5864 Automobile Club of Southern California, Los Angeles. Baja California. Los Angeles, 1978. Colored. 108 x 45 cm. (Map, 2400, 2401) Scale ca. 1:800,000.

Printed on both sides of sheet. Relief shown by shading and spot heights. Includes text, distance chart, and index. Insets: Tijuana; Ensenada; Mexicali; La Paz.

5865 Cardoza V., Ramón and Francisco Takaki. Fresnillo, Zac.; Zonificación agropecuaria y forestal. México, Comisión de Estudios del Territorio Nacional, 1976. Colored. 24 x 42 cm. Scale 1:250,000.

Agriculture and forestry map. Cover title: "La Información CETENAL en la Zonificación Agropecuaria y Forestal, con Fines de un Mejor Aprovechamientos de los Recursos Naturales." Relief shown by contours and spot heights. Shows Fresnillo region. Accompanied by text (34 p.). Bibliography in accompanying text.

5866 Esparza Torres, Héctor F. Yucatan. México, Librería Patria, 1977? Colored. 47 x 68 cm. Scale 1:600,000 (Mapas de los estados. Serie patria, 30)

Includes text, index, and inset of "Zona Arqueológica de Chichen-Itza." Text, tourist information, distance chart, map of Mérida region, and indexed map of Mérida on verso.

5867 Gastil, R. Gordon and Daniel Krummenacher. Reconnaissance geologic map of coastal Sonora between Puerto Lobos and Bahía Kino. Prepared by R. Gordon Castil, Daniel Krummenacher, and students at San Diego State Univ., 1974. Boulder, Colo., Geological Society of America, 1976. Colored. 113 x 39 cm. Scale 1:150,000 (Map and chart series MC-16)

For sources and acknowledgements see Geological Society of America Bulletin (Vol. 88, No. 1).

5868 Jalisco (state), Mexico. Departamento de Economía y Hacienda. Uso del agua por cuencas hidrológicas: Jalisco, subregión Ocotlán, Estados Unidos Mexicanos. Guadalajara, Mex., 1976? Colored. 63 x 125 cm. Scale 1:100,000.

Water supply map of Mexico with relief shown by contours.

5869 León González, Carlos García de.
Carta general del Estado de Michoacán. México, UNAM, Instituto de Geografía, 1977. Colored. 60 x 86 cm. Scale 1:500,000.
One of a series of detailed state maps of Mexico with relief shown by contours.

5870 Mexico. Secretaría de Asentamientos Humanos y Obras Públicas. Centro SAHOP: Yucatán. Mérida, Mex., 1978.
Planimetric map showing transportation network.

5871 Miller, Tom and **Elmar Baxter.** The Baja book II: a complete new mapguide to today's Baja California. Huntington Beach, Calif., Baja Trail Publications, 1977. 180 p., colored illus., colored maps; 25 cm.
Guide book and road atlas to Baja California.

5872 The Sea of Cortez—Gulf of California—and the Baja California Peninsula. Los Angeles, Calif., Triumph Press, 1975. Colored. 45 x 57 cm. (Kym's guide, 6) Scale not given.
Outdoor recreation map with relief shown by shading. Includes key map and distance charts. Text, recreation information, list of accommodations, and colored illustrations on verso.

5873 Yucatan (state), *Mexico.* **Departamento de Turismo.** Peninsula de Yucatán. Mérida, Yucatan, 1977? Colored. 22 x 26 cm. on sheet 44 x 40 cm.
Good tourist map of Yucatan. Includes maps of Chichen Itza and Yucatan, indexed map of "Archaeological Site: Uxmal," colored illustrations and distance list. Text and colored illustrations on verso.

CITIES

5874 Asociación Nacional Automovilística, *Mexico.* Ciudad de México; Mexico City. 5. ed. México, 1977. 84 x 65 cm. Scale ca. 1:40,000.
Folded title: "Guía Plano ANA de la Ciudad de México—Mexico City Guide." Copyright: Carlos Encinas. Includes four insets and indexes to points of interest. Map of downtown Mexico City, list of subway stations, and indexes on verso.

5875 Asorva (firm), *Guadalajara, Mex.*
Mazatlan: map and commercial guide (Mazatlan: plano y guía comercial). Guadalajara, Mex., 1978. Colored. 39 x 61 cm. Scale not given (Serie del Caribe, 78)
Relief shown by contours. Includes index to hotels and advertisements. Text, tourist information, commercial guide, and advertisements on verso.

5876 Guía Roji, S.A., *Mexico.* Alrededores. México, 1976. Colored. 62 x 43 cm.
Mexico City transit system. On verso: Area Central. Accompanied by: Guía Completa de Transportes, Distrito Federal y sus Alrededores (14 p., illus.; 23 cm.).

5877 ——, ——. Ciudad de México, zonas postales. México, 1978. Colored. 114 x 80 cm.
Detailed city plan including postal zones. Indexes and advertisements on verso. Accompanied by sheet of maps: "Mexico Central: Centro de la ciudad de México" (one leaf; colored maps; on sheet 27 x 37 cm.).

5878 ——, ——. Guadalajara. México, 1976. Colored. 66 x 91 cm. fold. to 23 x 12 cm. Scale 1:25,000.
Relief shown by shading. Tourist map. Indexed for points of interest. Index and indexed road map of Mexico with inset of Mexico City region and distance chart on verso.

5879 Irvine, Carlos. Mazatlán. Mazatlán, Mex., 1977. Colored. 34 x 55 cm. fold. to 14 x 11 cm.
Folded title: *Carlos Irvine's Guide & map of Mazatlán: official map and guide of the city of Mazatlán.* Relief shown by form lines. Shows locations of points of interest. Includes text, inset, and advertisements. Descriptive indexes to points of interest, telephone directories, map, illustrations, and advertisement on verso.

5880 Libromex (firm), *Mérida, Mex.* Plano actualizado de la Ciudad de Mérida y del Estado de Yucatán, 1976–77. Mérida, Mex., 1976. 43 x 56 cm.
Spanish and English. Includes text and index to points of interest. Map of Yucatan with distance list and text on verso.

5881 Mexico. Comisión de Estudios del Territorio Nacional (CETENAL).

Aguascalientes. México, 1976. 2 colored maps; 58 x 72 cm. (CETENAL carta temática urbana) Scale 1:10,000.

Very detailed urban land use maps.

5882 ——. ——. Mapa urbano: Puebla. México, 1975. 16 colored maps; 82 x 62 cm. or smaller. Scale 1:5,000.

Very detailed contour relief maps with legends in Spanish and English. This and the following map description are representative samples of two new series of excellent large-scale and very detailed map series designed, for urban areas of Mexico, to provide thematic and topographic information. Most medium and large urban areas have been mapped in this way.

NICARAGUA

5883 **Nicaragua. Dirección General de Caminos. Departamento de Ingeniería.** Red vial de Nicaragua. Managua, 1976. 31 x 34 cm. Scale ca. 1:1,750,000 (not "1:500,000").

General road map.

5884 **Rand McNally** (firm), *Chicago, Ill.* Nicaragua. Chicago, Ill., Texaco, 1978. Colored. 44 x 61 cm. Scale ca. 1:1,140,480.

Detailed road map with relief shown by shading and spot heights. Includes colored illustrations, text, index, two island insets, and distance chart. Insets: León; Granada; Managua. Indexed map of Central America, colored illustrations, island inset, distance chart, advertisements, and text in Spanish and English on verso.

PANAMA

5885 **Panama. Dirección General de Recursos Minerales.** Mapa geológico. Panamá, 1976. Colored. 36 x 66 cm. Scale 1:1,000,000.

Accompanied by: "Notas sobre la Geología de Panamá" (7 l.).

5886 ——. **Instituto Geográfico Nacional Tommy Guardia.** Atlas to the 1977 Panama Canal Treaty. Washington, 1977. 16 maps.

Maps of the land and water areas for the operation and defense of the Panama Ca-

nal, referred to in the agreements in implementation of Articles III and IV of the Panama Canal Treaty. The map atlas is deposited in the archives of the Department of State where it is available for reference. There is also a copy at the Library of Congress. Includes the following large scale maps prepared in cooperation with the U.S. Defense Mapping Agency: 1) General Map of the Land and Waters of the Panama Canal Treaty; 2) Mount Hope; 3) Rainbow City; 4) Ancón; 5) Balboa Heights; 6) Balboa; 7) Balboa: Industrial Area; 8) La Boca; 9) Diablo Heights; 10) Los Ríos; 11) Gamboa; 12) Gatún; 13) Margarita; 14) Pedro Miguel; 15) Paraíso; and 16) Rainbow City. See also item **5888.**

5887 ——. ——. República de Panamá. 3. ed. Panamá, 1976. Colored. 25 x 56 cm. Scale ca. 1:1,175,000.

Folded title: "Síntesis Geográfica." Relief shown by spot heights. Includes inset and illustrations. Statistical data, maps of "Coordenadas Geográficas Extremas del Istmo de Panamá" and "Ciudad de Panamá," and distance diagram on verso.

5888 ——. ——. República de Panamá: mapa general de las tierras y aguas del Tratado del Canal de Panamá (Republic of Panama: general map of the lands and waters of the Panama Canal Treaty). Washington, 1977.

Detailed topographical map with relief shown by contours and spot heights. Depths shown by contours and soundings. Same as Attachment No. 1 to the map atlas (see item **5886**) compiled to illustrate the agreements in implementation of Articles III and IV of the Panama Canal Treaty between the US and Panama, signed Washington 7 Sept. 1977.

5889 ——. ——. República de Panamá, mapa político. Panamá, 1977. Colored. 55 x 134 cm. on 2 sheets 57 3 73 cm. (Its Serie E462) Scale 1:500,000.

Good general political map. Relief shown by spot heights. Includes coat of arms and flag.

5890 **Rand McNally** (firm), *Chicago, Ill.* Panama. Chicago, Ill., Texaco, 1976. Colored. 44 x 61 cm. Scale ca. 1:1,125,000.

General road map. Relief shown by

shading and spot heights. Includes colored illustrations, text, distance chart, indexes, and insets of "Colón" and "Panamá." Map of "Central America," text in Spanish and English, index, colored illustrations, distance chart, and advertisements on verso.

5891 United Nations Regional Cartographic Conference for Latin America, I, *Panama, 1976.* Conferencia Cartográfica Regional de las Naciones Unidas para las Américas, Panama, 8 al 19 de marzo de 1976. Panamá?, 1976. 2 colored maps on sheet 40 x 75 cm. Scale 1:12,500 and 1:30,654.

General city map. Shows central city and metropolitan area. Indexed for points of interest.

PARAGUAY

5892 Guía General de Asunción e Interior del Paraguay (firm), *Asunción.* Plano actualizado de la ciudad de Asunción. Asunción?, 1976. Colored. 49 x 78 cm. Scale 1:40,000.

Detailed city plan. Shows points of interest. Includes descriptive lists of points of interest. Indexes, "Plano de la Ciudad de Asunción (Centro) con flechas indicadoras del sentido de circulación de sus calles," and advertisements on verso.

PERU

5893 Editorial Navarrete (firm), *Lima.* Mapa político del Perú. Lima, 1977. Colored. 101 x 71 cm. Scale 1:2,400,000.

General political map. Includes location map, coats of arms, tables of statistics, and distance chart.

5894 Góngora Perea, Amadeo. Plano de la ciudad de Lima metropolitana. Lima, 1978. Colored. 61 x 88 cm. Scale ca. 1:25,000.

Relief shown by hachures. Accompanied by: "Indice de Avenidas y Jirones" (1 l., 43 cm.).

5895 Peru. Instituto de Geología y Minería. Mapa geológico de Perú. Lima, 1976. Colored. 209 x 149 cm. on 4 sheets 110 x 78 cm. (*Boletín*, 28) Scale 1:1,000,000.

Depths shown by gradient tints. Includes location map and inset of "Fuentes de Información Geológica." Accompanied by: "Sinopsis Explicativa del Mapa Geológica del Perú" (1977, 41 p.).

5896 ———. Instituto Geográfico Militar. Departamento de Lambayeque: mapa físico, político. Lima, 1974. Colored. 78 x 57 cm. Scale 1:300,000.

Good example of general department maps. Relief shown by gradient tints and spot heights. Includes statistical data, coat of arms, and location map.

5897 ———. ———. Mapa vial del Perú. Lima, Petróleos del Perú [and] Ministerio de Transportes y Comunicaciones, 1975. Colored. 96 x 67 cm. Scale ca. 1:2,250,000.

Relief shown by shading and spot heights. Includes location map and distance chart. Indexed maps of "Lima Metropolitana" and "Centro de Lima," 20 city maps, and map of "Esquema Vial" on verso.

5898 ———. Oficina General de Catastro Rural. Mapa de regiones naturales y zonas agrarias. Lima, 1976? Colored. 106 x 74 cm. Scale 1:2,000,000.

Indexed map showing physical geography of Peru.

5899 ———. ———. Perú; cartografía a escala grande. Lima, 1977. Colored. 44 x 30 cm. Scale 1:5,000,000.

Shows areas to be mapped for agricultural planning.

5900 ———. Oficina Nacional de Evaluación de Recursos Naturales (ONERN). Mapa ecológico del Perú. Lima, 1976. 209 x 149 cm. Scale 1:1,000,000.

Relief shown by spot heights. Shows vegetation and climate. Includes three "Diagramas Bioclimáticos para la Clasificación de Zonas de Vida en el Mundo," inset of "Regiones Latitudinales," and location map.

5901 Touring y Automóvil Club del Perú, *Lima.* Circuito turístico del altiplano. Lima, 1977? Colored. 33 x 44 cm. Scale ca. 1:460,625.

Good example of tourist mapping. Relief shown by spot heights. Includes colored illustrations. On verso: Juliaca, Puno and Sur Turístico.

PUERTO RICO

**5902 Puerto Rico. Highway Authority.
Area of Transportation Planification.**
Mapa de carreteras estatales de Puerto Rico.
San Juan, 1977. 37 x 94 cm. Scale ca.
1:205,000.
Detailed road map. Shows distances.
Insets: Isla de Culebra and Isla de Vieques.
Distance chart and "Guía de Carreteras, Vías
Principales" on verso.

5903 United States. Geological Survey.
Mapa de unidad hidrológica—1974:
Región del Caribe (Hydrologic unit map—
1974: Caribbean region). Reston, Va., 1975. 5
colored maps on sheet 72 x 134 cm.
Drainage map showing hydrologic
units which also shows Puerto Rico. Includes
explanatory note and table showing hydrologic units. Also includes: Navassa Island;
Serrana Bank; Roncador Bank; Canal Zone;
and Virgin Islands.

5904 ——. National Ocean Survey. Puerto Rico, Virgin Islands: local aeronautical chart. Washington, 1974. Colored.
51 x 137 cm. fold. to 26 x 13 cm. Scale
1:250,000.
General aeronautical chart. Relief
shown by contours, gradient tints, and spot
heights. Includes inset of "Isla Mona" and
explanatory notes. Map of "Gulf of Mexico
and Caribbean Planning Chart," directory of
aerodromes, and text on verso.

SURINAM

**5905 Surinam. Centraal Bureau Lucht-
kaartering.** Kaart van de Republiek
Suriname (Map of the Republic of Suriname.
Uitgave Centraal Bureau Luchtkartering). 5.
ed. Paramaribo, 1975. Colored. 68 x 58 cm.
Scale 1:1,000,000.
General map with relief shown by gra-
dient tints and spot heights.

TRINIDAD AND TOBAGO

**5906 Trinidad and Tobago. Surveys Divi-
sion.** Trinidad. 3. ed. Port of Spain,
1975. Colored. 64 x 81 cm. Scale 1:150,000.
Detailed general map showing recreational areas and road network.

URUGUAY

**5907 Uruguay. Dirección Nacional de
Turismo.** Plano de la ciudad de Montevideo. Montevideo, 1975? Colored. 49 x 79
cm.
Detailed city plan. Relief shown by
land form drawings. Indexed for points of interest. Map of Montevideo metropolitan
area, colored illustrations, and text on verso.

VENEZUELA

5908 Aeromapas Seravenca (firm), *Caracas.* Mapa de carreteras de Venezuela.
Caracas, 1977. Colored. 66 x 113 cm. Scale
1:1,500,000.
Good general road map. Relief shown
by shading and spot heights. Includes index,
distance chart, and four insets. On verso,
with index: "Plano de Caracas."

5909 La Capitanía General de Venezuela:
1777–1778. Caracas, Consejo Municipal del Distrito Federal, 1977. 87 p., illus.,
maps, plates. 41 cm.
Facsimiles of early (1777–78) maps of
Venezuela's Federal District. Includes cop-
ies of letters and patents.

5910 Proyectos y Promociones Continente
(firm), *Caracas.* Cumaná. Caracas,
1976. Colored. 52 x 76 cm.
This entry serves as an example of excellent city plans for many other Venezuelan cities. Folded title: "Super Plano Informativo; Cumaná, Carúpano, Estado Sucre."
Relief shown by contours. Includes text in
English, colored illustrations, inset of "Futuro Aeropuerto." Maps of "Estado Sucre"
and "Carúpano," text, colored illustrations,
location map of Sucre, and advertisements
on verso.

5911 ——, ——. Estado de Aragua.
Caracas, 1976. Colored map 37 x 45
cm. Scale ca. 1:37,000.
Detailed general map of Aragua state
exemplifies the sort of map that is available
for each Venezuelan state. Includes text, colored illustrations, and advertisements. Map
of Maracay (1:15,000).

**5912 Venezuela. Corporación Venezolana
de Guayana** (CVG). Key to the developments in Venezuela: Ciudad Guayana.

Ciudad Guayana, Ven., 1976. 56 x 44 cm.
Economic map of Ciudad Guayana region. Scale not given. Both Spanish and English editions of this map are available.

5913 ———. ———. Ferrominera Orinoco.
Sistema de manejo de mineral y planta de trituración, secado y clasificación de mineral de hierro: Puerto Ordaz, Ciudad Guayana, Estado de Bolívar, Venezuela. Ciudad Guayana, Ven., 1977. Colored. 62 x 93 cm.
Perspective map not drawn to scale showing mining operations. Bird's eye-view. Oriented with north towards upper left. Indexed. Accompanied by map showing navigable routes to Puerto Ordaz with 150 km radial distances and map showing navigable route to Atlantic Ocean from Puerto Ordaz with inset.

5914 ———. **Dirección de Cartografía Nacional.** Mapa de las regiones administrativas de Venezuela según Decreto Ejecutivo No. 1.331 de fecha 16 de diciembre de 1975. Caracas, 1976. Colored. 75 x 93 cm. Scale 1:200,000 (Edición 1-DCN)
Administrative map. Relief shown by shading. Includes coat of arms, inset of "Isla de Aves," and location map.

5915 ———. ———. Mapa físico de la República de Venezuela. Caracas, 1975. Colored. Relief model 111 x 140 cm. Scale 1:1,250,000; escala vertical exagerada 5 veces.
Good general map on molded plastic relief model.

5916 ———. **Ministerio de Minas e Hidrocarburos. Dirección de Geología.** Mapa geológico estructural de Venezuela. Caracas, Ediciones FONINVES, 1976. 29 sheets. Scale 1:500,000.
Includes inset maps and location index. Excellent and detailed series of geology maps for the country based on detailed topographical maps. Geographical coverage complete in 23 sheets. Includes: five sheets of explanatory text and detailed diagrams and a geomorphological map of the country. In portfolio with title sheet.

5917 ———. **Ministerio de Obras Públicas. Dirección General de Vialidad. Oficina de Planeamiento.** Mapa de las carreteras de Venezuela, con otros datos de comunicaciones terrestres, marítimas y aéreas: Región

Norte de la República de Venezuela. Caracas, Maraven, 1977. Colored. 69 x 99 cm. Scale 1:1,00,000.
Official road map. Relief shown by shading and spot heights. Includes distance chart and inset of "Mapa Político de la República de Venezuela."

5918 ———. ———. ———. Mapa vial con otros datos de comunicaciones terrestres, marítimas y aéreas: Región Norte de la República de Venezuela. Caracas, Maraven, 1976. Colored. 69 x 99 cm. Scale 1:1,000,000.
Detailed road map with relief shown by shading and spot heights. Includes distance chart and inset of "Mapa Político de la República de Venezuela," as well as another inset.

JOURNAL ABBREVIATIONS
GEOGRAPHY

AAA/AE American Ethnologist. American Anthropological Association. Washington.

AAAS/S Science. American Association for the Advancement of Science. Washington.

AAG/A Annals of the Association of American Geographers. Lawrence, Kans.

ACCEFN/R Revista de la Academia Colombiana de Ciencias Exactas, Físicas y Naturales. Bogotá.

AGF/B Bulletin de l'Association de Géographes Français. Paris.

AGS/GR The Geographical Review. American Geographical Society. N.Y.

AI/A Anthropos. Anthropos-Institut. Psoieux, Switzerland.

AI/I Interciencia. Asociación Interciencia. Caracas.

BAS/SPA Bulletin of the Atomic Scientists. Science and public affairs. Educational Foundation for Nuclear Science *with the cooperation of the* Adlai Stevenson Institute of International Affairs. Chicago, Ill.

BBAA B.B.A.A. Boletín Bibliográfico de Antropología Americana. Instituto Panamericano de Geografía e Historia, Comisión de Historia. México.

BDG Boletim do Departamento de Geografia. Faculdade de Filosofia, Ciências e Letras de Presidente Prudente. Presidente Prudente, Brazil.

BNB/REN Revista Econômica do Nordeste. Banco do Nordeste do Brasil, Depto. de Estudos Econômicos. Fortaleza, Brazil.

CEPAC/REP Revista de Estudios del Pacífico. Consejo Coordinador Universitario de Valparaíso, Centro de Estudios del Pacífico. Valparaíso, Chile.

COIGN/BG Boletín Geológico. Ministerio de Minas y Petróleos, Instituto Geológico Nacional. Bogotá.

CU/EG Economic Geography. Clark Univ. Worcester, Mass.

DRG/BG Boletim Geográfico do Estado do Rio Grande do Sul. Diretório Regional de Geografia [and] Secção de Geografia. Porto Alegre, Brazil.

EJ Explorers Journal. N.Y.

FDD/NED Notes et Études Documentaires. Direction de la Documentation. Paris.

FFCLM/EH Estudos Históricos. Faculdade de Filosofia, Ciência e Letras, Depto. de História. Marília, Brazil.

FJB/BH Boletín Histórico. Fundación John Boulton. Caracas.

GEB/E Die Erde. Zeitschrift der Gesellschaft für Erdkunde zu Berlin. Walter de Gruyter & Co. Berlin.

GGDDR/GB Geographische Berichte. Geographischen Gesellschaft in der Deutschen Demokratischen Republic. Berlin.

GH Geographica Helvetica. Schweizerische Zeitschrift für Länder- und Völkerkunde. Kümmerly & Frey, Geographischer Verlag. Bern.

GM The Geographical Magazine. London.

GR Geographische Rundschau. Zeitschrift für Schulgeographie. Georg Westermann Verlag. Braunschweig, FRG.

GV/GR Geologische Rundschau. Internationale Zeitschrift für Geologie. Geologische Vereinigung. Ferdinand Enke Verlag. Stuttgart, FRG.

GZ Geographische Zeitschrift. Franz Steiner Verlag. Wiesbaden, FRG.

HAHR Hispanic American Historical Review. Duke Univ. Press *for the* Conference on Latin American History of the American Historical Association. Durham, N.C.

HU/BHR Business History Review. Harvard Univ., Graduate School of Business Administration. Boston, Mass.

IAA Ibero-Amerikanisches Archiv. Ibero-Amerikanisches Institut. Berlin, FRG.

IAEERI/E Estrategia. Instituto Argentino de Estudios Estratégicos y de las Relaciones Internacionales. B.A.

IAMEA Inter-American Economic Affairs. Washington.

IASI/E Estadística. Journal of the Inter American Statistical Institute. Washington.

IBGE/R Revista Brasileira de Geografia. Conselho Nacional de Geografia, Instituto Brasileiro de Geografia e Estatística. Rio.

ICEM/IM International Migration [Migrations Internationales. Migraciones Internacionales]. Quarterly review of the Intergovernmental Committee for European Migration [and] Research Group for European Migration Problems. Geneva, Switzerland.

IHGB/R Revista do Instituto Histórico e Geográfico Brasileiro. Rio.

III/AI América Indígena. Instituto Indigenista Interamericano. México.

INAH/A Anales del Instituto Nacional de Antropología e Historia. Secretaría de Educación Pública. Méxio.

IOC/M Memórias do Instituto Oswaldo Cruz. Rio.

IPE/EE Estudos Econômicos. Univ. de São Paulo, Instituto de Pesquisas Econômicas. São Paulo.

JDA The Journal of Developing Areas. Western Illinois Univ. Press. Macomb.

JEHM/R Revista de la Junta de Estudios Históricos de Mendoza. Mendoza, Arg.

JLAS Journal of Latin American Studies. Centers or institutes of Latin American studies at the universities of Cambridge, Glasgow, Liverpool, London and Oxford. Cambridge Univ. Press. London.

JPHC/R Revista de la Junta Provincial de Historia de Córdoba. Archivo Histórico Monseñor P. Cabrera. Córdoba, Arg.

JW Journal of the West. Los Angeles, Calif.

JWTL Journal of World Trade Law. Crans, Switzerland.

LARR Latin American Research Review. Univ. of North Carolina Press *for the* Latin American Studies Association. Chapel Hill.

LI/IA Ibero-Americana. Research news and principal acquisitions of documentation on Latin America in Denmark, Finland, Norway and Sweden. Latinamerika Institutet. Stockholm.

MEC/C Cultura. Ministério da Educação e Cultura, Diretoria de Documentação e Divulgação. Brasília.

MH Mundo Hispánico. Madrid.

NGS/NGM National Geographic Magazine. National Geographic Society. Washington.

NJGP Neues Jahrbuch für Geologie und Paläontologie. Stuttgart.

NS NS NorthSouth NordSud NorteSur NorteSul. Canadian journal of Latin American studies. Canadian Association of Latin American Studies. Univ. of Ottawa. Ottawa.

NSCI New Scientist. London.

OAS/CI Ciencia Interamericana. Organization of American States, Dept. of Scientific Affairs. Washington.

OCEANUS Oceanus. Oceanographic Institution. Woods Hole, Mass.

OGG/M Mitteilungen der Österreichischen geographischen Gesellschaft. Verleger, Herausgeber und Eigentümer. Vienna.

OLI/ZLW Zeitschrift für Lateinamerika Wien. Österreisches Lateinamerika-Institut. Wien.

PAIGH/G Revista Geográfica. Instituto Panamericano de Geografía e Historia, Comisión de Geografía. México.

PAIGH/RC Revista Cartográfica. Instituto Panamericano de Geografía e Historia, Comisión de Cartografía. México.

RGS/GJ The Geographical Journal. The Royal Geographical Society. London.

RIIA/WT The World Today. Royal Institute of International Affairs. Oxford Univ. Press. London.

SAA/HO Human Organization. Society for Applied Anthropology. N.Y.

SBPC/CC Ciência e Cultura. Sociedade Brasileira para o Progresso da Ciência. São Paulo.

SDHS/J The Journal of San Diego History. The San Diego Historical Society. San Diego, Calif.

SESC/PB Problemas Brasileiros. Revista mensal de cultura. Conselho Regional do Serviço Social do Comércio (SESC). São Paulo.

SGB/COM Les Cahiers d'Outre-Mer. Société de Géographie de Bordeaux; Institute de Géographie de la Faculté des Lettres de Bordeaux; Institut de la France d'Outre-Mer *avec le concours du* Centre National de la Recherche Scientifique et de la VI^{ieme} section de l'École Pratique des Hautes Études. Bordeaux, France.

SMHN/R Revista de la Sociedad Mexicana de Historia Natural. México.

SSAG/GA Geografiska Annaler. Svenska Sällskapet för Antropologi och Geografi. Stockholm.

SSG/RGI Rivista Geografica Italiana. Società di Studi Geografici e Coloniali. Firenze, Italy.

TESG Tijdschrift voor Economische en Sociale Geographie. Netherlands journal of economic and social geography. Rotterdam, The Netherlands.

UA Urban Anthropology. State Univ. of New York, Dept. of Anthropology. Brockport.

UASD/R Revista Dominicana de Antropología e Historia. Univ. Autónoma de Santo Domingo, Facultad de Humanidades, Depto. de Historia y Antropología, Instituto de Investigaciones Antropológicas. Santo Domingo.

UBGI/E Erdkunde. Archiv für Wissenschaftliche Geographie. Univ. Bonn, Geographisches Institut. Bonn, FRG.

UC/A Anales de la Universidad de Cuenca. Cuenca, Ecua.

UC/EDCC Economic Development and Cultural Change. Univ. of Chicago, Research Center in Economic Development and Cultural Change. Chicago, Ill.

UCIG/IG Informaciones Geográficas. Univ. de Chile, Facultad de Filosofía y Educación, Instituto de Geografía. Santiago.

UCR/RBT Revista de Biología Tropical. Univ. de Costa Rica [and] Consejo Nacional de Investigaciones Científicas y Tecnológicas (CONICIT). San José.

UFP/BPG Boletim Paranaense de Geociências. Univ. Federal do Paraná, Depto. de Geociências, Centro de Documentação e Informações, Setor de Tecnologia. Paraná, Brazil.

UFP/EB Estudos Brasileiros. Univ. Federal do Paraná, Setor de Ciências Humanas, Centro de Estudos Brasileiros. Curitiba, Brazil.

UJSC/ECA Estudios Centro-Americanos. Revista de extensión cultural. Univ. José Simeón Cañas. San Salvador.

UM/JIAS Journal of Inter-American Studies and World Affairs. Univ. of Miami Press for the Center for Advanced International Studies. Coral Gables, Fla.

UMG/RBEP Revista Brasileira de Estudos Políticos. Univ. de Minas Gerais. Belo Horizonte, Brazil.

UN/ISSJ International Social Science Journal. United Nations Educational, Scientific and Cultural Organization. Paris.

UNAM/RMS Revista Mexicana de Sociología. Univ. Nacional Autónoma de México, Instituto de Investigaciones Sociales. México.

UNECLA/B Economic Bulletin for Latin America. United Nations, Economic Commission for Latin America. N.Y.

UNLP/E Económica. Univ. Nacional de La Plata, Facultad de Ciencias Económicas, Instituto de Investigaciones Económicas. La Plata, Arg.

UTIEH/C Caravelle. Cahiers du monde hispanique et luso-brésilien. Univ. de Toulouse, Institut d'Études Hispaniques, Hispano-Americaines et Luso-Brésiliennes. Toulouse, France.

UW/LE Land Economics. A quarterly journal of planning, housing and public utilities. Univ. of Wisconsin. Madison.

UWI/CQ Caribbean Quarterly. Univ. of the West Indies. Mona, Jam.

ZG Zeitschrift für Geomorphologie. Gebrüder Borntraeger. Berlin.

GOVERNMENT AND POLITICS

GENERAL

7001 Almeyda Medina, Clodomiro. Sociologismo e ideologismo en la teoría revolucionaria. Prólogo de Gonzalo Martínez Corbalá. México, Fondo de Cultura Económica, 1976. 137 p. (Archivo del fondo, 69)

Author uses UP experience in Chile to discuss two fundamental problems facing Marxism in Latin America: 1) the value-free reserve of sociological theoreticians which prevents them from perceiving "deepest popular sentiments," and 2) dogmatism which precludes an examination of "fact" in matters relating to any given area's specific form of social conflict. Important statement relevant not only to Latin American Marxism but to political theory in general. [W.R. Garner]

7002 Aníbal Gómez, Luis. La agencia latinoamericana de noticias (CONAC/RNC, 39:232, julio/agosto 1977, p. 76–96, bibl.)

Discussion of rationale for establishing a Latin America controlled international news service by Venezuelan journalist. Offers reasons, ranging from the "foreignness" of major statebased agencies to the role they play as spokesmen for multinational interests. Includes history of Latin American meetings convened to discuss the topic, and of Latin American and Third World positions presented at UNESCO meetings. [P.B. Taylor, Jr.]

7003 Blachman, Morris J. and **Ronald G. Hellman** eds. Terms of conflict: ideology in Latin American politics. Philadelphia, Pa., Institute for the Study of Human Issues, 1977. 275 p., tables (Inter-American politics series, 1)

Collection of essays on the relationship between ideology and politics with emphasis on the general characteristics and historical foundations of four different ideological currents: Christian Democracy, corporatism, liberalism, and Marxism. Some fine essays in normative analysis suggests a rejection of liberalism in Latin America and the adoption of ideologies based on corporatist technocracy. Original and insightful analysis. [D.W. Dent]

7004 Boersner, Demetrio. Democracia representativa y transformación social en América Latina (NSO, 3, nov./dic. 1972, p. 18–31, plate)

Although dated in descriptive analysis, the examination of different paths to social transformation reveals that representative democracy is not as effective as violent or revolutionary modes of bringing about meaningful progress to the region. Most of the conclusions remain suspect since they appear to rest on a few cases such as Cuba and Peru. [D.W. Dent]

7005 Caldera Rodríguez, Rafael. Especificidad de la Democracia Cristiana. 5. ed. Prólogo de Pedro Pablo Aguilar. Epílogo de Eduardo Frei M. Caracas, Ediciones Nueva Política, 1977. 154 p., bibl.

Essentially a primer, this small book defines political Christian Democracy: doctrine, practice, organization, political effect. Christian Democratic parties in Latin America are listed and the linkages of the group are noted. The breadth of the movement is indicated by the variety of views Christian Democrats have held and acted upon. Includes valuable bibliography from world sources as well as Latin American. [P.B. Taylor, Jr.]

7006 Calderón, Enrique Santos. Las agencias de prensa y la distorsión de la noticia en los países dependientes: un caso, América Latina (USB/F, 19:57, sep./dic. 1977, p. 380–400)

Colombian journalist views the international gathering and dissemination of news as detrimental to Latin America and the Third World. Author cites numerous cases of distortion and bias based on the fact that the US controls more than 65 percent of the flow of information and ideas that circulate in the world. The nature of this control contributes to political and cultural stereotypes which serve to maintain patterns of domination and to distort the reality of Latin American development. One of the few attempts to investigate a much neglected area of research. [D.W. Dent]

7007 Cardoso, Fernando Henrique. The consumption of dependency theory in the United States (LARR, 12:3, 1977, p. 7–24)

A critical view of the ways in which *dependency* as a concept has been turned into paradigms, dogmas and means for escape from qualitatively respectable research—and also the ways in which it has pointed the way to new understandings. A revision of a lecture, this short paper is essential reading for all concerned with development and Latin America. [P.B. Taylor, Jr.]

Carta Política. See item **7469.**

7008 Centro de Información, Documentación y Análisis Latinoamericano (CIDAL), *Caracas.* Bibliografía demócrata-cristiana latinoamericana. Caracas, n.d. 1 v. (Unpaged) (Documentos. Entrega, 30)

Contains approximately 400 citations on Christian Democracy in Latin America. [P.B. Taylor, Jr.]

7008a Centro Interamericano de Investigación y Documentación sobre Formación Profesional (CINTERFOR), *Montevideo.* Proyecto 079: participación del movimiento sindical en la formación profesional; seminario efectuado en Montevideo, Uruguay, 10–14 de abril de 1972. Montevideo, 1973. 123 p. (Informes, 48)

Report of a seminar in Montevideo (International Labor Organization auspices) for labor union representatives from Argentina, Brazil, Chile, Paraguay, Peru, Uruguay. Includes discussions on training procedures for vocational education in Argentina, Chile, Colombia, Paraguay, Venezuela and Uruguay. Volume includes final report and recommendations of the meeting, and annexed papers reporting practices in these countries. [P.B. Taylor, Jr.]

7009 Chaparro, Patricio. Conducta política de los militares en América Latina. Santiago, Univ. Católica de Chile, Instituto de Ciencia Político, 1972. 36 p., bibl. (Documento de trabajo, 2)

This publication, though somewhat out of date (published 1972), includes predictions concerning the future role of the Latin American military which have proved essentially accurate. [W.R. Garner].

Chinchilla, Norma Stoltz. Mobilizing women: revolution in the revolution. See item **7389.**

7010 Conference on Energy and Nuclear Security in Latin America, *VI, St. John's, Antigua, 1978.* Conference on energy and nuclear security in Latin America. Muscatine, Iowa, Stanley Foundation, 1978. 48 p., plates.

Report of a small conference held in April 1978, of 20 persons from the Americas and Western Europe. The contents are more suggestive than informative. [P.B. Taylor, Jr.]

7011 Consejo Episcopal Latinoamericano (CELAM), *Bogotá.* La iglesia y la integración andina: solidaridad, nacionalismo, armamentismo. Introducción de Renato Poblete Barth. Bogotá, 1976. 256 p. (Documento CELAM, 27)

Representatives of CELAM's Dept. of Social Action discuss problems of integration among Andean Pact nations. They believe Andean Group goals of social and economic justice are jeopardized by: 1) ideological conflicts; 2) authoritarianism; 3) nationalism and armaments rivalry; and 4) a "system which serves capital over labor." As a "Liberationist" theological/public policy statement, it sheds light on the varied meanings of Liberationism as well as on the specific role of CELAM (Latin American Council of Catholic Bishops). [W.R. Garner]

7012 ———, ———. Socialismo y socialismos en América Latina. Presentación de Alfonso López Trujillo. Introducción de Renato Poblete Barth. Bogotá, 1977. 372 p. (Documento CELAM, 30)

Collection of studies requested by the XVI Assembly of CELAM to ascertain "the significative differences among different types of socialism in the world and specially in Latin America." It has more to say about the world than Latin America. [A. Suárez]

7013 Córdova, Arnaldo. Los orígenes del estado en América Latina (CP, 14, oct./dic. 1977, p. 23–43)

The Latin American state is seen as the product of economic and political circumstances surrounding independence from Spain. Author argues that the "oligarchical state" that has emerged in Latin America is the consequence of deep social cleavages, ideological conflicts over the nature of the state, and a long history of economic dependency. Thoughtful, but no new ground is broken. [D.W. Dent]

7014 Cornelius, Wayne A. Introduction (in Cornelius, Wayne A. and Robert V. Kemper eds. Metropolitan Latin America: the challenge and the response [see item 9016] p. 7–24, bibl., tables)

Introduction to vol. 6 of the Latin American Urban Research series (see HLAS 39:9016 for previous volumes) in which case studies of nine major Latin American and Caribbean cities are presented. Editor identifies some of the general patterns and trends found in contemporary metropolitan Latin America: metropolitan primacy and its social costs, the role of national government policy, the international context of metropolitan development, the critical problems facing these areas, and the kinds of governmental responses they have elicited. The record of governmental performance to date gives little cause for optimism. [D. W. Dent]

7015 Dessau, Adalbert. Theoretische Probleme der Analyse und Kritik nichtmarxistischer ideologischer Strömungen der Gegenwart in Lateinamerika (Asien, Afrika, Lateinamerika [Deutscher Verlag der Wissenschaften, Berlin, GDR] 6:1, 1978, p. 94–105)

East German author examines non-Marxist ideological currents in Latin America as well as the crisis of bourgeois ideology. He denotes specific traits and evolution of these currents. [M. Kossok]

7016 DiBacco, Thomas V. ed. Presidential power in Latin American politics. N.Y., Praeger Publishers, 1977. 122 p., bibl. (Praeger special studies in international politics and government)

Volume based on the Latin American portion of a 1976 conference (American Univ.) on the presidential system of government. The first two chapters focus on the historical evolution of the Latin American presidential system and the efforts to restrain presidential power. Individual chapters on Mexico, Colombia, Costa Rica, and Venezuela focus on the key determinants of presidential power. Does presidential authority stem from cultural, legal, personal, or technocratic sources? The democratic systems under examination reveal a growing institutionalization of a presidential role constrained by legal-constitutional procedures, powerful interest groups, and values embedded in the political culture. Strong presidents will continue to rule but with less of the free-wheeling style evident in the *caudillos* of the past. A concise and well-written set of chapters on a topic that is often neglected. [D.W. Dent]

7017 Dvorak, Ladislav. Latinská Amerika: armáda a revolucní proces. Praha, n.p., 1976. 326 p.

Czech author discusses roles of armies and military dictatorships in Latin America. Evaluates the present military regimes from a strict Marxist perspective. [G.J. Kovtun]

7018 Encuentro Latinoamericano de Periodistas, Caracas, 1974. Encuentro latinoamericano de periodistas, Caracas, Venezuela, 17–20 octubre, 1974. La Habana, Partido Comunista de Cuba, Comité Central, Depto. de Orientación Revolucionaria, 1975. 53 p.

Highly partial document resulting from a conference cosponsored by the Venezuelan Newspapermen's Association and the Publisher's Syndicate of Mexico, and attended by 153 journalists from 16 countries. Contains a statement by Ernesto Vera, of the Cuban delegation, and resolutions adopted by the meeting, including one condemning the Inter-American Press Association as an imperialist tool. [P.B. Taylor, Jr.]

7019 Drechsler, Horst. Die Völker Lateinamerikas im Kampf gegen den Imperialismus (Jahrbuch Asien Afrika Lateinamerika [Bilanz und Chronik des Jahres 1976. Deutscher Verlag der Wissenschaften, Berlin, GDR] 1976 [i.e. 1977] p. 279–305)

East German author offers a one-year chronology (1976) of the "anti-imperialist struggle" in Latin America. [M. Kossok]

7020 Fagen, Richard R. Studying Latin American politics: some implications of a *dependencia* approach (LARR, 12:2, 1977, p. 3–26)

Principal writer and subscriber to the *dependencia* interpretation of Latin American politics backs away for a critical historical, theoretical and analytical look at the literature this approach has generated over the past two decades. US specialists have not necessarily dealt realistically with problems affecting the region, and "rewards"—material as well as institutional—often have been given for work reflecting this lack of realism. Writer argues that dependency reflects Latin American reality. Moreover, the sheer volume and power of US influence in the area forces American scholars to recognize that they, too, partake of that influence. [P.B. Taylor, Jr.]

7021 Fontaine, Roger W. The Andean Pact: a political analysis. Beverly Hills, Calif., Sage Publications, 1977. 72 p., map, tables (The Washington papers, 45)

Descriptive paper concerning the Pact: inception, members' views and "romantic" aspirations, and possibilities for longterm results. The writer sees many problems, and contemplates its failure. [P.B. Taylor, Jr.]

Frei M., Eduardo. América Latina: opción y esperanza. See item **7402**.

Galjert, Benno. Movilización campesina en América Latina. See item **7404**.

7022 González, Heliodoro. The Latin American press and the UNESCO maneuvers (IAMEA, 32:3, Winter 1978, p. 77–94)

Comments concerning the UNESCO Declaration on a free flow of world news. [A. Suárez]

7023 Gordon, Lincoln. International stability and North-South relations. Muscatine, Iowa. The Stanley Foundation, 1978. 33 p., tables (Occasional paper, 17)

General policy proposal, based on a quick overview of the needs of Third World countries, for future action by the US. The discussion is very general but includes some reference to Brazil. [P.B. Taylor, Jr.]

7024 Grigulewitsch, J. Die Armee und der revolutionäre Prozess in Lateinamerika (Sowjetwissenschaft [Gesellschaft

Wissenschaftliche Beiträge, Berlin, GDR] 27:6, 1974, p. 629–644)

East German article discusses the historical development of Latin American armies and their role vis-à-vis the revolutionary process in Latin America. [M. Kossok]

7025 Hackethal, Eberhard. Faschismus und faschistische Ideologie in Lateinamerika (Asien, Afrika, Lateinamerika [Deutscher Verlag der Wissenchaften, Berlin, GDR] 5:4, 1977, p. 646–658)

East German analysis of what is Latin American "fascism," its causes, possibilities, limitations and its class base. [M. Kossok]

7026 Halperin, Ernst. Terrorism in Latin America. Beverly Hills, Calif., Sage Publications *for* Georgetown Univ., The Center for Strategic and International Studies, Washington, 1976. 90 p., map (The Washington papers, 4:33)

Concentrating on Argentina, Uruguay and Brazil, author proposes that fear is a most important variable in the success of Latin American terrorism. Various reasons are given for the phenomenon including a "schizoid collective psychosis" at once protective of and antagonistic to traditional Hispanic values. Intriguing study. [W.R. Garner]

7027 Hammergren, Linn A. Corporatism in Latin American politics: a reexamination of the "Unique" tradition (CUNY/CP, 9:4, July 1977, p. 443–461)

In a careful examination of the value of the corporatist model as a guide to political analysis, author seeks to refute the notion of a unique tradition by showing that recent political trends are primarily responses to the problem of building political cohesion in fragmented, poorly integrated societies with little consensus on political rules. Valuable for understanding the imperfect fit of the corporatist model to contemporary politics in Latin America. [D.W. Dent]

7028 Hennessy, Alistair. Fascism and populism in Latin America (*in* Laqueur, Walter *ed.* Fascism, a reader's guide: analyses, interpretations, bibliography. Berkeley, Univ. of California Press, 1976, p. 255–294)

Why didn't fascism take root in Latin America as it did in some parts of Europe between World Wars I and II? In a provocative treatment of this question, author stresses non-economic variables that prevented the rise of fascism but set the preconditions for the growth of populist parties and leaders in the post-Depression era. Case studies of Brazil, Argentina, Chile, and Peru demonstrate a solid grasp of the literature. Highly recommended to political scientists and historians who have struggled with the terms "fascism" and "populism." [D.W. Dent]

7029 Hodges, Donald C. The legacy of Che Guevara: a documentary study. Documents translated by Ernest C. Rehder and others. London, Thames and Hudson, 1977. 216 p., bibl.

Useful collection of documents issued by Latin American guerrilla movements. The introduction differentiates Castroism from "Guevarism," and identifies ideologies of guerrilla movements as varieties of the latter. [A. Suárez]

7030 Hughes, Arnold and Martin Kolinsky. "Paradigmatic fascism" and modernization: a critique (PSA/PS, 24:4, Dec. 1976, p. 371–396)

Authors challenge the assumption made by Gregor in 1974 *World Politics* article that Africa and other Third World areas are developing fascist governments in the post-war era. Article provides stimulating critique by arguing that sub-Saharan regimes ought not to be perceived as "fascist" or "neo-fascist" but rather as mutations of authoritarianism bordering on "bureaucratic-caesarism" regardless of whether the regime is military or civilian. Interesting and original piece. [W.R. Garner]

7031 Iglesia latinoamericana, política y socialismo. Prólogo de Gustavo Sucre. Caracas, Univ. Católica Andrés Bello, 1977. 227 p. (Col. Manoa, 2)

Collection of four documents: Paul VI's letter on the LXXX anniversary of the Encyclica *Rerum Novarum*; and doctrinal/political statements by the Bishops of Chile (1971), the Plenary Episcopal Assembly of Chile (1973) and the Bishops of Colombia (1976). [P.B. Taylor, Jr.]

7032 Jackman, Robert W. Politicians in uniform: military governments and social change in the Third World (APSA/R, 70:4, Dec. 1976, p. 1078–1097, tables)

Author investigates three hypotheses concerning nature of military government, that they are: 1) progressive forces; 2) "reactionary inhibitors" of social change; and 3) responsible for positive influence on size of nation's middle class and rate of industrialization. Using quantitative analysis, Jackman argues that there is no discernible relation between military governments and social, economic and political change. Important contribution. [W.R. Garner]

7033 Jaquaribe, Helio. Dependency and autonomy in Latin America (*in* Congreso Interamericano de Planificación, VII, Lima, 1968. Latin America in the year 2000. Edited by Joseph S. Tulchin. Reading, Mass., Addison-Wesley, 1975, p. 190–224)

In part a description of efforts by Latin American social scientists to create a model of Latin American development and integration, the paper is also a useful exercise in the weighing of evidence, the stating of historical and contemporary alternatives, and the meaning of concepts and terms. [P.B. Taylor, Jr.]

7034 Johnson, Kenneth F. Research perspectives on the revised Fitzgibbon-Johnson index of the image of political democracy in Latin America, 1945–75 (*in* Wilkie, James W. and Kenneth Ruddle *eds.* Quantitative Latin American studies, methods and findings: statistical abstract of Latin America. Los Angeles, UCLA, Latin American Center Publications, 1977, p. 87–91, tables [Supplement, 6])

Some of the methodological problems in measuring political democracy in Latin America are divulged in a revised index which seeks to measure political "distances" between country ranks and the effect of US aid on democratic political development. Optimistic in tone despite the inevitability of ethnocentric influence on one's measuring rod. [D.W. Dent]

Kistanov, Valeri. Cabeza de playa de los monopolios japoneses en América Latina. See item **7552.**

7035 Kohl, James and John Litt. Urban guerrilla warfare in Latin America. Cambridge, Mass., MIT Press, 1974. 425 p., bibl., maps.

Good collection of documents published by guerrilla movements in Brazil,

Uruguay, and Argentina. Not easily available in other sources. Introductory essays for each of the three countries under study, chronologies, and bibliography enhance the edition. [A. Suárez]

7036 Kossok, Manfred. Probleme einer vergleichenden Analyse der lateinamerikanischen Unabhängigkeitsrevolution (ZFG, 25:2, 1977, p. 143–155)

Analysis by East German historian of the independence movements in 19th-century Latin America, both from a regional and international perspective. He compares them with 20th-century revolutionary movements and discusses their common and distinct traits. [M. Kossok]

7037 Kucuk, Ejub. The socio-class determinants of militarism (Socialist Thought and Practice [Belgrad] 17:11, 1977, p. 91–123)

Yugoslav sociologist offers dialectical analysis of militarism in democratic and nondemocratic types of political systems. He argues that only a self-managing socialist society can transcend the negative consequences of a military organization which has historically defended class interests. [D.W. Dent]

7038 Kübler, Jürgen. Das Ringen der Arbeiterklasse Lateinamerikas um Aktionseinheit im Kampf gegen Imperialismus, Faschismus und Oligarchie (*in* Jahrbuch Asien Afrika Lateinamerika [Deutscher Verlag der Wissenschaften, Berlin, GDR] 1976 [i.e. 1975] p. 237–261)

Autor de Alemania Oriental describe "problemas de la lucha de la clase obrera en Latinoamérica contra el imperialismo y el fascismo durante el año 1975." [M. Kossok]

7039 ———. Der Kampf der Arbeiterklasse Lateinamerikas und ihrer Verbündeten gegen Imperialismus und Faschismus (*in* Jahrbuch Asien Afrika Lateinamerika. [Bilanz und Chronik des Jahres 1977. Deutscher Verlag der Wissenschaften, Berlin, GDR] 1978, p. 253–273)

Autor de Alemania Oriental analiza la situación en América Latina en 1977. La relación de fuerzas entre "la reacción y el movimiento revolucionario," la posición de Cuba y su desarrollo socialista, el movimiento obrero y estudiantil en Latinoamérica, papel de la Iglesia católica y de los ejércitos en varios países latinoamericanos. [M. Kossok]

7040 Latin American Symposium, *III,* *Meadville, Pa., 1978.* The state, social change and economic development: Latin America in the 1970 s. Edited by Giles Wayland-Smith. Meadville, Pa., Allegheny College, 1978. 33 p.

Consists of papers by Carlos Vilas of the Univ. of B.A., Ricardo Israel Zipper of the Univ. of Essex, and Hernán Rosenkranz-Schikler of the Univ. of Liverpool. The papers on Argentina, Chile, and Peru address the issue of the role of the state in economic development, and the stimulation/regulation of social change. The authors are Tinker Fellows at the Univ. of Pittsburgh. [P.B. Taylor, Jr.]

7041 *The Latin American Yearly Review.* American College in Paris. Vol. 1, 1973- . Paris.

A modest summary volume of highly selected events in Latin America during the year. [P.B. Taylor, Jr.]

7042 Latorre Cabal, Hugo. The revolution of the Latin American Church. Translated from the Spanish by Frances K. Hendricks and Beatrice Berler. Norman, Univ. of Oklahoma Press, 1978. 192 p., table.

The title is somewhat misleading. Book merely recounts episodes throughout the region reflecting the conflict between traditionalists and progressives in the contemporary Latin American Church. Critical of traditionalists. [A. Suárez]

7043 Lavretsky, I. Ernesto Che Guevara. Moscow, Progress Publishers, 1976. 311 p., plates.

Soviet biography of Che designed to restore the real meaning of Guevara's revolutionary life and to confound imperialist designs to make "an anti-Soviet hero" of him. The sovietization of the hero is so thorough that even his visits to China are omitted. Biography includes many factual errors (e.g., refers in Portuguese to Ingenieros' book *Las fuerzas morales,* published in B.A.). [A. Suárez]

7043a Levi, Georgina *ed.* Il fascismo dipendente in America Latina: una nuova fase dei rapporti fra oligarchia e imperialismo. Bari, Italy, De Donato Editore, 1976. 274 p., bibl.

Collection of papers delivered at a symposium organized by the Regional Council of Piedmont, Italy. The papers address Latin American authoritarianism and attempt to analyze it in the light of the fascist experience. Some of the papers are strictly political, others more analytical. Among the first kind, one should note the study by Luis Carlos Preste "Brasile: Base Continentale del Neofascismo;" among the second type, there are Luis Gonzaga de Souza Lima's "Il Fascismo Dipendente come Categoria de Analisi Política: il Brasile," and Osvaldo Fernández' "Esiste il Fascismo in Cile?" [M. Carmagnani]

7044 Linares Quintana, Segundo V. Sistemas de partidos y sistemas políticos: el gobierno de las leyes y el gobierno de los hombres. B.A., Editorial Plus Ultra, 1976. 693 p., tables.

A magisterial piece of typological comparisons beginning with Herodotus and continuing through contemporary theorists and describers. The writer's span is prodigious and includes all nationalities and theories, from western to Soviet, as well as Argentine and other Latin American. A useful survey piece. [P.B. Taylor, Jr.]

7045 López Trujillo, Alfonso. Liberation or revolution?: an examination of the priest's role in the socioeconomic class struggle in Latin America. Huntington, Ind., Our Sunday Visitor, 1977. 128 p.

Colombian Bishop ponders the role of priests in Latin American development following the doctrine of "theology of liberation" enunciated at Medellín in 1968. According to López Trujillo, the priest's role should avoid political struggles and work toward liberation of the community without class struggles. One of the Church's strongest critics of liberation theology sets the agenda for CELAM III at Puebla, Mexico. Spanish ed.: ¡Liberación o revolución? (Bogotá, Ediciones Paulinas, 1975). [D.W. Dent]

7046 Loveman, Brian and **Thomas M. Davies, Jr.** eds. The politics of antipolitics: the military in Latin America. Lincoln, Univ. of Nebraska Press, 1978. 309 p., bibl., tables.

Admirable and wide-ranging volume containing 44 individual articles, speeches, and short collections of documents. Bulk of the volume consists of (often deeply) edited scholarly studies on the armed forces but also includes one section of public statements and documents by military leaders themselves

and another section of papers which reviews the results of military "antipolitics" in five selected countries: Argentina, Bolivia, Brazil, Chile and Peru. Some of the pieces are relatively obscure, others discuss the countries in terms of 19th- and early 20th-century European influence, the inter-war period, and the era of largest US influence. The volume is enormously ambitious and although intended principally for teaching purposes, it is a useful reader for all specialists. Contributing editors are: Charles D. Corbett, Frederick M. Nunn, Marvin Golwert, Warren Schiff, Wm. S. Dudley, Víctor Villanueva, Robert A. Potash, Wm. H. Brill, Herbert S. Klein, Ronald M. Schneider, Raymond J. Barrett, John Saxe Fernández, John Thompson, David Rock, Albert Fishlow, Peter Flynn, Thos. G. Sanders, Abraham F. Lowenthal, and Julio Cotler. The Latin American military officers are: Juan Carlos Onganía, Jorge Rafael Videla, Alfredo Ovando Candia, Hugo Banzer Suárez, Humberto Castello Branco, Ernesto Geisel, Augusto Pinochet, Juan Velasco Alvarado, Francisco Morales Bermúdez, and Juan José Torres. [P.B. Taylor, Jr.]

7047 Lowy, Michael. The Marxism of Che Guevara: philosophy, economics, and revolutionary warfare. N.Y., Monthly Review Press, 1973. 127 p., bibl.

Translation of the French ed. published 1970. The aim of the book is "to show that Guevara's ideas constitute a coherent whole, and are built on the basic premises of Marxism-Leninism. . . ." [A. Suárez]

7048 Martínez Moreno, Carlos; Alberto Baeza Flores; Jorge Mario Quinzio; and **Jottin Cury.** Temas para el socialismo democrático latinoamericano. San José, Centro de Estudios Democráticos de América Latina (CEDAL), 1972. 75 p. (Col. Seminarios y documentos)

Papers by Chilean, Uruguayan and Dominican writers of uneven quality which, nonetheless, treat major problems facing traditional/transitional societies. Policy alternatives are given in the context of democratic socialism. [W.R. Garner]

7049 Myer, John. A crown of thorns: Cardoso and counter-revolution (LAP, 2:1, Spring 1975, p. 33–48, bibl.)

Fernando Henrique Cardoso's work is examined for detail and implications. The writer concludes that Cardoso, despite use of the language of Marx and Lenin, is not of their persuasion at all. Rather, Cardoso's ideas are expressions of bourgeois nationalism that do not contribute to the struggle against imperialism. The paper is a thorough wringing-out of topics within the dependency context. [P.B. Taylor, Jr.]

7050 Natsionalizm v Latinskoi Amerike: politicheskie i ideologicheskie techeniia (Nationalism in Latin America: political and ideological currents). Moscow, Izdatel'stvo "Nauka," 1976. 368 p.

Broad Soviet survey of nationalism in Latin America, including national-reformist movements, mass groups, national feelings in the Anglo- and Francophone Antilles, the position of the Church and attitudes in the armed forces. Attention is given to Indianismo, Argentinidad, etc. Bourgeois and ultra-left nationalisms are deprecated and the striving of Communist and workers' parties for progressive and anti-imperialist unity is emphasized. [R.V. Allen]

7051 Needler, Martin C. The closeness of elections in Latin America (LARR, 12:1, 1977, p. 115–121, tables)

Author names various causes for trend toward numerical closeness in Latin American elections including alienation from incumbents, technological and ideological sophistication (producing "minimal winning coalitions"), attraction of previously apathetic voters. Ascribes tendency toward violence to increasingly prevalent tally challenges which pose a constant threat to the legitimacy usually accruing to the winning party or coalition. Novel contribution. [W.R. Garner]

7052 ———. An introduction to Latin American politics: the structure of conflict. Englewood Cliffs, N.J., Prentice-Hall, 1977. 358 p., bibl., maps, tables.

Concise introduction to the Latin American political process which treats structural institutions and relevant factors in contemporary context. The first part of volume is integrated into a geographic section. Interesting concluding remarks on influence of both private and public US forces in Hemisphere. A good introductory text. [W.R. Garner]

7053 O'Donnell, Guillermo. Reflections on the patterns of change in the bu-

reaucratic-authoritarian state (LARR, 13:1, 1978, p. 3–38, bibl., tables)

Drawings on a broad sweep of literature, experience, and reflective observation, the author describes the changes that occur within bureaucratic-authoritarian states in the years and decades after their establishment. Although his chief examples are Argentina, Brazil and Mexico, he also refers to Cuba, Spain and the relevant literature for many other regions. See also item **7054**. [P.B. Taylor, Jr.]

7054 ———. Reflexiones sobre las tendencias generales de cambio en el estado burocrático-autoritario. Lima, Taller de Estudios Políticos, 1975. 79 p., table (Serie: Procesos políticos latinoamericanos, 3)

Original version of article written for a "Seminar on History and Human Sciences" (São Paulo, 1975) and later published in the *Latin American Research Review* (13:1, 1978) and entitled "Reflections on the Patterns of Change in the Bureaucratic-Authoritarian State." Examines the conditions which have fostered such (BA) regimes and the dynamics or stages of these regimes once they have been implanted and the structure and change ("deepening process") after international capital takes hold. Also discusses further efforts to refine the typology and meaning of political-economic change in Latin America. Examples are drawn mainly from Argentina and Brazil. See also item **7053**. [D.W. Dent]

7055 Parra E., Ernesto and **Isabel Aguirrezábal T.** Suramérica 76: modelos militares de desarrollo. Bogotá, Centro de Investigación y Educación Popular (CINEP), 1976. 84 p., tables (Controversia, 46)

Neo-Marxist analysis of three types— Brazilian, Peruvian, and Chilean—of military governments in terms of their main characteristics, achievements, and consequences for the working classes. Peruvian experiment is given relatively high marks until the rise of Gen. Morales Bermúdez in 1975. [D.W. Dent]

7056 Peguševa, L.V. Die Entwicklung der christlichen Gewerkschaftsbewegung in Lateinamerika (UR/L, Spring 1976, p. 5–17)

East German analysis of the role of Christian Democratic labor unions in Latin

America and how they relate to the "revolutionary struggle." [M. Kossok]

Phillips, David Atlee. The night watch. See *HLAS 40:2216.*

7057 Pizzorno, Alessandro; Marcos Kaplan; and Manuel Castells. Participación y cambio social en la problemática contemporánea. B.A., Ediciones Sociedad Interamericana de Planificación, 1975. 173 p. (SIAP/Planteos)

Three neo-Marxist essays on political participation that argue that unless there is more equality within and among nations, the act of participating in politics will remain an exercise in futility. General in scope but with some applicability to Latin America as part of the Third World. [D.W. Dent]

7058 *Política.* Fundação Milton Campos. No., 4, abril/junho 1977- . Brasília.

Significant intellectual review dating from 1976. This issue consists of articles in the social sciences and university education. [P.B. Taylor, Jr.]

7059 Pollack, John Crothers. An anthropological approach to mass communication research: the U.S. press and political change in Latin America (LARR, 13:1, 1978, p. 158–172, table)

US reporting of Latin America does not only reflect misinformation, bias or hostility. Author hypothesizes that news output is related to "systemic" perspectives typified by him as colonial, technocratic, and hegemonic. A research report. No data. [A. Suárez]

7060 Price, H. Edward, Jr. The strategy and tactics of revolutionary terrorism (CSSH, 19:1, Jan. 1977, p. 52–66, bibl.)

Theoretical treatment of the strategies and tactics of revolutionary terrorism in three types of socio-political systems: nation-state, colonial territory, and a single territory of dominant and subordinate ethnic groups. The Tupamaro movement in Uruguay is examined for strategies, tactics, and reasons for defeat. Author maintains that the Tupamaros failed because the violence of the Uruguayan government was seen as more legitimate than that of the revolutionary terrorists. [D.W. Dent]

7061 Puhle, Hans-Jürgen. "Revolution" von oben und Revolution von unten in Lateinamerika (UB/GG, 2:2, 1976, p. 143–159)

Author discusses Latin American revolutions from "above" and from "below" and comes to conclusion that there have been only three true revolutions in Latin America: the Mexican, Bolivian and Cuban. He notes that decisive impetus for all three came from "above" because populations are still too powerless for spontaneous action. [R.V. Shaw]

7062 Quijano, Aníbal. Clase obrera en América Latina. San José, Editorial Universitaria Centroamericana (EDUCA), 1976. 101 p. (Col. Aula)

Marxist theoretician sees problem of proletarian consciousness as a failure to achieve separate and distinct *national* mobilization for the working class in Latin America's corporate societies. [W.R. Garner]

7063 Rachum, Ilan. The Latin American revolutions of 1930: a non-economic interpretation (CLAPCS/AL, 17, 1976, p. 3–17)

Reexamination of the causes of the revolutions of 1930 with special emphasis on Peru, Argentina, and Brazil. Author finds these political events related more to generational conflicts, changes in elite attitudes, and the growth of radical political ideologies after World War I than to the economic impact of the depression of 1929 and its aftermath. Notable for its effort to go beyond economic explanations of these events. [D.W. Dent]

7064 Ramm, Hartmut. The Marxism of Régis Debray: between Lenin and Guevara. Lawrence, Kans., The Regents Press of Kansas, 1978. 240 p.

An exercise in revolutionary scholasticism. Although Debray himself has slighted his contribution to revolutionary strategy, the author thinks it is worthwhile to register minutely the discrepancies between the masters, Lenin and Che, and the novice, Debray. [A. Suárez]

7065 Rangel, Carlos. Del buen salvaje al buen revolucionario: mitos y realidades de América Latina. Prólogo de Jean-François Revel. Caracas, Monte Avila Editores, 1976. 257 p. (Col. Perspectiva actual)

An insightful and well-written historical account of the causes of Latin America's retarded development within the "sphere of influence" of the US. By contrasting the factors associated with Latin American and US development, author attempts to debunk the myths of the "good savage" and the "good revolutionary." Latin America's weaknesses appear to be rooted in a weak sense of national identity and the absence of any real consensus on the rules of the political game. [D.W. Dent]

7066 Remmer, Karen L. Evaluating the policy impact of military regimes in Latin America (LARR, 13:2, 1978, p. 39–54, bibl., table)

Do military and civilian regimes differ in their policies and performance records? Recent empirical studies are scrutinized in an attempt to link regime type with public policy. Findings suggest that conflicting results are often the result of inappropriate research strategies. The complexity of civil-military relations is reaffirmed, while author suggests that future research efforts concentrate on the characteristics that have been imputed to military and civilian regimes rather than attempting to measure the impact of regime type on public policy using a civilian-military dichotomy. A careful assessment with valuable insights for future research. [D. W. Dent]

7067 Rodríguez, Horacio Daniel. Che Guevara: ¿aventura o revolución? Barcelona, Plaza & Janes, 1976. 317 p. (Col. Manantial)

Argentinian author tells the story of the man—not the hero—and it is rather critical. Reprint of original published in 1968 which only used Spanish sources available at the time. [A. Suárez]

7068 Ruhl, J. Mark. Social mobilization and political instability in Latin America: a test of Huntington's theory (IAMEA, 29:2, Autumn 1975, p. 3–21, tables)

Brief mathematical testing of the theory by use of statistical data from 18 Latin American countries. The theory is modified somewhat in this paper, to include the variable of distribution as a major factor. Author concludes that Huntington's theory, as revised, does stand up for the present time and space. [P.B. Taylor, Jr.]

7068a Russell Tribunal on Repression in Brazil, Chile, and Latin America, *II,*

Rome, 1976. Controrivoluzione in America Latina: enversione militare e strumentalizzazione dei sindacati, della cultura, delle chiese. Introduction by Lelio Basso. Milano, Italy, La Pietra, 1976. 148 p., tables.

Collection of five papers presented to the Russell Tribunal, dealing with the following topics: military counterrevolution in Latin America, the situation in Argentina, the conditions of unions in the US, political action in Latin America, cultural imperialism, and imperialist penetration of the Church in Latin America. The authors are Italian, French, Chilean and American. [P.B. Taylor, Jr.]

7069 Sauvage, Leó. Che Guevara: the failure of a revolutionary. Translated from the French by Raoul Frémont. Englewood Cliffs., N.J., Prentice Hall, 1973. 272 p.

Shrewd scrutiny of Guevara's revolutionary activities using his own works and, mostly, Cuban sources. Good familiarity with the pertinent materials, although author may infer too much from the sources. Very critical. [P.B. Taylor, Jr.]

7070 Schmidt, Steffen W. Political participation and development: the role of women in Latin America (CU/JIA, 30:2, Fall/Winter 1976, p. 243–260, tables)

An important article concerning the changing role of women in Latin American development. Author finds that the dominant roles that women play in economic and political life often differ from the ideal norm of the patriarchal model. Questions of theory, method, and future research needs are also presented. For historian's comment, see *HLAS 40:2402.* [D.W. Dent]

7071 Seminario Latinoamericano La Democracia en Crisis, *Santa Bárbara de Heredia, C.R., 1974.* Latinoamérica: la democracia en crisis, en busca de un análisis de sus causas. Introducción de Alberto Baeza Flores and others. San José, Centro de Estudios Democráticos de América Latina (CEDAL), 1974. 55 p., bibl., tables (COL. Cuadernos CEDAL, 1)

A "working document" prepared for a conference, 26–31 May 1974, of Latin American specialists from the entire region. The theme is the failure of political democracy in Latin America. Also explores economic causes, with some attention to social outcomes of the presence and distribution of economic interests (both internal and international). A useful, if very brief, presentation of an agenda. [P.B. Taylor, Jr.]

7071a Senese, Salvatore. La trasformazione delle strutture giuridiche in América Latina (MULINO, 25:246, luglio/agosto 1976, p. 529)

The legal/juridical structure has been changed fundamentally in recent years in Latin America in the name of "national security," with the armed forces playing a major role. The paper addresses the situation in Brazil, Chile, Bolivia and Uruguay. The author finds that US examples are used for changing details of laws affecting civil rights of individuals as well as practices of security forces. Latin American dependency on the US encourages this tendency. This is a strong and persuasive paper but written in a biased tone. Prepared for and presented to the II Russell Tribunal meeting, Jan. 1976. See also item **7068a.** [P.B. Taylor, Jr.]

7072 Shokina, I.E. Die lateinamerikanischen Kommunisten über die Rolle der nationalistischen, "populistischen" Massenbewegungen in der antiimperialistischen Einheit (UR/L, Fall 1975, p. 5–16)

East German analysis of the strategies of Communist parties in Latin America vis-à-vis populist and nationalist movements. [M. Kossok]

7073 Silgado, Manuel Román de. Burocracia y cambio social. Lima, Univ. del Pacífico, Depto. de Ciencias Sociales y Políticas, Centro de Investigación, 1975. 327 p., tables (Serie: Departamento académicos, 2)

Author presents useful insights for the theorist of public administration based on works of Weber, Merton, Gouldner and Selznick. Distinguishes between two Weber models: 1) when the majority of groups within a society are already organized or psychologically prepared for mobilization; and 2) where such mobilization or mental preparedness for it does *not* exist. This is an incisive analysis of administration forms which combines modern with more traditional public administration theory. [W.R. Garner]

7074 Silvert, Kalman H. Essays in understanding Latin America. Foreword by Joel M. Jutkowitz. Philadelphia, Pa., Institute

for the Study of Human Issues, 1977. 240 p., table.

A collection of the author's writings chosen by him before his untimely death. Thoughtful and penetrating, they reveal a thorough knowledge of Latin America, and a deep commitment to the improvement of the human condition therein. [A. Suárez]

7075 Singelmann, Peter. Los movimientos campesinos y la modernización política en América Latina: apuntes críticos (CEDLA/B, 20, junio 1976, p. 34–53, bibl.)

Argues that established social science theory on role of peasants in modernization process is founded on inadequate equilibrium model; should be replaced with conflict model. This should stress search for obstacles to modernization that are located in domination of some classes by others. Discusses traditional mechanisms of domination that persist in 20th century, along with their opposites in structural changes which produced national state and national-populist politics. Locates new systems of domination in dependence of peasants on "intermediaries," particularization of class relations, and more effective repression. Concludes that view which holds that incorporation of peasants into national politics as an autonomous pressure group signifies political modernization is untenable because peasants always have been incorporated into wider political system, though in a dependent form and as a group internally divided into vertical alliances. Suggests that modernization be contrasted with revolutionary mobilization. Important critique of the modernization framework as applied to agrarian politics. [V.C. Peloso]

Smith, W.H. International terrorism: a political analysis. See item **8596.**

7076 Sousa Wahrlich, Beatriz M. de. La reforma administrativa en la América Latina: similitudes y diferencias entre cinco experiencias nacionales (*in* Seminario Interamericano de Reforma Administrativa, I, Rio, 1973/1974. Reforma administrativa: experiencias latinoamericanas. Mexico, Instituto Nacional de Administración Pública, 1975, p. 445–483)

In a tight comparative analysis, author discusses the similarities and differences in administrative reform among the countries of Brazil, Colombia, Venezuela, Panama and Mexico. The goals, problems/obstacles, and achievements of each country reveal more similarities than differences while the modern civil servant is quite distant from the present situation. [D.W. Dent]

7077 ———. Reforma administrativa na América Latina: semelhanças e diferencias entre cinco experiências nacionais (FGV/RAP, 8:4, 1974, p. 5–47)

Mexico, Panama, Venezuela, Colombia and Brazil are examined briefly by a professor in the Brazilian School of Public Administration. Material on each is divided as follows: history of administrative reform, concept and strategy, methodology, principal obstacles, results. Their experience shows some similarities, which are pointed out. Includes brief English language summary. [P.B. Taylor, Jr.]

Spalding, Hobart A., Jr. Organized labor in Latin America: historical case studies of workers in dependent societies. See *HLAS 40:2408.*

Sterling, Claire. The terrorist network. See item **8600.**

7078 Street, James H. The internal frontier and technological progress in Latin America (LARR, 12:3, 1977, p. 25–56, tables)

Substantial paper on the political economy of Latin America. It begins and ends with discussion of the role of energy, but in between it examines the social, demographic, technological, agricultural and other variables affecting prosperity and development in the region. [P.B. Taylor, Jr.]

7079 Sussman, Leonard R. Mass news media and the Third World challenge. Beverly Hills, Calif., Sage Publications, 1977. 80 p. (The Washington papers, 46)

A practicing journalist and official of Freedom House, the author's interest and activity lead logically to this short work. Describes principal complaints of Third World nations about transnational news services and recounts events in these countries' efforts toward attaining official control. While this is a general overview, it is still an excellent starting place for the student. Latin America is discussed as a region distinct from other Third World areas and the role ideology plays therein is also examined. [P.B. Taylor, Jr.]

7080 Tannahill, R. Neal. The performance of military and civilian governments in South America: 1948–1967 (NIU/JPMS, 4:2, Fall 1976, p. 233–244, bibl.)

Author believes basic disparities between military and civilian governments are "political." Neither type correlates decisively either to higher or lower rates of economic growth. The military, however, has produced higher industrialization and monetary stabilization rates. An important contribution to military studies. [W.R. Garner]

7081 Vanden, Harry E. The peasants as a revolutionary class: an early Latin American view (UM/JIAS, 20:2, May 1978, p. 101–209, bibl.)

The "early view" comes from José Carlos Mariátegui whom author perceives as a forerunner in discovering the revolutionary potentialities of the peasantry. [A. Suárez]

7082 Welch, Charles E., Jr. Civilian control of the military: theory and cases from developing countries. Albany, State Univ. of New York Press, 1976. 337 p., bibl., tables.

Selection of ten papers presented at an Inter-University Seminar on Armed Forces and Society held at SUNY/Buffalo in 1974. Latin American countries discussed are Guyana (as compared to Malaysia) by Cynthia H. Enloe; Mexico by Lt. Col. Franklin D. Margiotta; and Chile by Albert L. Michaels. [P.B. Taylor, Jr.]

7083 Wiarda, Howard J. Corporatist theory and ideology: a Latin American development paradigm (BU/JCS, 20:1, Winter 1978, p. 29–56)

As part of the Iberic-Latin political culture, corporatism represents a paradigm for development in Latin America in response to the sociopolitical change of the 19th century. Author discusses the Roman Catholic intellectual roots of corporatism and why it found a fertile ground in the ambiente of Latin America which tended to reject liberalism and Marxist socialism. As a response to modernization, corporatism is purported to serve as an alternative path to national development. What appears as a master plan and cohesive structure for dealing with national development to some, however, can be explained in alternative theoretical models by others who reject these cultural-ideological explanations. [D.W. Dent]

7084 Williams, Edward J. and **Freeman J. Wright.** Latin American politics: a developmental approach. Palo Alto, Calif., Mayfield Pub. Co., 1975. 480 p., bibls., map, plates, tables.

Introductory text based on a developmental model of politics. Using such concepts as secularization, integration, mobilization, participation, and institutionalization, authors investigate the developmental significance of traditional (e.g., landed oligarchy, military, Church) and modern (e.g., political parties, labor unions, etc.) power contenders. The rather optimistic conclusions concerning modernizing change will not be universally accepted but the analytical effort is commendable. The conceptual terminology in the first chapter may hinder the student's ability to grasp the nuances of Latin American politics and thereby restrict his or her understanding of how the political game is played in Latin America. [D.W. Dent]

7085 Wolpin, Miles D. Marx and radical militarism in the developing nations (AFS, 4:2, Winter 1978, p. 245–264, bibl.)

Attack on Marxist stereotype of military as reactionary and necessarily divorced from serious Marxist policy. In both long- and short-range philosophical perspective, existence of "leftist" militaries refutes any "suprahistorical Marxist orthodoxy" and confirms Marx's pragmatism and empiricism. Interesting think-piece. [W.R. Garner]

7086 Wynia, Gary W. The politics of Latin American development. Cambridge, U.K., Cambridge Univ. Press, 1978. 335 p., bibl., maps, tables.

In this introductory text, politics is viewed as a game with certain rules, players, and contests for power. The clarity and organization of this approach to understanding Latin American politics is a welcome addition to an area with few core textbooks. The emphasis on various types of political systems—populist, democratic reformist, military, and revolutionary—and an excellent chapter on economic strategies employed in Latin America should provide a solid foundation for students interested in the components and dynamics of the political process. Major theme is Latin America's inability to generate an agreement on fundamental rules of the political game. [D.W. Dent]

MEXICO, CENTRAL AMERICA, THE CARIBBEAN, AND THE GUIANAS

ANDRES SUAREZ, *Professor of Political Science, Center of Latin American Studies, University of Florida*

A FEW YEARS AGO GABRIEL A. ALMOND WROTE: "A mood of disillusionment appears to be sweeping the field of comparative politics . . ." The literature annotated for this section tends to substantiate Almond's assertion. With the exception of the suggestive contribution by Archibald R. M. Ritter (item **7214a**), the paper by R. S. Milne (item **7264**), and the final chapter in Susan Eckstein's book (item **7108a**), there are very few books annotated below which are explicitly comparative or that contribute significantly to the discipline.

Among country studies, there are four items that should not be overlooked by the Cuban specialist. Carlos Franqui's *Diary* (item **7198**) is probably the most important source yet published on the days of the struggle, particularly in the Sierra Maestra guerrilla campaign where Franqui was a participant. The book by Mario Llerena (item **7207**) offers penetrating glimpses of the actors involved and the events leading to the organization of the "26th of July Movement." The contribution by Carlos Rafael Rodríguez (item **7216**) makes available, to the foreign reader for the first time, a work that has been circulating in Cuba in restricted form. In it, Rodríguez explains, from the point of view of a top official, the political economy implemented during the period of transition to socialism. And finally, the standard sources used for the identification and quantification of the Cuban peasantry are subjected to close scrutiny and criticism in a provocative paper by Brian Pollit (item **7214**).

On Mexico, the collection edited by José Luis Reyna and Richard W. Weinert discusses the points of convergence between the Mexican system and the authoritarian model elaborated to explain the recent military governments to the south (item **7137**); Ariel José Contreras offers a well-researched and insightful analysis of one crucial event in recent Mexican politics: Avila Camacho's election (item **7104**); and Merilee S. Grindle relies on her knowledge of the bureaucracy to identify "políticos" and "técnicos" (item **7115**).

As has been noted in previous volumes, works on the politics and government of the English-speaking Caribbean are invariably few. This time, however, we are pleased to acknowledge Carl Stone's contributions on Jamaica which live up to the high quality of his previous works (items **7238–7241**) and the proceedings of a conference held in 1974 entitled *Implications of independence for Grenada* (item **7242**). This publication is not only of a high intellectual caliber but opportune as well, appearing at a time when there is urgent need for some explanation for the emergence of a radical government on this tiny island.

MEXICO

7087 Acevedo de Silva, María Guadalupe.
Crisis del desarrollismo y transformación del aparato estatal: México, 1970–1975 (UNAM/RMCPS, 21:82, oct./dic. 1975, p. 133–163, table)
Tries to explain how "changes in the state apparatus" during Echeverría's administration reflect "changes in the class struggle."

7088 Aguirre Avellaneda, Jerjes. La política ejidal en México. Prólogo de José Sánchez Cortés. México, Instituto Mexicano de Sociología, 1976. 200 p., bibl., tables.
The evolution of the ejido and policies implemented by the government to regulate the institution.

Aguilera Gómez, Manuel. El eterno problema de la tierra en México. See *HLAS 40:2682.*

7089 Aldana, Talavera. Organizaciones sindicales obreras de la rama textil: 1935–1970 (UNAM/RMCPS, 21:83, enero/marzo 1976, p. 227–299, fold. tables, maps, tables)
Very detailed description with substantial amounts of data.

7090 Alvarez, Alejandro and **Elena Sandoval.** Desarrollo industrial y clase obrera en México (CP, 4, abril/junio 1975, p. 6–24, tables)
The purpose is to study the industrial

proletariat, "the natural representative of the oppressed," and its future vanguard. Some data. Less than an introduction to the topic.

7091 Arguedas, Ledda. El movimiento de liberación nacional: una experiencia de la izquierda mexicana en los sesentas (UNAM/RMS, 39:1, enero/marzo 1977, p. 229–249)
Historical concept, program, activities and demise of the M.L.N. (1961–64).

7092 Bartra Muria, Roger. Y si los campesinos se extinguen . . . : reflexiones sobre la coyuntura política de 1976 en México (UNAM/RMS, 38:2, abril/junio 1976, p. 323–337)
The PRI, sexennial elections, etc., are nothing else but gimmicks to disguise the real fact: in Mexico the bourgeoisie is in power. No data. No footnotes. No bibliography. Pure "dialectics."

7093 Bernal García, Cristina and **Patricia Salcido Cañedo.** El proletariado, sus luchas y la política laboral en México: hemerografía (UNAM/RMCPS, 21:83, enero/marzo 1976, p. 301–311)
Consists only of articles and documents available at the Centro de Documentación de la Facultad de Ciencias Políticas y Sociales.

7094 Bernal Sahagún, Víctor M. Anatomía de la publicidad en México: monopolios, enajenación y desperdicio. México,

Editorial Nuestro Tiempo, 1974. 201 p., tables (Col. Temas de actualidad)

Marxist interpretation of multinational corporations and strong criticisms of the role they play. Good data on advertising business in Mexico.

Blasier, Cole and **Carmelo Mesa-Lago** *eds.* Cuba in the world. See item **8713.**

Boils, Guillermo. Los militares y la política en México: 1915–1974. See *HLAS 40:2693.*

7095 Burgoa, Ignacio and others. El régimen constitucional de los partidos políticos. Presentación de Héctor Fix-Zamudio. México, UNAM, Instituto de Investigaciones Jurídicas, 1975. 125 p., table (Serie G: estudios doctrinales, 12)

Discusses the constitutionalization of political parties in Latin America. Some data on the constitutional status of political parties in several Latin American countries.

7096 Busto, Emiliano. La administración pública de México: breve estudio comparativo entre el sistema de administración de Hacienda en Francia y el establecido en México, 1889. 2. ed. México, Secretaria de la Presidencia, Dirección General de Estudios Administrativos, 1976. 252 p., tables (Col. Fuentes para el estudio de la administración pública mexicana. Serie B: bibliográfica, 1)

Reprint of first systematic study of Mexican national public administration (1889). Representative of current massive publication program on the subject. Offers considerable detail with description of treasury structure, practices and procedures in both Mexico and France. [P.B. Taylor, Jr.]

Camp, Roderic Ai. Autobiography and decision-making in Mexican politics. See *HLAS 40:2696.*

7097 ———. La campaña presidencial de 1929 y el liderazgo político en México (CM/HM, 27:2, 1977, p. 231–259, bibl., tables)

The purpose of the paper is to evaluate the impact of José Vasconcelos, the defeated presidential candidate in 1929, upon a new generation of political leaders, some of them supporters and members of President Alemán's administration in 1946.

7098 ———. Losers in Mexican politics: a comparative study of official party pre-candidates for gubernatorial elections,

1970–75 (*in* Wilkie, James W. and Kenneth Ruddle *eds.* Quantitative Latin American studies, methods and findings: statistical abstract of Latin America. Los Angeles, UCLA, Latin American Center Publications, 1977, p. 23–34, tables [Supplement, 6])

Compares losing pre-candidates with successful contenders for the official party nomination in each of the 20 gubernatorial elections held during the term of office of President Echeverría. Uses three variables: career experience, camarilla membership, and qualifications suited to the context of the situation in the state. Author believes that pre-candidates with national political experience will become increasingly successful.

7099 ———. Mexican political biographies: 1935–1975. Foreword by Peter H. Smith. Tucson, The Univ. of Arizona Press, 1976. 468 p.

Biographies of "top political influentials" as defined, mainly, by Frank Brandenburg. The biographical information is organized in 12 different categories. Appendix discusses available sources. Painstaking work whose author deserves to be congratulated.

7100 ———. Review essay: autobiography and decision-making in Mexican politics (UM/JIAS, 19:2, May 1977, p. 275–283, bibl.)

Reviews seven autobiographies published recently by Mexican politicians and scholar-políticos (e.g., Jesús Silva Herzog, Jaime Torres Bodet, Eduardo Villaseñor). Interesting observations by a specialist in the Mexican political elite.

7101 ———. The role of economists in policy-making: a comparative case study of Mexico and the United States. Foreword by Edward J. Williams. Tucson, The Univ. of Arizona Press, The Institute of Government Research, College of Liberal Arts, 1977. 78 p., bibl.

Compares the roles played by economist/administrators or *técnicos* in two presidential decisions: the US Council of Economic Advisers and President Kennedy in their attempt to reduce income taxes (1963), and Mexican economists who advised President López Mateos to join LAFTA (1960). Author analyzes stages in the process of policy formulation in both countries.

7102 ———. El sistema mexicano y las decisiones sobre el personal político (CM/FI, 17:1, julio/sept. 1976, p. 51–83)

Discusses the presidential role in the selection of his own successor and the appointment of officials during his mandate. Personalism and camarillas are emphasized. Particularly interesting is the attempt to identify the camarillas headed by Presidents Cárdenas and Alemán.

7103 Caso, Andrés and **Alejandro Carrillo Castro.** La reforma administrativa en México (*in* Seminario Interamericano de Reforma Administrativa, I, Rio, 1973/1974. Reforma administrativa: experiencias latinoamericanas. México, Instituto Nacional de Administración Pública, 1975, p. 47–61)

Discusses in very general and introductory terms the administrative reforms institutionalized by President Echeverría in 1971.

7104 Contreras, Ariel José. México, 1940: industrialización y crisis política; estado y sociedad civil en las elecciones presidenciales. México, Siglo XXI Editores, 1977. 219 p. table (Sociología y política)

On the basis of contemporary press sources and available bibliography, the author has written a very competent analysis of events leading to the crucial election of Avila Camacho. Work exemplifies a creative application of a neo-Marxist approach.

7105 Corbett, John G. Role conflict as a local level constant in decision-making in Mexico (PCCLAS/P, 5, 1976, p. 77–85)

Includes data collected through interviews with over 100 current and former municipal office-holders. Part of a larger project on political change in Mexican communities, article discusses how intra-role and inter-role conflicts influence system-level performance.

7106 Cornelius, Wayne A. A structural analysis of urban caciquismo in Mexico (UA, 1:2, Fall 1972, p. 234–261, bibl.)

The origins, bases, internal and external roles, and durability or urban caciquism are discussed in this meaningful paper, based on the study of three squatter-settlements in Mexico City.

7107 Cosío Villegas, Daniel. La sucesión: desenlace y perspectivas. 2. ed. México,

Editorial Joaquín Mortiz, 1976. 118 p. (Cuadernos de Joaquín Mortiz)

El destapamiento de don José López Portillo as seen by Cosío Villegas. Not substantial but short, witty, and well written.

7108 Davis, Charles L. Social mistrust as a determinant of political cynicism in a transitional society: an empirical examination (JDA, 11:1, Oct. 1976, p. 91–102, tables)

Based on questionnaires completed by 345 randomly selected adults living in metropolitan Mexico City. Although most respondents were mistrustful of people in general, a substantial majority indicated trust in political leaders. Suggests explanations for these findings.

DelliSante, Angela. La intervención ideológica de la empresa transnacional en países dependientes: el caso de México. See item **8617.**

7108a Eckstein, Susan. The poverty of revolution: the state and the urban poor in Mexico. Princeton, N.J., Princeton Univ. Press, 1977. 300 p., bibl., maps, plates, tables.

Uses data from three low-income areas of Mexico City: 1) a traditional city slum; 2) a semi-rural one; and 3) a government-financed planned community. An Appendix elaborates on the method and ethic of research conducted in 1967–68. In the final chapter the Mexican experience is examined from a cross-national perspective. Author tries to show "how the state regulates lower-class city-dwellers in the basic interest of the capital."

7109 Fagen, Richard R. and **William S. Tuohy.** Politics and privilege in a Mexican city. Stanford, Calif., Stanford Univ. Press, 1972. 209 p., tables (Stanford studies in the comparative politics, 5)

The city of Jalapa. Based on interviews with elite members and adult Jalapeños. When the results are contrasted with a normative model derived "from three tenets of classic democratic theory," the authors conclude: "something is very wrong in Mexico." Could the model be unsound? A good contribution.

7110 Goldfrank, Walter L. Inequality and revolution in rural Mexico (UWI/SES, 25:4, Dec. 1976, p. 397–410, bibl., tables)

Author notes that ". . . rural revolt in

Mexico suggests no easy or linear correlations between inequality and discontent, or between discontent and revolt." The political capacity of the dispossessed and the flexibility of the rulers are the crucial conditions that explain the Mexican Revolution of 1910. A perceptive article.

7111 González Luna, Efraín. Revolución y espíritu burgués y otros ensayos: escritos diversos publicados de 1929 a 1934. Compilación, ordenamiento, anotaciones y prólogo de Pedro Vázquez Cisneros. México, Editorial Jus, 1976. 180 p., facsim., plate (Obras de Efraín González Luna, 7)

Literary essays written by the late leader of the Partido Acción Nacional.

7112 González Torres, José. Campaña electoral. México, Editorial Jus, 1976. 341 p.

Speeches delivered by the Presidential candidate of Acción Nacional during the 1964 campaign.

Grindle, Merilee S. Bureaucrats, politicians, and peasants in Mexico: a case study in public policy. See *HLAS 40:2719.*

7113 ———. Patrons and clients in the bureaucracy: career networks in Mexico (LARR, 12:1, 1977, p. 37–66, bibl., tables)

Elaborates on topics discussed in Chap. 2 and 3 of the author's 1977 book *Bureaucrats, politicians, and peasants in Mexico: a case study in public policy* (see *HLAS 39:7125*).

7114 ———. Policy change in an authoritarian regime (UM/JIAS, 19:4, Nov. 1977, p. 523–555, bibl., tables)

How economic policies were altered under President Echeverría to reflect his greater concern for agricultural development. Based on interviews with government officials and other informants.

7115 ———. Power, expertise and the *técnico*: suggestions from a Mexican case study (SPSA/JP, 39:2, May 1977, p. 399–426, tables)

Uses previous research in Mexico and the public administration literature available on Latin America. Finds difficult to differentiate *técnicos* from *políticos*, since the former require political skills for successfully performing their function. Required reading. For historian's comment, see *HLAS 40:2721.*

7116 Gutiérrez, Jorge. El sistema político y la burguesía rural en México: el caso del Valle del Mezquital (UNAM/RMS, 39:3, julio/sept. 1977, p. 901–919, bibl.)

Discusses caciquismo in three municipios of the Mezquital Valley as mediatory structures and mechanisms for political control. "Informants" are mentioned by name, but without any other identification (e.g., numbers, characteristics, etc.).

7117 Handelman, Howard. Oligarchy and democracy in two Mexican labor unions: a test of representation theory (CU/ILRR, 30:2, Jan. 1977, p. 205–218, tables)

Study based on an attitudinal survey of middle-level leaders and the rank-and-file of two Mexican labor unions. Tries to test hypotheses concerning the relationship between both: How representative are the leaders?

7118 Hellman, Judith Adler. Mexico in crisis. N.Y., Holmes & Meier [and] Heinemann Educational Books, London, 1978. 229 p., bibl., plates.

Covers Mexico's crisis from the Revolution to the end of Echeverría's period. Lacks any discussion of the most recent literature on Mexican authoritarianism. An introduction for the general reader.

7119 Huacuja R., Mario and José Woldenberg. Estado y lucha política en el México actual. México, Ediciones El Caballito, 1976. 281 p., bibl., tables.

Study applies the ideological "line" Marx-Poutlanzas to the study of Echeverría's administration. The protagonists are: the bureaucracy, several factions of the bourgeoisie, the popular movements, and imperialism. Fortunately, study does not suffer from the unrelenting determinism characteristic of this approach. Thus, the denoument remains open, making the reading more palatable. Finally, authors' skillful use of political information holds the reader's attention.

7120 Labastida Martín del Campo, Julio. Proceso político y dependencia en México: 1970–1976 (UNAM/RMS, 39:1, enero/marzo 1977, p. 193–227, bibl.)

Author believes the contemporary Mexican state was generated through gradual transformation, not "rupture," like Brazil and Argentina. Hence Mexico does not quite fit the bureaucratic-authoritarian model elaborated by O'Donnell. Includes a good analysis of Echeverría's administration.

7121 León, Samuel. Notas sobre la burocracia sindical mexicana (UNAM/RMCPS, 21:82, oct./dic. 1975, p. 121–131, table)

Title promises more than it delivers.

7122 Lerner de Sheinbaum, Bertha and Susana Ralsky de Cimet. El poder de los presidentes: alcances y perspectivas, 1910–1973. México, Instituto Mexicano de Estudios Políticos, 1976. 504 p., bibl., tables.

After a first chapter on regional caudillism (Zapata and Villa), and a second one on national caudillism (Carranza, Obregón, Calles), author examines successive presidential administrations, including Echeverría's from 1970 to 1973. A few final pages attempt to point out general trend which are hardly original.

7123 Marquet Guerrero, Porfirio. La estructura constitucional del Estado Mexicano. México, UNAM, Instituto de Investigaciones Jurídicas, 1975. 437 p., bibl. (Serie G: estudios doctrinales, 9)

Legalistic discussion of the "fundamental principles" stated in the present Mexican constitution: people's sovereignty, representation, human rights, division of power, Church-state relations, federalism and the municipality. Also examines the background of such principles in previous Mexican constitutions.

7124 Márquez, Javier *ed.* Pensamiento de México en los periódicos: páginas editoriales, 1976. Cuerpo de jurado: Pablo Aveleyra and others. México, Editorial Tecnos, 1977. 592 p.

Selection of editorials published by seven newspapers of Mexico City in 1976 (previous volume covers 1975). Organized in five sections: government, politics and administration; education; social problems; agriculture, economy; and international relations. Each section is preceded by an introduction.

7125 Martínez de la Vega, Francisco. ¿Crisis del sistema mexicano? (CAM, 208:5, sept./oct. 1976, p. 29–35)

Reflections on the "Monarquía Sexenal" under Echeverría. The title is misleading. For historian's comment, see *HLAS 40:2747*.

————. El sistema mexicano sobrevive. See *HLAS 40:2750*.

7126 Martínez Saldaña, Tomás and Leticia Gándara Mendoza. Política y sociedad en México: el caso de Los Altos de Jalisco. Presentación de Gustavo del Castillo V. México, Secretaría de Educación Pública (SEP), Instituto Nacional de Antropología e Historia (INAH), Centro de Investigaciones Superiores, 1976. 289 p., bibl., maps, tables.

Social-anthropological studies of two communities in the state of Jalisco, noted by their geographical isolation, lack of Indian influence, and strong traditionalism. In both communities there is a similar process: the emergence of local oligarchies, their mechanisms for self-perpetuation and adaptation, and bargaining with the national government. Recommended.

7127 Mexico. Presidencia. Secretaría. Departmento Editorial. Justicia en la libertad. México, 1976. 123 p., plates.

Speeches by European and Latin American leaders with a social democratic orientation who visited Mexico, in 1976, to express their solidarity with President Echeverría.

7128 Mumme, Stephen P. Mexican politics and the prospects of emigration policy: a policy perspective (IAMEA, 32:1, Summer 1978, p. 67–94)

Author believes that perceptual attitudes of Mexican policy-makers, the nature of the political system, policy-context, and policy-capabilities, make it highly improbable that emigration to the US will be addressed in a direct and specific way by the Mexican government. A well argued paper.

7129 Olguin Pérez, Palmira. Los militares en México: bibliografía introductoria (UNAM/RMS, 38:2, abril/junio 1976, p. 453–490, bibl.)

Bibliography which covers years 1950–76 and includes material from the catalogue of the Library of Congress, available at libraries in the Federal District, including that of the Secretariat of National Defense.

7130 Pacheco Méndez, Guadalupe; Arturo Anguiano Orozco; and Rogelio Vizcaíno A. Cárdenas y la izquierda mexicana: ensayo, testimonios, documentos. México, Juan Pablos Editor, 1975. 391 p., bibl.

Interviews with ex-leaders of the Mexican Communist Party (e.g., Miguel Velasco, Valentín Campa, José Revueltas) plus Communist and Trotskyist documents published in the 1930s. Authors' purpose is to clarify the relationships between the labor parties, Lázaro Cardenas and the organization of the Confederación de Trabajadores Mexicanos (CTM).

7131 Pellicer, Olga. La crisis mexicana: hacia una nueva dependencia (CP, 14, oct./dic. 1977, p. 45−55)

Notes how the 1976 devaluation and other symptoms of economic crisis have reduced the room for maneuver of the Mexican government, especially concerning its relations with the US. Under such conditions, oil discoveries could increase Mexican vulnerability instead of decreasing dependence.

7132 Portes, Alejandro. Legislatures under authoritarian regimes: the case of Mexico (NIUJ/JPMS, 5:2, Fall 1977, p. 185−201, bibl.)

Author believes authoritarian regimes set the highest priority on strategies for political recruitment, regulation of popular demand and integration. Legislatures help to perform these functions by transmitting messages, granting symbolic rewards, serving as brokers between the masses and their leaders, and by gratifying traditonal expectations of legitimacy.

7133 Raby, David L. Mexican political and social development since 1920 (NS, 1:1/2, 1976, p. 24−45)

Good review article but confined to a partial examination of the literature. Apparently written by a historian.

7134 Revueltas, José. México: democracia bárbara; posibilidades y limitaciones del mexicano. 2. ed. México, Editorial Posada, 1975. 158 p., illus., plates (Col. Ideas políticas)

Originally published in 1958, this edition includes a new introduction written by the author in 1975. A Marxist critique of the Mexican regime plus a brief discussion of "lo mexicano."

7135 Reyes Esparza, Ramiro; Enrique Olivares; Emilio Leyva; and Ignacio Hernández Gutiérrez. La burguesía mexicana: cuatro ensayos. 2. ed. México, Editorial Nuestro Tiempo, 1976. 206 p., tables.

Contributions to a future "revolutionary theory." Only Marx, Lenin, and Poutlanzas are considered relevant social theorists. The data is short and already available in other sources.

7136 Reyna, José Luis. Control político, estabilidad y desarrollo en México. 2. ed. México, El Colegio de México, Centro de Estudios Sociológicos, 1976. 30 p. (Cuadernos del CES, 3)

Short and intelligent analysis of the Mexican political system emphasizing the role of "political control." In this context the role of the army is also briefly discussed.

7137 ——— and Richard S. Weinert *eds.* Authoritarianism in Mexico. Preface by Ronald G. Hellman. Philadelphia, Pa., Institute for the Study of Human Issues, 1977. 241 p., tables (Inter-American politics series, 2)

An excellent collection made up of significant contributions by Lorenzo Meyer, Susan Eckstein, Rosa Elena Montes de Oca, René Villarreal, Richard S. Weinert, Peter H. Smith, José Luis Reyna, Susan Kaufman Purcell, and Robert R. Kaufman.

7138 Rodríguez Araujo, Octavio. Una reforma política en México (CAM, 36 [214]:5, sept./oct. 1977, p. 7−18)

Author discusses prospective political reforms and how to increase the number of legal political parties, from the point of view of working interests and the constraints imposed by the Mexican state. The nature of this state is capitalistic and bonapartist. Good characterization of what potential political parties could be legalized.

Ross, Stanley R. La protesta de los intelectuales ante México y su Revolución. See *HLAS 40:2770.*

7139 Schryer, Frans J. Faccionalismo y patronazgo del PRI en un municipio de la Huasteca Hidalguense. México, El Colegio de México, Centro de Estudios Sociológicos, 1976. 35 p., bibl., tables (Cuadernos del CES, 16)

Politics in a rural and backward Mexican municipio. PRI exercises its power monopoly by manipulating conflicts among the well-to-do and by coopting peasant demands. The outcome is the preservation of the status-quo.

7140 **Segovia, Rafael** and others. Las fronteras del control del Estado Mexicano. México, El Colegio de México, Centro de Estudios Internacionales, 1976. 175 p., tables (Col. Centro de estudios internacionales, 16)

Consists of four informative, insightful and relevant essays: Rafael Segovia's "Tendencias Políticas en México;" Carlos Arriola's "Los Grupos Empresariales frente al Estado, 1973–75;" and Samuel I. del Villar's "Depresión en la Industria Azucarera Mexicana."

Shapira, Yoram. Mexico: the impact of the 1968 student protest on Echeverría's reformism. See *HLAS* 40:2774.

7141 **Siller Rodríguez, Rodolfo.** La crisis del Partido Revolucionario Institucional. Nota preliminar de Alfonso Corona del Rosal. México, B. Costa-Amic, 1976. 219 p. (Col. Ciencias sociales, 15)

Another analysis of PRI's crisis, written this time by a professional politician and party leader, apparently close to the faction led by Alfonso Corona del Rosal. His suggestions on how to strengthen the party are not impressive.

7142 **Suárez, Luis.** Lucio Cabañas, el guerrillero sin esperanza. México, Roca, 1976. 338 p., facsim., plates.

Taped interviews and other materials related to the life of the guerrilla leader from the state of Guerrero who was killed in a 1974 Army skirmish.

7143 **Suárez-Iñiguez, Enrique.** El futuro de la Revolución mexicana: Benítez, Flores Olea, Fuentes y Paz (UNAM/RMCPS, 22:85, julio/sept. 1976, p. 185–217, bibl.)

Effort to summarize the visions of four prestigious Mexican intellectuals.

7144 **Talavera, Fernando** and **Juan Felipe Leal.** Organizaciones sindicales obreras de México: 1948–1970; enfoque estadístico (UNAM/RMS, 39:4, oct./dic. 1977, p. 1251–1286, tables)

Consists of 24 tables with data on trade union membership collected from official sources. Cut-points are 1948, 1954, 1960, and 1970. Useful compilation but lack of analysis makes for laborious consultation.

7145 **Trejo, Raúl.** La prensa marginal. México, Ediciones El Caballito, 1975. 174 p., bibl., tables.

Interesting analysis of the marginal press, defined as "printed papers published by the political opposition" and qualitatively different from the commercial press. The appendix names more than 100 marginal papers published in Mexico from 1972–74.

7146 **Tribuna de la Juventud,** *México.* Confrontación nacional. t. 1, La Constitución, la economía nacional, política exterior, política laboral y movimiento sindical; t. 2, Educación y desarrollo, política agraria, desarrollo regional. Presentación de Nazario Alvarado Morales. Comentario de Esteban M. Garaiz. Prólogo de Carlos Monsiváis. México, 1977. 2 v. (416, 415 p.) tables.

The Constitution, the economy, foreign and social policies, the trade union movement, education and development, agrarian policies, and regional development, are the topics discussed here with the participation of Mexican intellectuals, social scientists, academicians and political and trade union leaders. More relevant to Mexicans than to foreign students. See also item **7147.**

7147 ———, ———. Polémica nacional. Prólogo de Froylán N. López Narváez. México, Ediciones El Caballito, 1976. 408 p. (Col. Fragua mexicana, 23)

Speeches delivered by Mexican politicians and intellectuals from Tribuna de la Juventud (see item **7146**) a forum established to discuss contemporary national and international issues. Among the speakers, Lombardo Toledano, Madrazo, Cuáuthemoc Cárdenas, Cossío Villegas, Portes Gil, etc.

United States. Library of Congress. Congressional Research Service. Mexico's oil and gas policy: an analysis. See item **8654.**

7148 **Vázquez, Verónica.** Selección bibliográfica sobre los principales partidos políticos mexicanos: 1906–1970 (UNAM/RMS, 39:2, abril/junio 1977, p. 677–715)

Covers 17 political parties. Followed by a short chronology. Useful.

7149 **Villegas, Abelardo.** La ideología del movimiento estudiantil de México (NS, 1:1/2, 1976, p. 130–147)

Scattered but occasionally insightful reflections on the topic, written by the well-known historian. Implicit intent to demythologize the students' movement.

Welch, Claude E., Jr. *ed.* Civilian control of the military: theory and cases from developing countries. See *HLAS 40:2414.*

CENTRAL AMERICA
GENERAL

7150 Torres-Rivas, Edelberto and **Vinicio González.** Naturaleza y crisis del poder en Centro-américa. Documentos. Caracas, Centro de Información, Documentación y Análisis Latinoamericano (CIDAL), n.d. 40 l. (Entrega, 33)

Well-informed but radical analysis of Central American politics. Concludes that the model of associated development which is used to explain Mexico and Brazil, is not applicable in this region, where any perceived economic growth is only "weak, relative and dependent" implying high political costs.

COSTA RICA

7151 Aguilar Bulgarelli, Oscar. La Constitución de 1949: antecedentes y proyecciones. Prólogo de Mario Hernández-Sánchez Barba. San José, Editorial Costa Rica, 1973. 188 p., bibl.

Supported by the findings of a previous book, *Costa Rica y sus hechos políticos de 1948* (1969), the author places the 1949 document in the context of Costa Rica's general and constitutional history. The analysis of the text, however, is legalistic.

7152 Benavides, Enrique. Nuestro pensamiento político en sus fuentes. San José, Editorial Costa Rica, 1976. 226 p.

Journalistic interviews with political leaders: Manuel Mora, Rodrigo Carazo, José Joaquín Trejos, Fernando Trejos, Alfonso Carro, Luis Alberto Monge, Mario Echandi, Daniel Oduber y José Figueres.

7153 Carvajal, Manuel J. *ed.* Políticas de crecimiento urbano: la experiencia de Costa Rica. San José, Dirección General de Estadísticas y Censos, 1977. 288 p., maps, tables.

Contributions by Costa Rican and American scholars on infrastructure, productive processes, land and housing markets, and public policies. A good number of tables, graphics and maps enhance the publication.

7154 Cerdas Cruz, Rodolfo. La crisis de la democracia liberal en Costa Rica: interpretación y perspectiva. 2. ed. San José, Editorial Universitaria Centroamericana (EDUCA), 1975. 191 p., bibl., tables.

Neo-Marxist interpretation of Costa Rican history. An emergent sector called "burguesía gerencial" is challenging the traditional coffee-and-cattle interests. "Liberación Nacional" appears unable to protect the traditional group or to recruit adherents from the new sector. Author believes the only available answer to the present crisis is a new state of national democracy. Interesting perspective but the concept of "burguesía gerencial" needs considerable more elaboration.

7155 DeWitt, R. Peter, Jr. The Inter-American Development Bank and political influence with special reference to Costa Rica. N.Y., Praeger, 1977. 197 p., bibl., tables (Praeger special studies in international economics and development)

Tries to answer three central questions: the impact of the US' national interest on the IDB, the Bank's impact on Costa Rican development, and the linkages between both. Dependency theory is the conceptual framework.

7156 Goodsell, Charles. An empirical test of "legalism" in administration (JDA, 10:4, July 1976, p. 485–494)

Characterizes "legalism" in Latin American administration using a paragraph written by an American author in 1958. Then compares the levels of "legalism" in the Costa Rican and US postal services. A remarkable comparison since, among other things, there are no mail-carriers in Costa Rica.

7157 Jiménez Castro, Wilburg. Análisis electoral de una democracia: estudio del comportamiento político costarricense durante el período 1953–1974. San José, Editorial Costa Rica, 1977. 43 p., maps, tables.

Results of six elections: 1953, 1958, 1962, 1966, 1970 and 1974. Organized by provinces: registered voters, votes, abstentions, null and black ballots. Maps. Useful information on the institutional framework of electoral politics in Costa Rica. A helpful tool.

7158 Jiménez Quesada, Mario Alberto. Desarrollo constitucional de Costa Rica. 2.

ed. San José, Editorial Costa Rica, 1973. 170 p., bibl., plate.

Second ed. of book written in 1951. A competent survey of the topic and possibly the best text available for the layman. The author's approach is historical and legalistic and the 1949 Constitution is only briefly discussed.

7159 Rosenberg, Mark B. Thinking about Costa Rica's political future: a comment (IAMEA, 31:1, Summer 1977, p. 89–94)

These are, in fact, comments on two recent papers by Oscar Arias, Minister of National Planning under President Oduber. Author calls Arias "a scholar and persistent critic of Costa Rican politics." He should have added: persistent aspirant to the presidency as well.

7160 Seligson, Mitchell A. Agrarian policies in dependent societies: Costa Rica (UM/JIAS, 19:2, May 1977, p. 201–232, bibl., tables)

Outline of the major policies formulated and implemented in the agrarian sector in Costa Rica from the colonial days up to the present. It also tries to ascertain the impact of foreign dependency upon such policies.

7161 Trejos Fernández, José Joaquín. Ocho años en la política costarricense: ideales políticos y realidad nacional. t. 1, Principios fundamentales y orientación política, convivencia humana: relaciones entre las naciones, Administración pública y planeamiento; t. 2, Educación y desarrollo humano, Una política social para nuestra época: 1965–1970; t. 3, Producción nacional, economía y su infraestructura, Política monetaria, fiscal y crediticia; t. 4, Política electoral y de partidos. San José, Editorial Hombre y Sociedad, 1973/1974. 4 v. (330, 286, 457, 387 p.) tables (Col. Ciencia política)

Compilation of articles and speeches by the President of Costa Rica from 1966 to 1970. Includes some of the Presidential messages sent to the Congress during his mandate.

EL SALVADOR

López-Trejo, Roberto. Realidad dramática de la República: 25 años de traición a la Fuerza Armada y a la patria. See *HLAS 40:2895.*

7162 Richter, Ernesto. Proceso de acumulación en la formación socio-política salvadoreña. San Pedro de Montes de Oca, C.R., Programa Centroamericano de Ciencias Sociales, 1976. 169 l., tables (Serie informes de investigación, 16)

Marxist interpretation of the origins of the so-called Football war between Honduras and El Salvador, 1969.

GUATEMALA

7163 Jenkins, Brian and **Caesar D. Sereseres.** U.S. military assistance and the Guatemalan Armed Forces (AFS, 3:4, Summer 1977, p. 575–594)

To what extent has American military aid influenced intervention in political and domestic affairs by Guatemalan military personnel? Author offers answer in the context of civilian-military relations from 1956–74. Well researched and well balanced.

7164 Política y Sociedad. Univ. de San Carlos de Guatemala, Facultad de Ciencias Jurídicas y Sociales, Escuela de Ciencia Política, Instituto de Investigaciones Políticas y Sociales. Número extraordinario, Epoca 2, abril 1978- . Guatemala.

Issue dedicated to Guatemala. Analyzes the role of political parties since 1944 by applying a modified version of the concept "Bloque Histórico" suggested by Nicos Poulantzas.

7165 Problèmes de'Amérique Latine XLIII. Série de Notes et Etudes Documentaires. La Documentation Française. Nos. 4366/4367, 15 fév. 1977- . Paris.

Two parts. Pt. 1 reports on the Cuban process of institutionalization up to the installation of the Popular National Assembly. Pt. 2 is made of several contributions on the Guatemalan economy, agrarian problems, and the conditions of Indian life.

HONDURAS

7166 Congreso Nacional del Partido Comunista Marxista-Leninista de Honduras, II, *Tegucigalpa, 1976.* Informes sobre el Partido: la situación nacional, la situación internacional. Tegucigalpa, Partido Communista Marxista-Leninista de Honduras, 1976. 118 p.

Reports of Honduras' pro-Chinese party. They strongly denounce Soviet social-imperialism. No mention is made of Cuba.

7167 Murga Franssinetti, Antonio. Estado y burguesía industrial en Honduras (UNAM/RMS, 39:2, abril/junio 1977, p. 595–609, tables, bibl.)

Although this article states that it is based on 57 interviews with industrial entrepeneurs and leaders, the data is disclosed only partially to support the argumentation.

7168 ——— and others. Lecturas sobre la realidad nacional. Tegucigalpa, Univ. Nacional Autónoma de Honduras, Centro Univ. de Estudios Generales, Depto. de Ciencias Sociales, 1977. 145 p., tables.

Six contributions by two Hondurans, two Americans and one Peruvian. Emphasis on the socioeconomic aspects of Honduras and their linkages with the international economy. Essential work for those interested in the country.

7169 Ramírez, Asdrúbal. Línea general política del PCH. Tegucigalpa, Ediciones el Militante, 1975. 65 p., tables.

Publication of the Honduran Communist Party (PCH) which supports the Soviet line and favors a national and democratic front in domestic politics. The means of struggle are to be decided by the masses themselves.

7170 ———. El maoismo en Honduras. Tegucigalpa, Ediciones Compol, 1974. 140 p.

Describes the involvement of the Communist Party of Honduras in the organization of a guerrilla front, the subsequent factional split, and the emergence of a Maoist group. This is the version of the pro-Soviet Communist party.

NICARAGUA

7171 Frente Sandinista de Liberación Nacional (FSLN), *Managua.* Nicaragua: violaciones de los derechos humanos y de las garantías ciudadanas (OCLAE, 4, 1977, p. 24–38, illus., plates)

Describes assassinations, tortures, concentration camps, and other flagrant violations of human rights under Somoza. Supported by documents, photos, and evidence furnished by some of the victims.

7172 NACLA's Latin America & Empire Report. North American Congress on Latin America. Vol. 10, No. 2, Feb. 1976- . N.Y.

Issue devoted to Nicaragua which offers a very handy and timely introduction to the contemporary crisis that afflicts this country. Provides good background beginning with the emergence of Sandino and Somoza. Unfortunately, the informative thoroughness is marred by dogmatic interpretations which are characteristic of NACLA's publications.

PANAMA

7173 León Tapia, Ricardo A. de. La reforma administrativa en Panamá (*in* Seminario Interamericano de Reforma Administrativa, I, Rio, 1973. Reforma administrativa: experiencias latinoamericanas. México, Instituto Nacional de Administración Pública, 1975, p. 63–192, illus.)

Discusses the country's programs for administrative reform drafted 1954–71. The prevailing orientation is to study formulation, not implementation.

THE CARIBBEAN
GENERAL

7174 Andrianov, V. Caribbean problems (IA, 4, April 1978, p. 50–55)

Soviet author discusses the problems of the non-Spanish Caribbean. Notices that "the socialist concepts proclaimed by the leaders of Jamaica and Guyana are extremely vague and indefinite." Reminds these leaders that positive changes will not come about without "radical shifts in the international situation." Emphasizes increasing Cuban influence.

7175 Cuthbert, Marlene and others. Caribbean women in communication for development: report on workshop held at the University of the West Indies, Mona Campus, Jamaica, June 13–15, 1975. Bridgetown, Cedar Press, 1975. 61 p.

Participants came from the Commonwealth Caribbean plus Cuba. One of the recommendations was to form a "regional organization of communicators aimed at projecting the problems of the underprivileged, to be known as the Caribbean Progressive Communicators Association."

7176 DaBreo, D. Sinclair. Lessons from the Caribbean revolutions: to peace, justice, equality and equal opportunity for all the people of the Caribbean. St. Lucia, West Indies, The Author, 1975. 120 p., plates.

Superficial and eccentric. Covers Cuba, Trinidad-Tobago, Granada, Dominica, Antigua, Guyana and Jamaica. Difficult to determine if text is fanciful or factual.

7177 Demas, William G. Change and renewal in the Caribbean. Bridgetown?, CCC Publishing House, 1975. 60 p. (Challenges in the new Caribbean, 2)

The former Secretary-General of the Caribbean Community, an economist deeply familiar with the area, has collected here some of his speeches (1970–73) which examine the problem of Caribbean identity, roles of youth, school, and labor, and the process of decolonization.

7178 Duncan, W. Raymond. Caribbean leftism (USIA/PC, 27:3, May-June 1978, p. 33–56, maps, plates, tables)

Defines leftism as "a desire to change existing social and economic conditions to the advantage of the Caribbean's 'common man'." After discussing general currents in the area concentrates on Guyana and Jamaica. Pays only cursory attention to the work being done by the principal spokesman for leftism: members of the intelligentsia.

7179 Jagan, Cheddi. Culture as a unifying force (NHAC/K, 14, July 1976, p. 28–31)

"CARICOM can only become a viable instrument for meaningful change if each territory turns to socialism-scientific socialism as expounded by Marx and Lenin." Advances arguments in support of this proposition.

7180 Johnson, Howard. The West Indies and the conversion of the British official classes to the development idea (ICS/JCCP, 15:1, March 1977, p. 55–83)

Background to the *Report of the West Indian Royal Commission of 1938–39.* One consequence of the West Indian disturbances 1937–38 was a more precise formulation of new approaches to colonial development by British bureaucrats.

7181 Jones, Edwin and G.E. Mills. Institutional innovation and change in the Commonwealth Caribbean (UWI/SES, 25:4, Dec. 1976, p. 323–346, bibl.)

Authors believe administrative innovation requires both institutional creativity and commitment to a radical socio-economic transformation. They criticize methods of institution-building in the area but offer no solutions.

7182 Lent, John A. Third World mass media and their search for modernity: the case of Commonwealth Caribbean, 1717–1796. Lewisburg, Pa., Bucknell Univ. Press [and] Associated Univ. Presses, London, 1977. 405 p., bibl., facsims., map, plates, tables.

Examines "historical, cultural, economic, and political aspects of all Commonwealth Caribbean mass media, from the time of the first newspaper in 1717 until 1972." As far as I know this is the first well researched and serious study of the topic. Excellent addition to the knowledge of the region.

7183 Wallace, Elisabeth. The British Caribbean: from the decline of colonialism to the end of Federation. Toronto, Canada, Univ. of Toronto Press, 1977. 262 p.

Primary concern of this study is to examine constitutional developments in 12 British Caribbean territories during the first 60 years of the 20th century. Also includes discussion of unions and parties, as well as of the rise and fall of the Federation.

CUBA

Asociación Cubana de las Naciones Unidas, *New York.* Nueva división político-administrativa de Cuba. See item **5820.**

7184 Azicri, Max. Las estrategias de gobierno y la descentralización del poder en Cuba (AR, 3:1, Summer 1976, p. 4–11, plates)

Contends mass organizations have played a much more important role than is generally attributed by observers. Author mentions data collected for his dissertation, corroborates this but does not include it here.

7185 Baloyra, Enrique A. Democratic versus dictatorial budgeting: the case of Cuba with reference to Venezuela and Mexico (*in* Wilkie, James W. *ed.* Money and politics in Latin America. [see item **2935**] p. 3–17, tables)

Author has refined the method James W. Wilkie applied to Mexico, using budgetary expenses to differentiate between revolutionary governments. This study applies the method to Cuba and compares the periods under Prío (1948–52) and Batista (1953–58).

7186 Black, Jan Knippers and others. Area handbook for Cuba. 2. ed. Washington, U. S. Government Printing Office (GPO), Superintendent of Documents, 1976. 550 p., bibl., maps, table.

First ed. published in 1971. The usual format of these manuals. Comprehensive but also tedious. No footnotes. Tables do not identify the sources. An extensive bibliography.

Boersner, Demetrio. Democracia representativa y transformación social en América Latina. See item **7004.**

7187 Castro, Fidel. Discursos. t. 2. La Habana, Instituto Cubano del Libro, Editorial de Ciencias Sociales, 1975. 242 p.

Speeches delivered 1972–74. No introduction or notes.

7188 ———. Informe Central presentado al Partido Comunista de Cuba. B.A., Editorial Anteo, 1976. 248 p.

Report delivered by Castro at the I Congress of the Cuban Communist Party. This is required reading for anyone interested in the Cuban revolutionary process.

7189 ———. Obras escogidas. t. 1, 1953–1962; t. 2, 1962–1968. Madrid, Editorial Fundamentos, 1976. 2 v. (256, 231 p.) (Col. Ciencia)

Speeches by the Cuban leader which have appeared before in *Granma* and other publications. The criteria applied to select them is not specified.

7190 ———. La primera revolución socialista en América. México, Siglo XXI Editores, 1976. 327 p.

Castro's Report to the I Congress of the Cuban Communist Party plus opening and closing speeches. A handy edition.

7191 ——— and **Raúl Castro.** Selección de discursos acerca del Partido. La Habana, Instituto Cubano del Libro, Editorial de Ciencias Sociales, 1975. 262 p.

Useful collection which includes at least one speech by Raúl Castro (4 May 1973) to cadre and Cuban Communist Party officials. Not easily available elsewhere.

7192 ——— and others. Legalidad y poder popular en Cuba: con el texto completo de la constitución cubana. Presentación y selección de Juan Rosales. B.A., Editorial Convergencia, 1976. 254 p., tables (Col. Legislación para el cambio)

Valuable collection of texts (e.g., Raúl Castro, Blas Roca, etc.) including excerpts from *Moncada*, the magazine published by the Ministry of the Interior which is not available in the US.

Os Comités de Defesa da Revolução. See *HLAS 40:3009.*

7193 Congrés du Parti Communiste de Cuba, I, La Havane, 1975. Le 1ᵉʳ [i.e. premier] Congrès du Parti Communiste de Cuba: La Havane, 17–22 décembre 1975. Moscow, Editions de l'Agence de Presse Novosti, 1976. 109 p.

Excerpts of Castro's report and closing speech; greetings from the Soviet Communist Party; Brezhnev's message; and speech by Soviet representative, M.A. Suslov, at the Congress.

Debray, Régis. Che's guerrilla war. See *HLAS 40:3585.*

7193a Domínguez, Jorge I. The armed forces and foreign relations (*in* Blasier, Cole and Carmelo Mesa-Lago *eds.* Cuba in the world. [see item **8713**] p. 53–86, tables)

This paper deals with Cuban military capabilities and doctrine, military aid (including Angola), policies of subversion, the military connection with the Soviet Union, Cuban potentialities as a military threat, and the future of US-Cuban military relations.

7194 ——— and **Christopher N. Mitchell.** The roads are not taken: institutionalization and political parties in Cuba and Bolivia (CUNY/CP, 9:2, Jan. 1977, p. 173–195)

Compares the Cuban and Bolivian revolutionary regimes focusing on three variables: institutionalization, mobilization, and political criticism.

7195 Duncan, W. Raymond. Cuba: national communism in the global setting (CIIA/IJ, 32:1, Winter 1976/1977, p. 156–177)

Regards Cuba as a hybrid form of Communism which requires constant changes in foreign policy. Author tests this proposition against some particular policies and discusses Angola within this framework. Written for the general public.

7196 Fagen, Richard R. Cuba and the Soviet Union (WQ, 2:1, Winter 1978, p. 69–81, bibl., tables)

After a recent visit to Cuba, where he found "minimal Soviet presence," the author claims that Cuba would have been in Angola "with or without the Soviets." Since author does not differentiate among levels of involvement, number of soldiers, and scale of logistics, his argument is irrefutable.

Fernández Retamar, Roberto. Nuestra América y Occidente. See *HLAS 40:6710.*

7197 Fitzgerald, Frank T. A critique of the "Sovietization of Cuba" thesis (SS, 42:1, Spring 1978, p. 1–32)

Cuban economic policies since 1970 do not reflect increasing Sovietization, but are rational answers to domestic problems. Moreover, they stress both material and moral incentives, in balanced proportions. Author argues his case more persuasively than Cuban officials.

7198 Franqui, Carlos. Diario de la Revolución Cubana. Barcelona, Ediciones R. Torres, 1976. 754 p.

Collection of notes, taped interviews, letters, documents, etc., all related to the Cuban Revolution. Poorly organized and lacking any introduction to guide the reader. Nevertheless, this is undoubtedly the most important source concerning the period 1952–58 that has appeared in recent years. Franqui helped to organize the 26th of July Movement, he also was in the Sierra, and after victory served as editor of *Revolution.* He left Cuba in 1968. Required reading for Cubanologists.

7198a González, Edward. Institutionalization, political elites, and foreign policies (*in* Blasier, Cole and Carmelo Mesa-Lago *eds.* Cuba in the world. [see item **8713**] p. 3–36, tables)

Institutionalization has led to a "reconcentration" of power into the hands of the leader. Nevertheless there are three elite groups or "tendencies." Foreign policy now reflects the interests of the two predominant

groups: 1) the politico-revolutionary headed by Fidel; and 2) the military associated with brother Raúl. Author notes that Cuba did not act in Angola as a Soviet surrogate, although her interests coincided and supported the African country.

7199 Guevara, Ernesto. El socialismo y el hombre nuevo. Prólogo por José Aricó. México, Siglo XXI Editores, 1977. 429 p., plates (Col. América nuestra)

Useful collection. Includes some of the articles written by Guevara and others during the debate on economic incentives (e.g., Fernández Font, Bettelheim, Mandel). Editor Aricó has appended 40 p. of notes.

7200 Hansen, Joseph. Dynamics of the Cuban Revolution: the Trotskyist view. N.Y., Pathfinder Press, 1978. 393 p.

Articles and internal documents of the US Socialist Workers Party written before 1970 on questions such as "the class nature of the Cuban state" and the Stalinist deformation of the Cuban regime. Useful for those interested in Leftist polemics.

7201 Harnecker, Marta *ed. and comp.* Cuba: ¿dictadura o democracia? México, Siglo XXI Editores, 1975. 254 p., bibl. (Historia inmediata)

Based on recorded interviews with officials, delegates, and voters involved in drafting the Constitution of Popular Power at Matanzas province. A short introduction explains how, under the supervision of the Communist Party, popular participation in decision-making is beginning to flourish in Cuba. This amalgam is referred to as democratic-centralism.

7202 Horowitz, Irving Louis. Cuban communism. 3. ed. New Brunswick, N.J., Transaction Books, 1977. 576 p., tables.

Author has added new contribution and most of his previous highly idiosyncratic articles to this ed., a total of 152 p.

7203 King, Marjorie. Cuba's attack on women's second shift: 1974–1976 (LAP, 4[12/13]:1/2, p. 106–119, bibl.)

"Second shift" refers to the fact that in many countries women carry their full eight-hour workday load plus domestic chores and child-rearing responsibilities. Author offers some data supporting the contention that Cubans have started a successful struggle against this problem. "Cuban women have, in the person of Fidel Castro, the single most influential individual advocate for women's equality."

7204 LeoGrande, William M. A bureaucratic approach to civil-military relations in Communist political systems: the case of Cuba (*in* Herspring, Dale R. and Ivan Volgyes *eds.* Civil-military relations in Communist systems. Boulder, Colo., Westview Press, 1978, p. 201–218)

Author analyzes what he perceives as conflict between civilian and military in Cuba. Concludes that neither the conflictual model (Kolkowicz) nor the consensual one (Odom), used for the study of civil-military relations in Communist systems, applies to Cuba. Suggests the application of a bureaucratic model taken from Allison.

7205 ———. Continuity and change in the Cuban political elite (UP/CSEC, 8:2, July 1978, p. 1–32)

Author identifies elites as members of the National Directorate (1962), and the two Central Committees of the Communist Party (1965 and 1975). Uses institutional affiliations to compare the three bodies. Explores the presence of some cleavages to conclude that increasing internal unity is the trend. The Soviet influence is never discussed.

7206 Lewis, Oscar; Ruth M. Lewis; Susan M. Rigdon. Living the Revolution: an oral history of contemporary Cuba. v. 1, Four men; v. 2, Four women. Chicago, Univ. of Illinois Press, 1977. 2 v. (538, 443 p.) bibl., maps, plates.

Study based on research done in Cuba (1969–70). The purpose was to examine the impact of the Revolution upon the daily lives of eight Cubans, using the technique of taperecorded interviews. These two volumes and one more to follow attempt to structure 24,500 p. of transcriptions collected before the Government stopped the research. For historian's comment, see *HLAS 40:3013.*

7207 Llerena, Mario. The unsuspected revolution: the birth and rise of Castroism. Foreword by Hugh Thomas. London, Cornell Univ. Press, 1978. 324 p., facsims., plates.

The only true intellectual who was close to the original leadership of the 26th July Movement is the author of this sincere and moving testimony. Llerena resigned his

post as head of the Committee in Exile in Aug. 1958. His memoir constitutes an indispensable source on the murky origins of "the unsuspected revolution." Concludes by warning middle-class reformers against cooperation with radical revolutionaries.

7208 Macaulay, Neill. The Cuban Rebel Army: a numerical survey (HAHR, 58:2, May 1978, p. 284–295, tables)

Author evaluates different sources and offers tentative figures.

7209 Martin, Lionel. The early Fidel: roots of Castro's communism. Secaucus, N.J., Lyle Stuart, 1978. 269 p.

Written by a journalist after 16 years in Cuba. Attempts to substantiate premise of Castro's close Communist identification before 1959 by collecting mostly insignificant pieces or fragments. Author's primary evidence are interviews which Blas Roca and Carlos Rafael Rodríguez granted him in the 1970s and which contradict what both have previously written. Apparently, this book's chief purpose is to prove that British historian Hugh Thomas is wrong.

7210 Mesa-Lago, Carmelo. Building socialism in Cuba: romantic versus realistic approach (LAP, 3[11]:4, Fall 1976, p. 117–121, bibl.)

Answers previous criticism by Terry Karl concerning moral and material incentives in Cuba: "my position is that they are in conflict and that in certain stages of the revolution one has become predominant . . ."

7211 ———. Cuba in the 1970s: pragmatism and institutionalization. Rev. ed. Albuquerque, Univ. of New Mexico Press, 1978. 187 p., tables.

After offering a five-stage approach to the study of the Revolution since 1959, author concentrates on economics, institutionalization and foreign policy in the 1970s. The book closes with an analysis of the past and a forecast of the future. A competent and fair treatment.

7211a ———. The economics of U.S.— Cuban rapprochement (*in* Blasier, Cole and Carmelo Mesa-Lago *eds.* Cuba in the world. [see item **8713**] p. 199–224, tables)

Another excellent analysis of this problem by a keen observer of the Cuban economy.

7211b ———. The economy and international economic relations (*in* Blasier, Cole and Carmelo Mesa-Lago *eds.* Cuba in the world. [see item **8713**] p. 169–198, tables)

Another detailed and rigorous discussion by the author of many significant contributions to the study of the Cuban economy.

7212 Morais, Fernando. A ilha: um repórter brasileiro no país de Fidel Castro. Prefácio de Antonio Callado. São Paulo, Editora Alfa-Omega, 1976. 126 p. (Biblioteca alfaomega de cultura universal. Série 2:3)

Impressions of a visit to Cuba in 1974: the press, the schools, the courts, economy and rationing, etc. Probably written with a market, the Brazilian, in mind. Only very superficially informed about the island.

Pérez, Louis A., Jr. Army politics in Cuba: 1898–1958. See *HLAS 40:3037*.

7213 ———. Army politics in socialist Cuba (JLAS, 8:2, Nov. 1976, p. 251–271)

Despite the fact that the Rebel Army, according to the author, was small, mostly illiterate, and lacking in technical qualifications, it became a "disciplined and well-organized politico-military institution" after the victory on 1 Jan. 1959. Its chief role since then is a consequence of this experience and its level of institutionalization. A somewhat contradictory article. For author's book on army politics in Cuba prior to the Revolution, see *HLAS 40:3037*.

7214 Pollitt, Brian. Some problems of enumerating the "peasantry" in Cuba (JPS, 4:2, Jan. 1977, p. 162–180)

A landmark contribution. This is the first rigorous examination of serious errors and omissions in the standard data-sources used for the identification and quantification of Cuban peasants, e.g., Population Censuses, Agricultural Census, Lowry Nelson's *Survey of 1945*, the Rural Survey of Agrupación Católica, and the survey of rural families in Las Villas (1958).

Problèmes d'Amérique Latine XLIII. See item **7165**.

7214a Ritter, Archibald R. M. The transferability of Cuba's revolutionary development model (*in* Blasier, Cole and Carmelo Mesa-Lago *eds.* Cuba in the world. [see item **8713**] p. 313–336)

Author elaborates a socioeconomic development model based on two Cuban revolutionary experiences which he regards as particularly relevant for developing countries: 1) the basic dynamic model, characterized by emphasis on income distribution and access to opportunities; and 2) another model which has been evolving since the 1970s. The author's examination of the viability of both models for developing countries makes this an interesting contribution.

7215 Rivero Collado, Carlos. La contrarevolución cubana: los sobrinos del Tío Sam. Madrid, Akal Editor, 1977. 382 p. (Akal 74)

Published originally in Cuba. The author, an active participant in the "counter-revolution" defected to Cuba in 1974. Later, he reappeared in Colombia with some queer story. The vulgarity of this author is appalling; his style, atrocious; and the information highly questionable.

7216 Rodríguez, Carlos Rafael. Cuba en el tránsito al socialismo: 1959–1963. Lenin y la cuestión colonial. México, Siglo XXI Editores, 1978. 233 p.

The only leader of the Partido Socialista Popular, presently member of the Partido Comunista de Cuba, who is known to be a qualified Marxist. His first essay analyzes the transitional period of Cuba from neocolonialism to socialism. Although he does not deviate from Soviet orthodoxy, author suggests that after Cuba the role of the petite-bourgeoisie must be reconsidered. Also, there was no trace of a Castro-PSP pact, tacit or explicit, before 1959, after which the PSP simply surrendered. Unimaginative but indispensable work.

7217 Rodríguez, Ernesto E. Public opinion and the press in Cuba (UP/CSEC, 8:2, July 1978, p. 51–65, bibl., tables)

Uses Letters-to-the-Editor reported, not reproduced, by *Granma*, from 24 June 1974 to 30 June 1976. Of a total of 389, 36 percent are evaluated as negative, 54 percent as service-seeking and 10 percent as positive.

7218 Schroeder, Richard D. Cuban expansionism (Editorial Research Reports [Congressional Quarterly Inc., Washington] 1:19, 20 May 1977, p. 375–392, bibl., map, table)

Cuba's role in the Caribbean, America's Caribbean interests, and US responses to the Cuban challenge are the main questions discussed in this paper.

7218a Sobel, Lester A. *ed.* Castro's Cuba in the 1970s. Contributing writers: Joanne Edgar; Christopher Hunt; and John Miner. Indexed by Grace M. Ferrara. N.Y., Facts on File, 1978. 244 p., map, plate, tables (Checkmar books)

Useful reference tool. Covers the period 1970–77. Sources are not always identified. Includes several appendixes, e.g., the Cuban Constitution and a Report on Repression & Political Prisoners (1975).

7219 Turull, Toni. Cuba, hoy: una revolución en marcha. Barcelona, Aymá Editora, 1977. 277 p., plates, tables.

Written by a Catalan, Professor of Hispanic American Studies at the Univ. of Bristol, U.K., after two visits to Cuba. Filled with admiration for Cuba and lacking in usefulness for the social scientist. Appendixes include the new Constitution and the Family Code (90 p.)

7220 Useem, Bert. Peasant involvement in the Cuban Revolution (JPS, 5:1, Oct. 1977, p. 99–111)

Based almost entirely on English sources. A bibliography with more than 50 titles has only two in Spanish. Contends that organizational factors explain peasant involvement better than psychological factors. Author's knowledge of Cuban peasants and rural conditions is far from satisfactory.

7221 Valdés, Nelson P. Cuba: ¿socialismo democrático o burocratismo colectivista? 2. ed. Bogotá, Ediciones Tercer Mundo, 1973. 106 p. (Cuadernitos ¡que despierte del leñador!, 15. Série azul)

Author critizes labor militarization and other coercive policies applied by the regime at the end of the 1960s. First ed.: Paris, Aportes, 1972.

7222 Vázquez, Adelina and others. Apuntes de la prensa clandestina y guerrillera del período 1952–1958. La Habana, Unión de Periodistas de Cuba, 1973. 106 p., facsims., plates.

An introductory and descriptive study based on interviews with some of the editors.

Weiss, Judith A. *Casa de las Américas:* an intellectual review of the Cuban Revolution. See *HLAS 40:3018.*

7223 Zeuske, Max. Militärische Traditionen der kubanischen Revolution (Militärgeschichte [Deutscher Militärverlag, Berlin, GDR] 16:3, 1977, p. 339–348)

East German analysis of military traditions in the strategy of the Cuban Revolution. [M. Kossok]

DOMINICAN REPUBLIC

7224 Análisis del Movimiento Revolucionario Dominicano: bases para la unidad (Realidad Contemporánea [Editora Alfa y Omega, Santo Domingo] 1:5/7, n.d., p. 11–53, illus.)

Analysis of the Dominican Left from 1941 to the present. Informative and objective. Concludes by acknowledging the "immense" difficulties involved in organizing both a proletarian party and a united front. Important contribution to the study of the Dominican Left.

7225 Diederich, Bernard. Trujillo: the death of the goat. Boston, Mass., Little, Brown, 1978. 264 p., map, plate.

The Mexican Bureau Chief of *Time* magazine interviewed survivors of conspiracies and relatives of the scores of individuals butchered after the dictator was executed. This "thriller" is based on these interviews.

7226 Gutiérrez, Carlos María. The Dominican Republic: rebellion and repression. Translated by Richard E. Edwards. N.Y., Monthly Review Press, 1972. 172 p., bibl., table.

Leftist journalist denounces the senseless cruelty of Dominican political life in 1971. He indicts the CIA, Falcombridge, and Alcoa and almost absolves President Balaguer. Includes interviews with Bosch and other leaders of the fragmented Radical Left.

7227 Kryzanek, Michael J. Political party decline and the failure of liberal democracy: the PRD in Dominican politics (JLAS, 9:1, May 1977, p. 115–143)

Repression and internal squabbles between politicos and ideologues, the generational gap, and personalism vs. democracy have seriously debilitated the PRD. Nevertheless, the party won the presidential elections one year after this paper was published. For historian's comment, see *HLAS 40:3053.*

7228 Latorre, Eduardo. Política dominicana contemporánea. Prólogo de Miguel A. Heredia B. Santo Domingo, Editora Cosmos, 1975. 407 p., bibl., table.

An insightful and well-documented analysis of contemporary Dominican politics written by a political scientist born in that country. Covers span from Trujillo's death to the second election of Joaquín Balaguer (1970).

7229 *NACLA's Latin America & Empire Report.* North American Congress on Latin America. Vol. 9, No. 3, April 1975–. N.Y.

Issue devoted to conflict in Dominican Republic (1965–75) consists of two parts. Pt. 1: US interests in the Dominican Republic ten years later. Pt. 2: trade union imperialism in the Dominican Republic. Second part includes a not very pleasant profile of Sacha Volman.

Pierre-Charles, Gérard *ed.* Política y sociología en Haití y la República Dominicana: coloquio dominico-haitiano de ciencias sociales. See item **7231.**

HAITI

7230 Brisson, Gerald. Las vías de establecimiento de la Alianza Obrero-Campesina en Haití (Realidad Contemporánea [Editora Alfa y Omega, Santo Domingo] 1:3/4, julio/dic. 1976, p. 107–122)

The "Partie Entente Popular d'Haïti" marches once again along the well-trodden, strategic path opened by Lenin at the beginning of the century.

7231 Pierre-Charles, Gérard *ed.* Política y sociología en Haití y la República Dominicana: coloquio dominico-haitiano de ciencias sociales. México, UNAM, Instituto de Investigaciones Sociales, 1974. 169 p.

Compilation of valuable papers delivered at a colloquium of Haitian and Dominican social scientists held in 1971. Some of these studies reflect a revisionist trend in the study of the relations between both countries. The papers are: Gérard Pierre-Charles' "Génesis de las Naciones Haitiana y Dominicana;" Susy Castor's "El Impacto de la

Ocupación Norteamericana en Haití (1915–1934) y en la República Dominicana (1916–1924);" André Corten's "Migración e Intereses de Clases;" Lil Despradel's "Las Etapas del Anti-Haitianismo en la República Dominicana: el Papel de los Historiadores;" Arismendi Díaz Santana's "Desarrollo y Descomposición de la Economía Dominicana;" and Hector Cary's "Fascismo y Subdesarrollo: el Caso de Haití."

JAMAICA

7232 Charles, Pearnel. Detained: 283 days in Jamaica's detention camp, struggling for freedom, justice and human rights! Preface by Ulric Simmonds. Kingston, Kingston Publishers, 1977. 207 p., illus., plates.

Jamaican trade-unionist, Senator and political activitist, tells his disturbing experience under Prime Minister Michael Manley. Appendixes describe similar cases.

7233 Hamilton, B. St. John. Bustamante: anthology of a hero. Kingston, Publications and Productions, 1977? 162 p., facsims., illus., plates.

Author was Permanent Secretary to the "hero" when he was Prime Minister of Jamaica. The book describes the bizarre traits of Bustamante's personality which were plenty: "even in detention Bustamante was diet-conscious, ordering tomato juice and cod-liver oil."

7234 Hill, Frank *ed.* and *comp.* Bustamante and his letters. Kingston, Kingston Publishers *in association with* Matalon Group of Companies [and] Radio Jamaica, 1976. 126 p., plates, table.

Letters and other writings by the late Jamaican leader from 1935–38 and published in the *Daily Gleaner.* Editor includes an introduction and a short biographical and admirative essay. For historian's comment, see *HLAS 40:3051.*

7235 Payne, Anthony. From Michael with love: the nature of socialism in Jamaica (ICS/JCCP, 14:1, March 1976, p. 82–100)

Author believes that factors such as strong legitimacy of bi-partisan politics, the multiclass integration of both parties, and the leader's ideology make any significant redistribution of economic power under Manley highly improbable.

7236 Robertson, Paul D. Ruling class attitudes in Jamaica: the bureaucratic component (in Singham, A.W. ed. The Commonwealth Caribbean into the seventies: proceedings of a conference held on 28–30 September, 1973, Howard University, Washington. Montreal, Canada, McGill Univ., Center for Developing-Area Studies in co-operation with Howard Univ., Committee on Caribbean Studies, Washington, 1975, p. 94–118, tables [Occasional papers series, 10])

Author mentions in a footnote a questionnaire administered to a sample of 100 bureaucrats selected randomly from the top four levels of the civil service. Study's findings seem to indicate the persistence of the colonial syndrome among Jamaican bureaucrats.

7237 Robinson, Robert V. and **Wendell Bell.** Attitudes towards political independence in Jamaica after twelve years of nationhood (BJS, 29:2, June 1978, p. 208–233, tables)

Follow-up study of Jamaican leaders after 12 years of independence. Basic data: 24 interviews held in 1962 plus 83 for the present period. Authors report changes in elite attitudes toward political independence and the emergence of an increasing minority of Restive Nationalists.

7238 Stone, Carl. Class and institutionalization of two-party politics in Jamaica (ICS/JCCP, 14:2, July 1976, p. 177–196)

Follow-up to author's previous works published in 1973: Class, race, and political behaviour in urban Jamaica (see HLAS 37:1296) which should be required reading for specialists.

7239 ———. The 1976 parliamentary election in Jamaica (ICS/JCCP, 15:3, Nov. 1977, p. 250–265, tables)

Competent analysis which covers campaign strategies, mobilization, issues, and voting patterns.

7240 ———. Urban social movements in post-war Jamaica (in Singham, A.W. ed. The Commonwealth Caribbean into the seventies: proceedings of a conference held on 28–30 September, 1973, Howard University, Washington. Montreal, Canada, McGill Univ., Centre for Developing-Area Studies in co-operation with Howard Univ., Committee on Caribbean Studies, Washington, 1975, p. 71–93, bibl., tables [Occasional papers series, 10])

Analyzes labor and movements towards mass political participation and black national consciousness. Study uses data from a sample survey of 605 urban residents in middle working class and slum districts of Kingston.

7241 ——— and **Aggrey Brown** eds. Essays on power and change in Jamaica. Kingston, Jamaica Publishing House, 1977. 207 p., tables.

Collection of radical essays written by Jamaican-based social scientists at the Univ. of the West Indies, Mona. Organized in two parts: 1) Political Economy and Policies, and 2) Challenges for Change. Pt. 2 discusses policies articulated by the PNP government since 1972.

LESSER ANTILLES

7242 Conference on the Implications of Independence for Grenada, St. Augustine, Trinidad, 1974. Independence for Grenada: myth or reality? Edited by Conference Committee. Introduction by Selwyn Ryan. St. Augustine, Univ. of the West Indies, Institute of International Relations, 1974. 159 p., bibl., tables.

A collection of valuable studies which includes contributions from Archie Singham, Basil Ince, Vaughan Lewis, etc. Divided into three parts: 1) Grenada: A Social and Political Profile; 2) Independence: Legal and Political Aspects; and 3) The Role of Agriculture in the Economic Development of Grenada.

7243 Williams, Marion. Aspects of public policy in Barbados: 1964–1976 (UWI/SES, 26:4, Dec. 1977, p. 432–445, bibl., tables)

Author examines the impact of budgetary policies on the economy, but her lack of adequate data leads to very tentative conclusions.

PUERTO RICO

7244 Bayrón Toro, Fernando. Elecciones y partidos políticos de Puerto Rico: 1809–1976. Prólogo de Francisco Lluch Mora. Mayagüez, P.R., Editorial Isla, 1977. 284 p., illus., maps, plates, tables.

Study compiles the names of officials

elected, not electoral data. The portion devoted to each election is preceded by a summary on "the general situation" and the parties involved.

7245 Blaut, James. Are Puerto Ricans a national minority? (MR, 29:1, May 1977, p. 35–55)

An exercise in Marxist scholasticism. After comparing the concepts of "nationalism" and "national minorities" in the writings of Stalin and Lenin, author concludes by suggesting that Puerto Ricans in the US should be identified as "colonial minorities."

7246 Dietz, James. The Puerto Rican political economy (LAP, 3[10]:3, Summer 1976, p. 3–16, bibl.)

An introduction to this issue of *Latin American Perspectives* is dedicated to Puerto Rico. The assumption implicit in it, and the contributions, can be easily surmised from the journal's own statement that the status question cannot be settled by voting: "it is a question of what is best for the Puerto Rican people."

7247 Fromm, Georg H. César Andreu Iglesias: aproximación a su vida y obra. Río Piedras, P.R., Ediciones Huracán, 1977. 149 p., plates.

Iglesias, author of *Los Derrotados*, died in 1976. This is an outline of political and trade union activities by the novelist and veteran member of the Puerto Rican Communist Party.

7248 Lewis, Gordon K. Notes on the Puerto Rican revolution: an essay on American dominance and Caribbean resistance. N.Y., Monthly Review Press, 1974. 288 p.

With characteristic exhuberance and brillance, the author has expanded his prologue to *Puerto Rico: freedom and peace in the Caribbean* published in 1964 (see HLAS 27:1070). Recommends that Puerto Ricans who desire independence strive to overcome their present "opportunistic ambivalence."

7249 Maldonado-Denis, Manuel. Aproximación crítica al fenómeno nacionalista en Puerto Rico (CDLA, 17:102, mayo/junio 1977, p. 13–28)

A different version of the paper published in *Latin American Perspectives* (Summer 1976) is preceded by a short discussion of the Marxist-Leninist interpretation of nationalism.

7250 ———. Prospects for Latin American nationalism: the case of Puerto Rico (LAP, 3[10]:3, Summer 1976, p. 36–45, bibl.)

Author examines the historical evolution of Puerto Rican nationalism and notes that it reflects the weaknesses of the national bourgeoisie. Thus, the only possibility of achieving national independence is for the proletariat to transcend nationalism by embracing proletarian internationalism.

7251 ———. Puerto Rico y Estados Unidos: emigración y colonialismo; un análisis sociohistórico de la emigración puertorriqueña. México, Siglo XXI Editores, 1976. 197 p., bibl., tables (Historia inmediata)

Marxist approach to the study of this phenomenon. Author perceives Puerto Rican emigration—not migration—to the US as the intentional consequence of developmental policies implemented by the leaders of the island's "colonial parties." Includes useful statistical appendix.

7252 *NACLA's Latin America & Empire Report.* North American Congress on Latin America. Vol. 10, No. 5, May/June 1976–. N.Y.

Issue devoted to US labor unions in Puerto Rico. Overview covers span from the American occupation to the 1970s. Pt. 3 offers interesting information on the role of the International Brotherhood of Teamsters in the island. Well researched.

7253 Quintero Rivera, Angel G. La clase obrera y el proceso político en Puerto Rico (UPR/RCS, 20:1, marzo 1976, p. 3–48, bibl., tables; 19:3, p. 261–300, bibl., tables)

Important contribution. These two articles are part of a lengthy study and cover the period of "disintegration of class politics," approximately 1924–40. Author combines Marxist tools, some quantitative data, and a thorough knowledge of Puerto Rican sources.

TRINIDAD & TOBAGO

7254 Best, Lloyd. The political alternative. Tunapuna, Trinidad & Tobago, Tapia House Publishing Co., 1974. 23 l., plates (Booklet, 9)

A political speech delivered at Tapia House, 17 Nov. 1974, explains the kind of participatory politics promoted by Tapia Assembly.

GUYANA

7255 Barnett, D.F. and **P.A. Della Valle.** An analysis of sugar production in a changing political environment (IAEA/DE, 14:1, March 1976, p. 85–96, bibl., tables)

Author discuss the effects of politics on sugar production in Guyana before and after independence (1966). Includes data on labor productivity, land yields, land-labor ration, and ton cane/ton sugar, as well as policy recommendations.

7256 Burnham, Forbes. Declaration of Sophia: address by the Leader of the People's National Congress, Prime Minister ... , at a special Congress of the People's National Congress, Sophia, Georgetown, 14th December, 1974. Georgetown, Guyana Printers, 1974? 38 p., plates.

"The Comrade Leader" reports on the reorganization of the party, the goals accomplished, and the tasks ahead. Also includes "A Code of Conduct for P.N.C. Leaders and Members."

7257 ———. On the road to socialism. Georgetown, Office of the Prime Minister, 1976. 24 p., plates.

Prime Minister's address delivered on the occasion of the celebration of the sixth anniversary of the Co-operative Republic of Guyana (22 Feb. 1976).

7258 ———. The pursuit of perfection. Georgetown, Guyana Printers, 1976. 44 p., plates.

In an address to the nation on the occasion of the tenth anniversary of independence (25 May 1976). Burnham announces the nationalization of Booker assets at a cost of 70 million dollars. He rejects suggestions by "political morons" not to pay a penny.

7259 ———. Reports to the nation on Guyana Broadcasting Service and Radio Demerara: January 10, 1976. Georgetown, Guyana Printers, 1976. 47 p.

"Comrade Leader" Burnham concurs with the statement made by a Guyanese leader at the I Congress of the Cuban Communist Party, in the sense that "the People's National Congress is seeking to lay the foundations for the establishment of a socialist society based on Marxism-Leninism" in Guyana.

7260 ———. Towards the socialist revolution. Georgetown, Office of the Prime Minister, 1975. 52 p., plates.

There is no mention of revolution in this address delivered by Burnham at the I Biennial Congress of the People's National Congress, Georgetown, 18 Aug. 1975. Instead, he considers the present situation of his Party and explicates his variety of "cooperative-socialism.'

7261 Collymore, Clinton and **Cheddi Jagan.** The superiority of scientific socialism. Georgetown, People's Progressive Party (PPP), Propaganda Committee, 1976. 56 p., tables.

Only the last 15 p. of this pamphlet are of interest. They articulate the policy of "critical support" adopted by the People's Progressive Party (PPP) towards the Government headed by Forbes Burnham.

7262 Jagan, Cheddi. Guyana: a reply to critics (MR, 29:4, Sept. 1977, p. 36–46)

Author argues that although there is racial polarization in Guyana, the presence of a Marxist-Leninist party in the opposition, (his own PPP) makes a great difference in comparison with Trinidad or Surinam. He is worried by the emergence of a bureaucratic bourgeoisie under the People's National Congress (PNC) and notes that "cooperative socialism is becoming cooperative capitalism."

7263 ———. The struggle for a socialist Guyana. Georgetown?, n.p., 1975. 26 p.

In a collection of journalistic articles, Jagan tries to prove that he is a better Marxist-Leninist than Burnham.

7264 Milne, R.S. Politics, ethnicity and class in Guyana and Malaysia (UWI/SES, 26:1, March 1977, p. 18–37, bibl.)

Countries whose politics are based on ethnic cleavages and who wish to develop a class basis have four possibilities. Author believes Guyana fits the one in which a governmental party wants to switch and find conditions are favourable. This analysis should be compared with those by Premdas (see items **7266** and **7267**).

7265 People's Progressive Party, *Georgetown.* Documents of the XIX Congress of the People's Progressive Party held at Tain, Correntyne, from July 31–August 2,

1976. Georgetown, 1976. 100 p., plates.
    Consists of a report by Jagan plus speeches and messages from "fraternal" parties, and some of the Resolutions adopted by the Congress.

7266 Premdas, Ralph R. Guyana: communal conflict, socialism and political reconciliation (IAMEA, 30:4, Spring 1977, p. 63–83, table)
    Author discusses the background and recent nationalizations and then points out six political patterns of communal conflict by using two variables: the communal structure of the society and leadership struggle. See also item **7267**.

7267 ———. Guyana: socialist reconstruction or political opportunism? (UM/JIAS, 20:2, May 1978, p. 133–164, bibl.)
    Author identifies factors and analyzes

processes leading to the adoption of a socialist program. Nationalizations have occurred almost "by accident" and do not seem to follow any explicit plan or project. An informative and shrewd analysis. See also item **7266**.

7268 *Thunder.* People's Progressive Party of Guyana. Vol. 6, No. 4, Oct./Dec. 1974–. Georgetown.
    Consists of documents generated by the XVIII Congress of the People's Progressive Party.

7269 Working People's Alliance Guyana, *Georgetown.* The crisis and the working people. Georgetown, 1976. 40 p.
    "The white Canadians have left Demba but the 'black Canadians', as the workers term them, have taken over Guyabau as the new ruling elite." A critical perspective of Burnham's socialism.

SOUTH AMERICA: WEST COAST
Colombia and Ecuador

DAVID W. DENT, *Associate Professor of Political Science, Co-Director, Latin American Studies Program, Towson State University*

THE BIENNIAL REVIEW OF THE LITERATURE on Colombia and Ecuador offers some new materials that fill important gaps in our knowledge of these two Andean countries although currents of previously discussed themes continue. Greater selectivity was applied in reviewing materials this time so that more items were discarded than was previously the case. Thus, the works cited in this volume are ones that contain important theoretical and empirical contributions for the student and specialist in these areas. In terms of output, the literature on Colombian politics continues to surpass that on Ecuador by a wide margin, and this will probably always be the case even though the military government in Ecuador and its policies related to petroleum production, coastal waters, OPEC, and other types of reform have generated considerable interest.

The bulk of material on Colombian politics falls into roughly three categories: 1) party politics, voting behavior, and policy-oriented studies of the National Front and its aftermath; 2) campesino politics; and 3) studies of the Catholic Church and its role in Colombian politics. Conflicting ideological perspectives continue to color the type of research and the conclusions and/or recommendations for future policy change or tactics. However, the work now being done at Los Andes Univ. in Bogotá and the Fundación para la Educación Superior y el Desarrollo (FEDESARROLLO) deserves special mention because of its objectivity and high quality. The works on Colombia that especially impressed this reviewer include the studies of the Colombian Congress and voting behavior by R. Losada (items **7295** and **7296**) and F. Leal (item **7289**). In addition, E. Revéiz's exhaustive study (item **7305**) of various kinds of information in the making of national, regional, and local decisions breaks new ground and deserves mention. The study of ANUC (Asociación Nacional de Usuarios Campesinos) by B. Bagley and F. Botero (item **7272**) is a highly competent and valuable analysis of peasant politics in Colombia. And the political biography of Jorge Eliécer Gaitán by R. Sharpless (item **7307**) is noteworthy for the new material it adds to this important figure, particularly the insights on Gaitanismo, Colombian populism, and the roots of *la violencia*.

The Catholic Church in Colombia continues to receive the attention of scholars interested in this important power contender in Colombian politics. The dilemma that the Church faces in translating political issues into social outcomes is addressed by D. Levine and A. Wilde (item **7290**) and S. Brzezinski (item **7273**) examines the reasons for the defeat of the Catholic Church on the issue of birth control and family planning. J. Díaz (item **7281**) offers considerable information on the plight of the Colombian peasantry but presents an overly optimistic view of the Church which in the end does not match the scholarly sophistication of the previous works.

Ecuadorian materials continue to be sparse; however, this should not mask the exceptional study of the military coup d'état by J. Fitch (item **7319**). Fitch's study is an excellent treatment of the military in Ecuadorian politics since 1948 and thus fills a major gap in our understanding of this Andean country while offering a theoretical model of considerable comparative value.

What needs to be done? Very little is being done on the Colombian military, the news media, or rural reform. The literature on urban Colombia is growing but the large cities—Bogotá, Medellín, and Cali—continue to receive the bulk of the attention. And now that drugs—principally marijuana and cocaine—have replaced coffee as the number one product for export in Colombia, more information is needed on the impact of this commodity on the economic and political system, as well as its relationship to the increase in urban and rural violence and internal migration patterns. We know far too little about the role of the Catholic Church and labor organizations in Ecuadorian politics.

For those who teach Latin American politics at the undergraduate or graduate levels, there are several books and articles that this reviewer found to be of particular significance. For example, G. Wynia's introductory text (item **7068**) offers a solid foundation for understanding the components and dynamics of the political process in Latin America by emphasizing various types of political systems. The volume edited by T. DiBacco (item **7016**) is an important contribution to understanding the presidential system of government and its historical evolution. For those who emphasize corporatism in their courses, two articles should not be ignored: H. Wiarda (item **7083**) discusses the intellectual roots of corporatist theory and ideology while L. Hammergren (item **7027**) argues that the corporatist model fits less well than some claim. The articles by A. Hennessy (item **7028**) and I. Rachum (item **7063**) are particularly helpful for understanding economic and political trends in Latin America since 1930. Hennessey examines the factors that prevented the rise of fascism in Latin America whereas Rachum offers new insights into the causes of the "revolutions" of 1930 in Peru, Argentina, and Brazil. Each of these is important and adds new materials, ideas, and organization for the difficult task of understanding the politics of Latin America and communicating this information to college students.

COLOMBIA

7270 Araoz, Santiago. Historia del Frente Nacional y otros ensayos. Bogotá?, Editorial Presencia, 1977. 133 p., tables.

Brief political history of the National Front stressing its positive achievements and the idea of a modernizing elite. Electoral abstention and external dependency are also discussed and it is noted that they have not totally undermined the productive economy, administrative efficiency, and the growth of democratic maturity that are bi-products of this political experiment.

7271 Arrubla, Mario. Síntesis de historia política contemporánea (in Colombia hoy. Bogotá, Siglo XXI Editores de Colombia, 1978, p. 186–220)

Neo-Marxist political history since 1930 with emphasis on modernization from above including the national bourgeoisie and foreign economic interests. Author sees a fundamental problem in the economic choices made by Colombian governments which have resulted in an economic system which has left the masses outside of the mainstream of Colombian politics.

7272 Bagley, Bruce Michael and **Fernando Botero Zea.** Organizaciones contemporáneas en Colombia: un estudio de la Asociación Nacional de Usuarios Campesinas, ANUC (CLACSO/ERL, 1:1, enero/abril 1978, p. 59–95, bibl.)

Excellent essay on the origin, development, and present status of Colombia's most important peasant organization since the beginning of the National Front. In discussing the interrelationship between economic and political change, inside and outside Colombia, this case study of ANUC reveals that peasant interests are so heterogeneous that effective organization and consciousness raising are virtually impossible. A highly competent analysis of peasant politics by two political scientists.

7273 Brzezinski, Steven. Church versus state: family planning in Colombia, 1966–1972 (BU/JCS, 18:3, Autumn 1976, p. 491–502)

Case study of family planning efforts by the Colombian government reveals an interesting alliance of interest-group elites in opposition to birth control and family plan-

ning. Despite secular support from the press (*El Siglo*), labor organizations, Marxists, and others, the Catholic Church was defeated albeit family planning in Colombia remains piecemeal and small in scale. Author attempts to explain the nature of conflict resolution through the use of Gamson's model of "authorities" and "potential partisans."

7274 Campo, Urbano. La urbanización en Colombia. Bogotá, Ediciones Armadillo, 1977. 207 p., maps, tables (Biblioteca marxista colombiana, 3)

Marxist analysis of Colombian demographic trends. [W.R. Garner]

7275 Castro Caycedo, Germán. Colombia amarga. Bogotá, Carlos Valencia Editores, 1976. 199 p.

The "bitterness" of everyday life in Colombia is chronicled in a series of short articles by a perceptive and probing Colombian journalist. Themes of violence, corruption, exploitation, deceit, and dispair reveal a myriad of weaknesses in the political and economic system.

7276 Cepeda Ulloa, Fernando. De la oposición . . . (Estrategia Económica y Financiera [Servicios de Información Ltda., Bogotá] 1, junio 1977, p. 20–22, plate)

Colombian political scientist remarks on some of the factors in the opposition's (Conservative Party) relationship with the Liberal administration of López Michelsen.

7277 ——— and Claudia González de Lecaros. Comportamiento del voto urbano en Colombia: una aproximación. Bogotá, Univ. de Los Andes, Facultad de Artes y Ciencias, Depto. de Ciencia Política, 1976. 61 p., bibl., tables.

Perceptive analysis of urban voting behavior in 21 Dept. capitals between 1958–74 reveals important shifts in Liberal and Conservative voting with increasing urbanization. While the major pattern is one of Liberal strength in the urban centers and Conservative strength in the rural areas, proportionately greater numbers of voters are abstaining from voting altogether. Authors foresee a situation in the near future where the increasing number of "non-captive" voters may be mobilized by either a leader or party of the right or left.

7278 Consuegra Higgins, José. Siempre en la trinchera. Bogotá, Ediciones Universidades Simón Bolívar, Medellín y Libre de Pereira, 1977. 162 p. (Col. Universidad y pueblo, 14)

Series of 20 essays, lectures and articles written over the past 10 years on numerous social, political, and economic topics by one of Colombia's best known socialists. Author speaks in the humanistic tradition of Marx and Martí while denouncing the evils of Colombian capitalism.

7279 *Controversia*. Centro de Investigación y Educación Popular (CINEP). No. 54, 1977– . Bogotá.

Journal examines crisis in the "political class" in "post-mortem" of National Front experiment. Focus is on entrenched vested interests and their increasing hold on the social and political system during the Front's existence. Study calls for major reform of Presidential office and the bureaucracy when forthcoming Assembly revises the constitutional structure. [W.R. Garner]

7280 ——. ——. Nos. 57/58, 1977– . Bogotá.

Comprehensive study of Leftist/Marxist parties published one year before the 1978 elections. Describes major priorities of 12 such groups. [W.R. Garner]

7281 **Díaz de G., Jesús Luis.** Liberación campesina en América Latina: una opción para el pueblo campesino. Bogotá, Cepla Editores, 1977. 195 p., bibl., tables (Col. Estudios sociales, 7)

Despite the inaccurate title, an insightful assessment of the plight of the Colombian peasantry by a parish priest who spent four years in Cesar Dept. (Colombia) with the Catholic Church's ACPO (Acción Cultural Popular) program. Few scholars would disagree with his analysis of the causes and consequences of the life of *campesinos*, but the prescription of liberation—evangelization—will hardly be accepted by many who have worked in this area. An overly optimistic view of the Catholic Church in Colombia given its historical role in matters of social change.

7282 **Gauhan, Timothy O'Dea.** Housing and the urban poor: the case of Bogotá, Colombia (UM/JIAS, 19:1, Feb. 1977, p. 99– 124, bibl.)

Examination of the low-income hous-

ing market emphasizing socioeconomic and political factors—population growth, patterns of economic development, government ineptness and neglect—that have contributed to ineffective public policies. Author's thoughtful conclusion agrues that future urban housing policies for the poor will require revenues acquired through increased taxation on urban real estate, more efficient use of existing land, elimination of legal bottlenecks in creating new barrios, and the creation of an urban aid program.

7283 **González G., Fernán E.** Colombia 1974. t. 1, La Política. Bogotá, Centro de Investigación y Acción Social, 1975. 189 p. (Controversia, 33)

Interesting leftist analysis of the political forces in the 1974 presidential election, the hypocrisy of the "Mandato Claro" of President López, and the sources of discontent among the Colombian citizenry.

7284 ——. Controversia: pasado y presente del sindicalismo colombiano. Bogotá, Centro de Investigación Social, 1975. 216 p., bibl.

Author recounts evolution of Colombian labor movement from Independence through López Michelsen's Presidency. Fundamentally a corporatist study of interest to students of Colombian labor during various administrations—especially those of the National Front. [W.R. Garner]

7285 ——. Partidos políticos y poder eclesiástico: reseña histórica, 1810– 1930. Bogotá, Editorial CINEP, 1977. 211 p., bibl.

Study of Church-state conflicts over the nature and pace of social change from the colonial period to the collapse of Conservative rule in 1930. Critical, but valuable, socio-political history of the Catholic Church with emphasis on its links to the party system.

7286 **Guillén Martínez, Fernando.** El modelo de "El Poder" (NS, 2:3/4, 1977, p. 1–20)

Starting with de Tocqueville's theory of association, author traces different patterns of association in Colombian history to demonstrate the relationship between the distribution of power and the nature of association. Valuable work for understanding Colombia's modernization from above and certain aspects of the deviant case of Antioquia as related to the concept of a "spirit of association" for development decision making.

7287 Holmes Trujillo, Carlos. Trayectoria de un pensamiento de izquierda. Cali, Colombia, Talleres de Gráficas Karinn, 1977. 269 p., plates.

Influential Liberal from Cali offers his views on a number of topics from international economics and constitutional law to political economy, socialism and the Third World. As a social democrat, Holmes tries to steer a middle road between moderate Liberals and Marxists in what appears to be a future quest for the presidency of the Republic.

7288 La izquierda y la participación electoral. Bogotá, Centro de Investigación y Educación Popular, 1976. 111 p. (Controversia, 43)

Brief treatment of the various leftist groups and parties concerning their positions on electoral strategies and tactics. Divisions within the left emerge along with the continuing debate over whether the left should participate in conventional ways.

7289 Leal Buitrago, Francisco. Estudio del comportamiento legislativo en Colombia. t. 1, Análisis histórico del desarrollo político nacional: 1930–1970. Bogotá, Ediciones Tercer Mundo, 1973. 306 p., tables (Col. Manuales universitarios, 7)

Vol. 1 of an extensive structural-functional analysis of national legislative behavior in Colombia since 1930. Pt. 1 includes a theoretical treatment of legislative power within the context of national development over the past 40 years. An historical analysis of four key legislative variables—functions, absenteeism, efficiency, and power—takes up the bulk of Pt. 2. A careful descriptive and analytical study with important implications for executive-legislative relations, political legitimacy, the distribution of power, and the frustration of governing in an economically dependent nation.

7290 Levine, Daniel H. and **Alexander W. Wilde.** The Catholic Church, "politics," and violence: the Colombian case (UND/RP, 39:2, April 1977, p. 220–249)

To what extent is the Catholic Church in Colombia political? After distinguishing between conflicting views of politics by contemporary ecclesiastical elites, authors con-

clude that despite attempts to substitute "pastoral" for "political action" (largely due to the legacy of the *violencia*), the institutional Church will continue to be involved in agenda-setting areas of politics. Important study for understanding the dilemmas that the Church faces in translating political issues into social outcomes.

7291 López Michelsen, Alfonso. El gobierno del mandato claro. t. 2, 7 de febrero de 1975–7 de agosto de 1975; t. 3, 7 de agosto de 1975–6 de febrero de 1976. Bogotá, Imprenta Nacional, 1976. 2 v. (320, 376 p.) map, plates, tables.

President's public statements over period of one year (during which nation was under state of seige powers). Stands as López Michelsen's *apologia* for his policies during this period. Most importantly, the collection indicates corporatist mold of politics during this first administration after expiration of National Front. [W.R. Garner]

7292 ———. Mensaje al Congreso Nacional. Bogotá, Presidencia de la República, Secretaría de Información, 1975. 195 p., tables.

President reviews the first year's accomplishments of the "Mandato Claro" and the problems/reforms of the post-National Front government. Interesting data from DAS on recent kidnappings are presented in an appendix.

7293 ———. Mensaje al Congreso Nacional. Bogotá, Ediciones del Banco de la República, 1976. 229 p., tables.

Traditional message to Congress by President López reviewing his second year in office. Although written in a self-serving manner, much can be gleaned from this executive document.

7294 ———. Mensaje al Congreso Nacional. t. 1. Bogotá, Ediciones del Banco de la República, 1977. 123 p.

Vol. 1 of President's annual review of his administration's accomplishments in numerous areas. Emphasis is placed on the successful "governmental bridge" between the years of the National Front and competitive politics. On the economic front, consequences of the "coffee bonanza" are discussed.

López Trujillo, Alfonso. Liberation or revolution?: an examination of the priest's role in the socioeconomic class struggle in Latin America. See item **7045**.

7295 Losada Lora, Rodrigo. Propiedades y disposiciones políticas de los congresistas y su relación con las funciones del Congreso: un modelo empírico. Bogotá, Univ. de los Andes, Facultad de Artes y Ciencias, Depto. de Ciencia Político, 1973. 50 l.

Structural-functional analysis of the Colombian Congress during the first 10 years of the National Front. Main function appears to be the legitimation of decisions stemming from the presidency and directorates of the major political parties. After delineating a number of basic political functions, author attempts to develop an empirical model based on socio-political characteristics and patterns of socialization. Theoretical value of model remains weak although ways of applying it to future research on political elites are suggested.

7296 ———— and **Gladys Delgado Lersundy.** Las elecciones de Mitaca en 1976: participación electoral y perspectiva histórica. Bogotá, Fundación para la Educación Superior y el Desarrollo, 1976. 32 p., map, tables.

Sophisticated methodological effort to explain levels of electoral participation during *mitaca* (congressional, at various levels) elections from 1958 to 1976. Findings reveal a pattern of lower overall participation in these elections regardless of sex, residence, or regional sub-culture. The authors theorize that the reason Colombian voters stay home during these elections is due to the dismal record of solving key issues in the legislature and the low prestige attached to law-making institutions in general.

7297 ———— and others. Colombia política: estadísticas, 1935–1970. Bogotá, Depto. Administrativo Nacional de Estadística (DANE), 1972. 398 p., bibl., facsims., maps, tables.

Valuable compilation of data on voting behavior and elections during a period of significant political change in Colombia. Emphasis is placed on the congressional and presidential elections of 1968 and 1970.

7298 Mena, Lucila Inés. Bibliografía anotada sobre el ciclo de la violencia en la literatura Colombiana (LARR, 8:3, 1978, p. 95–107)

The "novel of the *violencia*" is briefly

discussed including a 109-item bibliography of which 35 are annotated. The years 1949–76 are covered with particular attention to the works of Gabriel García Márquez and Eduardo Caballero Calderón. Author claims that literature on the *violencia* has been one of the dominant themes of the past several decades. For more fictional treatment of the *violencia*, see *HLAS 40:6766.*

7299 Miranda Ontaneda, Néstor and **Fernán E. González G.** Clientelismo, "democracia" o poder popular. Bogotá, Centro de Investigación y Educación Popular (CINEP), 1976. 243 p., bibl. (Controversia, 41/42)

Neo-Marxist analysis of clientelism and democracy which argues that any form of political participation that perpetuates class-cacique dominance prevents the lower classes from realizing their interests and goals and exercising authentic political power. Interesting theoretical discussion with numerous examples of clientelism in operation in various parts of Colombia.

7300 Morcillo, Pedro Pablo. La reforma administrativa en Colombia (*in* Seminario Interamericano de Reforma Administrativa, I, Rio, 1973/1974. Reforma administrativa: experiencias latinoamericanas. México, Instituto Nacional de Administración Pública, 1975, p. 7–46)

Administrative reform since 1958 is discussed in terms of rationale, problems/obstacles, and major achievements. Although written by one of President Pastrana's urban planners, the amount of detail lends itself primarily to the specialist in planning and public administration.

7301 Noriega, Carlos Augusto. Lo que pasó aquella noche, 19 de abril de 1970. Bogotá, Ediciones Tercer Mundo, 1977. 324 p., facsims., tables (Col. Tribuna libre)

Minister of Labor and Government under President Lleras R. defends his role in the events surrounding the most disputed presidential election in Colombian history. Author claims that early returns did show Gen. Rojas Pinilla ahead by 13,707 votes but later returns shifted to Pastrana who eventually won fair and square. Considerable blame is directed at the radio stations that played up a Rojas victory from the beginning with false information.

7302 Pastrana Borrero, Misael. Programa Integración Popular: 1970–1974. Bogotá, Ediciones Banco de la República, 1974. 215 p., plates, tables.

Colombia's last Conservative president reviews his program to foster the integration of the marginal sectors of society into the mainstream of national life. This partisan effort includes 21 social and economic programs.

7303 Pérez González-Rubio, Jesús. Reformar las instituciones. Bogotá, Presidencia de la República, Secretaría de Información, 1978. 101 p.

Critical statement in *negative* vein made by Secretary of the Council of Ministers (12 Jan. 1977) at opening session of Constitutional Assembly charged with drafting a reform charter for the country. Author calls for reform in organization of Congress and public administration. This carefully worded critique by one of Colombia's leading professors of Constitutional Law merits attentions. [W.R. Garner]

7304 Restrepo Piedrahita, Carlos. 25 [i.e. Veinticinco] años de evolución político-constitutional: 1950–1975. Prólogo de Alfonso López Michelsen. Bogotá, Publicaciones Univ. Externado de Colombia, 1976. 237 p., plate.

Recent Colombian constitutional history is recounted in legal, political, and behavioral terms. An innovative approach and a significant contribution to understanding changes before and during the National Front. Author concludes that legal-constitutional alterations have not contributed to the resolution of basic political and social ills.

7305 Revéiz, Edgar and others. Poder e información: el proceso decisorio en tres casos de política regional y urbana en Colombia. Bogotá, Univ. de Los Andes, Centro de Estudios sobre Desarrollo Económico (CEDE), Facultad de Economía *con la colaboración* del Depto. de Ciencia Política [and] la Facultad de Ingeniería, 1977. 425 p., bibl., fold. tables, tables.

What kinds of information are used in making decisions on regional and urban policy at the national, regional, and local (urban) levels? In a well-conceived interdisciplinary effort, three different cases are analyzed in terms of the groups involved, their ideas and plans, and the way in which information was used in the process of making the decision. Results uncover the importance of legitimizing sources of information and the increasing dependence on external sources of funding for national-level projects.

7306 Rojas Ruiz, Humberto and **Alvaro Camacho Guizado.** El Frente Nacional: ideología y realidad. Bogotá, Punta de Lanza, 1974. 187 p., bibl., tables.

Consists of two articles which are a continuation of a 1970 publication by Rodrigo Parra attacking the National Front. All three authors associate the Front with traditional ruling groups, underdevelopment, and international economic dependence. On balance, these continuations of the Parra argument are well documented with hard data and relatively little polemic. [W.R. Garner]

7307 Sharpless, Richard E. Gaitán of Colombia: a political biography. Pittsburgh, Pa., Univ. of Pittsburgh Press, 1978. 229 p., bibl., plate, tables (Pitt Latin American series)

Excellent analysis of the leader and ideology of a mass-based political movement that emerged in Colombia in the 1930s and 1940s to challenge the traditional oligarchy. Although there is little comparison with other populists and populism in Latin America, author concludes that this type of political system is not a long-term solution to Latin America's problems of dependency and underdevelopment. Why? Author argues that charismatic authority and the army's linkage with the traditional elites serves to undermine efforts to meet the needs of the dispossessed proletariat through legal channels and the power of the state. A balanced biography and a significant contribution to understanding Gaitanismo, la violencia, and the nature of populism in 20th-century Colombia. For historian's comment, see *HLAS 40:3436.*

7308 Sociedad Colombiana de Defensa de la Tradición, Familia y Propiedad, *Bogotá.* La iglesia del silencio en Chile: un tema de meditación para los católicos latinoamericanos. Bogotá, 1976. 495 p., illus., plates.

Publication originally stemming from work of the Chilean FTP (Chilean Society for the Defense of Tradition, Family and Property) aimed at Colombian leadership (see item **7374**). [W.R. Garner]

7309 **Tirado Mejía, Alvaro.** Colombia: siglo y medio de bipartidismo (*in* Colombia hoy. Bogotá, Siglo XXI Editores de Colombia, 1978, p. 102–185, bibl.)

Useful socio-political history of Liberal-Conservative domination of Colombia from Bolívar to the beginning of the National Front. The twists and turns of bipartisan rule are interpreted as part of the system of elite domination and the ability of the two major parties to coalesce under periods of internal upheaval. Emphasis is placed on the historical conflicts over the role of the Church and state, how to stabilize the economy, and the nature of power and its distribution.

7310 **Vélez R., Ricardo.** La filosofía política conservadora en Colombia (UM/R, 24, 1977, p. 95–108)

Conservative political philosophy is characterized by a set of values inimical to social experimentation and secularization. Author claims that the roots of Conservative Party thought are connected with the ideas of Francisco Suárez and later (e.g., the 19th century) jelled in the reactionary views of aristocratic landowners and the Church against the progressive views of the commercial and artisan class after 1848. Brief, and rather general, but a worthwhile effort.

7311 **Zuckova, G.E.** Sobre la práctica de las alianzas anti-imperialists en Colombia (UR/L, Spring 1975, p. 41–52)

East German analysis of political tendencies in Colombia, as of the 1970s. Discusses the National Front and relations between Colombia's Communist Party and ANAPO. [M. Kossok]

ECUADOR

7312 **Campo, Esteban del.** Populismus und Velasquismus (OLI/ZLW, 12, 1977, p. 114–128, bibl.)

An analysis of populism in Ecuador in which the rise to power of Velasco Ibarra is seen as a consequence of post-depression industrialization and the rise of an urban working class. Author argues that the policies of Velasco Ibarra were less of a challenge to traditional political elites than a ploy to prevent the radicalization of the urban masses and to sustain the power of an increasingly divided oligarchy.

7313 El Ecuador en la nueva coyuntura. El estado y las inquietudes privadas. Imagen del Ecuador en el exterior. Quito, Comité de Información y Contacto Externo (CICE), n.d. 190 p. (Biblioteca CICE, 3)

Three papers address current national problems. They reach interesting if at times questionable conclusions (e.g., foreign capital is *not* required for national development; Ecuadorian journalism must be controlled in light of "revolutionary" goals, etc.). Also proposes the elaboration of a comparative analysis of Venezuelan and Ecuadorian petroleum policies. And finally, holds West German social democracy as the model for the social, economic, and political organization of Ecuador. Varied and interesting collection of papers. [W.R. Garner]

7314 **Egas R., José María.** Ecuador y el gobierno de la junta militar. B.A., Tierra Nueva, 1975. 87 p., tables (Col. Procesos, 8)

Ecuadorian political scientist analyzes the military government of Rodríguez Lara as a regime type along the lines of the Peruvian model. Author's conclusions state that the model offers little in the way of distributive social and economic development and legitimacy for the political system.

7315 *Ficha de Información Sociopolítica.* Pontificia Univ. Católica del Ecuador. Depto. de Ciencias Políticas y Sociales. No. 13, nov. 1974– . Quito.

Monthly compilation of political, social, and economic data taken chiefly from Ecuadorian newspapers (*El Comercio, El Universo, El Tiempo, El Expreso, El Telégrafo,* etc.) and coded by category and sub-category for easy reference, e.g., Monthly Activities, International Relations, National Political Statements and Problems, Economic Development, Agrarian Reform and Peasant Problems, Petroleum Politics, Andean Integration, Educational Matters, etc. (see items **7316** and **7317**). Unfortunately, the presentation of the data in paragraph form does not facilitate comparative analysis or easy reference although the effort to assemble and organize this sort of data is commendable. In this issue, of particular interest are: Andean Integration, political party meetings and activities, general economic development data, and government petroleum policies.

7316 ———. ———. No. 15, enero 1975– . Quito.

Of particular interest in this issue are: the capture of "pirate" tuna boats from the US, the Ford administration's cancellation of trade preference against Ecuador as a result of the OPEC oil embargo, and economic development statistics.

7317 ———. ———. No. 20, junio 1975–. Quito.

Of particular interest in this issue are: the defense and criticism of the military government (Gen. Rodríguez Lara), international relations, economic development statistics, and government petroleum policies.

7318 ———. ———. No. 29, marzo 1976–. Quito.

Of particular interest in this issue are: the discussion of the "Plan de Institucionalización" for the return of constitutional government, demands for nationalization of the petroleum industry, Andean Pact issues and problems, and economic development statistics.

7319 Fitch, John Samuel. The military coup d'état as a political process: Ecuador, 1948–1966. Baltimore, Md., The Johns Hopkins Univ. Press, 1977. 243 p., bibl. (The Johns Hopkins Univ. studies in historical and political science, 1. Series 95)

A splendid piece of social science research on the role of the military coup d'état in contemporary Ecuadorian politics. The theoretical model of the coup d'état and the application of a diversity of empirical techniques make this essential reading for those interested in civil-military relations. Fitch develops a series of propositions that center on the notion that the military coup d'état provides a "means of resolving the periodic crises stemming from weak political institutions and fluctuating, externally dependent economy." Careful analysis with excellent results.

7320 Moore, Richard J. Urban problems and policy responses for metropolitan Guayaquil (in Cornelius, Wayne A. and Robert V. Kemper eds. Metropolitan Latin America: the challenge and the response [see item **9016**] p. 181–203, bibl., illus., tables)

Policy-oriented case study of current urban problems in Ecuador's largest city and government action to solve critical urban problems related to rapid urban expansion. The inability to adequately solve these problems is due to the lack of coordination of governmental programs, the treatment of urban problems as purely technical rather than socio-political, and the reactive rather than creative nature of government response. Author maintains that Guayaquil's major urban problem is the incomplete integration of *suburbio* into city life.

7321 *NACLA's Latin America & Empire Report.* North American Congress on Latin America. Vol. 9, No. 8, Nov. 1975–. N.Y.

Issue entitled "Ecuador: Oil up for Grabs" is a leftist account of the political economy of Ecuador focusing on developments since the military took power in 1972. Economic policies since 1972 have increased dependency by expanding opportunities for foreign investment and the establishment of capital-intensive industries. A well-documented case for understanding the consequences of late industrialization in Latin America and the politics of petroleum.

7322 Pyne, Peter. The role of Congress in the Ecuadorian political system and its contribution to the overthrow of President Velasco Ibarra in 1961. Glasgow, U.K., Univ. of Glasgow, Institute of Latin American Studies, 1973. 36 p., bibl. (Occasional papers, 7)

Original monograph published five years after most of the text appeared as an article in *Comparative Political Studies* (see *HLAS 39:7338*) on executive-legislative relations during the fourth *Velasquista* administration.

Peru, Bolivia, and Chile

WILLIAM R. GARNER, *Associate Professor of Political Science, Latin American Studies Advisory Committee, Southern Illinois University-Carbondale*

CHILEAN LITERATURE REVIEWED IN *HLAS* 37 and *HLAS* 39 generally reflected the immediate frenzy of right- and of left-wing reaction to the fall of Unidad Popular. In this section, however, the still formidable amount of material has evolved into a more reflective and sophisticated post-mortem of the Allende period. French journalist, Pierre Rieben, observed in 1974 that the UP experiment had, by Sept. 1973, evolved into nothing more than an "academic debate" and, under the Junta, that claim is still essentially correct. However, the *quality* of the present debate has improved and one detects a less emotional tone and a more reasoned approach in the literature.

Broad-range analyses of fundamental weaknesses bringing about the military coup are noted in an excellent study by Cusack (item **7395**) which investigates early Junta policy (through 1974) as well. Landsberger and McDaniel (item **7420**) emphasize the theme of "hypermobilization" as counter-productive and generally dysfunctional for the UP. Stallings, in an exceptionally "tight" study (item **7446**) offers complex economic analysis in historical perspective and blames deficiencies in supply/demand policies adopted during the Alessandri and Frei administrations as the most frustrating legacy left to Allende. Works by Kay (items **7416** and **7417**) represent sophisticated Marxist interpretations. Sigmund (item **7443**) offers the most comprehensive analysis of Allende's flawed program. The consequences of endemic factionalism in both the Chilean Socialist Party and the UP, which were predicted by Heller Rouassant in his 1973 study of heterogeneity (item **7409**), appear in retrospect to have been prophetic. Prats' memoir-like volume (item **7434**) also concerns variousareas of vulnerability for the regime which point to and explain the Pinochet succession.

Relatively subdued Leftist/Marxist "self-criticism" may be found in Arrate (item **7377**), Arrigada Herrera (item **7378**), and Boorstein (item **7382**). There are criticisms of the 1925 constitutional framework for revolution in Tapia Videla's study (item **7449**), and broadside attacks aimed at former President Frei and Christian Democratic policies in Chonchol (item **7390**), De Riz (item **7437**), and Garreton (item **7405**). Pollack's comparative study of the Chilean Communist and Socialist Parties (item **7433**) together with the two-volume collection of documents defining MAPU's position within the Allende coalition (item **7427**) are incisive contributions to a comprehensive analysis of the period.

Post-coup support for Pinochet is examined by Fontaine (item **7401**) and an invaluable set of papers presented at a Junta-sponsored seminar on "The Crisis of Democracy" are of considerable interest (item **7452**). Cuevas Ferrán (item **7394**) argues, from the vantage point of jurisprudence and philosophy, in a labored attempt to delineate conditions under which constitutional governments may be legitimately overthrown. Atroshenko's critique of Friedman's economic-policy models is of considerable importance (item **7379**) as are the views of Favereau on the referendum of 4 Jan. 1978 (item **7400**). Maldonado (item **7425**) and Rodríguez (item **7438**) make valuable observations on techniques developed by the Junta to restrict artistic and cultural activities within limits imposed by the military. By far, one of the most significant contributions to any assessment of the Junta's administrative and, specifically, economic policy is the article on corporatism by Paul Drake (item **7398**).

Debate on the Chilean Church's role (1970–73) is, for the first time, covered in detail. The Díaz collection of quotations from sermons and official pronouncements by Cardinal Silva Henríquez (item **7444**) and the historical study of the Church's position in Chilean society by Hinkelammert (item **7411**) are representative of pro-hierarchy sentiment. Arguments opposing Silva Henríquez and the hierarchy are found in Domic (items **7396** and **7397**) as well as in a large expensively-produced volume published by the Sociedad Chilena de Defensa de la Tradición, Familia y Propiedad (TFP) for Chileans (item **7388**) with special editions prepared for Bolivian (item **7374**) and Colombian (item **7308**) readers.

On the potential re-establishment of democratic institutions and/or overthrow of the military regime, there are works by Castillo Velasco (item **7384**), the Peruvian Marxist Víctor Villanueva (item **7456**), and an extraordinary example of political sensitivity and balance by Von Muhlenbrock (item **7428**).

Peru: The literature reviewed for Peru shows considerable improvement over that covered in *HLAS 39* and also general acceptance of "consolidation" for the Peruvian military's "leftist revolution." Philosophical argumentation of "the proper role of law in a revolutionary society" is an important contribution by Cornejo Chávez (item **7329**) as is Fernando Lecaros' essay on the concept of "social property" (item **7341**). There are important works by Lara Soto (item **7339**) and Rocca Torres (item **7356**) on the preconquest Inca model as the basis for a successful revolutionary policy.

With regard to the "revolution" itself, Kuczynski (item **7338**) and Webb (item **7364**) are able to present exceptionally fine analyses of the foundations for the 1968 Velasco coup because of their experiences as economic advisors to Belaúnde Terry. Three small volumes of quotes and fuller texts from Velasco's 1972 speeches (item **7361**) provide good references to the original goals of the former President. These goals, however, are "reinterpreted" in two 1976 volumes published under the supervision of Morales Bermúdez (items **7346** and **7347**). The "styles" of the two presidents are contrasted by Colin-Delavaud (item **7327**) and in Chap. 10, "The Coup within the Coup" of Alba's book (item **7323**). In two official documents, Morales explains the "Second Phase" and the economic recession of 1976–77, respectively (items **7346** and **7347**). Chronological, nonanalytical works by Pease-García (item **7349**) and Soenens (item **7359**) are valuable as research references for the 1968–78 period. A worthwhile study by Denis Sulmont (item **7360**) compares the "First" and "Second" phases of the "revolution."

Studies of peasant politicization by Atusparia (item **7325**), Bartra (item **7326**), and Renique (item **7354**) are important contributions and articles by Dietz analyzing urban (Limeño) slum-politics are of superior quality (items **7330–7332**). Negative remarks on press censorship by Peirano (item **7350**) and Rocca (item **7355**) with a *pro*-censorship study by Verbitsky (item **7362**) offer profitable insights. The Peruvian War College (CAEM) study by Villanueva (item **7363**) and an outstanding analysis of the IPC controversy by McIrwin (item **7342**) are noteworthy.

Bolivia: There is an improvement in the quality of the literature on Bolivia, compared to *HLAS 39*. Christopher Mitchell's book-length analysis of the MNR's demise (item **7372a**) and the Mitchell-Domínguez article focusing on errors committed by the Cuban and Bolivian revolutionary elites with regard to "timing" and "institutionalization" (item **7194**) are illuminating. Almáraz Paz and other members of Bolivia's professional sector give valuable interpretations concerning the increase of political violence in their country (item **7366**). A government publication (item **7370**) is of multifaceted interest as an historical study of the evolution of Bolivia's Supreme Court.

PERU

7323 Alba, Víctor. Peru. Boulder, Colo., Westview Press, 1977. 245 p., bibl.

Alba's interpretation of Peru's current problems is based on his perception of the nation as one ossified by psychological and geographical regionalism. He believes this has prevented development of a national consciousness. Book stresses all facets of culture and behavior with political analysis features in chap. 4, 9, and 10. Chap. 10 "The coup within the Coup," on the Velasco and Morales Bermúdez periods is probably the best section of this work.

7324 Alva Orlandini, Javier. Respuesta a la dictadura. Prólogo de Luis Felipe Alarco. Lima, Librería Editorial Minerva-Miraflores, 1978. 210 p. (El populista, 2)

Author offers defense of Belaúnde Terry and Acción Popular in historical perspective through Velasco and Morales Bermúdez regimes. Written in light of AP's potential in the 1978 elections and upcoming Constitutional Assembly.

7325 Atusparia, Pedro. La izquierda y la reforma agraria peruana: tres cuestiones fundamentales. Jesús María, Perú, Editorial Labor, 1977? 58 p.

Marxist theoretical analysis of Peruvian agrarian/peasant problems focusing on three "areas of urgency:" 1) the peasantry's potential as a true political force, 2) their role *if* such potential is activated, and 3) the possibility of a real alliance between the urban industrialized labor and the peasant class for common proletarian action.

7326 Bartra, Roger. Las estructuras políticas de mediación: ensayos sobre las raíces campesinas del poder despótico moderno. Presentación de Mariano Valderrama. Lima, Pontificia Univ. Católica, Programa Académico de Ciencias Sociales, Taller de Investigacion Rural, 1976? 125 l., tables (Cuaderno, 16)

Marxist-Gramsci discussion of the State and its role in dealing with the rural peasantry.

Boersner, Demetrio. Democracia representativa y transformación social en América Latina. See item **7004**.

7327 Collin-Delavaud, Claude. L'évolution du Regime Militaire Péruvien: 1975–1977 (FDD/NED [Problèmes d'Amérique Latine 47] 4457, fev. 1978, p. 11–69, tables)

French interpretation which contrasts policies and styles of Velasco and Morales Bermúdez regimes. Written from a historical perspective, it includes a thorough chronology of events from 1 Jan. 1975 to 31 Dec. 1977. Interesting and valuable reference work.

7328 Conferencia Nacional del Partido Comunista del Perú, VII, Lima, 1976. Viva la unidad de los comunistas peruanos: documentos. Lima, Ediciones Lucha de Clases, 1976. 99 p.

This collection of documents generated by the 1976 Congress of the Peruvian Communist Party (Marxist-Leninist and Moscow-oriented) shows how the Party is far more concerned with its separation from the Peking Marxists than with concrete proposals for confronting a military government in power. Good example of how the Moscow-Peking rivalry confounds the Communist movement throughout Latin America.

7329 Cornejo Chávez, Héctor. Derecho y revolución. Caracas, Centro de Información, Documentación y Análisis Latinoamericano (CIDAL), 1972? 15 l. (Documentos, 27)

Founder of Peru's Christian Democratic Party adopts an interesting stance by exploring the philosophical argument that law makes society—even a revolutionary one. In revolutionary societies, law should not be perceived as dogma but as a tool for social change under a novel form of governmental/societal restructuring.

Cuche, Denys. Pouvoir et participation dans les coopératives agraires de production au Pérou: les cas des coopératives cotonnières de la Côte Sud. See *HLAS 40:3509*.

7330 Dietz, Henry A. Land invasion and consolidation: a study of working-poor/governmental relations in Lima, Peru

(UA, 6:4, Winter 1977, p. 371–385, bibl., tables)

This 1967–71 case study of Lima's slum settlements (pueblos jóvenes) is an interesting analytical description of: 1) the formation of the "Primero de Enero Association" ("Primero de Enero" being the name of the settlement); 2) the Association's original planning before the land invasion; 3) the Association's techniques for establishing positive relations with government agencies; and 4) internal consolidation efforts necessary for stable community life. Important contribution.

7331 ———. Metropolitan Lima: urban problem-solving under military rule (*in* Cornelius, Wayne A. and Robert V. Kemper *eds*. Metropolitan Latin America: the challenge and the response [see item **9016**] p. 205–226, bibl., illus., tables)

Incisive picture of social, economic, migration, demographic, historical and administrative characteristics of Greater Lima with analysis of the more serious problems facing the urban complex and response of Peruvian military. Excellent study in description and policy analysis.

7332 ———. Urban poverty, participation and authoritarian rule: further data from Peru (UT/SSQ, 59:1, June 1978, p. 105–116, bibl., tables)

Case study of two Lima slum settlements: a pueblo jóven (illegal squatter cluster *outside* the city) and a callejón (inner-city slum). Generalizing, author notes that the latter type of slum has been less effective because it is not as obvious and is legal. The *pueblos jóvenes* have been more successful in commanding government attention because they are illegal and representing huge, "readily tapable" populations, they are "officially" recognized as an important "political resource."

7333 **Englund, Peter; Lars Heikensten;** and **Claes Nordström.** Generalernas Peru. Lund, Sweden, Akademisk Forlag, 1977. 227 p., illus., map (Studentlitteratur)

Authors of this fine survey (*The Generals' Peru*) are three young Swedish economists who spent a couple of months in the country in the fall of 1975. Whereas the account of pre-1968 Peru is too sketchy, the political and economic developments under the Junta government are carefully outlined. Small case studies (on the land reform at Casa Grande and in the Valley of Mantaro, an industry similar to Moraveco S.A.) are ably incorporated into the text. The evaluation is rather critical, from a perspective to the left of the present regime. It is, moreover, clear that the book was written at a juncture when the economic and political crisis of the "Peruvian revolution" was no longer in doubt. [M. Mörner]

Estado y política agraria: cuatro ensayos. See *HLAS 40:3512*.

Gargurevich, Juan. Introducción a los medios de comunicación en el Perú. See *HLAS 40:3519*.

7334 **Guerrero Martínez, Juan** *ed*. 7 [i.e. Siete] años de revolución. Lima, Talleres de Printcolores, 1976? 1 v. (Unpaged) illus., plates.

Continuation of propaganda disseminated by quasi-official press agency (PROPERSA) stressing government accomplishments in transition from the Velasco to Morales Bermúdez administrations (see also item **7353**).

7335 **Heysen, Luis E.** Temas y obras del Perú a la verdad por los hechos. 3. ed. Lima, Enrique Bracamonte Vera, 1977. 436 p., facsims., plates, tables.

Third ed. of large volume continues discussion of APRA and its relevance to 20th-century Peruvian history. This highly emotional book will make reader wonder whether author is more interested in his own "life with APRA" than in the life and thought of Haya de la Torre or, for that matter, the real potential of Aprismo. Nevertheless, of interest to all students of APRA. For more on author's recollections of APRA, see *HLAS 40:3526*.

Joes, Anthony James. Fascism in the contemporary world: ideology, evolution, resurgence. See item **7489**.

7336 **Klaiber, Jeffrey.** El APRA: religión y legitimidad popular (UP/A, 4:8, 1978, p. 49–58)

Author, a Jesuit priest, posits that the 1968 revolution was a flawed attempt to copy APRA's ideology at a time when APRA was incapable of presenting its ideology in the sort of religious context that would appeal to the

Peruvian masses. This failure along with Haya de la Torre's exclusion from leadership led to the failure of the military experiment. Provocative statement which perceives political "legitimacy" as a "religious movement."

———. Religion and revolution in Peru: 1824–1976. See HLAS 40:3529.

7337 Klarén, Peter F. Formación de las haciendas azucareras y orígenes del APRA. Presentación de Heraclio Bonilla. 2. ed. rev. y aumentada. Lima, Instituto de Estudios Peruanos (IEP), 1976. 298 p., bibl., map, tables (Serie Perú problema, 5)

Historian studies the evolution of Aprismo out of the northern land-holding provinces of Cajamarca, La Libertad, and Lambayeque—a constituency which Haya de la Torre was able to capture and hold as his own over several decades. Interesting analysis which should be perused by students of the APRA phenomenon. For historian's comment, see HLAS 40:3530.

7338 Kuczynski, Pedro-Pablo. Peruvian democracy under economic stress: an account of the Belaúnde administration, 1963–1968. Princeton, N.J., Princeton Univ. Press, 1977. 308 p., bibl., map, tables.

Author, former Director of the Peruvian Central Reserve Bank, points to the following 10 factors as leading to the 1968 Velasco coup: 1) the *economically* outdated 1933 Constitution; 2) legislative immobility due to proportional representation; 3) lack of national consciousness; 4) APRA's frustration with legislative activity (intensified by multipartyism in Congress); 5) lack of effective constitutional provisions for economic management and planning; 6) Belaúnde Terry's inability to "lead" Congress; 7) anger produced by land and taxation reforms; 8) inequitable distribution that favored the middle classes; 9) fragmentation within APRA and; 10) anger over IPC settlement and balance of payments problems in general. Exceptional book which constitutes the "definitive" study of the Belaúnde Administration.

7339 Lara Soto, Jesús. Revolución auténtica y revolución postiza. Lima, Ediciones Prensa Peruana, 1975. 61 p.

Author argues that any "authentic" Peruvian revolution must be identified with preconquest indigenous "communality." Inter-

esting "indigenista" argument published during the Morales Bermúdez administration.

Latin American Perspectives. See HLAS 40:3532.

7340 Lauer, Mirko ed. Frente al Perú oligárquico: 1928–1968. Miraflores, Perú, Mosca Azul Editores, 1977. 187 p.

Historical study of the Peruvian Communist Party and more recent radical groups from the 1920s through 1968. Of particular interest is the section titled, "Capitalist or Semi-Feudal?"

7341 Lecaros, Fernando. Propiedad social: teoría y realidad; problemas y perspectivas de la Vía Peruana al socialismo. Lima, Ediciones Rikchay Perú, 1975. 128 p., bibl., tables.

Author focuses on the Peruvian revolutionary concept of "social property," and provides a thorough discussion of this fundamental ideological tenet.

7342 McIrvin, Ronald R. Buying time: the International Petroleum Company's public relations campaign in Peru, 1946–1966 (SECOLAS/A, 8, March 1977, p. 94–105)

Good addition to the material on IPC nationalization crisis. Author suggests that the Company's successful public relations campaign plus a few bona fide improvements in the "company town" of Talara made it possible for IPC to continue its stance of historic insensitivity to Talara's needs for many more years than would have normally been the case. When finally ousted, the company was able to leave Peru "with no significant economic loss." Interesting conclusions.

Mejía, José Manuel and **Rosa Díaz Suárez.** Sindicalismo y reforma agraria en el Valle de Chancay. See HLAS 40:3547.

7343 Militares en Latinoamérica (Cuestionario [A. Peña Lillo Editor, B.A.] 1:1, mayo 1973, p. 18–19, illus.)

Briefly stated thoughts of Brazilian politician on the characteristics of the Peruvian military regime—in a context of such regimes throughout Latin America. [P.B. Taylor, Jr.]

7344 Moncloa, Francisco. Perú: ¿que pasó?: 1968–1976. Lima, Editorial Horizonte, 1977. 196 p., tables.

Exploration of two areas of conflict: 1)

the permanent tension between processes of rapid structural change and orthodox 19th-century liberal economics, and 2) the conflict between full participatory democracy and the government's systematic demobilization of a true popular mass-base through use of corporatist structures. Fascinating analysis.

7345 Mooney, Helen. The role of the Church in Peruvian political development (NS, 3:5/6, 1978, p. 1–22, tables)

Contrary to opinion that the Church is not utilizing its full potential for structural change, author holds that the Peruvian Church is committed to "progressivism" and a "liberationist theology . . . attuned to contemporary Peruvian realities" in dimensions that are normative, structural and attitudinal. Interesting study with controversial conclusions.

7346 Morales Bermúdez Cerrutti, Francisco. The Peruvian revolution, political and economic considerations of the present moment: speech delivered by the President of the Republic . . . Lima, Empresa Editora Perú, 1976. 39 p.

Presidential address (31 March 1976) concerned with the "Second Phase" of the revolution and in which Morales disputes criticism that government has become "less revolutionary." By enlarging channels of political comment and debate, "closed during [Velasco's] 'First Phase'," the press is no longer "a monotonous flatterer" of the government, but a forum for all "*organized*" popular groups to debate and criticize "in accordance with the appropriate decree laws." Thinly veiled statement indicating corporatist orientation of the Peruvian "revolution" during the Morales Bermúdez period. Of interest to those studying press relations in Peru.

7347 ———. La Revolución Peruana: segunda fase. Discurco pronunciado por el Señor Presidente de la República, General de División, . . . al clausurar CADE 76 en la ciudad de Arequipa, noviembre 21 de 1976. Lima, Oficina Central de Información (OCI), 1976? 23 p.

President's response to the recession of 1976–77 accompanying the "Second Phase" of the revolution. Good source of official explanation of the problems of this period.

7348 Ortiz de Zevallos, Javier. Ante el tribunal de la opinión pública: la

democracia peruana presenta pruebas. Lima, 1976. 366 p., facsims., plates.

Short analysis of Peruvian politics from 1954 through administration of Manuel Prado to the 1968 coup with a prognosis for political development. Author, a follower of Prado and Haya de la Torre, places emphasis on democratic institutions as most functional and, from this point of view, this study of the 1954–76 period is of value to Peruvianists who anticipate a return to democracy.

Parra E., Ernesto and **Isabel Aguirrezábal T.** Suramérica 76: modelos militares de desarrollo. See item **7568.**

7349 Pease García, Henry and others. Perú: cronología política. v. 1/3, 1968–1974; v. 4, 1975; v. 5, 1976. Lima, DESCO, Centro de Estudios y Promoción del Desarrollo, Area de Estudios Políticos, 1974 (i.e. 1977). 5 v. (Continuous pagination) (2389 p.) tables.

Chronological description of "revolutionary" Peru (1968–76) with little analysis. Compilers correctly state that their treatment of events during the period covered provides merely the documentary base for future propositions and analyses of Peruvian political life. Good reference set on government policy.

7350 Peirano, Luis and others. Prensa: apertura y límites. Lima, DESCO, Centro de Estudios y Promoción del Desarrollo, 1978. 241 p., tables.

Comparative study of leading Lima newspapers before and after press reforms initiated by Velasco. Of interest because it focuses both on news management by the press itself and by government. Decrees dealing with press behavior are included in annex to volume.

7351 Pennano, Guido and **Jürgen Schuldt.** Premisas y antecedentes para la evaluación del proyecto del Plan Tupac Amaru (UP/A, 3:6, 1977, p. 51–68, bibl.)

Critical of all "populist" regimes from that of Odría and Belaúnde to the present "revolutionary" military government, authors castigate the Armed Forces for their "pseudo-revolution" which has only perpetuated the power of the military and other internal/external groups. Peruvian "Third Way" is the "Great Illusion" which, because of inherent economic and political crises, moves inexorably toward Brazilian-type military repression. Interesting negative critique of Peruvian leftist military from the Left.

7352 Peru. Oficina Central de Información. Bases ideológicas de la revolución peruana. Lima, Editorial Desarrollo, 1976. 61 p.

Official government statement of purposes and ideological bases of the 1968 "revolution," written in charter or constitutional format. Interesting, brief reference work.

7353 Producciones del Perú (PROPERSA), *Lima.* 5 [i.e. Cinco] años de revolución. Lima, 1973. 1 v. (Unpaged) plates.

Photographic essay produced by quasi-government press demonstrating the "emancipation" of Peru by the Velasco regime through Oct. 1973. Includes some discussion but little scientific (or other) analysis. Of interest due to photographic efforts. Very much a pro-Velasco volume.

7354 Renique, Gerardo. Sociedad Ganadera del Centro: pastores y sindicalización en una hacienda alto andina; documentos, 1945–1948. Lima, Univ. Nacional Agraria, Depto. de Ciencias Humanas, Taller de Estudios Andinos, 1977? 77 p. (Serie Andes centrales, 3)

Study focuses on rural unionization on a large Andean cattle hacienda. Time period of 1940s may be reason for study's dated effect. However, author's acuity in recording *campesino* behavior during the sindicalization process is of permanent value for understanding rural psychology.

7355 Rocca Torres, Luis. Crítica de la ideología del gobierno de las Fuerzas Armadas. Lima, Univ. Ricardo Palma, 1975. 294 p., bibl.

Author focuses on gap between dogmatic Marxism and Peruvian realities and concludes that Peruvian "socialism" is eclectic and indigenous and that no apology is needed for its past or future deviance from dogmatic assumptions. Complex but intriguing study.

7356 ———. El gobierno militar y las comunicaciones en el Perú. Lima, Ediciones Populares los Andes (EPASA), 1975. 127 p., bibl., tables (Col. Fondo de cultura popular, 35)

A "before and after" study of communications policy stressing governmental strictures after 1968. Thorough statement of policy concerning radio, television, newspaper and movie industries and aimed at enforced compliance with revolutionary ideology and planning through PUBLIPERÚ (agency for supervision and control of media).

7357 Rubio, Marcial. La actuación del Poder Ejecutivo y la estructura del orden jurídico (UP/A, 4:8, 1978, p. 81–98)

Systematic attempt to present problems of contemporary Peruvian military government in light of a "rationally organized" view of public administration. Of interest to Peruvianists who anticipate a return to constitutional government and democratic practice.

7358 Samarkina, J.K. Die Bauern der Comunidades und der revolutionäre Prozess in Peru (UR/L, Spring 1976, p. 39–55)

Article in East German journal analyzes revolutionary struggles of the Peruvian peasantry as well as the nature and consequences of Peru's 1969 agrarian reform. [M. Kossok]

7359 Soenens, Guido. El proceso revolucionario peruano, primera fase: bibliografía (UP/A, 3:6, 1977, p. 99–124)

Extensive, if not exhaustive, reference source for the 1968–77 period. Recommended for those interested in researching the leftist "revolution."

Souza, Herbet de. The world capitalist system and militarism in Latin America: a comparative analysis of the Brazilian and Peruvian models. See item **7583.**

7360 Sulmont, Denis. El movimento sindical en el Perú: 1968–1976. Lima, Pontificia Univ. Católica, Programa Académico de Ciencias Sociales, Taller de Estudios Urbano-Industriales, 1976. 32 l., tables (Serie Estudios sindicales, 5)

Incisive analysis of unionization under Velasco and Morales Bermúdez stressing SINAMOS administrative behavior, the "First" and "Second" phases of the revolution, foreign capital attraction, and monetary devaluation. Paper gives considerable attention to reorganization of the unions under Morales. Of permanent interest as a case study in mass mobilization of a country's work force.

Valderrama, Mariano. 7 [i.e. Siete] años de reforma agraria peruana: 1969–1976. *HLAS* 40:3565.

Vanden, Harry E. The peasants as a revolutionary class: an early Latin American view. See item **7081**.

7361 Velasco Alvarado, Juan. La política del gobierno revolucionario: discursos pronunciados por el General de División Don . . . , Presidente del Perú. v. 9/11. Lima, Oficina Nacional de Información, 1972. 3 v. (90, 147, 76 p.)

Government document presenting quotes and text of speeches by President Velasco Alvarado in the hope that Peruvian readers will "spread their meaning" throughout the nation. Touches the "ideology of the revolution," problems relative to "independent" international relations and the future role of the Armed Forces in formation of a "new Peru." Each volume is a compilation of quotes and speeches from a certain time period (v. 9, Jan. through July 1972; v. 10, Aug. through Dec. 1972; and v. 11, Jan. through July 1973).

7362 Verbitsky, Horacio. Prensa y poder en Perú. México, Extemporáneos, 1975. 182 p., tables (A pleno sol, 41)

Author studies how the press works by examining *El Comercio* and a select group of newspapers outside Lima. In his analysis of censorship, Verbitsky assumes the necessity of "taking from a small number of hands the immense power of dissemination of . . . dangerous ideas." Somewhat politically naive when speaking of Peru's "new democracy" but an interesting pro-censorship study.

7363 Villanueva, Víctor. EL CAEM y la revolución de la Fuerza Armada. Presentación de Julio Cotler. Lima, Instituto de Estudios Peruanos (IEP) [and] Campodónico Ediciones, 1972. 249 p., bibl.

Excellent study examines growth of CAEM (Center for Advanced Military Studies) from its founding in 1950 through the first years of the military government. Author stresses original intent in establishment of the Center by defining its ideological priorities: 1) national security and general welfare; 2) internal security; and 3) national power. All three concepts, however, were deeply influenced by the mostly civilian faculty employed at the Center. Includes description of new strategies called for by the Cuban revolution and skirmishes with the Peruvian oligarchy during the Prado Administration. The support

structures for CAEM in the 1968–71 period are clearly and dispassionately discussed.

7364 Webb, Richard Charles. Government policy and the distribution of income in Peru: 1963–1973. Cambridge, Mass., Harvard Univ. Press, 1977. 239 p., tables.

This work complements Kuczynski's study (see item **7338**). Webb presents a short but convincing analysis drawing on his experience as economic advisor to Belaúnde Terry. The problem, he believes, is not merely the gulf between the rich and poor, but the fact that the "middle classes" are the largest recipients of the benefits of Peruvian modernization. He notes, however, that these middle groups also bear the brunt of taxation. Webb suggests that more government money and planning must be transferred from urban to rural areas whose poor inhabitants must no longer be perceived as "objects of compassion" but as citizens with legal rights. Such a transfer, he believes, would lead to a more equitable distribution of national income. Provocative study.

7365 Zuzunaga Florez, Carlos *ed.* and *comp.* Liberalismo, desarrollismo y revolución. Lima, Editorial Universo, 1976. 290 p. (Serie Ensayos)

This compilation of legitimate conservative thought is aimed at what the editor-compiler concludes is a deficient revolutionary process. Although he believes in change he opts for one based on the Mexican "bloodless" (?) model, the sort which is not monopolized by the Armed Forces. Ideally, an effective and well organized combination of all national groups must work with the military (but presumably *not* in the corporatist sense).

BOLIVIA

7366 Almaraz Paz, Sergio and others. La violencia en Bolivia. La Paz, Editorial Los Amigos del Libro, 1976. 134 p., plates (Mini col. un siglo y medio)

General investigation of political violence, with special reference to Bolivia, which apportions the blame for it to: 1) a privileged, "culpable" Church; 2) Bolivian tradition; 3) inhumane treatment of labor (especially in the mines); 4) Bolivian racial characteristics (according to a La Paz psychiatrist); 5) the importation of a violent tradition from Southern Europe; and 6) themes of violence in the Bolivian novel. Revealing statements from a select elite of Bolivian professionals.

7367 Arauco, Fernando. La lucha del pueblo boliviano (UNAM/RMCPS, 21:82, oct./dic. 1975, p. 57–69)

Leftist critique of labor organization under the MNR (beginning 1952–53) extoling both present and past virtues of the Central Obrera Boliviana (COB).

7368 ———. Sobre la Central Obrera Boliviana (CP, 4, abril/junio 1975, p. 93–100)

Interview with Arauco traces development of "proletarian consciousness" and organization through the Central Obrera Boliviana (COB) after the Banzer coup (1971). Includes historical treatment of labor organizations since 1950 with particular emphasis on the 1952–53 MNR "revolutionary" experiment. As a spokesman for Bolivian organized labor, Arauco's position is stringently anti-Banzer.

7369 Banzer Suárez, Hugo. La revolución metalúrgica: objetivo y realidad del gobierno nacionalista. La Paz, Presidencia de la República, Secretaría de Prensa e Informaciones (SPI), 1976. 29 p.

President's proclamation of five-year development plan for regulation of minerals industry (in the interest of all Bolivians and not just for a "few wealthy families"). Interesting official statement in light of the abortive 1978 elections.

7370 Bolivia. Corte Suprema de Justicia. Sesquicentenario, 1827–16 de julio-1977. Sucre, Bol., 1977. 68 p., illus., map, plate, tables.

Government publication describing major shifts in development of the Supreme Court. Includes valuable Bolivian interpretation of original jurisdiction of Audiencia of Charcas as well as a descriptive statement of substantive and procedural areas of jurisdiction. Students of Chaco dispute should note p. 21–27. Written under "general supervision" of Secretary to President Banzer.

7371 Combo, Juan. Bolivia: bajo el modelo de Banzer (Controversia [Centro de Investigación y Educación Popular (CINEP), Bogotá] 55, 1977, p. 6–65, bibl., tables)

Pro-MNR, pro-Torres (anti-Barrientos and anti-Banzer) account of Bolivian labor development in face of the "siege of [US] imperialism." Sophisticated Leftist description of Banzer corporatist model for labor economics.

Dandler, Jorge. "Low classness" or wavering populism?: a peasant movement in Bolivia, 1952–1953. See *HLAS 40:3584*.

Domínguez, Jorge I. and **Christopher N. Mitchell.** The roads not taken: institutionalization and political parties in Cuba and Bolivia. See item **7194**.

7372 Font, Carlos. El movimiento, estudiantil lucha y se reorganiza en Bolivia (OCLAE, 5, 1978, p. 22–26, plates)

Account of student organization and action against Banzer regime from 1971–76. Indicating that most of the article's data comes from Havana's Continental Organization of Students (OCLAE), author describes Banzer regime in Cuban hyperbolic style as "German Hitlerian."

Gudmunson K., Lowell. El populismo y la integración de las clases obreras en Bolivia: 1952–1957. See *HLAS 49:3591*.

7372a Mitchell, Christopher N. The legacy of populism in Bolivia: from the MNR to military rule. N.Y., Praeger, 1977. 167 p., bibl., map (Praeger special studies in international politics and government)

Author posits that Bolivian "revolution" ceased being functional once it found its real support in the disenchanted middle class. Conservative control of middle class behavior caused all MNR programs to founder and set the stage for protective/preventive intervention by military on *behalf of the middle class* —a situation which will make it increasingly impossible for formation of broad-based populace and/or truely democratic coalitions. An important section gives conceptual statements concerning populism and the form(s) of Latin American populace movement.

7373 Saignes, Thierry and others. El país tranca: la burocratización de Bolivia. Introducción de Mariano Baptista Gumucio. La Paz, Editorial los Amigos del Libro, 1976. 95 p., illus., table (Col. Un siglo y medio)

Articles by various authors written to

demonstrate the insensitivity of the Bolivian bureaucracy (*tranca* meaning "boarded up" in the context of this volume). Includes case studies illustrating negative mass perception of government's performance. Interesting polemic.

7374 Sociedad Chilena de Defensa de la Tradición, Familia y Propiedad, *Bogotá.* La Iglesia del silencio en Chile: la TFP proclama la verdad entera. La Paz, Ediciones Cristiandad, 1977. 180 p., facsims., plates.

Attempt by the TFP to get its message across to the Bolivian readership. Consists of a special summary of materials found in the larger edition (see item **7308**).

7375 Viscarra Pando, Gonzalo. Prensa y país. La Paz, Editorial e Imprenta Crítica, 1977. 253 p.

Volume describes and evaluates present state of Bolivian media (radio, newspapers, and publishing in general) as well as those groups traditionally responsible for dissemination of news and quality of media coverage. Study traces theme from Independence through the Barrientos, Ovando and Torres regimes; promises sequel covering Banzer's policies. An excellent contribution to literature on Bolivian communications.

CHILE

Altamirano, Carlos. Diálectica de una derrota. See *HLAS 40:3609.*

7376 Um ano de fascismo no Chile. Tradução de Francisco de Melo. Lisboa, Editorial Estampa, 1974. 151 p., tables (Col. Praxis, 26)

Collection of Marxist statements translated for Portuguese readers denouncing the Pinochet government as a fascist conspiracy "against human rights," "democratic liberties" and Chilean traditions of military non-intervention. Includes appendices noting the number of prisoners held by the Junta (as of 1974), their occupational classifications with percentages, names of important individuals within the Chilean labor movement either assassinated or in prisons. An interesting leftist contribution to information—even if some of it is questionable—on the fate of the Chilean labor movement and its leadership.

7377 Arrate, Jorge. Apuntes para una autocrítica: ¿fué correcta la política de la izquierda chilena ante las fuerzas armadas? Barcelona, Agermanament, 1977. 28 p.

Study of attempts at "self-criticism" carried out at a conference of Marxist theoreticians held at the Univ. of Bologna (Italy, April 1977). Interesting example of Marxist behavior in the wake of UP's fall.

7378 Arriagada Herrera, Genaro and **Claudio Orrego Vicuña.** Leninismo y democracia: un debate a partir del caso chileno. Santiago, Ediciones Aconcagua, 1976. 214 p. (Col. Lautaro)

Symposium of articles by leading Marxist theoreticians. One of the more sophisticated contributions to the flow of post-UP debate.

7379 Atroshenko, A. The socio-economic "model" of Chilean fascism (IA, 2, Feb. 1978, p. 51–58)

Soviet author of pro-Allende study centers on negative critique of Milton Friedman's socio-economic stabilization model used during post-coup period. Interesting, if somewhat polemical, Marxist analysis of Pinochet's "monetarist" economic policy.

7380 Barros Charlín, Raymundo. Consideraciones sobre la integración latinoamericana en el siglo XIX, con particular referencia a la política en Chile. Santiago, Univ. de Chile, Depto. de Estudios Internacionales, 1975. 76 p. (Serie de publicaciones especiales, 8)

Historical study published by Pinochet government's Dept. of International Studies with special emphasis on Chile's role in Latin American integration planning during 1800s. Good reference from Chilean perspective.

7381 Bizzarro, Salvatore. Rigidity and restraint in Chile (CUH, 74:434, Feb. 1978, p. 66–69, 83)

After recounting repressive features of the Pinochet government, author optimistically predicts that pressures applied by former-President Frei and the Christian Democrats, US President Carter, the OAS, the UN, Amnesty International and the Chilean Church will lessen the harshness of the regime.

7382 Boorstein, Edward. Allende's Chile: an inside view. N.Y., International Publishers, 1977. 277 p.

Author is US economist and former advisor to Allende as well as member of Cuba's Ministry of Foreign Commerce. UP failure was due to "slow and cautious" movement by the government allowing massive opposition much time for organization. Moreover, the very weakness of the government which should have encouraged "intellectual boldness," led instead to factional disputes within the government and to wasted attempts to break up the Christian Democrats. In the end, "the forces of fascism prevailed."

Borón, Atilio Alberto. Notas sobre las raíces histórico-culturales de la movilización política en Chile. See *HLAS 40:3615.*

7383 Cantero, Manuel. Rolle und Charakter der äusseren Faktoren (Probleme des Friedens und des Sozialismus [Zeitschrift der kommunistischen und Arbeiterparteien. Dietz Verlag, Berlin, GDR] 20:8, 1977, p. 1047–1054)

East-German journal article analyzes foreign factors which affected the Chilean revolutionary process in 1977. [M. Kossok]

7384 Castillo Velasco, Jaime. Los caminos de la revolución. Santiago, Editorial del Pacífico [and] Instituto de Estudios Políticos (IEP), 1972. 436 p.

Philosophical essay on bases for "necessary dialogue" toward reestablishment of Christian Democracy in Chile. Fairly intensive treatment of concepts of democracy, liberal capitalism, and totalitarian collectivism. The "communitarian reply of Christianity in the twentieth century" and the "conflict of Christian humanism and Marxism" are the major themes of this study.

7385 Chile. Presidencia de la República. Comisión Nacional de la Reforma Administrativa (CONARA). Chile hacia un nuevo destino: su reforma administrativa integral y el proceso de regionalización. Santiago, 1976. 515 p., bibl., fold. maps, maps, plates, tables (Documento, 2)

First official report of the National Committee on Administrative Reform (CONARA). Physically massive, expensively produced volume with potential reference value. Published by the Office of the President (Pinochet).

7386 Chile: Klasskamp och stretegi, 1970–73. Stockholm, Förbundet Kommunist, 1974? 76 p. (Förbundet Kommunist's skriftserie, 6)

Booklet designed to explain to Swedish communists why the Popular Front strategy failed in Chile. Consists of one essay by the Organización Comunista de España Bandera Roja, and two others by members of Chile's MIR, an extremist group which opposed Allende's UP of coalition in favor of "armed struggle." [R.V. Shaw]

7387 Chile y su Presidente Augusto Pinochet Ugarte. Montevideo, Biblioteca del Poder Legislativo, 1976. 137 l., bibl., plates, tables.

Commemorative document by the Uruguayan Government includes biographical sketch of President Pinochet, the Junta's 11 Sept. 1973 statement on assumption of power and draft of Chilean-Uruguayan accord signed by Presidents Bordaberry and Pinochet. Includes other bilateral agreements. Of interest because of the relations between both military governments and their perceptions of their role.

7388 The Chilean Society for the Defense of Tradition, Family and Property, *Santiago.* The Church of silence in Chile. Cleveland, Ohio, Lumen Mariae Publications, 1976. 442 p., illus., plates.

This volume, a translation of original Chilean edition, is a broadside indictment of the Chilean Catholic hierarchy as the explicitly "silent" accomplice in Allende's coming to power in 1970. Most of the criticism is aimed at Cardinal Silva Henríquez who actively encouraged "Leftist-Catholic" ferment. Text also denounces former President Frei's "Christian-Socialist-Kerenskian" administration; Church's support of "Communist-Progressivism" as preparation for UP takeover; and the hierarchy's attempt to silence anti-Communist Catholics. Notes how the Church not only committed itself to the "moral and economic destruction of a Catholic nation," but acted "subversively" against the Junta after 1973 and continues to do so. The conclusion entitled "In Defense of the Church and the Country," states that TFP is the true representative of Chilean Christianity. An interesting if astonishing publication.

7389 Chinchilla, Norma Stoltz. Mobilizing women: revolution in the revolution

(LAP, 4:[15]4, Fall 1977, p. 83–102, bibl.)

What is the relationship between women's movements and class movements for revolutionary change? Author sees the necessity of a close relationship between the two and the need for a strategy of mobilization which includes issues of women's oppressions and societal inequalities. Most of the empirical examples are drawn from the case of Chile (1970–73) although the effort to develop a general theory leaves much to be answered about mobilizing women for revolutionary change. [D.W. Dent]

7390 Chonchol, Jacques. El sistema burocrático: instrumento y obstáculo en el proceso de reforma agraria chilena (CDAL, 15, 1977, p. 87–100)

Author argues that a "traditional" bureaucracy was, in the main, responsible for UP's failure at implementing a thorough agrarian reform. Problems lay in regime's inability to select qualified agents for agrarian transformation, individuals who could have interacted in a politically sensitive manner with peasant groups.

7391 Chronologie du Chile: septembre 1973-décembre 1976 (FDD/NED [Problèmes d'Amérique Latine, 45] 4421/4423, 21 oct. 1977, p. 21–52)

Extensive—almost daily—chronological treatment of Junta activity from Sept. 1973 through Dec. 1977. Of value for reference to dates and official actions.

7392 Corossacz, Anna ed. I mille giorni di Allende: l'azione del Governo di Unidad Popular in 125 documenti. Prefazione di Luciano Cafagna. Roma, Grafica Editrice Romana, 1975. 441 p. (Quaderni di mondoperaio. Nueva serie, 3)

Useful collection of documents, both official and unofficial, pertaining to the Allende government (1970–73). Supported by a glossary of terms and actors, and chronology. Very short introductory essays preface the 21 segments of the collection. [P.B. Taylor, Jr.]

7393 Corvalán, Luis. Revolution auf dem Weg des nichtbewaffnetan Kampfes: Wie er sich in unserem Lande gestaltete (Probleme des Friedens und des Sozialismus [Zeitschrift der kommunistischen und Arbeiterparteien. Dietz Verlag, Berlin, GDR] 21:1, 1978, p. 32–41)

Article by prominent Chilean Communist leader in an East German journal analyzes the causes of the UP defeat and weighs the prospects for the "vía pacífica" of the Chilean Revolution. [M. Kossok]

7394 Cuevas Ferrán, Gustavo. Cuando la rebelión es un derecho: el caso de Chile durante la UP. Introducción de Gisela von Muhlenbrock. Santiago, Univ. Católica de Chile, Instituto de Ciencia Política, 1976. 32 l. (Cuadernos, 5)

Author is Director of the Institute of Political Science and Professor of Constitutional Law at Catholic Univ. Discusses various criteria by which any democratic polity may rebel against constitutional authority. Similar to arguments in US Declaration of Independence's list of grievances against George III and John of Salisbury's justifications of "tyrannicide." A provocative piece of writing.

7395 Cusack, David F. Revolution and reaction: the internal dynamics of conflict and confrontation in Chile. Denver, Colo., Univ. of Denver, Graduate School of International Studies, 1977. 146 p., plates, tables (Monograph series in world affairs, 14. Studies in conflict issues in four troubled regions of today's world, 3)

Study of Chilean political development to time of the Allende regime (based on author's PhD dissertation). The UP's fall, according to Cusack, was not the result of US destabilization efforts but the consequence of more fundamental weaknesses and "internal contradictions" within Chilean society itself. During the period just before the coup and, after the events of 11 Sept. 1973, rationality and compromise as well as democratic sentiments were virtually non-existent in the country. Even the Junta looked about in "cautious shock" at what had been done. As for the author's perception of the US role, he contends that Washington "clearly placed world politics, anti-Communism, foreign investments, and balance of power over the defense and promotion of democracy." Provocative study by individual who lived in Chile from 1969 to 1974 doing research and teaching at Catholic Univ.

7396 Domic J., Juraj. Fundamentos de la praxis marxista-leninista en Chile. Santiago, Editorial Vaitea, 1977. 505 p., tables (Col. Ciencia política)

Detailed essay dealing with continued threat of Communism (equated with Marxist-Leninism) in Chile under Junta. An interesting statement touching the bases for development of Chilean Marxism, evolution of the UP under Allende and the continued existence of ideological and political threat of the Chilean Communist (*not* the Socialist) Party.

7397 ———. Participación de los trabajadores en el socialismo. Santiago, Editorial Vaitea, 1975. 55 p., tables (Col. Ciencia Política)

Author indicts the Chilean Church, the Soviet Union, and the Chilean Communist Party for being responsible for the crises of UP period. Specifically, Domic concerns himself with the use of Russian model for worker organization, asserting that it was inapplicable to the Chilean situation.

Donoso Letelier, Crescente. Notas sobre el origen, acatamiento y desgaste del régimen presidencial: 1925–1973. See *HLAS 40:3627.*

7398 **Drake, Paul W.** Corporatism and functionalism in modern Chilean politics (JLAS, 10:1, May 1978, p. 83–116)

Author traces two models of Chilean economic administration: 1) functionalism as practiced by sindicatos and gremios, and 2) corporatism (as general organic working of state and society). Distinction is made between "*natural*" and "*state*" corporatism; between *inclusionary* (quasi-populist) and *exclusionary* (repressive, "quasi-fascist") state corporatism. The exclusionary form is noted as apparent direction of Pinochet government. This study is a valuable, thoroughly documented, contribution to Southern European and Latin American political theory.

7399 **Enerstvedt, Regi Th.** and **Robert Feiring.** Chile og den frie Presse: *Aftenposten* og *Neues Deutschland*'s forhold til demokratiet og fascismen. Oslo, Univ. I Oslo, Instituttet for Sosiologi, 1975. 473 p., tables (Skriftserie, 30)

Norwegien sociologists present quantitative analysis of how two newspapers covered Chile's military coup: 1) the *Aftenposten* of Oslo (circulation: 201,476); and 2) the *Neues Deutschland* of East Germany (circulation: 100,000). Concludes that the East German paper gave much more space to events in Chile whereas the Norwegian paper

only increased coverage after Allende's assassination. [R.V. Shaw]

7400 **Favereau, Julio Retamal.** Le référendum chilean (NRDM, 5:12, mai 1978, p. 349–356)

The referendum of 4 Jan. 1978 was a significant demonstration (in its ratification of the Pinochet regime) of a desire to be free from international pressures. Nevertheless, it also consisted of a great deal of window dressing on the part of the Junta. Interesting study.

7401 **Fontaine A., Arturo** and others. Nuestro camino. Santiago, Ediciones Encina, 1976. 259 p.

Valuable collection of papers identifying the most crucial sources of support for the Armed Forces in the post-Allende period. Important contribution to the literature on contemporary Chilean political culture. Note especially the articles by Mac Hale and Domic.

7402 **Frei M., Eduardo.** América Latina: opción y esperanza. Barcelona, Editorial Pomaire, 1977. 299 p.

Former Chilean President describes Latin American society as plagued by two basic conflicts: 1) North American versus Latin value orientation, and 2) rich versus poor polarization accentuated by southern European influence in Latin America. Discusses how these conflicts are related to the "military industrial-complex" (in the words of Eisenhower) but does not suggest remedies. Study is most interesting in what it reflects of Frei's past and present attempts at theorizing.

7403 ———. El mandato de la historia y las exigencias del porvenir. Caracas, Ediciones Nueva Política, 1976. 106 p.

Concise statement of former Chilean President Frei's views in the post-Allende period. Value lies in potential for understanding recent Christian Democratic events as well as Frei's own political thinking.

7404 **Galjert, Benno.** Movilización campesina en América Latina (CEDLA/B, 12, junio 1972, p. 2–19, bibl.)

Using Chilean case study author generalizes on "functional" peasant mobilization. Basic conclusions focus on categorization according to labor type, land tenure system, power instruments of landholder class, educational opportunities and development levels of peasant political organizations. Novel but somewhat weak analysis due to heavy reliance on Chilean data for hemispheric generalization.

7405 Garreton M., Manuel Antonio. Continuidad y ruptura y vacío teórico ideológico: dos hipótesis sobre el proceso político chileno, 1970–1973 (UNAM/RMS, 39:4, oct./dic. 1977, p. 1289–1308)

The Frei administration failed to alter the Chilean tradition of capitalist "dependency" which excluded emerging middle sectors (both urban and rural). The incoming UP, however, was equally unable to reverse the trend but for different reasons: fragmentation of the Left combined with difficulties in total social and political reorganization. Interesting analysis.

7406 Greenfield, Michael G. Creating a climate of opinion: the *Los Angeles Times* and Salvador Allende (PCCLAS/P, 5, 1976, p. 57–68)

Author argues that the *Los Angeles Times* created a climate of apathy "in face of clear evidence" that the US government and powerful private groups were engaged in deliberate attempts to destabilize the Allende government. Intriguing study of an *uncontrolled* press' impact on public opinion and government policy (reverse structural-functionalism!)

7407 Guistet, Louis. Le Chile du Onze Septembre (FDD/NED [Problèmes d'Amérique Latine, 45] 4421/4423, 21 oct. 1977, p. 7–20, maps)

Chronological treatment of the Pinochet government (Sept. 1973 through Summer 1977) with biographical sketch of the President. Good reference on the regime and on personal background of Pinochet.

7408 Hackethal, Eberhard. Kreuzweg Chiles, Christen Kirche und Klassenkampf vor und nach dem Militärputsch. Berlin, GDR, Union Verlag, 1976. 189 p.

East German study analyzes the role of the Catholic Church in the political and social struggles of Chile, before and after the military coup of 1973. [M. Kossok]

7409 Heller Rouassant, Claude. Política de unidad en la Izquierda Chilena: 1956–1970. México, El Colegio de México, Centro de Estudios Internacionales, 1973. 144 p., bibl., tables (Jornadas, 73)

In study written before UP's fall, author notes that its greatest strength lies in its syndicalist beginning and broad "party development" of syndicates (a questionable assumption). Notes how UP's heterogeneity (in 1973) constituted both a great asset and a great weakness, especially in a constitutional-democratic setting. Perceives the most virulent factionalism as that of the Socialist Party. In hindsight, much of author's arguments appear to have been correct.

7410 Henfrey, Colin and **Bernardo Sorj** *eds.* Chilean voices: activists describe their experiences of the Popular Unity period. Atlantic Highlands, N.J., Humanities Press, 1977. 197 p., map, plates (Marxist theory and contemporary capitalism)

British author's assessment of UP through use of translated and edited recordings of interviews with Chilean exiles. Of interest to those who share the anti-US sentiments voiced by those interviewed or to those attracted by the method of data collection.

7411 Hinkelammert, Franz Josef. Ideología de sometimiento: la Iglesia Católica chilena frente al golpe, 1973–1974. San Juan, P.R., Editorial Universitaria Centro Americana (EDUCA), 1977. 176 p. (Col. DEI [Depto. Ecuménico de Investigaciones])

Historical study of the role of Catholic Church during the Allende regime. Volume explores the crucial position of Cardinal Silva Henríquez, Archbishop of Santiago, factionalism in the Chilean hierarchy and military threats to Silva. Author calls for return to democratic institutions.

Horowitz, Irving Louis *ed.* The rise and fall of Project Camelot: studies in the relationship between social science and practical politics. See *HLAS 40:3636.*

7412 Hudson, Rexford A. The role of the constitutional conflict over nationalization in the downfall of Salvador Allende (IAMEA, 31:4, Spring 1978, p. 63–79)

Author argues that Allende was far from "legalist" in dealing with constitutional issues and legislative procedure. In the case of "The Three Areas," author argues Allende proposed an anti-constitutionalist, opportunist stance.

7413 Huneeus, Pablo and others. Chile: el costo social de la dependencia ideológica. Santiago, Editorial del Pacífico [and] Instituto de Estudios Políticos (IDEP), 1973. 255 p.

Collection of papers by five university professors who argue that UP's failure and subsequent economic and political crises were result of superimposition of a foreign ideological model which was contrary to Chilean societal reality. An important contribution.

7414 Institut E. Vandervelde, *Brussels.* Le Front de la Gauche Chilienne. Brussels, 1974. 10 p. (Note de documentation, 13)

Statement by French Radical Party on the fall of UP and coming to power of "fascist" Pinochet. Interest lies in the leftist language employed by one of France's more pragmatic "centrist" parties. French Radical Party language notwithstanding, the Pinochet-Radical party gulf is wide.

7415 Insunza, Jorge. Wege der Revolution (Probleme des Friedens und des Sozialismus [Zeitschrift der kommunistischen und Arbeiter parteien, Dietz Verlag, Berlin, GDR] 20:5, 1977, p. 662–670)

East German article analyzes the possible routes for a future Chilean Revolution (e.g., the possibility of the peaceful route in view of internal and external factors, the army's role, class struggle, etc.). [M. Kossok]

7416 Kay, Cristóbal. Agrarian reform and the transition to socialism in Chile: 1970–1973 (JPS, 2:4, July 1975, p. 418–445, bibl.)

Author attributes failure of UP's Agrarian Reform and fall of peasant support in 1972 to deficiencies of the Allende regime in mobilization techniques, public administration and economic strategy. If "petty bourgeois" behavior had been stemmed by replacing private markets with those under strict state control (thus eliminating the black market and other "uncontrollables"), the peasant economy would not have expanded at the expense of the collective one.

7417 ———. Chile: the making of a coup d'état (SS, 39:1, Spring 1975, p. 3–25)

Analysis of the Sept. 1973 coup which blames both the forces of the right as well as deficient UP policy. A solid study. For historian's comment, see *HLAS 40:3639.*

7418 Kolm, Serge-Christophe. Chile-Portugal: vers une théorie des processus revolutionnaires modernes (AESC, 31:6, nov./déc. 1976, p. 1245–1261, tables)

Incisive comparative analysis of Chilean, Portuguese and French "revolutionary" (transitional) economic behavior in post-World War II period.

7419 Kudachkin, Mikhail Fedorovich and others. Chiliiskaia revoliutsiia: opyt i znachenie (The Chilean Revolution: experience and significance). Moscow, Izdatel'stvo politicheskoi literatury, 1977. 206 p.

Soviet study of Chile from Allende's victory in 1970 to his fall in 1973, based on authors' own experiences as well as on the literature. [R.V. Allen]

7420 Landsberger, Henry A. and **Tim Mac-Daniel.** Hypermobilization in Chile: 1970–1973 (PUCIS/WP, 28:4, July 1976, p. 502–541)

Authors attribute UP's failure at mass mobilization to "lack of spontaneity" and failure to make the experiment attractive. When mobilization occurred, it resulted in factionalism and diminished discipline especially where economic goals were at stake. Likewise, "hypermobilization" became so dynamic that groups were prone to exhaust themselves during the immediate phases of political activity. Provocative piece.

7421 Lehmann, David. Allende's Chile: the judgment of history and the verdict of foreign-Marxism (JDS, 14:2, Jan. 1978, p. 249–253)

Excellent review article of two recent volumes on the Allende regime: Philip O'Brien *ed. Allende's Chile* (N.Y., Praeger, 1976) and the Roxborough, O'Brien, and Roddick book *Chile: the state and revolution* (see *HLAS 39:7494*). To appreciate both works and to understand their strengths and weaknesses, Chileanists should take note of this brief but important essay.

7422 Leuchter, W. Zur Rolle der staatlichen Investitionspolitik im Rahmen der Strategie und Taktik der herrschenden Klassen Chiles in den fünfziger und sechziger Jahren (UR/L, Herbstsemester 1975, p. 49–57)

East German author examines state policies of investment during the administrations of President Ibáñez, Alessandri, and Frei. [M. Kossok]

7423 López Pintor, Rafael. Satisfacción en el trabajo y formalismo como fenómenos burocráticos: un análisis de actitudes en Chile (REOP, 44, abril/junio 1976, p. 101–145, tables)

This is one of the better statistical analyses of Chilean public opinion and should be carefully read by political behavior specialists in the US and Western Europe. It is rare to find such high quality in a quantitative analytic work.

7424 MacHale, Tomas P. Poder político y comunicación en Chile: marzo a setiembre de 1973. Santiago, Univ. Católica de Chile, Instituto de Ciencia Política, 1977. 70 l., tables (Cuadernos del Instituto de Ciencia Política, 14)

While author focuses on the last seven months before the coup, he acknowledges on final page (of 64 p. of text) the "subtle and covert suppression" of the communications media, without naming the Junta. Noteworthy statement by former editor of *El Mercurio*.

7425 Maldonado, Carlos. La Unidad Popular y el proceso cultural chileno (CAM, 36 [214]:5, sept./oct. 1977, p. 177–188)

Comparative study of artistic control during the UP and Pinochet periods. Pro-Allende in bias, author nevertheless gives an exhaustive coverage of Chilean music, theater and literature during the 1970–73 years.

7426 Marin, Gladys. Die Arbeiterklasses und ihre Bünd Bündnispolitik (Probleme des Friedens und des Sozialismus [Zeitschrift der kommunistischen und Arbeiterparteien, Dietz Verlag, Berlin, GDR] 20:7, 1977, p. 920–929)

East German article analyzes the policies of the Chilean Communist Party towards its allies during the UP Government and at present. [M. Kossok]

7427 Movimiento de Acción Popular Unitario (MAPU), *Santiago.* El primer año del Gobierno Popular [and] El segundo año del Gobierno Popular. With an introduction by Ben Hahm. Philadelphia, Pa., Institute for the Study of Human Issues (ISHI), 1977. 385 p. (Documentos of the Chilean road to socialism, 1/2)

Important volumes in that they investigate the roll of an important party in the Allende coalition, MAPU (Movement of United Popular Action). As a splinter party

originally part of the Christian Democratic organization, MAPU—while delivering few votes to the UP—was symbolic of the "revolution in liberty" sentiment that led so many intellectuals and students to adopt the Christian Democratic position in 1964. Author sees major contribution of the Party in its insistence that the UP was not really "foreign" or an "aberration," but firmly in the mainstream of Chilean democratic political thought. Important volume on role of former left-wing of Christian Democratic movement during the Allende years.

7428 Muhlenbrock, Julio von. La concepción de una nueva democracia para Chile. Santiago, Univ. Católica de Chile, 1976. 35 l. (Cuadernos del Instituto de Ciencia Política, 11)

Author walks the thin line between "reasonable" statements and proper deference to the Armed Forces government in calling for conditions within which Chilean democracy may be quickly revived. An exceptional study indicating brilliant political sensitivity.

7429 Nunn, Frederick M. Militares chilenos: desarrollo institucional; relaciones cívico-militares; consideraciones de política. Santiago, Univ. Católica de Chile, 1977. 19 l. (Cuadernos del Instituto de Ciencia Política, 13)

This paper was originally presented to the American Historical Association and is here translated and published by the Catholic Univ. of Chile. As usual, Nunn has presented cogent analysis of the conflicts between military corporatism and civilian democracy. For author's book on the subject, see *HLAS 40:3654.*

7430 Olivares B., Augusto. Reportero de la revolución. Prólogo de Hernán Uribe. n.p., n.p., 1974? 91 p.

Collection of articles written by Chilean journalist who died on 11 Sept. 1973, "by the side of Allende." Published as memorial to Olivares, his articles of June-Sept. 1973, are the most significant as are the details of Olivares' behavior on the day of his death described by Jorge Timossi (see item 7451). Whether fact or fiction the Timossi section together with the collection of Olivares' writings are of considerable interest.

7431 Organization of American States. Comisión Especial de Consulta sobre

Seguridad contra la Acción Subversiva del Comunismo Internacional (CECS). El proceso marxista-lenista en Chile: estudio preparado por la CECS en su vigésimo primero período de sesiones extraordinarias, 1974. Washington, 1974. 347 p., facsims., plates, tables (OEA/Ser.L/X/11.36)

Official statement of findings by OAS Special Council studying Allende Administration as threat to Hemispheric peace. Includes arguments that were given. Good reference.

Parra E., Ernesto and **Isabel Aguirrezábal T.** Suramérica 76: modelos militares de desarrollo. See item **7568.**

7432 Pike, Frederick B. Chilean local government and some reflections on dependence (IAMEA, 31:2, Autumn 1977, p. 63–70)

Basically a review essay of Arturo Valenzuela's *Political brokers in Chile: local government in a centralized polity* (see item **7454**). While the criticism is very positive, author has much to add from the historical perspective which clarify points raised in the study, especially those relating to internal Chilean client-patron relations.

7433 Pollack, Benny. The Chilean Socialist Party: prolegomena to its ideology and organization (JLAS, 10 [pt. 1] May 1978, p. 117–152, illus.)

Thorough analysis of the development of the Chilean Socialist Party in comparison with the Chilean Communist Party. Examines socialist autonomy relative to the CCP, experimentation with internal organization, its commitment to Marxism as a *general* orientation but *not* as dogma, and nationalism (the most compelling base for its anti-Soviet stance).

7434 Prats González, Carlos. Una vida por la legalidad. México, Fondo de Cultura Económica, 1976. 137 p. (Col. Popular, 162)

Autobiographical accounts of Prats' life during and immediately after the Allende period. Study would be of interest to those who perceive Prats' participation in the Marxist government as crucial in hastening the Sept. coup.

7435 Remmer, Karen L. Chile and the "peaceful" road to socialism (*in* Remmer, Karen L. and Gilbert W. Merkx *eds*. New

perspectives on Latin America [see *HLAS 39:7077*] p. 264–285, bibl., tables)

How did Allende come to power, what were his goals, how did he fail, and what was the strategy of UP? Author holds that strategy was the weakest link in the armor, and led to eventual failure—although the military was the obvious agent of that failure. The paper rejects some American leftist explanations and accounts as contrary to facts. [P.B. Taylor, Jr.]

7436 Rieben, Pierre. Chili: un an après le coup d'état. Lausanne, Switzerland, Editions CEDIPS, 1974. 110 p., tables.

Author is leftist French journalist who lived in Chile from March 1973 to April 1974, when he was arrested, imprisoned and tortured for not revealing his sources. Ultimately expelled from the country, he concludes that UP failure was due to general ineptitude and vastly diminished popular support. Notes that instead of engaging in real work, the UP devoted its energies to endless academic debate.

7437 Riz, Liliana de. La política agraria de la Unidad Popular y la lucha de clases en el campo (UNAM/RMS, 39:3, julio/sept. 1977, p. 873–884)

Marxist analysis of what author regards as Allende's failure to organize the rural peasantry. She assumes that the 1967 Agrarian Reform Law of the Christian Democrats—within which the "legalist" Allende was trapped—forced UP to attempt creation of a landless, "middle class," bourgeois grouping of farmers instead of a rural proletariat. Hence, author feels "socialist reconstruction" became impossible.

7438 Rodríguez, Abelandia. El papel de los medios masivos en la política cultural de la Junta Militar Chilena (CYC, 4, 1975, p. 15–53)

Excellent reference article on Pinochet Junta's suppression of cultural media which did not conform to official policy. Author favors the regulatory policies of the Allende period.

7439 Rodríguez Grez, Pablo. ¿Democracia liberal o democracia orgánica? Santiago, Univ. Católica de Chile, Instituto de Ciencia Política, 1977. 27 l. (Cuadernos del Instituto de Ciencia Política, 12)

Author's statement of preference for organic-corporatist "democracy" is so provocative one wonders whether he offers it "tongue in cheek."

7440 Rybácek-Mlýnková, Jirina comp. Chile under Allende: a bibliographical survey (CLAPCS/AL, 17, 1976, p. 32–69, bibl.)

Dispassionate bibliographical essay divided into appropriate topics according to the author's functional interpretation of the 1970–73 Allende experiment. A finely-honed reference work.

7441 Salvadori, Roberto Giuliano. Il Cile nell a pubblicistica e negli studi italiani (Annali della Fondazione Luigi Einaudi [Torino, Italy] 9, 1975, p. 217–282, bibl.)

Excellent critical analysis of the existing bibliography in Italian on the evolution of Chilean society, politics, and economics. [M. Carmagnani]

7442 Sánchez, Roberto. Las capas medias y la coyuntura política actual en Chile (NSO, 15, nov./dic. 1974, p. 52–67, tables)

Author attempts to analyze the role of Chile's middle groups during the Allende and Pinochet periods. Useful if at times confusing study which is one of the few to focus on the middle sectors "outside" the Marxist context.

7443 Sigmund, Paul E. The overthrow of Allende and the politics of Chile: 1964–1976. Pittsburgh, Pa., Univ. of Pittsburgh Press, 1977. 326 p., plates, tables.

Sigmund's list of factors causing fall of UP include: 1) Allende's realization that he was not President of all Chileans—a "class-oriented Marxism" being the real ideological and political basis for policy; 2) UP's attempt at fundamental change through democratic structures; 3) printing of money which produced inflation and severe economic crises; and 4) various severe internal problems which caused the Allende regime to collapse from within. "External forces:" namely, the CIA, ITT, Cuban and Russian influence were *not* crucial in UP failure but only exacerbated other *internal efforts* at destabilization. Author concludes that constitutional and democratic traditions deterred the military from intervention until all legal means were exhausted. The Chilean Congress, Supreme Court and bureaucracy "practically invited" the military to take power in a hopeless situation.

7444 Silva Henríquez, Raúl. El pensamiento social del Cardenal . . . [Edited by] Louis Antonio Díaz H. Prólogo de Joseph L. Bernardin. n.p., n.p., 1976. 268 p., facsim., plates.

Socioeconomic and political orientation of Cardinal Archbishop Silva of Santiago presented in excerpts from letters and speeches. Interesting source for those looking for data on the controversial "supporter" of Allende and UP. Compilation made by a priest close to the Cardinal.

7445 Soto, Francisco. Fascismo y Opus Dei en Chile: estudios de literatura e ideología. Barcelona, Editorial Avance, 1976. 260 p. (Textos de apoyo, 15)

Poetry, textbooks, and children's literature are subjected to author's analysis to determine the presence of "Hispanic authoritarianism" in Chilean culture, the extent of Opus Dei ideology coming from Spanish writers, and idealization of fascist syndicalism/corporatism.

7446 Stallings, Barbara. Class conflict and economic development in Chile: 1958–1973. Stanford, Calif., Stanford Univ. Press, 1978. 295 p., tables.

In the comparative study of three Chilean regimes (Alessandri, Frei and Allende) author notes that in failing to modify the country's Keynesian economics to stress *supply* and deemphasize demand, crises were inevitable for the three governments. All three lacked sufficient planning and project implementation structures to bring about increases in "collective" (vs. private) consumption. While the US government and the American private sector (ITT) were instrumental in bringing about the UP downfall, they should be described more accurately as tools of the Chilean national bourgeoisie who had everything to lose by a completion of the six-year Allende term. Analysis is complex and provocative but also very important for Chileanists of all disciplines and ideological tendencies.

7447 Steenland, Kyle. Agrarian reform under Allende: peasant revolt in the south. Albuquerque, Univ. of New Mexico Press, 1977. 241 p., bibl., maps, tables.

On the scene report of case study in expropriation and agrarian reform on a southern Chilean farm in Cautín prov. Analysis based on personal interviews and observation.

7448 Symposium sobre la Transición al Socialismo y la Experiencia Chilena, Santiago?, 1971. Transición al socialismo y experiencia chilena. Presentación de Roberto Pizarro and Manuel Antonio Garreton M. B.A., Rodolfo Alonso Editor, 1974. 332 p. (Col. Argumentos latinoamericanos)

Papers by leading Marxist thinkers from 1971 conference held at the Univ. of Chile. Issues touched are: 1) legality, democracy, and institutional arrangements (especially those for the Judiciary); 2) the dilemmas of Chilean economics; and 3) agrarian reform and peasant participation—all three within the context of the state's "anarchic" apparatus. Excellent Marxist discussion before the 1973 coup.

7449 Tapia Videla, Jorge I. The Chilean Presidency in a developmental perspective (UM/JIAS, 19:4, 1977, p. 451–481, bibl.)

According to author the "weak" Chilean Presidency is the result of "preoccupation with political philosophy," too rigid a boundary maintenance between President and Congress, commitment to parliamentary democracy (albeit corporatist in nature) and enhancement of pluralism by the 1925 Constitution. After analyzing the Frei and Allende administrations, author concludes that the 1973 crisis was unavoidable owing to constitutional peculiarities in the system.

7450 ——— and Luis Quirós Varela. Cambio político y la elección parlamentaria de marzo de 1973: antecedentes de una elección crítica-límite. Santiago, Univ. Católica de Chile, Instituto de Ciencia Política, 1974. 96 p., tables (Serie documentos de trabajo, 4:2)

Important analysis of major factors influencing the parliamentary elections of March 1973.

7451 Timossi, Jorge. Grandes alamedas: el combate del Presidente Allende. La Habana, Instituto Cubano del Libro, Editorial de Ciencias Sociales, 1974. 242 p., map, plates (Ediciones políticas)

Fragmentary notes taken by a close aide during the last weeks of Allende's (and UP's)

life. Interest lies in possible insights into the President's personal life-style, especially during the last months of Aug. and Sept. 1973.

7452 Universidad de Chile, Santiago. **Departamento de Derecho del Estado y de los Organismos Públicos.** ¿Crisis de la democracia?: conferencias de derecho público 1974. Santiago, Ediciones Revista de Derecho Público, 1975. 236 p., illus., tables.

Compendium of 10 papers by pro-Junta professors of law at the National Univ. originally presented at government-sponsored conference on the subject of democracy. Stress is on difficulties in definition of concept and democracy's unworkability in various situations such as the French Third and Fourth Republics. Calling past Chilean democratic experience a "pretense," the general thrust of collection may be inferred from the title of the first paper: "Why Democracy?: a Final View."

7453 Uroki Chili (The lessons of Chile). Moscow, Izdatel'stov "Nauka," 1977. 408 p.

Soviet study sponsored by the Institute of the International Workers' Movement of the Academy of Sciences of the USSR. Consists of essays by several authors on events in Chile 1970–73, including themes such as the role of the Communist movement, the attitude of the Church and of other parties, tactics of the "counter-revolution," and the continuing struggle against oppression in Chile. Includes detailed chronology of events up to the death of President Allende. [R.V. Allen]

7454 Valenzuela, Arturo. Political brokers in Chile: local government in a centralized polity. Durham, N.C., Duke University Press, 1977. 272 p., bibl., tables.

Study based on field research (1969) focuses on local officials—most importantly mayors—as prime linkages providing cohesion in a fragmented polity of many parties, factions and socioeconomic sectionalisms. The Chilean people are seen as recipients of demanded goods and services only in so far as they utilize the intricate network of local client-patron structures. Sub-system dominance is indicated in relation to the national bureaucracy and Congress. Provocative and novel study. For Frederick B. Pike's discussion of this work, see item **7432**.

7455 ———. Political participation, agriculture, and literacy: communal versus provincial voting patterns in Chile (LARR, 21:1, 1977, p. 105–114, tables)

From analysis of aggregative data, the author presents tentative conclusions that the rural participant in Chilean politics has a *lower* propensity to vote in predominantly rural areas while in urban settings he is more apt to vote and, in general, participate in political process. Author promises more data to strengthen these interesting propositions.

7456 Villanueva, Víctor. Modelo contrarevolucionario chileno. Lima, Editorial Horizonte, 1976. 199 p., bibl.

Peruvian Marxist presents possibilities for the overthrow of Pinochet government by the Chilean Left. Naively optimistic in tone but with sections giving a solid historical analysis—from the Marxist perspective—of the development of 20th-century Chilean military and its ideological determination to crush the Allende regime.

7457 Vuscovic, Pedro and others. El golpe de estado en Chile. Presentación de Víctor Flores Olea. México, UNAM, Facultad de Ciencias Políticas y Sociales, Centro de Estudios Latinoamericanos [and] Fondo de Cultura Económica, 1975. 324 p., tables (Col. Popular, 140)

Collection of papers by faculty and research staff at the UNAM which, in addition to naming reasons for UP collapse, also stress leftist factionalism (mainly in the universities) and political repression against intellectuals.

7458 Wetch, Chris. Introduction to Chile: a cartoon history. Illustrations by Chris Wetch. Text by Larry Wright and A. Mago. London, Bolivar Publications, 1976. 1 v. (Unpaged) facsim., illus., map, plates.

Recent Chilean political history "captured" in cartoon form. British compiler refers to various pro-Chile organizations (all leftist or neo-Marxist). Author's obvious leftist bias must be assumed by the reader who is likely to find the material interesting if a bit infantile.

7459 Williams, Lee H., Jr. *comp.* The Allende years: a union list of chilean imprints, 1970–1973, in selected North American libraries, with a supplemental holdings list of books published elsewhere for the same period by Chileans or about Chile or Chileans. Boston, Mass., G. K. Hall, 1977. 339 p.

Important single-volume bibliographic reference source. For bibliographer's comment, see *HLAS 39:12.*

7460 Zeitlin, Maurice; W. Lawrence Neuman; and **Richard Earl Ratcliff.** Class segments: agrarian property and political leadership in the capitalist class of Chile (ASA/ASR, 41:6, Dec. 1976, p. 1006–1029, bibl., tables)

Study focuses on representation function among dominant groups of Chilean "capitalist class." Specifically, authors ask *who* in this grouping, or segments of it, seek governmental positions through political party organizations? Authors find that representatives of large landholding interests are more likely to seek national political office(s) than are urban executives (even if their family/oligarchic groups hold power in both urban and rural enterprises).

SOUTH AMERICA: EAST COAST
Argentina, Brazil, Paraguay, Uruguay, and Venezuela

PHILIP B. TAYLOR, JR., *Professor of Political Science, University of Houston*

IN THIS BIENNIUM AS IN THE LAST ONE there is virtually no serious literature on one of the countries covered in this section, Paraguay. There is very little from a second, Uruguay, and less than in the past from a third, Venezuela. Argentina and Brazil are well-represented by both national and foreign writers among which European authors and institutes contribute useful additional materials.

The majority of Uruguay's publications have been put out by the fascist regime. Former President Bordaberry's betrayal is chronicled in his own words (item **7597**). The armed forces contribute a huge and rather frightening volume which attempts to justify their behavior in the 1970s (item **7611**). Several writers based in Mexico apply a dependency analysis although reputable Uruguayan leftist scholars have argued against the appropriateness of such an analysis (see *HLAS 37:8620*). Possibly the most interesting work is a piece by the octagenarian durable Dr. Demicheli (item **7598**), who considers the future from the vantage point of six decades of experience.

Several excellent pieces from Venezuela should be mentioned. Brewer-Carías and Izquierdo's essays on the decentralization of public administration (item **7616**). Asociación Pro-Venezuela, a right-nationalist business organization of substantial influence, is described in much detail by its prime mover: Cervini (item **7614**). Rangel leads a discussion group of important spokesmen of differing views who offer a lively debate on the armed forces (item **7633**).

The literature on Argentina is useful and provoking. Granted the country's dismal and worsening civil liberties record, one wonders how much could have been said. Most of the following pieces were published outside the country, although a critique of the media as biased reported in the López Rega affair is published in-country by Schmucler and Zires (item **7501**). Out of country papers include: Newton (item **7497**); Schoultz (items **7502** and **7503**); Rivera Echénique (item **7500**); and O'Donnell (item **7498**). Finally, a separate but related work by Wynia (item **7508**) marks the appearance in the literature of comparative politics of a most promising scholar whose excellent writing style is a boon as well.

The literature on Brazil easily leads in both volume and quality. Much of it also was published in-country. Coelho on the army's self-image (item **7528**); Fleischer on political recruitment (item **7536**); Queiroz on local authority structures (item **7573**); Martins on state capitalism (item **7559**), Durandin and Oliveira on national security doctrine (items **7531** and **7566**); and Frederico on workers' attitudes (item **7541**) all deserve mention. Among foreign scholars the best are Dulles with another monumental biography (item **7530**); Flynn with a major broad-gauge country analysis (item **7538**); Graham (item **7545**); and Erickson (item **7533**) with distinguished monographs.

Although much of the literature is still traditional in style, many works are supported by the tauter conceptualization available through comparative methods and contemporary mathematical modeling and processing.

This contributor concludes 22 years' association with the *Handbook* with his contribution to this volume. While *pensadores* still publish throughout the hemisphere (some having found a fashionable and inferentially militant genre in *dependencia*) the generational change in Latin American universities that began in the 1960s now produces regularly more insightful, perceptive and careful studies. The qualitative and quantitative improvement in the US is also notable. In Europe, however, few institutes and scholars in Europe have attained this level. The coming of age of literature on Latin America can be attributed to scholarly competition, based on the substantial change in the environment fostered by professional organizations such as the Latin American Studies Association, and to the ever-increasing number of active researchers.

It is therefore likely that, with the passage of time, the literature on Latin American government and politics will attain the level of sophistication and the wealth of specialization that is characteristic of western European bibliographies today.

ARGENTINA

Agosti, Héctor Pablo. Prosa política. See *HLAS 40:3675*.

7461 Allub, Leopoldo. Estado y sociedad civil: patrón de emergencia y desarrollo del Estado Argentino. México, Colegio de México, Centro de Estudios Sociológicos (CES), 1974. 85 p., tables (Cuadernos, 6)

Brief essay reexamines the history of economic development in Argentina. Argues from the base of a model postulating that the early constitutional structure of a country can hamper or encourage later establishment of democratic use of political power. In Argentina, a pluralistic society, the development of autonomies did not occur primarily because of the combination of a Buenos Aires-based dependent capitalist system and the rise of a centralizing bureaucracy. Although this made the unification of Argentina possible, it also limited the state's freedom to act as mediator of conflicts arising from external economic influences upon the society. The analysis is supported by a number of statistical tables.

7462 Apuntes del Peronismo Auténtico. B.A.?, Ediciones del Peronismo Auténtico, 1975. 46 p., facsims., map, plates.

Political recounting of events 1973–75, dwells on a theme of betrayal by malefactors rather than on the effects of change and decay. The material is presented in short propagandistic statements, with many photographs of events and personalities.

7463 Argentina. Congreso de la Nación. Oficina de Información Parlamentaria. Síntesis periodística. B. A., 1976. 413 p., illus., tables.

A log of all news stories in newspapers of the Federal District for the period Jan./March 1975 (Año 2, No. 5), prepared in the Office of Parliamentary Information. Some items are synthesized in about five lines; in a few cases they are printed entirely. The criteria are not stated. A useful index of stories, but arranged *only* chronologically.

Argentine: chronologie de la Présidence de Perón; la prise du pouvoir par la Junte Militaire, chronique du coup d'etat, 24–31 mars 1976. See *HLAS 40:3689*.

7464 Badeni, Gregorio *ed.* Constitución de la Nación Argentina. B.A., Editorial Plus Ultra, 1976. 61 p.

A new edition, useful for its indication of sections amended by the Estatuto Fundamental of 24 Aug. 1972, which makes a large number of changes, some of major importance.

7465 Bartolomé, Leopoldo J. Populismo y diferenciación social agraria: las ligas agrarias en Misiones, Argentina (UTIEH/C, 28, 1977, p. 141–168, bibl., tables)

Vigorous agrarian movements have appeared in the northern Argentine provinces in the 1970s. The paper describes the principal characteristics of this mobilization in Misiones, and explains them as part of the process of social differentiation occurring in the agrarian structure of the provinces. Author examines the socio-political nature of the movement as well as processes contributing to its alliance, mobilization, opposition and splintering. Study employs census data (1969 national farm census) for a number of useful statistical measurements for 17 depts. of the prov.

7466 Beinstein, Jorge. Argentina: dependent capitalism (Social Thought and Practice [Belgrade, Yugoslavia] 16:12, Dec. 1976, p. 103–116)

Marxist analysis, published in Yugoslav journal, of how Peron ruined a relatively affluent and smug bourgeois capitalist society in two installments. In the broader sense, of course, the writer is demonstrating that dependent capitalism is always the handmaiden of tyranny.

7467 Camilion, Oscar. Realidad política y actividad política (*in* Cultura Nacional. B.A., Ediciones Crisol, 1976, p. 241–272)

Author discusses how politics contributed to the formation of a unique national culture—in all its multiform characteristics. His chapter interprets political history (of Argentina) in terms of this thesis, i.e., organization, leadership, urban-rural distinctions, etc. He discusses their effects on style and behavior, but not in any systematic social science sense.

7468 Cantón, Darío and **Jorge R. Jorrat.** Occupation and vote in urban Argentina: the March 1973 presidential election (LARR, 13:1, 1978, p. 146–157, tables)

Research note from data collected on the occasion of elections in the cities of B. A., Rosario, La Matanza, Córdoba, and Tucumán. The method of the study is briefly stated and findings reported. Many tables support the latter.

7469 *Carta Política*. Informe político, económico cultural, internacional. Persona a Persona, S.A. No. 46, agosto 1977– . B.A.

High quality monthly news magazine. Half of each issue is usually devoted to long, descriptive and analytical articles. Also includes shorter pieces on Argentina's economy, national defense, scientific and cultural developments.

7470 Casares, Manuel. Dopo Perón: guerra civile. Milan, Italy, Sapere Edizioni, 1974. 96 p. (Materiali nuovi, 12)

Italian Marxist analyzes Perón's legacy to Argentina which the author regards as ambivalent and destructive of democratic problem-solving. He considers Perón a front for capitalism and its allies, although in his absence much confusion arose.

7471 Ciria, Alberto. Argentina at the crossroads (UM/JIAS, 20:2, May 1978, p. 211–220)

Useful review essay which discusses five recent books on Argentina: 1) Jeane J. Kirkpatrick's *Leader and vanguard in mass society: a study of Peronist Argentina* (see *HLAS 35:7959*); 2) Donald C. Hodges' *Argentina 1943–1976: the national revolution and resistance* (see item **7485** and *HLAS 40:3782*); 3) Mark Falcoff and Ronald H. Dolkart eds. *Prologue to Perón: Argentina in depression and war* (see *HLAS 39:7657*); 4) David Rock's *Politics in Argentina, 1890– 1930* (see *HLAS 38:3830*); and 5) also by Rock *Argentina in the twentieth century* (see *HLAS 38:3831*).

7472 Cirino, Julio Alberto. Argentina frente a la guerra marxista: análisis y causas de un largo conflicto. B.A., Editorial Rioplatense, 1974. 167 p., bibl.

Author is more concerned with description and analysis of guerrilla warfare ("Marxist" by definition) than with a simple description of the situation in Argentina. An interesting traditionalist and conservative examination, but one that does not suggest much that is new for the specialist.

7473 *Croissance des Jeunes Nations*. Georges Hourdin, ed. No. 196, juin 1978– . Paris.

Issue contains eight pieces supporting the lead editorial's title "Argentina in 1978: Return to Barbarism." Other papers refer to non-Latin American topics.

7474 Dorrego, Alejandro and **Victoria Azurduy** eds. El caso argentino: hablan sus protagonistas. B.A., Editorial Prisma, 1977. 313 p., tables (Serie América Latina: los actores)

Consists of 11 extended interviews by the two editors with persons who played significant roles as political activists, most of them forced into exile by governmental pursuit or about such persons after their deaths. The collection sheds much light on the Argentine version of revolutionary politics against a repressive regime.

7475 Dowie, Mark. The general and the children (Mother Jones [Foundation for National Progress, San Francisco, Calif.] 3:6, July 1978, p. 37–40, 42, 46–48, plates)

A highly detailed report of Argentine official torture and murder: the experience of the Santucho family of Santiago del Estero prov. Santucho was the leader of the ERP guerrilla faction.

7476 Dulevich, José Miguel. Caos social y crisis cívica: hacia la formación de un Partido Nacional. B.A., Artes Gráficas Bartolomé U. Chiesino, 1975. 125 p.

Participating founder of the Partido Demócrata Nacional in 1931, the author writes of the country's continuing need for such a party. His conservative viewpoint is amply expressed in a piece reflective of a lifetime of modest activism.

7477 Ferré, Dominique. Le Péronisme: un passé en quête de futur (UHB/EHA, 10, 1975, p. 83–100)

Written for French readers who consider *peronismo* an enigma as well as fascist. There is a dearth of information available in the French language. Author seeks the movement's roots and central ideas in the period 1943–55, and cites among other things the central decree-laws as well as the propaganda levelled by peronists and anti-peronists. The article is useful for general readers as well as specialists.

7478 Floria, Carlos A. and **Marcelo Montserrat** eds. Pensar la república. B.A., Fundación Piñero Pacheco, 1977. 476 p., bibl., tables.

Consists of 28 essays commissioned by the publishing foundation who asked 29 authors to think about the (Argentine) republic. The editors include brief biographical notes about each author. A provocative volume whose writers were selected on the basis of intellectual ability and not because of their opinions.

7479 Frigerio, Rogelio. La crisis argentina: sus causas, los responsables, sus soluciones. B.A., Movimiento de Integración y Desarrollo (MID), Juventud Nacional, 1975. 24 p.

A former government official examines the country's economic problems, and offers solutions, in a collection of previously-published newspaper articles.

7480 Frischknecht, Federico. Gobierno. B.A., Editorial Pleamar, 1976. 109 p., bibl.

Professor of Business Administration, who served as Secretary of the Presidency in the Onganía government, applies administrative criteria to governmental organization and behavior. There is relatively little of politics in this and much of the rules and uses of administrative power.

7481 Frondizi, Arturo. El movimiento nacional: fundamentos de su estrategia. B.A., Editorial Losada, 1975. 180 p. (Cristal del tiempo)

Former Argentine President Frondizi writes a methodologically and strategically-oriented manual for party leaders. How shall Argentine reality be interpreted at this time in light of changing attitudes within the movement? What techniques and criteria shall be applied to research and interpretation?

7482 Gabancho, Abelardo F. Hacia la conciencia nacional. Prólogo de Raúl Carlos Migone. B.A., Movimiento de Superación Nacional, 1976. 158 p.

Humanistic—rather than religious—tract, directed toward the renewal of conscience and responsibility, this small volume hopes to establish a new commitment to an Argentine "social renaissance." Includes some comparative materials (e.g., the case of contemporary Catalan nationalists).

7483 García Costa, Víctor O. Un capítulo de una negra historia: la CIADE. B.A., Ediciones FE.SO.PO.CA., 1975. 59 p., bibl. (Libritos del militante, 3)

Socialist party reactions to the announcement that CIADE (Compañía Italo-Argentina de Electricidad) will be nationalized. An historical recounting (of both the company and the party's claims against it) is followed by warnings of how the government's intent had been misdirected.

7484 Guevara, Juan Francisco. Proyecto XXI: mañana se hace hoy. B.A., Editorial Ancora, 1975. 238 p.

Personal interpretations and conclusions concerning Argentina's past and present, and needs for the future—if present (i.e., 1975) chaos is to be ended. This is largely a thoughtful and moderate conservative's thoughts and prescriptions.

7485 Hodges, Donald C. Argentina, 1943–1976: the national revolution and resistance. Albuquerque, Univ. of New Mexico Press, 1976. 206 p., bibl., table.

This is a detailed account of the partisan political events of the indicated period which also seeks to propose the Argentine peronist revolutionary model, with its antimilitarist and populist/labor characteristics, as useful for the Latin American region as a whole. The author has an extended personal record of Marxist activism, in both Argentina and the outside world, and the thrust of the work reflects this position. For historian's comment, see *HLAS 40:3782.*

7486 Imaz, José Luis de and others. La Argentina posible. Introducción de Avelino José Porto. B.A., Editorial de Belgrano para la Educación, la Ciencia y la Tecnología, 1976. 335 p., tables (Cátedra del pensamiento argentino)

Consists of 28 short papers presented during the meetings of the "Cátedra del Pensamiento Argentino," held in 1976 by the Univ. de Belgrano. The book also includes questions put to the writers by the series moderator, Emilio Stevanovitch. The papers cover the entire range of contemporary Argentine issues in concise and useful form. This is a valuable work for a general reader.

7487 James, Daniel. The peronist left, 1955–1975 (JLAS, 8:2, Nov. 1976, p. 273–296)

A useful sorting out of groups and forces. The known events, in which the country fell into an irregular civil war, are explicable in part as a result of this paper. For historian's review, see *HLAS 40:3789*.

7488 ———. Power and politics in peronist trade unions (UM/JIAS, 20:1, Feb. 1978, p. 3–36)

Focusing on peronist unions in the period while Perón was out of the country (1955–1973) the paper discusses leadership toward power goals (both internal and on the national political scene) rather than toward economic goals. Data are introduced throughout in much detail, but the principal contribution is an attempt to develop an explanatory framework for the formation of oligarchic leadership.

Jelin, Elizabeth. Conflictos laborales en la Argentina: 1973–1976. See *HLAS 40:3792*.

———. Spontanéité et organisation dans le mouvement ouvrier: le cas de l'Argentine, du Brésil, et du Mexique. See *HLAS 40:3793*.

7489 Joes, Anthony James. Fascism in the contemporary world: ideology, evolution, resurgence. Foreword by A. James Gregor. Boulder, Colo., Westview Press, 1978. 238 p., bibl. (A Westview special study)

Comparative and theoretical examination of fascism compares ten countries (including Argentina, Brazil and Peru), and theoretically seeks a definition of "fascism" that is relevant to initiating socio-political system characteristics in late-developing countries. Since several examples are European, the work is not confined to the Third World. But the author expects that other Third World examples will develop with time. The virtue of the author's general concept notwithstanding, his Latin American examples are quite superficial.

Kohl, James and **John Litt.** Urban guerrilla warfare in Latin America. See item **7035**.

7490 Kratochwil, G. *comp.* Probleme der argentinischen Gegenwart. Hamburg, FRG, Institut für Iberoamerika-Kunde, 1976. 130 p., bibl. (Arbeitsunterlagen und Diskussionsbeiträge, 3)

Papers delivered by D. Boris, P. Hiedl, O. Bayer, and D. Reichardt at meeting held in Hamburg's Institute of Ibero-American Studies on Argentina's political situation. Discussion covers history, Peronista movement, unions, guerrilla movement, the military, economy, etc. Authors conclude that Argen-

tina's future looks unpredictable and confusing. [R.V. Shaw]

7491 Lanusse, Alejandro A. Mi testimonio. B.A., Lasserre Editores, 1977. 34 p. " . . . This is how I see my self in the mirror" observes the writer, who was for a period a military President of Argentina. A useful first person account of events to his taking of power, and during his regime.

7492 Lázara, Alberto Simón. Cultura de la dependencia a la censura. Prólogo de Jorge Selser. Introducción de Octavio Getino. B.A.?, Centro de Estudios del Socialismo Nacional (CESN), 1973? 42 p.

Discusses censorship of film in Argentina, principally in B.A. It is argued that censorship imposed becomes an end in itself. The short statement includes much data on actual censorship practice, institutions, and effects on the national culture. Also records effort of the Socialist Party delegation in 1973 in Congress to change both policy and institutions.

7493 Llorente, Ignacio. Alianzas políticas en el surgimiento del peronismo: el caso de la provincia de Buenos Aires (IDES/DE, 17:65, abril/junio 1977, p. 61–88, tables)

Author focuses on the 1944–46 period and disregards argument that the indifference of traditional parties to newly-available majorities in B.A. made them available for mobilization. Author emphasizes voting behavior in 1946 and on the basis of this data he concludes that the rise of peronismo, at least in the province, is a more complex phenomenon than ordinarily believed. The paper is a significant contribution to the literature.

7494 Merkx, Gilbert W. Charisma in Latin American politics: some general comments and the case of Juan Domingo Perón (*in* Remmer, Karen L. and Gilbert W. Merkx *eds.* New perspectives on Latin America [see *HLAS 39:7077*] p. 164–181)

Author rephrases Weber's term *charisma*, and measures its applicability to Latin American political leadership, particularly in the case of Perón. After using him as an illustrative case, author determines that Weber's definition is, indeed, appropriate. The paper concludes by applying several of Weber's generalizations, and holds that charismatic leaders appear throughout Latin American history.

Molina, Carlos A. and **Emilio A. García Méndez.** El imperialismo y los "enemigos buenos:" Alvear, Lonardi, Frondizi. See *HLAS 40:3816.*

7495 Movimiento de Integración y Desarrollo (MID), *Argentina.* Comité de la Capital Federal ¿Qué es y qué piensa el desarrollismo? B.A., 1974? 24 p., illus.

Consists of proposal for the formation of a new party and a National Front in order to achieve development of the country and true national liberation.

Navarro, Marysa. The case of Eva Perón. See *HLAS 40:3820.*

7496 Neustadt, Bernardo. La Argentina y los argentinos. B.A., Emecé Editores, 1976. 403 p.

Transcript of some 80 television interviews, (Monday night programming, 1975–76) with 132 persons, including 74 from the government, 35 opposed to it, and 23 neutrals. As the interviewer Neustadt observes, this work may not be a "book" but it presents Argentine life and politics as it was at the time. The program was shut off by Executive Decree in early 1976.

7497 Newton, Ronald C. Social change, cultural crisis and the origins of Nazism within the German-speaking community of Buenos Aires (NS, 1:1/2, 1976, p. 62–105)

Case study which the writer perceives as paradoxical. The mass of the German community was anti-elitist and anti-capitalist, but the upper-class was capitalist and monarchist. Thus, although outwardly the community's support of Nazism appeared monolithic, there existed a deep split. The long paper is published in two sections; pre-World War I and post-World War II periods. For author's book on the subject, see *HLAS 40:3821.*

7498 O'Donnell, Guillermo. Estado y alianza en la Argentina, 1956–1976 (IDES/DE, 64:16, enero/marzo 1977, p. 523–554, tables)

Author presents an abridged version of his developing theory of Argentina's political-economic experience. Within the context of the country's cyclical economic change, he discusses the principal power-holding groups and the alliances they seek in order to main-

tain their influence. He notes that as the state's reliance on such groups increases its capacity to act independently diminishes. The result is that the Argentine state has now become largely the instrument of these groups. For more on the author's reflections on bureaucratic-authoritarian patterns, see item **7053.**

———. Reflexiones sobre las tendencias generales de cambio en el burocrático-autoritario. See item **7054.**

Perón, Juan Domingo. Organización peronista. See *HLAS 40:3833.*

7499 Ramírez Bosco, Luis. La función de los sindicatos: los sindicatos y la defensa del interés profesional como función de las asociaciones profesionales de trabajadores. Prólogo de Jorge Rodríguez Mancini. B.A., Editorial Universidad, 1976. 230 p.

Based on doctoral thesis in labor law, this work considers the role of labor organizations in establishing and defending the interests of workers.

7500 Rivera Echenique, Silvia. Militarismo en la Argentina: golpe de estado de junio de 1966. México, UNAM, Facultad de Ciencias Políticas y Sociales, 1976. 123 p., bibl. (Serie estudios, 50)

Author offers a National Security/Development model as the basis for his analysis of Argentine events from the fall of Perón to the preparation for his return. Until the start of the US Vietnam adventure, the author posits, Latin America was regarded (by the US) as part of its hegemonic area of capitalist ideological control. As Vietnam soured and US national power sagged, Brazil became in 1964 the first designated client for the new model, and Argentina in 1966 was scheduled to become the second. However, the strength of the Argentine working-class in Argentina pushed this plan off the rails. How then did the model progress under the military regimes of Onganía, Levingston and Lanusse? The work focuses on this period and question. Based on documents of the period. For historian's comment, see *HLAS 40:3846.*

7501 Schmucler, Héctor and **Margarita Zires.** El papel político-ideológico de los medios de comunicación: Argentina 1975 la crisis del Lopezreguismo (CYC, 5, marzo 1978, p. 119–178, tables)

The resignation, and subsequent disappearance from the political scene, of José López Rega marked the end of peronista power in Argentina. This very long and carefully structured paper recounts these events, by focusing on the Press as recorder and intepreter. Some newspapers (*La Prensa*) played down ("hid") the crisis in the view of the authors, others promoted it. Many major newspapers clearly recorded events from the view of the traditional oligarchy. The writers believe that many of the principal newspapers presented the events from their own peculiar standpoints and concluded that "Finally we state that we have thus denied any innocence to the media . . . "

7502 Schoultz, Lars. Political normlessness in comparative perspective (SPSA/JP, 40:1, Feb. 1978, p. 82–111, tables)

Author defines "political normlessness" as an aspect of alienation. He notes that in certain societies behaviors which otherwise would not be approved become permissible when certain political goals are perceived as necessary. Author shares the impression of other Latin Americanists that such behavior is widespread throughout the region. His paper tests the concept with Argentine data largely collected by Jeanne Kirkpatrick (see *HLAS 35.7959.*)

7503 ———. The socio-economic determinants of popular-authoritarian electoral behavior: the case of peronism (APSA/R, 71:4, Dec. 1977, p. 1423–1446, tables)

Study draws its data from elections in Greater B.A. (1942–73) and examines six hypotheses regarding the concept of a popular-authoritarian vote. The first hypothesis is conventional and attributes voting patterns to class-oriented behavior, the latter five examine why others voted for popular-authoritarian candidates. Multivariate analysis of the data leads to the explanation that 80 percent of the variation in peronist voting behavior can be attributed to socioeconomic variables. The paper is intensely machine-data oriented, but helpful writing makes the conclusions and reasoning accessible.

7504 Suárez, Carlos Oscar. Argentina: la crísis del proyecto peronista (UNAM/RMCPS, 21:80, abril/junio 1975, p. 121–130)

A radical, nationalist and populist interpretation of Argentine political and economic history from 1943 to present. Author argues that by the time Perón returned, he was so out of touch with the changed reality that he succumbed to those imperialist forces which prevent the liberation of the country.

7505 Tadioli, Pedro. Unir todas las voluntades democráticas, populares y patrióticas para derrotar a los enemigos de la Nación: informe central a la Conferencia de Delegados del Comité de la Provincia de Buenos Aires del Partido Comunista, realizada el 13 y 14 de febrero en el Teatro Roma, Avellaneda. La Plata, Arg., Ediciones Frente Unido, 1976. 59 p., maps, plates, table.

Report to the Communist Party's Central Committee, Buenos Aires prov.

7506 Villar Araújo, Carlos. Argentina: de Perón al golpe militar. Madrid, Ediciones Felmar, 1976. 216 p., bibl., tables (Col. Punto crítico, 14)

From self-imposed exile, a journalist offers his analysis of Argentina's political and economic history in the middle 20th century.

7507 Wiñar, David L. Poder político y educación: el peronismo y la Comisión Nacional de Aprendizaje y Orientación Profesional. B.A., Instituto Torcuato di Tella, Centro de Investigaciones en Ciencias de la Educación (CICE), 1970. 61 p., tables (Documento de trabajo, 3)

This work constitutes the first, concept-building stage of the author's final study concerning educational policy from pre-World War II through 1955. Author believes that since this policy is linked closely to the country's social and economic processes, it also is closely related to the country's external dependency. Most of the paper deals with the social and political strategy of peronist control of technical education (1945–55).

7508 Wynia, Gary W. Argentina in the postwar era: politics and economic policy making in a divided society. Albuquerque, Univ. of New Mexico Press, 1978. 289 p., bibl., tables.

Argentina (as of 1943) is subjected to a policy-oriented analysis, in a carefully-plotted and literate work. Author attributes the failure of Argentina's individual regimes to: 1) their elitism; 2) the strong competition of interests playing for zero-sum gains; 3) the absence of legitimating support-groups; and 4) the lack of political skill. Author examines political and economic failures, after careful research in documents and contemporary (and somewhat fugitive) publications.

BRAZIL

7509 Abreu, Alcides. Análise sistêmatica de partidos políticos. Porto Alegre, Brazil, Editora Movimento *em co-edição com a* Univ. para o Desenvolvimento do Estado de Santa Catarina (UDESC), Florianópolis, Brazil, 1977. 125 p., bibl., tables (Col. Ensaios, 16. Col. Santa Catarina, 11)

An essay in systematic analysis of political parties, drawing on Parsons, Huntington, Julied Freund, Almond, Powell, Drucker, Kissinger, and a number of other influences. Very little on Brazil, but much eclectic theorizing.

7510 Anderson, Robin L. Brazil's military regime under fire (CUH, 74:434, Feb. 1978, p. 61–65, 87)

Useful popular reporting of events in the period 1977, primarily at the national level, with somewhat pessimistic conclusions for the last year of the Geisel government.

7511 Azevedo, Thales de. Igreja e estado em tensão e crise: a conquista espiritual e o padroado na Bahia. São Paulo, Editora Atica, 1978. 179 p., bibl. (Ensaios, 51)

Critical historical analysis of the Church in Brazil, from the original settlement to 1930. Author discusses tensions and the political consequences implied in the title. He demonstrates that the clergy's humanistic sensitivities were skewed, however, and thus partial.

7512 Barman, Roderick and Jean Barman. The prosopography of the Brazilian Empire (LARR, 13:2, 1978, p. 78–97)

A methodological statement concerning the use of biographical materials for the study of elites of the Empire. Extensive bibliography as well as description of collection, bibliographical and analytical methods. See also item **7545.**

————— and —————. The role of the law graduate in the political elite of imperial Brazil. See *HLAS 40:4065.*

7513 Bath, Sérgio F. Guarischi. A formação do diplomata brasileiro (UMG/RBEP, 47, julho de 1978, p. 245–251)

Brief but informative report of the Instituto Rio Branco, the Academy of the Brazilian Foreign Service.

7514 Benevides, Maria Victoria de Mesquita. O Governo Kubitschek: desenvolvimento econômico e estabilidade política, 1956–1961. Prefácio de Celso Lafer. Rio, Editora Paz e Terra, 1976. 294 p., bibl., tables (Col. Estudos brasileiros, 8)

Based on MA thesis in contemporary political history at the Univ. of São Paulo, 1975. The work reflects the rising level of scholarship in this university, and makes a useful contribution to the reexamination of the topic.

7515 Beyna, Jean-Michel. Crise de l'énergie et développement régional au Brésil (FDD/NED [Problèmes d'Amerique Latine, 48] 4478, 13 juillet 1978, p. 65–118, maps, tables)

Highly useful long article, discusses trade-offs of energy. Gasoline, electricity and nuclear energy are examined in some detail in individual pieces as are the outcomes for energy usage and pricing in terms of the regional, industrial and transportation uses of energy.

7516 Braga, Roberto Saturnino. Discurso aos democratas. Rio, Editora Artenova, 1977. 107 p.

Short essay by active politician with service in the bureaucracy and a seat from the opposition party in the National Congress. His "bases for a new economic-social model", a programmatic proposal for the MDB, comprises the bulk of the book. A useful example, too, of constructive criticism of the present regime's creative and distributive policies.

7517 Brazil. Câmara dos Deputados. Centro de Documentação e Informação. Deputados brasileiros: repertório biográfico dos membros de Câmara dos Deputados da Sétima Legislatura, 1971–1975. Brasília, 1971/1974. 2 v. (630, 34 p.) plates.

Biographical register of Deputies of the Brazilian National Chamber of Deputies.

7518 —————. Ministério da Educação e Cultura. Conselho Federal de Cultura. Aspectos da política cultura brasileira. Apre-

sentação de Ney Braga. Rio, 1976. 114 p.
Cultural (i.e., education and mass culture) policy of the government of Brazil. A useful overview of laws, institutions and content. The implications of such planning are left unsaid.

7519 ———. **Presidência da República. Secretaria de Planejamento. Secretaria de Modernização e Reforma Administrativa** (SEMOR). Cadastro da administração federal, 1975. v. 11, Ministério do Interior. Brasília, 1976. 398 p.
Detailed job specification of the Ministry of the Interior. All legislative authorizations are also indicated.

7520 Bret, Bernard. L'agriculture du Brésil: expansion agricole et crise agraire (FDD/NED [Problèmes d'Amerique Latine, 44] 4391/4393, 17 juin 1977, p. 64–86, maps, tables)
Author reports the place of agriculture in national development planning and analyzes the obstacles to its success in his discussion of finance, land distribution and expansion, cropping and labor policies.

7521 Brossard [de Souza Pinto], Paulo. E hora de mudar. Porto Alegre, Brazil, L&PM Editores, 1977. 120 p.
Criticisms of the "revolution", in the form of an extended statement delivered in the National Senate, by an MDB senator from Rio Grande de Sul.

7522 Brunn, Gerhard. Die Revolution von 1930 als Ausgangsplunkt konservativer Modernisierung in Brasilien (UB/GG, 2:2, 1976, p. 217–233)
Author is dubious about the "modernization" of Brazil when only top 20 percent of the population are integrated into the 20th century. [R.V.Shaw]

7523 Caldeira, José Ribamar C. Estabilidade social e crise política o case do Maranhão (UMG/RBEP, 46, jan. 1978, p. 55–101, tables)
In the period 1956–76 a series of intrastate political crises occurred. Author analyzes the reasons for continuing civil stability during this period on the basis of a theoretical model, proposed by himself. Much material on parties and elections of their period is included.

7524 Castello Branco, Carlos. Os militares no poder. Rio, Editora Nova Fronteira, 1977. 680 p. (Col. Brasil Século, 20)
Collection of writer's daily columns in *O Jornal do Brasil*, from the golpe of April 1964 to 15 March 1967. The columns are of interest because of the author's professionalism, his perception and the immediacy of his response. They lack, however, as is obvious, the sense of retrospective overview.

7525 Chacon, Vamireh. Estado e povo no Brasil: as experiências do Estado Novo e da democracia populista: 1937–1964. Rio, Livraria José Olympio Editora *em convenio com a* Câmara dos Deputados, Brasília, 1977. 259 p. (Col. Documentos brasileiros, 181)
A scholarly interpretation of the period from Vargas' mid-term palace coup through the military coup of 1964. Exhaustive notes, bibliography, and index make this useful to the specialist. The writer seeks to place events within a conceptual context, establishing the ideological frame of the Vargas period, and seeking to demonstrate its continuity through the Goulart period.

7526 Chico Pinto: teoria e práctica de um político (VOZES, 20:8, out. 1976, p. 55–63)
A twice-sanctioned politician (by the government) and active member of Movimento Democrático Brasileiro is interviewed in some depth. The questions probe political ethics, party behavior, parliamentary usefulness in existing circumstances, and other useful concepts.

7527 Christo, Carlos Alberto Libanio. Against principalities and powers: letters from a Brazilian jail. Translated by John Drury. Maryknoll, N.Y., Orbis Books, 1977. 241 p.
Interspersed with a young man's reports of his personal struggle to find Christian salvation are the chilling accounts of totalitarian imprisonment. Released after many months before and after judgment for an act that would be considered a crime only by a tyrannical regime, the writer elected to become a lay Dominican brother.

7528 Coelho, Edmundo Campos. Em busca de identidade: o exército e a política na sociedade brasileira. Rio, Editora Forense-Universitária, 1976. 207 p., bibl., tables (Col. Brasil: análise e crítica)

The profession of arms in Brazil is subjected to detailed examination. What is the Army's self-image? What should it be? What is the view held by soldiers themselves? Changing attitudes since 1964 are questioned. Study is based on a substantial volume of useful data, as well as conceptual introspection.

7529 Droulers, Martine. Les paysans du Maranhão (FDD/NED [Problèmes d'Amérique Latine, 48] 4478, 13 juillet 1978, p. 119–136, maps, tables)

Short descriptive paper concerning the rural areas of the state of Maranhão. The emphasis is in fact on crops and money income, with a short concluding statement on the indigenous population.

Dudley, William S. Professionalization and politization as motivational factors in the Brazilian Army coup of 15 November 1889. See *HLAS 40:4096.*

7530 Dulles, John W.F. Castello Branco: the making of a Brazilian president. Foreword by Roberto de Oliveira Campos. College Station, Texas A&M Univ. Press, 1978. 487 p., bibl., maps, plates.

Careful and nearly monumental biography of the first military president of Brazil who took over after the coup of 1964. Somewhat more than half of the book is devoted to his army career prior to 1960. The book ends with his inauguration in 1964. Only Campos' introduction alludes to the presidency itself.

7531 Durandin, Catherine. L'idéologie de la sécurité nationale au Brésil (FDD/NED [Problèmes d'Amérique Latine, 44] 4391/4393, 17 juin 1977, p. 5–18, map)

Author analyzes Brazilian national security theory and policy since the military coup of 1964. The piece is useful for specialists. Appendix includes a discussion of the South African proposed military treaty of the South Atlantic.

7532 *Ensaios de* Opinião. 1– . Rio, Editora Inúbia, 1975– .

Intellectual monographic series composed of essays, short studies, documents, principally in the social sciences. Vol. 1, this issue, devotes 40 percent of the space to Vargas: his role in founding the Brazilian Labor Party, public statements, a recounting of events leading to his suicide, his roles and attitudes concerning popular music, etc. Also

includes essays on the importance of Jorge Amado and Erico Verissimo, Brazil's first foreign loans (from Portugal), etc.

7533 Erickson, Kenneth Paul. The Brazilian corporative state and working-class politics. Berkeley, Univ. of California Press, 1977. 225 p., bibl., map, tables.

Comprehensive reevaluation and reworking of dissertation material which, although a decade old, has been updated with the aid of experience and perspective. The author presents a useful and careful examination of the role of Brazilian labor in political change, a role which turned out to be less powerful than had been anticipated by the unions. For historian's comment, see *HLAS 40:4098.*

7534 Ferreira Filho, Manoel Gonçalves. A democracia possível. 3 ed. rev. São Paulo, Edição Saraiva, 1976. 129 p.

Thoughtful essay on democracy as a form of government, set of institutions, and system of values, with attention to the peculiar nature of democracy in Brazil. The writer suggests the need for a new constitution for Brazil, since the current revolutionary viewpoint is not properly represented nor contained by the existing document.

7535 ———. Sete vezes democracia. São Paulo, Editora Convívio, 1977. 181 p.

Seven papers and lectures by the author, who has been Professor of Constitutional Law (São Paulo), governmental official at both the state and national level, and is an ARENA party activist and leader. An interesting selection on liberty and democracy in Brazil, delivered 1969–76.

7536 Fleischer, David V. A bancada federal mineira: trinta anos de recrutamento político, 1945/1975 (UMG/RBEP, 45, julho 1977, p. 7–58, illus., map, tables)

Highly focused study of political recruitment, of Deputies in Brazil's National Congress, after Vargas. Also describes career patterns as well as the role of parties.

7537 ———. Concentração e dispersão eleitoral: um estudo da distribuição geográfica do voto en Minas Gerais, 1966–1974. Brasília, Univ. de Brasília, Depto. de Ciências Sociais, 1975. 28 l., maps, tables (Série política, 2)

Privately-circulated draft briefly examines distribution of votes in three parliamentary elections. The data are applied to the question: Would the successful candidates be strengthened by a single-member electoral system (in contrast to the actually-employed PR system)? author concludes that while state-level candidates would benefit, federal-level candidates would not. A useful paper by a recognized specialist in voting patterns of this major Brazilian state.

7538 Flynn, Peter. Brazil: a political analysis. London, Ernest Benn [and] Westview Press, Boulder, Colo., 1978. 564 p., bibl., maps, plates, tables (Nations of the modern world)

Major and noteworthy chronologically-arranged political treatment of Brazil. Flynn opens with the question, Why has the system failed to provide well for its majority? The theme carries through, implemented by exhaustive scholarly apparatus.

————. The Brazilian development model: the political dimension. See item **5625**.

7539 Fragoso, Antônio and others. A firmeza-permanente: a forca da não violência. Apresentação de Paulo Evaristo. São Paulo, Edições Loyola [and] Edições Vega, 1977. 247 p., plates.

Consists of 14 statements of various lengths which address nonviolence and the Christian approach to the solution of social and political issues in Brazil. Some are theoretical, others more specific offer concrete examples.

7540 Franco, Alvaro da Costa. O Brasil e a atual conjuntura econômica mundial (UMG/RBEP, 47, julho de 1978, p. 195–210)

Straightforward statement on Brazil's current position in international economic terms.

7541 Frederico, Celso. Consciência operária no Brasil. São Paulo, Editora Atica, 1978. 140 p., bibl., tables (Col. Ensaios, 39)

Based on direct personal observation of workers in the suburbs of São Paulo city, this short work explores their grievances, their adjustments and their tactics of struggle for improved status. The concluding chapter discusses the specific effects of the "long night" after the coup of 1964.

7542 Freire, Marcos. Nação oprimida. Prefácio de Barbosa Lima Sobrinho. Rio,

Editora Paz e Terra, 1977. 187 p.

Senator from Pernambuco (late 1960s to early 1970s) presents a root-and-branch condemnation of the present regime as authoritarian, deceitful and corrupt. The work is more useful than most of its genre because of the experience and stature of its author.

7543 Góes, Walder de. O Brasil do General Geisel: estudo do processo de tomada de decisão no regime militar-burocrático. Prefácio de Carlos Castello Branco. Rio, Editora Nova Fronteira, 1978. 185 p. (Col. Brasil: século 20)

Useful effort by an experienced journalist to trace, by both anecdote and analysis, the uses of power and the making of decisions under Geisel. Topics include domestic policies, candidate selection, compliance with initiatives and pressure from foreign sources (including the US) and military questions.

7544 Gomes, S. O Brasil como base do fascismo na América Latina (UR/L, Spring 1975, p. 63–73)

East German analysis of the 1964 military coup and of its place in the political strategy of the US. [M. Kossok]

7545 Graham, Richard. Governmental expenditures and political change in Brazil, 1880–1899: who got what (UM/JIAS, 19:3, Aug. 1977, p. 339–368, tables)

After examining government expenditures in the period bridging the Monarchy's overthrow, the writer takes a tentative look at who were the gainers from the establishment of the Republic. Author agrees with existing conclusions but cast doubt on others. For historian's comment, see *HLAS 40: 4109*.

7546 Greenfield, Sidney M. Patronage, politics, and the articulation of local community and national society in pre-1968 Brazil (UM/JIAS, 19:2, May 1977, p. 139–172, bibl.)

Descriptive and conventional/analytical examination of the relationship between patronage relationships and political events, drawn from two municipios in the state of Minas Gerais, in 1965. The material is anecdotal, deals with specific personalities, and recounts specific events.

7547 Harrigan, John J. Political economy and the management of urban development in Brazil (*in* Cornelius, Wayne A. and

Felicity M. Trueblood *eds.* Urbanization and inequality [see *HLAS 39:9016*] p. 207–220, bibl.)

Paper advances and tests an hypothesis: the nature of the political economy of Brazil leads invariably to incompatibilities between urban development planning and national economic development planning. The writer briefly examines literature in four areas: 1) existing development policies; 2) possible incompatibilities between urban and national planning; 3) how theoretical considerations of polar or broad management can help resolve these incompatibilities; and 4) how can practical and theoretical outcomes be predicted from these policies? Although brief, this ambitious paper offers useful roadmarkers.

7548 Hart, Jeffrey A. Cognitive maps of three Latin American policy makers (PUCIS/WP, 30:1, Oct. 1977, p. 115–140, illus., tables)

The casual beliefs or assertions of an individual are, in this paper, defined as his cognitive map. Venezuelan President Carlos Andrés Pérez, Brazilian Finance Minister Roberto de Oliveira Campos, and Brazilian War Minister Gen. Aurelio de Lyra Tavares are the persons examined. The paper is sharply focused on methodology; its policy implications are confined to the ability of the method to compare the individual's policy choices with his declared intents, and to determine the explanatory and predictive ability of the method.

7549 Jakubs, Deborah L. Police violence in times of political tension: the case of Brazil, 1968–1971 (*in* Bayley, David H. Police and society. Beverly Hills, Calif., Sage Publications, 1977, p. 85–106)

Author examines in some detail the "Squadron of Death" phenomenon in São Paulo and suggests hypotheses concerning its emergence. She also discusses the historical experience of Brazil's toleration of violence as an accepted form of retribution by official authority.

Joes, Anthony James. Fascism in the contemporary world: ideology, evolution, resurgence. See item **7489**.

7550 Jorge, Fernando. As diretrizes governamentais do Presidente Ernesto Geisel: subsídios e documentos para a história do Brasil contemporâneo. São Paulo, The Author,

1976. 351 p., bibls., facisms., plates.

Despite its obviously sycophantic aspects, this work has much useful information for the specialist. It includes a version of Brazil's political history with many direct excerpts from Geisel's statements. Contrary to the title's implication, the work is only partially confined to Geisel's cabinet.

7551 Kacowicz, Mateus and others. Desenvolvimento e política urbana. Apresentação de Diogo Lordello de Mello. Rio, Instituto Brasileiro de Administracão Municipal (IBAM), 1976. 231 p., tables.

Consists of 12 papers, plus transcript of roundtable, on Brazilian urban problems by personnel of the Brazilian Institute of Municipal Administration. While a number are rather abstract pieces drawing on theory or on experience in other countries, several specifically deal with Brazilian issues and experience.

7552 Kistanov, Valeri. Cabeza de playa de los monopolios japoneses en América Latina (URSS/AL, 1, 1977, p. 45–66)

Soviet author describes the "offensive" of Japanese capital in Latin America but devotes most of the article to long-term Japanese influence in Brazil, and the welcoming policy of military regimes since 1964. Does this variety of imperialism contribute to the specific Brazilian image in Latin America? The question is raised, from the Soviet perspective.

Kohl, James and **John Litt.** Urban guerrilla warfare in Latin America. See item **7035**.

7553 Konstantinova, Natalia. El nacionalismo brasileño: una nueva etapa (URSS/AL, 2, 1977, p. 99–116)

Soviet author denounces Brazil's reactionary bourgeois nationalism, which attacks the nationalism of the revolutionary vanguard as well as (in the past few years) the US. Such confusion serves to validate Lenin's theory concerning nationalism.

Langguth, A.J. Hidden terrors. See item **7603**.

7554 Leal, Víctor Nunes. Coronelismo: the municipality and representative government in Brazil. Translated by June Henfrey. With an introduction by Alberto Venancio Filho. Cambridge, U.K., Cambridge Univ. Press, 1977. 237 p., bibl. (Cambridge Latin American studies, 28)

Classic study of local government in Brazil appears in excellent English translation. Written in 1948 in a "concurso" for a university chair in Rio, it has not been updated. The comparatively unchanging nature of power at the local level, and in local-national relationships in Brazil, is thus affirmed by this useful publication. For Portuguese original *Coronelismo, exada e voto* published in 1949, see *HLAS 14:1611.*

7555 Machado Horta, Raúl. Os dereitos individuais na Constituicão (UMG/RBEP, 47, julho 1978, p. 49–75)

This is a legal-constitutional review of individual rights spelled out in constitutions in general and Brazilian constitutions in particular, especially those of the post-World War II era, including the 1967 draft. Author compares them with those of the US and the Federal Republic of Germany and remarks on political problems which arise when authoritarian regimes suspend individual rights.

7556 Malloy, James M. Social insurance policy in Brazil: a study in the politics of inequality (IAMEA, 30:3, Winter 1976, p. 41–67, bibl.)

Preliminary research note of the Brazilian phase of a multi-national study of Latin American policies and outcomes of social insurance as an income distributive device. The overall study hypothesizes that such systems have regressive effects on income distribution and suggests variables so far identified and studied. This is a largely descriptive piece of substantial strength with some impressive analysis.

7557 ———. Social security policy and the working class in twentieth-century Brazil (UM/JIAS, 19:1, Feb. 1977, p. 35–60, bibl.)

Social insurance policy which dates from the 1920s, began as a paternalistic response to the emergence of an urban industrial working class beyond the control of an earlier system that was private and paternalistic. Since then, the policy has been used as a device for controlling this class for the benefit of authoritarian regimes. Author perceives the present system as a logical result of earlier tendencies.

7558 Martínez-Alier, Verena and **Armando Bioto Júnior.** The hoe and the vote: rural labourers and the national election in Brazil in 1974 (JPS, 4:3, April 1977, p. 147–170, tables)

This study, based on a substantial amount of field interviewing, is studded with verbatim quotes illustrating points made by the authors concerning attitudes. The study overturns the view that rural workers have no opinions about politics and that they vote as they are told. The contrary, note the authors, is not only true but men and women have quite different attitudes about issues. A provocative article that should interest all readers.

7559 Martins, Carlos Estevam. Capitalismo de estado e modelo político no Brasil. Rio, Edicões do Graal, 1977. 428 p. (Biblioteca de ciências sociais. Brasil em foco, 1)

This dense and sophisticated examination of the political economy of Brazil, principally since the military golpe of 1964, is based on a detailed construction and application of socioeconomic models. The book concludes with a short examination of the linkage of foreign with domestic policy. Author contends that Brazilian state capitalism, centered on a nationalist view of national security, is the logical product of the operation of capitalism.

7560 Maurer, Harry. Is Brazil on the brink of democracy? (The New York Review of Books [N.Y.] 25:14, 28 Sept. 1978, p. 43–48, illus.)

Popular reporting of the general mood in Brazil centering on one topic: the return of democracy. Chiefly an anecdotal piece which ends with detailed and explicit pessimism.

Mendes, Cândido. Beyond populism. See *HLAS 40:2199.*

7561 Molotnik, J.R. Politics and popular culture in Brazil (TMR, 17:3, Autumn 1976, p. 507–524)

A lively and detailed report of the way in which contemporary Brazilian culture (not all of it really at the popular level) has been censored, distorted, or barred by the present regime. The resourcefulness (and counter-resourcefulness) of the players is convincingly set forth.

7562 Movimento Democrático Brasileiro (MDB), *Brazil.* Posição do MDB no Paraná. Curitiba, Brazil, Editora Hoje, 1976. 385 p., plates.

A handbook of the MDB organized according to the following: 1) the election of national officials from Paraná; 2) the election of regional, state, and municipal officials; and 3) what activities and offices are held by the party. The volume is introduced by the text of the Organic Law of the Parties (Federal); and by MDB's statutes, platform and code of ethics.

7563 *NACLA's Latin America & Empire Report.* North American Congress on Latin America (NACLA). Vol. 9, No. 4, May/June 1975 –. N.Y.

Issue devoted to "Brazil: the Continental Strategy" perceives Brazil as the rising imperialist power in South America, partly as agent of the US, partly as pursuing its own national interests. The bulk consists of a single article by Gustavo V. Dans "Brazil on the Offensive" (p. 5–30, illus., maps, plates).

7564 Nascimento, Alcino João do and others. Mataram o Presidente!: memórias do pistoleiro que mudou a história do Brasil. Apresentação de Mylton Severiano da Silva. São Paulo, Editora Alfa-Omega, 1978. 135 p. (Biblioteca Alfa-Omega de comunicações e artes. Série 1: história imediata, 4)

Contribution to the record of the suicide of Vargas. Some of this may be apocryphal, but of some interest to specialists.

7565 Ochs, Smil and **Aluizio Laureiro Pinto**. Modernización y reforma administrativa del gobierno federal brasileño (*in* Seminario Interamericano de Reforma Administrativa, I, Rio, 1973/1974. Reforma administrativa: experiencias latinoamericanas. México, Instituto Nacional de Administración Pública, 1975, p. 285–348, illus., tables)

The paper offers a brief review of reorganizational plans prior to 1969, with their premises, and follows with a statement of the impact of interests on and within the bureaucracy. Includes the texts of laws and constitutional provisions concerning ministerial supervision. Also discusses reform plans developed and organized by the Secretariat of Modernization and Administrative Reform: structure, criteria, action, links to budgeting, effects on domestic technical assistance programs.

O'Donnell, Guillermo. Reflexiones sobre las tendencias generales de cambio en el estado burocrático-autoritario. See item **7054**.

7566 Oliveira, Eliézer Rizzo de. As forças armadas: política e ideologia no Brasil, 1964–1969. Petrópolis, Brazil, Editora Vozes, 1976. 133 p. (Col. Sociologia brasileira, 6)

Systematic and serious study of national security doctrine and practice, under the guidance of the Escola Superior de Guerra, in the period indicated. The study draws on both academic works by other authors and on the specific experiences of military involvement in politics since 1964. A serious and worthwhile volume, with distinct insights to a not-so-simple phenomenon.

7567 Packenham, Robert A. Trends in Brazilian national dependency since 1964 (*in* Roett, Riordan ed. Brazil in the seventies. Washington, American Enterprise Institute for Public Policy Research, 1976, p. 89–115)

Is Brazil moving toward dependency or autonomy? Granting that there are proponents for both positions, this writer holds that the concept of dependency itself is complex and has been handled poorly in most of the literature. He focuses on one aspect, national dependency, and introduces five primarily economic features for analytical purposes. He concludes, somewhat diffidently, that during the period under study (1964–75) dependency decreased.

7568 Parra E., Ernesto and **Isabel Aguirrezábal T.** Suramérica 76: modelos militares de desarrollo. Perú: se derechiza la revolución?; Brasil: el fin del "milagro;" Chile: tres años después de Allende. Bogotá, Centro de Investigación y Educación Popular (CINEP), 1976. 84 p. (Controversia, 46)

Interesting, if extremely brief, effort to describe and discuss two models of economic development: the capitalist one in Brazil and Chile and the participatory one in Peru. Authors believe that the latter model strikes a midpoint between capitalism and communism. Both of course, exist under military auspices.

7568a Paupério, Artur Machado. Teoria democrática do Estado. Rio, Editora Pallas, 1976. 277 p., map, tables (Teoria democrática do poder, 1)

Author analyzes the problem of democracy and discusses the problem with respect to Brazil and other countries. While not an apologist for any regime, he clearly emphasizes that parliamentary democracy poses a problem for Brazil as does any attempt to copy other systems. [C.N. Ronning]

7569 Pedreira, Fernando. A liberdade e a ostra. Prefácio de Carlos Castello Branco. 2. ed. Revisão de Nildon Ferreira. Rio, Editora Nova Fronteira, 1977. 193 p. (Col. Brasil: século 20)

Series of political comments and essays, arranged into chapters addressing the belief patterns of Brazilians in authority. Final chapters examine current policy and leadership. A worthwhile piece by an experienced journalist and respected intellectual.

7570 Pereira, Potyara A.P. Burocracia e planejamento regional no Amazônia (UMG/RBEP, 46, jan. 1978, p. 127–157)

Short study of bureaucratic mores and interests against a backdrop of regional planning and development. The examination of bureaucracy occurs in the light of attempts by a regional authority, SUDAM (Superintendência do Desenvolimento da Amazônia), to achieve a series of goals often dimly perceived, as contrasted with the structure and attitudes of a national administration.

7571 Petrow, A. Das Ende des brasilianischen "Wirtschaftswunders" (IIB/DA, 22:4, 1977, p. 39–51)

East German article analyzes what are the basic elements and weaknesses of the "Brazilian economic miracle" [M. Kossok]

7572 Prado Júnior, Caio. A revolução brasileira. 5. ed. São Paulo, Editora Brasiliense, 1977. 269 p.

This revised edition includes author's replies to criticisms of the first ed. published in 1966 (see HLAS 29:6477). After a decade, he adds a short retrospective view of the regime as well as of his own work.

7573 Queiroz, Maria Isaura Pereira de. O mandonismo local na vida política brasileira e outros ensaios. São Paulo, Editora Alfa-Omega, 1976. 230 p., bibls. (Biblioteca alfa-omega de ciências sociais. Série sociologia, 1:5)

Although this study is described as sociology, a North American scholar would consider it cultural anthropology designed to analyze the political implications of local power and practices. Distinctly a book for the specialist, but of interest to generalists as well.

Rachum, Ilan. Feminism, woman suffrage, and national politics in Brazil: 1922–1937. See HLAS 40:4156.

Reis Júnior, Pereira. Os Presidentes do Brasil: sínteses biográficas. See HLAS 40:4159.

7574 Rio Grande do Sul (state), Brazil. **Tribunal Regional Eleitoral. Serviço de Estatística e Divulgação.** 30 [i. e. Trinta] anos de justiça eleitoral. Porto Alegre, Brazil, 1976. 73 p., tables.

Statistical summary of votes cast, by candidate, office, etc., in the period 1945–74 in the state of Rio Grande do Sul.

7575 Roett, Riordan. Brazil: politics in a patrimonial society. N.Y., Praeger, 1978. 197 p., bibl., map, tables.

Extensively revised and updated edition of a relatively simple but useful and intelligent text. For original version published 1972, see HLAS 35:7878.

7576 Santos, José Lopes dos. Votos e discursos. Goiânia, Brazil, Cannes Publicidade, Depto. de Edições, 1973. 179 p.

Collection of documents and statements by the author who served as judge in the regional electoral tribunal of Piauí state. Some merely discuss the roles of elections and of the tribunal, others urge reforms. Includes official decisions concerning votes and candidacies following the elections.

7577 Schooyans, Michel. Demain, le Brésil?: militarisme et technocratie. Paris, Les Editions Du Cerf, 1977. 169 p., bibl. (Col. Terres de feu, 20)

Professor who taught in the Catholic Univ. of São Paulo for 10 years writes a brief introduction to Brazil for French readers. Author's evaluations are at least as important in the body of the work as his selection of topics. He makes clear that an alliance of soldiers and technicians rules the country for closely defined purposes.

7578 Seminário de Estudos Mineiros, IV, Belo Horizonte, Brazil, 1976. Seminario de estudos mineiros. Belo Horizonte, Brazil, Univ. Federal de Minas Gerais, 1977. 260 p., illus., tables.

Seminar convened to discuss culture in Minas Gerais. Some papers are essentially historical: Afonso Arinos de Melo Franco's "Continuidade e Atualidade Política de

Minas" and his "A Autobiografia Poética e Ficcional na Literatura de Minas", Ivo Porto de Menezes's "Visão Atual do Ambiente Cultural Artístico de Minas Gerais;" Washington Peluso Abino de Souza's "As Lições das Vilas e Cidades de Minas Gerais"; and Antônio Aureliano Chaves de Mendoça's "Minas: Centro de Equilíbrio do Desenvolvimento Nacional."

7579 Seminário sobre Modernização Legislativa e Desenvolvimento Político, *I, Brasília, 1976.* Anais. Brasília, Senado Federal, Subsecretária de Edições Técnicas, 1976. 139 p., plates, table.

Consists of papers delivered at a five-day seminar on the 150th anniversary of the first meeting of the Brazilian Senate. Participants included professionals from all areas in Brazil plus Prof. James Heaphey of SUNY-Albany. Discussion topics covered legislatures as locales for political transactions, issues of public misunderstanding, reforms, and Senate history.

7580 Simon, Pedro. MDB: uma opção democrática. Prefácio de Fernando Henrique Cardoso. Porto Alegre, Brazil, L&PM Editores, 1976. 277 p., tables (Col. Política, 2)

President of the Directive Committee of the Movimento Demócrata Brasileiro in Rio Grande do Sul argues that democracy can occur in Brazil. The work deals with selected public policy issues as well as with theory and practice of democracy and responsible government.

7581 Siqueira, Moema Miranda de. O papel da função administrativa na evolução urbana de Belo Horizonte (UMG/RBEP, 44, jan. de 1977, p. 103–138, tables)

Short examination of the role played by administrative functions in the growth of a city and its bureaucracy.

7582 Soares, Gláucio Ari Dillon. Notas metodológicas sobre as consequencias políticas da migração interna (UMG/RBEP, 54, julho 1977, p. 59–92, tables)

This is a broadly conceived paper, partly methodological and partly analytical of the Brazilian case. A substantial cross-national content allows comparative conclusions with other Latin American countries. Specific examination of the effect on political parties cites Brazilian data.

7583 Souza, Herbet de. The world capitalist system and militarism in Latin America: a comparative analysis of the Brazilian and Peruvian models. Translated from the Spanish by Barbara Shepard. Toronto, Canada, Brazilian Studies, 1974. 52 p., tables.

Wide-ranging paper emphasizes the rising dominance of soldier-politicians, with their nationalist-leftist goals as well as their international hostilities. Although the author speaks in terms of "models" as the basis for his analysis, his paper is not tightly structured analytically. Of little interest.

7584 Souza, Maria do Carmo C. Campello de. Estado e partidos políticos no Brasil: 1930 a 1964. Prefácio de Victor Nunes Leal. São Paulo, Editora Alfa-Omega, 1976. 178 p. bibl., tables (Biblioteca alfa-omega de ciências sociais. Série 1: política, 3)

Careful and scholarly study of the roots, rise, decay and fall of parties during the indicated period.

Uricoechea, Fernando. A formação do estado brasileiro no século XIX. See *HLAS 40:4180.*

7585 Valle, Alvaro. As novas estruturas políticas brasileiras. Apresentação de Elysio Condé. Rio, Editorial Nórdica, 1977. 250 p., bibl.

Is it possible for Brazil to create a unique political system, benefitting from its own experience as well as from that of historic world intellectual currents? The work based on substantial research and recent Brazilian political history, addresses this question.

7586 Velloso, João Paulo dos Reis. Brasil: a solução positiva. São Paulo, Abril-Tec Editora, 1977. 238 p., bibl., tables.

A career bureaucrat, Director of the Planning Office of the Presidency, discusses economic and social growth in Brazil. The Brazilian "model" of development is discussed in detail and the author addresses its appropriateness for problem-solving.

7587 Viana Filho, Luís. O Govêrno Castello Branco. t. 1/2. Rio, Biblioteca do Exército [and] Livraria José Olympio Editora, 1975. 2 v. (284, 571 p.) facsims., plates (Biblioteca, 447. Col. General Benício, 125/126)

The Chief of the Presidential Personal Staff (Casa Civil) describes in detail the work, policies and personality of his Chief. This is a serious if, somewhat uncritical report of the period.

7588 Vianna, Luiz Werneck. Liberalismo e sindicato no Brasil. Rio, Editora Paz e Terra, 1976. 288 p., tables (Col. Estudos brasileiros, 12)

The work traces government labor policy through the period 1889–1950s with very slight mention made of events since 1964. Includes useful and original interpretation of Vargas' period as one of formalized corporatism, intended to create some interclass harmony while encouraging industrialization and capital growth.

7589 Vieira, Evaldo Amaro. Oliveira Vianna e o estado corporativo: um estudo sobre corporativismo e autoritarismo. São Paulo, Editorial Grijalbo, 1976. 149 p., bibl. (Col. Brasil ontem e hoje)

Critical analysis of the work of Oliveira Vianna, a principal ideologue of authoritarian and corporatist nationalism in the Vargas period. A valuable contribution to the intellectual history of Brazil.

7590 Vilhena, Paulo Emílio Ribeiro de. Região metropolitana e estrutura sindical brasileira (UMG/RBEP, 47, julho de 1978, p. 115–163)

From a primarily legal and constitutional viewpoint author briefly examines the questions that arise for labor organizations in large urban areas. While the long introduction is largely historic, the latter and major portion of the paper addresses Brazilian concerns in both theoretical and case terms.

7591 Wahrlich, Beatriz M. de Sousa. La reforma administrativa federal brasileira: pasado y presente (*in* Seminario Interamericano de Reforma Administrativa, I, Rio, 1973/1974. Reforma administrativa: experiencias latinoamericanas. México, Instituto Nacional de Administración Pública, 1975, p. 235–284)

Paper reports on the general issue of administrative reform, both before and after the major decree-laws of Feb. 1967. First portion of study refers almost entirely to formal structures of administration and their placement in hierarchies. The laws of 1967 are discussed in greater detail, both as to provisions and applications. The paper concludes with some theoretical, as well as practical,

considerations regarding personnel administration in Brazil.

7592 Weffort, Francisco Corrêa. O populismo na política brasileira. Rio, Editora Paz e Terra, 1978. 181 p., tables (Col. Estudos brasileiros, 25)

While the first section of this book is built on three previously published articles of the 1960s, the longer second part is new and addresses the characteristics and effects of urban populism. Author's principal argument is that the mass, influenced by populist leadership, will not rally to the summons of class reformist leaders or government figures.

Williams, Margaret Todaro. Church and State in Vargas' Brazil: the politics of cooperation. See *HLAS 40:4186.*

PARAGUAY

7593 Argaña, Luis María. Perfiles políticos: perfiles doctrinarios e ideológicos de los partidos y de los movimientos políticos en el Paraguay. Asunción, Asociación Nacional Republicana (Partido Colorado), 1977. 234 p., bibl., map, table.

Useful volume for generalists which presents (semi-officially) the party line on virtually all discussable political issues affecting the country. Because of the unique nature of the regime other topics are not discussed. The author, a Professor of the National Univ. in Asunción, suggests this book is a free effort despite its content and author's link with the Paraguayan Army as Professor in the Command and General Staff School. One wonders if this is so.

7594 La reforma agraria en el Paraguay: pautas políticas y administrativas, 1963–1973. Asunción, Instituto de Bienestar Rural (IBR), n.d. 256 p., map, plates, tables.

Relatively comprehensive volume on the declared goals of the Instituto de Bienestar Rural consists of excerpts from annual reports of the period since 1963 (e.g., presidential messages, documents, etc.).

7595 Romero Pereira, Tomás. Una trayectoria republicana: discursos políticos. [Edited by] Nelson Mendoza. Asunción, Ediciones Nelson Mendoza, 1976. 215 p.

Speeches by a supporter of the regime delivered over a 20-year period.

7596 Stroessner, Alfredo. Política y estrategia del desarrollo. Asunción, Instituto Colorado de Cultura, 1977. 463 p., tables (Biblioteca colorados contemporáneos, 1)

Since in one respect Stroessner *is* Paraguay the work has much value. But it is, one must observe, the mirror image of the man.

URUGUAY

7597 Bordaberry, Juan María. Hacia una doctrina política nacional. Montevideo, Presidencia de la República, 1974. 58 p., plate.

Collection of statements (speeches, decrees, an interview) from latter 1973 by Uruguayan President Bordaberry following the palace coup which closed the General Assembly and installed the Council of State. Steps on the road to totalitarian government in Uruguay.

7598 Demicheli, Alberto. Reforma constitucional: democracia participativa; representación del trabajo, del capital y la cultura. Montevideo, Barreiro y Ramos, 1976. 83 p.

An experienced conservative intellectual from Uruguay who is well versed in politics suggests a number of constitutional changes for the post-military regime. The intrinsic importance of this issue and Demicheli's stature and influence make this work central to any discussion of future possibilites.

7599 Dossier. No. 1– . Heverlée-Louvain, Belgium [and] Caracas, Información Documental de América Latina (INDAL), 1971– .

Very useful monographic series published by INDAL in Belgium (but printed in Caracas). The following monographs of this series concern Uruguay: Dossier No. 2 "Partido Comunista del Uruguay y Formación del Frente de Izquierda;" Dossier No. 6 "Las Medidas Prontas de Seguridad en el Uruguay;" Dossier No. 7 "Tortura, Libertad de Prensa y Tupamaros en el Uruguay."

7600 Gari, Juan José. Dinero y soberanía. Montevideo, Barreiro y Ramos, 1977. 109 p.

Radio broadcasts (June–Dec. 1976) on CX4 Radio Rural by the leader of *Ruralismo*, the old populist movement initiated by Benito Nardone. The 19 talks develop the point

that national sovereignty is threatened by the country's monetary instability. But then, author continues, so is the stability of the social structure, and this has led to current problems. Useful if somewhat vague examination from a populist/conservative viewpoint.

7601 ———. Orientalidad y nacionalismo. Montevideo, Barreiro y Ramos, 1976. 98 p.

More radio broadcasts (see item **7600**) by the heir of Nardone's *ruralistas*. He appeals for a radically nationalist and conservative reorientation of internal economic and finance policy, under the aegis of the armed forces; thus, an interestingly pragmatic adaptation.

7602 Gitli, Eduardo. Uruguay: del fin de la utopía a la dependencia fascista (CAM, 208: 5, sept./oct. 1976, p. 7–28, bibl., tables)

Uruguay, states the author, is today one of the principal examples of *fascist dependency*. Following arguments developed in earlier papers, he argues that subversion did not create the crisis but fed on it and worsened it. Further, while the economy floundered because of past bad practices, the application of mechanistic and inappropriate economic models aggravated the tensions. A useful overview, written with substantial objectivity.

Kohl, James and **John Litt.** Urban guerrilla warfare in Latin America. See item **7035**.

7603 Langguth, A.J. Hidden terrors. N.Y., Pantheon Books, 1978. 339 p.

The kidnap-murder of Dan Mitrione is used as a reference point for examining the role of the US government—Pentagon, CIA, State Dept. and police advisors—in the overthrow of Goulart in Brazil and the war against the Tupamaros in Uruguay. The author, a former *New York Times* reporter, exposes an ideological struggle between the right and left which reveals the disturbing role of the US to maintain conservative and capitalist regimes in Latin America. The torture chambers of Brazil and Uruguay are treated in considerable detail; however, the reader must look elsewhere to find the explanations for US policy initiatives, the nature of urban guerrilla warfare, and the brutality employed to achieve these "victories." [D.W. Dent]

7604 Lerin, François and **Cristina Torres.** La politique économique du governement uruguayen 1973–1977 (FDD/NED, [Problèmes d'Amerique Latine, 49] 4485–4486, 6 nov. 1978, p. 59–105, tables)

This article discusses in detail development plans, and the tenure of two Ministers of Economics (Vegh Villegas and Arismendi). Authors offer brief evaluative conclusions based on a multitude of useful statistical tables and charts.

7605 —— and ——. Les transformations institutionelles de l'Uruguay, 1973–1977 (FDD/NED [Problèmes d'Amerique Latine, 49] 4485/4486, 6 nov. 1978, p. 9–57, map)

Article consists of a detailed political chronicle of events in Uruguay in the indicated period. This is an indispensable reference for those interested in Uruguayan politics for which there is virtually no reliable and objective material available.

7606 Minello, Nelson. La militarización del estado en América Latina: un análisis del Uruguay. México, El Colegio de México, Centro de Estudios Sociológicos (CES), 1976. 41 p., table (Cuadernos del CES, 17)

Uruguay's system, analyzed in this short paper through 1974, is interpreted as essentially militaristic with slight fascist overtones; and militarists always end up by serving imperialism. Although useful, the paper is neither exciting, innovative, nor convincing.

7607 ——. Uruguay: la consolidación del estado militar (UNAM/RMS, 39:2, abril/junio 1977, p. 575–594, bibl., tables)

Author perceives the Uruguayan system as passing through the following phases: from clientelist-bourgeois dependency to protecting class dominance to institutionalized militarism. Author essentially repeats arguments of item **7606**, but with the useful addition (for the non-specialist) of historical material from the 19th and early 20th centuries. Unfortunately, author disdains to argue his class-analysis case.

7608 Organization of American States, *Washington.* **Inter-American Commission on Human Rights.** Reports on the situation of human rights in Uruguay. Washington, 1978. 70 p. (mimeo.)

Report of the Commission, approved for submission 31 Jan. 1978. Report demonstrates in substantial detail evidence of systematic violation by the Uruguayan government of a host of legal and moral norms concerning human rights: those of the OAS, of general international law, and of Uruguay's own constitutional and domestic law. The report was prepared without the cooperation of the Uruguayan government. The case against it is meticulously built. Report contains the texts of many documents cited, and details of specific cases.

Price, H. Edward, Jr. The strategy and tactics of revolutionary terrorism. See item **7060**.

7609 Sierra, Gerónimo de. L'emigration massive des travailleurs uruguayens de 1960 a 1976: en particulier vers l'Argentine (FDD/NED [Problèmes d'Amerique Latine, 49] 4485/4486, 6 nov. 1978, p. 107–134, tables)

Paper includes much comparative material (by time periods) to demonstrate the economic and political effects impelling migration to the neighboring country. Although more suggestive than one would like, the paper offers interesting insights.

7610 Sociedad Uruguaya de Defensa de la Tradición, Familia y Propiedad, *Montevideo.* **Comisión de Estudios.** Izquierdismo en la Iglesia: "Compañero de ruta" del comunismo, en la larga aventura de los fracasos y de las metamorfosis. Montevideo, 1976. 382 p., plates.

This Uruguayan conservative society believes that the Church, both in Uruguay and in the Vatican, has been captured by a tendency that is "soft on communism." This is a hard-line document, whose arguments relate only coincidentally to the country's present government.

7611 Uruguay. Junta de Comandantes en Jefe. Las Fuerzas Armadas al Pueblo Oriental. t. 1, pts. 1/2, La subversión. Montevideo, 1976. 2 v. (782 p.) (Continuous pagination) facsims., fold. map, fold. table, plates, tables.

By any measure this is an extraordinary publication. It is divided into two major segments: leftist subversion/terrorism in the world as a whole and in Uruguay in particular. The latter has the virtue of listing for the reader the names of all the communist-subversives—including many one might not have known until now. Documentation includes lists of thousands of individual armed attacks, both in Uruguay and in Latin America (and even in Europe). One cannot doubt the self-conscious seriousness of the armed forces in presenting this collection. The threat of subversion is its reason for existence at this time. This work was originally published as ten newsprint pamphlets.

7612 Zubillaga, Carlos. Herrera: la encrucijada nacionalista. Montevideo, Arca Editorial, 1976. 213 p., bibl.

A retrospective over a period of 67 years on Luis Alberto de Herrera, the second most important Uruguayan politician, a maker and shaker of political groups and leaders. Victimized by historians because of his opportunism, Herrera must be understood as the central figure of this century's political formation to his death in 1959.

VENEZUELA

7613 Albornoz, Orlando. Higher education and the politics of development in Venezuela (UM/JIAS, 19:3, Aug. 1977, p. 291–314, tables)

Leading Venezuelan specialist on his country's higher educational structure and capability recounts economic, technological and political changes of recent years and how the education community reacted to them. He does not find that the products of Venezuelan higher education have been supportive of the country's need for concerned and qualified leadership. Still, he recognizes that moderate reorganizational efforts have been made to correct the deficiency.

7614 Asociación Pro-Venezuela, *Caracas.*

Pensamiento y acción: pronunciamientos y declaraciones a los medios de comunicación social; intervenciones del Dr. Reinaldo Cervini, Presidente de Pro-Venezuela; Lapso, 20 de octubre de 1967/31 de julio de 1973. Caracas, 1974. 1031 p., tables.

Cervini has been an official, in varying capacities, of APV in the period indicated. The volume obviously casts his words in stone as do so many other self-serving pieces from Latin America. But since he is the spokesman for the country's unique nationalist and simultaneously belligerently private sector organization, it is worth reading this

work. The material is indexed three ways, for the purpose of quick reference.

7615 Blanco Múñoz, Agustín. Manifestaciones de la lucha de clases en la Venezuela actual (UCV/NC, 1:1, enero/abril 1975, p. 137–187)

Author departs from the axiom that the class struggle is the propelling force of history and declares that Venezuela demonstrates this. This long paper is a useful spelling out of the thesis within the national context.

7616 Brewer-Carías, Allan Randolph and **Norma Izquierdo Corser.** Estudios sobre la regionalización en Venezuela. Caracas, Univ. Central de Venezuela, La Biblioteca, 1977. 472 p., tables (Col. Ciencias económicas y sociales, 21)

Collected essays promoting the decentralization of administration in Venezuela, written between 1969–74. The principal author was President of the now-defunct Commission on Public Administration, and the second was a senior staff member. Profusely supported with tabular and graphic material, and annexes, this is an essential volume on regional problems.

7617 Caldera, Rafael. Towards a new hemispheric treatment. Caracas, Oficina Central de Información (OCI), Dirección de Publicaciones, 1970? 79 p., plates.

Consists of four speeches of President Rafael Caldera of Venezuela, on the occasion of his visit to Washington, D.C., in June 1970, and delivered at the reception held by President Nixon on the White House lawn and at the White House dinner in his honor; to the National Press Club; and to the Joint Session of the US Congress.

Carrillo Batalla, Tomás Enrique. Historia de las finanzas públicas en Venezuela. See *HLAS 40:3443.*

7618 Ewell, Judith. The extradition of Marcos Pérez Jiménez, 1959–63: practical precedent for enforcement of administrative honesty? (JLAS, 9, pt. 2, Nov. 1977, p. 291–313)

Careful and highly detailed examination of the case of Pérez in the US District Court allows the writer to raise, quite justifiably, questions as to the political, legal and foreign-policy advisability of efforts to extradite overturned Presidents. For historian's comment, see *HLAS 40:3448.*

7619 Frielich de Segal, Alicia. La vene-democracia. Caracas, Monte Avila Editores, 1978. 255 p., plates (Col. Estudios)

Consists of lengthy interviews with many great names of the post-Pérez Jiménez period (e.g., Betancourt, Caldera, Villalba, Machado, Márquez, Barrios, Prieto, Martin). Author analyzes what she considers Venezuela's unique type of democracy with two professors, Carlos Guerón and Humberto Njaim. Although hardly profound, this work is informative of these politicians' self-image a decade after the facts.

Fuenmayor, Juan Bautista. Historia de la Venezuela política contemporánea: 1899–1969. See *HLAS 40:3449.*

7620 García Ponce, Guillermo. Relatos de la lucha armada: 1960–67. v. 1, La insurrección: 1960–62. Valencia, Ven., Vadell Hermanos Editores, 1977. 194 p.

Active participant retells the extreme leftist attacks on the Betancourt government (1960–62) in this first of three proposed volumes. The detailed and comprehensive material is presented in the form of a long dialogue.

7621 González Oropeza, Hermann *ed.* and *comp.* Iglesia y Estado en Venezuela. Presentación de José Humberto Cardenal Quintero. Caracas, Univ. Católica Andrés Bello, 1977. 325 p., bibl. (Col. Manoa, 1)

Consists of some 75 documents (laws, letters, Bulls, etc.) relating to Church and State relations in Venezuela. Forenotes to chronologically-arranged sections are very short and place the collected materials in time periods. Indispensable collection for the specialist.

7622 Grosscors, Guido and **Miguel García Mackle.** La política informativa del gobierno. Caracas, Fracción Parlamentaria de Acción Democrática, 1976. 52 p. (Foro parlamentario, 1)

Consists of selected speeches by two Deputies delivered in the Chamber of Representatives in response to interpellation by COPEI of Grosscors, Minister of State, concerning the AD's public information policies and behavior toward the media.

Hart, Jeffrey A. Cognitive maps of three Latin American policy makers. See item **7548.**

7623 Larrazábal, Radamés. Venezuela: lo nuevo que plantea la nacionalización petrolera (URSS/AL, 1, 1977, p. 104–114)

Member of the Political Bureau of the Communist Party of Venezuela interprets the nationalization of petroleum as a step toward noncapitalist and nationalist development.

7624 ———. La vía del socialismo en Venezuela: o proceso a Petkoff. Prólogo de Jesús Sanoja Hernández. n.p., Gráfica Río Orinoco, 1977. 95 p.

Author believes the Venezuelan Communist party has been robbed of its ideas. Instead he notes "AD and Betancourt have introduced communism with vaseline." So why not the Movimiento al Socialismo? This pamphlet discusses the ideas of Teodoro Petkoff, leader of MAS, whom author regards as the most intelligent theoretician of the communist movement in Venezuela.

7625 Martz, John D. Policy-making and the quest for consensus: nationalizing Venezuelan petroleum (UM/JIAS, 19:4, p. 483–508, bibl., charts)

The politics and policy process of nationalization. The paper demonstrates that President Pérez's announced strategy of consensus in support of the action was poorly handled and that the government took action authoritatively. Author describes the technical aspects of the outcome which he believes are likely to endure.

7626 Myers, David J. Caracas: the politics of intensifying primacy (*in* Cornelius, Wayne A. and Robert V. Kemper *eds.* Metropolitan Latin America: the challenge and the response [see item **9016**] p. 227–258, bibl., maps, tables)

Substantial paper discusses the politics of increasing dominance of Caracas, and the problems resulting from this physical expansion and growing economic, social and political advantage relative to the rest of the country. Conclusions are brief and suggestive of further research.

7627 Njaim, Humberto and others. El sistema político venezolano. Caracas, Univ. Central de Venezuela, Facultad de Derecho, Instituto de Estudios Políticos, 1975. 101 p., bibl., tables.

Textbook-type introduction to Venezuelan government and politics. Useful for introductory purposes, not for specialists.

7628 Pérez, Carlos Andrés. Acción de gobierno. Caracas, n.p., 1973. 78 p.

Campaign statement by the author during the 1973 presidential campaign.

7629 Pérez Alfonzo, Juan Pablo and **Domingo Alberto Rangel.** El desastre. Entrevista polémica realizada por Pedro Duno. Con la colaboración de Fernando Martínez and others. 2. ed. Valencia, Ven., Vadell Hermanos, 1976. 345 p., plates.

Consists of dialogue held between Nov. 75 and Jan. 1976 in the form of a round-table discussion between the authors (Pérez Alfonzo and Rangel) and Pedro Duno; Fernando Martínez G.; Kim Fuad; and Ivan Loscher. The discussion ranges from the conduct of petroleum policy throughout the country's history to the structure of society, economy and values. A necessary book for both specialist or generalist, expressing the thoughts of two very tough-minded men.

7630 La prensa política venezolana del siglo XX. v. 2. Caracas, Ediciones Asociación Venezolana de Periodistas, n.d. 1 v. (Unpaged) facsims. (Col. Periodismo político siglo XX)

Useful volume of radical newspapers and journals of the period (1925–28). Contains the first 15 numbers of *Libertad* published by Salvador de la Plaza in Mexico, and one issue of *Venezuela Libre,* published in Havana.

7631 Les problèmes agraires au Venezuela (FDD/NED [Problèmes d'Amérique Latine, 47] 4457, 24 fev. 1978, p. 101–128, bibl., maps, tables)

Contains two articles: Noëlle Demyk's "Aspects Régionaux de l'Agriculture Venezueliene" (p. 103–110); and Marc Dufumier's "L'Agriculture au Venezuela" (p. 113–126). The presentation is essentially geographical and historical, with comparatively little innovative material or treatment.

7632 Rangel, José Vicente and **Juvencio Pulgar.** ¿Quién encubre a los culpables? Prólogo de Manuel Vicente Ledezma. Introducción de Héctor Rodríguez Bauza. Caracas, Ediciones Parlamento y Socialismo, 1975. 165 p., facsims., plates, tables (Col. Parlamento y socialismo)

Two Deputies of the left offer summaries of public knowledge of corruption and misbehavior in government by both COPEI and Acción Democrática.

7633 ———; Teodoro Petkoff; and Germán Lairet. El año chucuto. Caracas, Ediciones Parlamento y Socialismo, 1975. 225 p., plates, tables (Col. Parlamento y socialismo)

Criticism of government policy by members of Movimiento al Socialismo (MAS). The bulk of the publication is composed of statements in parliamentary debates, but also includes speeches to the party faithful in other forums.

7634 ——— and others. Militares y política: una polémica inconclusa. Caracas, Ediciones Centauro, 1976. 149 p.

Lively and pointed compilation whose writers represent a number of viewpoints, on the role of the military in Venezuelan development and maturation. Rangel begins by pointing out that no consideration of change can occur without taking for granted the central role of the armed forces. Anyone interested in the country, at any level, should know this work.

7635 Rodríguez, Gumersindo. La democracia venezolana y el surgimiento del capitalismo de estado (ACPS/B, 36:69/70, abril/sept. 1977, p. 45–74)

State capitalism has fomented political democracy, the writer argues. The Venezuelan experience since 1958 is reviewed for evidence of unique circumstances that have supported the increased affluence not only of the mass but of the managerial bourgeoisie. He concludes, however, that none of this is possible without skilled, dedicated, ethical and humble leadership.

7636 Silva Bascuñán, Alejandro and others. Democracia participativa. Prefacio de Guillermo Yepes Boscan. Caracas, Centro de Información, Documentación y Análisis Latino-americano (CIDAL), 1972? 1 v. (Various pagings)

A private publication for the Instituto de Formación Demócrata Cristiana (IFEDEC), the Venezuelan Christian Democratic Party's training school in Caracas for young leaders. Consists of 10 individual papers by individual writers who explore the fundamentals of a curriculum in political sociology. As a training manual this is a significant volume.

Suárez Figueroa, Naudy *ed.* Programas políticos venezolanos de la primera mitad del siglo XX. See *HLAS 40:3460.*

7637 Trejo, Hugo. La revolución no ha terminado . . . ! Prólogo de Evilio Gilmon Báez. Valencia, Ven., Vadell Hermanos Editores, 1977. 255 p.

Author was an active participant in the overthrow of Pérez Jiménez in 1958, and later in the year sought, from a rightist military base, to overthrow the nascent constitution-seeking provisional government. He spent many subsequent years in "gilded exile"—as Venezuelan military attaché (and representative at the Inter American Defense Board). This is a highly personal document which illustrates the psychosis of praetorian dogmas that still slow Latin American development.

7638 Venezuela. 5 [i.e. Cinco] años de cambio: pacificación y desarrollo en el Gobierno de Rafael Caldera, 1969–1974. Caracas, n.p., 1975. 325 p., facsim., plates, tables. tables.

Handsome volume with many photographs reports the presidential term of Caldera. The volume contains his address to the Congress on 1 Jan. 1974, and summarizes policies and individual acts in all ministries.

JOURNAL ABBREVIATIONS
GOVERNMENT AND POLITICS

ACPS/B Boletín de la Academia de Ciencias Políticas y Sociales. Caracas.

AESC Annales: Économics, Sociétés, Civilisations. Centre National de la Recherche Scientifique *avec le concours de la* VIe Section de l'École Pratique des Hautes Études. Paris.

AFS Armed Forces and Society. An interdisciplinary journal on military institutions, civil-military relations, arms control and peace-keeping, and conflict management. Univ. of Chicago. Chicago, Ill.

APSA/R American Political Science Review. American Political Science Association. Columbus, Ohio.

AR Areito. Areíto, Inc. N.Y.

ASA/ASR American Sociological Review. American Sociological Association. Menasha, Wis.

BJS British Journal of Sociology. London School of Economics and Political Science. London.

BU/JCS A Journal of Church and State. Baylor Univ., J. M. Dawson Studies in Church and State. Waco, Tex.

CAM Cuadernos Americanos. México.

CDAL Cahiers des Amériques Latines. Paris.

CDLA Casa de las Américas. Instituto Cubano del Libro. La Habana.

CEDLA/B Boletín de Estudios Latinoamericanos. Centro de Estudios y Documentación Latinoamericanos. Amsterdam.

CIIA/IJ International Journal. Canadian Institute of International Affairs. Toronto.

CLACSO/ERL Estudios Rurales Latinoamericanos. Consejo Latinoamericano de Ciencias Sociales, Secretaría Ejecutiva y de la Comisión de Estudios Rurales. Bogotá.

CLAPCS/AL América Latina. Centro Latino-Americano de Pesquisas em Ciências Sociais. Rio.

CM/FI Foro Internacional. El Colegio de México. México.

CM/HM Historia Mexicana. El Colegio de México. México.

CONAC/RNC Revista Nacional de Cultura. Consejo Nacional de Cultura. Caracas.

CP Cuadernos Políticos. Revista trimestral. Ediciones Era. México.

CSSH Comparative Studies in Society and History. An international quarterly. Society for the Comparative Study of Society and History. The Hague.

CU/ILRR Industrial and Labor Relations Review. Cornell Univ. *for the* New York State School of Industrial and Labor Relations. Ithaca.

CU/JIA Journal of International Affairs. Columbia Univ., School of International Affairs. N.Y.

CUH Current History. A monthly magazine of world affairs. Philadelphia, Pa.

CUNY/CP Comparative Politics. The City

Univ. of New York, Political Science Program. N.Y.

CYC Comunicación y Cultura. La comunicación masiva en el proceso político-latinoamericano. Editorial Galerna. B.A. [and] Santiago.

FDD/NED Notes et Études Documentaires. Direction de la Documentation. Paris.

FGV/RAP Revista de Administração Pública. Fundação Getúlio Vargas, Escola Brasileira de Administração Pública. Rio.

HAHR Hispanic American Historical Review. Duke Univ. Press *for the* Conference on Latin American History of the American Historical Association. Durham, N.C.

IA International Affairs. A monthly journal of political analysis. Moskova.

IAEA/DE The Developing Economies. Institute of Asian Economic Affairs. Tokyo.

IAMEA Inter-American Economic Affairs. Washington.

ICS/JCCP Journal of Commonwealth and Comparative Politics. Univ. of London, Institute of Commonwealth Studies. London.

IDES/DE Desarrollo Económico. Instituto de Desarrollo Económico y Social. B.A.

IIB/DA Deutsche Aussenpolitik. Institut für Internationale Beziehungen. Berlin, GDR.

JDA The Journal of Developing Areas. Western Illinois Univ. Press. Macomb.

JDS The Journal of Development Studies. A quarterly journal devoted to economics, politics and social development. London.

JLAS Journal of Latin American Studies. Centers or institutes of Latin American studies at the universities of Cambridge, Glasgow, Liverpool, London and Oxford. Cambridge Univ. Press. London.

JPS The Journal of Peasant Studies. Frank Cass & Co. London.

LAP Latin American Perspectives. Univ. of California. Riverside.

LARR Latin American Research Review. Univ. of North Carolina Press *for the* Latin American Studies Association. Chapel Hill.

MR Monthly Review. An independent Socialist magazine. N.Y.

MULINO Il Mulino. Rivista mensile de cultura e politica. Bologna, Italy.

NHAC/K Kaie. National History and Arts Council of Guyana. Georgetown.

NIU/JPMS Journal of Political and Military Sociology. Northern Illinois Univ., Dept. of Sociology. DeKalb.

NRDM La Nouvelle Revue des Deux Mondes. Paris.

NS NS NorthSouth NordSud NorteSul. Canadian journal of Latin American Studies. Canadian Association of Latin American Studies. Univ. of Ottawa. Ottawa.

NSO Nueva Sociedad. Revista política y cultural. San José.

OCLAE OCLAE. Revista mensual de la Organización Continental Latinoamericana de Estudiantes. La Habana.

OLI/ZLW Zeitschrift für Lateinamerika Wien. Österreichisches Lateinamerika-Institut. Wien.

PCCLAS/P Proceedings of the Pacific Coast Council on Latin American Studies. Univ. of California. Los Angeles.

PSA/PS Political Studies. Political Studies Association of the United Kingdom. Oxford, U.K.

PUCIS/WP World Politics. A quarterly journal of international relations. Princeton Univ., Center of International Studies. Princeton, N.J.

REOP Revista Española de la OPINIÓN PÚBLICA. Instituto de la Opinión Pública. Madrid.

SECOLAS/A Annals of the Southeastern Conference on Latin American Studies. West Georgia College. Carrollton.

SPSA/JP The Journal of Politics. The Southern Political Science Association *in cooperation with the* Univ. of Florida. Gainesville.

SS Science and Society. N.Y.

TMR The Massachusetts Review. A quarterly of literature, the arts and public affairs. Amherst College; Mount Holyoke College; Smith College; and the Univ. of Massachusetts. Amherst.

UA   Urban Anthropology. State Univ. of New York, Dept. of Anthropology. Brockport.

UB/GG   Geschichte und Gesellschaft. Zeitschrift für Historische Sozialwissenschaft. Univ. Bielefeld, Fakultät für Geschichtswissenschaft. Bielefeld, FRG.

UCV/NC   Nueva Ciencia. Revista cuatrimestral. Univ. Central de Venezuela, Facultad de Economía, Instituto de Investigaciones. Caracas.

UHB/EHA   Études Hispano-Américaines. Univ. de Haute Bretagne, Centre d'Études Hispaniques, Hispano-Américaines et Luso-Brésiliennes. Rennes, France.

UM/JIAS   Journal of Inter-American Studies and World Affairs. Univ. of Miami Press *for the* Center for Advanced International Studies. Coral Gables, Fla.

UM/R   Revista Universidad de Medellín. Centro de Estudios de Posgrado. Medellín, Colombia.

UMG/RBEP   Revista Brasileira de Estudos Políticos. Univ. de Minas Gerais. Belo Horizonte, Brazil.

UNAM/RMCPS   Revista Mexicana de Ciencias Políticas y Sociales. Univ. Nacional Autónoma de México, Facultad de Ciencias Políticas y Sociales. México.

UNAM/RMS   Revista Mexicana de Sociología. Univ. Nacional Autónoma de México, Instituto de Investigaciones Sociales. México.

UND/RP   The Review of Politics. Univ. of Notre Dame. Notre Dame, Ind.

UP/A   Apuntes. Univ. del Pacífico, Centro de Investigación. Lima.

UP/CSEC   Cuban Studies/Estudios Cubanos. Univ. of Pittsburgh, Univ. Center for International Studies, Center for Latin American Studies. Pittsburgh, Pa.

UPR/RCS   Revista de Ciencias Sociales. Univ. de Puerto Rico, Colegio de Ciencias Sociales. Río Piedras.

UR/L   Lateinamerika. Univ. Rostock. Rostock, GDR.

URSS/AL   América Latina. Academia de Ciencias de la URSS [Unión de Repúblicas Soviéticas Socialistas]. Moscú.

USB/F   Franciscanum. Revista de las ciencias del espiritú. Univ. de San Buenaventura. Bogotá.

USIA/PC   Problems of Communism. United States Information Agency. Washington.

UT/SSQ   Social Science Quarterly. Univ. of Texas, Dept. of Government. Austin.

UTIEH/C   Caravelle. Cahiers du monde hispanique et lusobrésilien. Univ. de Toulouse, Institute d'Études Hispaniques, Hispano-Americaines et Luso-Brésiliennes. Toulouse, France.

UWI/SES   Social and Economic Studies. Univ. of the West Indies, Institute of Social and Economic Research. Mona, Jam.

VOZES   Vozes. Revista de cultura. Editora Vozes. Petrópolis, Brazil.

WQ   The Wilson Quarterly. Woodrow Wilson International Center for Scholars. Washington.

ZFG   Zeitschrift für Geschichtswissenschaft. Veb Deutscher Verlag der Wissenschaften. Berlin, GDR.

INTERNATIONAL RELATIONS

YALE H. FERGUSON, *Professor of Political Science, Rutgers University, Newark*
C. NEALE RONNING, *Professor of Political Science, New School for Social Research*

SURVEYING THE LITERATURE TWO YEARS ago in *HLAS 39*, we noted that no new approaches or subjects had as yet evoked the widespread interest which "dependence," "bureaucratic politics," and the multinational corporation had previously done; and, indeed, that many items simply "recycled" earlier fashions, often to lesser effect. The same might be said of the present period under review, except that the recycling has markedly declined. Diversity is the principal characteristic of the literature today, perhaps reflecting the complexity and flux of the contemporary international relations of Latin America. The traditional "special relationship" with the US has largely evaporated, pan-Latin Americanism has borne only a few fruits of major consequence, and cooperation with Nonaligned and Third World groupings has yielded little real progress toward a "new international economic order." New multilateral ties and institutions are by no means inconsequential, but there appears to be a renewed emphasis on foreign policy as an instrument of nationalism and on bilateral relationships.

After years of ritualistic assertions by many authors of the general threat to national development posed by dependency and the multinationals in particular, the present trend seems to be toward case studies of the historical or current situation in specific countries and/or with regard to certain national/multilateral actors, economic sectors, or enterprises (items **8515, 8634, 8636, 8642** and **8744**). Political and "ideological" forms of dependency are no longer as neglected as they were formerly, eclipsed by an over-emphasis on economics (items **8515, 8563, 8587, 8612** and **8617**). If the trend toward case studies continues, in due course we may have a better appreciation for the many varieties and degrees of dependency, the amount of influence which even "dependent" countries have on some international issues, the hard bargaining to safeguard their respective interests that continues to take place between governments and foreign firms in many countries, and perhaps—heresy?—the positive contributions that the multinationals can yet make where appropriate conditions prevail. These subtleties will not be welcomed by Marxists and other strident critics of "imperialism," who take "bourgeoise *dependencistas*" to tasks for allegedly ignoring class conflict and failing to examine seriously the possibility of foregoing foreign direct investment entirely (items **8528** and **8545**).

Among the noteworthy works appearing in the present time-frame is a commendable diplomatic history (item **8524**), written "both from a general Latin American viewpoint and from the national viewpoints of the several nations." Another volume with a similar perspective, but focusing on Latin America and the contemporary world economy, is a collection of high-quality essays edited by Joseph Grunwald (item **8544**). Still other works concern regional economic relations and the integration process. Schmitter (item **8591**) makes a new contribution to theory, with Latin American illustrations, while others look at practical experience in the region and various subregions (items **8502, 8509, 8562, 8566, 8693** and **8746**). F. Parkinson,

Ricardo Ffrench-Davis (ANCOM), and Francisco Alejo and Héctor Hurtado (SELA) outline some of the accomplishments to date. However, the tone of most of these writings is far from optimistic. Edward Milenky, for example, observes that neither a stress on increasing regional/subregional trade (as in LAFTA) nor "developmental nationalism" (ANCOM) has produced a wholly viable basis for cooperation. Robert Bond and Mary Jane Reid Martz are equally pessimistic about the prospects for SELA. Looking at the CACM, Royce Shaw reminds us that the barriers to integration are as much political as economic.

Several items shed additional light on significant historical periods in the evolution of US politics toward Latin America. Lester Langley (item **8553**) points out that "inter-American distrust" emerged in part because of active Jackson administration efforts to extend US commerce and influence south of the border. David Pletcher (item **8580**) unearths a sort of time capsule, a State Department survey of hemisphere trade undertaken nearly 20 years before James Blaine finally succeeded in launching a series of inter-American conferences. Gene Sessions (item **8594**) insists that the Clark Memorandum had virtually no impact on the Hoover and Roosevelt administrations' gradual subscription to the principal of non-intervention. Michael Francis (item **8805**) explores the complexities of US relations with Argentina and Chile during World War II.

Carter administration policies, not surprisingly, have generated considerable written comment. Among the best early surveys and critiques are those by Abraham Lowenthal (item **8558**) and Richard Fagen (item **8530**). See also several analyses appearing in a special issue of the Colégio de México's *Foro Internacional* (item **8531**) and the interesting new journal of Mexico's CIDE, *Estados Unidos*.

Carter came to office when US concern for Latin America and some aspects of the US role in the area had been on the ebb for a decade. Writing in 1977, for example, Jerome Slater (item **8595**) viewed US influence as "undeniable, . . . though declining . . . and nowhere near substantial enough to justify the term 'imperialism'." Lowenthal characterizes the Carter posture toward Latin America as a "not-so-special relationship." Carter decision-makers have asserted that they approach Latin America primarily in the context of global policies, with certain adjustments made for the Caribbean and key bilateral relationships. However, most observers agree that the Carter team has at least increased the amount of time and attention devoted to hemisphere affairs.

The administration receives credit for spotlighting human rights, achieving a settlement on the Panama Canal, avoiding confrontations with leftist governments in Jamaica and Guyana, taking further steps toward a normalization of relations with Cuba, and attempting to formulate a coherent policy for the Caribbean (items **8743** and **8745**). On the other hand, there seems to be something of a consensus that policy-makers were not hard enough on Somoza (because of fear of the *Sandinistas*), over-reacted to some aspects of Cuban involvement in Africa, and inadequately followed through on promises for the general Caribbean. More fundamental are the criticisms leveled by Lowenthal, that the Carter administration has failed to address effectively most of the demands for a new international economic order (item **8539**); and by Fagen, that such an emphasis would logically entail acceptance of, even support for, "radical, nationalist, and potentially 'anti-American' regimes."

The Carter human rights campaign raises a number of important questions, which bridge the subfields of international relations and comparative politics. Among these is the question of whether the civil and political liberties that have been the administration's primary concern are entirely applicable to Latin America. Howard

Wiarda (item **8610**) argues that " . . . in Iberia and Latin America, key terms like 'representation,' 'participation,' 'pluralism,' 'democracy' and 'rights' frequently have quite different meanings, carry different connotations, or imply different expectations from those predominant in the Anglo-American context." However, Latin American proponents of such liberal-democratic values would be quite indignant at the notion that what they have been struggling for, whatever its historical origins, is other than absolute in concept and probably universal in application. Indeed, one might maintain that much of the political instability in the region from independence to the present has resulted from the *competition* (rather than the melding, as Wiarda suggests) between Anglo-American institutions and values and an often-predominant authoritarian tradition and values (*caudillismo, personalismo,* etc.) with roots in the Indo-Hispanic past. To illustrate, the fact that a "corporatist" military regime rigs elections should not be taken as evidence that no one in that country knows what a genuinely free election is; moreover, given the two traditions, the rigging itself greatly subtracts from the legitimacy the regime reaps from the electoral process. For that matter, considering the current range of "authoritarian" regimes in Latin America—Mexico (item **8645**), Brazil, Paraguay, Guatemala, Cuba (item **8726**), and so on—a case might well be made that it is the authoritarian tradition, rather than the Anglo-American, which carries different meanings, connotations, and expectations.

Another question suggested by the Carter human rights record to date is whether economic and social rights should be given greater stress. Economic and social rights are much less clearly defined and accepted by governments than civil and political rights (items **8511** and **8555**), partly because they are even more threatening to existing elites. Taken seriously, such rights would seem to imply redistribution policies that would constitute at least radical reform and perhaps a full-scale "revolution." Herein lies a dilemma which proponents of this kind of change, like Fagen, tend to glass over—the potential conflict between civil and political, and economic and social rights. In many countries socioeconomic change of great magnitude cannot be accomplished rapidly without an authoritarian state and severe repression. Therefore, unless one is willing to wait for results achieved via painfully slow reform-mongering, a choice of priorities between the two types of rights must be made.

Policy choices are limited not only by conditions abroad but also by the very process(es) through which the choices are made. This holds true for human rights policies and obviously for other policies too. Fagen acknowledges that no US administration has ever been able to bring itself to identify with radical change to the extent that he advocates. In fact, given constraints like ideological blinders, bureaucratic inertia, and the increasingly conservative mood of Congress and the general public, there is literally no chance that the Carter administration, or any other administration, will do so in the foreseeable future. The same applies to Lowenthal's advocacy of a more effective response to demands for a new international economic order.

Lowenthal does attempt to explain, in terms of the policy-making process, why so many of the good resolves of new administrations usually come to naught. Explanations like this are entirely too rare in the literature, no doubt because few authors know or care enough about the process to write about it. The reader should recall our initial comment that interest in bureaucratic politics seems to be on the decline: There is only one item in this category (item **8734**), and this is critical of the approach! However, whether bureaucratic behavior is central or not, we urgently need some studies of policy-making. Researchers should not stop at the national level, insofar as multilateral institutions are also making and implementing policies. For instance, LeBlanc (item **8555**), while discussing the useful role of the OAS Commission on Human Rights in investigating and publicizing violations of civil and political rights, suggests some of the limits of what can be accomplished in a multilateral setting.

Another issue that has prompted a great deal of literature is the Panama Canal. Among the most significant documents for future historians are, of course, those of major hearings in the US Senate and House. In preparation for the ratification debate, the Congressional Research Service collected a massive volume of background documents that is of lasting value for reference (item **9699**). Wayne Bray produced an excellent annotated bibliography (item **8661**), as well as an interesting case study of the common law zone in Panama (item **8660**). The Panamanian Mission to the UN compiled reprints of magazine articles, newspaper editorials, and other materials favorable to Panama's negotiating positions (item **8687**). Richard Falk's complaint that the new treaties are insufficiently favorable to Panama (item **8668**) is refreshing, although he does not go so far as to assert that "better" agreements could have been wrung out of the US Senate. Had the Senate failed to ratify, a Panamanian monograph (item **8657**) outlining possible grounds for the formal "denunciation" of the 1903 treaty might have become a best-seller.

Yet another issue with global, regional, bilateral, and US policy dimensions has been nuclear power development in Latin America and its implications for weaponry. On this topic, see the publications emanating from the Stanley Foundation (item **8584**) and the regional agency, OPANAL (items **8541** and **8543**); also item **8548**.

Work on the history of Mexico's foreign policy and bilateral relations has proceeded apace, encouraged by the increasing availability of archival sources. Items reviewed in this section concern relations with the US (item **8613**) and France (item **8643**) in the early 19th century; the diplomacy of the Maximillian era (item **8615** and **8652**); Díaz administration agents in the US (item **8623**); the Wilsonian intervention in the Mexican Revolution (items **8624** and **8630**), and the British (item **8628**) and Japanese (item **8631**) responses; and the nationalization of oil (item **8634**).

Currently, after the Echeverría administration, Mexican foreign policy seems to be assuming a lower profile and pragmatic character. The retrospective view, which is well-articulated by Colegio de México scholars and others (items **8626**, **8638**, **8641** and **8649**) seems to be that Echeverría's *política tercermundista* was of minimal consequence; that it drew attention and material resources, perhaps deliberately, from the solution of much more pressing domestic problems.

More than Echeverría's activism, the discovery of major new resources of oil and gas has greatly enhanced Mexico's international stature. Mexico City and Washington early-on became engaged in a sharp controversy over natural gas pricing (item **8627**). Analysts agree that Mexico is now in a much stronger bargaining position than ever before and will not hesitate to use the additional leverage vis-à-vis the US on issues like trade, emigration (item **8635**), external financing, and access to technology (items **8654** and **8655**). The US-Mexico borderlands are the concerns of a useful collection of essays edited by Stanley Ross, and an article by John Sloan and Jonathan West is a pioneering examination of policy-making in five twin cities along the border. On the problem of Colorado River salinity, see items **8616**, **8618** and **8633**.

Castro's support for African revolutionaries has heightened interest in Cuban foreign policy. The indispensable book on this subject to date is a comprehensive collection of first-rate essays edited by Cole Blasier and Carmelo Mesa-Lago (item **8713**). Two other articles, by Jorge Domínguez (item **8724**) and Edward González (item **8732**) respectively, also offer excellent overviews. In addition, there have appeared several helpful Cuban chronologies (items **8718**, **8722** and **8747**). Donald Schulz pieces together available evidence on CIA plots against Castro (items **8707** and **8751**) and a possible "Cuban connection" in the JFK assassination. Gerald Bender (item **8708**) examines the African campaign, and Lynn Bender (item **8709**), Cuban sugar, both as problems in the process of normalizing relations with the US.

Cole Blasier (item **8712**) sees Cuba as increasingly enmeshed in a triangular relationship with the USSR and the US. Analysts have had a challenge trying to explain the apparent contradictions in Cuban policies, cultivating better relations with the US while jeopardizing this goal through the intervention in Africa. González views these diverse tendencies as reflecting the priorities of different elites in Cuba. A closely related matter is Soviet influence over Cuba, the extent of which is assessed by various observers (items **8728**–**8729**, **8740**, **8752** and **8756**–**8757**). In separate essays, Richard Fagen and Frank Fitzgerald respond to the "Sovietization of Cuba" thesis that, despite the Soviet presence in Cuba and a coincidence of interests with the USSR in Africa, domestic and foreign policies remain fundamentally "Cuban." Clearly, in this case as in some others, "dependency" or the absence thereof is in the eye of the beholder.

On Cuban involvement in the Angolan civil war, see especially articles by Jorge Domínguez (item **8725**) and Charles Ebinger (item **8727**). Domínguez believes that the costs to Cuba have been sufficient to discourage a future combat role in Africa, but the benefits have been adequate to encourage continued military assistance short of combat. Castro's own explanations for the African campaign may be found in items **8715** and **8716**. The Havana propaganda mill has generated additional material in the classic "capitalist dog" school that one might have thought had died with Mao (item **8758**). Only a shade better is the account by none other than Gabriel García Márquez (item **8731**). As an aside, the image of Cuban "independence" from the USSR is definitely not strengthened by the regime's fawning adulation of everything Soviet, extending in the present materials to a detailed account of the first Soviet ship to visit Cuba in 1925! (item **8738**).

The foreign and domestic policies of the small states of the British Caribbean are the subject of a good book of essays that came from a 1974 conference at the Univ. of the West Indies (item **8720**). An article by the President of the Caribbean Development Bank (item **8723**) sets forth various characteristics of the countries of the Caribbean and what they might have to gain from the new international economic order agenda. Also, James O'Flaherty (item **8745**) discusses the problem the Manley government in Jamaica poses for the US, which he argues can best be resolved in the context of a general Caribbean policy.

Turning elsewhere in the Caribbean, we might note the appearance of the first major collection of essays specifically on Venezuela's international role (item **8775**). Additional items focus on the Venezuelan oil industry and its recent nationalization (items **8773** and **8855**). As yet, however, Venezuelan foreign policy has received much less attention than its importance would appear to merit or, for example, compared with that devoted to Mexico. A number of excellent works have appeared on Venezuelan diplomatic history. Some of them are chiefly documentary but others include interpretations (e.g., Fermín Toro Jiménez, Armando, Rojas and collections by the Ministry of Foreign Affairs).

Among South American writers, boundary and territorial claims still occupy a major place in the literature, e.g., Antarctic claims, Bolivia's quest for an outlet to the sea, the Argentine-Chilean conflicts, the Venezuelan-Colombian dispute and the extent and nature of jurisdiction over adjacent waters.

Brazil and Argentina understandably receive the most attention among South American states. Brazil as an emerging world power has been the focus of much study. Schneider's outstanding work should be noted (item **8879**) as well as others by Perry Williams, Edward Wonder, Thomas Skidmore, and Wayne Selcher.

Argentine writers are concerned about Brazil's nuclear development as well as what they see as expansionist tendencies in Brazilian foreign policy. The reader should consult any issue of the Argentine publication *Estrategia* (item **8798**) for numerous examples. This might have something to do with the widespread interest in geopolitics which one finds among Argentine writers. See for example the collection by Juan Angel Chamero and others (item **8781**). The best general work on Argentine foreign policy is Edward Milenky's *Argentina's foreign policies* (item **8844**).

General

8501 Aftalión, Marcelo E. La política exterior norteamericana y América Latina (IEP/RPI, 154, nov./dic. 1977, p. 145–157)

Perceptive early assessment of the Carter administration's Latin American policies. Detecting the potential for more interest in Latin American affairs than was demonstrated during the Kissinger years, Aftalión urges Latin American governments to avoid confrontation tactics and prepare themselves for serious negotiation on key issues. [F.]

8502 Alejo, Francisco Javier and **Héctor Hurtado.** El SELA: un mecanismo para la acción. México, Fondo de Cultura Económica, 1976. 76 p. (Archivo del fondo, 58)

Short volume reviewing the "necessity" for SELA (Sistema Económico Latinoamericano) and the structure and initial activities of the new organization. Documents are appended. [F.]

8503 Alexander, Robert J. Latin America: U.S. policy lights some sparks (Freedom at Issue [Freedom House, N.Y.] 44, Jan./Feb. 1978, p. 36–38)

Brief retrospect of developments relative to political democracy and civil liberties in Latin America during 1977. In Alexander's view, there was modest progress and some of this was probably attributable to pressures from Washington. [F.]

8504 Arosemena, Justo. Estudio sobre la idea de una Liga Americana. Edición y prólogo de Ricaurte Soler. Panamá, Ediciones de la *Revista Tareas* [and] Ministerio de Relaciones Exteriores, 1974. 108 p., facsim.

Reissue of a book written by a participant from Colombia in the 1864 Lima conference, arguing that the Latin American countries should form a pan-Latin American association. Interesting historical document. [F.]

8505 Assmann, Hugo *ed.* Carter y la lógica del imperialismo. t. 1/2. San José, Editorial Universitaria Centroamericana (EDUCA), 1978. 2 v. (330, 475 p.) bibl. (Col. DEI [Depto. Ecuménico de Investigaciones])

Extensive collection of documents and previously published essays (and excerpts) by Noam Chomsky and others who are of various ideological persuasions, relating to the Carter administration's Latin American policies. The title comes from an essay by James Petras, arguing that Carter's human rights campaign is essentially an effort to bolster the image of an "imperialism" that is in deep crisis. [F.]

8506 Astiz, Carlos A. U.S. policy and Latin American reaction (CUH, 74:434, Feb. 1978, p. 49–52, 89)

Astiz suggests that, public pronouncements aside, Carter's Latin American policy is merely a continuation of the "benign neglect" that characterized previous administrations (a misreading, in this reviewer's opinion). However, Astiz believes that this is "not only prudent, but perhaps in the best interest of all concerned" and is generally accepted by Latin American governments. Private entrepreneurs have filled the vacuum, especially in increasing their lending in the area. [F.]

Baily, Samuel L. The United States and the development of South America: 1945–1975. See *HLAS 40:2381*.

8507 Baklanoff, Eric N. The expropriation of United States investments in Latin America, 1959–74: a study of international conflict and accommodation (SECOLAS/A, March 1977, p. 48–60, tables)

Examining the record of investment disputes affecting US companies in Latin America over 15-year period, as well as the OPIC insurance program, Baklanoff recommends that the US government stop directly encouraging investment in the area and instead adopt a policy of "prudential neutrality." [F.]

Bhagwati, Jagdish N. The new international economic order: the North-South debate. See item **2766**.

8508 Bizelli, Edimilson. La política norteamericana para América Latina (UCV/ECS, 15:1/4, enero/dic. 1973, p. 204–223)

Reasonably objective, brief survey of US policies toward Latin America during Nixon's first term. [F.]

8509 Bond, Robert D. Regionalism in Latin America: prospects for the Latin American Economic System—SELA (WPF/IO, 32:2, Spring 1978, p. 401–423)

Analysis of the emergence, institutions, and political dynamics of SELA, including its role as influence-enhancer for Mexico and Venezuela. Bond expects the accomplishments of the new organization to be modest, at best. [F.]

8510 Bosch García, Carlos. La base de la política exterior estadounidense. México, UNAM, Colegio de Historia, Facultad de Filosofía y Letras, 1975. 165 p., bibl. (Col. Opúsculos, 72. Serie investigación)

A slap dash survey of 19th-century US Manifest Destiny and imperialism. There are only six books in the bibliography. [F.]

8511 Brookens, Benoit Otis. Diplomatic protection of foreign economic interests: the changing structure of international law in the new international economic order (UM/JIAS, 20:1, Feb. 1978, p. 37–67, bibl.)

Excellent review by State Dept. lawyer of evolving US policy regarding the international norms applicable to expropriations of the property of US firms abroad, compared with the norms embodied in the Charter of the Economic Rights and Duties of States (passed by the UN General Assembly in

1974). The latter he regards as "de facto non-universal." [F.]

8512 Chichique, Bruno. La crisis petrolera (USCG/E, 13:44, abril/junio 1976, p. 45–73, tables)

Yet another article predicting the eventual "ultimate collapse" of imperialism, of which (according to this author) the energy crisis of the 1970s is but a forerunner. [F.]

8513 Child, John. Latin America: military strategic concepts (AF/AUR, 27:6, Sept./Oct. 1976, p. 27–42, maps)

Child identifies eight military-strategic concepts which he believes have been dominant in different periods since the mid-19th century. Missing, unfortunately, is any serious critique of these concepts or real analysis of what the author views as a possible ninth concept, "the mature military partnership." [F.]

8514 Chomsky, Noam and **Edward S. Herman.** The United States versus human rights in the Third World (MR, 29:3, July/Aug. 1977, p. 22–45, tables)

The authors complain that "the Carter human rights campaign—mainly one of words rather than deeds, in any case—has been relatively strong on Soviet violations of civil rights and weak or nonexistent on human rights in U.S. client states." A diatribe with a foregone conclusion that fails to capture the subtleties of US policy relating to this issue. [F.]

8515 Claxton, Robert H. ed. Dependency unbends: case studies in inter-American relations. Carrolton, West Georgia College, 1978. 112 p. (Studies in the social sciences, 17)

Rather good collection of historical case studies of US influence and/or lack thereof in Peru, Honduras, Brazil, Chile, Cuba, Panama, and Mexico. The editor's introduction argues the need for just such case studies as a means of refining dependency theory. Unfortunately, there is no effort made to draw general theoretical "lessons" from the cases. [F.]

8516 Colard, Daniel. Vers l'établissement d'un nouvel ordre économique international. Paris, La Documentation Française, 1977. 84 p., bibl. (Notes et études documentaires, 4412/4414)

Short monograph examining the evolution of Third World positions on economic questions in various international conferences from World War II through the mid-1970s. [F.]

8517 Collins, Terry. Pan American Airways and Latin American hotel development: 1946–1956 (HSWS/H, 18, May 1977, p. 48–55)

Interesting historical footnote on the activities of Pan Am-Intercontinental Hotel combines in the first decade after World War II, prior to the emergence of substantial US-based competition. [F.]

8518 Conference on Conflict, Order, and Peace in the Americas, *Austin, Tex., 1976.* Conflict, order, and peace in the Americas. pt. 1, Dialogues on central issues. Edited by Norman V. Walbek and Sidney Weintraub. Preface by Kenneth E. Boulding. Austin, Univ. of Texas, Lyndon B. Johnson School of Public Affairs, 1978. 125 p.

Well-conceived, interesting, and occasionally profound "dialogues" from a 1976 Univ. of Texas conference. Jacques Chonchol, Allende's Minister of Agriculture, debates ex-CIA chief William Colby; Arnold Harberger, a Univ. of Chicago economist talks with Enrique Iglesias, Executive Secretary of ECLA; and economist Kenneth E. Boulding confronts Oslo professor Johan Galtung. [F.]

Conferencia sobre Cooperación Económica entre Países en Desarrollo, *México, 1976.* Declaraciones, resoluciones, recomendaciones y decisiones adoptadas en el sistema de las Naciones Unidas y otros foros interregionales relacionados con la cooperación económica entre países en desarrollo. See item **2787.**

8519 Corti, Arístides Horacio M. and **Virgilio Martínez de Sucre.** Multinacionales y derecho. B.A., Ediciones de la Flor, 1976. 387 p. (Col. Cuestionario)

Examines the legal maneuvers of multinational corporations, as well as national legislation and judicial decisions concerning them (primarily in Argentina). Because the focus is unusual, this volume is more notable than many on the subject of foreign firms and "dependency." [F.]

8520 *Cuadernos Semestrales.* Publicación semestral de *Estados Unidos: Perspectiva Latinoamericana.* Centro de Investigación Docencia Económica (CIDE). No. 1, abril 1977–. México.

First issue of an important new Mexican journal dedicated to publishing essays, research notes, and documents interpreting US domestic and foreign policies—including the policy-making process—for a Latin American audience. The items in this issue are of high quality; written, about half, by Latin Americans and the others, by prominent North American scholars. [F.]

8521 Cuadra Moreno, Héctor. La polémica sobre el colonialismo en las Naciones Unidas: el caso de Namibia. México, UNAM, Instituto de Investigaciones Jurídicas, 1975. 138 p., map (Serie G: Estudios doctrinales, 13)

Analysis by a Mexican law professor of UN debates and resolutions regarding Namibia (Southwest Africa). [F.]

8522 Cueva, Agustín. A summary of "Problems and Perspectives of Dependency Theory" (LAP, 3[11]:4, Fall 1976, p. 12–16, bibl.)

Summary of a longer article that appeared in a Mexican publication. The author argues that dependency theory erred in attributing Latin American domestic problems to links with world capitalism rather than the other way around. He feels that if more Latin American countries would adopt the course of Marxism-Leninism, as did Cuba, they would no longer be "dependent." In his view, implicitly, dependence on the Eastern bloc is fraternalism rather than dependency. [F.]

8523 Cuevas Mardones, Gualterio. La CIA sin máscara. Introducción de Guillermo Cuevas Mardones. B.A., Ediciones Reflexión, 1976. 158 p., bibl.

Another Latin American account, intended for a popular audience, of CIA activities in the region. Draws heavily on previous exposés by V. Marchetti and J.D. Marks, and P. Agee. [F.]

8524 Davis, Harold Eugene; John J. Finan; and **F. Taylor Peck.** Latin American diplomatic history: an introduction. Baton Rouge, Louisiana State Univ. Press, 1977. 301 p., bibl.

Solid short history of Latin American diplomacy, best—as "histories" so often are—on the years prior to the close of World War II. The authors state that they have attempted "to present this history both from a general Latin American viewpoint and from the national viewpoints of the several nations, rather than from the outside." In this aim they have largely succeeded. Recommended for the classroom. [F.]

8525 Dependencia y liberación en el Tercer Mundo. B.A., Centro Editor de América Latina, 1974. 288 p., facsims., plates, tables.

Profusely illustrated articles on colonialism, political developments, and "liberation" struggles in the Third World. Although Latin American events (the Mexican Revolution, the Panama Canal, the Torres government in Bolivia) are included, the volume appears oriented mainly to Africa and Asia. [F.]

8526 Díaz Müller, Luis. Henry Kissinger: la política exterior de los Estados Unidos y América Latina. Santiago, Univ. de Chile, Instituto de Estudios Internacionales, 1976. 104 p., bibl. (Serie de publicaciones especiales, 15)

Analysis of the ideological premises and policies of Henry Kissinger. The author concludes that after 1968 US policy was more self-consciously Realpolitik and that Kissinger believed Latin America to be a low-priority region for the US. [F.]

8527 Domínguez, Jorge I. Consensus and divergence: the state of the literature on inter-American relations in the 1970s (LARR, 13:1, p. 87–126, bibl., tables)

Thoughtful survey of the literature, which finds more divergence than consensus. Concludes with table comparing eight "perspectives" on inter-American relations. [F.]

8528 Droucopoulos, Vassilis. Radical in spite of itself: a review of Constantine V. Vaitsos' *Intercountry income: distribution and transnational enterprises* (LAP, 3[11]:4, Fall 1976, p. 86–96, bibl.)

Droucopoulos likes Vaitsos' book because it provides considerable evidence that the multinational corporation is not an "agent of development." However, he regrets that Vaitsos never examines the notion that a country might develop without any appreciable foreign direct investment. [F.]

8529 Espinosa, J. Manuel. Inter-American beginnings of U.S. cultural diplomacy: 1936–1948. Foreword by John Richardson, Jr. Washington, U.S. Dept. of State, Bureau of Educational and Cultural Affairs, 1976. 365 p.,

map, tables (Cultural relations programs of the U.S. Dept. of State. Historical studies, 2. Dept. of State publication, 8854. International information and cultural series, 110)

Useful, meticulously documented study filling a gap in the literature on the early, relatively halcyon years of inter-American cultural exchange. An "afterword" sketches developments after 1948, including some of the pressures of the McCarthy period.

8530 Fagen, Richard. The Carter Administration and Latin America: business as usual? (CFR/FA, 57:3, 1978, p. 652–669)

Special issue on "America and the World 1978." Generally excellent survey and critique of the Carter policies over the first two years. Fagen concedes that "the overall political record of the Carter Administration is better than its immediate predecessors," although he faults the Carter team for its handling of the Cuba and Nicaragua issues. He is pleased by some progress on human rights regarding civil and political liberties, by the "modus vivendi" sought with leftist English-speaking Caribbean states, and the Panama Canal settlement. However, Fagen strongly condemns the administration for failing to give adequate attention to economic and social rights, which he believes would have to lead to acceptance or even support for "much more radical, nationalist, and potentially 'anti-American' politics and economics than this or any other Administration has been willing to countenance." Fagen does *not* explain how such a posture, even if desirable, could be achieved given the constraints in the US policy-making process. [F.]

Faro, José Salvador. Nova Ordem Econômica Internacional: ilusões e realidades. See item **2807**.

Fernández Retamar, Roberto. Nuestra América y Occidente. See *HLAS 40:6710*.

8531 Foro Internacional. Revista trimestral. El Colegio de México. Vol. 17, no. 4 [suplemento de *Foro Internacional 68*] abril/junio 1977–. México.

Special supplement to vol. 68, entitled "Perspectives on the Foreign Policy of the Carter Administration." Intelligent early analyses by Mexican scholars of the new US administration and its policies toward Latin America and the Third World.

8532 Francis, Michael J. Military assistance and influence: some observations. Carlisle, Pa., U.S. Army War College, Strategic Studies Institute, 1977. 19 p. (Military issues research memorandum)

Francis concludes the "potential for influence" via US military assistance "varies . . . according to the [recipient] military's institutional nature, its role in the political system, the type of aid provided, and the nature of the issue." [F.]

8533 ———. United States policy toward Latin America: an immoderate proposal (FPRI/O, 20:4, Winter 1977, p. 991–1006)

Recognizing that he may be offering a "shout in the subway," Francis nevertheless suggests to US policy-makers "an influenceless 'new' " Latin American policy: 1) de facto recognition; 2) Latin American rather than North American initiatives; 3) aid aimed at quality of life, extended without distinction for regime; and 4) hands-off attitude toward US business interests. [F.]

8534 Fraser, Donald M. Freedom and foreign policy (FP, 26, Spring 1977, p. 140–156)

Retiring congressman from Minnesota, long a champion of human rights on Capitol Hill, offers his thoughts on this issue shortly after Jimmy Carter took office. He urges support for democratic governments and arms-length treatment for authoritarian regimes of both the right and the left, and he suggests institutional mechanisms—internal bureaucratic and international—that might assist such a policy. [F.]

8535 Galli, Rosemary E. The United Nations development program, "development," and multinational corporations (LAP, 3[11]:4, Fall 1976, p. 65–85, bibl.)

Galli maintains that UN assistance in all its form (World Bank, etc.) is too bound up with international capitalism to be of much help to anyone. [F.]

8536 García Robles, Alfonso and others. Terminología usual en las relaciones internacionales. v. 1, Organismos internacionales; v. 2, Derecho international público; v. 3, Derecho diplomático y tratados. México, Secretaría de Relaciones Exteriores, 1976. 3 v. (87, 60, 87 p.) (Col. del Archivo Histórico Diplomático Mexicano, 3. Serie Divulgación, 4/6)

Three-volume set issued by Mexico's Secretariat of Foreign Relations. Vol. 1 consists of a handbook of short descriptions of various international institutions and conferences; vol. 2 is a mini-dictionary of terms such as *Doctrina Drago, mar patrimonial, reconocimiento de facto,* etc.; vol. 3 is a handbook of international legal terms concerning diplomatic relations and treaties. [F.]

8537 Gaspar, Edmund. United States-Latin America: a special relationship? Washington, American Enterprise Institute for Public Policy Research [and] Stanford Univ., Hoover Institution on War, Revolution and Peace, Stanford, Calif., 1978. 90 p. (AEI-Hoover policy studies, 26. Hoover Institution studies, 63).

An entirely too brief and superficial review of past and present policies. Gaspar concludes that Latin Americans must now "choose between their affective cultural and economic bonds with the West and the magnetism of a leading role in the Third World." Query: if the Third World movement in most respects continues to be largely symbolic, need such a choice be made? Gaspar believes that a "special relationship" between the US and Latin America can be maintained but offers few imaginative recommendations toward this end. [F.]

8538 Gidengil, Elisabeth L. Centres and peripheries: an empirical test of Galtung's theory of imperialism (JPR, 15:1, 1978, p. 51–66, tables, diagrams)

Gidengil concludes: "The results of this cluster analysis suggest that many nations of the world do, in fact, form groups in terms of the dimensions that Galtung identifies as defining his centerperiphery distinction." [F.]

8539 González Aguayo, Leopoldo. Modelos invertidos y visita presidencial a Washington (UNAM/RI, 4:15, oct./dic. 1976, p. 41–46)

The author complains that whatever shift on human rights has characterized the Latin American policies of the Carter administration, the administration has done little to lift trade restrictions or otherwise to help even "democratic" Latin American countries financially. [F.]

8540 González Alberdi, Paulino and others. El mito de los "Dos imperialismos."

B.A., Ediciones Centro de Estudios, 1975. 114 p., tables.

This slim volume consists of three essays, each by a different author. The first compares the EEC and other capitalist integration movements unfavorably with integration in the Eastern bloc. The second argues against the notion that Soviet internationalism is "imperialism." The third urges developing countries to import technology from socialist rather than capitalist countries, so as to avoid "dependency." [F.]

8541 González de León, Antonio. La renuncia al uso de la fuerza, la proscripción de las armas nucleares por zonas y el Tratado de Tlatelolco. México, Organismo para la Proscripción de las Armas Nucleares en la América Latina (OPANAL), 1976. 52 p. (Serie Estudios y monografías, 4)

Discusses the rationale for the regional zone prohibiting nuclear weapons and the Treaty of Tlatelolco in this context. Published by the organization (OPANAL) created to oversee the administration of the treaty and related matters. [F.]

Gordon, Lincoln. International stability and North-South relations. See items **7023.**

8542 Gouré, Leon and **Morris Rothenberg.** Soviet penetration of Latin America. Miami, Fla., Univ. of Miami, Center for Advanced International Studies, 1975. 204 p., tables (Monographs in international affairs)

An analysis of Soviet policies (to 1975) toward Latin America generally and with special attention to Cuba, "progressive" military regimes, and Allende's Chile. Careful survey of Soviet doctrine and positions, based largely on Russian sources, that is only slightly marred by a somewhat hostile, Cold War tone. The authors conclude that the Soviet Union "still represents a relatively minor, if growing, factor" in Latin American affairs. "Whatever happens elsewhere, the consolidation of a pro-Soviet regime in Cuba guarantees a continuing Soviet role in the Southern Hemisphere." [F.]

8542a Grabendorff, Wolf. Lateinamerikas Rolle in der Weltpolitik (BESPL, 1:4, März/April 1976, p. 27–32)

Analyzes the changing nature of Latin America's role in international politics and its increasing importance to Western Europe. Presents Latin America as the logical link between developed and developing parts of the world. [G.M. Dorn]

8543 Gros Espiell, Héctor. La desnuclearización militar de la América Latina y la sucesión de estados en materia de tratados (UCEIA/H, 18, 1977, p. 593–603)

Article by the Secretary-General of OPANAL, analyzing some of the legal problems arising from the accession of non-member states to the Treaty of Tlatelolco and Protocols I and II. [F.]

8544 Grunwald, Joseph ed. Latin America and world economy: a changing international order. Beverly Hills, Calif., Sage Publications, 1978. 323 p. (Latin American international affairs series, 2)

Important collection of essays by leading North American and Latin American authorities. Subjects include: Latin American bilateral economic relations with the US, Britain, West Germany, and Japan; the foreign economic policies of Mexico and Brazil; regional integration in the Andean countries and Central America; Latin America and the Third World; and the two major issues of external financing for development and the multinational corporation. [F.]

Halperin, Ernst. Terrorism in Latin America. See item **7026.**

8545 Harding, Timothy F. Dependency, nationalism and the state in Latin America (LAP, 3[11]:4, Fall 1976, p. 3–11, bibl.)

According to Harding, a "serious weakness" of "bourgeois dependencistas" is "their tendency to ignore class conflict." On the other hand, class conflict is the very focus of Marxist doctrine, even when Marxists themselves disagree on strategies for achieving socialism. [F.]

8546 Hechos del Tercer Mundo. B.A., Centro Editor de América Latina, 1974. 256 p., map, plates.

Articles with numerous pictures on Bolivian political history, the Chinese Revolution, Perón, Bangladesh, the Mau Mau, and other "Third World" subjects. [F.]

Hersch, Robert. The transfer of modern weapons and expertise. See *HLAS 40:2358.*

8547 Hopkins, Jack W. Latin America in world affairs: the politics of inequality.

Woodbury, N.Y., Barron's Educational Series, Inc., 1977. 226 p., bibl., maps, tables (Politics in government series)

Very basic introduction to the subject, aimed at the uninitiated "general reader" rather than the specialist. As such, not bad. [F.]

8548 Huacuz V., Jorge M. El debate nuclear y sus implicaciones en América Latina (O debate nuclear e suas implicações na América Latina) (AI/I, 2:5, sep./oct. 1977, p. 264–274, bibl.)

Opponent of nuclear energy reviews reports of inherent dangers and argues that the Third World should resist pressures from the developed countries for the introduction of this technology. [F.]

8549 Infantino, Lorenzo. Alle origini della teoria del'imperialismo (Rassegna Italiana de Sociologia [Societa Editrice Il Mulino, Bologna, Italy] 17:3, luglio/set. 1976, p. 387–420)

Basically an essay in intellectual history, tracing theoretical positions relevant to "imperialism"—pro and con—from Smith and Malthus to Myrdal. [F.]

8550 Jaguaribe, Helio. La condición imperial (FCE/TE, 45[1]:177, enero/marzo 1978, p. 21–50)

Jaguaribe reviews and critiques historical theories of imperialism, and offers his own revised theory. Maintaining that the US economy and society are currently in a state of "crisis" and that US citizens do not generally favor imperialism, he believes that it is at least within the realm of possibility that the present age will see the emergence of a more egalitarian international order sponsored by the UD. [F.]

8551 Jiménez, Roberto and **P. Zeballos.** América Latina y el mundo desarrollado: bibliografía comentada sobre relaciones de dependencia. Bogotá, Centro de Estudios para el Desarrollo e Integración de América Latina (CEDIAL), 1977. 315 p., bibl.

The author sets forth both CEPAL's early criticism of the prevailing international economic order and the later critique of CEPAL's analysis and prescriptions by dependency theorists. Two-thirds of the book is annotated bibliography, particularly useful for Latin American items. [F.]

8552 Kleiman, Ephraim. Cultural ties and trade: Spain's role in Latin America (KYKLOS, 31:2, 1978, p. 275–290, tables)

Kleiman finds that, despite presumed constant cultural affinities, Spain's trade with Latin America (and especially with certain countries in the region) increased substantially between the early 1960s and the early 1970s. This increase was both in absolute terms and relative to Spanish trade elsewhere in the world. For economist's comment, see item **2850**. [F.]

8553 Langley, Lester D. The Jacksonians and the origins of inter-American distrust (IAMEA, 30:3, Winter 1976, p. 3–21)

Langley "explores Jackson's efforts to expand American commerce and influence in Spanish Cuba, Central America, and South America, an ambitious program that marred the political relationship between the United States and the emerging republics." A significant essay since the US has usually been regarded as having retreated into isolationism soon after the Monroe Doctrine was declared and not to have been seen by Latin America with quite this much distrust until the Manifest Destiny period. For historian's comment, see *HLAS 40:2361*. [F.]

8554 LeBesnerais, Jean-Marie. L'Amérique Latine et le Droit de la Mer (FDD/NED [Problèmes d'Amérique Latine, 41] 4316/4318, 27 sept. 1976, p. 70–96, bibl.)

Consists of a detailed analysis of contemporary Latin American positions on the Law of the Sea. [F.]

8555 LeBlanc, Lawrence J. Economic, social, and cultural rights and the interamerican system (UM/JIAS, 19:1, Feb. 1977, p. 61–82, bibl.)

Not-very-interesting article on an important subject. LeBlanc traces the history of the concept of economic, social, and cultural rights in the inter-American system and concludes—merely stating the obvious—that these rights have not yet received unequivocal support. For historian's comment, see *HLAS 40:2193*. [F.]

8556 ———. The OAS and the promotion and protection of human rights. The Hague, Netherlands, Martinus Nijhoff, 1977. 179 p., tables.

Revised Ph.D. dissertation. Scholarly

and useful account of the human rights issue in the OAS—especially the work of the OAS Commission on Human Rights—through early 1976. Hopefully, LeBlanc will write at least an additional article assessing the subsequent impact in OAS circles of the Carter human rights policy. [F.]

Levi, Georgina ed. Il fascismo dipendente in America Latina: una nuova fase dei rapporti fra oligarchia e imperialismo. See item **7043a**.

8557 Lillich, Richard B. and **Thomas E. Carbonneau.** The 1976 Terrorism Amendment to the Foreign Assistance Act of 1961 (GWU/JILE, 2:2, 1977, p. 223–236)

Analysis of a 1976 amendment requiring cut-off of aid ("except where the President finds national security to require otherwise") to any country granting sanctuary to terrorists. Examining the legislative history of the amendment and various objections raised to the measure, the author concludes that it might have at least a modest positive impact. [F.]

8558 Lowenthal, Abraham F. Latin America: a not-so-special relationship (FP, 32, Fall 1978, p. 107–126)

Perhaps the best early assessment of the Carter policies. Lowenthal gives the Carter team reasonably high marks on the Panama Canal, human rights, Cuba, and Jamaica-Guyana; at the same time, pointing to some of the problems encountered. He is particularly critical of what he sees as the administration's failure to address effectively the "new international economic order" demands of Latin Americans and the South generally. What makes this essay especially enlightening, however, is Lowenthal's effort to explain—in terms of the US domestic policy-making process—why so little often comes of the resolve of new administrations to improve inter-American relations. [F.]

8559 Lubbock, Michael R. Canada and Latin America (NS, 1:1/2, 1976, p. 19–23)

The author decries what he regards as Canada's unfortunate neglect of commercial opportunities; and he discusses approvingly the activities of the Canadian Association for Latin America (CALA), founded in 1969 by a small group of businessmen and partly funded by the OAS and the IDB. [F.]

8560 McGovern, George. Perspectives on Latin America: report of a study mission to Costa Rica, Panama, Peru, and Venezuela. Report to the United States Senate Committee on Foreign Relations. Washington, GPO, 1978. 51 p.

McGovern's report on his late-1977 "study mission" to four countries, for the Senate Foreign Relations Committee. A shade more intelligent than some such reports, but one wonders whether the taxpayer's money was well-spent.

Mamalakis, Markos J. Minerals, multinationals and foreign investment in Latin America: review article. See item **2857**.

8561 Mansilla, H.C.F. Latin America and the Third World: similarities and differences in development concepts (FFES/V, 68, juni 1977, p. 119–135, bibl.)

Comparing development patterns and concepts, Mansilla finds one similarity between Latin America and the Third World generally: " . . . despite attempts by the peripheral societies to redefine national identity and establish an alternative course of development, they have not succeeded in drawing up a real contrast program and a qualitative alternative to Western capitalism and Eastern state socialism." [F.]

8562 Martz, Mary Jeanne Reid. SELA: the Latin American economic system: "ploughing the seas?" (IAMEA, 32:4, Spring 1979, p. 33–64)

Excellent assessment of the current status of SELA. The author points out that there have been few accomplishments to date and is pessimistic about the organization's prospects. SELA's weakness, she argues, stems mainly from changes in domestic and international conditions since it was founded. [F.]

8563 Mattelart, Armand. Hacia la formación de los aparatos ideológicos del "Estado Multinacional" (CYC, 4, 1975, p. 73–115)

Mattelart alleges that US-based advertising agencies, publishers, foundations, and government propaganda agencies are involved in a "new ideological offensive" in Latin America. Whether one buys the conspiracy interpretation or not, the article includes some interesting information about the activities of various US enterprises. [F.]

8564 Medina Echavarría, José. Latin America in the possible scenarios of détente (CEPAL/R, 2:2, 1976, p. 9–92)

Very long-winded and unenlightening "thought piece" on détente, its possible and probable forms, and the implications of each form for Latin America. [F.]

8565 Melo Lecaros, Luis. El resurgimiento de la Guerra Fría. Prólogo de Sergio Fernández Larraín. Santiago, Editorial Vaite, 1976. 93 p., bibl. (Col. Ciencia política)

Historical analysis of the Cold War, peaceful coexistence, and détente in light of American foreign policy, Marxist strategy, Russian imperialism. Includes discussion of the manner in which democratic nations must combat communism together. [R.]

8566 Milenky, Edward S. Latin America's multilateral diplomacy: integration, disintegration and interdependence (RIIA/IA, 53:1, Jan. 1977, p. 73–96)

Reviewing the evolution of LAFTA, ANCOM, and other Latin American institutions, Milenky observes that neither "integration" nor "developmental nationalism" has produced a "viable base for regional co-operation." Nor is he optimistic about SELA. Failure of cooperation, he believes, heralds a return to a strategy of "pragmatic opportunism," with bilateral and multilateral dimensions. [F.]

Mizuno, Hajime. Colaboración económica entre América Latina y Japón. See item **2863**.

8567 Montiel Argüello, Alejandro. Artículos sobre Derecho del Mar. Presentación de Lorenzo Guerrero. Managua, Ministerio de Relaciones Exteriores, 1971. 135 p.

Survey of major aspects of the Law of the Sea, written by a distinguished Nicaraguan jurist and diplomat. [F.]

8568 Morrow, Charles W. Une approche globale de la coopération entre le Canada et l'Amérique Latine (NS, 1:1/2, 1976, p. 9–18)

Short discussion of Canada's development assistance to Latin America from 1970 through 1976. [F.]

8569 Murray, Tracy and Ingo Walter. Quantitative restrictions, developing countries, and GATT (JWTL, 2:5, Sept./Oct. 1977, p. 391–421, tables)

Excellent analysis of the issue of quantitative restrictions placed by developed countries (DCs) on less-developed country imports, one of the remaining non-tariff barriers to expanded DC-LCD trade now that generalized preference arrangements have been widely adopted. [F.]

8570 NACLA's Latin America & Empire Report. North American Congress on Latin America. Vol. 9, No. 2, March 1975–. N.Y.

Issue on "The Politics of U.S. Arms Sales to Latin America," featuring good lead essay by Michael Klare. Klare traces what he sees as stepped-up efforts on the part of US weapons exporters, and he attempts to refute the arguments for removing constraints on US arms sales to Latin America. [F.]

8571 Nálevka, Vladimír. Československo o Latinská Amerika v letech druhé světové války. Praha, Univ. Karlova, 1972. 160 p. (Acta Universitatis Carolinae. Philosophica et historica monographia, 40)

Study of Czech-Latin American relations during World War II as seen from Czech perspective. Includes English and Spanish summaries. [G.J. Kovtun]

8572 Naudon de la Sota, Carlos. La proliferación nuclear: ensayo sobre la diseminación de la muerte. Santiago, Univ. Católica de Chile, Instituto de Ciencia Política, 1976. 37 p., map, tables (Cuadernos del Instituto de Ciencia Política, 7)

Brief superficial synthesis of the impact of nuclear proliferation on the relations among nations; discusses various agreements and treaties, and calculated war verses accidental nuclear war. [R.]

8573 Nitsch, Manfred. Latin America in the Third World (FFES/V, 68, juni 1977, p. 91–105, bibl.)

Noting that Latin Americans have traditionally been reluctant to be identified with the Third World, Nitsch nevertheless points out that such identification is less demanding today than it was prior to the oil crisis of 1973. Query: Is this the case for Latin American states with inadequate domestic sources of petroleum? In any event, Nitsch also traces Latin American participation in Third World forums like the Non-Aligned and Group of 77. [F.]

8574 O'Farrell, Justino M. América Latina: cuáles son tus problemas? B.A., Editora

Patria Grande, 1976. 278 p. (Col. Amanece, 3)
Latin America's problems, according to
the author, are basically a matter of imperialism. When the continent is one *patria
grande* of socialist peoples, there will be no
problems. Repeated references to the role of
the Church in the struggle for "liberation." [F.]

Ogelsby, J.C.M. Gringos from the far north:
essays in the history of Canadian-Latin American relations, 1866–1968. See *HLAS
40:2206*.

8575 Organization of American States.
Comisión General para el Estudio de las
Enmiendas a la Carta de la OEA y al "Pacto
de Bogotá." Actas. v. 3/4. Washington, 1975?
2 v. (438, 387 p.) (Documentos oficiales.
OEA/Ser. GCP/CG-673/76)
Minutes of the meetings of the OAS
committee responsible for formulating pro-
posed changes in the OAS Charter and Pact of
Bogotá. [F.]

8576 Ortolí, François Xavier. La Carta y la
cooperación internacional (PPO, 23:90,
oct. 1976, p. 215–228)
Commentary by the President of the
European Communities on the Charter of the
Economic Rights and Duties of States. [F.]

8577 Paz del Río Urrejola, María and others. América Latina y la política
mundial. Santiago, Instituto de Estudios Sociales, Económicos y Culturales, 1974. 205 p.,
tables (Estudios internacionales)
Six essays by Chilean scholars on a
variety of subjects, including the foreign policies of the US and the USSR, the post détente
era, and the international monetary crisis.
Competent but not especially noteworthy. [F.]

Petras, James. Latin America agro-transformation from above and outside and its social
and political implications. See item **2874**.

8578 ———. El mito de la decadencia de
los Estados Unidos como poder capitalista mundial (FACES [Univ. Central de
Venezuela, Facultad de Ciencias Económicas y
Sociales, Caracas] 1, agosto/sept. 1976, p.
12–24, illus., plate)
Petras concludes that the "decline" of
the US can easily be overestimated. Europe
and Japan are not providing all that much
competition; the US Government and US
firms are still major influences in the Third
World; and client regimes have generally been

adaptable to changing conditions. Would
knowledge of subsequent events in Iran have
modified any part of this assessment? [F.]

8579 ——— and **Robert Rhodes.** La compe-
tencia y la dominación entre las
potencias capitalistas mundiales
(UNAM/RMS, 38:2, abril/junio 1976, p. 389–
410, bibl.)
The authors review the recent economic problems and progress of the major
developed countries, as well as their continued penetration of the Third World.
Although Petras and Rhodes acknowledge
some setbacks for nationalist movements in
Latin America and elsewhere, they believe
that there are new opportunities which the
left can and should exploit. [F.]

8580 Pletcher, David M. Inter-American
trade in the early 1870s: a State Department survey (AAFH/TAM, 33:4, April 1977,
p. 593–612, table)
Pletcher examines what he calls "an
early effort at reconnaissance for the expansionist campaign which came to be called
dollar diplomacy," an 1870–71 State Dept.
survey of hemisphere trade and the problems
that US merchants faced in competing with
Europeans. Intriguing glimpse of commercial
relationships on the eve of transition. For historian's comment, see *HLAS 40:2367*.

8581 Pollock, David H. and **Michael Zuntz.**
The United States and Latin American
development: some thoughts on the problems of a newly-emerging "middle income"
region. Ottawa, Carleton Univ., The Norman
Paterson School of International Affairs,
1978. 23 p. (Current comment, 12)
Paper by the Director of ECLA's Washington Office (Pollock) and an OAS Senior
Economist (Zuntz). They point out that neither the "big few" nor the "many smaller"
(though not "poor") countries of Latin America find their problems adequately addressed
by the international community today. [F.]

Powelson, John P. The balance sheet on
multinational corporations in less developed
countries. See item **2876**.

Prats, Raymond. Une économie marginale,
périphérique et dominée. See item **2878**.

Prebisch, Raúl. Desarrollo y político comercial internacional. See item **2879**.

Price, H. Edward, Jr. The strategy and tactics of revolutionary terrorism. See item **7060**.

8582 Rangel, Carlos. The Latin Americans: their love-hate relationship with the United States. N.Y., Harcourt Brace, Jovanovich, 1977. 301 p.

Provocative book by Venezuelan writer and former diplomat, who finds most of the reasons for Latin America's problems are indigenous—the region's particular history, values, and social structures. Useful corrective to some of the excesses in the dependency literature, although Rangel does not suggest that all US influence has been benign. [F.]

8583 Ravines, Eudocio. Derrota mundial del comunismo. México, Editor Gustavo de Anda, 1977. 337 p.

Philosophical "refutation" of Marxism and paean of praise to capitalism's virtues. [F.]

8584 Redick, John R. Regional restraint: U.S. nuclear policy and Latin America (FPRI/O, 22:1, Spring 1978, p. 161–200)

Redick details the Carter policy and nuclear capabilities of various Latin American states. Given nationalist sensitivities, he maintains, countries (like Brazil and Argentina) with the most immediate nuclear potential should be encouraged to become more actively involved themselves in suggesting means of control. [F.]

8585 Reid, John Turner. Spanish American images of the United States: 1790–1960. Gainesville, The Univ. Presses of Florida, 1977. 298 p., bibl., tables (A University of Florida book)

Enjoyable and useful survey of the written comments of Spanish Americans who visited the US. Three sections cover, respectively, the periods 1790–1825, 1826–90, and 1891–1960. [F.]

8586 Relaciones Internacionales. UNAM, Facultad de Ciencias Políticas y Sociales, Centro de Relaciones Internacionales. Vol. 5, No. 16, enero/marzo 1977–. México.

Reflections by several Mexican scholars on the systematic study of international relations, including the potential and utility of theory in this field. Interesting as rare Latin American counterpart to some of the concerns of US social scientists of the "behavioral" school. [F.]

8587 Reyes Matta, Fernando. América Latina, Kissinger y la UPI: errores y omisiones desde México (CYC, 4, 1975, p. 55–72)

Analysis of "errors and omissions" in United Press International's coverage of the 1974 OAS Meeting of Foreign Ministers in Tlatelolco, Mex., when Kissinger sounded his "new dialogue" theme. The author's intention is to demonstrate reporting bias, which he has done rather convincingly, as others before him with regard both to UPI and other North American media. [F.]

Russell Tribunal, Roma. Le multinazionali in America Latina. See item **2899**.

Russell Tribunal on Repression in Brazil, Chile, and Latin America, II, Rome, 1976. Controrivoluzione in America Latina: eversione militare e strumentalizzazione dei sindacati, della cultura, delle chiese. See item **7068a**.

8588 Sagrera, Martín. Poder blanco y negro: el conflicto racial estadounidense y su repercusión mundial. Ensayo. Caracas, Monte Avila Editores, 1970. 209 p., bibl. (Col. Continente)

Rambling reflections on historical and contemporary problems of race in the US, including the observation that these problems make it a little harder for the US to be a successful imperialist power in a world that is to a large extent non-white. Less than profound. [F.]

8589 Sánchez, Walter G. ed. Panorama de la política mundial. Santiago, Univ. de Chile, Instituto de Estudios Internacionales, 1977. 305 p. (Col. Estudios internacionales)

Essays emanating from the reconstructed Institute of International Studies of the Univ. of Chile. Subjects include the foreign policies of the US, the USSR, Chile, Europe, and Japan; the energy crisis; transfer of science and technology; the Angolan civil war; transnationalism; Latin American integration; and the Chilean position on Bolivia's desire for an outlet to the sea. [F.]

8590 Schiller, Herbert I. Decolonization of information: efforts toward a new international order (LAP, 5:1, Winter 1978, p. 35–48)

Reviewing UNESCO and other initiatives aimed at establishing a "new international information order"—e.g., a press pool serving the nonaligned states—Schiller argues the necessity of extending "the battleground of anti-imperialism . . . to the cultural sector." [F.]

8591 Schmitter, Philippe C. Intercambio, poder y lealtad en la integración internacional: nuevas perspectivas de teoría y medición (INTAL/IL, 2:10, enero/feb. 1977, p. 5–28, tables)

One of the earliest North American writers on Latin American integration revisits the subject, incorporating and extending some of the general theory he and others have developed in the interim. Schmitter argues that "exchange theory" provides a "unifying paradigm" for the analysis of integration. A major article. [F.]

8592 Schröder, Hans-Jürgen. Hauptprobleme der deutschen Lateinamerikapolitik: 1933–1941 (JGSWGL, 12, 1975, p. 408–433)

Examination of commercial relations between the National Socialist government in Germany and various Latin American countries prior to the outbreak of World War II. Schröder makes clear that Washington opposed an expansion of those relations because of their threat to US business, as well as strategic interests. [F.]

8593 Selser, Gregorio and **Carlos Díaz.** El Pentágono y la política exterior norteamericana. B.A., Editorial del Noroeste, 1975. 80 p., plates, tables (Cuadernos de crisis, 20)

Pictures the US as a one-dimensional society—purely militaristic. Furthermore this characteristic is presented as becoming ever more dangerous to Latin America. [R.]

8594 Sessions, Gene A. The Clark Memorandum myth (AAFH/TAM, 34:1, July 1977, p. 40–58)

Intriguing revisionist piece arguing that the actual importance of the Clark Memorandum has been much exaggerated by historians. According to Sessions, it had little influence either on Hoover or Roosevelt administration policies. [F.]

8595 Slater, Jerome. The United States and Latin America: the new radical orthodoxy (UC/EDCC, 25:4, July 1977, p. 747–761)

Provocative review-essay, a no-holds-barred attack on the concepts of "imperial-

ism" and "dependence." Slater maintains: "That the United States continues to have *influence* in Latin America is obviously undeniable, though it is a declining influence and nowhere near substantial enough to justify the term 'imperialism.' It seems reasonable to conclude that it is not U.S. imperial power and wealth that accounts for the continuing appeal of the imperialist model to Latin American and U.S. radicals but simply the existence of *unequal* power and wealth." [F.]

8596 Smith, W.H. International terrorism: a political analysis (LIWA/YWA, 31, 1977, p. 138–157)

Good survey of tactics and counter-tactics associated with domestic and international terrorism. Smith observes: "Although the possibility of eliminating international terrorism is minimal, so too is its potential for precipitating major disruptions in world politics." [F.]

8597 Smyth, Douglas C. The global economy and the Third World: coalition or cleavage? (PUCIS/WP, 29:4, July 1977, p. 584–609, tables)

Analyzing UN voting patterns, Smyth concludes that Third World countries—though "distinct" from Western and Eastern developed countries—are far from "homogenous." Moreover, they are somewhat unpredictable in their divergence on issues. Perhaps a more interesting finding is that, at least in terms of voting, there is no "Fourth World." [F.]

Solari, Aldo E. *comp.* Poder y desarrollo: América Latina. See item **9046.**

8598 Stankovich, Radivoj. El otro camino: hacia la solidaridad mundial. México, B. Costa-Amic Editor, 1975. 223 p. (Col. Ciencias sociales, 13)

Philosophical monograph which essentially argues that if humanity could only put aside its ideological divisions—for example, capitalism or Marxism—and work together to solve basic human problems, all would be better off. This is Stankovich's "otro camino." Why didn't we think of this solution before? [F.]

8599 Steinsleger, José. Imperialismo y sindicatos en América Latina. Puebla, Méx., Univ. Autónoma de Puebla, Escuela de Filosofía y Letras, 1976. 55 p., bibl., table.

Discusses several regional labor organizations (CTAL, ORIT, and others) and their links to "Yankee imperialism" (US labor, the CIA, the multinationals, etc.). [F.]

8600 Sterling, Claire. The terrorist network (The Atlantic Monthly [Boston] 242:5, Nov. 1978, p. 37–47, plates)

Intriguing, unsensational article about the significant links between various terrorist organizations. Includes discussion of the roles of (among others) Castro's Cuba, Argentina's Montoneros, Venezuela's "Carlos," and the Soviets (who the author believes are somewhat worried about the recent escalation in terrorism) in a worldwide "network." [F.]

Tambs, Lewis A. Fatores geopolíticos na América Latina. See item **8892**.

8601 ———. Latin American geopolitics: a basic bibliography (PAIGH/G, 73, dez. 1970, p. 75–105)

Useful chronological reference source for works in various languages published from 1874 through the late 1960s. [F.]

8602 Theberge, James David and **Roger W. Fontaine.** Latin America: struggle for progress. Foreword by William J. Ronan. Lexington, Mass., Lexington Books, 1977. 205 p., map, tables (Critical choices for Americans, 14)

One of a series of volumes to come out of the Commission on Critical Choices for Americans, "a nationally representative bipartisan group of forty-two prominent Americans" brought together by Nelson Rockefeller. The material is useful as an indication of the thinking and attitudes of "prominent Americans." Among the many interesting conclusions: "Few Latin American countries will remain as dependent on the U.S. as they once were in the first half-century between 1915 and 1965." [R.]

8603 Trías, Vivian. La guerra del petróleo y la crisis económica internacional. B.A., Ediciones de Crisis, 1975. 251 p., tables.

The author recounts the events surrounding the 1974 Arab oil boycott, which "petroleum war" she regards as a major positive development in a continuing struggle of dependent peoples against "imperialism." [F.]

8604 ———. Historia del imperialismo norteamericano. t. 1, La pugna por la hegemonía: 1776–1918. B.A., A. Peña Lillo

Editor, 1975. 195 p. (Biblioteca de estudios americanos, 11)

As the title might suggest, this is hardly an objective "history" of the role of the US in Latin America from independence through World War I. The author wishes to inflame rather than inform. [F.]

8605 Vantage Conference on Energy and Nuclear Security in Latin America, *St. John's, Antigua, 1978.* Vantage conference report on energy and nuclear security in Latin America, April 25–30, 1978. Muscatine, Iowa, The Stanley Foundation, 1978. 48 p.

Conference Chairman C. Maxwell Stanley's opening address and the Rapporteur's Report (by Richard H. Stanley and John R. Redick) are quite informative. Similar to the report on the Stanley Foundation's 1976 conference (see item **8606**) but less emphasis on US policy. Participants favored regional control centers for nuclear development. [F.]

8606 Vantage Conference on U.S. Nuclear Policy and Latin America, *Charlottesville, Va., 1976.* Vantage conference report on U.S. nuclear policy and Latin America, December 10–12, 1976. Muscatine, Iowa, The Stanley Foundation, 1976. 36 p.

The Rapporteur's (John R. Redick's) Report is a useful short survey of the main issues, existing policies, and institutions affecting nuclear development and nuclear weapon potential in the region. [F.]

8607 Villagrán Kramer, Francisco. Del mar patrimonial a la zona económica: confluencia del Tercer Mundo (USC/U, 6:2, 1975, p. 13–61)

A professor from the Univ. of San Carlos in Guatemala examines in detail the evolution of Third World positions on the Law of the Sea, emphasizing the largely independent but gradually confluent (no pun intended) Latin American and African practice. This essay includes a useful country-by-country summary of the current laws of Caribbean states regarding territorial waters, conservation, etc. [F.]

8608 Vincent, R.J. Kissinger's system of foreign policy (LIWA/YWA, 31, 1977, p. 8–26)

Vincent characterizes Kissinger's basic assumptions about world politics as "traditionally American . . . fashioned by an American among Americans" and Kissinger, as a "deep structural conservative," "not a twentieth century man." Vincent fails to identify contrary trends in America's past, e.g., genuine liberalism, Wilsonian "idealism," etc. [F.]

8609 Weede, Erich. U.S. support for foreign governments or domestic disorder and imperial intervention: 1958–1965 (CPS, 10:4, Jan. 1978, p. 497–528, bibl., tables)

Highly sophisticated quantitative essay, proving conclusively that there is a "close relationship between [a country's] domestic conflict, instability, or disorder and becoming a target of foreign intervention." We are deeply indebted for this startling insight. [F.]

8610 Wiarda, Howard J. Democracy and human rights in Latin America: toward a new conceptualization (FPRI/O, 22:1, Spring 1978, p. 137–160)

According to Wiarda: " . . . in Iberia and Latin America, key terms like 'representation,' 'participation,' 'pluralism,' 'democracy,' and 'rights' frequently have quite different meanings, carry different connotations, or imply different expectations from those predominant in the Anglo-American context." Reviewer's query: Has it been primarily a matter of different expectations or, rather, *competition* between liberal-democratic values and an often-predominant authoritarian tradition and values? [F.]

Mexico

8611 Annual Meeting of the National Wildlife Federation, XXXVI [and] **North American Wildlife and Natural Resources Conference,** *XXXVII, Mexico, 1972.* Aspectos internacionales de los recursos renovables de México. México, Instituto Mexicano de Recursos Renovables, 1972. 118 p., bibl.

An unusual item. Papers presented at a 1972 conference dealing with the conservation of Mexico's flora and fauna.

8612 Benjamin, Thomas. International Harvester and the henequen marketing system in Yucatan, 1898–1915: a new perspective (IAMEA, 31:3, Winter 1977, p. 3–19, tables)

Benjamin contests the traditional explanation for the fall of Yucatán henequen prices during the 1900s. Falling prices, he says, are not primarily attributable to the International Harvester Company's land monopoly, rather to several other factors at work in Yucatán and throughout the world.

8613 Bosch García, Carlos. Historia de las relaciones entre México y los Estados Unidos: 1819–1848. México, Secretaría de Relaciones Exteriores, 1974. 225 p., bibl. (Col. del Archivo Histórico Diplomático Mexicano. Serie obras monográficas, 3)

In contrast to the author's other work on 19th-century US foreign policy (see item 8510), this is an exceptionally well-documented and balanced account of the events

leading up to, and including, the war of Texas independence and the Mexican War. Bosch García draws heavily on Mexican archives, and his study is one of a series published by Mexico's Secretariat of Foreign Relations.

8614 Colina, Rafael de la. El Protocolo de Reformas al Tratado Interamericano de Asistencia Recíproca: participación de México. México, Secretaría de Relaciones Exteriores, 1977. 238 p., bibl., fold. maps, table (Cuestiones internacionales contemporáneas, 9)

Background and documents on the Mexican proposals for revision in the Rio Treaty, considered by the OAS in the mid-1970s. Particularly troublesome from the US point of view was the notion of incorporating a concept of "collective economic security."

8615 Cortada, James W. España y Estados Unidos ante la cuestión mexicana: 1855–1868 (CM/HM, 27:3, 1978, p. 387–426, bibl.)

Well-researched essay highlighting Spain's attitude toward the French-Maximillian venture into Mexico. According to Cortada, Spain—in contrast to its attempt to reincorporate Santo Domingo—did not seek to re-establish colonial control over Mexico, but would have been pleased to provide a king if Mexico were to opt for one. Contrary to the US assessment of the situation during this period, Paris and Madrid did not always cooperate on issues of foreign policy. See also author's bibliography on Spanish diplomatic history, *HLAS 40:21*.

8616 Cruz Miramontes, Rodolfo. El problema del Río Colorado y el Acta 242 de la Comisión Internacional de Límites y Aguas (UNAM/RFD, 25:97/98, enero/junio 1975, p. 25–60, bibl.)

Analysis of the background, negotiations, and terms of existing agreements between the US and Mexico concerning the de-salinization of the Colorado River.

8617 Delli Sante, Angela. La intervención ideológica de la empresa transnacional en países dependientes: el caso de México (UNAM/RMS, 39:1, enero/marzo 1977, p. 303–323, bibl.)

Case study of an advertising boycott engineered by foreign multinationals against the Mexican newspaper, *Excélsior*, in retaliation for its editorial support of Allende. The second half of the article lists other examples of the multinationals' "ideological influence" in Mexico. Definitely worth reading.

8618 Enríquez Coyro, Ernesto. El Tratado entre México y los Estados Unidos de América sobre Ríos Internacionales: una lucha nacional de noventa años. t. 1. México, UNAM, Facultad de Ciencias Políticas y Sociales, 1975. 671 p., fold. maps (Serie Estudios, 47)

US-Mexican interactions from 1843–1943 over the Rio Bravo (or Grande del Norte), Colorado, and Tijuana. The year 1943 marked a major treaty between the two countries, and the author participated in the negotiations leading thereto. Useful background on river issues, several of which have persisted into the 1970s.

8619 Fomento Cultural Banamex, *México*. Dos revoluciones: México y los Estados Unidos. México, Editorial Jus, 1976. 222 p.

Volume issued under the joint auspices of the Colegio de México and the American Historical Association, on the occasion of the US bicentennial. Includes several essays and commentaries on various aspects of the histories of Mexico and the US, some comparing the two countries.

8620 Fontaine, André. Justicia económica internacional: la batalla de México por la racionalidad y la justicia (PPO, 22:86, junio 1976, p. 227–236)

Paen of praise to Echeverría's Charter of the Economic Rights and Duties of States. Spanish translation of the prologue to a French publication of essays on the subject.

8621 Gabaldón Márquez, Edgard. El mexicano Jorge Flores Díaz y la historia diplomática en nuestro continente. Caracas, Archivo General de la Nación, 1975. 14 p. (Biblioteca venezolana de historia, 23)

Text of a brief essay hailing the work of the author's colleague, Mexican historian Flores Díaz, in investigating his country's archives. The Venezuelan Library of History obviously thought his was an example worth emulating.

8622 Gheorghiu, Mihnea. La Carta Echeverría por el Desarme y la Paz (PPO, 22:88, agosto 1976, p. 499–514, table)

Article of interest mainly because the author is President of the Rumanian Academy of Social and Political Science and a Professor at the Univ. of Bucharest. Gheorghiu notes, among other things, that the Mexican and Rumanian delegations co-authored no less than 31 resolutions at the UN from 1970–73.

8623 Gibbs, William E. Díaz' executive agents and United States foreign policy (UM/JIAS, 20:2, May 1978, p. 165–190, bibl.)

Interesting account of Latin American "domestic manipulation" in the US. Díaz succeeded in getting recognition by "awakening from its semidormant condition in the United States an expression of commercial interest in Mexico."

8624 Gilderhus, Mark T. Diplomacy and revolution: U.S.-Mexican relations under Wilson and Carranza. Tucson, Univ. of Arizona Press, 1977. 159 p., bibl., map, tables.

Gilderhaus justifies his study of the Wilson administration's relations with Carranza, by pointing out that previous analysts have almost exclusively explained Wilson's actions as motivated by idealism *or* (the New Left view) a desire for capitalist expansion. As he demonstrates, N. Gordon Levin's characterization of Wilson as a "liberal capitalist" provides a means of integrating the two explanations. According to Gilderhaus, Wilson himself was torn between the two goals when events in Mexico proved that, to some extent, they conflicted. For historian's comment, see *HLAS 40:2390*.

8625 Gill, Mario. México y la Revolución de Octubre. México, Ediciones de Cultura Popular, 1975. 210 p. (El libro popular. Biblioteca del militante, 3)

The cover blurb suggests that the essays in this collection have "a special utility for today's militant democrat and revolutionary." Given the heavy Moscow line, the "special utility" is the *only* utility.

8626 Grabendorff, Wolf. Mexico's foreign policy indeed a foreign policy? (UM/JIAS, 20:1, Feb. 1978, p. 85–92)

Review-essay focusing on four books by Colegio de Mexico scholars. Grabendorff suggests that since Mexico uses its foreign policy as a "factor of internal stabilization," "it can hardly qualify as a *real* foreign policy." This characterization is tenuous at best, considering all that social scientists have written about "linkages" and the fact that most governments shape foreign policy to some extent for domestic consumption. On the other hand, the domestic function of foreign policy is perhaps a bit more obvious in the Mexican case than some others.

8627 Grayson, George W. Mexico and the United States: the natural gas controversy (IAMEA, 32:3, Winter 1978, p. 3–27)

Excellent account of the Carter administration's clash with Mexico on the issue of natural gas pricing. Grayson, drawing in part on interviews, covers both the background of the issue and the domestic politics involved.

8628 Grieb, Kenneth J. Sir Lionel Carden and the Anglo-American confrontation in Mexico: 1913–1914 (IAA, 1, 1975, p. 201–216, bibl.)

"The principal British objective in Mexico in 1913," says Grieb, "was maintaining the flow of Mexican oil to the royal navy which was then . . . converting to oil powered vessels." This led the British to support Huerta, which, in turn, increased Anglophobia in the US. Sir Lionel Carden was the new British minister to Mexico appointed in Oct. 1913, who was subsequently ordered out of the country when Carranza triumphed on the battlefield. For historian's comment, see *HLAS 40:2718*.

8629 Guillén, Fedro. Estados Unidos y América Latina: recuerdos de la XVI Interpalamentaria (CAM, 210:2, marzo/abril 1977, p. 54–62)

Address delivered at the 1976 joint meeting of Mexican and US legislators, the XVI Interparliamentary Conference. If the speech is any indication, it wasn't much of a meeting.

8630 Harper, James W. Hugh Lenox Scott y la diplomacia de los Estados Unidos hacia la Revolución Mexicana (CM/HM, 27:3, 1978, p. 427–445, bibl.)

Harper concludes that Gen. Scott, one of Wilson's leading negotiators with Mexico during the Revolution, was not seeking so much US commercial advantages as a Mexico that was "orderly and cordial." In this respect, he was inclined neither to "old-style imperialism" nor to the "U.S. as guardian of the world" posture of later years. Harper thinks more attention should be given to an "imperialism of idealism."

Jones, Errol D. and **David Lafrance.** Mexico's foreign affairs under President Echeverría: the special case of Chile. See *HLAS 40:2731*.

8631 Lyon, Jessie Sanders. Huerta and Adachi: an interpretation of Japanese-Mexican relations, 1913–1914 (AAFH/TAM, 34:3, April 1978, p. 476–489)

Lyon focuses on a little-known aspect of the confrontation between Huerta and Wilson. Huerta courted the Japanese as something of an economic counterweight to the US, and Japan—in the person of its Minister to Mexico, M. Adachi—allowed itself to be courted. Lyon believes that Japan was motivated as much by irritation over the California Alien Land Act (prohibiting Japanese ownership of land) as it was by commercial ambitions in Mexico.

Martínez de la Vega, Francisco. Nunca estuvo México alejado de España. See *HLAS 40:2749*.

8632 Medina Peña, Luis. El sistema bipolar en tensión: la crisis de octubre de 1962. México, El Colegio de México, Centro de Estudios Internacionales, 1971. 114 p., bibl. (Jornadas, 69)

Analysis of the 1962 Missile crisis from the perspective of Latin America, particularly that of Mexico. Discussion of bipolarity, the role of the US and the USSR, and an evaluation of the role of the UN. [R.]

8633 México. Secretaría de Relaciones Exteriores. La salinidad del Río Colorado:

una diferencia internacional. México, 1975.
171 p., maps (Col. del Archivo Histórico Diplomático Mexicana. Serie documental, 13)

Highly useful publication of the Mexican Secretariat of Foreign Relations, summarizing the ongoing negotiations between the US and Mexico over the issue of Colorado River salinity. Includes relevant documents.

8634 Meyer, Lorenzo. Mexico and the United States in the oil controversy: 1917–1942. Austin, Univ. of Texas Press, 1977. 367 p.

Scholarly study in a dependency framework. Based largely on archival sources in the two countries, some never before utilized. Meyer, a professor at Colegio de México, sees the nationalization as an early example of a Latin American government seizing control of a leading economic sector. He notes, however, that although Mexico's "dependence" was lessened in the short range by the nationalization, dependence soon reemerged in another form when transnational corporations became active in other areas of the economy. Spanish original of this study was published in 1968 and revised and reissued by El Colegio de México in 1972 as *México y los Estados Unidos en el conflicto petrolero, 1917–1942.* For historian's comment, see *HLAS 40:2395.*

8635 Mumme, Stephen P. Mexican politics and the prospects for emigration policy: a policy perspective (IAMEA, 32:1, Summer 1978, p. 67–94)

Mumme argues that because it reflects badly on the performance of the Mexican system, Mexican policy-makers are unlikely to give the emigration issue much public acknowledgement or priority. To do so, he feels, would not only run counter to PRI politics of consensus but, more basically, would call into question the government's continued emphasis on economic development over redistributive policies. For another comment, see item **7128.**

8636 *NACLA's Latin America & Empire Report.* North American Congress on Latin America. Vol. 10, No. 6, July/Aug. 1976–. N.Y.

Issue focuses on "Agro-Imperialism in Mexico's Northwest." The most interesting is Sec. II on "The Big Tomato Deal," which discusses the link between US interests and local growers in the production of tomatoes, com-

petition from Florida, and related matters.

8637 Noriega Ondovilla, Raúl. Política y diplomacia. Edición rev. y autorizada por los herederos del autor. México, Editorial Superación, 1975. 190 p., plate.

Writings on diverse subjects relating to international law and conference diplomacy by a former Mexican Ambassador to the UN and compiled by his heirs. Not a memoir.

O'Brien, Dennis J. Petróleo e intervención relaciones entre los Estados Unidos y México: 1917–1918. See *HLAS 40:2397.*

8638 Ojeda, Mario. Alcances y límites de la política exterior de México. México, El Colegio de México, 1976. 220 p., bibl., tables (Col. Centro de estudios internacionales, 17)

Excellent analysis by a Colegio de México scholar of the foreign policy of Mexico over the years, especially but not exclusively as it has related to the US. Emphasis on the economic and political, external and internal constraints on Mexico's international role. The Echeverría activist international posture is criticized as neglecting grave domestic problems.

8639 ———. La realidad geopolítica de México (CM/FI, 17:1, julio/sept. 1976, p. 1–9)

Short summary of the benefits and problems stemming from Mexico's geographical location next to the US.

8640 Paz Cabrera, Graciela. México en la ONU: la descolonización, 1946–1973. México, Secretaría de Relaciones Exteriores, 1974. 70 p., tables (Col. del Archivo Histórico Diplomático Mexicana. Serie documental, 6)

Annotated checklist of UN documents relevant to Mexico's positions on colonial questions from 1946–73.

Pellicer de Brody, Olga. La crisis mexicana: hacia una nueva dependencia. See item **7131.**

8641 ———. Las relaciones comerciales de México: una prueba para la nueva política exterior (CM/FI, 17:1, julio/sept. 1976, p. 37–50)

A leading analyst of Mexican foreign policy surveys recent economic trends and concludes that "la política tercermundista" has been of decidedly limited utility in solving the country's major problems. Much more urgent, she feels, is a vigorous "internal" policy to diminish dependency, increase the efficiency of industry, and boost production for export.

8642 Peñaloza, Tomás. Mecanismos de la dependencia: el caso de México, 1970–1975 (CM/FI, 17:1, julio/sept. 1976, p. 10–36, tables)

Careful examination of economic relations between the US and Mexico over a five-year period, including exports, imports, tourism, frontier transactions, and capital flows.

8643 Penot, Jacques. Primeros contactos diplomáticos entre México y Francia: 1808–1838. México, Secretaría de Relaciones Exteriores, 1975. 139 p., bibl. (Col. del Archivo Histórico Diplomatico Mexicano. Serie de obras monográficas, 6)

Well-documented, intriguing study of French interest in, and contacts with, Mexico during the country's early years as a sovereign entity. Important background for understanding the later Maximillian experience.

Raat, William D. The diplomacy of suppression: *Los revoltosos,* Mexico, and the United States. See *HLAS 40:2651.*

8644 Rabasa, Emilio O. Las relaciones internacionales de México en los últimos 25 años (UNAM/RI, 4:15, oct./dic. 1976, p. 15–25)

Brief review of some of the milestones and patterns in Mexican foreign relations over the previous quarter-century. Unexceptional but for the fact that the essay is written by one who helped shape Mexico's policies, a former Secretary of Foreign Affairs and Ambassador to the US.

8645 Reyna, José Luis and Richard S. Weinert *eds.* Authoritarianism in Mexico. Preface by Ronald G. Hellman. Philadelphia, Pa., Institute for the Study of Human Issues (ISHI), 1977. 241 p., tables (Inter-American politics series, 2)

Excellent collection of essays on contemporary Mexico. A key theme is that the political system of Mexico resembles, yet differs substantially from, "corporatist" systems like post-1964 Brazil. It has been corporatism with a more "populist" orientation and has been somewhat more stable because considerable "institutionalization" was achieved prior to the onset of industrialization.

8646 Robledo, Ricardo *ed.* México y el nuevo orden económico internacional: documentos. México, Partido Revolucionario Institucional (PRI), Comisión Nacional, 1976. 142 p. (Serie documentos)

Commentary and documents on the Echeverría administration's initiatives relating to a "New International Economic Order," including the Charter of the Economic Rights and Duties of States passed by the UN General Assembly in 1974.

8647 Ross, Stanley R. *ed.* Views across the border: the United States and Mexico. Foreword by Richard W. Weatherhead. Albuquerque, Univ. of New Mexico Press *in cooperation with* The Weatherhead Foundation, N.Y., 1978. 456 p., bibls., map, tables.

Useful collection of essays from a 1975 conference in San Antonio, Tex., sponsored by the Weatherhead Foundation. The essays collectively profile the US-Mexico borderlands and examine various issues concerning them.

8648 Sayles, Stephen. The Romero-Frelinghuysen convention: a milestone in border relations (UNM/NMHR, 51:4, Oct. 1976, p. 295–311)

The story of "the beginning of a long and profitable relationship between *El Porfirato* (the Díaz administration) and the US," the negotiation of an 1882 agreement granting a "Reciprocal Right to Pursue Savage Indians Across the Border Line." For historian's comment, see *HLAS 40:2658.*

Sepúlveda, César. La frontera norte de México: historia, conflictos, 1762–1975. See *HLAS 40:2446.*

8649 Shapira, Yoram. Mexico's foreign policy under Echeverría: a retrospect (IAMEA, 31:4, Spring 1978, p. 29–61)

The author contends that Echeverría's "activist-'radical' foreign policy was, to a large extent, an outgrowth of his frustrated domestic reformism."

8650 Sloan, John W. and Jonathan P. West. The role of informal policy making in U.S.-Mexico border cities (UT/SSQ, 58:2, Sept. 1977, p. 270–282, bibl., tables)

Interesting study based on 724 interviews in 1974–75 of leading public officials in five twin-city complexes on the Texas-Mexico border. The authors explore some of the attitudes of officials, the particular policy areas that are the subject of interaction, and the factors that produce cooperation.

8651 Toney, William T. A descriptive study of the control of illegal Mexican migration in the southwestern U.S. San Francisco, Calif., R&E Research Associates, 1977. 118 p., bibl., maps, tables.

Useful, factual and analytical study of what will probably be an increasingly troublesome problem. Contains statistical information in appendix tables and graphs. [R.]

8652 Topete, María de la Luz. Labor diplomática de Matías Romero en Washington: 1861–1867. México, Secretaría de Relaciones Exteriores, 1976. 459 p., bibl., facsims. (Col. del Archivo Histórico Diplomático Mexicano. Serie obras monográficas, 8)

Documentary collection of the correspondence of the Mexico legation in Washington during the years 1861–67. Invaluable resource for the diplomatic historian interested in this critical era, including the conflict over the Maximillian government.

8653 Torre Villar, Ernesto de la. Los Estados Unidos de Norteamérica y su influencia ideológica en México (UCEIA/H, 18, 1977, p. 439–474)

Analysis of the impact of North American ideas on 19th-century Mexican intellectuals and politicians. According to the author, the love-hate relationship began early.

8654 United States. Library of Congress. Congressional Research Service. Mexico's oil and gas policy: an analysis. Washington, GPO, 1979. 67 p., tables.

Extremely useful, detailed information on Mexico's resources and a thoughtful section on the likely impact of new discoveries on US-Mexican relations. The analysis suggests that Mexico, now in a much stronger bargaining position, will seek to use its leverage primarily on the issues of trade and emigration.

8655 Williams, Edward J. Oil in Mexican-U.S. relations: analysis and bargaining scenario (FPRI/O, 22:1, Spring 1978, p. 201–216)

Williams sees the Mexican government using its newly expanded oil and gas resources as a bargaining tool to obtain more trade, financing, technology, and a satisfying resolution of the *bracero* issue from the US.

Central America

8656 Ardón, Juan Ramón. Honduras: objetivo rojo en Centro América. Tegucigalpa, Imprenta Bulnes, 1975? 136 p.

A passionate "exposé" by a Honduran conservative of a Communist plot to take over his country through patently subversive measures like agrarian reform. The cover depicts several Halloween-style goblins with fists up-raised and brandishing a blood-drenched hammer-and-sickle.

8657 Arosemena G., Diógenes A.; Carlos A. López Guevara; and Julio E. Linares. La denuncia como medio de liberación nacional. Panamá, Consejo Nacional de la Empresa Privada, Comisión de Divulgación Nacional, 1975. 68 p. (Serie La cuestión canalera)

Three Panamanian authorities on international law outline several possible grounds for their country's formal "denun-

ciation" of the 1903 treaty. Had the US failed to ratify the negotiated treaties, this might have been a very relevant book.

8658 ———; ———; Rogelio E. Alfaro; and Carlos Iván Zúñiga G. La cuestión canalera de 1903 a 1936. v. 1. Panamá, Litho-Impresora Panamá, 1975. 94 p., bibl.

Essays on the negotiation and content of the 1903 treaty and several subsequent agreements affecting the status of the Canal.

8659 Bona Fide [pseud. for Camilo O. Pérez]. Anatomía de un rechazo. Panamá?, Ediciones Autodeterminación, 1974? 79 p., fold. facsims.

A Univ. of Panama law professor, writing under a pseudonym, chronicles the events of 1947, when the National Legislature was in the process of ratifying a postwar agreement giving the US new military bases in Panama. He praises popular demonstrations at the time against the agreement as the effective beginning of the struggle for Panamanian dignity.

8660 Bray, Wayne D. The common law zone in Panama: a case study in reception with some observations on the relevancy thereof to the Panama Canal Treaty controversy. Introduction by Gustavo A. Mellander. Prólogo de Alfonso L. García Martínez with an English translation. San Juan, P.R., Inter American Univ. Press, 1977. 150 p., bibl., plates.

Scholarly, delightfully written "full-dress study of the jurisprudential consequences flowing from the turnover of jurisdiction in the Canal Zone in 1904." As Bray comments: "If what is past is prologue, the story of how the Common Law came into the Zone (on little cat's feet?) must contain some lessons as the time approaches for the Civil Law to return [when the Zone] reverts to the jurisdiction of Panama."

8661 —— comp. The controversy over a new canal treaty between the United States and Panama: a selective annotated bibliography of United States, Panamanian, Colombian, French, and international organization sources. Washington, The Library of Congress, 1976. 70 p. (U.S. GPO stock number 030-001-00074-5)

Splendid annotated bibliography of books, articles, even private papers relating to the Panama Canal. An invaluable reference tool for those interested in this subject, covering the early years to just prior to the battle over the new treaties. For bibliographer's comment, see *HLAS 39:16*.

8662 Burns, E. Bradford. Panama: new treaties or new conflicts? (CUH, 74:434, Feb. 1978, p. 74–76, 87–88, map)

Summary of the main arguments for the treaties prior to Senate ratification.

8663 Castro Herrera, Guillermo. Panamá: 1977. Panamá, Centro de Estudios Latinoamericanos Justo Arosemena, 1978. 23 p., tables (Cuaderno, 5)

The author regards the new Canal treaties as generally a step forward for Panama, but only an initial step in a continuing struggle against "the bourgeoisie" and "imperialism."

8664 Cuevas Cancino, Francisco M. Del Congreso de Panamá a la Conferencia de Caracas. Caracas, Gobierno de Venezuela, Oficina Central de Información (OCI), 1976. 530 p. (Serie del sesquicentenario del Congreso de Panamá)

Reissue—to commemorate the 150th anniversary of the Congress of Panama—of a work originally published in 1955. The book traces the evolution of the inter-American system from 1826 through the Caracas Conference of 1954.

8665 DeWitt, R. Peter, Jr. The Inter-American Development Bank and political influence: with special reference to Costa Rica. N.Y., Praeger, 1977. 197 p.

Good analysis of the continuing influence of the US over the IDB's programs and priorities, with a case study of the IDB's role in Costa Rica. DeWitt is intent on demonstrating that "multilateral" institutions can be instruments of dependency.

8666 *ECA: Estudios Centroamericanos.* Revista de extensión cultural. Univ. Centroamericana José Simeon Cañas. Año 32, Nos. 339/340, enero-feb. 1977–. San Salvador.

Special issue with several good articles on the dynamics of the integration process in Central America, including problems encountered to date.

8667 EPICA (Ecumenical Program for Inter-American Communication and Action) **Task Force,** *Washington.* Panama, sovereignty for a land divided: a people's primer. Washington, 1976. 127 p., bibl., illus., maps, plates, tables.

Slick, NACLA-style, profusely illustrated collection of short essays and documents arguing for a new Panama Canal treaty.

8668 Falk, Richard A. Panama Treaty trap (FP, 30, Spring 1978, p. 68–82)

The essence of this article is captured in its opening paragraph: "The new arrangements for the Panama Canal are regressive and unwise, if not utterly imperial. They make no genuine adjustment to changing international realities, and thus they are unlikely to remain acceptable to the Panamanian people for long, nor should they." Interestingly enough, Falk does not go so far as to suggest that the Carter administration could have gotten a "better" treaty through the US domestic political process.

8669 **Fallas Monge, Carlos Luis.** Alfredo González Flores. Presentación de Oscar Aguilar Bulgarelli. San José, Ministerio de Cultura, Juventud y Deportes, Depto. de Publicaciones, 1976. 377 p., bibl., tables (Serie: ¿Quien fue y qué hizo?)

History and documents on the Costa Rican presidency of Alfredo González Flores, with emphasis on the local economic and political impact of World War I.

8670 **Galich, Manuel.** A ciento cincuenta años del Congreso de Panamá: bolivarismo y panamericanismo (CDLA, 16:96, mayo/junio 1976, p. 4–17)

Galich hails Bolívar and the 1826 Congress of Panama as initiating the idea of Pan-Latin Americanism, Latin American unity against external threats. In Galich's view, from the founding of the alternative Pan American movement in the late 19th century, the principle threat has been Yankee imperialism.

8671 **Galindo Pohl, Reynaldo.** Paso inofensivo y libre navegación. Regimen para la exploración y explotación de la zona internacional de los fondos marinos. Solución de controversias relacionadas con el Derecho del Mar. San Salvador, Ministerio de Relaciones Exteriores, 1977? 155 p.

Three treatises (in one volume) on various aspects of the law of the sea. Written by El Salvador's Ambassador to the OAS.

8672 **Gerome, Frank.** Secretary of State Philander C. Knox and his good will tour of Central America: 1912 (SECOLAS/A, 8, March 1977, p. 72–83)

Gerome asserts that there is no evidence that the "tour" improved Knox's understanding of the [Central American] nations . . . nor did it change his imperious attitude toward Latin American leaders. Nor did it "lessen Latin American fears and suspicions of 'dollar diplomacy'." For historian's comment, see *HLAS 40:2878.*

Goytía, Víctor Florencio. Capítulo séptimo: Costa Rica. See *HLAS 40:2881.*

———. El siglo XIX en Panamá: escenarios abruptos. See *HLAS 40:2882.*

8673 **Gravel, Mike.** The Panama Canal: a reexamination. A report to the United States Senate's Committee on Environment and Public Works. Washington, GPO, 1977. 46 p., maps, tables (Serial, 95–6)

Brief by the Alaska Senator for a Panama Canal settlement and a new sea-level canal across Panama, which Gravel sees as "a very viable and cost-effective alternative for moving Alaskan oil and gas surpluses to markets on the east and gulf coasts."

8674 **Grieb, Kenneth J.** Guatemala and the Second World War (IAA, 3:4, 1977, p. 377–394)

Well-documented study of the problems which the loss of German trade and the presence of an influential domestic German community in Guatemala caused the pro-Allied Ubico government during World War II. See also *HLAS 40:2885.*

8675 **Guatemala. Ministry of Foreign Affairs.** A brief resumé of Guatemala's dispute with Great Britain over the Belize territory: 1783–1977. Guatemala, 1977? 34 p., maps.

Useful official summary of the Guatemalan case.

8676 **Herrera Cáceres, H. Roberto.** El diferendo hondureño-salvadoreño: su evolución y perspectivas. Prólogo de José Oswaldo Ramos Soto. Tegucigalpa, Univ. Nacional Autónoma de Honduras (UNAH), Facultad e Ciencias Jurídicas y Sociales, 1976. 215 p. (Col. Investigaciones jurídicas)

Analysis by a Honduran law professor of the dispute with El Salvador. Legalistic but reasonably objective.

8677 ———. Honduras y la problemática del Derecho Internacional Público del Mar. Prólogo de Víctor M. Padilla. Tegucigalpa, Univ. Nacional Autónoma de Honduras, 1975. 264 p. (Col. Investigaciones jurídicas)

All any reader would ever want to know about Honduran positions and legislation relating to the Law of the Sea. Seriously, a scholarly treatise of real value to students of national and subregional practice in this field.

Hirschman, Charles. Prior U.S. residence among Mexican immigrants. See item **9082.**

8678 **Howe, Ramón Ernesto.** Una geometría para la toma de decisiones respecto a un nuevo Tratado del Canal de Panamá (USMLA/LA, 6:8, mayo 1977, p. 9–15, illus.)

Curious attempt to construct a logical model from the Kissinger-Tack principles on the Panama Canal. The model at least illustrates the interrelated and interdependent qualities of some of the principles.

8679 Jaramillo Levi, Enrique *ed.* and *comp.* Una explosión en América: el Canal de Panamá. México, Siglo XXI Editores, 1976. 380 p., bibl., plates (Historia)

Extensive anthology of essays and documents on the Panama Canal: historical antecedents, the economic and political structures of the Canal Zone, the ownership issue, and negotiations (to 1976) for a new treaty. For historian's comment, see *HLAS 40:2889*.

Jenkins, Brian and **Caesar D. Sereseres.** U.S. military assistance and the Guatemalan Armed Forces. See item **7163**.

8680 Jiménez, Eddy E. La guerra no fué de futbol: mención ensayo. La Habana, Casa de las Américas, 1974. 164 p., fold. tables, tables (Col. Premio)

The best thing about this little book is its title. Jiménez purports to explain that the 1969 "Soccer War" between El Salvador and Honduras was really a war caused by hunger, local and international oligarchies, North American imperialism, etc.

8681 Levine, Isaac Don. Hands off the Panama Canal: an anatomy of the Soviet threat in the Caribbean and its violation of the Monroe Doctrine revealed in the light of the aggression of the Russian-Cuban Axis in Angola. Washington, Monticello Books, 1976. 98 p.

A right-wing author's "attempt to break through the debilitating fog which is paralyzing the Western World and prostrating the will of the United States" and "to save the free world from the advancing dark forces of serfdom."

López-Trejo, Roberto. Realidad dramática de la República: 25 años de traición a la fuerza armada y a la patria. See *HLAS 40:2895*.

8682 *Lotería.* Lotería Nacional de Beneficencia. Nos. 266/267, abril/mayo 1978–. Panamá.

This special issue reprints part of the Ministry of Foreign Relation's report to the Panamanian Assembly in Oct. 1977, which

detailed the status of negotiations with the US on the Canal issue.

McCullough, David G. The path between the seas: the creation of the Panama Canal, 1870–1914. See *HLAS 40:2899*.

8683 Maechling, Charles, Jr. The Panama Canal: a fresh start (FPRI/O, 20:4, Winter 1977, p. 1007–1023)

Writing during the negotiations that followed the 1974 Kissinger-Tack agreement, Maechling attacks—not at all persuasively, in this reviewer's opinion—Panamanian claims to "sovereignty" over the Canal and the notion that the 1903 Treaty was imposed on a "supine" Panama. Although his arguments might have served a "defend our Canal" position, Maechling urges that the US seek some form of internationalization of the Canal. What he particularly fears is confrontations with Panama, either before or after a new regime is established for the Canal.

8684 Martínez de la Vega, Francisco. Panamá: soberanía y negociación (CAM, 36[214]: 5, sept./oct. 1977, p. 47–53)

Not-especially-noteworthy discussion of some of the negotiations leading up to the Panama Canal settlement.

8685 Maza, Emilio. Belice en la geopolítica antillana (IEP/RPI, 154, nov./dic. 1977, p. 101–112)

This Guatemalan author is convinced that the Soviet Union and Cuba want Belize as a base for subversion and possible military intimidation of the rest of Central America. Refreshing perspective, at least alongside of some of the turgid legal arguments for the Guatemalan claim.

8686 Osborne, Alfred E., Jr. On the economic cost to Panama of negotiating a peaceful solution to the Panama Canal question (UM/JIAS, 19:4, Nov. 1977, p. 509–521, bibl., tables)

After examining the economic benefits flowing to Panama from the Canal from 1965–74, Osborne analyzes how much more Panama would have received had a toll-sharing formula proposed in 1970 been adopted.

Panama. Instituto Geográfico Nacional Tommy Guardia. Atlas to the 1977 Panama Canal Treaty. See item **5886**.

————. ————. República de Panamá: mapa general de las tierras y aguas del Tratado del Canal de Panamá. See item **5888**.

8687 Panama Mission to the United Nations, *New York.* Update: Panama. Paper no. 1, The issues in brief; Paper no. 2, The Political issues. N.Y., Permanent Mission of Panama to the U.N., 1977. 2 pamphlets (Unpaged) facsims., maps, plates, tables.

Well-chosen collection of reprints of magazine articles, newspaper editorials, and other materials favorable to the Panamanian position on the Canal. Assembled, with commentary, by the Panamanian Mission to the UN. Excellent public relations job.

8688 Parada, Alfredo. El proceso de la agresividad hondureña. San Salvador, Editorial Ahora, 1974. 71 p.

Another tract from El Salvador tracing the recent history of that country's stormy relations with Honduras, including the 1969 Soccer War, and condemning alleged aggressive tendencies in Honduras.

8689 Reunión Internacional Euro-Centroamericana y Panamá, *I, San Salvador, 1974.* Primera reunión internacional euro-centroamericana y Panamá, San Salvador, 5–8 de noviembre de 1974. San Salvador, Instituto Italo-Latinoamericano, 1975? 240 p., plate, tables.

Speeches, committee reports, and other documents emanating from a 1974 conference organized in El Salvador to discuss increasing economic ties between the EEC and Central America. The conference was attended from the European side mainly by representatives from Italy.

Richter, Ernesto. Proceso de acumulación y dominación en la formación socio-política salvadoreña. See item **7162.**

8690 Salamin, Judith de and **Marcel A. Salamin C.** La concepción oligárquica de las negociaciones entre Panamá y los Estados Unidos. pt. 1, 1903–1955. Panamá, Univ. de Panamá, Escuela de Diplomacia, 1976. 84 p., bibl., tables.

Analysis for the Diplomatic School of the Univ. of Panama of the 1903 Treaty, related laws, and the direct and indirect economic benefits flowing to the US and Panama from the Canal. Much of the exegesis is for the purpose of condemnation.

8691 Salisbury, Richard V. United States intervention in Nicaragua: the Costa Rican role (Prologue [National Archives, Washington] 9:4, Winter 1977, p. 209–217, map, plate)

The role of Costa Rica in Central America has been considerable, in spite of an isolationist posture, particularly with regard to US intervention policies. [R.C. Eidt]

8692 Selser, Gregorio. El rapto de Panamá: de cómo los Estados Unidos se apropiaron del Canal. 2. ed. corregida y aumentada. B.A., Granica Editor, 1975. 319 p., bibl., illus. (Col. Nuestra América)

Propagandistic account (first published in 1964) of the history of the Panama region through the 1903 Treaty.

8693 Shaw, Royce Q. Central America: regional integration and national political development. Boulder, Colo., Westview Press, 1979. 242 p.

Up-to-date look at the domestic politics of regional integration in Central America. Shaw demonstrates that the political barriers to integration have been as formidable as the economic ones, although the two have, of course, been closely interrelated.

8694 Sibaja Chacón, Luis Fernando. Nuestro límite con Nicaragua: estudio histórico. San José, Comisión Nacional de Conmemoraciones Históricas, 1974. 279 p., bibl., maps, tables.

Historical, legal and geographic study of Costa Rican boundary dispute with Nicaragua from the Costa Rican perspective. [W.R. Garner]

8695 United States. Congress. House of Representatives. Committee on International Relations. A new Panama Canal Treaty: a Latin American imperative. Report of a study mission to Panama, November 21–23, 1975, pursuant to House Resolution 315 authorizing the Committee on International Relations to conduct thorough studies and investigations on all matters coming within the jurisdiction of the Committee. Washington, GPO, 1976. 30 p. (94th Congress, 2nd Session)

Report outlining the Study Mission's reasons for supporting a new treaty.

8696 ————. ————. ————. Committee on Merchant Marine and Fisheries.

Subcommittee on the Panama Canal. Hearings on United States' interests in the Panama Canal, July 25–27, 1977. Washington, GPO, 1977. 583 p. (95th Congress, 1st Session)

Hearings before the House Subcommittee that early-on attempted to assert a role for itself (and the House) in the ratification of the new treaties and, after their ratification, tried to sabotage implementing legislation. Most of the testimony, however, is strongly favorable to a new regime for the Canal.

8697 ——. ——. Senate. Committee on Foreign Relations. Hearings on the Panama Canal Treaty and the Treaty Concerning the Permanent Neutrality and Operation of the Panama Canal. pt. 1, Administration witnesses, Sept. 26, 27, 29, 30 and Oct. 19, 1977; pt. 2, Congressional witnesses, Oct. 4 and 5, 1977; pt. 3, Public witnesses, Oct. 10, 11, 12, 13 and 14, 1977; pt. 4; Congressional and public witnesses, Jan. 19, 20, and 25, 1978; pt. 5, Markup, Jan. 26, 27, and 30, 1978. Washington, GPO, 1977/1978. 5 v. (679, 425, 722, 597, 146 p.) fold. treaties in pocket, tables (95th Congress, 1st/2nd Sessions)

The final hearings in the Senate prior to the ratification of the Panama Canal treaties. Obviously, (an) important historical document(s).

8698 ——. Department of Defense. Is the Panama Canal a vital installation? Are New York City and the State of Alaska vital? (IAMEA, 31:3, Winter 1977, p. 93–95)

Quotation from testimony of Brig. Gen. Irwin Graham from the Joint Chiefs of Staff before the House Subcommittee on the Panama Canal. Graham is led by right-wing congressman Dornan into a semantic discussion as to what "vital interest" means, a game the general is obviously not very good at. For balance, it is regrettable that the Editor of *Inter-American Economic Affairs* did not see fit to print other testimony in the same hearing, characterizing the need for revised treaties as a "vital interest" of the US.

8699 ——. Library of Congress. Congressional Research Service. Background documents relating to the Panama Canal. Prepared for the United States Senate Committee on Foreign Relations. Foreword

by John Sparkman. Washington, GPO, 1977. 1688 p., facsim., maps, tables.

Lengthy compendium of documents which should not be overlooked by students of the Panama Canal issue.

8700 Unterkoefler, Ernest. El caso del Canal: los E.U. y la integración latinoamericana (USMLA/LA, 5:7, nov. 1976, p. 25–30)

Speech made by the Bishop of Charlestown, S.C., at a conference in Panama.

8701 Uribe, Antonio José. Colombia y los Estados Unidos de América: el Canal Interoceánico; la separación de Panamá; política internacional económica; la cooperación. Actualizado por Antonio José Uribe Portocarrero. Medellín, Colombia, Imprenta Depto. de Antioquia, 1976. 515 p., table.

Account (originally published in 1931) of the tri-cornered negotiations surrounding the separation of Panama from Colombia, the construction of the Canal, and subsequent diplomacy. This volume was originally written by a former Colombia Minister of Foreign Relations and has now been updated by his son, with material about Panama's attempts to gain full control of the Canal.

8702 Valdés, Eduardo. The roots of the problem: a positive approach to the Panama Canal issue. English translation by Agustín de la Guardia, Jr. N.Y., Vantage Press, 1977. 66 p., plate.

Valdés, a prominent Panamanian lawyer and jurist, appeals to both sides in the negotiations for a truly "creative" solution to the problem of the future of the Canal.

8703 Velasco, Jesús Agustín. Torrijos por la liberación latinoamericana. Introducción de Federico L. Salazar Naváez. Tuxla Gutiérrez, Mex., Univ. Autónoma de Chiapas (UACH), 1976. 38 p., facsims., plates.

Glowing tribute to Torrijos on the occasion of his visit to Mexico to meet with President Echeverría. Authored by a professor at the Univ. Autónoma de Chiapas.

8704 Velásquez Díaz, Max. Las cuestiones pendientes entre Honduras y El Salvador. Tegucigalpa, n.p., 1976. 40 p., fold. maps, maps.

Pamphlet in three parts: 1) analysis of

the general treaty between Honduras and El Salvador signed after the 1969 "Soccer War;" 2) chronology of the frontier disputes between the two countries from 1742–1976; 3) examination of the frontier zones still in dispute as of 1976 (useful map appended).

8705 Zelaya U., José M. De los sistemas hegemónicos, estudio de caso: Tratado Bárcenas Meneses-Esguerra; ejemplo del sistema hegemónico en el Caribe. N.Y., Hispanic Printing Corp., 1974? 153 p., bibl., map (Administración patrimonial, 1)

Defense of the position that Nicaragua is entitled to exploit the natural resources of its continental shelf in the Caribbean, despite contrary claims by Colombia

based on a 1928 treaty between the two countries. Nicaragua insists that the 1928 treaty is inherently invalid because it was imposed by the US.

8706 Zúñiga Guardia, Carlos Iván. El panameño: su vocación de libertad y las negociaciones. Panamá, Cartillas Patrióticas, 1975. 40 p. (Ediciones, 3)

Strong statement by a Panamanian Deputy demanding a treaty with the US that will finally recognize Panama's full sovereignty. He traces the history of the Canal and also speaks out against a new canal at sea level. The statement was made in the Panamanian National Assembly in 1965. [R.]

Caribbean and the Guianas

Andrianov, V. Caribbean problems. See item 7174.

8707 Ayers, Bradley Earl. The war that never was: an insider's account of CIA operations against Cuba. Indianapolis, Ind., The Bobbs-Merrill Co., 1976. 235 p.

Ayers' story covers his personal involvement in CIA training of Cuban exiles in the Florida Keys and raids on Cuba in 1963–64. Few surprises for those who know the historical record, but the book captures the atmosphere of the time and the mind-set of patriotism, romanticism, and fanatical anti-Communism among those who participated.

8708 Bender, Gerald J. Angola, the Cubans, and American anxieties (FP, 31, Summer 1978, p. 3–30)

According to Bender, an initial Carter non-alarmist and flexible posture on the issue of the Cuban presence in Angola has now hardened. He attributes this primarily to the influence of National Security Adviser Zbigniew Brzezinski, a "globalist" who emphasizes the East-West rather than local implications of African conflicts. Bender argues that African governments, aware of the "multifaceted and often constructive" Cuban role in Angola, find US opposition lacks credibility; and he urges the Carter administration to clarify for itself and others "precisely what it finds objectionable about the Cuban-Angolan relationship."

8709 Bender, Lynn Darrell. Cuba, the United States, and sugar (UPR/CS, 14:1, 1975, p. 155–160)

Excellent analysis of the importance of sugar to the Cuban economy; Cuba's current trade in sugar with the Soviets and others; and the problem of reintegrating Cuban sugar into the US market in the event of a normalization in US-Cuban political relations.

8710 Benjamin, Jules Robert. The New Deal, Cuba, and the rise of a global foreign economic policy (HU/BHR, 51:1, Spring 1977, p. 57–78)

Benjamin points out that, although such general policies of the Roosevelt administration as "nonintervention" did respond in part to a mood of isolationism in the US, its economic ties with Cuba did intensify in this period. He believes that this experience foreshadowed more active policies in external trade and lending after World War II. For historian's comment, see HLAS 40:3043.

8711 ———. The United States & Cuba: hegemony and dependent development, 1880–1934. Pittsburgh, Pa., Univ. of Pittsburgh Press, 1977. 266 p., bibl. (Pitt Latin American series)

A noteworthy study of US influence in Cuba from 1880 to 1934, the year the Platt Amendment was abrogated. According to Benjamin, the US gradually transfered its support from the old conservative elite to the moderate wing of the nationalist movement and thus maintained its hegemony (despite the temporary rise to power of radical nationalists after Machado's fall in 1933). US co-opting of moderate nationalism at the outset, he believes, was an important reason why pre-Castro civilian governments lacked legitimacy. For historian's comment, see *HLAS 40:3044.*

8712 Blasier, Cole. The Cuban-U.S.-Soviet triangle: changing angles (UP/CSEC, 8:1, Jan. 1978, p. 1–9)

Blasier's point is that Cuba is increasingly engaged in a triangular relationship, between the USSR and the US. In the longer term, he believes, Cuba "is likely to expand its ties not only with the United States but also with many other Latin American and extra-hemispheric governments."

8713 —— and **Carmelo Mesa-Lago** *eds.* Cuba in the world. Pittsburgh, Pa., Univ. of Pittsburgh Press, 1979. 343 p. (Pitt Latin American series)

Splendid collection of essays by most of the leading analysts of Cuban foreign policy, which together comprise the single most valuable volume on this subject to appear to date. The 15 essays—emanating from a 1976 Univ. of Pittsburgh conference—are organized into two sections, focusing on Cuba's political and economic roles in world affairs, respectively. Among the topics covered are: the foreign-policy role of domestic elites in Cuba; the Angolan venture; Castro's pronouncements on the Puerto Rican and Arab-Israeli issues; and Cuba's relations with the Soviets, COMECON, the English-speaking Caribbean, the Nonaligned Movement, and hemisphere multinational organizations and programs.

Carré Lazcano, Elío. Girón: una estocada a fondo. See *HLAS 49:3007.*

8714 Casal, Lourdes and **Marifeli Pérez-Stable.** Sobre Angola y los negros de Cuba (AR, 3:1, Summer 1976, p. 32–33)

Article written to refute an allegation that the Angolan campaign was an outgrowth of Fidel's effort to control Cuba's own black population. The authors concede that "Cuba is not a paradise of utopian racial equality" but assert that the Revolu-

tion has destroyed the socio-economic bases of racism.

8715 Castro, Fidel. Angola: African Girón. La Habana, Editorial de Ciencias Sociales, 1976. 30 p., plates (Ediciones políticas)

English version of Fidel Castro's speech of 19 April 1976, commemorating the 15th anniversary of the Bay of Pigs (Playa Girón) and likening that victory to the one in Angola.

8716 ——. Estamos cumpliendo un elemental deber internacionalista cuando apoyamos al pueblo de Angola (UCE/A, 354, 1976, p. 167–171)

Text of Castro's speech on 22 Dec. 1975 to the I Congress of the Cuban Communist Party. The speech defends the Cuban role in Angola.

8717 ——. Imperialismo, Tercer Mundo y Revolución. Edición y notas de Bernardo Municsa. Barcelona, Editorial Anagrama, 1975? 136 p. (Cuadernos Anagrama, 113. Serie Ciencia política)

Excerpts from Fidel's speeches on various subjects (1966–74).

8718 Chronology of U.S.-Cuban rapprochement: 1977 (UP/CSEC, 8:1, Jan. 1979, p. 36–43)

Very useful chronology of events in the nine months prior to 1 Sept. 1977 establishment of mutual interest sections. See also item **8722.**

8719 Clarke, Colin G. The quest for independence in the Caribbean: review article (JLAS, 9:2, Nov. 1977, p. 337–345)

Not-very-illuminating review of a number of books on the independence of various Caribbean states. One of those essays where the book citations themselves are more useful than the reviewer's comments.

8720 Conference on the Independence of Very Small States with Special Reference to the Caribbean, *Cave Hill, Barbados, 1974.* Size self-determination and international relations: the Caribbean. Edited by Vaughan A. Lewis. Mona, Jam., Univ. of the West Indies, Institute of Social and Economic Research (ISER), 1976. 358 p., bibl., map, tables.

Collection of quality essays, emanating from a 1974 Univ. of the West Indies

(Barbados) conference, on the domestic politics and foreign policies of the British Caribbean.

8721 *Cuba Review.* Cuba Resource Center. Vol. 8, Nos. 3/4, Oct. 1978–. N.Y.
Special issue devoted to "Cuba and Africa" of a journal published by the CRC (a group "funded by Protestant and Roman Catholic Church groups") is unabashedly sympathetic to Cuba. Includes transcript of interesting roundtable discussion involving (among others) S. Brown, M. Finley, I. Wallerstein.

8722 Cuban chronology: a reference aid. Washington, Central Intelligence Agency, National Foreign Assessment Center, 1979. 137 p. (Doc. no. RP79-10162 April 1979)
CIA chronological listing of international and domestic events affecting Cuba from 1 Jan. 1975 to 31 Dec. 1978. Extremely useful reference source for students of Cuban foreign policy. Also cries out for "event data" analysis. See also item **8718.**

8723 Demas, William G. The Caribbean and the new international economic order (UM/JIAS, 20:3, Aug. 1978, p. 229–263, tables)
In a lengthy and fact-filled article, the President of the Caribbean Development Bank discusses various characteristics of the countries of the Caribbean (political system, population, etc.)—a useful chart is appended—and what they stand to gain both from NIEO proposals generally and regional economic integration.

Domínguez, Jorge I. The armed forces and foreign relations. See item **7193a.**

8724 ——. Cuban foreign policy (CFR/FA, 57:1, Fall 1978, p. 83–108)
Excellent overview of the external policies of the Cuban government as of mid-1978. Domínguez terms those policies possibly "the outstanding success of the Cuban Revolution." Their primary (although not exclusive) aim, he feels, has been to ensure the survival of the revolutionary government. Relations with the Soviets, the African venture, and normalization of relations with the US are discussed in this context.

8725 ——. The Cuban operation in Angola: costs and benefits for the armed forces (UP/CSEC, 8:1, Jan. 1978, p. 10–21)
Domínguez writes: "... the costs are high enough that Cuba will not lightly commit its troops to another operation on the scale of the Angolan war, but ... the benefits are sufficiently high to encourage continued exercise of influence through foreign military assistant short of a combat role."

8726 Duncan, W. Raymond. Cuba: national communism in the global setting (CIIA/IJ, 32:1, Winter 1976/1977, p. 156–177)
Duncan examines Fidel's personal leadership role, Cuban nationalism, and increasing institutionalization as facets of a "hybrid form of communism" in Cuba. For another comment, see also item 7195.

8727 Ebinger, Charles K. External intervention in internal war: the politics and diplomacy of the Angolan civil war (FPRI/O, 20:3, Fall 1976, p. 669–699)
Article based primarily on field interviews conducted by the author in 1974–75. Useful less for its coverage of the Cuban role in the Angolan civil war than for its explication of the total domestic and international context at the time, which helps put Cuban involvement in perspective.

8728 Fagen, Richard R. Cuba and the Soviet Union (WQ, 2:1, Winter 1978, p. 69–81, bibl., tables)
Fagen argues: "... the Soviet presence in Cuba is both substantial and special. But equally noteworthy is how Cuban, how unSoviet, how independent Fidel Castro's regime has remained throughout this long and tangled relationship." In the author's view, both the successes and the "mistakes" of the Revolution have been inherently Cuban. For another comment, see item **7196.**

8729 Fitzgerald, Frank T. A critique of the "Sovietization of Cuba" thesis (SS, 42:1, Spring 1978, p. 1–32)
Fitzgerald maintains that the view that the Cuban Revolution was "Sovietized" after 1970 fails to recognize that there were good indigenous reasons for some of the policy and ideological shifts; that some hallmarks of the "earlier" Cuba like "moral incentives," have been maintained (though in altered form and mixed, as was to some extent the case previously, with material incentives); and that Cuba seeks to integrate

with Latin America more than with the Soviet Union, insofar as there exist regimes in
the area receptive to the idea. A noteworthy
critique of the "Sovietization" thesis, although not entirely convincing to this reviewer. For another comment, see item **7197**.

8730 Franco, José Luciano. La política de
expansión imperialista norteamericana
en el Caribe. La Habana, Univ. de La
Habana, Centro de Información Científica y
Técnica, 1975. 31 p. (Humanidades. Serie
ciencias sociales, 1 : 5)
Short monograph by a Univ. of Havana
professor surveying the "history" of US involvement in the Caribbean from the early
1700s to 1940.

8731 García Márquez, Gabriel. Operación
Carlota. Lima, Mosca Azul Editores,
1977. 31 p., map, plates.
Although one would never guess, this
pamphlet account of Cuba's role in the Angolan war was apparently authored by the famous Colombian writer.

8732 González, Edward. Complexities of
Cuban foreign policy (USIA/PC, 26 : 6,
Nov./Dec. 1977, p. 1–15, plates, table)
An important essay. González relates
the apparent contradictions in recent Cuban
foreign policy—seeking accommodation
with the US while pursuing a controversial
interventionist policy in Africa—to "the
alignment of [three different] elites within
the Cuban leadership." The three groups are
Fidel and his closest associates, civilian
technocrats, and the military.

—————. Institutionalization, political elites,
and foreign policies. See item **7198a**.

Gouré, Leon and **Morris Rothenberg.** Soviet
penetration of Latin America. See item **8542**.

**8733 Guyana. Office of the Prime Minis-
ter.** Review: a pictorial review of
Prime Minister Forbes Burnham's visits to
China, Cuba and Romania. Georgetown,
1976. 44 p., plates.

8734 Hafner, Donald L. Bureaucratic politics and "those frigging missiles:" JFK,
Cuba and U.S. missiles in Turkey (FPRI/O,
21 : 2, Summer 1977, p. 307–333)
A revisionist study of US policy-making during the Cuban Missile Crisis. Hafner
argues that the role of bureaucracies in this
case has been greatly exaggerated by students

of "bureaucratic politics." He then launches
into an attack on the bureaucratic politics
perspective itself. His main contention is
that the approach places entirely too much
emphasis on the obstructionism of bureaucracies and too little on their positive
impact on US foreign policy. One need not
share Hafner's faith in bureaucracies to recognize that his is an important critique of
post-Graham Allison conventional wisdom.

8735 *International Policy Report.* Center
for International Policy. Vol. 3, No. 3,
Nov. 1977–. Washington.
This issue includes two essays: Patricia Weiss Fagen examines the past and
present status of US relations with Castro's
Cuba, concluding that the most serious
obstacle to a normalization continues to be
"an unyielding 'anticommunism'" among certain influential groups both within and outside the U.S. government." Christy Macy
briefly reviews the record of CIA activities
against Castro in the early 1960s and the current problems posed by still-active Cuban
exile "terrorists."

8736 Ireland, Gordon. Boundaries, possessions, and conflicts in Central and
North America and the Caribbean. N.Y., Oc-
tagon Books, 1971. 432 p., maps.
Reprint of a 1941 volume, compan-
ion to another on South America published in
1938. Still useful for background and historical reference.

8737 James, Ariel. La United Fruit Company y la penetración imperialista en
el área del Caribe (OCLAE, 10 : 3, 1976, p. 12–
21, illus.)
Short diatribe about the company's
expansion and activities, mainly in pre-
Revolution Cuba. This "Ariel" is not Rodó.

8738 Jiménez de la Cal, Arnaldo. El primer
barco soviético que visitó nuestro país.
La Habana, Partido Comunista de Cuba,
Comité Central, Depto. de Orientación Revo-
lucionaria, 1975. 44 p., bibl., facsims., plates
(Concurso de historia primero de enero)
Account of the first Soviet ship to visit
Cuba—the Vatslav Vorovski, in 1925.

8739 Joseph, Cedric L. The strategic importance of the British West Indies:
1882–1932 (UWI/JCH, 6/7, May/Nov. 1973, p.
23–67)
Discussion, based largely on archival

research, of the declining strategic importance of the British West Indies to Britain and its increasing importance to the US, as the US gradually replaced Britain as the leading power in the Western Hemisphere.

Langley, Lester D. Struggle for the American Mediterranean: United States-European rivalry in the Gulf-Caribbean, 1776–1904. See *HLAS 40:2190*.

8740 Levesque, Jacques. L'URSS et la Révolution Cubaine. Montréal, Canada, Fondation National des Sciences Politiques [and] Univ. de Montréal, 1976. 219 p., bibl., tables (Travaux et recherches de science politique, 42)

Study by a French Canadian professor of the Soviet Union's relations with Castro's Cuba, in three stages: 1) "From Prudence to Enthusiasm" (1959–63); 2) "From Enthusiasm to Disillusionment" (1963–68); and 3) "From Disillusionment to Accommodation" (1969–75). Solid work, drawing partly on Soviet sources, although few genuinely new insights.

8741 Maldonado Denis, Manuel. Las perspectivas del nacionalismo latinoamericano: el caso de Puerto Rico (UNAM/RMS, 38[38]:4, oct./dic. 1976, p. 799–810)

Brief history of the Puerto Rican nationalist movement, concluding that all will be well when the "working class" in that "country" gets moving as Marx commands.

8742 Marrero, Juan. El rostro de la victoria del socialismo. La Habana, Instituto Cubano del Libro, Editorial Arte y Literatura, 1975. 238 p., bibl.

A short, adulatory account of the Russian Revolution and the evolution of the USSR to modern times, including a travelfolder glimpse of some of the Soviet provinces. Two chapters discuss Soviet assistance to the Cuban Revolution and Vietnam. Where Is Mao?

8743 Martin, John Bartlow. U.S. policy in the Caribbean. With a foreword by M.J. Rossant. Boulder, Colo., Westview Press, 1978. 420 p., bibl., tables (A Twentieth Century Fund essay)

An important book. Includes a generally excellent analysis of US relations with the Caribbean, organized chronologically, with emphasis on the years 1952 to the present: US Latin American policies, the policy-making process (Martin was often an "insider" and privy to bureaucratic battles), and domestic conditions in each Caribbean country are discussed enroute. Martin summarizes (p. 277): "It is the underlying thesis of this book that the United States has vitally important economic, political, and strategic interests in the Caribbean; that we have neglected the Caribbean for at least a decade; that during that time much of the Caribbean has been transforming itself radically; that it has been detaching itself from us politically and making economic demands on us, some of them legitimate, to which we have responded inadequately; and that it is now time to adopt a whole new set of Caribbean policies." The recommended policies are intelligent, although few are new or surprising proposals. If there is one major deficiency in the book, it is that the "vital interest" thesis is accepted a little too readily.

Mesa-Lago, Carmelo. The economics of U.S.-Cuban rapprochement. See item **7211a.**

———. The economy and international economic relations. See item **7211b.**

8744 *NACLA: Report on the Americas.* North American Congress on Latin America. Vol. 12, No. 3, May/June 1978–. N.Y.

Useful data on the Jamaican bauxite industry in this issue.

8745 O'Flaherty, J. Daniel. Finding Jamaica's way (FP, 31, Summer 1978, p. 137–158)

O'Flaherty commends the Carter administration for improving relations with Manley's Jamaica. However, he believes that Jamaica's problems must be addressed in the context of a general US policy for the Caribbean, promised but not yet fully delivered by Carter. Such a policy might, among other benefits, shield US-Jamaican relations from rightist critics of Manley's friendly posture toward Castro's Cuba.

8746 Parkinson, F. International economic integration in Latin America and the Caribbean: a survey (LIWA/YWA, 31, 1977, p. 236–256)

Helpful comparison of LAFTA, CACM, ANCOM, and CARICOM as to liberalization of internal trade, common external tariff, control of foreign investments, industrialization, and finance. SELA is not discussed.

8747 Pérez-López, Jorge F. and **René G. Pérez-López.** A calendar of Cuban bilateral agreements, 1959–1975: description and uses (UP/CSEC, 7:2, July 1977, p. 167–182, tables)

Discussion of the methodology and utility of a forthcoming "calendar" of Cuban bilateral agreements, with an analysis of patterns in the year 1973 as an example.

8748 Puerto Rican Socialist Party, *San Juan.* The economic importance of Puerto Rico for the United States (LAP, 3[10]:3, Summer 1976, p. 46–65, tables)

After objectively reviewing Puerto Rico's economic links with the US and the performance of the Puerto Rican economy in recent years, this study concludes—optimistically, from the vantagepoint of its authors—that "in Puerto Rico and worldwide, capitalism is clearly on the decline."

8749 Rivero Collado, Carlos. Los sobrinos del Tío Sam. La Habana, Instituto Cubano del Libro, Editorial de Ciencias Sociales, 1976. 382 p., plates.

Vitriolic denunciation of exile plots against the Castro government.

8750 Ronfeldt, David F. Superclients and superpowers: Cuba-Soviet Union/Iran-United States. Santa Monica, Calif., The Rand Corporation, 1978. 29 p. (The Rand paper series)

Interesting comparison of independence/dependence of "superclients" Cuba and Iran from/on their respective superpowers, the USSR and the US. Special attention to the "benefits" of normalization of relations with the USSR in the case of the Shah, as an indication that Castro could accommodate with the US and thereby strengthen his position vis-à-vis the Soviets and domestic elites opposed to Soviet dominance. Subsequent fall of the Shah casts something of a pall over this analysis.

Schroeder, Richard D. Cuban expansionism. See item **7218.**

8751 Schulz, Donald E. Kennedy and the Cuban connection (FP, 26, Spring 1977, p. 57–64)

Effort to pull together available infor-

mation on CIA plots to assassinate Castro, Kennedy's interest in a possible normalization of relations, and the "Cuban connection" in the JFK assassination. Schulz believes it is unlikely, but not impossible, that Castro had a hand in Kennedy's death. He is quite critical of the Warren Commission proceedings and supportive of new congressional inquiries into political assassinations.

8752 Shapira, Yoram and **Edy Kaufman.** Cuba's Israel policy: the shift to the Soviet line (UP/CSEC, 8:1, Jan. 1978, p. 22–35)

According to the authors: "Although semi-official anti-Zionism had already surfaced in Cuba in the mid-1960s, Castro did not fully develop his attacks until the Algiers Conference in late 1973. Since then, stepped-up anti-Israeli pronouncements and virulent anti-Zionist declarations have become Cuba's major means of mobilizing Arab support in international organizations and Third World forums. Occasionally, pro-Palestinian pronouncements even go beyond the Soviet stance, which does not deny Israel's right to exist." Shapira and Kaufman also suggest that a future Middle East armed conflict might find Cuba participating, "most likely on the Syrian-Israeli front."

8753 Sherwin, Martin J. and **Peter Winn.** The U.S. and Cuba (WQ, 2:1, Winter 1978, p. 57–68, illus., map)

Unexceptional brief historical summary of US-Cuba relations from the 19th century to the present.

8754 Soderlund, Walter C. United States intervention in the Dominican Republic, 1916 and 1965: a comparative case study (NS, 2:3/4, 1977, p. 87–108)

The "comparison" yields the conclusions that the US has been a major actor in some Latin American domestic systems, that the US still uses force in pursuit of its foreign policy goals (albeit in 1965 under an OAS canopy), and that neither intervention established real democracy in the Dominican Republic. Why was this article written?

8755 Somoza Debayle, Anastasio. Communist-Cuban aggression versus the socio-economic development of Nicaragua. Managua, Presidencia de la República, Secretaría de Información y Prensa, 1977. 30 p., plates, tables.

In this speech (delivered 26 Jan. 1977), as its title suggests, Somoza extols his own accomplishments and blames unrest in his country exclusively on Castroist subversion. An adulatory introduction is offered by the President of the American-Nicaraguan Chamber of Commerce, Walter Duncan.

8756 United States. Congress. House of Representatives. Committee on International Relations. Subcommittee on Inter-American Affairs. Hearings on the impact of Cuban-Soviet ties in the western hemisphere, March 14 and 15; April 5 and 12, 1978. Washington, GPO, 1978. 199 p., bibl., tables (95th Congress,. 2nd Session)

Includes testimony of a variety of government and academic experts on recent links between the USSR and Cuba, Cuba's involvement in Africa, and the implications for the Western Hemisphere. Most witnesses stress the distinctiveness of Cuban foreign policy, despite a convergence of interests with the Soviets in Africa, and the limited activity of the Castro regime in Latin America today. Roger Fontaine is almost alone in warning about a continuing Cuban subversive threat in the Western Hemisphere, although even he admits this area is one of "less priority" for Castro and the Soviets.

8757 ———. ———. ———. ———. Subcommittee on International, Political

and Military Affairs. Hearings on Soviet activities in Cuba. Pts. 6/7, Communist influences in the Western Hemisphere, Oct. 7, 1975; June 15 and Sept. 16, 1976. Washington, GPO, 1976. 127 p. (94th Congress. 1st/2nd Sessions)

Statements mainly by Defense Intelligence Agency analysts on the Soviet naval presence in Cuba, the Angolan case, and Cuban influence (or lack thereof) in Latin America. The testimony of William H. Luen, Deputy Assistant Secretary of State for Inter-American Affairs, is a good summary of the Dept. of State's views on the problem of Cuba in the closing months of Kissinger's reign.

8758 Valdés Vivó, Raúl. Angola: fin del mito de los mercenarios. La Habana?, Imprenta Federico Engels de la Empresa de Medios de Propaganda, 1976. 127 p., plates.

Propagandistic Cuban account of the role of mercenaries in the Angola war. The imaginative cover shows four such soldiers marching under a flag that is a US hundred-dollar bill.

8759 Walters, Barbara. An interview with Fidel Castro (FP, 28, Fall 1977, p. 22–51, plates)

Partial text of Ms. Walter's 1977 interview with Castro, including much that was not aired on television. Worth reading.

South America

8760 L'Accord Nucléaire Germano-Brésilien et Washington (FDD/NED [Problèmes d'Amérique Latine, 44] 4391/4393, 17 juin 1977, p. 19–36)

Thorough discussion of the nuclear purchases by Brazil from the Federal Republic of Germany, and US opposition to this transaction. Article also includes the text of several documents, including the Brazilian "White Book" of March 1977, and a statement of President Carter's position on nuclear transfers. [P.B. Taylor, Jr.]

Aguilera, Jesús Antonio. Las fronteras de Venezuela. See item **5563.**

8761 Alcivar Castillo, Gonzalo. Estudios internacionales. Nota preliminar de Francisco Salazar Alvarado. Prólogo de Alfonso Barrera Valverde. Quito, Editorial Casa de la Cultura Ecuatoriana, 1977. 364 p., plate.

Texts of speeches and memoranda written by the author present his philosophy of international law. He discusses the questions involved in the Cyprus situation, international security, law, aggression and the UN; and analyzes territorial and maritime economic zones and political limits of nations.

8762 Amarante, José Alberto Albano do. O Acordo Nuclear Brasil-Alemanha: um reexame após 21 meses (SESC/PB, 15 : 167, julho 1977, p. 28–35, bibl., table)

A Brazilian scientist explains why Brazil needs nuclear energy, the reason for the agreement with West Germany, the nature of that agreement, the measures taken under the agreement (until 1977), Brazil's refusal to sign the non-proliferation treaty and comments briefly on future developments.

8763 Argentina. Ministerio de Cultura y Educación. Dirección de Bibliotecas Populares. Soberanía: contribución bibliográfica a la afirmación de derechos argentinos sobre las Malvinas, Islas y Sector Antártico. B.A., 1975. 15 p.

Very useful but unannotated bibliography of 278 sources on Argentina's interests in the Malvinas and the Antarctic.

8764 ———. Ministerio de Relaciones Exteriores y Culto. Argentina y la plataforma continental. B.A., 1974. 39 l.

Examines Argentina's interest in the international legal aspects of jurisdiction over continental shelf; discusses historical background, natural resources; and inter-American legal precedents.

8765 Asociación Pro-Venezuela, *Caracas.* El Presidente Pérez, La Nación Venezolana, y la guerra del petróleo declarada por Mr. Ford. Compilación hemerográfica de la . . . Presentación de Reinaldo Cervini. Caracas, Ediciones Centauro, 1974. 230 p.

Useful collection of source materials on contemporary US-Venezuelan relations. Includes the most important statements by US and Venezuelan officials (including Presidents Gerald M. Ford and Carlos Andrés Pérez) with respect to oil prices and the energy crisis. Covers reaction in the Venezuelan press and other segments of Venezuelan opinion.

8766 Atroshenko, A. Brazil: problems of development (IA, 3, March 1977, p. 62–68)

Soviet critic argues that Brazilian development cannot serve as a model for developing countries. It has opened up the country to foreign monopolies and intensified the exploitation of the working people.

8767 Báez, René. El panorama internacional: un enfoque crítico. Quito, Ediciones Crítica, 1977. 119 p.

Collection of brief newspaper articles of Marxist orientation, some of which were published in *El Sol de México* between Oct. 1976 and May 1977, when the political orientation of the paper changed. The articles are of more interest for this reason than for any new information or insight offered.

8768 Baily, Samuel L. The United States and the development of South America: 1945–1975. N.Y., Franklin Watts, New Viewpoints, 1976. 246 p., bibl., map, tables.

The book deals with South America because, as the author shows, the US has treated that area somewhat differently than other parts of Latin America. It focuses critically on the broad outline of US-South American relations with representative countries, is factual and has few if any axes to grind.

8769 Balderrama, Joel. El Puerto imposible para Bolivia. Prólogo de Manuel Frontaura Argandona. Cochabamba, Bol., Univ. Boliviana Mayor de San Simón (UMSS), 1976. 128 p.

Analysis of the many plans to resolve Bolivia's lack of access to the Pacific Ocean, lost as a result of the War of the Pacific (1879–83) that had its roots in the disputed boundary between Bolivia and Chile. Discusses Bolivia's relations with Chile, and includes 18th- and 19th-century documents dealing with the dispute. Proposes solution to the issue.

8770 Banzer Suárez, Hugo. Bolivia: contexto internacional y perspectiva interna. La Paz, Presidencia de la República, Secretaría de Prensa e Informaciones (SPI), 1976. 30 p.

Brief statement of what Bolivian President Banzer claimed were the major outlines of his administration's policy. The reference to 1980 as the date when Bolivia will begin its stage of "definitive institutionalization" is interesting in the light of what has followed since that time.

8771 Baptista Gumucio, Mariano. En lugar del desastre: Bolivia y el conflicto peruano-chileno. La Paz, Editorial Los Amigos del Libro, 1975. 105 p., illus., map, tables (Mini Col. Un siglo y medio)

A wide ranging discussion of Bolivia's history and problems. The conflict between Peru and Chile is only part of the analysis.

Bartley, Russell H. The inception of Russo-Brazilian relations: 1808–1828. See *HLAS 40:3962.*

8772 Bath, Sérgio F. Guarischi. A formação do diplomata brasileiro (UMG/RBEP, 47, julho 1978, p. 245–251)

Very brief but contains useful information on the Instituto Rio Branco and its role in training Brazilian diplomats with data as late as 1977.

8773 Betancourt, Rómulo. Venezuela's oil. Boston, Allen & Unwin, 1978. 275 p.

The country's leading statesman and the author of an early (1956) book on the Venezuelan oil industry reflects on its subsequent evolution—the problems and potential of the industry, and national and international policies relating thereto.

8774 Bibliografía sobre la frontera entre Venezuela y Colombia (UCAB/M, 5, 1976, p. 1131–1143)

This seemingly complete bibliography is arranged chronologically (1927–73). A valuable reference.

8775 Bond, Robert D. *ed.* Contemporary Venezuela and its role in international affairs. N.Y., New York Univ. Press, 1977. 267 p., tables (A Council on Foreign Relations book)

Contains six articles on or closely related to Venezuelan foreign policy. An excellent introductory chapter on the Venezuelan political system provides the context for the making of Venezuelan policy. Venezuela's policies in Latin America and toward the US, its role in international affairs and its role in OPEC are among the areas of interest to students of international affairs and Latin American studies. This is a very useful collection.

Bowers, Claude G. Chile through embassy windows: 1939–1953. See *HLAS 40:3616.*

8776 Bratzel, John F. The Chaco Dispute and the search for prestige (*in* Bratzel, John F. and Daniel M. Masterson *eds.* The underside of Latin American history. East Lansing, Michigan State Univ., The Latin American Studies Center, 1977, p. 88–106 [Monograph series, 16])

Useful analysis of personal and idiosyncratic aspects of international relations.

Caicedo Castilla, José Joaquín, Historia diplomática. See *HLAS 40:3420.*

8777 Calderón, Horacio. Argentina judía: reflexiones sobre la política exterior argentina en la cuestión israelita y palestinense. 2. ed. B.A., Editorial Legión, 1976. 200 p., bibl., facsims, tables.

"Argentina and Palestine were the targets selected by Judaism in order to install the state of Israel . . . with the manifest support of the Great Powers . . ."

8778 Campos, Roberto de Oliveira. O mundo que vejo e não desejo. Rio, Livraria José Olympio Editora, 1976. 251 p., plate.

Collection of short essays (including speeches) written by Roberto Campos between 1969–74. Although Dr. Campos has not been the most popular intellectual in liberal circles, his insight and perception in matters Brazilian as well as international are undeniable. As a figure closely associated with Brazilian domestic and foreign policy, his ideas are worthy of close attention on these grounds alone.

8779 Castro, Therezinha de. Rumo à Antártica. Prefácio de C. Delgado de Carvalho. Rio, Livraria Freitas Bastos, 1976. 172 p., fold. maps.

Studies questions relevant to Brazil posed by the Treaty of Antarctica (1959); discusses geography, climate, marine life of Antarctica; historic claims to the Falkland (or Malvinas) Islands; economic and political problems caused by historic and geopolitical claims of Chile, Argentina, Australia, New Zealand, Norway, Japan, South Africa, USSR and US. Includes text of Treaty and Brazil's official position.

8780 Cavelier, Germán. Memoria histórico-jurídica sobre el asunto de Los Monjes. Bogotá, Editorial Kelly, 1977. 543 p., bibl., maps.

Los Monjes are defined as "ten small islands, or keys, emerging from the Colombian continental shelf" so the author, not surprisingly, considers them Colombian territory. The study is, however, a thorough presentation of the Colombian case and highly recommended for anyone interested in this jurisdictional dispute.

Cerda Catalán, Alfonso. La misión de Jacinto Albístur al Perú en 1865. See *HLAS 40:3505.*

8781 Chamero, Juan Angel and others. Hacia donde va el mundo. v. 1, Ubicación argentina en este contexto; v. 2, Emergencia geopolítica argentina. B.A., Fundación Latina, 1976/1977. 2 v. (121, 106 p.) tables.

Vol. 1 consists of a series of essays explaining the political, economic, social, philosophical, and religious factors affecting the future development of Argentina. Vol. 2 analyzes the country's geopolitical significance, its strategic importance, human and natural resources and problems of national security.

8782 Cline, William R. Brazil's emerging international economic role (*in* Roett, Riordan *ed.* Brazil in the seventies. Washington, American Enterprise Institute for Public Policy Research, 1976, p. 63–87, tables)

After seven years of success in expanding exports (1967–74), Brazil will find future export expansion more difficult. Given its importance among LDCs "Brazil occupies a position of natural economic leadership among the developing countries. It is most likely to exploit this position in the pursuit of limited pragmatic goals directly affecting its own economic interests, rather than in advocacy of generalized measures for benefitting poor countries."

8783 Colombia. Ministerio de Educación Nacional. Oficina de Relaciones Internacionales. Convenios culturales bilaterales. Presentación de Juan Jacobo Muñoz Delgado. Bogotá, 1974. 207 p., bibl.

Contains the texts of bilateral "cultural conventions" between Colombia and 24 other countries throughout the world, covering a period from 1885 to 1973. The treaties cover a great variety of subjects, i.e., language teaching, exchange of scholars, protection of "intellectual property."

8784 Conference of Heads of State or Governments of Non-Aligned Countries, *IV, Algiers, 1973.* El Perú y el no alineamiento, Argel, 1973. Lima, Ministerio de Relaciones Exteriores, Dirección de Relaciones Públicas y Prensa, 1973? 139 p., plates.

Discusses Peru's official position concerning non-alignment as a working principle of Peruvian foreign policy and its role as part of the Third World. Also includes texts of official statements and resolutions adopted at this Algerian Conference on Non-Aligned Nations.

8785 Correa, Marcos Sá. 1964 [i.e. Mil novecentos e sessenta e quatro] visto e comentado pela Casa Branca. Porto Alegre, Brazil, L&PM Editores, 1977. 160 p., facsims.

Contains numerous documents from the Lyndon Johnson Library showing US knowledge, concern and involvement in what was happening in Brazil during 1964 (including documents from 1963–65). There is very little introduction or explanation of the documents. For a better and more complete study of this period, see *HLAS 39:8796.*

Corti, Arístides Horacio M. and **Virgilio Martínez de Sucre.** Multinacionales y derecho. See item **8519.**

Couyoumdjian, Ricardo. El mercado del salitre durante la Primera Guerra Mundial y la post-guerra, 1914–1921: notas para su estudio. See *HLAS 40:3625.*

8786 Cuevas Cancino, F. Del Congreso de Panamá a la Conferencia de Caracas. Nota editorial de Diógenes de la Rosa. Caracas, Oficina Central de Información (OCI), 1976. 530 p. (Serie del sesquicentenario del Congreso de Panamá)

A factual and analytical history of the inter-American system from 1826 to 1954. It is critical but not polemic with respect to US policy which, in any event, does not dominate the study to the exclusion of other members of the system.

8787 Cunha, Pedro Penner da. A diplomacia da Paz: Rui Barbosa em Haia. Apresentação de Homero Senna. Rio, Ministério de Educação e Cultura, Fundação Casa de Rui Barbosa, 1977. 66 p.

Consists of a discussion of Rui Barbosa's role at The Hague Conference, of Brazil's policies with respect to the issues raised, and of the Conference itself.

8788 Dans, Gustavo V. NACLA's Brasil a la ofensiva: la estrategia continental del imperialismo. Lima, Editorial DIPSA, n.d. 59 p. (Cuadernos de política mundial, 1)

Includes some interesting observations on Brazilian "subimperialism" despite the author's angry prose style.

8789 D'Eça, Florence L. The diary of a Foreign Service wife: assignment to Brazil. Tauton, Mass., William S. Sullwold Publishing, 1977. 333 p.

Describes the experiences of 11 years (1947–58) in the Brazilian cities of Recife, Rio, and Belo Horizonte. The work is divided into three parts, appropriately titled "cultural shock," "acceptance" and "adaptation." It offers insight into Brazilian culture and a few references to political events.

8790 Destefani, Laurio Hedelvio. El Alférez Sobral y la sobernía Argentina en la Antártida. B.A., Centro Naval, Instituto de Publicaciones Navales, 1974. 269 p., bibl., fold. maps, inserted maps, maps, plates, tables (Col. Historia, 6)

Alférez Sobral was the first Argentine to visit the Antarctic, accompanying a Swedish expedition there (1901–03). This is a biography of Sobral and a detailed account of the expedition. The connection between all of this and Argentine sovereignty is not clear.

8791 Díaz Albónico, Rodrigo *ed.* El mar en seis dimensiones: científica, técnica, política, jurídica, histórica, estratégica. Santiago, Univ. de Chile, Instituto de Estudios Internacionales, Editorial Universitaria, 1976. 114 p., maps, tables (Estudios internacionales)

The six "dimensions" described here are technical, scientific, judicial, political, historical and strategic. Each "dimension" is the subject of a separate and informative article.

8792 Díaz de Molina, Alfredo. Las Islas Malvinas y una nueva diplomacia. B.A., Editorial Platero, 1976. 84 p., plate.

Employs UN documents, diplomatic correspondence, newspaper arguments and reports to defend the national claim of Argentina to the Malvinas (Falkland) archipelago (1968–74).

8793 Dikó, Nicolás and others. Los recursos del Océano Pacífico y la paz del mundo. Prólogo de Orión Alvarez and Jorge Ganem. Presentación de Ana de Consuegra. Bogotá, Ediciones Universidades Simon Bolívar, Medellín y Libre de Pereira, 1977. 156 p., plates (Col. Universidad y pueblo, 14)

Consists of a series of lectures on problems and issues posed in exploring and utilizing the sea and its resources. Scholars from Latin America and the Academy of Sciences of the USSR, students and scientists from all nations bordering on the Pacific Ocean, discuss ecology and the role of the "Revolution" in protecting these natural resources.

8794 *Documentos.* Revista de información política. Univ. Central de Venezuela, Facultad de Ciencias Jurídicas y Políticas, Instituto de Estudios Políticos. No. 55, oct./dic. 1973–. Caracas.

Massive document collection for the year 1973 published by the Institute of Political Studies of the Central Univ. of Venezuela. Covers the UN, regional organizations, international conferences, inter-American relations, Venezuelan domestic politics and foreign policy. There are also chronologies of major events in the last three months of 1973, for the international system, Latin America, and Venezuela. [F.]

8795 Drago, Luis María. La República Argentina y el caso de Venezuela. Caracas, Oficina Central de Información (OCI), 1976. 237 p.

With focus on Venezuela, the Drago Doctrine is examined as a fundamental principle of public International Law. Discusses the relations of Venezuela with Germany, England and Italy, when the European nations threatened the political sovereignty and territorial integrity of Venezuela, at the beginning of the 20th century. Includes texts of Drago Doctrine, Presidential statements from Venezuelan Government, and opinions from Argentina, England, the French Institute of International Law; the relationship of the Drago and Monroe Doctrines; and the press opinion from newspapers in the Western Hemisphere.

Durandin, Catherine. L'idéologie de la sécurité nationale au Brésil. See item **7531.**

8796 Escobari Cusicanqui, Jorge. Historia diplomática de Bolivia: política internacional. 2. ed. Presentación de Jorge Siles Salinas. La Paz, Litografías e Imprentas Unidas, 1975. 519 p.

This is the most comprehensive history of Bolivia's international relations to come to this reader's attention. Understandably, the maritime problem and the question of the Lauca River are given emphasis but most of the work deals with many other themes. Peru, Paraguay, Argentina and Brazil are discussed in separate chapters (in addition to Chile).

8797 Escovar Salom, Ramón. Nuevas alternativas para la solidaridad internacional. Caracas, Ministerio de Relaciones Exteriores, 1976. 45 p.

Contains text in English, French and Spanish of the speech delivered by Ramon Escovar Salom, Foreign Minister of Venezuela before the UN General Assembly, 13th Session, 2379th Meeting, N.Y., 8 Oct. 1975. Escovar discusses his nation's views on the function and future of the UN in the development of Third World nations.

8798 *Estrategia.* Publicación bimestral. Instituto Argentino de Estudios Estratégicos y de las Relaciones Internacionales (INSAR). Nos. 31/32, nov. 1974/feb. 1975 [through] No. 50, nov. 1977/feb. 1978–. B.A.

Argentine journal devoted to issues of geopolitics and international relations with frequent contributions by military officers. Articles of interest are found in the following issues: Nos. 31/32 (nov. 1974/feb. 1975) includes articles on the future of the Antarctic and compares the policies of Brazil and Argentina in the southern cone; No. 33 (marzo/abril 1975) has an article on Brazilian "imperialism" in the Amazon region; Nos. 34/35 (mayo/agosto 1975) contain article by Argentine general on the significance of the Brazilian-West German treaty on nuclear energy and the possibility of nuclear weapons; No. 36 (sept./oct. 1975) includes two interesting articles on Argentine-Brazilian relations, emphasizing Brazil's expansionist tendencies vis-à-vis Argentina; No. 39 (marzo/abril 1976) includes two articles on Brazilian "Manifest Destiny" and the geopolitical ideas of Brazilian Gen. Golbery do Couto e Silva; Nos. 40/41 (mayo/agosto 1976) include a discussion of geopolitics and Bolivia and possible conflicts in the South Atlantic arising over exploitation of manganese nodules; Nos. 43/44 (nov. 1976/feb. 1977) contain 11 articles relating to Argentina and the South Atlantic with emphasis on the Malvinas Islands and the Antarctic; Nos. 49/50 (nov. 1977/feb. 1978) include articles on Argentine boundary or territorial

questions and the inevitable forebodings on Brazilian imperialism and expansionism.

8799 Estructura y reglamento de los organismos del Convenio Andrés Bello. Bogotá, Secretaría Ejecutiva Permanente del Convenio Andrés Bello (SECAB), 1976. 92 p., tables (SECAB/D, 56)

Careful and important analysis of the Andrés Bello Agreement which was signed in Bogotá on 31 Dec. 1970. This treaty seeks closer integration in the fields of education, science and culture for countries of the Andean region which signed it: Bolivia, Colombia, Chile, Ecuador, Peru and Venezuela.

8800 Etchepareborda, Roberto. Historia de las relaciones internacionales argentinas. B.A., Editorial Pleamar, 1978. 277 p., bibl. (Testimonios nacionales)

This book might more properly be called "Episodes in Argentine Foreign Relations: 1870–1920." It is, however, no less important for that reason. The author has selected important episodes in Argentine diplomacy with emphasis on the Southern Cone (Chile, Brazil, Paraguay). A well documented and useful work by a competent historian. Contains an excellent bibliography.

8801 Faura Gaig, Guillermo S. El mar peruano y sus límites. Lima, Editorial Imprenta Amauta, 1977. 338 p., bibl., fold. maps.

Pt. 1 summarizes the work and results of national and international efforts to deal with the question of national jurisdiction over adjacent waters, with emphasis on the Peruvian case. Pt. 2 deals with "oceanographic" matters but apart from "declarations" there is little to indicate much concern for conservation or environmental protection.

8802 Fernández Cendoya, Andrés. Bolivia-Chile: epílogo de un siglo de malas relaciones (IAEERI/E, 37/38, nov./feb. 1975/ 1976, p. 36–50)

Examines the conflict between Bolivia and Chile and their relations in the 20th century. Discusses possible solutions, including Plan Valdés and Proyecto Guevara and those involving Brazil and Argentina.

8803 Ferrigni, Yoston; Carlos Gueron; and **Eva de Gueron.** Hipótesis para el estudio de una política exterior. Caracas, Univ.

Central de Venezuela, 1973. 371 p., bibl.
(Estudio de Caracas, 8:2. Gobierno y política)
Analysis of Venezuelan international relationships which employs an hypothesis akin to linkage theory. This work should be of fundamental importance to specialists. [P.B. Taylor, Jr.]

Ficha de Información Sociopolítica. See item **7316.**

8804 Fleming Mendoza, Héctor. Frenemos a Mr. Ford. Caracas, Tipografía Sorocaima, 1975. 119 p., illus., plates (Col. Quadrum)
Propagandistic polemic presented in a series of letters addressed to a fictitious person, in which the anti-imperialistic and anti-US position of the Venezuelan Communist Party is clearly stated. Biased discussion of what fine examples Castro, Torrijos, Che Guevarra, are for "the cause." Exhorts Venezuelan people to follow their leadership.

8805 Francis, Michael J. The limits of hegemony: United States relations with Argentina and Chile during World War II. Notre Dame, Ind., Univ. of Notre Dame Press, 1977. 292 p. (International studies of the Committee on International Relations)
Definitive and well-written account of two troublesome cases in a period when the US was emerging as a superpower and beginning to forge what was to be a postwar "special relationship" with Latin America. Draws heavily on primary sources. [F.]

8806 ———. The United States and Chile during the Second World War: the diplomacy of misunderstanding (JLAS, 9:1, May 1977, p. 91–113)
Argues that the apparent conflict between the US and Chile during World War II stemmed from differing perceptions of their international responsibilities. The discussion also suggests that a uniform policy for all of Latin America is unwise. For historian's comment, see *HLAS 40:3633.*

8807 Frankel, Benjamin A. Venezuela y los Estados Unidos: 1810–1888. Traducción de Vicente de Amézaga. Revisada por Manuel Pérez Vila y Nelson Giannini. Prólogo de Manuel Pérez Vila. Caracas, Ediciones de la Fundación John Boulton, 1977. 404 p., tables.
Scholarly, comprehensive and well-

written study based on author's dissertation at Univ. of California, Berkeley. It makes an important contribution to the study of the foreign policy of smaller states among which Venezuela has recently received much attention.

8808 Fuchs, Friedrich-Wilhelm. Ökonomische Aktivitäten der BRD in Brasilien (IIB/DA, 22:7, 1977, p. 94–104)
East German author analyzes the scope and influence of West German capital in Brazil and how it has affected Brazilian domestic and foreign policies. [M. Kossok]

8809 Galindo Quiroga, Eudoro. Litoral andino: retrospección y perspectivas en torno al problema marítimo. Cochabamba, Bol., Editorial Los Amigos del Libro, 1977. 204 p., bibl., maps, plates, tables.
Traces the unfortunate events leading to Bolivia's loss of its seacoast, the attempts to recover it and the important link between these efforts and Bolivia's aspirations for development.

8810 Gallardo, Víctor A. Chile's national interest in the oceans. Santiago, Univ. of Chile, Institute of International Studies, 1976. 110 p., tables (Special publications series, 10)
Essentially a study of the extent to which Chile has perceived and utilized its marine interests. Concludes that potential has not been utilized. Conservation and pollution problems are discussed. A very careful study.

8811 García Amador, F.V. América Latina y el Derecho del Mar. Santiago, Univ. de Chile, Instituto de Estudios Internacionales, Editorial Universitaria, 1976. 197 p. (Col. Estudios internacionales)
Useful summary of the development of Latin American claims to extended jurisdiction over coastal waters. The relevant national legislation is reprinted as are all the "subregional instruments" up until 1972. It is interesting to note that conservation was the original objective stated in early claims yet there is little to suggest any subsequent justifications along these lines. Dr. García is perhaps the foremost contemporary jurist to write on the subject.

8812 Gómez Rueda, Héctor O. Teoría y doctrina de la geopolítica. Prólogo de

Osiris G. Villegas. B.A., Editorial Astrea de Alfredo y Ricardo Depalma, 1977. 328 p., bibl., maps, tables.

Good example of the recent interest in the concept of geopolitics. While much of this study treats the subject generally, a lengthy annex and several parts of the main text give special attention to Argentina, Paraguay, Bolivia and Uruguay. The author is Argentine.

8813 Gravil, Roger. The Anglo-Argentine connection and the War of 1914–1918 (JLAS, 9:1, May 1977, p. 59–89, tables)

An effective challenge to André Gunder Frank's thesis that the most important recent industrial development of Latin American countries (including Argentina) took place during the two world wars "when their ties to their metropolis [were] weakest." This study questions the applicability of Gunder Frank's thesis to Argentina during the War of 1914–18. For historian's comment, see HLAS 40:3772.

8814 Greno Velasco, José Enrique. El Acuerdo Brasil-RFA y el Principio de No-Proliferación Nuclear (IEP/RPI, 154, nov./dic. 1977, p. 113–143)

Analysis of the pros and cons of the agreement between Brazil and West Germany to bring nuclear technology to Brazil; with emphasis on the objections of the US to the proliferation of nuclear know-how in Latin America. Examines implications of the implementations of nuclear energy on the economic and social development of Brazil; and briefly discusses the effects on other Latin American nations.

8815 Grondona, Mariano. South America looks at detente—skeptically (FP, 26, Spring 1977, p. 184–203)

"When [the military regimes of the southern cone observe the U.S.] contacts with Moscow, [and] its censuring of regimes that are combatting communism within their own borders, there is a strong temptation for those in power today . . . to accuse U.S. leaders of abandoning their allies and of forsaking their historical role."

8816 Grow, Michael. The Good Neighbor Policy and Paraguay (in Bratzel, John F. and Daniel M. Masterson eds. The underside of Latin American history. East Lansing, Michigan State Univ., The Latin American

Studies Center, 1977, p. 67–87 [Monograph series, 16])

Factual-historical treatment of one of the lesser known areas of US foreign policy. The title might well have been "The Wartime Policy of the United States in Paraguay."

8817 Guachalla, Luis Fernando. La cuestión portuaria y las negociaciones de 1950. La Paz, Editorial Los Amigos del Libro, 1976. 111 p. (Un siglo y medio)

Concerns itself with the position of the Bolivian Government with the problem of providing Bolivia with a corridor to the sea; focuses on negotiations of 1950; includes background position of Bolivia; some texts of diplomatic exchanges between the Foreign Office of Chile and that of Bolivia.

8818 Gugliamelli, Juan E. Argentina, Brasil y la bomba atómica. B.A., Tierra Nueva, 1976. 105 p., maps, tables (Col. Proceso, 12)

Series of essays analyzing the economic and political impact of the use of nuclear energy in Brazil and Argentina; discusses pros and cons of the development of nuclear armaments; effect on alliance structure in southern South America; implications for Argentina's national and foreign policies and boundary difficulties.

8819 ———. Argentina, política nacional y política de fronteras: crisis nacional y problemas fronterizos (IAEERI/E, 37/38, nov./feb. 1975/1976, p. 5–21, maps)

Discusses the problem of nation building in Argentina with respect to the establishment of internationally recognized land and maritime frontiers, national political culture, foreign relations with neighboring nations, and defense of frontiers. Also examines relevant problems and possible solutions.

8820 Gutiérrez Alfaro, Tito. La Corte Internacional de Justicia y el diferendo colombo-venezolano (ACPS/B, 36:71, oct./dic. 1977, p. 129–132)

Examines the legal-political role of the International Court of Justice (the Hague) in the dispute between Colombia and Venezuela concerning claims to territorial waters and natural resources in the Gulf of Venezuela.

8821 Herrera Oropeza, José. Política y conflictos internacionales. Caracas, Ediciones del Congreso de la República, 1976. 308 p., bibl.

Using international law as a basis, the author discusses contemporary problems in international policies—inequality/equality of states; war/just war; Vietnam and Indo-China; colonialism and violence; and the role of Latin America in the contemporary international political scene.

8822 Hickey, John. Keep the Falklands British?: the principle of self-determination of dependent territories (IAMEA, 31:1, Summer 1977, p. 77–88)

A brief, well-written account of major economic and political events that were shaping the British-Argentine dispute over the Falkland (Malvinas) in 1976 and 1977.

8823 Hilton, Stanley E. Suástica sobre o Brasil: a história da espionagem alemã no Brasil, 1939–1944. Rio, Editora Civilização Brasileira, 1977. 357 p., facsims., plates, tables (Col. Retratos do Brasil, 105)

This study is based almost exclusively on archival sources from the US and Brazil (which include sources from other archives). Its thorough documentation and scope make it essential reading for students of Brazilian foreign policy and related topics.

8824 Holmberg, Adolfo María. ¿Cree Ud. que los ingleses nos devolverán las Malvinas?: yo, no. Prólogo de Ricardo R. Caillet-Bois. B.A., Editorial Grandes Temas Argentinos, 1977. 139 p., maps, plate.

Argues that despite negotiations and agreements between Argentina and Great Britain concerning the Malvinas (Falkland) archipelago; and the fact that they are an integral portion of the national territory of Argentina, Great Britain will not give them up.

8825 Homenaje al Doctor Luis M. Drago. Caracas, Oficina Central de Información (OCI), 1976. 446 p., bibl., plate.

Contains writings of Luis M. Drago on international policies including texts of Drago Doctrine. Essays by other authors analyze the Drago Doctrine and its historical implications.

Horowitz, Irving Louis ed. The rise and fall of Project Camelot: studies in the relation-

ship between social science and practical politics. See *HLAS 40:3636.*

8826 Hoyos Osores, Guillermo. Política internacional del Perú: 7 años de desvaríos. Lima, n.p., 1977. 271 p.

Discusses the "mistaken direction" of Peruvian foreign policy since 1968 and the disaster to which it inevitably brought the country. The author is a former Peruvian diplomat and Minister of Justice. The book also contains information on the foreign policies of other Latin American countries.

8827 Husbands, Jo L. Non-aligned nations in the Eighteen National Disarmament Conference: Mexico, Brazil and Argentina, 1962–1975. Pittsburgh, Pa., Univ. of Pittsburgh, Univ. Center for International Studies, Center for Arms Control and International Security Studies, 1976? 24 l., bibl., tables (Working paper series)

Mediation provides "a good starting point and a reasonable description of the behavior of at least some of the non-aligned" states in this particular conference.

8828 Illarramendi, Ramón Adolfo. Proyección venezolana en el exterior por vía cultural (Nueva Política [Grupo Residencial San Souci, Caracas] 5, julio/sept. 1972, p. 11–56, tables)

Analysis of the political culture, colonial heritage, and nationalism in Venezuela and their effect on the nation's foreign relations.

Kistanov, Valeri. Cabeza de playa de los monopolios japoneses en América Latina. See item **7552.**

8829 *Kollasuyo.* Revista de estudios bolivianos. Editora Universo. No. 88, 1975–. La Paz.

Special issue contains much historical material on Bolivia's maritime problems. An article on the 1904 Treaty with Chile is especially useful.

8830 Lafer, Celso. Evolução da política externa brasileira (IBRI/R, 18:69/72, 1./2. semestre 1975, p. 59–65)

Emphasizes the increasing importance of various government agencies in the formation of Brazilian foreign policy. Brazil's concern with development and trade, for example, has led to a greater importance of the Central Bank, The Ministry of Industry and Commerce and the National Monetary Council. Bases argument on 19th- and 20th-century documents, including those of the UN, correspondence, and texts of agreement.

8831 Laino, Domingo. Paraguay: fronteras y penetración brasileña. Asunción, Ediciones Cerro Cora, 1977. 227 p., tables.

Author believes Paraguay has become a dependency of Brazil not only in the economic sphere but also in the cultural one where Brazil is fast erasing Paraguayan identity.

8832 Lamounier, Bolívar. Brasil: la formación de un pensamiento político autoritario en la primera república; una interpretación (IDES/DE, 16:62, julio/sept. 1976, p. 253–280)

Analysis of the political ideas operative in the First Republic in Brazil (1889) as an ingredient in state building. Examines the social, economic and political ideology of the Brazilian Republic; corporatism, the role of technology and the conflicts engendered between the requirements for building nation-states, and the vision of the state as an authoritarian patrimonial society.

8833 Landovský, Vladimír. Argentina. Praha, Svoboda, 1974. 183 p.

Basic facts on Argentina for Czech audience which includes lengthy discussion of Czech-Argentine relations. [G.J. Kovtun]

8834 Leu, Hans-Joachim and **Freddy Vivas.** Las relaciones interamericanas: una antología de documentos. Caracas, Univ. Central de Venezuela, Facultad de Derecho, Instituto de Estudios Políticos, 1975. 340 p. (Documentos, 2)

Useful collection of the most important documents from the Monroe Doctrine (1828) to the Nuclear Non-Proliferation Treaty (1967).

8835 Londoño Paredes, Julio. Cuestiones de límites de Colombia. Bogotá, Banco de la República, 1975. 111 p., facsim., fold. maps (Breviarios colombianos, 4)

Contains a brief description of each of Colombia's boundary questions, past and present. A definition and historical look at the principle of *uti possidetis* and the inclusion of maps are a useful addition.

8836 ———. Geopolítica de Suramérica. Bogotá, Las Fuerzas Militares, 1977.

285 p., bibl., maps (Col. De oro del militar colombiano, 8)

Brief study of the geography of each of the South American countries with a discussion of the geographical, historical and political aspects of past and potential associations—Greater Colombia, the Confederation of the Pacific, The Plata Basin, Brazil and a confederation of the Guianas.

8837 Louscher, David J. The rise of military sales as a U.S. foreign assistance instrument (FPRI/O, 20:4, Winter 1977, p. 933–964, tables)

Argues that the US Congress has paid relatively little attention to arms sales abroad in the past. Now, however, Congress is aware that sales in a particular area *are* the foreign policy for that area. It is likely, therefore, that more attention will be paid to military sales in the future.

8838 Luder, Italo Argentino. Argentina en Latinoamérica y en el mundo. B.A., Editorial Universitaria de Buenos Aires, 1976. 101 p. (Cuestiones de geopolítica)

Contains the texts of reports concerning the foreign relations of Argentina with various nations, including those of Latin America, Europe, Japan. Also discusses Argentinian sovereignty and conflicts over territorial waters and argues for importance of understanding geopolitical factors in Argentina's international politics.

McIrvin, Ronald R. Buying time: the International Petroleum Company's public relations campaign in Peru, 1946–1966. See item **7342.**

8839 Mamalakis, Markos. The new international economic order (UM/JIAS, 20:3, Aug. 1978, p. 265–295, bibl., tables)

The author breaks down the NIEO into production, distribution, and investment, and he examines how Venezuela has affected and been affected by changes in these fields since 1973. He cautions that, in order for Venezuela to reap long-term gains from the recent oil price-rises, the country must convert profits into "scarce human, physical, and technological capital" and "achieve a permanent petroboom" by developing its Orinoco resources. [F.]

8840 Martinière, Guy. La politique africaine du Brésil: 1970–1976 (FDD/NED

[Problèmes d'Amérique Latine, 48] 4478, 13 juillet 1978, p. 7–64, map, tables)

The long article is handled in two sections: 1) 1970–73, search for conciliation between "white" and "black" power in Africa; and 2) 1974–76, the "second wind," in which the failures of the first effort were remedied. [P.B. Taylor, Jr.]

8841 Marull Bermúdez, Federico. Mar de Chile y Mar Andino: antecedentes para una política oceánica común. Santiago, Univ. de Chile, Depto. de Estudios Internacionales, 1975. 51 p., bibl. (Serie de publicaciones especiales, 7)

Calls for a common and unifying maritime policy among the Andean Pact countries.

Mata Mollejas, Luis. La revolución petrolera y la política venezolana. See item 3158.

8842 Melo Lecaros, Luis. El resurgimiento de la Guerra Fría. Prólogo de Sergio Fernández Larraín. Santiago, Editorial Vaite, 1976. 93 p., bibl. (Col. Ciencia política)

Discusses elements which constitute the Cold War, from Yalta and Potsdam, the sovietization of Eastern Europe, through Vietnam and the foreign policy of the US.

8843 Mercado Jarrín, Edgardo. El Perú y su política exterior: recopilación de los principales discursos pronunciados por El Ministro de Relaciones Exteriores General de División E.P. Edgardo Mercado Jarrín, del 24 nov. 1968 al 28 abril 1971. Lima, Ministerio de Relaciones Exteriores, n.d. 464 p., plates.

Texts of statements and speeches relating to the foreign policy of Peru as presented by its Foreign Minister (1968–71). Includes positions relating to the US, USSR, other Latin American nations; CECLA, Andean Pact; Law of the Sea and maritime and territorial jurisdiction; terrorism; etc.

8844 Milenky, Edward S. Argentina's foreign policies. Boulder, Colo., Westview Press, 1978. 345 p., bibl., tables (A Westview replica edition)

Excellent study, clearly the best on this subject in the literature. Comprehensive scope includes Argentina's domestic, economic and military capabilities and policymaking process, as well as the country's relations with the US, Latin American coun-

tries, non-Western Hemisphere states, and multilateral institutions. [F.]

8845 Mont'Alegre, Omer. Estrutura dos mercados de produtos primários. Rio, Ministério da Indústria e Comércio (MIC), Instituto do Açúcar e do Alcool, Depto. de Informática, Divisão de Informações e Documentação, 1976/1977. 268 p., map, plates, tables.

The book is essentially economic in focus but the final section "Politics of Primary Products" will interest students of international affairs. It is also somewhat of a synthesis of the book.

Morley, Morris and **Steven Smith.** Imperial "reach:" U.S. policy and the CIA in Chile. See item 9247.

8846 Mota, Deusdá Magalhães. Relações entre os Estados Unidos e a América Latina durante a Guerra de Sucessão: mudança operada em 1861 (USP/RH, 54:108, out./dez. 1976, p. 555–562)

The US Civil War convinced Latin Americans of two things: 1) the importance of a strong, united North American Republic to prevent European interventions such as that in Mexico; and 2) the importance of a Latin American union to contain the powerful Northern Republic.

8847 Moxon, Richard W. Harmonization of foreign investment laws among developing countries: an interpretation of the Andean Group experience (JCMS, 16:1, Sept. 1977, p. 22–52, tables)

"The Andean Group foreign investment code is the first effort in harmonizing foreign investment laws among developing countries. It has demonstrated that progress in this area is possible, but that effective implementation of common rules is very difficult. It also shows that a more flexible approach may be needed."

8847a *NACLA's Latin America & Empire Report.* North American Congress of Latin America (NACLA). Vol. 10, No. 10, Dec. 1976–. N.Y.

Issue titled "Time of Reckoning: the U.S. and Chile" consists of individual articles on the various types of US public and private aid to the military government of Chile. Chile's economic problems continue to grow, however, and continued US aid seems to be the only hope for the regime's survival.

Nava, Juan Carlos. Los ingleses no devolverán las Malvinas. See *HLAS 40:3819*.

8848 Nogueira Batista, Paulo. A un año del Acuerdo Nuclear Brasileño-Alemán (IAEERI/E, 42, sept./oct. 1976, p. 63–69)

The President of *Nuclebrás* summarizes (in an interview) what has happened in the first year since the signing of the nuclear agreement between Brazil and West Germany. Future plans are also mentioned.

Nweihed, Kaldone G. La delimitación marítima al noroeste del Golfo de Venezuela. See item **5576**.

O'Donnell, Guillermo. Estado y alianzas en la Argentina, 1956–1976. See item **7498**.

Organization of American States, Washington. **Inter-American Commission on Human Rights.** Report on the situation of human rights in Uruguay. See item **7608**.

8849 Orrego Vicuña, Francisco. Los fondos marinos y oceánicos: jurisdicción nacional y régimen internacional. Presentación de Arvid Pardo. Prólogo de F.V. García-Amador. Santiago, Editorial Andrés Bello, 1976. 451 p., plates, tables.

Pt. 1 contains a standard treatment of national claims and international activities. Pt. 2 is of more interest in that it discusses the area clearly beyond national control and the question of "patrimonio común de la humanidad." A very important work.

8850 ———. Las políticas latinoamericanas sobre el Derecho del Mar (CEPAC/REP, 9, enero 1975, p. 7–20, bibl.)

Analysis of the politics of the conference which negotiated a viable UN Law of the Sea Agreement, in Caracas, Venezuela, July-Aug. 1974. Includes the various positions of Brazil, Ecuador, El Salvador, Panama, Peru, and Uruguay concerning the 200-mile economic zone; the jurisdictional dispute between Argentina and Chile concerning the Straits of Magellan; the control of the continental shelf and its resources; scientific investigations; implications for economic development.

8851 Pereira, Osny Duarte. La seudorivalidad argentino-brasileña: pro y contra de Itaipú. Traducción de Neiva Moreira.

B.A., Ediciones Corregidor, 1975. 328 p., bibl. (Serie mayor)

Examines the politics of international energy involved in the construction of the reservoir and hydroelectric plant Itaipú on the Rio de la Plata, between Brazil and Argentina. Discusses the Brazilian point of view as well as that of Argentina. Includes documents, opinions of neighboring Latin American nations, the Treaty of Itaipú, and a brief discussion of the significance of the situation for the inter-American system. Translated from the Portuguese, *Itaipú: pros e contras* (Rio, Paz e Terra, 1974).

8852 Pérez, Carlos Andrés. Discursos de Carlos Andrés Pérez, Presidente de Venezuela, en su gira al exterior, 15-XI al 1-XII-1976: ONU, Roma, Vaticano, Londres, Moscú, Ginebra, Madrid, Lisboa. Caracas, Imprenta Nacional, 1977. 175 p.

Contains text of speeches delivered by President Carlos Andrés Pérez in 1976 to the UN; officials in Portugal, Spain, Italy, the International Socialist Movement, the Vatican, and his own nation.

8853 Perón, Juan Domingo. Doctrina universal: continentalismo, ecología, universalismo. Prólogo y selección por Eduardo Astesano. B.A., Ministerio de Cultura y Educación, Secretaría de Estado de Cultura, 1975. 192 p. (Ediciones culturales argentinas)

Excerpts from Perón's speeches, messages and interviews which help to bring up to date (1948–74) his ideas on a number of topics, including the Third World, ecology, and Argentina's place in the world.

8854 Perry, William. Contemporary Brazilian foreign policy: the international strategy of an emerging power. Beverly Hills, Calif., Sage Publications [and] Foreign Policy Research Institute, Philadelphia, Pa., 1976. 89 p. (The foreign policy papers, 2:6)

Concludes that "even under the most favorable circumstances, Brazil's growth relative to that of today's superpowers will only be gradual. By the end of this century, she could only realistically aspire to achievement of predominance on the South American Continent with a secondary, but still important, role on the wider international stage."

8855 Petras, James F.; Morris Morley; and Steven Smith. The nationalization of

Venezuelan oil. N.Y., Praeger, 1977. 175 p.

Interesting study of the nationalization from the perspectives of Venezuelan society and domestic politics, as well as the reactions of the foreign oil companies and the US Government. [F.]

8856 Pike, Fredrick B. The United States and the Andean Republics: Peru, Bolivia, and Ecuador. Foreword by Edwin O. Reischauer. Cambridge, Mass., Harvard Univ. Press, 1977. 493 p., maps (The American foreign policy library)

The book offers more than the title suggests. It is also a useful comparative political history and a study of the political culture of three Andean republics. The treatment is generally chronological. For historian's comment, see *HLAS 40:3554.*

8857 Pino, Norman; Luis Enrique Berrizbeitia; and René Arreaza. La OPEP: hacia un nuevo orden económico internacional. Caracas, Oficina Central de Información (OCI), 1975. 81 p., bibl., tables (Col. La alquitrana, 2)

Discusses the background, structure and functions of OPEC and Venezuela's role within that organization. Appended are 17 tables including much useful information and a chronological list of the date and place of the first 45 conferences (including special conferences) held until Sept. 1975.

8858 Pinochet de la Barra, Oscar. Base Soberanía y otros recuerdos antárticos chilenos: 1947–1949. B.A., Editorial Francisco Aguirre, 1977. 153 p., maps, plates (Biblioteca Francisco de Aguirre, 61. Col. Cruz del sur, 12)

Memoirs of a newspaperman with impressive legal credentials, who participated in the Chilean expedition to the Antarctic, and the establishment of Sobernía Base (1947–49). Also discusses claims of Chile to portions of Antarctic.

8859 Ponce Caballero, Jaime. Geopolítica chilena y mar boliviano. La Paz?, Ponce Caballero, 1976. 64 p., bibl.

Past and present geopolitical ambitions of Chile cast suspicion on that country's discussions concerning Bolivia's access of a corridor to the sea.

8860 Proceso de integración de la Cuenca del Plata. n.p., n.p., n.d. 23 p., tables. Brief but useful summary of the objec-

tives of recent efforts to integrate the Plata Basin, a description of the area, organizational efforts, principal resolutions and projects under way.

8861 Quagliotti de Bellis, Bernardo. Uruguay en el cono sur: destino geopolítico. B.A., Tierra Nueva, 1976. 207 p., bibl., maps, tables (Col. Proceso, 5/6)

Geopolitical study of the relationship of Uruguay to its neighbors. Emphasizes the possibilities of restructuring political action in the best interest of the people and nation of Uruguay and more in keeping with the nation's geopolitical realities. Discusses geopolitics of Brazil, Argentina, Bolivia and Paraguay in an effort to extract variables which can be applied to the Uruguayan situation.

8862 Ramírez Faría, Carlos. La clase gobernante y la frontera de Venezuela con Colombia. Caracas, Talleres de Litho formas, 1976. 146 p., bibl.

Discusses the historical processes which led to the frontier difficulties between Venezuela and Colombia; examines the social and political circumstances in Venezuela which led to the problem. Includes bibliography.

8863 Rapoport, Mario. La política británica en la Argentina a comienzo de la década de 1940 (IDES/DE, 16:62, julio/sept. 1976, p. 203–228, tables)

Analysis of British foreign policy toward Argentina during the 1930s and World War II. Examines economic and commercial relations; and attempts by Great Britain to preserve and expand trade with Argentina as an alternative source of supplies. Also discusses conflict with the US over trade and commerce with Argentina, with emphasis on the political and economic implications of exporting beef to Great Britain. For historian's comment, see *HLAS 40:3842.*

8864 Rasseli, Luiz Antônio. Mar territorial de 200 milhas. Prefácio de Artur José Almeida Diniz. Belo Horizonte, Brazil, Imprensa Oficial, 1976. 204 p., bibl.

Pt. 1 of the book offers a rather standard treatment of the subject. The chapters on Brazilian policy and especially on "The 200 Miles and their Advantage for Brazil" are worth noting. Relevant documents and a bibliography are included.

8865 *Resenha de Política Exterior do Brasil.* Revista trimestral. Ministério das Relações Exteriores. Ano 1, No. 1, março/junho 1974–. Brasília.

Quarterly of the Brazilian Foreign Ministry. Gives a brief summary of important aspects of Brazilian policy during the period, major documents, agreements signed and speeches by Brazilian diplomats. This journal is an important source of information and should be in all libraries where students of Brazilian foreign policy do research.

8866 **Reunião de Chanceleres dos Países da Bacia do Prata,** *VIII, Brasília, 1976.* VIII [i.e. Oitava] Reunião de Chanceleres dos Países da Bacia do Prata, Brasília, dezembro de 1976 (VIII Reunión de Cancilleres de los Países de la Cuenca del Plata, Brasília, diciembre de 1976). Brasília?, n.p., 1976? 450 p.

Text in Spanish and Portuguese. Contains the treaty and antecedents of the meeting of the Plata Basin countries (Argentina, Brazil, Paraguay, and Uruguay) to promote "the harmonious development and physical integration of the Plata Basin" and related areas. The documents are complete but there is no introductory or explanatory material.

8867 *Revista Argentina de Relaciones Internacionales.* Revista cuatrimestral. Centro de Estudios Internacionales Argentinos (CEINAR). Año 3, No. 8, mayo/agosto 1977–. B.A.

Contains articles concerning themes of importance to Latin American nations: Bolivia's access to the sea, the role of Latin America in world affairs, educational and social development, North-South dialogue, UN, Latin America and the Law of the Sea.

8868 *Revista de la Escuela de Diplomácia.* Univ. de Guayaquil. Año 2, No. 2, 1974–. Guayaquil, Ecua.

Contains articles on issues of importance to Ecuador: national integration, geopolitical position of Ecuador, politics of the air commerce of Ecuador, study of the Protocol of Rio, and the Conference concerning the Law of the Sea in Santiago.

8869 **Reyno Gutiérrez, Manuel.** Algunos antecedentes históricos sobre la contraposición peruana para otorgar una salida al Pacífico a Bolivia (SCHG/R, 144, 1976, p. 7–20)

Places the blame on Peru for the failure of a tripartite arrangement (Bolivia-Chile-Peru) that would give Bolivia direct access to the sea.

8870 **Rodríguez Berrutti, Camilo Hugo.** Malvinas, última frontera del colonialismo: hechos, legitimidad, opinión; documentos. Prólogo de Alfredo H. Rizzo Romano. B.A., EUDEBA, 1975. 144 p., bibl. (Cuestiones de geopolítica)

Although this study is by no means objective, it is one of the most inclusive. It deals with law, politics, diplomacy, history and economics. It is well documented and contains a bibliography.

Rodríguez Campos, Manuel. Venezuela, 1902: la crisis fiscal y el bloqueo; perfil de una soberanía vulnerada. See item **3170.**

8871 **Rojas, Armando.** Los creadores de la diplomacia venezolana. Presentación de Ramón Escovar Salom. 2. ed. Caracas, Ediciones de la Presidencia de la República, 1976. 340 p., illus., maps, plates (Serie historia. Col. Relaciones internacionales de Venezuela, 2)

This is one of the more useful works relating to the diplomatic history of Latin America to come to this reviewer's attention (first ed. 1965). In addition to valuable biographical material on major Venezuelan diplomats, there is material on Venezuelan diplomatic history, publications of the Foreign Office and the regional and global context of that country's policy.

8872 **Sabaté Lichtschein, Domingo.** Problemas argentinos de soberanía territorial. B.A., Cooperadora de Derecho y Ciencias Sociales, 1976. 315 p., maps.

Competent discussion of Argentina's contemporary territorial claims and controversies, including the continental shelf, the territorial sea, and the Antarctic. Presumably at least one, a minor question with Uruguay, was resolved in 1961.

8874 **Saint-John, Ronald Bruce.** The end of innocence: Peruvian foreign policy and the United States, 1919–1942 (JLAS, 8:2, Nov. 1976, p. 325–344)

"On the whole, United States foreign policy seldom equaled Peruvian expectations throughout the period, and its failure to do so precipitated or accelerated the growth of major new tenets in Peruvian foreign policy." For historian's comment, see *HLAS 40: 3561.*

8875 ———. *Hacia el mar*: Bolivia's quest for a Pacific port (IAMEA, 31:3, Winter 1977, p. 41–73)

The article contains not only a good summary of the historical material but discusses also the national and regional implications of this long-standing dispute. For historian's comment, see *HLAS 40:3600.*

8876 Sánchez G., Walter. The metropolis and the Latin American periphery in structural relations: theory and practice. Santiago, Univ. of Chile, Institute of International Relations, 1976. 49 p., table (Special publications series, 20)

Argues that Latin Americans have far more negotiating power than they have always been willing or able to use with respect to the industrialized metropolis. A major problem for ruling elites has been and will be an understanding of how to use that power most effectively.

8877 ——— *ed.* Panorama de la política mundial. Santiago, Univ. de Chile, Instituto de Estudios Internacionales, 1977. 305 p., bibls., tables (Estudios internacionales)

Most of the book is devoted to general and regional international politics. Two chapters deal with Latin America generally—one on integration and the other on "new directions" in Latin American policy.

Sanders, G. Earl. The quiet experiment in American diplomacy: an interpretive essay on U.S. aid to the Bolivian Revolution. See *HLAS 40:3603.*

8878 Santos, Theotonio dos. La crisis norteamericana y América Latina. Caracas, Univ. Central de Venezuela, Facultad de Ciencias Económicas y Sociales, División de Publicaciones, 1974. 170 p., illus. (Col. Libros)

"The period . . . from 1968 to 1972 was the period of defensive negotiation [on the part of world capitalism] and the loss of the relative positions of imperialism. The period now beginning [1973] will be a period of definition, maintenance and extension of popular gains."

Sanz, Pablo R. El espacio argentino. See *HLAS 40:3857.*

Scenna, Miguel Angel. Braden y Perón. See *HLAS 40:3861.*

8879 Schneider, Ronald M. Brazil: foreign policy of a future world power. Boulder, Colo., Westview Press, 1976. 136 p., map (Westview special studies on Latin America)

The most complete and sophisticated study of Brazilian foreign policy to appear to date. The author sees Brazil as an emerging world power and emphasizes its policy and policy-making process. The chapter on "Critical Continuing Questions" suggests some reservations to an otherwise generally optimistic picture of Brazil's future world role.

Secretaría Ejecutiva Permanente del Convenio Andrés Bello (SECAB), *Bogotá.* Tratados internacionales de integración de los países andinos. See item **2907.**

8880 Seidl-Hohenveldern, Ignaz. Chilean copper nationalization cases before German Courts (ASIL/J, 69:1, Jan. 1975, p. 110–119)

A German professor of international law comments critically on a decision of the Hamburg Superior Court which denied a motion for attachment of a cargo of copper by a "split company" of the nationalized former Chilean company SMETSA.

8881 Selcher, Wayne A. Brazilian relations with Portuguese Africa in the context of the elusive Luso-Brazilian community (UM/JIAS, 18:1, Feb. 1976, p. 25–58, bibl., tables)

Critical study of Brazil's relations with Portugal's former African colonies. "While events of 1974–1975 gave to the Foreign Ministry a more accurate image of Portuguese Africa . . . Brazil still has done little to prepare itself for an important role in the new countries and has very limited area expertise to draw upon." Interesting in view of numerous previous writings by Brazilians in which Brazil's "natural" affinity with Africa was emphasized.

8882 ———. Brazil's multilateral relations between First and Third Worlds. Boulder, Colo., Westview Press, 1978. 301 p., tables (A Westview replica edition)

Very good discussion of Brazil's somewhat "uneasy" position between First and

Third Worlds. In general it is keeping with Schneider's thesis (see item **8879**) on Brazil as a country moving upward in the world power structure. The chapter on Brazil's participation in the OAS will be of special interest to students of that organization.

8883 Selser, Gregorio. De cómo Nixinger desestabilizó a Chile. B.A., Hernández Editor, 1975. 238 p.

Focuses on the role and responsibility of the Nixon Administration—including Secretary of State Kissinger, and the Central Intelligence Agency—in the toppling of the regime of President Salvador Allende of Chile, between 1970–73.

8884 Seminario Internacional sobre la Formulación de la Política Oceánica, *Santiago, 1976.* Política oceánica. [Edición de] Francisco Orrego Vicuña. Santiago, Univ. de Chile, Instituto de Estudios Internacionales, 1977. 414 p., tables (Col. Estudios internacionales)

Fortunately this book goes beyond the tired subject of jurisdiction over coastal waters. Most of it deals with the more vital topics of scientific investigation, exploration of resources, marine pollution and international cooperation in protection and utilization of resources.

Seminario Internacional sobre Preservación del Medio Ambiente Marino, *Santiago, 1975.* Preservación del medio ambiente marino: estudios. See item **5485.**

8885 Seminario sobre el Nuevo Orden Internacional, *Bogotá, 1977.* Hacia un nuevo orden internacional. [Edición de] Indalecio Liévano Aguirre and others. Prólogo de Patricia Uribe Arango. Bogotá, Asociación Nacional de Instituciones Financieras (ANIF), 1978. 140 p., bibl., tables (Biblioteca ANIF de economía, 12)

Collection of papers presented at a Colombian seminar held to discuss and define the "new international order." The papers set out to discuss cultural, political, juridical and economic aspects of the "new order" but deal much more with the "old order." The participants are identified only as "a group of young people."

Senese, Salvatore. La trasformazione delle strutture giuridiche in América Latina. See item **7071a.**

8886 Sepúlveda, César. Las fuentes del Derecho Internacional Americano: una encuesta sobre los métodos de creación de reglas internacionales en el hemisferio occidental. 2. ed. México, Editorial Porrúa, 1975. 153 p.

Distinguished jurist writes on the old question of an American International Law. The book is also a useful contribution to the study of "sources" of international law generally. The role of the inter-American system in the process of creating law is emphasized. A chapter on the correlation between regional and general sources of law is especially interesting.

8887 Shackelton, E.A.A., *Lord;* **R.J. Storey;** and **R. Johnson.** Prospect of the Falkland Islands (RGS/GJ, 143, pt. 1, March 1977, p. 1–13, maps)

An important study that has added new dimensions to the Falkland (Malvinas) Islands dispute. Should be read in connection with item **8870.**

8888 Silenzi de Stagni, Adolfo. El nuevo Derecho del Mar: controversia entre las potencias navales y el Tercer Mundo. B.A., Juárez Editor, 1976. 327 p., maps, tables.

Contains most of the usual material on the Law of the Sea. Much useful material on the deep seabed. It is especially useful as one presentation of a "Third World" view of the controversy between them and the naval powers of the world.

8889 Sindicato de Mecánicos y Afines del Transporte Automotor de la República Argentina (SMATA), *B.A.* Enfoque político-doctrinario del gobierno popular para la gestación de su política exterior. B.A.?, 1973? 7 p. (Cursos de capacitación política: política exterior, 2)

Strongly pro-Peronist policy statement by an Argentine labor group. Serves as a useful brief summary of what pro-Peronists claimed or assumed to be Perón's foreign policy.

8890 Skidmore, Thomas E. Brazil's changing role in the international system: implications for U.S. policy (*in* Roett, Riordan *ed.* Brazil in the seventies. Washington, American Enterprise Institute for Public Policy Research, 1976, p. 9–40)

"We should not dismiss the influence of tradition and expectations in U.S.-Brazilian relations. Aside from the deliberate calculation of interests on both sides, policy makers in Brasília and Washington continue to believe in a special relationship between their countries . . . On the other hand, economic dependence has forced Brazil to acknowledge that despite trade and credit diversification, the stakes remain very high in Brazilian connections with the United States."

8891 Soberón A., Luis. Las operaciones del capital extranjero en el contexto de su desarrollo global: el caso de W.R. Grace & Co. (Debates en Sociología [Univ. Católica del Perú, Depto. de Sociología, Lima] 1 : 1, feb. 1977, p. 83–108, tables)

Study of the evolution of operations of W.R. Grace & Co. (1950–70) resulting from its transformation within the world corporate structure. The corporation has directed a decreasing share of its resources to Latin America (almost completely retiring from Peru) in exchange for greater concentration in Western Europe.

Stols, Eddy. O Brasil se defende da Europa: suas relações com a Belgica: 1830–1914. See *HLAS 40:4177.*

8892 Tambs, Lewis A. Fatores geopolíticos na América Latina (ADN, 65 : 679, set./out. 1978, p. 45–62, bibl.)

Geopolitical survey of contemporary Latin America, noting some of the changes since the author first wrote on this subject in the mid-1960s. Emphasis on Brazil, not surprisingly since this is a Brazilian publication. [F.]

8893 ———. Five times against the system: Brazilian foreign military expeditions and their effect on national politics (*in* Keith, Henry H. and Robert A. Hayes *eds.* Perspectives on armed politics in Brazil. Tempe, Arizona State Univ., Center for Latin American Studies, 1976, p. 117–205, plates)

Highly useful and interesting discussion of, among other things, the ways in which military officers were motivated to engage in political activity at home as a result of their experiences in foreign expeditions.

8894 Tavares, Aurélio de Lyra. Aspectos conjunturais da França: visita da Escola Superior de Guerra à Embaixada do

Brasil em Paris, junho 1973; exposição do Embaixador . . . Paris, The Author, 1973. 21 p.

Contains some interesting commentary on France but the most interesting section is a brief discussion of traditional French views of Brazil and of the efforts and success of the government in changing these views since 1964.

8895 Thomas, Larry P. The Colombian Supreme Court decision on the Andean Foreign Investment Code and its implications for the Law of Treaties (The Journal of International Law and Economics [George Washington Univ., National Law Center, Washington] 8 : 1, June 1973, p. 113–128)

Critical review of the recent decision of the Colombian Supreme Court holding invalid an executive decree implementing the Andean Foreign Investment Code. The article is of interest both in terms of Colombian constitutional law and politics as well as International Law—especially questions arising under the Vienna Convention on the Law of Treaties.

8896 Toro Jiménez, Fermín. La política de Venezuela en la Conferencia Interamericana de Consolidación de La Paz, Buenos Aires, 1936. Prólogo de Hans-Joachim Leu. Caracas, Univ. Central de Venezuela, Facultad de Ciencias Jurídicas y Políticas, 1977. 247 p., bibl. (Monografías de la Escuela de Estudios Políticos y Administrativos)

More than a study of Venezuela's participation in the 1936 conference, this is also a study of the context of the conference itself. This kind of detailed work sheds much light on the study of Venezuela's foreign policy and one hopes that similar studies will be made for other countries and other conferences.

8897 Townsend Ezcurra, Andrés. El Congreso Antifictiónico de Panamá y su significación actual para los países latinoamericanos. Lima, Univ. Nacional Federico Villarreal, Programa Académico de Educación, Depto. de Ciencias Históricas Sociales, 1976. 19 p. (Publicaciones, 1)

Brief critical analysis of the principles articulated at the Congress of Panama of 1824; their implications for the future political, and economic relations among Latin American nations. Author also discusses international relations, lack of supranational structures based on integrated political, economic and social policy, and other weaknesses.

8898 Trejo, Hugo. Basta de concesiones a Colombia. Prólogo de Aquiles Monagas. Presentación de Héctor Rodríguez Bauza. Caracas?, Ediciones Venezuela Contemporánea, 1975. 204 p., facsims., maps (Col. Venezuela contemporánea)

A Venezuelan military officer warns of the dangers of Colombian incursions on Venezuelan sovereignty and the failure of Venezuela to respond forcefully. Interesting study of small-power relations and role of the military in foreign policy.

8899 Uruguay. Centro de Navegación Transatlántica. Río de La Plata y Océano Atlántico: delimitación de la jurisdicción nacional. Montevideo, 1974. 28 l., table (Circular, 4438)

Recent documents relating to Uruguay's river and maritime boundaries with Argentina and Brazil. They will be of interest to anyone studying problems arising from the extension of maritime jurisdiction.

8900 ———. Ministerio de Relaciones Exteriores. Instituto Artigas del Servicio Exterior. El Tratado del Río de la Plata y su frente marítimo. Prólogo de Edison González Lapeyre. Montevideo, 1975. 93 p., fold. maps, tables.

Discusses various aspects of the Treaty of Rio de la Plata and Territorial Waters, with particular emphasis on its historical value in the development of relations between Argentina and Uruguay. Includes text of treaty, and various statements concerning treaty by the chief executives of the nations involved.

8901 Valla, Víctor V. Subsídios para uma melhor compreensão da entrada do Brasil na Primeira Guerra Mundial (FFCLM/EH, 15, 1976, p. 29–46)

Emphasizes the importance of Brazil in gaining support (or preventing neutrality) for the US and the Allies in World War I.

8902 Van Cleve, John V. The Latin American policy of President Kennedy: a reexamination case: Peru (IAMEA, 30:4, Spring 1977, p. 29–44)

"Inter-American relations were not drastically altered by the Kennedy Administration . . . [its] desire to hinder the forces of radical nationalism and communism,

while simultaneously presenting U.S. policy in the best possible light, led to its inconsistent policy with regard to military coups d'état." For historian's comment, see *HLAS 40:3566.*

8903 Venezuela. Ministerio de Relaciones Exteriores. Anales diplomáticos de Venezuela. t. 5, Relaciones con la Santa Sede; t. 6/7, Relaciones con los Estados Unidos. Prólogo de Carlos Felice Cardot. Caracas, 1975. 3 v. (343, 493, 582 p.)

Three more volumes in this useful collection devoted to Venezuelan diplomatic history. Vol. 5 includes documents dated 1824–1920 which shed much light on "Vatican diplomacy" and Church-state relations in Venezuela. Vols. 6/7, on US-Venezuelan relations, includes documents dated 1810–95 which have been inaccessible until now. Carlos Felice Cardot has written valuable introductions for both topics.

8904 Villacres Moscoso, Jorge W. El Ecuador y la causa venezolana por la Guyana Esequiba (ACPS/B, 36:71, oct./dic. 1977, p. 185–193)

Legal-historical analysis of the territorial dispute between Venezuela and Guyana, concerning the pros and cons of establishing the Esequibo River as their common boundary. Also examines the situation existing between the claim of Venezuela based on Spanish colonial boundaries at independence (1810), and Great Britain's colonial interest in their colony, British Guyana.

8905 ———. Geoeconomía internacional del estado ecuatoriano (CCE/CHA, 24:41, 1974, p. 13–76)

Wide-ranging discussion of Ecuador's foreign economic relations from colonial times but with emphasis on post-World War II period and on regional aspects, especially the Andean Pact.

8906 Villamil Bueno, Guillermo. La solución de los conflictos en el Pacto Andino. Bogotá, Pontificia Univ. Javeriana, Facultad de Ciencias Jurídicas y Socioeconómicas, 1976. 103 p.

Examines historical origins of the Andean Pact, including The Treaty of Montevideo (1960), The Declaration of Bogotá (1966), The Cartagena Agreement (1969). Discusses juridical aspects of Andean Pact:

sovereignty, economic integration, boundaries, and the Pact's impact.

8907 Vinces Zevallos, Fausto and **Antonio Kuljevan Pagador.** Estructura jurídica del Acuerdo de Cartagena. t. 1/2. Lima, Oficina Nacional de Integración (ONIT), 1974. 2 v. (903 p.) (Continuous pagination) tables.

Comprehensive collection of all the arguments for the Andean Pact (beginning with antecedents such as the Montevideo Treaty) and the decisions of its Comisión del Acuerdo de Cartagena through Sept. 1972.

Whitaker, Arthur P. The United States and the southern cone: Argentina, Chile, and Uruguay. See *HLAS 40:3882.*

8908 Wilhelmy, Manfred. La política exterior chilena y el Grupo Andino (CPU/ ES, 10, dic. 1976, p. 16–27)

Argues that five considerations of foreign policy (ideological orientation, anticommunism, geopolitics, nationalism, and direct diplomacy, in addition to the usual economic variable) explain Chile's withdrawal from the Andean group.

8909 Wonder, Edward. Nuclear commerce and nuclear proliferation: Germany and Brazil, 1975 (FPRI/O, 21:2, Summer 1977, p. 277–306)

One of the best brief discussions of this issue to come to this reviewer's attention. Emphasis is on German rather than Brazilian policy. Argues that "domestic socioeconomic factors, rather than politicomilitary factors at the international level," explain West German nuclear-export policy.

8910 Zeballos, Estanislao S. Diplomacia desarmada. Prólogo de Gustavo Ferrari. B.A., Editorial EUDEBA, 1974. 277 p. (Cuestiones de geopolítica)

Reprint of a work originally written in 1854 by a former Argentine Minister of Foreign Relations. The book focuses on Argentina's rivalry with Brazil and includes an "anthology" of comments by various statesmen on President Mitre's foreign policy. [F.]

8911 Zorraquín Becú, Ricardo. Inglaterra prometió abandonar las Malvinas: estudio histórico y jurídico del conflicto anglo-español. B.A., Instituto de Investigaciones de Historia del Derecho [and] Librería Editorial Platero, 1975. 200 p.

Detailed and documented study of the original Anglo-Spanish conflict over the Malvinas (Falklands). This is an important study inasmuch as the Spanish claims are indeed the starting point for subsequent Argentine claims.

JOURNAL ABBREVIATIONS
INTERNATIONAL RELATIONS

AAFH/TAM The Americas. A quarterly publication of inter-American cultural history. Academy of American Franciscan History. Washington.

ACPS/B Boletín de la Academia de Ciencias Políticas y Sociales. Caracas.

ADN A Defesa Nacional. Revista de assuntos militares e estudo de problemas brasileiros. Rio.

AF/AUR Air University Review. The professional journal of the United States Air Force. Maxwell Air Force Base, Ala.

AI/I Interciencia. Asociación Interciencia. Caracas.

AR Areito. Areíto, Inc. N.Y.

ASIL/J American Journal of International Law. American Society of International Law. Washington.

CAM Cuadernos Americanos. México.

CCE/CHA Cuadernos de Historia y Arqueología. Casa de la Cultura Ecuatoriana, Núcleo del Guayas. Guayaquil, Ecua.

CDLA Casa de las Américas. Instituto Cubano del Libro. La Habana.

CEPAC/REP Revista de Estudios del Pacífico. Consejo Coordinador Universitario de Valparaíso, Centro de Estudios del Pacífico. Valparaíso, Chile.

CEPAL/R CEPAL Review/Revista de la CEPAL. Naciones Unidas, Comisión Económica para América Latina. Santiago.

CFR/FA Foreign Affairs. Council on Foreign Relations. N.Y.

CIIA/IJ International Journal. Canadian Institute of International Affairs. Toronto, Can.

CM/FI Foro Internacional. El Colegio de México. México.

CM/HM Historia Mexicana. El Colegio de México. México.

CPS Comparative Political Studies. Northwestern Univ., Evanston, Ill. [and] Sage Publications, Beverly Hills, Calif.

CPU/ES Estudios Sociales. Corporación de Promoción Universitaria. Santiago.

CUH Current History. A monthly magazine of world affairs. Philadelphia, Pa.

CYC Comunicación y Cultura. La comunicación masiva en el proceso político latinoamericano. Editorial Galerna. B.A. [and] Santiago.

FCE/TE El Trimestre Económico. Fondo de Cultura Económica. México.

FDD/NED Notes et Études Documentaires. Direction de la Documentation. Paris.

FFCLM/EH Estudos Históricos. Faculdade de Filosofia, Ciências e Letras, Depto. de História. Marília, Brazil.

FFES/V Vierteljahresberichte. Probleme der entwicklungsländer. Forschungs-institut der Friedrich-Ebert-Stiftung. Hannover, FRG.

FP Foreign Policy. National Affairs, Inc. [and] Carnegie Endowment for International Peace. N.Y.

FPRI/O Orbis. A journal of world affairs. Foreign Policy Research Institute, Philadelphia, Pa., *in association with the* Fletcher School of Law and Diplomacy, Tufts Univ., Medford, Mass.

GWU/JILE Journal of International Law and Economics. George Washington Univ., The National Law Center. Washington.

HSWS/H The Historian. The undergraduate journal of research and scholarship. History Society of Washington Square [and] New York Univ., Univ. College. N.Y.

HU/BHR Business History Review. Harvard Univ., Graduate School of Business Administration. Boston, Mass.

IA International Affairs. A monthly journal of political analysis. Moskova.

IAA Ibero-Amerikanisches Archiv. Ibero-Amerikanisches Institut. Berlin, FRG.

IAEERI/E Estrategia. Instituto Argentino de Estudios Estratégicos y de las Relaciones Internacionales. B.A.

IAMEA Inter-American Economic Affairs. Washington.

IBRI/R Revista Brasileira de Política Internacional. Instituto Brasileiro de Relações Internacionais. Rio.

IDES/DE Desarrollo Económico. Instituto de Desarrollo Económico y Social. B.A.

IEP/RPI Revista de Política Internacional. Instituto de Estudios Políticos. Madrid.

IIB/DA Deutsche Aussenpolitik. Institut für Internationale Beziehungen. Berlin, GDR.

INTAL/IL Integración Latinoamericana. Instituto para la Integración de América Latina. B.A.

JCMS Journal of Common Market Studies. Oxford, U.K.

JGSWGL Jahrbuch für Geschichte von Staat, Wirtschaft und Gesellschaft Lateinamerikas. Köln, FRG.

JLAS Journal of Latin American Studies. Centers or institutes of Latin American studies at the universities of Cambridge, Glasgow, Liverpool, London and Oxford. Cambridge Univ. Press. London.

JPR Journal of Peace Research. International Peace Research Institute. Universitetforlaget. Oslo.

JWTL Journal of World Trade Law. Crans, Switzerland.

KYKLOS Kyklos. International review for social sciences. Basel, Switzerland.

LAP Latin American Perspectives. Univ. of California. Riverside.

LARR Latin American Research Review. Univ. of North Carolina Press *for the* Latin American Studies Association. Chapel Hill.

LIWA/YWA The Yearbook of World Affairs. London Institute of World Affairs. London.

MR Monthly Review. An independent Socialist magazine. N.Y.

NS NS NorthSouth NordSud NorteSur NorteSul. Canadian journal of Latin American Studies. Canadian Association of Latin American Studies [and] Univ. of Ottawa. Ottawa.

OCLAE OCLAE. Revista mensual de la Organización Continental Latinoamericana de Estudiantes. La Habana.

PAIGH/G Revista Geográfica. Instituto Panamericano de Geografía e Historia, Comisión de Geografía. México.

PPO Pensamiento Político. Cultura y ciencia política. México.

PUCIS/WP World Politics. A quarterly journal of international relations. Princeton Univ., Center of International Studies. Princeton, N.J.

RGS/GJ The Geographical Journal. The Royal Geographical Society. London.

RIIA/IA International Affairs. Royal Institute of International Affairs. London.

SCHG/R Revista Chilena de Historia y Geografía. Sociedad Chilena de Historia y Geografía. Santiago.

SECOLAS/A Annals of the Southeastern Conference on Latin American Studies. West Georgia College. Carrollton.

SESC/PB Problemas Brasileiros. Revista mensal de cultura. Conselho Regional do Serviço Social do Comércio (SESC). São Paulo.

SS Science and Society. N.Y.

UC/EDCC Economic Development and Cultural Change. Univ. of Chicago, Research Center in Economic Development and Cultural Change. Chicago, Ill.

UCAB/M Montalbán. Univ. Católica Andrés Bello, Facultad de Humanidades y Educación, Institutos Humanísticos de Investigación. Caracas.

UCE/A Anales de la Universidad Central del Ecuador. Quito.

UCEIA/H Humanitas. Boletín ecuatoriano de antropología. Univ. Central del Ecuador, Instituto de Antropología. Quito.

UCV/ECS Economía y Ciencias Sociales. Univ. Central de Venezuela, Facultad de Economía. Caracas.

UM/JIAS Journal of Inter-American Studies and World Affairs. Univ. of Miami Press

for the Center for Advanced International Studies. Coral Gables, Fla.

UMG/RBEP Revista Brasileira de Estudos Políticos. Univ. de Minas Gerais. Belo Horizonte, Brazil.

UNAM/RFD Revista de la Facultad de Derecho. Univ. Nacional Autónoma de México. México.

UNAM/RI Relaciones Internacionales. Revista del Centro de Relaciones Internacionales. Univ. Nacional Autónoma de México, Facultad de Ciencias Políticas y Sociales. México.

UNAM/RMS Revista Mexicana de Sociología. Univ. Nacional Autónoma de México, Instituto de Investigaciones Sociales. México.

UNM/NMHR New Mexico Historical Review. Univ. of New Mexico [and] Historical Society of New Mexico. Albuquerque.

UP/CSEC Cuban Studies/Estudios Cubanos. Univ. of Pittsburgh, Univ. Center for International Studies, Center for Latin American Studies. Pittsburgh, Pa.

UPR/CS Caribbean Studies. Univ. of Puerto Rico, Institute of Caribbean Studies. Río Piedras.

USC/U Universidad de San Carlos de Guatemala. Guatemala.

USCG/E Economía. Univ. de San Carlos de Guatemala, Facultad de Ciencias Económicas, Instituto de Investigaciones Economicas y Sociales. Guatemala.

USIA/PC Problems of Communism. United States Information Agency. Washington.

USMLA/LA La Antigua. Univ. de Santa María La Antigua, Oficina de Humanidades. Panamá.

USP/RH Revista de História. Univ. de São Paulo, Faculdade de Filosofia, Ciências e Letras, Depto. de História [and] Sociedade de Estudos Históricos. São Paulo.

UT/SSQ Social Science Quarterly. Univ. of Texas, Dept. of Government. Austin.

UWI/JCH The Journal of Caribbean History. Univ. of the West Indies, Dept. of History [and] Caribbean Universities Press. St. Lawrence, Barbados.

WPF/IO   International Organization. World Peace Foundation [and] Univ. of Wisconsin Press. Madison.

WQ   The Wilson Quarterly. Woodrow Wilson International Center for Scholars. Washington.

SOCIOLOGY

GENERAL

9001 Almeida, Fernando Lopes de. A especificidade da diferença entre a formação social africana e a formação social latino-americana (VOZES, 69:1, jan./fev. 1975, p. 45–57)

This work draws parallels between the evolution of African and Latin American societies. Although the author does not imply that their social structures are identical, he notes how Africa and Latin America suffered the effects of European expansionism and influences. He perceives the process of development in both regions as an attempt to attain freedom from these linkages. [J.F.B. Dasilva]

9002 Arbeláez, Fernando. La infraestructura invisible: ensayo sobre la mujer campesina de América Latina. Bogotá?, Banco Interamericano de Desarrollo?, 1976. 137 l., tables.

Written by an employee of the Inter-American Development Bank it has been described by the author as "an approximation to the subject." It presents the thesis that female labor in the rural area has been essential to the exploitation and development of agriculture. No concrete cases are given, nor any field research presented, rather it uses some secondary sources and novels, concentrating on the pre-national period. [N.P. Valdés]

9003 Archetti, Eduardo P. Una visión general de los estudios sobre el campesinado (CLACSO/ERL, 1:1, enero/abril 1978, p. 7–31, bibl.)

First published in 1976 in Howard Newby ed., *International research rural studies: progress and prospects* (Sussex, UK, John Wiley and Sons), the author reviews the recent literature on peasants noting the different definitions and methodologies. He points to the absence of a consistent theory of peasant economy and the need for empirical studies

that would address the question of modes of production (including the debate on simple commodity production). [N.P. Valdés]

9004 Argüello, Omar and others. Migración y desarrollo. v. 2, Consideraciones teóricas y aspectos socioeconómicos y políticos; v. 3, Análisis históricos y aspectos relacionados a la estructura agraria y al proceso de urbanización. B.A., Consejo Latinoamericano de Ciencias Sociales (CLACSO), Comisión de Población y Desarrollo, Grupo de Trabajo sobre Migraciones Internas, 1974. 2 v. (124, 173 p.) bibl., tables (Serie población. Informe de investigación)

Vol. 2 is series of papers on internal migrations prepared by a CLACSO working group which considers the following themes: a review of the literature on the relationship between migration and structural change; internal migration in Argentina; the relationship between migration and urban development; the effect of migration on occupational mobility in Mexico; and the political consequences of migration. Vol. 3 is another series of essays on internal migration, prepared by a working group of CLACSO. Topics analyzed cover the relationship between agrarian structure and internal migrations, development and migration, marginality and urban poverty, and different aspects of internal migration in Brazil and Mexico. [C.H. Waisman]

9005 Arriagada, Irma. Las mujeres pobres latinoamericanas: un esbozo de tipología (ACEP/EP, 2:8, Aug. 1977, p. 38–53, tables)

After describing the educational, occupational, and economic status of women in many Latin American nations, the author presents a typology of Latin American women of low socioeconomic status. [L. Pérez]

9006 Balán, Jorge ed. Las historias de vida en ciencias sociales: teoría y técnica. B.A., Ediciones Nueva Visión, 1974. 217 p., bibl., tables (Cuadernos de investigación social)

A collection of papers dealing with the utilization of life stories as a technique for the analysis of social structure. The introduction to the volume and the first part cover general methodological issues, such as the intersection between biography and social structure, the use of life stories for the validation of hypotheses, and the like. The articles in the second part discuss the utilization of life stories in relation to specific methods and substantive areas: conventional surveys, oral history, and anthropological analysis. Finally, the third part consists of two substantive studies, one on occupational histories, and the other on the life of a Bolivian miner. Useful as a textbook. [C.H. Waisman]

9007 Benítez Zenteno, Raúl ed. Clases sociales y crisis política en América Latina; Seminario de Oaxaca. México, Siglo XXI Editores, 1977. 454 p. (Sociología y política)

A symposium on social classes and political crisis in Latin America, organized by UNAM's Institute of Social Research. The volume is organized around three papers, which are discussed by the participants: 1) Torres Rivas' work deals with the crisis of bourgeois rule in Latin America. The focus of the essay is the conceptualization of hegemonic crises, and the application of this conceptualization to the post-1930 period. In particular, two frustrated bourgeois revolutions are discussed: Guatemala in the 1940s and Bolivia in the 1950s; 2) The paper by Quijano is a detailed study of the effect of external hegemony on class-rule in Peru during the "oligarchical" period. The discussion focuses on the relationship between classes and the state; 3) Finally, Cardoso examines general methodological issues in the conceptualization of the relationship between the class system and political processes, and explores the processes of class formation during colonial and contemporary capitalism in Latin America (for Roger Bartra's comment on how Cardoso's views apply to Mexico, see item **9057**). The papers, as well as some of the comments, are highly sophisticated. This book is an example of the best sociology being produced in the region. [C.H. Waisman]

9008 Blachman, Morris J. and **Ronald G. Hellman** eds. Terms of conflict: ideology in Latin American policies. Philadelphia, Pa., Institute for the Study of Human Issues (ISHI) [and] Center for Inter-American Relations, N.Y., 1977. 275 p. (Inter-American politics series, 1)

A collection of essays exploring the relationship between ideology and politics in Latin America. Most papers examine the effects of a specific ideology in a specific country: Dos Santos and Jacquette discuss liberalism in Brazil and Peru; Weinstein and Corradi analyze corporatism in Uruguay and Argentina; and Wilhelmy and Peppe deal with Christian Democratic and Socialist ideologies in Chile. On the other hand, Ferguson examines the ideological aspects of US policy towards Latin America in the postwar period. There are two more general chapters: Jutkowitz's deal with ideologies and their historical contexts, and Bennet's is a discussion of methodological issues in the analysis of ideologies. An interesting volume. For political scientist's comment, see item **7003**. [C.H. Waisman]

9009 *Boletín Documental sobre las Mujeres.* Publicación trimestral. Comunicación Intercambio y Desarrollo Humano en América Latina (CIDHAL). Asociación Civil Mexicana. Año 60, Vol. 6, No. 1, enero 1976–. Cuernavaca, Mex.

Issue entitled "La Mujer en la Religión: Pasado, Presente y Futuro," offers a rather superficial discussion of diverse feminist issues relevant to Latin America. A good theoretical article by M. Van de Melenbroke-Cahier de Grif (Brussels) is the most worthwhile contribution. [P.F. Hernández]

9010 Brackett, James. W. Family planning in four Latin American countries: knowledge, use, and unmet need: some findings from the World Fertility Survey (International Family Planning Perspectives and Digest [Alan Guttmacher Institute for the Planned Parenthood Federation of America, N.Y.] 4:4, Winter 1978, p. 116–123, bibl., illus., tables)

From the perspective of the author and the Planned Parenthood Federation, the message in this article is an optimistic one. Evidence from four countries (Colombia, Costa Rica, Dominican Republic, and Panama) indicates that fertility has declined substantially and that contraceptive use and knowledge have increased. The author does note, however, that there is still a considerable amount of "unmet need" for family-planning services. [L. Pérez]

9011 Brathwaite, Edward. Race and the divided self (UPR/CS, 14:3, Oct. 1974, p. 127–139)

The author writes a "cultural psychoanalysis" of Margaret Mead and James Baldwin using the book, *A rap on race* in which both spoke of the "plural societies" in very general terms, often clashing with each others' world-view. [N.P. Valdés]

9012 Centro Paraguayo de Estudios Sociológicos, *Asunción.* **Centro Paraguayo de Documentación Social. Grupo de Trabajo de Migraciones Internas.** Las migraciones en América Latina: bibliografía. B.A., Consejo Latinoamericano de Ciencias Sociales (CLACSO), 1976. 76 p. (Serie población. Informe de investigación)

A bibliography on internal migration in Latin America. Includes documents and monographs. Has a detailed analytical index. [C.H. Waisman]

9013 Cerase, Francesco P.; Luis M. Razeto; and Francesco P. Consoli. Classi ed istituzioni in America Latina: proposte di analisi en interpretazioni. Roma, Beniamino Carucci Editore, 1977. 269 p., bibl.

El volumen reune cuatro estudios sociológicos sobre las teorías y la formación del estado. De especial interés es el estudio de Consoli, en el cual el autor se esfuerza en demostrar la especificidad del caso venezolano en lo que concierne la interrelación entre la formación del estado y el desarrollo de las tensiones sociales. [M. Carmagnani]

9014 Colomina de Rivera, Marta. La Celestina mecánica: estudio sobre la mitología de lo femenino, la mujer y su manipulación a través de la industria cultural. Caracas, Monte Avila Editores, 1976. 433 p., bibl., illus., plates, tables (Col. Temas venezolanos)

Title, cover, and illustrations would lead one to believe this is a shallow and rhetorical attack on male-dominated society. But, on the contrary, the work is an interesting and well-grounded analysis of the exploitation and manipulation of women by the popular media of Latin America. The analysis includes a study of the depiction of women in the "fotonovelas" (see also items **9023** and **9329**). Author regards the advertising industry as the culprit. [L. Pérez]

9015 Consejo Episcopal Latinoamericano (CELAM), *Bogotá.* Iglesia y religiosidad popular en América Latina: ponencias y documento final. Introducción de Alfonso López Trujillo. Bogotá, 1977. 417 p. (Documento CELAM, 29)

A compilation of 24 papers presented by different Catholic authors treating the theme of popular religiosity (or the religious piety of the poor) from an historical, anthropological, theological, pastoral and devotional perspective. [N.P. Valdés]

9016 Cornelius, Wayne A. and Robert V. Kemper *eds.* Metropolitan Latin America: the challenge and the response. Beverly Hills, Calif., Sage Publications, 1978. 346 p., bibl., maps, tables (Latin American urban research, 6)

Outstanding compilation of articles by sociologists, political scientists, geographers, economists, anthropologists, etc. Vol. 6 of this excellent series lives up to the high standards of predecessor volumes (for vols. 1/5 see *HLAS 36:1716–1717, HLAS 37:9625, HLAS 38:2378,* and *HLAS 39:9016*). All contributions to this work are entered under authors' names. For Cornelius' introduction, see item **7014**. For piece on Guadalajara by John Walton, see item **9098**. For study of Mexico City by Gustavo Garza and Martha Schteingart, see item **9076**. For piece on Bogotá by Alan Gilbert, see item **3095**. For article on Medellín by David W. Dent, see item **9211**. For study of Port-au-Prince by Simon M. Fass, see item **9152**. For piece on Guayaquil by Richard J. Moore, see item **7320**. For article on Lima by Henry A. Dietz, see item **7331**. For study of Caracas by David J. Myers, see item **7626**. For work on Rio by V. Metter and Ana Maria Brasileiro, see item **5714**. [Ed.]

9017 Davis, Stanley M. and Louis Wolf Goodman *eds.* Workers and managers in Latin America. Lexington, Mass., D.C. Heath, 1972. 308 p., tables.

Important collection of articles. Topics range from description of workers and managers in Latin America to the sub-cultures of industry in both Latin America and the US.

Also includes discussion of social security, social welfare, workmen's compensation, unions, etc. A useful book for courses in business administration and intercultural programs. [P.F. Hernández]

9018 Delacroix, Jacques and **Charles Ragin.** Modernizing institutions, mobilization, and Third World development: a cross-national study (UC/AJS, 84:1, July 1978, p. 123–150, bibl., tables)

Test of Alejandro Portes' thesis that when modernization is Westernization, economic development is retarded. Authors, using panel regression analysis, agree. They note that education furthers economic progress in poor countries, regardless of political context; but the situation is more complex with respect to exposure to cinema. Statistical analysis covers 49 countries. [N.P. Valdés]

9019 Despradel, Lil. Notes sur la condition féminine en Amérique Latine (ULB/RIS, 3/4, 1975, p. 387–399, bibl., tables)

An extremely general article on the status of women in Latin America. Author believes Latin American women have, overall, the lowest status in the entire world, and then proceeds to discuss standards of sexuality and reproduction as well as the socialization of children. [L. Pérez]

9020 Edmonston, Barry and **Frank William Oechsli.** Fertility decline and socioeconomic change in Venezuela (UM/JIAS, 19:3, Aug. 1977, p. 369–392, tables)

Fertility and natality rates are falling in Venezuela as socioeconomic gains occur. The authors anticipate greater attention in the future, by the government, to immigration policy as immigrants contribute more importantly to technological and professional improvement. Raw statistical summaries to the contrary, Venezuela's demographic experience does not differ greatly from that of neighboring Caribbean countries. [P.B. Taylor, Jr.]

9021 Equipo del SEREM. Corrientes migratorias en América Latina (JLAIS/CS, 12:39, 1974, p. 87–90)

This is only a basic summary—and very gross figures—of major migratory movements (mostly Anglo-Saxon and Mediterranean) in and out of Latin America. For laymen. [P.F. Hernández]

9022 Estado y sociedad. Montevideo, Centro Latinoamericano de Economía Humana (CLAEH), 1978. 64 l. (Serie estudios, 8)

Two essays on the relationship between state and society are included in this volume. The first one is an examination of the political consequences of industrialization, with focus on the social forces generated in each state of development. The second article is a discussion of the "social state," which is an adaptation of the traditional state to the conditions of industrial and postindustrial society. [C.H. Waisman]

9023 Flora, Cornelia Butler and **Jan L. Flora.** The fotonovela as a tool for class and cultural domination (LAP, 5:1, Winter 1978, p. 134–150, plates)

Fascinating analysis of the functions and plot devices of those widely-read *fotonovelas*. Authors show how the *fotonovelas*, such an important part of the popular culture of the working classes, mirror and lend support to the multinational capitalistic industry that produces them. [L. Pérez]

9023a Fukui, Lia. Estudos clásicos de sociologia agrária: comunidades, estruturas agrárias, caracterização da camada camponesa (SBPC/CC, 27:6, junho 1975, p. 607–612)

Author reviews the most significant studies of agrarian sociology for the period 1950–60 and discusses their fundamental limitations: 1) a proliferation of ethnographies of limited scope; 2) a lack of theoretical frameworks and the use instead of schema which are too general, superficial and inadequate for an understanding of rural societies and their phenomena; 3) critical attitudes derived from theoretical schema imported from other societies which hamper theoretical innovation. The author, however, does mention a few studies of agrarian societies which transcend these limitations. [J.F.B. Dasilva]

9024 Galjert, Benno. Movilización campesina en América Latina (CEDLA/B, 12, junio 1972, p. 2–19, bibl.)

The possibilities of peasant mobilization for the attainment of common objectives is analyzed largely in the context of the man-land system. Particular emphasis is placed on the influence of tenure arrangements and concentration of land ownership on the capacity of peasants to mobilize. For political scientist's comment, see item **7404**. [L. Pérez]

9025 Germani, Gino. Autoritarismo, fascismo e classi sociali. Bologna, Italy, Società Editrice Il Mulino, 1975. 306 p., bibl.

Recopilación de algunos estudios del conocido sociólogo ítalo-argentino, actualmente en Italia. De los seis estudios contenidos en el volumen, dos de ellos—el rol del populismo en la modernización política y tradiciones políticas y mobilización social en los orígenes de un movimiento nacional popular—se refieren específicamente a América Latina. En estos dos estudios el autor presenta sus bien conocidas hipótesis sobre el populismo, en general, y el peronismo, en particular. [M. Carmagnani]

9026 Gouldner, Alvin W. Los intelectuales revolucionarios(UNAM/RMCPS, 22/85, julio/sept. 1976, p. 7–61)

Explores four themes: 1) the role of intellectuals in revolutions; 2) the socio-historical mechanisms that contribute to the radicalization of intellectuals; 3) what makes intellectuals revolutionaries; and 4) why intellectuals are essential to revolutions. The author is an exponent of the American "radical social critique" school. It does not deal with Latin America. [N.P. Valdés]

9027 Grau M., Ilda Elena. La mujer en la sociedad latinoamericana: su papel y su situación (III/AI, 38:2, abril/junio 1978, p. 475–513, bibl.)

Thoroughly annotated, contains citations of works published in the 1970s. The bibliography has three sections: 1) women in the labor force (13 citations); 2) women and social organization (30 citations); and 3) women, ideology and education (14 citations). It includes an appendix of bibliographies already published (49 citations). [N.P. Valdés]

9028 Janvry, Alain de and **Carlos Garramón.** The dynamics of rural poverty in Latin America (JPS, 4:3, April 1977, p. 206–216)

The authors argue that the fundamental economic and social dualism (subsistence and commodity-producing sectors) is an objective outcome of the dynamics of capitalism. Subsistence agriculture exhibits contradictions which derive from this binomial. For

economist's comment, see item **2842**. [L. Pérez]

9029 Kaplan, Marcos. La investigación latinoamericana en ciencias sociales. México, Consejo Latinoamericana de Ciencias de Estudios Sociológicos, 1973. 86 p. (Jornadas, 84)

In an examination of the crisis of social research in Latin America, the author discusses the broader context of research, the effects of the crisis on the institutional contexts in which social science is practiced—universities, government agencies, international organizations—and three typical responses to the crisis among social scientists: neutralism, technocratism, and radicalized engagement. [C.H. Waisman]

Knaster, Meri. Women in Latin America: the state of research, 1975. See *HLAS 40:2392.*

9030 Kovar, B. and others. Estructura clasista de América Latina. Bogotá, Ediciones Suramérica, 1975. 137 p., tables (Col. América Latina)

Significant compilation because of the insights it provides into how Soviet social scientists view Latin American society. Originally published in the USSR journal *América Latina,* the articles cover the following topics: class structure, nature of both working and middle classes, migration and urbanization, family planning, unemployment, and population problems. [L. Pérez]

9031 Lagos Matus, Gustavo and **Horacio H. Godoy.** Revolution of being: a Latin American view of the future. N.Y., The Free Press, 1977. 226 p., tables (Preferred worlds for the 1990's)

A book in a series of "Preferred Worlds for the 1990's," resulting from the World Order Models project. The authors' aim is to elaborate a desirable world model, from a Latin American perspective. Pt. 1 is an examination of the international system of stratification and of the place of Latin America in that system. Pt. 2 discusses the preferred world model and describes it from a "humanistic" perspective, whose principles are solidarity, an ethics of liberation, a new rationality, a new conception of peace, and a new legitimacy. The aim would be to generate a new society, whose members will be "multi-dimensional persons." The different dimensions of the new society—education, economy, polity—are explored. Pt. 3 focuses on the transition to the new society. The analysis of the emergence of prospective actors is particularly interesting. [C.H. Waisman]

9032 Lambert, Claire M. *ed.* and *comp.* Village studies: data analysis and bibliography. v. 2, Africa, Middle East and North Africa, Asia (excluding India), Pacific Islands, Latin America, West Indies and the Caribbean, 1950–1975. Brighton, UK, Univ of Sussex, Institute of Development Studies, Village Studies Programme, 1978. 319 p.

A most useful tool, the work excluded from the main section studies in which village data was not disaggregated. Primary emphasis given to land use. The authors coded the information about each village and the range of the data. There are 96 items on Latin America. [N.P. Valdés]

9033 Leacock, Eleanor. Women, development, and anthropological facts and fictions (LAP, 4[12/13]:1/2, Winter and Spring 1977, p. 8–17, bibl.)

An essay on the assumptions fostered in the social sciences that hinder women's organization. [L. Pérez]

9034 Maru, Rushikesh M. and others. The organization of family planning programs: India, China, Costa Rica, Venezuela, Lebanon. Foreword by M.C. Shelesnyak and John T. Holloway. Introduction by Amparo Menéndez Carrión. Washington, Smithsonian Institution, International Program for Population Analysis, Interdisciplinary Communications Program (ICP), 1976. 234 p., bibls., tables (Occasional monograph series, 8. ICP work agreement reports)

John T. McNelly tries to answer how people relate issues of population growth in general to their own personal situations and the impact of the mass media on individual values in urban Venezuela. M.J. Carvajal, David T. Geithman, and Lydia B. Neuhauser survey family planning and their activities in Costa Rica. They argue that fertility has been reduced in a major way by family planning. [N. Valdés]

Mörner, Magnus. Los movimientos campesinos de Latinoamérica y del Caribe en la investigación histórica. See item **9173**.

9035 Moreno Fraginals, Manuel *ed.* Africa en América Latina. México, Siglo XXI

Editores [and] UNESCO, 1977. 436 p., bibl., illus., tables.

An exceptional work that brings together noteworthy contributions by a number of scholars on African culture in Latin America on music and dance to the visual arts, literature, and food. Of particular interest to social scientists are the contributions on: social organization in the Caribbean, slavery, the plantation system, Afro-American religion by several notable authors such as Manuel Moreno Fraginals, Octavio Ianni, Jean Benoist, and Sidney Mintz. [L. Pérez]

9036 Nash, June; Juan Corradi; and **Hobart Spalding, Jr.** Ideology & social change in Latin America. N.Y., Gordon and Breach, 1977. 305 p.

A series of papers dealing with ideology and political action in Latin American labor and peasant movements. Most essays are case studies. A useful collection. A preliminary (mimeo) version of this book was annotated in the *HLAS* humanities volume (see *HLAS 38:2394*). Articles by individual authors are entered and annotated separately in the social sciences volume, *HLAS 39*. [C.H. Waisman]

9037 Ordóñez, José Guillermo. Familia y sociedad. Córdoba, Arg., Editorial Cóndor, 1975. 94 p.

A conservative Catholic defense of the traditional view of the family. Opposes feminism and divorce, and supports traditional religion and the protection of the family by the state. An ideological work. [C.H. Waisman]

9038 Paz, Juan Gervasio and **Emiliano Galende.** Psiquiatría y sociedad: hacia una psiquiatría materialista. B.A., Granica Editor, 1975. 206 p. (Col. Psiquiatría y sociedad)

An orthodox Marxist discussion of the relationship between psychiatry and society. In the style of the traditional Latin American essay, the authors look into some general issues, such as the linkages between science and praxis, the concept of ideology, the infrastructural determination of science; as well as more specific topics, such as the Marxist critique of psychoanalysis and other orientations in psychiatry, the ideological effects of psychiatric practice, the functions of mental health, institutions, and the foundations of a "materialist psychiatry." Sophisticated, but with the twin limitations of the approach—the "two sciences theory" lingers in the analysis—and of the genre. [C.H. Waisman]

Pescatello, Ann M. Power and pawn: the female in Iberian families, societies, and cultures. See *HLAS 40:2213.*

9039 Poviña, Alfredo. Diccionario de sociología a través de los sociólogos. v. 1/2. B.A., Editorial Astrea de Alfredo y Ricardo Depalma, 1976. 2 v. (1283 p.) (Continuous pagination)

A valuable reference tool, this biographic dictionary of sociologists summarizes the life and sociological contributions of more than 300 sociologists. They are arranged alphabetically, regardless of chronology and nationality, and anywhere from 2 to 20 p. are dedicated to each. The emphasis is on Europeans and North Americans, both classic and contemporary, while many contemporary Latin Americans are excluded. [L. Pérez]

9040 Quijano, Aníbal. Dependencia, urbanización y cambio social en Latinoamerica. Lima, Mosca Azul Editores, 1977. 242 p.

A series of essays, written in the 1960s, on urbanization in Latin America. The author interprets the urbanization process in the context of the development of capitalism, as a modality of the liberation of labor power. The peculiarities of Latin American urbanization are a consequence of the "unequal and combined" nature of dependent development. The author insists on the conception of "imperialism" as an internal aspect of peripheral social formations. [C.H. Waisman]

9041 ———. Imperialismo y marginalidad en América Latina. Lima, Mosca Azul Editores, 1977. 287 p.

A discussion of the concept of marginality, and an interpretation of the process of marginalization in Latin America. The author reviews the different uses of the term "marginality," and endeavors to elaborate a theoretically grounded definition, within the Marxist framework. The phenomenon of marginality is considered in the context of Capital Accumulation and the generation of relative overpopulation. Marginality is analytically distinct from the labor reserve army, for it refers to that segment of the labor force that cannot be absorbed by the productive apparatus. Latin American marginality is interpreted within the context of the specific type of capitalist development that took place in Latin America. A serious attempt to conceptualize a diffuse problem. [C.H. Waisman]

Race and class in post-colonial society: a study of ethnic group relations in the English-speaking Caribbean, Bolivia, Chile and Mexico. See item **9182.**

9042 Rico, José M. Crimen y justicia en América Latina. México, Siglo XXI Editores, 1977. 403 p., bibl., tables (Nueva criminología)

An interesting piece of work in a neglected area: criminal behavior. Pt. 1 is an examination of statistical data on several types of criminal activity, and of some of the factors that affect the variability of deviant behavior. Pt. 2 is a very useful discussion of social control mechanisms in Latin America: penal law, the police, courts, prisons, and post-prison assistance. Highly recommended. [C.H. Waisman]

9043 Safa, Helen. Modificaciones en la composición social de la fuerza laboral femenina en América Latina (ACEP/EP, 1:2, nov. 1976, p. 597–607, bibl.)

The principal argument of the author is that the kind of development that predominates in Latin America, foreign-dependent capitalism, is not conducive to the incorporation of women into the labor force, especially working-class women. [L. Pérez]

9044 Salazar, José Miguel and **Gerardo Marín.** National stereotypes as a function of conflict and territorial proximity: a test of the mirror image hypothesis (JSP, 101:1, Feb. 1977, p. 13–19, bibl., tables)

An article of special interest to psychologists. The mirror image hypothesis is supported if only the "evaluative" stereotype is considered. [L. Pérez]

Samaniego, Carlos and **Bernardo Sorj.** Articulaciones de modos de producción y campesinado en América Latina. See item **2903.**

Shaw, R. Paul. Land tenure and the rural exodus in Chile, Colombia, Costa Rica, and Peru. See *HLAS 40:2404.*

9045 Silva de Mejía, Luz María. Realidades y fantasías de las computadoras: un punto de vista sociológico. México, UNAM, Facultad de Ciencias Políticas y Sociales, 1976. 144 p., bibl. (Serie estudios, 46)

Valuable sociological reflections on the subjects of technology and human values. [P.F. Hernández]

Singelmann, Peter. Los movimientos campesinos y la modernización política en América Latina: apuntes críticos. See item **7075.**

Soeiro, Susan A. Recent work on Latin American women: a review essay. See *HLAS* 40:2236.

9046 Solari, Aldo E. *comp.* Poder y desarrollo: América Latina. Estudios sociológicos en homenage a José Medina Echavarría. México, Fondo de Cultura Económica, 1977. 429 p. (Sección de obras de sociología)

A Festschrift for José Medina Echavarría. Includes a biographical sketch and a presentation of Medina's work, and 11 original essays, written by leading Latin Americanists. Cardoso's paper is an excellent methodological discussion of the conceptualization of social classes. Fernandes examines the autocratic variant of the capitalist state, with special reference to Brazil. Franco summarizes the Marxist perspectives on international economic relations, ranging from Marx and Engels' views on colonialism to contemporary arguments about unequal exchange. Graciarena focuses on the consequences of the emergence of the authoritarian technocratic state for university activities and intellectual life in general. Marsal describes the evolution of sociology in Spain since the civil war. Jaguaribe analyzes the political implications of economic development, on the basis of different models and approaches that became popular in the 1960s and 1970s: the Pearson, Peterson and Rockefeller reports, the "Consensus of Viña del Mar," and the Prebisch report. Silva Michelena considers the relationship between modes of underdevelopment and international relations, from colonial times to the present. Silvert and Jutkowitz report data from three survey studies conducted in Chile in the 1960s, among teachers and students. These studies deal with the relationship among education, values, and openness to change. Steger describes the evolution of university systems in Europe and Latin America since the French revolution. Touraine discusses, in an excellent article, the

relationship between class and dependency analyses. The apparently limited value of class analysis in Latin America is the consequence of the "disorganization" of class relations. This disorganization arises from the fact that the center of economic power is external to the society. Wolfe, finally, examines different "options" for development. One of the best collections of essays published in the past decade, some unevenness notwithstanding. [C.H. Waisman]

9047 ———**; Rolando Franco; and Joel Jutkowitz.** Teoría, acción social y desarrollo en América Latina. México, Siglo XXI Editores, 1976. 637 p. (Textos del Instituto Latinoamericano de Planificación Económica y Social [ILPES]. Sociología y política)

A textbook of Latin American sociology prepared by social scientists from ILPES, the Latin American Institute for Economic and Social Planning. Pt. 1 deals with different interpretations of Latin American development. Pt. 2 is a very good summary of existing research on social classes and strata: upper class, urban marginals, and peasants. The focus is on the role of each of these groups as an agent of change or stability. Pt. 3 is devoted to intra-national heterogeneity and to international economic relations. Finally, pt. 4 is a discussion of the Latin American political system. Topics include the relationship between economic development and democracy, Marxist perspectives, populism, the role of the state in planning. This is a very useful book: It is the only comprehensive textbook of the dominant approach in Latin America, and reflects the "state-of-the-art" in the mid 1970s. The contents are restricted to sociology generated in Latin America by Latin Americans. Even though this limitation can be justified in terms of coherence, a broader perspective would have allowed a more comprehensive discussion of some topics, political processes in particular. Highly recommended. [C.H. Waisman]

9047a Sotelo, Ignacio. Sociología de América Latina: estructuras y problemas. Madrid, Editorial Tecnos, 1975. 214 p. (Col. De ciencias sociales. Serie de sociología)

Excellent overview of the history, nature and prospects of sociology in Latin America. Pt. 1, *Sociology and history*, covers the philosophical background of Latin American sociology, the question of feudalism vs.

capitalism, and includes a discussion of the typology of Latin American colonization. Pt. 2, *Basic structures*, examines social structures and agrarian reform, urbanization, industrialization, marginality and dependency. Pt. 3, *Agents of change*, analyzes the urban working class, the peasantry and the middle classes. An incisive epilogue makes two fundamental points: 1) the great differences among Latin American countries will increase rather than diminish; and 2) the middle, not the working classes will be the promoters of Latin American socialism. [Ed.]

9048 Stavenhagen, Rodolfo; John Saxe-Fernández; and Ignacio Sotelo. El futuro de América Latina. B.A., Ediciones Nueva Visión, 1975. 153 p., tables (Col. Fichas, 52)

Three essays on the future of Latin America. Stavenhagen's paper deals with underdevelopment as a structure, rather than as an indicator of relative backwardness vis-à-vis advanced countries, and considers the major disequilibria in that structure: the latifundio-minifundio complex, urbanization, marginality. The author also describes the main characteristics of dependent development based on import substitution, and discusses the failure of liberal democracy, and the emergence of "popular" movements and of military regimes. In the second essay, Saxe Fernández examines the use of social science research in counterinsurgency planning in the US, including the Camelot project and ulterior developments. Finally, Sotelo summarizes the development of "scientific sociology" in Latin America, and criticizes it for its alleged reliance on the traditional-modern continuum. [C.H. Waisman]

9049 A study of the economic and social classification of the Latin American countries (UNECLA/B, 17:2, 1972, p. 26–97, bibl., tables)

The article presents an up-dating of the "Typology of Latin American Countries" by R. Vekemans and T.L. Segundo, (OAS Pan-American Union, 1960), with a simpler, perhaps also more accurate methodology and certainly with new and better sources. Very relevant even at this preliminary stage. [P.F. Hernández]

9050 Stycos, J. Mayone. Recent trends in Latin American fertility (LSE/PS, 31:3, Nov. 1978, p. 407–425, tables)

One of the best and most comprehen-

sive analyses of the recent decline in fertility in Latin American countries. The author looks at the role played in that decline by social and economic development versus organized family-planning programs. Data are primarily from Costa Rica, Colombia, and Mexico. [L. Pérez]

9051 Touraine, Alain. Les classes sociales dans une société dépendente: la société latino-américaine (UP/TM, 16:61, janvier/ mars 1975, p. 235–256)

Social classes (middle and lower) which most suffer from social inequality also play a leading role in the major social processes of Latin America. The author offers a sociological analysis of this contradiction along the lines inspired by Benítez's collective work *Clases sociales en América Latina* (1974–75). [P.F. Hernández]

Turner, Frederick C. The rush to the cities in Latin America. See item **2924**.

9052 Vázquez Figueroa, Onel. La substancia de la sociología empírica: apuntes sobre un problema (UPR/RCS, 19:3, sept. 1975, p. 301–349, bibl., illus., tables)

An overview of empirical sociology. Notes that a real social science requires manipulation and verification. Argues empirical sociology is essentially typological and descriptive. Reviews work of Weber, Durkheim, Thomas, Znaniecki, Park, Lazarsfeld and Merton. Does not deal with Latin American sociologists. [N.P. Valdés]

9053 Walton, John. Elites and economic development: comparative studies on the political economy of Latin American cities. Austin, Univ. of Texas, Institute of Latin American Studies, 1977. 257 p., bibl., tables (Latin American monographs, 41)

Working from an empirical basis of field work in four cities and interviews with over 300 members of political and economic elites, Walton presents a major contribution toward our theoretical understanding of the theories of underdevelopment and economic dependency. [L. Pérez]

Wilkie, James W. and **Edna Monzón de Wilkie.** Dimensions of elitelore: an oral history questionnaire. See *HLAS 40:2415*.

9054 Wöhlcke, Manfred. Strukturelle Besonderheiten der gegenwärtigen Dependenzsituation Lateinamerikas (BESPL, 1:6, Juli/August 1976, p. 13–22)

Excerpt from author's dissertation in sociology at the Univ. of Erlangen–Nürnberg. It outlines the changing concepts of the de- pendency theory as it has been applied to Latin America and the diverse ideology components prompting various interpretations. [G.M. Dorn]

MEXICO AND CENTRAL AMERICA

PEDRO F. HERNANDEZ, *Associate Professor of Sociology, Loyola University*

ONE OF THE MOST IMPORTANT BOOKS on Latin American sociology published in the 1970s is Ignacio Sotelo's *Sociología de América Latina* (see item **9047a**). Sotelo's observations about development in the field are valid and timely, especially with regard to Mexico and Central America. He notes that Latin American sociology has become progressively more and more theoretical as exemplified by many interesting works recently published on the sociology of religion and the theology of liberation.

The majority of works annotated in this section reveal a number of trends: there is a rising interest in the roles of the public sector as well as in strategies of adaptation of certain social structures under hegemonic regimes. Other topics of interest in this biennium are ethnographical descriptions of subcultures and isolated communities, the problem of internal migration among the rural and urban poor (see items **9056, 9072** and **9075**), as well as urbanization and various demographic issues. In addition to the excellent work of the Colegio de Mexico, there are now other institutes conducting rigorous social research, the Centro de Estudios del Tercer Mundo and Estudios Transnacionales, both located in Mexico City.

MEXICO

9055 Ackerman, Kenneth. Politics and the migrant poor in Mexico City (UCL/CD, 9:1, 1977, p. 134–139, bibl.)

This is a review article where Ackerman evaluates Wayne Cornelius' book *Politics and the migrant poor in Mexico City* (see *HLAS 39:7115*). Ackerman's criticism makes a valuable complement to Cornelius' work. He notes some ideological inconsistencies and generalizations but corroborates that Cornelius' field-work (conducted in six poor barrios of Mexico City) supports his hypothesis concerning the relation between type of settlement and political awareness among the migrant poor.

Andrews, George Reid. Toward a reevaluation of the Latin American family firm: the industry executives of Monterrey. See *HLAS 40:2685*.

9056 Arizpe, Lourdes. La mujer en el sector de trabajo informal en ciudad de México: ¿un caso de desempleo o de elección voluntaria? (ACEP/EP, 1:2, nov. 1976, p. 627–645, bibl., tables)

There have been many approaches towards understanding informal labor among women in Mexico: most of them emphasize, one way or the other, the division of traditional feminine values. This study looks at the phenomenon from the perspective of economic development and growth, with special reference to labor policies in Mexico.

9057 Bartra, Roger. Clases sociales y crisis política en México (*in* Benítez Zenteno, Raúl *ed*. Clases sociales y crisis política en América Latina [see item **9007**] p. 261–283)

This study of Mexico constitutes an excellent theoretical complement to Fernando Henrique Cardoso's article (see item **9007**) about the relationship between the class system and political processes in Latin America as a whole.

9058 ——. Estructura agraria y clases sociales en México. México, UNAM, Instituto de Investigaciones Sociales [and] Ediciones Era, 1974. 182 p., bibl. (Serie popular Era, 28)

Excellent summary of the literature on the subject with good insights on Marxist-Leninist theory of class formation in rural Mexico.

9059 Berninger, Dieter George. La inmigración en México: 1821–1857. Traducción de Roberto Gómez Ciriza. México, Secretaría de Educación Pública (SEP), 1974. 198 p., bibl. (SepSetentas, 144)

This is the best synopsis of the literature and bibliography on the subject. Author recounts how Mexican conservatives and liberals, since the days of the first independent government to the beginnings of the Revolution, have been much interested in immigration policies and concerned with trying to improve Mexican agriculture by bringing in European and Asian immigrants. He also notes how the failure of these policies helped the growth of nationalism.

9060 *Cahiers des Amériques Latines.* Univ. de la Sorbonne Nouvelle, Institut des Hautes Études de l'Amérique Latine. No. 12, Semestre 2, 1975–. Paris.

Much of this issue is devoted to problems of urban migration into Mexico City and to the region around Patzcuaro (Michoacán state). A team of scholars from the Colegio de México and the Sorbonne's Institut des Hautes Etudes d'Amérique Latine have produced an excellent compilation of articles of high caliber. Recommended.

9061 Cámara Barbachano, Fernando. El mestizaje en México: planteamiento sobre problemáticas socio-culturales (UY/R, 18:106, julio/agosto 1976, p. 13–69, maps)

Study which has been published before (see *Revista de Indias*, enero/junio 1964). Nevertheless, it should be of interest to the younger generation of students. Author combines a good grasp of theoretical thinking on mestizaje with a careful if often succinct analysis of the major Indian groups of Mexico.

9062 —— and **Teófilo Reyes Couturier.** Los santuarios y las peregrinaciones:

una expresión de relaciones sociales en una sociedad compleja: el caso de México (BBAA, 35[2]:44, 1972, p. 29–45, bibl., tables)

The authors combine a basic typology of Indian societies with a description of "peregrinaciones" to the national shrine of Guadalupe in order to understand the degree of cohesiveness and of social interrelatedness (complexity of interrelation) of various strata.

9063 Campos Sevilla, Marcia J. Investigación sobre el desarrollo de la niñez en México: informe psicológico (INAH/B, 2:17, abril/junio 1976, p. 51–58, bibl., illus.)

A large interdisciplinary endeavor of the Instituto Nacional de Antropología e Historia (INAH) of Mexico has been the establishment of major bio-psychometric indexes for Mexican children in elementary schools. This article summarizes the most important psychological results of the project up until the 1970s.

9064 Casados, Alfonso J.B. Las clases sociales y el medio rural mexicano (CNC/RMA, 8:2, abril/junio 1975, p. 107–138)

The author has produced an excellent summary of sociological literature coupled with a sober examination of the dynamics of the various class-strata under the conditions of Mexican capitalism.

9065 Casas Guerrero, Rosalba. La investigación en las ciencias sociales en México: 1973–1974 (UNAM/RMS, 37:1, enero/marzo 1975, p. 185–215, tables)

Article consists of a summary of social science projects currently underway and sponsored by the CONACYT (the Mexican Board of Science and Technology). Trends worth noting are the predominance of historical and linguistic research and the commanding leadership of the federal government.

9066 Castells, Manuel. Apuntes para un análisis de clase de la política urbana del estado mexicano (UNAM/RMS, 39:4, oct./dic. 1977, p. 1161–1191, tables)

An introductory piece but still a valuable contribution to a subject that is, to this day, largely unexplored by Mexican scholars. For a worthy and rigorous study of a related topic (the phenomenal growth of Mexico City), see item **9076.**

9067 Chávez de Sánchez, María Isabel and others. Drogas y pobreza: estudio etnográfico del fenómeno de la farmacodependencia en una colonia situada de la Ciudad de México. México, Editorial Trillas, 1977. 135 p., bibl., tables.

The first years of President Echeverría's administration stimulated a number of fact-finding studies in Mexico. Among them was an investigation of "farmacodependencia" (drug-addiction) in the country. This is a case-study of one of the many proletarian "colonies" of Mexico City where the use of drugs is widespread.

9068 Cohen, Calman J. Beyond the pathological approach to Mexican family research: a study of authority relations in family and polity (in International Congress of Mexican History, IV, Santa Monica, Calif., 1973. Contemporary Mexico [see *HLAS 40:2730*] p. 367–388)

Author deplores the shortcomings of certain biased psychological approaches to the study of the Mexican family. He offers an interesting and reasonable review of the literature and stresses the importance of examining the interplay between family values and government policies.

9069 Cornelius, Wayne A. Out-migration from rural Mexican communities (in The dynamics of migration: international migration. Washington, Smithsonian Institution, Interdisciplinary Communications Program, 1976, p. 1–40, bibl., tables [Occasional monograph series, 5:2])

Study based on field work conducted in the region of Los Altos de Jalisco. Author concludes that government help to rural communities will not be effective unless a village's economy meets certain structural conditions.

———. A structural analysis of urban caciquismo in Mexico. See item **7106**.

Davies, Shane; Richard Blood; and Melvin Albaum. The settlement pattern of newly-arrived migrants in Guadalajara. See item **5342**.

Davis, Charles L. Social mistrust as a determinant of political cynicism in a transitional society: an empirical examination. See item **7108**.

9070 ——— and **Kenneth M. Coleman.** Discontinuous educational experiences and political and religious non–conformity

in authoritarian regimes: Mexico (SSQ, 58:3, Dec. 1977, p. 489–497, bibl., table)

Authors attribute the contradictory attitudes of Mexicans to the nation's long-line of anti-clerical regimes and their erratic and incoherent policies. Although modest, the authors' sample yields conclusive insights.

Díaz Polanco, Héctor. Economía y movimientos campesinos. See *HLAS 40:3048*.

9071 Díaz Ronner, Lucila M. and **María Elena Muñoz Castellanos.** La mujer asalariada en el sector agrícola (III/AI, 38:2, abril/junio 1978, p. 327–339)

Although only 4.7 percent of the Mexican agricultural wage force consists of women workers, this article asserts that the demand as well as the supply of female labor depends strictly on the crop. To support this premise while trying to answer the obvious question—Why some crops and not others?—the authors undertook a study of the vineyard region of Aguas Calientes in 1975. They discovered that women were not hired for special ability or suitable patience for a job but because of the necessity for intensive labor not demanding strength. [N.P. Valdés]

Dysart, Jane. Mexican women in San Antonio, 1830–1860: the assimilation process. See *HLAS 40:2429*.

9072 Eckstein, Susan. The poverty of revolution: the state and the urban poor in Mexico. Princeton, N.J., Princeton Univ. Press, 1977. 300 p., bibl., maps, plates, tables.

Extraordinarily insightful analysis of the poor classes of Mexico City based on careful, in-depth interviews. Most of the author's conclusions apply as well to the urban poor throughout the country, not just Mexico City. She notes how a populist revolution with a heavy agrarian orientation turned into a curious mixture of leftist politics and corporate capitalism which has defied all classical explanations and resulted in the subjugation of the poor it was supposed to liberate. For political scientist's comment, see item **7108a**.

9073 Elmendorf, Mary. The dilemma of peasant women: a view from a village in Yucatan (in Tinker, Irene and Michele Bo Bramsen eds. Women and world development. Washington, Overseas Development Council, 1976, p. 88–94)

Study of cases at Chan-Kom, a Maya village close to Can-cun, Yucatan. Although far from conclusive, the study provides a number of valuable insights into the modernization of the roles of peasant women.

9074 Exter, Thomas Gray. Rural community structure and migration: a comparative analysis of Acatic and Actlan de Juárez in Jalisco, Mexico. Ithaca, N.Y., Cornell Univ., 1976. 188 p., bibl., tables (Latin American studies program dissertation series, 71)

Doctoral dissertation whose relevance and novelty lie in the following factors: 1) author's unusual choice of topic, i.e. "comunidades de origen;" 2) determination of discrepancies within different levels of demographic analyses which author found in previous studies; and 3) linkages established by the author between migratory movements and larger frames of societal change.

Fagen, Richard R. and **William S. Tuohy.** Politics and privilege in a Mexican city. See item **7109.**

Frost, Melvin J. Mormon settlements in Mexico: a study in the hazards of foreign colonization. See item **5346.**

9075 García Mora, Carlos. La migración indígena a la Ciudad de México (III/AI, 37:3, julio/sept. 1977, p. 657–669, bibl., plates)

This article provides an abridged version of the experiences of five Indian communities: one Otomí and four Mazahua. The original and larger study was undertaken by A. Iwanska, Lourdes Arizpe and others who analyzed the migratory currents towards Mexico City. For the longer version, see *América Indígena* (33:2, abril/junio 1973) and *Diálogos* (El Colegio de México, 8, 1972)

9076 Garza, Gustavo and **Marta Schteingart.** Mexico City: the emerging megalopolis (in Cornelius, Wayne A. and Robert V. Kemper eds. Metropolitan Latin America: the challenge and the response [see item **9016**] p. 51–85, bibl., maps, tables)

An excellent study of what is fast becoming one of the world's largest cities and, surprisingly, one of the least studied in this context. This introductory work provides a long-overdue and rigorous analysis of the economic and spatial structure of Mexico City.

A useful series of tables and maps convey the dimension and significance of the problem. [Ed.]

9077 Gómez Tagle, Silvia. Organizaciones de las Sociedades de Crédito Ejidal de La Laguna. México, El Colegio de México, 1977. 46 p., bibl.

Brief but well documented study of the origins and performance of ejido credit societies around Torreón. It complements classic studies such as those by C. Senior and others.

9078 González Calzada, Manuel. México vasco. México, B. Costa–Amic Editor, 1975. 233 p., bibl.

Thorough, erudite and witty book written in an engaging style. However, the author does not share his knowledge of bibliographic sources.

9079 González Navarro, Moisés. Población y sociedad en México: 1900–1970. t. 1/2. México, UNAM, Facultad de Ciencias Políticas y Sociales, 1974. 2 v. (420, 391 p.) fold. tables, plates, tables (Serie estudios, 42)

Outstanding contribution to the study of Mexican demography. This work is a veritable landmark and includes exhaustive information on the population of Mexico (e.g., health, fertility, mortality, etiology, migration, housing, etc.). Highly recommended.

Griffin, Ernst C. and **Larry R. Ford.** Tijuana: landscape of a culture hybrid. See item **5348.**

9080 Guerra Guerra, Armando Javier ed. El alcoholismo en México. México, Fondo de Cultura Económica, 1977. 176 p., tables (Archivo del fondo, 73)

Compilation of articles for the layman on alcoholism in Mexico from a sociological and psychological perspective by Alcoholics Anonymous and other contributors. Topics are: alcoholism as drug-addiction, alcoholism as a community health problem; alcoholism and traffic accidents; definition, causes, and extent of alcoholism in Mexico; etc.

9081 Higgins, Michael James. Relaciones sociales entre los pobres de la ciudad de Oaxaca (III/AI, 37:4, oct./dic. 1977, p. 997–1018, bibl., tables)

Marxian but well documented analysis of inter–relationships among the poor of Oaxaca in various contexts (fiestas, family life, etc.).

9082 Hirschman, Charles. Prior U.S. residence among Mexican immigrants (SF, 56:4, June 1978, p. 1179–1203, bibl., tables)

This article is part of a larger study about the assimilation of Latin American minorities in the US undertaken by Alejandro Portes and commissioned by NIH and HSF. This overview of residence patterns among Mexican "illegals" provides a good introduction to understanding one of the major problems of the US-Mexican border.

9083 Kemper, Robert V. Campesinos en la ciudad: gente de Tzintzuntzan. Traducción de Poli Délano. México, Secretaría de Educación Pública (SEP), 1976. 157 p., bibl., plates, tables (SepSetentas, 270)

A most interesting and relevant complement to Foster's classic monographic study of Tarascan society in Tzintzuntzan. Provides many insights into the results of recent migratory movements and resulting structural changes.

9084 Levy, Ignacio. Los movimientos rurales en México y la reforma agraria: estudio de cuatro ejidos (UNAM/RMS, 39:3, julio/sept. 1977, p. 951–984)

Author emphasizes the importance of language and semantics for understanding the Mexican agrarian reform. This is a provocative and scholarly study.

Lynch, Kevin *ed.* Growing up in cities: studies of the spatial environment of adolescence in Cracow, Melbourne, Mexico City, Salta, Toluca, and Warszawa. See item **9269.**

9085 Marroquín, Enrique. La contracultura como protesta: análisis de un fenómeno juvenil. México, Editorial Joaquín Mortiz, 1975. 187 p. (Cuadernos de Joaquín Mortiz, 37/38)

A study of the "counter–culture" in Mexico. Author discusses many social issues and social groups, particularly among the poor. More general than specific.

Martínez, Oscar J. Chicanos and the border cities: an interpretive essay. See *HLAS 40:2746.*

Martínez Saldaña, Tomás and **Leticia Gándara Mendoza.** Política y sociedad en México: el caso de Los Altos de Jalisco. See item **7126.**

9086 Montes de Oca, Rosa Elena. La cuestión agraria y el movimiento campe-

sino: 1970–1976 (CP, 14, oct./dic. 1977, p. 57–71, tables)

Article synthesizes the various points of view of Mexican peasants who live on subsistence agriculture and oppose the big landowners. Another indication that President Echeverría's administration did not have the answers to the nagging problems of Mexico's agrarian reform.

Mumme, Stephen P. Mexican politics and the prospects for emigration policy: a policy perspective. See item **8635.**

9087 Olson, Jon L. Women and social change in a Mexican town (UNM/JAR, 33:1, Spring 1977, p. 73–88, bibl., table)

Study of the thrust of women's organizational efforts and their new roles in the predominantly peasant societies of northern Mexico. The emergence of matrifocal patterns attest to the transitional nature of rural structures. Article includes much information on the process of modernization underway throughout rural Mexico.

9088 Páez Oropeza, Carmen Mercedes. Los libaneses en México: asimilación de un grupo étnico. México, Escuela Nacional de Antropología e Historia, 1976. 266 p., bibl., maps, tables.

Based on author's Ph.D. dissertation, this work combines much sociological and anthropological information on a very important and little-studied immigrant group: the Lebanese-Mexicans.

9089 Paré, Luisa. El proletariado agrícola en México: campesinos sin tierra o proletarios agrícolas? México, Siglo XXI Editores [and] UNAM, Instituto de Investigaciones Sociales, 1977. 255 p., bibl., tables (Sociología y política)

A very insightful and provocative study of agricultural capitalism in modern Mexico illustrated by a series of case-studies in the Mezquital Valley. One of the best modern surveys of Mexico's rural proletariat.

9090 Pontones, Eduardo. La migración en México (*in* International Congress of Mexican History, IV, Santa Monica, Calif., 1973. Contemporary Mexico: papers [see *HLAS 40:2730*] p. 135–163, tables)

Attempt to combine the basic data of the censuses (by states and regions) with that on land redistribution (agrarian reform) and information on salary indexes. Lacks a methodological attempt to integrate such varied parameters.

9091 Portes, Alejandro. Legislatures under authoritarian regimes: the case of Mexico (NIU/JPMS, 5:2, Fall 1977, p. 185–201, bibl.)

Although author does not believe in the so-called "corporatism" of the Mexican government, he notes that the legislature plays a significant role in mediating between the society and the state. The article, however, does not provide a thorough analysis of the Mexican legislative process. For political scientist's comment, see item **7132**.

9092 Ramos G., Sergio. Urbanización y servicios públicos en México. México, UNAM, Instituto de Investigaciones Sociales, 1972. 192 p., fold. tables, tables.

This study (facts and trends of the Mexican process of urbanization) summarizes the basic characteristics of the country's public services and discusses their accountability for purposes of development and planning. A very useful tool for research on Mexican demography.

Rengert, Arlene C. and **George F. Rengert.** Does out-migration hinder agricultural development?: a view from rural Mexico. See item **5366**.

9093 Rollwagen, Jack R. Tuxtepec, Oaxaca: an example of rapid growth in Mexico (Urban Anthropology [State Univ. of New York, Brockport, N.Y.] 2:1, Spring 1973, p. 80–92, bibl.)

Comprehensive study of this particular city which allows the researcher to draw meaningful comparisons with other examples of urban growth throughout Mexico.

9094 Sabloff, Paula L.W. El caciquismo en el ejido post revolucionario (III/AI, 37:4, oct./dic. 1977, p. 851–881, bibl., tables)

Study of the cacique phenomenon in the ejidos of Yucatan. Includes case studies and good analysis of how the agrarian laws are implemented.

Seminario sobre Problemas del Empleo en América Latina, La Plata, Arg., 1975. El empleo en América Latina: problemas económicos, sociales y políticos. See item **9283**.

9095 Serron, Luis A. Escasez, explotación y pobreza en México: conclusiones

(UNAM/RMS, 39:4, oct./dic. 1977, p. 1143–1160, bibl., tables)

Author regards overpopulation as the consequence of poverty and capitalist exploitation.

9096 Sloan, John W. and **Jonathan P. West.** Community integration and policies among elites in two border cities: los dos Laredos (UM/JIAS, 18:4, Nov. 1976, p. 451–474, bibl., tables)

Examination of the case of Laredo (or rather, the two Laredos of the title) in which the high degree of economic integration has resulted in a sort of new international community whose identity transcends boundaries.

———— and ————. The role of informal policy making in U.S.-Mexico border cities. See item **8650**.

9097 Van Arsdol, Maurice D., Jr. and others. Migration and population redistribution in the state of Mexico (in The dynamics of migration: internal migration and migration and fertility. Washington, Smithsonian Institution, Interdisciplinary Communications Program, 1976, p. 133–176, bibl. [Occasional monograph series, 5:1])

Although questions of population size, distance, and their relation to economic stimuli are not examined, this article provides a useful review of previous works on the subject of the title and proposes an interesting migration model.

Walton, John. Elites and economic development: comparative studies on the political economy of Latin American cities. See item **2979**.

9098 ————. Guadalajara: creating the divided city (in Cornelius, Wayne A. and Robert V. Kemper eds. Metropolitan Latin America: the challenge and the response [see item **9016**] p. 25–50, bibl., illus., tables)

Insightful and valuable article on the contradictory results of government efforts to better the lot of the poor Guadalajara. The author's thorough acquaintance and deep understanding of the city facilitate his analysis of the paradoxical results of official plans which, in the case of Guadalajara, led to more rather than less class polarization.

9099 Ward, Peter W. The squatter settlement as slum or housing solution: evidence from Mexico City (UW/LE, 52:3,

Aug. 1976, p. 330–346, bibl., map, tables)

Study which shows how the squatter settlements of Mexico serve not only as indicators of vital growth but also as effective if elementary initiations in the urban economy and its marketing processes. Author believes government planning and social welfare agencies should assume responsibility for these settlements. A valuable study which shows a thorough command of the topic.

9100 Warman, Arturo. . . . Y venimos a contradecir: los campesinos de Morelos y el estado nacional. Edited by Victoria Miret and Miguel Angel Guzman. México, INAH, Centro de Investigaciones Superiores, 1976. 251 p., bibl., map (Ediciones de la casa chata, 2)

Good study of the peasants of Morelos provides much information on the dialectics of structural change in rural Mexico.

Wenzens, Gerd. Junge Wandlungen in der Agrarlandschaft der Comarca Lagunera, Nordmexico. See item **5376.**

CENTRAL AMERICA

9101 Arosemena R., Jorge. Los panameños negros descendientes antillanos: ¿un caso de marginalidad social? (CSUCA/ESC, 5:13, enero/abril 1976, p. 9–34, tables)

Article discusses the lack of assimilation of blacks of British–Caribbean descent into the mainstream of Panamanian society. Despite countless nationalist campaigns and other efforts launched by the government of Panama, this group maintains a separate identity and culture. Author attributes this lack of assimilation to their urban concentration in specific nuclei and to their persistent preference and use of the English over the Spanish language.

9102 Astorga Lira, Enrique and **Dora Suárez.** Evaluación de los asentamientos y cooperativas campesinas en Honduras. 2. ed. Colonia Alameda?, Hon., Instituto Nacional Agrario (INA), 1975. 1 v. (Various pagings) plates, tables.

Partial and laconic but important overview of the production of peasant cooperatives in the 1970s, a movement which affects the lives of more than 100,000 people. Little analysis of structural effects of social and economic issues.

9103 Barlett, Peggy F. Labor efficiency and the mechanism of agricultural evolution (UNM/JAR, 32:2, Summer 1976, p. 124–140, bibl.)

In periods of rapid population growth, an agricultural region may experience a decline in labor productivity because of the loss of soil fertility. This is contrary to the expectations of those who advocate capital-intensive techniques. This study of Costa Rican agriculture shows that farmers tend to choose labor-intensive techniques under adverse conditions as a mechanism of evolution.

9104 ———. The structure of decision-making in Paso (AAA/AE, 4:2, May 1977, p. 285–307, bibl., tables)

Exploration of the factors which influence decision-making in a Costa Rican community.

9105 Bataillon, Claude and **Ivon Lebot.** Migración interna y empleo agrícola temporal en Guatemala (CSUCA/ESC, 5:13, enero/abril 1876, p. 35–67, maps, tables)

Outstanding contribution. An inter-disciplinary analysis of man and land on the Guatemalan highlands. Thoroughly documented and filled with information.

9106 Bauer Paiz, Alfonso. La revolución guatemalteca del 20 de octubre de 1944 y sus proyecciones económico-sociales (CDLA, 14:84, mayo/junio 1974, p. 77–88)

Journalistic-type discussion of the impact of the Arbenz reforms on Guatemalan society. Special attention is devoted to educational and agrarian reforms.

9107 Biesanz, John and **Mavis Biesanz.** Costa Rican life. Preface by Robert Redfield. San José, Librería Lehmann, 1976. 272 p., bibl., plates.

Readable, modest yet scholarly account of the major social institutions of Costa Rica up to the 1950s (e.g., the family, political institutions, types of leisure, etc.). Authors base their conclusions on close interaction with Costa Ricans of all types.

9108 Calvo Pardo, Alonso. Liberia: un proyecto de investigación en sociología urbana (UCR/R, 38, julio 1974, p. 39–58, facsims., plate)

Historical and sociological analysis of the urban development of Liberia, C.R., a provincial city.

9109 Carvajal, M.J.; David T. Geithman; and Lydia B. Neuhauser. The Costa Rican Family Planning Program (in The organization of family planning programs: India, China, Costa Rica, Venezuela, Lebanon. Washington, Smithsonian Institution, Interdisciplinary Communications Program, 1976, p. 225–234, bibl., tables [Occasional monographs series, 8])

A useful overview of Costa Rica's National Family Planning Program complemented with basic data on services and the characteristics of the women participants.

9110 Cersosimo, Gaetano. Los estereotipos del costarricense: un análisis de estereotipos sociales como instrumento de control y dominación. Presentación de Daniel Camacho. San José, Univ. de Costa, Facultad de Ciencias Sociales, Instituto de Investigaciones Sociales, 1977. 131 p., bibl. (Avances de investigación, 23)

Rigorous, enlightening study of "Costa Rican stereotypes," as presented and promoted by the mass media. Although not based on extensive interviewing, the study tends to corroborate the author's hypothesis of social controls.

9111 Colby, Benjamin N. and Pierre L. Van Den Berghe. Ixiles y ladinos: el pluralismo social en el altiplano de Guatemala. Versión castellana de Gloria Li and Fernando Cruz. Guatemala, Ministerio de Educación, Editorial José de Pineda Ibarra, 1977. 217 p., bibl., plates, tables (Seminario de integración social guatemalteca, 37)

Excellent ethnographic portrayal of three municipalities in the highlands of Guatemala which discusses their structural aspects and major consequences of social pluralism.

9112 Demyk, Michel. La coopérativism au Guatémala (IEC/REC, 190:4, 1977, p. 101–119, map)

Examination of the history and activities of peasant cooperatives in four areas of the Chichicastenango Valley of Guatemala. Author analyzes their successful experiences and compares them to other ventures at the national level.

9113 Díaz López, Laurentino. La mujer delincuente en Panamá. Leon, Nic., Instituto Técnico La Salle, 1976. 277 p., bibl., tables.

An adequate study of a much neglected topic (female delinquency). The book discusses trends and facts concerning sexual deviance, prostitution, illegitimacy, and family life in Panama. Much of the text, however, is devoted to lengthy (and often doctrinaire) discussion of the nature of criminology and delinquency.

9114 Durston, John W. La estructura de poder en una región ladina en Guatemala: el Departamento de Jutiapa. Guatemala, Editorial José de Pineda Ibarra [and] Ministerio de Educación, 1972. 178 p., bibl. (Estudios centroamericanos, 7)

Good description of the emergence of social power in ladino structures and of how it works in daily life. Based on a combination of participant observations and "references" (i.e., opinions of the town's "knowledge-ables").

9115 Figueroa Ibarra, Carlos. Acerca del proletariado rural en Guatemala (USCG/PS, 2:3, enero/junio 1977, p. 29–44, tables)

Useful examination of the major characteristics of the Guatemalan peasantry which is, unfortunately, buried in much Marxist analysis of the doctrinaire type.

9116 Fouillet M., Jean and Anamaría Diéguez A. El desarrollo del comercio y sus efectos en la economía rural del altiplano occidental de Guatemala (USCG/PS, 2:3, enero/junio 1977, p. 45–95, tables)

Excellent description and detailed account of patterns of commercialization and product distribution in an important area in the Guatemalan highlands covering more than 100 municipios (93 percent of which were carefully surveyed).

9117 Gehler Mata, Carlos. Marginalidad rural en Guatemala y desarrollo comunitario (USC/U, 6:2, 1975, p. 63–96, bibl.)

In a series of analytical steps, author describes rural "marginalidad" in Guatemala. He believes the vicious circle of development/underdevelopment can be broken, "marginalidad" transcended and a stage of true communitarianism arrived at via a process of Christian liberation.

9118 Koch, Charles W. Jamaican blacks and their descendants in Costa Rica (UWI/SES, 26:3, Sept. 1977, p. 339–361, tables)

Author believes that despite claims to the contrary, racist policies still persist in Costa Rica today. However, this perceptive study of a black minority (of Jamaican descent) shows that important changes have occurred and that they reflect more progressive attitudes. Includes a relevant bibliography on the subject.

Loveland, Christine. Rural-urban dynamics: the Miskito coast of Nicaragua. See item 5327.

9119 Meléndez, Dania. Algunos resultados de encuesta de opinión sobre la mujer panameña (USMLA/LA, 5:7, nov. 1976, p. 15–24)

Report of a 1975 survey of urban, middle-aged Panamanian women. Questions asked concerned human development and women rights. Answers revealed that women regarded political participation and the strengthening of the family as the two most important issues.

9120 Mencia, Miguel Angel. Organización y funcionamiento de las empresas campesinas comunitarias en Honduras. Tegucigalpa, Instituto Nacional Agraria (INA), Depto. de Promoción y Organización Campesina, 1977. 25 l., bibl.

Despite methodological shortcomings and sketchy data, this is a worthwhile study because of the dearth of available information on both the subject and Honduras in general.

9121 Molina Chocano, Guillermo. Población, estructura productiva y migraciones internas en Honduras: 1950–1960 (CSUCA/ESC, 4:12, sept./dic. 1975, p. 9–39, bibl., tables)

Author discusses how the capitalist development of Honduran agriculture has produced a number of significant changes in the agrarian structure (social relations, social mobility, etc.). These changes have been largely beneficial for the people in regions which have greater potential for opening of new lands and the diversification of crops.

9122 Neupert, Ricardo. Manual de investigación social. Tegucigalpa, Editorial Universitaria, 1977. 213 p., bibl.

Interesting and well-designed handbook on the methodology of sociological research. Perhaps less comprehensive than Pardinas' *Manual* (México, Siglo XXI Editores), but adequate for introductory courses.

9123 Peek, Peter and **Pedro Antolinez.** Migration and the urban labour market: the case of San Salvador (WD, 5:4, April 1977, p. 291–302, tables)

Study which compares rural-urban and urban-urban migrants in El Salvador. Authors conclude that although both groups gain from the migratory process, upward mobility is more frequent among the urban-urban migrants.

9124 Porras Mendieta, Nemesio. Operativos campesinos. Presentación de Allan Fajardo. Tegucigalpa, Programa de Capacitación Campesina para la Reforma Agraria (PROCCARA), 1976. 168 p., facsims., illus., plates.

Compilation of all the internal reports on leadership development among peasants, a program sponsored by the UN Program for Development (PNUD) and FAO. Book also includes information on the Honduran National Assn. of Peasants (as of 1962).

9125 Quan R., Julio. Una interpretación sociogeográfica de Guatemala (USCG/ES, 5, 1972, p. 79–87, map)

Sober, insightful study of the land-tenure system of Guatemala. The author uses class-analysis and his basic typology constitutes a very good operational tool for further sociological research.

Rose, Susan O. The United Fruit Company in Tiquisate, Guatemala. See item 5322.

9126 Rosenberg, Mark B. La política del seguro social y los grupos de presión en Costa Rica (CSUCA/ESC, 4:10, enero/abril 1975, p. 57–62)

The summary nature of this paper does not allow the author the space in which to present a causal analysis of pressure groups and their impact on social security laws.

9127 Salguero, Miguel. Así vivimos los ticos. San José, Editorial Universitaria Centroamericana, 1976. 398 p., illus.

Excellent portrait of Costa Rican society. The interviews which range from priests to prostitutes and from criollos to mestizos convey the extraordinary variety of types that make up the "ticos." What emerges from the book are not only the personal qualities of the people (e.g., their passion, humor, optimism, etc.) but the highly developed political and civic qualities of this nation which are exceptional for Central America.

9128 Thiel, Bernardo A. and others. Población de Costa Rica y orígenes de los costarricenses. Presentación de Luis Demetrio Tinoco. San José, Editorial Costa Rica, 1977. 404 p., maps, tables (Biblioteca patria, 5)

Thorough work on Costa Rican demography. The author analyzes important censuses which took place between 1864 and 1893. Includes very useful maps, graphs and tables but lacks a bibliography. Still, a most valuable contribution to the study of Costa Rica's population.

9129 Torres Rivas, Edelberto. Notas sobre la estructura social del campo centroamericano (CPES/RPS, 9:23, enero/abril 1972, p. 36–98, tables)

Scholarly, valuable summary of the literature on the subject. The author has coordinated surveys of rural sociology in each Central American country. This study shows the origins, complexity and socioeconomic consequences of the concentration of property in the region.

9130 Universidad Nacional Autónoma de Honduras (UNAH), *Tegucigalpa.* **Centro Universitario de Estudios Generales (CUEG). Departamento do Ciencias Sociales.** Textos para sociología: material auxiliar para estudio de la asignatura. Prefácio de Laszlo Nemez N. Tegucigalpa, 1976. 376 p., bibl., facsims., tables.

Because of the dearth of sociological literature on Honduran society, this compilation is valuable. Most of the authors are from other Latin American nations and the most interesting article is Molina Chocano's analysis of the national situation of Honduras.

9131 Varela, Pablo. Los universitarios y la fe (USMLA/LA, 5:7, nov. 1976, p. 49–85)

Scholarly attempt to examine religious attitudes among students of Antigua Univ., Panama City. Author concludes the impact of industrialization, traditionalism, the extent and/or lack of participation, apathy, etc. on the religious life of the students.

9132 Zúñiga, Melba. La familia campesina. Tegucigalpa, Instituto de Investigaciones Socio-Económicas (IISE), 1975. 60 p., (Col. Argumentos para actuar)

Collection of field-work notes with incomplete bibliographical references. Nevertheless, the study provides good insights into the values and the lives of rural families in Honduras.

THE CARIBBEAN AND THE GUIANAS

NELSON P. VALDES, *Assistant Professor of Sociology, University of New Mexico*

THE TREND FOR SOCIOLOGY IN THE CARIBBEAN has changed somewhat in the last two years. Family-related studies continue to be dominant for Jamaica, Barbados, Trinidad, Costa Rica, and the Dominican Republic where investigations have concentrated on family planning, fertility and internal roles within this primary unit. However, as in previous years, there is an increasing interest in the complexity of social stratification as affected by race, occupation, property and education. Trinidad-and-Tobago, Barbados, Jamaica, Grenada and, to a lesser degree Puerto Rico, have been the only countries studied. Works on internal migration or migration to other countries continue as always to attract the interest of scholars even if most of these pieces now have (and this is new) a Marxist rather than functionialist perspective. Interestingly, migration studies, especially those involving migrants to the US, concentrate on assimilation and acculturation processes; this, however, is not the case with the studies of scholars who analyze migration from one Latin American country to another (e.g., from Haiti to the Dominican Republic).

There has been a notable increase in the quantity but not the quality of works on women. Studies of villages, crime and delinquency are gaining in importance. Dependency is still a concept widely used although seldom specified (or even defined).

Interest is on the wane for studies of religion, modernization or urban settlements.

The most notable work published during this period (1978) was the last two volumes of Manuel Moreno Fraginals' trilogy *El ingenio, complejo económico social cubano del azúcar* (item **9175**). The first volume was published in Spanish in 1964 (see *HLAS 27:2026*) and in English in 1976 (see *HLAS 39:1239*). Moreno Fraginals has written a thorough, rich, and magnificently perceptive set which will be recognized as the best statement on the Cuban plantation system. This work raises the level of Cuban social science to an unprecedented new stage of growth and development. It is, in brief, a classic.

9133 Abrahams, Roger. The West Indian tea meeting: an essay in civilization (*in* Pescatello Ann M. *ed.* Old roots in new lands: historical and anthropological perspectives on black experiences in the Americas. Westport, Conn., Greenwood Press, 1977, p. 173–208 [Contributions in Afro-American and African studies, 31])

The tea meeting, consciously imposed by white missionaries to teach a Christian way of worship, became a pattern of African performance in content and form. Traces description of the practice over time.

9134 Alcántara Almánzar, José. Encuesta sociológica de la ciudad de Santo Domingo (Ciencia [Univ. Autónoma de Santo Domingo, Dirección de Investigaciones Científicas] 2:3, julio/sept. 1975, p. 3–30, illus., tables)

Descriptive chapter from a thesis dealing with class structure and mobility in Santo Domingo. The author used official government data, and sample surveys given at random in about 75 percent of the city's districts. A total of 19 high-school students administered the questionnaires. No theoretical discussions, but useful hard data. Basically an empiricist approach.

9135 Angrosino, Michael V. Sexual politics in the East Indian family in Trinidad (UPR/CS, 16:1, April 1976, p. 44–66)

General study of 211 residences in rural village of Zenobia from 1970–71 and in 1973. Author suggests the family has been an adaptive mechanism which has changed with transformations in social and economic conditions or status. Female family roles (what author calls sexual politics) have changed also. Author sees three different family types in Trinidad.

9136 Arana-Soto, Salvador. Puerto Rico: sociedad sin razas y trabajos afines. Barcelona, Artes Gráficas Medinaceli, 1976. 96 p.

Puerto Rican physician using some newspaper reports and his own observations maintains there is no racism, nor racial violence in the island. He traces the origins of this to the "benign slave code" imposed by Spain. He agrees there is some "malestar racial" but only from the non-white population, and he explains it as due to psychological complexes. Polemical, lacking in scholarship.

9137 Belaval, Emilio S. Los problemas de la cultura puertorriqueña. Prólogo de Luis Rafael Sánchez. Río Piedras, P.R., Editorial Cultural, 1977. 96 p.

In the early 20th century tradition of pensadores "à la Ortega y Gasset" the author has a subjectivist interpretation of Puerto Rican culture. The essay calls for reconciling national culture with the Hispanic origins of the island. He wants a culture "culta," "viril" and "espiritual." The book is curiosity with no contribution to our sociological knowledge of Puerto Rico.

9138 Belcher, John C.; Kelly W. Crader; and Pablo B. Vázquez-Calcerrada. Style of life, social class and fertility in the rural Dominican Republic (YU/IJCS, 17:1/2, March/June 1976, p. 19–29, bibl., tables)

This study is modeled after one made of Puerto Rico. The authors investigated the relationship between consumer behavior (designated as life-style) and fertility rates. Methods used included sampling, interview surveys. They collected 2100 interviews and organized the data according to the Hollingshead Index of Social Position. Finding: fertility declined as consumption of commercial products increased.

9139 Bretón, Minerva; Nelson Ramírez; and Pablo Tactux. La migración interna en la República Dominicana. Santo Domingo, Fondo para el Avance de las Ciencias Sociales [and] Consejo Nacional de Población y Familia (CONAPOFA), 1977. 311 p., maps, tables.

Useful work pulling together all the findings of the fourth Encuesta Demográfica Nacional (Feb./March 1971), and comparing the data with previous materials on internal migration (particularly from rural to urban areas). Descriptive, no thesis is tested.

9140 Brody, Eugene B.; Frank Ottey; and Janet La Granade. Couple communication in the contraceptive decision making of Jamaican women (UM/JNMD, 159:6, Dec. 1974, p. 407–412, tables)

Study stresses the importance, in the Jamaican case, of joint decision-making in family planning as opposed to unilateral, single-decision by one marriage partner. [P.F. Hernández]

9141 ———; ———; and ———. Fertility-related behavior in Jamaica (in Cultural factors and population in developing countries. Washington, Smithsonian Institution, Interdisciplinary Communications Program, 1976, p. 15–30, bibl., tables [Occasional monograph series, 6])

Confined to Kingston, the study covered 283 men and 150 women. The authors tried to ascertain the psychological and cultural factors contributing to the regulation of fertility (by early and late contraceptive users). Relied on personality evaluation tests and interviews. Fertility declines with mother-daughter communication, sexual discussion of couples, and self determination of women.

9142 Brown, Susan. Variaciones de la composición familiar en una aldea dominicana (EME, 6:32, sept./oct. 1977, p. 28–44, bibl.)

Field research made from 1969–71 in a village containing 162 families in the Cebao valley. Author traces the origins of family structure in the area, develops a typology of families, and connects the types (depending on residence and marriage patterns) to economic conditions and ways of making a living.

9143 Campos, Ricardo and Frank Bonilla. Industrialization and migration: some effects on the Puerto Rican working class (LAP, 3[10]:3, Summer 1976, p. 66–108, bibl., tables)

Two essays in one, the first is in English and defines the composition of the PR working class, and how it has changed over time as the process of capitalist industrializa-tion unfolded. It distinguishes between productive and unproductive labor. The second essay, written in Spanish, concentrates on migration and the socioeconomic forces producing it (i.e., mode of production). Class relations in Puerto Rico are a reproduction of the US power.

9144 Carvajal, M.J. and David T. Geithman. Migration flows and economic conditions in the Dominican Republic (UW/LE, 52:2, May 1976, p. 207–220, tables)

Internal migration is "strongly affected" by economic conditions in the area of origin and destination; often helping to "equalize initial economic differences" between the areas of out-migration and those of in-migration. The findings showed a far greater variation in in-migration than in out-migration rates. For economist's comment, see item **3025**.

Casal, Lourdes and Marifeli Pérez-Stable. Sobre Angola y los negros de Cuba. See item **8714**.

9145 Cooney, Rosemary Santana and María Alina Contreras. Residence patterns of Social Register Cubans: a study of Miami, San Juan, and New York SMSAs (UP/CSEC, 8:2, July 1978, p. 34–49, bibl., tables)

Examination of residential segregation and socioeconomic characteristics of upper middle-class areas in which they reside. Shows that in Miami and N.Y. the upper middle-class Cubans live in higher quality areas, while in Puerto Rico they are not as socially distinct. Treats the impact these Cubans had on the demographic and ecological makeup of each city.

9146 Cordero, Walter; Ana Teresa Oliver; Fermín Garrido M.; and Otto Fernández. Actitudes de los directores de los medios de comunicación de masas frente a la planificación familiar. Santo Domingo, Consejo Nacional de Población y Familia, 1976. 65 p., tables.

Study measured attitudes toward family planning of those who control the mass media in the Dominican Republic (Oct. 1974 to May 1975). Results showed that 70.8 percent approved of reducing population growth.

9147 Corten, Andrés; Carlos María Vilas; Mercedes Acosta; and Isis Duarte. Azucar y política en la República Dominicana.

2. ed. Santo Domingo, Ediciones de Taller, 1976. 234 p., tables (Biblioteca Taller, 71)

These four authors use a "materialist method" in their analysis of the structure of domination. Their approach is original, creative, and rich in theoretical arguments. The work consists of four essays of which three nicely connect with one another. Corten, Acosta, and Duarte in "Las Relaciones de Producción en la Economía Azucarera Dominicana" illustrate how sugar production permeates all facets of the society, and tie this to the exploitation of Haitian labor—the major source of surplus. Corten, in the next essay, "Haiti: Estructura Agraria y Migración de Trabajadores a los Centrales Azucareros Dominicanos" explores the structural reasons forcing migration from Haiti to the Dominican Republic. Finally, Mercedes Acosta's "Azúcar e Immigración Haitiana" studies the economic and political dimensions of anti-Haitian racism. The work by Carlos María Vilas on imperialist mechanisms of socio-political control from a dependency perspective does not fit well with the other pieces. Useful and interesting compilation.

Cuthbert, Marlene and others. Caribbean women in communication for development: report on workshop held at the University of the West Indies, Mona Campus, Jamaica, June 13–15, 1975. See item **7175.**

9148 Dodd, David J. and Michael Parris. Socio-cultural aspects of crime and delinquency in Georgetown, Guyana. Mona, Jam., Univ. of the West Indies, Institute of Social and Economic Research, 1976. 57 1., bibl., tables (Working paper, 12)

Attempt to integrate the social anthropology of plantation societies with the prevailing American sociological literature on delinquency in order to explain delinquent behavior in Guyana. Thesis: the growth in Georgetown crime rates is due to drastic changes in traditional social relations. Findings are preliminary.

9149 Ebanks, G. Edward; P.M. George; and Charles E. Nobbe. Fertility and number of partnerships in Barbados (LSE/PS, 28:3, Nov. 1974, p. 449–461, tables)

Contrary to previous findings, the authors believe that stability of sexual unions does not affect fertility in a significant way. Despite stabilizing patterns that have in-

creased over the last 20 years in Barbados, societal fertility has decreased. [P.F. Hernández]

9150 Encuentro Nacional de Sociología y Ciencias Sociales, I, *Santo Domingo,* *1977.* Las ciencias sociales en la República Dominicana: una evaluación. Santo Domingo?, Asociación para el Desarrollo, 1977. 77 p., bibl.

This small book contains the papers presented by six authors (José del Castillo, César A. García, Modesto Reynoso, Ezequiel Garcia, Manuel M. Ortega, and Julio Brea Franco) who review the state of sociology, social anthropology, political science and demography in the Dominican Republic. Two papers deal with the role of the private social investigator, and another discusses the problems of financing and administering research. Overall, a descriptive and general overview with no discussion of sociological currents or prevailing paradigms. Papers were delivered at a meeting organized by the Fondo para el Avance de las Ciencias Sociales, 19 March 1977.

9151 Encuentro Nacional sobre la Investigación Demográfica en la República Dominicana, *Santo Domingo, 1977.* La investigación demográfica en la República Dominicana: una evaluación. Santo Domingo, Asociación para el Desarrollo, 1977. 80 p., bibls., table.

This small book consists of papers presented by eight social scientists reviewing demographic studies for the Dominican Republic. The topics are: British statistics (Nelson Ramírez); family planning methods (Leovigildo Báez); population policy (excellently analyzed by Manuel Ortega); socioeconomic characteristics of the population (Minerva Bretón, who used 1950, 1960, and 1970 censuses); demographic history (Francisco A. de Moya Espinal and José Miguel Guzmán, who began with the 1845 Ley de Ayuntamientos); mortality and morbidity (Méjico Angeles); and finally, Pablo J. Tactuk who briefly analyzes migration studies since 1958.

9152 Fass, Simon M. Port–au–Prince: awakening to the urban crisis (*in* Cornelius, Wayne A. and Robert V. Kemper *eds.* Metropolitan Latin America: the challenge and the response [see item **9016**] p. 155–180, bibl., illus., tables)

Detailed appraisal of the urban history and prospects of Port-au-Prince. Concentrates on employment, housing, water and erosion controls, sanitation, health, energy, transportation as well as financial and administrative resources. Author suggests urban plans to be "realistically conservative."

9153 Fischer, Michael M.J. Value assertion and stratification: religion and marriage in rural Jamaica, pt. 2 (UPR/CS, 14:3, Oct. 1974, p. 7–35, bibl.)

Pt. 2 of two-part article which attempts to describe the dynamics and inter-relations among religion, respectability, and superstition and their manifestations in the marriage union. For pt. 1 of this article, see *HLAS 39:1208.*

9154 Forsythe, Dennis. Race, colour and class in the British West Indies (*in* Singham, A.W. *ed.* The Commonwealth Caribbean into the seventies: proceedings of a conference held on 28–30 September, 1973, Howard Univ., Washington. Montreal, Canada, McGill Univ., Centre for Developing-Area Studies *in cooperation with* Howard Univ., Committee on Caribbean Studies, Washington, 1975, p. 16–42, table [Occasional papers series, 10])

Author notes that the determinants of life chances and differential status for blacks have changed since the 17th century. In the 17th century ascribed social factors (color, features) determined social position; this continued into the 18th century. By the 19th century the caste system evolved into a class system where wealth, property, income, occupation and education were also important. By the 20th century, ideational factors (respectability, refinement, foreign residence, "culture") further added to the complexity of differential status. The latter is an expression of continuing cultural colonialism.

9155 Forsythe, Victor. Trends towards a national communication policy in the Co-operative Republic of Guyana. Georgetown?, n.p. 1976. 16 1.

Position paper outlining how Guyana's communications system must be consistent with the social, economic, political and cultural system of the country, and contribute to national development.

9156 García-Carranza, Araceli *comp.* Homenaje XV Aniversario de la Federación de Mujeres Cubanas: muestra bibliográfica sobre la mujer (BNJM/R, 18:1, enero/abril 1976, p. 163–191, bibl.)

Consists of 193 items by Cuba's foremost bibliographer. No annotations. Covers 19th-century poets, letter collections, novels, theater, participants in war of independence. Largest section covers women writers from 1902–58.

9157 Gaviria, Moisés and **Ronald M. Wintrob.** Supernatural influences in psychopathology: Puerto Rican folk beliefs about mental illness (Canadian Psychiatric Association Journal [Canadian Psychiatric Assn., Ottawa] 21:6, Oct. 1976, p. 361–369, tables)

Consists of three parts: 1) authors' exploration of concepts of mental disorders among Puerto Ricans (spiritism, witchcraft, fate—main reasons for illness); 2) their evaluation of the relative importance of cultural, social and economic characteristics in mental disorder; and finally 3) their attempt to answer why Puerto Ricans under-utilize existing mental health facilities (since source is supernatural, folk-healers rather than modern healers are used). Based on interviews with 20 Puerto Rican patients and 40 non-patients, residing in two Connecticut urban areas.

9158 Girvan, Norman. White magic: the Caribbean and modern technology (NEA/RBPE, 8:2, Winter 1978, p. 153–166)

Thought piece with no documentary evidence. Thesis: Importation of western technology is not the answer to the socioeconomic and cultural problems of the area. Moreover, the technology is too costly, inappropriate and perpetuates dependency.

9159 Gomes, Ralph C. A social psychology of leadership: elite attitudes in Guyana (*in* Singham, A.W. *ed.* The Commonwealth Caribbean into the seventies: proceedings of a conference held on 28–30 September, 1973, Howard Univ., Washington. Montreal, Canada, McGill Univ., Centre for Developing-Area Studies *in cooperation with* Howard Univ., Committee on Caribbean Studies, Washington, 1975, p. 119–142, tables [Occasional papers series, 10])

Links attitudes held by Guyanese elite on the nationalization of large foreign-owned industries to one of three reference groups the elite members identify with. Author interviewed 308 persons who held positions at/or near the "top of the major institutions of society."

Gouraige, Ghislain. La Diaspora d'Haïti et l'Afrique. See *HLAS 40:7796.*

9160 Hidalgo, Ariel. Orígenes del movimiento obrero y del pensamiento socialista en Cuba. La Habana, Instituto Cubano del Libro, Editorial Arte y Literatura, 1976. 153 p. (Col. Pluma en ristre)

Traces history of labor movement from 1860s until early 20th century, focusing on tobacco workers. Heavy reliance on labor newspapers. Descriptive, no analysis.

9161 Instituto de Historia del Movimiento Comunista y la Revolución Socialista en Cuba, *La Habana.* El movimiento obrero cubano: documentos y artículos. La Habana, Instituto Cubano del Libro, Editorial de Ciencias Sociales, 1975/1977. 2 v. (465, 894 p.)

Vol. 1 covers the period 1865–1925. Vol. 2 includes the years 1925–35. These two volumes are the most thorough and complete collection of documents and essays dealing with the Cuban labor movement up to date. The documents have introductory notes. Interestingly, the editors include all socialist trends. Vol. 3 is forthcoming.

9162 Instituto Dominicano de Estudios Aplicados (IDEA), *Santo Domingo.* La drogadicción en Santo Domingo. Santo Domingo, 1977. 91 p., bibl., map, tables.

First analysis of 50 drug addicts in a rehabilitation center in Santo Domingo. The study focuses on the following variables: sex, age, educational level, occupation, social environment, family situations, cause for using drugs, drug use customs, most used drugs and frequency, and factors leading to drug consumption. The investigation relied on written questionnaires and in-depth interviews. Although limited in scope and lacking a general picture of what the situation is in the capital or other urban areas, the study is well presented and logically discussed.

9163 James, Alice. Economic adaptations of a Cuban community (NYAS/A, 293, July 15, 1977, p. 194–205, bibl., table)

A brief anthropological study (fieldwork information) of factors which influenced the economic adaptation of the Cuban communities in Tarrytown and North Tarrytown, N.Y. The essay attempts to answer the questions "Which strategies were used by Cubans in achieving financial independence? What motivated and sustained their economic struggle?" The author suggests the two most important factors in the process to be 1) preadaptation, mainly through the lack of strong middle-class identification in Cuba, of the refugees to enter the US work force; 2) transplantation to the US of the extended family, "their most important social institution."

9164 James, Ariel. Banes: imperialismo y nación en una plantación azucarera. La Habana, Editorial de Ciencias Sociales, 1976. 315 p., plates, tables (Nuestra historia)

Traces the local history of Banes, Oriente prov., and the impact of the sugar plantation over the area's institutions. Of particular interest is the treatment given to the United Fruit Co. Author used the company's archives in Cuba. Thoroughly researched.

9165 Jimenes Grullón, Juan, Isidro. Sociología política dominicana: 1844–1966. v. 1, 1844–1898; v. 2, 1898–1924. Presentación de Jottin Cury. 2. ed. Santo Domingo, Editora Taller, 1976. 2 v. (442, 524 p.) (Biblioteca Taller, 50)

The author of *La República Dominicana: análisis de su pasado y presente* (published in 1940, see *HLAS 6:3288*) and of *La República Dominicana: una ficción* (1965) provides us now with the first two volumes of a planned trilogy. The work is defined by the author as a sociology of politics which relies on a "dialectical Marxist" approach. He also claims to break with the country's traditional historiography. This is a polemical, global picture, relying on secondary sources and utilizing Marxist terminology, but lacking in method. There are frequent jumps in the political narrative which is mixed with discussions of theoretical issues. One basic weakness: an absence of operational definitions (such as "patriarcalismo" or charisma).

9166 Jones, H.R. Metropolitan dominance and family planning in Barbados (UWI/SES, 26:3, Sept. 1977, p. 327–338, tables, maps)

Paper presents data supportive of the ecological theory of metropolitan dominance in which urban norms and values of family planning are diffused from the urban areas to the hinterland.

9167 **King, Marjorie.** Cuba's attack on women's second shift: 1974–1976 (LAP, 4[12/13]:1/2, p. 106–119, bibl.)

The incorporation of women into social production is not sufficient to emancipate them if they also have to take care of the home (the second shift). The new Cuban legislation or Family Code, by calling upon men to help working women with household chores, tries to solve this problem. Author does not feel sexual equality has been achieved yet in Cuba. For political scientist's comment, see item **7203**.

9168 **Kolk, Charles J. Vander.** Physiological reactions of blacks, Puerto Rican, and white students in suggested ethnic encounters (JSP, 104, first half, Feb. 1978, p. 107–114)

A total of 88 male and female students were tested with questions suggesting ethnic interactions with one another. Study examined levels of stress each group experienced in relation to whites. Whites showed greater stress vis-à-vis Puerto Ricans than did blacks: whites generally felt more stress vis-à-vis blacks than vis-à-vis Puerto Ricans.

9169 **LaGuerre, John.** Afro-Indian relations in Trinidad and Tobago: an assessment (UWI/SES, 25:3, Sept. 1976, p. 291–306, bibl.)

Traces history of Afro-Indian relations from 1870s to 1970s, including discussions of the Black Power Movement. Uses secondary sources and newspaper reports.

9170 **Latorre, Eduardo** and others. Bonao: una ciudad dominicana. t. 1/2. Santiago de los Caballeros, R.D., Univ. Católica Madre y Maestra, 1972. 2 v. (444, 399 p.) bibl., tables (Col. Estudios, 11)

This book is the byproduct of the "Proyecto Bonao" a research project undertaken by a research team of 130 persons under the auspices of the Univ. Católica Madre y Maestra, and the Falconbridge Dominicana in 1968. The object of the study: to analyze the impact of massive capital investment (by Falconbridge) on an urban settlement with 18,000 inhabitants. Bonao was compared with Bani and Mao, towns of approximately the same socioeconomic characteristics. The two were used as controls. The investigation relied on questionnaires and in-depth interviews of family heads (in Bonao, 243 families were studied; in Mao, 80 families; and in Bani, 63 families). The impact of the investment on

demography, migration, social stratification, occupational structure, health, education, production, housing, government, services, communication and transport was *not* ascertained since the two volumes merely set the stage of what was the situation *before* the capital had been invested. Rigorous use of methodology and clearly stated hypotheses.

9171 **Leo Grande, William M.** Continuity and change in the Cuban political elite (UP/CSEC, 8:2, July 1978, p. 1–31, bibl.)

Study of the changing patterns of institutional relationships in the Cuban political system since 1959. Analyzes different cleavages from 1960s to 1970s noting that factionalism declined as the importance of the Communist Party increased. Confronts clientelist explanations of Cuban politics.

Lewis, Oscar; Ruth M. Lewis; and **Susan M. Rigdon.** Living the Revolution: an oral history of contemporary Cuba. See *HLAS 40:3013*.

9172 **Lindsay, Louis** ed. Methodology and change: problems of applied social science research techniques in the Commonwealth Caribbean. Mona, Jam., Univ. of the West Indies, Institute of Social and Economic Research, 1977. 370 p., bibl. (Working paper, 14)

Organized into eight sessions this volume contains the papers and statements of 35 participants from the Caribbean who attempted to answer a number of important issues relating to methodology and its application. The essays and discussions revolved around models of analysis, the need for a theoretical framework, empiricism, the problems of obtaining and/or using documentary evidence, the nature of social knowledge and what is objectivity.

9173 **Mörner, Magnus.** Los movimientos campesinos de Latinoamérica y del Caribe en la investigación histórica (CNC/RMA, 8:2, abril/junio 1975, p. 139–159)

A helpful review-of-the-literature essay in which the author highlights attempts by social scientists to define the nature of the Latin American peasantry. Author points out that most of the studies center on peasant movements' political motivations and that the "human aspects" of peasant history of the national period up to 1920 are virgin territory for social science research as are most outside of the rather exhausted Mexico, Chile,

Peru and Anglo-Caribbean islands. Includes good bibliographical footnotes.

9174 Moreno, José A. The Dominican Revolution revisited. Erie, Pa., Northwestern Pennsylvania Institute for Latin American Studies (ILAS) [and] Mercyhurst College, 1978. 32 1. (Latin American monograph series, 7)

Re-statement of the author's 1970 book, *Barrios in arms: revolution in Santo Domingo* (see *HLAS 33:7838*). Thesis: the 1965 revolution was an attempt to put an end to the internal dictatorship permitting US imperialist control of the country. The US intervention occurred when the internal dictatorship was overthrown, thus threatening imperial domination.

9175 Moreno Fraginals, Manuel. El ingenio: complejo económico social cubano del azúcar. v. 2/3. La Habana, Instituto Cubano del Libro, Editorial de Ciencias Sociales, 1978. 2 v. (245, 270 p.) bibl., illus., maps, plates, tables.

Beautifully printed and illustrated volumes whose quality corroborates Moreno Fraginals' well-deserved reputation as Cuba's foremost socioeconomic historian. These vols. 2/3 complete his opus on the Cuban sugar mill (for vol. 1, published in 1964, see *HLAS 27:2026*). Vol. 2 consists of two sections. Sec. 1, *Trabajo y Sociedad*, deals with: "El Hombre como Equipo;" "Controles de Trabajo: Tecnología y Trabajo;" "Sexo y Producción;" "Funche, Esquifaciones, Barracón;" "Hipócrates Negrero;" and "El Buen Tratamiento" Sec. 2, *Paréntesis Comercial*, covers: "Las Etapas, Económicas, Ciclo de Predominio Manufacturero en el Azúcar Cubano (1788–1873);" "Estructuración del Nuevo Orden Económico Social (1788–1819);" "La Plantación Esclavista Agota sus Posibilidades Productivas (1815–1842);" "Crecimiento por Involución y Crisis Definitiva (1838–1873)." Vol. 3 has three parts. Sec. 1 is a compilation of statistical tables covering world sugar and beet production, Cuban sugar exports, production by zones, and provinces. There are commentaries added to all the tables. Sec. 2 provides a glossary of terms used in the sugar industry. Sec. 3 is a "Mínima Bibliografía" containing 365 items all of which are thoroughly annotated. The author used libraries in Cuba, England, Spain, Mexico, France, Sweden, and the US as well as archives in Spain,

Cuba and England. For English translation annotated by anthropologist, see *HLAS 39:1239*; by historian, see *HLAS 40:2985*.

9176 *NACLA: Report on the Americas*. North American Congress on Latin America. Vol. 11, No. 8, Nov./Dec. 1977–. N.Y.

The entire issue is devoted to the subject of the hiring of Caribbean labor to work in US capitalist agriculture. The essays describe Caribbean workers as a "reserve army of labor that transcends national boundaries" and/or as "a colonized foreign work force." In either case, Caribbean laborers are compelled to work in the US because of the nature of international capitalism. The report concentrates on West Indians in Florida, Puerto Ricans in the East coast and Jamaicans in Virginia.

9177 Pascal-Trouillot, Ertha. Droit et privilèges de la femme dans la législation civile et sociale d'Haiti (IFH/C, 124, août 1974, p. 9–21, bibl.)

Brief but important resumé of the legal rights and privileges of women in the Haitian culture. [P.F. Hernández]

9178 Pérez de Jesús, Manuel. La transformación desigual de Puerto Rico y ensayos teóricos sobre Freud, Marx, y Parsons. n.p., n.p., 1977. 284 p., bibl.

Two books in one. Only the first part relates to Puerto Rico. The author attempts to trace problems of the society since 1940 resulting from economic changes. Among the problems discussed in a general way are: health, food, population growth, income inequality, unemployment, illiteracy, political corruption, and neocolonialism. Thesis: modernization solves some problems and creates others.

9179 Phillips, W.M., Jr. Race relations in Cuba: some reflections (NEA/RBPE, 8:2, Winter 1978, p. 173–183)

An impressionistic account of race relations by a black American sociologist who visited the island in Dec. 1977. Reports on conversation with Pedro Serviat, the 1976 Constitution and race, and the absence of an Afro-Cuban identity among blacks (who perceive themselves as Cubans).

9180 Portes, Alejandro; Juan M. Clark; and **Robert L. Bach.** The new wave: a statistical profile of recent Cuban exiles to the

United States (UP/CSEC, 7:1, Jan. 1977, p. 1–32, bibl., tables)

Descriptive profile of a sample of recently arrived Cubans. Concentrates on age, race, area of origin, education, social mobility, difficulties confronted and basic ideals. Sample consisted of 590 family heads between the ages of 18–60 residing in Miami. Data collected during fall 1973 and spring 1974.

9181 Presser, Harriet B. Sterilization and fertility decline in Puerto Rico. Berkeley, Univ. of California (UCLA), Instituto de Estudios Internacionales, 1973. 211 p., tables (Population monograph series, 13)

Explains and documents the uniqueness of the Puerto Rican experience by referring to medical, economic and political factors and compares them to factors in other countries as late as the mid 1970s. [P.F. Hernández]

9182 Race and class in post-colonial society: a study of ethnic group relations in the English-speaking Caribbean, Bolivia, Chile and Mexico. Paris, UNESCO, 1977. 458 p., bibls., illus., tables (Race and society)

Authors study the complex impact of colonialism on social stratification. Rich in theoretical suggestions and conclusions, the main thesis of the book is that ethnicity is not merely a cultural phenomenon but also a consequence of relations of exploitation. Class relations take the appearance of and operate through ethnic relations. Worthwhile. Includes essays on Barbados, Grenada and Jamaica.

9183 Randall, Margaret. We need a government of men and women . . !: notes on the Second National Congress of the Federación de Mujeres Cubanas, November 25–29, 1974 (LAP, 2:4 [issue 7] 1975, p. 111–117)

Interesting document on the history of women's liberation in Cuba. [P.F. Hernández]

9184 Roberts, George W. and **Sonja A. Sinclair.** Women in Jamaica: patterns of reproduction and family. Introduction by Vera Rubin. Millwood, N.Y., Kraus-Thomson Organization, KTO Press, 1978. 346 p., tables (The Caribbean: historical and cultural perspectives)

Thorough and scholarly. Traces the formation of families, their structure and types, and relative stability of each type. Also studies reproduction (pregnancy wastage, infant

mortality, menstrual patterns, sexual knowledge) and child-care (breast-feeding, family planning). Addresses the question of the social and cultural factors affecting fertility. Interviewed 626 women from Montego Bay, Mandeville, Kingston and St. Andrew.

Robertson, Paul D. Ruling class attitudes in Jamaica: the bureaucratic component. See item **7236.**

Robinson, Robert V. and **Wendell Bell.** Attitudes towards political independence in Jamaica after twelve years of nationhood. See item **7237.**

9185 Rogg, Eleanor Meyer. The assimilation of Cuban exiles: the role of community and class. N.Y., Federal Legal Publications, 1974. 241 p., bibl., tables.

Functionalist study of the adjustment of 250 Cuban families to life in West New York, N.Y. The author tests two hypotheses: 1) that if a community of immigrants recreates a strong ethnic-traditional culture in a new milieu it may find adjustment easier to the new country, but acculturation is slowed down. She provides evidence to prove the point. The strong ethnic community reduced adjustment problems, while assimilation has been slowed down "to a manageable pace;" 2) That class origins affect the process of adjustment and acculturation; the lower classes finding assimilation much more difficult. Among lower classes occupational adjustment preceded acculturations, it was the reverse in the higher social classes.

9186 Sharpe, Kenneth. El campesino de la sierra: el problema de vivir (EME, 21, nov./dic. 1975, p. 23–57, tables)

In this study of the problems faced by the various types of Dominican peasants of the Jaida Arriba region, the author notes the constant lack of sufficient land and capital which plagues all classes of peasants. Because of these basic difficulties, the relations of production vary greatly from one peasant segment to another. Author does not define size requirements of land for each sector of the peasantry he describes. Includes monthly income/output charts for four families.

9187 Sheppard, Jill. A historical sketch of the poor whites of Barbados: from indentured servants to redlegs (UPR/CS, 14:3, Oct. 1974, p. 71–94)

Historical account of Barbados "Redlegs" from the 17th century to 1961 based on primary and secondary sources. For author's book on the subject, see *HLAS 40:2954*.

9188 Sio, Arnold A. Race, colour, and miscegenation: the free coloured of Jamaica and Barbados (UPR/CS, 16:1, April 1976, p. 5–21)

Pt. 1 deals with the similarities and differences in the socioeconomic, political, and legal aspects of the status of "free coloured" in Jamaica and Barbados up to the 1830s. Pt. 2 uses Winthrop Jordan's model to interpret his material. Thesis: the interaction of culture and demography shaped attitudes toward miscegenation and toward free coloured.

Stone, Carl. Class and institutionalization of two-party politics in Jamaica. See item **7238**.

9189 ———. Class and status voting in Jamaica (UWI/SES, 26:3, Sept. 1977, p. 279–293, tables, figures)

Reassesses class voting studies in Jamaica. Thesis: voting mirrors class struggle or status awareness. Notes that class voting has increased in an unstable pattern, while status voting showed a secular decline.

———. Urban social movements in post-war Jamaica. See item **7240**.

——— and **Aggrey Brown** *eds*. Essays on power and change in Jamaica. See item **7241**.

9190 Sylvain, Jeanne G. Notes sur la famille haitienne (IFH/C, 124, août 1974, p. 23–34)

Article consists of a series of insightful but far from comprehensive vignettes on the nature of the Haitian family. [P.F. Hernández]

9191 Toro González, Carlos del. Algunos aspectos económicos sociales y políticos del movimiento obrero cubano: 1933–1958. La Habana, Instituto Cubano del Libro, Editorial Arte y Literatura, 1974. 474 p., bibl.

The work is divided in three sections: 1) "Economic Aspects" covers employment, occupational structure, internal and external migration, wages and cost of living, and housing; 2) "Social Aspects" deals with the technical level of the work force, social se-

curity and assistance, and legislation; and 3) "Political Aspects" merely reviews the main labor congresses since 1933. The author maintains that the work force was shaped by the permanent structural crisis of an economy controled by imperialism. Only a revolution could end the crisis. Good use of available secondary sources, magazines and newspapers of the period. No primary sources.

9192 Universidad de La Habana. Escuela de Letras y Artes, Equipo. Informe sobre el trabajo realizado en La Yaya: octubre de 1972–agosto de 1973 (UH/U, 200, 1973, p. 28–41)

Describes the means by which the "typical behavior" of the small agricultural producer changes as he becomes integrated into new state production plans while the revolutionary authorities implement a cultural policy aimed at wiping out the traditional value system. Cites some of the works the community reads and discusses with the local mass organizations. No information on the social characteristics of the population.

9193 ———. ———. Informe sobre la comunidad "El Tabloncito," Municipio de Cumanayagua, Regional Escambray (UH/U, 200, 1973, p. 42–59)

Report of a study made in new rural settlement in which 26 families work in milk production. Describes process of building the community and organizing it. Apparently, authors interviewed "heads of families" (i.e., males), but did not state what if any particular method was used. Although social origins were diverse (peasant, tenant farmer, rural worker) the study made no assessment of this question. Notes that this type of community is not viable, and that young people abandon it.

———. **Instituto de Economía. Centro de Estudios Demográficos** (CEDEM). La población de Cuba. See item **3083**.

Vitier, Cintio. Ese sol del mundo moral para una historia de la eticidad cubana. See *HLAS 40:6745*.

Young, Ruth C. The structural context of Caribbean agriculture: a comparative study. See item **5291**.

SOUTH AMERICA: ANDEAN COUNTRIES
(Venezuela, Colombia, Ecuador, Peru, Bolivia, and Chile)

LISANDRO PEREZ, Associate Professor of Sociology, Louisiana State University
QUENTIN JENKINS, Professor of Sociology, Louisiana State University

JUDGING FROM THE WORKS WE RECEIVED and considered for inclusion in this section, Colombia has apparently been the hub of sociological research in the past few years in the Andean region. This is reflected in the disproportionately large number of works on that country which are annotated in this section. The plethora of works on Colombia is particularly noticeable in the literature produced by North Americans. Perhaps this is to be expected since, in comparison with the other five nations of the Andean region, Colombia combines the social, economic, and political conditions (especially the latter) which have always attracted US social scientists.

Overall, sociological works on the Andean region continue the patterns we indicated in volumes 37 and 39 of the *Handbook*. There is still a discernible emphasis on population, particularly fertility control and migration (items **9010, 9194, 9197, 9203, 9205, 9219–9220, 9223–9224** and **9242**) and rural conditions and development (items **9024, 9028, 9225–9226** and **9235**). Nevertheless, it is apparent that several areas of research regarded as tentative until recently now dominate much of the literature. The number of works received and reviewed which deal with the structure and problems of urban areas are staggering. This is particularly true of the literature on Colombia: one is tempted to conclude that in the mid–1970s two of every five persons walking the streets of Colombian cities (especially Bogotá) were social scientists doing field work (items **9202, 9206–9207, 9211, 9214–9215, 9218** and **9221–9222**). Two additional research topics emphasized in recent years are the family and the status of women (items **9005, 9014, 9019, 9033, 9043, 9198, 9201, 9216–9217, 9228, 9230–9232, 9240–9241** and **9243–9244**).

It is interesting to note that there has been a noticeable shift in works dealing with rural development. In the past, the emphasis was on the need for reform in rural areas. Now that some reforms have been implemented, at least on a limited basis, the emphasis is on evaluating whether or not they have attained the desired development goals (items **9227, 9292, 9236, 9239** and **9250**).

The Chilean debacle continues to haunt some of the works related to Chile or social change in the region in general (item **9247** and **9251**). With regard to Peru, there are some interesting analysis of the social consequences of the Velasco government (items **9229** and **9235–9236**). One development which is also worthy of mention is the increasingly high quality of the works written from the perspective of historical materialism. Up to a few years ago, such works were more polemical than substantive. It is now apparent from recent studies that Marxists know their Marx, and many of their works are among the best, with rigorous empirical applications of this frame of reference (items **9014, 9023, 9195, 9212–9213, 9215, 9237** and **9247**).

VENEZUELA

9194 **Bamberger, Michael; Mara del Negro; and George Gamble.** Employment and contraceptive practice in selected barrios of Caracas (*in* Recent empirical findings on fertility: Korea, Nigeria, Tunisia, Venezuela, Phillipines. Washington, Smithsonian Institution, Interdisciplinary Communications Program, 1976, p. 115–143, tables [Occasional monograph series, 7])

An analysis of the determinants of labor force participation and contraceptive practice in four *barrios* in Caracas. Principal finding: no strong evidence of a link between employment and use of contraceptives.

9195 Blanco Muñoz, Agustín. Clases sociales y violencia en Venezuela. Caracas, Univ. Central de Venezuela, Facultad de Ciencias Económicas y Sociales, División de Publicaciones, 1976. 253 p., plates (Col. Libros)

Noteworthy work because of its rigorous application of historical materialism to the study of a Latin American society. The focus is on class struggle, with emphasis on its violent consequences.

———. Manifestaciones de la lucha de clases en la Venezuela actual. See item **7615**.

9196 Brito Figueroa, Federico. La formación de las clases sociales en Venezuela. Caracas, Editorial La Enseñanza Viva, 1976. 58 p. (Col. De Bolsillo)

A concise work on the historical development of the Venezuelan class structure.

Cerase, Francesco P.; Luis M. Razeto; and **Francesco P. Consoli.** Classi ed istituzioni in America Latina: proposte di analisi en interpretazioni. See item **9013**.

9197 Conaway, Mary Ellen. Circular migration in Venezuelan frontier areas (ICEM/IM, 15:1, 1977, p. 35–42, bibl.)

Circular migration into and within the region of the Orinoco in Venezuela is examined in light of government efforts at national integration which disrupt indigenous social systems. Circular migration among the Guahibo is viewed as an attempt to continue to form part of the traditional society and at the same time participate in the new economic structure being introduced into the area. For geographer's comment, see item **5568**.

9198 Consejo Venezolano del Niño, *Caracas*. **Oficina de Planificación y Presupuesto. Departamento de Organización y Métodos.** Familia y abandono de menores. Caracas, Cooperación Fondo de las Naciones Unidas para la Infancia (UNICEF), 1973. 357 p., bibl., fold. tables, tables.

This monograph presents the results of a massive (3,000 households) and rigorous survey conducted in Caracas under the auspices of the Consejo Venezolano del Niño. The findings contain a good general picture of the family in Caracas, although most of the analysis focuses on family situations which are conducive to child neglect and abandonment, a major problem in Caracas.

9199 Hallström, A. and **M. Linares.** Las estadísticas oficiales sobre la delincuencia en Venezuela: un análisis crítico. Caracas, Univ. Central de Venezuela, Facultad de Derecho, Instituto de Ciencias Penales y Criminológicas, 1972. 100 p., tables (Col. Cuadernos, 1)

A very informative book which offers a critical analysis and overview of official Venezuelan statistics on crime and delinquency.

Maru, Rushikesh M. and others. The organization of family planning programs: India, China, Costa Rica, Venezuela, Lebanon. See item **9034**.

9200 Pollak-Eltz, Angelina. Vestigios africanos en la cultura del pueblo venezolano. Caracas, Univ. Católica Andrés Bello, Instituto de Investigaciones Históricos, 1972. 171 p., bibl.

This monograph is the culminating work which synthesizes many of the author's previous contributions to the field of Afro-Venezuelan culture (see *HLAS 37:1208, 1280, 1281* and *1380* and *HLAS 39:9192*). Her contributions are highly significant, because we simply do not know as much about Afro-Venezuelan syncretism as we know about the equivalent cultural complex in the Caribbean and Brazil.

Ruddle, Kenneth and **Ray Chesterfield.** Education for traditional food procurement in the Orinoco Delta. See item **5578**.

9201 Schmink, Marianne. Dependent development and the division of labor by sex: Venezuela (LAP, 4[12/13]:1/2, Spring 1977, p. 153–179, bibl., tables)

An analysis of the possibility of women's emancipation in a situation of economic development. Growth in Venezuela brought about an increasing concentration of female employment in tertiary activities. For economist's comment, see item **3173**.

Urdaneta, Lourdes. Distribución del ingreso: análisis del caso venezolano. See item **3183**.

COLOMBIA

Alvarez Díaz, Enrique. Herencia colonial en la vida rural colombiana. See *HLAS 40:269.*

9202 Ashton, Guy T. The differential adaptation of two slum subcultures to a Colombian housing project (Urban Anthropology [State Univ. of New York, Brockport, N.Y.] 1:2, Fall 1972, p. 176–195, bibl.)

Interesting comparison between highland mestizos (antioqueños) and lowland blacks in their adaptation to life in a new housing project in Cali. Suggests that efforts at slum relocation in the future should consider the influence of cultural differences within target populations.

9203 Asociación Colombiana para el Estudio de la Población (ACEP), *Bogotá.* La población de Colombia. Bogotá, 1975. 183 p., illus., maps, tables.

Published under the auspices of the Committee for International Coordination of National Research in Demography, this is one of the most comprehensive works available on the population of Colombia. The available sources of data were pooled in order to present analyses of population characteristics, fertility, mortality, migration (internal and international), labor force characteristics, income distribution, population growth, and population projections. One shortcoming of the work is that it is somewhat dated, since it does not contain the results of the 1973 census of population. For geographer's comment, see item **5489**.

Bagley, Bruce Michael and **Fernando Botero Zea.** Organizaciones contemporáneas en Colombia: un estudio de la Asociación Nacional de Usuarios Campesinas, ANUC. See item **7272**.

9204 Bahamón Guerra, Marta Lucía and **Olga Helo Helo.** El divorcio en Colombia. Bogotá, Ministerio de Justicia, Fondo Rotatorio, 1977. 94 p., bibl.

A published doctoral dissertation presented to the Faculty of Legal and Socioeconomic Sciences of the Univ. Javeriana, this work details the development and current status of legal provisions relating to marital

disintegration and dissolution in Colombia, a topic that has received little attention in the past.

9205 Bailey, Jerald. La encuesta básica de Profamilia: un estudio de fecundidad y anticoncepción en una zona rural de Colombia (ACEP/EP, 2:4, April 1977, p. 32–58, bibl., illus., tables)

Presents an analysis of the results of a basic fertility-related survey conducted under the auspices of Profamilia in the coffee-growing areas of the depts. of Nariño, Santander, and Norte de Santander. The analysis of the following variables is emphasized: fertility levels; ideal family size; contraceptive knowledge; use of contraceptives; and specific sources of contraceptives.

9206 Berry, R. Albert. A positive interpretation of the expansion of urban services in Latin America, with some Colombian evidence (JDS, 14:2, Jan. 1978, p. 210–231, tables)

One of the most rigorous analyses available supporting the "positive" perspective on Latin American urbanization. Author argues convincingly against the widely-held notion that the expansion of metropolitan areas of Latin America is a pathological and inefficient trend. Utilizes Colombian data.

Brzezinski, Steven. Church versus state: family planning in Colombia, 1966–1972. See item **7273**.

9207 Castillo, Carlos comp. Urbanismo y vida urbana. Bogotá, Instituto Colombiano de Cultura, 1977. 542 p., maps, tables (Biblioteca básica colombiana, 30)

A general book of readings on urban life in Colombia. Virtually all the readings are by Colombians in various social sciences and therefore focus on a wide variety of subjects, e.g., housing; planning; urban policy; architecture; urban development, *gamines*; marginal urban settlements; affluent residential areas; etc.

9208 Chaney, Elsa M. Colombian migration to the United States: pt. 2 (in The dynamics of migration: international migration. Washington, Smithsonian Institution, Interdisciplinary Communications Program, 1976, p. 87–141, bibl., tables [Occasional monograph series, 5:2])

Although it is on the same general topic as pt. 1 (see item **9210**), the specific focus of this work is on the adaptation of Colombian immigrants in the US, particularly the characteristics of a Colombian ethnic neighborhood in Queens, N.Y.

Christie, Keith H. Antioqueño colonization in western Colombia: a reappraisal. See item **5493**.

9209 Colombia. Instituto Geográfico Agustín Codazzi. Estudio social aplicado de la Alta y Media Guajira. Préfacio de Carlos Roberto Pombo Urdaneta. Bogotá, 1975. 126 p., bibl., fold. maps, maps, plates, tables.

Typical of the publications that carry the name of the Instituto Geográfico Agustín Codazzi, this is a carefully-done, high-quality work. It presents the findings and recommendations of a multidisciplinary research project designed to investigate the social, economic, and geographic characteristics of the Guajira which are relevant to a development project for that isolated region of Colombia.

9210 Cruz, Carmen Ines and **Juanita Castano.** Colombian migration to the United States: pt. 1 (*in* The dynamics of migration: international migration. Washington, Smithsonian Institution, Interdisciplinary Communications Program, 1976, p. 41–86, bibl., tables [Occasional monograph series, 5:2])

A highly significant article. Colombians constitute one of the most important Latin American nationality groups currently migrating to the US. Authors analyze the demographic and socioeconomic selectivity of that migration through a survey of prospective migrants who filed immigrant visa applications with the US Consular Offices in Bogotá. For pt. 2, see item **9208**.

9211 Dent, David W. Urban development and governmental response: the case of Medellín (*in* Cornelius, Wayne A. and Robert V. Kemper *eds.* Metropolitan Latin America: the challenge and the response [see item **9016**] p. 127–153, bibl., illus., tables)

The rather unique success of the city of Medellín in contending with the many barriers to development is traced by the author to cooperation between private and public sector leaders. A major concern is how to cooperate and deal with the concentration of power in Bogotá.

9212 Fals Borda, Orlando. Capitalismo, hacienda y poblamiento: su desarrollo en la costa atlántica. 2. ed. Bogotá, Editorial Punta de Lanza, 1976. 70 p., fold. map, maps, plates.

A very brief monograph with many pictures and maps, in which the author traces the history of the major agrarian forms of production on Colombia's Atlantic coast. It starts with the communal modes of the indigenous population and ends with the rise of capitalism in the 20th century. It is written primarily for a general audience so as to help them understand "phenomena which today pass before our eyes without our knowledge of where they originate."

9213 ———. Historia de la cuestión agraria en Colombia. Bogotá, Fundacíon Rosca de Investigación y Acción Social, 1975. 160 p., bibl., illus., maps, plates (Publicaciones de la rosca. Nueva serie)

This general work although intended for a popular audience is of importance to the social sciences. An agrarian history of Colombia, it is also another result of Fals Borda's determination, through the Fundación Rosca de Investigación y Acción Social (see item **9212** and also *HLAS 39:9202*) to reshape sociological research into a tool for the peasant revolution or into a "social science of the proletariat . . . a science that can equip the exploited classes so that they will organize and act in an efficient manner within the historical process."

Fields, Gary S. Educación y movilidad económica en Colombia. See item **3091**.

Gauhan, Timothy O'Dea. Housing and the urban poor: the case of Bogotá, Colombia. See item **7282**.

9214 Grimes, Orville F., Jr. and **Gill C. Lim.** Employment, land values and the residential choice of low-income households: the case of Bogotá, Colombia (UW/LE, 52:3, Aug. 1976. p. 347–354, bibl., tables)

An interesting study of the factors affecting the choice of residential location among lower-class families in Bogotá. The findings suggest that although proximity to the city center continues to be important, economic realities force low-income families to remain on the periphery.

9215 Grupo de Estudios José Raimundo Russi, *Medellín, Colombia*. Luchas de clases por el derecho a la ciudad: historia de las luchas de los Barrios Orientales de Bogotá contra la Avenida de los Cerros. Medellín, Colombia, Editorial 8 de Junio, 1976? 241 p., tables.

A fascinating analysis of a most interesting phenomenon: the conflict that occurred in the mid-1970s in Bogotá over the proposed construction of the "Avenida de los Cerros," a project designed to benefit the elite residential areas. The issue is presented here as a case of class conflict and analyzed in a 22 June 1978 Marxist framework.

9216 Gutiérrez de Pineda, Virginia. Estructura, función y cambio de la familia en Colombia. v. 2. Bogotá, Asociación Colombiana de Facultades de Medicina, División de Medicina Social y Población, 1976. 277 p. tables.

Based on the same survey analyzed in vol. 1 (see *HLAS 39:9206*), except that the focus is on a different set of variables, primarily of an interactional nature: communication between family members, marital satisfaction, authority, socialization, and reproduction.

9217 ———. Familia y cultura en Colombia: tipologías, funciones y dinámica de la familia; manifestaciones múltiples a través del mosaico cultural y sus estructuras sociales. Bogotá, Instituto Colombiano de Cultura, Subdirección de Comunicaciones Culturales, 1975. 528 p., bibl., maps (Biblioteca básica colombiana, 3)

A valuable work which gives a description of differences in the family institution and household composition between different geo-cultural regions of Colombia.

9218 López de Rodríguez, Cecilia and **Hernando Gómez Buendía.** Familia y consumo en la ciudad colombiana. Bogotá, Fundación para la Educación Superior y el Desarrollo, 1977. 231 p., bibl., tables.

A survey of family budgets and expenditures in Bogotá, Barranquilla, Medellín, and Cali are the basis of this extensive analysis of the relation between family structure and patterns of consumption.

9219 Potter, Joseph E.; Myriam Ordoñez G.; and **Anthony R. Measham.** El rápido descenso de la fecundidad colombiana (ACEP/EP, 2:1, Jan. 1977, p. 35–51, bibl., illus., tables)

Documents and analyzes the widely-discussed recent fertility decline in Colombia. One notable feature of the article is that it represents one of the first analyses of the fertility data from the controversial 1973 census of the population of Colombia.

Rosenberg, Terry J. Individual and regional influences on the employment of Colombian women. See item **3114**.

9220 Samper, Diego Giraldo. Migración interna y salud en Colombia. Bogotá, Asociación Colombiana de Facultades de Medicina, División de Medicina Social y Población, 1976. 171 p., tables.

One in a long series of monographs published in the past few years by the Asociación Colombiana de Facultades de Medicina on health-related demographic phenomena. This work focuses on the differences in morbidity and mortality between zones that are characterized by heavy out-migration and those which experience heavy in-migration. A comprehensive and detailed study.

9221 Vargas G., Enrique and **Luis Ignacio Aguilar Z.** *eds.* Planeación urbana y lucha de clases: los circuitos viales. Bogotá, Centro de Investigación y Educación Popular, 1976. 107 p., fold. tables (Controversia)

As a response to the controversy created by the Avenida de los Cerros (see item **9215**), the municipal government of Bogotá encouraged the formulation of a comprehensive plan for building and enlarging thoroughfares in the city. This monograph is an attempt to present a balanced analysis of the political context of various plans for urban improvement in the Colombian capital.

Walton, John. Elites and economic development: comparative studies on the political economy of Latin American cities. See item **2979**.

9222 Whiteford, Andrew Hunter. An Andean city at mid-century: a traditional urban society. East Lansing, Michigan State Univ., 1977. 352 p., bibl., illus., map, plates, tables (Latin American studies center monograph series, 14)

A fascinating and entertaining work by the senior Whiteford which presents in one volume the field work which he conducted in 1950 in Popayán. Despite the fact that more than a quarter of a century has elapsed, the observations concerning life in Popayán, especially the descriptions of the various social classes, are valuable contributions to the literature on urban Latin America. The author's son Michael continues his father's interest in the study of that interesting Colombia city (see *HLAS 37:1553–1554* and *HLAS 39:9219*).

9223 Williams, Lynden S. and **Ernst G. Griffin.** Rural and small town depopulation in Colombia (AGS/GR, 68:1, Jan. 1978, p. 13–30, maps, tables)

A significant study which focuses on a frequently overlooked aspect of urbanization and city growth, rural and small-town depopulation. Most of the data analyzed are from the 1951 and 1964 population censuses. For geographer's comment, see item **5525**.

9224 Wills Franco, Margarita. Diferencias regionales de la fecundidad en Colombia. Bogotá, Asociación Colombiana de Facultades de Medicina (ASCOFAME), División de Medicina Social y Población, 1976. 106 p., map, tables.

A study of regional fertility differentials in Colombia. The emphasis is on the specific regional, cultural and economic factors as well as characteristics of the family institution which largely shape the observed fertility differentials. Particular emphasis is placed on interregional comparisons in the relative value placed on children.

ECUADOR

9225 Guerrero, Andrés. Renta diferencial y vías de disolución de la hacienda precapitalista en el Ecuador (UTIEH/C, 28, 1977, p. 47–72, bibl., tables)

A serious study of both the demise and the remnants of the "precapitalist" hacienda in Ecuador. The demise of that agricultural system is attributed to the elimination of the exploitative labor system (the *huasipungo*) on which the haciendas depended.

9226 Hurtado, Osvaldo and **Joachim Herudek.** La organización popular en el Ecuador. Quito, Instituto Ecuatoriano para el Desarrollo Social (INEDES), 1974. 136 p.

A brief, but valuable, work on the structure and functioning of organizations in rural Ecuador. Three basic types are discussed:

1) community-based organizations (4-F, communes, women's groups); 2) cooperatives; and 3) labor organizations. There is also a brief discussion of the public, semi-public, and private organizations or bureaucracies that are relevant to agriculture in Ecuador.

Moore, Richard J. Urban problems and policy responses for metropolitan Guayaquil. See item **7320**.

9227 Redclift, M.R. Agrarian class formation and the state: the Ecuadorian case (SBPC/CC, 29:12, dez. 1977, p. 1404–1416, bibl.)

A study of the social consequences of state intervention in the agricultural production process. Social power and the changes in its distribution among landlords, peasants, and the state are the focus of the study.

9228 Romoleroux de Morales, Ketty. Situación jurídica y social de la mujer en el Ecuador. Guayaquil, Ecua., Univ. de Guayaquil, Depto. de Publicaciones, 1975. 248 p.

The author's explicit purpose is "consciousness raising" among the women and progressive men of Ecuador. This is a highly informative study of the historical development of women's social and legal status in that country, although the analysis starts with family institutions in "primitive" times and in feudal Europe.

PERU

9229 Alberti, Giorgio; Jorge Santistevan; and **Luis Pasara.** Estado y clase: la comunidad industrial en el Perú. Lima, Instituto de Estudios Peruanos, 1977. 348 p. (Perú problema, 16)

This is an important book for those who are interested in the analysis of the impact of a "corporatist" revolution on the industrial segment of society. For economist's comment, see item **3243**.

9230 Bourque, Susan C. and **Kay B. Warren.** Campesinas and comuneras: subordination in the Sierra (WRU/JMF, 38:4, Nov. 1976, p. 781–788, bibl.)

Three explanations of the subordinate roles of women in the Sierra are evaluated through analysis of data from the Cornell-Peru VICOS project. Little support is found for the subordination of women especially in view of their performance of work which is the equal of men's and equally valued by both.

Cuche, Denys. Pouvoir et participation dans les coopératives agraires de production au Pérou: les cas des coopératives cotonnières de la Côte Sud. See *HLAS 40:3509.*

9231 Deere, Carmen Diana. Changing social relations of production and Peruvian peasant women's work (LAP, 4[12/13]:1/2, Spring 1977, p. 48–69, bibl.)

A well documented analysis of changes in the nature, duration and intensity of women's work as rural Peru has moved from pre-capitalism to the present day.

9232 ———. La división por sexo del trabajo agrícola: un estudio de la Sierra del Perú (ACEP/EP, 2:9, Sept. 1977, p. 14–29, bibl., tables)

A survey of peasant families in the prov. of Cajamarca provides support for the author's argument that women provide a significant portion of the labor performed by the peasant family. The survey also showed that the extent of female agricultural labor varies inversely with the economic status of the peasant family.

Dietz, Henry A. Land invasion and consolidation: a study of working-poor/governmental relations in Lima, Peru. See item **7330.**

———. Metropolitan Lima: urban problem-solving under military rule. See item **7331.**

9233 ———. Urban poverty, participation and authoritarian rule: further data from Peru (UT/SSQ, 59:1, June 1978, p. 105–116, bibl., tables)

Squatter settlements and central-city slums are distinctive despite the poverty they share. In Lima the squatter settlement is shown to be the much better organized and more politically active of the two types. For political scientist's comment, see item **7332.**

Gargurevich, Juan. Introducción a la historia de los medios de comunicación en el Perú. See *HLAS 40:3519.*

9234 Hernández Urbina, Alfredo. Compendio de sociología peruana: texto universitario. 4. ed. Lima, Ediciones Raíz, 1976. 192 p.

Fourth ed. of an introductory sociology text which chiefly concerns Peruvian so-

ciety. In the discussion of broader social concepts, Peruvian social structure and specific problems are presented.

Latin American Perspectives. See *HLAS 40:3532.*

9235 Matos Mar, José. Yanaconaje y reforma agraria en el Perú: el caso del Valle de Chancay. Lima, Instituto de Estudios Peruanos, 1976. 278 p., bibl., tables (Perú problema, 15)

The history of the institution of yanaconaje in rural Perú, a system of exploitation of both land and labor, goes back to prehispanic times. Matos Mar shows brilliantly how that institution has been modified through time to serve the interests of the colonial landowner, and eventually of the capitalist hacienda. Also documents the end of the yanaconaje during the past 20 years. For historian's comment, see *HLAS 40:3545.*

——— ed. Hacienda, comunidad y campesinado en el Perú. See *HLAS 40:3546.*

Mejía, José Manuel and **Rosa Díaz Suárez.** Sindicalismo y reforma agraria en el Valle del Chancay. See *HLAS 40:3547.*

Morisset, Jean. Puno: a geography of social and development ambivalence. See item **5550.**

9236 Pásara, Luis. El proyecto de Velasco y la organización campesina (UP/A, 4:8, 1978, p. 59–80, bibl.)

In 1968 the government of Gen. Velasco instituted an agrarian reform. The large landholding of the members of the Sociedad Nacional Agraria were nationalized and "cooperatives" were formed. In this study the consequences of these government actions on peasant organization are explored, such as changes in class affiliation.

Ponce, Fernando. La ciudad en el Perú. See *HLAS 40:3556.*

Pozuzo: un paraíso en los Andes peruanos. See item **5555.**

9237 Quijano, Aníbal. Imperialismo, clases sociales y estado en el Perú: 1895–1930 (*in* Benítez Zenteno, Raúl ed. Clases sociales y crisis política en América Latina [see item **9007**] p. 113–205)

A valuable contribution to Latin American thought on the role of imperialism and dependence on the development of class structure in Latin America. What makes this work particularly valuable is that Quijano's historical analysis of imperialism and dependence in Peru is followed by lengthy commentaries by Octavio Ianni, Orlando Fals Borda, José Luis Reyna, and Manuel Villa (p. 151–205) which, in addition to making constructive criticisms of Quijano's work, also extend his analysis to other Latin American nations.

Renique, Gerardo. Sociedad Ganadera del Centro: pastores y sindicalización en una hacienda alto andina; documentos, 1945–1948. See item **7354.**

Skeldon, Ronald. The evolution of migration patterns during urbanization in Peru. See item **5557.**

Valderrama, Mariano. 7 [i.e. Siete] años de reforma agraria peruana: 1969–1976. See *HLAS 40:3565.*

9238 Weller, Robert. La asimilación estructural de los inmigrantes en Lima (IASI/E, 30:114, julio 1976, p. 50–67, tables)

In order to reach some conclusion about the migrants' adjustment to the city, the author uses data from an official survey of families in Lima and compares the city's native population to in-migrants, primarily in terms of labor-force participation and educational levels.

9239 Whyte, William Foote and **Giorgio Alberti.** Power, politics and progress: social change in rural Peru. N.Y., Elsevier, 1976. 307 p., bibl., tables.

It is a pleasure to see this book from one of the best known and successful programs of social science research in Latin America. The Instituto de Estudios Peruanos and Cornell Univ. have been conducting cooperative research in rural Perú since 1964. This book is an attempt to distill what has been learned from such research for English-speaking readers. An important and valuable work.

BOLIVIA

Balán, Jorge *ed.* Las historias de vida en ciencias sociales: teoría y técnica. See item **9006.**

Bolivia. Comité Nacional del Sesquicentenario de la República. Monografía de Bolivia. See *HLAS 40:3580.*

Dandler, Jorge. "Low classness" or wavering populism?: a peasant movement in Bolivia, 1952–1953. See *HLAS 40:3584.*

Díaz Polanco, Héctor. Economía y movimientos campesinos. See *HLAS 40:3048.*

Gudmunson K., Lowell. El populismo y la integración de las clases obreras en Bolivia, 1952–1957. See *HLAS 40:3591.*

9240 Martínez, Joaquín and **Mari Odena.** Matrimonio y familia en Bolivia: estudio comparativo del matrimonio y vida de familia en el altiplano, los valles y el trópico. La Paz, Editorial Los Amigos del Libro, 1976. 269 p., bibl.

This work draws primarily upon the experience of social workers, and especially on the experience of the senior author, a priest who has apparently worked extensively with marital problems, to present a picture of marriage and the family in Bolivia. The emphasis is on interregional differences.

9241 Seminario la Promoción Femenina y la Participación de la Mujer Boliviana en el Desarrollo Nacional, *La Paz, 1975.* La promoción femenina y la participación de la mujer boliviana en el desarrollo nacional. La Paz, Centro Piloto de Formación Femenina, 1975. 86 p., plates (Publicación CODEX)

A compilation of papers presented at a conference on the participation of Bolivian women in the nation's development. The emphasis is on the role of social action agencies and social workers in raising the status of women.

Stearman, Allyn MacLean. The highland migrant in lowland Bolivia: multiple resource migration and the horizontal archipelago. See item **5454.**

9242 Velagapudi, Gunvor. La encuesta demográfica de Bolivia: algunas reflexiones sobre su contenido ocupacional. La Paz, Presidencia de la República, Ministerio de Planeamiento y Coordinación, Instituto Nacional de Estadística, 1976. 14 I., tables (Documento de trabajo. PREALC, 106)

Contains a brief analysis, as well as some data tables on the labor force taken from results of the 1975 Encuesta Demográfica

Nacional de Bolivia. The significance of this brief monograph stems primarily from the dearth of Bolivian demographic data: the last census was taken in 1950.

CHILE

9243 Andreas, Carol. The Chilean woman: reform, reaction, and resistance (LAP, 4[15]:4, Fall 1977, p. 121–125)

A rather caustic reaction to events involving Chilean women since 1970, from a radical-feminist perspective.

Chinchilla, Norma Stoltz. Mobilizing women: revolution in the revolution. See item **7389.**

9244 Crummett, María de los Angeles. El poder femenino: the mobilization of women against socialism in Chile (LAP, 4[15]:4, Fall 1977, p. 103–113, bibl.)

Ten interviews with leaders of the women's opposition movement (to President Allende's government) are presented and analyzed. It is evident that the actions of these women were important factors in the fall of the Allende government.

9245 Espinosa, Juan Guillermo. The experience of worker participation in the management of industrial firms: the case of the social ownership area in Chile, 1970–1973. Ithaca, N.Y., Cornell Univ., Latin American Studies Program, 1975. 423 p. (Latin American studies program dissertation series, 62)

Although the author is an economist, students of complex organizations, industrial sociology, and political sociology will find this dissertation useful and informative. The author has a strongly pro-"worker participation" point of view.

9246 Menanteau-Horta, Darío; George A. Donohue; and Freddy Fortuoul V. eds. El rol del sociólogo: análisis y perspectivas. Santiago, Editorial Universitaria, 1977. 228 p., tables.

Presents the papers, as well as a synopsis of the discussions, of a conference of Chilean sociologists. The conference held in 1977 was sponsored by the Centro de Sociología del Desarrollo Rural de la Univ. Austral de Chile. The papers focus primarily on the roles of sociologists in a variety of academic and nonacademic settings within Chile, and on the state of the discipline in that country. Among the participants were Hernán Godoy, Dagmar Raczynski, Domingo Sánchez, Raúl Urzúa, and Oscar Valenzuela S.

9247 Morley, Morris and Steven Smith. Imperial "reach:" U.S. policy and the CIA in Chile (NIU/JPMS, 5:2, Fall 1977, p. 203–216, bibl.)

While this article provides little new information on the role of the CIA in recent Chilean history, it does contain an excellent summary of the series of covert actions by the agency before and during the Allende administration. Those actions are viewed and interpreted within the author's theoretical perspective, which is explicitly Marxist-Leninist.

9248 Porteus, J. Douglas. Urban symbiosis: a study of company town camp followers in the Atacama Desert (NS, 3:5/6, 1978, p. 210–221, map)

A description of the lives and problems of the marginal groups which collected around the Chilean copper mines. For geographer's comment, see item **5477.**

9249 Rothhammer, Francisco and Elena Llop. Amerindian descent and intellectual performance in Chilean university students (WSU/HB, 48:3, Sept. 1976, p. 455–464, bibl., tables)

A brief article on the relationship between intellectual performance (measured by academic record and aptitude tests) and a number of independent variables (including an "indigeneity index"). Conclusion: "Amerindian descent" and other variables are far less important than sex in determining intellectual performance.

Soto, Francisco. Fascismo y Opus Dei en Chile: estudios de literatura e ideología. See item **7445.**

Stallings, Barbara. Class conflict and economic development in Chile: 1958–1973. See item **7446.**

Steenland, Kyle. Agrarian reform under Allende: peasant revolt in the south. See item **7447.**

9250 Vera, Hernán and Raúl Santoyo. The unequal exchange of mutual expectations: a neglected dimension of rural development (RSS/RS, 43:4, Winter 1978, p. 610–617, bibl.)

The focus of this article is on the interaction between peasants who are the subjects of rural development programs and the functionaries in charge of such programs. "Based on programs directed to Chilean *asentados* and Mexican *ejidatarios*, the analysis reveals a passivity and submission of peasants hard to reconcile with the stated goals of rural development programs. It is proposed that the interaction of peasants with agents be conceived of as an unequal exchange of mutual expectations.

9251 Zapata, Francisco. Las relaciones entre el movimiento obrero y el gobierno de Salvador Allende. 2. ed. corregida y aumentada. México, El Colegio de México, Centro de Estudios Sociológicos, 1976. 93 p., bibl., tables (Cuadernos del CES, 4)

A highly significant work which presents in detail the relationship between the labor movement and the Allende government. More importantly, it places that relationship into a historical perspective, for a basic thesis of the writer is that the situation during the Allende administration was the culmination of a long historical process. In an epilogue, the author discusses the labor policy of the current government.

9252 Zeitlin, Maurice; W. Lawrence Neuman; and Richard Earl Ratcliff. Class segments: agrarian property and political leadership in the capitalist class of Chile (ASA/ASR, 41:6, Dec. 1976, p. 1006–1029, bibl., tables)

The major issue confronted concerns the relationship between large landownership and political hegemony in the capitalist class. An incisive analysis of the political behavior of landed corporate executives and principal owners of capital as contrasted to their non-landed counterparts. For political scientist's comment, see item **7460**.

SOUTH AMERICA: THE RIVER PLATE
(Argentina, Paraguay, and Uruguay)

CARLOS H. WAISMAN, *Assistant Professor of Sociology, University of California, San Diego*

POPULATION, ESPECIALLY POPULATION MOVEMENTS, theoretical studies of social structure, and the social bases of politics are still the main concern of sociologists, both professional and amateur, in the Southern Cone. The reason this section does not fully reflect the antipathy to social research which one finds in the region today, is due to the fact that many of the works reviewed here were published prior to the 1976 military coup in Argentina, the country which generates about 80 percent of the entries. It is worth noting that the Sociology Department of the Fundación Bariloche, one of the few institutions in which competent sociological research was conducted—at least six of the entries in this section were produced there—was closed after the coup.

The composition of the Argentine subsection mirrors the social-science picture in the country as a whole. Most of the works written by professional social scientists—about half of the total number of entries—can be divided into analyses of social structure and politics, and demographic studies. The latter are competent pieces but, unfortunately, very descriptive. It is true that a rigorous description is the first step of research, but my impression is that Argentine demographers have already at their disposal the mass of data and the theoretical apparatus required for the development of more analytical population studies. Works on social structure and politics, on the other hand, have overcome this limitation. Several entries in this section successfully combine competent empirical research and social theory. The most significant of these works is Germani's book (item **9263**), undoubtedly a major contribution to the study of the structural determinants of fascist and national-populist regimes. Mora y Araujo's articles on the social bases of peronism (items **9273** and **9274**) are also serious pieces of research in political sociology. The papers by Accinelli and Borro (item **9253**), Aznar and Catterberg (item **9255**), and Hadis (item **9264**) are detailed studies of social structure, at the local and provincial level. It is the accumulation of studies of this type, rather than the endless speculations on dualism and overdetermination, that will advance our knowledge of the peculiarities of peripheral social formations. Gaudio and Pilone's paper (item **9262**) is also a good example of theoretically guided empirical research.

About half of the literature from Argentina consists of not professional social science but journalistic works, pieces written by amateurs—some of them tolerably good—and essays on social questions, in the traditional Latin American and Hispanic style. Most works in the latter category are heavily ideological, and entries cover the whole spectrum: right-wing radicalism, left-wing populism, and orthodox Marxism. The significance of these pieces as sources for the study of ideology outweighs whatever cognitive value they might have.

There are only two works received from Uruguay, and these are traditional essays. Intellectual life seems to have been stifled by the authoritarian regime there. On the other hand, it is ironic that solid—but noncontroversial—research is being conducted somewhere in the interstices of the Stroessner regime: the works by Paraguayan sociologists on housing and population are descriptive but competent.

ARGENTINA

9253 Accinelli, María Martha and **María del Carmen Borro.** Pequeña propiedad en la ganadería pampeana: el caso de los subfamiliares del partido de Ayacucho. B.A., Centro de Investigaciones en Ciencias Sociales (CICSO), n.d. 67 p., tables (Cuadernos de CICSO)

A study of small cattle-breeding agriculture in Ayacucho, a district of Buenos Aires prov., where interviews with farmers were conducted. On the basis of questionnaires and of aggregate data, the authors look into the weight of small agriculture in the society, the cleavage between breeders and fatteners, land tenure in Ayacucho, and cattle breeding as a capitalist enterprise—the use of capital, manpower, land, and credit, the profitability of cattle breeding, etc. A useful case study.

Alén Lascano, Luis. Desarrollo histórico socioeconómico de la Provincia de Santiago del Estero. See *HLAS* 40:3678.

9254 Alsogaray, Alvaro. La democracia de masas y la crisis en países del mundo libre. Santiago, Univ. Católica de Chile, Instituto de Ciencia Política, 1976. 19 l. (Cuadernos, 4)

A defense of military rule by a leading Argentine "liberal" economist. Argues that mass democracy is incompatible with the "economic order of freedom."

9255 Aznar, Luis and **Edgardo Catterberg.** Estructura de producción, estructura social y conflicto socio-político en el Alto Valle del Río Negro. San Carlos de Bariloche, Arg., Fundación Bariloche, Depto. de Ciencias Sociales, 1975. 36 l., tables.

A study of the agrarian structure of the Río Negro Valley, a fruit-producing region, in southern Argentina. The authors discuss the different social groups involved in this type of agriculture—farmers, wage laborers, packers—and the lines of conflict among them, particularly between farmers and packers. There is also a discussion of the role of the state in the articulation of interests of different groups. A very good case study.

9256 Badeni, Gregorio. Comportamiento electoral en la Argentina. Prólogo de Segundo V. Linares Quintana. B.A., Editorial Plus Ultra, 1976. 216 p., bibl., maps, tables.

A standard description of the electoral systems used in Argentina, and results, by department, of the 1973 election. Electoral data are just shown, without analysis.

Bartolomé, Leopoldo J. Populismo y diferenciación social agraria: las ligas agrarias en Misiones, Argentina. See item **7465**.

9257 Beveraggi Allende, Walter Manuel.
Del Yugo Sionista a la Argentina posible: esquema económico de la dependencia y la liberación argentina. B.A.?, Editorial Confederación Nacionalista Argentina, 1976. 136 p.

An anti-semitic and anti-liberal tract, written by an economist and addressed to the military.

9258 Catholic Church. Conferencia Episcopal Argentina. Centro de Estadísticas y Documentación del Episcopado (CEDE). Estadísticas de la Iglesia Argentina: 1970. v. 1, Región del Nordeste: Diócesis de Posadas, Corrientes, Goya, Reconquista, Sáenz Peña y Formosa; v. 2, Regiones Comahué: Diócesis de Bahía, Blanca, Viedman, Santa Rosa y Neuquén [and] Región Patagonia: Diócesis de Comodoro Rivadavia y Río Gallegos. B.A., 1971. 2 v. (122, 123 p.) maps, tables.

Vol. 1 consists of statistical information on the Catholic dioceses in northeastern Argentina. Includes statistics on church staff—bishops, priests, seminarians—and also on population characteristics, education, health and land tenure in the region. Data on clerics contain demographic information and date of ordination. Unfortunately, figures on church attendance and participation in religious rituals by the population are not given. Vol. 2 provides the same information for the regions of Comahué and Patagonia, in southern Argentina.

9259 Catterberg, Edgardo R. Actitudes de las elites argentinas hacia la creación y el desarrollo del Mercado Común Latinoamericano. San Carlos de Bariloche, Arg., Fundación Bariloche, Depto. de Sociología, 1974. 18 l., tables.

On the basis of questionnaires applied to a small sample (N=57), the author explores the attitudes of members of the Argentine elite toward a Latin American Common Market. Elite pertinence was determined by positional criteria. Business and trade union leaders, military officers, politicians, civil servants, and journalists were included in the sample. The main finding is that the elite seems to be fragmented in relation to this issue. Support for a common market is very low among military officers and politicians,

and relatively low in other groups. Only among other union leaders support exceeds 50 percent. The author also finds that the elite has very inadequate information about the nature of a common market. Most respondents seem to have defined a common market as a free trade zone. These results are very tentative, due to sample size.

9260 Cervera, Felipe Justo. Sociología de la dependencia interna. Santa Fe, Arg., Ediciones Colmegna, 1974? 91 p., tables.

The author distinguishes between external dependency, i.e., the conceptualization of a nation as a periphery in relation to an external center, and internal dependency, i.e., the analysis of center-periphery relations within a nation. He then looks into regional imbalances in Argentina, as an instance of internal dependency. The economic and political mechanisms that create these imbalances are considered—patterns of trade, control of credit, government spending, industrial policy, administrative centralization, etc.

9261 Elizalde, Diva. La migración interna en la Argentina: 1960–70. B.A., Instituto Nacional de Estadística y Censos (INDEC), n.d. 75 p., tables (Serie investigaciones demográficas, 5)

A study of internal migration in Argentina during the 1960s. Includes estimates of net migration by province, a classification of provinces into expellers and recipients of migration flows, and an analysis of the migrant population by sex and age.

9262 Gaudio, Ricardo and **Jorge Pilone.** Estado y relaciones obrero-patronales en los orígenes de la negociación colectiva en Argentina. B.A., Centro de Estudios de Estado y Sociedad (CEDES), 1976. 71 l., tables (Estudios sociales, 5)

A study of the origins of the pattern of collective bargaining under government control. The authors show that state intervention in labor management relations existed prior to Peronism: since the 1930s, the government began considering mediation in social and economic issues as one of its legitimate functions. The labor movement did not oppose this development, and attempted to benefit from it. A careful historical study.

9263 Germani, Gino. Authoritarianism, fascism, and national populism. New

Brunswick, N.J., Transaction Books, 1978. 292 p., tables.

One of the most important contributions to the study of the relationship between modernization and authoritarianism. Germani examines the concept of authoritarianism, the political consequences of social mobilization, and the social bases of fascist and national-populist regimes. These theoretical developments are applied to the analysis of the Argentine case. The failed attempts at establishing a fascist regime in Argentina, and formation of Peronism, a typical instance of national-populism, are discussed, and the process of social mobilization in Argentina is compared to that of Italy. On the basis of that comparison, the author tests propositions about the determinants of emergence of these two types of regimes, fascism and national-populism. The book also includes a chapter on political socialization of youth in Fascist Italy and in Franco's Spain. Some of these materials have been published before, but they were available in different places and in different languages. This book is a unified presentation of Germani's contributions to political sociology.

Goldberg, Marta B. La población negra y mulata de la ciudad Buenos Aires: 1810–1840. See *HLAS 40:3767.*

9264 Hadis, Benjamín F. La estructura ocupacional y la emigración en Santiago del Estero. San Carlos de Bariloche, Arg., Fundación Bariloche, Depto. de Ciencias Sociales, 1975. 53 l., tables.

A study of the process of emigration from Santiago del Estero, a "poor" province in northwestern Argentina. The author carefully examines the evolution of the occupational structure of the province, and concludes that emigration is the consequence of the penetration of capitalist social relations in the countryside. A solid piece of work.

9265 Hernández, Raúl Augusto. Bases para un modelo societal patagónico. San Carlos de Bariloche, Arg., Fundación Bariloche, Depto. de Sociología, 1974. 16 l., bibl., tables.

An attempt to elaborate a mathematical model of sociological processes in the region of Patagonia, in southern Argentina. Elements are: social structure, as determined by the productive system, subregional inter-

actions, and forces of change (both extra-and intra-systemic).

9266 Imaz, José Luis de. Los hundidos: evaluación de la población marginal. B.A., Ediciones La Bastilla, 1974. 164 p., tables (Serie campo minado)

An estimate of the incidence of marginality in Argentina. Marginality is diffusely defined as the opposite of participation, in all areas of social life, so that its manifestations range from illegitimate birth to urban poverty. On the basis of different indicators—personal status, occupation, education, housing, health, social and political participation—the size of the marginal population was estimated at 2,500,000 in 1970. Figures by province are given.

9267 Kandel, Pablo and **Mario Monteverde.** Entorno y caída. B.A., Editorial Planeta Argentina, 1976. 234 p., plates (Col. Textos)

A rather detailed journalistic account of Isabel Perón's presidency. Useful for the understanding of the events that led to the military coup of 1976.

9268 Luca de Tena, Torcuato. Yo, Juan Domingo Perón: relato autobiográfico. Barcelona, Editorial Planeta, 1976. 285 p., plates (Espejo del mundo, 2)

This book is based on a series of tapes recorded by Perón when he was in exile in Spain. Only excerpts, edited and with comments by Spanish journalists, are presented here. Since the tapes are available to researchers, these transcripts constitute the most reliable memoirs produced by Perón. The book contains as autobiographical sketch, Perón's defense of his administration, and rather candid opinions on a variety of subjects. These revealing opinions provide much insight into Perón's underlying ideology and his approach to policy-making. A useful source.

9269 Lynch, Kevin *ed.* Growing up in cities: studies of the spatial environment of adolescence in Cracow, Melbourne, Mexico City, Salta, Toluca, and Warszawa. From the reports of Tridib Banerjee and others. Cambridge, Massachusetts Institute of Technology (MIT) [and] UNESCO, Paris, 1977. 177 p., bibl., illus., maps, plates, tables.

A study of the city as an environment of childhood and adolescence. On the basis of interviews in cities in four countries (Salta, Arg.; Melbourne, Australia; Toluca and

Ecatepec, Mexico; and several locations in Poland) the author and his co-workers look into different aspects of the perception of the physical environment on children's everyday life. These aspects include: the image of the city, the use of space, time budgets, boredom and engagement, attraction to wastelands, conceptions about beauty and ugliness, etc.

9270 Mafud, Julio. La vida obrera en la Argentina. B.A., Editorial Proyección, 1976. 254 p., bibl., tables.

A vivid account of Argentine working-class life in the first decades of the century. The author surveys working and living conditions in different types of agrarian and industrial settings, including the organization of labor, wages paid, sanitary aspects, housing, life in working class neighborhoods, diet, sex differences, deviant behavior, etc.

9271 Martín, Enrique. Malthus y el control de la natalidad. B.A., Ediciones Acción, n.d. 79 p., bibl., plates (Ediciones acción, 4)

Two different essays on population. The first one deals with Malthusianism and its contemporary manifestations, and the second one, under the title of "Population Policy in Argentina," comments on the 1970 census, and on immigration, brain drain, and demographic disequilibria. Ideological and amateurish.

9272 Mignone, Emilio Fermín. Estudio de la realidad social argentina. B.A., Ediciones Coliseo, 1974. 3 v. (190, 198, 198 p.) illus., plates.

School text in social studies, in three volumes, corresponding to the third to fifth years of Argentine high school. The subject is "Argentine Social Reality," in 1973, when the Peronists took power. The aim of the course was "to describe and critically analyze" the political, social and economic structure of the country, "and to establish criteria for its transformation, according to the ideals of justice, common good, freedom and participation." The three volumes deal with the organization of the policy, the society and the economy, from a left-wing Peronist perspective.

9273 Mora y Araujo, Manuel. La estructura social del peronismo: un análisis electoral interprovincial. San Carlos de Bariloche, Arg., Fundación Bariloche, Depto. de Sociología, 1974. 29 l., tables.

A study of the social basis of Peronism, on the basis of an ecological analysis of the 1973 elections. The focus is the relationship between the degree of development of the provinces, measured by per-capita product, urbanization, education and industrialization, and the vote for FREJULI, th Peronist coalition. The main conclusion is that the social basis of Peronism varied according to the degree of modernization. Support for FREJULI was negatively correlated with the degree of development and with the rate of economic growth of the provinces. The author also finds a negative correlation between size of the working class and vote for FREJULI. This is due to the fact that, in the most developed provinces, Peronism was a working-class movement, while in the peripheral provinces it had a heterogeneous social base. A solid piece of electoral analysis.

9274 ———. Una primera caracterización sociopolítica de las provincias patagónicas. San Carlos de Bariloche, Arg., Fundación Bariloche, Depto. de Sociología, 1974. 9 l., bibl., tables.

An analysis of the social bases of politics in the Patagonia region of Argentina, on the basis of the 1973 electoral results. The main cleavage in this region was similar to the one at the national level: on the one hand, there was a "populist" coalition, based on lower and middle rural strata, lower urban strata, the labor movement, and a segment of the urban middle class; and on the other, the upper strata, both rural and urban, and a segment of the middle classes.

9275 Movimiento de Sacerdotes para el Tercer Mundo, Buenos Aires. El pueblo: ¿donde está? B.A., 1975. 153 p.

An ideological statement by the "Third World Priests" movement in Argentina. Focuses on the analysis of the concept of "people," and discusses the different meanings of this term, as well as topics more directly related to political strategy: "the people" and its enemies, "people's organizations," etc. A populist-nationalist political platform.

9276 Müller, María S. La mortalidad en Buenos Aires entre 1855 y 1960. B.A., Instituto Torcuato di Tella, Centro de Investigaciones Sociales [and] Centro Latinoamericano de Demografía, 1974. 141 p., bibl., tables (Serie naranja: sociología)

A study of mortality in B.A., from 1855 to 1960. The author measures mortality rates at ten points in time, analyzes the evolution of these rates according to sex, age, and origin of the population, and looks into causes of death. She finds that the decrease in the mortality rate was caused by the control of infectious and respiratory diseases.

Newton, Ronald C. Social change, cultural crisis and the origins of Nazism within the German-speaking community of Buenos Aires. See item **7497.**

9277 Pithod, Abelardo. La revolución cultural en la Argentina. B.A., Cruz y Fierro Editores, 1974. 89 p., illus.

A radical right-wing critique of contemporary culture. An attack on psychoanalysis, which the author considers to be an instrument of communism, and on liberal Catholicism, which is also alleged to be infiltrated by Marxism. These trends are seen, in a conspiratorial manner, as different aspects of a revolutionary strategy whose aim is the "liquidation of the Christian order." This decline, which would have begun in the 13th century, is indicated, for the author, by feminism, the liberalization of sexual norms, and other aspects of contemporary culture. A rare codification of the world-view of the most radical segment of the Argentine right.

9278 Portes, Alejandro. Perón and the Argentine national elections. Austin, Univ. of Texas, Institute of Latin American Studies, 1973. 18 p., facsim.

A good discussion of the social and political background of the return of Peronists to power. The author describes the political evolution of Argentina since the overthrow of Perón in 1955, and examines the changing nature of the Peronist movement.

9279 Recchini de Lattes, Zulma L. Aspectos demográficos de la urbanización en la Argentina: 1869–1960. B.A., Instituto Torcuato di Tella, Centro de Investigaciones Sociales, Programa de Actividades Demográficas, 1973. 99 p., bibl., map, tables (Serie naranja: sociología)

A description of the process of urbanization in Argentina from 1869 to 1960. Aspects considered include: demographic differentials between rural and urban populations, urban growth trends, rates of urban migration by age and sex.

9280 ——— and Alfredo E. Lattes comps. La población de Argentina. B.A., Ministerio de Economía, Instituto Nacional de Estadística y Censos (INDEC), 1975. 212 p., bibl., maps, tables (Serie investigaciones demográficas, 1)

A series of descriptive papers on aspects of the Argentine population: demographic evolution of the country in the past century, changes in the composition of the population, ecological distribution, urbanization, economically active population, and projections until the end of the century. Compendium is useful summary of information available elsewhere.

9281 Rojo, Alejandro. Las villas de emergencia. Introducción de José Luis de Imaz. B.A., Editorial El Coloquio, 1976. 159 p., map, tables (Col. Hombre y sociedad)

A discussion of health and educational conditions in Argentine shanty-towns—which are piously called "emergency villages" by officials. The book is based on first-hand knowledge, and includes useful statistical information.

9282 Sagrera, Martín. Argentina superpoblada: la inflación poblacional argentina y los traficantes de hombres. B.A., Libros de América, 1976. 220 p.

The author expounds the unusual thesis that, in view of existing economic conditions, Argentina is an overpopulated country. He also claims that this alleged overpopulation was artificially produced by the elite in order to continue their exploitation of the people.

Schmucler, Héctor and Margarita Zires. El papel político-ideológico de los medios de comunicación: Argentina 1975, la crisis del Lopezreguismo. See item **7501.**

9283 Seminario sobre Problemas del Empleo en América Latina, La Plata, Arg., 1975. El empleo en América Latina: problemas económicos, sociales y políticos. Edited by Víctor E. Tokman and Paulo Renato Souza. México, Siglo XXI Editores, 1976. 450 p., tables (Economía y demografía)

A series of papers presented at a CLACSO meeting on problems of employment in Latin America. The issues discussed include: the urban marginal sector, the relationship between education and occupational mobility, youth unemployment, technological unemployment, the use of production functions, and the Phillips curve. Argentina and Mexico are the countries analyzed in greater detail. The prevailing approach is that labor markets are split, and that the processes that determine the supply of and the demand for labor are different in each segment of the market. Competent papers.

Slater, Paul B. Internal migration regions of Argentina and Brazil: application of hierarchical clustering to doubly standardized lifetime migration tables. See item **9400.**

Szuchman, Mark D. The limits of the melting pot in urban Argentina: marriage and integration in Córdoba, 1869–1909. See *HLAS 40:3872.*

9284 Tedesco, Juan Carlos. Clases sociales y educación en la Argentina. Rosario, Arg., Ediciones Centro de Estudios, 1973? 1 v. (Unpaged) table.

An interpretation of the educational policies of different ruling groups in Argentina: the liberal elite that held power until 1916, the middle-class radicals, and the Peronists. Rather ideological, yet useful.

9285 Zito Lema, Vicente. Conversaciones con Enrique Pichon Rivière: sobre el arte y la locura. B.A., Timerman Editores, 1976. 166 p., facsim., illus., plates.

A series of interviews to Pichon Rivière, one of the leaders of Argentine psychoanalysis. Contains autobiographical references and Pichon Rivière's opinions on a variety of subjects, both professional and non-professional, these ranging from the training of analysts and the limits of analysis to the work of Lautréamont and Artaud.

PARAGUAY

9286 Baade, Perla. La vivienda en el Paraguay: situación y perspectivas. Asunción Centro Paraguayo de Estudios Sociológicos (CPES) [and] Sociedad Interamericana de Planificación (SIAP), 1976. 49 p., tables.

A description of the quality of housing in Paraguay, including information on construction materials used, the supply of basic services, such as water, electricity, and waste disposal; density and property status. Belongs to same series as item **9290.**

9287 Laterza, Gustavo. Políticas del estado sobre tierra y vivienda. Asunción, Centro Paraguayo de Estudios Sociológicos (CPES) [and] Sociedad Interamericana de Planificación (SIAP), n.d. 84 p., bibl.

A study of housing and urban land tenure policies in Paraguay. Includes an historical analysis of these policies, and a description of current legal norms and practices regarding housing. Part of the same series as item **9290.**

9288 Rivarola, Domingo M. and **José N. Morinigo.** La vivienda en el Paraguay: sus condicionantes socio-económicos. Asunción, Centro Paraguayo de Estudios Sociológicos (CPES) [and] Sociedad Interamericana de Planificación (SIAP), 1976. 86 p., bibl., tables.

A very good descriptive study of housing in Paraguay, from a sociological perspective. Authors explore the demographic, economic, and social determinants of the allocation of housing, including references to the effects of migration, urbanization, the rural economy, the occupational structure and income distribution in urban areas, social stratification, and market factors. Based on solid statistical information. Belongs to same series as item **9290.**

9289 ——— and others. La población del Paraguay. Asunción, Centro Paraguayo de Estudios Sociológicos, 1974. 194 p., bibl., maps, tables.

A historical study of the population of Paraguay. The authors discuss fecundity, mortality, immigration, composition of the population by age and sex, ecological distribution, internal migration, and characteristics of the economically active population such as size, distribution by age, occupational composition, and unemployment. A useful compendium.

9290 Rivarola, María Magdalena. Datos y estudios sobre la vivienda en el Paraguay. Asunción, Centro Paraguayo de Estudios Sociológicos (CPES), 1976. 35 p.

An annotated bibliography of sources on housing in Paraguay. Includes detailed information on the contents of statistical sources. Part of a series of studies sponsored by the Centro Paraguayo de Estudios Sociológicos and the Sociedad Inter-Americana de Planificación.

URUGUAY

9291 Machado Bonet, Ofelia. Status de la mujer en el Uruguay. Montevideo, n.p. 1977. 14 p., tables.

A description of the status of women in Uruguay. Subjects covered include: demographic characteristics, participation in the economy, education, legal rights.

Minello, Nelson. Uruguay: la consolidación del estado militar. See item **7607.**

Prost, Gérard. Structures agraires en Uruguay: l'example du Départment d'Artigas. See item **5561.**

Sierra, Gerónimo de. L'emigration massive des travailleurs uruguayens de 1960 a 1976: en particulier vers l'Argentine. See item **7609.**

Suárez Radillo, Carlos Miguel. El teatro experimental penitenciario uruguay . . . See *HLAS 40:7393.*

BRAZIL

JOSE FABIO BARBOSA DA SILVA, *Professor of Sociology, University of Notre Dame*

THE MATERIALS INCLUDED FOR REVIEW in this bibliography are highly selective and were taken from an extensive list of titles mostly published during the past two years. The application of strict selection criteria which is *Handbook* policy is designed to narrow down such a list to works which, in the judgement of the contributing editor, are of permanent record value.

As reported in previous volumes of the *Handbook,* there has been a notable increase in the publication of works on Brazilian sociology by local writers as well as by foreigners appearing in translation. The expansion of the university population and a growing middle class provide the market for the new publishing industry. This trend is exemplified by the boom in the publication of specialized collections of titles by well-known scholars as, for instance, those published by the Univ. of São Paulo Press, or by Editora Atica of São Paulo which parallel similar collections published by the Univ. of Chicago Press of major social thinkers such as Lenin, Habermas, Gadamer, Kojeve, and others. In addition to this scholarly trend, there has been a notable increase in the publication of titles on popular social themes of wide interest such as sexuality, crime, juvenile delinquency, communication, etc.

Of the material annotated below, I would like to single out a number of works for special consideration which are divided into four categories: a) works of theory; b) research studies of a general nature; c) research studies of southern Brazil; and d) works on population and urbanization. Among theoretical works of note, I would include: Paulo Edmur de Souza Queiroz's *Sociologia política de Oliveira Viana* (item **9383**) which adds significant materials and analysis to the exegesis of that author; Roberto Cardoso de Oliveira's *Identidade, etnia e estrutura social* (item **9364**) which gives a preliminary summation to the long stream of research works published by that well-known author; Roger Bastide's ideas are discussed in an article in his honor (item **9301**); and a volume records a series of interviews with Paulo Freire entitled *Concientización y liberación* (item **9333**); and finally two articles by the well-known sociologist Florestan Fernandes (items **9322–9323**).

In the second group which consists of specific research studies, one should single out a work (already reviewed in the Archaeology section, see *HLAS 37:855*) by Donald Pierson *O homen no Vale do São Francisco.* This detailed monograph in three large volumes was written in collaboration with a number of noted specialists such as Fernando Altenfelder Silva, Levy Cruz, Octavio da Costa Eduardo, and others. This is certainly a basic contribution for all future research in the area.

The third group consists of the large number of studies of the southernmost states of Brazil, particularly Rio·Grande do Sul. The growing number of well-qualified specialists working in this area have contributed significantly to an understanding of the sociocultural characteristics of the region. Among their works one should mention: Rovílio Costa's *Antropologia visual da imigração italiana* (item **9316**), a fascinating and innovative analysis which consists of many historical photographs of Italian immigrants and their world; Eliezer Pacheco's *Colonização e racismo* (item **9370**); Walter F. Piazza's *A colonização italiana em Santa Catarina* (item **9373**); Eloy Lacava Pereira's *O Brasil do imigrante* (item **9372**); Manoelito Ornellas' *Gaúchos e beduínos* (item **9367**); Francisco Ferraz and others' *Perfil socio-econômico das populações urbanas de baixas rendas no Rio Grande do Sul* (item **9324**); Laudelino Medeiros' *Formação da sociedade Rio-Grandense* (item **9346**); and Claudio Moreira Bento's *O negro e descendentes na sociedade do Rio Grande do Sul* (item **9302**).

Finally, among the last group or studies of population and urbanization, one should mention the study by Candido Procopio Ferreira de Camargo and Fernando Henrique Cardoso entitled *São Paulo, 1975: crescimento e pobreza* (item **9309**); Manoel T. Berlinck's careful monograph *Marginalidade social e relações de classe em São Paulo* (item **9304**); Manoel Augusto Costa's *Urbanização e migração urbana no Brasil* (item **9315**); and from the Fundação de Economia e Estatistica do Rio Grande do Sul's *Indicadores sociais do Rio Grande do Sul: migrações internas* (item **9332**).

All of these studies attest to the fact that sociology has outlived the turbulent stage and stagnant phase which hampered the field in the past and has emerged as one of the most dynamic and creative research areas in Brazil today.

9292 Adonias Filho [*pseud. for* **Adonias Aguiar**]. Sul da Bahia: chão cacau: uma civilização regional. Rio, Civilização Brasileira, 1976. 112 p., bibl.

On the basis of socio-historical data, the author discusses the processes that developed the peculiar cultural character of the regional area of cacau in northern Brazil. He analyzes social components, economic cycles, cultural elements, social types, politics, the interaction between religion and politics, and regional consciousness.

9293 Aguiar, Neuma. Totem e tabu no Nordeste: uma mediação sociológica entre a antropologia social e a antropologia clínica. Rio, Instituto Universitário de Pesquisas [and] Sociedade Brasileira de Instrução, 1973. 32 1.

Author applies theoretical notions derived from sociology and social and clinical anthropology to his analysis of religious phenomena peculiar to the Northeast. He examines the portrayal of mythical relations between human beings and the transformation of humans into animals in the popular literature of the region.

9294 Albuquerque, J. A. Guilhon *ed.* Classes médias e política no Brasil. Río, Editora Paz e Terra, 1977. 174 p., tables (Col. Estudos brasileiros, 17)

A collection of seven papers, some (the more comprehensive and theoretical pieces) previously published or read at international meetings, and three which report on unpublished research on the Brazilian middle-class. Collectively they deal with issues (definition, principal characteristics, and methodology for the study) of or about the middle class in developing countries, especially Latin America. Two papers on Brazil not previously published study university students, on the basis of interview data. The volume is a valuable compilation of otherwise inaccessible materials. [P.B. Taylor, Jr.]

9295 Alves, Henrique Losinskas *comp.* Bibliografia afro-brasileira: estudos sobre o negro. Apresentação de José Honório Rodrigues. São Paulo, Edições H, 1976. 154 p.

Lists more than 2,000 titles dealing with the study of blacks in Brazil. Although unannotated, this is an invaluable compilation for specialists.

Amado, Janaina. Contribuição au estudo da imigração alemã Rio Grande do Sul: São Leopoldo, 1824–1874. See *HLAS 40:4057.*

9296 Ammann, Safira Bezerra. Participação social. São Paulo, Cortez & Moraes, 1977. 139 p., bibl., tables.

Theoretical analysis of social participation in general and in Brasília in particular. The last section discusses "direct participation" (income as an index, formal organizations, participation in education and health etc.) as well as "indirect participation" (voluntary groups and their characteristics).

9297 Angelini, Arrigo Leonardo. Aspectos atuais da profissão de psicólogo no Brasil (Cadernos de Psicologia Aplicada [Univ. Federal do Rio Grande do Sul, Centro de Orientação e Seleção Psicotécnica, Porto Alegre, Brazil] 3:1, 1975, p. 35–52, bibl.)

Article based on a lecture which discusses the role and profession of psychologists in Brazil. Author calls for an expansion of psychological assistance in various areas such as labor and particularly education. Author believes in a preventive rather than therapeutic approach.

Bacha, Edmar Lisboa and **Roberto Mangabeira Unger.** Participação, salário, e voto: um projeto de democracia para o Brasil. See item **3436.**

Baer, Werner and others. Industrialização, urbanização e a persistência das desigualdades regionais do Brasil. See item **3439.**

9298 Baptista, Myrian Veras. Desenvolvimento de comunidade: estudo da integração do planejamento do desenvolvimento de comunidade no planejamento do desenvolvimento global. São Paulo, Cortez & Moraes, 1976. 170 p., bibl., tables.

Author provides a theoretical framework that will permit the coordination or integration of community projects (usually under the supervision of social workers) with national projects (usually managed by government officials). Although the author realizes that the main obstacles to such a coordination are political, she believes that if a certain level of technical integration between the local and national level can be achieved, it will minimize serious conflicts and discontinuities.

9299 Barroso, Carmen Lúcia de Melo. A participação da mulher no desenvolvimento científico brasileiro (SBPC/CC, 27:6, junho 1975, p. 613–620, bibl., tables)

An analysis of the Brazilian situation reveals what is also characteristic of other countries or that the full participation of women will not be easily achieved. The author, however, is optimistic and she singles out some promising symptoms.

9300 ———. Por que tão poucas mulheres exercem atividades científicas? (SBPC/CC, 27:7, julho 1975, p. 703–710, bibl.)

The process of socialization of girls hinders the development of characteristics typical of scientists. Women who choose a scientific career must face low expectations of success and the few who do succeed must, in turn, encounter discrimination barring access to promotion. Moreover, a woman's career is often handicapped by family obligations and by emotional conflicts arising from her "deviant" status as a female-professional.

9301 Bastide, Roger; Charles Beylier; and **Paul Arbousse-Bastide.** Bastidiana (AISCD, 40, juillet/dec. 1976, p. 5–62)

An article in honor of French scholar Roger Bastide who was active in Brazil for many years. It includes two lectures by him: "The Development of Brazil" and "For Pluralism in Development;" one of his first research reports "Images of the Mystical Northeast in Black and White;" and reminiscences of Bastide by his friend and colleague, Paul Arbousse-Bastide.

9302 Bento, Cláudio Moreira. O negro e descendentes na sociedade do Rio Grande do Sul: 1635–1975. Porto Alegre, Brazil, Grafosul em convênio com o Instituto Estadual do Livro, 1976. 288 p., bibl., facsim., maps, plates, tables (Série biênio da colonização e imigração, 5)

A social history of the role of blacks in the development of Rio Grande do Sul beginning with the bandeiras period in 1635. Includes discussion of blacks in the literature of the state.

9303 Bergmann, Michel. Nasce um povo: estudo antropológico da população brasileira; como surgiu, composição racial, evolução futura. Petrópolis, Brazil, Editora Vozes, 1977. 204 p., bibl., maps, tables (Publicações CID. História, 5)

Ethnographic exploration of the nature of the Brazilian population. The author's socio-historical analysis devotes special attention to the role and status of ethnic minorities, particularly blacks and Amerindians. A book designed chiefly for courses on "Brazilian Problems."

9304 Berlinck, Manoel T. Marginalidade social e relações de classes em São Paulo. Petrópolis, Brazil, Editora Vozes, 1975. 152 p., tables (Col. Sociologia brasileira, 1)

In this study of marginality, the author discusses the relationship between urbanism and industrialization. He also examines the connection between the process of capital accumulation and the expansion of the working class in São Paulo. He concludes by noting the existence of institutional mechanisms which foster marginality and identifies the organizations which support this process.

9305 Bono, Ernesto. Nós, a loucura e a antipsiquiatria. Rio, Pallas, 1975. 188 p.

Book of essays on the influence of Laing and Cooper, notions of "anti-psychiatry" and the author's professional experience in Rio's mental-health centers. Also includes critical reevaluations of Freud and Reich.

9306 Brazil. Fundação Nacional do Bem-Estar do Menor (FUNABEM). Assessoria de Relações Públicas. A revolução e o problema do menor. Brasilia?, 1974. 32 l.

This report makes public three documents: 1) a summary of the agreements reached between FUNABEM and various government agencies during the first three years of the military governments (1964–67); 2) a report detailing technical and financial cooperation between the Federal government and state and private institutions; and 3) a press release which provides basic information on child abandonment in Brazil.

————. Ministério do Interior (MINTER). Superintendência do Desenvolvimento do Nordeste (SUDENE). Departamento de Agricultura e Abastecimento (DAA). Suprimento de gêneros alimentícios de Caruaru. See item **3448.**

9307 Cadaval, Mauricio. Notas para um debate sobre mercado de trabalho e orientações no ensino da sociologia (SBPC/CC, 28:7, julho 1976, p. 746–749)

A plea for the reformulation of the sociology curriculum at Brazilian universities given the limited demand for the work of professional sociologists in the country at large.

9308 *Cadernos do CEAS.* Centro de Estudos e Ação Social. No. 36, março/abril 1975–. Salvador, Brazil.

This issue of *Cadernos do CEAS* includes two articles of interest: 1) Victor Thomas' "Colonization of the Amazon," an analysis of field-research recently conducted on current colonization programs in the Amazon region; and 2) Gerard Fourez' "Church-State: Brazilian Catholicism in a Period of Transition," a review essay of the existing literature on the topic.

9309 Camargo, Cândido Procópio Ferreira de and others. São Paulo, 1975: crescimento e pobreza. São Paulo, Edições Loyola, 1976. 155 p., plates, tables.

An unusual book of essays on the development and role of the city of São Paulo. In an attempt to show the linkages between development and poverty, the authors examine the growth of the city from the perspective of the laboring classes which constitute the majority of its inhabitants.

9310 Cardoso, Lycurgo Francisco. Ninguem vive impunemente as delícias dos extremos: ensaio político-sócio-econômico sobre o nosso e outros desenvolvimentos históricos e similares. Porto Alegre, Brazil, Grafosul, 1976. 605 p.

Polemical book about groups in Brazil who advocate development and their stands on various political, social and economic issues. For the general reader.

9311 Carvalho, J.A.M. Regional trends in fertility and mortality in Brazil (LSE/PS, 28:3, Nov. 1974, p. 401–421, maps, tables)

This study reviews: 1) fertility estimates for Brazil in 1970; 2) fertility and distribution of population for the periods 1930–40, 1940–50, and 1950–60; 3) fertility estimates for the period 1930–70 with other estimates; 4) mortality estimates for Brazil; 5) mortality patterns for Brazil; 6) comparisons between national and regional patterns; and 7) regional inequalities in mortality.

9312 Carvalho, Maria Luiza de. A mulher no mercado de trabalho brasileiro (VOZES, 66:6, agosto 1972, p. 41–48, tables)

Article which analyzes the role of Brazilian women in the labor market. Because of technological changes, the work of women is perceived as subsidiary and their participation in the more productive sectors has declined. Moreover, even though the educational level of Brazilian females is higher than that of males, salaries are higher for males even at the university level. Finally, author concludes that education for females is inadequate given today's labor market conditions.

9313 Carvalho, Rodrigues de. Lampião e a sociologia do Cangaço. Prefácio de Gastão Pereira da Silva. Rio, Gráfica Editora do Livro, 1976. 379 p., bibl., plates.

A detailed socio-historical analysis of a major popular and cultural hero of the arid Northeast. Although concerned basically with the elucidation of *Lampião* as an individual, the data and discussions attempt to shed light on the phenomena of rural banditry.

Coelho, Edmundo Campos. Em busca de identidade: o exército e a política na sociedade brasileira. See item **7528.**

Coleção Nosso Brazil: Estudos Sociais. See item **5614.**

9314 Cossard-Binon, Gisèle. Origines lointaines du syncrétisme afro-catholique au Brésil et perspectives d'avenir (UFB/AA, 12, junho 1976, p. 161–166, bibl.)

Discussion of Afro-Catholic syncretism in Brazil. The author calls attention to the early origins of this phenomenon by noting a fact supported by historical documents or how large numbers of slaves from the Congo and Angola had been baptized in Africa prior to their deportation to Brazil.

9315 Costa, Manoel Augusto. Urbanização e migração urbana no Brasil. Rio, Instituto de Planejamento Econômico e Social, Instituto de Pesquisas (IPEA/INPES), 1975. 198 p., bibl., tables (Série monográfica, 21)

On the basis of special tabulation generated by IBGE, the author analyzes a series of differentials between urban migrants and non-migrants at the regional level. He concludes by noting the socio-demographic effects of migration in the receiving areas.

Costa, Rovílio; Irineu Costella; Pedro A. Salame; and Paulo J. Salame. Imigração italiana no Rio Grande do Sul: vida, costumes e tradições. See *HLAS 40:4086.*

9316 ——— and others. Antropologia visual da imigração italiana. Caxias do Sul, Brazil, Univ. de Caxias [and] Escola Superior de Teologia São Lourenço de Brindes, Porto Alegre, Brazil, 1976. 221 p., bibl., facsims., plates (Col. Centenário da imigração italiana, 13)

A most original illustrated history of Italian immigration in the state of Rio Grande do Sul. Includes many valuable photographs and other illustrations of many aspects of the immigrants' lives, e.g. household organization, religious practices, work, leisure, crafts, etc. For authors' book on the subject, see *HLAS 40:4086.*

9317 Cunningham, Isabella C.M.; William H. Cunningham; and Russell M. Moore. Social class and consumption behavior in São Paulo, Brazil. Austin, Univ. of Texas, Bureau of Business Research, 1976. 177 p., bibl., tables (Studies in marketing, 23)

Monograph based on extensive surveys conducted in São Paulo during the summer 1972. Authors believe that the consumption behaviour of São Paulo residents has been influenced by five factors: 1) changes in the political and economic structure; 2) increasing importance of formal education; 3) rapid population increase; 4) rapid urbanization; and 5) development of new marketing institutions.

9318 Curitiba (city), *Brazil.* **Instituto de Pesquisa e Planejamento Urbano de Curitiba** (IPPUC). **Companhia de Habitação Popular de Curitiba** (COHAB/CT). **Departamento de Bem-Estar Social** (PMC). Política habitacional de interesse social: plano de desfavelamento; documento final. Curitiba, Brazil, 1976. 69 l., maps, tables.

Research report on the *favelas* (shantytowns) of the city of Curitiba. Data covers physical, social and economic factors. The discussion deals with possible policies to be adopted by the municipal authorities.

9319 Delhaes-Guenther, Dietrich von. La influencia de la inmigración en el desarrollo y composición étnica de la población de Rio Grande do Sul (JGSWGL, 13, 1976, p. 420–433, illus., tables)

A demographic and historical analysis on the influence of immigration on the development and ethnic composition of the population of Rio Grande do Sul. Author concludes that immigration (particularly in the period 1824–1914) led to a decline of the Luso-Brazilian component of the total population. As a result, today only one in three individuals is of Portuguese descent.

9320 Della Cava, Ralph. Catholicism and society in twentieth-century Brazil (LARR, 11:2, 1976, p. 7–50, illus.)

Author explores the Brazilian experience of half a century (1914–64) in order to establish what are the determinants and constraints of Catholicism in a modern Latin American society. He first summarizes the principal tenets of the literature on the Church as an agent of change; he examines the history of the Church since World War II; and finally, he assesses whether the history of the Church in one country (e.g., Brazil) corroborates the alleged capacity for reform of Latin American Catholicism as indicated by certain social science projections. For historian's comment, see *HLAS 40:4092*.

9321 Donnangelo, Maria Cecília F. Medicina e sociedade: o médico e seu mercado de trabalho. São Paulo, Livraria Pioneira Editora, 1975. 174 p., tables (Biblioteca pioneira de ciências sociais. Sociologia)

The book results from the elaboration of field research materials on the medical profession. It focuses on modalities of medical work as specialized subject, participating in the labor market and linked to the unit of production of services and health. The origins and modalities of state intervention on the medical sector are also discussed in detail.

Droulers, Martine. Les paysans du Maranhão. See item **7529.**

Faé, Walter José. Italianos do Rio Grande do Sul: 1875–1975. See item **5622.**

9322 Fernandes, Florestan. Beyond poverty: the Negro and the mulatto in Brazil (*in* Toplin, Robert Brent *ed*. Slavery and race relations in Latin America. Westport, Conn., Greenwood Press, 1974, p. 277–298, tables [Contributions in Afro-American and African studies, 17])

Another essay which documents the plight of Afro-Brazilians after abolition. Author contends that racial views in Brazil evolved over the centuries and as a result of slavery. Thus, they cannot be considered the product of "outside influences" or as "im-

ports." He does admit, however, that 19th-century European racial attitudes reinforced Brazilian views. All these factors prevented black mobility after abolition.

9323 ———. Entrevistas: sobre o trabalho teórico (Trans/Form/Ação [Faculdade de Filosofia, Ciências e Letras de Asis, Assis, Brazil] 2, 1975, p. 5–86)

Interviews with a number of São Paulo intellectuals who lived through a number of political difficulties since 1964. Questions range from societal problems to personal experiences. Of special significance are the comments by Florestan Fernandes and Octavio Ianni.

9324 Ferraz, Francisco; Hélgio Trindade; Judson de Cew; and Eduardo Aydos. Perfil sócio-econômico das populações urbanas de baixas rendas no Rio Grande do Sul. v. 1. Porto Alegre, Brazil, Pontificia Univ. Católica do Rio Grande do Sul, Instituto de Estudos Sociais, Políticas e Econômicas [and] Univ. Federal do Rio Grande do Sul, Insituto de Filosofia e Ciências Humanas, 1975. 336 p., tables.

Research report on the socio-economic conditions of the low-income urban population of the state of Rio Grande do Sul commissioned by state planners. Data was collected through a survey including a questionnaire and interviews with a random sample of the target population. Most of the report concerns the socioeconomic status of the population including analyses of life-patterns (e.g., occupation, migration, education, housing, etc.).

9325 Figueiredo, Ariosvaldo. O negro e a violência do branco: negro em Sergipe. Prefácio de Clóvis Moura. Rio, José Alvaro, 1977. 120 p., bibl., tables.

On the basis of historical documents, this work analyzes race relations between blacks and whites during slavery in the state of Sergipe. Author concludes that Sergipe did not differ from other areas in the cruelty and violence of the prevailing system of race domination.

9326 Fleisher, David V. O Poder Legislativo em Minas Gerais: uma análise da composição sócio-econômica, recrutamento e padrões de carreira, 1947–1977. Brasília, Univ. de Brasília, Depto. de Ciências Sociais,

1977. 93 1., bibl., map, tables (Série sociologia, 8)

Research monograph based on fieldwork conducted in the period 1947–77 among 322 state representatives of the state of Minas Gerais. The author analyzes their social and educational backgrounds: types of political careers; political recruitment; the recruitment styles of the various political parties; changes instituted by the 1964 revolution; the two party system; and the effects of extended service on political careers.

Frederico, Celso. Consciência operária no Brasil. See item **7541.**

9327 **Freyre, Gilberto.** Antologia. Madrid, Ediciones Cultura Hispánica, 1977. 257 p. bibl.

A collection of essays by the well-known Brazilian sociologist on literature, history, biography, autobiography, anthropology, philosophy, travel, poetry, etc. Includes short comments by Maria Elisa Dias Collier.

9328 ———. Brasil como nação hispanotropical: suas constantes e suas projeções transnacionais. São Paulo, Club Athlético Paulistano, 1975. 32 p., plate.

A conference which expounds the author's well-known theory of "Lusotropicalism" as a viable sociopolitical ideology.

Goodman, D.E. Rural structure, surplus mobilization and modes of production in a peripheral region: the Brazilian Northeast. See item **3475.**

Greenfield, Sidney M. Patronage, politics, and the articulation of local community and national society in pre-1968 Brazil. See item **7546.**

Grossi, Maria das Graças. Minas Gerais: del estancamiento al boom; una réplica local del modelo brasileño. See item **3476.**

9329 **Habert, Angeluccia Bernardes.** Fotonovela e indústria cultural: estudo de uma forma de literatura sentimental fabricada para milhões. Petrópolis, Brazil, Editora Vozes, 1974. 140 p., bibl., plates, tables (Col. Vozes do mundo moderno, 11)

This is the first analysis published in Brazil of that Latin American phenomenon known as the "fotonovela" (sentimental literature or soap operas which are illustrated by photographs printed in sequential frames, comic-book style). The study discusses various aspects: editorial policy; sociological and psychological features; the mass culture context; use of language; implicit "message;" etc. For another good study of the fotonovela, see item **9014.**

9330 **Hasenbalg, Carlos A.** Diagnóstico sobre as desigualdades raciais no Brasil: notas para uma história social do negro brasileiro (NS, 3:5/6, 1978, p. 119–137, tables)

The author contends that the dynamics of slavery and the ensuing process of internal migration after abolition led to an unbalanced distribution of blacks throughout Brazil. They became isolated from more promising regions with better financial opportunities. Because of these historical parameters, black mobility in Brazil has been differential. The Southeast emerges as the most advantageous region, but even there color discrimination perpetuates a structure of inequality.

9331 **Ibiapina, João Nonon de Moura Fontes.** Passarela de marmotas. Ilustrações de Bernardino. Teresina, Brazil, Companhia Editora do Piauí (COMEPI), 1975. 168 p., illus.

Collection of notes discusses mythical figures prevalent in the folklore of the state of Piauí.

9332 *Indicadores Sociais RS*. Fundação de Economia e Estatística. Ano 4, No. 4, out. 1976–. Porto Alegre, Brazil.

A study of internal migration in the state of Rio Grande do Sul incorporates data from the decenial censuses and data collected by SUDESUL. Analyzes relations between urbanization and migration; profiles of migrants; and delineation of pull-push areas for the state. Other issues such as the problems of urban marginality and the relation between urbanization and the labor market are also briefly examined.

9333 **Instituto de Acción Cultural,** *Geneva.* Concientización y liberación. Rosario, Arg., Editorial Axis, 1975. 214 p. (Col. Documentos, 2)

This work consists of a long interview with the well-known pedagogue Paulo Freire. It is organized into the following topics: conscientization and liberation; help to the Third World; the role of women's liberation; and political education based on the Peruvian experience.

9334 Joanides, Hiroito de Moraes. Boca do lixo. Prefácios de Percival de Souza e Orlando Criscuolo. São Paulo, Edições Populares, 1977. 207 p. (Col. Problemas brasileiros. Série depoimento, 1)

After interviewing a famous criminal who for years dominated the São Paulo underworld, the author offers a report and analysis of the meaning of "criminality" and "deviance" in the Brazilian context. A useful book for courses on Brazilian problems.

9335 Karasch, Mary C. The African heritage of Rio de Janeiro (in Pescatello, Ann M. *ed.* Old roots in new lands: historical and anthropological perspectives on black experiences in the Americas. Westport, Conn., Greenwood Press, 1977, p. 36–76, tables [Contributions in Afro-American and African studies, 31])

A study which focuses on the initial experience and adaptation of imported African slaves to the city of Rio. The description of their resistance to slavery and the gradual loss of their cultural heritage illuminates the trauma experienced by slaves who were brought to the New World. For historian's comment, see *HLAS 40:3985*.

9336 Kujawski, Gilberto de Mello. O projeto político. Petrópolis, Brazil, Editora Vozes, 1976. 99 p.

Author contrasts the conception of a "political model" as perceived by the Brazilian establishment with a "political project" a more encompassing social concept. The author uses this theoretical discussion to define the nature of politics in today's Brazil.

9337 Leite, Geraldo Lourenço de Oliveira.
A terapia centrada no cliente, do ponto de vista da teoria da informação (Symposium [Revista da Universidade Católica de Pernambuco, Recife, Brazil] 15:2, 1973, p. 47–51, bibl.)

A short note, within the context of information theory, on what constitutes "patient-oriented" therapy in Brazil today.

9338 Lima, Vivaldo da Costa. O conceito de Nação nos candomblés da Bahia (UFB/AA, 12, junho 1976, p. 65–90, bibl.)

Author explains that *candomblé* is a term used in Bahia to denote a religious group whose divinities are known as *orishas* (i.e., saints) and who believe in the phenomenon of possession or mystical trance. Author de-

scribes how the term *nação* (i.e., nation) as used by *candomblé* groups connotes the ideological/ritual aspects of their cult, its significance being more theological than political.

9339 Lopes, José Sérgio Leite. O vapor do diabo: o trabalho dos operários do açúcar. Rio, Editora Paz e Terra, 1976. 220 p., bibl. (Col. Estudos brasileiros, 10)

Anthropological study of working conditions in the Brazilian sugar industry based on field research conducted in 1972 in Pernambuco. Author sheds light on changing aspects of the sugar plantation.

Lopes, Juarez Rubens Brandão. Développement capitaliste et structure agraire au Brésil. See item **3483**.

Loureiro, Maria Rita Garcia. Parceria e capitalismo. See item **3486**.

McDowell, Bart. Brazil's golden beachhead. See item **5668**.

9340 Maciel, Marco Antônio. Aspectos sócio-políticos da urbanização brasileira (Política [Fundação Milton Campos, Brasília] 6, out./dez. 1977, p. 38–45)

General analysis of sociopolitical aspects of urbanization in Brazil. Author's ultimate goal is to influence Brazilian policymakers while there is still time to control the expansion and proliferation of cities. A sensible policy of urbanization would foster better living conditions for urban population.

9341 Makler, Harry M. Labor problems of native, migrant, and foreign-born members of the Recife industrial elite (JDA, 9:1, Oct. 1974, p. 27–51, tables)

Author finds that geographic mobility constitutes an important determinant of attitudes and behavior. He also compares interrelations of native, migrant and foreign-born and the economic conditions of their businesses or firms.

9342 Malloy, James M. Social insurance policy in Brazil: a study in the politics of inequality (IAMEA, 30:3, Winter 1976, p. 41–67, bibl.)

Author argues that there is no chance of building a "socialist society" in Brazil given the interventionist nature of the Brazilian state. The latter seeks, instead, to develop a sort of "state-capitalism" whereby the state can intervene to regulate the capitalist market without abolishing it. Author believes the system of social insurance exemplifies this policy having, therefore, a "negative effect on working men and women." For political scientist's comment, see item **7556**.

————. Social security policy and the working class in twentieth-century Brazil. See item **7557**.

Manfroi, Olívio. A colonizaçõ italiana no Rio Grande do Sul: implicações económicas, políticas e culturais. See item **5665**.

9343 ————. Religion d'attestation et créativité communautaire: l'immigration italienne au Rio Grande do Sul, 1875– 1914 (CNRS/ASR, 21:41, jan./juin 1976, p. 55–75)

Author establishes analogy between the religious beliefs and practices of two groups: Italian immigrants to Rio Grande do Sul and Afro-Brazilians as analyzed by Roger Bastide. Common features are: use of religion as a psychological prop; the rise of spontaneous communities of worship; construction of churches; choice and role of lay priests; etc.

9344 Margolis, Maxine. Historical perspectives on frontier agriculture as an adaptive strategy (AAA/AE, 4:1, Feb. 1977, p. 42–64, bibl.)

Careful examination of ecological and economic factors which result in resource depletion of a certain type of agricultural frontier (i.e., cash crop). Author argues that adaptive strategies typical of frontier cultivators are analogous to "fugitive strategies" characteristic of certain non-human species. These strategies account for the exploitative nature of frontier agriculture, one which leads to partial resource depletion or long-term ecological destruction. For geographer's comment, see item **5667**.

Martínez-Alier, Verena and **Armando Bioto Júnior.** The hoe and the vote: rural labourers and the national election in Brazil in 1974. See item **7558**.

9345 Martins, Carlos Estevam. Integración social y movilización política de la clase baja urbana del Brasil (FLACSO/RLCP, 2:1, abril 1971, p. 47–72, tables)

Purpose of study was to examine how "marginal populations" such as exist in Brazil function vis à vis the rest of society. Author concludes that they operate very much like

other sectors or as an integral part of the whole. He based his data on representative samples from 14 favelas in Rio and 16 in São Paulo, encompassing a total of 1,500 individuals.

9346 Medeiros, Laudelino Teixeira de. Formação da sociedade rio-grandense: ensaios. Porto Alegre, Brazil, Edições URGS (Univ. Federal do Rio Grande do Sul), 1975. 118 p., bibl., tables.

Three essays, two socio-historical and one demographic, analyze the socio-cultural characteristics of Rio Grande do Sul.

9347 Medina, C.A. de and **M. L. Rodrigues de Almeida.** Estudo das condições culturais da realidade nacional (CLAPCS/AL, 16, 1973/1975, p. 123–167, tables)

Examines the role played by radio, TV, newspapers, movies, theaters, museums, and libraries in the major Brazilian municipalities. The authors use data available for the years 1967 and 1972. The most significant factor for the existence, or lack thereof, of cultural activities was the presence or absence of a "cultural elite."

9348 ———— and ————. Hábitos de leitura: uma abordagem sociológica (CLAPCS/AL, 17, 1976, p. 70–129, tables)

Study which explores the development of reading habits among children. Informants were members of 50 families who lived in Rio and were selected on the basis of their socioeconomic status and children's age. Authors conclude that the family context influences the development of reading habits.

9349 ———— and others. Condições socioculturais do relacionamento familiar na transformação da sociedade brasileira (CLAPCS/AL, 16, 1973/1975, p. 3–37, tables)

On the basis of data gathered in three Rio boroughs (*municípios*) among high-school senior and high-school graduates, authors evaluate the Brazilian educational system and how the family transmits cultural values. In families where the chief priority is economic survival, sons are sent out into the job market very early, while daughters are kept at home for protection. In more traditional families, both boys and girls are sent to school. One interesting conclusion of the study is that neither school nor family play the principal role in transmitting cultural values. The media (TV, radio) appears to be the real teacher.

9350 ——— and others. Estudo das condições de programas de aperfeiçoamento cultural num contexto de comunicação
intergeracional (CLAPCS/AL, 16, 1973/1975,
p. 56–85, illus.)

Study which attempts to define the role
of the school as a cultural institution, based
on an examination of teacher activity and
community attitudes. High school seniors and
their teachers were the principal informants.
Authors conclude that the media is increasingly more relevant in both school and
home; that school and family are both increasingly more concerned with job opportunities; and that the young feel that only by
generating their own activities will they participate in the larger world of culture.

9351 Melatti, Delvair Montagner. Aspectos
da organização social dos Kaingáng
Paulistas. São Paulo?, Fundação Nacional do
Indio [and] Depto. Geral de Planejamento
Comunitário, Divisão de Estudos e Pesquisas,
1976. 172 p., bibl., maps, plates, tables.

Report on the few systematic studies
based on the Kaingang Indians who live in
Vanuire, São Paulo state. Field work used anthropological techniques to report on the
group's history, social organization, economic
and political life, the supernatural, health,
etc.

9352 Mello, Sylvia Leser de. Psicologia e
profissão em São Paulo. São Paulo, Editora Atica, 1975. 152 p., bibl., tables
(Ensaios, 16)

Study which analyzes the profession of
psychologist as practiced in Brazil today. Author is concerned with the limited scope of
the profession, especially in São Paulo, and
describes the causes which led to existing conditions. She attributes them to historical
processes and to the professional environment.

9353 Melo, José Marques de. Subdesenvolvimento, urbanização e comunicação. Petrópolis, Brazil, Editora Vozes,
1976. 89 p., bibl., tables (Col. Estudos
brasileiros, 5)

A collection of six essays discuss
"means of communication" in Brazil. The author analyzes their historical, social and
cultural context. The author's theoretical concerns are designed to serve as a basis for
discussion as well as for use in communications programs.

9354 ——— comp. Comunicação/inco-
municação no Brasil. São Paulo, Edições
Loyola, 1976. 207 p., tables (Biblioteca universitária de comunicação, 1)

Collection of essays by some of the
best-known living Brazilian scholars (e.g.,
Manuel Diégues, Jr., Oliveiros S. Ferreira, Antonio Fausto Neto, etc.). The subject is the
question of communication in Brazil and aspects discussed are: decadence of regional
culture; the crisis of the small newspaper; the
authenticity of folk-processes of communication; the "fatalism" which prevades rural
communication; the cultural universe of poverty; etc.

9355 Meneghini, L.C. A sombra do Plâtano.
Porto Alegre, Brazil, 1974. 198 p., bibl.,
plates.

Book of essays by well-known neu-
rologist from Rio Grande do Sul reminiscing
about his clinical experiences in the course
of 20 years of professional life. Has many
worthwhile observations for those interested
in the social history of medical care and mental health in southern Brazil.

9356 Minicucci, Agostinho. Análise transa-
cional pela imagem. São Paulo, Cortez
& Moraes, 1976. 114 p., illus., tables.

This work intends to disseminate notions from transactional analysis through the
use of cartoons by a well-known Brazilian
artist. For the general public.

9357 Miranda, Glaura Vasques de. Participación de la mujer en la fuerza de
trabajo de una sociedad en vía de desarrollo: el
caso del Brasil (ACEP/EP, 1:2, nov. 1976, p.
608–626, bibl., tables)

This analysis of the participation of
women in the job market reveals that education is a major factor in female employment.
Despite the great expansion of the educational
sector in recent years, women make up a
small segment of the Brazilian labor force.
Moreover, author concludes, the economic development of dependent capitalism does not
promote the creation of additional jobs in the
primary and secondary sectors where lower-
class women (with the least education) are
mostly employed.

Molotnik, J.R. Politics and popular culture in
Brazil. See item **7561**.

9358 Montenegro, Abelardo Fernando. O
feminismo no Ceará (DPB/RICS, 27/28,
1976, p. 277–285)
Historical account of feminism in the
state of Ceará. After a brief narrative of its
development and an examination of the roles
of female characters in key literary works,
author concludes that there exists a trend
away from dependency, exploitation and isolation towards a revolutionary consciousness
which is visible in contemporary literature.

9359 ———. Soriano de Albuquerque: um
pioneiro da sociologia no Brasil. 2. ed.
Fortaleza, Brazil, Univ. Federal do Ceará, Imprensa Universitária, 1977. 155 p., plate.
A biographical work, with brief critical
analysis, of the life-and-works of a pioneer
sociologist born in the state of Ceará in 1877.

9360 Montero, Paulo and Renato Ortiz.
Contribuição para um estudo quan-
titativo da religião umbandista (SBPC/CC,
28:4, abril 1976, p. 407–416, tables)
The authors regard this study as an
"identity card" for the study of *umbanda* in
Brazil. They provide a quantitative profile
derived from a survey of 590 participants,
members of 35 nuclei, in the greater São Paulo
area. Authors also discuss the nature of *umbanda* trances, recruitment and education as
well as the development of the cult.

9361 Mota, Mauro. Cara e c'roa: uma fase
do Instituto Joaquim Nabuco de Pesquisas Sociais. Recife, Brazil, Dialgraf, 1974.
144 p., illus.
Short monograph chronicles the period
1956–70 in the life of the Instituto Joaquim
Nabuco for Social Research located in Recife.
Includes statement of policy, list and description of the many research activities,
publications, and curricula.

9362 O'Gorman, Frances. Aluanda. Rio,
Livraria Francisco Alves Editora, 1977.
108 p.
Short, ethnographic monograph of the
umbanda religious cult center in the state of
Santa Catarina. Interestingly, this state which
is among the least influenced by African traditions, is now undergoing a great upsurge of
Afro-Brazilian cults which have, until now,
been traditional of Bahía.

9363 Oliveira, Nei Roberto da Silva. A juventude como status permanente

(CLAPCS/AL, 15, 1973/1975, p. 86–122, bibl.,
tables)
This study is based on data compiled
via a survey administered to 221 students of
both sexes from three Rio universities. After
analyzing their opinion on drugs, generational
conflict, family relations, and personal aspirations, the author concludes that these
students perceive "youth" not as a stage of life
but as a permanent condition.

9364 Oliveira, Roberto Cardoso de. Identidade, etnia e estrutura social. São Paulo,
Livraria Pioneira Editora, 1976. 118 p., bibl.
(Biblioteca Pioneira de ciências sociais.
Sociologia)
Examination of "ethnicity" as an ideological concept and as a mode of "collective
representation." Author examines the question of "identity," its links with social
structure, and how the mechanism of this
linkage conditions minority behavior and determines ideological formulations. Through
this analysis, author unveils new ways of perceiving ethnic minorities and their reactions
with dominant societies. Although the empirical data concerns Amerindian-European
relations in Brazil, the author's analytic and
interpretative model has a wider theoretical
applicability.

9365 Oliven, Ruben George. Integração sócio-cultural de grupos sociais em Porto
Alegre (SBPC/CC, 26:9, set. 1974, p. 831–
834)
This article reports the conclusion of
two research projects on sociocultural integration of social groups in Porto Alegre. The
first project analyzed upward social mobility;
the second, designed to clarify the first, examines this issue by studying five different
groups on the basis of income.

9366 ———. A integração sócio-cultural
dos moradores da Vila Farrapos na
Cidade de Pôrto Alegre (UMG/RBEP, 38, jan.
1974, p. 181–191, tables)
Research note dealing with the integration of villagers to the city of Porto Alegre.
Includes brief discussion of the problem, its
frame, schemas for data analysis, and methodology questions.

9367 Ornellas, Manoelita de. Gaúchos de
beduínos: a origem étnica e a formação
social do Rio Grande do Sul. Prefácio de
Erico Veríssimo. 3. ed. Rio, Livraria José

Olympio Editora *em convênio com o* Instituto Nacional do Livro, Brasília, 1976. 309 p., bibl., plates (Col. Documentos brasileiros, 57)

Reprint of book originally published in 1948 (see *HLAS 14:2302*) which traces the historical origins of the Brazilian *gaúcho* by discussing its Portuguese origins and the influence of *maragatos* (Rio Grande do Sul revolutionaries of the 1890s). Most important of all, however, is author's parallel between the gaúcho and the Arabic Bedouin who also roams the land and shares many common traits (i.e., myths, superstitions, customs, clothing, attitude towards the horse, traditions, etc.).

9368 Ortiz, Renato. Reflexões sobre o Carnaval (SBPC/CC, 28:12, dez. 1976, p. 1407–1412)

Sociological essay on Bahía's Carnaval which perceives the festival as structured along a series of different times (e.g., hot/cold; static/dynamic; etc.). Author uses lyrics and roles traditional in the Bahía Carnaval to substantiate his analysis.

9369 Osório, Carlos. Absorção dos migrantes na região metropolitana do Recife (BNB/REN, 7:4, out./dez. 1976, p. 581–603, tables)

Analysis of the effects of migration on the sectorial structure of the labor market in metropolitan Recife which shows that participation in the labor market is very different for natives and migrants and that incomes are higher among the latter.

9370 Pacheco, Eliezer. Colonização e racismo: relações raciais em uma zona de colonização européia. Rio, Editora Artenova *em co-edição com* Fidene, 1976. 46 p., bibl., tables.

Short monograph examines the existence of ethnic prejudice among descendants of Italians and Germans in Rio Grande do Sul, comparable to similar groups in Salvador, Bahía. Data compiled by the author (some of which reveals that elementary school children are among the least prejudiced of all) leads him to conclude that ethnic prejudice is more closely related to age than to educational level.

9371 Pebayle, Raymond. Une typologie de l'innovation rurale au Brésil (SGB/COM, 27:108, oct./dic. 1974, p. 338–355)

Sociological analysis of rural inno-

vation in Brazil, a topic more studied by geographers. Author defines "rural innovation" as a change that transforms, in a more or less radical fashion, the traditional occupation and use of the land. He offers a typology of innovations on the basis of their complexity, modalities of adoption, and patterns of spatial diffusion. Author includes a comparative table which illustrates his attempt at establishing a new typology for rural innovation in Brazil.

9372 Pereira, Eloy Lacava. Brasil do imigrante. Caxias do Sul, Brazil, Tipografia São Paulo, 1974. 137 p., bibl.

Collection of essays on the impact of Italian immigration on Brazilian society. Author discusses the Italian contribution and cultural complex and compares them with those of the original Portuguese colonizers and their descendants.

9373 Piazza, Walter Fernando. Colonização italiana em Santa Catarina. Florianópolis, Brazil, Govêrno do Estado de Santa Catarina, 1976. 89 p., plate, tables.

Short monograph discusses many aspects of the Italian colonization of Santa Catarina (e.g., reasons for the migration from Italy towards Brazil; evolution of the population of Santa Catarina since 1835; a case-study of the origins of the Italian colony known as Nova Italia; the general conditions of the population of Italian descent in today's Santa Catarina; etc.).

9374 Queiroz, Maria Isaura Pereira de. Classes sociais no Brasil: 1950–1960 (SBPC/CC, 27/7, julho 1975, p. 735–756, bibl.)

Analysis of social classes in Brazil for the period 1950–60. After a discussion of what constitutes "social class" in Brazil, the author analyzes many aspects of the problem (e.g., stratification of the rural sector; classes in the urban sector; mechanisms of their dynamics and interactions; etc.). Author concludes by noting that during the period in question Brazil did not have "homogeneous stratification" (the combination of a traditional economic with a more "social" differentiation). She attributes this to the heterogeneity of labor organizations and the diversity peculiar to the country.

9375 ———. Coletividades negras: ascensão sócio–econômica dos negros no

Brasil e em São Paulo (SBPC/CC, 29:6, junho 1977, p. 647–663, bibl.)

Analysis of what is "ethnic coexistence" in the Brazilian context. Author examines the many contradictory notions of "race," "caste," and "class" in the case of Brazilian blacks. This article is also available in French as "Collectivités Noires et Montée Socio-Economique des Noirs au Brésil," *Caravelles* (Univ. de Toulouse, 22, 1974, p. 105–131).

9376 ———. A condição feminina no Brasil: problemas atuais (SBPC/CC, 24:10, out. 1972, p. 933–937)

Brief report on a symposium held on "The Condition of Women in Brazil." Some of the data submitted at this meeting contradicted traditional perceptions of what constitutes "women's work" and their position in the labor market.

———. O mandonismo local na vida política brasileira e outros ensaios. See item **7573**.

9377 ———. Messiahs, miracle workers and "Catholic duality" in Brazil (UN/ISSJ, 29:2, 1977, p. 298–312, bibl.)

Author disputes the adequacy of dual taxonomies for the study of religious or other social phenomena. She contends that such dychotomies (e.g., "Catholic duality in Brazil") stem from ideological concepts which distort social reality to fit preconceptions. Instead, she advocates systematic theoretical thinking which will, in turn, lead to a rigorous and coherent analysis of social reality.

9378 ———. Mythes des paysans brésiliens (UP/TM, 15:57, jan./mars 1974, p. 205–216)

Article which analyzes the myths of Brazilian peasants and raises a number of questions in this context (e.g., possible universality of peasant myths; nature of their dynamics, cyclical or linear; conflicting goals, reformist or revolutionary; cognitive impact, visions of the world and/or notions of time; etc.).

9379 ———. Notas sociológicas sobre o cangaço (SBPC/CC, 27:5, maio 1975, p. 495–516)

Author contributes additional thoughts to the subject of the *cangaço* in the Brazilian Northeast (life-style of its regional outlaws). She focuses on the historical and cultural explanations of this phenomenon and concludes by comparing the rather narrow, sociological interpretation of the *cangaço* with political explanations and its portrayals in literature and art.

9380 ———. Novas orientações da sociologia no Brasil (SBPC/CC, 26:7, julho 1974, p. 637–641)

There is at present a growing interest in rural sociology in Brazil. The author attributes this to increasing socioeconomic pressures and an intensified search for new means of development.

9381 ———. Singularidades sócio-culturais do desenvolvimento brasileiro (USP/RIEB, 16, 1975, p. 62–81, bibl.)

The author notes that current studies of Brazilian development can be compared to Jacques Berque's studies of the Arab countries of the Maghreb. The introduction of significant changes into agrarian societies do not bring about a new being. On the contrary, changes in this context tend to reinforce existing differences turning development into a far more complex process than anticipated.

9382 ———. A sociologia brasileira na década de 40 e a contribuição de Roger Bastide (SBPC/CC, 29:12, dez. 1977, p. 1353–1361)

The author discusses the contributions of Roger Bastide to Brazilian sociology in the 1940s. She contends that social reality consists of oppositions, tensions, and conflicts which, in turn, lead to changes in that reality.

9383 Queiroz, Paulo Edmur de Souza. A sociologia política de Oliveira Vianna. São Paulo, Editora Convívio, 1975. 142 p., bibl.

This is the first systematic critical evaluation of the work of Oliveira Vianna, a classic of Brazilian political sociology. Author focuses on Vianna's theory of historical reconstruction of political structures, conjunctures, and their transformations.

9384 Rattner, Henrique. Tradição e mudança: a comunidade judaica em São Paulo. São Paulo, Editora Atica, 1977. 198 p., bibl., tables (Ensaios, 27)

Study of the establishment, development and dynamics of the Jewish community of São Paulo. Author has collected field data and is especially interested in inter-group relations, socioeconomic mobility, and cultural survival.

9385 Requixa, Renato. O lazer no Brasil. São Paulo, Editora Brasiliense, 1977. 111 p.

A book about the sociology of leisure in Brazil, the first on the subject. Author discusses the role of play in the formation of Brazilian ethnic groups; industrialization, urbanization, and their impact on leisure; contemporary manifestations of leisure in Brazil; etc.

9386 Reynolds, Clark W. and Robert T. Carpenter. Housing finance in Brazil: towards a new distribution of wealth (in Cornelius, Wayne A. and Felicity M. Trueblood eds. Urbanization of inequality [see HLAS 39:9016] p. 147–174, bibl., tables)

In Latin America a transfer of wealth among groups is often a consequence of certain phenomena associated with urbanization (e.g., migration, urban growth, expansion of urban infrastructures, real estate speculation, etc.). This article examines how Brazil's Housing Finance System has operated to redistribute wealth since the mid-1960s. The authors are especially interested in the impact which the flow of funds has had on the society as a whole.

9387 Ribeiro, Joaquim. Os brasileiros. Rio, Editora Pallas em convênio com o Instituto Nacional do Livro, Brasília, 1977. 593 p.

Book which consists of descriptions of the major social types in the various cultural regions of Brazil (e.g., praieiros; jangadeiros; caiçaras; roceiros; sertanejos; vaqueiros da caatinga; vaqueiros da chapada; vaqueiros do pantanal; montanheses; igariteiros da Amazônia; guascas do pampa; garimpeiros; etc.). Final discussion examines Brazilian mysticism and messianism as well as sensuality and leisure.

9388 Ribeiro, Jorge. Aspectos sociológicos do problema do menor abandonado (FREA/BES, 1, dez. 1972, p. 29–40, bibl.)

Examination of the extent of child neglect in Brazil and of the social-welfare mechanisms designed to cope with the problem. Author believes confinement of the children is not the solution. He attributes the anomalous personalities of these abandoned youngsters to lack of family environment or notions of kinship, minimal education and/or training, and the indifference to their plight of a mass society. He believes these children are doomed to a precarious existence without eventual participation in the community.

9389 Rio Grande do Sul (state), *Brazil*. **Secretaria do Trabalho e Ação Social. Unidade de Serviços Sociais.** Marginalização em Cachoeira do Sul: pesquisa realizada nas vilas Bom Retiro, Cavalheiro, Cristo Rei, Marques Ribeiro, Nosso Senhora Aparecida e Tupinambá. Porto Alegre, Brazil, 1974. 54 p., tables.

Study of social marginality in the município of Cachoeira do Sul commissioned by the state government of Rio Grande do Sul, in order to formulate a welfare-policy program. Data was compiled on the basis of interviews with 400 families.

9390 Rizzini, Jorge. O sexo nas prisões. São Paulo, Nova Epoca Editorial, 1976. 109 p.

Short look on the sex life of Brazilian prison inmates. It reports the result of several round tables on the topic which were held in São Paulo. Also discusses legal aspects and pronouncements by jurists of relevance to the subject.

Roche, Jean. A colonização alemã no Espírito Santo. See HLAS 40:4163.

9391 Rossini, Rosa Ester. Estado de São Paulo: a intensidade das migrações e do êxodo rural/urbano (SBPC/CC, 29:7, julho 1977, p. 779–803, tables)

Author calls for vigorous government action to deal with the rural exodus which is occurring in Brazil. She reviews data on population and migration, especially for the 1960–70 decade in the state of São Paulo. She believes that, unless adequate measures are adopted, short and long-term problems of difficult solution will arise.

Russell-Wood, A.J.R. Women and society in colonial Brazil. See HLAS 40:4045.

9392 Saffioti, Heleieth Iara Bongiovani. A mulher na sociedade de clases: mito e realidade. Petrópolis, Brazil, Editora Vozes, 1976. 383 p., bibl. (Col. Sociologia brasileira, 4)

Study of Brazilian women in three parts. Pt. 1 examines the relation of women and capitalism; pt. 2, the evolution of women in Brazil; and pt. 3, the contemporary mystique regarding the role of women. Author follows the theoretical approach and methodology of Durkheim.

9393 ———. Profissionalização de sociólogos (SBPC/CC, 28:6, junho 1976, p. 625–640, tables)

Study contends that, after a certain stage in their careers, social-science students in Brazil perform as if they lived in a constant "state of ambiguity." Author attributes this to the curricula's undue stress on theory which leads to an overemphasis on theoretical speculation as the supreme intellectual pursuit.

9394 **Saito, Hiroshi.** The integration and participation of the Japanese and their descendants in Brazilian society (ICEM/IM, 14:3, 1976, p. 183–199, bibl., tables)

The article describes the arrival of the first Japanese immigrants to Brazil in 1908 and changes in attitude and behaviour since that date. The Brazilian population of Japanese extraction is estimated today at 750,000. The majority work in agriculture (57.2 percent); commerce (40 percent); and services. The establishment of large Japanese business enterprises began about 1969 and by 1973 there were 300 Japanese-owned businesses in Sao Paulo alone. Indeed, in large urban centers such as São Paulo, Japanese integration into the general population is already a fact. The process, however, is taking longer in smaller cities and rural areas, where Japanese-Brazilians still keep to themselves. For geographer's comment, see item 5695.

9395 **Sartori, Luís Maria A.** O encontro humano dentro da empresa: a empresa a caminho de ser comunidade. São Paulo, Edições Paulinas, 1976. 108 p., bibl. (Col. Encontros do operário com Cristo)

Brazilian Catholic publication analyzes labor relations in industry and provides a general introduction to the layman on the topic.

9396 **Siegel, Bernard J.** The Contestado Rebellion, 1912–16: a case study in Brazilian messianism and regional dynamics (UNM/JAR, 33:2, Summer 1977, p. 202–213, bibl., map)

An essay which reevaluates the well-known messianic movement of southern Brazil. Author believes the Contestado Rebellion demonstrated the strength of regional politics during the Republic but notes that the political environment of "coronelismo" proved weak in the long run by failing to assimilate important outside influences (i.e. international enterprise, influx of foreigners, growth of native population, etc.). For historian's comment, see *HLAS 40:4171*.

9397 **Sigaud, Lygia.** The idealization of the past in a plantation area: the Northeast of Brazil (*in* Nash, June and Juan Corradi *eds*. Ideology and social change in Latin America [see *HLAS 38:2394*] v. 1, p. 167–182)

Anthropological survey of how rural workers perceive advantages and drawbacks of modernization and commercialization of agricultural labor since early 1960s. [R.J. Barman]

9398 **Silva, Aguinaldo.** O crime antes de festa: a história de Angela Diniz e seus amigos. Rio, Editora Lidador, 1977. 136 p.

A social report which provides a detailed analysis of a crime that took place in Buzios (Rio de Janeiro state). Author attempts to explore the social and economic factors which led to the tragedy. Addressed to the layman.

Singer, Paul and others. Capital e trabalho no campo. See item **3525**.

9399 **Siqueira, Moema Miranda de.** O papel da função administrativa na evolução urbana de Belo Horizonte (UMG/RBEP, 44, jan. 1977, p. 103–125, tables)

Study of the role of public administration in the development of the city of Belo Horizonte. Includes discussion of trade; banking; financial institutions; administrative services; consulting and publicity services; education; health; recreational facilities; etc. Concludes that public administration has played a key role in the urban transformation of Belo Horizonte.

9400 **Slater, Paul B.** Internal migration regions of Argentina and Brazil: application of hierarchical clustering to doubly standardized lifetime migration tables (IASI/E, 30:114, julio 1976, p. 3–12, tables)

Application of cluster analysis to regions of internal migration in Brazil reveals that the city of Rio and Guanabara constitute the strongest pair and are, in a sense, analogous to the City of Buenos Aires (Capital Federal) and the outlying suburbs (Gran Buenos Aires). Author groups São Paulo with the southern rather than southeastern states. Minas Gerais merges, at a slightly higher threshold, with this cluster rather than with Rio, Guanabara and Espírito Santo. Another well defined combination is made up of Rio Grande do Norte, Paraíba, Pernambuco, and Alagoas. The largest and clearly distinct cluster, however, is the southern one.

9401 Soares, Gláucio Ari Dillon. Notas metodológicas sobre as conseqüências políticas da migração interna (UMG/RBEP, 45, julho 1977, p. 59–92, tables)

Author notes that the study of the political consequences of migration is still limited. He attributes this to the fact that it is difficult to distinguish the levels of analysis in published studies (e.g., underpopulation; direct and indirect effects; meanings implicit in concepts such as "radicalization;" etc.). The author offers some guidelines to deal with this problem.

9402 Souza, João Crisóstomo de. Teorias do subdesenvolvimento e comprensão crítica da sociedade brasileira (Cadernos do CEAS [Centro de Estudos e Ação Social, Salvador, Brazil] 31, maio/junho 1974, p. 22–41)

An article which examines whether three different theories of development (i.e., linear, dualist, and dependency) contribute to our understanding of Brazilian society. Author notes that all three represent ideological exercises which do not bear much relation to reality. In fact, he attributes the lack of rigorous criticism and the extent of ideological overlapping to the prevalence of these interpretations.

9403 Souza, Percival de. A prisão: histórias dos homens que vivem no maior presídio do mundo. São Paulo, Editora Alfa-Omega, 1977. 128 p. (Biblioteca Alfa-Omega de comunicação e artes. Série 1. História inmediata, 1)

Consists of interviews conducted by a journalist with the inmates of one of Brazil's largest prisons (the Detention House of São Paulo, pop. 6,300). The material is mostly descriptive but rich in insights into the men's lives, their involvement with crime, attitudes towards the police and society, etc.

9404 Studart, Heloneida and Wilson Cunha. A primeira vez . . . à brasileira. Rio, Ediçoes Nosso Tempo, 1977. 231 p.

Attempt to provide data on the sexual lives of Brazilian women. Consists of short interviews with females of various social and economic strata, most of them recounting their first sexual experience.

9405 Tavares-Neto, José and Eliane S. Azevêdo. Racial origin and historical aspects of family names in Bahia, Brazil (WSU/HB, 49:3, Sept. 1977, p. 287–299, bibl., tables)

Analysis of racial origins and history of family names in the state of Bahía. Using documents from the 18th and 19th centuries, the authors culled 6,002 names from a mixed population. Their investigation revealed that since the majority of slaves had only first names those who used surnames after abolition had selected devotional ones or, in some instances, their master's. For historian's comment, see *HLAS 40:4019.*

Tsukuba Daigaku. Latin America Tokubetsu Kenkyu Project. Jumbi Iinkai. Burajiru to Nippon. See item **5711.**

9406 Universidade do Vale do Rio dos Sinos, *São Leopoldo, Brazil.* **Centro de Documentação e Pesquisa.** População e família: a dinâmica populacional brasileira (VOZES, 66:6, agôsto 1972, p. 57–60, tables)

Study of the lack of family-planning facilities and services for the Brazilian public in general and the poor in particular. The study attributes this lack to religious and political prejudices.

9407 Valladares, Lícia do Prado. Associações voluntárias na favela (SBPC/CC, 29:12, dez. 1977, p. 1390–1403)

Attempt to describe and analyze the internal organization of the Brazilian shantytown *(favela).* Author notes how different elements or groups in the favelas interact among each other and with the society as a whole. She shows that there exists indeed a local dynamics but one that is largely dependent on outside support. These external linkages (with external support groups) reinforce and define local power groups.

9408 Velho, Gilberto *ed.* Arte e sociedade: ensaios de sociologia da arte. Rio, Zahar Editores, 1977. 169 p., bibl., music (Biblioteca de antropologia social)

Collection of essays on art and society including three by Brazilian scholars: Gilberto Velho's "Avant-Garde and Deviation;" José Sergio Leite Porto's "Kinship Relations and Property Relations in the 'Sugar-Cane' Novels of José Lins do Rego;" and Alfredo Wagner B. de Almeida's "A Genealogy of Euclides da Cunha."

9409 Wanderley, Maria de Nazareth Baudel.
Algumas reflexões sobre o campesinato do Nordeste: conceito e realidade (SBPC/CC, 29:5, maio 1977, p. 537–544)

In pre-capitalist economies, the peasantry constitutes one of the principal productive classes whose configuration is determined by certain elements. Using this frame of reference, author analyzes the peasantry of the Northeast.

9410 Weber, Silke. Formação escolar e funções profissionais do sociólogo (SBPC/CC, 28:7, julho 1976, p. 758–761)

A short paper on the professional training of Brazilian sociologists. Data was collected from a survey of second-year social-science students at the Univ. of Pernambuco. Author concludes that professional training is affected by both the political process and the labor market.

9411 Wirth, John D. and Robert L. Jones
eds. Manchester and São Paulo: problems in rapid urban growth. Stanford, Calif., Stanford Univ. Press, 1978. 234 p., bibl., tables.

Collection of papers about two cities which share structural similarities. The topics are: 1) changing city-hinterland relations, including migration; 2) spatial organization problems; 3) changing patterns of production and labor organization; 4) problems of adapting to city life; 5) changing political strategies of city elites; and 6) intellectuals' and artists' perceptions of phenomena without precedent. Authors are: historian Richard Morse; literary critic Iumna Maria Simon; economist Martin T. Katzman; and anthropologists Robert W. Shirley and Peter Fry. [Ed.]

JOURNAL ABBREVIATIONS
SOCIOLOGY

AAA/AE American Ethnologist. American Anthropological Association. Washington.

ACEP/EP Estudios de Población. Asociación Colombiana para el Estudio de la Población. Bogotá.

AGS/GR The Geographical Review. American Geographical Society. N.Y.

AISCD Archives Internationales de Sociologie de la Coopération et du Développement. Paris.

ASA/ASR American Sociological Review. American Sociological Association. Menasha, Wis.

BBAA B.B.A.A. Boletín Bibliográfico de Antropología Americana. Instituto Panamericano de Geografía e Historia, Comisión de Historia. México.

BESPL Berichte zur Entwicklung in Spanien, Portugal, Lateinamerika. München, FRG.

BNB/REN Revista Econômica do Nordeste. Banco do Nordeste do Brasil, Depto. de Estudos Econômicos do Nordeste. Fortaleza, Brazil.

BNJM/R Revista de la Biblioteca Nacional José Martí. La Habana.

CDLA Casa de las Américas. Instituto Cubano del Libro. La Habana.

CEDLA/B Boletín de Estudios Latinoamericanos. Centro de Estudios y Documentación Latinoamericanos. Amsterdam.

CLACSO/ERL Estudios Rurales Latinoamericanos. Consejo Latinoamericano de Ciencias Sociales, Secretaría Ejecutiva y de la Comisión de Estudios Rurales. Bogotá.

CLAPCS/AL América Latina. Centro Latino-Americano de Pesquisas em Ciências Sociais. Rio.

CNC/RMA Revista del México Agrario. Confederación Nacional Campesina. México.

CNRS/ASR Archives de Sociologie des Religions. Centre Nationale de la Recherche Scientifique. Paris.

CP Cuadernos Políticos. Revista trimestral. Ediciones Era. México.

CPES/RPS Revista Paraguaya de Sociología. Centro Paraguayo de Estudios Sociológicos. Asunción.

CSUCA/ESC Estudios Sociales Centroamericanos. Consejo Superior de Universidades Centroamericanas, Confederación Universitaria Centroamericana, Programa Centroamericana de Ciencias Sociales. San José.

DPB/RICS Revista del Instituto de Ciencias Sociales. Diputación Provincial de Barcelona. Barcelona, Spain.

EME Revista Eme-Eme. Estudios dominicanos. Univ. Católica Madre y Maestra. Santiago de los Caballeros, R.D.

FLACSO/RLCP Revista Latinoamericana de Ciencia Política. Facultad Latinoamericana de Ciencias Sociales, Escuela Latinoamericana de Ciencia Política y Administración Pública. Santiago.

FREA/BES Boletim de Estudos Sociais. Fundação Regional Educacional de Avaré. São Paulo.

IAMEA Inter-American Economic Affairs. Washington.

IASI/E Estadística. Inter-American Statistical Institute. Washington.

ICEM/IM International Migration [Migrations Internationales] [Migraciones Internacionales]. Quarterly review of the Intergovernmental Committee for European Migration [and] Research Group for European Migration Problems. Geneva.

IEC/REC *See* IFC/REC.

IFC/REC Revue des Études Coopératives. Institut Français de la Coopération. Paris.

IFH/C Conjonction. Institut Français d'Haïti. Port-au-Prince.

III/AI América Indígena. Instituto Indigenista Interamericano. México.

INAH/B Boletín del Instituto Nacional de Antropología e Historia. Secretaría de Educación Pública. México.

JDA The Journal of Developing Areas. Western Illinois Univ. Press. Macomb.

JDS The Journal of Development Studies. A quarterly journal devoted to economics, politics and social development. London.

JGSWGL Jahrbuch für Geschichte von Staat, Wirtschaft und Gesellschaft Lateinamerikas. Köln, FRG.

JLAIS/CS Cristianismo y Sociedad. Junta Latino Americana de Iglesia y Sociedad. Montevideo.

JPS The Journal of Peasant Studies. Frank Cass & Co. London.

JSP Journal of Social Psychology. The Journal Press. Provincetown, Mass.

LAP Latin American Perspectives. Univ. of California. Riverside.

LARR Latin American Research Review. Univ. of North Carolina Press *for the* Latin American Studies Association. Chapel Hill.

LSE/PS Population Studies. London School of Economics, The Population Investigation Committee. London.

NEA/RBPE The Review of Black Political Economy. National Economic Association [and] Atlanta Univ. Center. Atlanta, Ga.

NIU/JPMS Journal of Political & Military Sociology. Northern Illinois Univ., Dept. of Sociology. DeKalb.

NS NS NorthSouth NordSud NorteSur NorteSul. Canadian journal of Latin American studies. Canadian Association of Latin American Studies. Univ. of Ottawa.

NYAS/A Annals of the New York Academy of Sciences. N.Y.

RSS/RS Rural Sociology. Rural Sociological Society [and] New York State College of Agriculture. Ithaca.

SBPC/CC Ciência e Cultura. Sociedade Brasileira para o Progresso da Ciência. São Paulo.

SF Social Forces. Williams & Wilkins Co. *for the* Univ. of North Carolina Press. Baltimore, Md.

SGB/COM Les Cahiers d'Outre-Mer. Institut de Géographie de la Faculté des Lettres de Bordeaux; Institut de la France d'Outre-Mer; Société de Géographie de Bordeaux *avec le concours du* Centre National de la Recherche Scientifique [and] VI. Section de l'École Pratique des Hautes Études. Bordeaux, France.

SSQ Social Science Quarterly. Southwestern Social Science Association. Austin, Tex.

UC/AJS American Journal of Sociology. Univ. of Chicago. Chicago, Ill.

UCL/CD Cultures et Développement. Revue internationale des sciences du développement. Univ. Catholique de Louvain *avec le concours de la* Fondation Universitaire de Belgique. Louvain, Belgium.

UCR/R Revista de la Universidad de Costa Rica. San José.

UFB/AA Afro-Asia. Univ. Federal Bahia, Centro de Estudos Afro-Orientais. Bahia, Brazil.

UH/U Universidad de La Habana. La Habana.

ULB/RIS Revue de l'Institut de Sociologie. Univ. Libre de Bruxelles. Bruxelles.

UM/JIAS Journal of Inter-American Studies and World Affairs. Univ. of Miami Press *for the* Center for Advanced International Studies. Coral Gables, Fla.

UM/JNMD Journal of Nervous and Mental Disease. Univ. of Maryland, Psychiatric Institute. Baltimore, Md.

UMG/RBEP Revista Brasileira de Estudos Políticos. Univ. de Minas Gerais. Belo Horizonte, Brazil.

UN/ISSJ International Social Science Journal. United Nations Educational, Scientific and Cultural Organization. Paris.

UNAM/RMCPS Revista Mexicana de Ciencias Políticas y Sociales. Univ. Nacional Autónoma de México, Facultad de Ciencias Políticas y Sociales. México.

UNAM/RMS Revista Mexicana de Sociología. Univ. Nacional Autónoma de México, Instituto de Investigaciones Sociales. México.

UNECLA/B Economic Bulletin for Latin America. United Nations, Economic Commission for Latin America. N.Y.

UNM/JAR Journal of Anthropological Research. Univ. of New Mexico, Dept. of Anthropology. Albuquerque.

UP/A Apuntes. Univ. del Pacífico, Centro de Investigación. Lima.

UP/CSEC Cuban Studies/Estudios Cubanos. Univ. of Pittsburgh, Univ. Center for International Studies, Center for Latin American Studies. Pittsburgh, Pa.

UP/TM Tiers Monde. Problèmes des pays sous-développés. Univ. de Paris, Institut d'Étude du Développement Économique et Social. Paris.

UPR/CS Caribbean Studies. Univ. of Puerto Rico, Institute of Caribbean Studies. Río Piedras.

USC/U Universidad de San Carlos de Guatemala. Guatemala.

USCG/ES Estudios. Univ. de San Carlos de Guatemala, Facultad de Humanidades, Depto. de Historia. Guatemala.

USCG/PS Política y Sociedad. Univ. de San Carlos de Guatemala, Facultad de Ciencias Jurídicas y Sociales, Escuela de Ciencia Política, Instituto de Investigaciones Políticas y Sociales. Guatemala.

USMLA/LA La Antigua. Univ. de Santa María La Antigua, Oficina de Humanidades. Panamá.

USP/RIEB Revista do Instituto de Estudos Brasileiros. Univ. de São Paulo, Instituto de Estudos Brasileiros. São Paulo.

UT/SSQ Social Science Quarterly. Univ. of Texas, Dept. of Government. Austin.

UTIEH/C Caravelle. Cahiers du monde hispanique et luso-brésilien. Univ. de Toulouse, Institut d'Études Hispaniques, Hispano-Americaines et Luso-Brésiliennes. Toulouse, France.

UW/LE Land Economics. A quarterly journal of planning, housing and public utilities. Univ. of Wisconsin. Madison.

UWI/SES Social and Economic Studies. Univ. of the West Indies, Institute of Social and Economic Research. Mona, Jam.

UY/R Revista de la Universidad de Yucatán. Mérida, Mex.

VOZES Vozes. Revista de cultura. Editora Vozes. Petrópolis, Brazil.

WD World Development. Pergamon Press. Oxford, U.K.

WRU/JMF Journal of Marriage and the Family. Western Reserve Univ. Cleveland, Ohio.

WSU/HB Human Biology. Official publication of the Human Biology Council. Wayne State Univ., School of Medicine. Detroit, Mich.

YU/IJCS International Journal of Comparative Sociology. York Univ., Dept. of Sociology and Anthropology. Toronto, Canada.

INDEXES

ABBREVIATIONS AND ACRONYMS

Except for journal acronyms which are listed at: a) the end of each major disciplinary section, (e.g., Anthropology, Economics, etc.); and b) after each serial title in the *Title List of Journals Indexed*, p. 675.

a	annual
ABC	Argentina, Brazil, Chile
A.C.	antes de Cristo
ACAR	Associação de Crédito e Assistência Rural, Brazil
AD	Anno Domini
A.D.	Acción Democrática, Venezuela
ADESG	Associação dos Diplomados de Escola Superior de Guerra, Brazil
AGI	Archivo General de Indias, Sevilla
AGN	Archivo General de la Nación
AID	Agency for International Development
Ala.	Alabama
ALALC	Asociación Latinoamericana de Libre Comercio
ANAPO	Alianza Nacional Popular, Colombia
ANCARSE	Associação Nordestina de Crédito e Assistência Rural de Sergipe, Brazil
ANCOM	Andean Common Market
ANDI	Asociación Nacional de Industriales, Colombia
AP	Acción Popular
APRA	Alianza Popular Revolucionaria Americana
Arg.	Argentina
Ariz.	Arizona
Ark.	Arkansas
ASA	Association of Social Anthropologists of the Commonwealth, London
ASSEPLAN	Assesoria de Planejamente e Acompanhamento, Recife, Brazil
Assn.	Association
Aufl.	Auflage (edition, edición)
AUFS	American Universities Field Staff Reports, Hanover, N.H.
Aug.	August, Augustan
b.	born (nacido)
B.A.	Buenos Aires
Bar.	Barbados
BBE	Bibliografia Brasileira de Educação
b.c.	indicates dates obtained by radio-carbon methods
BC	Before Christ
bibl.	bibliography
BID	Banco Interamericano de Desarrollo
BNDE	Banco Nacional de Desenvolvimento Econômico, Brazil
BNH	Banco Nacional de Habitação, Brazil
Bol.	Bolivia
BP	before present
b/w	black-and-white
C14	Carbon 14
ca.	circa
C.A.	Centro América, Central America

CACM	Central American Common Market
CADE	Conferencia Anual de Ejecutivos de Empresas, Peru
CAEM	Centro de Altos Estudios Militares, Peru
Calif.	California
CARC	Centro de Arte y Comunicación
CARICOM	Caribbean Common Market
CARIFTA	Caribbean Free Trade Association
CBD	central business district
CD	Christian Democrats, Chile
CDI	Conselho de Desenvolvimento Industrial
CEBRAP	Centro Brasileiro de Análise e Planejamento, São Paulo
CECORA	Central de Cooperativas de la Reforma Agraria, Colombia
CEDAL	Centro de Estudios Democráticos de América Latina, Costa Rica
CEDE	Centro de Estudios sobre Desarrollo Económico, Univ. de los Andes, Bogotá
CEDEPLAR	Centro de Desenvolvimento e Planejamento Regional, Belo Horizonte, Brazil
CEDES	Centro de Estudios de Estado y Sociedad, Buenos Aires
CELADE	Centro Latinoamericano de Demografía
CEMLA	Centro de Estudios Monetarios Latinoamericanos, México
CENDES	Centro de Estudios del Desarrollo, Venezuela
CENIDIM	Centro Nacional de Información, Documentación e Investigación Musicales, Mexico
CEPADE	Centro Paraguayo de Estudios de Desarrollo Económico y Social
CEPA-SE	Comissão Estadual de Planejamento Agrícola, Sergipe, Brazil
CEPAL	*See* ECLA.
CES	constant elasticity of substitution
cf.	compare
CFI	Consejo Federal de Inversiones, B.A.
CGE	Confederación General Económica, Argentina
CGTP	Confederación General de Trabajadores del Perú
ch., chap.	chapter
CHEAR	Council on Higher Education in the American Republics
Cía.	compañía
CIA	Central Intelligence Agency
CIDA	Comité Interamericano de Desarrollo Agrícola
CIE	Centro de Investigaciones Económicas, Buenos Aires
CIP	Conselho Interministerial de Preços
CLACSO	Consejo Latinoamericano de Ciencias Sociales, Secretaría Ejecutiva, Buenos Aires
CLASC	Confederación Latinoamericana Sindical Cristiana
CLE	Comunidad Latinoamericana de Escritores, México
cm	centimeter
CNI	Confederação Nacional da Industria, Brazil
Co.	company
COBAL	Companhia Brasileira de Alimentos
Col.	collection, colección, coleção
Colo.	Colorado
COMCORDE	Comisión Coordinadora para el Desarrollo Económico, Uruguay
comp.	compiler
CONDESE	Conselho de Desenvolvimento Econômico de Sergipe, Brazil
Conn.	Connecticut
COPEI	Comité Organizador Pro-Elecciones Independientes, Venezuela
CORFO	Corporación de Fomento de la Producción, Chile
CORP	Corporación para el Fomento de Investigaciones Económicas, Colombia
Corp.	Corporation
C.R.	Costa Rica
CUNY	City University of New York

CVG	Corporación Venezolana de Guayana
d.	died
DANE	Departamento Nacional de Estadística, Colombia
DC	developed country; Demócratas Cristianos, Chile
d.C.	después de Cristo
Dec.	December, décembre
Del.	Delaware
dept.	department
depto.	departamento
dez.	dezembro
dic.	diciembre
DNOCS	Departamento Nacional de Obras Contra as Sêcas, Brazil
D.R.	Dominican Republic
Dra.	Doctora
ECLA	Economic Comission for Latin America
ECOSOC	UN Dept. of Economic and Social Affairs
Ecua.	Ecuador
ed(s).	edition(s), edición(es), editor(s), redactor(es)
EDEME	Editora Emprendimentos Educacionais Florianópolis, Brazil
Edo.	Estado
EEC	European Economic Community
EFTA	European Free Trade Association
e.g.	exempio gratia [for example]
El Sal.	El Salvador
ELN	Ejército de Liberación Nacional, Colombia
estr.	estrenado
et al	et alia [and others]
ETENE	Escritório Técnico de Estudios Econômicos do Nordeste, Brazil
ETEPE	Escritório Técnico de Planejamento, Brazil
EUDEBA	Editorial Universitaria de Buenos Aires
EWG	Europaische Wirtschaftsgemeinschaft. See EEC.
facsim.	facsimile
FAO	Food and Agriculture Organization of the United Nations
feb.	February, febrero
FEDECAFE	Federación Nacional de Cafeteros, Colombia
fev.	fevreiro, février
ff.	following
FGTS	Fundo do Garantia do Tempo de Serviço, Brazil
FGV	Fundação Getúlio Vargas
FIEL	Fundación de Investigaciones Económicas Latinoamericanas, Argentina
film.	filmography
fl.	flourished, floresció
Fla.	Florida
FLACSO	Facultad Latinoamercana de Ciencias Sociales, Buenos Aires
fold. map	folded map
fold. table	folded table
fols.	folios
FRG	Federal Republic of Germany
ft.	foot, feet
FUAR	Frente Unido de Acción Revolucionaria, Colombia
Ga.	Georgia
GAO	General Accounting Office, Washington
GATT	General Agreement on Tariffs and Trade
GDP	gross domestic product
GDR	German Democratic Republic
Gen.	General

GMT	Greenwich Meridian Time
GPA	grade point average
GPO	Government Printing Office
Guat.	Guatemala
h.	hijo
ha.	hectares, hectáreas
HLAS	*Handbook of Latin American Studies*
HMAI	*Handbook of Middle American Indians*
Hond.	Honduras
IBBD	Instituto Brasileiro de Bibliografia e Documentação
IBRD	International Bank of Reconstruction and Development
ICA	Instituto Colombiano Agropecuario
ICAIC	Instituto Cubano del Arte e Industria Cinematográficas
ICCE	Instituto Colombiano de Construcción Escolar
ICSS	Instituto Colombiano de Seguridad Social
ICT	Instituto de Crédito Territorial, Colombia
IDB	Inter-American Development Bank
i.e.	id est [that is]
IEL	Instituto Euvaldo Lodi, Brazil
IEP	Instituto de Estudios Peruanos
IERAC	Instituto Ecuatoriano de Reforma Agraria y Colonización
III	Instituto Indigenista Interamericano, Mexico
IIN	Instituto Indigenista Nacional, Guatemala
Ill.	Illinois
illus.	illustration(s)
ILO	International Labour Organization, Geneva
IMES	Instituto Mexicano de Estudios Sociales
in.	inches
INAH	Instituto Nacional de Antropología e Historia, México
INBA	Instituto Nacional de Bellas Artes, México
Inc.	incorporated
INCORA	Instituto Colombiano de Reforma Agraria
Ind.	Indiana
INEP	Instituto Nacional de Estudos Pedagógicos, Brazil
INI	Instituto Nacional Indigenista, Mexico
INIT	Instituto Nacional de Industria Turística, Cuba
INPES/IPEA	Instituto de Planejamento Econômico e Social, Instituto de Pesquisas, Brazil
IPA	Instituto de Pastoral Andina, Univ. de San Antonio de Abad, Seminario de Antropología, Cuzco, Peru
IPEA	Instituto de Pesquisa Econômico-Social Aplicada, Brazil
IPES/GB	Instituto de Pesquisas e Estudos Sociais, Guanabara, Brazil
IPHAN	Instituto do Patrimônio Histórico e Artístico Nacional, Brazil
ir.	irregular
ITT	International Telephone and Telegraph
Jam.	Jamaica
jan.	January, janeiro, Janvier
JLP	Jamaican Labour Party
JUCEPLAN	Junta Central de Planificación, Cuba
Jul.	juli
Jun.	Juni
Kans.	Kansas
km	kilometers, kilómetros
Ky.	Kentucky
l.	leaves, hojas (páginas impresas por una sola cara)
La.	Louisiana
LASA	Latin American Studies Association

LDC	less developed country
Ltda.	Limitada
m	meters, metros, monthly
M	mille, mil, thousand
MAPU	Movimiento de Acción Popular Unitario, Chile
MARI	Middle American Research Institute, Tulane University, New Orleans
Mass.	Massachusetts
MCC	Mercado Común Centro-Americano
MCN	multinational corporation
Md.	Maryland
MDB	Movimento Democrático Brasileiro
MDC	more developed countries
MEC	Ministério de Educação e Cultura, Brazil
Mex.	Mexico
Mich.	Michigan
mimeo	mimeographed, mimeografiado
min.	minutes, minutos
Minn.	Minnesota
MIR	Movimiento de Izquierda Revolucionaria, Chile
Miss.	Mississippi
MIT	Massachusetts Institute of Technology
MLN	Movimiento de Liberación Nacional
mm.	millimeter
MNR	Movimiento Nacionalista Revolucionario, Bolivia
Mo.	Missouri
MOIR	Movimiento Obrero Independiente y Revolucionario, Colombia
MRL	Movimiento Revolucionario Liberal, Colombia
ms.	manuscript
msl	mean sea level
n.	nacido (born)
N.C.	North Carolina
n.d.	no date
N. Dak.	North Dakota
Nebr.	Nebraska
neubearb.	neurbearbcitet (revised, corregida)
Nev.	Nevada
n.f.	neue Folge
N.H.	New Hampshire
Nic.	Nicaragua
NIEO	new international economic order
NIH	National Institutes of Health, Washington
N.J.	New Jersey
N. Mex.	New Mexico
no(s).	number(s), número(s)
NOSALF	Scandinavian Committee for Research in Latin America
Nov.	noviembre, November, novembre, novembro
n.p.	no place, no publisher
NSF	National Science Foundation
NY	New York
NYC	New York City
OAS	Organization of American States
oct.	October, octubre
ODEPLAN	Oficina de Planificación Nacional, Chile
OEA	Organización de los Estados Americanos
OIT	See ILO.
Okla.	Oklahoma

Okt.	Oktober
op.	opus
OPANAL	Organismo para la Proscripción de las Armas Nucleares en América Latina
OPEC	Organization of Petroleum Exporting Countries
OPEP	Organización de Países Exportadores de Petróleo
OPIC	Overseas Investment Corporation
Oreg.	Oregon
ORIT	Organización Regional Interamericana del Trabajo
out.	outubro
p.	page
Pa.	Pennsylvania
Pan.	Panama
PAN	Partido Acción Nacional, Mexico
Par.	Paraguay
PC	partido comunista
PCR	Partido Comunista Revolucionario, Chile and Argentina
PCV	Partido Comunista de Venezuela
PDC	Partido Demócrata Cristiano, Chile
PEMEX	Petróleos Mexicanos
PETROBRAS	Petróleo Brasileiro
PIP	Partido Independiente de Puerto Rico
PLANAVE	Engenharia e Planejamento Limitada, Brazil
PLANO	Planejamento e Assesoria Limitada, Brazil
PLN	Partido Liberación Nacional, Costa Rica
PNM	People's National Movement, Trinidad and Tobago
PNP	People's National Party, Jamaica
pop.	population
PPP	purchasing power parities
P.R.	Puerto Rico
PRD	Partido Revolucionario Dominicano
PRI	Partido Revolucionario Institucional, Mexico
PROABRIL	Centro de Projetos Industriais, Brazil
Prof.	Professor
PRONAPA	Programa Nacional de Pesquisas Arqueológicas, Brazil
prov.	province, provincia
PS	Partido Socialista, Chile
pseud.	pseudonym, pseudónimo
pt(s).	part(s), parte(s)
PUC	Pontificia Universidade Católica, Rio
PURSC	Partido Unido de la Revolución Socialista de Cuba
q.	quarterly
R.D.	República Dominicana
rev.	revisada, revista, revised
R.I.	Rhode Island
Rio	Rio de Janeiro
S.a.	semiannual
SALALM	Seminar on the Acquisition of Latin American Library Materials
S.C.	South Carolina
sd.	sound
S. Dak.	South Dakota
SDR	special drawing rights
Sec.	section, sección
SELA	Sistema Económico Latinoamericano
SENAC	Serviço Nacional de Aprendizagem Comerical, Rio
SENAI	Serviço Nacional de Aprendizagem Industrial, São Paulo

Sept.	September, septiembre, septembre
SES	socio-economic status
SESI	Serviço Social de Industria, Brazil
set.	setembre
SIECA	Secretaría Permanente del Tratado General de Integración Centroamericana
SIL	Summer Institute of Linguistics
SINAMOS	Sistema Nacional de Apoyo a la Movilización Social, Peru
S.J.	Society of Jesus
SNA	Sociedad Nacional de Agricultura, Chile
SPVEA	Superintendência do Plano de Valorização Econômica da Amazônia, Brazil
sq.	square
SUDAM	Superintendência do Desenvolvimento da Amazônia, Brazil
SUDENE	Superintendência do Desenvolvimento do Nordeste, Brazil
SUFRAMA	Superintendência da Zona Franca de Manaus, Brazil
SUNY	State Universities of New York
t.	tomo, tome
T. and T.	Trinidad & Tobago
TAT	Thematic Apperception Test
TB	tuberculosis
Tenn.	Tennessee
Tex.	Texas
TG	transformational generative
TL	Thermoluminescent
TNP	Tratado de No Proliferación
trans.	translator
U.K.	United Kingdom
UN	United Nations
UNAM	Universidad Nacional Autónoma de México
UNCTAD	United Nations Conference on Trade and Development
UNDP	UN Development Programme
UNEAC	Unión de Escritores y Artistas de Cuba
UNESCO	United Nations Educational, Scientific and Cultural Organization
univ.	university, universidad, universidade, université, universität
uniw.	uniwersytet
UP	Unidad Popular, Chile
URD	Unidad Revolucionaria Democrática
URSS	Unión de Repúblicas Soviéticas Socialistas
Uru.	Uruguay
US	United States of America
USIA	United States Information Agency, Washington
USSR	Union of Soviet Socialist Republics
UTM	Universal Transverse Mercator
v.; vol.	volume, volumen
Va.	Virginia
Ven.	Venezuela
V.I.	Virgin Islands
viz.	videlicet, that is, namely
vs.	versus
Vt.	Vermont
W.I.	West Indies
Wis.	Wisconsin
Wyo.	Wyoming
yr.	the younger, el joven, year

TITLE LIST OF JOURNALS INDEXED*

Acta Geneticae Medicae et Gemellologiae. Instituto Gregorio Mendel. Roma. (IGM/AGMG)

Afro-Asia. Univ. Federal da Bahia, Centro de Estudos Afro-Orientais. Bahia, Brazil. (UFB/AA)

Air University Review. The professional journal of the United States Air Force. Maxwell Air Force Base, Ala. (AF/AUR)

Aisthesis. Revista chilena de investigaciones estéticas. Pontificia Univ. Católica de Chile, Instituto de Estética. Santiago.

Allpanchis Phuturinqa. Univ. de San Antonio de Abad, Seminario de Antropología, Instituto de Pastoral Andina. Cuzco, Peru. (IPA/AP)

Amazonia Peruana. Centro Amazónico de Antropología y Aplicación Práctica. Lima.

América Indígena. Instituto Indigenista Interamericano. México. (III/AI)

América Latina. Academia de Ciencias de la URSS [Unión de Repúblicas Soviéticas Socialistas]. Moscú. (URSS/AL)

América Latina. Centro Latino-Americano de Pesquisas em Ciências Sociais. Rio. (CLAPCS/AL)

American Anthropologist. American Anthropological Association. Washington. (AAA/AA)

American Antiquity. The Society for American Archaeology. Menasha, Wis. (SAA/AA)

American Economic Review. American Economic Association. Evanston, Ill. (AEA/AER)

American Ethnologist. American Anthropological Association. Washington. (AAA/AE)

American Indian Quarterly. Southwestern American Indian Society [and the] Fort Worth Museum of Science and History. Hurst, Tex. (SAIS/AIQ)

American Journal of Clinical Nutrition. American Society for Clinical Nutrition. N.Y. (ASCN/J)

American Journal of Human Genetics. The American Society for Human Genetics. Baltimore, Md. (ASHG/J)

American Journal of International Law. American Society of International Law. Washington. (ASIL/J)

American Journal of Physical Anthropology. American Association of Physical Anthropologists [and] The Wistar Institute of Anatomy and Biology. Philadelphia, Pa. (AJPA)

American Journal of Public Health and the Nation's Health. The American Public Health Assocation. Albany, N.Y. (APHA/J)

American Journal of Sociology. Univ. of Chicago. Chicago, Ill. (UC/AJS)

American Political Science Review. American Political Science Association. Columbus, Ohio. (APSA/R)

American Sociological Review. American Sociological Association. Menasha, Wis. (ASA/ASR)

The Americas. A quarterly publication of inter-American cultural history. Academy of American Franciscan History. Washington. (AAFH/TAM)

Amérique Latine. Bulletin analytique de documentation. Groupe des Recherches sur l'Amérique Latine (GRAL), Toulouse, France; Groupe des Recherches et d'Études Economiques et Sociales sur l'Amérique Latine (GRESAL), Grenoble, France; and Centre des Recherches Scientifiques, Institut des Hautes Études de l'Amérique Latine (IHEAL), Paris.

Anais. Academia Brasileria de Ciências. Rio.

Anais da Biblioteca Nacional. Divisão de Obras Raras e Publicações. Rio. (BRBN/A)

Anais do Museu de Antropologia. Univ. Federal de Santa Catarina. Florianopolis, Brazil.

Anales de Antropología. Univ. Nacional Autónoma de México, Instituto de Investigaciones Históricas. México. (UNAM/AA)

Anales de Geografía. Univ. Nacional Autónoma de México, Facultad de Filosofía y

* Journals that have been included in the *Handbook* as individual items are listed alphabetically by title in the Author Index.

Letras, Centro de Investigaciones Geográficas. México.

Anales de la Academia de Geografía e Historia de Costa Rica. San José. (AGHCR/A)

Anales de la Universidad Central del Ecuador. Quito. (UCE/A)

Anales de la Universidad de Cuenca. Cuenca, Ecua. (UC/A)

Anales de la Universidad del Norte. Antofagasta, Chile.

Anales del Instituto de Investigaciones Estéticas. Univ. Nacional Autónoma de México. Mexico. (IIE/A)

Anales del Instituto Nacional de Antropología e Historia. Secretaría de Educación Pública. México. (INAH/A)

Anales del Museo Nacional David J. Guzmán. San Salvador. (MNDJG/A)

Annales: Économies, Sociétés, Civilisations. Centre National de la Recherche Scientifique *avec le concours de la* VIe Section de l'École Pratique des Hautes Études. Paris. (AESC)

Annali della Fondazione Luigi Einaudi. Torino, Italy.

Annals of Carnegie Museum. Pittsburgh, Pa.

Annals of Human Biology. Taylor and Francis Publishers. London.

Annals of Human Genetics (Annals of Eugenics). Univ. College, Galton Laboratory. London. (UCGL/AHG)

Annals of the Association of American Geographers. Lawrence, Kans. (AAG/A)

Annals of the New York Academy of Sciences. N.Y. (NYAS/A)

Annals of the Southeastern Conference on Latin American Studies. West Georgia College. Carrollton. (SECOLAS/A)

Anthropological Linguistics. A publication of the Archives of the Languages of the World. Indiana Univ., Anthropology Dept. Bloomington. (IU/AL)

Anthropological Quarterly. Catholic Univ. of America, Catholic Anthropological Conference. Washington. (CUA/AQ)

Anthropology. State Univ. of New York, Dept. of Anthropology. Stonybook.

Anthropos. Anthropos-Institut. Psoieux, Switzerland. (AI/I)

La Antigua. Univ. de Santa María La Antigua, Oficina de Humanidades. Panamá. (USMLA/LA)

Antropología Andina. Centro de Estudios Andinos. Cuzco, Peru.

Antropología Ecuatoriana. Casa de la Cultura Ecuatoriana. Quito.

Antropología y Prehistoria. Univ. de La Habana, Escuela de Ciencias Biológicas. La Habana.

Antropológica. Fundación La Salle de Ciencias Naturales, Instituto Caribe de Antropología y Sociología. Caracas. (FSCN/A)

Anuario Bibliográfico Uruguayo de 1977. Biblioteca Nacional. Montevideo.

Anuário de Divulgação Científica. Univ. Católica de Goiás, Instituto Goiano de Pré-História e Antropologia. Goiânia, Brazil.

Anuario de Geografía. Univ. Nacional Autónoma de México, Facultad de Filosofía y Letras. México. (UNAMCG/A)

Anuario de Letras. Univ. Nacional Autónoma de México, Facultad de Filosofía y Letras. México. (UNAM/AL)

Apuntes. Univ. del Pacífico, Centro de Investigación. Lima. (UP/A)

Archaeology. Archaeological Institute of America. N.Y. (AIA/A)

Archeometry. Oxford Univ. U.K.

Archiv für Völkerkunde. Museum für Völkerkunde in Wien und von Verein Freunde der Völkerkunde. Wien. (MVW/AV)

Archives de Sociologie des Religions. Centre Nationale de la Recherche Scientifique. Paris. (CNRS/ASR)

Archives Internationales de Sociologie de la Coopération et du Développement. Paris. (AISCD)

Arctic and Alpine Research. Univ. of Colorado, Institute of Arctic and Alpine Research. Boulder.

Areito. Areíto, Inc. N.Y. (AR)

Armed Forces and Society. An interdisciplinary journal on military institutions, civil-military relations, arms control and peacekeeping, and conflict management. Univ. of Chicago. Chicago, Ill. (AFS)

Arqueología en América Latina. Boletín trimestral dedicado a los estudios arqueológicos en América Latina en el Caribe. Huancayo, Peru.

Arqueológicas. Museo Nacional de Antropología y Arqueología, Instituto Nacional de Cultura. Lima. (MNAA/A)

Årstryck. Etnografiska Museum. Göteborg, Sweden. (EM/A)

Art International. Zurich, Switzerland. (AI)

Artes de México. Revista bimestral. México. (ARMEX)

Asien, Afrika, Lateinamerika. Deutscher Verlag der Wissenschaften. Berlin, GDR.

Asien, Afrika, Lateinamerika. Zeitschrift des Zentralen Rates für Asien-, Afrika- und Lateinamerikawissenschaften in der DDR. Deutscher Verlag der Wissenschaften. Berlin, GDR.

The Atlantic Monthly. Boston, Mass.

B.B.A.A. Boletín Bibliográfico de Antropología Americana. Instituto Panamericano de Geografía e Historia, Comisión de Historia. México. (BBAA)

Baessler-Archiv. Museums für Völkerkunde. Berlin, FRG. (MV/BA)

Bank of London and South America Review. Lloyds Bank Group Publication. London.

Behavior Genetics. Greenwood Periodicals. Westport, Conn.

Berichte zur Entwicklung in Spanien, Portugal, Lateinamerika. München, FRG. (BESPL)

Bibliografía Económica de México. Indice general. Banco de México, Subdirección de Investigación Económica y Bancaria. México.

Bibliografía Histórica Mexicana: 1976–1978. El Colegio de México, Centro de Estudios Históricos. México.

Bibliografía Nacional. Libros, artículos de revistas y periódicos. Biblioteca Nacional. Lima.

Bijdragen tot de Taal-, Land- en Volkenkunde. Koninklijk Instituut voor Taal-, Land- en Volkenkunde. Leiden, The Netherlands. (KITLV/B)

Boletim Bibliográfico. Biblioteca Mário de Andrade. São Paulo. (BMA/BB)

Boletim Bibliográfico da Biblioteca Nacional. Biblioteca Nacional. Rio.

Boletim de Estudos Sociais. Fundação Regional Educacional de Avaré. São Paulo. (FREA/BES)

Boletim do CEPE. Univ. para o Desenvolvimento do Estado de Santa Catarina (UDESC), Faculdade de Educação, Centro de Estudos e Pesquisas Educacionais. Florianópolis, Brazil.

Boletim do Departamento de Geografia. Faculdade de Filosofia, Ciências e Letras de Presidente Prudente. Presidente Prudente, Brazil. (BDG)

Boletim do Museu Paraense Emílio Goeldi. Nova série: antropologia. Conselho Nacional de Desenvolvimento Científico e Tecnológico, Instituto Nacional de Pesquisas da Amazônia. Belém, Brazil. (MPEG/B)

Boletim Geográfico do Estado do Rio Grande do Sul. Diretório Regional de Geografia [and] Secção de Geografia. Porto Alegre, Brazil. (DRG/BG)

Boletim Paranaense de Geociências. Univ. Federal do Paraná, Depto. de Geociências, Centro de Documentação e Informações, Setor de Tecnologia. Paraná, Brazil. (UFP/BPG)

Boletín. Banco de la República, Museo del Oro. Bogotá.

Boletín de Educación. Publicación semestral. UNESCO, Oficina Regional de Educación. Santiago.

Boletín de Estudios Geográficos. Univ. Nacional de Cuyo, Facultad de Filosofía y Letras, Instituto de Geografía. Mendoza, Arg.

Boletín de Estudios Latinoamericanos. Centro de Estudios y Documentación Latinoamericanos. Amsterdam. (CEDLA/B)

Boletín de la Academia de Ciencias Políticas y Sociales. Caracas. (ACPS/B)

Boletín de la Academia Nacional de la Historia. Caracas. (VANH/B)

Boletín de la Sociedad Geográfica de Lima. Lima. (SGL/B)

Boletín de la Sociedad Venezolana de Espeleologia. Caracas.

Boletín de Legislación Educativa Venezolana. Univ. del Zulia, Facultad de Humanidades y Educación, Centro de Documentación e Investigación Pedagógica (CEDIP). Maracaibo, Ven.

Boletín del Centro de Investigaciones Biológicas. Univ. del Zulia. Maracaibo, Ven.

Boletín del Instituto de Geografía. Univ. Nacional Autónoma de México, Instituto de Geografía. México.

Boletín del Instituto Nacional de Antropología e Historia. Secretaría de Educación Pública. México. (INAH/B)

Boletín del Museo del Hombre Dominicano. Santo Domingo. (MHD/B)

Boletín del Seminario de Arqueología. Pontificia Univ. Católica del Perú, Instituto Riva Agüero. Lima. (PUCIRA/BSA)

Boletín Documental sobre las Mujeres. Publicación trimestral. Comunicación Intercambio y Desarrollo Humano en América Latina (CIDHAL). Asociación Civil Mexicana. Cuernavaca, Mex.

Boletín Geológico. Ministerio de Minas y Petróleos, Instituto Geológico Nacional. Bogotá. (COIGN/BG)

Boletín Histórico. Fundación John Boulton. Caracas. (FJB/BH)

Boletín Indigenista Venezolano. Ministerio de Justicia, Comisión Indigenista. Caracas. (VMJ/BIV)

Boletín Nicaragüense de Bibliografía y Documentación. Banco Central de Nicaragua, Biblioteca. Managua. (BNBD)

Brazilian Economic Studies. Instituto de Planejamento Econômico e Social, Instituto de Pesquisas (IPEA/INPES). Rio.

British Journal of Sociology. London School of Economics and Political Science. London. (BJS)

Bulletin. Société Suisse des Américanistes. Geneva. (SSA/B)

Bulletin de la Sécretarie d'Etat des Finances et des Affaires Economiques. Direction des Affaires Economiques, Division Études et Statistiques. Port-au-Prince.

Bulletin de l'Association de Géographes Français. Paris. (AGF/B)

Bulletin de l'Institut Français d'Études Andines. Lima. (IFEA/B)

Bulletin de Musées Royaux d'Art et d'Histoire. Bruxells.

Bulletin of the Atomic Scientists. Science and Public Affairs. Educational Foundation for Nuclear Science with the cooperation of the Adlai Stevenson Institute of International Affairs. Chicago, Ill. (BAS/SPA)

Bulletin of the New York Academy of Medicine. N.Y.

Bulletin of the Pan American Health Organization. Washington. (PAHO/B)

Business History Review. Harvard Univ., Graduate School of Business Administration. Boston, Mass. (HU/BHR)

Cadernos de Arqueologia. Univ. Federal do Paraná, Museu de Arqueologia e Artes Populares. Paranaguá, Brazil. (UFP/CA)

Cadernos de Psicologia Aplicada. Univ. Federal do Rio Grande do Sul, Centro de Orientação e Seleção Psicotécnica. Porto Alegre, Brazil.

Cadernos do CEAS. Centro do Estudo e Ação Social. Salvador, Brazil.

Cahiers des Amériques Latines. Univ. de la Sorbonne Nouvelle, Institut des Hautes Études de l'Amérique Latine. Paris. (CDAL)

Les Cahiers d'Outre-Mar. Sociéte de Géographie de Bordeaux; Institut de Géographie de la Faculté des Lettres de Bordeaux; Institut de la France d'Outre-Mer avec le concours du Centre National de la Recherche Scientifique et de la VIème Section de l'Ecole Pratique des Hautes Études. Bordeaux, France. (SGB/COM)

Canadian Psychiatric Association Journal. Canadian Psychiatric Association. Ottawa.

Caravelle. Cahiers du monde hispanique et luso-brésilien. Univ. de Toulouse, Institut d'Études Hispaniques, Hispano-Americaines et Luso-Brésiliennes. Toulouse, France. (UTIEH/C)

Caribbean Quarterly. Univ. of the West Indies. Mona, Jam. (UWI/CQ)

Caribbean Studies. Univ. of Puerto Rico, Institute of Caribbean Studies. Río Piedras. (UPR/CS)

The CARICOM Bibliography. Caribbean Community, Secretariat, Library. Georgetown.

Carta Económica. Banco Nacional de Panamá. Asesoría Económica y de Planificación. Panamá.

Carta Informativa. Secretaría Permanente del Tratado General de Integración Económica Centroamericana (SIECA). Guatemala.

Carta Política. Informe político, económico, cultural, internacional. Persona a Persona, S.A. B.A.

Casa de las Américas. Instituto Cubano del Libro. La Habana. (CDLA)

CEPAL Review/Revista de la CEPAL. Naciones Unidas, Comisión Económica para América Latina. Santiago. (CEPAL/R)

Cespedesia. Boletín científico. Depto. del Valle del Cauca, Colombia.

Ciencia. Univ. Autónoma de Santo Domingo, Dirección de Investigaciones Científicas. Santo Domingo.

Ciência e Cultura. Sociedade Brasileira para o Progresso da Ciência. São Paulo. (SBPC/CC)

Ciencia Interamericana. Organization of American States, Dept. of Scientific Affairs. Washington. (OAS/CI)

Ciencias Administrativas. Univ. Nacional de La Plata, Facultad de Ciencias Económicas, Instituto de Investigaciones de Ciencias Administrativas. La Plata, Arg. (UNLP/CA)

Cladindex. Resúmen de documentos CEPAL/ILPES. Organización de las Naciones Unidas. Comisión Económica para

América Latina (CEPAL), Centro Latino-americano de Documentación Económica y Social (CEDES). Santiago.

Columbia Journal of World Business. Columbia Univ. N.Y. (CJWB)

Comentarios sobre la Situación Económica. Univ. de Chile, Facultad de Ciencias Económicas y Administrativas, Depto. de Economía. Santiago.

Comercio Exterior. Banco Nacional de Comercio Exterior. México. (BNCE/CE)

Comparative Education Review. Comparative Education Society. N.Y. (CES/CE)

Comparative Political Studies. Northwestern Univ., Evanston, Ill. [and] Sage Publications. Beverly Hills, Calif. (CPS)

Comparative Politics. The City Univ. of New York, Political Science Program. N.Y. (CUNY/CP)

Comparative Studies in Society and History. An international quarterly. Society for the Comparative Study of Society and History. The Hague. (CSSH)

Comunicación y Cultura. La comunicación masiva en el proceso político latinoamericano. Editorial Galerna. B.A. [and] Santiago. (CYC)

Comunicaciones Proyecto Puebla-Tlaxcala. Fundación Alemana para la Investigación Científica. Puebla, Mex. (FAIC/CPPT)

Comunidad. Revista de la U.I.A. Cuadernos de difusión cultural. Univ. Iberoamericana. México. (UIA/C)

Conjonction. Institut Français d'Haïti. Port-au-Prince. (IFH/C)

Controversia. Centro de Investigación y Educación Popular (CINEP). Bogotá.

Coyuntura Económica Andina. Univ. de Chile, Depto. de Economía, Santiago [and] Fundación para la Educación Superior y el Desarrollo, Bogotá [and] Fundación para la Educación y el Desarrollo, Quito. Santiago.

Cristianismo y Sociedad. Junta Latino Americana de Iglesia y Sociedad. Montevideo. (JLAIS/CS)

Croissance des Juennes Nations. Paris.

Cuadernos Americanos. México. (CAM)

Cuadernos de Economía. Univ. Católica de Chile. Santiago. (UCC/CE)

Cuadernos de Historia y Arqueología. Casa de la Cultura Ecuatoriana, Núcleo del Guayas. Guayaquil, Ecua. (CCE/CHA)

Cuadernos de la CEPAL. Naciones Unidas. Comisión Económica para América Latina. Santiago.

Cuadernos de la C.V.F. Corporación Venezolana de Fomento. Caracas.

Cuadernos de Marcha. México.

Cuadernos del Cendia. Univ. Autónoma de Santiago Domingo. Santo Domingo.

Cuadernos Hispanoamericanos. Instituto de Cultura Hispánica. Madrid. (CH)

Cuadernos Políticos. Revista trimestral. Ediciones Era. México. (CP)

Cuadernos Semestrales. Publicación semestral de *Estados Unidos*: Perspectiva Latinoamericana. Centro de Investigación Docencia Económica (CIDE). México.

Cuba Review. Cuba Resource Center (CRC). N.Y.

Cuban Studies/Estudios Cubanos. Univ. of Pittsburgh, Univ. Center for International Studies, Center for Latin American Studies. Pittsburgh, Pa. (UP/CSEC)

Cuestionario. A. Peña Lillo Editor. B.A.

Cultura. Ministério da Educação e Cultura, Directoria de Documentação e Divulgação. Brasília. (MEC/C)

Culture, Medicine and Psychiatry. D. Reidel. Dordrecht, The Netherlands.

Cultures et Développement. Revue internationale des sciences du développement. Univ. Catholique de Louvain *avec le concours de la* Foundation Universitaire de Belgique. Louvain, Belgium. (UCL/CD)

Current Anthropology. Univ. of Chicago, Chicago, Ill. (UC/CA)

Current History. A monthly magazine of world affairs. Philadelphia, Pa. (CUH)

Debates en Sociología. Univ. Católica del Perú, Depto. de Sociología. Lima.

A Defesa Nacional. Revista de assuntos militares et estudo de problemas brasileiros. Rio. (ADN)

Demografía y Economía. El Colegio de México. México. (CM/D)

Desarrollo Económico. Instituto de Desarrollo Económico y Social. B.A. (IDES/DE)

Deutsche Aussenpolitik. Institut für Internationale Beziehungen. Berlin, GDR. (IIB/DA)

Deutsche Bauzeitung. Stuttgart, FRG.

The Developing Economies. Institute of Asian Economic Affairs. Tokyo, (IAEA/DE)

Diálogos. Artes/Letras/Ciencias humanas. El Colegio de México. México. (CM/D)

Discusión Antropológica. Univ. Nacional Mayor de San Marcos. Lima.

Docencia. Univ. Autónoma de Guadalajara, Comunidad Académica. Guadalajara, Méx.

Documentação Amazônica: catàlogo coletivo. Superintendência do Desenvolvimento da Amazônia (SUDAM). Rede de Bibliotecas da Amazônia (REBAM). Belém, Brazil.

Documentación Socioeconómica Centroamericana. Confederación Universitaria Centroamericana (CSUCA), Programa Centroamericano de Ciencias Sociales, Centro de Documentación Económica y Social de Centroamerica (CEDESC). San José.

Documentos. Revista de información política. Univ. Central de Venezuela, Facultad de Ciencias Jurídicas y Políticas, Instituto de Estudios Políticos. Caracas.

El Dorado. Univ. of Northern Colorado. Greeley.

Dyn. Durham Univ., Anthropological Society. Durham, U.K.

ECA: Estudios Centroamericanos. Revista de extensión cultural. Univ. Centroamericana José Simeon Cañas. San Salvador.

Economía. Univ. de San Carlos de Guatemala, Facultad de Ciencias Económicas, Instituto de Investigaciones Económicas y Sociales. Guatemala. (USCG/E)

Economía de América Latina. Centro de Investigación y Docencia Económicas. México.

Economia Internazionale. Instituto di Economia Internazionale. Genova, Italy. (IEI/EI)

Economía y Ciencias Sociales. Univ. Central de Venezuela, Facultad de Ciencias Económicas y Sociales. Caracas. (UCV/ECS)

Economía y Desarrollo. Univ. de La Habana, Instituto de Economía. La Habana. (UH/ED)

Economic Botany. Devoted to applied botany and plant utilization. New Botanical Garden *for the* Society for Economic Botany. N.Y. (SEB/EB)

Economic Bulletin for Latin America. United Nations, Economic Commission for Latin America. N.Y. (UNECLA/B)

Economic Development and Cultural Change. Univ. of Chicago, Research Center in Economic Development and Cultural Change. Chicago, Ill. (UC/EDCC)

Economic Geography. Clark Univ. Worcester, Mass. (CU/EG)

Económica. Univ. Nacional de la Plata, Facultad de Ciencias Económicas, Instituto de Investigaciones Económicas. La Plata, Arg. (UNLP/E)

Economie et Développement. Secrétarie d'Etat des Finances et des Affaires Economiques, Unité de Programmation. Port-au-Prince.

Economundo. Informe de la economía internacional. Secretaría de Hacienda y Crédito Público. México.

Ediciones Educación y Desarrollo. Comisión Nacional de Reforma de la Educación, Secretaría de Educación Pública. Tegucigalpa.

Editorial Research Reports. Congressional Quarterly, Inc. Washington.

La Educación. Organización de los Estados Americanos (OEA), Secretaría General, Depto. de Asuntos Educativos. Washington.

Educación. Revista trimestral. Ministerio de Educación. La Habana.

Educación Popular. Instituto de Investigación Cultural para la Educación Popular. Oruro, Bol.

Educación U.P.B. Univ. Pontificia Bolivariana. Medellín, Colombia.

Encuentro. Revista de la Univ. Centroamericana. Managua.

Encuesta de Hogares. República Oriental del Uruguay, Ministerio de Economía y Finanzas, Dirección General de Estadística y Censos. Montevideo.

English Langue Teaching. London.

Ensayos ECIEL. Programa de Estudios Conjuntos sobre Integración Económica Latinoamericana, Brookings Institution. Washington. (ECIEL)

Ensayos Económicos. Banco Central de la República Argentina. B.A. (BCRA/EE)

Environmental Conservation. Elsevier Sequoia, Lausanne, Switzerland *with the collaboration of the* International Union for Conservation of Nature and Natural Resources and others *for the* Foundation of Environmental Conservation. Geneva.

Die Erde. Zeitschrift der Gesellschaft Für Erdkunde zu Berlin. Walter de Gruyter & Co. Berlin. (GEB/E)

Erdkunde. Archiv für Wissenschaftliche Geographie. Univ. Bonn, Geographisches Institut. Bonn, FRG. (UBGI/E)

Estadística. Inter-American Statistical Institute. Washington. (IASI/E)

Estrategia. Publicación bimestral. Instituto Argentino de Estudios Estratégicos y de las Relaciones Internacionales (INSAR). B.A. (IAEERI/E)

Estrategia Económica y Financiera. Servicios de Información, Ltda. Bogotá.

Estudios. Instituto de Estudios Económicas so-

bre la Realidad Argentina y Lati-
noamericana. Córdoba, Arg. (IEERAL/E)
Estudios. Univ. de San Carlos de Guatemala,
Facultad de Humanidades, Depto. de Histo-
ria. Guatemala. (USCG/ES)
Estudios Andinos. Univ. of Pittsburgh, Latin
American Studies Center. Pittsburgh, Pa.
(UP/EA)
Estudios Arqueológicos. Univ. Católica, Cen-
tro de Investigaciones Arqueológicas. Quito.
Estudios Centro-Americanos. Revista de ex-
tensión cultural. Univ. José Simeón Cañas.
San Salvador. (UJSC/ECA)
Estudios de Arqueología. Museo Arqueológico
de Chachi. Arg.
Estudios de Cultura Maya. Univ. Nacional
Autónoma de México, Centro de Estudios
Mayas. México. (CEM/ECM)
Estudios de Economía. Univ. de Chile, Fa-
cultad de Ciencias Económicas y Admi-
nistrativas, Depto. de Economía. Santiago.
(UC/EE)
Estudios de Población. Asociación Colom-
biana para el Estudio de la Población.
Bogotá. (ACEP/EP)
Estudios Paraguayos. Univ. Católica Nuestra
Señora de la Asunción. Asunción.
(UCNSA/EP)
Estudios Rurales Latinoamericanos. Consejo
Latinoamericano de Ciencias Sociales
(CLACSO), Comisión de Estudios Rurales.
Bogotá. (CLACSO/ERL)
Estudios Sociales. Corporación de Promoción
Universitaria. Santiago. (CPU/ES)
Estudios Sociales Centroamericanos. Consejo
Superior de Universidades Cen-
troamericanas, Confederación Universitaria
Centroamericana, Programa Cen-
troamericana de Ciencias Sociales. San José.
(CSUCA/ESC)
Estudos Brasilciros. Univ. Federal do Paraná,
Setor de Ciências Humanas, Centro de Es-
tudos Brasileiros. Curitiba, Brazil. (UFP/EB)
Estudos CEBRAP. Centro Brasileiro de Análise
e Planejamento [and] Editora Brasiliense.
São Paulo.
Estudos Econômicos. Univ. de São Paulo
(USP), Instituto de Pesquisas Econômicas
(IPE). São Paulo. (IPE/EE)
Estudos Históricos. Faculdade de Filosofia,
Ciência e Letras, Depto. de História. Ma-
rília, Brazil. (FFCLM/EH)
Ethnic Groups. Gordon and Breach. N.Y.
Ethnologia Americana. Düsseldorfer Institut

für Americanische Völkerkunde. Düssel-
dorf, FRG.
Ethnology. Univ. of Pittsburgh. Pittsburgh, Pa.
(UP/E)
Ethnos. Statens Etnografiska Museum. Stock-
holm. (SEM/E)
Etnía. Museo Etnográfico Municipal Dámaso
Arce. Municipalidad de Olavarría, Provincia
de Buenos Aires, Arg. (MEMDA/E)
Études Hispano-Américaines. Univ. de Haute
Bretagne, Centro d'Études, Hispano-Améri-
caines et Luso-Brésiliennes. Rennes, France.
(UHB/EHA)
Ex Horreo. Univ. van Amsterdam Albert
Egges Giffen, Instituut voor Prae-en Pro-
tohistoire.
Explorers Journal. N.Y. (EJ)

FACES. Univ. Central de Venezuela, Facultad
de Ciencias Económicas y Sociales. Caracas.
Ficha de Información Sociopolítica. Pontificia
Univ. Católica del Ecuador, Depto. de Cien-
cias Políticas y Sociales. Quito.
Fieldana: Anthropology. Field Museum of
Natural History. Chicago, Ill.
Folklore Americano. Organización de los Es-
tados Americanos, Instituto Panamericano
de Geografía e Historia, Comisión de Histo-
ria, Comité Interamericano de Folklore.
Lima. See IPGH/FA. (CIF/FA)
Foreign Affairs. Council on Foreign Relations.
N.Y. (CFR/FA)
Foreign Policy. National Affairs, Inc. [and]
Carnegie Endowment for International
Peace. N.Y. (FP)
Foro Internacional. Revista trimestral. El Co-
legio de México. México. (CM/FI)
Foundation News. Inter-American Founda-
tion. Arlington, Va.
Franciscanum. Revista de las ciencias del es-
piritú. Univ. de San Buenaventura. Bogotá.
(USB/F)
Freedom at Issue. Freedom House. N.Y.

Gaceta Médica de México. Academia Nacio-
nal de Medicina. México. (MANM/G)
Gayana: Zoología. Univ. de Concepción, Ins-
tituto de Biología. Concepción, Chile.
Genetics. Genetics, Inc. [and] Univ. of Texas.
Austin.
Geografiska Annaler. Svenska Sällskapet för
Antropologi och Geografi. Stockholm.
(SSAG/GA)
Geographica Helvetica. Schweizerische

Zeitschrift für Länder- und Völkerkunde. Kümmerly & Fray, Geographischer Verlag. Bern. (GH)

The Geographical Journal. The Royal Geographical Society. London. (RGS/GJ)

The Geographical Magazine. London. (GM)

The Geographical Review. American Geographical Society. N.Y. (AGS/GR)

Geographical Review of Japan. Association of Japanese Geographers. Tokyo.

Geographische Berichte. Geographischen Gesselschaft in der Deutschen Demokratischen Republic. Berlin. (GGDDR/GB)

Geographische Rundschau. Zeitschrift für Schulgeographie. Georg Westermann Verlag. Braunschweig, FRG. (GR)

Geographische Zeitschrift. Franz Steiner Verlag. Wiesbaden, FRG. (GZ)

Geologische Rundschau. Inernationale Zeitschrift für Geologie. Geologische Vereinigung. Ferdinand Enke Verlag. Stuttgart, FRG. (GV/GR)

The Gerontologist. Gerontological Society. St. Louis, Mo.

Geschichte und Gessellschaft. Zeitschrift für Historische Sozialwissenschaft. Univ. Bielefeld, Fakultät für Geschichtswissenschaft. Bielefeld, FRG. (UB/GG)

Ginecología y Obstetricia de México. Federación Mexicana de Asociaciones de Ginecología y Obstetricia. México.

Growth and Change: A Journal of Regional Development. Univ. of Kentucky, College of Business Economics. Lexington.

Guatemala Indígena. Instituto Indigenista Nacional. Guatemala.

Guyanese National Bibliography. National Library of Guyana. Georgetown.

Harvard Library Bulletin. Harvard Univ. Cambridge, Mass.

Hemoglobin. Marcel Dekker Journals. N.Y.

Hispanic American Historical Review. Duke Univ. Press *for the* Conference on Latin American History of the American Historical Association. Durham, N.C. (HAHR)

Historia Mexicana. El Colegio de México. México. (CM/HM)

The Historian. The undergraduate journal of research and scholarship. History Society of Washington Square [and] New York Univ., Univ. College. N.Y. (HSWS/H)

Histórica. Univ. Autónoma del Estado de México, Instituto de Investigaciones Históricas. México. (UAEM/H)

Hojas Universitarias. Revista de la Fundación Univ. Central. Bogotá. (HU)

Hombre y Cultura. Univ. Nacional, Centro de Investigaciones Antropológicas. Panamá. (UNCIA/HC)

Human Biology. Official publication of the Human Biology Council. Wayne State Univ., School of Medicine. Detroit, Mich. (WSU/HB)

Human Ecology. Plenum, N.Y.

Human Genetics. Excerpta Medica Foundation. Amsterdam.

Human Heredity. Basel, Switzerland. (HH)

Human Organization. Society for Applied Anthropology. N.Y. (SAA/HO)

Humanitas. Boletín ecuatoriano de antropología. Univ. Central del Ecuador, Instituto de Antropología. Quito. (UCEIA/H)

Humanitas. Univ. Nacional de Tucumán, Facultad de Filosofía y Letras. Tucumán, Arg. (UNT/H)

Ibero-Americana. Research news and principal acquisitions of documentation on Latin America in Denmark, Finland, Norway and Sweden. Latinamerika Institutet. Stockholm. (LI/IA)

Ibero-Amerikanisches Archiv. Ibero-Amerikanisches Institut. Berlin, FRG. (IAA)

Iberoromania. Zeitschrift für die iberoromanischen Sprachen und Literaturen in Europa und Amerika. Max Niemeyer Verlag. Tübingen, FRG.

Indiana. Beiträge zur Volker-und Sprachenkunde, Archäologie und Anthropologie des Indianischen Amerika. Ibero-Amerikanisches Institut. Berlin, FRG. (IAI/I)

Indicadores Económicos. Banco Central de Nicaragua. Depto. de Estudios Económicos. Managua.

Indicadores Sociais RS. Fundação de Economia e Estatística. Porto Alegre, Brazil.

Indice CENATE. Catálogo de teses universitarias brasileiras. Informações, Microformas e Sistemas, Centro Nacional de Teses. São Paulo.

Indice de Artículos sobre Educación y Adiestramiento. Servicio Nacional ARMO. México.

Indice de Ciências Sociais. Instituto Universitario de Pesquisas do Rio de Janeiro. Rio.

Industrial and Labor Relations Review. Cornell Univ. *for the* New York State School of Industrial and Labor Relations. Ithaca, N.Y. (CU/ILRR)

Informaciones. Univ. Nacional de La Plata, Biblioteca Pública. La Plata, Arg.

Informaciones Arqueológicas. Ediciones Catequil. Lima.

Informaciones Geográficas. Univ. de Chile, Facultad de Filosofía y Educación, Instituto de Geografía. Santiago. (UCIG/IG)

Integración Latinoamericana. Instituto para la Integración de América Latina. B.A. (INTAL/IL)

Inter-American Economic Affairs. Washington. (IAMEA)

Interciencia. Asociación Interciencia. Caracas. (AI/I)

International Affairs. A monthly journal of political analysis. Moskova. (IA)

International Affairs. Royal Institute of International Affairs. London. (RIIA/IA)

International Development Review. The Society for International Development. Washington. (SID/IDR)

International Family Planning Perspectives and Digest. Alan Guttmacher Institute for the Planned Parenthood Federation of America. N.Y.

International Journal. Canadian Institute of International Affairs. Toronto. (CIIA/IJ)

International Journal of American Linguistics. Indian Univ. *under the auspices of the* Linguistic Society of America, American Anthropological Association *with the cooperation of the* Joint Committee on American Native Languages. Waverly Press, Inc. Baltimore, Md. (IU/IJAL)

International Journal of Comparative Sociology. York Univ., Dept. of Sociology and Anthropology. Toronto, Canada. (YU/IJCS)

International Journal of Social Psychiatry. London. (IJSP)

International Migration (Migrations Internationales. Migraciones Internacionales). Quarterly review of the Intergovernmental Committee for European Migration [and] Research Group for European Migration Problems. Geneva, Switzerland. (ICEM/IM)

International Organization. World Peace Foundation [and] Univ. of Wisconsin Press. Madison. (WPF/IO)

International Policy Report. Center for International Review. Washington.

International Review of Education. United Nations Educational, Scientific and Cultural Organization, Institute for Education. Hamburg, FRG. (UNESCO/IRE)

International Social Science Journal. United Nations Educational, Scientific and Cultural Organization. Paris. (UN/ISSJ)

International Studies Quarterly. Sage *for* International Studies Association. Beverly Hills, Calif.

Jahrbuch Asien Afrika Lateinamerika. Bilanz und Chronik des Jahres 19 . . Deutscher Verlag der Wissenschaften. Berlin, GDR.

Jahrbuch für Geschichte von Staat, Wirtschaft und Gesellschaft Lateinamerikas. Köln, FRG. (JGSWGL)

Jamaica Journal. Institute of Jamaica. Kingston.

Journal de la Société des Américanistes. Paris. (SA/J)

Journal of American Folklore. American Folklore Society. Austin, Tex. (AFS/JAF)

Journal of Anthropological Research. Univ. of New Mexico, Dept. of Anthropology. Albuquerque. (UNM/JAR)

Journal of Applied Physiology. The American Physiological Society. Washington.

Journal of Biosocial Science. Blackwell Scientific Publications. Oxford, U.K.

The Journal of Caribbean History. Univ. of the West Indies, Dept. of History [and] Caribbean Universities Press. St. Lawrence, Barbados. (UWI/JCH)

A Journal of Church and State. Baylor Univ., J. M. Dawson Studies in Church and State. Waco, Tex. (BU/JCS)

Journal of Common Market Studies. Oxford, U.K. (JCMS)

Journal of Commonwealth and Comparative Politics. Univ. of London, Institute of Commonwealth Studies. London. (ICS/JCCP)

Journal of Dental Research. International Association for Dental Research. St. Louis, Mo.

The Journal of Developing Areas. Western Illinois Univ. Press. Macomb. (JDA)

The Journal of Development Studies. A quarterly journal devoted to economics, politics and social development. London. (JDS)

The Journal of Experimental Education. The Helen Dwight Reid Education Foundation. Washington.

Journal of Field Archaeology. Boston Univ. Boston, Mass.

Journal of Heredity. American Genetic Association. Washington.

Journal of Historical Geography. Academic Press. London.

Journal of Inter-American Studies and World

Affairs. Univ. of Miami Press *for the* Center for Advanced International Studies. Coral Gables, Fla. (UM/JIAS)

The Journal of International Law and Economics. George Washington Univ., National Law Center. Washington. (GWU/JILE)

Journal of Latin American Lore. Univ. of California, Latin American Center. Los Angeles. (UCLA/JLAL)

Journal of Latin American Studies. Centers or institutes of Latin American studies at the universities of Cambridge, Glasgow, Liverpool, London and Oxford. Cambridge Univ. Press. London. (JLAS)

Journal of Marriage and the Family. Western Reserve Univ. Cleveland, Ohio. (WRU/JMF)

Journal of Nervous and Mental Disease. Univ. of Maryland, Psychiatric Institute. Baltimore, Md. (UM/JNMD)

Journal of New World Archaeology. Univ. of California, Institute of Archaeology. Los Angeles.

Journal of Peace Research. International Peace Research Institute. Universitetforlaget. Oslo. (JPR)

The Journal of Peasant Studies. Frank Cass & Co. London. (JPS)

Journal of Political and Military Sociology. Northern Illinois Univ., Dept. of Sociology. DeKalb. (NIU/JPMS)

Journal of Political Economy. Univ. of Chicago. Chicago, Ill. (JPE)

The Journal of Politics. The Southern Political Science Association *in cooperation with the* Univ. of Florida. Gainesville. (SPSA/JP)

The Journal of San Diego History. The San Diego Historical Society. San Diego, Calif. (SDHS/J)

Journal of Social Psychology. The Journal Press. Provincetown, Mass. (JSP)

Journal of the Caribbean Society of Educational Administrators (CARSEA). Univ. of the West Indies, School of Education. Mona, Jam.

Journal of the Hellenic Diaspora. Pella Publishing Co. N.Y.

Journal of the West. Los Angeles, Calif. (JW)

Journal of World Trade Law. Crans, Switzerland. (JWTL)

Kaie. National History and Arts Council of Guyana. Georgetown. (NHAC/K)

Katunob. Univ. of Northern Colorado, Museum of Anthropology. Greeley, Colorado. (UNC/K)

Kollasuyo. Revista de estudios bolivianos. Editora Universo. La Paz.

Kyklos. International review for social sciences. Basel, Switzerland. (KYKLOS)

Land Economics. A quarterly journal of planning, housing and public utilities. Univ. of Wisconsin. Madison. (UW/LE)

Lateinamerika. Univ. Rostock. Rostock, GDR. (UR/L)

Lateinamerika Studien. Univ. Erlangen-Nürnberg, Sektion Lateinamerika. Nürnberg, FRG. (UEN/LS)

Latin America in Books. Univ. of New Orleans, Dept. of Anthropology and Geography. New Orleans, La.

Latin America Ronshu. Univ. Sofia, Sociedad Japonesa de Ciencias Sociales de Latinoamérica. Tokyo.

Latin American Digest. Arizona State Univ. Tempe.

Latin American Indian Literatures. Univ. of Pittsburgh, Dept. of Hispanic Languages and Center for International Studies, Center for Latin American Studies. Pittsburgh, Pa.

Latin American Perspectives. Univ. of California. Riverside. (LAP)

Latin American Research Review. Univ. of North Carolina Press *for the* Latin American Studies Association. Chapel Hill. (LARR)

The Latin American Times. José Font Castro. Bogotá.

The Latin American Yearly Review. American College in Paris. Paris.

Library Trends. Univ. of Illinois, Library School. Urbana.

El Libro Español. Instituto Nacional del Libro Español. Madrid.

Linguistics. An international review. Mouton. The Hague. (LING)

Lotería. Lotería Nacional de Beneficencia. Panamá. (LNB/L)

Man. A monthly record of anthropological science. The Royal Anthropological Institute. London. (RAI/M)

The Massachusetts Review. A quarterly of literature, the arts and public affairs. Amherst College; Mount Holyoke College; Smith College; and the Univ. of Massachusetts. Amherst.

The Masterkey. Southwest Museum. Los Angeles, Calif. (SM/M)

Mededelingen. Surinaáms Museum. Paramaribo.

Medical Anthropology. Redgrave. Pleas-
antville, N.Y.
Medical Anthropology. Society or Medical An-
thropology. Washington.
Memoria. Sociedad de Ciencias Naturales La
Salle. Caracas.
Memórias do Instituto Oswaldo Cruz. Rio.
(IOC/M)
México: Artículos Clasificados. Univ. Nacio-
nal Autónoma de México, Facultad de
Ciencias Políticas y Sociales, Centro de
Documentación. México.
Militärgeschichte. Deutscher Militärverlag.
Berlin, GDR.
Mitteilungen der Anthropologischen
Gesellschaft in Wien. Wien. (AGW/M)
Mitteilungen der Österreichischen
geographischen Gesselschaft. Verleger, Her-
ausgeber und Eigentümer. Vienna. (OGG/M)
Montalbán. Univ. Católica Andrés Bello, Fa-
cultad de Humanidades y Educación, Ins-
titutos Humanísticos de Investigación. Ca-
racas. (UCAB/M)
Monthly Review. An independent Socialist
magazine. N.Y. (MR)
Mother Jones. Foundation for National Prog-
ress. San Francisco, Calif.
Il Mulino. Rivista mensile di cultura e politica. Bologna, Italy. (MULINO)
Mundo Hispánico. Madrid. (MH)

NACLA: Report on the Americas. North
American Congress and Latin America.
N.Y.
NACLA's Latin America & Empire Report.
North American Congress on Latin Amer-
ica. N.Y.
NS NorthSouth NordSud NorteSur Norte Sul.
Canadian journal of Latin American studies.
Canadian Association of Latin American
Studies. Univ. of Ottawa. Ottawa. (NS)
National Geographic Magazine. National Geo-
graphic Society. Washington. (NGS/NGM)
Natural History. American Museum of Natu-
ral History. N.Y. (AMNH/NH)
Nature. A weekly journal of science. Mac-
Millan & Co. London (NWJS)
Ñawpa Pacha. Institute of Andean Studies.
Berkeley, Calif. (IAS/ÑP)
Neues Jahrbuch für Geologie und Paläon-
tologie. Stuttgart. (NJGP)
New Mexico Historical Review. Univ. of New
Mexico [and] Historical Society of New
Mexico. Albuquerque. (UNM/NMHR)

New Scientist. London. (NSCI)
The New York Review of Books. N.Y.
Nheengatu. Cadernos brasileiros de ar-
queologia e indigenismo. Instituto Superior
de Cultura Brasileira. Rio.
Nieuwe West-Indische Gids. Martinus Nijhof.
The Hague. (NWIG)
Norte Grande. Revista de estudios integrados
referentes a comunidades humanas del
Norte Grande de Chile, en una perspectiva
geográfica e histórico-cultural. Univ.
Católica de Chile, Instituto de Geografía,
Depto. de Geografía de Chile, Taller Norte
Grande. Santiago. (UCC/NG)
Notes et Études Documentaires. Direction de
la Documentation. Paris. (FDD/NED)
La Nouvelle Revue des Deux Mondes. Paris.
(NRDM)
Nueva Ciencia. Revista cuatrimestral. Univ.
Central de Venezuela, Facultad de Econo-
mía, Instituto de Investigaciones. Caracas.
(UCV/NC)
Nueva Política. Grupo Residencial San Souci.
Caracas.
Nueva Sociedad. Revista política y cultural.
San José. (NSO)

OCLAE. Revista mensual. Organización Con-
tinental Latinoamericana de Estudiante. La
Habana. (OCLAE)
Objets et Mondes. Musée de l'Homme. Paris.
(MH/OM)
Oceanus. Oceanographic Institution. Woods
Hole, Mass. (OCEANUS)
Orbis. A journal of world affairs. Foreign Pol-
icy Research Institute, Philadelphia, Pa. *in
association with the* Fletcher School of Law
and Diplomacy, Tufts Univ., Medford,
Mass. (FPRI/O)
Ornament VIA III. Univ. of Pennsylvania,
Graduate School of Fine Arts. Philadelphia.

Pacific Viewpoint. Victoria Univ. of Wel-
lington, Dept. of Geography. Wellington,
New Zealand.
Paideuma. Mitteilungen Zur Kulturkunde.
Deutsche Gesellschaft für kulturmor-
phologie von Frobenius Institut au der
Johann Wolfgang Goethe–Universität.
Wiesbaden, FRG. (PMK)
Papers in Anthropology. Univ. of Oklahoma,
Dept. of Anthropology. Norman.
El Papiro. Orgáno de la Asociación Domini-
cana de Bibliotecarios (ASODOBI). Santo
Domingo.

Pensamiento Político. Cultura y ciencia política. México. (PPO)

Pesquisa e Planejamento Econômico. Instituto de Planejamento Econômico e Social. Rio. (IPEA/PPE)

Phylon. Atlanta Univ. Atlanta, Ga. (AU/P)

Planejamento. Governo de Estado da Bahia, Secretaria do Planejamento, Ciência e Tecnologia. Salvador, Brazil.

Política. Fundação Milton Campos. Brasília.

Política y Sociedad. Univ. de San Carlos de Guatemala, Facultad de Ciencias Jurídicas y Sociales, Escuela de Ciencia Política, Instituto de Investigaciones Políticas y Sociales. Guatemala. (USCG/PS)

Political Studies. Political Studies Association of the United Kingdom. Oxford, U.K. (PSA/PS)

Population Studies. London School of Economics, The Population Investigation Committee. London. (LSE/PS)

Problemas Brasileiros. Revista mensal de cultura. Conselho Regional de Serviço Social do Comércio (SESC). São Paulo. (SESC/PB)

Probleme des Friedens und des Sozialismus. Zeitschrift der kommunistischen und Arbeiterparteien. Dietz Verlag. Berlin, GDR.

Problèmes d'Amérique Latine XLIII. Série de Notes et Études Documentaires. La Documentation Française. Paris.

Problems of Communism. United States Information Agency. Washington. (USIA/PC)

Proceedings of the American Philosophical Society. Philadelphia, Pa. (APS/P)

Proceedings of the National Academy of Sciences. Washington. (NAS/P)

Proceedings of the Pacific Coast Council on Latin American Studies. Univ. of California. Los Angeles. (PCCLAS/P)

Prologue. National Archives. Washington.

Quaderni Asnal. Associazione per gli Studi e la Documentazzione dei Problemi Socio-Religiosi dell'America Latina. Roma.

Quarterly Economic Review: Uruguay, Paraguay. The Economist Intelligence Unit (EIU). London.

Quarterly Review. Banca Nazionale del Lavoro. Rome. (BNL/QR)

Rassegna Italiana di Sociologia. Societa Editrice Il Mulino. Bologna, Italy.

Realidad Contemporánea. Editora Alfa y Omega. Santo Domingo.

Referativa. Ministerio de Educación, Centro de Documentación e Información Pedagógica. La Habana.

Relaciones de la Sociedad Argentina de Antropología. B.A. (SAA/R)

Relaciones Internacionales. Revista del Centro de Relaciones Internacionales. Univ. Nacional Autónoma de México, Facultad de Ciencias Políticas y Sociales. México. (UNAM/RI)

Research Reports: 1969 Projects. National Geographic Society. Washington.

Resenha de Política Exterior do Brasil. Revista trimestral. Ministerio das Relações Exteriores. Brasília.

Resuménes Analíticos en Educación. Centro de Investigación y Desarrollo de la Educación (CIDE), Servicio de Documentación. Santiago.

Resúmenes de Formación Profesional. Centro Interamericano de Investigación y Documentación sobre Formación Profesional (CINTERFOR). Montevideo.

The Review of Black Political Economy. National Economic Association [and] Atlanta Univ. Center. Atlanta, Ga. (NEA/RBPE)

The Review of Economics and Statistics. Harvard Univ. Cambridge, Mass.

The Review of Politics. Univ. of Notre Dame. Notre Dame, Ind. (UND/RP)

Revista Argentina de Relaciones Internacionales. Revista cuatrimestral. Centro de Estudios Internacionales Argentinos (CEINAR). B.A.

Revista Brasileira de Economía. Fundação Getúlio Vargas, Instituto Brasileiro de Economia. Rio. (IBE/RBE)

Revista Brasileira de Estudos Políticos. Univ. de Minas Gerais. Belo Horizonte, Brazil. (UMG/RBEP)

Revista Brasileira de Geografia. Conselho Nacional de Geografia, Instituto Brasileiro de Geografia e Estatística. Rio. (IBGE/R)

Revista Brasileira de Lingüística. Sociedade Brasileira para Professores de Lingüística. São Paulo. (SBPL/RBL)

Revista Brasileira de Mercado de Capitais. Instituto Brasileiro de Mercado de Capitais (IBMEC). Rio.

Revista Cartográfica. Instituto Panamericano de Geografía e Historia, Comisión de Cartografía. México. (PAIGH/RC)

Revista Chilena de Antropología. Univ. de Chile, Depto. de Antropología. Santiago.

Revista Chilena de Historia y Geografía. Sociedad Chilena de Historia y Geografía. Santiago. (SCHG/R)

Revista Coachuilense de Historia. Colegio Coahuilense de Investigaciones Históricas. Saltillo, Mex.

Revista Colombiana de Antropología. Ministerio de Educación Nacional, Instituto Colombiano de Antropología. Bogotá. (ICA/RCA)

Revista da Escola de Biblioteconomia. Univ. Federal de Minas Gerais. Belo Horizonte, Brazil.

Revista da Faculdade de Educação. Univ. de São Paulo, Faculdade de Educação. São Paulo.

Revista de Administração Pública. Fundação Getúlio Vargas, Escola Brasileira de Administração Pública. Rio. (FGV/RAP)

Revista de Antropología. Casa de la Cultura Ecuatoriana, Núcleo del Azuay. Cuenca. Ecua. (CCE/RA)

Revista de Biología Tropical. Univ. de Costa Rica [and] Consejo Nacional de Investigaciones Científicas y Tecnológicas (CONICIT). San José. (UCR/RBT)

Revista de Ciencias Sociales. Univ. de Puerto Rico, Colegio de Ciencias Sociales. Río Piedras. (UPR/RCS)

Revista de Economía Latinoamericana. Banco Central de Venezuela. Caracas. (BCV/REL)

Revista de Estudios Agro-Sociales. Instituto de Estudios Agro-Sociales. Madrid. (IEAS/R)

Revista de Estudios del Pacífico. Consejo Coordinador Universitario de Valparaíso, Centro de Estudios del Pacífico. Valparaíso, Chile. (CEPAC/REP)

Revista de Hacienda. Ministerio de Hacienda. Caracas.

Revista de Historia. Univ. de Concepción, Chile.

Revista de História. Univ. de São Paulo, Faculdade de Filosofia, Ciências e Letras, Depto. de História [and] Sociedade de Estudos Históricos. São Paulo. (USP/RH)

Revista de Indias. Instituto Gonzalo Fernández de Oviedo [and] Consejo Superior de Investigaciones Científicas. Madrid. (IGFO/RI)

Revista de la Academia Colombiana de Ciencias Exactas, Físicas y Naturales. Bogotá. (ACCEFN/R)

Revista de la Biblioteca Nacional José Martí. La Habana. (BNJM/R)

Revista de la Educación Superior. Publicación trimestral. Asociación Nacional de Universidades e Institutos de Enseñanza Superior. México.

Revista de la Escuela de Diplomacia. Univ. de Guayaquil. Guayaquil, Ecua.

Revista de la Facultad de Derecho. Univ. Nacional Autónoma de México. México. (UNAM/RFD)

Revista de la Junta de Estudios Históricos de Mendoza. Mendoza, Arg. (JEHM/R)

Revista de la Junta Provincial de Historia de Córdoba. Archivo Histórico Monseñor P. Cabrera.Córdoba, Arg. (JPHC/R)

Revista de la Sociedad Mexicana de Historia Natural. México. (SMHN/R)

Revista de la Universidad de Costa Rica. San José. (UCR/R)

Revista de la Universidad de Yucatán. Merida. (UY/R)

Revista de la Universidad del Zulia. Maracaibo, Ven. (UZ/R)

Revista de Política Internacional. Instituto de Estudios Políticos. Madrid. (IEP/RPI)

Revista del Archivo General de la Nación. B.A.

Revista del Centro de Investigación y Acción Social. B.A.

Revista del Instituto de Ciencias Sociales. Diputación Provincial de Barcelona. Barcelona, Spain. (DPB/RICS)

Revista del Instituto de Cultura Puertorriqueña. San Juan. (ICP/R)

Revista del Instituto de Investigaciones Educativas. B.A.

Revista del México Agrario. Confederación Nacional Campesina. México. (CNC/RMA)

Revista del Museo Nacional. Casa de la Cultura del Perú, Museo Nacional de la Cultura Peruana. Lima. (PEMN/R)

Revista do CEPA. Associação Pro-Ensino, Centro de Ensino e Pesquisas Arqueológicas. Santa Cruz do Sul, Brazil.

Revista do Instituto de Estudos Brasileiros. Univ. de São Paulo, Instituto de Estudos Brasileiros. São Paulo. (USP/RIEB)

Revista do Instituto Histórico e Geográfico Brasileiro. Rio. (IHGB/R)

Revista do Instituto Histórico e Geográfico de São Paulo. São Paulo. (IHGSP/R)

Revista do Museu Paulista. São Paulo. (MP/R)

Revista Dominicana de Antropología e Historia. Univ. Autónoma de Santo Domingo, Facultad de Humanidades, Depto. de Historia y Antropología, Instituto de Investigaciones Antropológicas. Santo Domingo. (UASD/R)

Revista Econômica do Nordeste. Banco do Nordeste do Brasil (BNB), Depto. de Estudos Econômicos do Nordeste (ETENE). Fortaleza, Brazil. (BNB/REN)

Revista Eme-Eme. Estudios dominicanos. Univ. Católica Madre y Maestra. Santiago de los Caballeros, R.D. (EME)

Revista Española de la OPINION PUBLICA. Instituto de la Opinión Pública. Madrid. (REOP)

Revista FELABAN. Federación Latinoamericana de Bancos. Bogotá.

Revista Geográfica. Instituto Panamericano de Geografía e Historia. Comisión de Geografía. México. (PAIGH/G)

Revista Geográfica. Univ. de los Andes, Facultad de Ciencias Forestales, Instituto de Geografía y Conservación. Mérida, Colombia.

Revista Geográfica de América Central. Univ. Nacional, Facultad de Ciencias de la Tierra y el Mar, Escuela Geográfica. Heredia, C.R.

Revista Geográfia de Chile. Terra Australis. Instituto Geográfico Militar. Comité Nacional de Geografía, Geodesia y Geofísica [and] Instituto Pan-Americano de Geografía e Historia, Sección Nacional. Santiago.

Revista Interamericana de Bibliografía [Inter-American Review of Bibliography]. Organization of American States. Washington. (RIB)

Revista Interamericana de Planificación. Bogotá.

Revista Interamericana de Psicología (Interamerican Journal of Psychology). Sociedad Interamericana de Psicología (Interamerican Society of Psychology). De Paul Univ., Dept. of Psychology. Chicago, Ill. (SIP/RIP)

Revista Latinoamericana de Ciencia Política. Facultad Latinoamericana de Ciencias Sociales, Escuela Latinoamericana de Ciencia Política y Administración Pública. Santiago. (FLACSO/RLCP)

Revista Latinoamericana de Psicología. Bogotá. (RLP)

Revista Médica de Chile. Sociedad Médica de Santiago. Santiago. (SMS/RMC)

Revista Mexicana de Ciencias Políticas y Sociales. Univ. Nacional Autónoma de México, Facultad de Ciencias Políticas y Sociales. México. (UNAM/RMCPS)

Revista Mexicana de Estudios Antropológicos. Sociedad Mexicana de Antropología. México. (SMA/RMEA)

Revista Mexicana de Sociología. Univ. Nacio-nal Autónoma de México, Instituto de Investigaciones Sociales. México. (UNAM/RMS)

Revista Nacional de Cultura. Consejo Nacional de Cultura. Caracas. (CONAC/RNC)

Revista Paraguaya de Sociología. Centro Paraguayo de Estudios Sociológicos. Asunción. (CPES/RPS)

Revista Pernambucana de Desenvolvimento. Insitituto de Desenvolvimento de Pernambuco (CONDEPE). Recife, Brazil.

Revista/Review Interamericana. Univ. Interamericana. San Germán, P.R. (RRI)

Revista Universidad de Medellín. Centro de Estudios de Posgrado. Medellín, Colombia. (UM/R)

Revue de l'Institut de Sociologie. Univ. Libre de Bruxelles. Bruxelles. (ULB/RIS)

Revue des Études Coopératives. Institut Français de la Coopération. Paris. (IFC/REC)

Revista Geografica Italiana. Società di Studi Geografici e Coloniali. Firenze, Italy. (SSG/RGI)

Rural Sociology. Rural Sociological Society [and] New York State College of Agriculture. Ithaca. (RSS/RS)

Saeculum. Jahrbuch für Universalgeschichte. München, FRG. (SJUG)

Sapiens. Museu Arqueológico Oswaldo F.A. Menghin. Chivilcoy, Provincia Buenos Aires.

Sarance. Revista del Instituto Otavaleño de Antropología. Otavalo, Ecua.

Science. American Association for the Advancement of Science. Washington. (AAAS/S)

Science and Society. N.Y.

Serie Documentos de Trabajo. Univ. de Chile, Depto. de Ciencias Sociales, Grupo de Arqueología y Museos. Sede Antofagasta.

Série Lingüística. Summer Institute of Linguistics. Brasília.

Smithsonian. Smithsonian Institution. Washington.

Social and Economic Studies. Univ. of the West Indies, Institute of Social and Economic Research. Mona, Jam. (UWI/SES)

Social Biology. Society for the Study of Social Biology. N.Y.

Social Forces. Williams & Wilkins Co. *for the* Univ. of North Carolina Press. Baltimore, Md. (SF)

Social Science and Medicine. N.Y.

Social Science Quarterly. Southwestern Social

Science Association. Austin, Tex. (SSQ)
Social Science Quarterly. Univ. of Texas, Dept. of Government. Austin. (UT/SSQ)
Socialist Thought and Practice. Belgrade, Yugoslavia.
Sociologie du Travail. Association pour le Développement de la Sociologie Travail. Paris. (ADST/SDT)
Sociologus. Zeitschrift für empirische Soziologie, sozialpsychologische und ethnologische Forschung (A journal of empirical sociology, social psychology and ethnic research). Berlin, FRG. (SOCIOL)
Sowjetwissenschaft. Gesellschaft Wissenschaftliche Beiträge. Berlin, GDR.
Staff Papers. International Monetary Fund. Washington. (IMF/SP)
Studies in Comparative International Development. Rutgers Univ. New Brunswick, N.J. (RU/SCID)
Studies in Physical Anthropology. Polish Academy of Sciences. Warsaw.
Stylo. Pontificia Univ. Católica de Chile. Temuco.
Suplemento Antropológico. Univ. Católica de Nuestra Señora de la Asunción, Centro de Estudios Antropológicos. Asunción. (UCNSA/SA)
Symposium. Universidade Católica de Pernambuco. Recife, Brazil.

Temas Administrativos. Univ. de Antioquia, Escuela de Administración y Finanzas e Instituto Tecnológico, Centro de Investigaciones. Medellín, Colombia. (UA/TA)
Temática Dos Mil. Revista de pensamiento. B.A.
Terra. Univ. Central de Venezuela, Facultad de Humanidades y Educación, Area de Geografía. Caracas.
Textile Museum Journal. Washington.
Thesaurus. Boletín del Instituto Caro y Cuervo. Bogotá. (ICC/T)
Thrombosis Research. Pergamon Press. Elmsford, N.Y.
Thunder. People's Progressive Party of Guyana. Georgetown.
Tiers Monde. Problèmes des pays sous-développés. Univ. de Paris, Institut d'Étude du Développement Economique et Social. Paris. (UP/TM)
Tijdschrift voor Economische en Sociale Geographie. Netherlands journal of economic and social geography. Rotterdam, The Netherlands. (TESG)

Tissue Antigens. Copenhagen.
Tokyo Geography Papers. Kyoiku Univ. Dept. of Geography. Tokyo.
Trans/Form/Ação. Faculdade de Filosofia, Ciências e Letras de Assis. Assis, Brazil.
Tribus. Veröffentlichungen des Linden-Museums. Museum für Länder- und Völkerkunde. Stuttgart, FRG. (MLV/T)
El Trimestre Económico. Fondo de Cultura Económica. México. (FCE/TE)
Troquel. Banco Central de Costa Rica. San José.

Universidad. Divulgación filosófica, científica y artística. Univ. Autónoma de Querétaro. Mexico.
Universidad. Univ. de Antioquia. Medellín, Colombia. (UA/U)
Universidad. Univ. Nacional del Litoral. Santa Fé, Arg. (UNL/U)
Universidad de La Habana. La Habana. (UH/U)
Universidad de San Carlos de Guatemala. Guatemala. (USC/U)
L'Universo. Revista bimestrale dell'Istituto Geografico Militare. Firenze, Italy. (IGM/U)
Universo. Univ. Autónoma de Santo Domingo, Facultad de Humanidades. Santo Domingo.
Urban Anthropology. State Univ. of New York, Dept. of Anthropology. Brockport. (UA)

Vierteljahresberichte. Probleme der entwicklungsländer. Forschungs-institut der Friederich-Ebert-Stiftung. Hannover, FRG. (FFES/V)
Vínculos. Revista de antropología. Museo Nacional de Costa Rica. San José. (MNCR/A)
Virgin Islands Archaeological Society Journal. St. Thomas.
Vozes. Revista de cultura. Editora Vozes. Petrópolis, Brazil. (VOZES)

Weltwirschaftliches Archiv. Zeitschrift des Instituts für Weltwirtschaft an der Christians-Albrechts-Univ. Kiel. Kiel, FRG. (CAUK/WA)
William and Mary Quarterly. College of William and Mary, Institute of Early American History and Culture. Williamsburg, Va.
The Wilson Quarterly. Woodrow Wilson International Center for Scholars. Washington. (WQ)
World Archaeology. Routledge & Kegan Paul. London.

World Development. Pergamon Press. Oxford, UK. (WD)

World Politics. A quarterly journal of international relations. Princeton Univ., Center of International Studies. Princeton, N.J. (PUCIS/WP)

The World Today. Royal Institute of International Affairs. Oxford Univ. Press. London. (RIIA/WT)

Yax-kin. Instituto Hondureño de Antropología e Historia. Tegucigalpa. (YAXKIN)

The Yearbook of World Affairs. London Institute of World Affairs. London. (LIWA/YWA)

Zeitschrift für Ethnologie. Deutschen

Gesellschaft für Völkerkunde. Braunschweig, FRG. (DGV/ZE)

Zeitschrift für Geomorphologie. Gebrüder Borntraeger. Berlin. (ZG)

Zeitschrift für Geschichtswinssenschaft. Veb Deutscher Verlag der Wissenschaften. Berlin, GDR. (ZFG)

Zeitschrift für Lateinamerika Wien. Österreisches Lateinamerika-Institut. Wien. (OLI/ZLW)

Zeitschrift für Missionswissenschaft und Religionswissenschaft. Lucerne, Switzerland. (ZMR)

Zeitschrift für Morphologie und Anthropologie. E. Nägele. Stuttgart, FRG. (ZMA)

SUBJECT INDEX

Pre-Columbian Cultures of the Lesser Antilles, 7th, Montreal, Canada (1978), 495. International Congress of Anthropological and Ethnological Sciences, 9th, Chicago, Illinois (1973), 767. Jornadas Peruano-Bolivianas de Estudio Científico del Altiplano Boliviano y del Sur del Perú, I, La Paz (1975), 619. Mesoamerica, 261–471. Mexican Expedition, 267a. Models, 554. "New Archaeology," 280, 554. New World, 259, 562–563, 5273. Research Methods, 637. South America, 562–878. State-of-the-Art, 365. Theories, 339.

ARCHITECTURE. *See also* Housing; Urban Planning. Andes Region, 791. Bibliography, 36. Central America, 36. Chile, 703. Colombia, 9207. Education, 4359. Fortresses, 852. Inca, 793. Maya, 264, 277, 290, 318, 335. Mesoamerica, 267, 282, 290, 297, 299, 318, 329, 334–335, 350, 356, 375–376, 385, 409. Mexico, 5364. Peru, 758, 793, 813, 836, 852. Precolumbian, 252, 562, 791. Tropical, 5688.

Archives. *See also* Libraries and Library Services; Manuscripts. Administration, 56. Archivo del Arzobispado de Córdoba (Argentina), 96. Archivo General de Indias, Seville (Spain), 78. Archivo General de la Nación (Mexico), 101. Archivo General del Estado de Nuevo León (Mexico), 85. Archivo Histórico de Hacienda (Mexico), 94. Argentina, 56. Bibliography, 2. Biblioteca Nacional (Brazil), 95. Congreso Nacional de Archivos de la República Argentina, 1st, Buenos Aires (1977), 56. Paraguay, 95. Tiradentes (Minas Gerais, Brazil), 76. Washington, D.C. Research Guide, 116.

Area Handbook for . . . *See* specific countries.

ARGENTINA. *See also* Antarctica; El Chaco; Malvinas, Islas; Patagonia; Territorio Nacional de la Tierra del Fuego.

Bibliography and General Works, 43, 96, 145, 151, 5429.

Anthropology.
  Archaeology, 578–609, 612, 701.
  Biological Anthropology, 1472, 1492–1493, 1603, 1612, 1615, 1639, 1655.
  Ethnology, 1191, 1230–1231.
  Linguistics, 1343, 1365, 1378, 1432, 1434.

Economics, 2862, 3365–3427, 7479, 7490, 7498.

Education, 4343, 4365–4390, 7507, 9258, 9284.

Geography, 5258, 5281, 5388, 5398–5444, 5734–5752.

Government and Politics, 7008a, 7026, 7028, 7035, 7040, 7053–7054, 7068a, 7120, 7461–7508, 9277.

International Relations, 8763–8764, 8777, 8779, 8781, 8790, 8792, 8796, 8798, 8800, 8802, 8805, 8812–8813, 8818, 8833, 8838, 8844, 8850, 8853, 8861, 8867, 8872, 8889, 8899, 8910.

Sociology, 9004, 9008, 9253–9285, 9400–9401.

Argentina and Brazil Relations, 8798, 9810.

Argentina and Chile Relations, 37.

Argentina and Czechoslovakia Relations, 8833.

Argentina and Europe Relations, 8838.

Argentina and Japan Relations, 8838.

Argentina and Latin America Relations, 8838, 8844.

Argentina and Middle East Relations, 8777.

Argentina and United Kingdom Relations, 8822, 8824, 8863.

Argentina and United States Relations, 3418, 8805, 8844, 8851.

Arhuacos (Indigenous Group), 1255, 1264.

Armed Forces. *See* Military.

Arms. *See also* Disarmament; Military; Military Assistance; National Security.

Archery, 1154. Argentina, 8818. Brazil, 1154, 8818. Nuclear, 8818. Precolumbian, 736. United States to Latin America, 8570, 8837.

ART. *See also* Architecture; Artifacts; Ceramics; Crafts; Film; Inscriptions; Literature; Museums; Music; Petroglyphs; Script; Sculpture; Symbolism. Archaeological Study Techniques, 652. Argentina, 592, 603. Artists, 9411. Aztec, 368, 373. Bibliography, 34, 36, 309, 506. Bolivia, 616. Brazil, 646, 675, 1152, 9408, 9411. Cave Paintings, 420. Central America, 36. Colombia, 716, 719, 722. Colonial Period, 747. Costa Rica, 529, 533, 535. Costumes and Ornaments, 394, 745, 890. Cuna, 926–927. Ecuador, 745, 747. Education, 4603. Fertility, 626. Funerary, 395. Huichol, 885. Human Mask-pectorals, 452. Iconography, 276, 300, 308, 317, 330–331, 337, 390, 392, 423, 425, 539, 545, 788, 804, 839, 924. Masks, 394, 716. Maya, 284a, 290, 318–319, 337. Maya Ballgame Objects, 273, 282. Mesoamerica, 284a, 290, 300, 308–309, 312, 318–319, 324, 328–331, 337, 368, 373, 388, 390, 392–393, 395, 403, 420, 423, 425, 429, 439, 449, 452–453. Mexico, 885. Mural Paintings, 390, 392, 453. Olmec, 276, 283. Panama, 529, 539, 545–546, 560, 924, 926. Peru, 46, 768–

669, 671, 672–673, 789, 841, 867. Societies, 1077. Venezuela, 867.

Burnham, Forbes, 7256, 8733.

Business Administration. *See also* Marketing and Product Distribution. Brazil, 9395. Budgeting, 3156. Chile, 9245. Industrial Relations, 9017. Journals, 75. Labor Relations, 9395. Latin America, 9017. Multinational Corporations, 2795. Peru, 3259. Venezuela, 3156. Worker Participation in Management, 9245.

Bustamante, William Alexander, 7233–7234.

Cabañas, Lucio, 7142.

Cabécar (Indigenous Group), 1652.

Caciques, 7106, 7116, 9094.

CACM. *See* Central American Common Market.

Cakchiquel (Indigenous Group), 985.

Caldera, Rafael, 3138, 7617, 7638.

Calendrics. Inca, 264. Mayan, 5356.

Calles, Plutarco Elías, 4520, 7122.

Campa (Indigenous Group), 1196.

Campesinos. *See* Peasants.

Campos, Roberto de Oliveira, 7548.

Canada and Latin America Relations, 8559, 8568.

Canadian Association for Latin America (CALA), 8559.

Canals. *See* Panama Canal; Transportation.

Cañaris (Indigenous Group), 1265, 1269, 1272.

Candomblé, 9338.

Canela (Indigenous Group), 1132, 1164.

Canelos Quichua (Indigenous Group), 1214.

Cannabis. *See* Drugs, marijuana and hashish.

Cannibalism. *See* Sacrifice.

Canoeiro (Indigenous Group), 1137.

Capital Goods. Mexico, 2967. Policy, 2967.

Capital Markets. Brazil, 3452, 3513. Colombia, 3120. Conference, 3357. Journals, 3511. Peru, 3260. Uruguay, 3357.

Capitalism, 8535, 9028. Amazonia, 5610. Brazil, 3438, 3452, 3486, 7559, 7583, 9046, 9342. Chile, 3234. Colombia, 3101, 3115, 9212. Latin America, 2762, 2887, 9040. Mexico, 976, 2969. Peru, 3251, 3293, 7583. Policies, 9342. State, 7559, 7635, 9342. United States Influence, 8578. Venezuela, 7635. and Women, 9392.

Cárdenas, Lázaro, 7130.

Cardoso, Fernando Henrique, 7049.

Cargo Systems. *See* Social Organization.

Carib Language Group, 1003, 1096.

CARIBBEAN. *See also* specific countries; Lesser Antilles; West Indies.

Bibliography and General Works, 8, 48, 54–55, 109, 128, 153, 1014, 1016, 1062. Anthropology, 1014.
   Archaeology, 48, 472–561.
   Biological Anthropology, 1472, 1591.
   Ethnology, 48, 515, 1015–1016, 1088, 1106, 5728.
   Linguistics, 48, 1349.
Economics, 55, 143, 1106, 2872, 3026–3028, 3036, 8746.
Education, 55, 1023, 4339, 4597–4599, 7177.
Geography, 48, 5287–5298, 5724–5726.
Government and Politics, 55, 7174–7269.
International Relations, 153, 7218, 8607, 8685, 8707–8759.
Sociology, 9032, 9035, 9133–9193, 9158, 9173, 9182, 9200.

Caribbean Community (CARICOM), 3040, 7179. Bibliography, 8. Compared, 2872, 8746. Haiti, 3031. Trade Statistics, 3023.

Caribbean Studies, 128, 1016, 1066.

Caribs (Indigenous Group), 481, 489, 516, 1003, 1088, 1096, 1107, 1138, 1578.

CARICOM. *See* Caribbean Community.

Carijona (Indigenous Group), 1003.

Carranza, Venustiano, 7122.

Cashibo (Indigenous Group), 1218.

Cartagena Agreement. *See* Andean Pact.

Carter, Jimmy, 8501, 8505–8506, 8514, 8530, 8558, 8708, 8745.

Cartography. *See* Maps and Cartography.

Cashinawa (Indigenous Group), 1133, 1161.

Castaneda, Carlos, 884, 988.

Castelauros (Ethnic Group), 942.

Castello Branco, Humberto, 7046, 7530, 7587.

Castro, Cipriano, 3170.

Castro, Fidel, 4454, 4457–4459, 7029, 7187–7193, 7198a, 7206, 8715–8717, 8749, 8751, 8759, 8804.

Castro, Raúl, 7191, 7198a.

Catalogs, card and book. Biblioteca de la Superintendencia de Bancos, Quito, Ecuador, 75. Biblioteca Pública del Estado de Jalisco, Mexico, 73. Catalog of Columbian Serial Titles in the University of Illinois Library at Urbana-Champaign, 84. Catalog of Serial Titles in Brazilian Research Collections, 67. Catálogo de obras manuscritas en Latín de la Biblioteca Nacional de México, 98. Fundação Getúlio Vargas, Biblioteca (Rio de Janeiro, Brazil), 77. Genealogical Society of Utah, 72. Universidade Federal de Bahia, Federico Edelweiss Library, 70. University of Texas at Austin, Latin American Collection Catalog Supplement, 66.

Comuneros. Peru, 9230.
Conflict. *See also* Boundary Disputes; Class Conflict. International, 8821.
Conscientization, 4303, 4347, 9333.
Conservation. *See also* Ecology; Natural Resources. Amazonia, 5600. Archaeological, 702. Brazil, 5600, 5635, 5638, 5708. Chile, 8810. Conference, 5277. Environmental, 3037, 5305, 5635, 5638, 5708. Flora and Fauna, 1172, 8611. Forests, 5649, 5676. Latin America, 1484, 8811, 8884. Marine Environments, 5307. Mexico, 906.
Constitutional History and Constitutionalism. Argentina, 7464. Brazil, 7555. Chile, 7394, 7412. Colombia, 7304. Congresses and Parliaments, 7579. Costa Rica, 7151, 7158. Cuba, 7201. Ecuador, 7318, 7322. Latin America, 7095. Mexico, 7123, 7146. Uruguay, 7598, 7608.
Consumption. Argentina, 3386, 3395. Brazil, 3448, 3495, 9317. Chile, 1609. Colombia, 9218. and Credit Industry, 3495. Cuba, 3082. Dominican Republic, 9138. Electric, 3395. Food, 1604–1609, 3448. Latin America, 2865. Mexico, 1604. Patterns, 9218. Price Statistics, 3339. Survey, 3448. Uruguay, 3339.
Contestado Rebellion, 9396.
Contraceptives. *See* Family Planning.
Contact. Brazil, 639. Colombia, 729. Costa Rica, 543. Eastern/Western Hemisphere, 1453. Europe/Mesoamerica, 916, 979. Europe/New World, 1472. Europe/Virgin Islands, 479. Linguistic, 1350, 1399. Mesoamerica, 342, 347, 433, 1453. South America, 1453. South America/Costa Rica, 534. South America/Mesoamerica, 866. Theories, 565, 5256. Transatlantic Migration Theory, 5256. Transoceanic, 1453. Transpacific, 320, 564–565, 738. Venezuela/Antilles, 876.
Convenio Andrés Bello. *See* Education.
COOPERATIVES. *See also* Agrarian Reform; Land Tenure; Peasants. Agricultural, 1077, 9102, 9112. Dominican Republic, 1089. Ecuador, 5539. Government Regulations and Legislation, 7088. Guatemala, 2990, 9112. Honduras, 2981, 9102. Jamaica, 1053. Mexico, 897, 5376, 7088, 9077, 9084, 9094. Panama, 922, 926, 929. Peru, 9236. Production, 9102. Venezuela, 3180.
Cooperativism. Peru, 3261, 3288.
Coras (Indigenous Group), 1575.
Coronelismo, 7554, 9396.

Corporación Andina de Fomento (CAF). *See* Andean Development Corporation.
Corporación Venezuela de Fomento (CVF). *See* Venezuelan Development Corporation.
Corporación Venezolana de Guayana (CVG). *See* Venezuelan Corporation of Guayana.
Corporatism. *See also* Authoritarianism; Dictatorships. Argentina, 9008. Brazil, 7588–7589, 8832. Chile, 7398. Latin America, 7003, 7027, 7083. Mexico, 9072. Model, 7027. Peru, 9229. Uruguay, 9008.
Corruption. Government, 7632. Puerto Rico, 9178. Venezuela, 7632.
Cosmology. Campa, 1196. Canelos Quichua, 1214. Maya, 539. Mexico, 274–275. Panama, 539. Peru, 1319. Precolumbian, 924.
COSTA RICA.
Bibliography and General Works, 23, 151, 528, 886.
Anthropology, 528.
Archaeology, 527, 529, 533–535, 541–542, 550–551, 555, 558–559.
Biological Anthropology, 1465, 1493, 1652.
Ethnology, 886, 893, 1045.
Economics, 2756, 2992.
Education, 4357, 4447–4452, 7161.
Geography, 5309–5313, 5817–5819.
Government and Politics, 7016, 7151–7161.
International Relations, 8560, 8665–8666, 8669, 8672, 8694.
Sociology, 9010, 9034, 9103–9104, 9107–9110, 9118, 9126–9127.
Costa Rica and Nicaragua Relations. *See* Boundary Disputes.
Costa Rica and United States Relations, 8691.
Costumes and Ornaments. *See* Art.
Council of Mutual Economic Assistance (COMECON). and Cuba, 3079, 8713.
Coup d'Etat. Argentina, 7506. Argentina (1966), 7500. Argentina (1976), 9267. Brazil (1964), 7525, 7541, 7544. Chile (1973), 7399, 7408, 7417, 7436, 7443, 7457. Ecuador, 7319. Uruguay (1973), 3351. and United States Foreign Policy, 8902.
CRAFTS. *See also* Artifacts; Ceramics; Textiles and Textile Industry. Argentina, 254. Basketry, 1150. Bibliography, 254. Bolivia, 1237. Ceramics, 1162. Colombia, 5811. Ecuador, 1275. Hammock-making, 938. Map, 5811. Mexico, 938. Panama, 254. Peru, 761, 843. Production Theory, 898. Silversmithing, 254. Stonework, 898. Surinam, 1037. Weaving, 254, 761, 1162, 1237, 1242, 1271.
Credit. *See also* Banking and Financial Institu-

tina, 3424. Brazil, 5670, 7568, 7586. Chile,
7379, 7568. Colombia, 1485. Common Ex-
ternal Duty, 3213. Cuba, 7214a. for
Development, 3207. International, 2764.
Latin America, 2771, 7033. Mexico, 2948.
Model for Measuring Change in the Social
Sciences, 3142. Mesoamerica, 336. Peruvian
Economy, 3246. Prebisch Models, 2796. Precolumbian, 336. Sunkel Model, 2768.
Uruguay, 7602.
Economic Planning. *See also* Economic Devel-
opment, planning. Brazil, 3436. Cuba, 3052,
3057, 3074. Venezuela, 3136, 3189.
Economic Policy. Argentina, 3372, 3378,
3387–3389, 3402, 3409, 7508. Brazil, 3450,
3467, 3527, 3529, 3531. Central America,
3014. Chile, 3202, 3207, 3221, 3227, 3236.
Colombia, 3120. Cuba, 3058, 3076–3078,
3082. Dominican Republic, 3029. Latin
America, 2829. Macroeconomic Policy,
3455. Mexico, 2948, 2960. Peru, 3265, 3292.
Uruguay, 3349, 3363. United States, 8710.
Venezuela, 3127, 3136, 3143, 3148, 3191.
Economic System of Latin America (SELA),
8502, 8509, 8562, 8566. and the United
States, 2878.
ECONOMICS (items 2751–3532). *See also*
Banking and Financial Institutions; Capital
Markets; Debt; Economic Development;
Economic History; Economic Integration;
Economic Policy; Fiscal Policy; Foreign In-
vestment; Foreign Trade; Imports and
Exports; Income Distribution; Industry and
Industrialization; Inflation; International
Economic Relations; Investment; Multina-
tional Corporations; New International
Economic Order; Private Enterprise; Projections, economic; Public Enterprise; Public
Finance; Research; Tariffs and Trade Policy;
Taxation; Teaching; specific countries, organizations and economic groups. Applied,
2984. Bibliography, 3, 17, 31, 49, 55. Conferences, 3116, 3505. Economists, 3081,
3409, 3509, 3523–3524, 7101. Journal Indexes, 106. Journals, 2780, 2789, 2800, 2805,
2985–2986, 3031, 3042, 3140, 3142, 3161–
3163, 3166–3167, 3209, 3234, 3253, 3328,
3449, 3505, 3511, 3514, 3516. Macroeconomic Theory, 3159. Statistics, 2968, 3182,
3186. Textbooks, 3068. Theory, 2771, 2796.
Economies. Bolivia, 3311. Brazil, 3485. Latin
America, 251, 2809, 2878, 2929, 3171.
Ecosystems. *See* Ecology.

ECUADOR.
Bibliography and General Works, 83, 151,
7315.
Anthropology.
Archaeology, 723, 731–749.
Biological Anthropology, 1444, 1502,
1530, 1657, 1666.
Ethnology, 1149, 1177, 1214, 1265–1276.
Linguistics, 1351, 1403, 1425.
Economics, 2756, 3122–3124, 8905.
Education, 4309, 4440, 4480, 4482.
Geography, 5378–5380, 5390, 5392, 5527–
5541, 5826–5833.
Government and Politics, 7312–7322.
International Relations, 7315, 8799, 8850,
8905.
Sociology, 9225–9228.
EDUCATION (items 4301–4633). *See also*
Educators; Literacy and Illiteracy; Mass Me-
dia; Public Policy; Students; Teaching;
Teacher Training; Television, educational;
Universities, University Reform; specific
disciplines; specific countries. Administra-
tion, 4319, 4383, 4443, 4461, 4497, 4598,
4606. Adult, 4314, 4411, 4414, 4442, 4453,
4475, 4488, 4491, 4539, 4549, 4557, 4611.
Bibliography, 55, 133, 4321, 4371, 4405,
4437, 4537, 4554, 4557, 4611, 9027. Centro
Interamericano de Investigación y Docu-
mentación sobre Formación Profesional
(CINTERFOR), 4334. Communist, 4461.
Comparative, 4385, 4502. Conferences,
4306, 4329, 4333, 4343–4344, 4349–4351,
4353, 4400, 4440, 4472, 4479, 4495, 4586.
Convenio Andrés Bello, 4309, 4440, 8799.
Curriculum, 4331, 4351, 4456, 4496, 4587.
Cost, 4588. Deficiencies, 4339. Dissertations, 4554. Educational Assistance to Latin
America, 4305. Enrollment, 4513, 4584.
Evauation of, 4393, 4502, 4555, 4625. Financing of, 4324, 4357, 4373, 4547. Foreign
Influence, 4452, 4553. Government Organizations, 4421, 4486, 4574, 4589. Government Regulations and Legislation, 4395,
4455, 4494, 4513, 4547, 4558, 4566, 4609,
4617. Growth, 4458–4459, 4477. History,
4377, 4524, 4535, 4553, 4576, 4630. Institutions and Schools, 4331, 4631. Journals,
4306, 4314–4316, 4341–4342, 4345, 4457–
4459, 4523, 4566, 4598, 4624. Mexico, 97.
Non-formal, 4322–4323, 4355, 4393, 4397,
4418, 4569, 4593, 4601. Occupational Training, 4321, 4332–4334, 4341–4342, 4456,
4460, 4496, 4539, 4586, 4593. Planning,
4463, 4487, 4582, 4594–4595, 4625, 7518.

El Salvador and Honduras Relations. *See*
Boundary Disputes.
El Salvador, Handbook for, 148
Emberá (Indigenous Group), 1158, 1256, 1263.
Emerillon (Indigenous Group), 1553.
Emigration. *See* Migration.
EMPLOYMENT. *See also* Labor and Unions;
Unemployment; Underemployment. Argentina, 3394, 9283. Bolivia, 3321. Brazil, 3449,
3491, 3530–3531. Caribbean Commonwealth, 3026. Chile, 3209. Colombia, 3114,
9214. Conferences, 4333, 9283. Costa Rica,
5310. Cuba, 3082. El Salvador, 3012–3013.
Haiti, 9152. Latin America, 2790, 2831,
9283. Mexico, 2963, 9283. Northeast, Brazil,
3518. Paraguay, 3328. Peru, 3250. Policy,
2816, 3321. Rural, 3491, 3518. Surveys,
3344. Uruguay, 3344. Venezuela, 3173,
9194, 9201. Women, 3114, 3173, 9201.
Enculturation, 975. Guajiro Girls, 1213. Latin
America, 260. Mexico, 916. Panama, 922.
Venezuela, 1213, 1216. Warao, 1216.
ENERGY SOURCES. *See also* Petroleum and
Petrochemical Industry. Amazonia, 5773.
Antarctica, 5415. Argentina, 3379, 3395–
3396, 5416, 5430, 5737, 7483. Atomic,
5660. Biomass Program, 5634. Bolivia, 5762.
Brazil, 3500, 4632, 4634, 5660, 5675, 5781,
7515. Colombia, 3110, 4416. Conferences,
7010, 8605. Cost, 5284. Cuba, 3070. and
Development, 5284. Electric, 3110, 3279,
3395–3396, 3500, 7515. Electric Companies, 7483. Electric Power Distribution,
5762, 5773, 5781, 5794, 5855. Gas, 5737.
Gasoline, 7515. Geothermal Energy, 3018,
3038, 3110, 5480, 5612. Haiti, 3033, 3038,
9152. Honduras, 2998. Hydroelectric, 2998,
3038, 3343, 5284, 5416, 5430, 5634, 8851.
and International Politics, 8851. Latin
America, 5271, 7078, 8605. Maps, 5737,
5762, 5773, 5781. Mexico, 2961, 5855,
8654–8655. Natural Gas, 5737, 8627, 8654–
8655. Nuclear, 3070, 4632, 5284, 5634,
5660, 7010, 7515. Peru, 3279. Policies, 3500,
5660, 8654–8655. Project Evaluation, 2961
Solar, 3037, 5634. Sugar, 3038, 5675. Uruguay, 3343. Venezuela, 3186. Wind, 3038.
Environmental Studies. *See* Ecology; Pollution.
Epidemiological Anthropology (items 1636–
1672). *See also* Disease; Folk Medicine;
Health Care; Public Health. Amazonia,
1665. Argentina, 1639, 1655. Bahamas,
1654. Brazil, 1636, 1640, 1643, 1649, 1659–
1661, 1663, 1665. Chile, 1658. Colombia,

1644. Costa Rica, 1652. Cuba, 1648. Ecuador, 1657, 1666. Guatemala, 1646, 1653,
1662, 1670, 1672. Haiti, 1664. Latin America, 1642, 1650. Mexico, 1647, 1651, 1667–
1669. Paraguay, 1637–1638, 1645. Puerto
Rico, 1656. Trinidad, 1671.
Ethnic Groups. *See* names of specific groups.
Ethnicity, 1011, 1036, 1065, 1071, 1263.
Ethnocide. Ecuador, 1276. Venezuela, 1170.
Ethnography. *See also* specific ethnic and indigenous groups. Brazil, 9303. Colombia,
1258.
Ethnological Projects. Bibliography of the Harvard University Chiapas Project, 983.
Harvard University Central Brazil Research
Project, 1174. Marandu Project (Paraguay),
1123, 1200.
Ethnohistory. Caribbean, 515, 1104. Dominica, 503. Latin America, 1104. Trinidad,
481.
ETHNOLOGY (items 879–1330). *See also*
Anthropology; Blacks; Caribs; Creoles; Indigenous Peoples; Kinship; Migration; Race
and Race Relations; Religion; Social Organization; and specific countries. Bibliography,
48, 1153, 1179, 1181, 1221. Paleoethnology,
641. Soviet School Map, 5728.
Europe and Latin America Relations. *See also*
specific countries. 8542a, 8589, 8838.
European Economic Community, 8540. and
Central America, 8689.
Exchange Rate Policy. Argentina, 3410.
Exchange Systems. *See* Trade, precolumbian.
Exploration and Expeditions. *See also* Travel
and Tourism. Amazonia, 1122. Antarctica,
5397, 8790, 8858. Archaeological Tour,
267a. Argentina, 5431, 8790. Brazil, 1152,
5608, 5631, 5664, 5693–5694. Chile, 5467.
Colombia, 5504. Easter Island (Chile), 5482.
Ecuador, 5380, 5536. Explorers, 8790. Mexico, 5359. New World, 5259. Panama, 5331.
Patagonia, 5418, 5432. Peru, 5553.
Export Promotion. *See also* Imports and Exports. Bibliography, 51. Brazil, 3508, 3532.
Chile, 3205, 3210, 3216. Conference, 2926.
Latin American Countries, 2926. Less Developed Countries, 2840, 2926. Mexico,
2945. Peru, 3291.
Exports. *See* Imports and Exports.
Expropriation. *See* Nationalization.
External Debt. *See* Debt.

Facio, Rodrigo, 4450.
FALKLAND ISLANDS. *See* Malvinas, Islas.
FAMILY AND FAMILY RELATIONSHIPS.

Fiscal Reform. Brazil, 3436. Chile, 3241. Venezuela, 3167.

FISH AND FISHING INDUSTRY. *See also* Law of the Sea; Marine Resources; Territorial Waters. Brazil, 5628, 5681. Central America, 5307. Colombia, 1111, 1158. Cuba, 3053. Dominican Republic, 1049. Food Industry, 5283, 5287, 5470. Grenada, 1022. Impact of Technological Change, 1022. Makuna, 1111. Panama, 1078. Peru, 1119, 5544. Puerto Rico, 1078. Seal Hunting, 5472. Whale Hunting, 5472.

FLORA AND FAUNA. *See also* Botany; Ecology; Fish and Fishing Industry; Forests and Forest Industry; Marine Resources; Natural Resources; Paleobotany; Paleontology. Alligators, 5575. Animal Domestication in the New World, 576, 775, 857. Argentina, 608, 5420, 5422, 5752. in Art, 768–769. Birds, 5580. Bolivia, 5761. Brazil, 653, 5611, 5629, 5649, 5651, 5664, 5719, 5772. Camelidae, 576, 775, 857. Central America, 5307. Chile, 5469, 5479. Colombia, 5488. Conferences, 5378, 8611. Conservation, 1172, 8611. Costa Rica, 5313. Crustacea, 5479. Cuba, 5292. Ecuador, 5378–5379, 5529, 5538. Ethnozoology, 480, 928, 1295. Faunal Remains, 857. Galapagos Islands (Ecuador), 5533–5534. Government Regulations and Legislation, 5292. Guinea Pigs, 576. Guyana, 1035. Hairless Dogs, 855. Introduction of Crops into the New World, 5719. Margarita Island (Venezuela), 5575. Marine, 5529. Mexico, 928, 5333, 5336, 5345, 5353, 5857, 8611. in Mythology, 924. Naturalists, 5422, 5612, 5664, 5693–5694. Origins of New World Crops, 573. Paleoethnozoology, 608. Panama, 544–545. Peru, 576, 775, 855, 1295, 5547–5548, 5900. Peru/Australia, 5396. Peru/Java, 5396. Plankton, 5469. Plants, 5378–5379, 5566. Plant Domestication in the New World, 572, 577. Precolumbian, 483, 547, 550, 615, 780–781, 806, 824, 863. Tortoises, 5534. Trees, 5307, 5313, 5420. Vegetation, 5336, 5353, 5379, 5538, 5547–5548, 5651. Vegetation Maps, 5752, 5761, 5772, 5857, 5900. Venezuela, 5566, 5580. Wildlife, 5422. Wild Ungulates, 5274.

Folk Healers. *See also* Shamanism. Brazil, 1643, 1654. Paraguay, 1637. Peru, 1318, 1321. Puerto Rico, 1047–1048, 1656. Trinidad and Tobago, 994.

FOLKLORE. *See also* Catholic Church, folk catholicism; Folk Medicine; Literature, folk; Music, folk. Brazil, 92, 9331, 9387.

Carib-speaking Indians, 1003. Dominican Republic, 998. Ecuador, 1288. Guatemala, 1653. Guyana, 1003. Jamaica, 1002. Mesoamerica, 319. Methodology, 998. Mexico, 928. Panama, 889. Peru, 1277, 1292, 1415. Quechua, 1277. Texts, 1365, 1415.

Folk Medicine. *See also* Drugs; Folk Healers; Shamanism. Andean region, 1223. Costa Rica, 1652. Ecuador, 1657. Ethnosemantics, 990. Guatemala, 1470, 1653, 1662, 1670. Guyana, 1013. Mesoamerica, 310. Mexico, 990, 1669. Midwifery, 1470. Paraguay, 1166, 1637. Peru, 1298, 1321, 1441. Puerto Rico, 1047–1048. Trinidad and Tobago, 994, 1671. Venezuela, 1206.

Fondo de Inversiones de Venezuela (FIV), Annual Report, 3144.

Food. *See also* Consumption; Malnutrition; Nutrition. Amazonia, 1192. Andean region, 827. Archaeological Remains, 844. Argentina, 3419. Bolivia, 3314. Brazil, 635, 3490. Colombia, 1111, 1158. Colonial Period, 485. Development Plan, 3278. Fruit Processing Industry, 3341. Indices of Agricultural Production in the Western Hemisphere, 142. Manioc, 635. Marine, 707. Mesoamerica, 421. Mexico, 1604, 1627. Paleoindian, 829. Panama, 552. Peru, 1119, 1133, 1614, 3278. Precolumbian Food Sources, 421, 547, 552, 707, 775. Prices, 3314. Puerto Rico, 9178. Taboos, 1172, 1192.

Ford, Gerald, 7316, 8765, 8804.

Foreign Aid. *See* Economic Assistance; Military Assistance.

FOREIGN INVESTMENT IN. Andean region, 2867, 2923, 8847. Argentina, 3418, 3421. Brazil, 5625. Central America, 2995. Chile, 3179, 3196. Colombia, 3086, 3090, 3099, 3105. Decision-making, 3157. Developing Countries from Other Developing Countries, 2934. Ecuador, 7321. Government Regulation and Legislation, 3188, 8847. Honduras, 3017. Latin America, 2818, 2857, 2863, 2929, 8507, 8511, 8891. Latin American Free Trade Association countries, 2836. Mexico, 2944. Nationalization, 2995. and Opinion Leaders, 3179. Peru, 8891. Policy, 2918. Textbook, 3157. Venezuela, 3151, 3157, 3179, 3188.

Foreign Policy. *See also* specific countries. Argentina, 8798, 8818, 8844, 8889, 8910. Brazil, 8544, 8779, 8798, 8808, 8823, 8830, 8840, 8854, 8865, 8879. British Caribbean, 8720. Chile, 8589, 8908. Cuba, 8722, 8724–8729, 8731–8732. Europe, 8589. Japan,

America, 2986. Chile, 3210, 3212. Commercialization, 3247. Directories, 3212. Ecuador, 2804. Export Finance, 2808, 2892. Export Policies, 2950. Haiti, 3022. Honduras, 3001. Industrial Sector, 3258. International Tin Agreement, 3302. Latin America, 2930. Latin American Dependency, 2886. Latin American Exports, 2837, 2879, 2929, 2932. Latin American Free Trade Association, 2834. Less Developed Countries, 8569. Mexico, 2950, 8641–8642. Paraguay, 3347. Peru, 1313, 3247–3248, 3257–3258, 3266. Policy, 2813. of Public Sector, 3248. United States Dominance, 2886. Uruguay, 3347. Venezuela, 3172. Wheat, 3266. Wool, 1313.

Incas, 597, 694, 703, 739, 748, 756, 787, 793, 806, 810, 815–817, 831, 853.

Income. Argentina, 3405. Bolivia, 3314. Brazil, 1613, 3433, 3469, 3516, 7529. Chile, 3199, 3229. Dominican Republic, 3020. Effects on Diet, 1613. El Salvador, 3013. and Food Prices, 3314. Honduras, 3020. Latin America, 2821, 2865. National Income, 2983, 3020, 3199, 3229, 3274, 3328. Nicaragua, 3003. Panama, 3011. Paraguay, 3328. Peru, 1320, 3274. Uruguay, 3358.

INCOME DISTRIBUTION. Andean region, 2873. Argentina, 3378, 3384, 3407. Brazil, 3429, 3436, 3455, 3480, 5625, 7556. Chile, 3218, 3220, 3235, 4404. Colombia, 9203. Costa Rica, 5310. Cuba, 3058, 3078, 7214a. Ecuador, 3122. and Education, 4404. El Salvador, 5315. Guatemala, 5322. Latin America, 2784, 2826, 2829, 2933. Mexico, 2974, 4540, 5345. Paraguay, 9288. Peru, 7364. Policies, 3078, 7364. Statistics, 3407. Survey of Research, 2942. Venezuela, 3183. World, 2941.

Independence Movements. See also Political Organization and Political Parties; Puerto Rican Status. Caribbean, 8719–8720. Conference, 8720. Grenada, 7242. Jamaica, 1006–1007, 1083, 7237. Latin American, 7036.

Indian Policy. See Public Policy, on Indians.

Indians. See Indigenous Peoples.

Indigenismo, 251, 879, 911.

Indigenous Civilizations. See Aztecs; Cultural Development; Incas; Mayas; Olmecs; Precolumbian Cultures; Toltecs; Zapotecs.

INDIGENOUS LANGUAGES. See also Bilingualism; Dictionaries; Language; Literature; individual countries and regions. Aguaruna, 1342. Andean region, 1331. Araucano, 1365. Arawak, 1430. Arekuna, 1356.

Argentina, 1365, 1378, 1432, 1434. Aymara, 19, 1331, 1370, 1391, 1438. Aweti, 1398. Baja California, 1395–1396. Barasano, 1360, 1424. Bari, 1387. Bibliography, 1352, 1363. Bolivia, 1332, 1378, 1427, 1434. Bora, 1388. Borderlands, 1375. Brazil, 1356, 1367, 1369, 1390, 1393, 1398, 1406, 1421–1423. Campa Ashaninca, 1388. Canamarí, 1369. Capanahua, 1388, 1415. Carib Languages, 1349, 1430. Caribbean, 478, 1349. Cashibo, 1388. Cashinahua, 1388. Catechisms, 113. Chibcha, 1392. Chile, 1378, 1429. Chocho, 1397. Chol, 1362. Chontal, 1436. Chuj, 1414. Classification Systems, 1351, 1412, 1436. Colombia, 1335, 1360, 1379, 1385, 1392, 1417, 1424. Conferences, 1368, 1375. Cora, 1348. Culina, 1388. Cuna, 1389. Discourse Analysis, 1368. Ecuador, 1351, 1403, 1425. Grammars, 1333, 1340, 1366, 1381, 1385, 1390, 1417, 1435. Guahibo, 1379. Guajiro, 1430. Guanano, 1435. Guaraní, 1345, 1352, 1357, 1399, 1409. Guaraqueçaba, 1393. Guatemala, 1358, 1420. Hokan-Yuman Languages, 1353, 1375, 1400, 1436. Honduras, 1359, 1404. Huave, 1426. Huitoto Murui, 1388. Inga, 1385. Jaqaru, 1370. Jicaque, 1404. Jívaro, 1363. Journals, 1383. Kadiwéu, 1367. Kiliwa, 1395–1396. Katukina, 1388. Kawki, 1370. Kaxuyâna, 1406. Mapuche, 1365, 1378, 1429. Mataco, 1432, 1434. Matlatzinca, 1340. Mayan Languages, 464–465, 1337–1339, 1413–1414, 1426, 1428. Mayo, 1386. Mayoruna, 1388. Mazatec, 1377, 1421. Mexico, 1333, 1337–1340, 1346, 1348, 1353, 1362, 1371, 1374–1377, 1386, 1394, 1397, 1400–1401, 1404, 1408, 1412, 1421, 1426, 1433. Mixtec-Zoque, 1426. Mohave, 1395. Morphology, 1371, 1403, 1426, 1434. Mosca, 1333. Moseten, 1427. Munduruku, 1423. Nahuatl, 1333, 1374, 1382. Orejón, 1388. Orthography, 1358, 1438. Oto-Manguean, 1426. Otopamean Languages, 1340, 1394, 1412. Paipai, 1395–1396. Panama, 1389, 1417. Panoan Languages, 1378. Paraguay, 1352, 1357, 1399, 1409, 1434. Parecis, 1416. Peru, 1363, 1378, 1384, 1388, 1405, 1415, 1437. Phonemes, 1394–1395, 1428. Phonology, 1354, 1356, 1359, 1361, 1371, 1376–1378, 1387, 1394, 1403, 1408, 1426, 1432, 1434. Pipil, 1371. Piro, 1388. Place Names, 478. Publications from Spain, 53. Quechua, 1331, 1343, 1366, 1384, 1388, 1403, 1405, 1437. Quiché, 1420. Seri, 1400–1401. South America, 1349, 1402. Subtiaba, 1404. Taino,

Promotion Law, 3356. Property Laws, 3501. Puerto Rico, 9143. Shoe Manufacturing, 5411. State Control, 7140. Statistics, 3307. Surveys, 3346. Technological Innovations, 3435, 3444. Tobacco Industry, 5411. Uruguay, 3340, 3342, 3346, 3356, 3358, 3362. United States/Mexico border, 5343. Venezuela, 2905, 3135, 3139–3140, 3150, 3176, 3191.

INFLATION. Argentina, 3214, 3373–3374, 3377, 3383, 3386, 3405, 3417, 3425. Bolivia, 2756. Brazil, 2756, 3455, 3459, 3474, 3488, 3507, 3509, 3513. Chile, 3214. Colombia, 2756, 3087, 3098, 3107, 3116. Costa Rica, 2756. Ecuador, 2756. Guatemala, 2994. Latin America, 2765, 2829, 2911, 2931. in Less Developed Countries, 2840. Mexico, 2958. Policy, 3214, 3373. Uruguay, 2756. Venezuela, 3146, 3148. World-wide, 2767.

Information Science. See also Library and Information Science. Mexican University Courses, 4515.

Inscriptions. See also Art, Petroglyphs. Brazil, 634, 676. Dominican Republic, 521. Maya, 264, 311, 458, 462, 464–465, 469–470, 1428. Mesoamerica, 430, 469–470. Peru, 779, 807. Pictographs, 521, 634, 676, 779, 807. Stelae, 462.

Insurance. Latin America, 8507.

Intellectual History, 8549, 9046. Brazil, 7589, 9411. Intellectual Revolutionaries, 9026. Intellectuals, 9323, 9411. Journals, 129. Uruguay, 134.

Inter American Development Bank (IDB). Costa Rica, 7155, 8665. Latin America, 7155. Non-regional Members, 2837. President's Speeches, 5272. United States Influence, 8665.

Inter-American Foundation (IAF). Credit to Rural Poor, 2913. Self-assessment, 2838.

Inter-American Relations. See also Inter-American System; specific countries or regions, 8527, 8553, 8582, 8794.

Inter American Research and Documentation Centre on Vocational Training, 4334.

Inter-American System. See also Inter American Development Bank; Organization of American States. Congresses, 8664, 8670, 8897. Economic, Social and Cultural Rights, 8555. History, 8785.

International Agreements. See also Bilateral Agreements; Trade Agreements; Treaties. of the Andean region, 2907. of Central America, 2986. Cultural Conventions, 8783.

International Bank for Reconstruction and Development. See World Bank.

International Court of Justice, 8820

International Economic Relations, 2793, 2828, 8603, 9046–9047. Brazil, 8782. Conferences, 2787–2788. Cuba, 3065, 3079. Journal, 3166. Latin America, 3171. Venezuela, 3131, 3152, 3175.

International Labor Organization (ILO), Mission to El Salvador, 3013.

International Law. See also specific subjects, 8761. International American Law, 8886.

International Organizations. See specific organizations. Handbook, 8536.

INTERNATIONAL RELATIONS (items 8501–8911). See also Boundary Disputes; Foreign Policy; Law of the Sea; Inter-American System; Territorial Claims; specific countries; specific international organizations; specific subjects. Bibliography and General Works, 37. Brazil, 5628. Conference, 8518. Gunder Frank Thesis, 8813. International Conflicts, 8821. Journals, 8520, 8530, 8570, 8586, 8666, 8682, 8721, 8735, 8794, 8798, 8829, 8865, 8867–8868. Marine Problems, 5485.

Interparliamentary Conference, 8629.

INVESTMENT. See also Foreign Investment. Argentina, 3389, 3418, 3420. Brazil, 3456, 3506, 3520, 3522. Chile, 3209, 7422. Cuba, 3048. Dominican Republic, 9170. Fondo de Inversiones de Venezuela (FIV), 3144. Government Regulations and Legislation, 3352, 3356. Guides, 3353. Institutional Investors, 3461. Mexico, 2967. Paraguay, 3325. Peru, 3258, 3283. Policy, 3356. Proyecto Bonao, 9170. Sociological Effects, 9170. Uruguay, 3331, 3352, 3356, 3362. Venezuela, 3144.

Irrigation. Andean region, 827. Argentina, 5258. Brazil, 5779. Colombia, 5258. Maps, 5779, 5861. Mesoamerica, 345, 416, 436. Mexico, 2952, 5258, 5332, 5861. Northeast, Brazil, 5655. Peru, 5258.

ISLA DE SAN LORENZO (Peru), 830.

Israel and Cuba Relations, 8752.

Itaipú Dam Project. See also Archaeological Projects, Itaipú. Argentine Press, 5416, 8851.

Italians in Latin America. Brazil, 5603, 5622, 5665, 5685, 9316, 9343, 9372–9373.

Ixiles (Ethnic Group), 9111.

Jagan, Cheddi, 7262–7263.

JAMAICA
Bibliography and General Works, 8, 151.

and Politics, 7093. Precolumbian Labor, 813. Puerto Rico, 7252. Rural, 9002, 9225–9227, 9232. Sociedad Ganadera del Centro (Peru), 7354. Statistics, 7144. Sugar Cane Cutters, 3289. Teachers Union, 4509. Textile Workers Union, 7089. Urban Market, 3012, 9123. Venezuela, 4571, 4577, 5565, 5570. Women, 9027, 9043, 9071, 9231–9232, 9312, 9376. Work Capacity, 1592. Worker-managed Enterprises, 3436. Workman's Compensation, 9017.

Lacandon (Indigenous Group), 1526.

Ladinos. Guatemala, 985, 9111, 9114. Mexico, 945, 965, 984. Power Structure, 9114.

LAFTA. See Latin American Free Trade Association.

Laming-Emperaire, Annette (Festschrift), 645.

LAND TENURE. See also Agrarian Reform; Cooperatives; Plantations. Argentina, 3390, 5408, 9253, 9258. Belize, 1008. Brazil, 3486, 3525, 7520. Central America, 3016. Chile, 3195, 9252. Colombia, 1256, 1264, 5506, 5512. Costa Rica, 9129. Dominica, 42. Dominican Republic, 1099, 9186. Ecuador, 5535, 9227. Guatemala, 9125. Honduras, 3017. Land Rentals, 3390. Landless Indigenous Groups, 1316. Latin America, 9024, 9048. Mexico, 907, 964, 1473, 2955, 5344. Nicaragua, 5329. Northeast, Brazil, 3475, 3517, 5672. Peru, 1291, 1316, 1327, 5558. Sharecropping, 3486, 3517. Uruguay, 5560–5561. Venezuela, 5570.

Land Use Patterns. See also Agrarian Reform; Agriculture; Land Tenure; Urban Planning. Amazonia, 5650, 5699. Belize, 1008. Bolivia, 5763. Brazil, 3499, 3503, 5607, 5630, 5632, 5642, 5666, 5772. Chile, 5798. Classification System, 5522. Colombia, 5501, 5522. Cuba, 5823. Latin America, 9032. Maps, 5763, 5772, 5798, 5823, 5881. Mesoamerica, 345. Mexico, 5881. Peru, 1282, 1327, 3296.

LANGUAGE. See also Bilingualism; Dictionaries; Indigenous Languages; Linguistics; Literature; Maps and Cartography; Methodology; Public Policy, on languages; Research; Teaching, languages; specific languages or language groups. Arawak, 1096. Carib, 1096. Creole Languages, 1004, 1096. Instituto Lingüístico de Verano, 1217. Jamaica, 1043. Peru, 1217, 1280. Quechua, 1280. Spanish, 1357. Trilingualism, 1333. West Indies, 1096.

Lanusse, Alejandro, 7491, 7500.

Latifundios. See Plantations.

LATIN AMERICA. See specific region or country.

Latin American Episcopal Council (Latin American Council of Catholic Bishops), 7011–7012.

Latin American Free Trade Association (LAFTA). Background, 2856, 2901, 8566, 8746. Banking Systems, 2854. Compared, 2872, 8746. Exports, 2834. Foreign Investment in LAFTA, 2836. Laws of Other Countries Pertaining to LAFTA, 2835. Preference Margins, 2833. Short-run Trade Effects, 2823. Venezuela, 3152.

Latin American Library Collections. See Libraries and Library Services.

Latin American Relations. See specific countries.

Latin American Studies. See also Caribbean Studies; Teaching. Directory of Latin Americanists in Kansas, 100. in Europe, 157. German Latin Americanists, 121. Journals, 27. Journal Index, 104. Latin Americanists, 128. Non-print Materials Research Guide, 137. Research Guides, 103, 116, 137–138. Review of United States Publications on Latin America, 122. Rocky Mountain Council on Latin American Studies, 25th, Tucson, Arizona (1977), 155. Union of Soviet Socialist Republics Survey of United States Institutions, 4352.

Law. See also Government regulations and legislation under specific subject terms; Territorial Law. Bolivia, 7370. Caribbean, 55. Colombia, 7289, 7303. Courts, 7212, 7370. Criminal, 9042. Cuba, 7212. Education, 4570. Law-making Bodies, 9091. Legislative Process, 7289, 7303. Legal/Juridical Structure Changes in Latin America, 7071a.

Law of the Sea. See also Territorial Waters. Andean Policy, 8841. Argentina, 8764, 8850. Brazil, 8850, 8864. Chile, 8850. Conference, 8850, 8868, 8884. Ecuador, 8850. El Salvador, 8850. Honduras, 8677. International, 8791. Latin America, 8554, 8567, 8811, 8849–8850, 8884. Panama, 8850, Peru, 8801, 8843, 8850. Policies, 8864. Third World Positions, 8607, 8888. Treaties, 8671. Uruguay, 8850.

Lebanese in Mexico, 9088.

Leisure. Brazil, 9385, 9387.

Lengua (Indigenous Group), 1574.

LESSER ANTILLES. See also Anguilla; Antigua; Aruba; Barbados; Barbuda; Bonaire; Curaçao; Dominica; Grenada; Guadeloupe; Martinique; Montserrat; Netherlands An-

lands, 5724. Central America, 5304, 5727–
5729, 5884. Chile, 5793–5802. Colombia,
5508, 5803–5816. Computer Mapping,
5689. Costa Rica, 5817–5819. Cuba, 59,
5293, 5820–5823. Dominican Republic,
5294. Ecuador, 5532, 5826–5833. El Salvador, 107, 5834–5836. Galapagos Islands,
5731. Guatemala, 5837–5841. Guyana,
5842. Haiti, 5843–5844. Historical, 5821,
5833, 5850, 5909. History, 5532. Honduras,
5845–5847. Latin America, 5721–5723,
5730. Linguistic, 1336, 1382. Mexico, 5347,
5848–5884. New World, 5259. Nicaragua,
130, 5329, 5883–5884. Panama, 5885. Paraguay, 5892. Peru, 5893–5901. Puerto Rico,
5902–5904. Reference Works, 112. Research
Guide, 116. School Maps of Latin America
(Arabic), 5730, (Chinese), 5722, (Russian),
5723, 5728. School Maps of Individual
Countries, 5839. South America, 5731–
5733. Strait of Magellan, 5473. Surinam,
5905. Textbook, 5657. Trinidad and Tobago,
5906. Uruguay, 5907. Venezuela, 5908–
5918. West Indies, 5727–5729.
Mapuche (Indigenous Group), 1249–1251.
MARAJO ISLAND (Brazil), Bibliography,
5673.
MARGARITA ISLAND (Venezuela), Geogra-
phy, 5575.
Marginality. Argentina, 9266. Brazil, 9304,
9345, 9389. Definition, 9041. Guatemala,
9117. Latin America, 251, 9041, 9047–9048.
Mexico, 939–940. Rural, 9117. Social, 9389.
Mariátegui, José Carlos, 14, 7081.
Marine Resoures. See also Fish and Fishing
Industry. Barbados, 3037. Chile, 8810. Ec-
uador, 5529. Food Source, 5283. Galapagos
Islands (Ecuador), 5527. International, 8791.
Pacific Ocean, 8793. Plant Life, 5529. Seal
Hunting, 5472. Whale Hunting, 5472.
MARKETING AND PRODUCT DISTRIBU-
TION. Agricultural Products, 3254, 3313,
3472. Amazonia, 5549. Argentina, 1230,
3375, 5411, 5428. Aztec, 352. Belize, 5308.
Bolivia, 3313, 5455. Brazil, 3472, 8845,
9317. Colombia, 1262, 5506. Dominican Re-
public, 1049. Guatemala, 5317, 9116.
International, 2798. Kogi, 1262. Mesoamerica, 303, 352. Mexico, 880, 897, 904,
906, 989, 5354, 8612. Multinational Corporations, 2795, 3005. Northeast, Brazil, 3475.
Peru, 3254. Precolumbian, 817. Uruguay,
3332, 5560. Yucatan, 8612.
Maroons (Ethnic Group), 489, 1032, 1040,
1046, 1104.

Marriage. See also Family and Family Relationships. Afro-Caribbean, 1085–1086. Andean region, 1221, 1225. Bolivia, 1235, 9240.
Brazil, 1205. Carib, 1107. Chile, 1495. Colombia, 1160. Curaçao, 1088. Dominica,
1026. Dominican Republic, 1099, 1474.
Guyana, 1107. Jamaica, 9153. Mate Selec-
tion Patterns, 1494–1495. Peru, 1197, 1279,
1293, 1300, 1308. Qolla, 1279. St. Vincent,
1085–1086. Trinidad, 1101. Venezuela,
1201.
MARTINIQUE.
Bibliography and General Works, 69, 151.
Anthropology.
    Ethnology, 1028, 1063, 1070.
Marxism, 7064. Chile, 4406, 7396, 7433. and
Education, 4360, 4461, 4474, 4504. Latin
America, 2762, 7001, 7003, 7047. Mexico,
938, 4504. Production Theory, 898, 938.
Mashco (Indigenous Group), 1140.
Masonry. See Religious Organizations.
MASS MEDIA. See also Communication;
Film; New International Information Order;
Press; Radio; Telecommunications; Televi-
sion. Argentina, 1612. Bibliography, 1.
Bolivia, 7375. Brazil, 7518, 9347, 9349.
Chile, 7424, 7438. Colombia, 4414. Com-
monwealth Caribbean, 7182. Costa Rica,
9110. Creation of Stereotypes, 9110. Cuba,
9. Dominican Republic, 9146–9147. and
Education, 9349. Educational, 4414, 4611.
Effects on Food Consumption, 1612.
Fotonovelas, 9014, 9023, 9329. Guyana,
9155. Guyana Broadcasting Service, 7259.
and National Development, 9155. Peru,
7356. Political Cartoons, 7458. Posters, 9.
Public Policy, 7622. United States/Latin
America, 8563. Venezuela, 7622, 9034. and
Women, 9014.
Mataco (Indigenous Group), 1191.
Mayan Languages. See also Codices; Inscrip-
tions, 459.
Mayas (Ancient). See also Mesoamerica, 264–
264a, 266, 269, 276, 282, 286, 289–291,
295, 298, 307, 311, 318–319, 327–328, 335,
341, 355, 363, 374, 378, 391, 393, 398–400,
433–435, 438–439, 445, 458–460, 462–
465, 5357. Collapse of the Maya Civiliza-
tion, 262. Origins of Maya Civilization, 261.
Quiché, 285
Mayas (Present-day), 890, 909, 950–951, 959,
970–971, 974, 978, 982, 1088, 1632.
Mayos (Indigenous Group), 899–900.
Mazatecos (Indigenous Group), 910.
McGovern, George, 8560.

Negros. *See* Blacks.
NETHERLANDS ANTILLES. *See also* specific islands.
Bibliography and General Works, 3, 128.
Anthropology.
Ethnology, 1088.
Geography, 5563.
NEVIS.
Bibliography and General Works, 8, 151.
Anthropology.
Ethnology, 1088.
New International Economic Order, 2766, 2779, 2798, 2807, 2828, 2878, 3027, 8511, 8516, 8550, 8558, 8646, 8723, 8839, 8857, 8885, 9031.
New International Information Order, 7002, 7022, 8590.
Newspapers. *See* Press.
NICARAGUA.
Bibliography and General Works, 44, 99, 151.
Anthropology.
Archaeology, 532, 548–549.
Ethnology, 1038.
Education, 4532.
Geography, 130, 5327–5330, 5883–5884.
Government and Politics, 7171–7172.
International Relations, 8694, 8755.
Nicaragua and Costa Rica Relations. *See* Boundary Disputes.
Nicaragua and United States Relations, 8530, 8691.
Nixon, Richard, 7617, 8508, 8883.
Non-aligned Nations, 8573, 8713, 8827. Conference, 8784.
Nonviolence. Brazil, 7539.
NORTHEAST, BRAZIL.
Anthropology.
Biological Anthropology, 1471.
Economics, 3467, 3475, 3514–3515, 3517.
Geography, 5592–5593, 5655, 5662, 5672, 5691, 5789.
Nuclear Energy. *See* Energy Sources, nuclear.
Nuclear Power. *See also* Arms; Disarmament; Energy Sources. Argentina, 8584, 8818. Brazil, 8584, 8818, 8848. Brazil/Federal Republic of Germany Accord, 8760, 8762, 8798, 8814, 8848, 8909. Conference, 8605–8606. Latin America, 8548, 8605–8606. Nuclear Non-Proliferation Treaty, 8834. Nuclear Proliferation, 8572, 8605, 8814, 8909. Policies, 8584, 8606, 8760. United States/Latin America, 8584, 8814.
NUTRITION. *See also* Food; Human Development; Malnutrition; Public Policy, on

nutrition. Amazonia, 5600. Andean region, 827. Antigua, 5289. Argentina, 1612. Barbados, 5289. Bolivia, 3306. Brazil, 1583, 1597, 1599, 1613, 1634, 4608, 5681. Caribbean, 490. Chile, 1600, 1609, 1628, 1631, 1658, 3231. Colombia, 1629–1630. Dominican Republic, 1601. Ecuador, 1657. El Salvador, 5289. Fish, 5283, 5287, 5470. Guatemala, 1607, 1624–1626, 1646. Haiti, 3033. Honduras, 1611. Jornadas Peruanas de Bromatología y Nutrición, 4th, Lima (1973), 1614. Latin America, 1484. Mexico, 1604–1605, 1622, 1627, 1667. Peru, 1608, 1614. Survey, 3433. Venezuela, 1583, 1633, 5578.

OAS. *See* Organization of American States.
Obregón, Alvaro, 4520, 7122.
Obsidian. *See also* Artifacts; Dating; Minerals and Mining; Trade, precolumbian. Production Methods, 301.
Occupational Training. *See* Labor and Unions.
Oceanography. *See also* Marine Resources. Argentina, 5736. Bathymetric Chart, 5736. Bottom Contours, 5741, 5744–5745. Currents, 5741. Ecology, 5485. International, 8791. South Atlantic, 5741, 5744–5745.
Oil. *See* Petroleum and Petrochemical Industry.
Olmecs, 271, 276, 333, 401, 566, 1445, 5356.
Onganía, Juan Carlos, 7046, 7480, 7500.
OPANAL. *See* Agency for the Prohibition of Nuclear Weapons in Latin America.
OPEC. *See* Organization of Petroleum Exporting Countries.
Organismo para la Proscripción de las Armas Nucleares en la América Latina. *See* Agency for the Prohibition of Nuclear Weapons in Latin America.
Organization of American States (OAS). American Treaty of Pacific Settlement (Pact of Bogotá), 8575. Brazil, 8882. Catalog of Publications, 86–87. Charter, 8575. Index to 1975 Documents List, 88. Inter-American Commission on Human Rights, 8556. Inter-American Committee on Agricultural Development, 3009. Inter-American Council for Education, Science, and Culture, 4329. Inter-American Treaty for Reciprocal Assistance (Rio Treaty), 8614. Press Coverage, 8587. Special Council on Security against Subversive Activity of International Communism, 7431. Uruguay, 7608.
Organization of Petroleum Exporting Countries (OPEC). *See also* Petroleum and Petrochemical Industry. 2916, 3151, 3158,

Guatemala, 1624. Labor Force, 2893. Latin America, 2821. Mexico, 2962, 2965, 4499, 5372. Military, 7009. Northeast, Brazil, 5606. Population, 2864, 2893, 2962, 3038, 5372, 5464, 5489–5490, 5586, 5606, 5683, 9203. Resources, 2864. Venezuela, 2893, 5586.

Prostitution. Panama, 9113.

Protestant Churches. Guatemala, 970. Jamaica, 1019. Martinique, 1063. Pentecostal, 1019. Protestantism, 970. Seventh-Day Adventists, 1063.

Psychiatry. *See also* Mental Health. Brazil, 9305, 9337. Negative Attitudes Toward Psychiatry, 9305. Patient-oriented Therapy, 9337. Psychiatrists, 9285. Psychoanalysis, 9038, 9285. Psychopathology, 9157. Puerto Rico, 9157. and Society, 9038.

Psychology. Argentina, 4385. Brazil, 1589, 9297, 9352. Education, 1589, 4556, 4565. National Stereotypes, 9044. Psychologists, 9297, 9352. Tests, 965, 1589, 4385, 4556, 4565. Transactional Analysis, 9356.

PUBLIC ADMINISTRATION. *See also* Banking and Financial Institutions; Political Leaders/Administrators; Political Organization and Political Parties; Public Finance; Public Health; Public Services; Public Works; Taxation; Urban Planning. Administrators' Attitudes, 7236. Argentina, 5439, 7480, 9260. Bolivia, 3319, 7373. Brazil, 92, 3434, 5700, 7076–7077, 7545, 7554, 7565, 7581, 7587, 7591. Budgeting, 2935. Chile, 7385, 7390, 7398, 7423. Colombia, 5490, 7076–7077, 7300, 7303. Commonwealth Caribbean, 7181. Conferences, 2909. Costa Rica, 7156, 7161. Cuba, 2935, 3058, 3069, 3074. French Antilles, 1028. French Guiana, 149 Geoadministrative Training, 5393. History, 5439. Jamaica, 7236. Mexico, 38, 2935, 5355, 7076–7077, 7087, 7096, 7103, 7113–7116, 7124. Model for Development, 2880. Panama, 7076–7077, 7173. Paraguay, 3327. and Politics, 2935. and Population, 5490. Regional Administration, 2909. Theory, 7073.

PUBLIC ENTERPRISE. *See also* Industry and Industrialization; Private Enterprise; Public Administration. Argentina, 3389. Brazil, 3436, 3441, 3468, 3481, 3513. Caribbean, 3030. Chile, 3233. Holding Companies, 3134. Mexico, 2883, 2953, 2955a, 2978. Peru, 3263. Venezuela, 3134.

Public Finance. *See also* Taxation. Bahamas, 3042. Barbados, 3042. Brazil, 3428. British Virgin Islands, 3042. Caribbean, 3042.

Chile, 3209. Commonwealth Caribbean, 3026. Guatemala, 2994. Haiti, 3031. Jamaica, 3042. Levies, 2855. Nicaragua, 3003. Surinam, 3042. Trinidad and Tobago, 3042. United States Virgin Islands, 3042. Venezuela, 3129.

Public Health. *See also* Health Care; Malnutrition; Nutrition. Argentina, 1655. Bolivia, 3306. Brazil, 1649, 3430, 3510. Chile, 1658. Colombia, 1479. Cuba, 3050, 3053, 3055, 3082. Haiti, 1009, 9052. Health Services, 3510, 9052. Latin America, 1618, 1642. Mexico, 1651, 1667. National Sanitation Plan (PLANASA, Brazil), 3430. Venezuela, 1503.

Public Opinion. Argentina, 7496. Bermuda, 1059. Chile, 7423. Cuba, 7217. Mexico, 7108. Surveys, 7108. Venezuela, 3185.

PUBLIC POLICY. *See also* Economic Policy; Fiscal Policy; Monetary Policy; Public Administration; Tariffs and Trade Policy; specific subjects. Argentina, 7508. Barbados, 7243. Brazil, 1125, 4629, 5660, 7518, 7543, 7547, 7580. Chile, 1251, 1628, 4404. Colombia, 7305. Costa Rica, 7153, 7160. on Drugs, 1647. Formulation, 7101, 7305. on Indians, 901, 1064, 1125, 1251. on Languages, 1331, 1357. Mexico, 1647, 4503, 7101, 7113–7115, 7146. on Nutrition, 1628, 1635. Peru, 7349, 7356, 7364. on Population, 1484. Policy-making, 2897. Under Different Types of Governments, 7066. Venezuela, 4583, 7625, 7629, 7633.

Public Services. *See also* specific services. Bibliography, 17. Colombia, 9206. Haiti, 9052. Latin America, 9206. Mexico, 17, 9092.

Public Works. Mexico, 5355.

Publishing Industry. *See also* Advertising Industry; Bookdealers; Censorship; Press; Printing. Argentina, 5410. Colombia, 79. Science and Technology, 4346. Spanish-language Publishers, 80.

Puerto Rican Status, 7246, 7248–7249.

Puerto Ricans in Continental United States, 32, 1011a, 4554, 7245, 9176.

PUERTO RICO.
Bibliography and General Works, 90.
Anthropology.
    Archaeology, 472, 475.
    Biological Anthropology, 1571, 1656.
    Ethnology, 961, 1021, 1047–1048, 1088, 1100, 1103, 1105.
Economics, 9178.
Education, 4304, 4553–4556.
Geography, 5296–5298, 5902–5904.

Researchers, 4371, 4502, 4507. Science and Technology, 4378, 4386, 4406, 4471, 4507, 4525. Social Sciences, 1056, 4590, 9029, 9048, 9065, 9150, 9361. Use of Film, 975. in the West Indies, 1056.

Research Aids. *See* Archives; Catalogs; Dissertations and Theses; Government Documents; Journals; Latin American Studies; Libraries and Library Services; Library and Information; Manuscripts; Maps and Cartography; National Bibliographies; Projections; Research; specific disciplines, methodology; specific subjects; bibliography; specific subjects, journals.

REVOLUTION AND REVOLUTIONARY MOVEMENTS. *See also* Bolivian Revolution; Cuban Revolution; Guatemalan Revolution; Guerrillas; Mexican Revolution; Peasants; Political Organization and Political Parties; Students. Argentina, 7063, 7485. Bolivia, 7194. Brazil, 7063, 7521, 7572. Caribbean, 7176. Chile, 7383, 7389, 7415, 7418. Cuba, 7194. Dominican Republic, 9174. Latin America, 2898, 7024, 7036, 7039, 7065, 7081. Mexico, 7110–7111, 9072. Peru, 3261, 7063, 7339, 7346–7347, 7359, 7365. Role of Intellectuals, 9026. and Social Change, 7004. Third World, 8717. Venezuela, 7620.

Rio Grande do Norte (State) Brazil. Geography, 5613.

Rio Grande do Sul (State) Brazil. Geography, 5602–5603, 5622, 5685.

Rituals. *See* Burial Rituals and Mortuary Customs; Festivals and Rituals; Folklore; Religion.

Road Maps. *See also* Street Maps; Transportation; Travel and Tourism. Argentina, 5738. Baja California, 5871. Brazil, 5764, 5769, 5788. Cayman Islands, 5724. Chile, 5793. Colombia, 5807, 5809, 5811. Costa Rica, 5817–5818. Ecuador, 5832. El Salvador, 5835. Guatemala, 5840. Haiti, 5843. Mexico, 5848–5849, 5859, 5860, 5862. Nicaragua, 5883–5884. Panama, 5890. Peru, 5897. Puerto Rico, 5902. Trinidad and Tobago, 5906. Venezuela, 5908, 5917–5918.

Rockshelters. *See* Housing.

Rodríguez Lara, Guillermo, 7314, 7317.

Rubber and Rubber Industry. Amazonia, 5617, 5692. Bibliography, 3273. Export, 3273. Peru, 3273. Precolumbian Uses, 498.

Rumania and Mexico Relations. Cooperation in the United Nations, 8622.

RURAL SETTLEMENT. *See also* Agrarian Reform; Land Tenure; Migration; Peasants. Amazonia, 1276, 5600, 5626, 5650, 5698–5699, 5706. Andean region, 5491. Argentina, 5382, 5388, 5402, 5407, 5417, 5419, 5421, 5436, 5439, 5441. Bibliography, 5602–5603, 9032. Bolivia, 5455. Brazil, 3478, 5382, 5589, 5615, 5642, 5645, 5648, 5671, 5685. El Chaco, 5543. Chile, 5388, 5457, 5467, 5477, 9248. Colombia, 1255, 5493, 5499, 5513, 5516. Company Melhoramentos Norte do Paraná, 5615, 5648. Company town, 9248. Cuba, 9193. Ecuador, 1276, 5535, 5827. Guyana, 5541. Latin America, 5473, 9032. Map, 5827. Mexico, 2945a, 5346, 5366–5367, 5369, 5371, 7108a, 9074. Nicaragua, 5327. Paraguay, 5382, 5388, 5543. Patagonia, 5403, 5419, 5431. Peru, 1294, 5547, 5553, 5555–5556. Social Structure, 9074. Standard of Living, 5341. Venezuela, 5388, 5571, 5587.

Russia. *See* Union of Soviet Socialist Republics.

Sacrifices. Aztec, 326, 1415–1452. Grenada, 1040. Human, 326, 367, 882, 1451–1452. Mesoamerica, 882, 1451–1452.

ST. CHRISTOPHER. Bibliography and General Works, 69.

Saint-Hilaire, Augustin François Cesar Provençal de, 5693–5694.

ST. KITTS Bibliography and General Works, 8. Anthropology Archaeology, 488. Ethnology, 1012.

ST. LUCIA Bibliography and General Works, 8. Anthropology Ethnology, 1065.

ST. THOMAS. *See* United States Virgin Islands.

ST. VINCENT. Bibliography and General Works, 8. Anthropology Ethnology, 1085–1086.

Salaries. *See* Wages.

Salcedo-Bastardo, José Luis, 13.

Salto Grande Project (Uruguay), 3343.

Sandinistas. *See* Political Organization and Political Parties, Frente Sandinista de Liberación Nacional (FSLN), Nicaragua.

Sandino, Augusto César, 7172.

San Martín, José de, 12.

Santucho, Mario Roberto, 7475.

São Paulo (State) Brazil, 5703.

SCIENCE AND TECHNOLOGY. *See also* Research; Technology Transfer; specific disciplines. Argentina, 3389, 4370, 4379, 8850. Barbados, 3037. Bibliography, 827. Brazil, 4626, 8832, 8850, 9299–9300. Brazil US Chemistry Program, 4619. Chile, 8850. Colombia, 3109. Conference, 4329, 4350, 8850. Costa Rica, 4452. Cuba, 3059. and Dependency, 4362. and Development, 4350. Dominican Republic, 3029. Ecuador, 8850. Education, 4362, 4424, 4452, 4499, 4597. El Salvador, 8850. Engineers, 4499. and Human Values, 9045. Policies, 3059, 4602. Publishing, 4346. Researchers, 4507. Role of Technology, 3389. Role of Women, 9299–9300. Technological Innovations, 3435. Technological Progress, 3399–3400. Uruguay, 8850.

Sculpture. Aztec, 429. Brazil, 674. Colombia, 710, 718. Easter Island, 697. Fertility Symbols, 374. Izapa, 325. Maya, 374, 417. Mesoamerica, 287, 291, 325, 374, 380, 388, 397, 400–402, 417, 423, 429, 453, 467. Olmec, 401, 467. Panama, 560. Peru, 842. Precolumbian, 252, 287, 291, 325, 374, 380, 388, 397, 400–402, 417, 423. Stone, 842. Uruguay, 674.

Secretaría Permanente del Tratado General de Integración Económica Centroamericana (SIECA). *See* General Treaty on Central American Economic Integration.

Security. *See also* Military; National Security; Organization of American States. Jamaica, 1051.

Sekoya (Indigenous Group), 1178.

SELA. *See* Economic System of Latin America.

Settlement. *See* Rural Settlement; Urbanization.

Settlement Patterns, precolumbian. Argentina, 602, 604, 606. Aztec, 352. Chile, 690, 694, 705. Colombia, 724. Costa Rica, 542. Inca, 694. Maya, 272, 288, 304. Mesoamerica, 272, 288, 304, 352, 358, 363, 379, 538. Peru, 784. Precolumbian, 549, 583, 602, 604, 606, 784. Theory, 784.

SEX AND SEXUAL RELATIONS. *See also* Family Planning; Fertility; Women. Barbados, 1095, 9149. Brazil, 1145, 5628, 9387, 9390, 9404. Caribbean, 1088. Central America, 1088. Chile, 1594. Colombia, 1629. Education, 4345. Incest, 1086. Mexico, 991. Panama, 9113. Peru, 1289. Precolumbian, 802. Prisoners, 9390. St. Vincent, 1086. Sex

Roles, 991. Sterilization, 9181. Women, 9404. Xingu, 1145.

Shamanism, 253, 842, 887, 910, 916, 988, 1003, 1120, 1145, 1166, 1202, 1215, 1220, 1318–1319, 1643.

Shanty Towns. *See* Slums.

Shells and Shell Middens. *See* Artifacts.

Shipibo (Indigenous Group), 1119.

Shuara (Indigenous Group), 1530.

SIECA. *See* General Treaty on Central American Economic Integration.

Silva Henríquez, Raúl, 7388, 7444.

Sindicalism. *See* Labor and Unions.

Sirionó (Indigenous Group), 1118.

Sistema Económico de Latinoamerica. *See* Economic System of Latin America.

Sites. *See* Archaeological Sites.

Slavery and Slave Trade. Barbados, 1034. Brazil, 24, 3508, 9322, 9325, 9330, 9335. Cuba, 1036. Guyana, 1064. Jamaica, 999. Latin America, 9035. Nicaragua, 1472.

Slums. *See also* Marginality. Argentina, 9281. Brazil, 9318, 9407. Colombia, 9202. Jamaica, 1073. Mexico, 939–940, 981, 7106, 7108a, 9055, 9099. Peru, 7330, 7332, 9233. and Political Awareness, 9055.

Sobral, Alférez, 8790.

Soccer War (1969). *See* Boundary Disputes, Honduras/El Salvador.

Social Development. *See also* Economic Development. Africa/Latin America, 9001. Bibliography, 52. Bolivia, 9241. Brazil, 9292, 9301, 9310, 9380–9381, 9402. British Virgin Islands, 1010. Comparisons, 9001. Guyana, 1074. Jamaica, 1023, 1098. Latin America, 52, 9046–9047. Maya, 346. Mesoamerica, 346, 376. Mexico, 956. Olmec, 346. Peru, 3285, 9239. Projects, 9209. Rural, 9381. Social Change, 9239. Theory, 9022, 9402. Trinidad, 997. and Women, 9033, 9241.

SOCIAL ORGANIZATION. *See also* Class Structure; Marginality. Africa/Latin America, 9001. Andean region, 255. Argentina, 9272–9273. Aymara, 1302. Barasana, 1157. Bibliography, 9027. Bolivia, 1239. Bororo, 1205. Brazil, 1195, 1205, 1219, 5645, 9296, 9346, 9351, 9365, 9407. Cargo Systems, 1267, 1317, 1324. Carib-speaking Groups, 1003. Caribbean, 1088, 9035. Cashinahua, 1161. Central America, 1088, 9129. Comparisons, 9001. Costa Rica, 9104, 9107, 9127. Decision-making, 9104. Dominican Republic, 1102. Ecuador, 1267, 9226. Grenada, 1040, 5295. Guadeloupe, 1004. Guatemala, 9111–9112. Guyana, 1069,

1087. Haiti, 1004. Jamaica, 999, 1041. Latin America, 9047a. Laymis, 1241. Machas, 1241. Maya, 295. Mesoamerica, 268, 295, 336, 349. Mexico, 902, 913, 948, 986, 9087. Mundurucú, 1185. Panama, 544. Peru, 1161, 1278, 1302, 1311, 1317, 1324, 5552. Quechua, 1239. Rural, 9226. Saraguro, 1267. Sociocultural Integration, 9365. Suyá, 1195. Voluntary Organization, 1102. Women, 9027, 9033, 9087. Xingú, 1219.

Social Participation. Brazil, 9296. Theory, 9296.

Social Sciences. *See also* Computers and Cumputerization; Methodology; Research; specific disciplines. Anthropology, 998. Bibliography, 2, 128. Brazil, 138. Caribbean, 55. Central America, 106. Conferences on, 9150. Education, 55. Japanese Journal on Latin America, 152. Journal Indexes, 106, 119. Projects in Mexico, 9065. in Puerto Rico, 1068. Research, 128. Research Guides, 116.

SOCIAL SECURITY. Argentina, 2862, 3393. Bolivia, 3306. Brazil, 7556–7557. Chile, 2862. Costa Rica, 9126. Cuba, 3082, 9191. Government Regulation and Legislation, 9126. Latin America, 9017. Mexico, 2862, 2883. Peru, 2862. Uruguay, 2862.

SOCIALISM AND SOCIALIST PARTIES, 8742. Chile, 3223, 7409, 7433, 9008, 9244. Colombia, 7278. Cuba, 3068, 3077, 9160–9161. Jamaica, 7235. Latin America, 7012, 7048, 9047a. Movimiento al Socialismo (MAS, Venezuela), 7624, 7633. Puerto Rico, 8748. US Socialist Workers Party, 7200. Venezuela, 3192. and Women, 9244. Yugoslav Model, 3192.

Sociological Models, 9265. World Order Models, 9031.

SOCIOLOGY (items 9001–9411). *See also* Children; Class Structure; Demography; Family and Family Relationships; Family Planning; Methodology; Migration; Race and Race Relations; Religion; Sex and Sexual Relations; Social Development; Social Organization; Urbanization; Women; Youth; specific countries; specific ethnic or national groups. Bibliography, 3. Brazil, 9380, 9410. Conferences, 9246. Empirical, 9052. Evolution in Spain, 9046. Journal Indexes, 106. Journal, 9332. Rural Sociology, 9380. Sociologists, 9039, 9359, 9382–9383, 9397, 9410. Textbook, 9047, 9130, 9234. Theory, 9382–9383, 9397.

Soils. *See also* Natural Resources. Amazonia, 5674, 5712–5713. Argentina, 3366. Arid Regions, 3366. Aztec, 5337. Brazil, 653, 5613, 5630, 5674, 5780. Central America, 5300. Chemical Analysis, 5501. Classification, 5674. Colombia, 5497–5501, 5506. Ecology, 5500. Ecosystems, 5300. Ecuador, 5828. Fertility, 9103. Haiti, 5844. Maps, 5780, 5828, 5844, 5857. Mexico, 5332, 5373, 5857. Semi-arid, 5613. Uruguay, 5560.

Somoza, Anastasio, 7171–7172, 8755.

SOUTH AMERICA. *See* specific region or country.

SOUTH SHETLAND ISLANDS. Geography, 5424.

Spain and Latin America Relations, 8552.

Spain and Mexico Relations, 8615.

Special Latin American Coordinating Commission (CECLA), 8843.

Spiritism. Puerto Rico, 1047.

Sports. Cuba, 3053, 3061, 3082, 4459. Fish, 3061.

Squatter Settlements. *See* Land Tenure; Rural Settlement; Slums; Urbanization.

Statistics. *See* specific subject. Brazil, 115.

Stelae. *See* Art; Inscriptions.

Stereotypes. Costa Rica, 9110. National, 9044.

Sterilization. *See* Family Planning.

Stock Market. *See also* Capital Markets. Brazil, 3441, 3461, 3512. Uruguay, 3333–3334.

Street Maps. Asunción, Paraguay, 5892. Bogotá, Colombia, 5807, 5812. Brasília, Brazil, 5778. Buenos Aires, Argentina, 5400, 5747–5748, 5750. Caracas, Venezuela, 5908. Cumaná, Venezuela, 5910. Guatemala City, Guatemala, 5837–5838. La Paz, Bolivia, 5756. Lima, Peru, 5894. Manaus, Brazil, 5790. Mazatlán, Mexico, 5875, 5879. Mérida, Mexico, 5866, 5880. Mexico City, Mexico, 5856, 5874. Montevideo, Uruguay, 5907. Panama City, Panama, 5891. Port-au-Prince, Haiti, 5843. Quito, Ecuador, 5830. San José, Costa Rica, 5817. Santo Domingo, Dominican Republic, 5824. Tegucigalpa, Honduras, 5847.

Stroessner, Alfredo, 7596.

STUDENTS. Academic Performance, 4412. Activism, 4526, 4531, 4562. Argentina, 4382. Attrition and Absenteeism, 4382, 4585, 4605. Barbados, 996. Bolivia, 7372. Chile, 4406, 4412, 9249. Colombia, 4429, 4433, 4441, 4446. Conferences, 4472. Cuba, 4468. Dominican Republic, 4472, 4476. Enrollment, 4446. Ethnic Background, 9249. Guyana, 996, 1023. Jamaica, 1023. Latin America, 7039. Mexico, 4526, 4528, 4531,

7149. Movements, 4406, 4468, 7039, 7149.
Organizations, 4335, 4564, 7372. Political
Perspectives, 996. Rights, 4327, 4528. Socioeconomic Background, 4382, 4398, 4408,
4410. Trinidad, 996. Venezuela, 4562, 4564,
4582. Vocational Interests, 4429.
SUDAM. *See* Superintendência do Desen-
volvimento da Amazônia.
SUFRAMA. *See* Superintendência da Zona
Franca de Manaus.
Sugar and Sugar Industry. Bibliography, 3154,
9175. Brazil, 8845, 9339. Caribbean, 54.
Cuba, 1036, 3047, 3072–3073, 3080–3081,
5823, 8709, 9164, 9175. Dominican Re-
public, 9147. International, 3080. Labor,
9147. Maps, 5823. Mexico, 7140. Northeast,
Brazil, 5672. Panama, 919. Peru, 3258, 3289,
7337. Policies, 3046, 8845. Production,
3047. Venezuela, 3154.
Superintendência da Zona Franca de Manaus
(Brazil), 5591.
Superintendência do Desenvolvimento da
Amazônia (SUDAM, Brazil), 5591, 5687,
7570.
SURINAM.
Bibliography and General Works, 39, 128,
151.
Anthropology, 1014.
Archaeology, 750–751, 754–755.
Ethnology, 1003, 1011, 1032, 1037, 1052,
1076, 1088, 1097, 1104, 1167, 1178
Economics, 143.
Geography, 5905.
Government and Politics, 7262.
Surui (Indigenous Group), 1125.
Suyá (Indigenous Group), 1195.
Symbolism. Amazonia, 731. Chile, 1254. Ec-
uador, 731. Guatemala, 985. Mesoamerica,
265, 302, 320, 395, 430. Mexico, 900.
Moche, 788. Peru, 763, 788. Riddles, 1224.

Taino (Indigenous Group), 474, 485, 496, 517,
724.
Tairona (Indigenous Group), 1260.
Tapirapé (Indigenous Group), 1207–1208.
Tarahumara (Indigenous Group), 913.
Tarasca (Indigenous Group), 892, 905, 1575.
Tariffs and Trade Policy. *See also* Balance of
Payments; Foreign Trade; Imports and Ex-
ports. Andean Pact, 3213. Argentina, 3376,
3396, 3410, 3426. Brazil, 3449. Colombia,
3085. Haiti/European Economic Commu-
nity, 3022. Haiti/United States, 3022, 3031.
Latin America, 2918. Less Development
Countries, 2840, 8569. Non-tariff Trade

Barriers, 2813, 8569. Uruguay, 3330. United
States/Latin America, 8539.
Taruma (Indigenous Group), 751.
Tavares, Aurelio de Lyra, 7548.
Taxation. Argentina, 3381, 3411, 3417, 3425.
Bolivia, 3309. Brazil, 3436, 3462, 3506. Cor-
porate Income Tax, 3411, 3462. Costa Rica,
5312. Developing Countries, 3035. Govern-
ment Regulations and Legislation, 3462.
Income Tax, 3436. Jamaica, 3035. Policy,
3411. Progressive Income Tax, 3425. Real
Estate, 5312. Tax Collection, 3417. Uruguay, 5560. Venezuela, 3160.
Teacher Training. *See also* Educators. Argentina, 4390. Brazil, 4630. Caribbean, 1023.
Conference, 4587. Latin America, 4351. Private School, 4615. Puerto Rico, 4304.
Teacher Qualifications, 4584. Training University Administrators, 4415.
Teaching. *See also* Education; Literacy and Illiteracy; Radio; Television; Universities;
specific discipline. Biology, 4501. Brazil,
9350, 9393, 9410. Business Administration,
2859. Chemistry, 4619. Economics, 2859,
4328. Information Science, 4515. Languages,
4491–4492, 4615. Latin American Culture,
4331. Latin American History, 4330, 4352.
Literacy, 4532. Materials, 4330. Natural Sciences, 4403. Nicaragua, 4532. Public
Relations, 4579. Qualitative Improvement,
4606. Science, 4616. Sociology, 9307, 9393,
9410. Techniques, 4331, 4345, 4426, 4552,
4600, 4610, 4616. University, 4312, 4581.
Technology Transfer. Andean region, 2867,
2938. Bibliography, 35. Brazil, 2938, 3501.
Colombia, 3086. Developing Countries,
2906, 2910. Government Regulation and
Legislation, 3188. Latin America, 2920,
3097, 8540, 8589. Mexico, 3501. Policy,
2937–2938. Third World, 2815. in the Tropics, 2847. Venezuela, 3188.
Tehuantepec Isthmus (Mexico), 5332, 5339.
Teixeira, Anísio, 4614.
Telecommunications. Amazonia, 5775. Ecuador, 5832. Maps, 5775, 5832.
Television. Argentina, 7496. Bibliography,
4310. Bolivia, 4402. Brazil, 9347, 9349. Censorship, 7496. Colombia, 4310, 4423. and
Education, 9349. Educational, 4310, 4313,
4402, 4423, 4485. El Salvador, 4485.
Territorial Claims. *See also* Boundary Disputes; Law of the Sea; Territorial Waters. on
Antarctica, 5397, 5444, 5735, 5797, 5800,
8763, 8779, 8798. by Argentina, 5444, 5735,
8763, 8779, 8792, 8798, 8818–8819, 8822,

Venezuelan Development Corporation. Agroindustrial Development, 3154.
Verissimo, Erico, 7532.
Vianna, Francisco José de Oliveira, 7589.
Videla, Jorge Rafael, 3414, 7046.
Villa, Pancho, 7122.
Villegas, Vegh, 7604.
Violence. See also Guerrillas; Military; Repression; Terrorism; Torture. Bolivia, 7366. Brazil, 7549. Colombia, 7275. Jamaica, 1051. and Politics, 1051. Venezuela, 9195.
La Violencia (Colombia), 7307. Bibliography, 7298. Effect on Agriculture, 3117.
Vocational Training. See Labor and Unions, occupational training.
Volcanoes. See Geology; Natural Disasters, volcanic eruptions.
Voodoo, 993, 1004, 1044, 1054, 1057, 7425.
Voting Patterns. See Elections and Electoral Traditions.

Wages. See also Income Distribution; Labor and Unions. Argentina, 3423. Brazil, 3431, 3530. Colombia, 3117. Forced Savings, 3431. Industrial Sector, 3423, 3530. Legislation, 3117. University Staff, 4372.
Wapishana (Indigenous Group), 1538.
Warao (Indigenous Group), 1215–1216, 1525.
Warfare. Bolivia, 1248. Chiriguanos, 1248. Trinidad, 487. Venezuela, 1169. Yanomamö, 1169.
Water Resources. See Energy Sources; Natural Resources.
Waurá (Indigenous Group), 665.
Wayampi (Indigenous Group), 1553.
Weapons. See Arms.
West Germany. See Federal Republic of Germany.
West Indians. Abroad, 1012, 1052. in the United Kingdom, 1024, 1052. in the United States, 1011a, 9176.
WEST INDIES. See also Cuba; Danish West Indies; Dominican Republic; Haiti; Jamaica; Lesser Antilles; Puerto Rico.
Bibliography and General Works, 131, 151.
Anthropology.
    Biological Anthropology, 1591.
    Ethnology, 992–1106.
    Linguistics, 1430.
Economics, 143, 3020–3045.
Education, 4597–4599.
Geography, 5727–5729.

Government and Politics, 7180, 7183.
International Relations, 8739.
Sociology, 9032, 9133, 9154.
Wildlife. See Flora and Fauna.
Witoto (Indigenous Group), 1143, 1178.
WOMEN. See also Family Planning; Feminism; Indigenous Peoples; Prostitution; Sex and Sexual Relations. Age of Menarche, 1621. Argentina, 123. Barbados, 999, 1095. Bibliography, 9027, 9156. Bolivia, 9241. Brazil, 123, 9299–9300, 9312, 9357, 9376, 9392, 9404. Capitalism, 9392. Caribbean, 515. Chile, 7389, 9243. Colombia, 1485, 3114. Commonwealth Caribbean, 7175. Conferences, 9376. Cuba, 7175, 7203, 9156, 9167, 9183. Depicted in Mass Media, 9014. Division of Labor, 9201. Economic Role, 905, 991. Ecuador, 9228. Education, 4314. Employment, 3114, 3173. and Development, 7070, 7175. Government Regulations and Legislation, 9167, 9177. Guatemala, 896. Haiti, 9177. History, 9183. Indigenous, 515, 881, 905, 909, 911, 929, 1212–1213. Jamaica, 1082, 1500. Journals, 9009. and Labor, 9043, 9071, 9357, 9376. Latin America, 9002, 9005, 9019, 9032. Liberation, 9183, 9333. Mexico, 881, 903, 905, 956, 991, 1499, 1621, 9056, 9071, 9073, 9087. Movements, 7389. Panama, 9113, 9118–9119. Peasants, 9002, 9073. Peru, 123, 9230–9232. Political Participation, 9119. Precolumbian, 515. and Religion, 9009. Research, 123. Uruguay, 9291. Venezuela, 123, 1212–1213, 9201.
World Bank. See also Project Evaluation. World Development Report, 2939.
World War I. Brazil, 8901.
World War II. and Guatemala, 8674. Impact on Brazilian Economy, 3451. United States/Argentina Relations, 8805. United States/Chile Relations, 8805–8806.

Xetá (Indigenous Group), 1194.
Xingú (Indigenous Group), 1108, 1145.
Xokleng (Indigenous Group), 1194.

Yagua (Indigenous Group), 1124, 1178.
Yanaconaje. Peru, 9235.
Yanomamö (Indigenous Group), 1112, 1127, 1168–1170, 1186, 1199, 1539, 1541, 1548, 1583, 1641.
Ye'kwana (Indigenous Group), 1003, 1150, 1541, 1549.

AUTHOR INDEX

Browning, David G., 5314
Brownrigg, Edwin Blake, 68
Brownrigg, Leslie Ann, 1268–1269
Brucher, Wolfgang von, 5491
Bruder, Claus J., 374
Brugada Guanes, Alejandro, 4536
Bruhn, Jan G., 615
Bruhns, Karen Olson, 713–715, 768–769
Brumbaugh, Robert C., 1118
Brunn, Gerhard, 7522
Brunner, Heinrich, 3047
Brush, Stephen B., 1282–1284
Bryan, Alan Lyle, 563, 633, 636
Bryant, Shasta M., 20
Bryant, Solena V., 2
Bryce-Laporte, Roy Simón, 889, 1011a
Brzezinski, Steven, 7273
Bubberman, F.C., 751
Buckingham, Beth, 265
Budowski, Gerardo, 5253
Bueno Mendoza, Alberto, 770
Buenos Aires (city), Arg., 5749
Buenos Aires (province), Arg. Ministerio de
    Economía. Dirección de Recurso, 5408
Buenos Aires (province), Arg. Ministerio de
    Educación. Instituto de Bibliografía, 4371
Buescu, Mircea, 3451, 3497
Büttner, Elizabeth Holt, 4505
Bulhões, Octavio Gouvêa de, 3452
Bulletin de la Sécretarie d'Etat des Finances
    et des Affaires Economiques, 3022
Bumgarner, Max, 33
Bunch, Roger, 890
Bunch Roland, 890
Burchard, Roderick E., 1285
Burger, Richard L., 771
Burggraaf, Winfield J., 3177
Burgoa, Ignacio, 7095
Burneo, José, 3250
Burnham, Forbes, 7256–7260
Burns, Donald H., 1403
Burns, E. Bradford, 8662
Burton, Richard Francis, 5608
Busby, L., 143
Buse, Rueben C., 2984
Bustamante, Kassem, 5803
Busto, Emiliano, 7096
Bustos, R., 5739
Butterworth, Douglas, 891
Byard, P.J., 1578

Caballero, Manuel, 4567
Cabieses Cubas, Hugo, 3251
Cabrera Castro, Rubén, 375
Cabrera Darquea, Javier, 772

Cáceres, Baldomero, 1286, 4541
Cáceres, Carlos, 5808
Cadaval, Mauricio, 9307
Cadernos do CEAS, 9308
Cadogan, León, 1345
Cafasso, José, 3379
Caggiano, Maria Amanda, 580
Cahiers des Amériques Latines, 9060
Cahlander, Adele, 1237
Caicedo, Elizabeth, 1600
Cail, Michèle, 5382
Caillavet, Sebastián Chantal, 808
Calamaro, Eduardo S., 5409
Calandra, Horacio A., 584
Caldeira, José Ribamar C., 7523
Caldera Rodríguez, Rafael, 7005, 7617
Calderón, Enrique Santos, 7006
Calderón, Horacio, 8777
Callegari Jacques, Sidia M., 1512
Calvo Pardo, Alonso, 9108
Camacho Guizado, Alvaro, 7306
Camacho Roldán, Salvador, 3089
Câmara, Antônio Alves, 5609
Cámara Barbachano, Fernando, 9061–9062
Camargo, Cândido Procópio Ferreira de, 9309
Camilion, Oscar, 7467
Camino, Alejandro, 1287
Camp, Roderic Ai, 7097–7102
Campal, Esteban F., 3453
Campbell, D.G., 1665
Campbell, Leon G., 21
Campbell, Lyle, 1346
Campbell, Pedro, 3135
Campello de Souza, Maria do Carmo C. See
    Souza, Maria do Carmo C. Campello de.
Campo, Esteban del, 7312
Campo, Urbano, 7274
Campos, Camilo, 4483
Campos, Renato, 5628
Campos, Ricardo, 9143
Campos, Roberta, 1119
Campos, Roberto de Oliveira, 3523, 8778
Campos Coelho, Edmundo. See Coelho,
    Edmundo Campos.
Campos e Silva, Antônio. See Silva, Antônio
    Campos e.
Campos Rivera, Jorge, 3248
Campos Sevilla, Marcia J., 9063
Canabrava Barreiros, Eduardo. See Barreiros,
    Eduardo Canabrava.
Cantero, Manuel, 7383
Cantón, Darío, 7468
Capdevila, Raymond, 5545
La Capitanía General de Venezuela: 1777–1778
Capote F., Fausto, 5567

tación Social. Grupo de Trabajo de Migraciones Internas, 9012
CEPAL Review, 2780
Cepeda Ulloa, Fernando, 7276–7277
Cerase, Francesco P., 9013
Cerdas Cruz, Rodolfo, 7154
Cereceda, Verónica, 1238
Cerososimo, Gaetano, 9110
Cerrolaza Asenjo, Alberto, 2781
Cervera, Felipe Justo, 9260
Céspedes Gutiérrez, Gerardo, 1443–1444
Cetrulo, Ricardo, 4303
Cew, Judson de, 9324
Chacon, Vamireh, 7525
Chahud, Carlos E., 779
Chakraborty, Ranajit, 1513
Chalout, Yves, 3460
Chambers, Erve, 894
Chamero, Juan Angel, 8781
Chance, John K., 895
Chaney, Elsa M., 9208
Chaparro, Patricio, 7009
Chapman, Anne, 582
Charles, Pearnel, 7232
Charlton, Thomas H., 279, 377
Chase-Sardi, Miguel, 1123
Chatwin, Bruce, 5410
Chaumeil, J., 1124
Chaumeil, J. P., 1124
Chautard, José Luiz, 3431
Chautard-Freire-Maia, E.A., 1514
Chaves de Azcona, Lilia, 1603
Chaves Mendoza, Alvaro, 716
Chaves Vargas, Luis Fernando, 3137
Chávez de Sánchez, María Isabel, 9067
Chayanov, A.V., 2782
Cheredeev, A.N., 1517
Chernick, Sidney E., 3026
Chesterfield, Ray, 5578
Chiappino, Jean, 1125
Chiara, Philomena, 672
Chiara, Wilma, 637, 1154. *See* also Chiara, Vilma.
Chichique, Bruno, 8512
Chico Pinto: teoria e práctica de um político, 7526
Child, John, 8513
Chile. Dirección de Vialidad. Departamento de Estudios. Sección Planificación, 5793
Chile. Empresa Nacional de Electricidad (ENDESA). Oficina de Información y Control de Resultados de Explotación, 5794
Chile. Instituto de Investigaciones Geológicas, 5795
Chile. Instituto Geográfico Militar, 5796

Chile. Instituto Nacional de Estadísticas, 5463–5464
Chile. Instituto Nacional de Estadísticas. Departamento de Geografía y Censos, 5797
Chile. Junta de Gobierno. Oficina de Planificación Nacional (ODEPLAN), 3196–3204
Chile. Ministerio de Agricultura. Oficina de Planificación Agrícola (ODEPA), 3205
Chile. Ministerio de la Vivienda y Urbanismo. Dirección de Planificación del Desarrollo Urbano. Departamento Area Metropolitana, 5798
Chile. Presidencia de la República. Comisión Nacional de la Reforma Administrativa (CONARA), 7385
Chile: Klasskamp och stretegi, 1970–73, 7386
Chile y su Presidente Augusto Pinochet Ugarte, 7387
The Chilean Society for the Defense of Tradition, Family and Property, *Santiago. See* Sociedad Chilena de Defensa de la Tradición Familia y Propiedad, *Bogotá.*
Chinchilla, Norma Stoltz, 896, 7389
Chmyz, Igor, 638–644
Chomsky, Noam, 8514
Chonchol, Jacques, 2783, 3206, 7390
Chong Díaz, Guillermo, 5465
Christiansen, Jens, 4308
Christiansen, Ole, 715
Christie, Keith H., 5493
Christinat, Jean Louis, 1289
Christo, Carlos Alberto Libanio, 7527
Chronologie du Chile: septembre 1973– décembre 1976, 7391
Chronology of U.S.–Cuban rapprochement: 1977, 8718
Chu, Ke-Young, 3383
Cicciamali de Souza, Maria Cristina. *See* Souza, Maria Cristina Cicciamali de.
Cifuentes, Malva, 3207
Cigliano, Eduardo Mario, 583–584
5 [i.e. Cinco] años de cambio: pacificación y desarrollo en el gobierno de Rafael Caldera, 1969–1974, 3138
Ciria, Alberto, 7471
Cirino, Julio Alberto, 7472
Ciudac, Adolfo, 3250
Civeira Taboada, Miguel, 101
Cladindex, 102
Clark, Juan M., 9180
Clark, Lawrence E., 1350
Clarke, Colin G., 1012, 8719
Clastres, Pierre, 1126
Clavijo, Fernando, 2948–2950

buros. Dirección de Geología, 5916
Venezuela. Ministerio de Obras Públicas. Dirección General de Vialidad. Oficina de Planeamiento, 5917–5918
Venezuela. Ministerio de Relaciones Exteriores, 8903
Venezuela. Ministry of Finance. Superintendency of Foreign Investment, 3188
Venezuela. Oficina Central de Coordinación y Planificación (CORDIPLAN), 3189
Venezuela. Oficina Central de Coordinación y Planificación. Dirección de Planificación Social y Cultural. Departamento de Recursos Humanos, 4595–4596
Venezuela. Presidencia de la República. Consejo Nacional de Recursos Humanos, 3190
Vera, Hernán, 9250
Vera Godoy, Rodrigo, 4384, 4390
Veras Baptista, Myrian. See Baptista, Myrian Veras.
Verbitsky, Horacio, 7362
Vergnes H., 1560
Versiani, Flávio Rabelo, 3528
Versteeg, A.H., 754–755
Verstraeten, Juan, 3413
Vetter, David M., 5714
Viagnoni, Lida, 5715
Vial, Alvaro, 3217
Viana Filho, Luís, 7587
Vianna, Luiz Werneck, 7588
Vicuña Izquierdo, Leonardo, 2929
Vidal, Luz Boelitz, 1203–1204
Vidal, Philippe, 5545
Vidaurre Retamoso, Enrique, 1248
Viedma, Pablo Franco, 3329
Vieira, Anna da Soledade, 64
Vieira, Evaldo Amaro, 7589
Viertler, Renate Brigitte, 1205
Vietmeyer, Noel D., 5396
Vilar, Pierre, 2762
Vilas, Carlos María, 2930, 9147
Vilhena, Paulo Emílio Ribeiro de, 7590
Vilhena de Moraes, Agueda. See Moraes, Agueda Vilhena de.
Vilhena Vialou, Agueda, 749
Villa M., Rosa Olivia, 2976
Villa Rojas, Alfonso, 982
Villacres Moscoso, Jorge W., 8904–8905
Villagómez V., Rafael, 4506
Villagrán Kramer, Francisco, 8607
Villalobos Paz, José, 4579
Villamañán, Adolfo de, 1206
Villamil Bueno, Guillermo, 8906
Villanueva, María, 1605
Villanueva, Víctor, 7363, 7456

Villar Araújo, Carlos, 7506
Villarreal, René, 2977–2978
Villarreal, Rocío R. de, 2978
Villavicencio Chumacero, Ismael, 3319
Villegas, Abelardo, 4531, 7149
Villegas A., Víctor Hugo, 1443–1444
Villela, Annibal V., 3529
Viloria R., Oscar, 3191
Viñas Urquiza, María Teresa, 1434
Viñaza, Cipriano Muñoz y Manzano, conde de la, 53
Vincent, M., 5261
Vincent, R.J., 8608
Vinces Zevallos, Fausto, 8907
Vinhas de Queiroz, Maurício. See Queiroz, Maurício Vinhas de.
Vining, James W., 5541
Viscarra Pando, Gonzalo, 7375
Visintini, Alfred A., 3395, 3427
Vita-Finzi, C., 5373
Vivas, Freddy, 8834
Vivas Terán, Abdón, 3192
Vizcaíno A., Rogelio, 7130
Vogel, Robert C., 2931
Vogel, Sonia, 5486
Vogt, Evon Z., 983–984
Volkov, Serguei, 3084
von Euw, Eric, 465
von Kanel, Alfred, 5716
von Winning, Hasso, 452–453
von Wuthenau, Alexander. See Wuthenau, Alexander von.
Voorhies, Barbara, 353, 361
Voydanoff, Patricia, 1101
Vreeland, James, 854
Vries, Barend A. de, 2932
Vuscovic, Pedro, 7457

Wagley, Charles, 1207–1208
Wagner, Catherine A., 1325
Wagner, Erika, 875–877, 1209
Wahrlich, Beatriz. See Sousa Wahrlich, Beatriz M. de.
Walalam, Aushi, 1112
Wald, Karen, 4469
Wales. See United Kingdom.
Walker, Malcolm T., 1102
Wallace, Elisabeth, 7183
Wallace de García Paula, Ruth. See Paula, Ruth Wallace de García.
Walter, Ingo, 8569
Walters, Barbara, 8759
Walters, Rudy Schmidt. See Schmidt Walters, Rudy.
Walton, John, 2979, 9053, 9098